KT-172-874

How do you want

Comprehensive

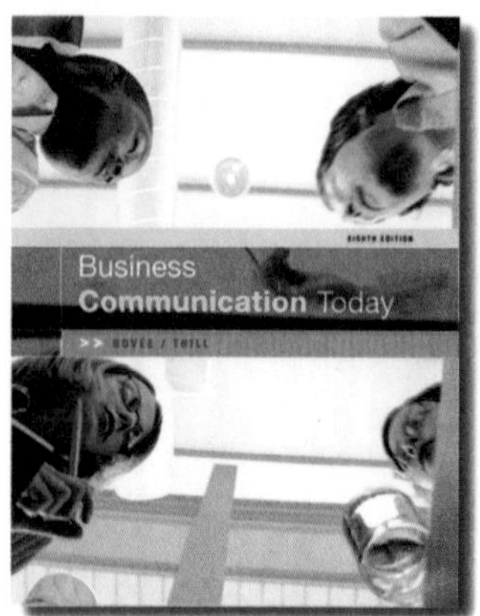

ISBN: 0-13-147845-1

Brief Paperback with Grammar Emphasis

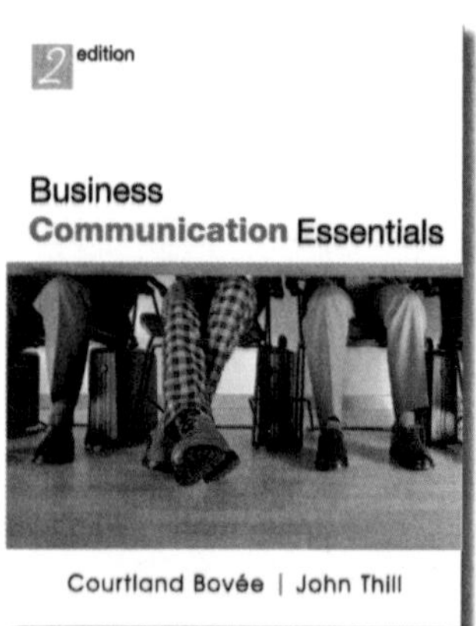

ISBN: 0-13-147245-3

Interactive Media Edition

ISBN: 0-13-041786-X

your Bovée/Thill?

Balanced Presentation of Fundamentals

ISBN: 0-13-141965-X

Business Communication Today Custom One-Color Option

The Core

\$40.00!

for the core nine chapters

- Net price to bookstore

Optional Chapters

\$5.00!

each additional chapter

- Net price to bookstore

Contact your local PH Rep for more information on the custom/core option.

BUSINESS

BUSINESS COMMUNICATION TODAY

Eighth Edition

COURTLAND L. BOVÉE

Professor of Business Communication
C. Allen Paul Distinguished Chair
Grossmont College

JOHN V. THILL

Chief Executive Officer
Communication Specialists of America

Pearson Education International

Acquisition Editor: David Parker
Editorial Assistant: Denise Vaughn
Marketing Manager: Anke Braun
Marketing Assistant: Patrick Dansozo
Senior Managing Editor (Production): Judy Leale
Production Editor: Cindy Durand
Permissions Supervisor: Charles Morris
Production Manager: Arnold Vila
Design Manager: Maria Lange
Art Director: Janet Slowik
Interior Design: Liz Harasymczuk
Cover Design: Liz Harasymczuk
Cover Illustration/Photo: Robert Daly/Image Bank/Getty Images, Inc.
Illustrator (Interior): ElectraGraphics, Inc.
Photo Researcher: Melinda Alexander
Image Permission Coordinator: Nancy Seise
Manager, Print Production: Christy Mahon
Composition/Full-Service Project Management: Lynn Steines, Carlisle Communications
Printer/Binder: Courier/Kendallville
Typeface: Minion 10.5 pt

Credits and acknowledgments for material borrowed from other sources and reproduced, with permission, in this textbook appear on page AC-1.

Pearson Education LTD.
Pearson Education Singapore, Pte. Ltd
Pearson Education, Canada, Ltd
Pearson Education–Japan
Pearson Education Australia PTY, Limited
Pearson Education North Asia Ltd
Pearson Educación de Mexico, S.A. de C.V.
Pearson Education Malaysia, Pte. Ltd
Pearson Education, Upper Saddle River, New Jersey

10 9 8 7 6 5 4 3 2 1
ISBN 0-13-196873-4

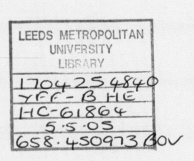

Contents in Brief

Contents

Learn How the Leading Text Blends with Technology to Create a Total Teaching and Learning Solution

Technology now plays a central role in business communication, and technology plays a central role in *Business Communication Today*, too—as both content and pedagogy. The eighth edition builds on 20 years of success with an extensive revision that integrates every vital form of technology that students will be expected to use on the job.

Technology is part of this book's mission to provide students with a solid background in communication fundamentals, a realistic look at the challenges of working in today's demanding business environment, and the skills they need to compete and succeed. From the opening chapter on communication concepts to the closing discussion of employment interviewing, *Business Communication Today* helps students use technology wisely, work quickly under time and budget constraints, and communicate with close attention to ethics and etiquette.

Moreover, only *Business Communication Today* helps instructors and students take full advantage of new advances in technology that can have a highly positive effect on learning. The blending of this textbook with technology, such as its "Document Makeovers" that are presented in an engaging multimedia environment, OneKey learning modules, and interactive website, make the text the most effective teaching and learning tool you'll find for a business communication course.

Because of its vivid insights into real-world communication situations and lively, conversational writing style, this text holds the interest of students and teachers alike. In the two decades since the first edition was published, millions of students have learned about business communication from *Business Communication Today*. The text has been awarded the prestigious Award of Excellence by the Text and Academic Authors Association and is the leading text in the field.

This textbook offers an extraordinary number of devices to simplify teaching, promote active learning, stimulate critical thinking, and develop career skills. As you'll see on the pages that follow, this edition of the text with its high-tech supplements make classes livelier, more relevant, and more enjoyable.

NEW CONTENT IN THIS EDITION

Integrated Approach to Technology

Technology is woven into the fabric of this book in every chapter to illustrate the changing ways people are communicating with each other. Students are introduced to the pervasive role of communication technology in a special four-page photo essay in Chapter 1, "Powerful Tools for Communicating Effectively." These cutting-edge topics throughout the book include the following:

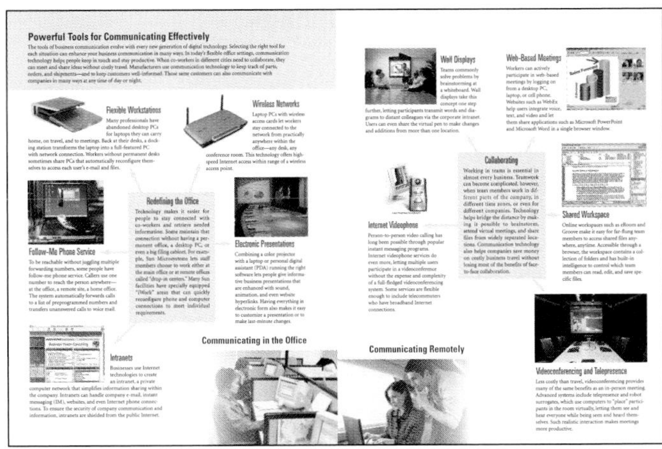

- computer animation
- corporate blogs
- digital rights
- electronic documents
- electronic forms
- electronic presentations
- electronic résumé production
- e-mail
- e-portfolios
- extranets
- graphic design software
- groupware and shared online workspaces
- idea-generation and document-planning software
- image processing tools
- instant messaging
- interactive media
- Internet telephony (VoIP)
- intranets
- linked and embedded documents
- multimedia documents
- multimedia presentations
- online chat systems for sales and customer support
- online research techniques
- online survey tools
- proposal-writing software
- résumé scanning systems
- RSS newsfeeds
- search and metasearch engines
- security and privacy concerns in electronic media (including e-mail hygiene)
- social networking applications
- streaming media
- templates and stylesheets
- translation software
- videoconferencing and telepresence
- virtual agents and bots
- virtual private networks (VPNs)
- web directories
- web publishing systems
- web-based virtual meetings
- webcasts
- website accessibility

Document Makeovers

In each chapter of the book, an assignment overview directs students to the OneKey website, where interactive exercises help them apply chapter concepts to an actual business document. "Document Makeovers" offer students an appealing opportunity to refine and reinforce their writing skills in a dynamic multimedia environment.

DOCUMENT MAKEOVER

IMPROVE THIS E-MAIL MESSAGE

To practice correcting drafts of actual documents, visit www.prenhall.com/onekey on the web. Click "Document Makeovers," then click Chapter 7. You will find an e-mail message that contains problems and errors relating to what you've learned in this chapter about routine, good-news, and goodwill messages. Use the Final Draft decision tool to create an improved version of this e-mail. Check the message for skilled presentation of the main idea, clarity of detail, proper handling of negative information, appropriate use of resale, and a courteous close.

Peak Performance Grammar and Mechanics

In each chapter, students are directed to the OneKey website to improve their skills with mechanics and specific parts of speech by using the "Peak Performance Grammar and Mechanics" module. Students can take the pretest to determine whether they have any weak areas; then they can review those areas in the module's refresher course. Students can also take a follow-up test. For an extra challenge or advanced practice, students can take the advanced test.

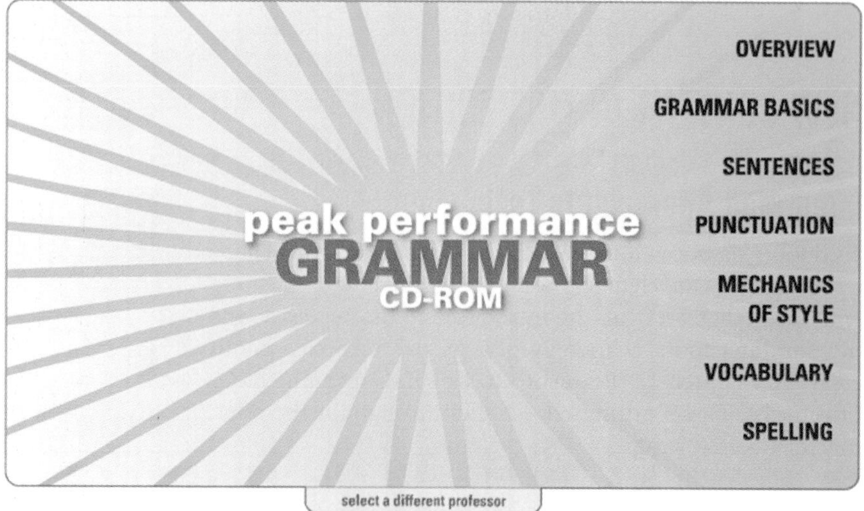

COMMUNICATION CLOSE-UP AT STONE YAMASHITA PARTNERS

www.stoneyamashita.com

If you've ever wondered what a typical business consultant really does, Keith Yamashita isn't the best example—but he may be the most interesting. His biggest fans are executives at IBM, Nike, Gap, HP, and other firms who have worked with Keith and his company, Stone Yamashita Partners (SYP).

Yamashita and designer Robert Stone started SYP in 1994, after working together at Apple Computer. Gradually, they assembled a diverse team that includes designers, writers, technologists, a poet, a sociologist, and a former lawyer—and very few MBAs. This eclectic group specializes in helping companies examine, revamp, and sometimes reinvent their strategy, image, culture, and vision.

That kind of fundamental change affects everyone in a company, from the grayest senior executive to the greenest new hire. Of course, most people resist change, at least initially; however, communication that is effective and compelling can help turn such resistance into commitment.

Communication is SYP's specialty, but Yamashita's team never relies on words alone. Instead, they use strong visual elements to paint a picture—sometimes literally—of a company's new direction. Everything they produce is full of compelling visual cues, whether it's a short video, an interactive website, a pocket-sized book, a giant story scroll, or a

Compelling visual messages are critical to the success of consulting partners Keith Yamashita and Robert Stone.

331

Communication Close-Up

These Communication Close-Ups offer a chapter-framing communication situation. This situation dramatizes the connection between the chapter's contents and life on the job. Reviewers were unanimous in their praise of the rich, engaging real-company examples used to illustrate the book to make communication concepts come alive. To give students the most current picture of business communication possible, all 18 Communication Close-Ups are new in this edition and highlight such intriguing organizations as Mark Burnett Productions (creators of *Survivor* and *The Apprentice*), Toyota Scion, Google, *Rolling Stone* magazine, and the *Complete Idiot's Guides* series.

Communication Solutions

Each chapter also contains one or more of these special margin notes that are adjacent to the principles in the text to which the solution relates and points to how the person featured in the vignette solved the problem described in the vignette.

Communication Solution

Balancing several message goals is the secret to Cone, Inc.'s successful use of positive messages in its work for ConAgra's Feeding Children Better program. Cone's messages help ConAgra maintain a positive image in the marketplace as they help solve the problem of childhood hunger.

Communication Challenges

These projects conclude each chapter and are related to the situation described in the Communication Close-Up. Each chapter has one individual challenge and one team challenge.

COMMUNICATION CHALLENGES AT CONE, INC.

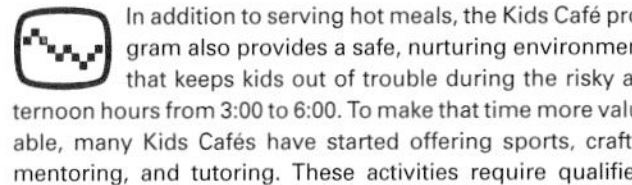

In addition to serving hot meals, the Kids Café program also provides a safe, nurturing environment that keeps kids out of trouble during the risky afternoon hours from 3:00 to 6:00. To make that time more valuable, many Kids Cafés have started offering sports, crafts, mentoring, and tutoring. These activities require qualified volunteers who are willing to spend a few hours each week working with the kids.

Individual Challenge: To staff the tutoring program, ConAgra has asked Cone to create a recruiting campaign that will attract volunteers qualified to help with math, English, and science homework. One of the most importa
will be a letter addressed to current moneta
them to give as little as three hours a month
you, her executive assistant, to draft the re
key points should you include in the introduction, body, and close of the letter? Make a brief outline for your instructor.

Team Challenge: It's nine months later and the recruiting program has been a success: most Kids Cafés are now offering more tutoring sessions. Carol now asks you to draft a letter of appreciation, which is reviewed by executives at ConAgra. During this review process, ConAgra executives have suggested using the letter to ask volunteers to increase the amount of time they spend tutoring each month. With a small group, discuss the pros and cons of adding this request to your letter. In a brief paragraph, explain your team's conclusions.

Special Feature Sidebars

Strategically placed within each chapter, special-feature sidebars extend the chapter material and center on four well-integrated themes: **Ethics Detective, Communication Miscues, Communication Across Cultures,** and **Connecting with Technology**. The sidebars are seamlessly integrated in the text and are an integral part of the learning experience. The Ethics Detective and Communication Miscues themes are both new, and **a total of 29 sidebars in this edition are new**.

Increased Coverage of Listening and Teams

To help students strengthen their communication skills, material on listening and working effectively in teams has been expanded and updated to include the latest information. Improved coverage provides students with skills they'll need to gain a competitive edge in today's workplace, including overcoming the tendency to prejudge, listening across cultural and language barriers, and using short-term memorization techniques that boost retention and reduce misinterpretation.

Increased Coverage of Business Etiquette

To obtain employment and succeed on the job, students need to understand and practice workplace etiquette in areas such as personal appearance, teamwork, face-to-face interactions, written correspondence (including maintaining etiquette in both negative and persuasive messages), research (such as respecting the privacy of interview subjects), instant messaging and e-mail, telephone interactions (receiving calls, making calls, reducing cell phone disruptions, and using voice mail), and job search and interviewing.

Business Communication Videos with Exercises

Entirely new, professionally produced videos cover topics such as ethics, technology, globalization, and intercultural communication. The videos feature real-world examples and are designed to effect a deeper understanding of the concepts and issues covered in the text. Each video is introduced with a synopsis, and exercises ask students to react to the videos by responding to questions, making decisions, and taking the initiative to solve real business communication problems. The following video case teaching guides for instructors are located at www.prenhall.com/bovee and in the instructor's manual:

- *Ethical Communication*, 2003, 11:40 minutes
- *Second City: Communication, Innovation, and Creativity*, 2005, 11:13 minutes
- *Communicating in the Global Workplace*, 2003, 11:12 minutes
- *Impact of Culture on Business*, 2004, 18:26 minutes
- *Technology and the Tools of Communication*, 2003, 5:13 minutes

TRADEMARK FEATURES—ALL UPDATED FOR THIS EDITION

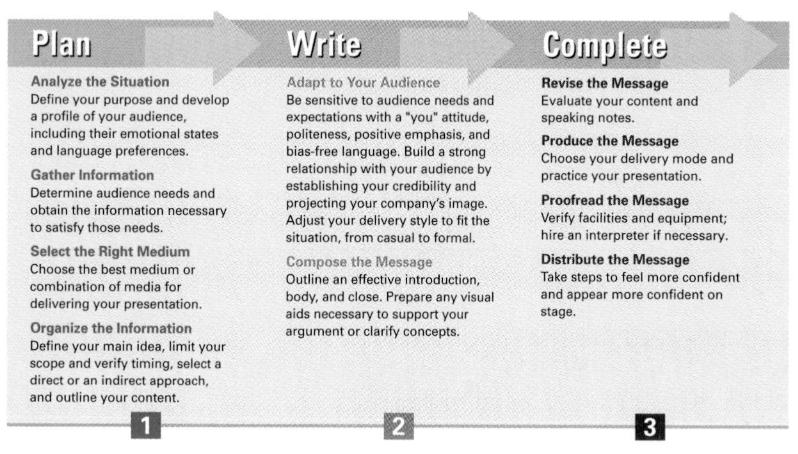

Emphasis on Process and Product

To help students write business messages quickly, easily, and effectively, chapters are organized into a series of three easy-to-follow steps (planning, writing, and completing business messages). In this eighth edition, the process has been further improved to present steps in a more logical order. A "Three-Step Writing Process" graphic not only illustrates the general process but is also applied to specific examples throughout the book.

Checklists

Useful during the course and even years after completion, checklists help students organize their thinking when they begin a project, make decisions as they write, and check their own work. Serving as reminders rather than "recipes," these checklists provide useful guidelines without limiting creativity. In the eighth edition, we've improved the checklists by making them more concise, action oriented, and tightly correlated with the wording of the text.

Sample Documents with Annotated Comments

Students can examine numerous sample documents, many collected by the authors in their consulting work at well-known companies. Some documents are accompanied by a three-step-writing-process graphic, and all documents include marginal annotations to help students understand how to apply the principles being discussed.

Documents for Analysis

Students have the opportunity in every chapter to critique and revise a wide selection of documents, including letters, memos, e-mail, graphic aids, and résumés. Hands-on experience in analyzing and improving sample documents helps students revise their own business messages.

Exercises and Cases

Hundreds of exercises challenge students with practical assignments like those they will most often face at work. Each exercise is labeled by type (such as "Team," "Ethical Choices," "Self-Assessment," or "Internet") to make it easier for instructors to assign specific types of homework activities. Exercises appear in each chapter of the book.

Real-world cases are generally based on actual organizations and appear in Chapters 7–9, 11–12, and 14–15. In Chapters 7–9, because instant messaging is rapidly becoming the preferred communication tool for many businesspeople, **instant messaging cases have been included, a first for a business communication text.**

ONEKEY ONLINE COURSES

OneKey offers the best teaching and learning online resources all in one place. OneKey is all instructors need to plan and administer their course. OneKey is all students need for anytime, anywhere access to online course material. Conveniently organized by textbook chapter, these compiled resources help save time and help students reinforce and apply what they have learned. OneKey for convenience, simplicity, and success. *OneKey is available in three course management platforms: Blackboard, CourseCompass, and WebCT.*

For the Student

- **Companion Website** for students includes a student version of the PowerPoint package, an online Quizzing, the English-Spanish Audio Glossary of Business Terms, the Handbook of Grammar, Mechanics and Usage Practice Sessions, and the Business Communication Study Hall—which allows students to brush up on several aspects of business communication—grammar, writing skills, critical thinking, report writing, résumés, and PowerPoint development.
- **OneKey Online Support:** Learning Modules are provided for each chapter and are divided into approximately four sections. Each section has a pretest of five questions, a summary for review, an online learning activity, and a post-test of 10 questions. Also included in the OneKey website are the Peak Performance grammar assessment tool and "Document Makeovers" that allow students to practice their revision skills.

Instructor's Resource Center available online, in OneKey or on CD-ROM

The Instructor's Resource Center, available on CD, at www.prenhall.com, or in your OneKey online course, provides presentation and other classroom resources. Instructors can collect the materials, edit them to create powerful class lectures, and upload them to an online course management system.

Using the Instructor's Resource Center on CD-ROM, instructors can easily create custom presentations. Desired files can be exported to the instructor's hard drive for use in classroom presentations and online courses.

With the Instructor's Resource Center, you will find the following faculty resources:

- **PowerPoints**
  Two PowerPoint packages are available with this text. The first is a fully developed, non-interactive set of instructor's PowerPoints. The second is an enhanced, interactive version of the first with video clips and Web links in each chapter. Both versions contain teaching notes.
- **TestGen Test-Generating Software**
  The printed test bank contains approximately 100 questions per chapter including multiple-choice, true/false, short-answer, and scenario-based questions. Short-answer questions are questions that can be answered in one-to-five sentences. Scenario-based questions are essay type questions developed around a short scenario. (*Print version also available.*)
- **Instructor's Resource Manual**
  This comprehensive supplement provides all the assistance any instructor would ever need. The manual includes a course planning guide, a cooperative learning guide for groups and small teams, a collaborative writing guide, diagnostic tests of English skills, a video guide, and chapter guides for each chapter in the text. The chapter guides include a chapter outline, lecture notes, answers to "Special Features," instructions for when to best use each overhead transparency, answers to all end-of-chapter questions and exercises, and suggested solutions in the form of fully formatted documents for every case in chapters 7, 8, and 9, plus selected cases in other chapters. (*Print version also available.*)
- **Test Item File (*Word file*)**
- **Art Files from the Text**

Transparencies

A set of color transparencies is available to instructors upon request. The acetates highlight text concepts and supply facts and information to help bring concepts alive in the classroom and enhance the classroom experience. (*In print only.*)

Student Study Guide

This study guide includes a chapter outline, review questions, and study quizzes. Page references to the review questions and quizzes are included.

Video Series with Teaching Guides

Topic videos highlight five key areas in business communication including culture and technology. All five clips are available on VHS and four selected clips are available on DVD.

Author's E-Mail Hotline for Faculty at hotline@leadingtexts.com

REVIEWERS

We especially want to thank the reviewers of this new, eighth edition. Their detailed and perceptive comments resulted in excellent refinements. These reviewers include the following:

Timothy Alder, *Pennsylvania State University—University Park*
Heather Allman, *University of West Florida*
Janice Cooke, *University of New Orleans*
Terry Engebretsen, *Idaho State University*
Joyce Hicks, *Valparaiso University*
Lynda Hodge, *Guilford Technical Community College*
Mary Humphrys, *University of Toledo*
Iris Johnson, *Virginia Commonwealth University*
Marsha Kruger, *University of Nebraska—Omaha*
Marianna Larsen, *Utah State University*
Anita Leffel, *University of Texas—San Antonio*
Richard Malamud, *California State University—Dominguez Hills*
Thomas Marshall, *Robert Morris University*
Leanne Maunu, *Palomar College*
Michael Mclane, *University of Texas—San Antonio*
Bronna McNeely, *Midwestern State University*
Holly Payne, *University of Southern Indiana*
Kathy Peacock, *Utah State University*
Folke Person, *Idaho State University*
Diza Sauers, *University of Arizona*
Lucinda Sinclair, *Longwood University*
Rodney Smith, *University of Dubuque*
Bruce Strom, *University of Indianapolis*
Dana Swesen, *Utah State University*
Dennielle True, *Florida Gulf Coast University*
Robyn Walker, *University of Arizona*
Judy Walton, *Howard University*

Thanks also to the many individuals whose valuable suggestions and constructive comments have contributed to the success of this book. The authors are deeply grateful for the efforts of the following:

Janet Adams, *Mankato State University*
Elaine Krajewski, *Louisiana State University*
Robert Allen, *Northwest Connecticut Community College*
John Lammers, *University of Illinois*
Lillie Anderton-Lewis, *North Carolina A&T State University*
Reva Leeman, *Portland Community College*
J. Douglas Andrews, *University of Southern California*
Pauline Ann Buss, *William R. Harper College*
Carol Lutz, *University of Texas—Austin*
Lois J. Bachman, *Community College of Philadelphia*
Ethel A. Martin, *Glendale Community College*
Jane Beamish, *North Country Community College*
Kenneth R. Mayer, *Cleveland State University*
Jane Bennett, *Dekalb College*
Gertrude M. McGuire, *University of Montevallo*
Mary Bresnahan, *Michigan State University*
Mary Meredith, *University of Louisiana*
Vivian Brown, *Laredo Community College*

Willie Minor, *Phoenix College*
Julian Caplan, *Borough of Manhattan Community College*
Evelyn P. Morris, *Mesa Community College*
Donald Crawford, *West Georgia College*
Glynna Morse, *Georgia College*
Susan Currier, *California Polytechnic State University*
Linda Munilla, *Georgia Southern College*
David P. Dauwalder, *California State University, Los Angeles*
Tom Musial, *Saint Mary's University*
Richard David Ramsey, *Southeastern Louisiana University*
Alexa North, *Georgia State University*
Carol David, *Iowa State University*
Devern Perry, *Brigham Young University*
Rod Davis, *Ball State University*
Paul Preston, *University of Texas, San Antonio*
Sauny Dills, *California Polytechnic State University*
Thomas P. Proietti, *Monroe Community College*
James Dubinsky, *Virginia Polytechnic Institute and State University*
Virgil R. Pufahl, *University of Wisconsin—Platteville*
Earl A. Dvorak, *Indiana University—Bloomington*
Nelda Pugh, *Jefferson State College*
Susan Eisner, *Ramapo College*
Claudia Rawlins, *California State University—Chico*
Nanette Clinch Gilson, *San Jose State University*
Sheryll Roeber, *University of Nebraska*
James L. Godell, *North Michigan University*
Lillian E. Rollins, *Dekalb College*
Kenneth Gorman, *Winona State University*
Jim Rucker, *Fort Hays State University*
Norma J. Gross, *Houston Community College*
W. J. Salem, *Central Michigan University*
Florence Grunkemeyer, *Ball State University*
Grant T. Savage, *Texas Tech University*
Francis N. Hamlet, *Longwood College*
Dorothy Sibley, *Brevard Community College*
Maxine Hart, *Baylor University*
Carla L. Sloan, *Liberty University*
Bill Hendricks, *California University, Pennsylvania*
Jeremiah J. Sullivan, *University of Washington*
William Hendricks, *Temple University*
Roberta M. Supnick, *Western Michigan University*
Susan Hilligoss, *Clemson University*
Rose Ann Swartz, *Ferris State University*
Louise C. Holcomb, *Gainesville Junior College*
Sumner B. Tapper, *Northeastern University*
J. Kenneth Horn, *Southwestern Missouri State University*
Vincent Trofi, *Providence College*
Randolph H. Hudson, *Northeastern Illinois University*
Linda N. Ulman, *University of Miami*
Edna Jellesed, *Lane Community College*
Dona Vasa, *University of Nebraska*
Elizabeth Jenkins, *Pennsylvania State University*
Dr. Colleen Vawdrey, *Utah Valley State College*
Kathryn Jensen White, *University of Oklahoma*
David Victor, *Eastern Michigan University*
Barbara Jewell, *Pierce College*

Ruth A.Walsh, *University of South Florida*
Betty Johnson, *Stephen F. Austin State University*
John L. Waltman, *Eastern Michigan University*
Paul J. Killorin, *Portland Community College*
William Wardrope, *Southwest Texas State University*
Lorraine Krajewski, *Louisiana State University*
Mimi Will, *Foothill College*

Reviewers of the Document Makeover feature:

Lisa Barley, *Eastern Michigan University*
Ellen Leathers, *Bradley University*
Marcia Bordman, *Gallaudet University*
Diana McKowen, *Indiana University*
Jean-Bush Bacelis, *Eastern Michigan University*
Bobbie Nicholson, *Mars Hills College*
Bobbye Davis, *Southern Louisiana University*
Andrew Smith, *Holyoke Community College*
Cynthia Drexel, *Western State College*
Jay Stubblefield, *North Carolina Wesleyan College*
Kenneth Gibbs, *Worcester State College*
Dawn Wallace, *Southeastern Louisiana University*

Personal Acknowledgments

Business Communication Today, Eighth Edition, is the product of the concerted efforts of a number of people. A heartfelt thanks to our many friends, acquaintances, and business associates who provided us with valuable advice and support.

We are also indebted to Krispy Kreme Doughnuts, Ace Hardware, Swiss Army Brands, Target, Office Depot, Qantas, Petsmart, General Nutrition, Discovery Communications, Host Marriott Services, Carnival Cruise Lines, National Geographic Society, Greyhound Lines, Herman Miller Inc., and Kelly Services for granting us permission to use materials from their companies. The model memos and letters that are shown in this textbook on company stationery have been included to provide realistic examples of company documents for educational purposes. They do not always represent actual business documents created by these companies.

A very special acknowledgment to George Dovel, whose superb knowledge of technology, distinguished background, and wealth of business experience helped assure the soundness of this project.

Also, we are grateful to Terry Anderson, whose outstanding communication skills, breadth of knowledge, and organizational ability contributed to this book's clarity and completeness; to Jackie Estrada for her remarkable talents and special skills; to Lianne Downey for her unique insights and valuable experience; to Stef Gould for her artistry and exceptional abilities; to Gail Olson, for her dedication and attention to detail; to Joe Glidden for his valuable research efforts; to Todd Landis for his expertise and great ability to motivate; and to John Cutchen and Pam LaBruyere for their wise counsel and sound judgment.

We want to extend our warmest appreciation to the devoted professionals at Prentice Hall. They include Jerome Grant, president; Jeff Shelstad, vice president and editor-in-chief; David Parker, editor; Anke Braun, marketing manager; Denise Vaughn, editorial assistant; Ashley Keim, media project manager; Melissa Yu, assistant editor; all of Prentice Hall Business Publishing, and the outstanding Prentice Hall sales representatives. Finally, we thank Judy Leale, senior managing editor, production, and Cindy Durand, production editor, for their dedication, and we are grateful to Lynn Steines, project manager at Carlisle Communications; Suzanne Grappi, permissions editor; Melinda Alexander, photo researcher and website permissions; Liz Harasymczuk, interior and cover designer; and Janet Slowik, art director, for their superb work.

Courtland L. Bovée
John V. Thill

Dedication

To the millions of students throughout the world who have learned about business communication from Business Communication Today

and

to the Text and Academic Authors Association, which awarded Business Communication Today *its prestigious Award for Excellence*

and

to the Association for Business Communication, whose meetings and publications provide a valuable forum for the exchange of ideas and professional growth

PART 1

Understanding the Foundations of Business Communication

chapter 1

Achieving Success Through Effective Business Communication

LEARNING OBJECTIVES

After studying this chapter, you will be able to

1. Explain why effective communication is important to your success in today's business environment
2. Identify seven communication skills that successful employers expect from their employees
3. Describe the five characteristics of effective business communication
4. List six factors that make business communication unique
5. Describe five strategies for communicating more effectively on the job
6. Explain four strategies for using communication technology successfully
7. Discuss the importance of ethics in business communication and differentiate between ethical dilemmas and ethical lapses

COMMUNICATION CLOSE-UP AT AMERICAN AIRLINES CREDIT UNION

www.aacreditunion.org

Does the convenience of electronic banking ever start to feel a bit too machine-like? After dealing with ATMs, automated phone systems, and online transactions, do you long for that personal touch? If so, you're not alone. Many of today's customers are happy to bank efficiently, conveniently, and electronically. However, many others find such impersonal dealings cold and distant. At American Airlines Credit Union (AACU), Carol Brown, vice president of member and lending services, is trying to give customers interactive communication with a live person.

Brown and her team face a big challenge as they try to connect with 220,000 members around the world and make their banking experiences more personal. To help its online service feel warmer, AACU added live instant messaging chat to its website, giving members a direct link to member-service representatives (MSRs). The idea was to provide the same level of service online that a customer would receive at a branch location.

Before launching the new chat function, Brown's team spent a month composing well-thought-out answers to common questions and storing them in the chat system. During a session, system software lets MSRs search, recall, and paste answers into a chat window. This effort not only ensures

American Airlines Credit Union uses instant messaging to add a human touch to its customer communication efforts.

high-quality responses but also minimizes typing time—no more than five MSRs are online at one time, but they handle roughly 2,500 chat sessions every month.

AACU's website traffic grew 75 percent during the first 12 months that chat was available. Moreover, the AACU was recently named Credit Union of the Year by the National Association of Federal Credit Unions. Brown is convinced that live chat has not only helped personalize AACU's online communication but also strengthened the credit union's relationships with its members and improved its standing in the industry—all major goals of effective business communication.[1]

1 LEARNING OBJECTIVE

Explain why effective communication is important to your success in today's business environment

ACHIEVING SUCCESS IN TODAY'S COMPETITIVE ENVIRONMENT

Professionals such as Carol Brown will tell you that to succeed in business today, you need the ability to communicate with people both inside and outside your organization. Whether you are competing to get the job you want or to win the customers your company needs, your success or failure depends to a large degree on your ability to communicate.

Your career success depends on effective communication.

Communication is the process of sending and receiving messages, whether you are exchanging e-mail, giving a formal presentation, or chatting with co-workers around the espresso machine. However, communication is considered *effective* only when others understand your message correctly and respond to it the way you want them to. Effective communication helps you manage your work flow, improves business relationships, enhances your professional image, and provides a variety of other important benefits (see Figure 1.1). In all these activities, the essence of successful communication is sharing—providing data, information, and insights in an exchange that benefits both you and the people with whom you are communicating.[2]

Effective communication provides numerous benefits.

Communication is vital to every company's success.

Effective communication is at the center of virtually every aspect of business because it connects the company with all its **stakeholders**, groups affected in some way by the company's actions: customers, employees, shareholders, suppliers, neighbors, the community, and the nation.[3] If you want to improve efficiency, quality, responsiveness, or innovation, you'll need to do so with the help of strong communication. Conversely, when communication breaks down, the results can be anything from time-wasting to tragic (see "Communication Miscues: The High Cost of Failure"). At every stage of your career, communication is the way you'll succeed, and the higher you rise in your organization, the

FIGURE 1.1
The Benefits of Effective Communication

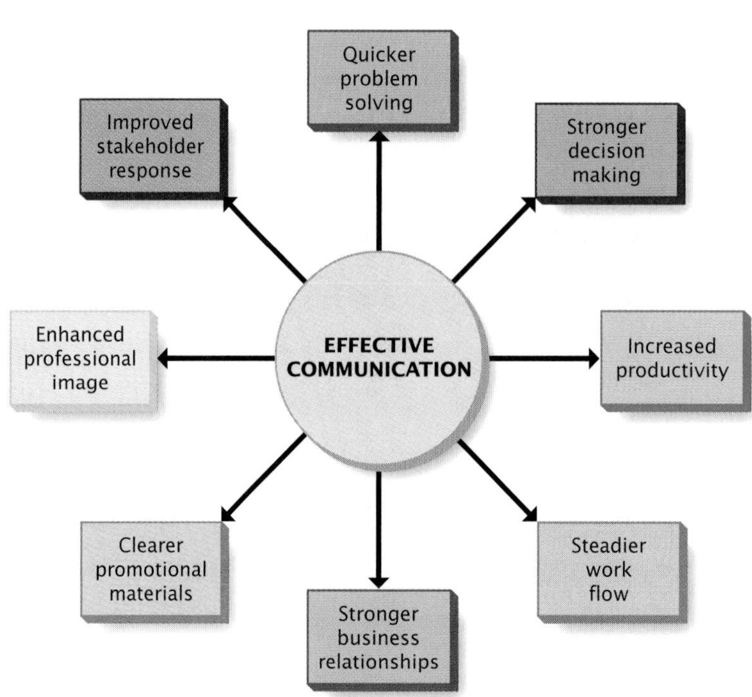

Communication Miscues

The High Cost of Failure

"No warning. Nothing. The train came and tried to kill us." That's how Ana Rosa Cabrera described the shock when 11 runaway cars from a Union Pacific freight train jumped the tracks and tore through her neighborhood east of Los Angeles in the summer of 2003.

After a series of errors and miscommunications, a string of 31 freight cars broke free in a switching yard in the town of Montclair on the morning of June 20. As the cars picked up speed on the downhill track, eventually traveling as fast as 86 miles per hour, railroad managers faced a tough decision. With no locomotive engine attached to the cars, they had no way to control or brake the runaways. Ahead on the track: other trains and downtown Los Angeles. Around noon, Union Pacific decided to switch the cars onto a siding track that led to another switching yard, hoping they'd make it that far and at least crash in a safer area. Unfortunately, the cars barreled over the switching device at more than three times the speed it was designed for. Eleven of them derailed and smashed into a residential neighborhood in the city of Commerce, demolishing several homes and damaging others. To everyone's amazement, no one was killed, but more than a dozen people received minor injuries.

Shock turned to anger when residents learned the cars had been diverted through Commerce on purpose and that Union Pacific had failed to warn local police, who might have had time to start evacuating homes in the cars' path. The railroad defended the decision to derail, saying it was the safest alternative in a tough situation, and government investigators reached the same conclusion.

The failure to warn anyone is another matter, of course, and Union Pacific's chief of railroad operations, Ted Lewis, acknowledges that: "We thought we had a system to notify in case we had an emergency, but we didn't."

CAREER APPLICATIONS

1. Are the residents of Commerce, California, stakeholders in Union Pacific? Please explain.
2. Can a complex business such as a railroad realistically plan a communication system that covers every possible situation like the one in Commerce? Please explain your answer.

more important it becomes. In fact, top managers spend as much as 85 percent of their time communicating with others.[4]

What Employers Expect from You

2 LEARNING OBJECTIVE

Identify seven communication skills that successful employers expect from their employees

No matter how good you are at accounting, law, science, or whatever professional specialty you pursue, most companies expect you to be competent at a wide range of communication tasks. Employers spend millions of dollars on communication training every year, but they expect you to come prepared with basic skills so that you can take full advantage of the learning opportunities they make available to you.

In fact, employers start judging your ability to communicate before you even show up for your first interview, and the process of evaluation never really stops. Improving your communication skills helps ensure that others will recognize and reward your talents and contributions. Fortunately, the specific skills that employers expect from you are the very skills that will help you advance in your career:

Employers are constantly evaluating your communication skills.

Employers expect you to maintain an acceptable level of basic communication skills.

- **Organizing ideas and information coherently and completely.** You'll often be required to find, process, and organize substantial amounts of raw data and random information so that others can easily grasp its significance.
- **Expressing and presenting ideas and information coherently and persuasively.** Whenever you're called on to offer an opinion or recommendation, you'll be expected to back it up with solid evidence. However, organizing your evidence well is only half the battle; you'll also need to convince your audience with compelling arguments.
- **Listening to others effectively.** Effective listening is not as easy as one might think. Amidst all the distractions on the job, you'll need to employ specific skills to find out what people are really trying to tell you. (For a more extensive discussion of listening, see Chapter 2.)

- **Communicating effectively with people from diverse backgrounds and experiences.** You'll often be called on to communicate across differences in gender, ethnic background, age, profession, and so on.
- **Using communication technologies effectively and efficiently.** Chances are you're already familiar with e-mail, **instant messaging** (an alternative to e-mail that allows two or more people to transmit text messages instantaneously), and online research. Increasingly, employers will also expect you to use web conferencing, electronic presentations, and a variety of other technological tools.
- **Communicating in a civilized manner that reflects contemporary expectations of business etiquette.** Even when the pressure is on, you'll be expected to communicate with courtesy and respect in a manner that is appropriate to the situation.
- **Communicating ethically, even when choices aren't crystal clear.** Whether you're simply reporting on the status of a project or responding to a complicated, large-scale crisis, you're certain to encounter situations that call for you to make sound ethical choices.

You'll have the opportunity to practice all these skills throughout this course—but don't stop there. Successful professionals continue to hone communication skills throughout their careers.

Characteristics of Effective Communication

You can have the greatest ideas in the world, but they're no good to your company or your career if you can't express them clearly and persuasively. As one project manager at NASA's Marshall Space Flight Center put it, "Knowledge may be power, but communication skills

FIGURE 1.2 Ineffective Communication

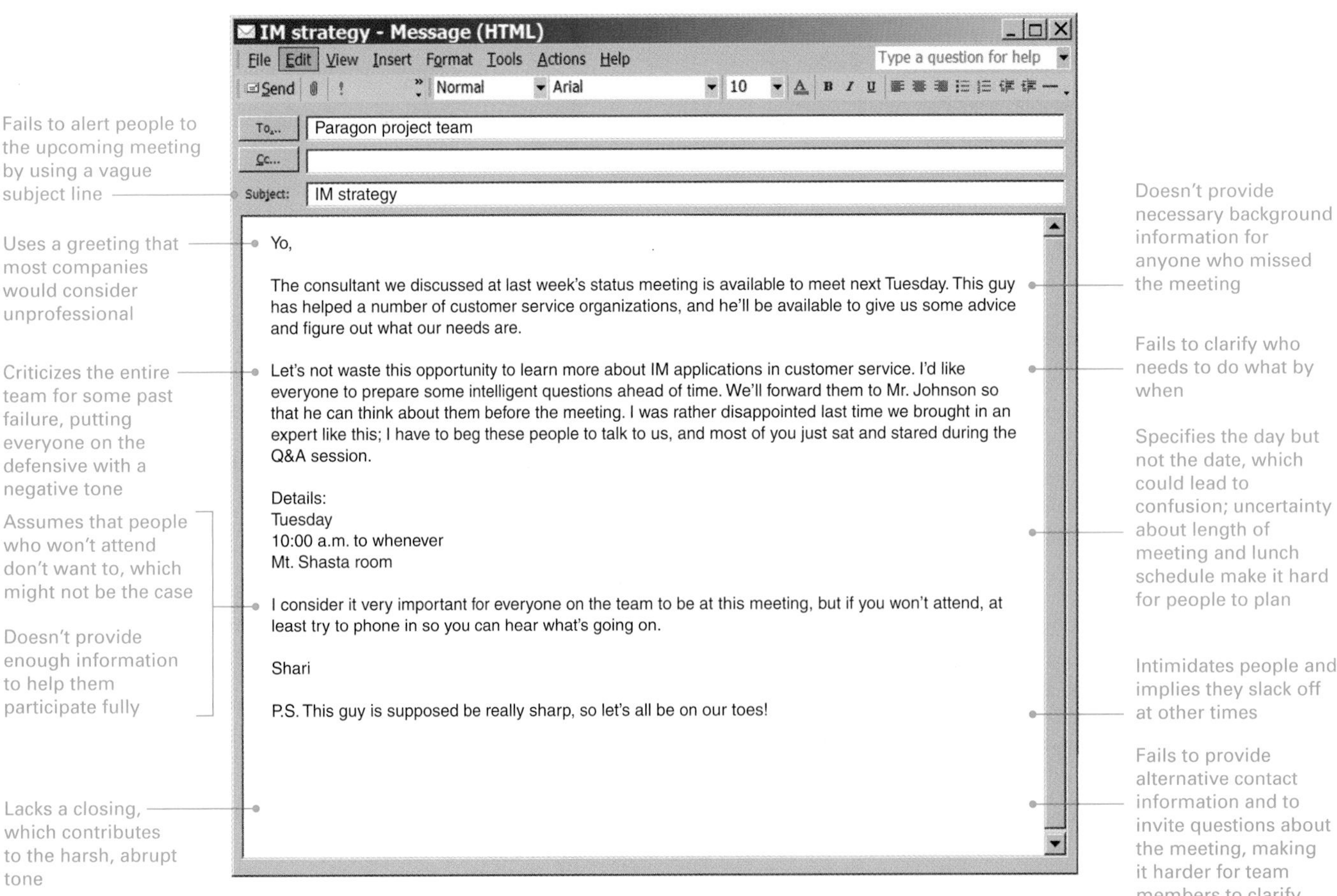

are the primary raw materials of good client relationships." Every job description for a new position on this manager's staff includes the following line: "Required—effective organization skills and mastery of the English language in written and oral forms."[5]

To make your messages effective, make them practical, factual, concise, clear about expectations, and persuasive:[6]

- **Provide practical information.** Give recipients useful information, whether it's to help them perform a desired action or understand a new company policy.
- **Give facts rather than impressions.** Use concrete language, specific detail, and information that is clear, convincing, accurate, and ethical. Even when an opinion is called for, present compelling evidence to support your conclusion.
- **Clarify and condense information.** Highlight the most important information, rather than dumping everything on the reader. Most business professionals find themselves wading in a flood of data and information. Messages that clarify and summarize are more effective than those that do not.
- **State precise responsibilities.** Write messages to generate a specific response from a specific audience. Clearly state what you expect from audience members or what you can do for them.
- **Persuade others and offer recommendations.** Show your readers precisely how they will benefit from responding to your message the way you want them to. Including reader benefits is the key to persuading employers, colleagues, customers, or clients to adopt a plan of action or purchase a product.

Keep these five important characteristics in mind as you review Figures 1.2 and 1.3. Both e-mails appear to be well-constructed at first glance, but Figure 1.2 is far less effective,

3 LEARNING OBJECTIVE

Describe the five characteristics of effective business communication

Effective business documents share five key attributes.

FIGURE 1.3 Effective Communication

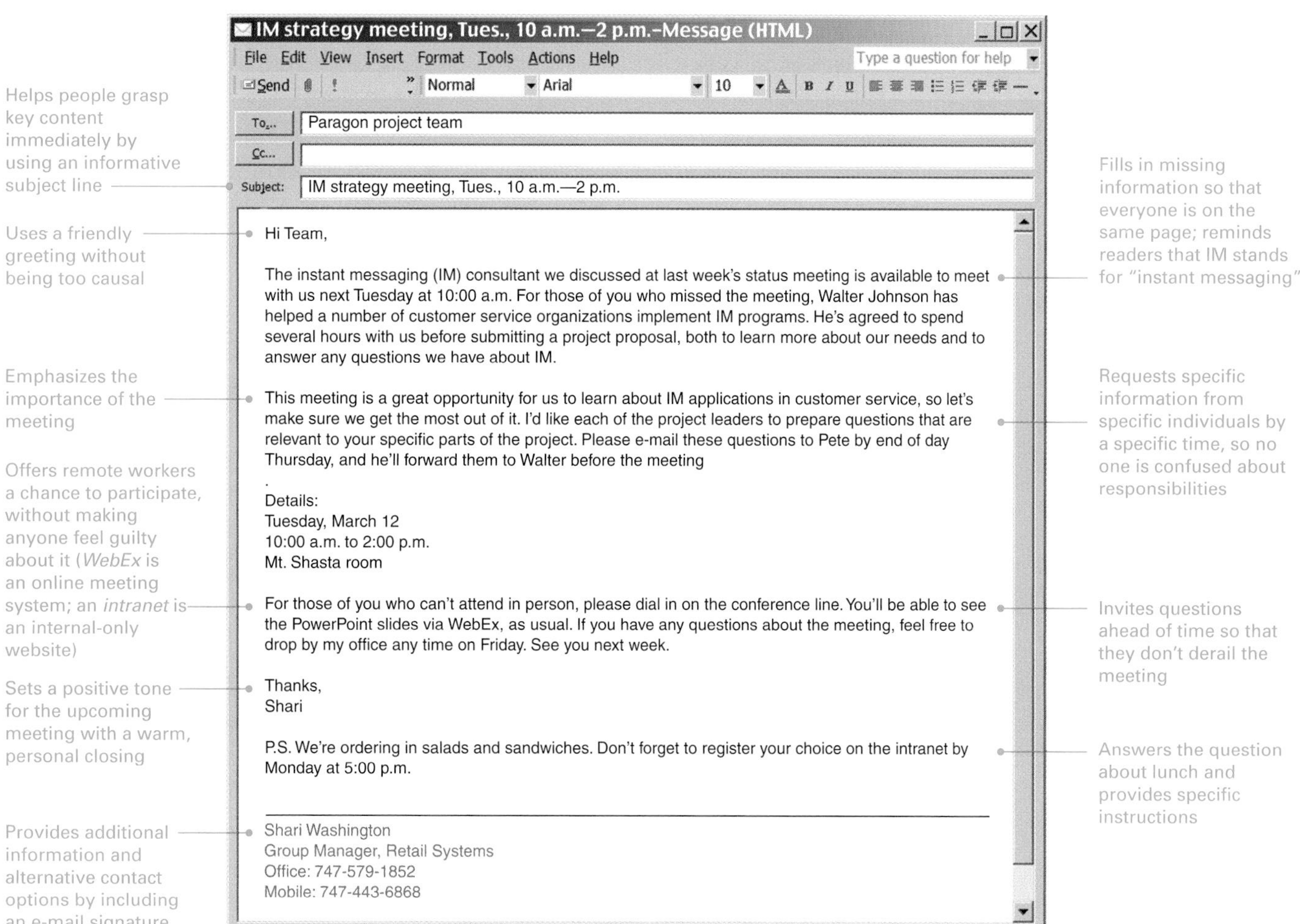

as explained in the margin comments. It shows the negative impact that poorly conceived messages can have on an audience. In contrast, Figure 1.3 shows how an effective message can help everyone work more efficiently (in this case, by helping them prepare effectively for an important meeting).

Communication in Organizational Settings

No matter what your level in the organization, you have an important communication role.

In every part of the business organization, communication provides the vital link between people and information. Whether you're a top manager or an entry-level employee, you have information that others need in order to perform their jobs, and others have information that is crucial to you. You exchange information with people inside your organization, called **internal communication**, and you exchange information and ideas with others outside your organization, called **external communication**. This information travels over both *formal* and *informal* channels (see Figure 1.4).

Formal and Informal Communication

Every organization has a **formal communication network,** in which ideas and information flow along the lines of command (the hierarchical levels) in your company's organization structure (see Figure 1.5). Throughout the internal formal network, information flows in three directions:

Formal communication flows in three directions.

- **Downward flow.** Downward communication flows from executives to employees, sharing executive decisions and providing information that helps employees do their jobs.
- **Upward flow.** Upward communication flows from employees to executives, providing accurate, timely reports on problems, trends, opportunities, grievances, and performance—thus allowing executives to solve problems and make intelligent decisions.
- **Horizontal flow.** Lateral or diagonal communication flows between departments to help employees share information and coordinate tasks. Such communication is especially useful for solving complex and difficult problems.[7]

Grapevines flourish when employees don't receive information they want or need.

Every organization also has an **informal communication network**—a *grapevine*—that operates anywhere two or more employees are in contact, from the lunchroom to the golf course to the company's e-mail and instant-messaging systems. Some executives are wary of the informal network, but savvy managers tap into it to spread and receive informal messages.[8] Grapevines tend to be most active when employees believe the formal network is not providing the information they want or need.

External communication flows into and out of the organization along formal lines (carefully prepared letters, announcements, e-mail messages, face-to-face meetings, and so on). It can also take place by informal means, such as discussing work with your friends, meeting potential sales contacts at industry gatherings, networking at social events, talking with customers, and so on. Although these interactions are informal, they

FIGURE 1.4
Forms of Communication

	Internal	External
Formal	Planned communication among insiders (letters, reports, memos, e-mail, instant messages) that follows the company's chain of command	Planned communication with outsiders (letters, reports, memos, speeches, websites, instant messages, and news releases)
Informal	Casual communication among employees (e-mail, instant messages, face-to-face conversations, and phone calls that do not follow the company's chain of command)	Casual communication with suppliers, customers, investors, and other outsiders (face-to-face conversations, e-mail, instant messages, and phone calls)

FIGURE 1.5 Formal Communication Network

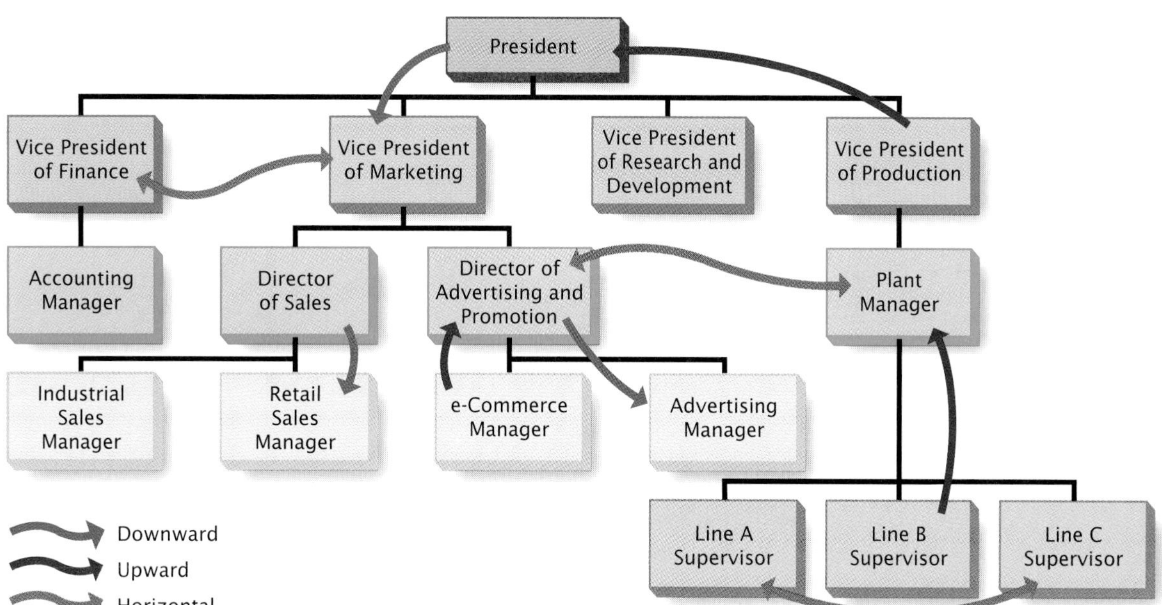

can still be vital to the company's success, so they require the same care and skill as formal communication.

In fact, these informal exchanges are considered so important that a new class of technology is springing up to enable them. *Social networking* software, such as Spoke Connect, and websites, such as LinkedIn.com and Ryze.com, help companies take advantage of all the connections their employees may have. These solutions typically work by indexing e-mail and instant-messaging address books, calendars, and message archives and then looking for connections between names. For instance, you might find that the sales lead you've been struggling to contact at a large customer might be a golf buddy of someone who works just down the hall from you.[9]

The Communication Process

Senders and receivers connect through a six-step process.

Whether you're having an impromptu exchange at lunch or making an elaborate multimedia presentation, the communication process connects sender and receiver (see Figure 1.6). The process consists of six phases:

1. **The sender has an idea.** You conceive an idea and want to share it.
2. **The sender encodes the idea.** When you put your idea into a message that your receiver will understand, you are **encoding** it. You decide on the message's form (words, facial expressions, gestures, illustrations, and so on), length, organization, tone, and style—all of which depend on your idea, your audience, and your personal style or mood.
3. **The sender transmits the message.** To transmit your message to your receiver, you select a **communication channel** such as the telephone, a letter, a memo, an e-mail—even a facial gesture. This choice of channel depends on your message, your audience's location, the media available to you, your need for speed, and the formality required.
4. **The receiver gets the message.** You have no guarantee that your message will actually get through. The receiver may not hear you, or your e-mail might get caught in an anti-spam filter. In fact, one of the biggest challenges you'll face as a communicator in today's crowded business environment is cutting through the clutter and noise in whatever medium you choose.
5. **The receiver decodes the message.** Your receiver tries to extract your idea from the message in a form that he or she can understand, a step known as **decoding**. If all goes well, the receiver interprets your message correctly, assigning the same meaning to your words as you intended and then responding in the way you desire.

FIGURE 1.6 The Communication Process

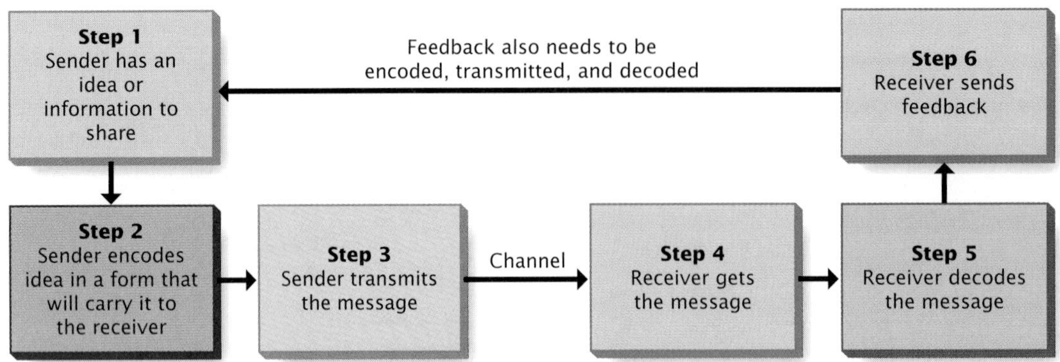

6. **The receiver sends feedback.** After decoding your message, the receiver has the option of responding in some way. This **feedback** enables you to evaluate the effectiveness of your message: Feedback often initiates another cycle through the process, which can continue until both parties are satisfied with the result. Successful communicators place considerable value on feedback, not only as a way to measure effectiveness but also as a way to learn.

Be aware that this is a simplified model; real-life communication is usually more complicated. Both sender and receiver might be talking at the same time, or the receiver might be trying to talk on the phone with one person while instant messaging with another, or the receiver may ignore your request for feedback, and so on.

UNDERSTANDING WHY BUSINESS COMMUNICATION IS UNIQUE

4 LEARNING OBJECTIVE

List six factors that make business communication unique

The complexity of business communication makes it vulnerable to factors such as
- Globalization and diversity
- Growing value of information
- Technology
- Teamwork
- Organizational structures
- Communication barriers

Business communication is far more demanding than the communication you typically engage in with family, friends, and school associates. Expectations are higher on the job, and the business environment is so complex that your messages can fail for reasons you've never even heard of before. Business communication is affected by factors such as the globalization of business and the increase in workforce diversity, the increasing value of information, the pervasiveness of technology, the growing reliance on teamwork, the evolution of organizational structures, and numerous barriers to successful communication.

The Globalization of Business and the Increase in Workforce Diversity

Chances are your career will involve communicating with colleagues or customers in other countries.

Today's businesses increasingly reach across international borders to market their products, partner with other businesses, and employ workers and executives—an effort known as **globalization.** A number of companies and brands that you may think of as U.S. organizations (including Ben & Jerry's, Dr. Pepper, Pillsbury, Carnation, and Shell Oil), are in fact owned by organizations based in other countries.[10] Likewise, many U.S. companies rely on exports for a significant portion of their sales, often more than 50 percent. Companies such as Boeing, Microsoft, Coca-Cola, and Ford, among many others, frequently communicate with customers and colleagues in other countries.

People with different cultural backgrounds and life experiences may have different communication styles.

As people and products cross borders, businesses of all shapes and sizes are paying more attention to **workforce diversity**—all those differences among the people you come into contact with on the job, including age, gender, sexual orientation, education, cultural background, life experience, and so on. Consider a 20-year-old man from a small town in the West and a 60-year-old woman from a large city on the East Coast. Even if they share the same ethnic background, they might have more trouble communicating than two next door neighbors of different ethnic background who grew up immersed in the same culture. As Chapter 3 discusses in more detail, successful companies realize two important facts: (1) the more diverse their workforce, the more attention they need to pay to communication, and (2) a diverse workforce can yield a significant competitive advantage by bringing more ideas and broader perspectives to bear on business challenges.

At Staples, managers must communicate clearly with the employees they supervise, regardless of differences in their age, gender, culture, or ethnic background.

The Increasing Value of Business Information

As competition for jobs, customers, and resources continues to grow, the importance of information continues to escalate as well. An organization's information is now every bit as important as its people, money, raw materials, and other resources. Even companies often not associated with the so-called Information Age, such as manufacturers, rely on **knowledge workers** at all levels of the organization, employees who specialize in acquiring, processing, and communicating information. The valuable information you'll be expected to communicate addresses such key areas as competitive insights, customer needs, and regulations and guidelines:

Information has become a company resource that is as important as any other.

Information deals with three areas of an organization's concerns.

- **Competitive insights.** Successful companies work hard to understand their competitors' strengths and weaknesses. The more you know about your competitors and their plans, the better you can adjust your own business plans.
- **Customer needs.** Most companies invest significant time and money in the effort to understand the needs of their customers. This information is collected from a variety of sources and needs to be analyzed and summarized so that your company can develop goods and services that better satisfy customer needs.
- **Regulations and guidelines.** Today's businesses must understand and follow a wide range of government regulations and guidelines covering such areas as employment, environment, taxes, and accounting. Your job may include the responsibility of researching and understanding these issues and then communicating them throughout the organization.

The Pervasiveness of Technology

Technology can help or hinder communication, depending on how it's designed and used.

Technology affects virtually every aspect of business communication. However, even those technological developments intended to enhance communication can actually impede it if they are not used intelligently. Moreover, staying on top of technology requires time, energy, and constant improvement of skills. If your level of technical expertise doesn't keep up with that of your colleagues and co-workers, the imbalance can put you at a disadvantage and complicate the communication process. For example, if instant messaging becomes popular in your organization but you resist or avoid it, you'll be excluded from an important communication channel.

For a concise overview of the technologies you're most likely to encounter, see "Using Technology to Improve Business Communication," later in this chapter. Throughout this course, you'll learn about numerous technological tools and systems, and it's important to have a general understanding of the Internet and its uses. If you'd like a brief introduction to the Internet and related technologies, click on "Internet Basics" at www.prenhall.com.bovee.

The Evolution of Organizational Structures

Organizations with tall structures may unintentionally restrict the flow of information.

As Figure 1.5 illustrates, every business has a particular structure that defines the relationships between the various people and departments within the organization. These relationships, in turn, affect the nature and quality of communication throughout the organization. Tall structures have many layers of management between the lowest and highest positions, so they can suffer communication breakdowns and delays as messages are passed up and down through multiple layers.

At Amy's ice cream parlors, the corporate culture of "fun" leads to an open communication climate and makes it easy for all employees to speak up.

To overcome such problems, many businesses are now adopting flatter structures that reduce the number of layers. The fewer the links in the communication chain, the less likely it is that misunderstandings will occur.[11] Moreover, flatter organizations help managers share information, pushing responsibility downward to give lower-level employees more responsibility for decision making, goal setting, and problem solving.[12] With fewer formal lines of control and communication in these organizations, you also take more responsibility for communication.

In the pursuit of speed and agility, some businesses have adopted flexible organizations that pool the talents of employees and external partners. For instance, when launching a new product, a company might supplement the efforts of internal departments with help from a public relations firm, an ad agency, a marketing consultant, a web developer, and a product distributor. With so many individuals and organizations involved in the project, everyone must share the responsibility for giving and getting necessary information, or else communication will break down.

Flatter organizational structures usually make it easier to communicate effectively.

Corporate cultures with an open climate benefit from free-flowing information and employee input.

Regardless of the particular structure a company uses, your communication efforts will also be influenced by the organization's **corporate culture**, the mixture of values, traditions, and habits that give a company its atmosphere and personality. Successful companies encourage employee contributions by making sure that communication flows freely down, up, and across the organization chart. Open climates encourage candor and honesty, helping employees feel free enough to admit their mistakes, disagree with the boss, and express their opinions. Of course, as with any honest relationship, sending or receiving negative news is not always easy. Employees need to be prepared not only to send negative news but also to hear constructive criticism from their supervisors. In fact, most employees want feedback from their managers so that they know what steps they must take to succeed.[13] Meanwhile, managers, need to overcome the natural inclination to smooth things over and avoid conflict; sometimes strong, negative feedback is a necessary first step to improvement.

The Growing Reliance on Teamwork

Roughly half of all North American companies now rely on teams extensively, and many others plan to do so in the future. Consequently, you'll probably find yourself on a number of teams throughout your career. As Chapter 2 discusses in detail, teams offer many potential advantages, from increasing employee satisfaction to improving an organization's flexibility and thus its ability to respond to competition.[14]

Working in a team makes you even more responsible for communicating effectively.

When teams replace or complement the formal channels in the organization chart, information may no longer be conveyed automatically, so every team member becomes more responsible for communication. This responsibility includes both sending and receiving messages; for example, you might seek out the information you need rather than waiting for someone to deliver it to you. In fact, you and your fellow team members may have to invent your own communication processes to make sure that everyone gets the right information at the right time. This extra attention to communication can pay off dramatically in higher performance and a more satisfying work experience.

Communication Solution

Carol Brown recognized that electronic conveniences such as ATMs were sometimes a barrier to effective communication between American Airlines Credit Union and its customers worldwide. The solution, ironically, was instant messaging—another electronic convenience, but one that supported human-to-human contact.

The Barriers to Effective Communication

Throughout your career, you'll find that perfectly effective messages can fail for a variety of reasons. Your attempts to transmit and receive messages can be disrupted, distorted, even blocked by **communication barriers** such as these:

- **Distractions.** Business messages can be interrupted or distorted by a wide variety of distractions. Physical distractions range from bad connections and poor acoustics to illegible printing and uncomfortable meeting rooms. Emotional distractions can affect

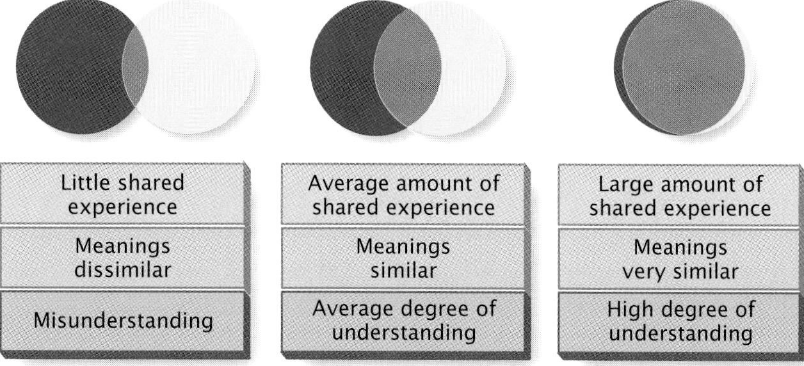

FIGURE 1.7
How Shared Experience Affects Understanding

the way you prepare and deliver messages and the way your audiences interpret those messages.

- **Information overload.** The sheer number of messages that people receive on the job can be distracting. Too many messages can result in **information overload**, which makes it difficult to discriminate between useful and useless information. E-mail traffic alone is mushrooming toward an estimated 60 billion messages a day, and you still have to contend daily with dozens of phone messages, traditional mail pieces, instant messages, and other interruptions. The chairman of Intel, Andy Grove, receives so much e-mail that it takes the equivalent of two or three people working full time just to handle it all.[15]
- **Perceptual differences.** Our minds organize incoming sensations into a mental map that represents our individual **perception** of reality. As a sender, you choose the details that seem important to you. As a receiver, you try to fit new details into your existing pattern; however, if a detail doesn't quite fit, you are inclined to distort the information rather than rearrange your pattern—a process known as **selective perception.**[16] The more experiences you share with another person, the more likely you are to share perception and thus share meaning (see Figure 1.7).
- **Language differences.** The very language we use to communicate can turn into a barrier if two people define a given word or phrase differently. When a boss asks for something "as soon as possible," does that mean within 10 seconds, 10 minutes, 10 days?
- **Restrictive environments.** Companies that restrict the flow of information, either intentionally or unintentionally, limit their competitive potential. With their many levels between top and bottom, tall hierarchies often result in significant loss of message quality in both directions.[17]
- **Deceptive tactics.** Given the difficulty of communication in the best of circumstances, deceptive communication is regrettably easy. Unscrupulous communicators can present opinions as facts, omit crucial information, exaggerate benefits, or downplay risks.

COMMUNICATING MORE EFFECTIVELY ON THE JOB

5 LEARNING OBJECTIVE

Describe five strategies for communicating more effectively on the job

No single solution will overcome all communication barriers. However, a careful combination of strategies can improve your ability to communicate effectively. For example, you can minimize distractions, adopt an audience-centered approach, improve your basic communication skills, make your feedback constructive, and be sensitive to business etiquette.

Minimizing Distractions

Overcome physical distraction by
- Using common sense and courtesy
- Sending fewer messages
- Informing receivers of your message's priority

Everyone in the organization can help overcome distractions. Start by reducing as much noise, visual clutter, and interruption as possible. A small dose of common sense and courtesy goes a long way. Turn off that cell phone before you step into a meeting. Don't talk across the tops of cubicles when people inside them are trying to work. Be sensitive to personal differences, too; for instance, some people may be able to work with music blaring, but many others can't.

Don't let e-mail, instant messaging, or telephones interrupt you every minute of the day. Set aside time to attend to messages all at once so that you can think and focus the rest of the time. In fact, one of the most important steps you can take is simply sending fewer messages.

Writer Richard Saul Wurman summed up the great irony of the Information Age nicely: Information used to be a precious commodity, but now it's "like crabgrass; something to be kept at bay."[18] You never want to undercommunicate, but sending unnecessary messages or sending the right message to the wrong people is almost as bad. E-mail is compounding this problem, making it so easy to send and forward messages to dozens or hundreds of people at once. Think before you click that "send" button.

In addition, if you must send a message that isn't urgent or crucial, let people know so that they can prioritize. If a long report requires no action from recipients, tell them up front so that they don't have to search through it looking for action items. Most e-mail and voicemail systems let you mark messages as urgent; however, use this feature only when it's truly needed. Too many so-called urgent messages that aren't particularly urgent will lead to annoyance and anxiety, not action.

Emotionally charged situations require extra care when communicating.

Try to overcome emotional distractions by recognizing your own feelings and anticipating responses from others.[19] When a situation might cause tempers to flare, choose your words carefully. As a receiver, avoid placing blame and reacting subjectively.

Adopting an Audience-Centered Approach

Communication Solution

For AACU, adopting an audience-centered approach to communication meant installing a completely new mode of communication and training a staff of service specialists to interact with customers via instant messaging.

An **audience-centered approach** means focusing on and caring about the members of your audience, making every effort to get your message across in a way that is meaningful to them. Learn as much as possible about the biases, education, age, status, style, and personal and professional concerns of your receivers. If you're addressing strangers and unable to find out more about them, then try to project yourself into their position by using your common sense and imagination.

Keeping your audience's needs in mind helps you ensure successful messages.

The more you know about the people you're communicating with, the easier it will be to concentrate on their needs—which, in turn, makes it easier for them to hear your message, understand it, and respond positively. For instance, the presentation slide in Figure 1.8 takes an audience-centered approach. Rather than trying to cover all the technical and legal details that are often discussed in insurance plans, this slide addresses the common fears and worries that employees might have as their company moves to a new health insurance plan.

If you haven't had the opportunity to communicate with a diverse range of people in your academic career so far, you might be surprised by the different communication styles you will surely encounter on the job. Recognizing and adapting to your audience's style will not only improve the effectiveness of your communication but the quality of your working

FIGURE 1.8
PowerPoint Slide Showing Audience-Centered Communication

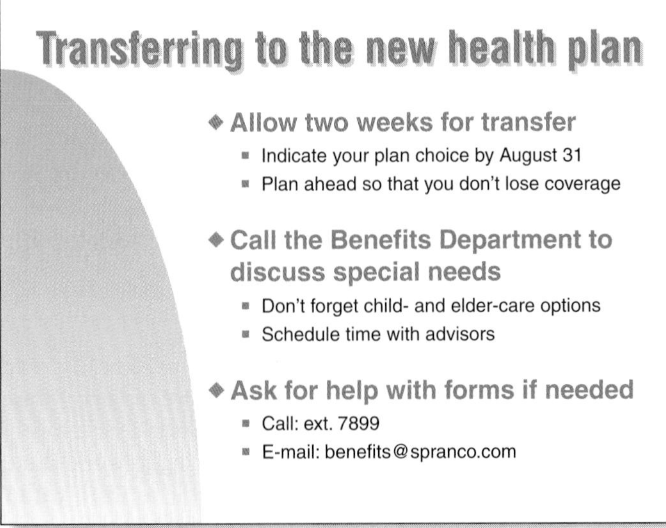

relationship as well.[20] The audience-centered approach is emphasized throughout this book, so you'll have plenty of opportunity to practice this approach to communicating more effectively.

Fine-Tuning Your Business Communication Skills

Your own skills as a communicator will be as much a factor in your business success as anything else. No matter what your skill level, opportunities to improve are numerous and usually easy to find. As mentioned earlier, many employers provide communication training in both general skills and specific scenarios, but don't wait. Use this course to begin mastering your skills now.

Work on your communication skills before you start your business career.

Lack of experience may be the only obstacle between you and effective communication. Perhaps you're worried about a limited vocabulary or uncertain about questions of grammar, punctuation, and style. If you're intimidated by the idea of writing an important document or appearing before a group, you're not alone. Everyone gets nervous about communicating from time to time, even people you might think of as "naturals." People aren't born writing and speaking well; they master these skills through study and practice. Someone who has written 10 reports or given 10 speeches is usually better at it than someone who has produced only two, so seek out opportunities to practice. Even simple techniques, such as keeping a reading log and writing practice essays, will improve not only your writing skills but also your scholastic performance.[21]

This course lets you practice in an environment that provides honest and constructive feedback. You'll have ample opportunity to plan and produce documents, collaborate in teams, listen effectively, improve nonverbal communication, and communicate across cultures—all skills that will serve your career well.

Giving—and Responding to—Constructive Feedback

Feedback doesn't end when you leave school, of course. While searching for employment and once on the job, you will encounter numerous situations in which you are expected to give and receive feedback. Whether giving or receiving criticism, be sure you do so in a constructive way. **Constructive feedback**, sometimes called *constructive criticism,* focuses on the process and outcomes of communication, not on the people involved (see Table 1.1). In contrast, **destructive feedback** delivers criticism with no effort to stimulate improvement.[22] For example, "This proposal is a confusing mess, and you failed to convince me of anything" is destructive feedback. Your goal is to be more constructive: "Your proposal could be more effective with a clearer description of the construction process and a well-organized explanation of why the positives outweigh the negatives." When giving feedback, avoid personal attacks and give the person clear guidelines for improvement.

Constructive feedback focuses on improvement, not personal criticism.

When you receive constructive feedback, resist the all-too-human impulse to defend your work or deny the validity of the feedback. Remaining open to criticism isn't always easy when you've poured your heart and soul into a project, but feedback is a valuable opportunity to learn and improve. Try to disconnect your emotions from the work and view it simply as something you can make better. Many writers also find it helpful to step back, think about the feedback for a while, and let their emotions settle down before diving in to make corrections. For all that, don't automatically assume that even well-intentioned feedback is necessarily correct. You have the responsibility for the final quality of the message, so make sure that any suggested changes are valid ones.

Try to react unemotionally when you receive constructive feedback.

Being Sensitive to Business Etiquette

In today's hectic, competitive world, the notion of **etiquette** (the expected norms of behavior in a particular situation) can seem outdated and unimportant. However, the way you conduct yourself can have a profound influence on your company's success and your career. When executives hire and promote you, they expect your behavior to protect the company's reputation. The more you understand such expectations, the better chance you have of avoiding career-damaging mistakes.

Understanding communication etiquette can help you avoid needless blunders.

TABLE 1.1 Giving Constructive Feedback

HOW TO BE CONSTRUCTIVE	EXPLANATION
Think through your suggested changes carefully	Since many business documents must illustrate complex relationships between ideas and other information, isolated, superficial edits can do more harm than good.
Discuss improvements rather than flaws	Instead of saying "this illustration is confusing," explain how it can be improved to make it clearer
Focus on controllable behavior	Since the writer may not have control over every variable that affected the quality of the message, focus on those things that the writer can control.
Be specific	Comments such as "I don't get this" or "Make this clearer" don't identify what the writer needs to fix.
Keep feedback impersonal	Focus comments on the message, not the person who created it.
Verify understanding	Ask for confirmation from the recipient to make sure that the person understood your feedback.
Time your feedback carefully	Make sure the writer will have sufficient time to implement the changes you suggested.
Highlight any limitations your feedback may have	If you didn't have time to give the document a thorough edit, or if you're not an expert in some aspect of the content, let the writer know so that he or she can handle your comments appropriately

Throughout this book, you'll encounter advice for a variety of business situations, but even if you don't know the specific expectations in a given situation, some general guidelines will get you through any rough spots. Start by being sensitive to the fact that people can have different expectations about the same situation. Something you find appalling or embarrassing might be business as usual for a colleague, and vice versa. At the same time, don't be overwhelmed by long lists of etiquette "rules." You'll never memorize all of them or remember to follow all of them in the heat of the moment.

Respect, courtesy, and common sense will get you through most etiquette challenges on the job.

Respect, courtesy, and common sense are three principles that will get you through just about anything; moreover, these principles will encourage forgiveness if you do happen to make a mistake. As you encounter new situations, take a few minutes to learn the expectations of the other people involved. Travel guidebooks are a great source of information about norms and customs in different countries. Don't be afraid to ask questions, either. People will respect your concern and curiosity. You'll gradually accumulate considerable knowledge, which will help you feel comfortable and be effective in a wide range of business situations.

Communication Solution

Technology by itself wasn't a complete solution to AACU's communication challenges; employees with solid communication skills and the motivation to help customers were just as important.

USING TECHNOLOGY TO IMPROVE BUSINESS COMMUNICATION

Today's businesses rely heavily on technology to improve the communication process. Companies and employees who use technology wisely can communicate more effectively and therefore compete more successfully.

Communicating in today's business environment nearly always requires some level of technical competence as well.

You will find that technology is discussed extensively throughout this book, with specific advice on using common tools to meet communication challenges. The four-page photo essay, "Powerful Tools for Communicating Efficiently" (pp. 18–21), offers an overview of the technologies that connect people in offices, factories, and other business settings. In addition, some aspects of communication technology are undergoing exciting changes almost daily. Technologies such as the following have the potential to dramatically enhance business communication:

Businesses use a variety of communication technologies to ensure the effectiveness of their messages.

- **Voice technologies.** The human voice will always be central to business communication, and it's being supplemented by a variety of new technologies. *Voice synthesis* regenerates a human speaking voice from computer files that represent words or parts of words. *Voice recognition* converts human speech to computer-compatible data. Both technologies continue to improve every year, gaining richer vocabularies and more human-sounding voices.

- **Virtual agents.** The dream of replicating or even surpassing human capabilities with computers has been driving artificial intelligence research for years. **Virtual agents** are a limited form of machine intelligence, also known as *bots* (derived from *robot*), *verbots*, and *V-reps*. These virtual operators are used in customer service departments and other areas where people tend to ask similar questions over and over. Through a combination of voice recognition, voice synthesis, and basic problem-solving skills, these virtual operators are some 40 percent faster than menu-based touch-tone calls, and they cost about half as much as a call handled by a human.[23] A variation on virtual phone communication is the virtual meeting, in which technology creates the illusion of sitting next to someone who might actually be thousands of miles away (see "Connecting with Technology: Extreme Telecommuting").
- **Mobile communication.** If you're accustomed to studying on the go, moving from dorm room to coffee shop to library, you'll fit right in with today's untethered work environments. In many cases, mobile workers don't even have traditional offices, using temporary cubicles at work, home offices, cars, airports, and even new Internet-equipped airplanes for office space.
- **Networking advances.** You might already be using four new networking technologies that are just now making serious inroads into the corporate world. Instant messaging lets two or more people connect virtually and exchange text instantaneously, without the delays of going through central e-mail servers. **Peer-to-peer (P2P) computing** extends this concept by letting multiple PCs communicate directly so that they can

(continued on page 22)

Connecting with Technology

Extreme Telecommuting

If traffic isn't too heavy, you might make it home from the airport in time for a few hours of sleep before turning around and heading right back for your next flight. The conference in Stockholm ran longer than expected, and now you need to hop another plane to Tokyo. A major customer wants to renegotiate your contract, and the situation is too sensitive and important for a mere phone call. You need to be there in person. As you crawl into bed, your sleepy brain remembers the telepresence system your office just installed. That'll do the trick, giving you an amazingly real presence in the meeting with your client—but without the 16-hour flight to get there. You unplug the alarm and sink deep into bed.

Telepresence systems start with the basic idea of videoconferencing but go far beyond with imagery so real that colleagues thousands of miles apart appear to be in the same room together. Business executives dissatisfied with the delays and image quality of conventional videoconferencing are turning to telepresence systems to stay connected with colleagues and customers—while avoiding the disruptions, costs, or perceived risks of travel.

Duke University's Fuqua School of Business installed a telepresence system to link its campuses in Durham, North Carolina, and Frankfurt, Germany. When meeting participants sit down at a table in one city, virtual participants from the other city appear to be sitting on the other side of the table. The effect is so real that some people think it's downright eerie. Not only can participants make eye contact across the Atlantic, but "you can stick your head in the room in Durham and hear the traffic of downtown Frankfurt," says Associate Dean Nevin Fouts.

Teliris is an early innovator in the technology and now offers telepresence to customers in major business centers around the world. Other developers are working on robotic telepresence, in which you'll be able to control a robot surrogate hundreds or thousands of miles away. Before long, you might be able to run your global empire from the conference room down the hall.

CAREER APPLICATIONS

1. Could an overreliance on telepresence affect business communications? Explain your answer.
2. What effect might telepresence have on the composition of the U.S. workforce?

Powerful Tools for Communicating Effectively

The tools of business communication evolve with every new generation of digital technology. Selecting the right tool for each situation can enhance your business communication in many ways. In today's flexible office settings, communication technology helps people keep in touch and stay productive. When co-workers in different cities need to collaborate, they can meet and share ideas without costly travel. Manufacturers use communication technology to keep track of parts, orders, and shipments—and to keep customers well-informed. Those same customers can also communicate with companies in many ways at any time of day or night.

Flexible Workstations

Many professionals have abandoned desktop PCs for laptops they can carry home, on travel, and to meetings. Back at their desks, a docking station transforms the laptop into a full-featured PC with network connection. Workers without permanent desks sometimes share PCs that automatically reconfigure themselves to access each user's e-mail and files.

Wireless Networks

Laptop PCs with wireless access cards let workers stay connected to the network from practically anywhere within the office—any desk, any conference room. This technology offers high-speed Internet access within range of a wireless access point.

Follow-Me Phone Service

To be reachable without juggling multiple forwarding numbers, some people have follow-me phone service. Callers use one number to reach the person anywhere—at the office, a remote site, a home office. The system automatically forwards calls to a list of preprogrammed numbers and transfers unanswered calls to voice mail.

Redefining the Office

Technology makes it easier for people to stay connected with co-workers and retrieve needed information. Some maintain that connection without having a permanent office, a desktop PC, or even a big filing cabinet. For example, Sun Microsystems lets staff members choose to work either at the main office or at remote offices called "drop-in centers." Many Sun facilities have specially equipped "iWork" areas that can quickly reconfigure phone and computer connections to meet individual requirements.

Electronic Presentations

Combining a color projector with a laptop or personal digital assistant (PDA) running the right software lets people give informative business presentations that are enhanced with sound, animation, and even website hyperlinks. Having everything in electronic form also makes it easy to customize a presentation or to make last-minute changes.

Intranets

Businesses use Internet technologies to create an intranet, a private computer network that simplifies information sharing within the company. Intranets can handle company e-mail, instant messaging (IM), websites, and even Internet phone connections. To ensure the security of company communication and information, intranets are shielded from the public Internet.

Communicating in the Office

Wall Displays

Teams commonly solve problems by brainstorming at a whiteboard. Wall displays take this concept one step further, letting participants transmit words and diagrams to distant colleagues via the corporate intranet. Users can even share the virtual pen to make changes and additions from more than one location.

Web-Based Meetings

Workers can actively participate in web-based meetings by logging on from a desktop PC, laptop, or cell phone. Websites such as WebEx help users integrate voice, text, and video and let them share applications such as Microsoft PowerPoint and Microsoft Word in a single browser window.

Collaborating

Working in teams is essential in almost every business. Teamwork can become complicated, however, when team members work in different parts of the company, in different time zones, or even for different companies. Technology helps bridge the distance by making it possible to brainstorm, attend virtual meetings, and share files from widely separated locations. Communication technology also helps companies save money on costly business travel without losing most of the benefits of face-to-face collaboration.

Internet Videophone

Person-to-person video calling has long been possible through popular instant messaging programs. Internet videophone services do even more, letting multiple users participate in a videoconference without the expense and complexity of a full-fledged videoconferencing system. Some services are flexible enough to include telecommuters who have broadband Internet connections.

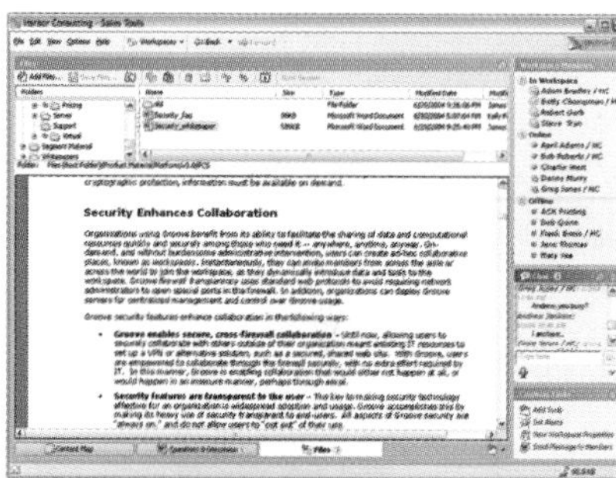

Shared Workspace

Online workspaces such as eRoom and Groove make it easy for far-flung team members to access shared files anywhere, anytime. Accessible through a browser, the workspace contains a collection of folders and has built-in intelligence to control which team members can read, edit, and save specific files.

Videoconferencing and Telepresence

Less costly than travel, videoconferencing provides many of the same benefits as an in-person meeting. Advanced systems include telepresence and robot surrogates, which use computers to "place" participants in the room virtually, letting them see and hear everyone while being seen and heard themselves. Such realistic interaction makes meetings more productive.

Warehouse RFID

In an effort to reduce the costs and delays associated with manual inventory reports, Wal-Mart requires its top suppliers to put radio-frequency identification (RFID) tags on all their shipping cases and pallets. These tags automatically provide information that was previously collected by hand via barcode scanners.

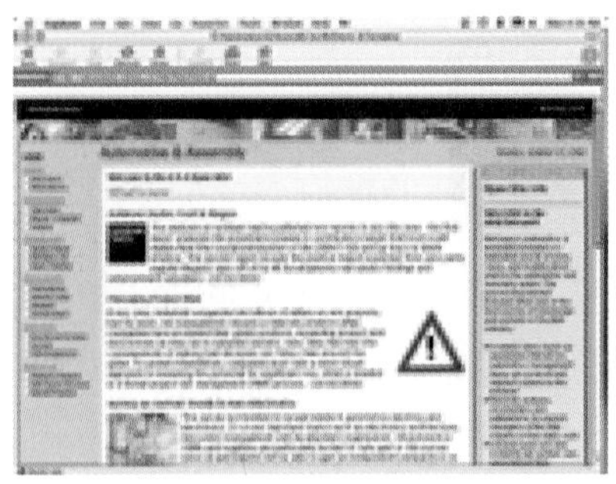

Extranet

Extranets are secure, private computer networks that use Internet technology to share business information with suppliers, vendors, partners, and customers. Think of an extranet as an extension of the company intranet that is available to people outside the organization by invitation only.

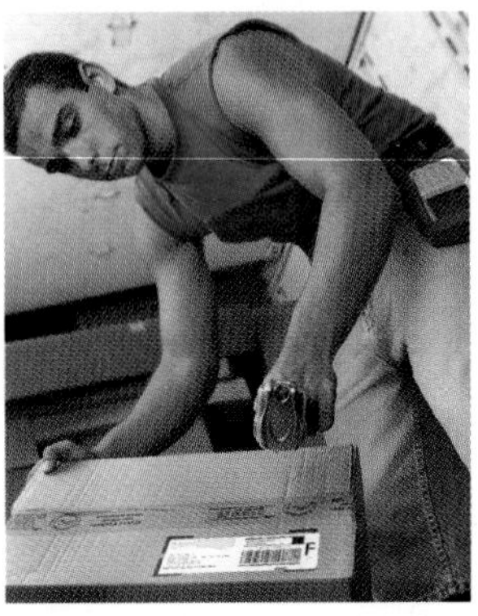

Wireless Warehouse

Communication technology is a key source of competitive advantage for shipping companies such as FedEx and UPS. Hand-worn scanners use wireless links to help warehouse personnel access instant information that lets them process more packages in less time at transit hubs. Currently, 300 package loaders at four UPS hub facilities are testing the new wireless application called UPScan. A pager-size cordless scanner worn on the loader's hand captures data from a package bar code and transmits the data via Bluetooth® wireless technology to a Symbol Technologies wireless terminal worn on the loader's waist.

Sharing the Latest Information

Companies use a variety of communication technologies to create products and services and deliver them to customers. The ability to easily access and share the latest information improves the flow and timing of supplies, lowers operating costs, and boosts financial performance. Easy information access also helps companies respond to customer needs by providing them timely, accurate information and service and by delivering the right products to them at the right time.

Package Tracking

Senders and receivers often want frequent updates when packages are in transit. Handheld devices such as the FedEx PowerPad enhance customer service by letting delivery personnel instantly upload package data to the FedEx network. The wireless PowerPad also aids drivers by automatically receiving weather advisories.

Supply Chain Management

Advanced software applications let suppliers, manufacturers, and retailers share information—even when they have incompatible computer systems. Improved information flow increases report accuracy and helps each company in the supply chain manage stock levels.

Communicating About Products and Services

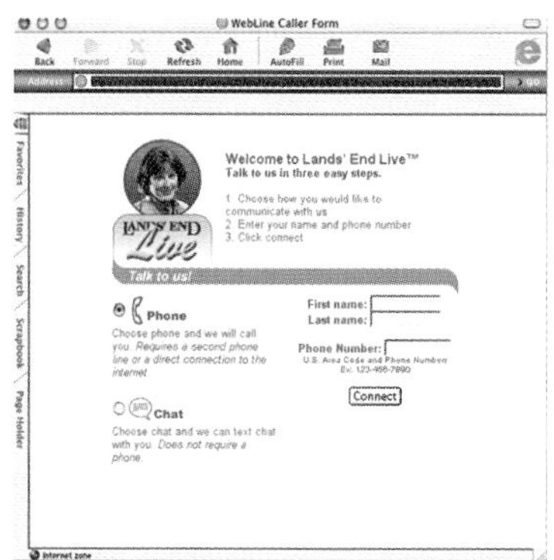

Over-the-Shoulder Support

For online shoppers who need instant help, many retail websites make it easy to connect with a live sales rep via phone or instant messaging. The rep can provide quick answers to questions and, with permission, can even control a shopper's browser to help locate particular items.

Help Lines

Some people prefer the personal touch of contact by phone. Moreover, some companies assign preferred customers special ID numbers that let them jump to the front of the calling queue. Many companies are addressing the needs of foreign-language speakers by connecting them with external service providers who offer multilingual support.

Interacting

Maintaining an open dialog with customers is a great way to gain a better understanding of their likes and dislikes. Today's communication technologies make it easier for customers to interact with a company whenever, wherever, and however they wish. A well-coordinated approach to phone, web, and in-store communication helps a company build stronger relationships with its existing customers, which increases the chances of doing more business with each one.

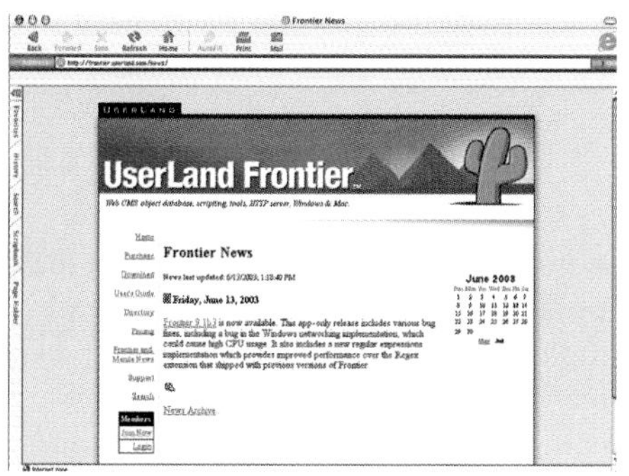

Corporate Blogs

Web-based journals let companies offer advice, answer questions, and promote the benefits of their products and services. Elements of a successful blog include frequent updates and the participation of knowledgeable contributors. Adding a subtle mix of useful commentary and marketing messages helps get customers to read or listen to them.

Retail RFID

Customers can't buy what they can't find, and manual reporting is often too slow for fast-paced retailing. To keep enough goods on the shelves, some retailers use RFID tags to monitor products on display. Clerks use wireless readers to scan tagged products and report stock data to a computerized inventory system that responds with an up-to-the-minute restocking order.

In-Store Kiosks

Staples is among the retailers that let shoppers buy from the web while they're still in the store. Web-connected kiosks were originally used to let shoppers custom-configure their PCs, but the kiosks also give customers access to roughly 8,000 in-store items as well as to the 50,000 products available online.

share files or work on large problems simultaneously. **Wireless networking**, commonly know as *Wi-Fi*, extends the reach of the Internet with wireless access points that connect to PCs and handheld devices via radio signals. **Short messaging service (SMS)** is a text communication feature that has been common on mobile phones in other parts of the world for several years and has recently gained a presence in North America. Instead of interrupting people with a voice call, you simply key in a text message and send it to another phone. The First National Bank in South Africa uses SMS to improve Internet banking security for its customers. Whenever an account is accessed online, the bank immediately sends a text message to the customer so he or she can verify that the access is legitimate.[24] (Note that while *instant messaging* and *text messaging* perform a similar function, and some people use the terms interchangeably, instant messaging is generally considered a computer-to-computer activity and text messaging is a phone-to-phone or computer-to-phone function.)

Even though such impressive enhancements are available, anyone who has used a computer knows that the benefits of technology are not automatic. When poorly designed or inappropriately used, technology can harm communication more than it helps. To communicate effectively, you need to keep technology in perspective, use technological tools productively, spend time and money on technology wisely, and disengage from the computer frequently to communicate in person.

6 LEARNING OBJECTIVE

Explain four strategies for using communication technology successfully

Keeping Technology in Perspective

Technology is an aid to interpersonal communication, not a replacement for it. This fact may seem obvious, but you can easily lose sight of it. Technology can't think for you or communicate for you, and if you lack some essential skills, technology probably can't fill in the gaps.

The spellchecker in your word processor is a great example. It's happy to run all your words through the dictionary, but it doesn't know whether you're using the correct words or the best words possible. Similarly, presentation software such as Microsoft PowerPoint can decorate your slide show with color, animation, sound bites, dancing text, and even video clips, but you have to provide the well-thought-out content.

Don't let technology overwhelm the communication process.

Technology is not always the answer to your communication needs. The sheer number of possibilities in many technological tools can get in the way of successful communication. For example, both senders and receivers may be distracted if they're having trouble configuring their computers to participate in an online meeting. Or the content of a message may be obscured if an electronic presentation is overloaded with visual effects. Moreover, if technological systems aren't adapted to a user's (or an organization's) needs, people won't adapt to the technology—they won't use it effectively, or worse, they won't use it at all.

Recent advances in technology make it possbile for all business communicators to create presentations that once required expensive professional equipment and specialized skills. With Visual Communicator from Serious Magic, you can easily combine audio, video, and PowerPoint slides to create multimedia presentations.

Using Technological Tools Productively

You don't have to become an expert to use most communication technologies effectively, but you will need to be familiar with the basic features and functions of the tools your employer expects you to use. If you don't know the basic functions of your word processor, you could spend hours trying to format a document that a skilled user could format in minutes. Similarly, if you can't figure out how to tell your phone or instant-messaging system that you don't want to be disturbed, your day will be full of interruptions.

People who are proficient at using their technological tools can produce impressive results, but the expectations of production quality seem to increase with every new capability. Only a few years ago, the norm for presentations was typed content on overhead transparencies. Today's standard is computer-based, full-color presentations on liquid crystal displays (LCDs). The presentations are certainly more attractive and sometimes more effective, but the technology has forced millions of businesspeople to learn a new set of skills. At some point in the future, you might have to learn how to program your virtual identity robot to attend meetings for you. Technology will always require some new skill to be learned. Whatever the tool, if you learn the basics, your work will be less frustrating and far more productive.

Develop at least a working knowledge of the technology your employer expects you to use.

Spending Time and Money on Technology Wisely

Computers and other technologies used in business communication are often promoted as time savers and efficiency boosters, but such benefits don't always materialize. No one using a typewriter ever lost a month's work because a hard drive crashed or ever wasted an hour trying to decide which font to use. You have a responsibility to invest your time—and your company's money—wisely. To do so, you may often need to make tough decisions, because you won't always have enough time to make everything perfect.

As with many of the tasks that you'll face on the job, you'll need to strike a balance between the importance of the communication activity and the time and money you invest in it. You'll need to consider potential consequences, both positive and negative, and then spend sufficient time and money to achieve acceptable results for each individual situation. Should you spend a couple of days planning and designing a presentation to fellow employees about the company picnic? No, but such an investment might well make sense if your presentation had to explain why the company needs to move to a new city. Such a message would generate considerable anxiety and plenty of questions, so it needs to be planned and presented with great care. Extra attention to planning and design will help calm nervous employees and reduce stress.

Balance the needs of each communication activity with the time and money you'll invest in its technology.

Reconnecting with People Frequently

In spite of technology's efficiency and speed, it may not be the best choice for every communication situation. For one thing, even in the best circumstances, technology can't match the rich experience of person-to-person contact. Technological tools such as e-mail, instant messaging, and voicemail can't always convey the necessary emotional and nonverbal aspects of communication, which can cause unnecessary confusion and aggravation.[25] Let's say you e-mail a colleague asking how she did with her sales presentation to an important client, and her answer comes back simply as "Fine." What does *fine* mean? Is an order expected soon? Did she lose the sale? Was the client rude and she doesn't want to talk about it? If you reconnect with her, perhaps visit her in person, she might provide additional information, or you might be able to offer advice or support during a difficult time.

No matter how much technology is involved, communication is still about people connecting with people.

For another thing, most human beings need to connect with other people. You can create amazing documents and presentations without ever leaving your desk or meeting anyone in person. But if you stay hidden behind technology, people won't get to know you nearly as well. You might be funny, bright, and helpful, but you're just a voice on the phone or a name on a document until people can interact with you in person. As technological options increase, people seem to need the human touch even more. When Alan Hassenfeld, the CEO of game maker Hasbro, recently implored his employees to interact more in person and rely less on technological communication, they gave him a standing ovation.[26]

MAKING ETHICAL COMMUNICATION CHOICES

7 LEARNING OBJECTIVE

Discuss the importance of ethics in business communication and differentiate between ethical dilemmas and ethical lapses

Ethics are the principles of conduct that govern a person or a group. Unethical people say or do whatever it takes to achieve an end. Ethical people are generally trustworthy, fair, and impartial, respecting the rights of others and showing concern about the impact of their actions on society. Former Supreme Court Justice Potter Stewart defined ethics as "knowing the difference between what you have a right to do and what is the right thing to do."[27]

Ethical behavior is a companywide concern, of course, but communication is the public face of a company. Communication efforts are therefore subjected to rigorous scrutiny from regulators, legislators, investors, consumer groups, environmental groups, labor organizations, and anyone else affected by business activities. **Ethical communication** includes all relevant information, is true in every sense, and is not deceptive in any way. In contrast, unethical communication can include falsehoods and misleading information (or withhold important information). Some examples of unethical communication include[28]

Any time you try to mislead your audience, the result is unethical communication.

- **Plagiarism.** Stealing someone else's words or other creative product and claiming it as your own
- **Selective misquoting.** Deliberately omitting damaging or unflattering comments to paint a better (but untruthful) picture of you or your company
- **Misrepresenting numbers.** Increasing or decreasing numbers, exaggerating, altering statistics, or omitting numerical data
- **Distorting visuals.** Making a product look bigger or changing the scale of graphs and charts to exaggerate or conceal differences

An ethical message is accurate and sincere. It avoids language and images that manipulate, discriminate, or exaggerate. On the surface, such ethical practices appear fairly easy to recognize, but deciding what is ethical can be a considerable challenge in complex business situations.

Distinguishing Ethical Dilemmas from Ethical Lapses

Every company has responsibilities to its stakeholders, and those various groups often have competing interests. In some situations, what's right for one group may be wrong for another.[29] Moreover, as you attempt to satisfy the needs of a particular group, you may be presented with an option that seems right on the surface but somehow feels wrong. When people must choose between conflicting loyalties and weigh difficult tradeoffs, they are facing a dilemma.

An ethical dilemma is a choice between alternatives that may all be ethical and valid.

An **ethical dilemma** involves choosing among alternatives that aren't clear-cut (perhaps two conflicting alternatives are both ethical and valid, or perhaps the alternatives lie somewhere in the gray area between clearly right and clearly wrong). Suppose you are president of a company that's losing money. You have a duty to your shareholders to try to cut your losses and to your employees to be fair and honest. After looking at various options, you conclude that you'll have to lay off 500 people immediately. You suspect you may have to lay off another 100 people later on, but right now you need those 100 workers to finish a project. What do you tell them? If you confess that their jobs are shaky, many of them may quit just when you need them most. However, if you tell them that the future is rosy, you'll be stretching the truth.

An ethical lapse is knowing that something is wrong and doing it anyway.

Unlike a dilemma, an **ethical lapse** is a clearly unethical or illegal choice. When someone in the marketing department at Sony Pictures invented a fake movie critic to generate quotes of lavish praise for several of its movies, there was no ethical gray area. It was a clear case of deception. Even Sony's own spokeswoman later called it "a case of incredibly bad judgment."[30] With both internal and external communication efforts, the pressure to produce results and justify decisions can make unethical communication a tempting choice. Although the deception isn't often as blatant as using quotes from an imaginary movie critic, the effect can be just the same. The memo in Figure 1.9 paints a sunny picture of a business decision by presenting selective facts, whereas the memo in Figure 1.10 portrays a rather depressing—but honest—picture of that decision by presenting all the facts.

Ensuring Ethical Communication

To ensure ethical business communications, three elements need to be in place: ethical individuals, ethical company leadership, and the appropriate policies and structures to support employees' efforts to make ethical choices.[31] Moreover, these three elements need to work together in harmony. If employees see company executives making unethical deci-

FIGURE 1.9 Unethical Communication

SunStar Sports

Confidential Memorandum

TO: Executive Committee
FROM: Darcy O'Leary & Bob Caruthers, Product Management
DATE: October 23, 2005
SUBJECT: Pegasus market confirmation

We're pleased to announce that the numbers are in, and as we predicted before the research began, consumers show strong support for the Pegasus product concept. The results validate the several months we've invested in product design and should give a green light to fund the completion of the project.

We're particularly pleased with the results in this case, since the research was directed by Sadie McMahon at Bowerman Research. She has conducted hundreds of research projects and is known for her keen insights into the consumer market. Only a third of the consumers surveyed expressed little or no interest in Pegasus, and Sadie said that doesn't worry her at all since few products ever appeal to the entire market. With a two-thirds majority in our favor, this looks to be a winner before we even bring it to market.

Given the momentum we've already built up, coupled with this powerful endorsement of the concept, we're confident the executive committee will reach the same strategic conclusion that we have and continue funding the project.

Thank you for your support.

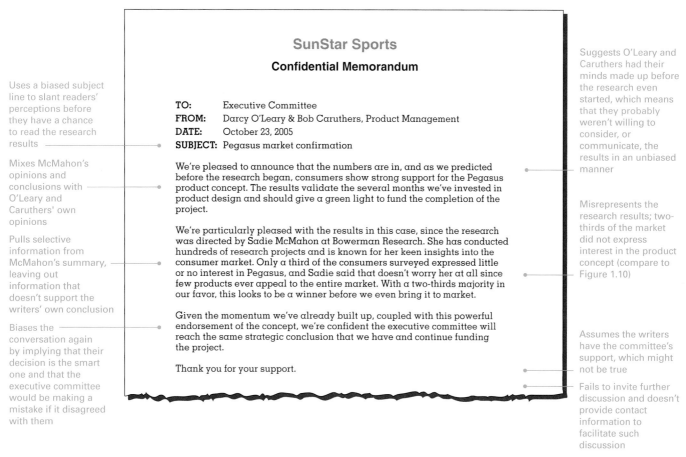

Uses a biased subject line to slant readers' perceptions before they have a chance to read the research results

Mixes McMahon's opinions and conclusions with O'Leary and Caruthers' own opinions

Pulls selective information from McMahon's summary, leaving out information that doesn't support the writers' own conclusion

Biases the conversation again by implying that their decision is the smart one and that the executive committee would be making a mistake if it disagreed with them

Suggests O'Leary and Caruthers had their minds made up before the research even started, which means that they probably weren't willing to consider, or communicate, the results in an unbiased manner

Misrepresents the research results; two-thirds of the market did not express interest in the product concept (compare to Figure 1.10)

Assumes the writers have the committee's support, which might not be true

Fails to invite further discussion and doesn't provide contact information to facilitate such discussion

sions and flouting company guidelines, they might conclude that the guidelines are meaningless and emulate their bosses' unethical behavior.

Employers have a responsibility to establish clear guidelines for ethical behavior, including business communication. Many companies establish an explicit ethics policy by using a written **code of ethics** to help employees determine what is acceptable. For example, the large aerospace and defense company Lockheed Martin developed a code of ethics that embodies six key principles: honesty, integrity, respect, trust, responsibility, and citizenship. All employees are expected to follow these principles, and the company offers a variety of resources to help employees make ethical decisions in specific situations.[32] In addition to ethics codes , many managers use **ethics audits** to monitor ethical progress and to point out any weaknesses that need to be addressed.

Responsible employers establish clear ethical guidelines for their employees to follow.

Whether or not formal guidelines are in place, every employee has the responsibility to communicate in an ethical manner. Although ethics can be a murky place to navigate, a good place to start is with the law. If something is illegal, you don't do it. No questions asked. Many companies have lawyers on staff or outside attorneys that you can call on for advice when necessary.

Unfortunately, the law doesn't cover every situation that you'll encounter in your career. Moreover, you may find yourself with a choice that is legal but still unethical. For years a debate has been raging over the labels on dietary supplements. Treating supplements more like food products than drugs, current laws don't require the same degree of disclosure regarding potential safety issues. In one analysis, 89 out of 100 supplement labels failed to provide any information

DOCUMENT MAKEOVER

IMPROVE THIS MEMO

To practice correcting drafts of actual documents, visit www.prenhall.com/onekey on the web. Click "Document Makeovers," then click Chapter 1. You will find a memo that contains problems and errors relating to what you've learned in this chapter about overcoming communication barriers in business messages. Use the Final Draft decision tool to create an improved version of this memo. Check the message for an audience-centered approach, ethical communication, efficient communication, and facilitation of feedback.

FIGURE 1.10 Ethical Communication

Tries not to "sell" the conclusion ahead of time, using an even-handed subject line

Offers full disclosure of all the background information

Provides the complete text of the researcher's summary

Separates the researcher's observations and opinions from the writers' own

Invites further discussion of the situation

SunStar Sports

Confidential Memorandum

TO: Executive Committee
FROM: Darcy O'Leary & Bob Caruthers, Product Management
DATE: October 23, 2005
SUBJECT: Market research summary

The market research for the Pegasus Project concluded last week with phone interviews of 236 sporting goods buyers in 18 states. As in the past, we used Bowerman Research to conduct the interviews, under the guidance of Bowerman's survey supervisor, Sadie McMahon. Sadie has directed surveys on more than two hundred consumer products, and we've learned to place a great deal of confidence in her market insights.

A complete report, including all raw data and verbatim quotes, will be available for downloading on the Engineering Department intranet by the end of next week. However, in light of the project-funding discussions going on this week, we believe the conclusions from the research warrant your immediate attention.

Sadie McMahon's research summary

Consumer interest in the new product, code-named Pegasus, is decidedly mixed, with 34 percent expressing little or no interest in the product but 37 percent expressing moderate to strong interest. The remaining 29 percent expressed confusion about the basic product concept and were therefore unable to specify their level of interest. The segment expressing little or no interest is not a cause for concern in most cases; few products appeal to the entire consumer market.

However, in my opinion, the portion of the market expressing confusion about the fundamental design of the product should sound an alarm bell. We rarely see more than 10 or 15 percent confusion at this stage of the design process. The much higher figure we measured for Pegasus suggests that the product design does not align with many consumers' expectations and that it might be difficult to sell if SunStar goes ahead with production.

Our recommendations

At \$7.6 million, the development costs for Pegasus are too high to proceed with this much uncertainty. The business case we prepared at the beginning of the project indicated that at least 50 percent consumer acceptance would be needed in order to generate enough sales to produce an acceptable return on the engineering investment. We would need to convince nearly half of the "confused" segment in order to reach that threshold. We recommend that further development be put on hold until the design can be clarified and validated with another round of consumer testing.

Please contact Darcy at ext. 2354 or Bob at ext. 2360 if you have any questions or concerns.

Emphasizes the skills of the researcher without biasing the readings regarding her conclusions

Alerts the executive committee to a situation that is relevant to another set of decisions occurring simultaneously

Illustrates clearly that the market expert is concerned about the project

States clearly and honestly that the project will not live up to original hopes

about adverse reactions or side effects, and 85 out of 100 failed to provide clear information about maximum doses. Even though the manufacturers may be following current laws, are they practicing sound ethics?[33]

In the absence of clear legal boundaries or ethical guidelines, ask yourself the following questions about your business communications:[34]

Certain questions can help you ensure that your communication is ethical.

- Have you defined the situation fairly and accurately?
- What is your intention in communicating this message?
- What impact will this message have on the people who receive it, or who might be affected by it?
- Will the message achieve the greatest possible good while doing the least possible harm?
- Will the assumptions you've made change over time? That is, will a decision that seems ethical now seem unethical in the future?
- Are you comfortable with your decision? Would you be embarrassed if it were printed in tomorrow's newspaper or spread across the Internet?

If all else fails, ask yourself what your mother would think. If you wouldn't be proud to describe your choice to someone you admire and respect—someone whose opinion of you matters—then you probably shouldn't be making it.

If you can't decide whether a choice is ethical, picture yourself explaining it to your mom, your spouse, or anyone whose opinion you care about.

COMMUNICATION CHALLENGES AT AACU

You land a summer internship with Carol Brown's team. You look forward to the opportunity because you know her reputation for effective, audience-centered communication. You spend the first month rotating through several departments, learning about their functions, products, and clients, gaining valuable skills each time. You spend your fifth week as a member services representative (MSR), using the online chat system to help actual clients. The Monday you start, the MSR supervisor, Howard, informs you that he is too busy to train you, saying simply, "You're a college kid; you'll figure it out." The chat function is easy to operate, but the FAQ database takes you two days to master. When your rotation ends on Thursday, Howard starts the review session by saying, "I know you're just an intern, but you did a lousy job this week."

Individual Challenge: Howard follows with some unfavorable statistics from the chat system and then shares his negative opinions about the internship program. After that unhappy prelude, he asks you for feedback about your week as "a pretend MSR." How do you overcome your defensive reaction? What kind of feedback should you provide?

Team Challenge: Every Friday, you meet with Brown to discuss your experiences from the week. Working with a small team, decide (1) what kind of feedback to provide about the MSR rotation and (2) how to deliver the message to Brown. Come up with at least four specific, constructive recommendations that will make things better for future interns.

SUMMARY OF LEARNING OBJECTIVES

1 **Explain why effective communication is important to your success in today's business environment.** Your ability to communicate will influence the perceptions that people have of you as a business professional. Moreover, because your communication plays a key role in efforts to improve efficiency, quality, responsiveness, and innovation, your communication affects your company's success. As your career advances and you achieve positions of greater responsibility with an organization, communication will become an increasingly visible and important part of your job.

2 **Identify seven communication skills that successful employers expect from their employees.** Employers expect employees to have skills such as organizing ideas and information coherently and completely, expressing and presenting ideas and information coherently and persuasively, listening to others effectively, communicating effectively with people from diverse backgrounds and experiences, using communication technologies effectively and efficiently, communicating in a civilized manner that reflects contemporary expectations of business etiquette, and communicating ethically—even when choices aren't crystal clear.

3 **Describe the five characteristics of effective business communication.** To be effective, business messages are practical. They provide the information that receivers need. Effective messages either leave out personal impressions or support such opinion with objective facts. Effective business communication is also concise. It clarifies and condenses information in a way that helps the receiver see and understand the most important issues. Effective messages are clear about expectations. They state precise responsibilities to eliminate confusion over who needs to do what next. Finally, effective messages are persuasive, when necessary, convincing others to accept your ideas or recommendations.

4 **List six factors that make business communication unique.** Business communication differs from social communication in six important ways: the ongoing globalization of business and the increasing recognition of the value of workforce diversity, the growing importance that many businesses place on information today,

the pervasiveness of technology throughout both internal and external communication, the growing reliance on teamwork, the evolution of organizational structures into flatter and more flexible arrangements, and numerous barriers to successful communication (including distractions, information overload, perceptual differences, language differences, restrictive environments, and deceptive tactics).

5 **Describe five strategies for communicating more effectively on the job.** To communicate more effectively on the job, use five strategies. First, reduce distractions in the work environment, including not sending unnecessary messages. Second, by adopting an audience-centered approach, you can focus on the needs of your audience and work to ensure successful transmission and reception of your messages. Third, you need to fine-tune your business communication skills. Fourth, by giving and receiving feedback that is constructive, rather than destructive, you will be able to focus on improvement rather than criticism. And fifth, by being sensitive to business etiquette, you reduce the chance of interpersonal blunders that might negatively affect communication.

6 **Explain four strategies for using communication technology successfully.** To use communication technology successfully, use strategies such as keeping technology in perspective. That way, you can make sure that it supports the communication effort, rather than overwhelming or disrupting it. Another strategy is to learn how to use technological tools productively. Doing so allows you to focus on communicating rather than on the tool being used. In addition, try to spend time and money wisely, at a level that reflects the importance of the communication effort. Finally, by reconnecting with people frequently, you ensure that communication is successful and that technology doesn't come between you and the people you need to reach.

7 **Discuss the importance of ethics in business communication and differentiate between ethical dilemmas and ethical lapses.** In addition to the general need to conduct business in an ethical manner, ethical communication is particularly important in business because communication is the public face of a company, which is why communication efforts are intensely scrutinized by company stakeholders. The difference between an ethical dilemma and an ethical lapse is a question of clarity. In a situation where two or more alternatives seem equally right or equally wrong, you face an ethical dilemma because the choice is unclear. In contrast, an ethical lapse occurs when a person makes a conscious choice that is clearly unethical.

Test Your Knowledge

1. What role will your communication skills play in your company's success?
2. What three principles will help you minimize missteps in business etiquette?
3. How does formal communication differ from informal communication?
4. In what directions can information travel within an organization's formal hierarchy?
5. What is the grapevine, and why should managers be aware of it?
6. In which of the six phases of the communication process do messages get encoded and decoded?
7. Why should communicators take an audience-centered approach to communication?
8. How is communication affected by information overload?
9. How can you make sure your feedback is constructive?
10. Why is ethical communication important?

Apply Your Knowledge

1. Why do you think good communication in an organization improves employee attitudes and performance? Explain briefly.
2. Is it possible for companies to be too dependent on communication technology? Explain briefly.
3. Would written or spoken messages be more susceptible to noise? Why?
4. As a manager, how can you impress on your employees the importance of strong business ethics when dealing with colleagues, customers, and the general public?
5. **Ethical Choices** Because of your excellent communication skills, your boss always asks you to write his reports for him. When you overhear the CEO complimenting him on his logical organization and clear writing style, he responds as if he'd written all those reports himself. What kind of ethical choice does this response represent? What can you do in this situation? Briefly explain your solution and your reasoning.

Practice Your Knowledge

Document for Analysis

Read the following document, then (1) analyze whether the document is effective or ineffective communication (be sure to explain why); and (2) revise the document so that it follows this chapter's guidelines.

It has come to my attention that many of you are lying on your time cards. If you come in late, you should not put 8:00 on your card. If you take a long lunch, you should not put 1:00 on your time card. I will not stand for this type of cheating. I simply have no choice but to institute an employee monitoring system. Beginning next Monday, video cameras will be installed at all entrances to the building, and your entry and exit times will be logged each time you use electronic key cards to enter or leave.

Anyone who is late for work or late coming back from lunch more than three times will have to answer to me. I don't care if you had to take a nap or if you girls had to shop. This is a place of business, and we do not want to be taken advantage of by slackers who are cheaters to boot.

It is too bad that a few bad apples always have to spoil things for everyone.

Exercises

For live links to all websites discussed in this chapter, visit this text's website at www.prenhall.com/bovee. Just log on, select Chapter 1, and click on "Featured Websites." Locate the page or the URL related to the material in the text.

1.1 **Effective Business Communication: Understanding the Difference** Bring to class a sales letter that you received in the mail or via e-mail. Comment on how well the communication

a. provides practical information
b. gives facts rather than impressions
c. clarifies and condenses information
d. states precise responsibilities
e. persuades others and offers recommendations

1.2 **Internal Communication: Planning the Flow** For the following tasks, identify the necessary direction of communication (downward, upward, horizontal), suggest an appropriate type of communication (casual conversation, formal interview, meeting, workshop, web conference, instant message, newsletter, memo, bulletin board notice, and so on), and briefly explain your suggestion.

a. As personnel manager, you want to announce details about this year's company picnic.
b. As director of internal communication, you want to convince top management of the need for a company newsletter.
c. As production manager, you want to make sure that both the sales manager and the finance manager receive your scheduling estimates.
d. As marketing manager, you want to help employees understand the company's goals and its attitudes toward workers.

1.3 **Communication Networks: Formal or Informal?** An old college friend phoned you out of the blue to say, "Truth is, I had to call you. You'd better keep this under your hat, but when I heard my company was buying you guys out, I was dumbfounded. I had no idea that a company as large as yours could sink so fast. Your group must be in pretty bad shape over there!" Your stomach suddenly turned queasy, and you felt a chill go up your spine. You'd heard nothing about any buyout, and before you could even get your college friend off the phone, you were wondering what you should do. Of the following, choose one course of action and briefly explain your choice.

a. Contact your CEO directly and relate what you've heard.
b. Ask co-workers whether they've heard anything about a buyout.
c. Discuss the phone call confidentially with your immediate supervisor.
d. Keep quiet about the whole thing (there's nothing you can do about the situation anyway).

1.4 **Ethical Choices** In less than a page, explain why you think each of the following is or is not ethical.

a. Keeping quiet about a possible environmental hazard you've just discovered in your company's processing plant
b. Overselling the benefits of instant messaging to your company's management; they never seem to understand the benefits of technology, so you believe it's the only way to convince them to make the right choice
c. Telling an associate and close friend that she'd better pay more attention to her work responsibilities or management will fire her
d. Recommending the purchase of excess equipment to use up your allocated funds before the end of the fiscal year so that your budget won't be cut next year

1.5 **The Changing Workplace: Always in Touch** Technologies such as instant messaging, cell phones, electronic mail, and voice mail are making businesspeople easily accessible at any time of day or night, at work, and at home. What kind of impact might frequent intrusions have on their professional and personal lives? Explain your answer in less than a page.

1.6 **Internet** Cisco is a leading manufacturer of equipment for the Internet and corporate networks and has developed a code of ethics that it expects employees to abide by. Visit the company's website at www.cisco.com and find the Code of Conduct. In a brief paragraph, describe three specific examples of things you could do that would violate these provisions; then list at least three opportunities that Cisco provides its employees to report ethics violations or ask questions regarding ethical dilemmas.

1.7 **Communication Etiquette** Potential customers frequently visit your production facility before making purchase decisions. You and the people who report to you in the sales department have received extensive training in etiquette issues because you deal with high-profile clients so frequently. However, the rest of the workforce has not received such training, and you worry that someone might inadvertently say or do something that would offend one of these potential customers. In a two-paragraph email, explain to the general manager why you think anyone who might come in contact with customers should receive basic etiquette training.

1.8 **Ethical Choices** Knowing that you have numerous friends throughout the company, your boss relies on you for feedback concerning employee morale and other issues affecting the staff. She recently approached you and asked you to start reporting any behavior that might violate company polices, from taking office supplies home to making personal long-distance calls. List the issues you'd like to discuss with her before you respond to her request.

1.9 **Formal Communication: Self-Introduction** Write a memo or prepare an oral presentation introducing yourself to your instructor and your class. Include such things as your background, interests, achievements, and goals. If you write a memo, keep it under one page, and use Figure 1.3 on page 7 as a model for the format. If you prepare an oral presentation, plan to speak for no more than 2 minutes.

1.10 **Teamwork** Your boss has asked your work group to research and report on corporate child-care facilities. Of course, you'll want to know who (besides your boss) will be reading your report. Working with two team members, list four or five other things you'll want to know about the situation and about your audience before starting your research. Briefly explain why each of the items on your list is important.

1.11 **Communication Process: Analyzing Miscommunication** Use the six phases of the communication process to analyze a miscommunication you've recently had with a coworker, supervisor, classmate, teacher, friend, or family member. What idea were you trying to share? How did you encode and transmit it? Did the receiver get the message? Did the receiver correctly decode the message? How do you know? Based on your analysis, identify and explain the barriers that prevented your successful communication in this instance.

1.12 **Ethical Choices** You've been given the critical assignment of selecting the site for your company's new plant. After months of negotiations with landowners, numerous cost calculations, and investments in ecological, social, and community impact studies, you are about to recommend building the new plant on the Lansing River site. Now, just 15 minutes before your big presentation to top management, you discover a possible mistake in your calculations: Site-purchase costs appear to be \$500,000 more than you calculated, nearly 10 percent over budget. You don't have time to recheck all your figures, so you're tempted to just go ahead with your recommendation and ignore any discrepancies. You're worried that management won't approve this purchase if you can't present a clean, unqualified solution. You also know that many projects run over their original estimates, so you can probably work the extra cost into the budget later. On your way to the meeting room, you make your final decision. In a few paragraphs, explain the decision you made.

1.13 **Communication Etiquette** In group meetings, some of your colleagues have a habit of interrupting and arguing with the speaker, taking credit for ideas that aren't theirs, and shooting down ideas they don't agree with. You're the newest person in the group and not sure if this is accepted behavior in this company, but it concerns you both personally and professionally. Should you go with the flow and adopt their behavior or stick with your own communication style, even though you might get lost in the noise? In two paragraphs, explain the pros and cons of both approaches.

Expand Your Knowledge

For live links to the websites that follow, visit this text's website at www.prenhall.com/bovee. When you log on, select Chapter 1, then select "Featured Websites," click on the URL of the featured website, and review the website to complete these exercises.

Exploring the Best of the Web

Check Out These Resources at the Business Writer's Free Library
www.mapnp.org/library/commskls/cmm_writ.htm
The Business Writer's Free Library is a terrific resource for business communication material. Categories of information include basic composition skills, basic writing skills, correspondence, reference material, and general resources and advice. Log on and read about the most common errors in English, become a word detective, ask Miss Grammar, review samples of common forms of correspondence, fine-tune your interpersonal skills, join a newsgroup, and more. Follow the links and improve your effectiveness as a business communicator.

1. What are some strategies for communicating with an uncooperative audience?
2. What is the value of diversity in the workplace?
3. Why is bad etiquette bad for business?

Exploring the Web on Your Own

Review these chapter-related websites on your own to learn more about achieving communication success in the workplace.

1. Netiquette Home Page, www.albion.com/netiquette index.html. Learn the dos and don'ts of online communication at this site, then take the Netiquette Quiz.
2. The Information and Communication Technology tutorial provided by Resource Discovery Network in Great Britain, www.vts.rdn.ac.uk, offers a free tutorial to improve your Internet skills (look under "Internet for Further Education"). Learn helpful techniques for searching the Internet, figure out what you can trust and what you can't, and find out how to use the Internet in your work.
3. 101 Best Websites for Writers, at www.writersdigest.com, points the way to great search engines and general reference sites. While aimed primarily at professional writers, the list has something to offer all business communicators. The site list is updated every year, so be sure to select the current year's list.

Learn Interactively

Interactive Study Guide

Go to the Companion Website at www.prenhall.com/bovee. For Chapter 1, take advantage of the interactive "Study Guide" to test your knowledge of the chapter. Get instant feedback on whether you need additional studying.

Also, visit this site's "Study Hall," where you'll find an abundance of valuable resources that will help you succeed in this course.

Peak Performance Grammar and Mechanics

To improve your skill with nouns and pronouns, visit www.prenhall.com/onekey, click "Peak Performance Grammar and Mechanics," click "Grammar Basics," then click "Nouns and Pronouns." Take the Pretest to determine whether you have any weak areas. Then review those areas in the Refresher Course. Take the Follow-Up Test to check your grasp of nouns and pronouns. For an extra challenge or advanced practice, take the Advanced Test. Finally, for additional reinforcement in nouns, go to www.prenhall.com/bovee, where you'll find "Improve Your Grammar, Mechanics, and Usage" exercises.

chapter 2

Communicating in Teams and Mastering Listening and Nonverbal Communication

LEARNING OBJECTIVES

After studying this chapter, you will be able to

1. Highlight the advantages and disadvantages of working in teams
2. Outline an effective approach to team communication
3. Explain how group dynamics can affect team effectiveness
4. Discuss the role of etiquette in team settings, both in the workplace and in social settings
5. Describe how meeting technologies can help participants communicate more successfully
6. Describe the listening process and explain how good listeners overcome barriers at each stage of the process
7. Clarify the importance of nonverbal communication and briefly describe six categories of nonverbal expression

COMMUNICATION CLOSE-UP AT THE CONTAINER STORE

www.containerstore.com

Are your possessions totally organized or completely chaotic? Either way, The Container Store can create the solution you need. Rallying around the slogan "Contain Yourself," the company uses a powerful mix of communication and teamwork to inspire its staff to help customers solve every storage problem imaginable—from sweaters to DVDs to rubber stamps—with an array of boxes, baskets, hangers, shelves, and more.

Helping people get organized is what founders Garrett Boone and Kip Tindell had in mind when they opened their first store in Dallas in 1978. Their founding principles focus on hiring talented people, then training and motivating them to be problem solvers who work well with customers and with each other.

Teamwork is reinforced twice a day, before opening and after closing, through staff gatherings called "huddles." Similar to a huddle in football, the goal is to "keep people on the same page," says Boone, by setting goals, sharing information, boosting morale, and bonding as a team. Morning sessions typically feature spirited discussions of sales goals, product training, and even a chorus of "Happy Birthday" for celebrating team members. Evening huddles include more team building and friendly competitions such as guessing the daily sales figures.

A wide selection of storage products attract customers to The Container Store, but teamwork and strong communication skills are just as important to the company's success.

In 2003, the founders' ongoing commitment to communication and teamwork was recognized with the annual Performance Through People Award, presented by Northwestern University. The company has also earned a spot on *Fortune* magazine's list of The 100 Best Companies to Work For, finishing number 1 twice and number 2 twice. Tindell believes that full, open communication with employees takes courage but says, "The only way that people feel really, really a part of something is if they know everything."[1]

IMPROVING YOUR PERFORMANCE IN TEAMS

Team members have a shared mission and are collectively responsible for their work.

Chances are good that your career will lead you to an organization such as The Container Store, where working in teams and small groups will put your communication skills to the test. A **team** is a unit of two or more people who share a mission and the responsibility for working to achieve their goals. Not all groups in an organization qualify as teams. For example, if the various employees in your department were working on separate projects with individual goals, they would not be considered a team.[2]

Organizations establish several types of teams, and each type may communicate a little differently. Companies can create *formal teams* that become part of the organization's structure, or they can establish *informal teams,* which aren't part of the formal organization but are formed to solve a problem, work on a specific activity, or encourage employee participation. Some teams stay together for years; others may meet their goals in just a few days and then disband.

Two popular types of informal teams are problem-solving teams and task forces.

Problem-solving teams and **task forces** are informal teams that assemble to resolve specific issues and then disband once their goal has been accomplished. Teams often include representatives of many departments so that those who have a stake in the outcome are allowed to provide input.[3] For example, a team at Mattel gathered input from artists, designers, and technical experts to reduce the development time for a new toy from 13 months to only 5.[4]

Effective communication is essential to every aspect of team performance.

Committees are formal teams that usually have a long life span and can become a permanent part of the organizational structure. Committees typically deal with regularly recurring tasks. For example, an executive committee may meet monthly to plan strategy and review results, and a grievance committee may be formed as a permanent resource for handling employee complaints and concerns.

Whether the task is to write reports, give oral presentations, produce a product, solve a problem, or investigate an opportunity, you and your fellow team members must be able to communicate effectively with each other and with people outside your team. As Chapter 1 points out, this ability often requires taking on additional responsibility for communication: sharing information with team members, listening carefully to their inputs, and crafting messages that reflect the team's collective ideas and opinions.

1 LEARNING OBJECTIVE

Highlight the advantages and disadvantages of working in teams

Advantages and Disadvantages of Teams

Teams are a popular form of organization in business today and when they are successful, they improve productivity, creativity, employee involvement, and even job security.[5] Teams are often at the core of **participative management**, the effort to involve employees in the company's decision making. Some companies even base pay raises and promotions on an employee's effectiveness as a team player.

To be an effective collaborator in a team setting, you and your colleagues should recognize that each individual brings valuable assets, knowledge, and skills to the team. Strong collaborators are willing to exchange information, examine issues, and work through conflicts that arise. They trust each other, working toward the greater good of the team and organization rather than focusing on personal agendas.[6] The most effective teams have a clear sense of purpose, communicate openly and honestly, reach decisions by consensus, think creatively, and know how to resolve conflict.[7] Learning these team skills takes time and practice, so U.S. companies now teach teamwork more frequently than on any other aspect of business.[8]

Communication Solution

Getting employees involved in the daily operation of their own stores is one of the central principles of participative management at The Container Store. Through effective team communications, managers and employees share vital business information every day.

In contrast, unsuccessful teamwork can waste time and money, generate lower-quality work, and frustrate both managers and employees alike. One of the most common reasons for failure is poor communication, particularly when teams have to operate across different cultures, countries, and time zones.[9]

Teams can play a vital role in helping an organization reach its goals, but they are not appropriate for every situation—and even when they are appropriate, you need to weigh both the advantages and disadvantages of a team-based approach. A successful team can provide advantages such as the following:[10]

- **Increased information and knowledge.** By pooling the resources of several individuals, teams bring more information to the decision-making process.
- **Increased diversity of views.** Team members bring a variety of perspectives to the decision-making process.
- **Increased acceptance of a solution.** Those who participate in making a decision are more likely to support the decision enthusiastically and encourage others to accept it.
- **Higher performance levels.** Working in teams can unleash new amounts of creativity and energy in workers who share a sense of purpose and mutual accountability. Furthermore, teams fill the individual worker's need to belong to a group, reduce employee boredom, increase feelings of dignity and self-worth, and reduce stress and tension between workers.

Companies in fast-moving industries, such as the Internet company Yahoo!, rely on teams to work closely and quickly to solve problems and capitalize on market opportunities.

Although teamwork has many advantages, it also has a number of potential disadvantages. At their worst, teams are unproductive and frustrating, and they waste everyone's time. This outcome is a particular risk with standing committees that have outlived their original purpose but continue to meet anyway. Teams need to be aware of and work to counter the following disadvantages:

Unsuccessful teams can waste time and generate lower-quality work.

Effective teams can pool knowledge, take advantage of diverse viewpoints, increase acceptance of solutions the team proposes, and enhance individuals' performance.

Teams need to avoid the negative impact of peer pressure, groupthink, hidden agendas, free riders, and excessive costs.

- **Peer pressure.** When individuals are pressured to conform, they may abandon their sense of personal responsibility and agree to ill-founded or even unethical plans. As a consequence, some teams may actually be counterproductive by generating bad decisions.
- **Groupthink.** A team may develop **groupthink** if individual members value team harmony more than they value effective decision making. They become willing to set aside their personal opinions and go along with everyone else.
- **Hidden agendas.** Some team members may have a **hidden agenda**—private motives that affect the group's interaction. Sam might want to prove that he's more powerful than you, you might be trying to share the risk of making a decision, and Laura might be looking for a chance to postpone doing "real" work. Each person's hidden agenda can detract from the team's effectiveness.
- **Free riders.** Some team members may be **free riders**—those who don't contribute their fair share to the group's activities. Perhaps these members aren't being held individually accountable for their work. Or perhaps they don't believe they'll receive adequate recognition for their individual efforts.
- **Cost.** Still another drawback to teamwork is the high cost of coordinating group activities. Aligning schedules, arranging meetings, and coordinating individual parts of a project can eat up a lot of time and money.

Team Communication

2 LEARNING OBJECTIVE

Outline an effective approach to team communication

Team presentations and reports can give an organization the opportunity to show off its brightest talent while capitalizing on each person's unique presentation and communication skills. In other words, you can take the collective energy and expertise of the team and create something that transcends what you could do otherwise.[11] Even so, collaborating on team messages requires special effort.

To begin with, team members coming from different backgrounds may have different work habits or concerns: A technical expert may focus on accuracy and scientific standards, whereas an editor might be more concerned about organization and coherence, and a manager might focus on schedules, cost, and corporate goals. In addition, team members will differ in writing styles and personality traits—two factors that can complicate the creative nature of communication.

To collaborate effectively, everyone involved must be flexible and open to other opinions, focusing on team objectives rather than on individual priorities.[12] Successful writers know that a given thought can be expressed in many ways, so they avoid the "my way is best" attitude. The following guidelines will help you collaborate more successfully on team messages:[13]

Successful collaboration requires a number of steps, from selecting the right partners and agreeing on project goals to establishing clear processes and avoiding writing as a group.

- **Select collaborators carefully.** Choose a combination of people who have the specific experience, information, and talent needed for the project; avoid blindly assigning some predefined group to take it on.
- **Agree on project goals before you start.** Starting without a clear idea of where you hope to finish inevitably leads to frustration and wasted time. Chapter 4 shows you how to plan messages successfully.
- **Give your team time to bond before diving in.** Even if a virtual team doesn't have the opportunity to meet in person, spend at least some of your time online socializing so that people are more comfortable working together.
- **Clarify individual responsibilities.** Since members will be depending on each other, make sure individual responsibilities are clear, including who is supposed to do what and by when.
- **Establish clear processes.** Make sure everyone knows how the work will be done, including checkpoints and decisions to be made along the way. For instance, if the team members will report their progress once a week, make this expectation obvious at the beginning so that everyone will be prepared.
- **Make sure tools and techniques are ready and compatible across the team.** Even minor details such as different versions of software can delay projects. If you plan to use technology for sharing or presenting materials, test the system before work begins.
- **Avoid writing as a group.** The actual composition is the only part of developing team messages that does not benefit from group participation. Group writing is usually a slow, painful process that delivers bland results. Plan, research, and outline together, but assign the actual writing to one person. If you must divide and share the writing for scheduling reasons, try to have one person do a final pass to ensure a consistent style.
- **Check to see how things are going along the way.** Don't assume everything is working just because you don't hear anything negative; periodically ask team members how they think the project is going.

3 LEARNING OBJECTIVE

Explain how group dynamics can affect team effectiveness

Group Dynamics

Group dynamics are the interactions and processes that take place in a team.

To accomplish their goals successfully, team members constantly connect with one another. The interactions and processes that take place between the members of a team are called **group dynamics**. Some teams are more effective than others simply because the dynamics of the group facilitate member input and the resolution of differences. To keep things moving forward, productive teams also tend to develop rules that are conducive to business. Often unstated, these rules become group **norms**—informal standards of conduct that members share and that guide member behavior. For example, some teams may develop a casual approach to schedules, with members routinely showing up 10 or 15 minutes late for meetings, while other teams may expect strict adherence to time commitments.

Teams with a strong sense of identity and cohesiveness can develop overly strong expectations for group behavior with little tolerance for deviations from those norms. Such strong identity can lead to higher levels of commitment and performance. Unfortunately, it can also lead to groupthink or make it difficult for new members to fit in. Group dynamics are affected by several factors: the roles that team members assume, the current phase of team development, the team's success in resolving conflict, and its success in overcoming resistance.

Assuming Team Roles

Each member of a group plays a role that affects the outcome of the group's activities.

Members of a team can play various roles, which fall into three categories (see Table 2.1). Members who assume **self-oriented roles** are motivated mainly to fulfill personal needs, so they tend to be less productive than other members. Far more likely to contribute to team

TABLE 2.1 Team Roles People Play

DYSFUNCTIONAL	FUNCTIONAL	
SELF-ORIENTED ROLES	**TEAM-MAINTENANCE ROLES**	**TASK-FACILITATING ROLES**
Controlling: Dominating others by exhibiting superiority or authority	**Encouraging:** Drawing out other members by showing verbal and nonverbal support, praise, or agreement	**Initiating:** Getting the team started on a line of inquiry
Withdrawing: Retiring from the team either by becoming silent or by refusing to deal with a particular aspect of the team's work	**Harmonizing:** Reconciling differences among team members through mediation or by using humor to relieve tension	**Information giving or seeking:** Offering (or seeking) information relevant to questions facing the team
Attention seeking: Calling attention to oneself and demanding recognition from others	**Compromising:** Offering to yield on a point in the interest of reaching a mutually acceptable decision	**Coordinating:** Showing relationships among ideas, clarifying issues, summarizing what the team has done
Diverting: Focusing the team's discussion on topics of interest to the individual rather than on those relevant to the task		**Procedure setting:** Suggesting decision-making procedures that will move the team toward a goal

goals are those members who assume **team-maintenance roles** to help everyone work well together, and those who assume **task-facilitating roles** to help solve problems or make decisions.

To a great extent, the roles that you assume in a team depend on whether you joined the group voluntarily or involuntarily and on your status in that group. Your status is determined by many variables, some substantive (expertise, past successes, education) and some superficial (personal attractiveness, age, social background, organizational position). Your status can also change over time, particularly when a team is just starting to form. In most teams, as people try to establish their relative status, an undercurrent of tension can get in the way of the real work. Until roles and status have stabilized, a team may have trouble accomplishing its goals.

Allowing for Team Evolution

Teams typically evolve through five phases: orientation, conflict, brainstorming, emergence, and reinforcement.

Teams can rarely jump right to work and start making decisions; you and your fellow team members need time to establish rapport and let natural leadership roles emerge. Teams typically evolve through five phases on their way to becoming productive (see Figure 2.1):[14]

1. **Orientation.** Team members socialize, establish their roles, and begin to define their task or purpose.
2. **Conflict.** Team members begin to discuss their positions and become more assertive in establishing their roles. If you and the other members have been carefully selected to represent a variety of viewpoints and expertise, disagreements are a natural part of this phase.
3. **Brainstorming.** Team members air all the options and discuss the pros and cons fully. At the end of this phase, members begin to settle on a single solution to the problem.
4. **Emergence.** Team members reach a decision. Consensus is reached when the team finds a solution that is acceptable enough for all members to support (even if they have reservations). This consensus happens only after all members have had an opportunity to communicate their positions and feel that they have been listened to.
5. **Reinforcement.** Group feeling is rebuilt, and the solution is summarized. Members receive their assignments for carrying out the group's decision, and they make arrangements for following up on those assignments.

These five phases almost always occur regardless of what task or what type of decision is being considered. Moreover, team members naturally use this process, even when they lack experience or training in teamwork.

FIGURE 2.1
Phases of Group Development

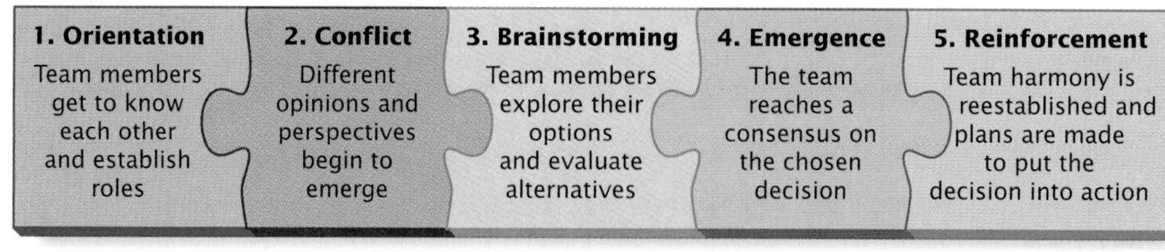
1. Orientation
Team members get to know each other and establish roles
2. Conflict
Different opinions and perspectives begin to emerge
3. Brainstorming
Team members explore their options and evaluate alternatives
4. Emergence
The team reaches a consensus on the chosen decision
5. Reinforcement
Team harmony is reestablished and plans are made to put the decision into action

Resolving Conflict

As mentioned earlier, team members are often chosen precisely because they hold differing views and opinions, which ensures a broader perspective of the project the team faces. Consequently, conflict is a natural part of any team experience. When handled poorly, conflict can lead to complete failure of a group's efforts; however, the right approach to conflict can push the team to better performance.

Conflict can arise for any number of reasons. Team members may believe that they need to compete for money, information, or other resources. Or members may disagree about who is responsible for a specific task (usually the result of poorly defined responsibilities and job boundaries). Also, poor communication can lead to misunderstandings about other team members, and intentionally withholding information can undermine trust. Basic differences in values, attitudes, and personalities may lead to arguments. Power struggles may result when one member questions the authority of another or when people or teams with limited authority attempt to increase their power or exert more influence. Conflict can also arise because individuals or teams are pursuing different goals.[15] To explore a common source of conflict, see "Ethics Detective: Taking Credit Where Credit Isn't Due: When 'We' Turns into 'I'."

Conflict in teams can be both constructive and destructive.

Conflict can be both constructive and destructive to a team's effectiveness. Conflict is constructive if it forces important issues into the open, increases the involvement of team members, and generates creative ideas for the solution to a problem. Conflict is destructive if it diverts energy from more important issues, destroys the morale of teams or individual team members, or polarizes or divides the team.[16]

Destructive conflict can lead to win-lose or lose-lose outcomes, in which one or both sides lose, to the detriment of the entire team. If you approach conflict with the idea that both sides can satisfy their goals to at least some extent (*win-win strategy*), no one loses. However, for the win-win strategy to work, everybody must believe that (1) it's possible to find a solution that both parties can accept, (2) cooperation is better for the organization than competition, (3) the other party can be trusted, and (4) higher status doesn't entitle one party to impose a solution.

One of the first steps to finding a win-win solution is to consider the other party's needs. Find out what is acceptable to the other people on the team. Keep your eyes and ears open; ask questions that will help you understand their needs. Search for mutually satisfactory solutions or compromises whose results are better for the team overall.[17] And remember that both sides can usually get what they want if both are willing to work together. In many cases, the resolution process is chiefly an exchange of opinions and information that gradually leads to a mutually acceptable solution.[18]

Here are seven measures that can help team members successfully resolve conflict:

- **Proaction.** Deal with minor conflict before it becomes major conflict.
- **Communication.** Get those directly involved in the conflict to participate in resolving it.
- **Openness.** Get feelings out in the open before dealing with the main issues.
- **Research.** Seek factual reasons for the problem before seeking solutions.
- **Flexibility.** Don't let anyone lock into a position before considering other solutions.
- **Fair play.** Don't let anyone avoid a fair solution by hiding behind the rules.
- **Alliance.** Get opponents to fight together against an "outside force" instead of against each other.

Ethics Detective

Taking Credit Where Credit Isn't Due: When "We" Turns into "I"

Your entire team has been looking forward to this meeting for weeks. When the company president assembled this team to find creative solutions to the company's cash flow problems, few people thought the team would succeed. However, through plenty of hard work, you and your colleagues found new sources of investment capital that should save the company. Now it's time to present your accomplishments to the board of directors. Because exposure in front of the board can be a major career boost, the team planned to present the results together, giving each person a few minutes in the limelight.

However, Jackson Mueller, the chief financial officer and the leader of your team, had a surprise for you this morning. He said he'd received word at the last minute that the board wants a short, concise presentation, and he says the only way to do this is with a single presenter. No one is happy about the change, but Jackson is the highest-ranking employee on the team and the only one with experience presenting to the board.

Unfortunately, disappointment turned to dismay as you and your teammates watched from the back of the conference room. Jackson deftly compressed your 60-minute presentation down to 20 minutes, and the board showered him with praise. However, he never introduced anyone else on the team, so your moment in the sun passed without recognition.

ANALYSIS

Did Jackson behave unethically by not introducing you and your colleagues to the board? Explain your answer. Later on, you complain to a colleague that by stressing "my team" so often, Jackson actually made the presentation all about him, not the team. But one of your colleagues argues that the team's assignment was to solve the problem, not score career points with the board, so that goal shouldn't have been such a top priority. Explain why you agree or disagree.

Overcoming Resistance

Resistance to change is a particular type of conflict that can often affect your work in teams. Some of this resistance is clearly irrational, such as when people resist any kind of change, whether it makes sense or not. Sometimes, however, the resistance is perfectly logical. A change might require someone to relinquish authority or give up comfortable ways of doing things. In any event, you can help overcome resistance with calm, reasonable give-and-take:

When you encounter resistance or hostility, try to maintain your composure and address the other person's emotional needs.

- **Express understanding.** Show that you sympathize. You might say, "I can understand that this change might be difficult, and if I were in your position, I might be reluctant myself." Help the other person relax and talk about his or her anxiety so that you have a chance to offer reassurance.[19]
- **Bring resistance out into the open.** When people are noncommittal and silent, they may be tuning you out without even knowing why. Continuing with your argument is futile. Deal directly with the resistance, without being accusing. You might say, "You seem cool to this idea. Have I made some faulty assumptions?" Such questions force people to face and define their resistance.[20]
- **Evaluate others' objections fairly.** Don't simply repeat yourself. Focus on what the other person is expressing, both the words and the feelings. Get the person to open up so that you can understand the basis for the resistance. Others' objections may raise legitimate points that you'll need to discuss, or they may reveal problems that you'll need to minimize.[21]
- **Hold your arguments until the other person is ready for them.** Getting your point across depends as much on the other person's frame of mind as it does on your arguments. You can't assume that a strong argument will speak for itself. By becoming more audience centered, you will learn to address the other person's emotional needs first.

4 LEARNING OBJECTIVE

Discuss the role of etiquette in team settings, both in the workplace and in social settings

Etiquette in Team Settings

Etiquette is particularly important in team settings because the ability to get along with teammates is vital to everyone's success. Nobody wants to spend weeks or months working with someone who is rude to colleagues or an embarrassment to the company in public.

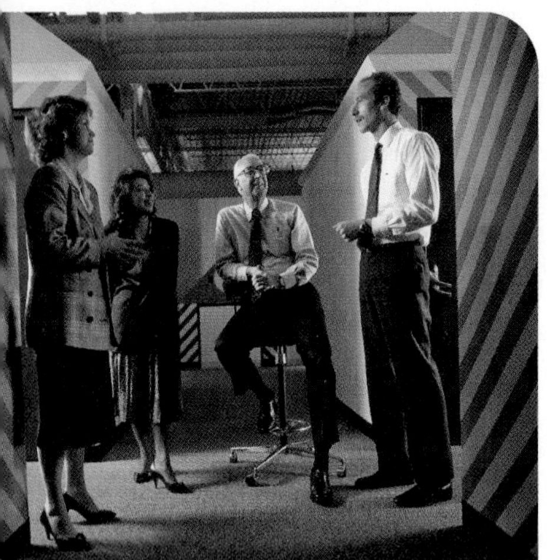

Even in informal and impromptu meetings, executives at Herman Miller recognize the importance of etiquette in business communication.

Here are some key etiquette points to remember when you're in the workplace and out in public. None of the following material is unique to team settings, of course; it's good advice for all your business efforts.

In the Workplace

During a typical workday, you'll have dozens of opportunities to make an impression on the people around you, and paying some attention to etiquette basics will help determine whether those impressions are positive or negative. Knowing how to behave and how to interact with people in business will help you appear polished, professional, and confident.[22] Understanding business etiquette also helps you put others at ease so that they are comfortable enough to do business with you.[23]

Attention to basic business etiquette will help your career at every stage.

For instance, your personal appearance has considerable impact on your career success—rightly or wrongly. Pay attention to the style of dress where you work and adjust your style to match, particularly if you work with people from diverse backgrounds and age groups. If you're not sure, dress moderately and simply—earn a reputation for what you can *do,* not for what you can wear.

Personal appearance can have considerable impact on your success in business.

Besides your clothing, personal grooming affects your workplace appearance. Pay close attention to cleanliness and avoid using products with lingering scents, such as perfumed soaps, colognes, shampoos, and after-shave lotions. Shampoo frequently, keep hands and nails neatly manicured, use mouthwash and deodorant, and make regular trips to a hair stylist.[24] Try to follow company policy regarding hairstyle.[25]

Fake smiles are easy to spot—and bad for your reputation.

Something as simple as your smile also affects the way people do business with you. When you smile, do so genuinely. A fake smile is obvious because the timing is off and the expression fails to involve all the facial muscles that a genuine smile would.[26] Repeated false smiling may earn you the reputation of being a phony. However, certain occasions require smiling, such as when you're introduced to someone, when you give or receive a compliment, and when you applaud someone.[27]

Phone skills have a definite impact on your success. Phone calls lack the visual richness of face-to-face conversations, but you can convey confidence and professionalism through your attitude and tone of voice. Make sure phones are answered quickly and courteously. Identify yourself and establish the caller's needs by asking how you can help. If you can't help, find someone who can, or promise to get back with an answer—always being careful not to make promises you can't keep. If you answer the phone for someone unable to take the call, take a brief but accurate message. Be sure to check your own voice mail frequently so that people know you are responsive.

Plan phone calls as carefully as you plan meetings.

When you place phone calls, plan them as carefully as you would plan a meeting. Be ready with relevant questions or information, and schedule calls for an opportune time. For example, avoid calling first thing in the morning, when many people like to answer e-mail and plan the day. Likewise, avoid calling near the end of the day, when most people are trying to wrap up business and leave the office.

Start your call with a clear introduction and then verify that you've called at a convenient time. After you've given or received the necessary information, close in a positive manner and clarify any unfinished tasks and responsibilities. If you need to leave a voice-mail message, keep it professional and brief but complete.[28] Many voice-mail systems let recipients forward messages to anybody in the company, and you could end up regretting an inappropriate message.

To minimize disruptions, many companies restrict cell phone usage in the workplace.

If you're accustomed to using your cell phone anywhere and everywhere, get ready to change your habits; many companies are putting restrictions on their use. Cell phones are causing so much disruption in the workplace that some senior executives now ban their use in meetings, even going so far as to fine employees whose phones ring during meetings. (The fines are typically donated to charity or used to buy team lunches.) As Ian Campbell of Nucleus Research puts it, "A cell phone has gone from a symbol of status to a device of scorn." Moreover, this problem of wireless interruptions is only going to get worse, with the proliferation of personal digital assistants (PDAs), laptop computers, and other devices with wireless access.[29]

In Social Settings

From business lunches to industry conferences, you represent your company when you're out in public, so make sure your appearance and actions are appropriate to the situation. First impressions last a long time, so get to know the customs of the culture when you meet new people. In North America, a firm handshake is expected when two people meet, whereas a respectful bow of the head is more appropriate in Japan. If you are expected to shake hands, be aware that the passive "dead fish" handshake creates an extremely negative impression. Also, women and men should shake hands on equal terms; the days of a woman offering just her fingertips are long gone in the business world. If you are physically able, always stand when shaking someone's hand.

You represent your company when you're out in public, so etiquette continues to be important.

When introducing yourself, include a brief description of your role in the company. When introducing two other people, speak both their first and last names clearly, then try to offer some information (perhaps a shared professional interest) to help these two people ease into a conversation.[30] Generally speaking, the lower-ranking person is introduced to the senior-ranking person, without regard to gender.[31] When you're introduced to someone, repeat the person's name as soon as possible. Doing so is both a compliment and a good way to remember it.[32]

Business is often conducted over meals, and knowing the basics of dining etiquette will make you more effective in these situations.[33] Choose foods that are easy to eat—you don't want to wrestle with a lobster while trying to carry on a conversation. If a drink is appropriate, save it for the end of the meal so that you can stay clear and composed. Leave business papers under your chair until entrée plates have been removed; the business aspect of the meal doesn't usually begin until then.

Misuse of mobile phones in restaurants and other public places is a common etiquette blunder. When you use your cell phone in public, you send the message that people around you aren't as important as your call and that you don't respect your caller's privacy.[34] Older colleagues who grew up without cell phones may find them particularly offensive in social settings. If it's not a matter of life and death—literally—wait until you're back in the office.

Business meals are a forum for business, period. Don't get on your soapbox about politics, religion, or any other topic likely to stir up emotions. Some light chatter and questions about personal interests is fine, but don't get too personal. Don't complain about work, avoid profanity, and be careful with humor—a joke that might entertain some people could offend others. In general, learn from co-workers who are respected by customers and colleagues. You'll find that they choose topics carefully, listen with respect, and leave a positive impression with everyone they meet.

DOCUMENT MAKEOVER

IMPROVE THIS E-MAIL MESSAGE

To practice correcting drafts of actual documents, visit www.prenhall.com/onekey on the web. Click "Document Makeovers," then click Chapter 2. You will find an e-mail message that contains problems and errors relating to what you've learned in this chapter about communicating in teams. Use the Final Draft decision tool to create an improved version of this e-mail. Check the message for clarity, relevance of topics to meeting participants, proper approach to group collaboration, and communication of meeting etiquette.

MAKING YOUR MEETINGS MORE PRODUCTIVE

Meetings are a primary communication venue for today's businesses, whether held in formal conference rooms or on the Internet as *virtual meetings*. Well-run meetings can help you solve problems, develop ideas, and identify opportunities. Much of your workplace communication will occur in small-group meetings; therefore, your ability to contribute to the company and to be recognized for those contributions will depend on your meeting participation skills.

Much of the communication you'll participate in will take place in meetings.

Unfortunately, many meetings are unproductive. In a recent study, senior and middle managers reported that only 56 percent of their meetings were actually productive and that 25 percent of them could have been replaced by a phone call or a memo.[35] The three most frequently reported problems with meetings are getting off the subject, not having an agenda, and running too long.[36] Given such demoralizing statistics and the high cost of meetings—which can run hundreds or thousands of dollars an hour in lost work time and

A single poorly run meeting can waste thousands of dollars.

travel expenses—it's no wonder that companies are focusing on making their meetings more productive. You'll help your company make better use of meetings by preparing carefully, conducting meetings efficiently, and using meeting technologies wisely.

Preparing for Meetings

Careful preparation helps you avoid the two biggest meeting mistakes: (1) holding a meeting when a memo or other message would do the job or (2) holding a meeting without a specific goal in mind. Before you even begin preparing for a meeting, make sure it's truly necessary. Once you're sure, proceed with four preparation tasks:

To ensure a successful meeting, decide on your purpose ahead of time, select the right participants, choose the time and facility carefully, and set a clear agenda.

- **Decide on your purpose.** Although many meetings combine purposes, most focus on one of two types: *Informational meetings* involve sharing information and perhaps coordinating action. *Decision-making meetings* involve persuasion, analysis, and problem solving. They often include a brainstorming session, followed by a debate on the alternatives. Moreover, decision-making meetings require that each participant be aware of the nature of the problem and the criteria for its solution. Whatever your purpose, make sure it is clear and clearly communicated to all participants.
- **Select participants for the meeting.** With a clear purpose in mind, it's easier to identify the right participants. If the session is purely informational and one person will do most of the talking, you can invite a large group. For problem-solving and decision-making meetings, invite only those people who are in a direct position to help the meeting reach its objective. The more participants, the more comments and confusion you're likely to get, and the longer the meeting will take. However, make sure you invite all the key decision makers, or your meeting will fail to satisfy its purpose.
- **Choose the time and the facility.** For working sessions, morning meetings are usually more productive than afternoon sessions. Also, consider the seating arrangements: Are rows of chairs suitable, or do you need a conference table or some other setting? Plus, give some attention to details such as room temperature, lighting, ventilation, acoustics, and refreshments; any of these seemingly minor details can make or break a meeting.
- **Set the agenda.** The success of any meeting depends on the preparation of the participants. Distribute a carefully written agenda to participants, giving them enough time to prepare as needed. A typical agenda format (see Figure 2.2) may seem overly formal, but it will help you start on time and stay on track. A productive agenda answers three key questions: (1) What do we need to do in this meeting to accomplish our goals? (2) What issues will be of greatest importance to all participants? (3) What information must be available in order to discuss these issues?[37] In addition to improving productivity, this level of agenda detail shows respect for participants and the other demands on their time.

Leading and Participating in Meetings

Everyone shares the responsibility for successful meetings.

Everyone in a meeting shares the responsibility for keeping the meeting productive and making it successful. If you're the designated leader of a meeting, however, you have an extra degree of responsibility and accountability. To ensure productive meetings, be sure to do the following:

- **Keep the meeting on track.** A good meeting draws out the best ideas and information the group has to offer. Good leaders occasionally guide, mediate, probe, stimulate, and summarize, but mostly they encourage participants to share. Experience will help you recognize when to be dominant and press the group forward, and when to step back and let people talk. If the meeting lags, you'll need to ask questions to encourage participation. Conversely, there will be times when you have no choice but to cut off discussion in order to stay on schedule.
- **Follow agreed-upon rules.** Business meetings run the gamut from informal to extremely formal, complete with detailed rules for speaking, proposing new items to discuss, voting on proposals, and so on. The larger the meeting, the more formal you'll need to be to maintain order. Formal meetings use **parliamentary procedure**, a time-

FIGURE 2.2
Typical Meeting Agenda

AGENDA

PLANNING COMMITTEE MEETING

Monday, October 21, 2005
10:00 A.M. to 11:00 A.M.

Executive Conference Room

	Person	Proposed Time
I. Call to Order		
II. Roll Call		
III. Approval of Agenda		
IV. Approval of Minutes from Previous Meeting		
V. Chairperson's Report on Site Selection Progress		
VI. Subcommittee Reports		
a. New Markets	Alan	5 minutes
b. New Products	Jennifer	5 minutes
c. Finance	Craig	5 minutes
VII. Old Business—Pricing Policy for New Products	Terry	10 minutes
VIII. New Business		
a. Carson and Canfield Data on New Product Sales	Sarah	10 minutes
b. Restructuring of Product Territories Due to New Product Introductions	Edith	10 minutes
IX. Announcements		
X. Adjournment		

tested method for planning and running effective meetings. The best-known guide to this procedure is *Robert's Rules of Order.* Whatever system of rules you employ, make sure everyone is clear about the expectations.

- **Encourage participation.** As the meeting gets under way, you'll discover that some participants are too quiet and others are too talkative. The quiet participants might be shy, they might be expressing disagreement or resistance, or they might be answering e-mail or instant messages on their laptop computers. Draw them out by asking for their input on issues that particularly pertain to them. For the overly talkative, simply say that time is limited and others need to be heard from.
- **Participate actively.** If you're a meeting participant, try to contribute to both the subject of the meeting and the smooth interaction of the participants. Use your listening skills and powers of observation to size up the interpersonal dynamics of the people; then adapt your behavior to help the group achieve its goals. Speak up if you have something useful to say, but don't monopolize the discussion.
- **Close effectively.** At the conclusion of the meeting, verify that the objectives have been met; if not, arrange for follow-up work as needed. Either summarize the general conclusion of the discussion or list the actions to be taken. Make sure all participants agree on the outcome and give people a chance to clear up any misunderstandings.

CHECKLIST: Improving Meeting Productivity

A. PREPARE CAREFULLY

- Make sure the meeting is necessary.
- Decide on your purpose.
- Select participants carefully.
- Choose the time and facility.
- Set the agenda.

B. LEAD EFFECTIVELY AND PARTICIPATE FULLY

- Keep the meeting on track.
- Follow agreed-upon rules.
- Encourage participation.
- Participate actively.
- Close effectively.

To review the tasks that contribute to productive meetings, refer to "Checklist: Improving Meeting Productivity."

For formal meetings, it's good practice to appoint one person to record the *minutes,* a summary of the important information presented and the decisions made during a meeting. In smaller or informal meetings, attendees often make their own notes on their copies of the agenda. In either case, a clear record of the decisions made and the people responsible for follow-up action is essential.

If your company doesn't have a specific format for minutes, follow the generic format shown in Figure 2.3. Key elements include a list of those present and a list of those who were invited but didn't attend, followed by the times the meeting started and ended, all major decisions reached at the meeting, all assignments of tasks to meeting participants, and all subjects that were deferred to a later meeting. In addition, the minutes objectively summarize important discussions, noting the names of those who contributed major points. Outlines, subheadings, and lists help organize the minutes, and additional documentation (such as tables or charts submitted by meeting participants) are noted in the minutes and attached. Many companies now post meeting minutes on an intranet site for easy reference. Whichever method you use, make sure that responsibilities are clear so that all issues raised at the meeting will be addressed.

Using Meeting Technologies

Virtual meeting technologies connect people spread around the country or around the world.

5 LEARNING OBJECTIVE

Describe how meeting technologies can help participants communicate more successfully

The high cost of travel, loss of valuable work time, increased security concerns, and growing reliance on global workforces and partnerships have all stimulated a number of advances in meeting technologies. Instead of hopping on a plane and spending a couple of days and a couple of thousand dollars for a meeting, you can now hop on the Internet and have that meeting for a fraction of the cost and time commitment. The rise of these technologies has spurred the emergence of **virtual teams**, whose members work in different locations and interact electronically through **virtual meetings**. People may work together for months or years and never meet face to face. At times, technology replaces meetings entirely, such as when team members use e-mail or instant messaging to interact over the course of several hours or days, rather than meet online or over the phone at a specific time.

As with most new technologies, electronic meeting tools are evolving rapidly, and the lines separating these tools have become blurred. For example, instant messaging and videoconferencing are both stand-alone capabilities; both are also common features in **groupware**, an umbrella term for systems that let people communicate, share files, present materials, and work on documents simultaneously.

Naturally, before you and your colleagues can interact electronically, you need some way to connect. Expect to encounter some combination of wired and wireless networking that uses both the public Internet and private corporate networks. Your company might have you connect via a *virtual private network (VPN),* a secure "tunnel" through the public Internet. VPNs let you connect from the office, from home, and from the road—costing much less than an actual private network and providing greater security than regular Internet access. Clothing maker Bernard Chaus replaced its private network and extensive use of postal mail with a VPN; its New York office now communicates with its offices in Hong Kong, South Korea, and Taiwan more effectively than before and at one-sixth the

FIGURE 2.3 Typical Minutes of a Meeting

Provides ample information in the heading about which meeting these minutes pertain to

Lists who did and did not attend the meeting

Gives the start and end times of the meeting

Organizes topics under convenient headings by using an outline format

Summarizes outcomes, not entire discussions:

- Reminds everyone of what took place
- Shows who is responsible for which follow-up tasks
- Summarizes all decisions and suggestions made

MINUTES
Planning Committee Meeting
Human Resources Employee Programs
Monday, October 10, 2005

Present: Tabitha Brown, Peter Crantz, Kathi Kazanopolis, Agatha Myers, Julie Owens, Bob Phelps, Judith Williams
Absent: Joseph Kingman, Maria Lopez

Meeting called to order by: Agatha Myers at 9:30 a.m. (ended at 11:45 a.m.)

1. **November program (speaker replacement)**
   - Kathi Kazanopolis offered to give a presentation about continuing education in job skills, to include detailed information about available workshops, online courses, etc.
   - Julie Owens volunteered to help Kathi with preparation: handouts, possible topics for small group discussions, research, etc.

2. **Future programs**
   - Bob Phelps contacted Edith Orlofsky, who teaches business communication courses at UCLA Extension, about giving a writing (or related) presentation to employees (possibly December). He is still waiting to hear back from her.
   - Tax program: Still targeted for January or February. Judith Williams will try to locate a tax attorney or tax accountant as speaker.
   - Tabitha Brown will contact Joan Mason to find out whether the "Nitty Gritty Grammar" authors (Edith Fine and Judith Josephson) are available in January or February.
   - Elizabeth Garfield asked for clarification about the specific topics to address in her presentation on marketing. She will be teaching a UCSD Extension class on marketing next month and might be able to present a shorter version to employees once the content has been developed (possibly March).

3. **December newsletter (quarterly)**
   - Calendar of upcoming events for December quarterly newsletter: Information needs to be sent to Julie Owens by November 21.
   - Bob Phelps will write up some information about the Bay Area HR Forum and their rates for their newsletter.
   - Employee Profiles: Maria Lopez's last employee profile will be published in the December newsletter. Joseph Kingman broke his arm and will be unable to help out in the interim, as originally proposed.
     - Tabitha Brown will ask Maria if she can recommend a replacement.
     - Peter Crantz will contact Dina Gaines about writing some profiles.
     - If the employee profiles do continue, Julie Owens suggested publishing the profiled member's photograph with the feature.

cost.[38] Whatever the network, you'll connect with colleagues and customers using technologies such as e-mail and instant messaging, shared workspaces, and virtual meetings.

E-Mail and Instant Messaging

In addition to their everyday communication uses, e-mail and instant messaging (IM) are now used extensively to both supplement and replace meetings. With the cost, hassles, and even risks of travel, more and more companies look to these tools to help teams interact without being in the same room together. By giving employees a fast, inexpensive way to communicate, e-mail and IM enhance information sharing and project collaboration.

Of the two technologies, e-mail is less effective for real-time communication because it forces you to check for incoming messages, which can be delayed for several seconds or even longer as they pass through the e-mail system. However, e-mail is still used to set up and supplement meetings. For example, the group scheduling capabilities in e-mail programs such as Microsoft Outlook make it easy for you to verify everyone's schedules and send out invitation messages. You can also use e-mail during teleconferences and videoconferences to share files. In a pinch, e-mail can even substitute for IM and face-to-face meetings, although it becomes unwieldy when more than two or three people are involved.

Instant messaging has become an important business technology, frequently replacing or supplementing meetings.

Instant messaging is a recent entry into the corporate communication scene, but it is catching on rapidly. Indeed, IM may soon surpass e-mail as the more commonly used tool for communicating with business associates and customers. Some businesses use the same consumer-oriented IM systems that you might already be familiar with, such as AOL Instant Messenger, Yahoo!, and MSN Messenger from Microsoft. However, many companies use business-oriented versions of these systems, or they choose systems designed specifically for business or even for a particular industry. For example, a custom-built IM network now connects thousands of users in the financial services industry, which is required by law to archive all written communication with customers (something a typical IM system can't do).

Various business IM systems offer a range of capabilities, including basic chat (see Figure 2.4), *presence awareness* (the ability to quickly see who's at their desks and available to IM), remote display of documents, video capabilities, remote control of other computers, and the bot capability you read about in Chapter 1.[39] All these capabilities can supplement both one-on-one conversations and group meetings and can even replace meetings in many cases.

The benefits of IM in meetings (and in the workplace in general) include its rapid response to urgent messages, lower cost than both phone calls and e-mail, ability to mimic conversation more closely than e-mail, and availability on a wide range of devices from PCs to phones to PDAs.[40]

The drawbacks include both technical and behavioral issues. The primary technical issues are security (one quarter of all U.S. corporations have blocked employee access to consumer IM systems because of worries that sensitive communications might be intercepted by outsiders), user authentication (making sure that online correspondents are really who they appear to be), the inability to log messages for later review and archiving, and incompatibility between competing IM systems.

Although developers will eventually solve all these problems, the human side of IM will be an ongoing concern. To use IM effectively for meetings, all users need to pay attention to some important behavioral issues: the potential for constant interruptions, the ease of accidentally mixing personal and business messages, the risk of being out of the loop (if a hot discussion or impromptu meeting flares up when you're away from your PC or other IM device), and the "vast potential for wasted time" (in the words of MIT labor economist David Autor). On top of all that, you're at the mercy of other people's typing abilities, which can make IM agonizingly slow.[41]

FIGURE 2.4
Yahoo! Business-Class Instant Messaging

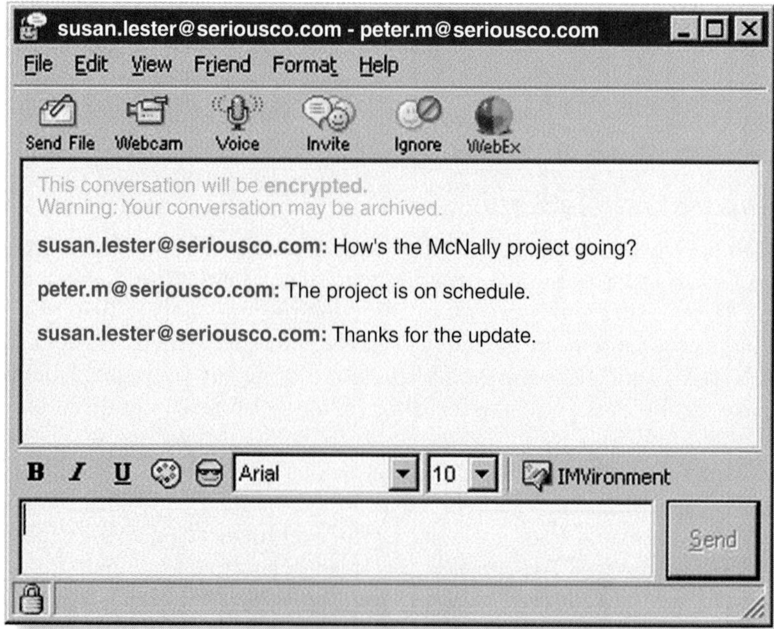

Regardless of the system you're using, you can make IM more efficient and effective for both meetings and general communication by following these tips:[42]

- Unless a meeting is scheduled, make yourself unavailable when you need to focus on other work.
- If you're not on a secure system, don't send confidential information.
- Be extremely careful about sending personal messages—they have a tendency to pop up on other people's computers at embarrassing moments.
- Don't use IM for important but impromptu meetings if you can't verify that everyone concerned will be available.
- Unless your system is set up for it, don't use IM for lengthy, complex messages; e-mail is better for those.
- If IM has become the primary communication channel in your company, particularly for important meetings, make sure everyone is comfortable with the technology and both capable and willing to use it.
- Try to avoid carrying on multiple IM conversations at once to minimize the chance of sending messages to the wrong people.
- Don't assume that whatever IM slang you might use in personal communications is appropriate for business messages; your colleagues may not be familiar or comfortable with it.
- If your IM system has filters for *spim,* the IM version of e-mail spam, make sure they're active and up to date.[43]

Shared Workspaces

Shared workspaces are "virtual offices" that give everyone on a team access to the same set of resources and information: databases, calendars, project plans, pertinent IM and e-mail exchanges, shared reference materials, and team-created documents (see Figure 2.5). Workspaces such as Documentum eRoom, Groove Workspace, Microsoft SharePoint, and IBM Lotus Team Workspace create a seamless, comprehensive environment for collaboration. Such workspaces make it easy for geographically dispersed team members to access shared files anytime, anywhere. Typically accessible through a web browser, the workspace lets you and your team organize its files into a collection of electronic folders.

Shared workspaces give team members instant access to shared resources and information.

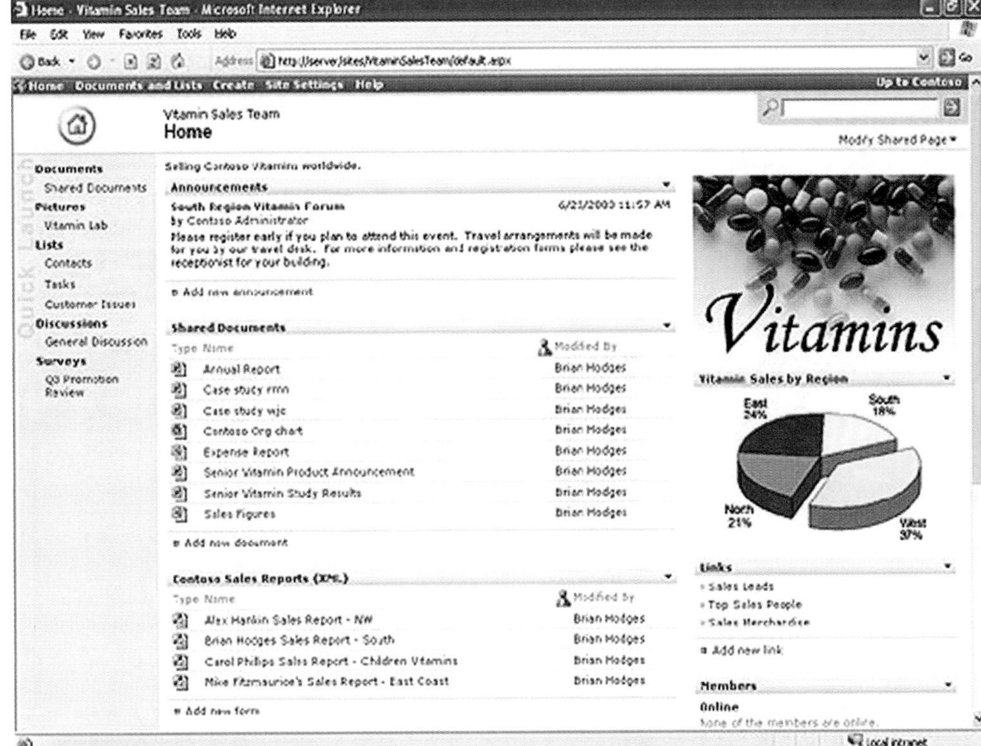

FIGURE 2.5
Shared Workspaces

Most systems also have built-in intelligence to control which team members can read, edit, and save specific files. *Revision control* goes one step further: it allows only one person at a time to check on a given file or document and records all the changes that person makes. This feature prevents two people from independently editing the same report at the same time, thus avoiding the messy situation in which a team would end up with two versions of the same document. Many systems also include the presence awareness offered by IM systems so that you can tell instantly which team members are online and available to chat or to attend an impromptu meeting.[44]

Virtual Meetings

Virtual meetings range from videoconferencing to web-based systems.

Virtual meeting technologies cover a wide range of tools that let team members in different locations interact at the same time without the hassle, risk, and cost of travel.[45] IM chat sessions and telephone conference calls are the simplest forms of virtual meetings. **Videoconferencing** combines audio communication with live video, letting team members see each other, demonstrate products, and transmit other visual information. Videoconferencing is available in two systems. *Room systems* require specialized conference room facilities but offer large-screen displays and the ability to accommodate more participants. *Desktop systems* typically use a webcam attached to each participant's PC, with the video displayed on the computer monitor and audio provided either over the Internet or a standard phone connection.

The most sophisticated **web-based meeting systems** combine the best of IM, shared workspaces, and videoconferencing with other tools such as *virtual whiteboards* that let teams collaborate in real time (see Figure 2.6). Attendees can log on from a desktop or laptop PC, PDA, or even a web-enabled cell phone from almost anywhere in the world.

Through web-based collaboration, far-flung teams can work together on documents, designs, and other materials as though they were in the same room. For instance, you and your team might have the task of laying out the floor plan of the company's new offices. Rather than trying to verbally describe visual ideas to one another, you can all make changes to the same graphic design file. One person has control of the cursor at a time, and he or she can add walls, move tables, and so on. If you then see a better way to arrange the

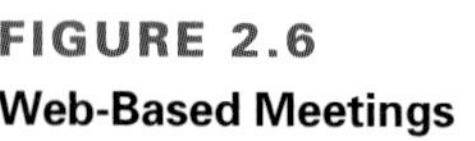
FIGURE 2.6
Web-Based Meetings

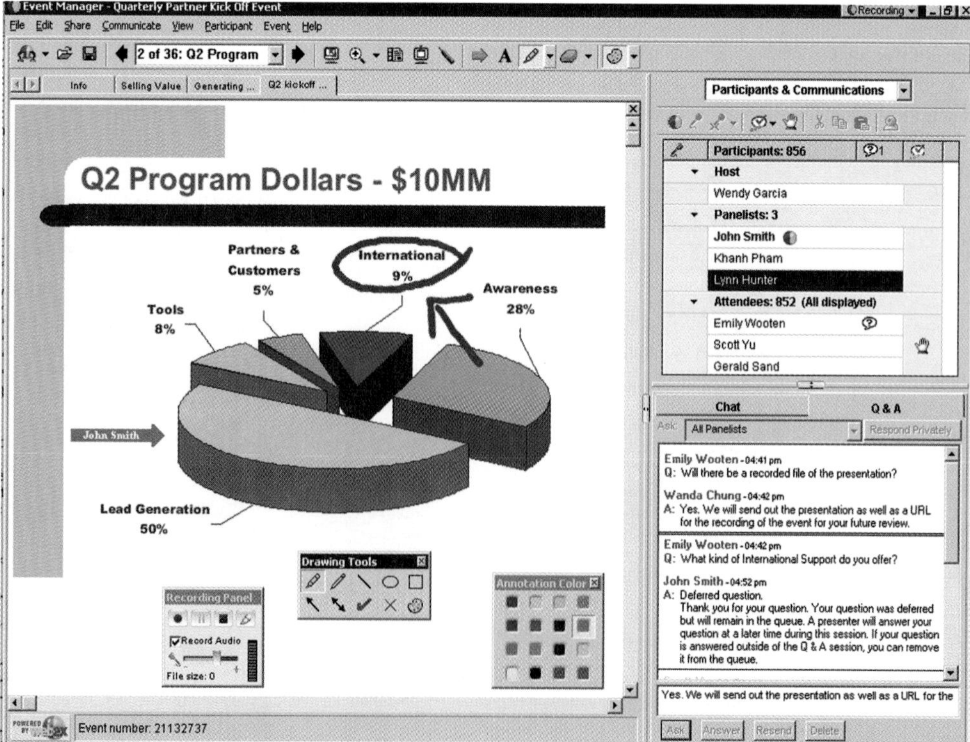

walls, you can ask for control of the cursor and then move the walls yourself. Not only does this level of interaction help the team work more closely, but the document or drawing is ready to go immediately. You don't have to wait for one person to incorporate everyone's inputs and produce a new version of the drawing.

The latest twist in online meetings are *darknets,* small, invitation-only networks that are typically more secure than other networks. Although they are popular with people sharing pirated music files, darknets have legitimate business uses as well, primarily to exchange highly confidential information.

IMPROVING YOUR LISTENING SKILLS

Listening is one of the most important skills in the workplace.

The success of meetings and teams, of individuals and companies, depends on effective listening. The importance of listening is self-evident: If a receiver won't or can't listen, the speaker's message simply won't get through. Some 80 percent of top executives say that listening is the most important skill needed to get things done in the workplace.[46]

Effective listening strengthens organizational relationships, enhances product delivery, alerts the organization to opportunities for innovation, and allows the organization to manage growing diversity both in the workforce and in the customers it serves.[47] Companies that listen effectively stay informed, up to date, and out of trouble; those that don't do so lose millions of dollars each year. Effective listening is vital to the process of building trust not only between organizations but also between individuals.[48] Throughout your own career, effective listening will give you a competitive edge, enhancing your performance and thus the influence you have within your company.

Recognizing Different Types of Listening

Understanding the nature of listening is the first step toward improving your listening skills. People listen in a variety of ways, and although how they listen is often an unconscious choice, it influences both what they hear and the meaning they extract. For instance, an employee who values teamwork and relationships will naturally be inclined to look for ways to bond with a speaker. In contrast, an action-oriented listener will listen more for information related to tasks that need to be completed.

To be a good listener, vary the way you listen to suit the situation.

In either case, relying on a single approach to listening limits your effectiveness. A people-oriented listener might miss important information about an upcoming deadline, whereas an action-oriented listener might miss an important clue that there's a personal problem brewing between two team members.[49] As you read the following paragraphs about the three types of listening, reflect on your own inclination as a listener, and consider how learning to use several methods could make your listening more effective.

The primary goal of **content listening** is to understand and retain the speaker's message. When you're listening for content, the emphasis is on information and understanding. Ask questions to clarify the material and probe for details. Since you're not evaluating at this point, it doesn't matter whether you agree or disagree, approve or disapprove—only that you understand. Try to overlook the speaker's style and any limitations in the presentation; just focus on the information.[50]

The goal of **critical listening** is to understand and evaluate the meaning of the speaker's message on several levels: the logic of the argument, the strength of the evidence, the validity of the conclusions, the implications of the message for you and your organization, the speaker's intentions and motives, and the omission of any important or relevant points. If you're skeptical, ask questions to explore the speaker's point of view and credibility. Be on the lookout for bias that might color the way the information is presented, and be careful to separate opinions from facts.[51]

The goal of **empathic listening** is to understand the speaker's feelings, needs, and wants so that you can appreciate his or her point of view, regardless of whether you share that perspective. By listening in an empathic way, you help the individual vent the emotions that prevent a calm, clear-headed approach to the subject. Sometimes the only thing an

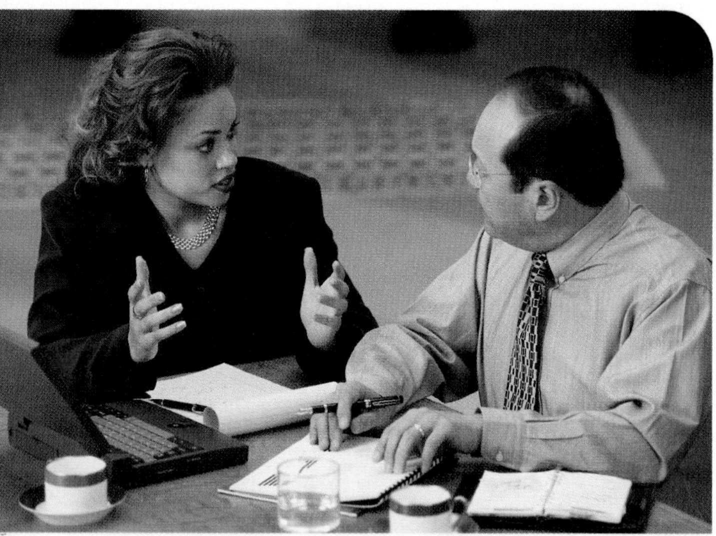
When you engage in empathic listening, you pay attention to feelings, needs, and wants—not just the spoken words.

upset colleague is looking for is somebody to listen, so avoid the temptation to jump in with advice unless the person specifically asks for it. Also, don't judge the speaker's feelings and don't try to tell people they shouldn't feel this or that emotion. Instead, let the speaker know that you appreciate his or her feelings and understand the situation. Once you establish that connection, you can then help the speaker move on to search for a solution.[52]

Understanding the Listening Process

No matter which mode of listening you use in a given conversation, it's important to recognize that listening is a far more complex process than most people think. As a consequence, most of us aren't very good at it. Given such complexity, it's no wonder most of us listen at or below a 25 percent efficiency rate, remember only about half of what's said during a 10-minute conversation, and forget half of that within 48 hours.[53] Furthermore, when questioned about material we've just heard, we are likely to get the facts mixed up.[54]

6 LEARNING OBJECTIVE

Describe the listening process, and explain how good listeners overcome barriers at each stage of the process

Why is such a seemingly simple activity so difficult? The answer lies in the complexity of the process. To listen effectively, you need to successfully complete five separate steps:[55]

Listening involves five steps: receiving, interpreting, remembering, evaluating, and responding.

- **Receiving:** You start by physically hearing the message and acknowledging it. Physical reception can be blocked by noise, impaired hearing, or inattention. Some experts also include nonverbal messages as part of this stage, since these factors influence the listening process as well.
- **Interpreting:** Your next step is to assign meaning to sounds, which you do according to your own values, beliefs, ideas, expectations, roles, needs, and personal history.
- **Remembering:** Before you can act on the information, you need to store it for future processing. First you need to capture it in *short-term memory,* which is your brain's temporary note pad. Information disappears from short-term memory quickly, though, so you need to transfer it to *long-term memory* for safekeeping.
- **Evaluating:** With the speaker's message captured, your next step is to evaluate it by applying critical thinking skills. Separate fact from opinion and evaluate the quality of the evidence.
- **Responding:** After you've evaluated the speaker's message, you now react. If you're communicating one-on-one or in a small group, the initial response generally takes the form of verbal feedback. If you're one of many in an audience, your initial response may take the form of applause, laughter, or silence. Later on, you may act on what you have heard.

If any one of these steps breaks down, the listening process becomes less effective or even fails entirely. For example, if you work in a noisy environment, you may never hear a message intended for you. If you do receive the message, a lack of shared meaning or shared language between you and the speaker might lead to a different interpretation than the speaker intended. Or you might've looked away when the person was speaking and thereby missed an important nonverbal clue that would've helped you decipher the intended meaning. And even if you did interpret the meaning as the speaker hoped, you might forget it before you get around to acting on the information.

As both a sender and receiver, you can reduce the failure rate by recognizing and overcoming a variety of physical and mental barriers to effective listening.

Overcoming Barriers to Effective Listening

Good listeners actively try to overcome the barriers to successful listening.

Good listeners look for ways to overcome potential barriers throughout the listening process (see Table 2.2). You are unlikely to have control over some barriers to physical

TABLE 2.2 Distinguishing Effective Listeners from Ineffective Listeners

EFFECTIVE LISTENERS	INEFFECTIVE LISTENERS
• Listen actively	• Listen passively
• Take careful and complete notes	• Take no notes or ineffective notes
• Make frequent eye contact with the speaker (depends on culture to some extent)	• Make little or no eye contact
• Stay focused on the speaker and the content	• Allow their minds to wander; are easily distracted
• Mentally paraphrase key points to maintain attention level and ensure comprehension	• Fail to paraphrase
• Adjust listening style to the situation	• Listen with the same style, regardless of the situation
• Give the speaker nonverbal cues (such as nodding to show agreement or raising eyebrows to show surprise or skepticism)	• Fail to give the speaker nonverbal feedback
• Save questions or points of disagreement until an appropriate time	• Interrupt whenever they disagree or don't understand
• Overlook stylistic differences and focus on the speaker's message	• Are distracted by or unduly influenced by stylistic differences; are judgmental
• Make distinctions between main points and supporting details	• Unable to distinguish main points from details
• Look for opportunities to learn	• Assume they already know everything that's important to know

reception, such as conference room acoustics, poor cell phone reception, background music, and so on. However, you can certainly control other barriers, such as interrupting speakers or creating distractions that make it hard for others to pay attention. If you have questions for a speaker, wait until he or she has finished speaking. And don't think that you're not interrupting just because you're not talking. Rustling papers, tapping on your PDA, checking your watch, making eye contact with someone over the speaker's shoulder—these are just a few of the many nonverbal behaviors that can interrupt a speaker and degrade physical reception.

Selective listening is one of the most common barriers to effective listening. If your mind wanders, you often stay tuned out until you hear a word or phrase that gets your attention once more. But by that time, you're unable to recall what the speaker *actually* said; instead, you remember what you *think* the speaker probably said.[56]

Your mind can process information much faster than most speakers talk.

One reason listeners' minds tend to wander is that people think faster than they speak. Most people speak at about 120 to 150 words per minute. However, studies indicate that, depending on the subject and the individual, humans can process audio information at around 500 words per minute.[57] In other words, your brain has a lot of free time whenever you're listening, and if left unsupervised, it will find a thousand other things to think about. Rather than listening part time, make a conscious effort to focus on the speaker, and use the extra time to analyze what you hear, prepare questions you might need to ask, and engage in other relevant thinking.

A common barrier to successful interpretation is prejudgment—making up your mind before truly hearing what another person has to say. Remember, assumptions that work in one situation or in one area of your life might be inappropriate for other situations. Similarly, some people listen defensively, always on the lookout for perceived personal attacks. To protect their self-esteem, they distort messages by tuning out anything that doesn't confirm their view of themselves.

Overcoming such interpretation barriers can be difficult because you might not even be aware of them. As Chapter 1 noted, selective perception leads listeners to mold a message to fit their own conceptual framework. The speaker's frame of reference may be quite

CHECKLIST: Overcoming Barriers to Effective Listening

- Control whatever barriers to physical reception you can (especially interrupting speakers by asking questions or by exhibiting disruptive nonverbal behaviors).
- Avoid selective listening by trying to focus on the speaker and analyzing what you hear.
- Keep an open mind by avoiding any prejudgment and by not listening defensively.
- Try to paraphrase the speaker's ideas, giving that person a chance to confirm or correct your interpretation.
- Don't count on your memory, but record, write down, or capture information in some other physical way.
- Improve your short-term memory by repeating information, organizing it into patterns, or breaking it into shorter lists.
- Improve your long-term memory by association, categorization, visualization, and mnemonics.

different from yours, so work hard to determine what the speaker really means. Listening with an open mind will help you overcome many interpretation barriers.

Even when your intentions are the best, you can still misinterpret incoming messages if you and the speaker don't share enough language or experience. Lack of common ground is why misinterpretation is so frequent between speakers of different native languages, even when they're trying to speak the same language. When listening to a speaker whose native language or life experience is different from yours, try to paraphrase that person's ideas. Give the speaker a chance to confirm what you think you heard or to correct any misinterpretation.

When information is crucial, don't count on your memory.

Overcoming memory barriers is a slightly easier problem to solve, but it takes some work. One simple rule: Don't count on your memory. If the information is crucial, record it, write it down, or capture it in some other physical way. However, if you do need to memorize something, you can capture information in short-term memory for a few seconds or a few minutes by repeating it to yourself (silently, if need be), organizing it into patterns (perhaps in alphabetical order or as steps in a process), and breaking a long list of items into several shorter lists. To store information in long-term memory, four techniques can help: (1) associate new information with something closely related (such as the restaurant in which you met a new client), (2) categorize the new information into logical groups (such as alphabetizing the names of products you're trying to remember), (3) visualize words and ideas as pictures, and (4) create mnemonics such as acronyms or rhymes. Note that all four techniques have an important factor in common: You have to *do* something to make the information stick.

If you can overcome all these barriers to effective listening, you're finally ready to evaluate what you hear and respond as needed. Your response might be simple, even automatic, such as laughing or thanking the speaker and following her directions to the office building around the corner. However, your response might require a far more rigorous process of analysis, such as interpreting the results of a series of in-depth market research interviews before making recommendations about future product development. For a reminder of the steps you can take to overcome listening barriers, see "Checklist: Overcoming Barriers to Effective Listening."

7 LEARNING OBJECTIVE

Clarify the importance of nonverbal communication, and briefly describe six categories of nonverbal expression

IMPROVING YOUR NONVERBAL COMMUNICATION SKILLS

The boss walks out of the conference room after explaining that your department needs to double its sales next year. You're skeptical, though. You turn to a colleague on your right and raise your eyebrows. She smiles and nods, sitting upright on the edge of her seat—she seems to relish the challenge. You turn to the left, but that colleague seems to dread what lies ahead, rolling his eyes and sighing. He is slumped so far down in his chair you wonder how he keeps from sliding off.

A complex conversation has just taken place, but not a single word was spoken. **Nonverbal communication** is the interpersonal process of sending and receiving information, both intentionally and unintentionally, without using written or spoken language. Nonverbal signals play three important roles in communication. The first is complementing verbal language. Nonverbal signals can strengthen a verbal message (when nonverbal signals match words), they can weaken a verbal message (when nonverbal signals don't match words), or they can replace words entirely.

Nonverbal communication supplements spoken language.

The second role for nonverbal signals is revealing truth. People find it much harder to deceive with nonverbal signals. You might tell a client that the project is coming along fine, but your sweaty brow and nervous eyes send a different message. In fact, nonverbal communication often conveys more to listeners than the words you speak—particularly when they're trying to decide how you really feel about a situation or when they're trying to judge your credibility and aptitude for leadership.[58] The third role for nonverbal signals is conveying information efficiently. Nonverbal signals can convey both nuance and rich amounts of information in a single instant, as the previous conference room example suggests.

Nonverbal clues help you ascertain the truth of spoken information.

Communication Solution

Rather than relying on memos, newsletters, or other common formats, The Container Store takes advantage of the immediate communication that comes with face-to-face contact. Effective listening by all team members is key to the success of small group meetings at the beginning and end of every business day.

Recognizing Nonverbal Communication

You've been tuned into nonverbal communication since your first contact with other human beings, but special attention to these signals in the workplace will enhance your ability to communicate successfully. Moreover, as you interact with business associates from other cultures, you'll discover that some nonverbal signals don't necessarily translate across cultures (see "Communicating Across Cultures: Actions Speak Louder Than Words All Around the World"). You'll learn more about cultural influences on nonverbal communication in Chapter 3. The range and variety of nonverbal signals is almost endless, but you can grasp the basics by studying five general categories:

Nonverbal signals include facial expression, gesture and posture, vocal characteristics, personal appearance, touch, and time and space.

- **Facial expression.** Your face is the primary site for expressing your emotions; it reveals both the type and the intensity of your feelings.[59] Your eyes are especially effective for

Actions Speak Louder Than Words All Around the World

"He wouldn't look me in the eye. I found it disconcerting that he kept looking all over the room but rarely at me," said Barbara Walters after her interview with Libya's Colonel Muammar al-Qadhafi. Like many people in the United States, Walters associated eye contact with trustworthiness, so when Qadhafi withheld eye contact, she felt uncomfortable. In fact, Qadhafi was paying Walters a compliment. In Libya, *not* looking conveys respect, and looking straight at a woman is considered nearly as serious as physical assault.

Nonverbal cues vary widely between cultures, as you can see by comparing just a few:

- Canadian listeners nod to signal agreement.
- Japanese listeners nod to indicate only that they have understood.
- British listeners stare at the speaker, blinking their eyes to indicate understanding.
- People in the United States are taught that it's impolite to stare.

To adjust your nonverbal communication to other cultures, learn as much as you can. Consult books, seminars, and motion pictures on cultural differences. Try renting movies and TV shows from other countries. Examine illustrations in news and business magazines to get an idea of expected business dress and personal space. Above all, remain flexible as you interact with people from other cultures.

CAREER APPLICATIONS

1. Explain how watching a movie from another country might help you prepare to interpret nonverbal behavior from that culture correctly.
2. One of your co-workers is originally from Saudi Arabia. You like him, and the two of you work well together. However, he stands so close when you speak with him that it makes you uncomfortable. Do you tell him of your discomfort or try to cover it up?

indicating attention and interest, influencing others, regulating interaction, and establishing dominance.[60]

- **Gesture and posture.** By moving or not moving your body, you express both specific and general messages, some voluntary and some involuntary. Many gestures—a wave of the hand, for example—have a specific and intentional meaning. Other types of body movement are unintentional and express a more general message. Slouching, leaning forward, fidgeting, and walking briskly are all unconscious signals that reveal whether you feel confident or nervous, friendly or hostile, assertive or passive, powerful or powerless.
- **Vocal characteristics.** Your voice also carries both intentional and unintentional messages. Consider the sentence "What have you been up to?" If you repeat that question, changing your tone of voice and stressing various words, you can consciously convey quite different messages. However, your voice can also reveal things of which you are unaware. Your tone and volume, your accent and speaking pace, and all the little *um*'s and *ah*'s that creep into your speech say a lot about who you are, your relationship with the audience, and the emotions underlying your words.
- **Personal appearance.** People respond to others on the basis of their physical appearance, sometimes fairly and other times unfairly. Although an individual's body type and facial features impose limitations, most people are able to control their appearance to some degree. Grooming, clothing, accessories, style—you can control all of these. If your goal is to make a good impression, adopt the style of the people you want to impress.
- **Touch.** Touch is an important way to convey warmth, comfort, and reassurance. Touch is so powerful, in fact, that it is governed by cultural customs that establish who can touch whom and how in various circumstances. In the United States and Great Britain, for instance, people usually touch less frequently than people in France or Costa Rica. Even within each culture's norms, however, individual attitudes toward touch can vary widely. A manager might be comfortable using hugs to express support or congratulations, but his or her subordinates might interpret those hugs as either a show of dominance or sexual interest.[61] Touch is a complex subject. The best advice: when in doubt, don't touch.
- **Time and space.** Like touch, time and space can be used to assert authority, imply intimacy, and send other nonverbal messages. For instance, some people try to demonstrate their own importance or disregard for others by making other people wait; others show respect by being on time. The manipulation of space works in a similar way. When top executives gather for lunch in a private dining room, they send a strong signal to all the employees crowding into the cafeteria downstairs. The decision to respect or violate someone's "private space" is another powerful nonverbal signal. Again, attitudes toward time and space vary from culture to culture (see Chapter 3).

Physical appearance is an important element of nonverbal communication. Dressing too formally or too casually for a particular setting could send a message that you don't understand or don't respect the situation.

Using Nonverbal Communication Effectively

Paying attention to nonverbal cues will make you both a better speaker and a better listener (see "Checklist: Improving Nonverbal Communication Skills"). When you're talking, be more conscious of the nonverbal cues you might be sending. Are they effective without being manipulative? Consider a situation in which an employee has come to you to talk about a raise. This situation is a stressful one for the employee, so don't say you're interested in what she has to tell you and then spend your time glancing at your computer or checking your watch. Conversely, if you already know you won't be able to give her the raise, be honest in expressing your emotions. Don't over-

CHECKLIST: Improving Nonverbal Communication Skills

A. UNDERSTAND THE ROLES THAT NONVERBAL SIGNALS PLAY IN COMMUNICATION

- Nonverbal signals complement verbal language by strengthening, weakening, or replacing words.
- Nonverbal signals reveal the truth, often conveying more to listeners than spoken words.

B. RECOGNIZE NONVERBAL COMMUNICATION SIGNALS

- Note that facial expressions (especially eye contact) reveal the type and intensity of a speaker's feelings.
- Watch for clues from gesture and posture.
- Listen for vocal characteristics that signal who the speaker is, the speaker's relationship with the audience, and the emotions underlying the speaker's words.
- Recognize that listeners are influenced by physical appearance.
- Be careful with physical contact; touch can convey positive attributes but can also be interpreted as dominance or sexual interest.
- Pay attention to the use of time and space.

compensate for your own stress by smiling too broadly or shaking her hand too vigorously. Both nonverbal signals would raise her hopes without justification. In either case, match your nonverbal cues to the tone of the situation.

Work to make sure your nonverbal signals match the tone and content of your spoken communication.

Also consider the nonverbal signals you send when you're not talking—the clothes you wear, the way you sit, the way you walk. Are you talking like a serious business professional but dressing like you belong in a nightclub or a frat house? The way you look and act sends signals too; make sure you're sending the right ones.

What signals does your personal appearance send?

When you listen, be sure to pay attention to the speaker's nonverbal clues. Do they amplify the spoken words or contradict them? Is the speaker intentionally using nonverbal signals to send you a message that he or she can't put into words? Be observant, but don't assume that you can "read someone like a book." Nonverbal signals are powerful, but they aren't infallible. Just because someone doesn't look you square in the eye doesn't mean he or she is lying, contrary to popular belief.[62] If something doesn't feel right, ask the speaker an honest and respectful question—doing so might clear everything up, or it might uncover issues you need to explore further.

COMMUNICATION CHALLENGES AT THE CONTAINER STORE

During one of your frequent visits to the local Container Store, the manager asks if you'd like to interview for a job (the company often hires its best customers). Three weeks later you report for work and attend your first huddle. Surprisingly, it isn't as energizing or informative as described in your communication textbook: the shift manager, Tamara, lets two people do most of the talking and does little to encourage input from others. Still, the huddle ends on time and everyone spreads out for another busy day.

Individual Challenge: A month later, cofounder Kip Tindell drops in for a visit—early enough to attend the morning huddle. As usual, Tamara leads another lackluster session, even with a co-founder attending. Tindell spends the morning wandering the store, talking to employees and customers. During his chat with you, Tindell describes what he observed during the huddle and asks what you would do to improve the situation. What will you suggest? Write out your ideas.

Team Challenge: Huddle-like meetings seem to be an effective communication tool in a retail operation such as The Container Store. In a small group, discuss the value of a huddle in (a) an electronics manufacturing company and (b) an advertising agency. In either company, how would you ensure the effectiveness of a huddle held via teleconference or online meeting? List your conclusions in writing.

SUMMARY OF LEARNING OBJECTIVES

1 **Highlight the advantages and disadvantages of working in teams.** Teams can achieve a higher level of performance than individuals because of the combined intelligence and energy of the group. Motivation and creativity flourish in team settings. Moreover, individuals tend to perform better because they achieve a sense of purpose by belonging to a group. Teams also bring more input and a greater diversity of views, which tends to result in better decisions. And because team members participate in the decision process, they are committed to seeing the results succeed. Teams are not without disadvantages, however. Poorly managed teams can be a waste of everyone's time. For example, if members are pressured to conform, they may develop groupthink, which can lead to poor-quality decisions and ill-advised actions. Some members may let their private motives get in the way. Others may not contribute their fair share, so certain tasks may not be completed.

2 **Outline an effective approach to team communication.** Collaborative communication is a great opportunity for teams to pool their diverse talents and knowledge to produce messages that are of higher quality than any single team member could produce on his or her own. However, collaborative writing requires close attention. Select team members carefully to balance talents and viewpoints, and be sure to agree on project goals at the outset to avoid confusion and wasted time. If the team hasn't worked together before, make sure they have time to get to know one another. Next, make sure that everyone clearly understands individual responsibilities, processes, and tools. Also, resist the temptation to write as a group; research and plan as a group, but assign the actual writing to one person, or at least assign separate sections to individual writers and have one person edit them all.

3 **Explain how group dynamics can affect team effectiveness.** When group dynamics encourage full participation and constructive resolution of conflict, teams communicate more effectively, both internally and externally. In contrast, when group dynamics are negative, communication breaks down within the team—whether from groupthink, too many members assuming dysfunctional self-oriented roles, or excessive levels of conflict. As a result, the team is also less able to communicate externally in a clear and coherent manner.

4 **Discuss the role of etiquette in team settings, both in the workplace and in social settings.** The ability of all members of the team to get along, day in and day out, is vital to every team's success. Etiquette plays an important part in this process. If team members get on each other's nerves through inconsiderate behavior, communication gradually breaks down and vital energy gets diverted away from the team's real mission. In the workplace, team members need to pay attention to factors such as personal appearance, grooming, and phone skills as they affect not only other team members but also the people with whom the team interacts. Team communication often extends into social settings, and each team member needs to keep in mind that they represent the company when out in public. Proper etiquette in these situations helps foster good communication, particularly when new people are introduced to the group.

5 **Describe how meeting technologies can help participants communicate more successfully.** Communication and groupware technologies such as e-mail, instant messaging, shared workspaces, and virtual meetings enhance communication by helping teams break down the barriers of time and distance. E-mail and instant messaging let employees communicate in real time or nearly real time, without the cost, time investment, and risks of travel. Shared workspaces give teams instant access to a common set of project resources, including documents, databases, schedules, and other materials. Virtual meetings combine several of these technologies with others (such as virtual whiteboards) to emulate in-person meetings over long distances.

6 **Describe the listening process, and explain how good listeners overcome barriers at each stage of the process.** The listening process involves five activities: (1) receiving (physically hearing the message), (2) interpreting (assigning meaning to what you hear), (3) remembering (storing the message for future reference), (4) evaluating (thinking about the message), and (5) responding (reacting to the message, taking action, or giving feedback). Several barriers can interfere with the listening process. To improve reception, minimize certain distractions by holding questions until the speaker finishes and avoiding distracting nonverbal behaviors, such as rustling papers, tapping on your PDA, or not looking at the speaker. To improve interpretation, avoid prejudgment and defensive listening by taking a patient, open-minded approach to listening. To improve remembering, capture information in some physical way, recording it or writing it down. Store information for the short term by repeating it to yourself, organizing it into patterns, or breaking a long list into several shorter lists. Also transfer information from short-term to long-term memory through association, categorization, visualization, and mnemonics. To improve evaluating, overcome selective listening by focusing on the speaker, taking careful notes, mentally paraphrasing what's being said, and analyzing the speaker's argument.

To improve responding, react naturally when appropriate and plan out any response to a more complex message.

7 **Clarify the importance of nonverbal communication, and briefly describe six categories of nonverbal expression.** Nonverbal communication is important because actions speak louder than words. Body language is more difficult to control than words and may reveal a person's true feelings, motivation, or character. Therefore, people believe nonverbal signals over words. In addition, nonverbal communication is more efficient; with a wave of your hand or a wink, you can streamline your thoughts and do so without much thought. Types of nonverbal expression include facial expression, gesture and posture, vocal characteristics, personal appearance, touching behavior, and use of time and space.

Test Your Knowledge

1. How can organizations and employees benefit from successful teamwork?
2. What steps should teams take to ensure successful communication results?
3. How do self-oriented team roles differ from team-maintenance roles and task-facilitating roles?
4. What is groupthink, and how can it affect an organization?
5. How can organizations help team members successfully resolve conflict?
6. Why is etiquette so important in team settings?
7. What questions should an effective agenda answer?
8. What are the main activities that make up the listening process?
9. How does content listening differ from critical listening and empathic listening?
10. In what six ways can an individual communicate nonverbally?

Apply Your Knowledge

1. How can nonverbal communication help you run a meeting? How can it help you call a meeting to order, emphasize important topics, show approval, express reservations, regulate the flow of conversation, and invite a colleague to continue with a comment?
2. Whenever your boss asks for feedback, she blasts anyone offering criticism, which causes people to agree with everything she says. You want to talk to her about it, but what should you say? List some of the points you want to make when you discuss this issue with your boss.
3. Is conflict in a team good or bad? Explain your answer.
4. At your last department meeting, three people monopolized the entire discussion. What might you do at the next meeting to encourage other department members to voluntarily participate?
5. **Ethical Choices** Strange instant messages occasionally pop up on your computer screen during your team's virtual meetings, followed quickly by embarrassed apologies from one of your colleagues in another city. You eventually figure out that this person is working from home, even though he says he's in the office; moreover, the messages suggest that he's running a sideline business from his home. IM is crucial to your team's communication, and you're concerned about the frequent disruptions, not to mention your colleague's potential ethical violations. What should you do? Explain your choice.

Practice Your Knowledge

Document for Analysis

A project leader has made notes about covering the following items at the quarterly budget meeting. Prepare a formal agenda by putting these items into a logical order and rewriting, where necessary, to give phrases a more consistent sound.

- Budget Committee Meeting to be held on December 12, 2005, at 9:30 A.M.
- I will call the meeting to order.
- Real estate director's report: A closer look at cost overruns on Greentree site.
- The group will review and approve the minutes from last quarter's meeting.
- I will ask the finance director to report on actual versus projected quarterly revenues and expenses.
- I will distribute copies of the overall divisional budget and announce the date of the next budget meeting.
- Discussion: How can we do a better job of anticipating and preventing cost overruns?
- Meeting will take place in Conference Room 3, with WebEx active for remote employees
- What additional budget issues must be considered during this quarter?

Exercises

For live links to all websites discussed in this chapter, visit this text's website at www.prenhall.com/bovee. Just log on, select Chapter 2, and click on "Featured Websites." Locate the page or the URL related to the material in the text.

2.1 **Teamwork** With a classmate, attend a local community or campus meeting where you can observe a group discussion, vote, or other group action. During the meeting, take notes individually and, afterwards, work together to answer the following questions.
   a. What is your evaluation of this meeting? In your answer, consider (1) the leader's ability to articulate the meeting's goals clearly, (2) the leader's ability to engage members in a meaningful discussion, (3) the group's dynamics, and (4) the group's listening skills.
   b. How did group members make decisions? Did they vote? Did they reach decisions by consensus? Did those with dissenting opinions get an opportunity to voice their objections?
   c. How well did the individual participants listen? How could you tell?
   d. Did any participants change their expressed views or their votes during the meeting? Why might that have happened?

e. Did you observe any of the communication barriers discussed in Chapter 1? Identify them.
f. Compare the notes you took during the meeting with those of your classmate. What differences do you notice? How do you account for these differences?

2.2 **Team Communication: Overcoming Barriers** Every month, each employee in your department is expected to give a brief oral presentation on the status of his or her project. However, your department has recently hired an employee with a severe speech impediment that prevents people from understanding most of what he has to say. As department manager, how will you resolve this dilemma? Please explain.

2.3 **Team Development: Resolving Conflict** Describe a recent conflict you had with a team member at work or at school, and explain how you resolved it. Did you find a solution that was acceptable to both of you and to the team?

2.4 **Ethical Choices** During team meetings, one member constantly calls for votes before all the members have voiced their views. As the leader, you asked this member privately about his behavior. He replied that he was trying to move the team toward its goals, but you are concerned that he is really trying to take control. How can you deal with this situation without removing the member from the group?

2.5 **Meeting Productivity: Analyzing Agendas** Obtain a copy of the agenda from a recent campus or work meeting. Does this agenda show a start time or end time? Is it specific enough that you, as an outsider, would be able to understand what was to be discussed? If not, how would you improve the agenda?

2.6 **Internet** Visit the PolyVision website at www.websterboards.com and read about electronic whiteboards. What advantages do you see in using this kind of whiteboard during a meeting? Draft a short internal memo to your boss outlining the product's advantages, using the memo format in Figure 1.10 on page 26.

2.7 **Listening Skills: Overcoming Barriers** Identify some of your bad listening habits and make a list of some ways you could correct them. For the next 30 days, review your list and jot down any improvements you've noticed as a result of your effort.

2.8 **Nonverbal Communication: Analyzing Written Messages** Select a business letter and envelope that you have received at work or home. Analyze their appearance. What nonverbal messages do they send? Are these messages consistent with the content of the letter? If not, what could the sender have done to make the nonverbal communication consistent with the verbal communication?

2.9 **Nonverbal Communication: Analyzing Body Language** Describe what the following body movements suggest when someone exhibits them during a conversation. How do such movements influence your interpretation of spoken words?
a. Shifting one's body continuously while seated
b. Twirling and playing with one's hair
c. Sitting in a sprawled position
d. Rolling one's eyes
e. Extending a weak handshake

2.10 **Listening Skills: Self-Assessment** How good are your listening skills? Use the following chart to rate yourself on each element of listening. Then examine your ratings to identify where you are strongest and where you can improve, using the tips in this chapter.

Element of Listening	Always	Frequently	Occasionally	Never
1. I look for areas of interest when people speak.	____	____	____	____
2. I focus on content rather than delivery.	____	____	____	____
3. I wait to respond until I understand the content.	____	____	____	____
4. I listen for ideas and themes, not isolated facts.	____	____	____	____
5. I take notes only when needed.	____	____	____	____
6. I really concentrate on what speakers are saying.	____	____	____	____
7. I stay focused even when the ideas are complex.	____	____	____	____
8. I keep an open mind despite emotionally charged language.	____	____	____	____

Expand Your Knowledge

For live links to the websites that follow, visit this text's website at www.prenhall.com/bovee. When you log on, select Chapter 2, then select "Featured Websites," click on the URL of the featured website, and review the website to complete these exercises.

Exploring the Best of the Web

Making Meetings Work
www.3m.com/meetingnetwork
The 3M Meeting Network contains a wide selection of articles on planning meetings, designing activities to build teamwork, and making better presentations. Click on "Articles and Advice," find the appropriate articles, and then answer the following questions:

1. How can you know if a meeting should be held or not?
2. How can good leaders show they trust the group's ability to perform successfully?
3. What are the advantages and disadvantages of "open space" meetings, which take place without formal agendas or facilitation?

Exploring the Web on Your Own

Review these chapter-related websites on your own to learn more about achieving communication success in the workplace.

1. CRInfo, www.crinfo.org, is a website dedicated to providing support for conflict resolution.
2. The Center for Collaborative Organizations, www.workteams.unt.edu, has many links, articles, and research reports on the subject matter of teams.
3. Symbols.com, www.symbols.com, offers a graphical search engine that explains the meaning of 2,500 graphical symbols. Find out what that unusual symbol on a foreign-language website means, or verify that the symbols you plan to use don't convey some inappropriate nonverbal meaning. The Word Index feature lets you see the graphical symbols associated with thousands of words and ideas.

Learn Interactively

Interactive Study Guide

Go to the Companion Website at www.prenhall.com/bovee. For Chapter 2, take advantage of the interactive "Study Guide" to test your knowledge of the chapter. Get instant feedback on whether you need additional studying.

Also, visit this site's "Study Hall," where you'll find an abundance of valuable resources that will help you succeed in this course.

Peak Performance Grammar and Mechanics

In Chapter 1 you were referred to the Peak Performance Grammar and Mechanics activities on the web at www.prenhall.com/onekey to improve your skill with nouns and pronouns. For additional reinforcement in pronouns, go to www.prenhall.com/bovee, where you'll find "Improve Your Grammar, Mechanics, and Usage" exercises.

chapter 3

Communicating Interculturally

LEARNING OBJECTIVES

After studying this chapter, you will be able to

1. Discuss the opportunities and challenges of intercultural communication
2. Define culture and explain how culture is learned
3. Define ethnocentrism and stereotyping; then give three suggestions for overcoming these limiting mindsets
4. Explain the importance of recognizing cultural variations, and list six categories of cultural differences
5. Outline strategies for studying other cultures
6. List seven recommendations for writing clearly in multilanguage business environments

COMMUNICATION CLOSE-UP AT E-SOFTSYS

www.e-softsys.com

It's tough enough to schedule meetings and coordinate team efforts when your partners work across the hall. Imagine what it's like when they work on the other side of the planet. The potential for misunderstandings, missed assignments, and mistrust could easily derail any project. And these are just some of the obstacles facing Kat Shenoy, president and CEO of E-SoftSys. His company employs offshore teams of engineers in two development centers located in Bangalore and Mangalore India, to develop software for other companies.

When potential customers think about using E-SoftSys for offshore software development, most need reassurance that the firm can successfully manage and monitor its far-flung team. As one customer asks: "How will it operate from so far away? Will we be able to communicate effectively?" To address their concerns and ensure effective teamwork, Shenoy offers customers a mix of human interaction and electronic collaboration (tools such as e-mail, instant messaging, and NetMeeting online software).

Keeping the project on track requires plenty of communication with the customer and within the team. Team members in the United States and India rely on frequent, informal communication to avoid misunderstanding one another, missing assignments, and forcing the project off schedule.

To succeed in today's marketplace, E-SoftSys relies on its team of programmers, who are spread across the globe, from the United States to Russia to India. Everyone in the company recognizes the challenges of communicating across cultures.

The project manager uses regular, formal communication with the customer—typically through daily/weekly status reports—to build trust and provide reassurance that the international team is making progress toward timely completion of the software.

However, technology can't address all the communication challenges. E-SoftSys teams often pull together people from diverse cultural backgrounds with different language abilities, and the company has found that face-to-face communication is critical when these teams are forming. For instance, during the early stages of most projects, either an India-based project manager travels to a customer's location in the United States, or a U.S.-based project manager travels to the E-SoftSys office in Bangalore, India, to collaborate with the Indian staff in designing the software and planning the work. By working side by side, even temporarily, these intercontinental colleagues establish a rapport that bridges time and space when the personnel return to their home office.[1]

1 LEARNING OBJECTIVE

Discuss the opportunities and challenges of intercultural communication

UNDERSTANDING THE OPPORTUNITIES AND CHALLENGES OF INTERCULTURAL COMMUNICATION

Effective intercultural communication
- Opens up business opportunities around the world
- Improves the contributions of employees in a diverse workforce

E-SoftSys's experience illustrates both the challenges of intercultural communication and the opportunities available for business professionals who know how to communicate across cultures. **Intercultural communication** is the process of sending and receiving messages between people whose cultural background could lead them to interpret verbal and nonverbal signs differently. Every attempt to send and receive messages is influenced by culture, so to communicate successfully, you'll need a basic grasp of the cultural differences you may encounter and how you might overcome them. Your efforts to recognize and surmount cultural differences will open up business opportunities throughout the world and maximize the contribution of all the employees in a diverse workforce.

The Opportunities in a Global Marketplace

You might be a business manager looking for new customers or new sources of labor. Or you might be an employee looking for new work opportunities. Either way, chances are good that you'll be looking across international borders sometime in your career.

You will probably communicate with people in other countries at some time in your career.

Thousands of U.S. businesses depend on exports for significant portions of their revenues. Every year, these companies export roughly $700 billion in materials and merchandise, along with billions more in personal and professional services. If you work in one of these companies, you may well be called on to visit or at least communicate with a wide variety of people who speak languages other than English and who live in cultures quite different from what you're used to. Of the top ten export markets for U.S. goods, only two (Canada and Great Britain) speak English as an official language, and Canada has two official languages, English and French.

In the global marketplace, most natural boundaries and national borders are no longer the impassible barriers they once were. Domestic markets are opening to worldwide competition as businesses of all sizes look for new growth opportunities outside their own countries. Automotive giant Ford markets to customers in more than 125 countries with websites that offer local information, usually in the local language.[2]

Even small companies in remote locations can sell and support their products on a global scale, thanks to e-mail, the Internet, and worldwide delivery services. Pygmy Boats is a small manufacturer of kayak kits in the equally small town of Port Townsend, Washington, and yet it reaches customers all over the world via its website.[3] Similarly, Pens.it, an Italian retailer of fountain pens, sells its products globally online as well.[4] Large or small, companies know that in the global marketplace, they face cultural and language barriers among customers and employees (see Figure 3.1).

Communication Solution

E-SoftSys's Kat Shenoy recognizes the economic advantages of employing the large pool of talented computer professionals in India and other countries, but he also understands that successful intercultural communication requires extra effort by everyone involved.

The Advantages of a Multicultural Workforce

Even if you never visit another country or transact business on a global scale, you will interact with colleagues from a variety of cultural backgrounds. Smart business leaders recog-

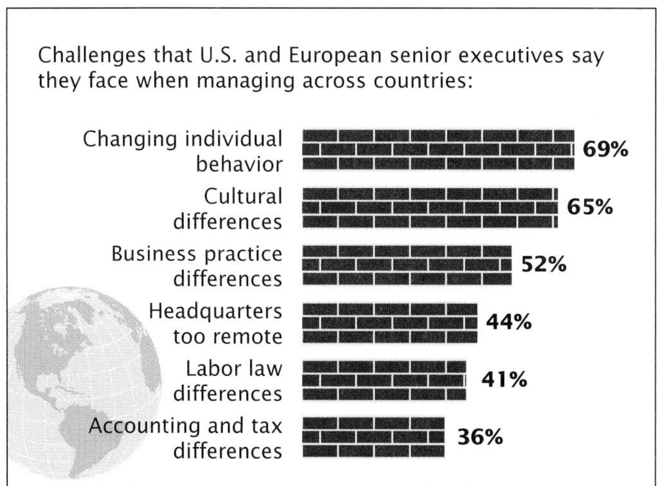

FIGURE 3.1
Going Global Has Its Barriers

nize the competitive advantages of a diverse workforce that has employees of different national, religious, and ethnic backgrounds—as well as different gender and age groups. Diverse workforces bring a broader range of viewpoints and ideas, help companies understand and identify with diverse markets, and enable companies to tap into the broadest possible pool of talent.

The diversity of today's workforce brings distinct advantages to businesses:

- A broader range of views and ideas
- An understanding of diverse markets
- A broad pool of talent from which to recruit

When Louis Gerstner, Jr., took over as CEO of IBM, workplace diversity became one of his top priorities—and it played a supporting role in the turnaround of IBM's faltering business. Under Gerstner's direction, IBM established executive-led task forces to represent women, Asian Americans, African Americans, Hispanic Americans, Native Americans, people with disabilities, and individuals who are gay, lesbian, bisexual, and transgender. Recommendations from these task forces helped transform IBM's recruiting, training, leadership, and development practices. Today, diversity is fostered at the employee level through 133 networking groups that unite people with a variety of talents and interests.[5]

Diversity is simply a fact of life for all companies. The United States has been a nation of immigrants from the beginning, and that trend continues today. The Western and Northern Europeans who made up the bulk of immigrants during the nation's early years now share space with people from across Asia, Africa, Eastern Europe, and other parts of the world. By 2010 recent immigrants will account for half of all new U.S. workers.[6] Nor is this pattern of immigration unique to the United States: Workers from Africa, Asia, and the Middle East are moving to Europe in search of new opportunities, while workers from India, the Philippines, and Southeast Asia contribute to the employment base of the Middle East.[7]

Putting more people of various ethnicities on the floor—and in executive positions—is commonplace for Wal-Mart, which was recently ranked by *Fortune* magazine as one of America's 50 best companies for Asian, African, and Hispanic Americans. This diverse group of Wal-Mart managers clearly understand the importance of being sensitive to others' cultures.

However, you and your colleagues don't need to be recent immigrants to constitute a diverse workforce. Differences in everything from age and gender to religion and ethnic heritage to geography and military experience enrich the workplace. Both immigration and workforce diversity create advantages—and challenges—for business communicators throughout the world.

The Challenges of Intercultural Communication

A company's cultural diversity affects how its business messages are conceived, composed, delivered, received, and interpreted.

Cultural diversity affects how business messages are conceived, planned, sent, received, and interpreted in the workplace. Today's increasingly diverse workforce brings with it a wide range of skills, traditions, backgrounds, experiences, outlooks, and attitudes toward work—all of which can affect employee behavior on the job. Supervisors face the challenge of communicating with these diverse employees, motivating them, and fostering cooperation and harmony among them. Teams face the challenge of working together closely, and companies are challenged to coexist peacefully with business partners and with the community as a whole.

Culture influences everything about communication, including
- Language
- Nonverbal signals
- Word meaning
- Time and space issues
- Rules of human relationships

The interaction of culture and communication is so pervasive that separating the two is virtually impossible. The way you communicate—from the language you speak and the nonverbal signals you send to the way you perceive other people—is influenced by the culture in which you were raised. The meaning of words, the significance of gestures, the importance of time and space, the rules of human relationships—these and many other aspects of communication are defined by culture. To a large degree, your culture influences the way you think, which naturally affects the way you communicate as both a sender and a receiver.[8] So you can see how intercultural communication is much more complicated than simply matching language between sender and receiver. It goes beyond mere words to beliefs, values, and emotions.

Throughout this chapter, you'll see numerous examples of how communication styles and habits vary from one culture to another. These examples are intended to illustrate the major themes of intercultural communication, not to give an exhaustive list of styles and habits of any particular culture. With an understanding of these major themes, you'll then be prepared to explore the specifics of any culture.

ENHANCING YOUR INTERCULTURAL SENSITIVITY

Your communication tends to be automatic.

The good news is that you're already an expert in culture, at least in the culture you grew up with. You understand how your society works, how people are expected to communicate, what common gestures and facial expressions mean, and so on. The bad news is that because you're such an expert in your own culture, your communication is largely automatic; that is, you rarely stop to think about the communication rules you're following. An important step toward successful intercultural communication is becoming more aware of these rules and of the way they influence your communication. A good place to start is to understand what culture is.

2 LEARNING OBJECTIVE

Define culture and explain how culture is learned

Understanding the Concept of Culture

Culture is a shared system of symbols, beliefs, attitudes, values, expectations, and behavior norms.

You belong to several cultures.

For the purposes of communication, **culture** can be defined as a shared system of symbols, beliefs, attitudes, values, expectations, and norms for behavior. In other words, your cultural background influences the way you prioritize what is important in life, helps define your attitude toward what is appropriate in any given situation, and establishes rules of behavior.[9]

Actually, you belong to several cultures. The most obvious is the culture you share with all the people who live in your own country. In addition, you belong to other cultural groups, including an ethnic group, probably a religious group, and perhaps a profession that has its own special language and customs. All members of a culture have similar assumptions about how people should think, behave, and communicate, and they all tend to act on those assumptions in much the same way. However, cultures differ widely from group to group and may vary in their rate of change, their degree of complexity, and their tolerance toward outsiders. These differences affect the level of trust and openness that you can achieve when communicating with people of other cultures.

Within a major culture such as the United States are other cultural groups, such as Mexican Americans, Californians, and science fiction fans. In fact, as a country with a large population and a long history of immigration, the United States is home to a vast array of cultures. Similarly, Indonesia is home to a wide variety of ethnic and religious cultures, whereas Japan is much more homogeneous, having only a few separate cultural groups.[10]

People learn about culture directly and indirectly from members of their group.

People learn culture directly and indirectly from other members of their group. As you grow up in a culture, you are taught who you are and how best to function in that culture by the group's members. For example, you might've been raised to address parental figures as "Ma'am and Sir," "Mother and Father," "Mom and Dad," or simply "Marge and Bob," depending on the degree of respect and formality that your culture expects of children.

Sometimes you are explicitly told which behaviors are acceptable; at other times you learn by observing which values work best in a particular group. This double-edged format for learning ensures that culture is passed on from person to person and from generation to generation.[11] It also ensures that, as stated earlier, you are often unaware of the influence of your own culture, acting and reacting automatically.

In addition to being automatic, established cultures tend to be coherent; that is, they are fairly logical and consistent throughout. For instance, the notion of progress is deeply embedded in the culture of the United States. From the country's early westward expansion to its support and admiration of entrepreneurs and innovators, U.S. culture generally views progress as a positive factor, and it rewards those who achieve it. Conversely, those who don't progress are sometimes considered underachievers, even if they live perfectly happy and contented lives. Such coherence generally helps a culture function more smoothly internally.

Cultures tend to be coherent.

Cultures also tend to be complete; that is, they provide most of their members with most of the answers to life's big questions. This idea of completeness dulls or even suppresses curiosity about life in other cultures. Therefore, such completeness can complicate communication with other cultures.[12]

Cultures tend to be complete.

Overcoming Ethnocentrism and Stereotyping

3 LEARNING OBJECTIVE

Define ethnocentrism and stereotyping; then give three suggestions for overcoming these limiting mindsets

The very nature of culture being automatic, coherent, and complete can lead the members of one culture to form negative attitudes about—and rigid, oversimplified views of—other cultures. **Ethnocentrism** is the tendency to judge all other groups according to your own group's standards, behaviors, and customs. When making such comparisons, people too often decide that their own group is superior.[13] An even more extreme reaction is **xenophobia**, a fear of strangers and foreigners. Clearly, businesspeople who take these views will not interpret messages from other cultures correctly, nor are they likely to send successful messages.

Ethnocentrism is the tendency to judge all other groups according to the standards, behaviors, and customs of one's own group.

As you recall from Chapter 1, selective perception leads people to rearrange incoming information to fit their existing beliefs.Thus, someone with a negative view of another culture is likely to continue holding that view, even if he or she sees evidence to the contrary.

Xenophobia is a fear of strangers.

Distorted views of other cultures or groups also result from **stereotyping**, assigning a wide range of generalized attributes to an individual on the basis of membership in a particular culture or social group, without considering the individual's unique characteristics. Whereas ethnocentrism and xenophobia represent negative views of everyone in a particular group, stereotyping is more a matter of oversimplifying and of failing to acknowledge individuality. For instance, assuming that an older colleague will be out of touch with the youth market or that a younger colleague can't be an inspiring leader is an example of stereotyping age groups. Many people in the United States have stereotypical views both of co-cultures within the United States and of cultures in other countries. Likewise, the people in these other countries sometimes exhibit stereotypical views of U.S. residents as well.

Stereotyping is assigning generalized attributes to an individual on the basis of membership in a particular group.

To show respect for other people and to communicate effectively in business, adopt a more positive viewpoint: **Cultural pluralism** is the practice of accepting multiple cultures on their own terms. When crossing cultural boundaries, you'll be even more effective if you move beyond simple acceptance and adapt your own communication style to that of the new cultures you encounter—even integrating aspects of those cultures into your own.[14] A few simple habits can help you avoid both the negativity of ethnocentrism and the oversimplification of stereotyping:

Cultural pluralism is the acceptance of multiple cultures on their own terms.

- **Avoid assumptions.** Don't assume that others will act the same way you do, that they will operate from the same values and beliefs, or that they will use language and symbols the same way you do.
- **Avoid judgments.** When people act differently, don't conclude that they are in error, that their way is invalid, or that their customs are inferior to your own.
- **Acknowledge distinctions.** Don't ignore the differences between another person's culture and your own.

To avoid ethnocentrism and stereotyping, develop a few simple habits.

4 LEARNING OBJECTIVE

Explain the importance of recognizing cultural variations, and list six categories of cultural differences

Recognizing Cultural Variations

Cultural differences lead to miscommunication.

When you communicate with someone from another culture, you encode your message using the assumptions of your own culture. However, members of your audience decode your message according to the assumptions of their culture, so your meaning may be misunderstood. The greater the difference between cultures, the greater the chance for misunderstanding.[15] Consider the differences in communication styles, personal values, and nonverbal symbols that led to the following cultural mishaps:

- When Hewlett-Packard (HP) brought its U.S. engineers together with its French engineers to design software, the U.S. engineers sent long, detailed e-mails to their counterparts in France. But the engineers in France viewed the lengthy messages as patronizing and replied with quick, concise e-mails. That response made the U.S. engineers believe that French engineers were withholding information. The situation spiraled out of control until HP hired a consulting firm to provide cultural training so that both sides could learn to work through their differences.[16]
- A Canadian employer rewarded a Polish-born engineer for his excellent job performance over the years with every possible award it could give him and a salary on the same level as many senior managers. However, in the engineer's view, the company should have rewarded him by putting him in charge of a large number of subordinates—as top performers are typically rewarded in his native Poland. Even though the company thought it was communicating its gratitude with pay and awards, the talented engineer left the company.[17]
- Exhibitors at a trade show could not understand why Chinese visitors were not stopping by their booth. The exhibitors were wearing green hats and giving them away as promotional items. They soon discovered that for many Chinese people, green hats are associated with infidelity: the Chinese expression "He wears a green hat" indicates that a man's wife has been cheating on him. As soon as the exhibitors discarded the green hats and started giving out T-shirts instead, the Chinese attendees began visiting the booth.[18]

Treat people the way they expect to be treated.

Communication breakdowns such as these arise when we assume, wrongly, that other people's attitudes and lives are like ours (see "Communicating Across Cultures: Test Your Intercultural Knowledge"). Part of the problem stems from treating others the way *you* want to be treated. The best approach when communicating with people from other cultures is to treat them the way *they* want to be treated.

You can begin to learn how people in other cultures want to be treated by recognizing and accommodating six main types of cultural differences: contextual, legal and ethical, social, nonverbal, age, and gender.

Contextual Differences

Cultural context is the pattern of physical cues, environmental stimuli, and implicit understanding that conveys meaning between members of the same culture.

Every attempt at communication occurs within a **cultural context**, the pattern of physical cues, environmental stimuli, and implicit understanding that convey meaning between two members of the same culture. However, cultures around the world vary widely in the role that context plays in communication (see Figure 3.2).

High-context cultures rely on implicit nonverbal actions and environmental setting to convey meaning, unlike low-context cultures, which rely heavily on explicit verbal communication.

In a **high-context culture** such as South Korea or Taiwan, people rely less on verbal communication and more on the context of nonverbal actions and environmental setting to convey meaning. A Chinese speaker expects the receiver to discover the essence of a message and uses indirectness and metaphor to provide a web of meaning.[19] In high-context cultures, the rules of everyday life are rarely explicit; instead, as individuals grow up, they learn how to recognize situational cues (such as gestures and tone of voice) and how to respond as expected.[20] Also, in a high-context culture, the primary role of communication is building relationships, not exchanging information.[21]

In a **low-context culture** such as the United States or Germany, people rely more on verbal communication and less on circumstances and cues to convey meaning. An English speaker feels responsible for transmitting the meaning of the message and often places sentences in chronological sequence to establish a cause-and-effect pattern.[22] In a low-context culture, rules and expectations are usually spelled out through explicit state-

Communicating Across Cultures

Test Your Intercultural Knowledge

Never take anything for granted when you're doing business in a foreign country. Here are several examples based on true stories about businesspeople who blundered by overlooking some simple but important cultural differences. Can you spot the erroneous assumptions?

1. You're tired of the discussion and you want to move on to a new topic. You ask your Australian business associate, "Can we table this for a while?" To your dismay, your colleague ignores the request and keeps right on discussing the topic.
2. You finally made the long trip overseas to meet the new German director of your division. Despite slow traffic, you arrive only four minutes late. His door is shut, so you knock on it and walk in. The chair is too far away from the desk, so you pick it up and move it closer. Then you lean over the desk, stick out your hand and say, "Good morning, Hans, it's nice to meet you." Why is his reaction so chilly?
3. Your meeting went better than you'd ever expected. In fact, you found the Japanese representative for your new advertising agency to be very agreeable; she said yes to just about everything. When you share your enthusiasm with your boss, he doesn't appear very excited. Why?

Here's what went wrong in each situation:

1. To "table" something in Australia means to bring it forward for discussion, the opposite of the usual U.S. meaning. The English that's spoken in Australia is closer to British than to U.S. English.
2. You've just broken four rules of German polite behavior: punctuality, privacy, personal space, and proper greetings. In time-conscious Germany, you should never arrive even a few minutes late. Also, Germans like their privacy and space, and they adhere to formal greetings of "Frau" and "Herr," even if the business association has lasted for years.
3. The word *yes* may not always mean "yes" in the Western sense. Japanese people may say *yes* to confirm they have heard or understood something but not necessarily to indicate that they agree with it. You'll seldom get a direct no. Some of the ways that Japanese people say no indirectly include "It will be difficult," "I will ask my supervisor," "I'm not sure," "We will think about it," and "I see."

ments such as "Please wait until I'm finished" or "You're welcome to browse."[23] Exchanging information is the primary task of communication in low-context cultures.[24]

Contextual differences are apparent in the way cultures approach situations such as decision making, problem solving, and negotiating:

Low-context cultures concentrate on every detail of a decision, whereas high-context cultures build relationships and trust.

- **Decision-making practices.** In lower-context cultures, businesspeople tend to focus on the results of the decisions they face, a reflection of the cultural emphasis on logic and progress. Will this be good for our company? For my career? In comparison, higher-context cultures emphasize the means or the method by which the decision will be made. Building or protecting relationships can be as important as the facts and information used in making the decisions.[25] For example, executives negotiating in a high-context culture such as China may spend most of their time together building relationships, rather than hammering out contractual details.
- **Problem-solving techniques.** In low-context cultures, businesspeople usually bring a problem out in the open, look for causes, and then often assign blame. Both problems and solutions can be handled in a highly individualized manner, assigning blame to those who cause problems and heaping credit on troubleshooters and problem solvers. However, in higher-context cultures businesspeople view problems more as part of the context in which the business is operating and less as the fault of any particular individual. The group works together to solve the problem.[26] Similarly, the tolerance for open conflict differs widely across cultures. Low-context U.S. businesspeople tolerate and sometimes even expect confrontation and debate, but high-context Japanese executives shun such tactics, even using an intermediary to avoid the unpleasant feelings that might result from open conflict.

Low-context cultures encourage open disagreement, whereas high-context cultures avoid confrontation and debate.

- **Negotiating styles.** A business negotiation is a complicated exchange of messages. Although the two sides are willing to work together, each is also asking the other to make concessions. Complex negotiations may involve many players on both sides, may

FIGURE 3.2 How Cultural Context Affects Business Communication

IN LOW-CONTEXT COMPANIES	IN HIGH-CONTEXT COMPANIES
Executive offices are separate with controlled access.	Executive offices are shared and open to all.
Workers rely on detailed background information.	Workers do not expect or want detailed information.
Information is highly centralized and controlled.	Information is shared with everyone.
Objective data are valued over subjective relationships.	Subjective relationship are valued over objective data.
Business and social relationships are discrete.	Business and social relationships overlap.
Competence is valued as much as position and status.	Position and status are valued much more than competence.
Meetings have fixed agendas and plenty of advance notice.	Meetings are often called on short notice, and key people always accept.

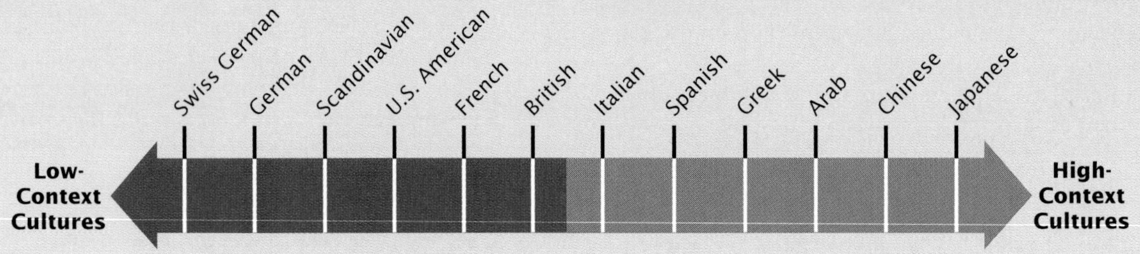

Note: These are generalized assessments of each culture; contextual variations can be found within each culture between individuals.

When negotiating, whereas low-context cultures view negotiations impersonally as a series of problems to be overcome. High-context cultures emphasize harmony and agreement, even when points remain to be worked out.

drag out over months, may cover a wide range of technical and financial details, and may require translation services. Negotiators from low-context cultures expect negotiations to be an impersonal affair and view the process as a series of problems to be overcome until mutual satisfaction is reached. This style conflicts with the high-context style of emphasizing harmony and agreement, even when all the points of the negotiation aren't yet settled. Open disagreement about a business issue can be perceived by people in a high-context culture as an attack on the businessperson.[27]

Whether you're making a decision, solving a problem, or negotiating a business deal, the communication tactics that work well in a high-context culture may backfire in a low-context culture, and vice versa. The key to success is understanding why the other party is saying and doing particular things and then adapting your approach accordingly.

Legal and Ethical Differences

Low-context cultures tend to value written agreements and interpret laws strictly, whereas high-context cultures view adherence to laws as being more flexible.

Cultural context also influences legal and ethical behavior. For example, because low-context cultures value the written word, they consider written agreements binding. But high-context cultures put less emphasis on the written word and consider personal pledges more important than contracts. They also tend to take a more flexible approach regarding adherence to the law, whereas low-context cultures would adhere to the law strictly.[28]

Legal systems differ from culture to culture.

As you conduct business around the world, you'll find that legal systems differ from culture to culture. In the United Kingdom and the United States, someone is presumed innocent until proved guilty, a principle rooted in English common law. However, in Mexico and Turkey, someone is presumed guilty until proved innocent, a principle rooted in the Napoleonic code.[29]

As discussed in Chapter 1, making ethical choices can be difficult, even within your own culture. When communicating across cultures, ethics can be even more complicated. What does it mean for a business to do the right thing in Thailand? In Nigeria? In Norway? What happens when a certain behavior is unethical in the United States but an accepted practice in another culture?

For example, in the United States, bribing officials is illegal, but Kenyans consider paying such bribes a part of life. To get something done right, they pay *kitu kidogo* (or "something small"). In China businesses pay *huilu,* in Russia they pay *vzyatka,* in the Middle East it's *baksheesh,* and in Mexico it's *una mordida* ("a small bite").[30]

The United States enacted the Foreign Corrupt Practices Act in 1977, making it illegal for U.S. companies to pay bribes, even in countries where the practice is accepted (or expected). To help level the playing field for U.S. businesses, the U.S. government lobbied other nations to also outlaw bribery. After nearly 20 years, the 29 member nations of the Organization for Economic Cooperation and Development, along with five nonmembers, finally signed a treaty that made payoffs to foreign officials a criminal offense. Of course, bribery won't end just because a treaty has been signed, but many of the signatory countries have ratified the treaty and passed supporting legislation.[31]

Ethical choices can be even more complicated when communicating across cultures; for example, bribing officials is viewed differently from culture to culture.

Making ethical choices across cultures can seem incredibly complicated, but doing so actually differs little from the way you choose the most ethical path in your own culture (see Chapter 1). When communicating across cultures, keep your messages ethical by applying four basic principles:[32]

Keep your messages ethical by actively applying four principles.

- **Actively seek mutual ground.** To allow the clearest possible exchange of information, both parties must be flexible and avoid insisting that an interaction take place strictly in terms of one culture or another.
- **Send and receive messages without judgment.** To allow information to flow freely, both parties must recognize that values vary from culture to culture, and they must trust each other.
- **Send messages that are honest.** To ensure that the information is true, both parties must see things as they are—not as they would like them to be. Both parties must be fully aware of their personal and cultural biases.
- **Show respect for cultural differences.** To protect the basic human rights of both parties, each must understand and acknowledge the other's needs and preserve each other's dignity by communicating without deception.

Social Differences

The nature of social behavior varies among cultures, sometimes dramatically. These behaviors are guided by rules. Some rules are formal and specifically articulated (table manners are a good example), and some are informal, learned over time (such as the comfortable standing distance between two speakers in an office or whether it's acceptable for male and female employees to socialize outside of work). The combination of both types of rules influences the overall behavior of everyone in a society, or at least most of the people most of the time. In addition to the factors already discussed, social rules can vary from culture to culture in the following areas:

Formal rules of etiquette are explicit and well defined, but informal rules are learned through observation and imitation.

- **Attitudes toward work and success.** Although the United States is home to millions of people having different religions and values, the major social influence is still the Puritan work ethic. Many U.S. citizens hold the view that material comfort earned by individual effort is a sign of superiority, and that people who work hard are better than those who don't. This view is reflected in the number of hours that U.S. employees work every year (see Figure 3.3). Workers in Australia, Japan, and Spain also average at least 1,800 hours of work per year, significantly more than workers in France, Germany, and Norway.

People from the United States emphasize hard work and individual effort more than many people in other countries do.

- **Roles and status.** Culture dictates, or at least tries to dictate, the roles that people play, including who communicates with whom, what they communicate, and in what way. For example, in many countries women still don't play a prominent role in business, so women executives who visit these countries may find that they're not taken seriously as businesspeople.[33] Culture also dictates how people show respect and signify rank. For example, people in the United States show respect by addressing top managers as "Mr. Roberts" or "Ms. Gutierrez." However, people in China are addressed according to their official titles, such as "President" or "Manager."[34]

Respect and rank are reflected differently from culture to culture in the way people are addressed and in their working environment.

- **Use of manners.** What is polite in one culture may be considered rude in another. For instance, asking a colleague "How was your weekend?" is a common way of making small talk in the United States, but the question sounds intrusive to people in cultures where business and private lives are seen as totally separate. In Arab countries it's

The rules of polite behavior vary from country to country.

FIGURE 3.3 Working Hours Vary from Culture to Culture

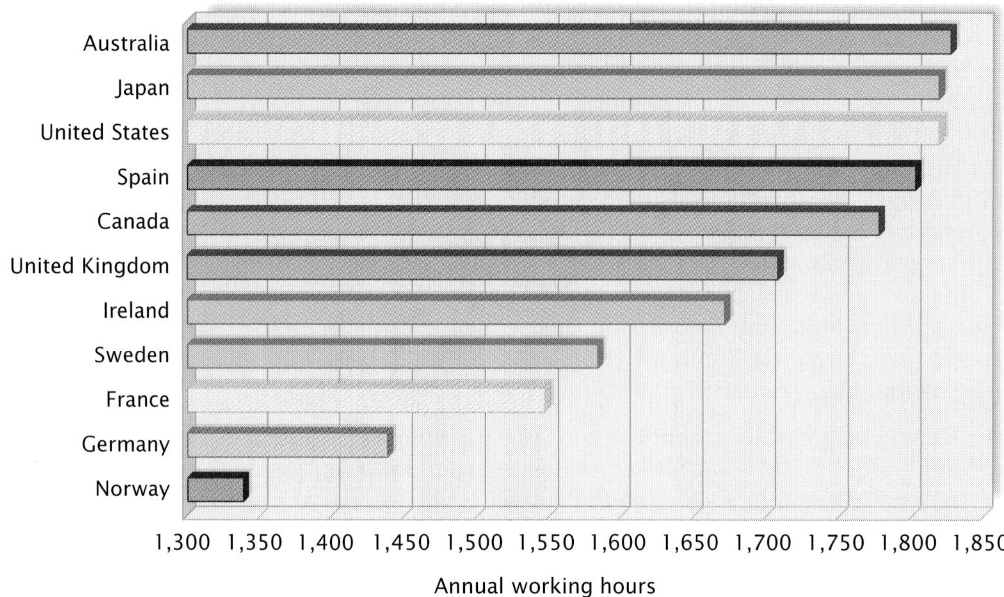

impolite to take gifts to a man's wife, but it's acceptable to take gifts to his children. In India, if you're invited to visit someone's home "any time," you should make an unexpected visit without waiting for a definite invitation. Failure to take the "any time" invitation literally would be an insult, a sign that you don't care to develop the friendship. Read about a country's expectations before you visit, then watch carefully and learn after you arrive.

Although businesspeople in the United States, Germany, and some other nations see time as a way to organize the business day efficiently, other cultures see time as more flexible.

- **Concepts of time.** Business runs on schedules, deadlines, and appointments, but these matters are regarded differently from culture to culture. People in high-context cultures see time as a way to plan the business day efficiently, often focusing on only one task during each scheduled period and viewing time as a limited resource. However, executives from low-context cultures often see time as more flexible. Meeting a deadline is less important than building a business relationship. So the workday isn't expected to follow a rigid, preset schedule.[35] Trying to coax a team into staying on a strict schedule would be an attractive attribute in U.S. companies but could be viewed as pushy and overbearing in other cultures.

Nonverbal Differences

As discussed in Chapter 2, nonverbal communication can be a reliable guide to determining the meaning of a message. However, this notion of reliability is valid only when the communicators belong to the same culture. For instance, the simplest hand gestures change meaning from culture to culture. A gesture that communicates good luck in Brazil is the equivalent of giving someone "the finger" in Colombia.[36] In fact, the area of gestures is so complicated that entire books have been written about it. Don't assume that the gestures you grew up with will translate to another culture; doing so could lead to embarrassing mistakes (see Figure 3.4).

From colors to facial expression, nonverbal elements add yet another layer of richness and complexity to intercultural communication. When you have the opportunity to interact with people in another culture, the best advice is to study the culture in advance, then observe the way people behave in the following areas:

Nonverbal differences may be observed in numerous areas.

- **Greetings.** Do people shake hands, bow, or kiss lightly (on one side of the face or both)?
- **Personal space.** When people are conversing, do they stand closer together or farther away than you are accustomed to?
- **Touching.** Do people touch each other on the arm to emphasize a point or slap each other on the back to show congratulation? Or do they refrain from touching altogether?

FIGURE 3.4 **Avoiding Nonverbal Mishaps**

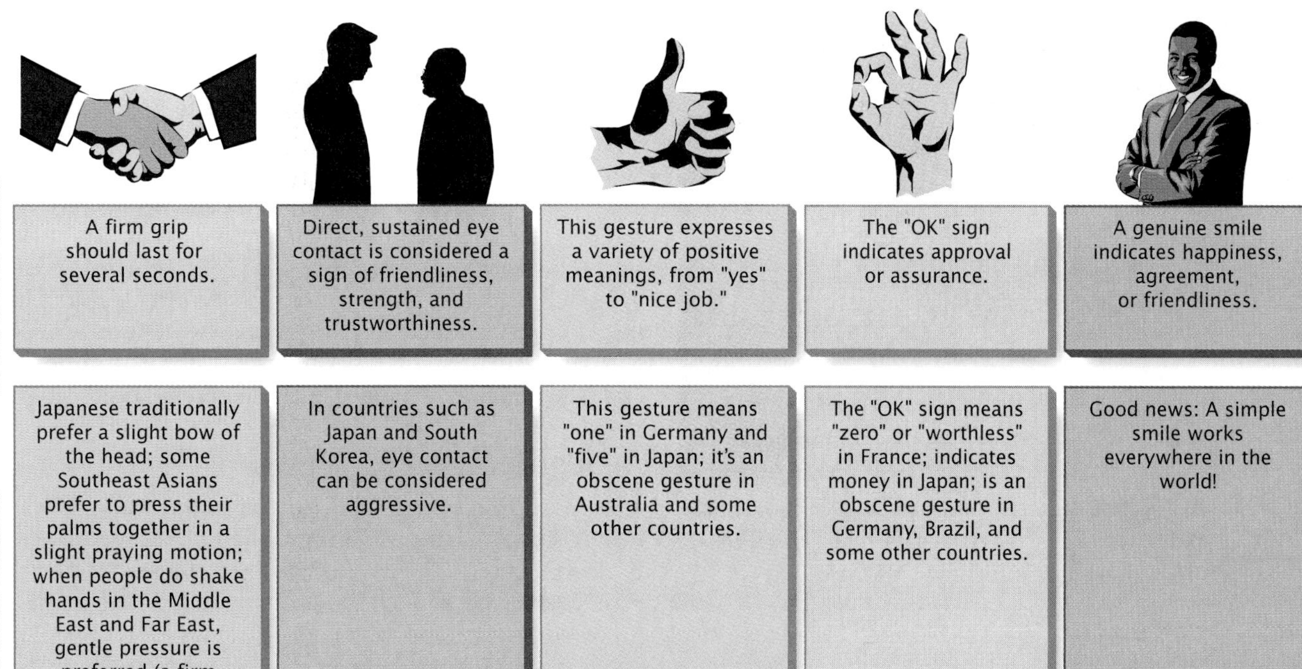

In the United States
A firm grip should last for several seconds.
Direct, sustained eye contact is considered a sign of friendliness, strength, and trustworthiness.
This gesture expresses a variety of positive meanings, from "yes" to "nice job."
The "OK" sign indicates approval or assurance.
A genuine smile indicates happiness, agreement, or friendliness.
In Other Cultures
Japanese traditionally prefer a slight bow of the head; some Southeast Asians prefer to press their palms together in a slight praying motion; when people do shake hands in the Middle East and Far East, gentle pressure is preferred (a firm handshake is considered aggressive).
In countries such as Japan and South Korea, eye contact can be considered aggressive.
This gesture means "one" in Germany and "five" in Japan; it's an obscene gesture in Australia and some other countries.
The "OK" sign means "zero" or "worthless" in France; indicates money in Japan; is an obscene gesture in Germany, Brazil, and some other countries.
Good news: A simple smile works everywhere in the world!

- **Facial expressions.** Do people shake their heads to indicate "no" and nod them to indicate "yes"? This is what people are accustomed to in the United States, but it's not universal.
- **Eye contact.** Do people make frequent eye contact or avoid it? Frequent eye contact is often taken as a sign of honesty and openness in the United States, but in other cultures it can be a sign of aggressiveness or lack of respect.
- **Posture.** Do people slouch and relax in the office and in public, or do they sit up straight?
- **Formality.** In general, does the culture seem more or less formal than yours?

Following the lead of people who grew up in the culture is not only a great way to learn but a good way to show respect as well.

Age Differences

The United States celebrates youth in general and successful young businesspeople in particular. The emphasis on youth is so strong that millions of older people spend millions of dollars every year trying to look or feel younger, whether it's dying that gray hair back to its original color or surgically reversing the effects of aging. Business publications frequently publish lists of successful young executives who are making their mark before age 30 or 40. Youth is associated with strength, energy, possibilities, and freedom, whereas age is too often associated with declining powers and a loss of respect and authority.[37] As a result, younger employees in U.S. companies often communicate with older colleagues as equals, even to the point of openly disagreeing with them.

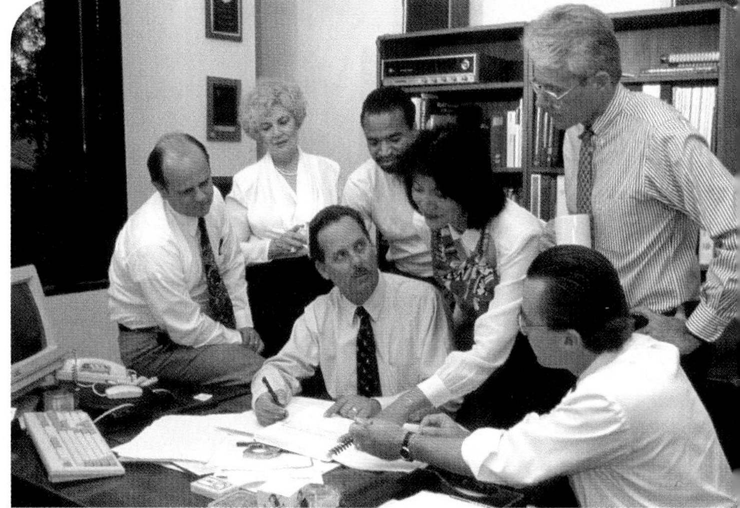

Expectations of personal space vary from culture to culture; not everyone is comfortable working in close quarters such as these.

However, in cultures that value age and seniority, longevity earns respect and increasing power and freedom. For instance, in many Asian societies, the oldest employees hold the most powerful jobs, the most impressive titles, and the

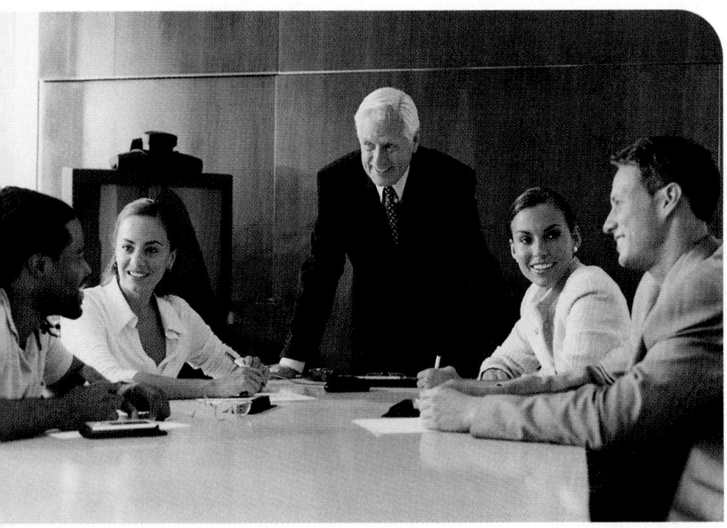

Communication styles and expectations can vary widely between age groups, putting extra demands on teams that include workers of varying ages.

greatest degree of freedom and decision-making authority. If a younger employee disagrees with one of these senior executives, the discussion is never conducted in public. The notion of "saving face," of avoiding public embarrassment, is too strong. Instead, if a senior person seems to be in error about something, other employees will find a quiet, private way to communicate whatever information they feel is necessary.[38]

Communicating between a youth-oriented culture and a seniority-oriented culture can require flexibility on both sides. For example, if you work for a U.S. company that is trying to influence a group of senior managers in Japan or China, they'll probably expect to communicate with peers of equivalent seniority or status. Sending the young hotshot over to close the deal may be viewed as a sign of disrespect.

Gender Differences

The perception of men and women in business also varies from culture to culture. In the United States today, women find a much wider range of business opportunities than existed just a few decades ago (even though differences in pay and access to top management positions still exist—with women holding fewer than 5 percent of the top executive positions in *Fortune 500* companies).[39] However, such opportunity is not the case in more tradition-oriented societies, where men tend to hold most or all of the positions of authority and women are expected to play a more subservient role. Female executives who visit other cultures may not be taken seriously until they successfully handle challenges to their knowledge, capabilities, and patience.[40]

In the United States, women are finding more opportunities in business than ever before.

As more women enter the workforce and take on positions of increasing responsibility, it's important for company leaders to revisit assumptions and practices.[41] For instance, company cultures that have been dominated by men for years may have adopted communication habits that some women have difficulty relating to—such as the constant use of sports metaphors or the acceptance of coarse language.

Whatever the culture, evidence suggests that men and women tend to have slightly different communication styles. Although the following broad generalizations might not apply in every case, understanding them can serve as a useful starting point for improving communication with the opposite sex:[42]

The communication styles of men and women differ on several points.

- **Workplace hierarchy influences communication.** Regardless of your opinions or beliefs, the simple fact remains that most businesses in most countries have been dominated by men for years; therefore, women face the challenge of finding a place for themselves within this hierarchy. When communicating within such a context, women may feel more pressure to adapt their communication styles to the prevailing style in the male-dominated environment.
- **Decision-making styles influence communication.** When making a decision, the differences between men and women are similar to the differences between low-context and high-context cultures. Men tend to value decisiveness over relationship quality, and their communication therefore emphasizes content—facts and figures, tasks, and results. In contrast, women tend to emphasize collaboration and the maintenance of positive business relationships, and their communication efforts generally reflect this concern. Even when a man and a woman reach the same conclusion in a given situation, their communication on the subject may differ as a result of these stylistic difference.
- **Problem-solving styles influence communication.** Particularly in the U.S. culture of success and progress, most men place great value on their ability to solve problems. In both their personal and professional lives, they have been conditioned to judge themselves by their ability to fix things. This conditioning can lead to misunderstandings when a woman voices frustration over a problem at work and a male colleague jumps

in with a potential solution. The woman may not have been asking her colleague for a solution, but merely trying to share her feelings. She may find her colleague's response to be controlling, misguided, even insulting.

Improving intercultural skills is a career-long effort.

IMPROVING INTERCULTURAL COMMUNICATION SKILLS

5 LEARNING OBJECTIVE

Outline strategies for studying other cultures

The better you are at intercultural communication, the more successful you'll be in today's business environment. However, communicating successfully from one culture to another requires a variety of skills (see Figure 3.5). You can improve your intercultural skills throughout your entire career. Begin now by studying other cultures and languages, respecting preferences for communication styles, learning to write and speak clearly, listening carefully, knowing when to use interpreters and translators, and helping others adapt to your culture.

Communication Solution

The teams at E-SoftSys realize that successful communication requires an understanding of cultural influences. To promote effective intercultural communication, the company encourages employees to learn more about each other's cultures through international assignments and constant communication.

Studying Other Cultures

Learning all you can about a particular culture will help you send and receive intercultural messages effectively. Unfortunately, a thorough knowledge of another culture and its language—or languages—can take years to acquire. Fortunately, you don't need to learn about the whole world all at once. Many companies appoint specialists for specific countries or regions, giving you a chance to focus on fewer cultures at a time.

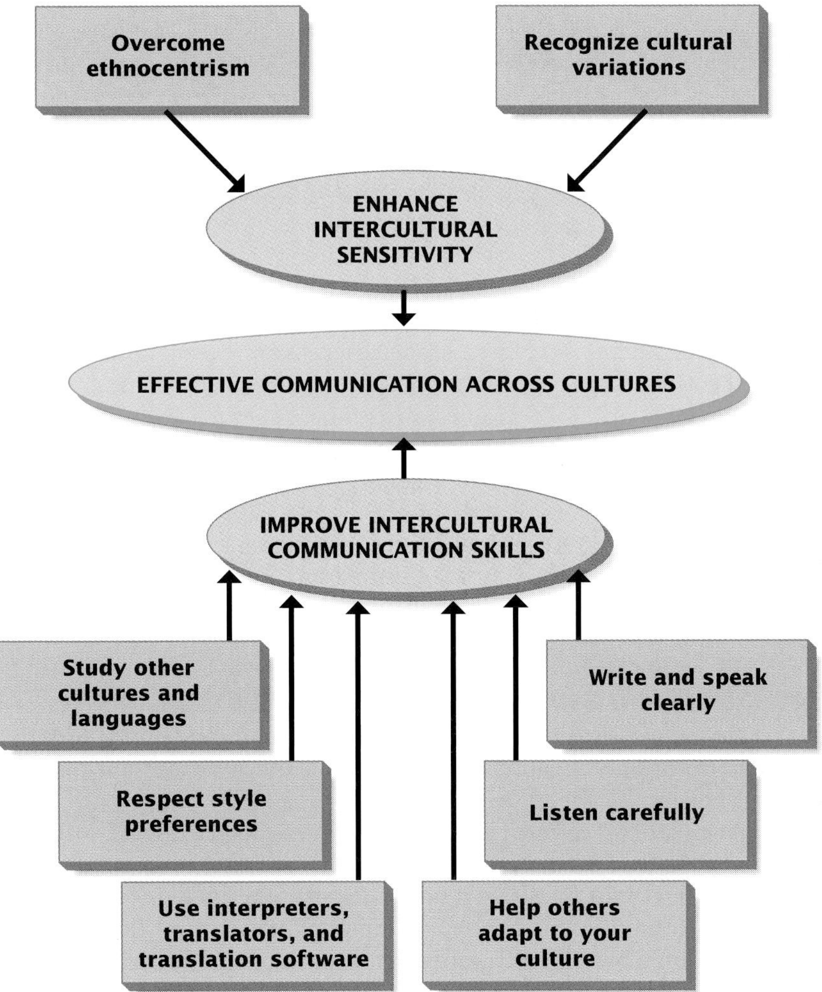

FIGURE 3.5
Components of Successful Intercultural Communication

Just a little research can help you grasp the basics of another culture.

Nor do you need to learn everything about a culture to ensure some level of communication success. Even a small amount of research will help you grasp the big picture and recognize enough communication basics to get through most business situations. In addition, most people respond positively to honest effort and good intentions, and many business associates will help you along if you show an interest in learning more about their cultures.

Mistakes will happen, and when they do, apologize (if appropriate), ask about the accepted way, and move on.

Try to approach situations with an open mind and a healthy sense of humor. You will make a mistake or two; at one point or another, everybody who tries to communicate across cultures makes mistakes. When it happens, simply apologize if appropriate, ask the other person to explain the accepted way, and then move on. As business becomes ever more global, even the most tradition-bound cultures are learning to deal with outsiders more patiently and overlook the occasional cultural blunder.[43]

If you try to learn nonverbal customs from a movie, remember that your resource is intended as entertainment.

Numerous websites and books offer advice on traveling to and working in specific cultures; they're a great place to start. Also try to sample newspapers, magazines, and even the music and movies of another country. For instance, a movie can demonstrate nonverbal customs even if you don't grasp the language. (However, be careful not to read too much into entertainment products. If people in other countries based their opinions of U.S. customs only on the silly teen flicks and violent action movies that the United States exports around the globe, what sort of impression do you imagine they'd get?) For some of the key issues to research before doing business in another country, refer to Table 3.1.

Studying Other Languages

English is the most prevalent language in international business, but it's a mistake to assume that everyone understands it.

With so many businesses stretched across national borders, successful employees commonly possess multilingual skills. Some countries have emphasized language diversity more than others over the years. For instance, businesspeople in the United States and United Kingdom often assume that people in other nations can speak enough English to get by in business, so there is less emphasis on learning other languages. In contrast, in a country such as the Netherlands, with its long history of international trade, fluency in multiple languages is considered an essential business skill.[44] The European Union, the international community of nations stretching across Europe, designated English as its official working language, but it actually has eleven official languages.[45] To simplify matters, some multinational companies ask all their employees to use English when communicating with employees in other countries, wherever they're located. Employees of Nissan, Japan's third-largest automaker, use English for internal e-mail and memos to colleagues around the world. When the company formed a strategic relationship with Renault, a French carmaker, the situation at Nissan headquarters became even more interesting, since English is not the native language of either Japanese or French employees.[46]

Many companies find that they must be able to conduct business in languages other than English.

Similarly, a number of U.S. companies are teaching their English-speaking employees a second language to facilitate communication with their co-workers. One out of every seven people in the United States now speaks a language other than English when at home. After English, Spanish is by far the most common spoken language, followed by French, German, Italian, and Chinese.[47] The Target retail chain is among those sponsoring basic Spanish classes for English-speaking supervisors of immigrant employees. Around the country, enrollment is growing in specialized classes such as health-care Spanish, firefighter Spanish, and Spanish for professionals.[48]

If you have a long-term business relationship with people of another culture, it is helpful to learn their language.

Even if your colleagues or customers in another country do speak your language, it's worth the time and energy to learn common phrases in theirs. Learning the basics not only helps you get through everyday business and social situations but also demonstrates your commitment to the business relationship. After all, the other person probably spent years learning your language.

Even if the same language is spoken in another country, don't assume that it is spoken the same way.

Don't assume that two countries speaking the same language speak it the same way. The French spoken in Quebec and other parts of Canada is often noticeably different from the French spoken in France. Similarly, it's often said that the United States and the United Kingdom are two countries divided by a common language (see Table 3.2 on p. 76.). Another complication to watch for is words that seem similar in different languages but in fact convey different degrees of intensity or different meanings entirely. The English word *formidable* (pronounced FOR-mid-a-bull or for-MID-a-bull) usually refers to something

TABLE 3.1 Doing Business Abroad

ACTION	DETAILS TO CONSIDER
Understand social customs	• How do people react to strangers? Are they friendly? Hostile? Reserved? • How do people greet each other? Should you bow? Nod? Shake hands? • How do you express appreciation for an invitation to lunch, dinner, or someone's home? Should you bring a gift? Send flowers? Write a thank-you note? • Are any phrases, facial expressions, or hand gestures considered rude? • How do you attract the attention of a waiter? Do you tip the waiter? • When is it rude to refuse an invitation? How do you refuse politely? • What topics may or may not be discussed in a social setting? In a business setting?
Learn about clothing and food preferences	• What occasions require special clothing? • What colors are associated with mourning? Love? Joy? • Are some types of clothing considered taboo for one gender or the other? • How many times a day do people eat? • How are hands or utensils used when eating? • Where is the seat of honor at a table?
Assess political patterns	• How stable is the political situation? • Does the political situation affect businesses in and out of the country? • What are the traditional government institutions? • Is it appropriate to talk politics in social or business situations?
Understand religious and folk beliefs	• To which religious groups do people belong? • Which places, objects, actions, and events are sacred? • Is there a tolerance for minority religions? • How do religious holidays affect business and government activities? • Does religion require or prohibit eating specific foods? At specific times?
Learn about economic and business institutions	• Is the society homogeneous or heterogeneous? • What languages are spoken? • What are the primary resources and principal products? • Are businesses generally large? Family controlled? Government controlled? • Is it appropriate to do business by telephone? By fax? By e-mail? • What are the generally accepted working hours? • How do people view scheduled appointments? • Are people expected to socialize before conducting business?
Appraise the nature of ethics, values, and laws	• Is money or a gift expected in exchange for arranging business transactions? • Do people value competitiveness or cooperation? • What are the attitudes toward work? Toward money? • Is politeness more important than factual honesty?

that is difficult or that arouses fear or dread. The identically spelled French word (pronounced for-mee-DAH-bluh) means terrific or wonderful.

Respecting Preferences for Communication Style

Communication style—including the level of directness, the degree of formality, preferences for written versus spoken communication, and other factors—varies widely from culture to culture. Knowing what your communication partners expect can help you adapt to their particular style. Once again, watching and learning is the best way to improve your skills; however, you can infer some generalities from what you already know about a culture. For instance, U.S. workers typically prefer an open and direct communication style; they find other styles frustrating or suspect. Directness is also valued in Sweden as a sign of efficiency, but unlike discussions in the United States, heated debates and confrontations are unusual. Italian, German, and French executives don't soften up colleagues with praise before they criticize—doing so seems manipulative to Europeans. However, professionals from high-context cultures, such as Japan or China, tend to be less direct.[49]

Communication style varies from culture to culture.

TABLE 3.2 U.S. Versus British English

U.S. ENGLISH	BRITISH ENGLISH
apartment	flat
eggplant	aubergine
cleaning lady	charwoman
elevator	lift
first floor	ground level
long-distance call	trunk call
organization	organisation
pharmacist	chemist
rare	underdone
roast	joint
string bean	French bean
sweater	pullover

International correspondence is often more formal than what U.S. businesspeople are used to.

In international correspondence, U.S. businesspeople will generally want to be somewhat more formal than they would be when writing to people in their own country. In many cultures, writers use a more elaborate style, so your audience will expect more formal language in your letter. The letter in Figure 3.6 was written by a supplier in Germany to a nearby retailer. The tone is more formal than would be used in the United States, but the writer clearly focuses on his audience. In Germany, business letters usually open with a reference to the business relationship and close with a compliment to the recipient. Of course, if you carry formality to extremes, you'll sound unnatural.

6 LEARNING OBJECTIVE

List seven recommendations for writing clearly in multilanguage business environments

Writing Clearly

In addition to learning the preferred style of your communication partners, you can help ensure successful messages by taking extra care with your writing. When sending written communication to businesspeople from another culture, familiarize yourself with their written communication preferences and adapt your approach, style, and tone to meet their expectations. To help you prepare effective written communications for multicultural audiences, follow these recommendations:[50]

- **Use simple, clear language.** Use precise words that don't have the potential to convey multiple meanings. For instance, the word *rich* has at least half a dozen different meanings, whereas *wealthy* has exactly one, leaving no room for ambiguity.
- **Be brief.** Use simple sentences and short paragraphs, breaking information into smaller chunks that are easier for your reader to capture and translate.
- **Use transitional elements.** Help readers follow your train of thought by using transitional words and phrases. Precede related points with expressions such as *in addition* and *first, second,* and *third.*
- **Address international correspondence properly.** Refer to Table 1.2 in Appendix A for an explanation of different address elements and salutations commonly used in certain foreign countries.
- **Cite numbers and dates carefully.** In the United States, 12-05-06 means December 5, 2006, but in France, Germany, and many other countries, it means May 12, 2006. Dates in Japan and China are usually expressed with the year first, followed by the month and then the day; therefore, to write December 5, 2006, in Japan, write it as 2006-12-05. Similarly, 1.000 means one with three decimal places in the United States and Great Britain, but it means one thousand in many European countries.

FIGURE 3.6 Effective German Business Letter (translated)

Furtwangen
Handcrafts
Kussenhofstrasse 150
Furtwangen, Germany

Mister
Karl Wieland
Business Leader
Black Forest Gifts
Friedrichstrasse 98
70174 Stuttgart
GERMANY

15.5.2005

Very honorable Mister Wieland,

Because the tourist season will begin soon, we would like to seize the opportunity to introduce our new line of hand-carved cuckoo clocks to you. Last year you were so friendly as to buy two dozen of our clocks. In recognition of our good business relationship, we now offer you the opportunity to select the new models before we offer this line to other businesses for purchase.

As you know, our artisans use only the best wood. According to time-honored patterns that are passed on from generation to generation, they carefully carve every detail by hand. Our clockworks are of superior quality, and we test every clock before it is painted and shipped. We give you a guarantee of five years on all Furtwangen Handcrafts clocks.

Enclosed you will find a copy of our newest brochure and an order form. To express our appreciation, we will take over the shipping costs if you order before 15 June.

We continue to wish you a lot of success in your new Stuttgart location. We are convinced that you will satisfy your regular clientele with your larger exhibition area and expanded stock and will gain many new visitors.

With friendly greetings

Frederick Semper

Frederick Semper

Literal translation of *Geschäfts-fürer* (Common English translation would be "managing director")

Refers to the ongoing business relationship

Uses language a bit more formally than U.S. letters do

Uses a complimentary close typical of German business letters

Shows concern for the audience

Ends with a compliment to the receiver

Includes no title in the typed name

- **Avoid slang, idiomatic phrases, and business jargon.** Everyday speech and writing is full of slang and **idiomatic phrases**, phrases that mean more than the sum of their literal parts. Many of these informal usages are so deeply ingrained that you may not even be aware that you're using them. Examples from U.S. English include phrases like "Off the top of my head," "Crossing the finish line," "More bang for the buck," and "Face the music." Your foreign correspondent may have no idea what you're talking about when you use such phrases.
- **Avoid humor and other references to popular culture.** If your everyday business correspondence is sprinkled with jokes, references to TV shows, and other cultural tidbits, make a conscious effort to avoid these when writing to people from another culture.

The correspondence shown in Figures 3.7 and 3.8 illustrates how intercultural correspondence can be improved by paying close attention to the guidelines offered in this chapter.

Speaking Clearly

Whether you're traveling to another country or teaming up with someone who is visiting or immigrating to your country, chances are good that sometime in your career you'll need

To gain insight into speaking more effectively in intercultural situations, think about what it's like to listen to someone whose native language is different from yours.

FIGURE 3.7 Ineffective Intercultural Letter

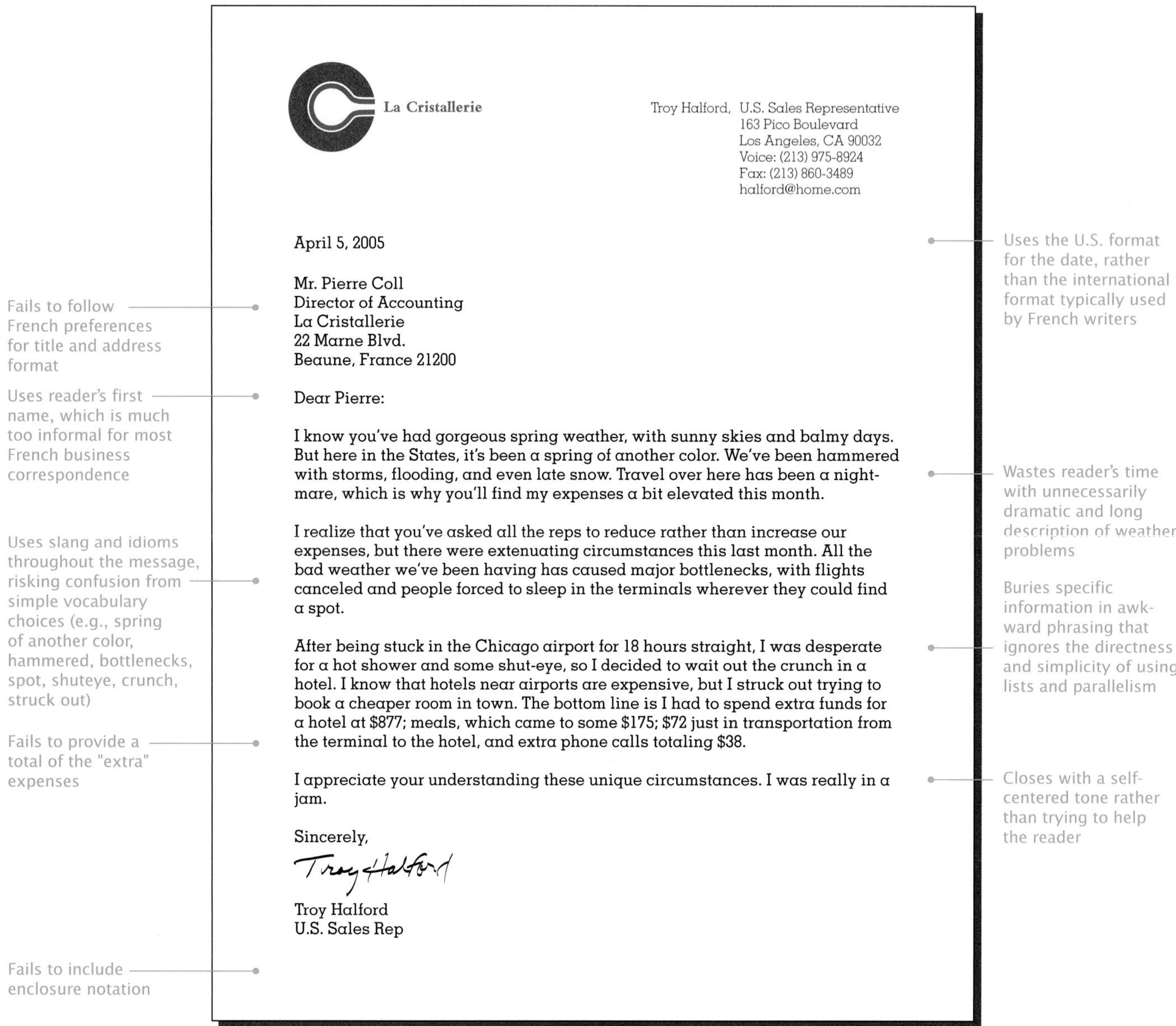

La Cristallerie

Troy Halford, U.S. Sales Representative
163 Pico Boulevard
Los Angeles, CA 90032
Voice: (213) 975-8924
Fax: (213) 860-3489
halford@home.com

April 5, 2005

Mr. Pierre Coll
Director of Accounting
La Cristallerie
22 Marne Blvd.
Beaune, France 21200

Dear Pierre:

I know you've had gorgeous spring weather, with sunny skies and balmy days. But here in the States, it's been a spring of another color. We've been hammered with storms, flooding, and even late snow. Travel over here has been a nightmare, which is why you'll find my expenses a bit elevated this month.

I realize that you've asked all the reps to reduce rather than increase our expenses, but there were extenuating circumstances this last month. All the bad weather we've been having has caused major bottlenecks, with flights canceled and people forced to sleep in the terminals wherever they could find a spot.

After being stuck in the Chicago airport for 18 hours straight, I was desperate for a hot shower and some shut-eye, so I decided to wait out the crunch in a hotel. I know that hotels near airports are expensive, but I struck out trying to book a cheaper room in town. The bottom line is I had to spend extra funds for a hotel at $877; meals, which came to some $175; $72 just in transportation from the terminal to the hotel, and extra phone calls totaling $38.

I appreciate your understanding these unique circumstances. I was really in a jam.

Sincerely,

Troy Halford

Troy Halford
U.S. Sales Rep

Fails to follow French preferences for title and address format
Uses reader's first name, which is much too informal for most French business correspondence
Uses slang and idioms throughout the message, risking confusion from simple vocabulary choices (e.g., spring of another color, hammered, bottlenecks, spot, shuteye, crunch, struck out)
Fails to provide a total of the "extra" expenses
Fails to include enclosure notation
Uses the U.S. format for the date, rather than the international format typically used by French writers
Wastes reader's time with unnecessarily dramatic and long description of weather problems
Buries specific information in awkward phrasing that ignores the directness and simplicity of using lists and parallelism
Closes with a self-centered tone rather than trying to help the reader

to converse with people whose native language is different from yours. You can gain some great insights into *speaking* more effectively in these situations by remembering what it's like trying to *listen* in these situations.

Every year, thousands of people around the world venture to other countries on business or personal travel, many of them eager to try the language skills they've been studying in a classroom. The result is often immediate confusion. You might ask where your hotel is or what time the meeting starts and get a response that is incomprehensible. All those words and phrases that made perfect sense in the classroom suddenly sound like an endless string of noise and gibberish.

Even when you know the vocabulary and grammar of another language, the ability to process everyday conversation can take years to master. People from the United States are notorious for stringing together multiple words into a single pseudo-word that mystifies non-native English speakers. "Did you eat yet?" becomes "Jeat yet?" and "Can I help you?" becomes "Cannahepya?" Similarly, the French language frequently uses a concept known as *liaison*, in which one word is intentionally joined with the next. Without a lot of practice, new French speakers have a hard time telling when one word ends and the next one begins.

FIGURE 3.8 Effective Intercultural Letter

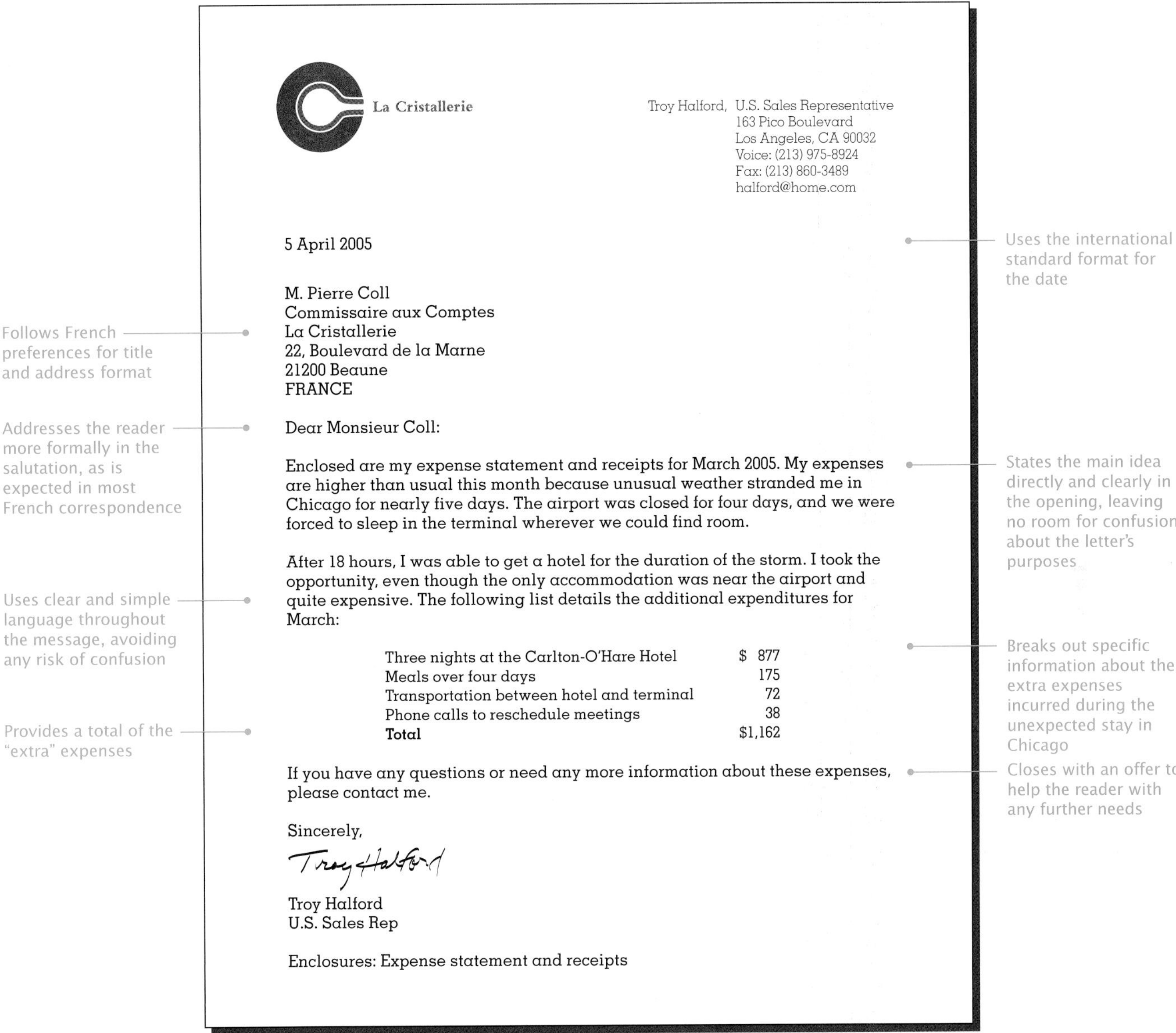

La Cristallerie
Troy Halford, U.S. Sales Representative
163 Pico Boulevard
Los Angeles, CA 90032
Voice: (213) 975-8924
Fax: (213) 860-3489
halford@home.com

5 April 2005

M. Pierre Coll
Commissaire aux Comptes
La Cristallerie
22, Boulevard de la Marne
21200 Beaune
FRANCE

Dear Monsieur Coll:

Enclosed are my expense statement and receipts for March 2005. My expenses are higher than usual this month because unusual weather stranded me in Chicago for nearly five days. The airport was closed for four days, and we were forced to sleep in the terminal wherever we could find room.

After 18 hours, I was able to get a hotel for the duration of the storm. I took the opportunity, even though the only accommodation was near the airport and quite expensive. The following list details the additional expenditures for March:

Three nights at the Carlton-O'Hare Hotel	$ 877
Meals over four days	175
Transportation between hotel and terminal	72
Phone calls to reschedule meetings	38
Total	$1,162

If you have any questions or need any more information about these expenses, please contact me.

Sincerely,

Troy Halford

Troy Halford
U.S. Sales Rep

Enclosures: Expense statement and receipts

Uses the international standard format for the date
Follows French preferences for title and address format
Addresses the reader more formally in the salutation, as is expected in most French correspondence
States the main idea directly and clearly in the opening, leaving no room for confusion about the letter's purposes
Uses clear and simple language throughout the message, avoiding any risk of confusion
Breaks out specific information about the extra expenses incurred during the unexpected stay in Chicago
Provides a total of the "extra" expenses
Closes with an offer to help the reader with any further needs

In addition to the advice provided in the preceding section on writing clearly, these guidelines will help you be more effective with intercultural conversations:

To speak more clearly in intercultural conversations, follow six guidelines.

- **Speak slowly and clearly.** Your listener may need time to consciously work through several steps—steps that you do automatically and nearly instantly in your language—from deciding what the sounds mean to translating individual words to even rearranging the order of words in a sentence, if necessary. Pronounce each word clearly, stop at distinct punctuation points, and make one point at a time. This pattern of speech might sound odd and even uncomfortable to you, but it's more sensitive to the needs of your conversation partner and faster and more effective in the long run.
- **Don't rephrase until it's necessary.** A common mistake is quickly rephrasing a statement or question if you think the other person doesn't immediately grasp what you've just said. Rather than helping, this often makes the situation worse because your listener now has two sets of words to translate and comprehend. Be patient while he or she tries to extract the meaning from your message. If you get a clear sign that he or she doesn't understand what you've said, then try another angle. And when you rephrase, choose simpler words and more concrete language if possible; don't fall into the common mistake of simply saying the same thing again but louder.

- **Look for—and ask for—feedback.** Be alert to signs of confusion in your listener. Realize that nods and smiles don't necessarily mean understanding. If the other person's body language seems at odds with the flow of the conversation, ask questions to see if your message is getting through.
- **Don't talk down to the other person.** Try not to overenunciate, don't simplify sentences to the point of spouting gibberish, and don't get frustrated with the listener for not understanding. Use phrases such as "Am I going too fast?" rather than "Is this too difficult for you?"
- **Learn foreign phrases.** Learn common greetings and a few basic phrases in the other person's native language. Even something as simple as knowing how to say "please" and "thank you" in the other language will show your good intentions and respect for others.
- **Clarify what will happen next.** At the end of the conversation, be sure that you and the other person agree on what has been said and decided. If appropriate, follow up by writing a letter or a memo that summarizes the conversation and thanks the person for meeting with you.

Experienced international speakers, such as Dell's CEO Michael Dell, are careful to incorporate cultural and language variations into their communication efforts.

Listening Carefully

Languages vary considerably in the significance of tone, pitch, speed, and volume. The English word *progress* can be a noun or a verb, depending on which syllable you accent. In Chinese, the meaning of the word *mà* changes depending on the speaker's tone; it can mean *mother, pileup, horse,* or *scold.* Arabic speech can sound excited or angry to an English-speaking U.S. listener, even though the speaker is simply asking a question without being either excited or angry.[51] Businesspeople from Japan tend to speak more softly than Westerners, a characteristic that implies politeness or humility to a Western listener.

With some practice, you can start to get a sense of vocal patterns. The key is simply to accept what you hear first, without jumping to conclusions about meaning or motivation. Let other people finish what they have to say. If you interrupt, you may miss something important. You'll also show a lack of respect. If you do not understand a comment, ask the person to repeat it. Any momentary awkwardness you might feel in asking for extra help is less important than the risk of unsuccessful communication.

To listen more effectively in intercultural situations, accept what you hear without judgment and let people finish what they have to say.

Using Interpreters, Translators, and Translation Software

Certain documents and situations require the use of an interpreter, translator, or translation software.

You may encounter business situations that require using an interpreter (for spoken communication) or a translator (for written communications). In addition, most customers expect to be addressed in their native language, particularly concerning advertising, warranties, repair and maintenance manuals, and product labels. These documents certainly require the services of a translator. Microsoft spends several hundred million dollars a year to make virtually all of its software products, websites, and help documents available in dozens of languages; the company is believed by some to be the world's largest purchaser of translation services.[52]

Professional interpreters and translators can be expensive (translators can earn up to $150 an hour or more for some languages), but skilled professionals provide invaluable assistance in business communication. For instance, an experienced translator can analyze a message, understand its meaning in the cultural context, consider how to convey the meaning in another language, and then use verbal and nonverbal signals to encode or decode the message for someone from another culture. If you use translators, you should meet with them ahead of time to give them a sense of what you are presenting and to discuss specific words or concepts that could be confusing.[53] Some companies use *back-translation* to ensure accuracy. Once a translator encodes a message into another language, a different translator retranslates the same message into the original language. This back-translation is then compared with the original message to discover any errors or discrepancies.

Back-translation is having a second translator decode the first translator's work back to the original language.

Connecting with Technology

The Gist of Machine Translation

What is the writer trying to say in the following sentence?

We have the need to balance for the barriers on this one or the market could draw well after us.

Can you figure it out? Here's the original sentence, which uses a tone that is overly casual and colloquial—a common problem in U.S. business documents:

We need to swing for the fences on this one or the market could shoot right past us.

When this sentence was run through a simple computerized translation service, from English to French and back to English, the software clearly had trouble with the "swing for the fences" and "shoot right past us" figures of speech.

Without hands-on intervention from experienced human translators, machine translation systems can produce results that are anywhere from amusing to nonsensical to downright dangerous. Whether you're using one of the automatic website translation services available from such sites as Alta Vista and Google, or a text translator such as the one available at WorldLingo (www.worldlingo.com), keep in mind that you won't get the same quality that you'd get from a human translator.

However, you won't always have the luxury of waiting for, or paying for, a human translator. For example, your sales department might receive an unexpected e-mail message from somebody who appears to be a potential customer in another country. You don't want the expense of hiring a translator this early in the relationship, but you don't want to let a big deal slip away either. By running the message through a basic machine translator, chances are you can get a basic idea of the message almost instantly. At the very least, you'll probably be able to tell whether the message is important enough to warrant the time and expense of a translator. And if you get results that make you scratch your head or laugh out loud, do call in a translator to make sure that you and the sender understand one another correctly.

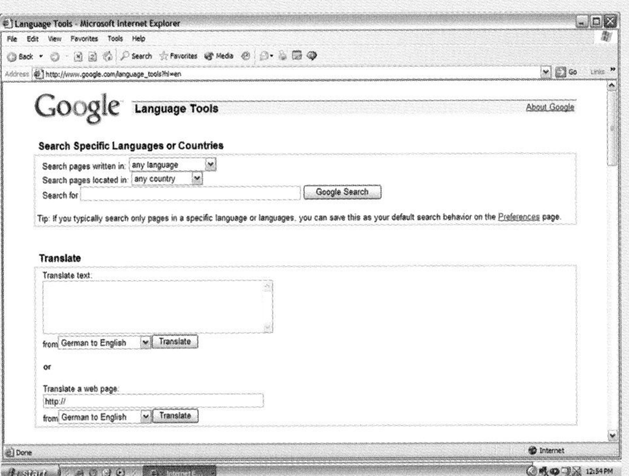

CAREER APPLICATIONS

1. Why do you think a computer might have trouble translating "swing for the fences" (a baseball phrase for trying as hard as one can to hit the ball out of the park)?
2. What are some examples of business documents that would probably be safe to read via machine translation? What are some that would be dangerous to trust to software?

Machine translation uses computerized intelligence to translate material from one language to another.

The time and cost required for professional translation has encouraged the development of **machine translation**, any form of computerized intelligence used to translate one language to another. Dedicated software tools and online services such as WorldLingo (www.worldlingo.com) and Alis Technologies (www.alis.com) offer some form of automated translation. Major search engines such as Alta Vista and Google let you request a translated version of the websites you find. Although none of these tools promises translation quality on a par with human translators, they can be quite useful with individual words and short phrases, and they can give you the overall gist of a message (see "Connecting with Technology: The Gist of Machine Translation").[54]

Don't rely on machine translation for important messages.

Even though translation technology is getting better, frequent errors make it risky to use for important business communications. A computer could translate every word perfectly and still present you with a new message that is wildly inaccurate, given differences in sentence structure, idiomatic usage, and other factors. If you want to create business documents that are accurate and truly localized, the only sure solution is using human translators who are native speakers of the target language.[55]

When people from other cultures try to communicate with you, try to help them by suggesting media such as e-mail, IM, or intranet sites.

Helping Others Adapt to Your Culture

Now that you have a good appreciation for the complexity of getting your message across to someone in another culture, you can also appreciate the challenge faced by people from

CHECKLIST: Improving Intercultural Communication Skills

- Study other cultures so that you can appreciate cultural variations.
- Study other languages.
- Help nonnative English speakers learn English.
- Respect cultural preferences for communication style.
- Write clearly, using brief messages, simple language, generous transitions, and appropriate international conventions.
- Avoid slang, humor, and references to popular culture.
- Speak clearly and slowly, giving listeners time to translate your words.
- Ask for feedback to ensure successful communication.
- Listen carefully and ask speakers to repeat anything you don't understand.
- Use interpreters and translators for important messages.

other cultures when they try to communicate with you. Whether a younger person is unaccustomed to the formalities of a large corporation or a colleague from another country is working on a team with you, look for opportunities to help people fit in and adapt their communication style. For more ideas on how to improve communication in the workplace, see "Checklist: Improving Intercultural Communication Skills."

Remember that speaking and listening are usually much harder in a second language than writing and reading. Oral communication requires participants to process sound in addition to meaning, and it doesn't provide any time to go back and reread or rewrite. So instead of asking a foreign colleague to provide information in a conference call, you could set up an intranet site where the person can file a written report. Similarly, using instant messaging and e-mail is often easier for colleagues with different native languages than participating in live conversations. An added plus with many of these technologies is overcoming the barrier of time zones. You can simply carry on a written conversation online, rather than participating in phone calls early in the morning or late at night.

Whatever assistance you can provide will be greatly appreciated. Smart businesspeople recognize the value of intercultural communication skills. Moreover, chances are that while you're helping others, you'll learn something about other cultures, too.

DOCUMENT MAKEOVER

IMPROVE THIS LETTER

To practice correcting drafts of actual documents, visit www.prenhall.com/onekey on the web. Click "Document Makeovers," then click Chapter 3. You will find a letter that contains problems and errors relating to what you've learned in this chapter about developing effective intercultural communication skills. Use the Final Draft decision tool to create an improved version of this letter. Check the message for a communication style that keeps the message brief, does not become too familiar or informal, uses transitional elements appropriately, and avoids slang, idioms, jargon, and technical language.

COMMUNICATION CHALLENGES AT E-SOFTSYS

After contributing to several successful projects, you were recently promoted to the position of project manager. You're now managing your first project, and Kat Shenoy has told you it's time to visit the office in Bangalore, India, to complete the software design, organize the work, and get acquainted with the local team. You're already nervous about leading your first project, and that feeling is compounded by your apprehension about working with an international team.

Individual Challenge: You have two weeks to prepare for the trip. Several of your U.S. co-workers have ample experience working with the Bangalore office, and several have traveled there for launch meetings. You also learn that a recently hired software engineer, Mahesh, is originally from Jaipur, a city about 945 miles (1,524 km) north of Bangalore. He has spent the last 6 years in the United States, earning his degree from the local university. Who would you ask for advice on communicating with Indian team members? Please explain your answer. Explain how you would approach Mahesh to ask for his help in learning about the Indian business culture.

Team Challenge: Mahesh is flattered that you approached him and agrees to help, even though he is quite busy. In a small group, create a prioritized list of the topics you should explore and the questions you would like to ask both Mahesh and your U.S. colleagues about your upcoming 6-week assignment in India.

SUMMARY OF LEARNING OBJECTIVES

1 **Discuss the opportunities and challenges of intercultural communication.** The global marketplace spans natural boundaries and national borders, allowing worldwide competition between businesses of all sizes. Therefore, today's businesspeople are likely to communicate across international borders with people who live in different cultures. Moreover, the world's domestic workforces are becoming more and more diverse, with employees having different national, religious, and ethnic backgrounds. Therefore today's companies benefit from a broader range of viewpoints and ideas, they have a better understanding of diverse markets, and they recruit workers from the broadest possible pool of talent. However, whether communicating with people around the world or at home, intercultural communication presents challenges as well, including motivating diverse employees to cooperate and to work together in teams, as well as understanding enough about how culture affects language to prevent miscommunication.

2 **Define culture and explain how culture is learned.** Culture is a shared system of symbols, beliefs, attitudes, values, expectations, and norms for behavior. Culture is learned by listening to advice from other members of a society and by observing their behaviors. This double-edged method uses direct and indirect learning to ensure that culture is passed from person to person and from generation to generation.

3 **Define *ethnocentrism* and *stereotyping*; then give three suggestions for overcoming these limiting mindsets.** Ethnocentrism is the tendency to judge all other groups according to the standards, behaviors, and customs of one's own group. Stereotyping is assigning a wide range of generalized attributes to individuals on the basis of their membership in a particular culture or social group, without considering an individual's unique characteristics. To overcome ethnocentrism and stereotyping, follow three suggestions: (1) avoid assumptions, (2) avoid judgments, and (3) acknowledge distinctions.

4 **Explain the importance of recognizing cultural variations, and list six categories of cultural differences.** People from different cultures encode and decode messages differently, increasing the chances of misunderstanding. By recognizing and accommodating cultural differences, we avoid automatically assuming that everyone's thoughts and actions are just like ours. Begin by focusing on six categories of cultural differences: contextual differences (the degree to which a culture relies on verbal or nonverbal actions to convey meaning), legal and ethical differences (the degree to which laws and ethics are regarded and obeyed), social differences (how members value work and success, recognize status, define manners, and think about time), nonverbal differences (differing attitudes toward greetings, personal space, touching, facial expression, eye contact, posture, and formality), and age differences (how members think about youth, seniority, and longevity).

5 **Outline strategies for studying other cultures.** Although a thorough knowledge of another culture and its language(s) can take years to acquire, conducting research will help you grasp the big picture and recognize enough basics to get through most business situations. Find websites and books that offer advice on traveling to and working in specific cultures. Also sample newspapers, magazines, music, and movies of the culture you're interested in to get an idea of dress, nonverbal customs, manners, and so on—always being careful not to read too much into entertainment products.

6 **List seven recommendations for writing clearly in multilanguage business environments.** Take extra care with your writing, adapting your approach, style, and tone to meet audience expectations. To write effectively to multicultural audiences, follow these recommendations: (1) use simple, clear language; (2) be brief; (3) use transitional elements; (4) address international correspondence properly; (5) cite numbers and dates carefully, (6) avoid slang, idiomatic phrases, and business jargon, (7) avoid humor and other references to popular culture.

Test Your Knowledge

1. How have market globalization and cultural diversity contributed to the increased importance of intercultural communication?
2. What are the potential advantages of a multicultural workforce?
3. How do high-context cultures differ from low-context cultures?
4. In addition to contextual differences, what other categories of cultural differences exist?
5. What is ethnocentrism, and how can it be overcome in communication?
6. What four principles apply to ethical intercultural communication?
7. Why is it a good idea to avoid slang and idioms when addressing a multicultural audience?
8. What are some ways to improve oral skills when communicating with people of other cultures?
9. What are the risks of using computerized translation when you need to read a document written in another language?

10. What steps can you take to help someone from another culture adapt to your culture?

Apply Your Knowledge

1. What are some of the intercultural differences that managers of a U.S.-based firm might encounter during a series of business meetings with a China-based company whose managers speak English fairly well?
2. What are some of the intercultural communication issues to consider when deciding whether to accept an overseas job with a firm whose headquarters are in the United States? A job in the United States with a local branch of a foreign-owned firm? Explain.
3. How do you think company managers from a country that has a relatively homogeneous culture might react when they do business with the culturally diverse staff of a company based in a less homogeneous country? Explain your answer.
4. Your company has relocated to a U.S. city where Vietnamese culture is strongly established. Many of your employees will be from this culture. What can you do to improve communication between your management and the Vietnamese Americans you are currently hiring?
5. **Ethical Choices** Your office in Turkey desperately needs the supplies that have been sitting in Turkish customs for a month. Should you bribe a customs official to speed up delivery? Explain your decision.

Practice Your Knowledge

Document for Analysis

Your boss wants to send a brief e-mail message welcoming employees recently transferred to your department from your Hong Kong branch. They all speak English, but your boss asks you to review his message for clarity. What would you suggest your boss change in the following e-mail message—and why? Would you consider this message to be audience centered? Why or why not?

I wanted to welcome you ASAP to our little family here in the States. It's high time we shook hands in person and not just across the sea. I'm pleased as punch about getting to know you all, and I for one will do my level best to sell you on America.

Exercises

For live links to all websites discussed in this chapter, visit this text's website at www.prenhall.com/bovee. Just log on, select Chapter 3, and click on "Featured Websites." Locate the page or the URL related to the material in the text.

3.1 **Intercultural Sensitivity: Recognizing Variations** You represent a Canadian toy company that's negotiating to buy miniature truck wheels from a manufacturer in Osaka, Japan. In your first meeting, you explain that your company expects to control the design of the wheels as well as the materials that are used to make them. The manufacturer's representative looks down and says softly, "Perhaps that will be difficult." You press for agreement, and to emphasize your willingness to buy, you show the prepared contract you've brought with you. However, the manufacturer seems increasingly vague and uninterested. What cultural differences may be interfering with effective communication in this situation? Explain.

3.2 **Ethical Choices** A U.S. manager wants to export T-shirts to a West African country, but a West African official expects a special payment before allowing the shipment into his country. How can the two sides resolve their different approaches without violating U.S. rules against bribing foreign officials? On the basis of the information presented in Chapter 1, would you consider this situation an ethical dilemma or an ethical lapse? Please explain.

3.3 **Teamwork** Working with two other students, prepare a list of 10 examples of slang (in your own language) that might be misinterpreted or misunderstood during a business conversation with someone from another culture. Next to each example, suggest other words you might use to convey the same message. Do the alternatives mean *exactly* the same as the original slang or idiom?

3.4 **Intercultural Communication: Studying Cultures** Choose a specific country, such as India, Portugal, Bolivia, Thailand, or Nigeria, with which you are not familiar. Research the culture and write a brief summary of what a U.S. manager would need to know about concepts of personal space and rules of social behavior in order to conduct business successfully in that country.

3.5 **Multicultural Workforce: Bridging Differences** Differences in gender, age, and physical abilities contribute to the diversity of today's workforce. Working with a classmate, role-play a conversation in which

a. A woman is being interviewed for a job by a male personnel manager
b. An older person is being interviewed for a job by a younger personnel manager
c. An employee who is a native speaker of English is being interviewed for a job by a hiring manager who is a recent immigrant with relatively poor English skills

How did differences between the applicant and the interviewer shape the communication? What can you do to improve communication in such situations?

3.6 **Intercultural Sensitivity: Understanding Attitudes** As the director of marketing for a telecommunications firm based in Germany, you're negotiating with an official in Guangzhou, China, who's in charge of selecting a new telephone system for the city. You insist that the specifications be spelled out in the contract. However, your Chinese counterpart seems to have little interest in technical and financial details. What can you do or say to break this intercultural deadlock and obtain the contract so that both parties are comfortable?

3.7 **Cultural Variations: Ability Differences** You are a new manager at K & J Brick, a masonry products company that is now run by the two sons of the man who founded it 50 years ago. For years, the co-owners have invited the management team to a wilderness lodge for a combination of outdoor sports and annual business planning meetings.

You don't want to miss the event, but you know that the outdoor activities weren't designed for someone with your physical impairments. Draft a short memo to the rest of the management team, suggesting changes to the annual event that will allow all managers to participate.

3.8 **Culture and Time: Dealing with Variations** When a company knows that a scheduled delivery time given by an overseas firm is likely to be flexible, managers may buy in larger quantities or may order more often to avoid running out of product before the next delivery. Identify three other management decisions that may be influenced by differing cultural concepts of time, and make notes for a short (two-minute) presentation to your class.

3.9 **Intercultural Communication: Using Interpreters** Imagine that you're the lead negotiator for a company that's trying to buy a factory in Prague, capital of the Czech Republic. Although you haven't spent much time in the country in the past decade, your parents grew up near Prague, so you understand and speak the language fairly well. However, you wonder about the advantages and disadvantages of using an interpreter anyway. For example, you may have more time to think if you wait for an intermediary to translate the other side's position. Decide whether to hire an interpreter, and then write a brief (two- or three-paragraph) explanation of your decision.

3.10 **Internet: Translation Software** Explore the powers and limitations of computer translation at AltaVista, www.altavista.com. Click on "translate" and enter a sentence such as "We are enclosing a purchase order for four dozen computer monitors." Select "English to Spanish" and click to complete the translation. Once you've read the Spanish version, cut and paste it into the "text for translation" box, select "Spanish to English," and click to translate. Try translating the same English sentence into German, French, or Italian and then back into English. How do the results of each translation differ? What are the implications for the use of automated translation services and back-translation? How could you use this website to sharpen your intercultural communication skills?

3.11 **Intercultural Communication: Improving Skills** You've been assigned to host a group of Swedish college students who are visiting your college for the next two weeks. They've all studied English but this is their first trip to your area. Make a list of at least eight slang terms and idioms they are likely to hear on campus. How will you explain each phrase? When speaking with the Swedish students, what word or words might you substitute for each slang term or idiom?

Expand Your Knowledge

For live links to the websites that follow, visit this text's website at www.prenhall.com/bovee. When you log on, select Chapter 3, then select "Student Resources," click on the URL of the featured website, and review the website to complete these exercises.

Exploring the Best of the Web

Cultural Savvy for Competitive Advantage
www.executiveplanet.com

Want to be more competitive when doing business across borders? Executive Planet offers quick introductions to expected business practices in a number of countries, from setting up appointments to giving gifts to negotiating deals. Visit www.executiveplanet.com and browse the country reports to answer the following questions.

1. What sort of clothes should you pack for a business trip to Mexico that will include both meetings and social events?
2. You've been trying to sell your products to a Saudi Arabian company whose executives treat you to an extravagant evening of dining and entertainment. Can you take this as a positive sign that they're likely to buy from you?
3. You collect antique clocks as a hobby, and you plan to give one of your favorites to the president of a Chinese company you plan to visit. Would such a gift likely help or hurt your relationship with this person?

Exploring the Web on Your Own

Review these chapter-related websites on your own to learn more about intercultural communication.

1. Background Notes, www.state.gov, provides helpful background information on every country with which the United States has an official relationship. This site is published by the U.S. State Department. Just click on Country Background Notes in the Travel and Living Abroad section.
2. Geert Hofstede Analysis, www.cyborlink.com/besite/hofstede.htm, offers insight into how various countries differ—sometimes widely—in the personal and social values that affect business.
3. Travlang, www3.travlang.com, can help you learn a foreign language. Check out the site's translating dictionaries and learn a new word in a foreign language every day.

Learn Interactively

Interactive Study Guide

Go to the Companion Website at www.prenhall.com/bovee. For Chapter 3, take advantage of the interactive "Study Guide" to test your knowledge of the chapter. Get instant feedback on whether you need additional studying.

Also, visit this site's "Study Hall," where you'll find an abundance of valuable resources that will help you succeed in this course.

Peak Performance Grammar and Mechanics

To improve your skill with verbs, visit www.prenhall.com/onekey, click "Peak Performance Grammar and Mechanics," click "Grammar Basics," then click "Verbs." Take the Pretest to determine whether you have any weak areas. Then review those areas in the Refresher Course. Take the Follow-Up Test to check your grasp of verbs. For an extra challenge or advanced practice, take the Advanced Test. Finally, for additional reinforcement in verbs, go to www.prenhall.com/bovee, where you'll find "Improve Your Grammar, Mechanics, and Usage" exercises.

PART 2

Applying the Three-Step Writing Process

chapter 4

Planning Business Messages

LEARNING OBJECTIVES

After studying this chapter, you will be able to

1. Describe the three-step writing process
2. Explain why it's important to define your purpose carefully, and list five questions that can help you test that purpose
3. Describe the importance of analyzing your audience, and identify the six factors you should consider when developing an audience profile
4. Discuss gathering information for simple messages, and identify three attributes of quality information
5. List factors to consider when choosing the most appropriate medium for your message
6. Explain why good organization is important to both you and your audience
7. Summarize the process for organizing business messages effectively

COMMUNICATION CLOSE-UP AT THE COMPLETE IDIOT'S GUIDES

www.idiotsguides.com

You can't wait to use that new computer—or digital camera, or mobile phone, or other innovative gadget—you've just purchased. It will simplify your life and give you amazing new capabilities. All too often, though, the device ends up gathering dust in your closet. Why? Because it's difficult to use and the manual is little or no help.

Joe Kraynak is on your side. A successful writer who sympathizes with consumers, Kraynak wrote *The Complete Idiot's Guide to Computer Basics.* He thinks people are right to criticize the manuals that come with PCs, phones, and other complex products. Many high-tech products make people feel, well, like idiots—which is why the *Complete Idiot's* series now covers hundreds of subjects. Kraynak and other experts know that the problem is often the user manual, not the user.

Too many product manuals are written with insufficient attention to the reader's real needs. The engineers or technicians who typically do the writing are intimately familiar with their product and its technology, and they often mistakenly assume that readers are, too. This disregard for what readers need can lead not only to inadequate explanations of new topics but also to overuse of befuddling jargon and acronyms. Moreover, too many manuals focus on descriptions of a product when readers really want explanations of

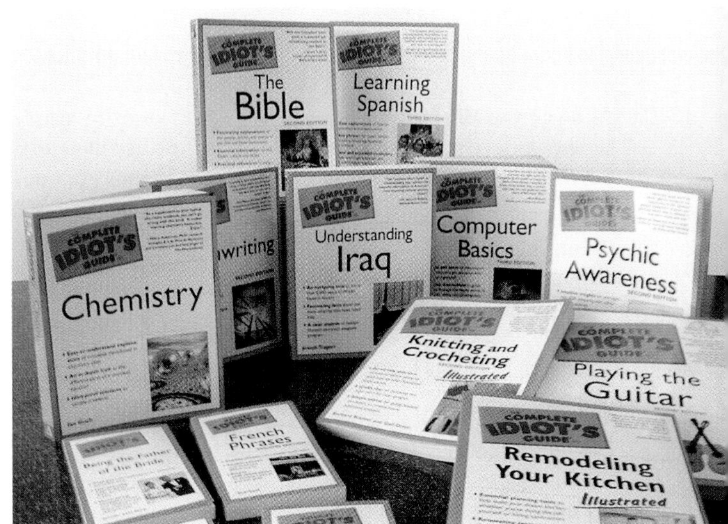

The Complete Idiot's Guides series has enjoyed widespread success through careful attention to audience needs.

how to use it. Such writer-focused problems aren't limited to technology, either; people writing about finances, government regulations, business processes, and other complex topics frequently fail to understand their readers' needs.

"I try to put myself in the shoes of a new user, to think like somebody I know," says Kraynak. He advises all writers to do the same. What essential information do your readers need first? Which details are less important? What style of writing will be most effective? In addition to explaining complex ideas, Kraynak tries to entertain and educate. Focusing on readers will keep your business messages from gathering dust like those high-tech products in your closet.[1]

1 LEARNING OBJECTIVE

Describe the three-step writing process

UNDERSTANDING THE THREE-STEP WRITING PROCESS

Like Joe Kraynak, you'll face a variety of communication assignments in your career, both oral and written. Some of your tasks will be routine, requiring little more than jotting down a few sentences on paper or keyboarding a brief e-mail message; others will be more complex, involving weeks of reflection, research, and careful document preparation.

As soon as the need to create a message appears, inexperienced communicators are often tempted to dive directly into writing. However, spending even a few minutes analyzing, organizing, adapting, and revising can often save you hours of rework later on—and help you generate much more effective messages. Successful communicators such as Kraynak follow a writing process that can be divided into three major steps (see Figure 4.1):

The three-step writing process consists of planning, writing, and completing your messages.

- **Planning business messages.** To plan any message, first *analyze the situation* by defining your purpose and developing a profile of your audience. Once you're sure what you need to accomplish with your message, *gather information* that will meet your audience's needs. Next, *select the right medium* (oral, written, or electronic) to deliver your message. With those three factors in place, you're ready to *organize the information* by defining your main idea, limiting your scope, selecting a direct or an indirect approach, and outlining your content. Planning messages is the focus of this chapter.
- **Writing business messages.** Once you've planned your message, *adapt to your audience* with sensitivity, relationship skills, and style. Be sensitive to your audience's needs by adopting the "you" attitude, being polite, emphasizing the positive, and using bias-

FIGURE 4.1 The Three-Step Writing Process

Plan

Analyze the Situation
Define your purpose and develop an audience profile.

Gather Information
Determine audience needs and obtain the information necessary to satisfy those needs.

Select the Right Medium
Choose the best medium for delivering your message.

Organize the Information
Define your main idea, limit your scope, select a direct or an indirect approach, and outline your content.

1

Write

Adapt to Your Audience
Be sensitive to audience needs with a "you" attitude, politeness, positive emphasis, and bias-free language. Build a strong relationship with your audience by establishing your credibility and projecting your company's image. Control your style with a conversational tone, plain English, and appropriate voice.

Compose the Message
Choose strong words that will help you create effective sentences and coherent paragraphs.

2

Complete

Revise the Message
Evaluate content and review readability; then edit and rewrite for conciseness and clarity.

Produce the Message
Use effective design elements and suitable layout for a clean, professional appearance.

Proofread the Message
Review for errors in layout, spelling, and mechanics.

Distribute the Message
Deliver your message using the chosen medium; make sure all documents and all relevant files are distributed successfully.

3

free language. Build strong relationships with your audience by establishing your credibility and projecting your company's image. Be sure to control your style by using a conversational tone, plain English, and the correct voice. Then you're ready to *compose your message* by choosing strong words, creating effective sentences, and developing coherent paragraphs. Writing business messages is discussed in Chapter 5.

- **Completing business messages.** After writing your first draft, *revise your message* by evaluating the content, reviewing readability, and then editing and rewriting until your message comes across concisely and clearly, with correct grammar, proper punctuation, and effective format. Next *produce your message.* Put it into the form that your audience will receive, and review all design and layout decisions for an attractive, professional appearance. *Proofread* the final draft for typos, spelling errors, and other mechanical problems. Finally, *distribute your message,* using the best combination of personal and technological tools. Completing business messages is discussed in Chapter 6.

Throughout this book, you'll see the three steps in this process applied to a wide variety of business messages: basic tasks for short messages (Chapters 4 to 6), additional tasks for longer messages (Chapters 12 to14), special tasks for oral presentations (Chapters 15 and16), and distinct tasks for employment messages (Chapters 17 and18).

Optimizing Your Writing Time

The more you practice the three-step writing process, the more intuitive and automatic it will become. As you become familiar with the process, you will develop messages faster and easier. You'll also get better at allotting your time for each task during a writing project.

As a general rule, try using roughly half your time for planning—for defining your purpose, getting to know your audience, immersing yourself in your subject matter, and working out media selection and organization. Try to use no more than about a quarter of your time for writing your document. Reserve the remaining quarter of your time for completing the project, so that you don't shortchange important completion steps such as revising, producing, proofreading, and distributing.[2]

As a starting point, try to use half your time for planning, one quarter for writing, and one quarter for completing your messages.

Of course, these time allotments will change significantly, depending on the project; for example, if you already know your material intimately, the planning step might take less than half your time. Then again, if you're delivering your message via complex multimedia such as CD-ROM or DVD, the completion step could take far longer than a quarter of your time. Simple efforts such as instant messages and interoffice memos take far less time and energy than long reports, websites, and other sophisticated projects.

Seasoned professionals understand that there is no right or best way to write all business messages. As you work through the writing process presented in Chapters 4, 5, and 6, try not to view it as a list of how-to directives but as a way to understand the various tasks involved in effective business writing.[3]

Planning Effectively

When writing important messages for important audiences, planning may take hours or days, but it'll pay for itself with the sort of compelling communication that makes careers. Whether your communication effort is simple, complex, or somewhere in between, planning will make it more effective and more efficient. Analyzing your audience helps you find and assemble the facts they're looking for and then deliver that information in a concise and compelling way. Planning reduces your indecision as you write and helps eliminate work as you review and revise.

When deadlines loom and assignments pile up, it's tempting to rush through the planning phase and jump directly into writing. However, more often than not, trying to save time up front costs you more time as you struggle to complete a message that wasn't well thought out. Even if you have only 20 or 30 minutes to prepare and send a message, work through all three steps quickly to ensure that your efforts aren't wasted.

Trying to save time by skimping on planning usually costs you more time in the long run.

2 LEARNING OBJECTIVE

Explain why it's important to define your purpose carefully, and list five questions that can help you test that purpose

ANALYZING YOUR SITUATION

A successful message starts with a clear purpose that connects the sender's needs with the audience's needs. Identifying your purpose and your audience is usually a straightforward task for simple, routine messages; however, this task can be more demanding in more intricate situations. For instance, if you need to communicate about a shipping problem between your Beijing and Los Angeles factories, your purpose might be simply to alert upper management to the situation, or it might involve asking the two factory managers to explore and solve the problem. These two scenarios have different purposes and different audiences; therefore, they yield dramatically different messages. If you launch directly into writing without clarifying both your purpose and your audience, you'll waste time and energy, and you'll probably generate a less-effective message.

Your general purpose may be to inform, to persuade, or to collaborate.

Defining Your Purpose

All business messages have a **general purpose**: to inform, to persuade, or to collaborate with your audience. This purpose helps define the overall approach you'll need to take, including the information you need to gather, your choice of media, and even the way you organize your message. The general purpose also determines both the appropriate degree of audience participation and the amount of control you have over your message.

Communication Solution

A clear purpose is key to the success of Joe Kraynak's work on *The Complete Idiot's Guide to Computer Basics;* he knows he isn't trying to turn readers into computer experts but rather helping them understand how to use their computer more successfully.

Informing your audience requires little interaction (see Figure 4.2). Audience members absorb the information and accept or reject it, but they don't contribute to message content; you control the message. To persuade your audience, you require a moderate amount of participation, such as giving people the chance to ask questions so that you can answer any doubts; nevertheless, you need to retain a moderate amount of message control. Finally, to collaborate with audience members, you need maximum participation. Your control of the message is reduced because you must adjust to new, unexpected input and reactions.

To determine the specific purpose, think of how the audience's ideas or behavior should be affected by the message.

Within the scope of its general purpose, each message also has a **specific purpose**, which identifies what you hope to accomplish with your message and what your audience should do or think after receiving your message. For instance, is your goal simply to update your audience on an event, or do you want them to take immediate action? State your specific purpose as precisely as possible, even identifying which audience members should respond, how they should respond, and when.

Defer a message, or do not send it at all, if

- Nothing will change as a result
- The purpose is not realistic
- The timing is not right
- You are not the right person to deliver the message
- The purpose is not acceptable to your organization

Once you have defined your specific purpose, you can decide whether that purpose merits the time and effort required for you to prepare and send it. Test your purpose by asking five questions:

- **Will anything change as a result of your message?** The change doesn't have to be dramatic; it might be as basic as bringing everyone up to date on a project they're all interested in. However, if your message changes nothing, ask yourself whether you should even be sending it. Unnecessary messages waste both your time and your audience's time, and sending too many of them will hurt your credibility.

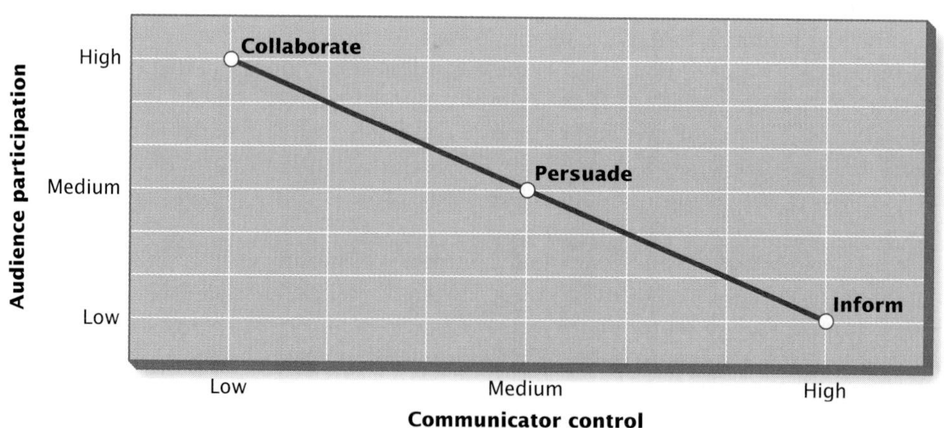

FIGURE 4.2
The Relation Between the General Purpose of a Business Message and Communicator Control

- **Is your purpose realistic?** If your purpose involves a radical shift in action or attitude, go slowly. Consider proposing a first step so that your message acts as the beginning of a learning process.
- **Is the time right?** Think through the potential impact of your message—both intentional and unintentional—to see whether this is a good time to send it. Many professions and departments have recurring cycles in their workloads, so messages sent during peak times might be ignored. Similarly, employees in departments that are in the midst of a reorganization, series of layoffs, or other changes won't be able to give your message their full attention.
- **Is the right person delivering your message?** Even though you may have done all the work, achieving your objective is usually more important than taking the credit. If your boss or even a respected senior colleague might be a more compelling messenger, consider asking this person to deliver your message.
- **Is your purpose acceptable to your organization?** If you receive an abusive letter that unfairly attacks your company, you might feel like firing back an angry reply. But your supervisors might prefer that you regain the customer's goodwill. Make sure that your response reflects the organization's priorities.

Once you are satisfied that (1) you have a clear and meaningful purpose and (2) now is a smart time to proceed, your next step is to understand the members of your audience and their needs.

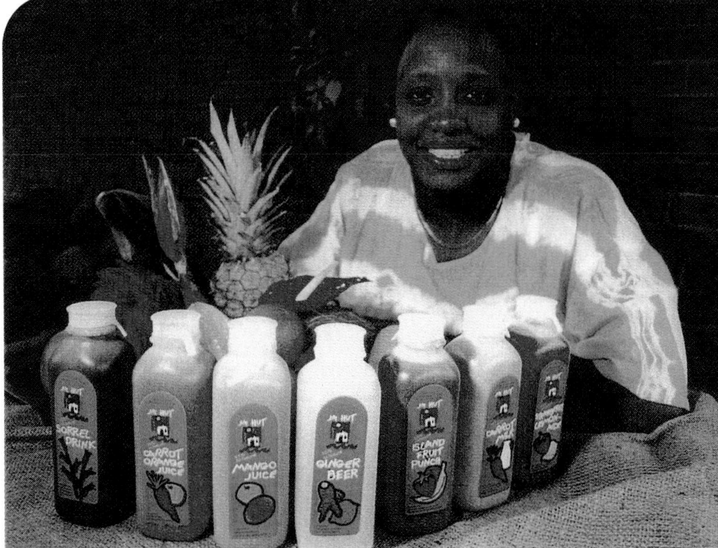

Nicola Shirley uses her Jamaican background and West Indian cooking talent to entice customers to eat at her restaurant or try her JaHut food products. But savory cooking is only one of her strengths. When it comes to communicating with customers, suppliers, or investors, Shirley gets results by making sure her message has a clear purpose and addresses her audience's information needs.

Developing an Audience Profile

How often do you toss out junk mail because it offers to solve problems you don't have and doesn't offer to solve the problems you do have? Before your own audiences will take the time to read or hear your messages, they need to be interested in what you're saying. They need to see what's in it for them—which of their problems will be solved by listening to your advice or doing what you ask. The more you know about your audience, their needs, and their expectations, the more effectively you'll be able to communicate with them.

If you're communicating with someone you know well, audience analysis is relatively easy. You can identify the person's needs and predict his or her reaction to any given message without a lot of research. On the other hand, your audience could be made up of strangers—customers or suppliers you've never met, a new boss, or new employees. In these situations, you'll need to learn more in order to adjust your message to meet the needs of your audience. For an example of the kind of information you need to compile in an audience analysis, see the planning sheet in Figure 4.3. To conduct an audience analysis:

3 LEARNING OBJECTIVE

Describe the importance of analyzing your audience, and identify the six factors you should consider when developing an audience profile

Ask yourself some key questions about your audience:

- Who are they?
- How many people do you need to reach?
- How much do they already know about the subject?
- What is their probable reaction to your message?

- **Identify your primary audience.** For some messages, certain audience members might be more important than others. Don't ignore the needs of less influential members, but make sure you address the concerns of the key decision makers.
- **Determine audience size and geographic distribution.** A message aimed at 10,000 people spread around the globe might require a different approach than one aimed at a dozen people down the hall.
- **Determine audience composition.** Look for both similarities and differences in culture, language, age, education, organizational rank and status, attitudes, experience, motivations, and any other factors that might affect the success of your message. For example, if you're reporting the results of a market research project, the vice president of sales will probably want to know what's happening right now, whereas the vice

FIGURE 4.3
Audience Analysis Helps You Plan Your Message

Audience Analysis Notes

Project: A report recommending that we close down the on-site exercise facility and subsidize private memberships at local health clubs.

- **Primary audience:** Nicole Perazzo, vice president of operations, and her supervisory team.
- **Size and geographic distribution:** Nine managers total; Nicole and five of her staff are here on site; three other supervisors are based in Hong Kong.
- **Composition:** All have experience in operations management, but several are new to the company.
- **Level of understanding:** All will no doubt understand the financial considerations, but the newer managers might not understand the importance of the on-site exercise facility to many of our employees.
- **Expectations and preferences.** They're expecting a firm recommendation, backed up with well-thought-out financial rationale and suggestions for communicating the bad news to employees. For a decision of this magnitude, a formal report is appropriate; e-mail distribution is expected.
- **Probable reaction.** From one-on-one discussions, I know that several of the managers receiving this report are active users of the on-site facility and won't welcome the suggestion that we should shut it down. However, some nonexercisers generally think it's a luxury the company can't afford. Audience reactions will range from highly positive to highly negative; the report should focus on overcoming the highly negative reactions since they're the ones I need to convince.

president of research might be more interested in how the market will look a year or two from now, when that department's new products will be ready to sell.

- **Gauge audience members' level of understanding.** If audience members share your general background, they'll probably understand your material without difficulty. If not, your message will need an element of education, and deciding how much information to include can be a challenge. Try to include only enough information to accomplish the specific purpose of your message. Everything else is irrelevant and risks overwhelming your audience and diverting attention from your important points. If the members of your audience have various levels of understanding, gear your coverage to your primary audience (the key decision makers).

If audience members have different levels of understanding of the topic, aim your message at the most influential decision makers.

- **Understand audience expectations and preferences.** Will members of your audience expect complete details or just a summary of the main points? Do they want an e-mail or will they expect a formal memo? In general, the higher up the organization your message goes, the fewer details people want to see, simply because they have less time to read them.
- **Forecast probable audience reaction.** As you'll read later in the chapter, audience reaction affects message organization. If you expect a favorable response, you can state conclusions and recommendations up front and offer minimal supporting evidence. If you expect skepticism, you can introduce conclusions gradually, with more proof. By anticipating the primary audience's response to certain points, you can vary the amount of evidence you'll need to address those issues.

A gradual approach and plenty of evidence are required to win over a skeptical audience.

GATHERING INFORMATION

With a clear picture of your audience and their needs, your next step is to assemble the information that you will include in your message. For simple messages, you may already have all the information at hand, but more complex messages can require considerable research and analysis before you're ready to begin writing. Chapter 10 explores formal techniques for finding, evaluating, and processing information, but you can often use a variety of informal techniques to gather insights and focus your research efforts:

- **Considering other viewpoints.** Putting yourself in someone else's position helps you consider what that person might be thinking, feeling, or planning.
- **Reading reports and other company documents.** Your company's files may be a rich source of the information you need for a particular memo or e-mail message. Consider annual reports, financial statements, news releases, memos, marketing reports, and customer surveys for helpful information. Find out whether your company has a *knowledge management system*, a centralized database that collects the experiences and insights of employees throughout the organization.
- **Talking with supervisors, colleagues, or customers.** Fellow workers and customers may have information you need, or they may know what your audience will be interested in. Conducting telephone or personal interviews is a convenient way to gather information.
- **Asking your audience for input.** If you're unsure of what audience members need from your message, ask them—whether through casual conversation (face-to-face or over the phone), informal surveys, or unofficial interviews. Admitting you don't know but want to meet their needs will impress an audience more than guessing and getting it wrong.

Gathering information from co-workers in conversations or informal interviews helps Levi Strauss editors determine how much detail about a project their audience expects in the company newsletter.

Uncovering Audience Needs

In many situations your audience's information needs are readily apparent, such as when a consumer sends you a letter asking a specific question. In other cases, your audience might be unable to articulate exactly what is needed. If someone makes a vague or broad request, ask questions to narrow the focus. If your boss says, "Find out everything you can about Interscope Records," ask which aspect of the company and its business is most important. Asking a question or two often forces the person to think through the request and define more precisely what is required.

If you're given a vague request, ask questions to clarify it before you plan a response.

Also, try to think of information needs that your audience may not even be aware of. Suppose your company has just hired a new employee from out of town, and you've been assigned to coordinate this person's relocation. At a minimum, you would write a welcoming letter describing your company's procedures for relocating employees. With a little extra thought, however, you might include some information about the city: perhaps a guide to residential areas, a map or two, brochures about cultural activities, or information on schools and transportation facilities. In some cases, you may be able to tell your audience something they consider important but wouldn't have thought to ask. Although adding information of this sort lengthens your message, it also creates goodwill.

Include any additional information that might be helpful, even though the requester didn't specifically ask for it.

Communication Solution

Joe Kraynak organizes his writing to overcome a common flaw in manuals for technical products: providing too little of the right information (how to use the equipment) and too much of the wrong information (how the equipment works).

Providing Required Information

Once you've defined your audience's information needs, be sure you satisfy those needs completely. One good way to test the thoroughness of your message is to use the **journalistic approach**: Check to see whether your message answers *who, what, when, where, why,* and *how.* Using this test, you can quickly tell whether a message fails to deliver—such as this letter requesting information from a large hotel:

Test the completeness of your document by making sure it answers all the important questions: who, what, when, where, why, and how.

> Dear Ms. Hill:
>
> I just got back from a great vacation in Hawaii. However, this morning I discovered that my favorite black leather shoes are missing. Since I wore them in Hawaii, I assume I left them at the Hawaii Sands Hotel. Please check the items in your "lost and found" and let me know whether you have the missing shoes.

4 LEARNING OBJECTIVE

Discuss gathering information for simple messages, and identify three attributes of quality information.

The letter fails to tell Hill everything she needs to know. The *what* could be improved by including a detailed description of the missing shoes (size, brand, distinguishable style or trim). Hill doesn't know *when* the writer stayed at the Hawaii Sands, *where* (in which room) the writer stayed, or *how* to return the shoes. Hill will have to write or call the writer to get the missing details, and the inconvenience may be just enough to prevent her from complying with the request.

Be Sure the Information Is Accurate

Be certain that the information you provide is accurate and that the commitments you make can be kept.

Inaccurate information communicated in business messages can cause a host of problems, from embarrassment and lost productivity to serious safety and legal issues. Inaccurate information might persist for months or years after you distribute it, or you might commit the organization to promises it isn't prepared or able to keep.

You can minimize mistakes by double-checking every piece of information you collect. If you are consulting sources outside the organization, ask yourself whether they are current and reliable. Be particularly careful when using sources you find on the Internet. As you'll see in Chapter 10, the simplicity of online publishing and frequent lack of editorial oversight call for extra care in using online information. If your sources are international, remember that various cultures can view accuracy differently. A German bank may insist on balancing the books to the last penny, whereas an Italian bank may be more lenient.[4] Be sure to review any mathematical or financial calculations. Check all dates and schedules, and examine your own assumptions and conclusions to be certain they are valid.

Be Sure the Information Is Ethical

Ethics should guide your decisions when determining how much detail to include in your message.

By working hard to ensure the accuracy of the information you gather, you'll also avoid many ethical problems in your messages. If you do make an honest mistake, such as delivering information you initially thought to be true but later found to be false, contact the recipients of the message immediately and correct the error. No one can reasonably fault you in such circumstances, and most people will respect your honesty.

Messages can also be unethical if important information is omitted (see "Ethics Detective: Telling Only Half the Story"). Of course, as a business professional, you may have legal or other sound business reasons for not including every detail about every matter. So just how much detail should you include? Make sure you include enough detail to avoid misleading your audience. If you're unsure about how much information your audience needs, offer as much as you believe best fits your definition of complete, and then offer to provide more upon request.

Be Sure the Information Is Pertinent

Try to figure out what points will especially interest your audience; then give those points the most attention.

When gathering information for your message, remember that some points will be of greater interest and importance to your audience than others. In a world overflowing with information, your audience will appreciate your efforts to prioritize the information they need and filter out the information they don't. For example, if you're summarizing a recent conversation you had with one of your company's oldest and best customers, the emphasis you give each point of the conversation will depend on your audience's concerns. The head of engineering might be most interested in the customer's reaction to your product's new design features, whereas the shipping manager might be most concerned about the customer's comments on recent delivery schedules. In other words, by focusing on the information that concerns your audience the most, you increase your chances of sending an effective message—one that will have the most impact on your audience.

Rely on common sense if you don't know enough about your audience to know exactly what will interest them.

If you don't know your audience, or if you're communicating with a large group of people with diverse interests, use your common sense to identify points of particular interest. Audience factors such as age, job, location, income, and education can give you a clue. If you're trying to sell memberships in a health club, you might adjust your message for athletes, busy professionals, families, and people in different locations or in different income brackets. The comprehensive facilities and professional trainers would appeal to athletes, whereas the low monthly rates would appeal to college students on tight budgets.

Ethics Detective

Telling Only Half the Story

Your company, Furniture Formations, creates a variety of home furniture products with extensive use of fine woods. To preserve the look and feel of the wood, your craftspeople use an oil-based finish that you purchase from a local building products wholesaler. The workers apply the finish with rags, which are thrown away after each project. After a news report about spontaneous combustion of waste rags in other furniture shops, you grow concerned enough to contact the wholesaler and ask for verification of the product's safety. The wholesaler knows that you've been considering a nonflammable water-based alternative from another source but assures you that as long as you dispose of the rags and other waste in a safe manner, you have no need to worry:

> "Seal the rags in an approved container and dispose of it according to local regulations. As you probably already know, county regulations require all commercial users of solvent-based materials to dispose of leftover finishes at the county's hazardous waste facility."

You're still not satisfied. After some further research, you visit the website of the manufacturer, Minwax, www.minwax.com/shoptalk/resources/faq.cfm, and find the following cautionary statement about the product you're currently using:

> "For some products, when oil-soaked rags and other porous waste are improperly discarded, heat can build up which may result in flames that immediately feed on the oil-soaked material. This phenomenon is known as spontaneous combustion and can be avoided simply by immersing all wood-finishing materials, including rags, steel wool and other waste, in a water-filled, metal container. Seal the container and dispose of in accordance with local regulations."

ANALYSIS

Was the wholesaler guilty of an ethical lapse in this case? If yes, explain what you think the lapse is and why you believe it is unethical. If no, explain why you think the statement qualifies as ethical.

As Figure 4.4 shows, your main goal is to tell audience members what they need to know—no more, no less.

SELECTING THE RIGHT MEDIUM

Selecting the best medium for your message can make the difference between effective and ineffective communication.[5] A **medium** is the form through which you choose to communicate your message. You may choose to talk with someone face to face, write a letter, send e-mail, or leave a voice-mail message—and there are many other media to choose from.

In fact, categorizing media has become increasingly blurred in recent years with the advent of so many options that include multimedia formats. For the sake of discussion, you can think of media as traditionally being either oral or written. Nowadays, electronic media extend the reach of both oral and written media, and even combine all three forms. Each type of media has advantages and disadvantages.

Oral Media

Primary oral media include face-to-face conversations, speeches, presentations, and meetings. You may think that most conversations are relatively informal; however, conversations such as employment interviews and performance evaluations are certainly more structured. Likewise, speeches, presentations, and meetings require careful planning and preparation.

Being able to see, hear, and react to each other can benefit communicators. Oral media have several advantages:

- They provide immediate feedback.
- They allow a certain ease of interaction.
- They involve rich nonverbal cues (both physical gesture and vocal inflection).
- They allow you to express the emotion behind your message.

Oral communication is best when you need to encourage interaction, express emotions, or monitor emotional responses.

FIGURE 4.4 An Audience-Centered Letter

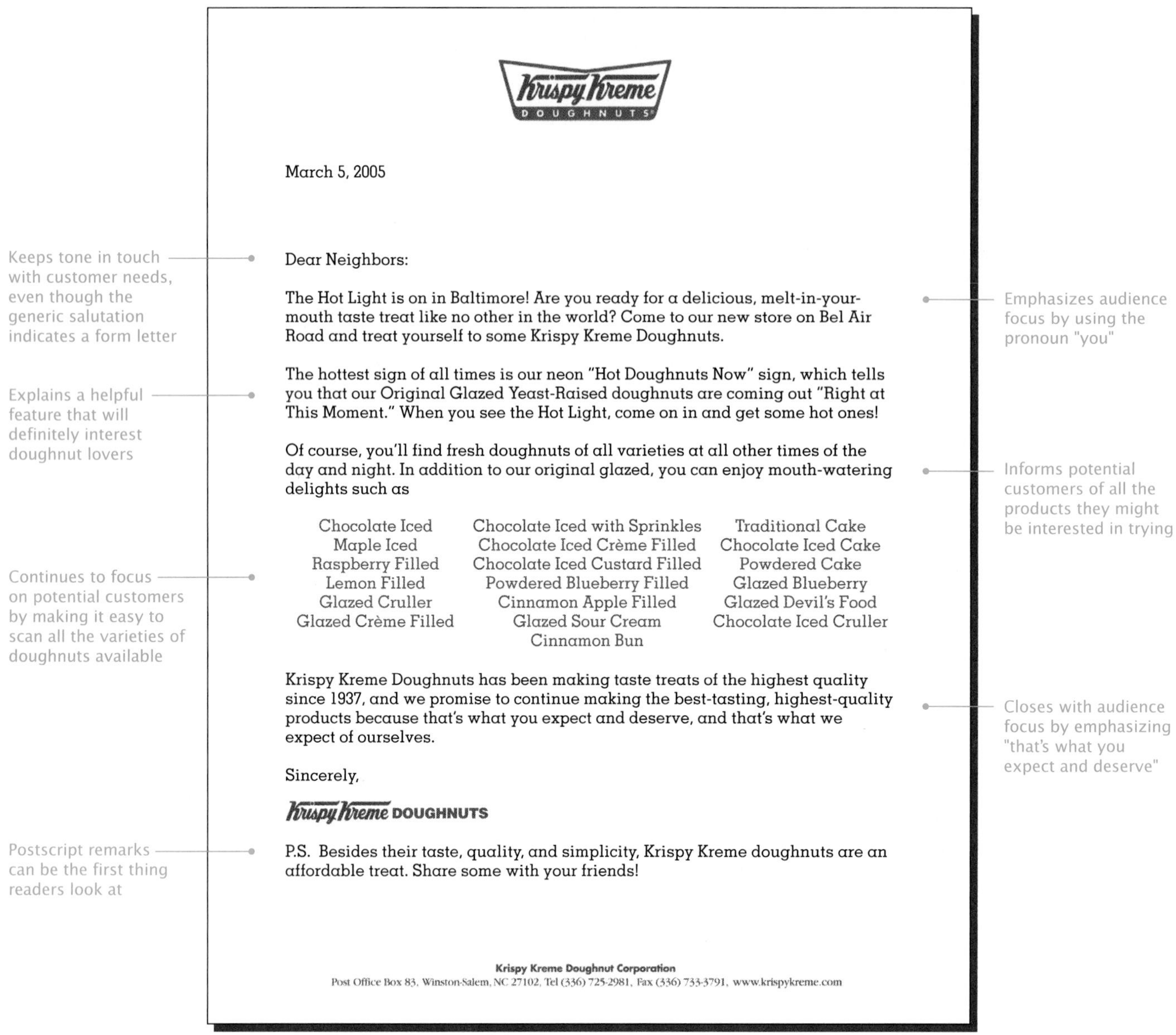

Krispy Kreme DOUGHNUTS

March 5, 2005

Dear Neighbors:

The Hot Light is on in Baltimore! Are you ready for a delicious, melt-in-your-mouth taste treat like no other in the world? Come to our new store on Bel Air Road and treat yourself to some Krispy Kreme Doughnuts.

The hottest sign of all times is our neon "Hot Doughnuts Now" sign, which tells you that our Original Glazed Yeast-Raised doughnuts are coming out "Right at This Moment." When you see the Hot Light, come on in and get some hot ones!

Of course, you'll find fresh doughnuts of all varieties at all other times of the day and night. In addition to our original glazed, you can enjoy mouth-watering delights such as

Chocolate Iced
Maple Iced
Raspberry Filled
Lemon Filled
Glazed Cruller
Glazed Crème Filled
Chocolate Iced with Sprinkles
Chocolate Iced Crème Filled
Chocolate Iced Custard Filled
Powdered Blueberry Filled
Cinnamon Apple Filled
Glazed Sour Cream
Cinnamon Bun
Traditional Cake
Chocolate Iced Cake
Powdered Cake
Glazed Blueberry
Glazed Devil's Food
Chocolate Iced Cruller

Krispy Kreme Doughnuts has been making taste treats of the highest quality since 1937, and we promise to continue making the best-tasting, highest-quality products because that's what you expect and deserve, and that's what we expect of ourselves.

Sincerely,

Krispy Kreme DOUGHNUTS

P.S. Besides their taste, quality, and simplicity, Krispy Kreme doughnuts are an affordable treat. Share some with your friends!

Krispy Kreme Doughnut Corporation
Post Office Box 83, Winston-Salem, NC 27102, Tel (336) 725-2981, Fax (336) 733-3791, www.krispykreme.com

Keeps tone in touch with customer needs, even though the generic salutation indicates a form letter
Explains a helpful feature that will definitely interest doughnut lovers
Continues to focus on potential customers by making it easy to scan all the varieties of doughnuts available
Postscript remarks can be the first thing readers look at
Emphasizes audience focus by using the pronoun "you"
Informs potential customers of all the products they might be interested in trying
Closes with audience focus by emphasizing "that's what you expect and deserve"

Traditional oral media are useful for getting people to ask questions, make comments, and work together to reach a consensus or decision. However, if you don't want or need all that interaction, then oral media can have several disadvantages:

Oral media limit participation to those who are present, reduce your control over the message, and make it difficult to revise or edit your message.

- They restrict participation to those physically present.
- They provide no permanent, verifiable record of the communication, without special recording equipment.
- They reduce the communicator's control over the message.
- They often rule out the chance to revise or edit your spoken words.

Written Media

From the scribbled notes that people use to jog their own memories to the elaborate, formal reports that rival magazines in graphic quality, written messages take many forms, including the traditional memos, letters, and reports. Appendix A discusses the accepted formats for these business documents. Most letters and memos are relatively brief documents, generally one or two pages, although some run much longer. Memos are used for the routine, day-to-day exchange of information within an organization. Because of their open construction and informal method of delivery (e-mail or interoffice mail), memos are less private than letters.

Letters are written messages sent to recipients outside the organization, so in addition to conveying a particular message, they perform an important public relations function in fostering good working relationships with customers, suppliers, and others. Many organizations rely on form letters to save time and money on routine communication. Form letters are particularly handy for such one-time mass mailings as sales messages about products, information about organizational activities, and goodwill messages such as seasonal greetings. Chapters 7 to 9 discuss shorter messages such as would be sent in a letter or memo.

Reports and proposals are often longer than letters and memos. These factual, objective documents may be distributed to insiders or outsiders, depending on their purpose and subject. They come in many formats, including preprinted forms, letters, memos, and manuscripts. In length, they range from a few pages to several hundred, and they are generally more formal in tone than a typical business letter or memo. Chapters 12 to 14 discuss reports and proposals in detail.

Written media have a number of advantages over oral media:

- They allow you to plan and control your message.
- They offer a permanent, verifiable record.
- They help you reach an audience that is geographically dispersed.
- They minimize the distortion that can accompany oral messages.
- They can be used to avoid immediate interactions.
- They de-emphasize any inappropriate emotional components.

Written media increase your control, help you reach dispersed audiences, and minimize distortion.

Even so, not everything about written media is positive. Disadvantages of written media include the following:

- Many are not conducive to speedy feedback.
- They lack the rich nonverbal cues provided by oral media.
- They often take more time and more resources to create and distribute.
- They can require special skills in preparation and production.

The disadvantages of written media include difficulty of feedback, lack of nonverbal cues, and the time and skill sometimes required to prepare written messages.

Electronic Media

Electronic media include choices such as e-mail, telephones, videotape, faxes, voice mail, instant messaging, websites, and many more. When you want to make a powerful impression on supervisors, customers, investors, or other key audiences, electronic media can increase the excitement and visual appeal with computer animation, video, even music. The growth of electronic communication options is both a blessing and a curse. You have more tools than ever to choose from, but the choice itself can complicate the communication process. The trick is to pick the tool that does the best overall job in each situation. Although no hard rules dictate which tool to use in each case, here are a few pointers that will help you determine when to select electronic over more traditional forms:[6]

- **Telephone calls** are still the lifeblood of many organizations, for both internal and external communication. But even the humble telephone has joined the Internet age, thanks to the emerging capability to place phone calls over the Internet. Known by the technical term VoIP (which stands for *Voice over IP*, the Internet Protocol), Internet-based phone service promises to offer cheaper long-distance service for businesses worldwide.[7]

In spite of numerous technological advances in recent years, the basic telephone remains one of the most important communication tools for businesses large and small. Whether you are taking orders, resolving problems, or screening new job applications, good telephone skills are essential to your success.

- **Voice mail** can replace short memos and phone calls that need no response. It's best for short, unambiguous messages. It solves time-zone difficulties and can reduce interoffice paperwork.[8] Voice mail is a powerful tool when you need to communicate your emotion or tone. It is especially useful for goodwill and other positive messages.
- **Teleconferencing and videoconferencing** are best for informational meetings and less effective for highly interactive meetings such as negotiation. New online meetings are less expensive than traditional videoconferencing.
- **Videotapes and DVDs** are often effective for sending a motivational message to a large number of people. By communicating nonverbal cues, they can strengthen the sender's image of sincerity and trustworthiness; however, they offer no opportunity for immediate feedback.
- **Electronic documents** let you send written materials over e-mail and instant messaging networks or on CD-ROM. Other than simple word processor files, Adobe's Portable Document Format (PDF) is the most popular type of electronic document. Computer users can view PDFs on screen with free reader software, and PDFs are more secure and less vulnerable to viruses than word processor files.
- **Faxes** can overcome time-zone barriers when a hard copy is required. They have all the characteristics of a written message, except (1) they lack the privacy of a letter, and (2) they may appear less crisp, even less professional, depending on the quality of the audience's machine. Internet-based fax services, such as eFax, lower the cost by eliminating the sender's need for a dedicated fax machine.
- **E-mail** offers speed, low cost, increased access to other employees, portability, and convenience (not just overcoming time-zone problems but reaching many receivers at once). It's best for brief, noncomplex information that is time sensitive. With such a quick turnaround time, e-mail tends to be more conversational than traditional media. However, e-mail's ease and speed can contribute to poorly conceived, confusing messages that waste more time than they save.[9] (Chapter 5 presents more advice on writing effective e-mail messages.)
- **Instant messaging** (IM) allows real-time, one-on-one and small-group text conversations. IM is more versatile than a phone call and quicker than e-mail. You can send a text message that is immediately displayed on your receiver's computer screen, and you often get a response back within seconds. Similarly, you can use IM to exchange documents or hold a virtual meeting online in a private chat area. Newer IM systems offer file attachments, streaming audio and video, and other enhancements.
- **Websites** offer interactive communication through hyperlinks, allowing readers to absorb information nonsequentially: Readers can take what they need and skip everything else. A website can tailor the same information for numerous readers by breaking it up into linked pages. However, web expectations differ around the world. Writing for the web is a specialized skill; you can learn more about these techniques at www.prenhall.com/bovee.

As you can see, electronic messages offer considerable advantages:

In general, use electronic media for speed, to reach widely dispersed audiences, and to take advantage of rich multimedia formats.

- They deliver messages with great speed.
- They reach audiences physically separated from you.
- They reach a dispersed audience personally.
- They offer the persuasive power of multimedia formats.
- They can increase accessibility and openness in an organization.

For all their good points, electronic media are not problem-free. Consider some of these disadvantages:

Electronic media can suffer from a lack of privacy and can reduce productivity when people send too many low-value messages.

- **They can inadvertently create tension and conflict.** Electronic messages can give the illusion of anonymity, so people sometimes say things in e-mail or IM that they would never say in person or in a traditional document.
- **They are easy to overuse.** Sending too many unnecessary messages to too many people can overload company networks and even result in lost messages or system crashes.

- **They often lack privacy.** Some people are careless about screening their distribution lists; plus, any recipient can easily forward your message to someone else. In addition, employers can legally monitor e-mail and voice mail, and both can be subpoenaed for court cases.
- **They can seriously drain employee productivity.** Employees can be easily distracted either by constant streams of e-mail, IM, voice mail, conference calls, and faxes or by surfing the web and visiting non-business-related websites during working hours. In one report, 31 percent of the businesses surveyed cited financial losses from reduced employee productivity as a result of Internet misuse alone.[10]

Factors to Consider When Choosing Media

5 LEARNING OBJECTIVE

List factors to consider when choosing the most appropriate medium for your message

When choosing a medium for your message, balance your needs with your audience's needs. You certainly want to select the medium whose advantages offer you the best fit with the situation and your audience (see Figure 4.5). Just as critical, however, is considering how your message is affected by important factors such as the following:

The more complicated the message, the richer the medium required.

- **Media richness.** Richness is a medium's ability to (1) convey a message through more than one informational cue (visual, verbal, vocal), (2) facilitate feedback, and (3) establish personal focus. The richest medium is face-to-face communication; it's personal, it provides immediate feedback (verbal and nonverbal), and it conveys the emotion behind a message.[11] At the other end of the richness continuum are the leanest media—unaddressed documents, such as fliers (see Figure 4.6). Use the richest media to send nonroutine, complex messages, to humanize your presence throughout the organization, to communicate caring to employees, and to gain employee commitment to company goals. Use leaner media to send simple, routine messages.
- **Message formality.** Your choice of media governs the style and tone of your message. For instance, you wouldn't write an e-mail message with the same level of formality that you would use in a letter. Thus, if your purpose were to share simple information with employees, such as changes in the cafeteria hours, you would probably send an e-mail message rather than write a formal letter or make a lengthy face-to-face presentation. Similarly, drafting a few notes for a conversation with an employee would be less formal than drafting a letter of reprimand.

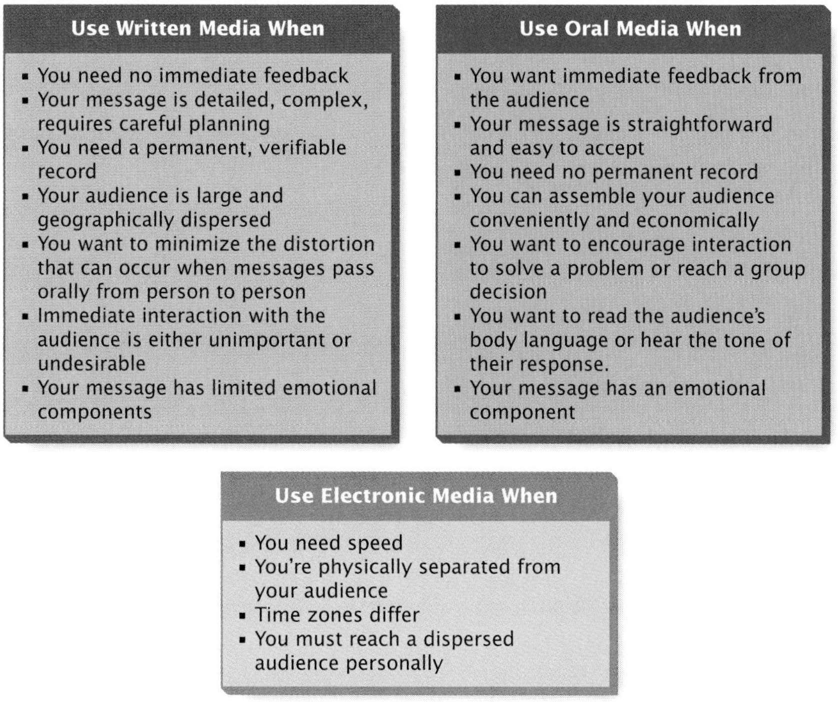

Use Written Media When

- You need no immediate feedback
- Your message is detailed, complex, requires careful planning
- You need a permanent, verifiable record
- Your audience is large and geographically dispersed
- You want to minimize the distortion that can occur when messages pass orally from person to person
- Immediate interaction with the audience is either unimportant or undesirable
- Your message has limited emotional components

Use Oral Media When

- You want immediate feedback from the audience
- Your message is straightforward and easy to accept
- You need no permanent record
- You can assemble your audience conveniently and economically
- You want to encourage interaction to solve a problem or reach a group decision
- You want to read the audience's body language or hear the tone of their response.
- Your message has an emotional component

Use Electronic Media When

- You need speed
- You're physically separated from your audience
- Time zones differ
- You must reach a dispersed audience personally

FIGURE 4.5
Choosing the Most Appropriate Medium

FIGURE 4.6
Media Richness

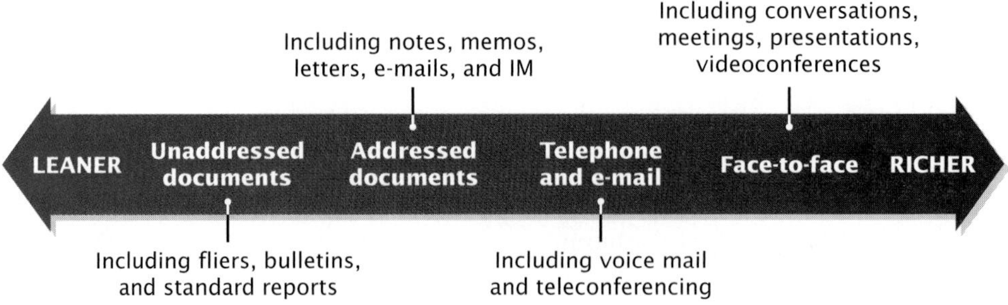

- **Media limitations.** Every medium has limitations. Although face-to-face communication is the richest medium, it's one of the most restrictive because you and your audience must be in the same place at the same time.[12] Or consider instant messaging; it's perfect for communicating simple, straightforward messages, but it is ineffective for sending complex ones.

Your intentions heavily influence your choice of medium.

- **Sender intentions.** Your choice of medium influences your audience's perception of your intentions. If you want to emphasize the formality of your message, use a more formal medium, such as a memo or a letter. To emphasize the confidentiality of your message, use voice mail rather than a fax, send a letter rather than a memo, or address the matter in a private conversation rather than during a meeting. To instill an emotional commitment to corporate values, consider a visual medium such as a personal speech or a video conference. For immediate feedback meet face-to-face, make a phone call, or use instant messaging.[13] However, if you need a written record, use one of the written media or an electronic equivalent such as an intranet posting.

Time and cost also affect medium selection.

- **Urgency and cost.** If your message is urgent, you'll probably use the phone or instant messaging. But don't forget to weigh cost against speed. For instance, you wouldn't think twice about telephoning an important customer in Australia if you just discovered that your company had erroneously sent the wrong shipment, but you'd probably choose to fax or e-mail a routine order acknowledgment to that same customer.

When choosing the appropriate medium, don't forget to consider your audience's expectations.

- **Audience preferences.** Make sure to consider which media your audience expects or prefers.[14] What would you think if your college tried to deliver your diploma by fax? You'd expect the college to hand it to you at graduation or mail it to you. In addition, some cultures tend to favor one channel over another. For example, the United States, Canada, and Germany emphasize written messages, whereas Japan emphasizes oral messages—perhaps because its high-context culture carries so much of the message in nonverbal cues and "between the lines" interpretation.[15]

Once you select the best medium for your purpose, your situation, and your audience, you are ready to start thinking about the organization of your message.

ORGANIZING YOUR INFORMATION

For anything beyond the simplest messages, organization can make the difference between success and failure. Consider this letter from Jill Saunders, the accounting manager at General Nutrition Corporation (GNC), which manufactures health-food products and nutritional supplements:

> General Nutrition Corporation has been doing business with ComputerTime since I was hired 6 years ago. Your building was smaller then, and it was located on the corner of Federal Avenue and 2nd N.W. Jared Mallory, our controller, was one of your first customers. I still remember the day. It was the biggest check I'd ever written. Of course, over the years, I've gotten used to larger purchases.
>
> Our department now has 15 employees. As accountants, we need to have our computers working so that we can do our jobs. The CD-RW drive we bought for my assistant, Suzanne, has been a problem. We've taken it in for repairs three times in

three months to the authorized service center, and Suzanne is very careful with the machine and hasn't abused it. She does like playing interactive adventure games on lunch breaks. Anyway, it still doesn't work right, and she's tired of hauling it back and forth. We're all putting in longer hours because it is our busy season, and none of us has a lot of spare time.

This is the first time we've returned anything to your store, and I hope you'll agree that we deserve a better deal.

Look closely at this letter, and you can distinguish four of the most common organization mistakes:

- **Taking too long to get to the point.** Saunders didn't introduce her topic, the faulty CD-RW drive, until the third paragraph. Then she waited until the final paragraph to state her purpose: requesting an adjustment. *Solution:* Make the subject and purpose clear, and get to the point without wasting the reader's time.
- **Including irrelevant material.** Does it matter that ComputerTime used to be smaller or that it was in a different location? Is it important that Saunders's department has 15 employees or that her assistant likes playing computer games during lunch? *Solution:* Include only information that is related to the subject and purpose.
- **Getting ideas mixed up.** Saunders tries to make five points: (1) Her company has money to spend, (2) it's an old customer, (3) it has purchased numerous items at ComputerTime, (4) the CD-RW drive doesn't work, and (5) Saunders wants an adjustment. However, the ideas are mixed up and located in the wrong places. *Solution:* Group similar ideas and present them in a logical way, where one idea leads to the next.
- **Leaving out necessary information.** ComputerTime may want to know the make, model, and price of the CD-RW drive; the date of purchase; the specific problems the machine has had; and whether the repairs were covered by the warranty. Saunders also failed to say what she wants the store to do: send her a new CD-RW drive of the same type, send her a different model, or simply refund her money. *Solution:* Include all the information necessary for the audience to respond as the writer wishes.

Most disorganized communication suffers from problems with clarity, relevance, grouping, and completeness.

Saunders can make her letter more effective by organizing all the necessary information in a sequence that helps ComputerTime understand the message (see Figure 4.7).

Understanding what good organization is can be helpful, but it is only half the battle. Knowing *how* to organize your messages well is the other half. As you'll see in the following chapters, various types of messages may require different organizational schemes. Nevertheless, in every case, you can organize your message in a logical and compelling way by recognizing the importance of good organization, defining your main idea, limiting your scope, choosing either a direct or an indirect approach, and outlining your content.

To organize a message,
- Define your main idea
- Limit the scope
- Choose the direct or indirect approach
- Group your points

Recognizing the Importance of Good Organization

6 LEARNING OBJECTIVE

Explain why good organization is important to both you and your audience

At best, poor organization creates unnecessary work for your readers, forcing them to piece your message together in a sensible way. At worst, poor organization leads readers to inaccurate conclusions, forces them to ask for clarification, and can even cause them to stop reading or listening. If you gain the reputation as a disorganized communicator who creates extra work for others, people will find ways to ignore or avoid your messages. In other words, sending messages that aren't well-organized is bad for business and bad for your career.

Organizing your message before you start writing helps you work better. It saves you time and consumes less of your creative energy. Your draft goes more quickly because you don't waste time putting ideas in the wrong places or composing material that you don't need. You might also use your organizational plan to get advance input from your audience. That way, you can be sure you're on the right track *before* you spend hours working on your draft. Furthermore, if you're working on a large, complex project, you can use your organization plan to divide the writing job among co-workers.

FIGURE 4.7 Letter with Improved Organization

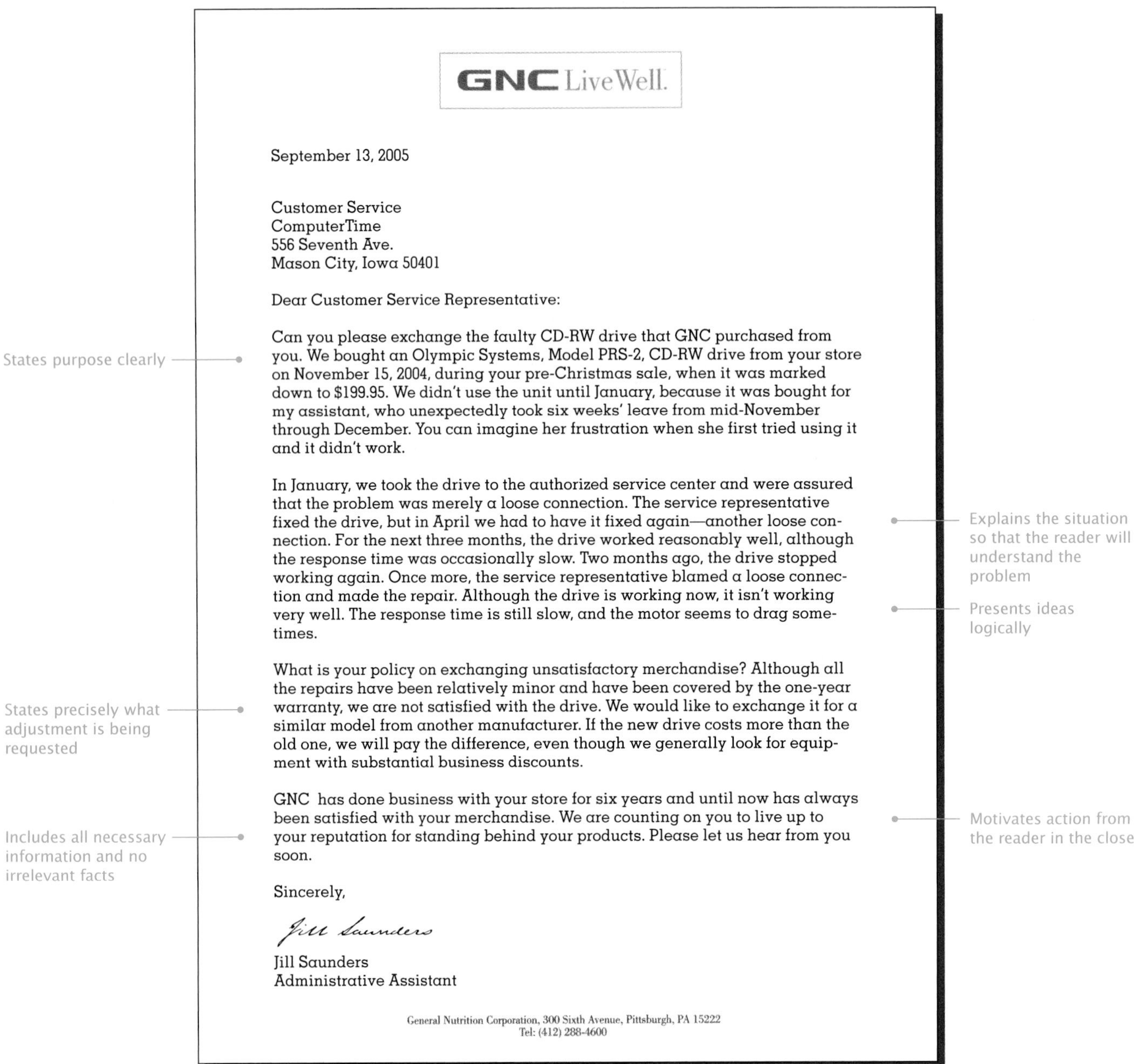

GNC LiveWell.

September 13, 2005

Customer Service
ComputerTime
556 Seventh Ave.
Mason City, Iowa 50401

Dear Customer Service Representative:

Can you please exchange the faulty CD-RW drive that GNC purchased from you. We bought an Olympic Systems, Model PRS-2, CD-RW drive from your store on November 15, 2004, during your pre-Christmas sale, when it was marked down to $199.95. We didn't use the unit until January, because it was bought for my assistant, who unexpectedly took six weeks' leave from mid-November through December. You can imagine her frustration when she first tried using it and it didn't work.

In January, we took the drive to the authorized service center and were assured that the problem was merely a loose connection. The service representative fixed the drive, but in April we had to have it fixed again—another loose connection. For the next three months, the drive worked reasonably well, although the response time was occasionally slow. Two months ago, the drive stopped working again. Once more, the service representative blamed a loose connection and made the repair. Although the drive is working now, it isn't working very well. The response time is still slow, and the motor seems to drag sometimes.

What is your policy on exchanging unsatisfactory merchandise? Although all the repairs have been relatively minor and have been covered by the one-year warranty, we are not satisfied with the drive. We would like to exchange it for a similar model from another manufacturer. If the new drive costs more than the old one, we will pay the difference, even though we generally look for equipment with substantial business discounts.

GNC has done business with your store for six years and until now has always been satisfied with your merchandise. We are counting on you to live up to your reputation for standing behind your products. Please let us hear from you soon.

Sincerely,

Jill Saunders

Jill Saunders
Administrative Assistant

General Nutrition Corporation, 300 Sixth Avenue, Pittsburgh, PA 15222
Tel: (412) 288-4600

States purpose clearly
Explains the situation so that the reader will understand the problem
Presents ideas logically
States precisely what adjustment is being requested
Includes all necessary information and no irrelevant facts
Motivates action from the reader in the close

Good organization helps audience members understand your message, accept your message, and save time.

In addition to helping you, good organization helps the members of your audience in three key ways. First, it helps your audience understand your message. By making your main point clear at the outset and by presenting information logically, a well-organized message satisfies your audience's need for information.

Second, it helps your audience accept your message. However, effective messages often require a bit more than simple, clear logic. A diplomatic approach helps receivers accept your message, even if it's not what they want to hear. By softening refusals and leaving a good impression, you enhance your credibility and authority. When ComputerTime responds to the GNC inquiry, the message is negative, but the letter is diplomatic and positive (see Figure 4.8).

Third, good organization saves your audience time. Well-organized messages are efficient. They contain only relevant ideas, and they are brief. Moreover, all the information in a well-organized message is in a logical place. Audience members receive only the information they need, and because that information is presented as accessibly and succinctly as possible, audience members can follow the thought pattern without a struggle. Before

FIGURE 4.8 Letter Demonstrating a Diplomatic Organization Plan

ComputerTime
247 Allison Avenue, Pittsburgh, PA 15202
(412)381-8870 / Comptime@netins.net

September 17, 2005

Ms. Jill Saunders
Administrative Assistant
General Nutrition Corporation
300 Sixth Ave.
Pittsburgh, PA 15222

Dear Ms. Saunders:

Thank you for letting us know about your experience with the Olympic CD-RW drive that you bought last November. It's important that we learn of unusual problems with the equipment we stock.

As you know, regularly priced equipment returned to ComputerTime within 30 days is covered by the unconditional refund that has been our tradition for 22 years. Your drive, however, is still covered by the manufacturer's warranty. Your needs will receive immediate attention if you write to

Mr. George Bender
Olympic Systems
P.O. Box 7761, Terminal Annex
Los Angeles, CA 90010

From experience, I know that the people at Olympic truly care about having satisfied customers.

We, too, value your business, Ms. Saunders. Please don't miss our holiday sale in early November, which will feature more of the low prices and high-quality equipment on which you've come to rely.

Sincerely,

Linda Davis

Linda Davis
Customer Service

hg

Avoids being objectionable to the reader by using a neutral opening

Links refusal with a solution to the reader's problem

Closes on an appreciative note

Supports neutral opening with a reason for gratitude

States refusal indirectly

Assures reader, giving her confidence in the suggested solution

Confidently assumes that the solution proposed in the letter is satisfactory and that the customer will continue to do business with ComputerTime

you can even begin arranging the information in your message, take a moment to define your main idea.

Defining Your Main Idea

The broad subject, or **topic**, of every business message is condensed to one idea, whether it's soliciting the executive committee for a larger budget or apologizing to a client for an incident of poor customer service. Your entire message supports, explains, or demonstrates your **main idea**—a specific statement about the topic of your message (see Table 4.1).

The topic is the broad subject; the main idea makes a statement about the topic.

Your main idea may be obvious when you're preparing a brief message with simple facts that have little emotional impact on your audience. If you're responding to a request for information, your main idea may be simply, "Here is what you wanted." However, defining your main idea is more complicated when you're trying to persuade someone or when you have disappointing information to convey. In these situations, try to define a main idea that will establish a good relationship between you and your audience. For example, you may choose a main idea that highlights a common interest you share with your audience or one that emphasizes a point you can both agree on.

Defining your main idea is more difficult when you're trying to persuade someone or convey disappointing information.

TABLE 4.1 Defining Topic and Main Idea

GENERAL PURPOSE	SPECIFIC PURPOSE	TOPIC	MAIN IDEA
To inform	Teach customer service reps how to file insurance claims.	Insurance claims	Proper filing by reps saves the company time and money.
To persuade	Get top managers to approve increased spending on research and development.	Funding for research and development	Competitors spend more than we do on research and development.
To collaborate	Solicit ideas for a companywide incentive system that ties wages to profits.	Incentive pay	Tying wages to profits motivates employees and reduces compensation in tough years.

In longer documents and presentations, you often need to unify a mass of material, so you'll need to define a main idea that encompasses all the individual points you want to make. Finding a common thread through all these points can be a challenge. Sometimes you won't even be sure what your main idea is until you sort through the information. For tough assignments like these, consider a variety of techniques to generate creative ideas:

- **Brainstorming.** Working alone or with others, generate as many ideas and questions as you can, without stopping to criticize or organize. After you capture all these pieces, look for patterns and connections to help identify the main idea and the groups of supporting ideas. For example, if your main idea concerns whether or not to open a new restaurant in Denver, you'll probably find a group of ideas related to financial return, another related to competition, and so on. Identifying such groups helps you see the major issues that will lead you to a conclusion you can feel confident about.
- **Journalistic approach.** Introduced earlier in the chapter, the journalistic approach asks *who, what, when, where, why,* and *how* questions to distill major ideas from piles of unorganized information.
- **Question and answer chain.** Start with a key question, from the audience's perspective, and work back toward your message. In most cases, you'll find that each answer generates new questions, until you identify the information that needs to be in your message.
- **Storyteller's tour.** Some writers find it easier to talk through a communication challenge before they try to write. Pretend you're giving a colleague a guided tour of your message and capture it on a tape recorder. Then listen to your talk, identify ways to tighten and clarify the message, and repeat the process. Working through this recording several times will help you distill the main idea down to a single, concise message.
- **Mind mapping.** You can also generate and organize ideas using a graphic method called mind mapping. Start with a main idea, and then branch out to connect every other related idea that comes to mind. For instance, the map in Figure 4.9 outlines the writer's own concerns about a report, her insights into the audience's concerns, and several issues related to writing and distributing the report. Some mind-mapping software can even automatically generate outlines in Microsoft Word and slides in Microsoft PowerPoint.

Communication Solution

Because computers are endlessly complicated devices that could fill an entire encyclopedia with descriptive detail, Joe Kraynak limits his scope carefully—providing only enough information to fulfill his specific purpose of helping people use computers more successfully.

Limiting Your Scope

The **scope** of your message is the range of information you present, the overall length, and the level of detail—all of which need to correspond to your main idea. For a report outlining your advice on whether to open a new restaurant in Denver, your message, including all supporting evidence, needs to focus on that question alone. Your plan for new menu selections and your idea for a new source of financing both would be outside the scope of your message.

Limit the number of support points; having fewer, stronger points is a better approach than many, weaker points.

Whether your audience expects a one-page memo or a one-hour speech, work within that framework to develop your main idea with major points and supporting evidence.

FIGURE 4.9 Using the Mind-Mapping Technique to Plan a Writing Project

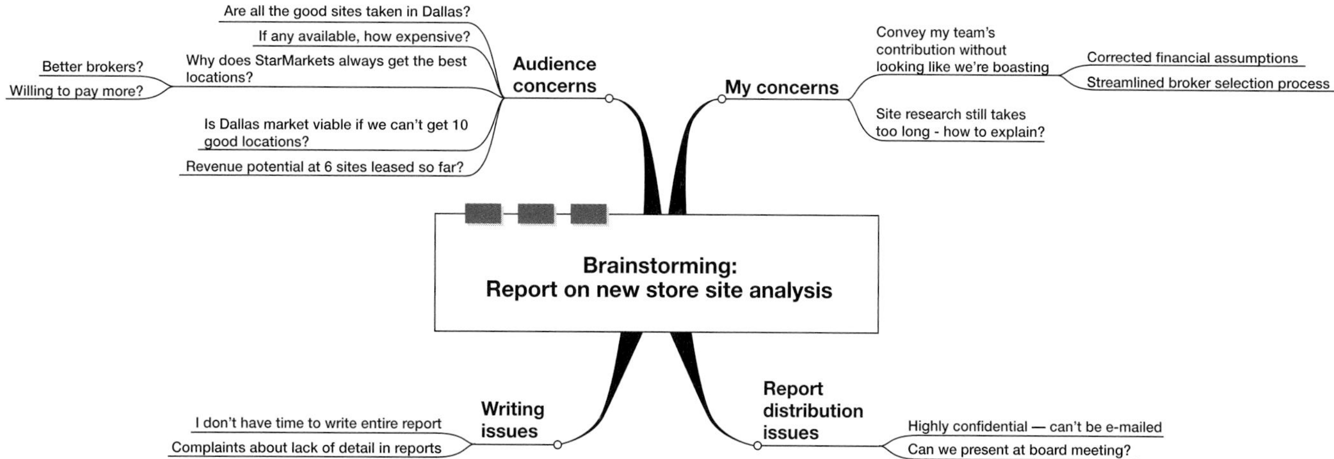

Once you have a tentative statement of your main idea, test it against the length limitations that have been imposed on your message. If you don't have enough time or space to develop your main idea fully, or if your main idea won't fill up the time and space allotted, you'll need to redefine it accordingly. If you don't have a fixed limit to work against, plan to make the document or presentation only as long as it needs to be to convey your main idea and critical support points.

Whatever the length of your message, limit the number of major support points to half a dozen—and if you can get your idea across with fewer points, all the better. Listing 20 or 30 support points might feel as if you're being thorough, but your audience will view such detail as disorganized and rambling. Instead, look for ways to group supporting points under major headings, such as finance, customers, competitors, employees, or whatever is appropriate for your subject. Just as you might need to refine you're main idea, you may also need to refine your major support points so that you have a small number with high impact.

If your message is brief (say, four minutes or one page), plan on only one minute or one paragraph each for the introduction, conclusion, and major points. Because the amount of evidence you can present is limited, your main idea will have to be both easy to understand and easy to accept. However, if your message is long (say, 60 minutes or 20 pages), you can develop the major points in considerable detail. You can spend about 10 minutes or 10 paragraphs (more than three pages of double-spaced, typewritten text) on each of your key points, and you'll still have room for your introduction and conclusion.

How much you can communicate in a given number of words depends on the nature of your subject, your audience members' familiarity with the topic, their receptivity to your conclusions, and your credibility. You'll need fewer words to present routine information to a knowledgeable audience that already knows and respects you. You'll need more time to build a consensus about a complex and controversial subject, especially if the members of your audience are skeptical or hostile strangers.

Choosing Between Direct and Indirect Approaches

After you've defined your ideas, you're ready to decide on the sequence you will use to present your points. You have two basic options:

- **Direct approach (deductive).** When you know your audience will be receptive to your message, start with the main idea (such as a recommendation, a conclusion, or a request), and follow that with your supporting evidence.
- **Indirect approach (inductive).** When your audience will be skeptical about or even resistant to your message, start with the evidence first and build your case before presenting the main idea.

Use the direct approach if the audience's reaction is likely to be positive and the indirect approach if it is likely to be negative.

To choose between these two alternatives, analyze your audience's likely reaction to your purpose and message. Bear in mind, however, that each message is unique. No simple

Audience reaction can range from eager to unwilling.

FIGURE 4.10 Choosing Between the Direct and Indirect Approaches

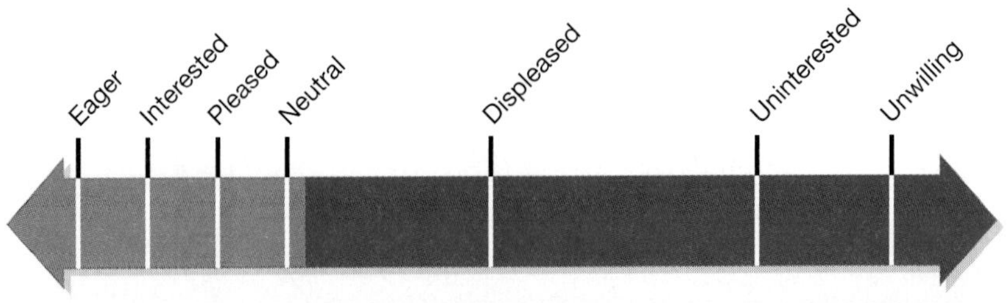

	Direct approach	Indirect approach	
Audience Reaction	**Eager/interested/ pleased/neutral**	**Displeased**	**Uninterested/unwilling**
Message Opening	Start with the main idea, the request, or the good news.	Start with a neutral statement that acts as a transition to the reasons for the bad news.	Start with a statement or question that captures attention.
Message Body	Provide necessary details.	Give reasons to justify a negative answer. State or imply the bad news, and make a positive suggestion.	Arouse the audience's interest in the subject. Build the audience's desire to comply.
Message Close	Close with a cordial comment, a reference to the good news, or a statement about the specific action desired.	Close cordially.	Request action.

formula will solve all your communication problems. For example, although an indirect approach may be best when you're sending bad news to outsiders, if you're writing a memo to an associate, you may want to get directly to the point, even if your message is unpleasant. The direct approach might also be a good choice for long messages, regardless of your audience's attitude—because delaying the main idea could cause confusion and frustration. Figure 4.10 summarizes how your approach may differ depending on the likely audience reaction. Also affecting your choice of a direct or an indirect approach is the type of message you are sending.

Routine and Positive Messages

The most straightforward business messages are routine and positive messages. If you're inquiring about products or placing an order, your audience will usually want to comply. If you're announcing a price cut, granting an adjustment, accepting an invitation, or congratulating a colleague, your audience will most likely be pleased to hear from you. If you're providing routine information as part of your regular business, your audience will probably be neutral, neither pleased nor displeased.

Aside from being easy to understand, routine messages are easy to prepare. In most cases you use the direct approach. In the opening, you state your main idea directly, without searching for some creative introduction. By starting off with your positive idea, you emphasize the pleasing aspect of your message. You put your audience in a good frame of mind and encourage them to be receptive to whatever else you have to say. The body of your message can then provide all necessary details. The close is cordial and emphasizes your good news or makes a statement about the specific action desired. Routine and positive messages are discussed in greater detail in Chapter 7.

Negative Messages

If you're refusing credit or denying a request for an adjustment, your audience will be disappointed. In such cases, it may be best to use the indirect approach—putting the evidence first and building up to the main idea. This approach strengthens your case as you go along, not only making the receiver more receptive to the eventual conclusion but also treating the receiver in a more sensitive manner, which helps you retain as much goodwill as possible. Astute businesspeople know that every person they encounter could be a potential customer, supplier, or contributor or could influence someone who is a customer, supplier, or contributor.

Successful communicators take extra care with their negative messages. They often open with a neutral statement that acts as a transition to the reasons for the bad news. In the body, they give the reasons that justify the negative answer, announcement, or information before they state or imply the bad news. And they are always careful to close cordially.

If you have bad news, try to put it somewhere in the middle, cushioned by other, more positive ideas.

The challenge of negative messages lies in being honest but kind. You don't want to sacrifice ethics and mislead your audience; nor do you want to be overly blunt. To achieve a good mix of candor and kindness, focus on some aspect of the situation that makes the negative news a little easier to take.

Keep in mind that the indirect approach is neither manipulative nor unethical. As long as you can be honest and reasonably brief, you're often better off opening a bad-news message with a neutral point and putting the negative information after the explanation. Then if you can close with something fairly positive, you're likely to leave the audience feeling at least okay—not great, but not hostile either (which is often about all you can hope for when you must deliver bad news). Negative messages are discussed further in Chapter 8.

The indirect approach should not be used to manipulate.

Persuasive Messages

Persuasive messages present a special communication challenge because you're asking your audience to give, do, or change something, whether it's buying a product or changing a belief or an attitude. Professionals who specialize in persuasive messages such as sales letters and other advertising spend years perfecting their craft, and the best practitioners command salaries on a par with many high-ranking executives. You might not have the opportunity to take your skills to this level, but you can learn some basic techniques to improve your own persuasive messages.

Persuasive messages have their own indirect pattern.

Before you try to persuade people to do something, capture their attention and get them to consider your message with an open mind. Make an interesting point, and provide supporting facts that encourage your audience to continue paying attention. In most persuasive messages, the opening mentions a reader benefit, refers to a problem that the recipient might have, poses a question, or mentions an interesting statistic. Then the body builds interest in the subject and arouses audience members' desire to comply. Once you have them thinking, you can introduce your main idea. The close is cordial and requests the desired action. Persuasive messages are discussed at greater length in Chapter 9.

Persuasive messages often employ a special plan relating to the indirect approach that you'll read about in Chapter 9.

Outlining Your Content

Once you have chosen the right approach, it's time to figure out the most logical and effective way to provide your supporting details. Even if you've resisted creating outlines in your school assignments over the years, try to get into the habit when you're preparing business documents and presentations. You'll save time, create better results, and do a better job of navigating through complicated business situations. Whether you use the outlining features provided with word-processing software or simply jot down three or four points on the back of an envelope, making a plan and sticking to it will help you cover the important details. For a look at some of the most powerful outlining tools available today, see "Connecting with Technology: Create and Collaborate with Powerful Outlining Tools."

> **DOCUMENT MAKEOVER**
>
> **IMPROVE THIS LETTER**
>
> To practice correcting drafts of actual documents, visit www.prenhall.com/onekey on the web. Click "Document Makeovers," then click Chapter 4. You will find a letter that contains problems and errors relating to what you've learned in this chapter about planning and organizing business messages. Use the Final Draft decision tool to create an improved version of this letter. Check the document for audience focus, the right choice of medium, and the proper choice of direct or indirect approach.

When you're preparing a longer, more complex message, an outline is indispensable, because it helps you visualize the relationships among the various parts. Without an outline, you may be inclined to ramble. As you're describing one point, another point may occur to you, so you describe it. One detour leads to another, and before you know it,

A good way to visualize how all the points will fit together is to construct an outline.

Connecting with Technology

Create and Collaborate with Powerful Outlining Tools

Experienced business communicators recognize the power of a well-planned outline. However, outlining doesn't have to be the dull exercise you might remember from book reports and other school projects. Today's outlining tools, such as Microsoft Word's outline mode, make it easy to organize and reorganize ideas quickly, and some can even help ignite your creativity and generate new ideas.

For example, by following a consistent scheme of headings and subheadings, you can quickly add, delete, and rearrange sections to make sure your overall structure is logical and coherent. Also, if you ever feel like you've gotten lost in a long document after you've started writing, you can find your way again by shifting to outline mode. Collapse the outline down to just the first-level headings, then expand one level at a time—it's a great way to rediscover the shape of the forest when you're lost in the trees. Outline software is also a powerful way to study the layout of a website because you can see the entire structure underneath the home page and make sure that your visitors won't get lost in or frustrated by confusing navigation.

For complex reports, you'll often need to collaborate on the outline with one or more colleagues, who might be in different locations around the world. Groupware collaboration tools let multiple people work on an outline at the same time, often with integrated instant messaging so that you can brainstorm and evaluate ideas on the fly. Rather then sending the outline around via e-mail and letting each person modify it individually—which can create endless rounds of revision and compromise—groupware outliners let everyone contribute, argue, and collaborate all at once.

CAREER APPLICATIONS

1. Assume your boss has asked you to deliver a presentation on a report you've just completed. She says you don't need to start from scratch, though. Figure out the steps needed to transfer your report structure from Microsoft Word to Microsoft PowerPoint.
2. Product designers use a process called *reverse engineering* to find out how a finished product is put together. You can do the same thing with finished articles and reports to see how they're organized. Cut and paste the text of a substantial online news article into your word processor, then distill it down to an outline. Do you see any ways to improve the organization of the article?

you've forgotten the original point and wasted precious time and energy. With an outline to guide you, however, you can communicate in a more systematic way. Following an outline also helps you insert transitions so that your message is coherent and your audience can understand the relationships among your ideas.

You're no doubt familiar with the basic outline formats that identify each point with a number or letter and that indent certain points to show which ones are of equal status. A good outline divides a topic into at least two parts, restricts each subdivision to one category, and ensures that each subdivision is separate and distinct (see Figure 4.11).

FIGURE 4.11
Two Common Outline Forms

ALPHANUMERIC OUTLINE

I. First Major Point
  A. First subpoint
  B. Second subpoint
    1. Evidence
    2. Evidence
      a. Detail
      b. Detail
    3. Evidence
  C. Third subpoint
II. Second Major Point
  A. First subpoint
    1. Evidence
    2. Evidence
  B. Second subpoint

DECIMAL OUTLINE

1.0 First Major Point
  1.1 First subpoint
  1.2 Second subpoint
    1.2.1 Evidence
    1.2.2 Evidence
      1.2.2.1 Detail
      1.2.2.2 Detail
    1.2.3 Evidence
  1.3 Third subpoint
2.0 Second Major Point
  2.1 First subpoint
    2.1.1 Evidence
    2.1.2 Evidence
  2.2 Second subpoint

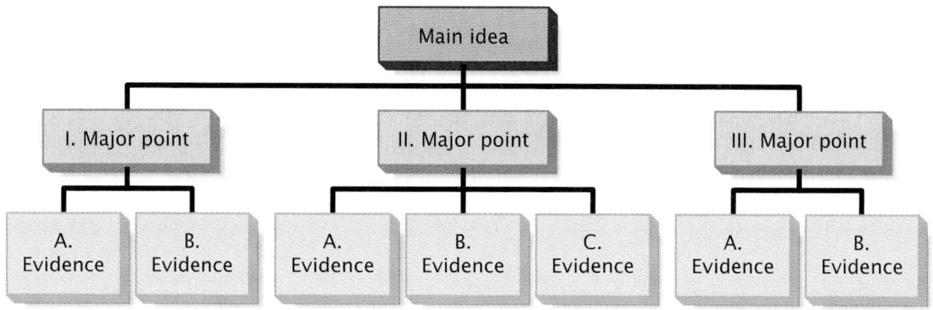

FIGURE 4.12
"Organization Chart" for Organizing a Message

Another way to visualize the outline of your message is to create a message "organization chart" similar to the charts used to show a company's management structure (see Figure 4.12). The main idea is shown in the highest-level box and, like a top executive, establishes the big picture. The lower-level ideas, like lower-level employees, provide the details. All the ideas are logically organized into divisions of thought, just as a company is organized into divisions and departments.[16] Using a visual chart instead of a traditional outline has many benefits. Charts help you (1) see the various levels of ideas and how the parts fit together, (2) develop new ideas, and (3) restructure your information flow. The mind-mapping technique used to generate ideas works in a similar way.

Try other organizational schemes in addition to traditional outlines.

Whichever outlining or organizing scheme you use, start your message with the main idea, follow that with major supporting points, and then illustrate these points with evidence.

Start with the Main Idea

7 LEARNING OBJECTIVE

Summarize the process for organizing business messages effectively

The main idea helps you establish the goals and general strategy of the message, and it summarizes two things: (1) what you want your audience to do or think and (2) why they should do so. Everything in your message either supports the main idea or explains its implications. As discussed earlier in this chapter, some messages state the main idea quickly and directly, whereas other messages delay the main idea until after the evidence is presented.

State the Major Points

Now it's time to support your main idea with the major points that clarify and explain your ideas in more concrete terms. If your purpose is to inform and the material is factual, your major points might be based on something physical or financial—something you can visualize or measure, such as activities to be performed, functional units, spatial or chronological relationships, or parts of a whole. When you're describing a process, the major points are almost inevitably steps in the process. When you're describing an object, the major points correspond to the components of the object. When you're giving a historical account, major points represent events in the chronological chain. If your purpose is to persuade or to collaborate, select major points that develop a line of reasoning or a logical argument that proves your central message and motivates your audience to act.

Major supporting points clarify your main idea.

You can divide major points according to physical relationships, the description of a process, the components of an object, or a historical chronology.

Illustrate with Evidence

After you've defined the main idea and identified supporting points, you're ready to illustrate each point with specific evidence that helps audience members understand and remember the more abstract concepts you're presenting. For example, if you're advocating that your company increase its advertising budget, you can support your major point by providing evidence that your most successful competitors spend more on advertising than you do. You can also describe a case in which a particular competitor increased its ad budget and achieved an impressive sales gain. Then you can show that over the past five years, your firm's sales have gone up and down in response to the amount spent on advertising.

TABLE 4.2 Six Types of Detail

TYPE OF DETAIL	EXAMPLE	COMMENT
Facts and figures	Sales are strong this month. We have two new contracts worth $5 million and a good chance of winning another worth $2.5 million.	Adds more credibility than any other type. Can become boring if used excessively. Most common type used in business.
Example or illustration	We've spent four months trying to hire recent accounting graduates, but so far, only one person has joined our firm. One candidate told me that she would love to work for us, but she can get $5,000 more a year elsewhere.	Adds life to a message, but one example does not prove a point. Idea must be supported by other evidence as well.
Description	Upscale hamburger restaurants target burger lovers who want more than the convenience and low prices of a McDonald's. These places feature wine and beer, half-pound burgers, and generous side dishes (nachos, potato skins). "Atmosphere" is key.	Helps audience visualize the subject by creating a sensory impression. Does not prove a point, but clarifies it and makes it memorable. Begins with overview of function; defines its purpose, lists major parts, and explains how it operates.
Narration	Under former management, executives worked in blue jeans, meetings rarely started on time, and lunches ran long. When Jim Wilson became CEO, he completely overhauled the operation. A Harvard MBA who favors Brooks Brothers suits, Wilson has cut the product line in half and chopped $12 million off expenses.	Works well for attracting attention and explaining ideas, but lacks statistical validity.
Reference to authority	I discussed this idea with Jackie Loman in the Chicago plant, and she was very supportive. As you know, Jackie has been in charge of that plant for the past 6 years. She is confident that we can speed up the number 2 line by 150 units an hour if we add another worker.	Bolsters a case while adding variety and credibility. Works only if "authority" is recognized and respected by audience.
Visual aids	Graphs, charts, tables	Helps audience grasp specific data. Used more in memos and reports than in letters.

If you're developing a long, complex message, you may need to carry the outline down several levels. Remember that every level is a step along the chain from the abstract to the concrete, from the general to the specific. The lowest level contains the evidence, the individual facts and figures that tie the generalizations to the observable, measurable world. The higher levels are the concepts that reveal why those facts are significant.

Each major point must be supported with enough specific evidence to be convincing, but not so much that it's boring.

Up to a point, the more evidence you provide, the more conclusive your case will be. If your subject is complex and unfamiliar, or if your audience is skeptical, you'll need a lot of facts and figures to demonstrate your points. On the other hand, if your subject is routine and your audience is positively inclined, you can be more sparing with the evidence. You want to provide enough support to be convincing but not so much that your message becomes boring or inefficient.

Another way to keep your audience interested is to vary the type of detail you include. As you draft your message, try to incorporate the methods described in Table 4.2. Switch from facts and figures to narration, add a dash of description, throw in some examples or a reference to authority. If it makes sense, you can reinforce all these details with visual aids. Think of your message as a stew: a mixture of ingredients seasoned with a blend of spices. Each separate flavor adds to the richness of the whole.

If your schedule permits, try to put aside your outline for a day or two before you begin composing your first draft. Then review it with a fresh eye, looking for opportunities to improve the flow of ideas. For a reminder of the planning tasks involved in preparing your messages, see "Checklist: Planning Business Messages."

CHECKLIST: Planning Business Messages

A. ANALYZE YOUR SITUATION

- Determine whether the purpose of your message is to inform, persuade, or collaborate.
- Identify what you want your audience to think or do.
- Make sure your purpose is worthwhile and realistic.
- Make sure the time is right for your message.
- Make sure the right person is delivering your message.
- Make sure your purpose is acceptable to your organization.
- Identify the primary audience.
- Determine audience size and composition.
- Estimate your audience's level of understanding and probable reaction to your message.

B. GATHER INFORMATION

- Decide whether to use formal or informal techniques for gathering information.
- Find out what your audience wants to know.
- Provide all required information and make sure it's accurate, ethical, and pertinent.

C. SELECT THE BEST MEDIUM FOR YOUR MESSAGE

- Understand the advantages and disadvantages of oral, written, and electronic media.
- Consider media richness, formality, media limitations, sender intentions, urgency, cost, and audience preference.

D. ORGANIZE YOUR INFORMATION

- Define your main idea.
- Limit your scope.
- Choose a direct or indirect approach.
- Outline content by starting with the main idea, adding major points, and illustrating with evidence.

COMMUNICATION CHALLENGES AT THE COMPLETE IDIOT'S GUIDES

Alpha Books has commissioned Joe Kraynak to write a new book titled *The Complete Idiot's Guide to the Motorokia Navitainer.* This new device combines the capabilities of a cell phone, a personal digital assistant (PDA), a global positioning system (GPS) receiver, an MP3 player, and a digital camera in one amazingly compact package. The purpose of the book is to quickly teach people how to use all of the product's major functions. You're working as Kraynak's assistant and are responsible for researching key topics and writing some sections of the book.

Individual Challenge: Alpha Books has provided a brief project summary that focuses on the audience's expectations and preferences, including clear, concise text that's humorous and easy to read; lists of key points; and lots of illustrations. Kraynak wants more detail about the readers—so your first assignment is to develop a detailed audience profile. What kinds of questions will you ask Megan, Kraynak's contact at Alpha, about the target audience for the book?

Team Challenge: Megan was able to provide plenty of descriptive information about the intended audience but very little about one essential point: their level of understanding of the component products. Kraynak has given you just four weeks to complete the audience profile. Working in a small group, brainstorm ways to gather information about the audience's level of understanding.

SUMMARY OF LEARNING OBJECTIVES

1 **Describe the three-step writing process.** (1) Planning consists of analyzing the situation (defining your purpose and profiling your audience), gathering the information to meet your audience's needs, selecting the best medium for the message and the situation, and organizing the information (defining your main idea, limiting your scope, selecting an approach, and outlining your content). (2) The writing step consists of two tasks: adapting to your audience and composing the message. Adapt your message to your audience by being sensitive to audience needs, building a strong relationship with your audience, and controlling your style. Compose your message by drafting your thoughts with strong words, effective sentences, and coherent paragraphs. (3) Completing your message consists of revising your message by evaluating content and then rewriting and editing for clarity and conciseness, producing your message by using effective design elements and suitable delivery methods, proofreading

your message for typos and errors in spelling and mechanics, and distributing it in a way that meets both your needs and your audience's needs.

2 **Explain why it's important to define your purpose carefully, and list five questions that can help you test that purpose.** You must know enough about your purpose to shape your message in a way that will achieve your goal. To decide whether you should proceed with your message, ask five questions: (1) Will anything change as a result of this message? (2) Is this message realistic? (3) Is it acceptable to my organization? (4) Is the right person delivering this message? (5) Is it being delivered at the right time?

3 **Describe the importance of analyzing your audience, and identify the six factors you should consider when developing an audience profile.** Analyzing your audience helps you discover who the members of your audience are, what their attitudes are, what they need to know, and why they should care about your purpose in communicating. An effective profile helps you predict how your audience will react to your message. It also helps you know what to include in your message and how to include it. To develop an audience profile, you need to determine your primary audience (key decision makers), the size of your audience, the makeup of your audience, the level of your audience's understanding, your audience's expectations, and their probable reaction.

4 **Discuss gathering information for simple messages, and identify three attributes of quality information.** Gathering the information that will fulfill your audience's needs is a vital step before attempting to organize your content. For more complex documents, you may need to plan a research project to acquire all the necessary information. However, for simple messages, if you don't already have all the information you need, you can gather it using other methods such as considering other viewpoints, reading existing reports and other company documents, talking with supervisors and others who have information and insight, and asking your audience directly for their input. To determine whether the information you've gathered is good enough, verify that it is accurate, ethical, and pertinent to the audience's needs.

5 **List factors to consider when choosing the most appropriate medium for your message.** The first factor to consider is media richness. Richness is determined by the medium's ability to (1) convey a message using more than one informational cue (visual, verbal, vocal), (2) facilitate feedback, and (3) establish personal focus. Other factors to consider when selecting media include the level of formality, the specific limitations of each medium, your intentions in sending the message, the level of urgency balanced with the cost of using a particular channel, and your audience's preferences.

6 **Explain why good organization is important to both you and your audience.** When you organize messages carefully, you save time and conserve creative energy because the writing process is quicker. You can also use your organization plan to get advance input from your audience members and to make sure you're on the right track. Finally, good organization can help you divide portions of the writing assignment among co-workers. Audiences also benefit from good organization in several ways. When audience members receive a message that is well organized, they don't have to read and reread a message to make sense of it, so they save time. They are also better able to understand the content, so they can accept the message more easily and make better decisions based on the information conveyed.

7 **Summarize the process for organizing business messages effectively.** To organize messages effectively, begin with recognizing the importance of good organization. Then define the main idea by making a specific statement about the topic. Limit the scope of the message by adjusting the space and detail you allocate to major points (which should number no more than half a dozen, and fewer if possible). To choose either a direct or an indirect approach, anticipate the audience's reaction to the message (positive, neutral, or negative) and match the approach to both message length (short or long) and message type (routine, positive, bad-news, or persuasive). Finally, group the points by constructing an outline to visualize the relationship between the ideas and the supporting material.

Test Your Knowledge

1. What are the three steps in the writing process?
2. What two types of purposes do all business messages have?
3. What do you need to know in order to develop an audience profile?
4. How can you test the thoroughness of the information you include in a message?
5. What is media richness and how is it determined?
6. What are the main advantages of oral media? Of written media?
7. What are the advantages and disadvantages of electronic media?
8. What is the process for organizing messages?
9. Why is it important to limit the scope of your message?
10. What three elements do you consider when choosing between a direct and an indirect approach?

Apply Your Knowledge

1. Some writers argue that planning messages wastes time because they inevitably change their plans as they go along.

How would you respond to this argument? Briefly explain.

2. As a member of the public relations department, what medium would you recommend using to inform the local community that your toxic-waste cleanup program has been successful? Why?
3. Would you use a direct or an indirect approach to ask employees to work overtime to meet an important deadline? Please explain.
4. Which approach would you use to let your boss know that you'll be out half a day this week to attend your father's funeral—direct or indirect? Why?
5. **Ethical Choices** The company president has asked you to draft a memo to the board of directors informing them that sales in the newly acquired line of gourmet fruit jams have far exceeded anyone's expectations. As purchasing director, you happen to know that sales of moderately priced jams have declined substantially (many customers have switched to the more expensive jams). You were not directed to add that tidbit of information. What should you do?

Practice Your Knowledge

Document for Analysis

A writer is working on an insurance information brochure and is having trouble grouping the ideas logically into an outline. Prepare the outline, paying attention to appropriate subordination of ideas. If necessary, rewrite phrases to give them a more consistent sound.

Accident Protection Insurance Plan

- Coverage is only pennies a day
- Benefit is $100,000 for accidental death on common carrier
- Benefit is $100 a day for hospitalization as result of motor vehicle or common carrier accident
- Benefit is $20,000 for accidental death in motor vehicle accident
- Individual coverage is only $17.85 per quarter; family coverage is just $26.85 per quarter
- No physical exam or health questions
- Convenient payment—billed quarterly
- Guaranteed acceptance for all applicants
- No individual rate increases
- Free, no-obligation examination period
- Cash paid in addition to any other insurance carried
- Covers accidental death when riding as fare-paying passenger on public transportation, including buses, trains, jets, ships, trolleys, subways, or any other common carrier
- Covers accidental death in motor vehicle accidents occurring while driving or riding in or on automobile, truck, camper, motor home, or nonmotorized bicycle

Exercises

For live links to all websites discussed in this chapter, visit this text's website at www.prenhall.com/bovee. Just log on, select Chapter 4, and click on "Featured Websites." Locate the page or the URL related to the material in the text.

4.1 **Message Planning Skills: Self-Assessment** How good are you at planning business messages? Use the following chart to rate yourself on each element of planning an audience-centered business message. Then examine your ratings to identify where you are strongest and where you can improve, using the tips in this chapter.

Element of Planning	Always	Frequently	Occasionally	Never
1. I start by defining my purpose.	___	___	___	___
2. I analyze my audience before writing a message.	___	___	___	___
3. I investigate what my audience wants to know.	___	___	___	___
4. I check that my information is accurate, ethical, and pertinent.	___	___	___	___
5. I consider my audience and purpose when selecting media.	___	___	___	___

4.2 **Planning Messages: General and Specific Purpose** Make a list of communication tasks you'll need to accomplish in the next week or so (for example, a job application, a letter of complaint, a speech to a class, an order for some merchandise). For each, determine a general and a specific purpose.

4.3 **Planning Messages: Specific Purpose** For each of the following communication tasks, state a specific purpose (if you have trouble, try beginning with "I want to . . .").

a. A report to your boss, the store manager, about the outdated items in the warehouse
b. A memo to clients about your booth at the upcoming trade show
c. A letter to a customer who hasn't made a payment for three months
d. A memo to employees about the department's high cell phone bills
e. A phone call to a supplier checking on an overdue parts shipment
f. A report to future users of the computer program you have chosen to handle the company's mailing list

4.4 **Planning Messages: Audience Profile** For each communication task below, write brief answers to three questions: Who is my audience? What is my audience's general attitude toward my subject? What does my audience need to know?

a. A final-notice collection letter from an appliance manufacturer to an appliance dealer, sent 10 days before initiating legal collection procedures
b. An unsolicited sales letter asking readers to purchase computer disks at near-wholesale prices
c. An advertisement for peanut butter

d. Fliers to be attached to doorknobs in the neighborhood, announcing reduced rates for chimney lining or repairs
e. A cover letter sent along with your résumé to a potential employer
f. A request (to the seller) for a price adjustment on a piano that incurred $150 in damage during delivery to a banquet room in the hotel you manage

4.5 **Meeting Audience Needs: Necessary Information** Choose an electronic device (such as a personal computer, MP3 player, or digital camera) that you know how to operate well. Write two sets of instructions for operating the device: one set for a reader who has never used that type of device and one set for someone who is generally familiar with that type of machine but has never operated the specific model. Briefly explain how your two audiences affect your instructions.

4.6 **Selecting Media: Defining the Purpose** List five messages you have received lately, such as direct-mail promotions, letters, e-mail messages, phone solicitations, and lectures. For each, determine the general and the specific purpose; then answer the following questions: (a) Was the message well timed? (b) Did the sender choose an appropriate medium for the message? (c) Did the appropriate person deliver the message? (d) Was the sender's purpose realistic?

4.7 **Selecting Media: Identifying an Audience** Barbara Marquardt is in charge of public relations for a cruise line that operates out of Miami. She is shocked to read a letter in a local newspaper from a disgruntled passenger, complaining about the service and entertainment on a recent cruise. Marquardt will have to respond to these publicized criticisms in some way. What audiences will she need to consider in her response? What medium should she choose? If the letter had been published in a travel publication widely read by travel agents and cruise travelers, how might her course of action differ?

4.8 **Teamwork: Audience Analysis** Your team has been studying a new method for testing the durability of your company's power tools. Now the team needs to prepare three separate reports on the findings: first, a report for the administrator who will decide whether to purchase the equipment needed for this new testing method; second, a report for the company's engineers who design and develop the hand tools; and third, a report for the trainers who will be showing workers how to use the new equipment. To determine the audience's needs for each of these reports, the team has listed the following questions: (1) Who are the readers? (2) Why will they read my report? (3) Do they need introductory or background material? (4) Do they need definitions of terms? (5) What level or type of language is needed? (6) What level of detail is needed? (7) What result does my report aim for? Working with two other students, answer the questions for each of these audiences:
a. The administrator
b. The engineers
c. The trainers

4.9 **Internet: Planning Your Message** Go to the PepsiCo website at www.pepsico.com and follow the link to the latest annual report. Then locate and read the chairman's letter. Who is the audience for this message? What is the general purpose of the message? What do you think this audience wants to know from the chairman of PepsiCo? Summarize your answers in a brief (one-page) memo or oral presentation.

4.10 **Message Organization: Outlining Your Content** Using the GNC letter in this chapter (Figure 4.7), draw an organizational chart similar to the one shown in Figure 4.12. Fill in the main idea, the major points, and the evidence provided in this letter. (Note: Your diagram may be smaller than the one provided in Figure 4.12 on p. 109).

4.11 **Message Organization: Limiting Scope** Suppose you are preparing to recommend that top management install a new heating system that uses the cogeneration process. The following information is in your files. Eliminate topics that aren't essential; then arrange the other topics so that your report will give top managers a clear understanding of the heating system and a balanced, concise justification for installing it.
- History of the development of the cogeneration heating process
- Scientific credentials of the developers of the process
- Risks assumed in using this process
- Your plan for installing the equipment in your building
- Stories about its successful use in comparable facilities
- Specifications of the equipment that would be installed
- Plans for disposing of the old heating equipment
- Costs of installing and running the new equipment
- Advantages and disadvantages of using the new process
- Detailed 10-year cost projections
- Estimates of the time needed to phase in the new system
- Alternative systems that management might wish to consider

4.12 **Message Organization: Choosing an Approach** Indicate whether a direct or an indirect approach would be best in each of the following situations; then briefly explain why. Would any of these messages be inappropriate for e-mail? Explain.
a. A letter asking when next year's automobiles will be put on sale locally
b. A letter from a recent college graduate requesting a letter of recommendation from a former instructor
c. A letter turning down a job applicant
d. An announcement that because of high air-conditioning costs, the plant temperature will be held at 78 degrees during the summer
e. A final request to settle a delinquent debt

4.13 **Message Organization: Audience Focus** If you were trying to persuade people to take the following actions, how would you organize your argument?
a. You want your boss to approve your plan for hiring two new people.
b. You want to be hired for a job.
c. You want to be granted a business loan.

d. You want to collect a small amount from a regular customer whose account is slightly past due.
e. You want to collect a large amount from a customer whose account is seriously past due.

4.14 **Ethical Choices: Providing Information** Your supervisor, whom you respect, has asked you to withhold important information that you think should be included in a report you are preparing. Disobeying him could be disastrous for your relationship and your career. Obeying him could violate your personal code of ethics. What should you do? On the basis of the discussion in Chapter 1, would you consider this situation to be an ethical dilemma or an ethical lapse? Please explain.

4.15 **Three-Step Process: Other Applications** How can the material discussed in this chapter also apply to meetings as discussed in Chapter 2? (Hint: Review the section headings in Chapter 4 and think about making your meetings more productive.)

Expand Your Knowledge

For live links to the websites that follow, go to www.prenhall.com/bovee. When you log on, select Chapter 4, then select "Featured Websites," click on the URL of the website you wish to visit, and review the website to complete these exercises.

Exploring the Best of the Web

Instant Insights into Instant Messaging
www.howstuffworks.com/instant-messaging.htm
Wondering what all the fuss is about instant messaging (IM)? Haven't had a chance to use ICQ, AIM, or one of the other popular IM services? Learn the basics of IM so you'll be ready to use IM on the job.

1. What are the key advantages of instant messaging?
2. What is the difference between a chat room and instant messaging?
3. Is instant messaging a secure way to communicate?

Exploring the Web on Your Own

Review these chapter-related websites on your own to learn more about achieving communication success in the workplace:

1. Learn more about the writing process, English grammar, style and usage, words, and active writing at Garbl's Writing Resources Online, www.garbl.com.
2. See how to put phone text messaging to work in business applications at Text.It, www.text.it (click on Text for Business).
3. Discover how e-mail works and how to improve your e-mail communications by following the steps at About Internet for Beginners—Harness E-Mail, www.learnthenet.com/english/section/email.html.

Learn Interactively

Interactive Study Guide

Go to the Companion Website at www.prenhall.com/bovee. For Chapter 4, take advantage of the interactive "Study Guide" to test your knowledge of the chapter. Get instant feedback on whether you need additional studying.

Also, visit this site's "Study Hall," where you'll find an abundance of valuable resources that will help you succeed in this course.

Peak Performance Grammar and Mechanics

To improve your skill with adjectives and adverbs, visit www.prenhall.com/onekey, click "Peak Performance Grammar and Mechanics," click "Grammar Basics," then click "Adjectives and Adverbs." Take the Pretest to determine whether you have any weak areas. Then review those areas in the Refresher Course. Take the Follow-Up Test to check your grasp of adjectives and adverbs. For an extra challenge or advanced practice, take the Advanced Test. Finally, for additional reinforcement in adjectives, go to www.prenhall.com/bovee, where you'll find "Improve Your Grammar, Mechanics, and Usage" exercises.

chapter 5

Writing Business Messages

LEARNING OBJECTIVES

After studying this chapter, you will be able to

1. Explain the importance of adapting your messages to the needs and expectations of your audience
2. Discuss four ways of achieving a businesslike tone with a style that is clear and concise
3. Briefly describe how to select words that are not only correct but also effective
4. Explain how sentence style affects emphasis within your message
5. List five ways to develop coherent paragraphs
6. Discuss the importance of effective e-mail subject lines and explain how to write them

COMMUNICATION CLOSE-UP AT ALGENIX

www.algenix.com

As a new employee, you face the challenge of building credibility: How do you convince colleagues and supervisors to believe in you and take your ideas seriously? If you were starting a new company, you would face a similar challenge—how to get investors, the news media, and target customers to believe in your organization and its products. Start-up Algenix faced this challenge when trying to establish its credibility in the medical field.

Algenix developed a "bioartificial liver" to assist patients who have serious liver disease. This external device processes toxins that are carried in the blood—but it uses pig-liver cells, which are quite similar to human cells. When Algenix was ready to recruit participants for clinical tests, it knew people would be skeptical about its product. So when the company decided to use its website as a recruiting tool, it engaged a consulting team from the nearby University of Minnesota, led by Laura Gurak, director of the Internet Studies Center.

Fortunately, Algenix had a well-defined audience: liver patients, their caregivers, and their loved ones. To clarify audience needs and expectations, Gurak's team monitored and surveyed Internet communities, such as listservs and

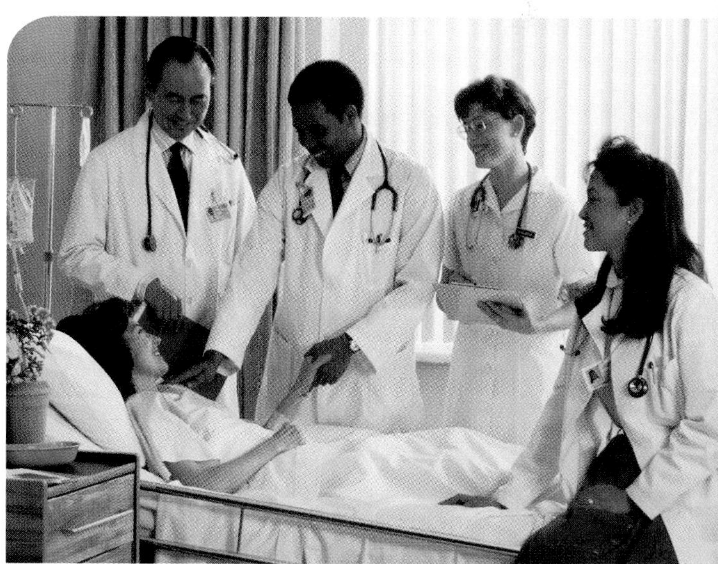

With their innovative and unusual product, executives at Algenix realize that they must work hard to build credibility with both patients and doctors.

Usenet news groups that address liver disease. The team used its findings to define webpage content that would demonstrate important elements of credibility, including competence and goodwill.

To highlight its competence, Algenix created a page that describes the education and experience of key staff members and company directors. To demonstrate goodwill, it linked to credible sources of information about liver disease, emphasizing respected government organizations and educational institutions. It also provided contact information for a doctor on its staff. Algenix communicated its complex message in just 14 pages and put a credible, caring face on the company as it prepared for its first wave of product tests. You may never discuss something as exotic as artificial organs in your own communication efforts, but building credibility with your audiences will be important in every phase of your business career.[1]

1 LEARNING OBJECTIVE

Explain the importance of adapting your messages to the needs and expectations of your audience

ADAPTING TO YOUR AUDIENCE

Audiences want to know how your messages will benefit them.

A good relationship with your audience is essential to effective communication.

Whether consciously or not, audiences greet most incoming messages with a question: "What's in this for me?" If your intended audience thinks a message does not apply to them or does not offer them anything useful or interesting, they'll be far less inclined to pay attention to it. By adapting your communication to the needs and expectations of your audience, you'll provide a more compelling answer to this question and improve the chances of your message being successful.

However, as Laura Gurak can attest, adapting your message is not always a simple task. Some situations will require you to balance competing or conflicting needs—for example, when you're trying to convince people to change their minds or when you're delivering bad news. Other situations may tempt you to adapt your personal style, but do so carefully. Although adjusting your style is a positive move, don't go so far that you come across as someone you're not. You won't be comfortable with this approach, and your audience will probably see through it.

A good relationship is vital to conveying your messages effectively, whether you're sending messages across the office via e-mail or to the other side of the planet in an online meeting. Like every relationship, successful communication meets the needs of both partners—you and your audience. The careful analysis you conducted during planning (see Chapter 4) will give you the insights to meet those needs. To adapt your message to your audience, try to be sensitive to your audience's needs, build a strong relationship with your audience, and control your style to maintain a professional tone.

Jenny J. Ming, president of Old Navy, combines her passion for fashion with the ability to communicate effectively with others. Ming recognizes that people's needs change as quickly as the latest fashion trends, so she takes extra care to focus on every audience's changing needs.

Being Sensitive to Your Audience's Needs

Even in simple messages intended merely to share information, it's possible to use all the right words and still not be sensitive to your audience and their needs. You can improve your audience sensitivity by adopting the "you" attitude, maintaining good standards of etiquette, emphasizing the positive, and using bias-free language.

Using the "You" Attitude

You are already becoming familiar with the audience-centered approach, trying to see a subject through your audience's eyes. Now you want to project this approach in your messages by adopting a **"you" attitude**—that is, by speaking and writing in terms of your audience's wishes, interests, hopes, and preferences.

On the simplest level, you can adopt the "you" attitude by replacing terms that refer to yourself and your company with terms that refer to your audience. In other words, use *you* and *yours* instead of *I, me, mine, we, us,* and *ours:*

INSTEAD OF THIS	USE THIS
To help us process this order, we must ask for another copy of the requisition.	So that your order can be filled promptly, please send another copy of the requisition.

We are pleased to announce our new flight schedule from Atlanta to New York, which is any hour on the hour.	Now you can take a plane from Atlanta to New York any hour on the hour.
We offer MP3 players with 10, 15, or 20 gigabytes of storage capacity.	Select your MP3 player from three models with 10, 15, or 20 gigabytes of storage capacity.

The "you" attitude is best implemented by expressing your message in terms of the audience's interests and needs.

When business messages use an "I" or "we" attitude, they risk sounding selfish and uninterested in the audience. The message tells what the sender wants, and the audience is expected to go along with it. Even so, using *you* and *yours* requires finesse. If you overdo it, you're likely to create some rather awkward sentences, and you run the risk of sounding overly enthusiastic and artificial.[2]

The "you" attitude is not intended to be manipulative or insincere. It's an extension of the audience-centered approach. In fact, the best way to implement the "you" attitude is to sincerely think about your audience when composing your message.

Nor is the "you" attitude simply a matter of using one pronoun rather than another; it's a matter of genuine empathy. You can use *you* 25 times in a single page and still ignore your audience's true concerns. In other words, it's the thought and sincerity that count, not the pronoun *you*. If you're talking to a retailer, try to think like a retailer; if you're dealing with a production supervisor, put yourself in that position; if you're writing to a dissatisfied customer, imagine how you would feel at the other end of the transaction. The important thing is your attitude toward audience members and your appreciation of their position.

Communication Solution

Even though the relatively formal tone of Algenix's website doesn't always address the reader as *you*, the "you" attitude is strongly evident in the way the company acknowledges the fears and concerns of patients with diminished liver function.

Be aware that on some occasions it's better to avoid using *you*, particularly if doing so will sound overly authoritative or accusing. For instance, instead of saying, "You failed to deliver the customer's order on time," you could minimize ill will by saying, "The customer didn't receive the order on time," or "Let's figure out a system that will ensure on-time deliveries."

Avoid using *you* and *yours* when doing so
- Makes you sound dictatorial
- Makes someone else feel guilty
- Goes against your organization's style

INSTEAD OF THIS	USE THIS
You should never use that type of paper in the copy machine.	That type of paper doesn't work very well in the copy machine.
You must correct all five copies by noon.	All five copies must be corrected by noon.

As you practice using the "you" attitude, be sure to consider the attitudes of other cultures and the policies of your organization. In some cultures, it is improper to single out one person's achievements because the whole team is responsible for the outcome; in that case, using the pronoun *we* or *our* (when you and your audience are part of the same team) would be more appropriate. Similarly, some companies have a tradition of avoiding references to *you* and *I* in their memos and formal reports. If you work for a company that expects a formal, impersonal style, confine your use of personal pronouns to informal letters and memos.

Maintaining Standards of Etiquette

Another good way to demonstrate interest in your audience and to earn their respect is to demonstrate etiquette in your messages. You know how it feels to be treated inconsiderately; when that happens, you probably react emotionally and then pay less attention to the offending message. By being courteous to members of your audience, you show consideration for them and foster a more successful environment for communication.

On those occasions when you experience frustration with co-workers, customers, or others you deal with, you might be tempted to say what you think in blunt terms. But venting your emotions rarely improves the situation and can jeopardize your audience's goodwill. Demonstrate your diplomatic skills by controlling your emotions and communicating calmly and politely:

Although you may be tempted now and then to be brutally frank, try to express the facts in a kind and thoughtful manner.

INSTEAD OF THIS	USE THIS
Once again, you've managed to bring down the website through your incompetent programming.	Let's go over what went wrong with the last site update so that we can find out how to improve the process.

You've been sitting on our order for two weeks, and we need it now!	Our production schedules depend on timely delivery of parts and supplies, but we have not yet received the order you promised to deliver two weeks ago. Please respond today with a firm delivery commitment.

Use extra tact when writing and when communicating with higher-ups and outsiders.

Of course, some situations require more diplomacy than others. If you know your audience well, a less formal approach might be more appropriate. However, when you are communicating with people who outrank you or with people outside your organization, an added measure of courtesy is usually needed.

Written communication generally requires more tact than oral communication. When you're speaking, your words are softened by your tone of voice and facial expression. Plus, you can adjust your approach according to the feedback you get. If you inadvertently offend someone in writing, you won't get the immediate feedback you would need to resolve the situation. In fact, you may never know that you offended your audience.

Keep these points in mind as you review Figures 5.1 and 5.2. Because of a death in the family, a restaurant owner closed his doors for three days over Labor Day weekend. Unfor-

FIGURE 5.1 Ineffective Response to Customer Request

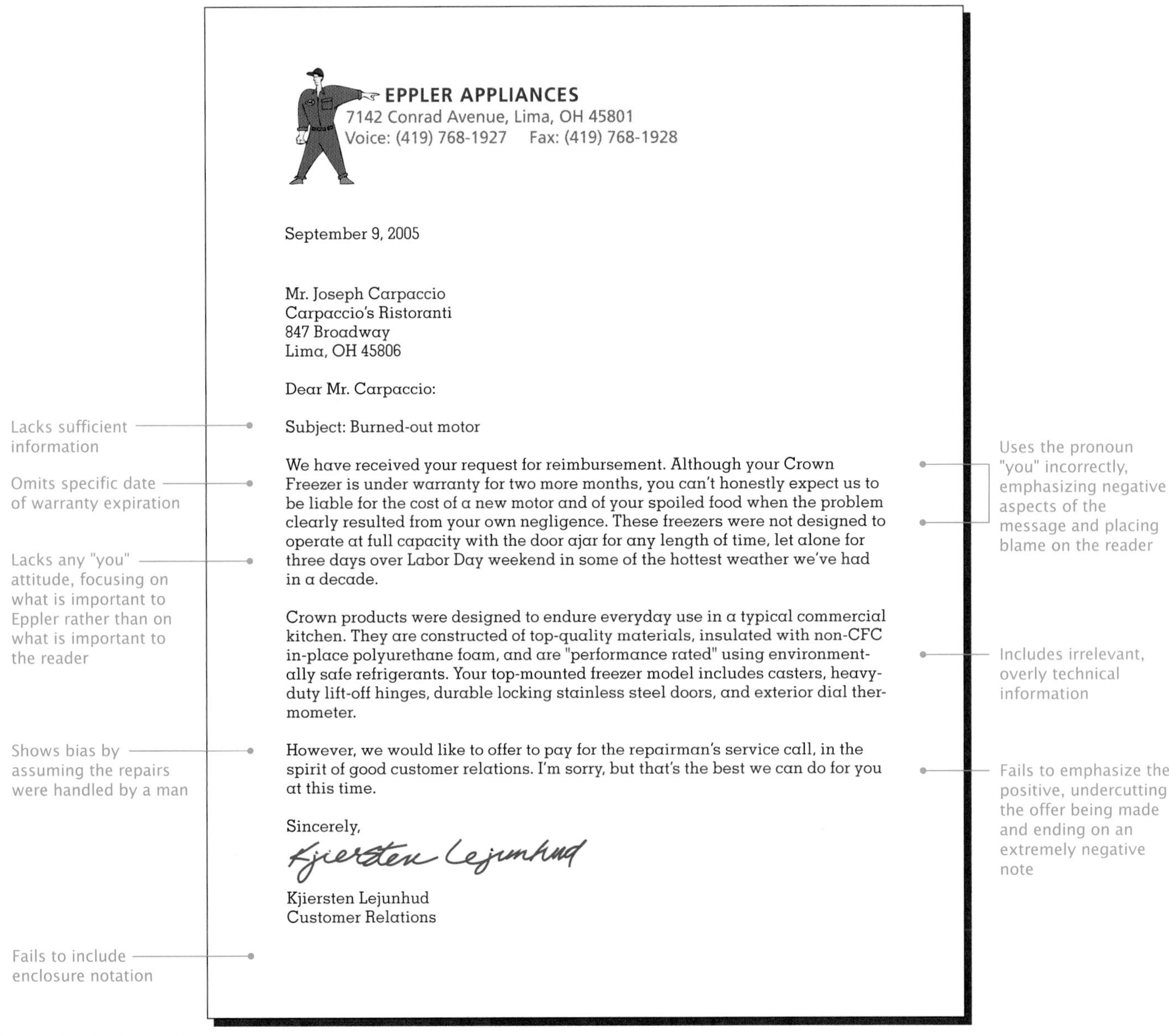

EPPLER APPLIANCES
7142 Conrad Avenue, Lima, OH 45801
Voice: (419) 768-1927 Fax: (419) 768-1928

September 9, 2005

Mr. Joseph Carpaccio
Carpaccio's Ristoranti
847 Broadway
Lima, OH 45806

Dear Mr. Carpaccio:

Subject: Burned-out motor

We have received your request for reimbursement. Although your Crown Freezer is under warranty for two more months, you can't honestly expect us to be liable for the cost of a new motor and of your spoiled food when the problem clearly resulted from your own negligence. These freezers were not designed to operate at full capacity with the door ajar for any length of time, let alone for three days over Labor Day weekend in some of the hottest weather we've had in a decade.

Crown products were designed to endure everyday use in a typical commercial kitchen. They are constructed of top-quality materials, insulated with non-CFC in-place polyurethane foam, and are "performance rated" using environmentally safe refrigerants. Your top-mounted freezer model includes casters, heavy-duty lift-off hinges, durable locking stainless steel doors, and exterior dial thermometer.

However, we would like to offer to pay for the repairman's service call, in the spirit of good customer relations. I'm sorry, but that's the best we can do for you at this time.

Sincerely,

Kjiersten Lejunhud

Kjiersten Lejunhud
Customer Relations

Lacks sufficient information
Omits specific date of warranty expiration
Lacks any "you" attitude, focusing on what is important to Eppler rather than on what is important to the reader
Shows bias by assuming the repairs were handled by a man
Fails to include enclosure notation
Uses the pronoun "you" incorrectly, emphasizing negative aspects of the message and placing blame on the reader
Includes irrelevant, overly technical information
Fails to emphasize the positive, undercutting the offer being made and ending on an extremely negative note

tunately, someone left the freezer door ajar, which burned out the motor and spoiled all the frozen food. The total cost to replace the motor and replace the food was over $2,000. The customer requested that Eppler Appliances cover these costs, but Eppler had to refuse. Compare the two letters for diplomacy.

Another simple but effective courtesy is to be prompt in your correspondence. If possible, answer voice mail, instant messages, and e-mail within 24 hours and answer regular mail within two or three days. If you need more time to prepare a reply, call or write a brief note to say that you're working on an answer. Your audience will appreciate the courtesy.

Promptness is a form of courtesy.

Emphasizing the Positive

During your career, you will also be required to communicate bad news—maybe dozens or hundreds of times. However, there is a big difference between delivering negative news and being negative. When the tone of your message is negative, you put unnecessary strain on business relationships, which can cause people to distance themselves from you and your ideas.

You can communicate negative news without being negative.

If you're facing a potentially negative situation, look for ways to soften the blow or emphasize positive aspects of a situation. For example, when Alaska Airlines instituted

FIGURE 5.2 Effective Response to Customer Request

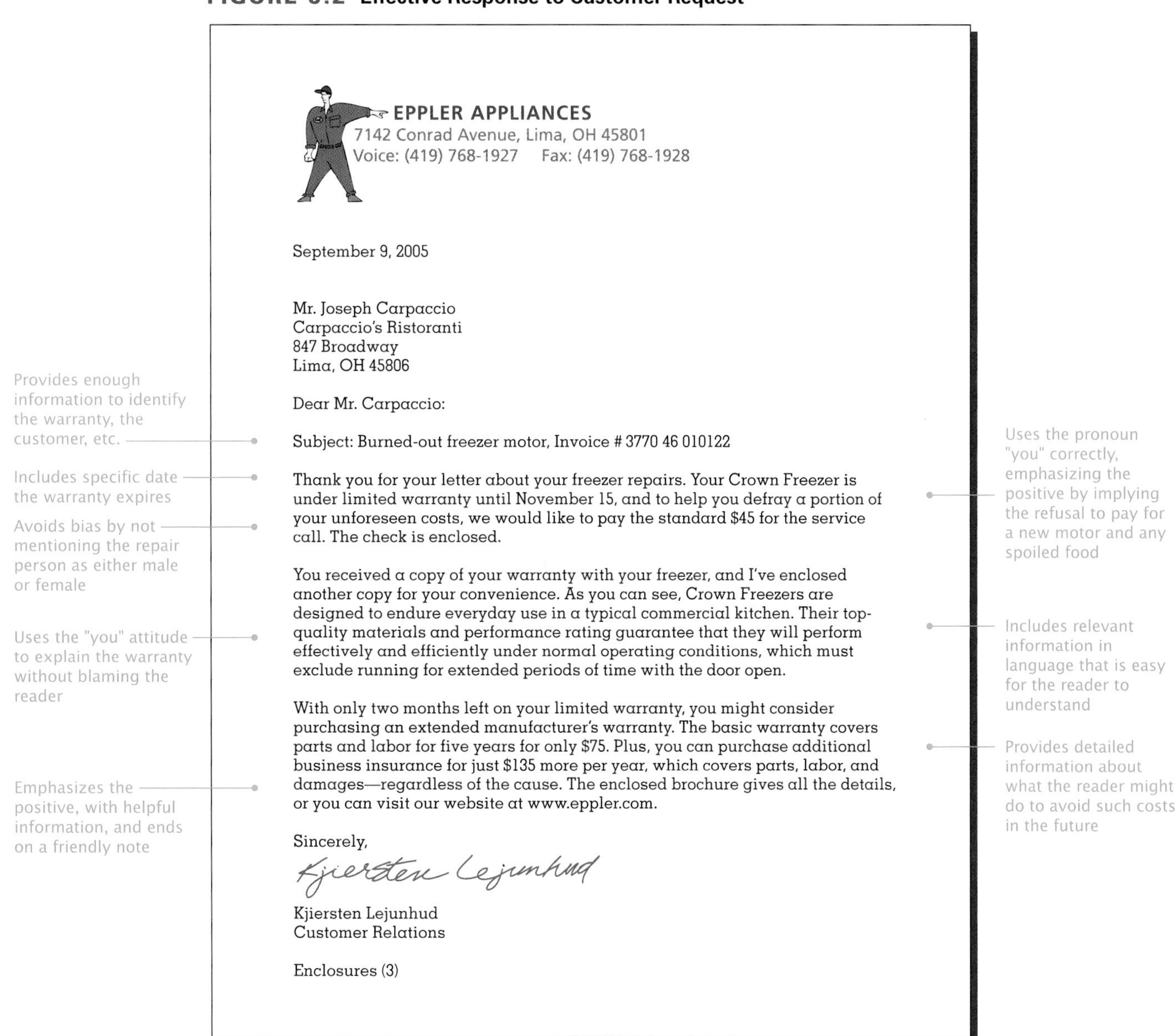

EPPLER APPLIANCES
7142 Conrad Avenue, Lima, OH 45801
Voice: (419) 768-1927 Fax: (419) 768-1928

September 9, 2005

Mr. Joseph Carpaccio
Carpaccio's Ristoranti
847 Broadway
Lima, OH 45806

Dear Mr. Carpaccio:

Subject: Burned-out freezer motor, Invoice # 3770 46 010122

Thank you for your letter about your freezer repairs. Your Crown Freezer is under limited warranty until November 15, and to help you defray a portion of your unforeseen costs, we would like to pay the standard $45 for the service call. The check is enclosed.

You received a copy of your warranty with your freezer, and I've enclosed another copy for your convenience. As you can see, Crown Freezers are designed to endure everyday use in a typical commercial kitchen. Their top-quality materials and performance rating guarantee that they will perform effectively and efficiently under normal operating conditions, which must exclude running for extended periods of time with the door open.

With only two months left on your limited warranty, you might consider purchasing an extended manufacturer's warranty. The basic warranty covers parts and labor for five years for only $75. Plus, you can purchase additional business insurance for just $135 more per year, which covers parts, labor, and damages—regardless of the cause. The enclosed brochure gives all the details, or you can visit our website at www.eppler.com.

Sincerely,

Kjiersten Lejunhud

Kjiersten Lejunhud
Customer Relations

Enclosures (3)

Provides enough information to identify the warranty, the customer, etc.
Includes specific date the warranty expires
Avoids bias by not mentioning the repair person as either male or female
Uses the "you" attitude to explain the warranty without blaming the reader
Emphasizes the positive, with helpful information, and ends on a friendly note
Uses the pronoun "you" correctly, emphasizing the positive by implying the refusal to pay for a new motor and any spoiled food
Includes relevant information in language that is easy for the reader to understand
Provides detailed information about what the reader might do to avoid such costs in the future

surcharges for heavy luggage in an attempt to reduce injuries to baggage handlers, the company presented the change to passengers with posters that said, "Pack Light & Save."[3] By presenting the situation as an opportunity to save money, rather than as an added cost of travel, Alaska worked to maintain a positive relationship with its customers. Never hide or shy away from negative news, but always be on the lookout for positive points that will foster a good relationship with your audience:[4]

INSTEAD OF THIS	USE THIS
It is impossible to repair your car today.	Your car can be ready by Tuesday. Would you like a loaner until then?
We apologize for inconveniencing you during our remodeling.	The renovations now under way will help us serve you better.
We wasted $300,000 advertising in that magazine.	Our $300,000 advertising investment did not pay off; let's analyze the experience and apply the insights to future campaigns.

When you are offering criticism or advice, focus on what the person can do to improve.

When you find it necessary to criticize or correct, don't dwell on the other person's mistakes. Avoid referring to failures, problems, or shortcomings. Focus instead on what the person can do to improve:

INSTEAD OF THIS	USE THIS
The problem with this department is a failure to control costs.	The performance of this department can be improved by tightening cost control.
You filled out the order form wrong.	Please check your color preferences on the enclosed card so that we can process your order.

Show your audience how they will benefit from complying with your message.

If you're trying to persuade the audience to buy a product, pay a bill, or perform a service for you, emphasize what's in it for them. Don't focus on why *you* want them to do something. An individual who sees the possibility for personal benefit is more likely to respond positively to your appeal:

INSTEAD OF THIS	USE THIS
I've been working on this proposal for six months, and I hope the time wasn't wasted.	This proposal identifies $4 million in potential savings companywide, without reducing staff.
We need your contribution to the Boys and Girls Club.	You can help a child make friends and build self-confidence through your donation to the Boys and Girls Club.

Avoid words with negative connotations; use meaningful euphemisms instead.

In general, try to state your message without using words that might hurt or offend your audience. Substitute *euphemisms* (mild terms) for those that have unpleasant connotations. You can be honest without being harsh. Gentle language won't change the facts, but it will make them more acceptable:

INSTEAD OF THIS	USE THIS
cheap merchandise	economy merchandise
used cars	resale cars
failing	underperforming
elderly	senior citizen
fake	imitation or faux

On the other hand, don't carry euphemisms to extremes. If you're too subtle, people won't know what you're talking about. "Derecruiting" workers to the "mobility pool" instead of telling them that they have six weeks to find another job isn't really very helpful. When using euphemisms, you walk a fine line between softening the blow and hiding the facts. It would be unethical to speak to your community about "relocating refuse" when you're really talking about your plans for disposing of toxic waste. Such an attempt to hide the facts would likely backfire, damaging your business image and reputation. In the end, people respond better to an honest message delivered with integrity than they do to a sugar-coated message filled with empty talk.

Using Bias-Free Language

Avoid biased language that might offend your audience.

Chapter 3 points out that you are often unaware of the influence of your own culture on your behavior, and this circumstance extends to the language you use. Any bias present in your culture is likely to show up in your language, often in subtle ways that you might not even recognize. However, chances are that your audience will. **Bias-free language** avoids words and phrases that unfairly and even unethically categorize or stigmatize people in ways related to gender, race, ethnicity, age, or disability. Moreover, since communication is all about perception, being fair and objective isn't enough; to establish a good relationship with your audience, you must also *appear* to be fair.[5] Good communicators make every effort to change biased language (see Table 5.1). Bias can come in a variety of forms:

- **Gender bias.** Avoid sexist language by using the same label for everyone (don't call a woman *chairperson* and then call a man *chairman*). Reword sentences to use *they* or to use no pronoun at all. Vary traditional patterns by sometimes putting women first (*women and men, she and he, her and his*). Note that the preferred title for women in business is *Ms*, unless the individual asks to be addressed as *Miss* or *Mrs.* or has some other title, such as *Dr.*
- **Racial and ethnic bias.** Avoid language suggesting that members of a racial or an ethnic group have stereotypical characteristics. The best solution is to avoid identifying people by race or ethnic origin unless such a label is relevant to the matter at hand—and it rarely is.
- **Age bias.** As with gender, race, and ethnic background, mention the age of a person only when it is relevant. Moreover, be careful of the context in which you use words that refer to age. Such words carry a variety of positive and negative connotations—and not only when referring to people beyond a certain age. For example, *young* can imply youthfulness, inexperience, or even immaturity, depending on how it's used.
- **Disability bias.** No painless label exists for people with a physical, mental, sensory, or emotional impairment. Avoid mentioning a disability unless it is pertinent. However, if you must refer to someone's disability, avoid terms such as *handicapped, crippled*, or *retarded*. Put the person first and the disability second.[6] Present the whole person, not just the disability, by showing the limitation in an unobtrusive manner.

Building Strong Relationships with Your Audience

Focusing on your audience's needs is vital to effective communication, but you also have your own priorities as a communicator. Sometimes these needs are obvious and direct, such as when you're appealing for a budget increase for your department. At other times, the need may be more subtle. For instance, you might want to demonstrate your understanding of the marketplace or your company's concern for the natural environment. Two key efforts help you address your own needs while building positive relationships with your audience: establishing your credibility and projecting your company's image.

Establishing Your Credibility

People are more likely to react positively to your message when they have confidence in you.

Your audience's response to every message you send depends heavily on their perception of your **credibility**, a measure of your believability based on how reliable you are and how much trust you evoke in others. With colleagues and long-term customers, you've already established some degree of credibility based on past communication efforts, and these people automatically lean toward accepting each new message from you because you haven't let them down in the past. With audiences who don't know you, however, you need to establish credibility before they'll listen fully to your message. Whether you're working to build credibility with a new audience, to maintain credibility with an existing audience, or even to restore credibility after a mistake, consider emphasizing the following characteristics:

TABLE 5.1 Overcoming Bias in Language

EXAMPLES	UNACCEPTABLE	PREFERABLE
GENDER BIAS		
Using words containing "man"	Mankind Man-made Manpower Businessman Salesman Foreman	Humanity, human beings, human race, people Artificial, synthetic, manufactured, constructed Human power, human energy, workers, workforce Executive, business manager, businessperson Sales representative, salesperson, clerk, sales agent Supervisor
Using female-gender words	Authoress, actress, stewardess	Author, actor, cabin attendant
Using special designations	Woman doctor, male nurse	Doctor, nurse
Using "he" to refer to "everyone"	The average worker . . . he	The average worker . . . he or she
Identifying roles with gender	The typical executive spends four hours of his day in meetings.	Most executives spend four hours a day in meetings.
	the consumer . . . she	Consumers . . . they
	the nurse/teacher . . . she	nurses/teachers . . . they
Identifying women by marital status	Phil Donahue and Marlo	Phil Donahue and Marlo Thomas
	Phil Donahue and Ms. Thomas	Mr. Donahue and Ms. Thomas
RACIAL/ETHNIC BIAS		
Assigning stereotypes	My black assistant speaks more articulately than I do.	My assistant speaks more articulately than I do.
	Jim Wong is an unusually tall Asian.	Jim Wong is tall.
Identifying people by race or ethnicity	Mario M. Cuomo, Italian American politician and ex-governor of New York	Mario M. Cuomo, politician and ex-governor of New York
AGE BIAS		
Including age when irrelevant	Mary Kirazy, 58, has just joined our trust department	Mary Kirazy has just joined our trust department.
DISABILITY BIAS		
Putting the disability before the person	Crippled workers face many barriers on the job.	Workers with physical disabilities face many barriers on the job.
	An epileptic, Tracy has no trouble doing her job.	Tracy's epilepsy has no effect on her job performance.

To enhance your credibility, emphasize such factors as honesty, objectivity, and awareness of audience needs.

- **Honesty.** Honesty is the cornerstone of credibility. No matter how famous, important, charming, or attractive you are, if you don't tell the truth most people will eventually lose faith in you. On the other hand, demonstrating honesty and integrity will earn you the respect of your colleagues and the trust of everyone you communicate with, even if they don't always agree with or welcome the messages you have to deliver.
- **Objectivity.** Audiences appreciate the ability to distance yourself from emotional situations and to look at all sides of an issue. They want to believe that you have their interests in mind, not just your own.
- **Awareness of audience needs.** Let your audience know that you understand what's important to them. If you've done a thorough audience analysis, you'll know what your audience cares about and their specific issues and concerns in a particular situation.

- **Credentials, knowledge, and expertise.** Every audience wants to be assured that the messages they receive come from people who know what they're talking about—that's why doctors hang their medical school diplomas on their office walls and why public speakers often arrange to be introduced with brief summaries of their experience and qualifications. When you need to establish credibility with a new audience, put yourself in their shoes and try to identify the credentials that would be most important to them. Is it your education, a professional certification, special training, success on the job? Express these qualifications clearly and objectively, without overshadowing the message. Sometimes it's as simple as using the right technical terms or mentioning your role in a successful project.
- **Endorsements.** If your audience doesn't know anything about you, you might be able to get assistance from someone they do know and trust. Once the audience learns that someone they trust in turn trusts you, they'll be more receptive to your messages.
- **Performance.** Who impresses you more, the person who always says, "If you ever need me, all you have to is call," or the one who actually shows up when you need to move or when you need a ride to the airport? It's easy to say you can do something, but following through can be much harder. That's why demonstrating impressive communication skills is not enough; people need to know they can count on you to get the job done.
- **Communication style.** If you support your points with evidence that can be confirmed through observation, research, experimentation, or measurement, audience members will recognize that you have the facts, and they'll respect you. On the other hand, trying to spice up your messages with terms such as *amazing, incredible, extraordinary, sensational,* and *revolutionary* strains your credibility unless you can support these terms with some sort of proof.

You also risk losing credibility if you seem to be currying favor with insincere compliments. Try to support compliments with specific points that show you are aware of a person's contributions and not just spouting off a generic thanks:

INSTEAD OF THIS	USE THIS
My deepest heartfelt thanks for the excellent job you did. It's hard these days to find workers like you. You are just fantastic! I can't stress enough how happy you have made us with your outstanding performance.	Thanks for the great job you did filling in for Sean at the convention on such short notice. Despite the difficult circumstances, you managed to attract several new orders with your demonstration of the new line of coffeemakers. Your dedication and sales ability are truly appreciated.

Even though arrogance turns listeners off, displaying too much modesty or too little confidence can hurt your credibility. If you lack faith in yourself, you're likely to communicate an uncertain attitude that undermines your credibility. The key to being believable is to believe in yourself. If you are convinced that your message is sound, you can state your case with authority so that your audience has no doubts. Avoid vague sentiments and confidence-draining words such as *if, hope,* and *trust:*

INSTEAD OF THIS	USE THIS
We hope this recommendation will be helpful.	We're glad to make this recommendation.
If you'd like to order, mail us the reply card.	To order, mail the reply card.
We trust that you'll extend your service contract.	By extending your service contract, you can continue to enjoy top-notch performance from your equipment.

Finally, keep in mind that credibility can take days, months, even years to establish—and it can be wiped out in an instant. An occasional mistake or letdown is usually forgiven,

Communication Solution

Many patients would naturally be skeptical of an unfamiliar solution such as a bioartificial liver, so Algenix takes care to build credibility on its website by sharing the clinical evidence in favor of its particular approach.

DOCUMENT MAKEOVER

IMPROVE THIS LETTER

To practice correcting drafts of actual documents, visit www.prenhall.com/onekey on the web. Click "Document Makeovers," then click Chapter 5. You will find a letter that contains problems and errors relating to what you've learned in this chapter about establishing a good relationship with your audience. Use the Final Draft decision tool to create an improved version of this letter. Check the document for a "you" attitude, positive language, communication etiquette, bias-free language, and phrases that establish credibility.

but major lapses in honesty or integrity can destroy your reputation. On the other hand, when you do establish credibility, communication becomes much easier because you no longer have to spend time and energy convincing people that you are a trustworthy source of information and ideas.

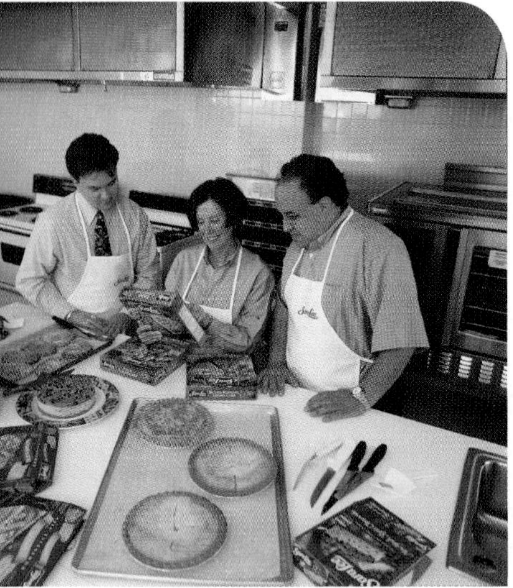

Before writing a letter or an e-mail message on behalf of your company, think about how you project the company image, says Elizabeth Taris (center), manager of consumer affairs at Sara Lee Bakery. "We want everyone to understand the high quality and high standards at Sara Lee—that's how we made our good name, and that's how we're going to keep it."

Projecting the Company's Image

When you communicate with outsiders, on even the most routine matter, you serve as the spokesperson for your organization. The impression you make can enhance or damage the reputation of the entire company. Thus, your own views and personality must be subordinated, at least to some extent, to the interests and style of your company.

Your company's interests and reputation take precedence over your personal communication style.

Many organizations have specific communication guidelines that show everything from the correct use of the company name to preferred abbreviations and other grammatical details. Specifying a desired style of communication is more difficult, however. Observe more experienced colleagues to see how they communicate, and never hesitate to ask for editorial help to make sure you're conveying the appropriate tone. For instance, with clients entrusting thousands or millions of dollars to it, an investment firm communicates in a style quite different from that of a clothing retailer. And a clothing retailer specializing in high-quality business attire communicates in a style different from that of a store catering to the latest trends in casual wear.

Controlling Your Style and Tone

2 LEARNING OBJECTIVE

Discuss four ways of achieving a businesslike tone with a style that is clear and concise

Style is the way you use words to achieve a certain **tone,** or overall impression. You can vary your style—your sentence structure and vocabulary—to sound forceful or objective, personal or formal, colorful or dry. The right choice depends on the nature of your message and your relationship with the reader. Although style can be refined during the revision phase (see Chapter 6), you'll save time and a lot of rewriting if you use a style that allows you to achieve the desired tone from the start.

When composing your message, you can vary the style to create a tone that suits the occasion.

Using a Conversational Tone

The tone of your business messages can range from informal to conversational to formal. If you're in a large organization and you're communicating with your superiors or with customers, your tone would tend to be more formal and respectful.[7] However, that formal tone might sound distant and cold if used with close colleagues.

Compare the three versions of the letter in Table 5.2. The first is too formal and stuffy for today's audiences, whereas the third is too casual for any audience other than close associates or friends. The second message demonstrates the conversational tone used in most business communication—using plain language that sounds businesslike without being stuffy or full of jargon. You can achieve a conversational tone in your messages by following these guidelines:

Most business messages aim for a conversational tone that is warm but still businesslike.

- **Avoid obsolete and pompous language.** Business language used to be much more formal than it is today, and some out-of-date phrases still remain. You can avoid using such language if you ask yourself, "Would I say this if I were talking with someone face to face?" Similarly, avoid using big words, trite expressions, and overly complicated sentences to impress others. Such pompous language sounds self-important (see Table 5.3).
- **Avoid preaching and bragging.** Few things are more irritating than people who think that they know everything and that others know nothing. If you do need to remind your audience of something obvious, try to work the information casually, perhaps in the middle of a paragraph, where it will sound like a secondary comment rather than a major revelation. Also, avoid bragging about your accomplishments or those of your organization (unless your audience is a part of your organization).
- **Be careful with intimacy.** Most business messages should avoid intimacy, such as sharing personal details or adopting a causal, unprofessional tone. However, when you do have a close relationship with your audience, such as among the members of a close-knit team, a more intimate tone is sometimes appropriate and even expected.

TABLE 5.2 Three Levels of Tone: Formal, Conversational, and Informal

FORMAL TONE (RESERVED FOR THE MOST FORMAL OCCASIONS)	CONVERSATIONAL TONE (PREFERRED FOR MOST BUSINESS COMMUNICATION)	INFORMAL TONE (RESERVED FOR COMMUNICATION WITH FRIENDS AND CLOSE ASSOCIATES)
Dear Ms. Navarro: Enclosed please find the information that was requested during our telephone communication of May 14. As was mentioned at that time, Midville Hospital has significantly more doctors of exceptional quality than any other health facility in the state. As you were also informed, our organization has quite an impressive network of doctors and other health-care professionals with offices located throughout the state. In the event that you should need a specialist, our professionals will be able to make an appropriate recommendation. You would be entitled to utilize the numerous programs that we provide to assist you and your family in achieving the highest level of health possible. We are especially proud of our health hotline, which allows you to speak with a registered nurse 24 hours a day, seven days a week. In the event that you have questions or would like additional information, you may certainly contact me during regular business hours. Most sincerely yours, Samuel G. Berenz	Dear Ms. Navarro: Here's the information you requested during our phone conversation on Friday. As I mentioned, Midville Hospital has the best doctors and more of them than any other hospital in the state. In addition, we have a vast network of doctors and other health professionals with offices throughout the state. If you need a specialist, they can refer you to the right one. You and your family can also participate in numerous health programs, such as smoking-cessation classes, health fairs, nutritional guidance, and a 24-hour hotline whose registered nurse can answer your questions seven days a week. If you would like more information, please call anytime between 9:00 and 5:00, Monday through Friday. Sincerely, Samuel G. Berenz	Hi Gabriella: How's it going? Just sending along the information you asked for. As I said on Friday, Midville Hospital has more and better doctors than any other hospital in the state. We also have a large group of doctors and other health professionals with offices close to you at work or at home. Need a specialist? They'll refer you to the right one. You and your family can get and stay healthy, thanks to our health fairs and numerous classes to improve your overall fitness. We even have a health hotline where you can get answers to your health questions all day, every day. Just give me a ring if you want to know more. Any time from 9:00 to 5:00 should do the trick. Take care, Sam

- **Be careful with humor.** Humor can be an effective tool to inject interest into dry subjects or take the sting out of negative news. However, use it with great care: the humor must be connected to the point you're trying to make. Business messages are not a forum for sharing jokes. Never use humor in formal messages or when you're communicating across cultural boundaries. Humor can easily backfire and divert attention from your message. If you don't know your audience well or you're not skilled at using humor in a business setting, don't use it at all. When in doubt, leave it out.

Using Plain English

Plain English is a way of presenting information in a simple, unadorned style so that your audience can easily grasp your meaning, without struggling through specialized, technical, or convoluted language. Because it's close to the way people normally speak, plain English is easily understood by anyone with an eighth- or ninth-grade education. The Plain English Campaign (a nonprofit group in England campaigning for clear language) defines plain English as language "that the intended audience can read, understand and act upon the first time they read it."[8] You can see how this definition supports using the "you" attitude and shows respect for your audience.

Audiences can understand and act on plain English without reading it over and over.

TABLE 5.3 Staying Up to Date and Down to Earth

OBSOLETE	UP TO DATE
in due course	today, tomorrow (or a specific time)
permit me to say that	(permission is not necessary)
we are in receipt of	we have received
pursuant to	(omit)
in closing, I'd like to say	(omit)
the undersigned	I; me
kindly advise	please let us know
we wish to inform you	(just say it)
attached please find	enclosed is
it has come to my attention	I have just learned; or, Ms. Garza has just told me
our Mr. Lydell	Mr. Lydell, our credit manager
please be advised that	(omit)
POMPOUS	**DOWN TO EARTH**
Upon procurement of additional supplies, I will initiate fulfillment of your order.	I will fill your order when I receive more supplies.
Perusal of the records indicates a substantial deficit for the preceding accounting period due to the utilization of antiquated mechanisms.	The records show a company loss last year due to the use of old equipment.

Few people argue with the value of plain English, but murky, pompous, and unnecessarily complex writing is still more common than it should be. Such writing is usually unsuccessful, failing to get the writer's message across. Moreover, poorly written documents create additional problems. As a nurse recently complained, a poorly written memo not only made her and her colleagues feel angry and inferior but also built a barrier between them and the writer.[9]

So why is unclear writing so pervasive when so many people don't like it? One reason is that writers are unsure about their own writing skills and about the impact their messages will have. They mistakenly believe that packaging simple ideas in complex writing makes their messages seem more impressive. Another reason is inadequate planning, which results in messages that meander in search of a conclusion. A third reason is that some writers intentionally try to create distance between themselves and their audiences. But whatever the cause, the result of unnecessarily complex writing is always the same: ineffective communication that wastes time, wastes money, and annoys everyone who comes in contact with it.

As frustration builds over confusing, grandiose writing, groups such as the Plain English Campaign are raising awareness of the costs of poor communication. A number of government agencies and businesses are also working to improve matters. To help financial managers write more clearly, the U.S. Securities and Exchange Commission (SEC; the agency in charge of monitoring financial markets) produced *A Plain English Handbook: How to Create Clear SEC Disclosure Documents.* Deloitte Consulting (a large management consulting firm) went so far as to create Bullfighter software, a tool that runs in Microsoft Word and PowerPoint to catch jargon, buzzwords, and other instances of poor writing.[10]

Even though plain English is intended for audiences who speak English as their primary language, plain English can also help you simplify the messages you prepare for audiences who speak English only as a second or even third language. For example, by choosing words that have only one interpretation, you will communicate more clearly with your

Communicating Across Cultures

Communicating with a Global Audience on the Web

Reaching an international audience on the web involves more than simply offering translations of the English language. Successful global sites address the needs of international customers in five ways:

1. **Consider the reader's perspective.** Many communication elements that you might take for granted may be interpreted differently by audiences in different countries. Should you use the metric system, different notations for times or dates, or even different names for countries? For example, German citizens don't refer to their country as *Germany;* it's *Deutschland* to them. Review the entire online experience and look for ways to improve communication, including such helpful tools as interactive currency converters and translation dictionaries.
2. **Take cultural differences into account.** For instance, since humor is rooted in cultural norms, U.S. humor may not be so funny to Asian or European readers. Avoid idioms and references that aren't universally recognized, such as "putting all your eggs in one basket" or "jumping out of the frying pan into the fire."
3. **Keep the message clear.** Use simple words and sentences and write in the active voice. Define abbreviations, acronyms, and words an international audience might not be familiar with.
4. **Complement language with visuals.** Use drawings, photos, and other visuals to help communicate when words can't.
5. **Consult local experts.** Seek the advice of local experts about phrases and references that might be expected. Even terms as simple as *homepage* differ from country to country. Spanish readers refer to the "first page," or *pagina inicial,* whereas the French term is "welcome page," or *page d'accuei.*

CAREER APPLICATIONS

1. Visit the World of Sony Music Entertainment at www.sonymusic.com/world and examine Sony's sites for Argentina, France, and Germany. How does Sony "localize" each country's site?
2. Compare Sony Music's international sites to IBM's global webpages at www.ibm.com. How does Sony's approach differ from IBM's? Do both corporations successfully address the needs of a global audience? Write a two-paragraph summary that compares the international sites of both companies.

intercultural audience (see "Communicating Across Cultures: Communicating with a Global Audience on the Web").[11]

For all its advantages, plain English does have some limitations. It sometimes lacks the precision or subtlety necessary for scientific research, engineering documents, intense feeling, and personal insight. Moreover, it doesn't embrace all cultures and dialects equally.

Communication Solution

Algenix uses plain English extensively in its communication efforts, defining unfamiliar medical terms whenever these specialized words are required for technical accuracy.

Selecting Active or Passive Voice

Your choice of active or passive voice also affects the tone of your message. You are using **active voice** when the subject performs the action, and the object receives the action: "John rented the office." You're using **passive voice** when the subject receives the action: "The office was rented by John." As you can see, the passive voice combines a form of the verb *to be* (was) with the past participle of the main verb (rented). When you use active sentences, your messages generally sound less formal and make it easier for readers to figure out who performed the action (see Table 5.4). In contrast, using passive voice de-emphasizes the subject and implies the action was done by something or someone.

Use the active voice to produce shorter, stronger sentences and make your writing more vigorous, concise, and generally easier to understand.[12] The passive voice is not wrong grammatically, but it is often cumbersome, is unnecessarily vague, and can make sentences longer. Nevertheless, using the passive voice can help you demonstrate the "you" attitude in some situations:

Active sentences are usually stronger than passive ones.

- When you want to be diplomatic about pointing out a problem or error of some kind (the passive version seems less like an accusation)
- When you want to point out what's being done without taking or attributing either the credit or the blame (the passive version leaves the actor completely out of the sentence)

Use passive sentences to soften bad news, to put yourself in the background, or to create an impersonal tone.

TABLE 5.4 Choosing Active or Passive Voice

AVOID PASSIVE VOICE IN GENERAL	USE ACTIVE VOICE IN GENERAL
The new procedure was developed by the operations team.	The operations team developed the new procedure.
Legal problems are created by this contract.	This contract creates legal problems.
Reception preparations have been undertaken by our PR people for the new CEO's arrival.	Our PR people have undertaken reception preparations for the new CEO's arrival.
SOMETIMES AVOID ACTIVE VOICE	**SOMETIMES USE PASSIVE VOICE**
You lost the shipment.	The shipment was lost.
I am analyzing the production line to determine the problem.	The production line is being analyzed to determine the problem.
We have established criteria to evaluate capital expenditures.	Criteria have been established to evaluate capital expenditures.

- When you want to avoid personal pronouns in order to create an objective tone (the passive version may be used in a formal report, for example)

The second half of Table 5.4 illustrates several situations in which the passive voice helps you focus your message on your audience.

COMPOSING YOUR MESSAGE

With these insights into how you can adapt to your audience, you're ready to begin composing your message. Composition is easiest if you've already figured out what to say and in what order (refer to the outlining advice in Chapter 4), although you may need to pause now and then to find the right word. You may also discover as you go along that you can improve on your outline. Feel free to rearrange, delete, and add ideas, as long as you don't lose sight of your purpose.

As you compose your first draft, try to let your creativity flow. Don't try to draft and edit at the same time or worry about getting everything perfect. Make up words if you can't think of the right word, draw pictures, talk out loud—whatever it takes to get the ideas out of your head and onto your computer screen or a piece of paper. You'll have time to revise and refine the material later.

If you get stuck and feel unable to write, try to overcome writer's block by jogging your brain in creative ways: skip to another part of the document (the opening paragraph is often the hardest to write, but you don't need to write it first), work on nontext elements such as graphics or your cover page, revisit your purpose and confirm your intent in writing the message, or give yourself a mental break by switching to a different project. Sometimes all you need to do is to start writing without worrying about what you're writing or how it sounds. Words will start flowing, your mind will engage, and the writing will come easier. The most successful messages have three important elements: strong words, effective sentences, and coherent paragraphs.

3 LEARNING OBJECTIVE

Briefly describe how to select words that are not only correct but also effective

Choosing Strong Words

Correctness is the first consideration when choosing words.

Effective messages depend on carefully chosen words, whether you select them during your first draft or edit them in later.[13] First, pay close attention to correctness. The "rules" of grammar and usage are constantly changing to reflect changes in the way people speak. Even editors and grammarians occasionally have questions about correct usage, and they sometimes disagree about the answers. For example, the word *data* is the plural form of *datum,* yet some experts now prefer to treat *data* as a singular noun when it's used in non-scientific material to refer to a body of information. You be the judge: Which of the following sentences sounds better?

Our market share data is consistent from region to region.

Our market share data are consistent from region to region.

Although debating the finer points of usage may seem like nitpicking, using words correctly is important. If you make grammatical or usage errors, you lose credibility with your audience—even if your message is otherwise correct. Poor grammar implies that you're unaware or uninformed, and audiences put less faith in an uninformed source. Even if an audience is broad-minded enough to withhold such a judgment, grammatical errors are distracting.

Correct grammar enhances your image.

If you have doubts about what is correct, look up the answer, and use the proper form of expression. Check the "Handbook of Grammar, Mechanics, and Usage" at the end of this book, or consult the many special reference books and resources available in libraries, in bookstores, and on the Internet. Most authorities agree on the basic conventions.

Just as important as selecting the correct word is selecting the most suitable word for the job at hand. Naturally, using the right words is important in life-and-death situations (see "Communication Miscues: When Words Kill: Hidden Dangers in Food Labels"). But even when you're dealing with less perilous circumstances, the right words can make all the difference in the success of your communication efforts. Word effectiveness is generally more difficult to achieve than correctness, particularly in written communication. Even professional writers with decades of experience continue to work at their craft to use functional and content words correctly and to find the words that communicate.

Effectiveness is the second consideration when choosing words.

Using Functional and Content Words Correctly

Words can be divided into two main categories. **Functional words** express relationships and have only one unchanging meaning in any given context. They include conjunctions, prepositions, articles, and pronouns. Your main concern with functional words is to use

Communication Miscues

When Words Kill: Hidden Dangers in Food Labels

When you see the phrase "May contain peanuts" on the label of a food product, chances are you don't give it a second thought. For the thousands of people allergic to peanuts, however, these warnings can literally mean the difference between life and death. Seven million people in the United States are allergic to one or more food ingredients. Every year 30,000 of these people end up in the emergency room after suffering an allergic reaction, and every year 200 of them die. Many of these tragic events are tied to poorly written food labels that either fail to identify dangerous allergens or use scientific terms that most consumers don't recognize.

With lives on the line, you might expect government regulations to call for strict, easy-to-understand disclosure of dangerous allergens. In fact, the Food and Drug Administration (FDA) does require labeling of many allergens, but it currently exempts spices, flavorings, and some coloring agents and additives. Even more troubling, an FDA study found that one quarter of all food manufacturers failed to list potentially fatal allergens, and nearly half failed to accurately portray all the ingredients in their products.

Many political leaders and groups such as the Food Allergy Initiative continue to push for labels that are not only more accurate and complete but also in plain English. A number of companies, including industry leaders General Foods and Kraft, opted not to wait for improved regulations; they established their own guidelines for safer production and better labeling. The changes are coming just in time, too, as occurrences of food allergies continue to multiply around the world.

CAREER APPLICATIONS

1. What steps should manufacturers take to ensure that consumers read, understand, and follow warnings on food products?
2. Do food manufacturers have a responsibility to educate consumers about potential allergens in food? Explain your answer.

Functional words (conjunctions, prepositions, articles, and pronouns) express the relationships among content words (nouns, verbs, adjectives, and adverbs).

them correctly. **Content words** are multidimensional and therefore subject to various interpretations. They include nouns, verbs, adjectives, and adverbs. These words carry the meaning of a sentence. In your sentences, content words are the building blocks, and functional words are the mortar that holds them together. In the following sentence, all the content words are underlined:

> Some objective observers of the cookie market give Nabisco the edge in quality, but Frito-Lay is lauded for superior distribution.

Both functional words and content words are necessary, but your effectiveness as a communicator depends largely on your ability to choose the right content words for your message.

Content words have both a denotative (explicit, specific) meaning and a connotative (implicit, associative) meaning.

Denotation and Connotation Content words have both a denotative and a connotative meaning. The **denotative meaning** is the literal, or dictionary, meaning. The **connotative meaning** includes all the associations and feelings evoked by the word.

The denotative meaning of *desk* is "a table used for writing." Some desks may have drawers or compartments, and others may have a flat top or a sloping top, but the literal meaning is generally well understood. The connotative meaning of *desk* may include thoughts associated with work or study, but the word *desk* has fairly neutral connotations—neither strong nor emotional. However, some words have much stronger connotations than others. For example, the connotations of the word *fail* are negative and can carry strong emotional meaning. So if you say that a student *failed* to pass a test, the connotative meaning suggests that the person is inferior, incompetent, below some standard of performance.

Business communicators are careful to avoid words with negative connotations.

In business communication, be careful with words that have multiple interpretations and are high in connotative meaning. By saying that a student achieved a score of 65 percent, you communicate the facts and avoid a heavy load of negative connotations. If you use words that have relatively few possible interpretations, you are less likely to be misunderstood. In addition, because you are trying to communicate in an objective, rational manner, you want to avoid emotion-laden comments.

The more abstract a word is, the more it is removed from the tangible, objective world of things that can be perceived with the senses.

Abstraction and Concreteness Words vary dramatically in the degree of abstraction or concreteness they convey. An **abstract word** expresses a concept, quality, or characteristic. Abstractions are usually broad, encompassing a category of ideas, and they are often intellectual, academic, or philosophical. *Love, honor, progress, tradition,* and *beauty* are abstractions. In contrast, a **concrete word** stands for something you can touch or see. Concrete terms are anchored in the tangible, material world. *Chair, table, horse, rose, kick, kiss, red, green,* and *two* are concrete words; they are direct, clear, and exact.

In business communication, use concrete, specific terms whenever possible; use abstractions only when necessary.

You might assume that concrete words are better than abstract words because they are more precise, but this isn't always the case. For example, try to rewrite this sentence without using the underlined abstract words:

> We hold these truths to be self-evident, that all men are created equal, that they are endowed by their Creator with certain unalienable Rights, that among these are Life, Liberty, and the Pursuit of Happiness.

As you can see, the Declaration of Independence needs abstractions, and so do most business messages. Abstractions let you rise above the common and tangible. They allow you to refer to concepts such as *morale, productivity, profits, quality, motivation,* and *guarantees.*

Even though they're indispensable, abstractions can be troublesome. They tend to be fuzzy and subject to many interpretations. Moreover, it isn't always easy to get excited about ideas, especially if they're unrelated to concrete experience. The best way to minimize such problems is to blend abstract terms with concrete ones, the general with the specific. State the concept, then pin it down with details expressed in more concrete terms. Save the abstractions for ideas that cannot be expressed any other way.

Because words such as *small, numerous, sizable, near, soon, good,* and *fine* are imprecise, try to replace them with terms that are more accurate. Instead of referring to a *sizable loss,* talk about a *loss of $32 million.*

TABLE 5.5 Finding the Words That Communicate with Power

AVOID WEAK PHRASES	USE STRONG TERMS
Wealthy businessperson	Tycoon
Business prosperity	Boom
Hard times	Slump
AVOID UNFAMILIAR WORDS	**USE FAMILIAR WORDS**
Ascertain	Find out, learn
Consummate	Close, bring about
Peruse	Read, study
Circumvent	Avoid
Increment	Growth, increase
Unequivocal	Certain
AVOID CLICHÉS	**USE PLAIN LANGUAGE**
Scrape the bottom of the barrel	Strain shrinking resources
An uphill battle	A challenge
Writing on the wall	Prediction
Call the shots	Be in charge
Take by storm	Attack
Cost an arm and a leg	Expensive
A new ballgame	Fresh start
Worst nightmare	Strong competitor; disaster
Fall through the cracks	Be overlooked

Finding Words That Communicate

By practicing your writing, learning from experienced writers and editors, and reading extensively, you'll find it easier to choose words that communicate exactly what you want to say. When you compose your business messages, think carefully to find the most powerful words for each situation (see Table 5.5).

Try to use words that are powerful and familiar.

- **Choose powerful words.** Choose words that express your thoughts most clearly, specifically, and dynamically. Nouns and verbs are the most concrete and should do most of the communication work in your messages. Verbs are especially powerful because they tell what's happening in the sentence, so make them dynamic and specific. For instance, you might replace *rise* or *fall* with *soar* or *plummet* if appropriate. Adjectives and adverbs have obvious roles, but if you find yourself using them often, you're probably trying to compensate for weak nouns and verbs.
- **Choose familiar words.** You'll communicate best with words that are familiar to both you and your readers. Moreover, trying to use an unfamiliar word for the first time in an important document can lead to embarrassing mistakes.
- **Avoid clichés.** Although familiar words are generally the best choice, beware of terms and phrases so common that they have lost some of their power to communicate. Because clichés are used so often, readers tend to slide right by them to whatever is coming next. Most people use these phrases not because they think it makes their message more vivid and inviting but because they don't know how to express themselves otherwise.[14]

Avoid clichés in your writing and use jargon only when your audience is completely familiar with it.

- **Use jargon carefully.** Handle technical or professional terms with care. Although jargon has a bad reputation in general, it's usually an efficient way to communicate within specific groups that understand their own special terms. After all, that's how jargon develops in the first place, as people with similar interests develop ways to communicate complex ideas quickly. For instance, when a recording engineer wants to communicate that a particular piece of music is devoid of reverberation and other sound effects, it's a lot easier to simply describe the track as "dry." Of course, to people who aren't familiar with such insider terms, jargon is meaningless and intimidating—one more reason it's so important to understand your audience before you start writing.

Remember, you improve your business writing skills through imitation and practice. As you read business journals, newspapers, and even novels, make a note of the words you think are effective and keep them in a file. Look through your file before drafting your next letter or report, and try using some of these words in your document. You may be surprised how they can strengthen your writing.

Creating Effective Sentences

Making every sentence count is a key step in creating effective messages. Start by selecting the optimum type of sentence, then arrange words to emphasize the most important point in each sentence.

Choosing from the Four Types of Sentences

A simple sentence has one main clause.

Sentences come in four basic varieties: simple, compound, complex, and compound-complex. A **simple sentence** has one main clause (a single subject and a single predicate), although it may be expanded by nouns and pronouns serving as objects of the action and by modifying phrases. Here's a typical example (with the subject underlined once and the predicate verb underlined twice):

Profits increased in the past year.

A compound sentence has two main clauses.

A **compound sentence** has two main clauses that express two or more independent but related thoughts of equal importance, usually joined by *and, but,* or *or.* In effect, a compound sentence is a merger of two or more simple sentences (independent clauses) that are related. For example,

Wage rates have declined by 5 percent, and employee turnover has been high.

The independent clauses in a compound sentence are always separated by a comma or by a semicolon (in which case the conjunction—*and, but, or*—is dropped).

A complex sentence has one main clause and one subordinate clause.

A **complex sentence** expresses one main thought (the independent clause) and one or more subordinate thoughts (dependent clauses) related to it, often separated by a comma. The subordinate thought, which comes first in the following sentence, could not stand alone:

Although you may question Gerald's conclusions, you must admit that his research is thorough.

A compound-complex sentence has two main clauses and at least one dependent clause.

A **compound-complex sentence** has two main clauses, at least one of which contains a subordinate clause:

Profits have increased in the past year, and although you may question Gerald's conclusions, you must admit that his research is thorough.

When constructing a sentence, choose the form that matches the relationship of the ideas you want to express. If you have two ideas of equal importance, express them as two simple sentences or as one compound sentence. However, if one of the ideas is less important than the other, place it in a dependent clause to form a complex sentence. For example, although the following compound sentence uses a conjunction to join two ideas, they aren't truly equal:

> The chemical products division is the strongest in the company, and its management techniques should be adopted by the other divisions.

By making the first thought subordinate to the second, you establish a cause-and-effect relationship. So the following complex sentence is much more effective:

> Because the chemical products division is the strongest in the company, its management techniques should be adopted by the other divisions.

To make your writing as effective as possible, strive for variety and balance using all four sentence types. If you use too many simple sentences, you won't be able to properly express the relationships among your ideas, and your writing will sound choppy and abrupt. If you use too many long, compound sentences, your writing will sound monotonous. On the other hand, an uninterrupted series of complex or compound-complex sentences is hard to follow.

Writing is more effective if it balances all four sentence types.

Using Sentence Style to Emphasize Key Thoughts

4 LEARNING OBJECTIVE

Explain how sentence style affects emphasis within your message

Sentence style varies from language to language. German sentences tend to be long and complex, with lots of modifiers; Japanese and Chinese languages don't even have sentences in the same sense that Western languages do.[15] English offers tremendous flexibility in saying what you want to say and in developing your own style. For most business audiences, clarity and efficiency take precedence over literary style, so strive for straightforward simplicity.

In every message, some ideas are more important than others. You can emphasize these key ideas through your sentence style. One obvious technique is to give important points the most space. When you want to call attention to a thought, use extra words to describe it. Consider this sentence:

Emphasize parts of a sentence by
- Devoting more words to them
- Putting them at the beginning or at the end of the sentence
- Making them the subject of the sentence

> The chairperson of the board called for a vote of the shareholders.

To emphasize the importance of the chairperson, you might describe her more fully:

> Having considerable experience in corporate takeover battles, the chairperson of the board called for a vote of the shareholders.

You can increase the emphasis even more by adding a separate, short sentence to augment the first:

> The chairperson of the board called for a vote of the shareholders. She has considerable experience in corporate takeover battles.

You can also call attention to a thought by making it the subject of the sentence. In the following example, the emphasis is on the person:

> *I* can write letters much more quickly using a computer.

However, by changing the subject, the computer takes center stage:

> The *computer* enables me to write letters much more quickly.

Another way to emphasize an idea is to place it either at the beginning or at the end of a sentence:

> **Less Emphatic:** We are cutting the *price* to stimulate demand.
>
> **More Emphatic:** To stimulate demand, we are cutting the *price*.

Dependent clauses can determine emphasis.

In complex sentences, the placement of the dependent clause hinges on the relationship between the ideas expressed. If you want to emphasize the idea, put the dependent clause at the end of the sentence (the most emphatic position) or at the beginning (the second most emphatic position). If you want to downplay the idea, bury the dependent clause within the sentence.

Most Emphatic: The electronic parts are manufactured in Mexico, *which has lower wage rates than the United States.*

Emphatic: *Because wage rates are lower there,* the electronic parts are manufactured in Mexico.

Least Emphatic: Mexico, *which has lower wage rates,* was selected as the production site for the electronic parts.

Techniques such as these give you a great deal of control over the way your audience interprets what you have to say.

5 LEARNING OBJECTIVE

List five ways to develop coherent paragraphs

Crafting Coherent Paragraphs

Paragraphs organize sentences related to the same general topic. Readers expect each paragraph to focus on a single unit of thought and to be a logical link in an organized sequence of the thoughts that make up a complete message. As with sentences, you can control the elements of each paragraph. Doing so helps your readers grasp the main idea of your document and understand how the specific pieces of support material back up that idea.

Even when reading online, readers expect each paragraph to address one main idea and all the paragraphs in a document to link together logically.

Elements of the Paragraph

Paragraphs vary widely in length and form. You can communicate effectively in one short paragraph or in pages of lengthy paragraphs, depending on your purpose, your audience, and your message. The typical paragraph contains three basic elements: a topic sentence, support sentences that develop the topic, and transitional words and phrases.

Most paragraphs consist of a topic sentence, related sentences, and transitional elements.

Topic Sentence Every properly constructed paragraph is *unified;* it deals with a single topic. The sentence that introduces that topic is called the **topic sentence**. In informal and creative writing, the topic sentence may be implied rather than stated. In business writing, the topic sentence is generally explicit and is often the first sentence in the paragraph. The topic sentence gives readers a summary of the general idea that will be covered in the rest of the paragraph. The following examples show how a topic sentence can introduce the subject and suggest the way that subject will be developed:

The topic sentence reveals the subject of the paragraph and indicates how the subject will be developed.

The medical products division has been troubled for many years by public relations problems. [In the rest of the paragraph, readers will learn the details of the problems.]

Relocating the plant in New York has two main disadvantages. [The disadvantages will be explained in subsequent sentences.]

To get a refund, you must supply us with some additional information. [The details of the necessary information will be described in the rest of the paragraph.]

Paragraphs are developed through a series of related sentences that provide details about the topic sentence.

Support Sentences In most paragraphs, the topic sentence needs to be explained, justified, or extended with one or more support sentences. These related sentences must all have a bearing on the general subject and must provide enough specific details to make the topic clear:

> The medical products division has been troubled for many years by public relations problems. Since 2002 the local newspaper has published 15 articles that portray the division in a negative light. We have been accused of everything from mistreating laboratory animals to polluting the local groundwater. Our facility has been described as a health hazard. Our scientists are referred to as "Frankensteins," and our profits are considered "obscene."

The support sentences are all more specific than the topic sentence. Each one provides another piece of evidence to demonstrate the general truth of the main thought. Also, each sentence is clearly related to the general idea being developed, which gives the paragraph its unity. A paragraph is well developed when (1) it contains enough information to make the topic sentence convincing and interesting and (2) it contains no extraneous, unrelated sentences.

Transitional Elements In addition to being unified and well supported, effective paragraphs are *coherent;* that is, they are arranged in a logical order so that the audience can understand the train of thought. When you complete a paragraph, your readers automatically assume that you've finished with a particular idea. You achieve coherence by using transitions that show the relationship between paragraphs and among sentences within paragraphs. Transitions are words or phrases that tie ideas together by showing how one thought is related to another. They not only help readers understand the connections you're trying to make but also smooth your writing. You can establish transitions in a variety of ways:

Because each paragraph covers a single idea, use transitional words and phrases to show readers how paragraphs relate to each other.

- **Use connecting words:** *and, but, or, nevertheless, however, in addition,* and so on.
- **Echo a word or phrase from a previous paragraph or sentence:** "A system should be established for monitoring inventory levels. *This system* will provide . . ."
- **Use a pronoun that refers to a noun used previously:** "Ms. Arthur is the leading candidate for the president's position. *She* has excellent qualifications."
- **Use words that are frequently paired:** "The machine has a *minimum* output of . . . Its *maximum* output is . . ."

Some transitional devices include
- Connecting words (conjunctions)
- Repeated words or phrases
- Pronouns
- Words that are frequently paired

Some transitional elements serve as mood changers; that is, they alert the reader to a change in mood from the previous paragraph. Some announce a total contrast with what's gone on before, some announce a causal relationship, and some signal a change in time. Transitional elements prepare your reader for what is coming. Here is a list of transitions frequently used to move readers smoothly between sentences and paragraphs:

Transitions move readers between sentences and paragraphs.

Additional detail:	moreover, furthermore, in addition, besides, first, second, third, finally
Causal relationship:	therefore, because, accordingly, thus, consequently, hence, as a result, so
Comparison:	similarly, here again, likewise, in comparison, still
Contrast:	yet, conversely, whereas, nevertheless, on the other hand, however, but, nonetheless
Condition:	although, if
Illustration:	for example, in particular, in this case, for instance
Time sequence:	formerly, after, when, meanwhile, sometimes
Intensification:	indeed, in fact, in any event
Summary:	in brief, in short, to sum up
Repetition:	that is, in other words, as I mentioned earlier

Although transitional words and phrases are useful, they're not sufficient in themselves to overcome poor organization. Put your ideas into a strong framework first, and then use transitions to link them together even more strongly.

Consider using a transition whenever it might help the reader understand your ideas and follow you from point to point. You can use transitions inside paragraphs to tie related points together and between paragraphs to ease the shift from one distinct thought to another. In longer reports, transitions that link major sections or chapters are often complete paragraphs that serve as mini-introductions to the next section or as summaries of the ideas presented in the section just ending. Here's an example:

> Given the nature of this product, the alternatives are limited. As the previous section indicates, we can stop making it altogether, improve it, or continue with the current model. Each of these alternatives has advantages and disadvantages, which are discussed in the following section.

This paragraph makes it clear to the reader that the analysis of the problem (offered in the previous section) is now over, and that the document is making a transition to an analysis of alternatives (to be offered in the next section).

Five Ways to Develop a Paragraph

Five ways to develop paragraphs:
- Illustration
- Comparison or contrast
- Cause and effect
- Classification
- Problem and solution

The coherence in your paragraph strongly depends on how you develop it, and the best way to do that is to use a structure that is familiar to your readers, appropriate to the idea you're trying to portray, and suited to your purpose. Five of the most common development techniques are illustration, comparison or contrast, cause and effect, classification, and problem and solution (see Table 5.6).

TABLE 5.6 Five Techniques for Developing Paragraphs

TECHNIQUE	DESCRIPTION	SAMPLE
Illustration	Giving examples that demonstrate the general idea	Some of our most popular products are available through local distributors. For example, Everett & Lemmings carries our frozen soups and entrees. The J. B. Green Company carries our complete line of seasonings, as well as the frozen soups. Wilmont Foods, also a major distributor, now carries our new line of frozen desserts.
Comparison or contrast	Using similarities or differences to develop the topic	In previous years, when the company was small, the recruiting function could be handled informally. The need for new employees was limited, and each manager could comfortably screen and hire her or his own staff. Today, however, Gambit Products must undertake a major recruiting effort. Our successful bid on the Owens contract means that we will be doubling our labor force over the next six months. To hire that many people without disrupting our ongoing activities, we will create a separate recruiting group within the human resources department.
Cause and effect	Focusing on the reasons for something	The heavy-duty fabric of your Wanderer tent probably broke down for one of two reasons: (1) a sharp object punctured the fabric, and without reinforcement, the hole was enlarged by the stress of erecting the tent daily for a week or (2) the fibers gradually rotted because the tent was folded and stored while still wet.
Classification	Showing how a general idea is broken into specific categories	Successful candidates for our supervisor trainee program generally come from one of several groups. The largest group, by far, consists of recent graduates of accredited data-processing programs. The next largest group comes from within our own company, as we try to promote promising clerical workers to positions of greater responsibility. Finally, we do occasionally accept candidates with outstanding supervisory experience in related industries.
Problem and solution	Presenting a problem and then discussing the solution	Selling handmade toys by mail is a challenge because consumers are accustomed to buying heavily advertised toys from major chains. However, if we develop an appealing catalog, we can compete on the basis of product novelty and quality. In addition, we can provide craftsmanship at a competitive price: a rocking horse of birch, with a hand-knit tail and mane; a music box with the child's name painted on the top; a real Indian teepee, made by Native American artisans.

In practice, you'll occasionally combine two or more methods of development in a single paragraph. To add interest, you might begin by using illustration, shift to comparison or contrast, and then shift to problem and solution. However, when combining approaches, do so carefully so that you don't lose readers partway through the paragraph. In addition, before settling for the first approach that comes to mind, consider the alternatives. Think through various methods before committing yourself. By avoiding the easy habit of repeating the same old paragraph pattern time after time, you can keep your writing fresh and interesting.

USING TECHNOLOGY TO COMPOSE AND SHAPE YOUR MESSAGES

Communication Solution

Algenix takes advantage of electronic communication technology with an interactive, web-based tutorial that shows potential patients how the bioartificial liver works.

As with every phase of business communication, careful use of technology can help you compose and shape better messages in less time. You're likely to use a variety of electronic tools to compose messages: software for creating regular web content that constitutes the bulk of most websites, *web logs* or *blogs* for frequently updated web postings, instant messaging (IM) for brief exchanges and support for online meetings, and e-mail and word processing for lengthier messages. You read about effective IM in Chapter 2, Chapter 6 highlights some of the ways blogs are being used to distribute business messages, and you can read about effective blog and web content development at www.prenhall.com/bovee. The following sections offer advice on crafting effective e-mail messages and using your word processors formatting features to full advantage.

Composing Effective E-Mail Messages

Even though e-mail messages may seem transitory, attention to detail is just as important for these messages as for any other type of business message. In addition to the principles and techniques already discussed in this chapter, remember to consider a few additional points when writing e-mail messages.

E-mail messages need as much care and attention as other business messages.

Following Company Guidelines—and Common Sense

Organizations need their employees to use e-mail in a responsible, businesslike manner. Thus, many companies actually train their employees in e-mail use. At the very least, most organizations develop e-mail guidelines to help you reduce unnecessary communication and confusion. Typical e-mail guidelines include the following:

Follow your company's e-mail guidelines, but use common sense, too.

- **Restrict e-mail usage to appropriate content.** In most organizations, e-mail is used for sharing information such as goals, schedules, research, company news, and the like. An electronic message is not the medium for delivering tragic news or for disciplining people. Such messages should be reserved for personal meetings.
- **Avoid sending personal messages at work.** In countless incidents, employees have been dismissed for sending personal e-mail—messages that criticize their company, discuss starting a new business, or mention a new position with another company. Moreover, many companies now archive all e-mail; therefore, that ill-considered message you zap out in a careless moment might live for a long time—whether personal or business related.
- **Respect the chain of command.** In many companies, any employee can e-mail anyone else, including the president and CEO. However, take care that you don't abuse this freedom. For instance, when corresponding with superiors, don't send an e-mail complaint straight to the top just because it's easy to do so. Your e-mail will usually be more effective if you follow the organizational hierarchy and give each person a chance to address the situation in turn.
- **Pay attention to e-mail hygiene.** *E-mail hygiene* refers to all the efforts that companies are making to keep e-mail clean and safe—from spam blocking and virus protection to content filtering.[16] Make sure you understand what your employer expects from you, and follow those guidelines. For example, to reduce the chances that spammers can find company e-mail addresses, some companies no longer put employee e-mail addresses on their websites.

Of course, company policies can't cover every aspect of e-mail or every situation. The extraordinary ease of e-mail is also its greatest potential shortcoming: it's far too easy to send too many needless messages. How many people would send jokes and photos around the company if they had to walk to the photocopier every time? Think twice before you create new messages, and think three times before you forward any. The things that annoy your recipients are the same things you find annoying—jokes, vacation photos, messages that have been forwarded so many times they have multiple screens full of useless header information, messages you've already read five times, angry complaints full of inappropriate language—so don't contribute to the problem. Let common sense be your guide.

Keep your emotions under control when creating and responding to e-mail.

Finally, never let your emotions get the best of you when you're composing e-mail. A message that contains insensitive, insulting, or critical comments is called a *flame*. If you're upset about something or angry with someone, compose yourself before composing your e-mail. If you're fuming, cool off before writing your e-mail message. If you do write an emotionally charged message, let it sit for at least a day. Ask yourself, "Would I say this to my audience face to face?" Remember that a live person is on the receiving end of your communication—and that your message can be forwarded easily and stored forever.

Arranging Your E-Mail Messages

Help your readers by including relevant parts of the original message in your response.

If you are responding to a question or a request for information, be sure to start your e-mail by inserting the original question into your reply. You can set most e-mail software packages to automatically include the sender's original message in your e-mail replies and forwards. Or you can cut and paste the message yourself. Either way, use this feature with care. You can save the reader time by editing the original message to include only the information that is directly applicable to your reply. In other words, include enough of the original message to refresh your audience's memory as to why you are sending the e-mail and how it addresses their specific needs.

If you are initiating a request for information, you might state the type of response you need or even ask for that response in your subject line. Then in the body of your message, if you state your request in a series of organized (perhaps numbered) questions, be sure to keep your questions simple. Restate compound requests into several single topics, and if possible, word them so that your audience can respond with a simple yes or no answer.

Finally, try to limit e-mail to one screen; otherwise, write like a reporter—starting with the "headline" and adding detail in descending order of importance.[17] That way you'll be sure to get your point across as early as possible, in case your reader doesn't have the time or interest to finish reading your message.

Adapting Your E-Mail Messages

Adjust the level of formality to your audience and the situation.

6 LEARNING OBJECTIVE

Discuss the importance of effective e-mail subject lines and explain how to write them

E-mail can be as informal and casual as a conversation between old friends. But it can also emulate "snail mail" by using conventional business language, a respectful style, and a more formal format—such as a traditional greeting, formalized headings, and a formal closing and signature.[18] As with any business communication, how formal you make your message depends on your audience and your purpose. Whatever level of formality you decide to use, be sure to include an informative subject line and to make your message personal.

Making E-Mail Subject Lines Effective An effective subject line is one of the most important parts of every e-mail message. When receivers look through their in-box to decide which messages to read and which of those to read first, they look at who sent each message, they check the subject lines, and they may even scan the first screen. A message with a blank subject line or a general subject line such as "Question" will probably go unread and will perhaps be deleted if the receiver doesn't know you.[19]

To capture your audience's attention, make sure your subject line is both informative and compelling. Do more than just describe or classify message content. Use the opportunity to build interest with key words, quotations, directions, or questions:[20]

INEFFECTIVE SUBJECT LINE	EFFECTIVE SUBJECT LINE
July sales figures	Send figures for July sales
Tomorrow's meeting	Bring consultant's report to Friday's meeting

Marketing report	Need budget for marketing report
Employee parking	Revised resurfacing schedule for parking lot
Status report	Warehouse remodeling is on schedule

If you are exchanging multiple e-mails with someone on the same topic, be sure to periodically modify the subject line of your message to reflect the revised message content. Most e-mail programs will copy the subject line when you click on Reply, so you need only revise it. When numerous messages have identical subject lines, trying to find a particular one can be confusing and frustrating. Moreover, some messages sharing the same subject line may actually have absolutely nothing to do with the original topic. Modifying the subject line with each new response will save you time and make it easier to locate a message at a later date.

Personalizing Your E-Mail Messages Adding a greeting to your e-mail message makes it more personal. Naturally, whether you use a formal greeting (*Dear Professor Ingersol*) or a more casual one (*Hi Marty*) depends on your audience and your purpose. Your closing and signature also personalize your e-mail message. In most cases, use simple closings, such as *Thanks* or *Regards,* rather than more traditional business closings such as *Sincerely yours.* However, you may want to use a more formal closing for international e-mail.

Use a greeting to make your e-mail more personal.

For your signature, you can simply type your name on a separate line. Or you may want to use a *signature file,* a short identifier that can include your name, company, postal address, fax number, other e-mail addresses, and sometimes the company's slogan or tagline. Once you create a signature file, you can save it in your mail program and add it to e-mail messages without retyping it. You can also use a digital copy of your handwritten signature, which is becoming acceptable as legal proof in business transactions, especially when accompanied by a date stamp, which is automatically inserted by your mail program.

Use a signature file to provide additional contact options.

Formatting Your E-Mail Messages

Most corporate e-mail systems have moved beyond plain text, giving you multiple options for fonts (complete sets of characters in a particular size and style of type), colors, bullet lists, and so on. Many even offer full HTML formatting, so you can send e-mail messages that are as extensively formatted as web pages. However, except for formal messages to external audiences (such as newsletters or marketing messages), most people don't expect anything beyond basic formatting. Also, some systems don't accept HTML formatting, so your message won't come through as you expect it to.

Unless you're preparing a company newsletter for customers or some other formal marketing message, then, stick with basic formatting. Use bulleted and numbered lists if needed, and perhaps use boldface or italics to emphasize headings and subheadings, but don't bother getting much fancier than that. Your e-mail audience wants information quickly and easily; they're not interested in your design skills.

For everyday messages, keep formatting simple and clear.

Some e-mail old-timers insist that spelling, grammar, capitalization, and punctuation are less important for e-mail than they are for printed messages.[21] But in business communication, e-mail needs to be as clear and as easy to understand as possible. So be sure to use correct spelling and proper grammar in these electronic messages:

- **Use proper capitalization.** Typing in all caps is considered shouting, and doing so brands you as a "newbie." At the other extreme, avoiding capital letters entirely is too informal for many business messages.
- **Use acronyms sparingly.** Your close colleagues might know that "IMHO" stands for "in my humble opinion," but important customers or nonnative English speakers might not. (By the way, if you need to decode an acronym that you don't know, simply search for "acronym dictionary" in any search engine and you'll probably find what you need.)
- **Use emoticons carefully.** Expressive characters such as the common smiley face are called *emoticons,* and they need to be used with care. Some people view them as unprofessional; however, between colleagues, emoticons can help overcome the emotional sterility of the medium and help avoid misunderstandings.

FIGURE 5.3 Ineffective E-Mail Message

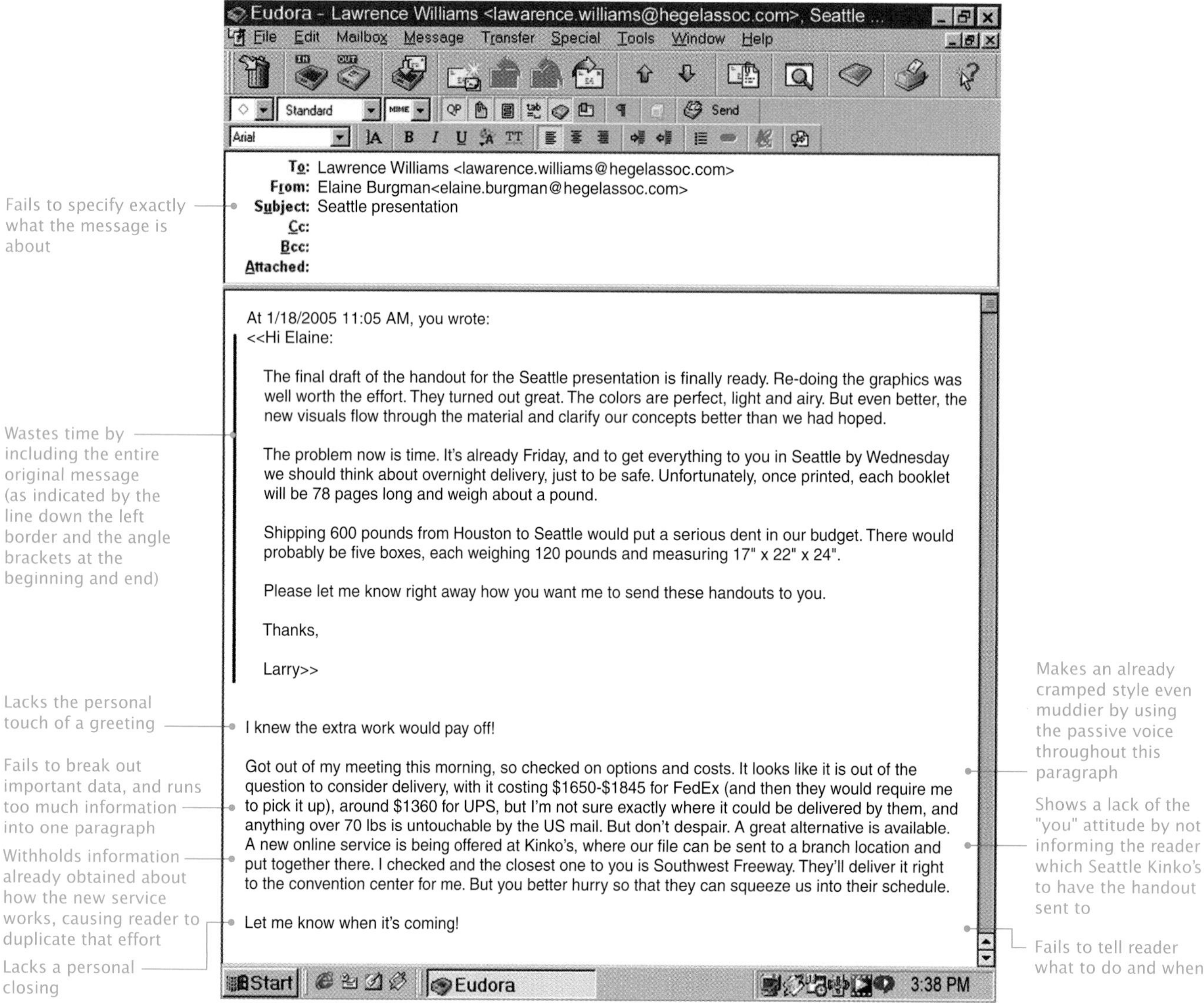

Eudora - Lawrence Williams <lawarence.williams@hegelassoc.com>, Seattle ...

File Edit Mailbox Message Transfer Special Tools Window Help

To: Lawrence Williams <lawarence.williams@hegelassoc.com>
From: Elaine Burgman<elaine.burgman@hegelassoc.com>
Subject: Seattle presentation
Cc:
Bcc:
Attached:

At 1/18/2005 11:05 AM, you wrote:
<<Hi Elaine:

The final draft of the handout for the Seattle presentation is finally ready. Re-doing the graphics was well worth the effort. They turned out great. The colors are perfect, light and airy. But even better, the new visuals flow through the material and clarify our concepts better than we had hoped.

The problem now is time. It's already Friday, and to get everything to you in Seattle by Wednesday we should think about overnight delivery, just to be safe. Unfortunately, once printed, each booklet will be 78 pages long and weigh about a pound.

Shipping 600 pounds from Houston to Seattle would put a serious dent in our budget. There would probably be five boxes, each weighing 120 pounds and measuring 17" x 22" x 24".

Please let me know right away how you want me to send these handouts to you.

Thanks,

Larry>>

I knew the extra work would pay off!

Got out of my meeting this morning, so checked on options and costs. It looks like it is out of the question to consider delivery, with it costing $1650-$1845 for FedEx (and then they would require me to pick it up), around $1360 for UPS, but I'm not sure exactly where it could be delivered by them, and anything over 70 lbs is untouchable by the US mail. But don't despair. A great alternative is available. A new online service is being offered at Kinko's, where our file can be sent to a branch location and put together there. I checked and the closest one to you is Southwest Freeway. They'll deliver it right to the convention center for me. But you better hurry so that they can squeeze us into their schedule.

Let me know when it's coming!

Start Eudora 3:38 PM

Fails to specify exactly what the message is about
Wastes time by including the entire original message (as indicated by the line down the left border and the angle brackets at the beginning and end)
Lacks the personal touch of a greeting
Fails to break out important data, and runs too much information into one paragraph
Withholds information already obtained about how the new service works, causing reader to duplicate that effort
Lacks a personal closing
Makes an already cramped style even muddier by using the passive voice throughout this paragraph
Shows a lack of the "you" attitude by not informing the reader which Seattle Kinko's to have the handout sent to
Fails to tell reader what to do and when

To see these principles in action, compare and contrast Figures 5.3 and 5.4. Pay close attention to the subject line, organization, word choice, tone, and sentence structure used in each e-mail message.

Shaping Your Documents with Word Processing Tools

Take full advantage of your word processor's formatting capabilities to help you produce effective, professional documents in less time.

As you probably know, today's word processing software provides a wide range of tools to help writers compose documents. Most of these tools take care of the "housekeeping chores" often associated with business document preparation, allowing you to focus on the creative aspects of writing. If you're not aware of all these capabilities in your word processing software, spend a few minutes with them to see how they can help:

- **Style sheets.** Most word processors offer some form of style sheets, which are master lists of predefined styles for headlines, paragraph text, and so on. Many organizations provide employees with approved style sheets to ensure a consistent look for all company documents. Style sheets can eliminate hours of design time by making many of your choices for you.
- **Templates.** A template provides standardization on a larger scale, defining such factors as page design, available fonts, and other features. Templates can include *boilerplate,* sections of text that are reused from document to document. For example, the last

FIGURE 5.4 Effective E-Mail Message

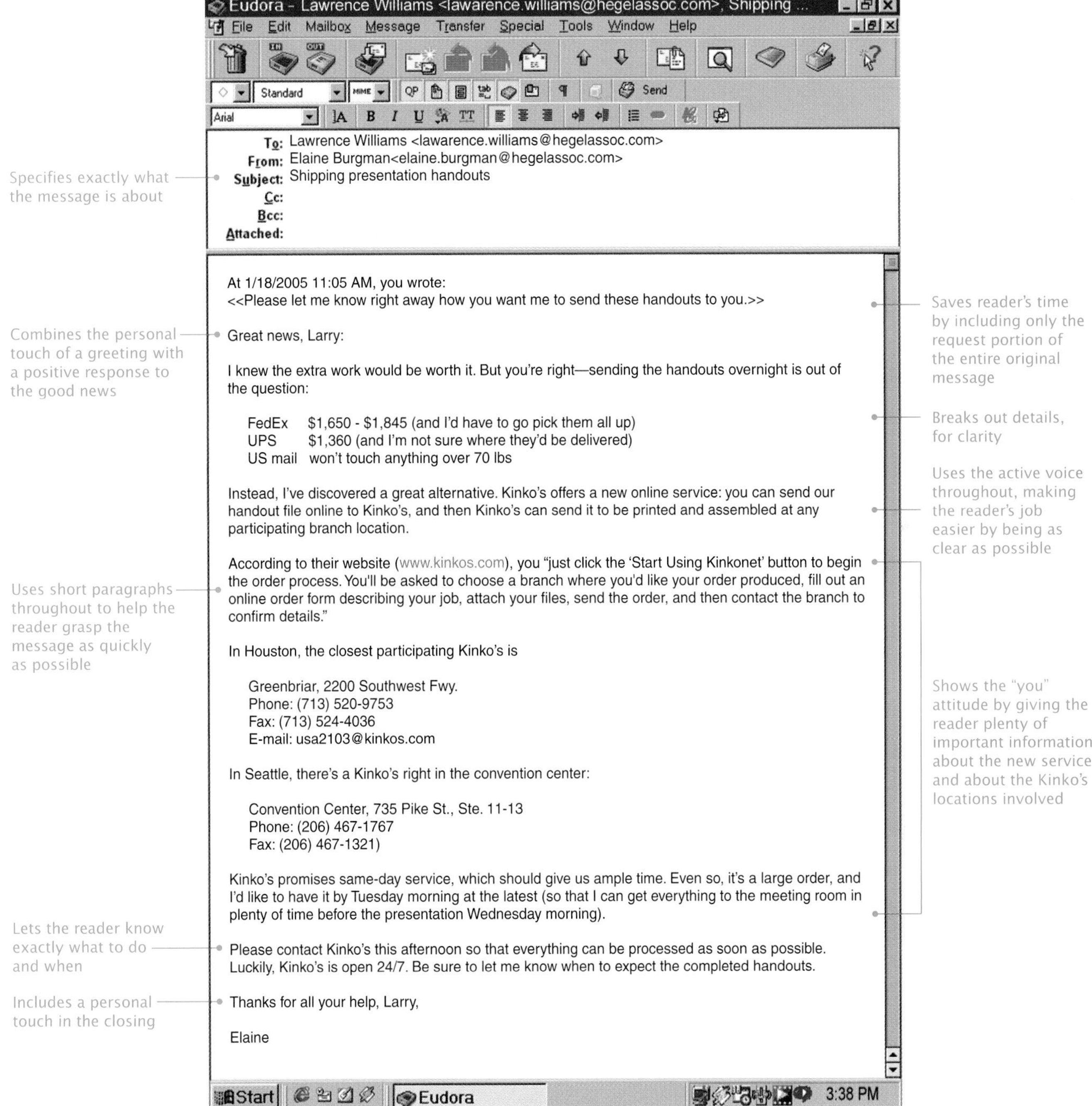

Eudora - Lawrence Williams <lawarence.williams@hegelassoc.com>, Shipping ...

To: Lawrence Williams <lawarence.williams@hegelassoc.com>
From: Elaine Burgman<elaine.burgman@hegelassoc.com>
Subject: Shipping presentation handouts
Cc:
Bcc:
Attached:

At 1/18/2005 11:05 AM, you wrote:
<<Please let me know right away how you want me to send these handouts to you.>>

Great news, Larry:

I knew the extra work would be worth it. But you're right—sending the handouts overnight is out of the question:

FedEx $1,650 - $1,845 (and I'd have to go pick them all up)
UPS $1,360 (and I'm not sure where they'd be delivered)
US mail won't touch anything over 70 lbs

Instead, I've discovered a great alternative. Kinko's offers a new online service: you can send our handout file online to Kinko's, and then Kinko's can send it to be printed and assembled at any participating branch location.

According to their website (www.kinkos.com), you "just click the 'Start Using Kinkonet' button to begin the order process. You'll be asked to choose a branch where you'd like your order produced, fill out an online order form describing your job, attach your files, send the order, and then contact the branch to confirm details."

In Houston, the closest participating Kinko's is

Greenbriar, 2200 Southwest Fwy.
Phone: (713) 520-9753
Fax: (713) 524-4036
E-mail: usa2103@kinkos.com

In Seattle, there's a Kinko's right in the convention center:

Convention Center, 735 Pike St., Ste. 11-13
Phone: (206) 467-1767
Fax: (206) 467-1321)

Kinko's promises same-day service, which should give us ample time. Even so, it's a large order, and I'd like to have it by Tuesday morning at the latest (so that I can get everything to the meeting room in plenty of time before the presentation Wednesday morning).

Please contact Kinko's this afternoon so that everything can be processed as soon as possible. Luckily, Kinko's is open 24/7. Be sure to let me know when to expect the completed handouts.

Thanks for all your help, Larry,

Elaine

paragraph of a press release is commonly boilerplate, providing a standard message regarding the company's background. Like style sheets, templates save you time by making choices for you in advance.

- **Autocompletion.** Software called *autocompletion* (or something similar) inserts a ready-made block of text when you type the first few characters. For example, instead of typing your company's name, address, phone number, fax number, e-mail address, and website URL, you can set the software to enter all this information as soon as you type the first three letters of the company name. This feature also reduces the chance of typos.
- **Autocorrection.** Another automatic feature in some programs instantly corrects spelling and typing errors and converts text to symbols, such as converting (c) to the © copyright symbol. Also, autocorrection may make changes that you *don't* want made, such as converting "nd," "st," or "th" to superscript characters when paired with numbers, as in

CHECKLIST: Writing Business Messages

A. ADAPT TO YOUR AUDIENCE
- Use the "you" attitude.
- Maintain good etiquette through polite communication.
- Emphasize the positive whenever possible.
- Use bias-free language.
- Establish your credibility in the eyes of your audience.
- Project your company's preferred image.
- Use a conversational but still professional and respectful tone.
- Use plain English for clarity.

B. COMPOSE YOUR MESSAGE
- Choose strong words that communicate efficiently.
- Make sure you use functional and content words correctly.
- Pay attention to the connotative meaning of your words.
- Balance abstract and concrete terms to convey your meaning accurately.
- Avoid clichés.
- Use jargon only when your audience understands it and prefers it.
- Vary your sentence structure for impact and interest.
- Develop coherent, unified paragraphs.
- Use transitional elements generously to help your audience follow your message.

"21st century." (Although this is common in word processing, many design professionals consider it poor typesetting.) In addition, depending on autocorrection to take care of your spelling errors can be risky. This feature catches only the most common typing mistakes. Plus, the autocorrection feature for your e-mail might have different capabilities from the one for your instant messaging system, so the two may not catch the same mistakes.

- **File merge, mail merge.** Today's software makes it easy to combine files—an especially handy feature when several members of a team write different sections of a report. For particularly complex reports, you can set up a master document that merges a number of subdocuments automatically when it's time to print. *Mail merge* lets you personalize form letters by inserting names and addresses from a database.
- **Endnotes, footnotes, indexes, and tables of contents.** Your computer can also help you track footnotes and endnotes, renumbering them every time you add or delete references. For a report's indexes and table of contents, you can simply flag the items you want to include, and the software assembles the lists for you.
- **Wizards.** Programs such as Microsoft Word offer *wizards* that step you through the process of creating letters, résumés, and other common documents. You still need to provide the content and perform the writing, of course, but the wizards can be helpful reminders of the various elements you need to include in the document.

As with every other communication technology, using these tools efficiently and effectively requires some balance. You need to learn enough about the features to be handy with them, without spending so much time that the tools distract the writing process. Chances are somebody in your organization has already figured out the feature you're trying to use and can offer advice.

For a reminder of the tasks involved in writing your messages, see "Checklist: Writing Business Messages."

COMMUNICATION CHALLENGES AT ALGENIX

To attract participants for a new clinical study, Algenix is expanding its recruiting efforts and plans to contact doctors directly. The company will send a marketing letter to members of the American Gastroenterological Association. (Gastroenterologists are the doctors who specialize in diseases of the digestive system, which includes the liver.)

Individual Challenge: You are a member of the Algenix marketing team, and you work with Dr. Timothy D. Sielaff, the principal investigator for the clinical study. He has asked you to draft the letter to doctors and has specified four things it must do: introduce the bioartificial liver and its main benefits, describe the clinical testing program, outline the ideal types of patients for the clinical study, and provide information that builds confidence in the company. You've completed the planning stage and are now sitting down to write the letter. Considering the audience you're addressing, what steps should you take to demonstrate sensitivity to audience needs? How can you use the letter to build a strong relationship with your audience? What style and tone are most appropriate for this letter? Write your thoughts in a brief e-mail to your instructor.

Team Challenge: In a small group, discuss the value of using jargon—and the importance of using it correctly—when one professional is communicating with another. Dr. Sielaff asks for a companion letter that will go to patients; how much jargon should that letter contain? Why? What style and tone will be most appropriate in a letter to patients? Summarize your team's conclusions in less than one page.

SUMMARY OF LEARNING OBJECTIVES

1 **Explain the importance of adapting your messages to the needs and expectations of your audience.** By adapting your communication to the needs and expectations of your audience, you provide more compelling answers to their questions and improve the chances that your messages will be received successfully. If your intended audience thinks a message does not apply to them or does not offer them anything useful or interesting, they'll be far less inclined to pay attention to it.

2 **Discuss four ways of achieving a businesslike style that is clear and concise.** To ensure that messages are businesslike, clear, and concise, start by using a conversational tone: avoid obsolete and pompous language, avoid preaching and bragging, avoid intimacy unless you have a close relationship with the audience, and use humor with great care. Support this conversational tone by using plain English, which is easily understood by anyone with an eighth- or ninth-grade education. Then select the best voice for your message. Use the active voice to emphasize the subject of the message and to produce shorter, stronger sentences; use the passive voice to be diplomatic, to avoid taking credit or placing blame, and to create an objective tone.

3 **Briefly describe how to select words that are not only correct but also effective.** To select the best words, first make sure they are correct by checking grammar and usage guides. Next, make sure they are effective by knowing how to use functional and content words. Choose words that have fewer connotations (to reduce the chance of misinterpretation) and no negative connotations (to reduce the chance of offending your audience). Blend abstract words with concrete ones, narrowing from the general to the specific, and select words that communicate clearly, specifically, and dynamically. Choose words that are strong, choose words that are familiar, avoid clichés, and use jargon only when your audience will understand it.

4 **Explain how sentence style affects emphasis within your message.** The order and placement of words within each sentence affects the emphasis your audience perceives. You can employ the following techniques to focus emphasis on specific parts of the sentence: give the idea the most emphasis by dedicating more words to it, add an additional sentence to clarify the key idea from the first sentence, or put the key idea at either the beginning or the end of the sentence.

5 **List five ways to develop coherent paragraphs.** Paragraphs can be developed by illustration (giving examples), by comparison and contrast (pointing out similarities or differences), by focusing on cause and effect (giving reasons), by classification (discussing categories), and by focusing on the solution to a problem (stating a problem and showing how to solve it).

6 **Discuss the importance of effective e-mail subject lines and explain how to write them.** When your e-mail message arrives in the recipient's mailbox, the subject line creates the first impression. E-mail subject lines can make the difference between a message being read right away, skipped over for later attention, or ignored entirely. To capture your audience's attention, make your subject line both informative and compelling. Go beyond simply identifying the content of the message by using key words, quotations, directions, or questions.

Test Your Knowledge

1. What is the "you" attitude and how does it differ from an "I" attitude?
2. Why is it important to establish your credibility when communicating with an audience of strangers?
3. How does using bias-free language help communicators establish a good relationship with their audiences?
4. How does the denotative meaning of a word differ from its connotative meaning?
5. What is style, and how do you decide on the appropriate style for a message?
6. How does an abstract word differ from a concrete word?
7. In what three situations is passive voice appropriate?
8. What is the purpose of the topic sentence?
9. What functions do transitions serve?
10. How do you use the subject line in an e-mail?

Apply Your Knowledge

1. How can you apply the "you" approach when you don't know your audience personally?
2. When composing business messages, how can you be yourself and project your company's image at the same time?
3. What steps can you take to make abstract concepts such as *opportunity* feel more concrete in your messages?
4. Considering how fast and easy it is, should e-mail replace meetings and other face-to-face communication in your company? Why or why not?
5. **Ethical Choices** One of the most unpleasant tasks in your role as human resources manager is delivering bad news to unsuccessful job applicants. How can you emphasize the positives in these situations without crossing the line into unethical communication?

Practice Your Knowledge

Document for Analysis

Read the following document, then (1) analyze the strengths and weaknesses of each sentence, and (2) revise the document so that it follows this chapter's guidelines.

> I am a new publisher with some really great books to sell. I saw your announcement in *Publishers Weekly* about the booksellers' show you're having this summer, and I think it's a great idea. Count me in, folks! I would like to get some space to show my books. I thought it would be a neat thing if I could do some airbrushing on T-shirts live to help promote my hot new title, *T-Shirt Art.* Before I got into publishing, I was an airbrush artist, and I could demonstrate my techniques. I've done hundreds of advertising illustrations and have been a sign painter all my life, so I'll also be promoting my other book, hot off the presses, *How to Make Money in the Sign Painting Business.*
>
> I will be starting my PR campaign about May 2005 with ads in *PW* and some art trade papers, so my books should be well known by the time the show comes around in August. In case you would like to use my appearance there as part of your publicity, I have enclosed a biography and photo of myself.
>
> P.S. Please let me know what it costs for booth space as soon as possible so that I can figure out whether I can afford to attend. Being a new publisher is mighty expensive!

Exercises

For live links to all websites discussed in this chapter, visit this text's website at www.prenhall.com/bovee. Just log on, select Chapter 5, and click on "Featured Websites." Locate the page or the URL related to the material in the text.

5.1 **Audience Relationship: Courteous Communication** Substitute a better phrase for each of the following:

- **a.** You claim that
- **b.** It is not our policy to
- **c.** You neglected to
- **d.** In which you assert
- **e.** We are sorry you are dissatisfied
- **f.** You failed to enclose
- **g.** We request that you send us
- **h.** Apparently you overlooked our terms
- **i.** We have been very patient
- **j.** We are at a loss to understand

5.2 **Audience Relationship: The "You" Attitude** Rewrite these sentences to reflect your audience's viewpoint.

- **a.** Your e-mail order cannot be processed; we request that you use the order form on our website instead.
- **b.** We insist that you always bring your credit card to the store.
- **c.** We want to get rid of all our CRT monitors to make room in our warehouse for the new LCD flat screen monitors. Thus we are offering a 25 percent discount on all sales this week.
- **d.** I am applying for the position of bookkeeper in your office. I feel my grades prove that I am bright and capable, and I think I can do a good job for you.
- **e.** As requested, we are sending the refund for $25.

5.3 **Audience Relationship: Emphasize the Positive** Revise these sentences to be positive rather than negative.

- **a.** To avoid the loss of your credit rating, please remit payment within 10 days.
- **b.** We don't make refunds on returned merchandise that is soiled.
- **c.** Because we are temporarily out of Baby Cry dolls, we won't be able to ship your order for 10 days.
- **d.** You failed to specify the color of the blouse that you ordered.
- **e.** You should have realized that waterbeds will freeze in unheated houses during winter. Therefore, our guarantee does not cover the valve damage, and you must pay the $9.50 valve-replacement fee (plus postage).

5.4 **Audience Relationship: Emphasize the Positive** Provide euphemisms for the following words and phrases:

- **a.** Stubborn
- **b.** Wrong

c. Stupid
d. Incompetent
e. Loudmouth

5.5 **Audience Relationship: Bias-Free Language** Rewrite each of the following to eliminate bias:
a. For an Indian, Maggie certainly is outgoing.
b. He needs a wheelchair, but he doesn't let his handicap affect his job performance.
c. A pilot must have the ability to stay calm under pressure, and then he must be trained to cope with any problem that arises.
d. Candidate Renata Parsons, married and the mother of a teenager, will attend the debate.
e. Senior citizen Sam Nugent is still an active salesman.

5.6 **Ethical Choices** Your company has been a major employer in the local community for years, but shifts in the global marketplace have forced some changes in the company's long-term direction. In fact, the company plans to reduce local staffing by as much as 50 percent over the next five to ten years, starting with a small layoff next month. The size and timing of future layoffs has not been decided, although there is little doubt more layoffs will happen at some point. In the first draft of a letter aimed at community leaders, you write that "this first layoff is part of a continuing series of staff reductions anticipated over the next several years." However, your boss is concerned about the vagueness and negative tone of the language and asks you to rewrite that sentence to read "this layoff is part of the company's ongoing efforts to continually align its resources with global market conditions." Do you think this suggested wording is ethical, given the company's economic influence in the community? Please explain your answer.

5.7 **Message Composition: Controlling Style** Rewrite the following letter to Mrs. Betty Crandall (1597 Church St., Grants Pass, OR 97526) so that it conveys a helpful, personal, and interested tone:

We have your letter of recent date to our Ms. Dobson. Owing to the fact that you neglected to include the size of the dress you ordered, please be advised that no shipment of your order was made, but the aforementioned shipment will occur at such time as we are in receipt of the aforementioned information.

5.8 **Message Composition: Selecting Words** Write a concrete phrase for each of these vague phrases:
a. Sometime this spring
b. A substantial saving
c. A large number attended
d. Increased efficiency
e. Expanded the work area
f. Flatten the website structure

5.9 **Message Composition: Selecting Words** List terms that are stronger than the following:
a. Ran after
b. Seasonal ups and downs
c. Bright
d. Suddenly rises
e. Moves forward

5.10 **Message Composition: Selecting Words** As you rewrite these sentences, replace the clichés with fresh, personal expressions:
a. Being a jack-of-all-trades, Dave worked well in his new general manager job.
b. Moving Leslie into the accounting department, where she was literally a fish out of water, was like putting a square peg into a round hole, if you get my drift.
c. I knew she was at death's door, but I thought the doctor would pull her through.
d. Movies aren't really my cup of tea; as far as I am concerned, they can't hold a candle to a good book.
e. It's a dog-eat-dog world out there in the rat race of the asphalt jungle.

5.11 **Message Composition: Selecting Words** Suggest short, simple words to replace each of the following:
a. Inaugurate
b. Terminate
c. Utilize
d. Anticipate
e. Assistance
f. Endeavor
g. Ascertain
h. Procure
i. Consummate
j. Advise
k. Alteration
l. Forwarded
m. Fabricate
n. Nevertheless
o. Substantial

5.12 **Message Composition: Selecting Words** Write up-to-date, less-stuffy versions of these phrases; write *none* if you think there is no appropriate substitute:
a. As per your instructions
b. Attached herewith
c. In lieu of
d. In reply I wish to state
e. Please be advised that

5.13 **Message Composition: Creating Sentences** Suppose that end-of-term frustrations have produced this e-mail message to Professor Anne Brewer from a student who believes he should have received a B in his accounting class. If this message were recast into three or four clear sentences, the teacher might be more receptive to the student's argument. Rewrite the message to show how you would improve it:

I think that I was unfairly awarded a C in your accounting class this term, and I am asking you to change the grade to a B. It was a difficult term. I don't get any money from home, and I have to work mornings at the Pancake House (as a cook), so I had to rush to make your class, and those two times that I missed class were because they wouldn't let me off work because of special events at the Pancake House (unlike some other students who just take off when they choose). On the midterm examination, I originally got a 75 percent, but you said in class that there were two different ways to answer the third question and that you would change the grades of students who used the "optimal cost" method and had been counted off 6 points for doing this. I don't think that you took this into account, because I got 80 percent on the final, which is clearly a B. Anyway, whatever you decide, I just want to tell you that I really enjoyed this class, and I thank you for making accounting so interesting.

5.14 **Message Composition: Creating Sentences** Rewrite each sentence so that it is active rather than passive:

a. The raw data are entered into the customer relationship management system by the sales representative each Friday.
b. High profits are publicized by management.
c. The policies announced in the directive were implemented by the staff.
d. Our computers are serviced by the Santee Company.
e. The employees were represented by Janet Hogan.

5.15 **Message Composition: Writing Paragraphs** In the following paragraph, identify the topic sentence and the related sentences (those that support the idea of the topic sentence):

Each year, McDonald's sponsors the All-American Band, made up of two high school students from each state. The band marches in Macy's Thanksgiving Day parade in New York City and the Rose Bowl Parade in Pasadena. Franchisees are urged to join their local Chamber of Commerce, United Way, American Legion, and other bastions of All-Americana. McDonald's tries hard to project an image of almost a charitable organization. Local outlets sponsor campaigns on fire prevention, bicycle safety, and litter cleanup, with advice from Hamburger Central on how to extract the most publicity from their efforts.[22]

Now add a topic sentence to this paragraph:

Our analysis of the customer experience should start before golfers even drive through the front gate here at Glencoe Meadows; it should start when they phone in or log onto our website to reserve tee times. When they do arrive, the first few stages in the process are also vital: the condition of the grounds leading up to the club house, the reception they receive when they drop off their clubs, and the ease of parking. From that point, how well are we doing with check-in at the pro shop, openings at the driving range, and timely scheduling at the first tee? Then there's everything associated with playing the course itself and returning to the club house at the end of the round.

5.16 **Teamwork** Working with four other students, divide the following five topics among yourselves and each write one paragraph on his or her selected topic. Be sure each student uses a different technique when writing his or her paragraph: One student should use the illustration technique, one the comparison or contrast technique, one a discussion of cause and effect, one the classification technique, and one a discussion of problem and solution. Then exchange paragraphs within the team and pick out the main idea and general purpose of the paragraph one of your teammates wrote. Was everyone able to correctly identify the main idea and purpose? If not, suggest how the paragraph might be rewritten for clarity.

a. Types of digital cameras (or dogs or automobiles) available for sale
b. Advantages and disadvantages of eating at fast-food restaurants
c. Finding that first full-time job
d. Good qualities of my car (or house, or apartment, or neighborhood)
e. How to make a dessert recipe (or barbecue a steak or make coffee)

5.17 **Internet** Visit the Security Exchange Commission's (SEC) plain-English website at www.sec.gov, click on "Online Publications," and review the online handbook. In one or two sentences, summarize what the SEC means by the phrase "plain English." Now read the SEC's online advice about how to invest in mutual funds. Does this document follow the SEC's plain-English guidelines? Can you suggest any improvements to organization, words, sentences, or paragraphs?

5.18 **Message Organization: Transitional Elements** Add transitional elements to the following sentences to improve the flow of ideas. (Note: You may need to eliminate or add some words to smooth out your sentences.)

a. Steve Case saw infinite possibilities in online business. Steve Case was determined to turn his vision into reality. The techies scoffed at his strategy of building a simple Internet service for ordinary people. Case doggedly pursued his dream. He analyzed other online services. He assessed the needs of his customers. He responded to their desires for an easier way to access information over the Internet. In 1992, Steve Case named his company America Online (AOL). Critics predicted the company's demise. By the end of the century, AOL was a profitable powerhouse.
b. Facing some of the toughest competitors in the world, Harley-Davidson had to make some changes. The company introduced new products. Harley's management team set out to rebuild the company's production process. New products were coming to market and the company was turning a profit. Harley's quality standards were not on par with those of its foreign competitors. Harley's costs were still among the highest in the industry. Harley made a U-turn and restructured the company's organizational structure. Harley's efforts have paid off.
c. Whether you're indulging in a doughnut in New York or California, Krispy Kreme wants you to enjoy the same delicious taste with every bite. The company maintains consistent product quality by carefully controlling every step of the production process. Krispy Kreme tests all raw ingredients against established quality standards. Every delivery of wheat flour is sampled and measured for its moisture content and protein levels. Krispy Kreme blends the ingredients. Krispy Kreme tests the doughnut mix for quality. Krispy

Kreme delivers the mix to its stores. Krispy Kreme knows that it takes more than a quality mix to produce perfect doughnuts all the time. The company supplies its stores with everything they need to produce premium doughnuts—mix, icings, fillings, equipment—you name it.

5.19 **Ethical Choices** Under what circumstances would you consider the use of terms that are high in connotative meaning to be ethical? When would you consider it to be unethical? Explain your reasoning.

Expand Your Knowledge

For live links to the websites that follow, go to www.prenhall.com/bovee. When you log on, select Chapter 5, then select "Featured Websites," click on the URL of the website you wish to visit, and review the website to complete these exercises.

Exploring the Best of the Web

Compose a Better Business Message
http://owl.english.purdue.edu
At Purdue University's Online Writing Lab (OWL), you'll find tools to help you improve your business messages. For advice on composing written messages, for help with grammar, and for referrals to other information sources, you'd be wise to visit this site. Purdue's OWL offers online services and an introduction to Internet search tools. You can also download a variety of handouts on writing skills. Check out the resources at the OWL homepage, then answer the following questions:

1. Explain why positive wording in a message is more effective than negative wording. Why should you be concerned about the position of good news or bad news in your written message?
2. What six factors of tone should you consider when conveying your message to your audience?
3. What points should you include in the close of your business message? Why?

Exploring the Web on Your Own

Review these chapter-related websites on your own to learn more about writing business messages.

1. Write it right by paying attention to these writing tips, grammar pointers, style suggestions, and reference sources at www.webgrammar.com.
2. Can't find the right word to use when writing about specialized topics? Check out one of the hundreds of subject-area glossaries available at www.glossarist.com.
3. Maximize your e-mail effectiveness by visiting A Beginner's Guide to Effective E-Mail, www.webfoot.com/advice/email.top.html.

Learn Interactively

Interactive Study Guide

Go to the Companion Website at www.prenhall.com/bovee. For Chapter 5, take advantage of the interactive "Study Guide" to test your knowledge of the chapter. Get instant feedback on whether you need additional studying.

Also, visit this site's "Study Hall," where you'll find an abundance of valuable resources that will help you succeed in this course.

Peak Performance Grammar and Mechanics

In Chapter 4 you were referred to the Peak Performance Grammar and Mechanics activities on the web at www.prenhall.com/onekey to improve your skill with adjectives and adverbs. For additional reinforcement in adverbs, go to www.prenhall.com/bovee, where you will find "Improve Your Grammar, Mechanics, and Usage" exercises.

chapter 6

Completing Business Messages

LEARNING OBJECTIVES

After studying this chapter, you will be able to

1. Discuss the value of careful revision and list the main tasks involved in completing a business message
2. List four writing techniques you can use to improve the readability of your messages
3. Describe the steps you can take to improve the clarity of your writing
4. Discuss why it's important to make your message more concise and give four tips on how to do so
5. Explain how design elements help determine the effectiveness of your documents
6. Highlight the types of errors to look for when proofreading
7. Discuss the most important issues to consider when distributing your messages

COMMUNICATION CLOSE-UP AT ROLLING STONE

www.rollingstone.com

The next time you pick up your favorite magazine, don't read it. Instead, flip through the pages and look at the design and presentation. What kinds of fonts are used for headlines and text? How many photos or illustrations appear with each article? How is color used? In all, how easy is it to read? Editors and designers use such design elements to connect with their readers and create the overall style of a magazine. *Rolling Stone* magazine is a classic example.

Born in the 1960s in San Francisco, *Rolling Stone* has remained relevant for decades because publisher and founder Jann Wenner has made dozens of changes over the years. The most recent makeover occurred in 2002. During the first half of that year, *Rolling Stone*'s newsstand sales fell 15 percent as newer magazines such as *Blender*, *FHM*, *Maxim,* and *Spin* gained popularity.

In response, Wenner wanted to make his magazine more relevant and more appealing to its target audience—without losing its core focus on music and culture. He started by hiring an editor from *FHM* and asking him to update the magazine's look, tone, and personality. The result was a major redesign that touched every aspect: cover logo, photography, article length, music reviews, and more.

Founder Jann Wenner has kept *Rolling Stone* on the cutting edge of culture with topical content and contemporary design.

"We're responding to an overall change in the media landscape and an overall change in the way people use and consume media," explained Wenner. Once again, *Rolling Stone* gathered no moss: Within a few months, its circulation figures were on the rise once again. By applying the same kind of attention to audience needs and design details, you can make your business messages more relevant and appealing, too.[1]

MOVING BEYOND YOUR FIRST DRAFT

First drafts are rarely as effective as they could be.

Once you've completed the first draft of your message, you may be tempted to breathe a sigh of relief and go on to the next project. Resist the temptation. Professional communicators like Jann Wenner recognize that the first draft is rarely good enough. Even if you successfully express the intended content of the message—which often isn't the case—the first draft is rarely as tight, clear, and compelling as it needs to be. You owe it to yourself and to your audience to review and refine your messages before producing and distributing them. In fact, many writing authorities suggest that when you revise a document, you go over it several times: one pass for content, organization, style, and tone; one for readability; and one for clarity and conciseness.

Look back at the diagram of the three-step writing process (Figure 4.1 on page 88). Completing your message consists of four tasks: not only revising your message but also producing, proofreading, and distributing it. As Figure 6.1 shows, you perform these tasks in top-down order—addressing the document as a whole before looking at details. Focusing on the big picture first is more efficient, since you won't be wasting time perfecting sections that you may eventually eliminate or change substantially.

1 LEARNING OBJECTIVE

Discuss the value of careful revision, and list the main tasks involved in completing a business message

You might wonder whether all this effort to fine-tune a message is worthwhile. If your message is a quick e-mail inviting your project team to lunch, you obviously wouldn't spend hours crafting and polishing it. But successful businesspeople care very much about saying precisely the right thing in precisely the right way. Their willingness to go over the same document several times shows just how important it is to communicate effectively.[2]

REVISING YOUR MESSAGE

Revision is a continual process for most writers.

Although the tendency is to separate revision from composition, revision is an ongoing activity that occurs throughout the writing process. You revise as you go along; then after you've completed the first draft, you revise again. You constantly search for the best way to

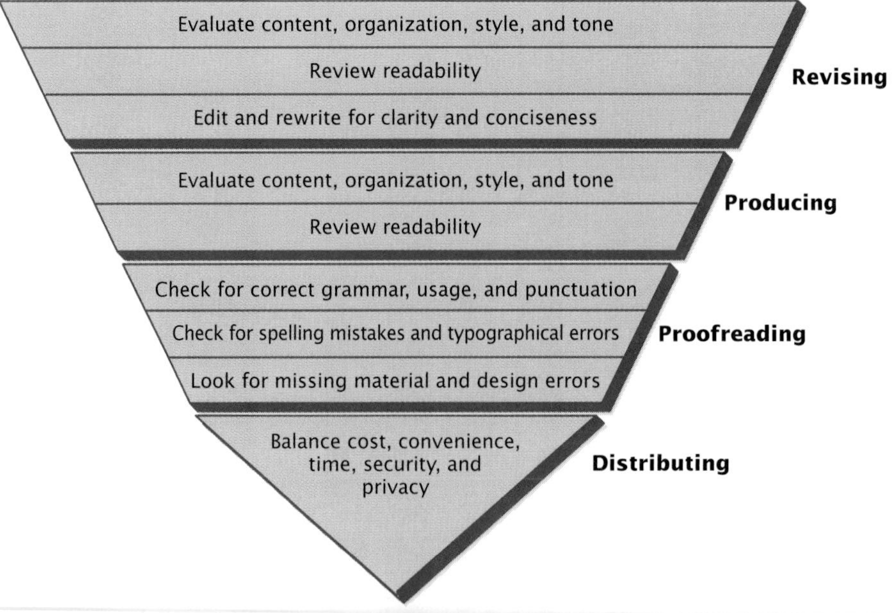

FIGURE 6.1
Completing Business Messages

say something, probing for the right words, testing alternative sentences, reshaping, tightening, and juggling elements that already exist. Ideally, you should put your draft aside for a day or two before you begin the revision process so that you can approach the material with a fresh eye. Then read through the document quickly to evaluate its overall effectiveness before moving to finer points such as readability, clarity, and conciseness.

If you have time, put your draft aside for a day or two before you begin the revision process.

As you complete the tasks shown in Figure 6.1, you'll find yourself rewriting sentences, passages, and even whole sections to improve their effectiveness. Of course, you're probably also facing a deadline, so try to stick to the schedule you set during the planning stage of the project. Do your best to revise and rewrite thoroughly but also economically. With a minimal amount of rewriting, you'll end up with a stronger document.

Look closely at Figure 6.2, the draft of a letter responding to Louise Wilson's request for information about the frequent-guest program at the Commerce Hotel. The draft has been edited using the proofreading marks shown in Appendix C. Now review the letter in Figure 6.3, which incorporates all the revisions. As you can see, Figure 6.3 provides the requested information more clearly, in a more organized fashion, with a friendlier style, and with precise mechanics.

FIGURE 6.2 Sample Edited Letter

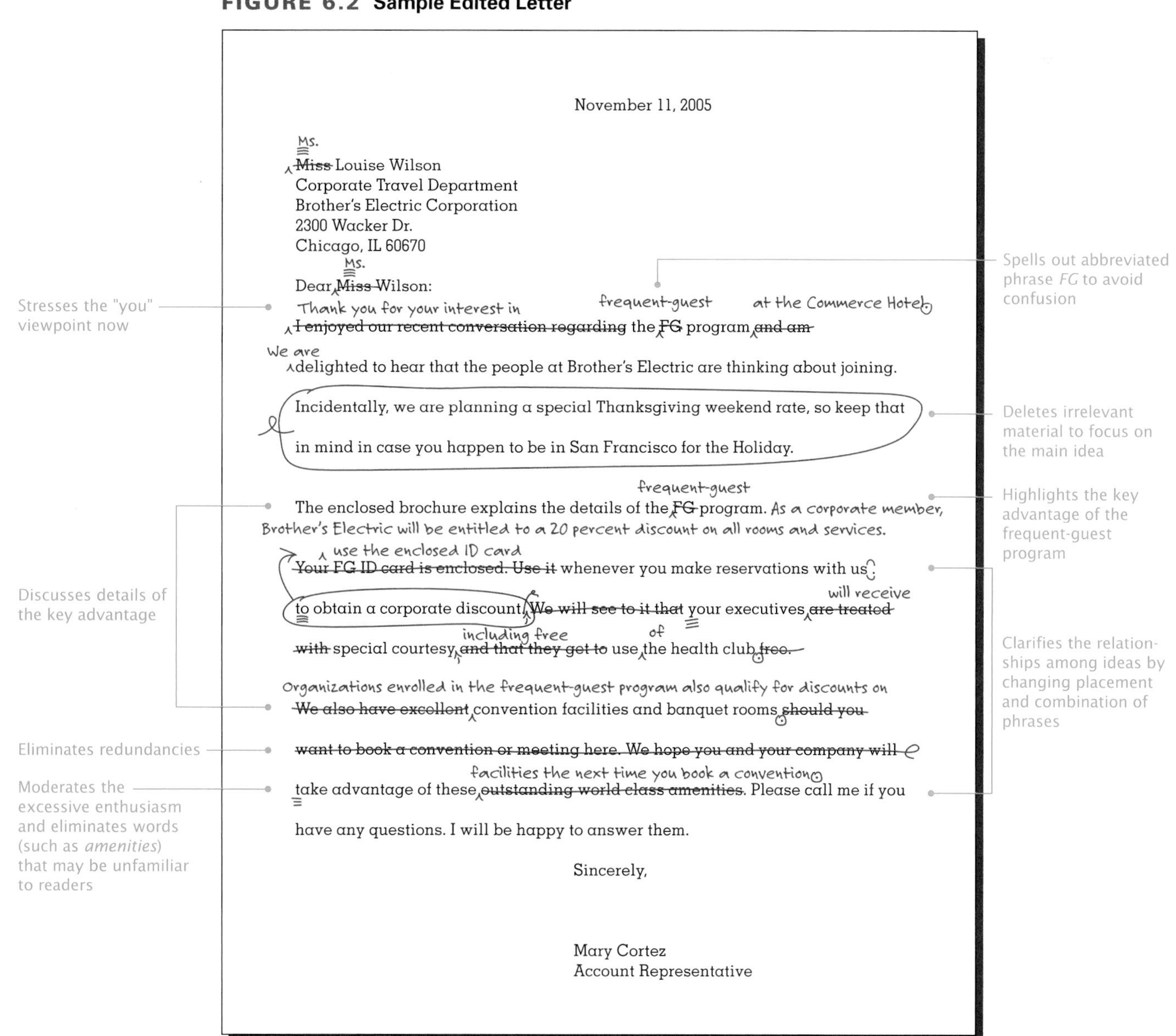

November 11, 2005

~~Miss~~ Ms. Louise Wilson
Corporate Travel Department
Brother's Electric Corporation
2300 Wacker Dr.
Chicago, IL 60670

Dear ~~Miss~~ Ms. Wilson:

~~I enjoyed our recent conversation regarding~~ Thank you for your interest in the ~~FG~~ frequent-guest program ~~and am~~ at the Commerce Hotel. We are delighted to hear that the people at Brother's Electric are thinking about joining.

Incidentally, we are planning a special Thanksgiving weekend rate, so keep that in mind in case you happen to be in San Francisco for the Holiday.

The enclosed brochure explains the details of the ~~FG~~ frequent-guest program. As a corporate member, Brother's Electric will be entitled to a 20 percent discount on all rooms and services. ~~Your FG ID card is enclosed. Use it~~ use the enclosed ID card whenever you make reservations with us; to obtain a corporate discount. ~~We will see to it that~~ your executives ~~are treated with~~ will receive special courtesy ~~and that they get to~~ including free use of the health club ~~free~~.

~~We also have excellent~~ Organizations enrolled in the frequent-guest program also qualify for discounts on convention facilities and banquet rooms ~~should you want to book a convention or meeting here. We hope you and your company will take advantage of these outstanding world class amenities~~ facilities the next time you book a convention. Please call me if you have any questions. I will be happy to answer them.

Sincerely,

Mary Cortez
Account Representative

FIGURE 6.3 Sample Revised Letter

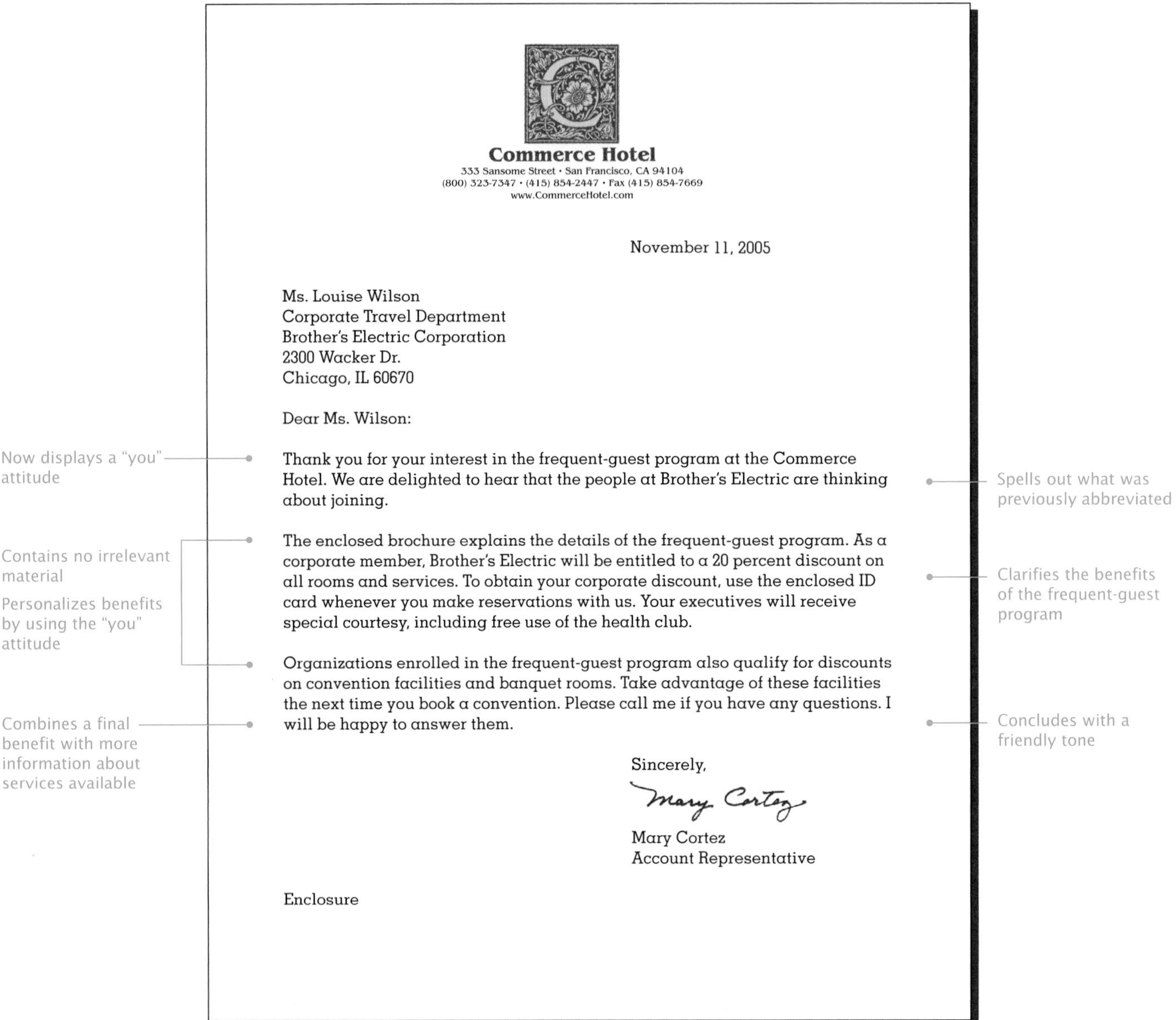

Commerce Hotel
333 Sansome Street • San Francisco, CA 94104
(800) 323-7347 • (415) 854-2447 • Fax (415) 854-7669
www.CommerceHotel.com

November 11, 2005

Ms. Louise Wilson
Corporate Travel Department
Brother's Electric Corporation
2300 Wacker Dr.
Chicago, IL 60670

Dear Ms. Wilson:

Thank you for your interest in the frequent-guest program at the Commerce Hotel. We are delighted to hear that the people at Brother's Electric are thinking about joining.

The enclosed brochure explains the details of the frequent-guest program. As a corporate member, Brother's Electric will be entitled to a 20 percent discount on all rooms and services. To obtain your corporate discount, use the enclosed ID card whenever you make reservations with us. Your executives will receive special courtesy, including free use of the health club.

Organizations enrolled in the frequent-guest program also qualify for discounts on convention facilities and banquet rooms. Take advantage of these facilities the next time you book a convention. Please call me if you have any questions. I will be happy to answer them.

Sincerely,

Mary Cortez

Mary Cortez
Account Representative

Enclosure

Now displays a "you" attitude
Contains no irrelevant material
Personalizes benefits by using the "you" attitude
Combines a final benefit with more information about services available
Spells out what was previously abbreviated
Clarifies the benefits of the frequent-guest program
Concludes with a friendly tone

Evaluating Your Content, Organization, Style, and Tone

When you begin the revision process, focus your attention on content, organization, style, and tone. To evaluate the content of your message, ask yourself these questions:

- Is the information accurate?
- Is the information relevant to your audience?
- Is there enough information to satisfy your reader's needs?
- Is there a good balance between the general and the specific?

Once you are satisfied with the content of your message, you can review its organization. Ask yourself another set of questions:

- Are all your points covered in the most logical order?
- Do the most important ideas receive the most space, and are they placed in the most prominent positions?
- Would the message be more convincing if it were arranged in another sequence?
- Are any points repeated unnecessarily?
- Are details grouped together logically, or are some still scattered through the document?

With the content in place and effectively organized, next consider whether you have achieved the right style and tone for your audience. Is your writing formal enough to meet the audience's expectations without being too formal or academic? Is it too casual for a serious subject? Does your message emphasize the audience's needs over your own?

In this first pass, spend a few extra moments on the beginning and ending of your message. These sections have the greatest impact on the audience. Be sure that the opening of your document is relevant, interesting, and geared to the reader's probable reaction. In longer documents, check to see that the first few paragraphs establish the subject, purpose, and organization of the material. Review the conclusion to be sure that it summarizes the main idea and leaves the audience with a positive impression.

The beginning and end of a message have the greatest impact on your readers.

Reviewing for Readability

Once you're satisfied with the content, organization, style, and tone of your message, make a second pass to look at its readability. Most professionals are inundated with more reading material than they can ever hope to consume, and they'll appreciate your efforts to make your documents easier to read. You'll benefit from this effort, too: If you earn a reputation for well-crafted documents that respect the audience's time, people will tend to pay more attention to your work.

The effort to make your documents more readable will pay for itself in greater career success.

You might be familiar with one of the many indexes that have been developed over the years in an attempt to measure readability. For example, the Flesch-Kincaid Grade Level score computes reading difficulty relative to the grade level achievement. A score of 10 suggests that a document can be read and understood by the average tenth-grader. Most business documents score in the 8–11 range. Technical documents often score in the 12–14 range. A similar scoring system, the Flesch Reading Ease score, ranks documents on a 100-point scale; the higher the score, the easier the document is to read. Both of these measurements are built into Microsoft Word, making them easy to use for most business communicators.

Readability indexes offer a useful reference point, but they are all limited by what they are able to measure: word length, number of syllables, sentence length, and paragraph length. They can't measure any of the other factors that affect readability, such as audience analysis, writing clarity, and document design. Compare these two paragraphs:

Readability formulas can give you a helpful indication, but they can't measure everything that affects readability.

> Readability indexes offer a useful reference point, but they are all limited by what they are able to measure: word length, number of syllables, sentence length, and paragraph length. They can't measure any of the other factors that affect readability, from "you" orientation to writing clarity to document design.
>
> Readability indexes can help. But they don't measure everything. They don't measure whether your writing clarity is good. They don't measure whether your document design is good or not. Reading indexes are based on word length, syllables, sentences, and paragraphs.

The first paragraph scores 12.0 on grade level and 27.4 on reading ease. The second paragraph scores much better on both grade level (8.9) and reading ease (45.8). However, the second example is choppy, unsophisticated, and poorly organized. As a general rule, then, don't assume that a piece of text is readable if it scores well on a readability index. It may still suffer from other problems. Conversely, if a piece of text scores poorly (with a high grade level or a low reading ease score), examine it carefully to see whether you can use simpler words or shorter sentences. Chances are you can make the piece easier to read without making it sound choppy or amateurish.

Successful business communicators know that beyond shortening words and sentences for readability measurements, they can improve readability of a message by making the document interesting and easy to scan. Most business audiences—particularly influential senior managers—skim most documents looking for key ideas, conclusions, and recommendations. Skimming also helps readers assess the worthiness of the document. If they determine that the document contains valuable information or requires a response, they will read it more carefully when time permits. You can adopt a number of techniques to make your message easier to skim: varying sentence length, using shorter paragraphs, using

2 LEARNING OBJECTIVE

List four writing techniques you can use to improve the readability of your messages lists and bullets instead of narrative, and adding effective headings and subheadings. These techniques also make your message more appealing and interesting to read.

Varying Your Sentence Length

To keep readers' interest, use both long and short sentences.

Variety is a creative way to make your messages interesting and readable. By choosing words and sentence structure with care, you can create a rhythm that emphasizes important points, enlivens your writing style, and makes your information appealing to your reader. For example, a short sentence that highlights a conclusion at the end of a substantial paragraph of evidence makes your key message stand out. Effective documents, therefore, usually use a mixture of sentences that are short (up to 15 words or so), medium (15–25 words), and long (more than 25 words).

Each sentence length has its advantages. Short sentences can be processed quickly and are easier for nonnative speakers and translators to interpret. Medium-length sentences are useful for showing the relationships among ideas. Long sentences are often the best way to convey complex ideas, list multiple related points, or summarize or preview information.

Of course, each sentence length also has disadvantages. Too many short sentences in a row can make your writing choppy. Medium sentences lack the punch of short sentences and the informative power of longer sentences. Meanwhile, long sentences are usually harder to understand than short sentences because they are packed with information that must all be absorbed at once. Since readers can absorb only a few words per glance, longer sentences are also more difficult to skim. Thus, the longer your sentence, the greater the possibility that the reader who skims it will not read enough words to process its full meaning.

By choosing the best sentence length for each communication need and remembering to mix sentence lengths for variety, you'll get your message across while keeping your documents lively and interesting.

Keeping Your Paragraphs Short

Short paragraphs are easier to read than long ones.

Unlike the variety needed in sentence length, the optimum paragraph length is short to medium in most cases. Large blocks of text can be intimidating. Unless you break up your thoughts somehow, you'll end up with a three-page paragraph that's guaranteed to intimidate even the most dedicated reader. Short paragraphs (of 100 words or fewer) are easier to read than long ones, and they make your writing look inviting. Short paragraphs help audiences read letters, memos, and e-mail more carefully. From time to time, you can emphasize an idea by isolating it in a short, forceful paragraph.

However, don't go overboard with short paragraphs. Be careful to use one-sentence paragraphs only occasionally and only for emphasis. When you want to package a big idea in short paragraphs, break the idea into subtopics and treat each subtopic in a separate paragraph—being careful to provide plenty of transitional elements. By breaking a large single paragraph into several shorter ones, you can make material more readable. Of course, many other approaches might be as effective. As you saw in Chapter 5, there is no "right" way to develop a paragraph.

Using Lists and Bullets to Clarify and Emphasize

Lists are effective tools for highlighting and simplifying material.

An effective alternative to using conventional sentences is to set off important ideas in a **list**—a series of words, names, or other items. Lists can show the sequence of your ideas, heighten their impact visually, and increase the likelihood that a reader will find your key points. In addition, lists provide readers with clues, simplify complex subjects, highlight the main point, break up the page visually, ease the skimming process for busy readers, and give the reader a breather. Consider the difference between the following two approaches to the same information:

NARRATIVE

Owning your own business has many advantages. One is the ease of establishment. Another advantage is the satisfaction of working for yourself. As a sole proprietor, you also have the advantage of privacy because you do not have to reveal your information or plans to anyone.

LIST

Owning your own business has three advantages:

- Ease of establishment
- Satisfaction of working for yourself
- Privacy of information

When creating a list, you can separate items with numbers, letters, or bullets (a general term for any kind of graphical element that precedes each item). Bullets are generally preferred over numbers, unless the list is in some logical sequence or ranking, or specific list items will be referred to later on. The following three steps need to be performed in the order indicated, and the numbers make that clear:

1. Find out how many employees would like on-site day-care facilities.
2. Determine how much space the day-care center would require.
3. Estimate the cost of converting a conference room for the on-site facility.

John Hutchison's (far right) success depends on clarity in all his business communication. For instance, his sales contracts for Golden Gate Insurance break out specific clauses in bulleted lists that are easy to locate, read, and understand.

Lists are easier to locate and read if the entire numbered or bulleted section is set off by a blank line before and after, as the preceding examples demonstrate. Furthermore, when using lists, make sure to introduce them clearly so that people know what they're about to read. One way to introduce lists is to make them a part of the introductory sentence:

> The board of directors met to discuss the revised annual budget. To keep expenses in line with declining sales, the directors voted to
>
> - cut everyone's salary by 10 percent
> - close the employee cafeteria
> - reduce travel expenses

If necessary, add further discussion after the lists to complete your thought. Another way to introduce a list is to precede it with a complete introductory sentence, followed by a colon:

> The decline in company profit is attributable to four factors:
>
> - Slower holiday sales
> - Increased transportation and fuel costs
> - Higher employee wages
> - Slower inventory turnover

Regardless of the format you choose, the items in a list should be parallel; that is, they should all use the same grammatical pattern. For example, if one list item begins with a verb, all list items should begin with a verb. If one item is a noun phrase, all should be noun phrases.

NONPARALLEL LIST ITEMS	PARALLEL LIST ITEMS
• Improve our bottom line	• Improving our bottom line
• Identification of new foreign markets for our products	• Identifying new foreign markets for our products
• Global market strategies	• Developing our global market strategies
• Issues regarding pricing and packaging size	• Resolving pricing and packaging issues

Parallel forms are easier to read and skim. You can create parallelism by repeating the pattern in words, phrases, clauses, or entire sentences (see Table 6.1).

Adding Headings and Subheadings

Use headings to grab the reader's attention and organize material into short sections.

A **heading** is a brief title that tells readers about the content of the section that follows. Headings are similar to the subject line in memos and e-mail correspondence. However, subject lines merely identify the purpose of the memo or e-mail, whereas headings and subheadings also advise the reader about the material included in the section to follow.

TABLE 6.1 Achieving Parallelism

METHOD	EXAMPLE
Parallel words:	The letter was approved by Clausen, Whittaker, Merlin, and Carlucci.
Parallel phrases:	We have beaten the competition in supermarkets, in department stores, and in specialty stores.
Parallel clauses:	I'd like to discuss the issue after Vicki gives her presentation but before Marvin shows his slides.
Parallel sentences:	In 2000 we exported 30 percent of our production. In 2001 we exported 50 percent.

Subheadings are subordinate to headings, indicating subsections with a major section. Headings and subheadings serve these important functions:

- **Organization.** Headings show your reader at a glance how the document is organized. They act as labels to group related paragraphs together and effectively organize your material into short sections.
- **Attention.** Informative, inviting, and in some cases intriguing headings grab the reader's attention, make the text easier to read, and help the reader find the parts he or she needs to read—or skip.
- **Connection.** Using headings and subheadings together helps readers see the relationship between main ideas and subordinate ones so that they can understand your message more easily. Moreover, headings and subheadings visually indicate shifts from one idea to the next.

Informative headings are generally more helpful than descriptive ones.

Headings fall into two categories. **Descriptive headings**, such as "Cost Considerations," identify a topic but do little more. **Informative headings**, such as "A New Way to Cut Costs," put your reader right into the context of your message.

Informative headings guide readers to think in a certain way about the topic. They are also helpful in guiding your work as a writer, especially if written in terms of questions you plan to address in your document. However, informative headings are more difficult to create. A well-written informative heading is self-contained. In other words, readers should be able to read your headings and subheadings and understand them without reading the rest of the document. For example, "Introduction" conveys little information, whereas the heading "The Economic Impact of Staffing Shortages in Finance and Accounting" gives the reader a key piece of information, catches the reader's attention, and sparks interest. Whatever types of headings you choose, keep them brief, and use parallel construction as you would for an outline, lists, or a series of words.

Use the same grammatical form for each heading.

Editing for Clarity and Conciseness

Clarity is essential to getting your message across accurately and efficiently.

Once you've reviewed and revised your message for readability, you'll want to make sure that your message is clear. Perhaps a sentence is so cluttered that readers can't unravel it. Its wording may be so vague that readers can interpret it in several ways. Perhaps pronouns or tenses switch midsentence so that readers lose track of who is talking or when an event took place. Sentence B may not be a logical sequel to sentence A, or an important word may be used incorrectly.[3]

3 LEARNING OBJECTIVE

Describe the steps you can take to improve the clarity of your writing

Ask yourself whether your sentences are easy to decipher. Do your paragraphs have clear topic sentences? Are the transitions between ideas obvious? Are your statements simple and direct? A clear sentence is no accident. Few sentences come out exactly right the first time. See Table 6.2 for examples of the following tips:

- **Break up overly long sentences.** Don't connect too many clauses with *and.* If you find yourself stuck in a long sentence, you're probably trying to make the sentence do more than it can reasonably do, such as express two dissimilar thoughts. You can often clarify your writing style by separating a string into individual sentences.

TABLE 6.2 Revising for Clarity

EXAMPLES	UNACCEPTABLE	PREFERABLE
OVERLY LONG SENTENCES Taking compound sentences too far	The magazine will be published January 1, and I'd better meet the deadline if I want my article included.	The magazine will be published January 1. I'd better meet the deadline if I want my article included.
HEDGING SENTENCES Overqualifying sentences	I believe that Mr. Johnson's employment record seems to show that he may be capable of handling the position.	Mr. Johnson's employment record shows that he is capable of handling the position.
UNPARALLEL SENTENCES Using dissimilar construction for similar ideas	Ms. Simms had been drenched with rain, bombarded with telephone calls, and her boss shouted at her.	Ms. Sims had been drenched with rain, bombarded with telephone calls, and shouted at by her boss.
	Ms. Reynolds dictated the letter, and next she signed it and left the office.	Ms. Reynolds dictated the letter, signed it, and left the office.
	To waste time and missing deadlines are bad habits.	Wasting time and missing deadlines are bad habits.
	Interviews are a matter of acting confident and to stay relaxed.	Interviews are a matter of acting confident and staying relaxed.
DANGLING MODIFIERS Placing modifiers close to the wrong nouns and verbs	Walking to the office, a red sports car passed her.	A red sports car passed her while she was walking to the office.
	Working as fast as possible, the budget was soon ready.	Working as fast as possible, the committee soon had the budget ready.
	After a three-week slump, we increased sales.	After a three-week slump, sales increased.
LONG NOUN SEQUENCES Stringing too many nouns together	The window sash installation company will give us an estimate on Friday.	The company that installs window sashes will give us an estimate on Friday.
CAMOUFLAGED VERBS Changing verbs and nouns into adjectives	The manager undertook implementation of the rules.	The manager implemented the rules.
	Verification of the shipments occurs weekly.	Shipments are verified weekly.
Changing verbs into nouns	reach a conclusion about make a discovery of give consideration to	conclude discover consider
SENTENCE STRUCTURE Separating subject and predicate	A 10 percent decline in market share, which resulted from quality problems and an aggressive sales campaign by Armitage, the market leader in the Northeast, was the major problem in 2005.	The major problem in 2005 was a 10 percent loss of market share, which resulted from both quality problems and an aggressive sales campaign by Armitage, the market leader in the Northeast.
Separating adjectives, adverbs, or prepositional phrases from the words they modify	Our antique desk is suitable for busy executives with thick legs and large drawers.	With its thick legs and large drawers, our antique desk is suitable for busy executives.
AWKWARD REFERENCES	The Law Office and the Accounting Office distribute computer supplies for legal secretaries and beginning accountants, respectively.	The Law Office distributes computer supplies for legal secretaries; the Accounting Office distributes those for beginning accountants.
TOO MUCH ENTHUSIASM	We are extremely pleased to offer you a position on our staff of exceptionally skilled and highly educated employees. The work offers extraordinary challenges and a very large salary.	We are pleased to offer you a position on our staff of skilled and well-educated employees. The work offers challenges and an attractive salary.

Don't be afraid to present your opinions without qualification.

- **Rewrite hedging sentences.** Sometimes you have to write *may* or *seems* to avoid stating a judgment as a fact. However, when you have too many such hedges, you risk coming across an unsure of what you're saying.

When you use the same grammatical pattern to express two or more ideas, you show that they are comparable thoughts.

- **Impose parallelism.** When you have two or more similar ideas to express, make them parallel. Repeating the same grammatical construction shows that the ideas are related, of similar importance, and on the same level of generality. Parallelism is discussed earlier in this chapter, in the section on lists and bullets.
- **Correct dangling modifiers.** Sometimes a modifier is not just an adjective or an adverb but an entire phrase modifying a noun or a verb. Be careful not to leave this type of modifier dangling, with no connection to the subject of the sentence. The first unacceptable example under "Dangling Modifiers" in Table 6.1 implies that the red sports car has both an office and the legs to walk there. The second example shows one frequent cause of dangling modifiers: passive construction.
- **Reword long noun sequences.** When multiple nouns are strung together as modifiers, the resulting sentence can be hard to read. You might be trying too hard to create the desired effect; first see if a single well-chosen word will do the job. If the nouns are all necessary, consider moving one or more to a modifying phrase as shown in Table 6.1. Although you add a few more words, your audience won't have to work as hard to understand the sentence.
- **Replace camouflaged verbs.** Watch for words that end in *-ion, -tion, -ing, -ment, -ant, -ent, -ence, -ance,* and *-ency.* These endings often change verbs into nouns and adjectives, requiring you to add a verb just to get your point across. To prune and enliven your messages, use verbs instead of noun phrases.

Subject and predicate should be placed as close together as possible, as should modifiers and the words they modify.

- **Clarify sentence structure.** Keep the subject and predicate of a sentence as close together as possible. When the subject and predicate are far apart, readers may need to read the sentence twice to figure out who did what. Similarly, adjectives, adverbs, and prepositional phrases usually make the most sense when they're placed as close as possible to the words they modify.
- **Clarify awkward references.** In an effort to save words, business writers sometimes use expressions such as *the above-mentioned, as mentioned above, the aforementioned, the former, the latter,* and *respectively.* These words cause readers to jump from point to point, which hinders effective communication. Use specific references, even if you must add a few more words.

Showing enthusiasm for ideas is fine, but be careful not to go so far that you sound unprofessional.

- **Moderate your enthusiasm.** An occasional adjective or adverb intensifies and emphasizes your meaning, but too many can degrade your writing and damage your credibility.

4 LEARNING OBJECTIVE

Discuss why it's important to make your message more concise, and give four tips on how to do so

In addition to clarity, readers appreciate conciseness in business messages. Many of today's business documents are swollen with words and phrases that add little or nothing to the message. In fact, three-fourths of the executives in one survey complained that most written messages are too long.[4] Executives are more likely to read documents that communicate efficiently, so it's especially important to weed out unnecessary material.

Most first drafts can be cut by as much as 50 percent.[5] By reorganizing your content, improving the readability of your document, and correcting your sentence structure for clarity, you will have already eliminated most of the excess. Now it is time to examine every word you put on paper. When you edit for conciseness, you eliminate every word that serves no function, replace every long word that could be a short word, and remove every adverb that adds nothing to the meaning already carried in the verb. To test whether every word counts, try removing a word or phrase that doesn't appear to be essential. If the meaning doesn't change, leave it out. For instance, *very* can be a useful word to achieve emphasis, but more often it's simply clutter. There's no need to call someone "very methodical." The person is either methodical or not. As you begin your editing task, simplify, prune, and strive for order. See Table 6.3 for examples of the following tips:

Make your documents tighter by removing unnecessary words.

- **Delete unnecessary words and phrases.** Some combinations of words have more efficient, one-word equivalents. In addition, avoid the clutter of too many or poorly placed relative pronouns (*who, that, which*). Even articles can be excessive (mostly too many *the*'s). However, well-placed relative pronouns and articles prevent confusion.

TABLE 6.3 Revising for Conciseness

EXAMPLES	UNACCEPTABLE	PREFERABLE
UNNECESSARY WORDS AND PHRASES		
Using wordy phrases	for the sum of	for
	in the event that	if
	on the occasion of	on
	prior to the start of	before
	in the near future	soon
	have the capability of	can
	at this point in time	now
	due to the fact that	because
	in view of the fact that	because
	until such time as	when
	with reference to	about
Using too many relative pronouns	Cars that are sold after January will not have a six-month warranty.	Cars sold after January will not have a six-month warranty.
	Employees who are driving to work should park in the underground garage.	Employees driving to work should park in the underground garage.
Using too few relative pronouns	The project manager told the engineers last week the specifications were changed.	The project manager told the engineers last week that the specifications were changed.
		The project manager told the engineers that last week the specifications were changed.
LONG WORDS AND PHRASES		
Using overly long words	During the preceding year, the company accelerated productive operations.	Last year the company sped up operations.
	The action was predicated on the assumption that the company was operating at a financial deficit.	The action was based on the belief that the company was losing money.
Using wordy phrases rather than infinitives	If you want success as a writer, you must work hard.	To be a successful writer, you must work hard.
	He went to the library for the purpose of studying.	He went to the library to study.
	The employer increased salaries so that she could improve morale.	The employer increased salaries to improve morale.
REDUNDANCIES		
Repeating meanings	absolutely complete	complete
	basic fundamentals	fundamentals
	follows after	follows
	reduce down	reduce
	free and clear	free
	refer back	refer
	repeat again	repeat
	collect together	collect
	future plans	plans
	return back	return
	important essentials	essentials
	end result	result
	actual truth	truth
	final outcome	outcome
	uniquely unusual	unique
	surrounded on all sides	surrounded
Using double modifiers	modern, up-to-date equipment	modern equipment
IT IS/THERE ARE STARTERS		
Starting sentences with *it* or *there*	It would be appreciated if you would sign the lease today.	Please sign the lease today.
	There are five employees in this division who were late to work today.	Five employees in this division were late to work today.

CHECKLIST: Revising Business Messages

A. EVALUATE CONTENT, ORGANIZATION, STYLE, AND TONE

- Make sure the information is accurate, relevant, and sufficient.
- Check that all necessary points appear in logical order.
- Verify that you present enough support to make the main idea convincing and interesting.
- Be sure the beginning and ending are effective.
- Make sure you've achieved the right tone.

B. REVIEW FOR READABILITY

- Consider using a readability index, being sure to interpret the answer carefully.
- Use a mix of short and long sentences.
- Keep paragraphs short.
- Use bulleted and numbered lists to emphasize key points.
- Make the document easy to scan with headings and subheadings.

C. EDIT FOR CLARITY

- Break up overly long sentences and rewrite hedging sentences.
- Impose parallelism to simplify reading.
- Correct dangling modifiers.
- Reword long noun sequences and replace camouflaged verbs.
- Clarify sentence structure and awkward references.
- Moderate your enthusiasm to maintain a professional tone.

D. EDIT FOR CONCISENESS

- Delete unnecessary words and phrases.
- Shorten long words and phrases.
- Eliminate redundancies.
- Recast "It is/There are" starters.

- **Shorten long words and phrases.** Short words are generally more vivid and easier to read than long ones. The idea is to use short, simple words, *not* simple concepts.[6] Plus, by using infinitives in place of some phrases, you not only shorten your sentences but also make them clearer.
- **Eliminate redundancies.** In some word combinations, the words tend to say the same thing. For instance, "visible to the eye" is redundant because *visible* is enough without further clarification; "to the eye" adds nothing.
- **Recast "It is/There are" starters.** If you start a sentence with an indefinite pronoun such as *it* or *there,* odds are that the sentence could be shorter.

As you rewrite, concentrate on how each word contributes to an effective sentence and on how that sentence develops a coherent paragraph. Be sure to consider the effect your words will actually have on readers (not just the effect you *plan* for them to have). Look for opportunities to make the material more interesting through the use of strong, lively words and phrases (as discussed in Chapter 5). For a reminder of the tasks involved in revision, see this chapter's "Checklist: Revising Business Messages."

Sometimes you'll find that the most difficult problem in a sentence can be solved by simply removing the problem itself. When you come upon a troublesome element, ask yourself, "Do I need it at all?" Possibly not. In fact, you may find that it was giving you so much grief precisely because it was trying to do an unnecessary job.[7] Once you remove the troublesome element, the afflicted sentence will spring to life and breathe normally. Of course, before you delete anything, you'll probably want to keep copies of your current version. Using a word processor, you can save the original and all revisions of your documents either for long-term reference or to rely on the "undo" function while you're editing.

DOCUMENT MAKEOVER

IMPROVE THIS LETTER

To practice correcting drafts of actual documents, visit www.prenhall.com/onekey on the web. Click "Document Makeovers," then click Chapter 6. You will find a letter that contains problems and errors relating to what you've learned in this chapter about revising messages. Use the Final Draft decision tool to create an improved version of this letter. Check the message for organization, readability, clarity, and conciseness.

Using Technology to Revise Your Message

When it's time to revise and polish your message, your word processor helps you add, delete, and move text with functions such as *cut and paste* (taking a block of text out of one section of a document and pasting it in somewhere else) and *search and replace* (tracking

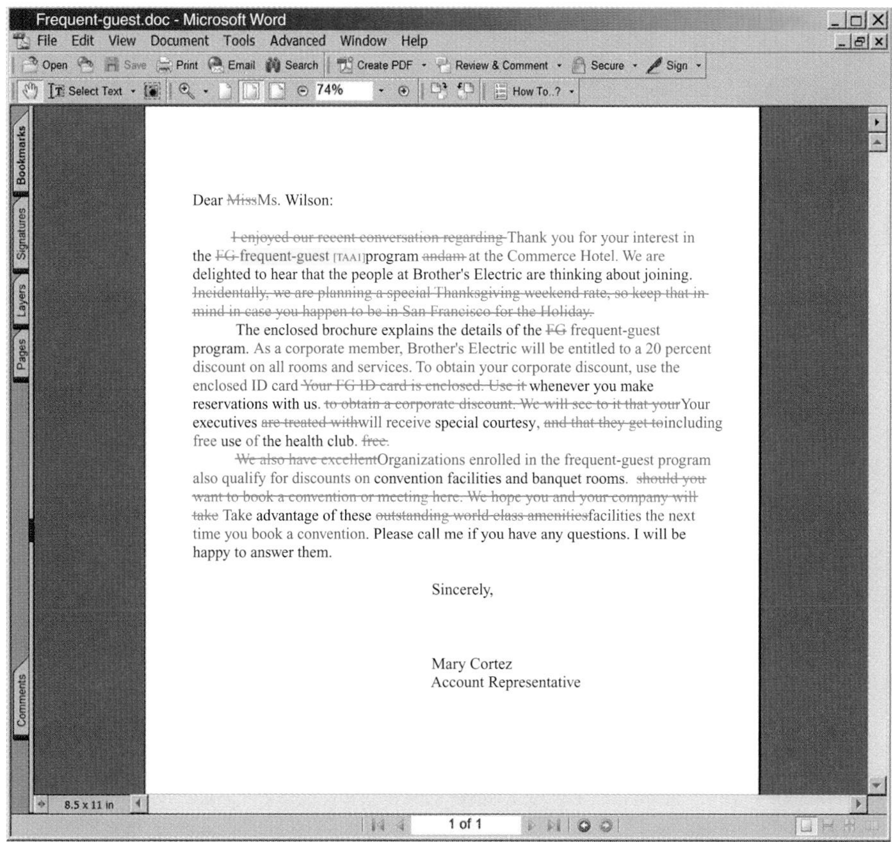

Dear ~~Miss~~Ms. Wilson:

~~I enjoyed our recent conversation regarding~~ Thank you for your interest in the ~~FG~~ frequent-guest [TAA1]program ~~andam~~ at the Commerce Hotel. We are delighted to hear that the people at Brother's Electric are thinking about joining. ~~Incidentally, we are planning a special Thanksgiving weekend rate, so keep that in mind in case you happen to be in San Francisco for the Holiday.~~

The enclosed brochure explains the details of the ~~FG~~ frequent-guest program. As a corporate member, Brother's Electric will be entitled to a 20 percent discount on all rooms and services. To obtain your corporate discount, use the enclosed ID card ~~Your FG ID card is enclosed. Use it~~ whenever you make reservations with us. ~~to obtain a corporate discount. We will see to it that your~~Your executives ~~are treated with~~will receive special courtesy, ~~and that they get to~~including free use of the health club. ~~free.~~

~~We also have excellent~~Organizations enrolled in the frequent-guest program also qualify for discounts on convention facilities and banquet rooms. ~~should you want to book a convention or meeting here. We hope you and your company will take~~ Take advantage of these ~~outstanding world-class amenities~~facilities the next time you book a convention. Please call me if you have any questions. I will be happy to answer them.

Sincerely,

Mary Cortez
Account Representative

FIGURE 6.4
Revision Marks

down words or phrases and changing them if you need to). Be careful using this feature though; choosing the "replace all" option can result in some unintended errors. For example, finding *power* and replacing all occurrences with *strength* will also change the word *powerful* to *strengthful.* In addition, the many word processing programs have an autocorrection feature that allows you to store words you commonly misspell or mistype, along with their correct spelling. So if you frequently type *teh* instead of *the,* AutoCorrect will automatically correct your typo for you.

Software tools such as *revision marks* and *commenting* keep track of proposed editing changes electronically and provide a history of a document's revisions. In Microsoft Word, the revisions appear in a different font color than the original text (see Figure 6.4), giving you a chance to review changes before accepting or rejecting them. (In Figure 6.4, "TAA" is the initials of the person who made a comment that appears in Word's comment pane, which is not shown here. Comments can be text or voice. Since this is the first comment, it is marked "1.") Adobe Acrobat lets you attach notes to Portable Document Format (PDF) files, a widely used format for sharing documents over the Internet (see Figure 6.5). Revision marks and commenting features are also a great way to keep track of editing changes made by team members. This feature is especially helpful if you are writing collaborative messages. Programs such as Microsoft Word let you choose different colors for different reviewers as well, so you can keep everyone's comments straight.

In addition to the many revision tools, four software functions can help bring out the best in your documents. First, a *spell checker* compares your document with an electronic dictionary, highlights unrecognized words, and suggests correct spellings. Spell checkers are a wonderful way to weed major typos out of your documents, but they are no substitute for good spelling skills. For example, if you use *their* when you mean to use *there,* your spell checker won't notice, because *their* is spelled correctly. If you're in a hurry and accidentally omit the *p* at the end of *top,* your spell checker will read *to* as correct. Or if you mistakenly type a semicolon instead of *p,* your spell checker will read *to;* as a correctly spelled word. Plus, some of the "errors" that the spell checker indicates may actually be proper names, technical words, words that you misspelled on purpose, or simply words that weren't

FIGURE 6.5
PDF File with Comments

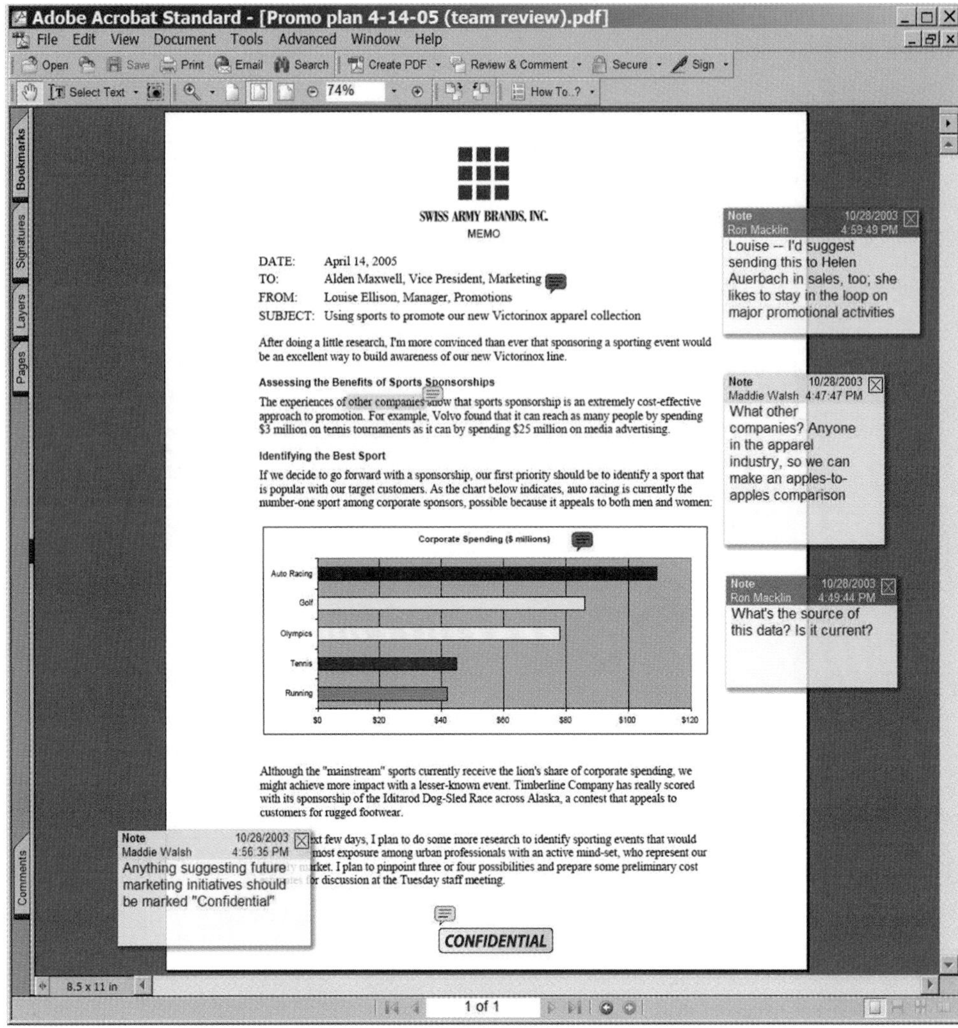

SWISS ARMY BRANDS, INC.
MEMO

DATE: April 14, 2005
TO: Alden Maxwell, Vice President, Marketing
FROM: Louise Ellison, Manager, Promotions
SUBJECT: Using sports to promote our new Victorinox apparel collection

After doing a little research, I'm more convinced than ever that sponsoring a sporting event would be an excellent way to build awareness of our new Victorinox line.

Assessing the Benefits of Sports Sponsorships

The experiences of other companies show that sports sponsorship is an extremely cost-effective approach to promotion. For example, Volvo found that it can reach as many people by spending $3 million on tennis tournaments as it can by spending $25 million on media advertising.

Identifying the Best Sport

If we decide to go forward with a sponsorship, our first priority should be to identify a sport that is popular with our target customers. As the chart below indicates, auto racing is currently the number-one sport among corporate sponsors, possible because it appeals to both men and women:

Although the "mainstream" sports currently receive the lion's share of corporate spending, we might achieve more impact with a lesser-known event. Timberline Company has really scored with its sponsorship of the Iditarod Dog-Sled Race across Alaska, a contest that appeals to customers for rugged footwear.

...xt few days, I plan to do some more research to identify sporting events that would ... most exposure among urban professionals with an active mind-set, who represent our ...arket. I plan to pinpoint three or four possibilities and prepare some preliminary cost ...r discussion at the Tuesday staff meeting.

included in the spell checker's dictionary. It's up to you to decide whether each flagged word should be corrected or left alone, and it's up to you to find the errors that your spell checker has overlooked.

Second, a computer *thesaurus* gives you alternative words, just as a printed thesaurus does. A computer thesaurus is much faster and lets you try multiple alternatives in just a few seconds to see which works best. The best uses of any thesaurus, printed or computerized, are to find fresh, interesting words when you've been using the same word too many times and to find the word that most accurately conveys your intended meaning. In contrast, don't fall into the temptation of using your thesaurus to find impressive "ten dollar" words to spice up your writing; if you're not comfortable using the word, it won't sound natural in your documents.

Third, the *grammar checker* tries to do for your grammar what a spell checker does for your spelling. The catch is that checking your spelling is much easier than checking your grammar. A spell checker simply compares each word in your document with a list of correctly spelled words. A grammar checker has to determine whether you're using words correctly and constructing sentences according to the complex rules of composition.

Because the program doesn't have a clue about what you're trying to say, it can't tell whether you've said it correctly. Moreover, even if you've used all the rules correctly, a grammar checker still can't tell whether your document communicates clearly. However, grammar checkers can perform some helpful review tasks and point out things you should consider changing, such as passive voice, long sentences, and words that tend to be misused or overused. Some programs even run readability formulas for you.

Fourth, a *style checker* can also monitor your word and sentence choices and suggest alternatives that might produce more effective writing. For instance, the style checking options in

Microsoft Word range from basic issues, such as spelling out numbers and using contractions to more subjective matters, such as sentence structure and the use of technical terminology.

By all means, use any software that you find helpful when revising your documents. Just remember that it's unwise to rely on spell checkers, grammar checkers, or style checkers to do all your revision work. What these programs can do is identify potential errors that you may have overlooked. It's up to you to decide what, if anything, needs to be done, and it's up to you to catch the mistakes that these computer programs can't.[8]

Spell checkers, grammar checkers, and computerized thesauruses can all help with the revision process, but they can't take the place of good writing and editing skills.

PRODUCING YOUR MESSAGE

5 LEARNING OBJECTIVE

Explain how design elements help determine the effectiveness of your documents

Now it's time to put your hard work on display. The *production quality* of your message—the total effect of page design, graphical elements, typography, paper, and so on—plays an important role in its effectiveness. A polished, inviting design not only makes your document more appealing but also conveys a sense of professionalism and attention to detail. When producing your message, look for effective ways to enhance your message with carefully chosen graphics, sound, video, and hypertext links. Also be sure to design your documents for readability, and use production technology wisely.

The quality of your document design affects both readability and audience perceptions.

Adding Graphics, Sound, Video, and Hypertext

Take advantage of your word processor's ability to incorporate other communication elements.

Fortunately, today's word processors and other software tools make it easy to produce impressive documents that enliven your text with full-color pictures, sound and video recordings, and hypertext links. The software for creating business visuals falls into two basic groups: *Presentation software* helps you create overhead transparencies and computerized slide shows (electronic presentations are discussed in Chapter 16). *Graphics software* includes products of varying complexity, ranging from simple tools that help you create straightforward diagrams and flowcharts (see Chapter 11) to comprehensive tools that are geared to handle the rigorous demands of artists and graphic designers. You can create your graphics from scratch, use *clip art* (collections of uncopyrighted images), or scan in drawings or photographs.

Adding sound bites or video clips to your documents is an exciting new way to get your message across. Several systems now allow you to record a brief message or other sound and attach it to particular places in a document. For instance, you can add sound annotations, instead of written ones. The reader clicks on the special speaker icon to play a recorded comment, such as "Please convert this paragraph to a bulleted list." To hear the sound or see the video, the person receiving the memo has to load the memo into his or her computer and must have a sound card installed.

You can also use hypertext markup language (HTML) to insert hyperlinks into your message. Readers can easily jump from one document to another by clicking on such a link. They can go directly to a website, jump to another section of your document, or go to a different document altogether. Say you're preparing a report on this year's budget. Rather than include pages and pages of budget details from prior years, you can submit your report on disk and include a hyperlink in the file. Then, when readers click on the hyperlink, they can access a document containing details of the prior years' budgets. By using hyperlinks, you can customize your documents to meet the individual information needs of your readers—just as you can on a webpage. Of course, you'll have to make sure that the file (or the software program used to open that file) is included with your electronic document, installed on the recipient's computer, or accessible via a network connection (see "Connecting with Technology: Linking to Endless Information").

Communication Solution

As younger readers began to show less interest in *Rolling Stone's* lengthy articles on politics and other serious issues, the magazine adjusted its editorial emphasis and reviewed the publication's overall readability.

Designing for Readability

The design of your document can make or break readability in two important ways. First, if done carefully, the various elements of visual design can improve the effectiveness of your message; if done poorly, design elements can act as barriers, blocking your communication. Second, the visual design itself sends a nonverbal message to the audience, influencing their perceptions of the communication before they read a single word. Compare the two

Design affects the impression your message makes.

Connecting with Technology

Linking to Endless Information

Word processors have come a long way since their invention as a replacement for the typewriter. With more and more businesspeople reading documents online, the word processor has evolved into a multimedia information delivery system. Not only can you provide rich, comprehensive information to your readers, but you can also make reading more efficient by providing a shorter overview document that gives each reader the opportunity to link to whatever additional information he or she might be interested in. With some creative thinking and careful planning, you can create multifaceted documents of virtually endless variety and depth. Consider the many ways you can use simple hyperlinks to help your readers access specific information:

- **Link to another location within the current document.** Instead of asking readers to "turn to page 23," simply insert a link that takes them right there. If your word processor allows *bookmarking*, you can even take your reader to a specific part of the page, avoiding any confusion or delay.
- **Link to another document, spreadsheet, or presentation file.** This feature can be particularly helpful if you or someone else has already created a file that provides complementary information.
- **Link to a website that provides additional information.** Send your readers to internal or external web sites that provide examples of points you're trying to make, background data that you don't want cluttering up your main document, or any other source of information that bolsters your message.
- **Create an e-mail message.** Looking for immediate feedback on your ideas? Simply insert a mail-to link in your document, and readers can send feedback while they're looking at the document.

CAREER APPLICATIONS

1. How might teams use hyperlinks to facilitate collaborative writing?
2. What are the possible risks of providing links to information in a document, rather than the information itself? Identify all the risks you can think of and explain why each might present a problem.

memos shown in Figures 6.6 (page 167) and 6.7 (page 168). They contain virtually the same information but send dramatically different messages to the reader. Figure 6.6 is crowded, uninviting, and difficult to read. In contrast, Figure 6.7 is open, inviting, and easy to either read entirely or scan quickly. This section explains why the two designs produce such different results and how you can improve the design of your documents.

Effective design helps you establish the tone of your document and helps guide your readers through your message. To achieve an effective design, pay careful attention to the following design elements:

For effective design, pay attention to
- Consistency
- Balance
- Restraint
- Detail

- **Consistency.** Throughout each message, be consistent in your use of margins, typeface, type size, and spacing (such as in paragraph indents, between columns, and around photographs). Figure 6.6 violates this rule in several ways, starting with too many fonts (three in the heading alone, all different from the font used for the text). It also uses too many type styles (screens, wavy underlines, different colors) and uses them inconsistently as well. Also be consistent when using recurring design elements, such as vertical lines, columns, and borders. In many cases, you'll want to be consistent not only within a message but also across multiple messages; that way, audiences who receive messages from you recognize your documents and know what to expect.
- **Balance.** To create a pleasing design, balance the space devoted to text, artwork, and white space. Balance is a subjective issue. One document may have a formal, rigid design in which the various elements are placed in a grid pattern, and another could have a less formal design where elements flow more freely across the page—and both could be in balance. However, the design in Figure 6.6 is out of balance and much less effective than the formal design used in Figure 6.7.
- **Restraint.** Strive for simplicity in design. Don't clutter your message with too many design elements, too much highlighting, or too many decorative touches. The numerous elements in Figure 6.6 are distracting.

Communication Solution

A key part of the *Rolling Stone* redesign was shifting the balance of text and visuals to make the magazine more appealing to readers accustomed to other popular entertainment magazines.

FIGURE 6.6 **Ineffective Document Design**

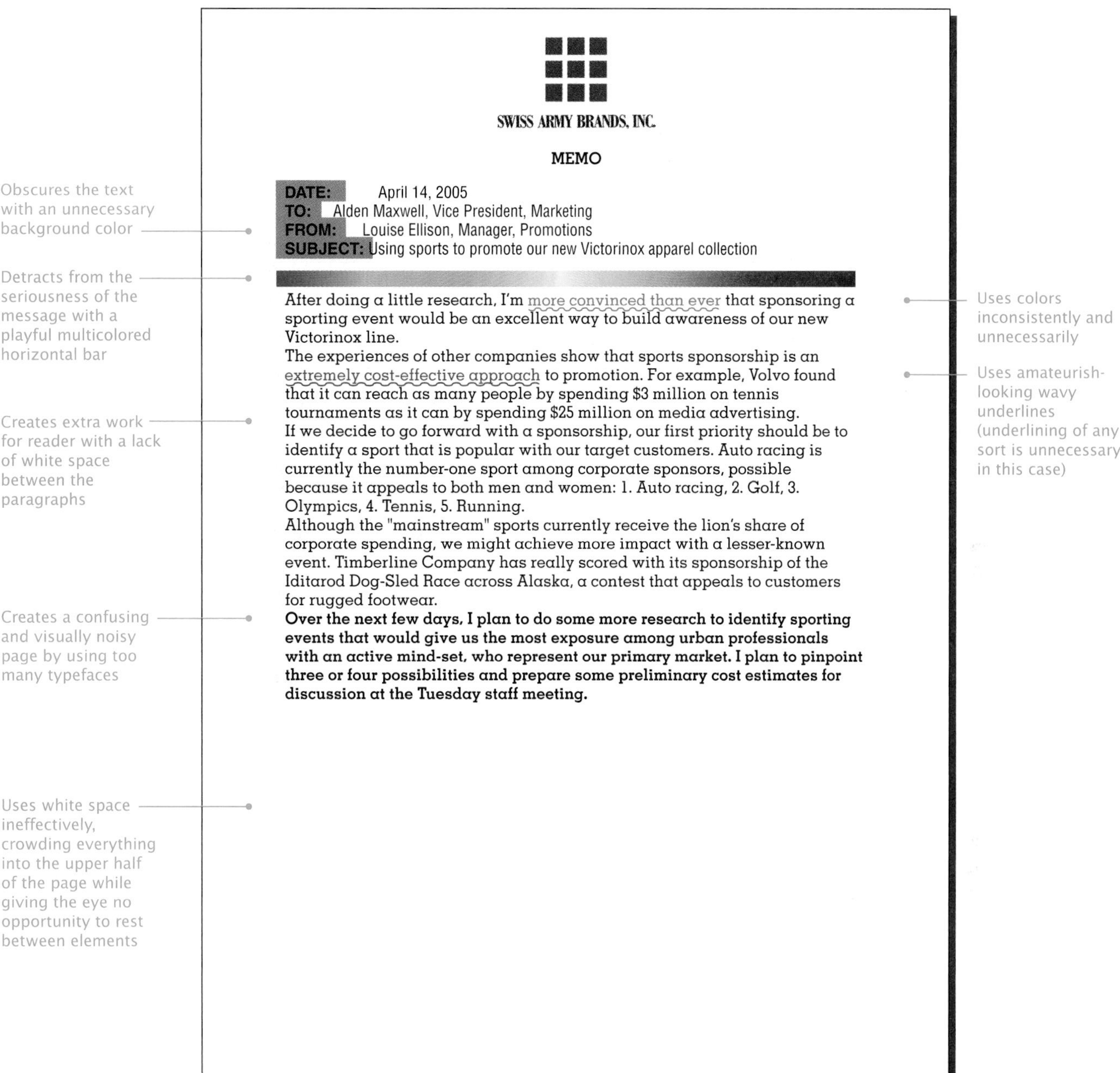
SWISS ARMY BRANDS, INC.

MEMO

DATE: April 14, 2005
TO: Alden Maxwell, Vice President, Marketing
FROM: Louise Ellison, Manager, Promotions
SUBJECT: Using sports to promote our new Victorinox apparel collection

After doing a little research, I'm more convinced than ever that sponsoring a sporting event would be an excellent way to build awareness of our new Victorinox line.
The experiences of other companies show that sports sponsorship is an extremely cost-effective approach to promotion. For example, Volvo found that it can reach as many people by spending $3 million on tennis tournaments as it can by spending $25 million on media advertising.
If we decide to go forward with a sponsorship, our first priority should be to identify a sport that is popular with our target customers. Auto racing is currently the number-one sport among corporate sponsors, possible because it appeals to both men and women: 1. Auto racing, 2. Golf, 3. Olympics, 4. Tennis, 5. Running.
Although the "mainstream" sports currently receive the lion's share of corporate spending, we might achieve more impact with a lesser-known event. Timberline Company has really scored with its sponsorship of the Iditarod Dog-Sled Race across Alaska, a contest that appeals to customers for rugged footwear.
Over the next few days, I plan to do some more research to identify sporting events that would give us the most exposure among urban professionals with an active mind-set, who represent our primary market. I plan to pinpoint three or four possibilities and prepare some preliminary cost estimates for discussion at the Tuesday staff meeting.

Obscures the text with an unnecessary background color
Detracts from the seriousness of the message with a playful multicolored horizontal bar
Creates extra work for reader with a lack of white space between the paragraphs
Creates a confusing and visually noisy page by using too many typefaces
Uses white space ineffectively, crowding everything into the upper half of the page while giving the eye no opportunity to rest between elements
Uses colors inconsistently and unnecessarily
Uses amateurish-looking wavy underlines (underlining of any sort is unnecessary in this case)

- **Detail.** Pay attention to details that affect your design and thus your message. For instance, headings and subheadings that appear at the bottom of a column or a page can annoy readers when the promised information doesn't appear until the next column or page. Also, narrow columns with too much space between words can be distracting.

If you will be designing a lot of documents that go beyond simple memos and reports, consider taking a course in page layout or design to make the most of your creative efforts. Otherwise, to make your messages look professional, interesting, and up to date, you can use a variety of design elements, such as white space, margins and line justification, typefaces, and type styles.

White Space

White space separates elements in a document and helps guide the reader's eye.

Any space free of text or artwork is considered **white space**, and it provides visual contrast for your readers and (perhaps even more important) gives them a resting point. White

FIGURE 6.7 Effective Document Design

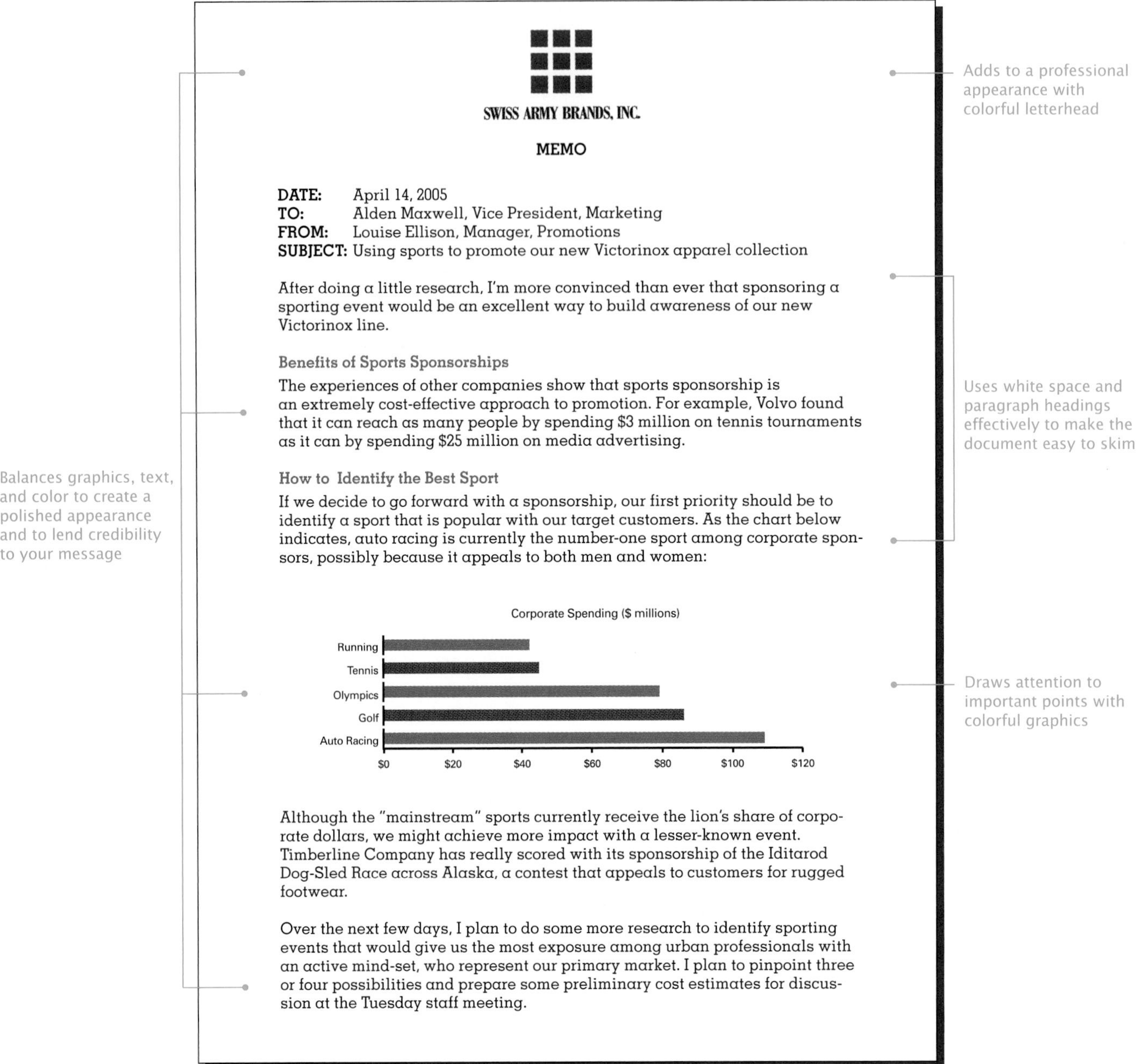

SWISS ARMY BRANDS, INC.

MEMO

DATE: April 14, 2005
TO: Alden Maxwell, Vice President, Marketing
FROM: Louise Ellison, Manager, Promotions
SUBJECT: Using sports to promote our new Victorinox apparel collection

After doing a little research, I'm more convinced than ever that sponsoring a sporting event would be an excellent way to build awareness of our new Victorinox line.

Benefits of Sports Sponsorships

The experiences of other companies show that sports sponsorship is an extremely cost-effective approach to promotion. For example, Volvo found that it can reach as many people by spending $3 million on tennis tournaments as it can by spending $25 million on media advertising.

How to Identify the Best Sport

If we decide to go forward with a sponsorship, our first priority should be to identify a sport that is popular with our target customers. As the chart below indicates, auto racing is currently the number-one sport among corporate sponsors, possibly because it appeals to both men and women:

Corporate Spending ($ millions)
Running
Tennis
Olympics
Golf
Auto Racing
$0
$20
$40
$60
$80
$100
$120
Adds to a professional appearance with colorful letterhead
Uses white space and paragraph headings effectively to make the document easy to skim
Balances graphics, text, and color to create a polished appearance and to lend credibility to your message
Draws attention to important points with colorful graphics

Although the "mainstream" sports currently receive the lion's share of corporate dollars, we might achieve more impact with a lesser-known event. Timberline Company has really scored with its sponsorship of the Iditarod Dog-Sled Race across Alaska, a contest that appeals to customers for rugged footwear.

Over the next few days, I plan to do some more research to identify sporting events that would give us the most exposure among urban professionals with an active mind-set, who represent our primary market. I plan to pinpoint three or four possibilities and prepare some preliminary cost estimates for discussion at the Tuesday staff meeting.

space includes the open area surrounding headings, margin areas, the vertical space between columns, the space created by ragged line endings, the paragraph indents or extra space between unindented paragraphs, and the horizontal space between lines of text. One of the reasons Figure 6.6 is so hard to read is the lack of white space; readers have to work to separate the various pieces of the document.

When placing headings and subheadings into your documents, remember that their purpose is to invite readers to become involved in your message. Centered heads should contain no more than two lines, because multiple lines will slow your readers as they search for the beginning of each line. To improve readability, position your headings "flush left" (aligned with the left-hand margin). You may even want to set them in a type size larger than the type used for text, and you may want to use a different typeface. Because headings and subheadings clue readers in to the organization of your message's content, link them as closely as possible to the text they introduce. You can do so by putting more space above the heading than below it.

Captions are often the most widely read part of a document. They tie photographs and illustrations into the rest of your message. Although usually placed below the exhibits they describe, captions can also be placed beside or above their exhibits. Make sure that the width of your captions is in proportion to the width of the exhibit, the surrounding white space, and the text.

Margins and Justification

Margins define the space around your text and between text columns. They're influenced by the way you place lines of type, which can be set (1) justified (flush on the left and flush on the right), (2) flush left with a ragged right margin, (3) flush right with a ragged left margin, or (4) centered. Justified type "darkens" your message's appearance, because the uniform line lengths lack the white space created by ragged margins. It also tends to make your message look more like a form letter and less like a personalized message. Justified type is often considered more difficult to read, because large gaps can appear between words and because more words are hyphenated. Excessive hyphenation is distracting and hard to follow. Even so, many magazines and newspapers use justified type because increased hyphenation can accommodate more text in a given space.

Flush-left, ragged-right type "lightens" your message's appearance. It gives a document an informal, contemporary feeling of openness. Spacing between words is the same, and only long words that fall at the ends of lines are hyphenated.

Most business documents use a flush left margin and a ragged right margin.

Centered type is rarely used for text paragraphs but is commonly used for headings and subheadings. Flush-right, ragged-left type is rarely used in business documents.

Typefaces

Typeface refers to the physical design of letters, numbers, and other text characters. Most computers offer innumerable choices of fonts or typefaces. Each typeface influences the tone of your message, making it look authoritative or friendly, businesslike or casual, classic or modern, and so on (see Table 6.4). Be sure to choose fonts that are appropriate for your message.

Serif typefaces have small crosslines (called serifs) at the ends of each letter stroke. Serif faces such as Times Roman are commonly used for text; they can look busy and cluttered when set in large sizes for headings or other display treatments. Typefaces with rounded serifs can look friendly; those with squared serifs can look official.

Serif typefaces are commonly used for text; sans serif typefaces are commonly used for headings.

Sans serif typefaces have no serifs. Faces such as Helvetica and Arial are ideal for display treatments that use larger type. Sans serif faces can be difficult to read in long blocks of text. They look best when surrounded by plenty of white space—as in headings or in widely spaced lines of text.

Whichever fonts you choose, limit the number of typefaces in a single document.[9] In general, avoid using more than two typefaces on a page. Many great-looking business documents are based on a single sans serif typeface (such as Arial) for heads and subheads,

TABLE 6.4 Typeface Personalities: Serious to Casual to Playful

SERIF TYPEFACES (BEST FOR TEXT)	SAN SERIF TYPEFACES (BEST FOR HEADLINES; SOME WORK WELL FOR TEXT)	SPECIALTY TYPEFACES (FOR DECORATIVE PURPOSES ONLY)
Bookman Old Style	Arial	ANNA
Century Schoolbook	**Eras Bold**	Bauhaus
Courier	Franklin Gothic Book	*Edwardian*
Garamond	Frutiger	*Lucida Handwriting*
Rockwell	Gill Sans	Old English
Times Roman	Tekton	**STENCIL**

with a second serif typeface (such as Times New Roman) for text and captions. Using too many typefaces clutters the document and can produce an amateurish look (as seen in Figure 6.6 on page 167).

Type Styles

Type style refers to any modification that lends contrast or emphasis to type. Most computers offer boldface, italic, underlining, and other highlighting and decorative styles. Using boldface type for subheads breaks up long expanses of text. You can also boldface isolated words in the middle of a text block to draw more attention to them. However, if you set too many words in boldface, you might create a "checkerboard" appearance within a paragraph, and you will darken the appearance of your entire message, making it look heavy and uninviting.

Use italic type for emphasis. Although italics are sometimes used when irony or humor is intended, quotation marks are usually best for that purpose. Italics can also be used to set off a quote and are often used in captions. Boldfaced type and italics are most effective when reserved for key words—those that help readers understand the main point of the text. A good example of using boldface type effectively is found in the document-revision tips listed under the heading "Editing for Clarity and Conciseness" on pages 158–162 of this chapter. Here the boldfaced type draws attention to the key tips, followed by a short, regular-typeface explanation of each tip.

Avoid using any type style that inhibits your audience's ability to read your messages.

As a general rule, avoid using any style that slows your audience's progress through your message. For instance, underlining or using all-uppercase letters can interfere with your reader's ability to recognize the shapes of words, improperly placed boldface or italicized type can slow down your reader, and shadowed or outlined type can seriously hinder legibility. So use these styles judiciously. Using all uppercase in e-mail can be especially annoying and is usually considered "shouting."

Make sure the size of your type is proportionate to the importance of your message and the space allotted. For most business messages, use a type size of 10 to 12 points (a point is approximately 1/72 of an inch). Resist the temptation to reduce your type size to squeeze in text or to enlarge it to fill up space. Smaller type is hard to read, whereas larger type looks unprofessional and, if squeezed into a small area, is hard to read and visually claustrophobic.

Using Technology to Produce Your Message

The production tools you'll have at your disposal might vary widely, depending on the software and systems you're using. Some IM and e-mail systems offer limited formatting and production capabilities, whereas most word processors now offer some capabilities that rival professional publishing software for many day-to-day business needs. Desktop publishing software such as Quark XPress, Adobe InDesign, and Microsoft Publisher go beyond word processing with more advanced layout capabilities that are designed to accommodate photos, technical drawings, and other elements. (Quark, InDesign, and similar products are used mainly by design professionals.) Microsoft PowerPoint is the most widely used software for electronic presentations, and it offers a wide range of tools for formatting and displaying your message. Companies with large websites frequently have web publishing systems that make it easy to produce web pages with graphics, animation, and other eye-catching features. Multimedia production tools such as Microsoft Producer let you combine slides, audio commentary, video clips, and other features into computer-based presentations that once cost thousands of dollars to create.

Your word processor will be your primary communication tool; learn to use it effectively.

However, most of your message production work is likely to be done with a word processor, such as Microsoft Word or Sun StarOffice. If you're not already familiar with the ins and outs of your software, a few hours of exploration on your own or an introductory training course can dramatically improve the production quality of your documents. At a minimum, you'll benefit from being proficient with the following features:

- **Templates and stylesheets.** As Chapter 5 noted, you can save a tremendous amount of time by using templates (which preset various aspects of page design such as margins) and stylesheets (which standardize formatting decisions for various headings, subheadings, paragraphs, captions, and so forth). Many companies provide templates and stylesheets to ensure a consistent look and feel for all company documents, thus relieving employees from making many of the organizational and formatting decisions discussed throughout this text.

- **Page setup.** Use page setup to control margins, orientation (*portrait* is vertical; *landscape* is horizontal), and the location of *headers* (text and graphics that repeat at the top of every page) and *footers* (similar to headers but at the bottom of the page). Use these controls to ensure adequate white space in your documents.
- **Column formatting.** Most business documents use a single column of text per page, but multiple columns can be an attractive format for documents such as newsletters. Columns are also a handy way to format long lists.
- **Paragraph formatting.** Take advantage of the various paragraph formatting controls to alter the look of your documents as needed. You can offset quotations by increasing margin width around a single paragraph, subtly compress line spacing to fit a document on a single page, use hanging indents to offset the first line of a paragraph, and make sure page breaks have no widows (such as a single line of text by itself at the beginning or end of a page). If you use your word processor only as a glorified typewriter—simply hitting the Enter key at the end of each line or hitting Enter multiple times to put space between lines or paragraphs—you miss out on some of the most powerful features a word processor has to offer. Get to know paragraph formatting.

Paragraph formatting gives you greater control over the look of your documents.

- **Font formatting.** In addition to typeface selection and the basics of bold, italics, and underlining, your word processor probably offers a way to expand or compress text horizontally. This feature can be a lifesaver, for instance, when you need to fit a header on a single line. However, use this expand/compress feature carefully, or it can produce amateurish results. As a general rule, avoid the "special font effects" your word processor might offer, such as blinking, sparkling, or shimmering text. They might be entertaining but they're out of place in any business document.
- **Numbered and bulleted lists.** Let your word processor do the busywork of formatting numbered and bulleted lists, too. It can also automatically renumber lists when you add or remove items, saving you the embarrassment of misnumbered lists.
- **Tables.** Tables are a great way to display any information that lends itself to rows and columns: calendars, numerical data, comparisons, and so on. Use paragraph and font formatting thoughtfully within tables for the best look.
- **Pictures, text boxes, and objects.** Your word processor probably lets you insert a wide variety of *pictures* (using one of the industry-standard formats such as JPEG or GIF). *Text boxes* are small blocks of text that stand apart from the main text (great for captions, callouts, margin notes, and so on). *Objects* can be anything from a spreadsheet to a sound clip to an engineering drawing. Used carefully, all these elements can enhance your documents.

Even though you may need a few hours and some practice to become proficient at using all these features, your time will be well spent. By improving the appearance of your documents, you improve your readers' impressions of you.

PROOFREADING YOUR MESSAGE

6 LEARNING OBJECTIVE

Highlight the types of errors to look for when proofreading

Although spelling, punctuation, and typographical errors seem trivial to some people, most readers view your attention to detail as a sign of your professionalism (see Figure 6.8). In addition to damaging your credibility, typos can wreak havoc ranging from upset customers to legal troubles. If you apply for a job with a typo-filled résumé, your résumé and your chances will probably head straight for the wastebasket. Whether you're writing a one-paragraph memo or a 500-page report, if you let mechanical errors slip through, your readers wonder whether you're unreliable in more important ways.

Your credibility is affected by your attention to the details of mechanics and form.

When you proofread your message, check it for correct grammar, usage, and punctuation (for a quick review, see the "Handbook of Grammar, Mechanics, and Usage" that is included at the end of this textbook). You'll also want to be on the lookout for common spelling errors and typographical errors. Check too for missing material: a missing source

The types of details to look for when proofreading include language errors, missing material, design errors, and typographical errors.

FIGURE 6.8
Why Accuracy in Proofreading Is Important

If you believe that 99.9% accuracy is acceptable, then

Every hour:
18,322 pieces of mail would be mishandled
22,000 checks would be deducted from the wrong bank account

Every day:
12 newborn babies would be given to wrong parents
55 incorrect drug prescriptions would be written

Every week:
500 incorrect surgical procedures would be performed
48,000 books would be shipped with the wrong cover

Every year:
81,000 faulty rolls of 35mm film would be loaded
2 million documents would be lost by the IRS

In addition:
320 entries in Webster's Third New International Dictionary of the English Language would be misspelled

99.9%

note, a missing exhibit, or even a missing paragraph. Look for design errors. For example, some headings and text might appear in the wrong typeface (Helvetica rather than Times New Roman, or Arial Black rather than Arial Narrow). One or two special elements may appear in the wrong type style (boldface instead of italic, or italic instead of underlined). Columns within tables and exhibits on a page might be misaligned. Graphic characters such as ampersands and percent signs may appear when they should be spelled out, and numerical symbols might be incorrect. Look closely at the type to spot problems, such as extra spacing between lines or between words, crowded type, a short line of type ending a paragraph at the top of a new page, a heading left hanging at the bottom of a page, or incorrect hyphenation.

Also give some attention to your overall format. Have you followed accepted conventions and company guidelines for laying out your pages (such as margin width, number of columns, headers)? Have you included all the elements that your audience is expecting? Have you been consistent in handling page numbers, heading styles, exhibits titles, source notes, and other details? (To resolve questions about format and layout, see Appendix A.)

Plan to spend more time proofing documents that are long, complex, and important.

The amount of time you need to spend on proofing depends on both the length and complexity of the document and the situation. A typo in a memo to your team might not be a big deal, but a typo in a financial report or a medical file certainly could be serious. As with every task in the writing process, practice helps—you become not only more familiar with what errors to look for but also more skilled in identifying those errors. For a quick review of items to look for when you proof, see "Checklist: Proofing Business Messages."

7 LEARNING OBJECTIVE

Discuss the most important issues to consider when distributing your messages

DISTRIBUTING YOUR MESSAGE

With the production finished, you're ready to distribute the message. As with every other aspect of business communication, your options for distribution multiply with every advance in technology. In some cases, the choice is obvious: just hit the Send button in your e-mail program, and your message is on its way. In other cases, such as when you have a

CHECKLIST: Proofing Business Messages

A. LOOK FOR WRITING ERRORS

- Typographical mistakes
- Misspelled words
- Grammatical errors
- Punctuation mistakes

B. LOOK FOR MISSING ELEMENTS

- Missing text sections
- Missing exhibits (drawings, tables, photographs, charts, graphs, and so on)
- Missing source notes, copyright notices, or other reference items

C. LOOK FOR DESIGN AND FORMATTING MISTAKES

- Incorrect or inconsistent font selections
- Column sizing, spacing, and alignment
- Margins
- Special characters
- Clumsy line and page breaks
- Page numbers
- Page headers and footers
- Adherence to company standards

100-page report with full-color graphics or a multimedia presentation that is too big to e-mail, you'll need to plan the distribution carefully so that your message is received by everyone who needs it and only those who need it (see "Communication Miscues: Sending Messages Where They Don't Belong"). When planning your distribution, consider the following factors:

Consider cost, convenience, time, security, and privacy when choosing a distribution method.

- **Cost.** Cost won't be a concern for most messages, but for lengthy reports or multimedia production, it might well be. Printing, binding, and delivering reports can be an expensive proposition, so weigh the cost versus the benefits before you decide. If you're trying to land a half-million-dollar client, then spending $1,000 on presentation materials could be a wise investment.
- **Convenience.** How much work is involved for you and your audience? Although it's easy to attach a document to an e-mail message, things might not be so simple for the people on the other end. They may not have access to a printer, might be accessing your message from a slow dial-up connection in a hotel, or might not have the software needed to open your file. If you're sending large files as IM or e-mail attachments, use a file compression utility such as WinZip or StuffIt to shrink the file first. For extremely large files, see whether your audience would prefer a CD-ROM instead.
- **Time.** How soon does the message need to reach the audience? Don't waste money on overnight delivery if the recipient won't read the report for a week.
- **Security and privacy.** The convenience offered by IM, e-mail, and other technologies needs to be weighed against security and privacy concerns. For the most sensitive documents, your company will probably restrict both the people who can receive the documents as well as the means you can use to distribute them. In addition, most computer users are wary of opening attachments these days. Instead of sending Word files (which might be vulnerable to macro viruses and other risks), consider using Adobe Acrobat to convert your documents to PDF files.

Distribution technologies continue to advance, so be on the lookout for new ways to put your messages in the hands of your audience. For example, blogs (see Chapter 5) offer an easy way to publish running commentaries on virtually any subject. *Fast Company* magazine features a blog on its website that gives company staff a forum for sharing ideas and information that either don't make it into the magazine itself or appear in between the monthly publication schedule. (Go to www.fastcompany.com, and click on "weblog" near the top of the page.) Editor-in-Chief John A. Byrne says the blog lets *Fast Company* respond to fast-breaking news and help involve readers in an ongoing discussion of important issues.

Another recent development, Rich Site Summary (RSS), provides a means to automatically retrieve new content from target websites (including blogs) and sends it to a software program known as a news aggregator. RSS-enabled websites make it easy for audiences to collect information they want without repeatedly visiting favorite blogs or subscribing to multiple e-mail newsletters and thus encountering the rampant spam

Communication Miscues

Sending Messages Where They Don't Belong

Mike Dosskey was shocked when the first fax arrived. He was downright angry by the time the third showed up. He isn't a doctor and has no connection with Providence Everett Medical Center in Everett, Washington. Nevertheless, between April and June 2003, the hospital mistakenly sent three separate patient reports to his home fax machine—a serious invasion of patient privacy.

How can such a mistake happen? In this case, someone transposed two digits when dialing the fax number for a local long-term care facility. One misdirected fax contained 13 pages of information about a 76-year-old patient with congestive heart failure. The report included the patient's name, medical history, and a list of prescribed medications.

Dosskey called the hospital after each of the first two misdirected faxes and was simply told to throw them away. Then the third fax arrived. "After calling them twice, I'm done calling," he told a newspaper reporter. "It's irritating me."

In response to these three incidents—and the unwanted newspaper coverage—Providence tightened up its fax policy and implemented a few important precautions:

- Within each department, only those employees trained in patient confidentiality requirements are allowed to send faxes that include patient information.
- These employees should double-check the phone number before sending any confidential fax.
- If a confidential fax goes astray, someone will be sent to retrieve the fax or, if it's long distance, the hospital will send a stamped, self-addressed envelope for return of the message.

Paula Bradlee, who is responsible for medical privacy issues at Providence, responded, "I wish it hadn't happened," referring to the third fax. "Now that it has, we had the opportunity to make changes, and we're making them."

CAREER APPLICATIONS

1. If these faxes had included a social security number, the mistake would've raised the risk of identity theft. What other risks might misdirected messages present?
2. Many hospitals send patient information via e-mail—and some have accidentally sent copies to multiple recipients who could easily forward the message. What kind of precautions should hospitals take to avoid improper transmission of e-mail?

problem associated with e-mail.[10] Technologies such as these can help you deliver the information your audiences want in ways that are most convenient and appealing to them. To learn more about the possibilities of blogging and RSS feeds, explore the following sites:

- Blogger (http://www.blogger.com)
- Blogarama (http://www.blogarama.com)
- Blogdex (http://blogdex.media.mit.edu)
- BlogStreet (http://www.blogstreet.com)

COMMUNICATION CHALLENGES AT ROLLING STONE

In addition to *Rolling Stone*, Wenner Media publishes *US Weekly* and *Men's Journal* magazines. Jann Wenner wants to investigate the possibility of launching a fourth magazine sometime next year. You recently joined Wenner Media's editorial projects team, and Wenner has asked you to help with the analysis of existing magazines.

Individual Challenge: A recent survey of people in the 18-to-25 age group identified several promising areas for new magazines: business, entertainment, fashion, music, sports, and technology. Your task is to pick a category and analyze an existing magazine such as *Business Week, People, Jane, Vibe, ESPN the Magazine,* or *Wired*. Look at the table of contents and the various sections that constitute the front, middle, and back portions of the magazine. Pick two or three articles from each section: How would you describe the style and tone of the headlines? How long is a typical article? How long are the paragraphs and sentences? How much does sentence length vary? Write down your observations for your instructor.

Team Challenge: With three or four people who looked at different magazines, compare your individual analyses. Among these magazines, which ones seem to be written for the 25-and-above crowd? How would you change the writing style to change a magazine in that category to appeal to the 18-to-25 audience? Summarize your team's conclusions for your instructor.

SUMMARY OF LEARNING OBJECTIVES

1 **Discuss the value of careful revision, and list the main tasks involved in completing a business message.** Revision is a vital step in producing effective business messages; even if the first draft conveys the necessary information, chances are it can be made tighter, clearer, and more compelling—making it more successful for you. Revision occurs throughout the writing process, again after you complete the first draft of your business message, and again after you produce the final version. Revision consists of three main tasks: (1) evaluating content, organization, style, and tone, (2) reviewing for readability and scannability, and (3) editing for clarity and conciseness. After you revise your message, you complete it by using design elements to give your message a professional look, proofreading the final version after it has been produced, and distributing it to your audience.

2 **List four writing techniques you can use to improve the readability of your messages.** The four techniques that improve readability are varying sentence length, keeping paragraphs short, using lists and bullets, and adding headings and subheadings. Varying sentence length helps keep your writing fresh and dynamic while giving you a chance to emphasize the most important points. Paragraphs, on the other hand, are usually best kept short to make it easier for readers to consume your information in manageable chunks. Lists and bullets are effective devices for delineating sets of items, steps in a procedure, or other collections of related information. Headings and subheadings organize your message, call attention to important information, and help readers make connections between related pieces of information.

3 **Describe the steps you can take to improve the clarity of your writing.** Clear writing doesn't happen the first time, so you need to revise your work. As you try to clarify your message, (1) break up overly long sentences, (2) rewrite hedging sentences, (3) impose parallelism, (4) correct dangling modifiers, (5) reword long noun sequences, (6) replace camouflaged verbs, (7) clarify sentence structure, (8) clarify awkward references, and (9) moderate your enthusiasm.

4 **Discuss why it's important to make your message more concise, and give four tips on how to do so.** Businesspeople are more likely to read documents that give information efficiently. So to make business messages more concise, try to include only necessary material and write clean sentences by (1) deleting unnecessary words and phrases, (2) shortening overly long words and phrases, (3) eliminating redundancies, and (4) recasting sentences that being with "It is" and "There are."

5 **Explain how design elements help determine the effectiveness of your documents.** White space provides contrast and gives readers a resting point. Margins define the space around the text and contribute to the amount of white space. Typefaces influence the tone of the message. Type styles provide contrast or emphasis. When selecting and applying design elements, you can ensure their effectiveness by being consistent throughout your document; balancing your space between text, art, and white space; showing restraint in the number of elements you use; and paying attention to every detail.

6 **Highlight the types of errors to look for when proofreading.** When proofreading the final version of your document, always keep an eye out for errors in grammar, usage, and punctuation. In addition, watch for spelling errors and typos. Make sure that nothing is missing (whether a source note, an exhibit, or text). Correct design errors such as elements that appear in the wrong typeface, elements that appear in the wrong type style, misaligned elements (columns in a table, exhibits on a page, etc.), and graphic characters (such as ampersands and percent signs) that appear in both symbol and spelled-out form. Look for typographical errors such as uneven spacing between lines and words, a short line of type at the top of a page, a heading at the bottom of a page, or incorrect hyphenation. In addition, make sure your layout conforms to company guidelines.

7 **Discuss the most important issues to consider when distributing your messages.** Consider cost, convenience, time, security, and privacy when choosing the method to distribute your messages. Cost isn't a major issue for most messages, although production, printing,

and distribution of lengthy or complex reports can be a concern. In general, balance the cost with the importance and urgency of the message. Make sure the distribution method is convenient for your audience; it might be easy for you to simply attach a document to an e-mail message, but that might not be the best approach for a given audience. As with cost, balance the time factor with your needs and the needs of your audience. Lastly, consider security and privacy issues before distributing documents that contain sensitive or confidential information.

Test Your Knowledge

1. What are the three main tasks involved in revising a business message?
2. How can you increase the readability of your paragraphs?
3. What functions do headings serve?
4. What are some ways you can make a document more concise?
5. What computer tools can you use when revising messages?
6. What is parallel construction, and why is it important?
7. Why is it a good idea to use verbs instead of noun phrases?
8. How do readers benefit from white space?
9. Why is proofreading an important part of the writing process?
10. What factors should you consider when choosing a distribution method for your messages?

Apply Your Knowledge

1. Why is it helpful to let a first draft "age" for a while before you begin the editing process?
2. Given the choice of only one, would you prefer to use a grammar checker or a spell checker? Why?
3. When you are designing a formal business letter, which design elements do you have to consider and which are optional?
4. Which distribution method would you choose for a highly confidential strategic planning report that needs to be sent to top executives at six locations in North America, Asia, and Europe? Explain your choice.
5. **Ethical Choices** What are the ethical implications of murky, complex writing in a document explaining how customers can appeal the result of a decision made in the company's favor during a dispute?

Practice Your Knowledge

Documents for Analysis

Read the following documents, then (1) analyze the strengths and weaknesses of each sentence, and (2) revise each document so that it follows the guidelines in Chapters 4 through 6.

Document 6.A

The move to our new offices will take place over this coming weekend. For everything to run smooth, everyone will have to clean out their own desk and pack up the contents in boxes that will be provided. You will need to take everything off the walls too, and please pack it along with the boxes.

If you have a lot of personal belongings, you should bring them home with you. Likewise with anything valuable. I do not mean to infer that items will be stolen, irregardless it is better to be safe than sorry.

On Monday, we will be unpacking, putting things away, and then get back to work. The least amount of disruption is anticipated by us, if everyone does their part. Hopefully, there will be no negative affects on production schedules, and current deadlines will be met.

Document 6.B

Dear Ms. Giraud:

Enclosed herewith please find the manuscript for your book, *Careers in Woolgathering*. After perusing the first two chapters of your 1,500-page manuscript, I was forced to conclude that the subject matter, handicrafts and artwork using wool fibers, is not coincident with the publishing program of Framingham Press, which to this date has issued only works on business endeavors, avoiding all other topics completely.

Although our firm is unable to consider your impressive work at the present time, I have taken the liberty of recording some comments on some of the pages. I am of the opinion that any feedback that a writer can obtain from those well versed in the publishing realm can only serve to improve the writer's authorial skills.

In view of the fact that your residence is in the Boston area, might I suggest that you secure an appointment with someone of high editorial stature at the Cambridge Heritage Press, which I believe might have something of an interest in works of the nature you have produced.

Wishing you the best of luck in your literary endeavors, I remain

Arthur J. Cogswell
Editor

Document 6.C

For delicious, air-popped popcorn, please read the following instructions: The popper is designed to pop 1/2 cup of popcorn kernels at one time. Never add more than 1/2 cup. A half cup of corn will produce three to four quarts of popcorn. More batches may be made separately after completion of the first batch. Popcorn is popped by hot air. Oil or shortening is not needed for popping corn. Add only popcorn kernels to the popping chamber. Standard grades of popcorn are recommended for use. Premium or gourmet type popping corns may be used. Ingredients such as oil, shortening, butter, margarine, or salt should never be added to the popping chamber. The popper, with popping chute in position, may be preheated for two minutes before adding the corn. Turn the popper off before adding the corn. Use electricity safely and wisely. Observe safety precautions when using the popper. Do not touch the popper when it is hot. The popper should not be left unattended when it is plugged into an outlet. Do not use the popper if it or its cord has been damaged. Do not use the popper if it is not working properly. Before using the first time, wash the chute and butter/measuring cup in hot soapy water. Use a dishcloth or sponge. Wipe the outside of the popper base. Use a damp cloth. Dry the base. Do not immerse the popper base in water or other liquid. Replace the chute and butter/measuring cup. The popper is ready to use.

Exercises

For live links to all websites discussed in this chapter, visit this text's website at www.prenhall.com/bovee. Just log on, select Chapter 6, and click on "Featured Websites." Locate the name of the page or the URL related to the material in the text.

6.1 Message Readability: Writing Paragraphs Rewrite the following paragraph to vary the length of the sentences and to shorten the paragraph so it looks more inviting to readers.

> Although major league baseball remains popular, more people are attending minor league baseball games because they can spend less on admission, snacks, and parking and still enjoy the excitement of America's pastime. Connecticut, for example, has three AA minor league teams, including the New Haven Ravens, who are affiliated with the St. Louis Cardinals; the Norwich Navigators, who are affiliated with the New York Yankees; and the New Britain Rock Cats, who are affiliated with the Minnesota Twins. These teams play in relatively small stadiums, so fans are close enough to see and hear everything, from the swing of the bat connecting with the ball to the thud of the ball landing in the outfielder's glove. Best of all, the cost of a family outing to see rising stars play in a local minor league game is just a fraction of what the family would spend to attend a major league game in a much larger, more crowded stadium.

6.2 Message Readability: Using Bullets Rewrite the following paragraph using a bulleted list:

> With our alarm system, you'll have a 24-hour security guard who signals the police at the suggestion of an intruder. You'll also appreciate the computerized scanning device that determines exactly where and when the intrusion occurred. No need to worry about electrical failure, either, thanks to our backup response unit.[11]

6.3 Revising Messages: Clarity Break these sentences into shorter ones by adding more periods:

a. The next time you write something, check your average sentence length in a 100-word passage, and if your sentences average more than 16 to 20 words, see whether you can break up some of the sentences.
b. Don't do what the village blacksmith did when he instructed his apprentice as follows: "When I take the shoe out of the fire, I'll lay it on the anvil, and when I nod my head, you hit it with the hammer." The apprentice did just as he was told, and now he's the village blacksmith.
c. Unfortunately, no gadget will produce excellent writing, but using a yardstick like the Fog Index gives us some guideposts to follow for making writing easier to read because its two factors remind us to use short sentences and simple words.
d. Know the flexibility of the written word and its power to convey an idea, and know how to make your words behave so that your readers will understand.
e. Words mean different things to different people, and a word such as *block* may mean city block, butcher block, engine block, auction block, or several other things.

6.4 Revising Messages: Conciseness Cross out unnecessary words in the following phrases:

a. Consensus of opinion
b. New innovations
c. Long period of time
d. At a price of $50
e. Still remains

6.5 Revising Messages: Conciseness Revise the following sentences, using shorter, simpler words:

a. The antiquated calculator is ineffectual for solving sophisticated problems.
b. It is imperative that the pay increments be terminated before an inordinate deficit is accumulated.
c. There was unanimity among the executives that Ms. Jackson's idiosyncrasies were cause for a mandatory meeting with the company's personnel director.
d. The impending liquidation of the company's assets was cause for jubilation among the company's competitors.
e. The expectations of the president for a stock dividend were accentuated by the preponderance of evidence that the company was in good financial condition.

6.6 Revising Messages: Conciseness Use infinitives as substitutes for the overly long phrases in these sentences:

a. For living, I require money.
b. They did not find sufficient evidence for believing in the future.
c. Bringing about the destruction of a dream is tragic.

6.7 Revising Messages: Conciseness Rephrase the following in fewer words:

a. In the near future
b. In the event that
c. In order that
d. For the purpose of
e. With regard to
f. It may be that
g. In very few cases
h. With reference to
i. At the present time
j. There is no doubt that

6.8 Revising Messages: Conciseness Condense these sentences to as few words as possible:

a. We are of the conviction that writing is important.
b. In all probability, we're likely to have a price increase.
c. Our goals include making a determination about that in the near future.
d. When all is said and done at the conclusion of this experiment, I'd like to summarize the final windup.
e. After a trial period of three weeks, during which time she worked for a total of 15 full working days, we found her work was sufficiently satisfactory so that we offered her full-time work.

6.9 Revising Messages: Modifiers Remove all the unnecessary modifiers from these sentences:

a. Tremendously high pay increases were given to the extraordinarily skilled and extremely conscientious employees.
b. The union's proposals were highly inflationary, extremely demanding, and exceptionally bold.

6.10 Revising Messages: Hedging Rewrite these sentences so that they no longer contain any hedging:

a. It would appear that someone apparently entered illegally.
b. It may be possible that sometime in the near future the situation is likely to improve.
c. Your report seems to suggest that we might be losing money.
d. I believe Nancy apparently has somewhat greater influence over employees in the word-processing department.
e. It seems as if this letter of resignation means you might be leaving us.

6.11 Revising Messages: Indefinite Starters Rewrite these sentences to eliminate the indefinite starters:

a. There are several examples here to show that Elaine can't hold a position very long.
b. It would be greatly appreciated if every employee would make a generous contribution to Mildred Cook's retirement party.
c. It has been learned in Washington today from generally reliable sources that an important announcement will be made shortly by the White House.
d. There is a rule that states that we cannot work overtime without permission.
e. It would be great if you could work late for the next three Saturdays.

6.12 Revising Messages: Parallelism Present the ideas in these sentences in parallel form:

a. Mr. Hill is expected to lecture three days a week, to counsel two days a week, and must write for publication in his spare time.
b. She knows not only accounting, but she also reads Latin.
c. Both applicants had families, college degrees, and were in their thirties, with considerable accounting experience but few social connections.
d. This book was exciting, well written, and held my interest.
e. Don is both a hard worker and he knows bookkeeping.

6.13 Revising Messages: Awkward References Revise the following sentences to delete the awkward references:

a. The vice president in charge of sales and the production manager are responsible for the keys to 34A and 35A, respectively.
b. The keys to 34A and 35A are in executive hands, with the former belonging to the vice president in charge of sales and the latter belonging to the production manager.
c. The keys to 34A and 35A have been given to the production manager, with the aforementioned keys being gold embossed.
d. A laser printer and a dot-matrix printer were delivered to John and Megan, respectively.
e. The walnut desk is more expensive than the oak desk, the former costing $300 more than the latter.

6.14 Revising Messages: Dangling Modifiers Rewrite these sentences to clarify the dangling modifiers:

a. Running down the railroad tracks in a cloud of smoke, we watched the countryside glide by.
b. Lying on the shelf, Ruby saw the seashell.
c. Based on the information, I think we should buy the property.
d. Being cluttered and filthy, Sandy took the whole afternoon to clean up her desk.
e. After proofreading every word, the memo was ready to be signed.

6.15 Revising Messages: Noun Sequences Rewrite the following sentences to eliminate the long strings of nouns:

a. The focus of the meeting was a discussion of the bank interest rate deregulation issue.
b. Following the government task force report recommendations, we are revising our job applicant evaluation procedures.
c. The production department quality assurance program components include employee training, supplier cooperation, and computerized detection equipment.
d. The supermarket warehouse inventory reduction plan will be implemented next month.
e. The State University business school graduate placement program is one of the best in the country.

6.16 Revising Messages: Sentence Structure Rearrange the following sentences to bring the subjects closer to their verbs:

a. Trudy, when she first saw the bull pawing the ground, ran.
b. It was Terri who, according to Ted, who is probably the worst gossip in the office (Tom excepted), mailed the wrong order.
c. William Oberstreet, in his book *Investment Capital Reconsidered,* writes of the mistakes that bankers through the decades have made.
d. Judy Schimmel, after passing up several sensible investment opportunities, despite the warnings of her friends and family, invested her inheritance in a jojoba plantation.
e. The president of U-Stor-It, which was on the brink of bankruptcy after the warehouse fire, the worst tragedy in the history of the company, prepared a press announcement.

6.17 Revising Messages: Camouflaged Verbs Rewrite each sentence so that the verbs are no longer camouflaged:

a. Adaptation to the new rules was performed easily by the employees.
b. The assessor will make a determination of the tax due.
c. Verification of the identity of the employees must be made daily.
d. The board of directors made a recommendation that Mr. Ronson be assigned to a new division.
e. The auditing procedure on the books was performed by the vice president.

6.18 Producing Messages: Design Elements Look back at your revised version of Document 6.C (see exercise under "Documents for Analysis" on page 176). Which design elements could you use to make this document more readable? Produce your revision of Document 6.C using your selected design elements. Then experiment by changing one of the design elements. How does the change affect readability? Exchange documents with another student and critique each other's work.

6.19 Web Design Visit the stock market page of Bloomberg's website at www.bloomberg.com and evaluate the use of design in presenting the latest news. What design improvements can you suggest to enhance readability of the information posted on this page?

6.20 Teamwork Team up with another student and exchange your revised versions of Document 6.A, 6.B, or 6.C (see exercises under "Documents for Analysis"). Review the assignment to be sure the instructions are clear. Then read and critique your teammate's revision to see whether it can be improved. After you have critiqued each other's work, take a moment to examine the way you expressed your comments and the way you felt listening to the other student's comments. Can you identify ways to improve the critiquing process in situations such as this?

6.21 Proofreading Messages: E-Mail Proofread the following e-mail message and revise it to correct any problems you find:

> Our final company orrientation of the year will be held on Dec. 20. In preparation for this sesssion, please order 20 copies of the Policy handbook, the confindentiality agreenemt, the employee benefits Manual, please let me know if you anticipate any delays in obtaining these materials.

6.22 Ethical Choices Three of your company's five plants exceeded their expense budgets last month. You want all the plants to operate within their budgets from now on. You were thinking of using broadcast faxing to let all five plants see the memo you are sending to the managers of the three over-budget plants. Is this a good idea? Why or why not?

Expand Your Knowledge

For live links to the websites that follow, go to www.prenhall.com/bovee. When you log on, select Chapter 6, then select "Featured Websites," click on the URL of the website you wish to visit, and review the website to complete these exercises.

Exploring the Best of the Web

Write it Right: Tips to Help You Rethink and Revise
www.powa.org

Are you sure that readers perceive your written message as you intended? If you want help revising a message that you're completing, use the Paradigm Online Writing Assistant (POWA). With this interactive writer's guide, you can select topics to get tips on how to edit your work, reshape your thoughts, and rewrite for clarity. Read discussions about perfecting your writing skills, and for practice, complete one of the many online activities provided to reinforce what you've learned. Or select the Forum to talk about writing. At POWA's website, you'll learn how to improve the final draft of your message. Explore POWA's advice then answer the following questions:

1. Why is it better to write out ideas in a rough format and later reread your message to revise its content? When revising your message, what questions can you ask about your writing?
2. Name the four elements of the "writing context." Imagine that you're the reader of your message. What questions might you ask?
3. When you revise a written message, what is the purpose of "tightening"? What is one way to tighten your writing as you complete a message?

Exploring the Web on Your Own

Review these chapter-related websites on your own to learn more about writing business messages.

1. Produce flawless messages by reviewing the material at the Guide to Grammar and Writing, http://ccc.commnet.edu/grammar.
2. Troubled by those tricky word choices that bother every writer? Not sure if "alternate" or "alternative" is the right choice? Visit the Grammar Slammer at http://englishplus.com/grammar and click on "Common Mistakes and Choices" for advice on dozens of common word choice dilemmas.
3. Learn the basics of page layout in Microsoft Word to make sure your documents are designed effectively. Visit http://office.microsoft.com, click on Assistance, find the link to browse assistance for Word, then click through the pages of advice on document formatting.

Learn Interactively

Interactive Study Guide

Go to the Companion Website at www.prenhall.com/bovee. For Chapter 6, take advantage of the interactive "Study Guide" to test your knowledge of the chapter. Get instant feedback on whether you need additional studying.

Also, visit this site's "Study Hall," where you'll find an abundance of valuable resources that will help you succeed in this course.

Peak Performance Grammar and Mechanics

To improve your skill with prepositions, conjunctions, and articles, visit www.prenhall.com/onekey, click "Peak Performance Grammar and Mechanics," click "Grammar Basics," then click "Prepositions, Conjunctions, and Articles." Take the Pretest to determine whether you have any weak areas. Then review those areas in the Refresher Course. Take the Follow-Up Test to check your grasp of prepositions, conjunctions, and articles. For an extra challenge or advanced practice, take the Advanced Test. Finally, for additional reinforcement in prepositions, conjunctions, and articles, go to www.prenhall.com/bovee, where you will find "Improve Your Grammar, Mechanics, and Usage" exercises.

PART 3

Writing Letters, Memos, E-Mails, and Instant Messages

CHAPTER 7
Writing Routine and Positive Messages

CHAPTER 8
Writing Negative Messages

CHAPTER 9
Writing Persuasive Messages

chapter 7

Writing Routine and Positive Messages

LEARNING OBJECTIVES

After studying this chapter, you will be able to

1 Apply the three-step writing process to routine and positive messages

2 Illustrate an effective strategy for writing routine requests

3 Explain how to ask for specific action in a courteous manner

4 Illustrate a strategy for writing routine replies and positive messages

5 Discuss the importance of knowing who is responsible when granting claims and requests for adjustment

6 Explain how creating informative messages differs from responding to information requests

7 Describe the importance of goodwill messages and explain how to make them effective

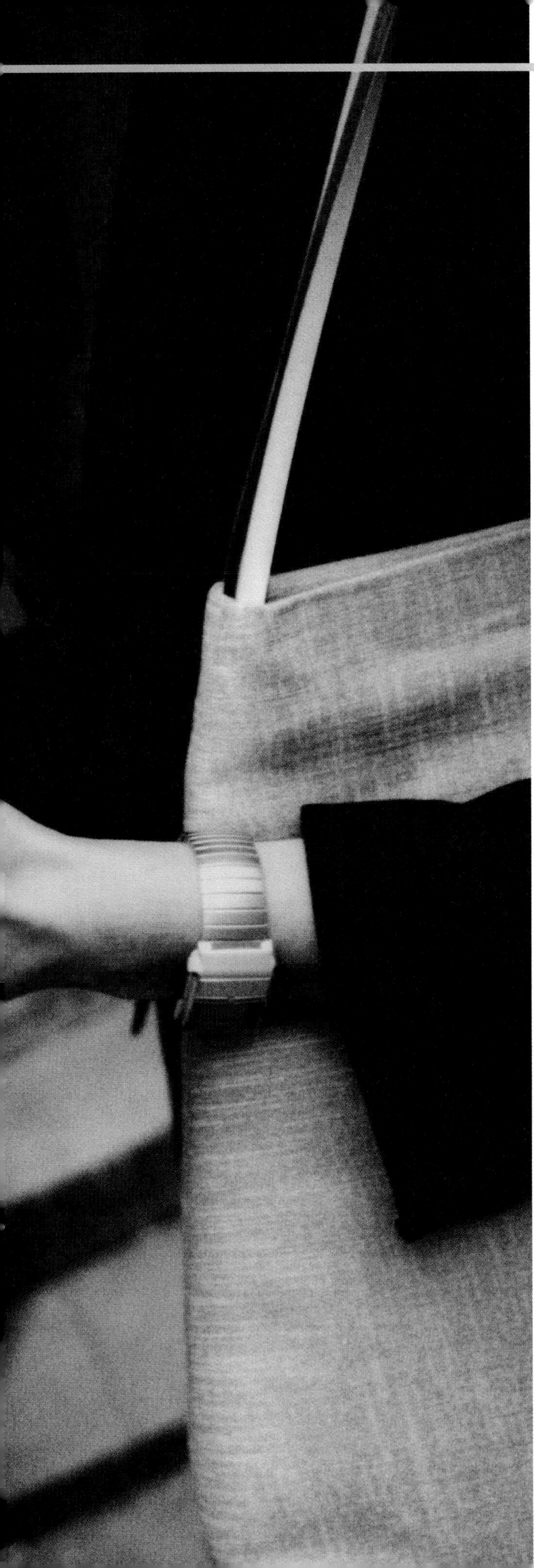

COMMUNICATION CLOSE-UP AT CONE, INC.

www.coneinc.com

Considering the number of corporate scandals in recent years, you might assume that all businesses are up to no good. Although a few companies fill headlines with bad news, thousands of other companies continue to conduct business ethically, and even more than that, they work to make significant contributions in their communities. Ready to help them in their efforts to help others is Cone, Inc., a Boston-based agency that specializes in "cause marketing." CEO Carol Cone explains: "Consumers no longer have trust in anything, so they look to companies for a lot more. They look to see what companies stand for."

One of Cone's clients, ConAgra Foods, took up the cause of child hunger in the United States through its Feeding Children Better program. By writing positive messages and news releases, Cone helps ConAgra spread the message about its program, which began when ConAgra became a national sponsor of Kids Cafés, an after-school program that serves free, hot, nutritious meals to kids in need. Company contributions funded over 130 new Kids

ConAgra's Feeding Children Better program supports thousands of children every year, and the company's public relations agency uses these successes to focus nationwide attention on the problem of childhood hunger.

Cafés, each one providing more than 10,000 meals a year. Then to improve distribution of food to the cafés, ConAgra bought 100 refrigerated trucks from Webvan (after the dot-com grocer failed) and donated them to America's Second Harvest, a national network of food banks and food-rescue programs that helps a variety of organizations, including Kids Cafés.

Cone focuses her news releases on the three main goals of ConAgra's Feeding Children Better program: (1) getting food to children who need it, (2) repairing breakdowns in food distribution, and (3) raising national awareness about child hunger. ConAgra and Cone have received numerous awards for their good work and effective communication, such as the 2002 Corporate Citizenship Award from the U.S. Chamber of Commerce and the 2003 Cause Marketing Halo Award.

What makes Cone's messages so effective? Simply trumpeting ConAgra's good deeds would be positive enough, but Cone puts her press releases to work by highlighting ConAgra's progress toward each goal. She focuses attention on ConAgra's activities to highlight the problems of childhood hunger, thereby helping her client accomplish even more positive outcomes through the use of positive messages.

Regardless of the subject matter of your business messages, you can make them more effective by following Cone's advice to stay focused on your overall business goals and to emphasize the audience's concerns whenever you write.[1]

1 LEARNING OBJECTIVE

Apply the three-step writing process to routine and positive messages

USING THE THREE-STEP WRITING PROCESS FOR ROUTINE AND POSITIVE MESSAGES

Like Carol Cone, chances are you will compose numerous routine and positive messages during the typical business day. Most of a typical employee's communication is about routine matters: orders, information, company policies, claims, credit, employees, products, operations, and so on. Such messages are rarely long or complex. Even so, to produce the best messages possible, you'll want to apply the three-step writing process.

Communication Solution

Balancing several message goals is the secret to Cone, Inc.'s successful use of positive messages in its work for ConAgra's Feeding Children Better program. Cone's messages help ConAgra maintain a positive image in the marketplace as they help solve the problem of childhood hunger.

Step 1: Plan Your Message

Even though planning routine and positive messages may take only a few minutes, the four tasks of planning still apply. First, analyze the situation, making sure that your purpose is clear and that you know enough about your audience to craft a successful message. Second, gather whatever information your audience needs to know. Even something as simple as a team meeting can involve dozens of details, from presentation setups to lunch arrangements to parking. Including all necessary information the first time saves you and your audience the time and trouble of additional messages to fill in the gaps. Third, select the right medium for the message and the audience. Both routine and positive messages are often sent via e-mail and instant messaging, but printed memos and letters are still common. Fourth, organize your information effectively. This task includes defining your main idea, limiting your scope, selecting a direct or an indirect approach, and outlining your content. Throughout this chapter, you'll learn more about performing all four of these tasks for a variety of routine and positive message types.

Step 2: Write Your Message

Start by adapting your approach to your audience. Be sensitive to your audience's needs by maintaining a "you" attitude, being polite, emphasizing the positive, and using bias-free language. To strengthen your relationship with your audience, establish your credibility and project your company's image. Also, even though your tone is usually conversational, some messages may need to be more formal than others. You'll want to use plain English and make your writing as active as possible.

With some practice, you'll be able to compose most routine messages quickly. In fact, the ability to generate such messages quickly is a key skill for most business executives. Your main idea is probably well defined already; just be sure you stick to it by limiting the scope of your message.

Communicating Across Cultures

How Direct Is Too Direct?

The direct mode of communication generally valued in the United States and other high-context cultures is often viewed as abrupt, rude, and intrusive in high-context cultures found in France, Mexico, Japan, Saudi Arabia, Italy, and the Philippines (see discussion of context in Chapter 3). When making requests in such cultures, determine whether to use a direct or an implied approach by considering audience attitudes toward destiny, time, authority, and logic:

- **Destiny.** Do audience members believe they can control events themselves? Or do they see events as predetermined and uncontrollable? If you're supervising employees who believe that fate controls a construction deadline, an e-mail asking them to stay on schedule might be confusing or even insulting.
- **Time.** Do audience members view time as precise and not to be wasted? Or do they see time as relative and relaxed? If you ask for a response by a specific time, is it reasonable to expect your audience to comply?
- **Authority.** Do audience members conduct business more autocratically or more democratically? In Mexico, rank and status are highly valued, so when communicating downward, you may need to be even more direct than you're used to being in the United States. And when communicating upward, you may need to be much less direct than usual.
- **Logic.** Do audience members pursue logic in a straight line, from point A to point B? Or do they communicate in circular or spiral patterns of logic? If you organize a speech or letter in a straightforward and direct manner, your message may be considered illogical, unclear, and disorganized.

By finding out how much or how little a culture tends toward high-context communication, you'll know whether to be direct or to rely on nuance.

CAREER APPLICATIONS

1. Research a high-context culture such as may be found in Japan, Korea, or China, and write a one- or two-paragraph summary of how someone in that culture would go about requesting information.
2. When you are writing in American English to someone in a high-context culture, would it be better to (a) make your request directly in the interest of clarity or (b) try to match your audience's unfamiliar logic and make your request indirectly? Explain your answer.

Also, your readers in most cases will be interested or at least neutral, so you can usually adopt the direct approach for routine and positive messages: Open with a clear statement of the main idea, include all necessary details in the body, and then close cordially. However, even though these messages are the least complicated to write, communicating across cultural boundaries can be a challenge, especially if you're not familiar with the cultural differences involved (see "Communicating Across Cultures: How Direct Is Too Direct?").

Step 3: Complete Your Message

No matter how brief or straightforward your message, maximize its impact by giving yourself plenty of time to revise, produce, proofread, and distribute it. First, revise your message by evaluating content and organization to make sure you've said what you want to in the order you want to say it. Review your message's readability. Edit and rewrite to make it concise and clear. Second, design your document to suit your purpose and your audience. Even simple e-mails and instant messages can benefit from careful font selection, the use of white space, and other design choices. Next, proofread the final version of your message, looking for typos, errors in spelling and mechanics, alignment problems, poor print quality, and so on. Finally, choose a distribution method that balances cost, convenience, time, security, and privacy. Increasingly, routine and positive messages are delivered electronically, on intranets (for internal audiences), extranets (for restricted external audiences), or websites (for general external audiences), or via e-mail and instant messaging.

Just as you do for other messages, you need to revise, produce, and proofread routine messages.

Perry Klebahn's firm, Atlas Snow-Shoe Company, sells high-end showshoes in more than 1,000 stores across the United States, ringing up annual sales of about $12 million. Klebahn tells his employees to establish a good relationship with their audience by learning what they need to know and by using language that is positive and polite.

MAKING ROUTINE REQUESTS

Making requests—for information, action, products, adjustments, or other matters—is a routine part of business. In most cases, you're audience will be prepared to comply, as long as you're not being unreasonable or asking someone to do something they would expect you to do yourself. By applying a clear strategy and tailoring your approach to each situation, you'll be able to generate effective requests quickly.

Strategy for Routine Requests

Like all business messages, routine requests have three parts: an opening, a body, and a close. Using the direct approach, open with your main idea (a clear statement of your request). Use the body to give details and justify your request. Then close by requesting specific action (see Figure 7.1).

For routine requests and positive messages
- State the request or main idea
- Give necessary details
- Close with a cordial request for specific action

2 LEARNING OBJECTIVE

Illustrate an effective strategy for writing routine requests

State Your Request Up Front

Begin routine requests by placing your request first—up front is where it stands out and gets the most attention. Of course, getting right to the point should not be interpreted as a license to be abrupt or tactless:

Take care that your direct approach doesn't come across as abrupt or tactless.

- **Pay attention to tone.** Even though you expect a favorable response, the tone of your initial request is important. Instead of demanding action ("Send me your latest catalog"), soften your request with words such as *please* and *I would appreciate.*
- **Assume your audience will comply.** An impatient demand for rapid service isn't necessary. You can generally make the assumption that your audience will comply with your request once the reason for it is clearly understood.
- **Punctuate questions and polite requests differently.** A polite request in question form requires no question mark: "Would you please help us determine whether Kate Kingsley is a suitable applicant for this position." A direct question within your message does require a question mark: "Did Kate Kingsley demonstrate an ability to work smoothly with clients?"
- **Be specific.** State precisely what you want. For example, if you request the latest market data from your research department, be sure to say whether you want a one-page summary or a hundred pages of raw data.

Explain and Justify Your Request

In the body of the request, give the details of your request.

Use the body of your message to explain your initial request. Make the explanation a smooth and logical outgrowth of your opening remarks. If possible, point out how complying with the request could benefit the reader. For instance, if you would like some assistance interpreting complex quality-control data, point out how a better understanding of quality-control issues would improve customer satisfaction and ultimately lead to higher profits for the entire company.

Whether you're writing a formal letter or a simple instant message, you can use the body of your request to list a series of questions. This list of questions helps organize your message and helps your audience identify the information you need. Just keep in mind a few basics:

Using lists help readers sort through multiple related items or multiple requests.

- **Ask the most important questions first.** If cost is your main concern, you might begin with a question such as "What is the cost for shipping the merchandise by air versus truck?" Then you may want to ask more specific but related questions about, say, discounts for paying early.
- **Ask only relevant questions.** To help expedite the response to your request, ask only those questions that are central to your main request. Doing so will generate an answer sooner and make better use of the other person's time.

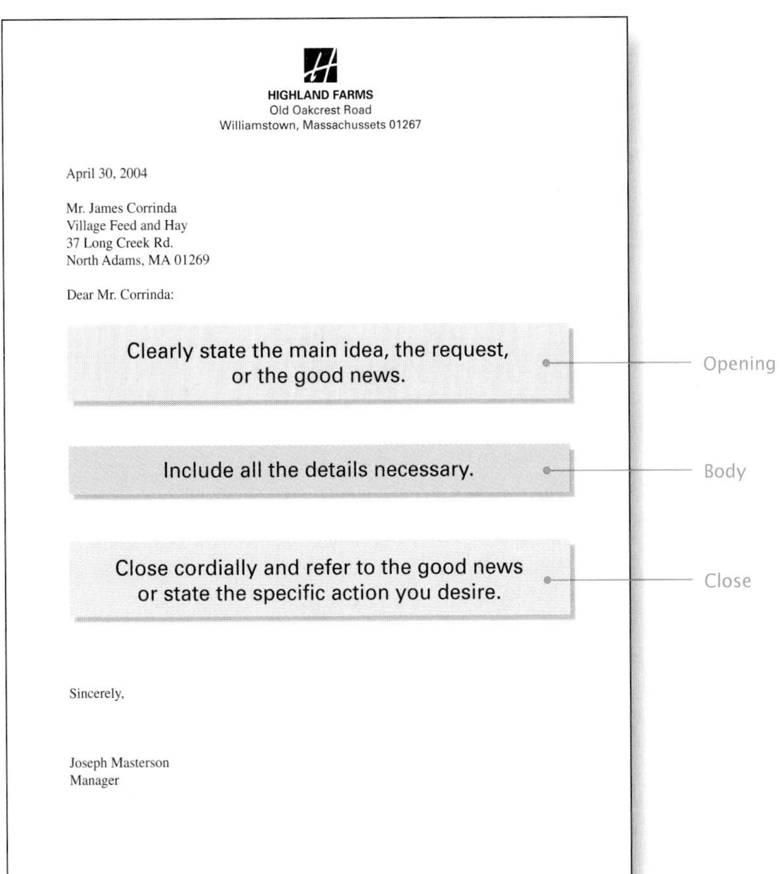
HIGHLAND FARMS
Old Oakcrest Road
Williamstown, Massachussets 01267

April 30, 2004

Mr. James Corrinda
Village Feed and Hay
37 Long Creek Rd.
North Adams, MA 01269

Dear Mr. Corrinda:

Sincerely,

Joseph Masterson
Manager

FIGURE 7.1
Organizing Routine and Positive Messages

- **Deal with only one topic per question.** If you have an unusual or complex request, break it down into specific, individual questions so that the reader can address each one separately. Don't put the burden of untangling a complicated request on your reader. This consideration not only shows respect for your audience's time but also gets you a more accurate answer in less time.

Request Specific Action in a Courteous Close

3 LEARNING OBJECTIVE

Explain how to ask for specific action in a courteous manner

Close your message with three important elements: (1) a specific request, (2) information about how you can be reached (if it isn't obvious), and (3) an expression of appreciation or goodwill. When you ask readers to perform a specific action, ask that they respond by a specific time, if appropriate ("Please send the figures by April 5 so that I can return first-quarter results to you before the May 20 conference"). Plus, by including your phone number, e-mail address, office hours, and other contact information, you help your readers respond easily.

Close with
- A request for some specific action
- Information about how you can be reached
- An expression of appreciation

Conclude your message by sincerely expressing your goodwill and appreciation. However, don't thank the reader "in advance" for cooperating. If the reader's reply warrants a word of thanks, send it after you've received the reply. To review, see "Checklist: Writing Routine Requests."

Common Examples of Routine Requests

The various types of routine requests are innumerable, from asking favors to requesting credit. However, many of the routine messages that you'll be writing will likely fall into a few main categories. The following sections discuss three of these categories: asking for information and action, asking for recommendations, and making claims and requesting adjustments.

CHECKLIST: Writing Routine Requests

A. STATE YOUR REQUEST UP FRONT

- Write in a polite, undemanding, personal tone.
- Use the direct approach, since your audience will probably respond favorably to your request.
- Be specific and precise in your request.

B. EXPLAIN AND JUSTIFY YOUR REQUEST

- Justify the request or explain its importance.
- Explain any potential benefits of responding.
- Ask the most important questions first.
- Break complex requests into individual questions that are limited to only one topic each.

C. REQUEST SPECIFIC ACTION IN A COURTEOUS CLOSE

- Make it easy to comply by including appropriate contact information.
- Express your gratitude.
- Clearly state any important deadlines for the request.

Jyoti Gupta, owner of Jyoti Cuisine India, doesn't spend her entire day making specialty frozen meals for passengers of British Airways and US Airways. Most of the time she's running her business and communicating with her suppliers, customers, and employees. Gupta routinely sends memos to these parties requesting information and action or responding to their information requests. For routine communications, Gupta uses a direct approach and a cordial tone.

Asking for Information and Action

When you need to know about something, to elicit an opinion from someone, or to request a simple action, you usually need only ask. In essence, simple requests say

- What you want to know or what you want readers to do
- Why you're making the request
- Why it may be in your readers' interest to help you

If your reader can do what you want, such a straightforward request gets the job done with a minimum of fuss. Follow the direct approach: Open with a clear statement of your reason for writing. In the body, provide whatever explanation is needed to justify your request. Then close with a specific account of what you expect, and include a deadline if appropriate. In more complex situations, readers might be unwilling to respond unless they understand how the request benefits them, so be sure to include this information in your explanation.

Naturally, you'll adapt your request to your audience and the situation. Requests to fellow employees are usually casual and sometimes spoken rather than written. However, as long as you avoid writing frequent, long, or unneeded messages, sending a thoughtfully written memo or e-mail message can save time and questions by helping readers understand precisely what you want. The memo in Figure 7.2 was sent to all employees of Ace Hardware. It seeks employee input about a new wellness and benefits program. The tone is matter-of-fact, and the memo assumes some shared background, which is appropriate when communicating about a routine matter to someone in the same company. (For more information on formatting memos and other business messages, see Appendix A.)

In contrast to requests sent internally, those sent to people outside the organization usually adopt a more formal tone. You'll most likely be in a position to ask businesses, customers, or others outside your organization to provide information or to take some simple action (attend a meeting, return an information card, endorse a document, confirm an address, supplement information on an order). Such requests are often in letter form, although some are sent via e-mail. These messages are usually short and simple, but still formal and professional, like the following request for information:

Makes overall request in polite (no question mark) question form

Would you please supply me with information about the lawn services you provide. Pralle Realty owns 27 pieces of rental property in College Station, and we're looking for a lawn service to handle all of them. We are making a commitment to provide

Plan

Analyze the Situation
Purpose is to request feedback from fellow employees.

Gather Information
Gather accurate, complete information on program benefits and local gyms.

Select the Right Medium
Office memo is appropriate for this message since the document needs to be signed and returned.

Organize the Information
The main idea is saving money while staying healthy. Save time and meet audience expectations by using a direct approach.

1

Write

Adapt to Your Audience
Show sensitivity to audience needs with a "you" attitude, politeness, positive emphasis, and bias-free language. Writer already has credibility as manager of the department.

Compose the Message
Style is conversational but still businesslike, using plain English and appropriate voice.

2

Complete

Revise the Message
Evaluate content and review readability; avoid unnecessary details.

Produce the Message
Simple memo format is all the design this message needs.

Proofread the Message
Review for errors in layout, spelling, and mechanics.

Distribute the Message
Deliver the message via the company's interoffice mail delivery system.

3

FIGURE 7.2 Effective Memo Requesting Action from Company Insiders

ACE Ace Hardware Corporation

INTERNAL MEMORANDUM

Routes message efficiently, with all needed information

TO: All Employees
FROM: Tony Ramirez, Human Resources
DATE: October 10, 2005
SUBJ: New Wellness Program Opportunity

States purpose in opening to avoid wasting busy readers' time

The benefits package committee has asked me to contact everyone about an opportunity to save money and stay healthier in the bargain. As you know, the committee has been to decide on changes in our benefits package. Last week, we sent you a memo detailing the Synergy Wellness Program.

Presents the situation that makes the inquiry necessary

In addition to the package as described in the memo (life, major medical, dental, hospitalization), Synergy has sweetened the pot by offering IDD a 10 percent discount. To meet the requirements for the discount, we have to show proof that at least 25 percent of our employees participate in aerobic exercise at least three times a week for at least 20 minutes. (Their actuarial tables show a resulting 10 percent reduction in claims.)

Lists reader benefits and requests action

After looking around, we discovered a gymnasium just a few blocks south on Haley Boulevard. Sports Midwest will give our employees unlimited daytime access to their indoor track, gym, and pool for a group fee that comes to approximately $4.50 per month per employee if at least half of us sign up.

In addition to using the track and pools, we can play volleyball, Jazzercise, form our own intramural basketball teams, and much more. Our spouses and children can also participate at a deeply discounted monthly fee. If you have questions, please e-mail or call me (or any member of the committee). Let us know your wishes on the following form.

Sign and return the following no later than Friday, October 29.

= =

Provides an easy-to-use response form

_____ Yes, I will participate in the Synergy Wellness program and pay $4.50 a month.
_____ Yes, I am interested in a discounted family membership.
_____ No, I prefer not to participate.

Signature ______________________________

Employee ID Number ______________________________

Keeps reader's interest by hinting at possibility of future business

quality housing in this college town, and we are looking for an outstanding firm to work with us.

Avoids making an overly broad request by using a series of specific questions

Itemizes questions in a logical sequence

Avoids useless yes-or-no answers by including open-ended questions

1. **Lawn care:** What is your annual charge for each location for lawn maintenance, including mowing, fertilizing, and weed control?
2. **Shrubbery:** What is your annual charge for each location for the care of deciduous and evergreen bushes, including pruning, fertilizing, and replacing as necessary?
3. **Contract:** How does Agri-Lawn Service structure such large contracts? What additional information do you need from us?

Specifies a time limit in the courteous close

Please let us hear from you by February 15. We want to have a lawn-care firm in place by March 15.

A more complex request might require not only greater detail but information on how responding will benefit the reader.

The purpose of some routine requests to customers is to reestablish communication.

Sometimes you may need to reestablish a relationship with former customers or suppliers. In many cases, when customers are unhappy about some purchase or about the way they were treated, they don't complain; they simply stay away from the offending business. Thus, a letter of inquiry might encourage customers to use idle credit accounts, offering them an opportunity to register their displeasure and then move on to a good relationship. In addition, a customer's response to such an inquiry may give you insights into ways to improve your products and customer service. Even if they have no complaint, customers still welcome the personal attention.

Asking for Recommendations

The need to inquire about people arises often in business. For example, before awarding credit, contracts, jobs, promotions, scholarships, and so on, some companies ask applicants to supply references. If you're applying for a job and your potential employer asks for references, you may want to ask a close personal or professional associate to write a letter of recommendation. Or, if you're an employer considering whether to hire an applicant, you may want to write directly to the person the applicant named as a reference.

Always ask for permission before using someone's name as a reference.

Companies ask applicants to supply references who can vouch for their ability, skills, integrity, character, and fitness for the job. Before you volunteer someone's name as a reference, ask that person's permission. Some people won't let you use their names, perhaps because they don't know enough about you to feel comfortable writing a letter or because they have a policy of not providing recommendations. In any event, you are likely to receive the best recommendation from people who agree to write about you, so check first.

Because requests for recommendations and references are routine, you can assume your reader will honor your request, and you can organize your inquiry using the direct approach. Open your message by clearly stating that you're applying for a position and that you would like your reader to write a letter of recommendation. If you haven't had contact with the person for some time, use the opening to recall the nature of the relationship you had, the dates of association, and any special events that might bring a clear, favorable picture of you to mind.

Refresh the memory of any potential reference you haven't been in touch with for a while.

If you're applying for a job, a scholarship, or the like, include a copy of your résumé to give the reader an idea of the direction your life has taken. After reading the résumé, your reader will know what favorable qualities to emphasize and will be able to write the recommendation that best supports your application. If you don't have a résumé, use the body of your letter to include any information about yourself that the reader might use to support a recommendation, such as a description of related jobs you've held.

Close your letter with an expression of appreciation and the full name and address of the person to whom the letter should be sent. When asking for an immediate recommendation, you should also mention the deadline. You'll make a response more likely if you enclose a stamped, preaddressed envelope, which is a considerate step in any event. The letter from Joanne Tucker in Figure 7.3 covers all these points and adds important

Plan

Analyze the Situation
Purpose is to request a recommendation letter from a college professor.

Gather Information
Gather information on classes and dates to help the reader recall you and to clarify the position you seek.

Select the Right Medium
The letter format gives this message an appropriate level of formality, although many professors prefer to be contacted by e-mail.

Organize the Information
Messages like this are common and expected, so a direct approach is best.

1

Write

Adapt to Your Audience
Show sensitivity to audience needs with a "you" attitude, politeness, positive emphasis, and bias-free language.

Compose the Message
Style is respectful and businesslike, while still using plain English and appropriate voice.

2

Complete

Revise the Message
Evaluate content and review readability; avoid unnecessary details.

Produce the Message
Emphasize a clean, professional appearance. Enclose your résumé and a preaddressed envelope.

Proofread the Message
Review for errors in layout, spelling, and mechanics.

Distribute the Message
Deliver the message via postal mail or e-mail if you have the professor's e-mail address.

3

FIGURE 7.3 Effective Letter Requesting a Recommendation

1181 Ashport Drive
Tate Springs, TN 38101
March 14, 2005

Professor Lyndon Kenton
School of Business
University of Tennessee, Knoxville
Knoxville, TN 37916

Dear Professor Kenton:

May I have a letter of recommendation from you? I recently interviewed with Strategic Investments and have been called for a second interview for their Analyst Training Program (ATP). They have requested at least one recommendation from a professor, and I immediately thought of you.

Opens with the request, assumes the reader will honor the request, and names the potential employer

As you may recall, I took BUS 485, Financial Analysis, from you in the fall of 2003. I enjoyed the class and finished the term with an "A." Professor Kenton, your comments on assertiveness and cold-calling impressed me beyond the scope of the actual course material. In fact, taking your course helped me decide on a future as a financial analyst.

Includes information in the opening to refresh reader's memory about this former student

My enclosed résumé includes all my relevant work experience and volunteer activities. But I'd also like to add that I've handled the financial planning for our family since my father passed away several years ago. Although initially, I learned by trial and error, I have increasingly applied my business training in deciding what stocks or bonds to trade. This, I believe, has given me a practical edge over others who may be applying for the same job.

Refers to résumé in the body and mentions experience that could set applicant apart from other candidates

If possible, Ms. Blackmon in Human Resources at Strategic Investment needs to receive your letter by March 30. For your convenience, I've enclosed a preaddressed, stamped envelope.

Gives a deadline for response in the closing and includes information about the person expecting the recommendation

I appreciate your time and effort in writing this letter of recommendation for me. It will be great to put my education to work, and I'll keep you informed of my progress.

Sincerely,

Joanne Tucker

Joanne Tucker

Enclosure

information about some qualifications that might be of special interest to her potential employer.

Making Claims and Requesting Adjustments

If you're dissatisfied with a company's product or service, you can opt to make a **claim** (a formal complaint) or request an **adjustment** (a claim settlement). In either case, it's important to maintain a professional tone in all your communication, no matter how angry or frustrated you might be. Keeping your cool will help you get the situation resolved sooner. In addition, be sure to document your initial complaint and every correspondence after that.

In your claim letter
- Explain the problem and give details
- Provide backup information
- Request specific action

In most cases, and especially in your first letter, assume that a fair adjustment will be made, and follow the plan for direct requests. Open with a straightforward statement of the problem. In the body, give a complete, specific explanation of the details. Provide any information an adjuster would need to verify your complaint. In your close, politely request specific action or convey a sincere desire to find a solution. And if appropriate, suggest that the business relationship will continue if the problem is solved satisfactorily.

Be prepared to document your claim. Send copies and keep the original documents.

Companies usually accept the customer's explanation of what's wrong, so ethically it's important to be entirely honest when filing claims. Also, be prepared to back up your claim with invoices, sales receipts, canceled checks, dated correspondence, catalog descriptions, and any other relevant documents. Send copies and keep the originals for your files.

Be as specific as possible about what you want to happen next.

If the remedy is obvious, tell your reader exactly what will return the company to your good graces—for example, an exchange of merchandise for the right item or a refund if the item is out of stock. In some cases you might ask the reader to resolve a problem. However, if you're uncertain about the precise nature of the trouble, you could ask the company to make an assessment. Supply your contact information so that the company can discuss the situation with you if necessary.

The following letter was written to a utility company. As you read it, compare its tone with the tone of the letter in Figure 7.4. If you were the person receiving the complaint, which version would you respond to more favorably?

FIRST DRAFT

We have been at our present location only three months, and we don't understand why our December utility bill is $815.00 and our January bill is $817.50. Businesses on both sides of us, in offices just like ours, are paying only $543.50 and $545.67 for the same months. We all have similar computer and office equipment, so something must be wrong.

Small businesses are helpless against big utility companies. How can we prove that you read the meter wrong or that the November bill from before we even moved in here got added to our December bill? We want someone to check this meter right away. We can't afford to pay these big bills.

Most people would react much more favorably to the version in Figure 7.4. A rational, clear, and courteous approach is best for any routine request. To review the tasks involved in making claims and requesting adjustments, see "Checklist: Making Claims and Requesting Adjustments."

CHECKLIST: Making Claims and Requesting Adjustments

- Maintain a professional tone, even if you're extremely frustrated.
- Open with a straightforward statement of the problem.
- Provide specific details in the body.
- Present facts honestly and clearly.
- Politely summarize desired action in the closing.
- Clearly state what you expect as a fair settlement, or ask the reader to propose a fair adjustment.
- Explain the benefits of complying with the request, such as your continued patronage.

FIGURE 7.4 Effective Claim Letter

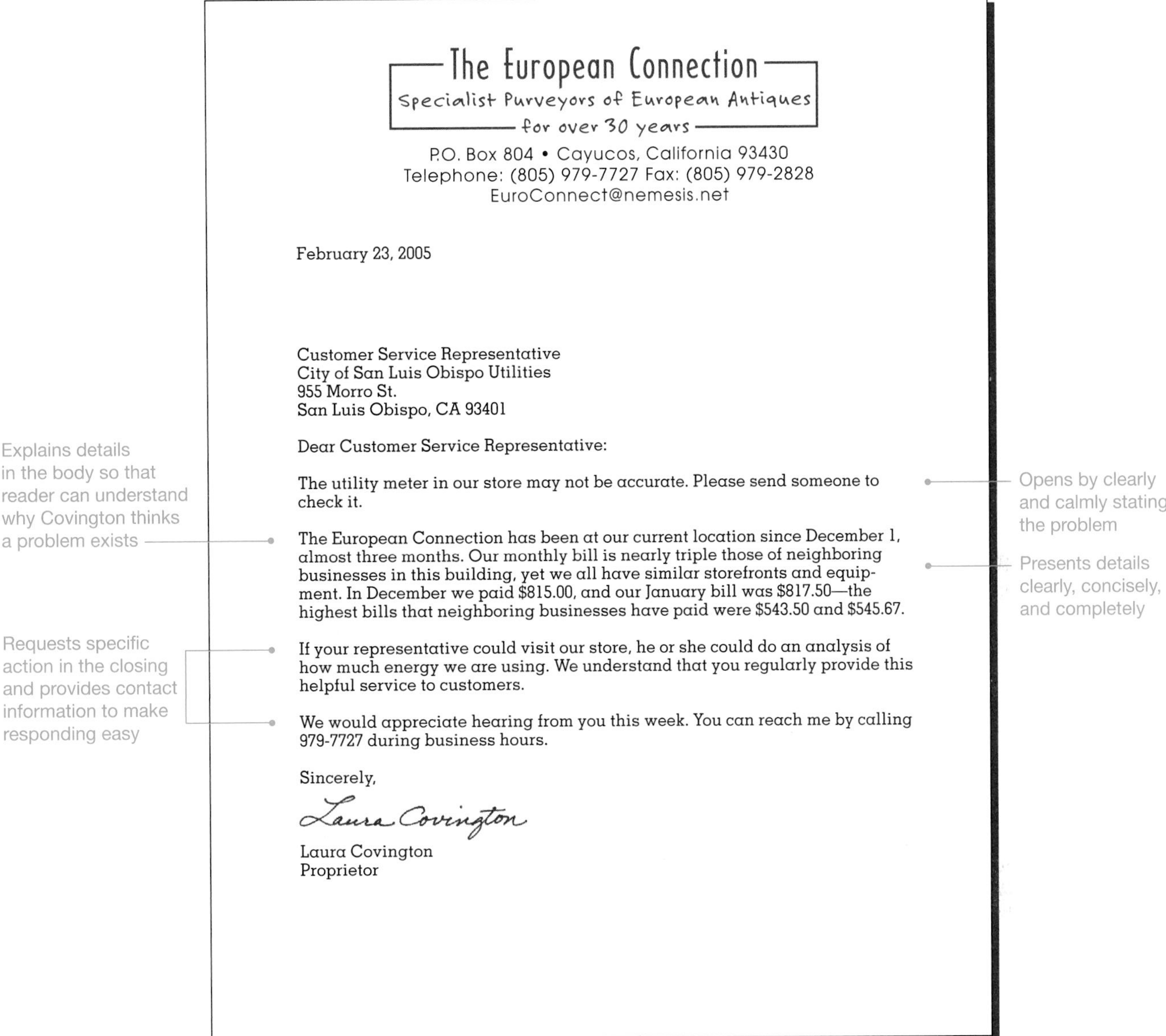

The European Connection
Specialist Purveyors of European Antiques
for over 30 years
P.O. Box 804 • Cayucos, California 93430
Telephone: (805) 979-7727 Fax: (805) 979-2828
EuroConnect@nemesis.net

February 23, 2005

Customer Service Representative
City of San Luis Obispo Utilities
955 Morro St.
San Luis Obispo, CA 93401

Dear Customer Service Representative:

The utility meter in our store may not be accurate. Please send someone to check it.

The European Connection has been at our current location since December 1, almost three months. Our monthly bill is nearly triple those of neighboring businesses in this building, yet we all have similar storefronts and equipment. In December we paid $815.00, and our January bill was $817.50—the highest bills that neighboring businesses have paid were $543.50 and $545.67.

If your representative could visit our store, he or she could do an analysis of how much energy we are using. We understand that you regularly provide this helpful service to customers.

We would appreciate hearing from you this week. You can reach me by calling 979-7727 during business hours.

Sincerely,

Laura Covington

Laura Covington
Proprietor

Explains details in the body so that reader can understand why Covington thinks a problem exists
Requests specific action in the closing and provides contact information to make responding easy
Opens by clearly and calmly stating the problem
Presents details clearly, concisely, and completely

SENDING ROUTINE REPLIES AND POSITIVE MESSAGES

Just as you'll make numerous requests for information and action throughout your career, you'll also respond to similar requests from other people. When responding positively to a request, sending routine announcements, or sending a positive or goodwill message, you have several goals: to communicate the information or the good news, answer all questions, provide all required details, and leave your reader with a good impression of you and your firm. Even though you may be doing someone a favor by responding to a request, you want to be courteous and upbeat and maintain a you-oriented tone.

Strategy for Routine Replies and Positive Messages

4 LEARNING OBJECTIVE

Illustrate a strategy for writing routine replies and positive messages

Like requests, routine replies and positive messages have an opening, a body, and a close. Since readers receiving these messages will generally be interested in what you have to say, you'll usually use the direct approach. Place your main idea (the positive reply or the good news) in the opening. Use the body to explain all the relevant details, and close cordially, perhaps highlighting a benefit to your reader.

Use the direct organizational plan for positive messages.

Prepare your audience for the detail that follows by beginning your positive message with the main idea or good news.

Start with the Main Idea

By opening your routine and positive messages with the main idea or good news, you're preparing your audience for the detail that follows. Try to make your opening clear and concise. Although the following introductory statements make the same point, one is cluttered with unnecessary information that buries the purpose, whereas the other is brief and to the point:

INSTEAD OF THIS	WRITE THIS
I am pleased to inform you that after deliberating the matter carefully, our human resources committee has recommended you for appointment as a staff accountant.	Congratulations. You've been selected to join our firm as a staff accountant, beginning March 20.

Before you begin, have a clear idea of what you want to say.

The best way to write a clear opening is to have a clear idea of what you want to say. Before you put one word on paper, ask yourself, "What is the single most important message I have for the audience?"

Provide Necessary Details and Explanation

The body of routine and positive messages is typically the longest. You need the space to explain your point completely so that your audience will experience no confusion or lingering doubt. In addition to providing details in the body, maintain the supportive tone established in the opening. This tone is easy to continue when your message is entirely positive, as in this example:

> Your educational background and internship have impressed us, and we believe you would be a valuable addition to Green Valley Properties. As discussed during your interview, your salary will be $4,300 per month, plus benefits. In that regard, you will meet with our benefits manager, Paula Sanchez, at 8 A.M. on Monday, March 21. She will assist you with all the paperwork necessary to tailor our benefit package to your family situation. She will also arrange various orientation activities to help you acclimate to our company.

Embed any negative information in a positive context.

However, if your routine message is mixed and must convey mildly disappointing information, put the negative portion of your message into as favorable a context as possible:

INSTEAD OF THIS	WRITE THIS
No, we no longer carry the Sportsgirl line of sweaters.	The new Olympic line has replaced the Sportsgirl sweaters that you asked about. Olympic features a wider range of colors and sizes and more contemporary styling.

The more complete description is less negative and emphasizes how the audience can benefit from the change. Be careful, though: You can use negative information in this type of message *only* if you're reasonably sure the audience will respond positively. Otherwise, use the indirect approach (discussed in Chapter 8).

If you are communicating to customers, you might also want to use the body of your message to assure the customer of the wisdom of his or her purchase selection (without being condescending or self-congratulatory). Talking favorably about something the customer has bought even though it may not have been delivered yet is a good way to build customer relationships. Such favorable comments are commonly included in order acknowledgments and routine announcements to customers, and they are most effective when they are relatively short and specific:

> The zipper on the carrying case you purchased is double-stitched and guaranteed for the life of the product.
>
> The Kitchen Aid mixer you ordered is our best-selling model. It should meet your cooking needs for many years.

CHECKLIST: Writing Routine Replies and Positive Messages

A. START WITH THE MAIN IDEA

- Be clear and concise.
- Identify the single most important message before you start writing.

B. PROVIDE NECESSARY DETAILS AND EXPLANATION

- Explain your point completely to eliminate any confusion or lingering doubts.
- Maintain a supportive tone throughout.
- Embed negative statements in positive contexts or balance them with positive alternatives.
- Talk favorably about the choices the customer has made.

C. END WITH A COURTEOUS CLOSE

- Let your readers know that you have their personal well-being in mind.
- If further action is required, tell readers how to proceed and encourage them to act promptly.

End with a Courteous Close

Your message is most likely to succeed if your readers are left feeling that you have their personal welfare in mind. You can accomplish this task either by highlighting a benefit to the audience or by expressing appreciation or goodwill. If follow-up action is required, clearly state who will do what next. See "Checklist: Writing Routine Replies and Positive Messages" to review the primary tasks involved in this type of business message.

Make sure the audience understands what to do next and how that action will benefit them.

Common Examples of Routine Replies and Positive Messages

As with routine requests, you'll encounter the need for a wide variety of routine replies and positive messages. You can expect to write letters for most routine messages directed to people outside the company, although e-mail and instant messaging (with live operators or automated bots) are gaining in popularity in customer-service applications. Most routine and positive messages fall into six main categories: answers to requests for information and action, grants of claims and requests for adjustment, recommendations, informative messages, good-news announcements, and goodwill messages.

Answering Requests for Information and Action

Every professional answers requests for information and action from time to time, and some business functions answer such requests many times a day. If the response to a request is a simple yes or some other straightforward information, the direct plan is appropriate. A prompt, gracious, and thorough response will positively influence how people think about you and the organization you represent. Depending on the resources your company offers, you might use letters, memos, e-mail, or instant messaging to answer these requests (see Figure 7.5)

Many requests can be similar. For example, a human resources department gets numerous routine inquiries about job openings. To handle repetitive queries like these quickly and consistently, companies usually develop form responses. To avoid coming across as cold and impersonal in such form messages, put extra care into the standardized wording of the message as you try to accommodate as many individual situations and concerns as you can. Thus, a computerized form letter prepared with care may actually be more personal and sincere than a hastily typed "personal" reply.

With a form message as the starting point, you can then personalize it for each recipient by using the mail merge capability in your word processor. For example, instead of addressing a form reply to "Dear Applicant," you can have the computer insert the recipient's name. If you have time and the message is important, go beyond this and revise the content of each letter with unique information about each recipient.

E-mail messages may be standardized as well. For example, when Julian Zamakis sent an e-mail to Herman Miller asking for information about employment opportunities, he received the encouraging e-mail reply in Figure 7.6 on page 195.

DOCUMENT MAKEOVER

IMPROVE THIS E-MAIL MESSAGE

To practice correcting drafts of actual documents, visit www.prenhall.com/onekey on the web. Click "Document Makeovers," then click Chapter 7. You will find an e-mail message that contains problems and errors relating to what you've learned in this chapter about routine, good-news, and goodwill messages. Use the Final Draft decision tool to create an improved version of this e-mail. Check the message for skilled presentation of the main idea, clarity of detail, proper handling of negative information, appropriate use of resale, and a courteous close.

FIGURE 7.5 Effective Instant Messaging Response to Information Request Using AOL's Instant Messenger

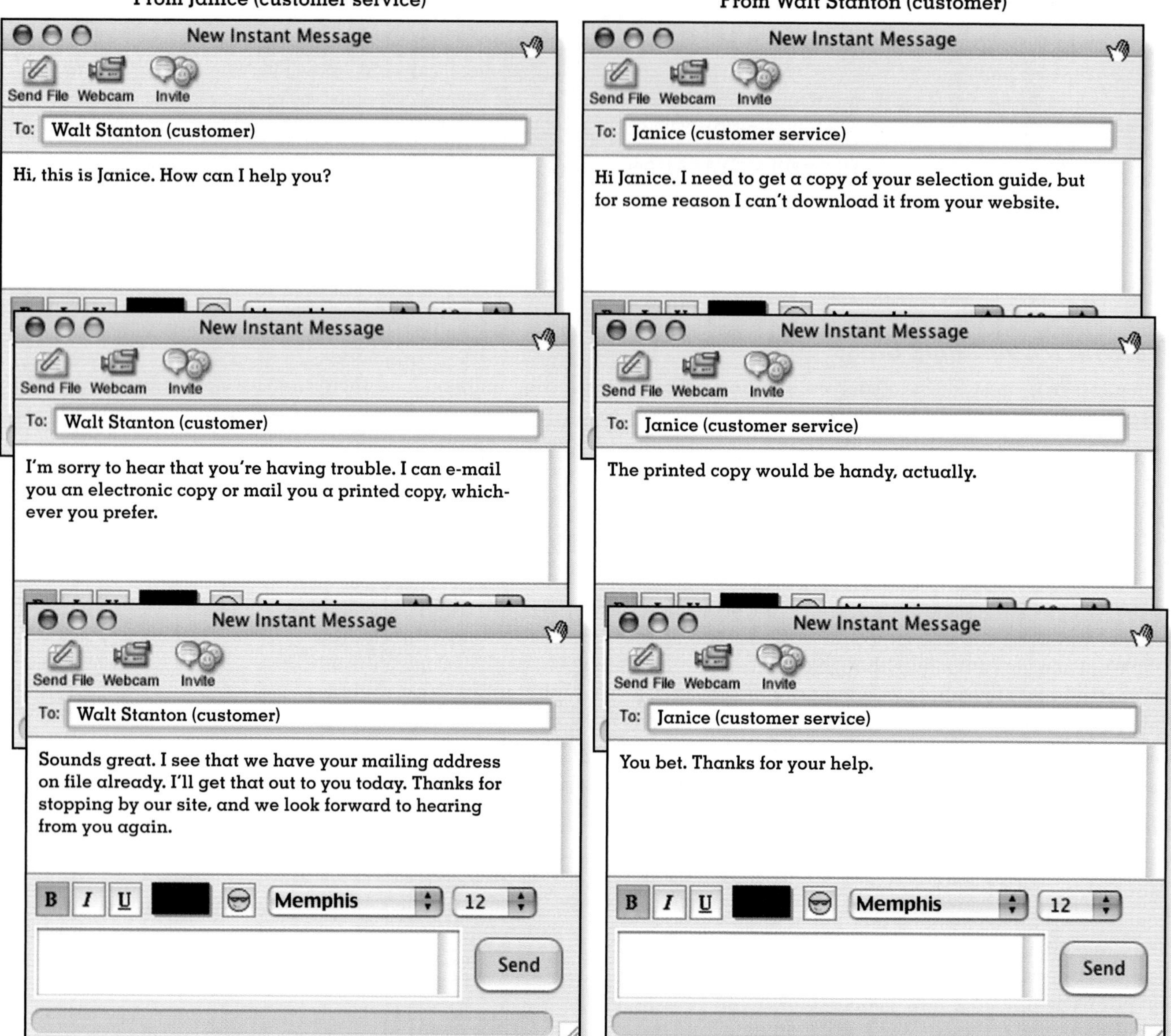

When you're answering requests and a potential sale is involved, you have three main goals: (1) to respond to the inquiry and answer all questions, (2) to leave your reader with a good impression of you and your firm, and (3) to encourage the future sale. The following letter meets all three objectives:

Starts with a clear, statement of the main point →

Here is the brochure "Entertainment Unlimited" that you requested. This booklet describes the vast array of entertainment options available to you with an Ocean Satellite Device (OSD).

Presents key information immediately, along with resale and sales promotion →

On page 12 of "Entertainment Unlimited" you'll find a list of the 338 channels that the OSD brings into your home. You'll have access to movie, sport, and music channels; 24-hour news channels; local channels; and all the major television networks. OSD gives you a clearer picture and more precise sound than those old-fashioned dishes that took up most of your yard—and OSD uses only a small dish that mounts easily on your roof.

FIGURE 7.6 Effective E-Mail Replying to Request for Information

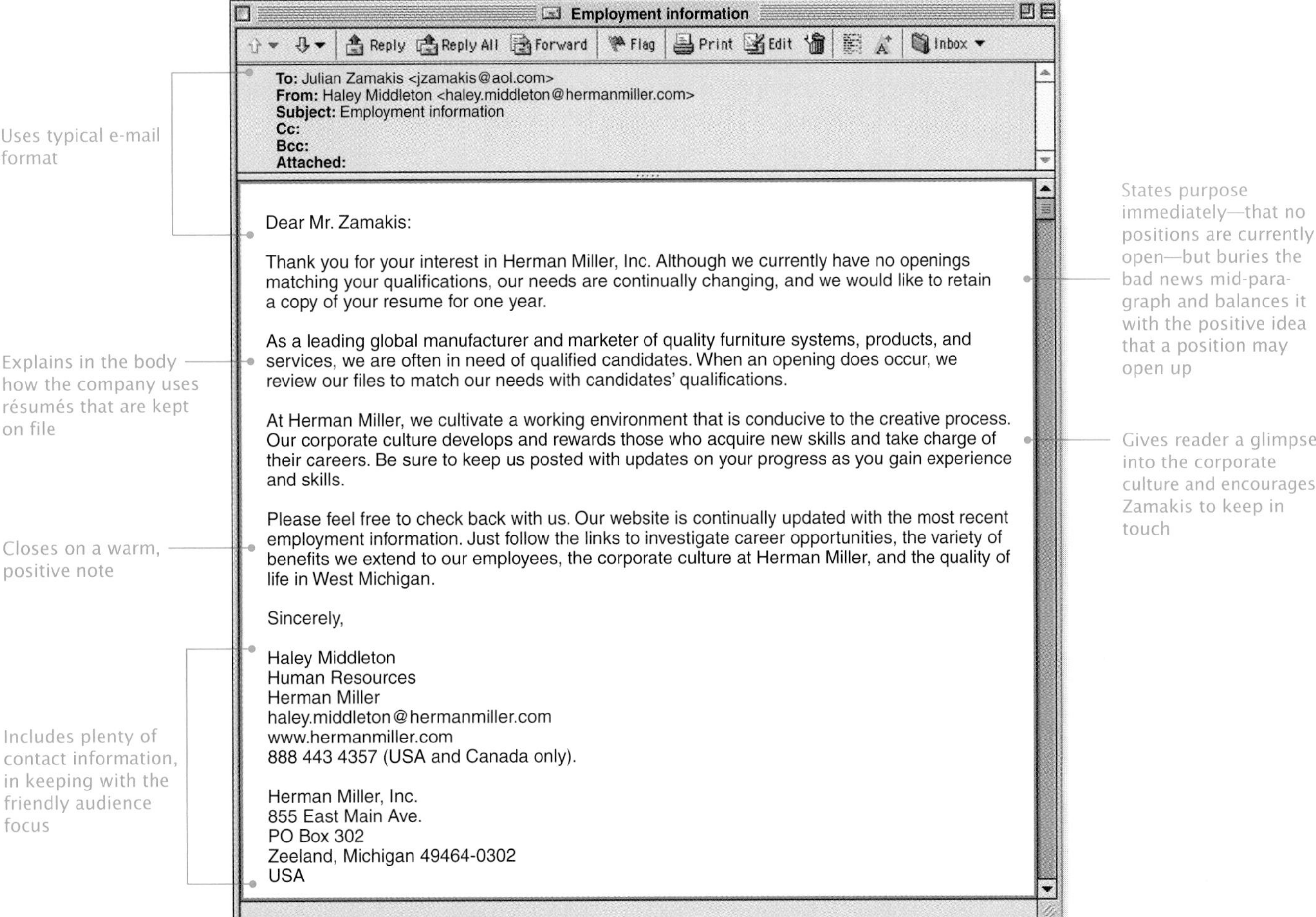
Employment information

To: Julian Zamakis <jzamakis@aol.com>
From: Haley Middleton <haley.middleton@hermanmiller.com>
Subject: Employment information
Cc:
Bcc:
Attached:

Dear Mr. Zamakis:

Thank you for your interest in Herman Miller, Inc. Although we currently have no openings matching your qualifications, our needs are continually changing, and we would like to retain a copy of your resume for one year.

As a leading global manufacturer and marketer of quality furniture systems, products, and services, we are often in need of qualified candidates. When an opening does occur, we review our files to match our needs with candidates' qualifications.

At Herman Miller, we cultivate a working environment that is conducive to the creative process. Our corporate culture develops and rewards those who acquire new skills and take charge of their careers. Be sure to keep us posted with updates on your progress as you gain experience and skills.

Please feel free to check back with us. Our website is continually updated with the most recent employment information. Just follow the links to investigate career opportunities, the variety of benefits we extend to our employees, the corporate culture at Herman Miller, and the quality of life in West Michigan.

Sincerely,

Haley Middleton
Human Resources
Herman Miller
haley.middleton@hermanmiller.com
www.hermanmiller.com
888 443 4357 (USA and Canada only).

Herman Miller, Inc.
855 East Main Ave.
PO Box 302
Zeeland, Michigan 49464-0302
USA

Reply
Reply All
Forward
Flag
Print
Edit
Inbox
Uses typical e-mail format
Explains in the body how the company uses résumés that are kept on file
Closes on a warm, positive note
Includes plenty of contact information, in keeping with the friendly audience focus
States purpose immediately—that no positions are currently open—but buries the bad news mid-paragraph and balances it with the positive idea that a position may open up
Gives reader a glimpse into the corporate culture and encourages Zamakis to keep in touch

More music, more cartoons, more experts, more news, and more sports are available to you with OSD than with any other cable or satellite connection in this region. Yes, it's all there, right at your fingertips. — *Encourages readers to take one more step toward a purchase by highlighting product benefits*

Just call us at 1-800-786-4331, and an OSD representative will come to your home to answer your questions. You'll love the programming and the low monthly cost. Call us today! — *Points toward the sale confidently*

Granting Claims and Requests for Adjustment

In some cases, even the best-run companies make occasional mistakes, from shipping the wrong order to billing the customer's credit card inaccurately. In other cases, the reason for a claim might be the fault of the customer who is asking your company for restitution. In still other cases, a third party may be the cause of a claim, such as a delivery company dropping a fragile package or a company's subcontractor assembling a product incorrectly. Whatever the reason, each of these events represents a turning point in your relationship with your customer. If you handle the situation well, your customer will likely be even more loyal than before because you've proven that you're serious about customer satisfaction. However, if a customer believes that you mishandled a complaint, you'll make the situation even worse—sometimes much worse. Dissatisfied customers often take their business elsewhere without notice; moreover, they tend to tell numerous friends and colleagues about the negative experience. A transaction that might be worth only a few dollars by itself could cost you many times that amount in lost business over time. In other words, every mistake is an opportunity to improve a relationship.

Few people go to the trouble of requesting an adjustment unless they actually have a problem, so most businesses start from the assumption that the customer is correct. From there, your response to the complaint depends on both your company's policies for resolving such issues and your assessment of whether the company, the customer, or some third party is at fault.

5 LEARNING OBJECTIVE

Discuss the importance of knowing who is responsible when granting claims and requests for adjustment

When Your Company Is at Fault Whenever you communicate about a mistake your company has made, do so carefully. Before you respond, make sure you know your company's policies in such cases, which might even dictate specific legal and financial steps to be taken. For serious problems that go beyond routine errors, your company should have a *crisis management plan* that outlines communication steps both inside and outside the organization (see Chapter 8).

Most routine responses should take your company's specific policies into account and address the following points:

- **Acknowledge receipt of the customer's claim or complaint.** Just knowing that somebody is listening goes a long way toward soothing frayed nerves. Even if you can't solve the problem immediately, at least let the other party know that you're listening and that you've heard the complaint.
- **Take (or assign) personal responsibility for setting matters straight.** Customers don't want their complaints to fall into a bureaucratic black hole. In larger companies with hundreds or thousands of transactions a month, identifying a specific person at this stage might be impossible.
- **Sympathize with the customer's inconvenience or frustration.** Letting the customer see that you're on his or her side helps defuse the emotional element of the situation.
- **Explain precisely how you have resolved, or plan to resolve, the situation.** The customer may have wasted time, lost money, or suffered in other ways, and he or she will want to know how you plan to make the situation right. If you are able to respond exactly as the customer requested, be sure to communicate that. If you can't respond exactly as the customer asked, explain the reasons behind your response, rather than leaving the customer to wonder why.
- **Take steps to repair the relationship.** Keeping your existing customers is almost always less expensive than acquiring new customers, so look for ways to go beyond simply granting the claim or fixing the problem. Many companies offer coupons or gift certificates that not only give the customer more than they asked for but also encourage continued business.
- **Keep the lines of communication open.** Make sure you haven't compounded the customer's frustration by solving the wrong problem or solving the right problem in the wrong way.
- **Follow-up to verify your response was correct.** Follow-up not only helps improve customer service but also gives you another opportunity to show how much you care about your customer.

In addition to these positive steps, maintain professional demeanor by avoiding some key negative steps as well:

- Don't blame anyone in your organization by name
- Don't make exaggerated apologies
- Don't imply that the customer is at fault
- Don't promise more than you can deliver

As with requests for information or action, some claims are likely to occur again and again, such as claims made against insurance policies or requests to correct orders. A form letter is an efficient way to begin the communication process. In the following example, a large mail-order clothing company created a form letter to respond to customers who complain that they haven't received exactly what was ordered. The form letter can easily be customized through word processing (perhaps to state the good news in the opening) and then individually signed:

Your letter concerning your recent Klondike order has arrived and has been forwarded to our director of order fulfillment. Your complete satisfaction is our goal, and a customer service representative will contact you within 48 hours to assist with the issues raised in your letter.

In the meantime, please accept the enclosed $5 gift certificate as a token of our appreciation for your business. Whether you're skiing or driving a snowmobile, Klondike Gear offers you the best protection from wind, snow, and cold—and Klondike has been taking care of customers' outdoor needs for over 27 years.

Thank you for taking the time to write to us. Your input helps us better serve you and all our customers.

Acknowledges receipt of the customer's communication

Explains what will happen next and when, without making promises the writer can't keep

Takes steps to repair the relationship and ensure continued business

Closes with statement of company's concern for all its customers

In contrast, a response letter written as a personal answer to a unique claim would open with a clear statement of the good news: the settling of the claim according to the customer's request. The following is a more personal response from Klondike Gear:

Here is your heather-blue wool-and-mohair sweater (size large) to replace the one returned to us with a defect in the knitting. Thanks for giving us the opportunity to correct this situation. Customers' needs have come first at Klondike Gear for 27 years.

I've enclosed our newest catalog and a $5 gift certificate that's good toward any purchase from it. Whether you are skiing or driving a snowmobile, Klondike Gear offers you the best protection available from wind, snow, and cold. Please let us know how we may continue to serve you and your sporting needs.

When the Customer Is at Fault Communication about a claim is a delicate matter when the customer is clearly at fault. You can (1) refuse the claim and attempt to justify your refusal or (2) simply do what the customer asks. If you refuse the claim, you may lose your customer—as well as many of the customer's friends and colleagues, who will hear only one side of the dispute. You must weigh the cost of making the adjustment against the cost of losing future business from one or more customers.

If you choose to grant the claim, you can open with the good news: You're replacing the merchandise or refunding the purchase price. However, the body needs more attention. Your job is to make the customer realize that the merchandise was mistreated, but you want to avoid being condescending ("Perhaps you failed to read the instructions carefully") or preachy ("You should know that wool shrinks in hot water"). The dilemma is this: If the customer fails to realize what went wrong, you may commit your firm to an endless procession of returned merchandise; but if you insult the customer, your cash refund will have been wasted because you'll lose your customer anyway. Close in a courteous manner that expresses your appreciation for the customer's business. Without being offensive, the letter in Figure 7.7 educates a customer about how to treat his in-line skates.

When complying with an unjustified claim, let the customer know that the merchandise was mistreated, but maintain a respectful and positive tone.

When a Third Party Is at Fault Sometimes neither your company nor your customer is at fault. An overnight delivery service could lose a package, or the windows that your construction company installed could fail to perform as the manufacturer promised. Even a simple transaction can involve several parties; for example, ordering a music CD from Amazon.com involves not only Amazon.com but also a distribution service such as Federal Express or the U.S. Postal Service, the manufacturer of the CD, and a credit card issuer. Any one of these other partners might be at fault, but the customer is likely to blame Amazon.com, since that is the entity that receives the customer's payment. In some transactions, the customer might not even be aware that third parties were involved.

No general scheme applies to every case involving a third party, so evaluate the situation carefully and know your company's policies before responding. An online retailer and the companies that manufacture its merchandise might have an agreement specifying that the manufacturers automatically handle all complaints about product quality. The retailer and its delivery company may have a separate agreement specifying that the delivery companies

When a third party is at fault, your response depends on your company's agreements with that organization.

Plan

Analyze the Situation
Purpose is to grant the customer's claim, tactfully educate him, and encourage further business.

Gather Information
Gather information on product care, warranties, and resale information.

Select the Right Medium
The letter format gives this message an appropriate level of formality, which shows respect for the reader.

Organize the Information
You're responding with a positive answer, so a direct approach is best.

1

Write

Adapt to Your Audience
Shows sensitivity to audience needs with a "you" attitude, politeness, positive emphasis, and bias-free language.

Compose the Message
Style is respectful while still managing to educate the customer on product usage and maintenance.

2

Complete

Revise the Message
Evaluate content and review readability; avoid unnecessary details.

Produce the Message
Emphasize a clean, professional appearance appropriate for a letter on company stationery.

Proofread the Message
Review for errors in layout, spelling, and mechanics.

Distribute the Message
Deliver the message via postal mail.

3

FIGURE 7.7 Effective Letter Responding to a Claim When the Buyer Is at Fault

Skates Alive!

20901 El Dorado Hills
Laguna Niguel, CA 92677
(714) 332-7474 • Fax: (714) 336-5297
skates@speed.net

February 7, 2005

Mr. Steven Cox
1172 Amber Court
Jacksonville, FL 32073

Dear Mr. Cox:

Thank you for contacting Skates Alive! about your in-line skates. Even though your six-month warranty has expired, Skates Alive! is mailing you a complete wheel assembly replacement free of charge. The enclosed instructions make removing the damaged wheel line and installing the new one relatively easy.

Acknowledges reader communication, keeps opening positive by avoiding words such as "problem," and conveys the good news right away

The "Fastrax" (model NL 562) you purchased is our best-selling and most reliable skate. However, wheel jams may occur when fine particles of sand block the smooth rotating action of the wheels. These skates perform best when used on roadways and tracks that are relatively free of sand. We suggest that you remove and clean the wheel assemblies (see enclosed directions) once a month and have them checked by your dealer about every six months.

Explains the problem without blaming the customer by avoiding the pronoun "you" and by suggesting ways to avoid future problems

Because of your Florida location, you may want to consider our more advanced "Glisto" (model NL 988) when you decide to purchase new skates. Although more expensive than the Fastrax, the Glisto design helps shed sand and dirt quite efficiently and should provide years of carefree skating.

Includes sales promotion in the body, encouraging the customer to "trade up"

Enjoy the enclosed copy of "Rock & Roll," with our compliments. Inside, you'll read about new products, hear from other skaters, and have an opportunity to respond to our customer questionnaire.

Adds value by enclosing a newsletter that invites future response from customer

We love hearing from our skaters, so keep in touch. All of us at Skates Alive! wish you good times and miles of healthy skating.

Closes positively, ending on a "feel good" note that conveys an attitude of excellent customer service

Sincerely,

Candace Parker

Candace Parker
Customer Service Representative

Enclosure

CHECKLIST: Granting Claims and Adjustment Requests

A. RESPONDING WHEN YOUR COMPANY IS AT FAULT

- Be aware of your company's policies in such cases before you respond.
- For serious situations, refer to the company's crisis management plan.
- Start by acknowledging receipt of the claim or complaint.
- Take or assign personal responsibility for resolving the situation.
- Sympathize with the customer's frustration.
- Explain how you have resolved the situation (or plan to).
- Take steps to repair the customer relationship.
- Verify your response with the customer and keep the lines of communication open.

B. RESPONDING WHEN THE CUSTOMER IS AT FAULT

- Weigh the cost of complying with or refusing the request
- If you choose to comply, open with the good news.
- Use the body of the message to respectfully educate the customer about steps needed to avoid a similar outcome in the future.
- Close with an appreciation for the customer's business.

C. RESPONDING WHEN A THIRD PARTY IS AT FAULT

- Evaluate the situation and review your company's policies before responding.
- Avoid placing blame; focus on the solution.

Regardless of who is responsible for resolving the situation, let the customer know what will happen to resolve the problem.

handle all complaints related to shipping. In other cases, the retailer might have a blanket policy of resolving all grievances itself. However, regardless of who eventually resolves the problem, if customers contact you, you need to respond with messages that explain how the problem will be solved. Pointing fingers is both unproductive and unprofessional. Resolving the situation is more important to customers than learning who made the mistake in the first place. See "Checklist: Granting Claims and Adjustment Requests" to review the tasks involved in these kinds of business messages.

Providing Recommendations

When writing a letter of recommendation, your goal is to convince readers that the person being recommended has the characteristics necessary for the job, project assignment, or other objective the person is seeking. A successful recommendation letter contains a number of relevant details:

- The candidate's full name
- The position or other objective the candidate is seeking
- The nature of your relationship with the candidate
- An indication of whether you're answering a request from the person or taking the initiative to write
- Facts and evidence relevant to the candidate and the opportunity
- A comparison of this candidate's potential with that of peers, if available (for example, "Ms. Jonasson consistently ranked in the top 10 percent of her class")
- Your overall evaluation of the candidate's suitability for the opportunity

As surprising as this might sound, the most difficult recommendation letters to write are often those for truly outstanding candidates. Your audience will have trouble believing uninterrupted praise for someone's talents and accomplishments. To enhance your credibility—and the candidate's—illustrate your general points with specific examples that point out the candidate's abilities and fitness for the job opening.

Most candidates aren't perfect, however, and you'll need to decide how to handle each situation that comes your way. Omitting a reference to someone's shortcomings may be tempting, especially if the shortcomings are irrelevant to the demands of the job in question. Even so, you have an obligation to refer to any serious shortcoming that could be related to job performance. You owe it to your audience, to your own conscience, and even to better-qualified candidates. You don't have to present the shortcomings as simple criticisms, however. A good option is to list them as areas for improvement, even as areas the person might be working on now.

A serious shortcoming cannot be ignored, but beware of being libelous:

- Include only relevant, factual information
- Avoid value judgments
- Balance criticisms with favorable points

A recommendation letter presenting negatives can be carefully worded to satisfy both the candidate and the person or company requesting information.

The danger in writing a critical letter is that you might inadvertently engage in libel, publishing a false and malicious written statement that injures the candidate's reputation. On the other hand, if that negative information is truthful and relevant, it may be unethical and illegal to omit it from your recommendation. So if you must refer to a shortcoming, you can best protect yourself by sticking to the facts, avoiding value judgments, and placing your criticism in the context of a generally favorable recommendation, as in Figure 7.8. In this letter, the writer supports all statements with facts and steers clear of vague, critical judgments.

You can also avoid trouble by asking yourself the following questions before mailing a recommendation letter:

- Does the person receiving this personal information have a legitimate right to it?
- Does all the information I've presented relate directly to the job or benefit being sought?
- Have I put the candidate's case as strongly and as honestly as I can?
- Have I avoided overstating the candidate's abilities or otherwise misleading the reader?
- Have I based all my statements on firsthand knowledge and provable facts?

FIGURE 7.8 Effective Recommendation Letter

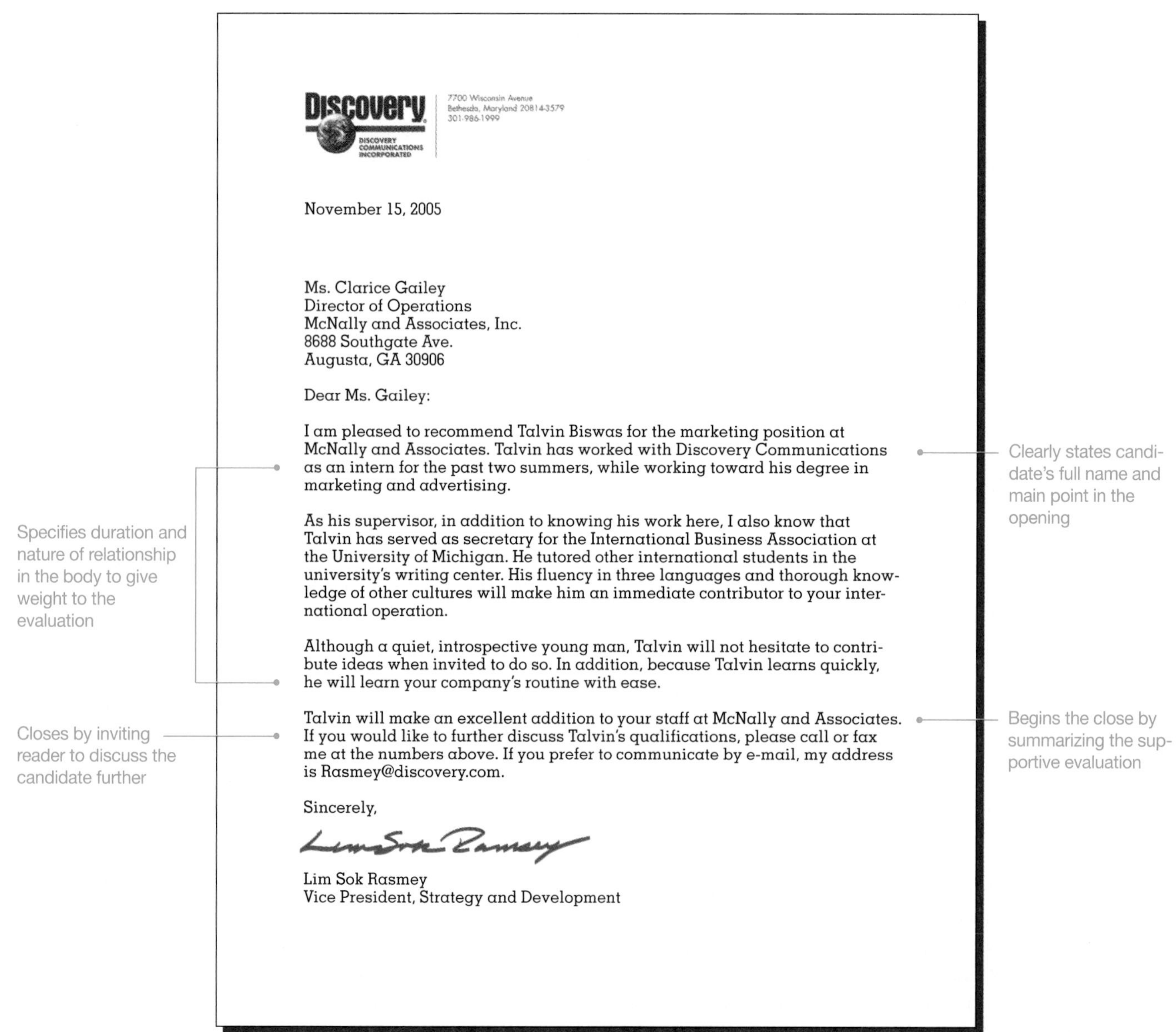

Discovery
DISCOVERY COMMUNICATIONS INCORPORATED
7700 Wisconsin Avenue
Bethesda, Maryland 20814-3579
301-986-1999

November 15, 2005

Ms. Clarice Gailey
Director of Operations
McNally and Associates, Inc.
8688 Southgate Ave.
Augusta, GA 30906

Dear Ms. Gailey:

I am pleased to recommend Talvin Biswas for the marketing position at McNally and Associates. Talvin has worked with Discovery Communications as an intern for the past two summers, while working toward his degree in marketing and advertising.

As his supervisor, in addition to knowing his work here, I also know that Talvin has served as secretary for the International Business Association at the University of Michigan. He tutored other international students in the university's writing center. His fluency in three languages and thorough knowledge of other cultures will make him an immediate contributor to your international operation.

Although a quiet, introspective young man, Talvin will not hesitate to contribute ideas when invited to do so. In addition, because Talvin learns quickly, he will learn your company's routine with ease.

Talvin will make an excellent addition to your staff at McNally and Associates. If you would like to further discuss Talvin's qualifications, please call or fax me at the numbers above. If you prefer to communicate by e-mail, my address is Rasmey@discovery.com.

Sincerely,

Lim Sok Rasmey

Lim Sok Rasmey
Vice President, Strategy and Development

Ethics Detective

Inflating the Truth for a Friend

You had bills to pay right after college, so you joined the marketing department of Durango Biotech. Your friend Jonathan declined two good job offers and spent six months backpacking around Europe.

Shortly after his return, Jonathan called you to exchange news. The long-winded retelling of his European adventures was just a prelude to the real reason for his call: He was applying for a software job at Durango and wanted you to write a letter of recommendation. You agreed, thinking, "It'd be great to have him working here."

When you started writing the letter, you were struck by a realization. In school, Jonathan's grades had fallen steadily as he lost interest in his programming classes and struggled with working in groups. At Durango, successful software projects depend on having team players who work well in small groups.

Ultimately, you decided to praise Jonathan's abilities as a team player. As evidence, you highlighted his team's success in the school's annual "Battling Robots" competition. After receiving your letter, the hiring manager, Tom, asked your boss, Sandra, about your judgment. Sandra praised your work habits and suggested that your recommendation be taken seriously. This helped Jonathan get the interview; he did well and was offered the job.

Shortly after Jonathan joined Durango, he started taking long lunch breaks, often asking you to go along. During one two-hour lunch, he boasted that the job at Durango was temporary: He was saving up enough cash to spend six months traveling in Asia.

Three months later, Tom stopped Sandra in the hall to tell her that your recommendation was way off the mark—and that he now doubted not only your credibility but hers as well. Jonathan had proven to be a poor team player and, worse, his lack of commitment was delaying an important project.

ANALYSIS

Was your recommendation ethical? Why or why not? How did your decision affect the company and your co-workers?

If the person's shortcomings are so pronounced that you don't think he or she is a good fit for the job, the only choice is to not write the letter at all. Unless your relationship with the person warrants an explanation, simply suggest that someone else might be in a better position to provide a recommendation.

Before you dash off any recommendation letter, even for someone you know closely and respect without reservation, keep in mind that every time you write a recommendation, you're putting your own reputation on the line (see "Ethics Detective: Inflating the Truth for a Friend"). Your recommendation influences a decision that has long-term consequences for the hiring organization as well as for the candidate, so make sure you truly believe what you'll be writing.

Creating Informative Messages

6 LEARNING OBJECTIVE

Explain how creating informative messages differs from responding to information requests

All companies send routine informative messages such as reminder notices and policy statements. You may need to inform employees of organizational changes, upcoming events, new procedures, and changing policies. Similarly, you may need to tell customers and suppliers about shipping and return policies, sales discount procedures, and company developments that might be helpful when doing business with your company or when using your company's products. When you write informative messages, use the opening of the message to state the purpose (to inform) and briefly mention the nature of the information you are providing. Unlike the replies discussed earlier, informative messages are not solicited by your reader, so make it clear up front why the reader is receiving this particular message. In the body, provide the necessary details and end your message with a courteous close.

When writing informative messages:

- State the purpose at the beginning and briefly mention the nature of the information you are providing
- Provide the necessary details
- End with a courteous close

Most informative communications are neutral. That is, they stimulate neither a positive nor a negative response from readers. For example, when you send departmental meeting announcements and reminder notices, you'll generally receive a neutral response from your readers (unless the purpose of the meeting is unwelcome). Simply present the factual information in the body of the message and don't worry too much about the reader's attitude toward the information.

Some informative messages may require additional care. For instance, policy statements or procedural changes may be good news for a company (perhaps by saving money); however, it may not be obvious to employees that such savings may make available additional employee resources or even raises. In instances where the reader may not initially view the information positively, use the body of the message to highlight the potential benefits from the reader's perspective.

Announcing Good News

A letter telling someone that she or he got the job is a legal document, so make sure all statements are accurate.

To develop and maintain good relationships, smart companies recognize that it's good business to spread the word about positive developments, whether the company is opening new facilities, appointing a new executive, introducing new products or services, or sponsoring community events. Because good news is always welcome, use the direct approach.

Writing to a successful job applicant is one of the most pleasant good-news messages you might have the opportunity to write. The following example uses the direct approach and provides information that the recipient needs:

Announces news in a friendly, welcoming tone

Welcome to Lake Valley Rehabilitation Center. A number of excellent candidates were interviewed, but your educational background and recent experience at Memorial Hospital make you the best person for the position of medical records coordinator.

Explains all necessary details

Explains first day's routine to ease new employee's uncertainty

As we discussed, your salary is $29,200 a year. We would like you to begin on Monday, February 1. Please come to my office at 9 a.m. I will give you an in-depth orientation to Lake Valley and discuss the various company benefits available to you. You can also sign all the necessary employment documents.

After lunch, Vanessa Jackson will take you to the medical records department and help you settle into your new responsibilities at Lake Valley Rehabilitation Center. I look forward to seeing you first thing on February 1.

Between her nationally syndicated television series, books on entertaining, three restaurants, and collection of products for the home, former fashion model B. Smith generates numerous informative messages. Like all successful communicators, she emphasizes efficient, objective transfer of information.

Although letters like these are pleasant to write, they constitute a legal job offer. You and your company may be held to any promises you make. So attorneys sometimes recommend stating salary as a monthly amount and keeping the timing of performance evaluations and raises vague; you want to avoid implying that the newly hired employee will be kept on, no matter what, for a whole year or until the next scheduled evaluation.[2] Your company's legal staff can provide specific advice and guidelines.

Good-news announcements are usually communicated via a letter or a **news release**, a specialized document used to share relevant information with the local or national news media. In most companies, news releases are usually prepared (or at least supervised) by specially trained writers in the public relations department (see Figure 7.9). The content follows the customary pattern for a positive message: good news, followed by details and a positive close. However, news releases have a critical difference: you're not writing directly to the ultimate audience (such as the readers of a newspaper); you're trying to interest an editor or reporter in a story, and that person will then write the material that is eventually read by the larger audience. To write a successful news release, keep the following points in mind:[3]

- Make sure your information is newsworthy and relevant. Editors at most media outlets are overwhelmed with news releases, so those with little or no news content quickly find their way into the recycling bin.
- Put your most important idea first. (Don't say "Calco's president James Grall announced today that the company will move its headquarters to the Main Street office." Instead, start with the news: "Calco will move its headquarters to the Main Street office, President James Grall announced today.")
- Be brief: Break up long sentences and keep paragraphs short.
- Eliminate clutter such as redundancy and extraneous facts.

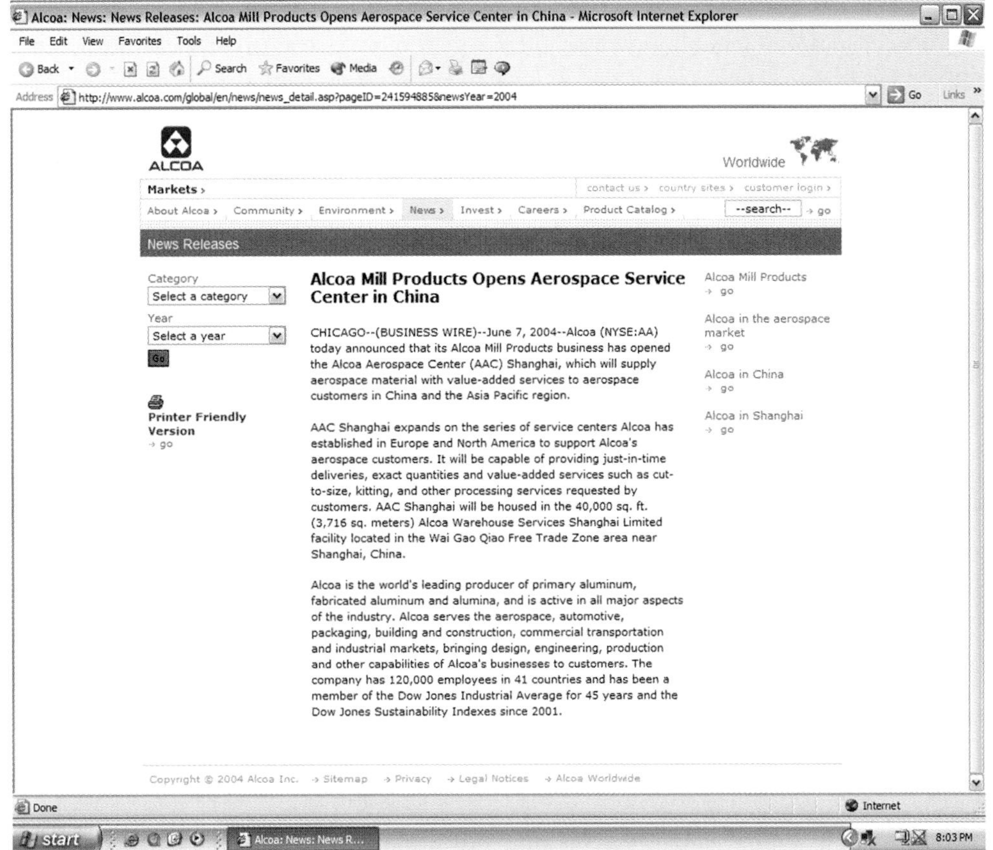

Alcoa Mill Products Opens Aerospace Service Center in China

CHICAGO--(BUSINESS WIRE)--June 7, 2004--Alcoa (NYSE:AA) today announced that its Alcoa Mill Products business has opened the Alcoa Aerospace Center (AAC) Shanghai, which will supply aerospace material with value-added services to aerospace customers in China and the Asia Pacific region.

AAC Shanghai expands on the series of service centers Alcoa has established in Europe and North America to support Alcoa's aerospace customers. It will be capable of providing just-in-time deliveries, exact quantities and value-added services such as cut-to-size, kitting, and other processing services requested by customers. AAC Shanghai will be housed in the 40,000 sq. ft. (3,716 sq. meters) Alcoa Warehouse Services Shanghai Limited facility located in the Wai Gao Qiao Free Trade Zone area near Shanghai, China.

Alcoa is the world's leading producer of primary aluminum, fabricated aluminum and alumina, and is active in all major aspects of the industry. Alcoa serves the aerospace, automotive, packaging, building and construction, commercial transportation and industrial markets, bringing design, engineering, production and other capabilities of Alcoa's businesses to customers. The company has 120,000 employees in 41 countries and has been a member of the Dow Jones Industrial Average for 45 years and the Dow Jones Sustainability Indexes since 2001.

Copyright © 2004 Alcoa Inc. → Sitemap → Privacy → Legal Notices → Alcoa Worldwide

FIGURE 7.9
Online News Release

- Be as specific as possible.
- Minimize self-congratulatory adjectives and adverbs; if the content of your message is newsworthy, the media professionals will be interested in the news on its own merits.

As with many aspects of business communication, the process of creating and distributing news releases and other media materials is continually improved by technological advances. Online distribution systems such as PR Newswire and BusinessWire make it easy for even the smallest companies to reach editors and reporters at the most prominent publications around the world. *Webcasts,* an online alternative to press conferences, lets you reach stock market analysts, reporters, and potential customers with a combination of *streaming audio* and *streaming video* presentations that bring voice and video to anyone with Internet access. Many companies also create special media pages on their websites that contain their latest news releases, background information on the company, and archives of past news releases.

7 **LEARNING OBJECTIVE**

Describe the importance of goodwill messages and explain how to make them effective

Fostering Goodwill

All business messages should be written with an eye toward fostering goodwill among business contacts, but some messages are written primarily and specifically to build goodwill. You can use these messages to enhance your relationships with customers, colleagues, and other businesspeople by sending friendly, even unexpected notes with no direct business purpose. Jack Welch, former CEO of General Electric, is known for his handwritten notes to all employees, from managers to hourly workers. He once wrote a note to one manager who had turned down a promotion because he didn't want to move his teenager to a different school: "Bill," wrote Welch, "we like you for a lot of reasons—one of them is that you are a very special person. You proved it again this morning. Good for you and your lucky family. . . ."[4]

Goodwill is the positive feeling that encourages people to maintain a business relationship.

Effective goodwill messages must be sincere and honest. Otherwise, you'll appear to be interested in personal gain rather than in benefiting customers, fellow workers, or your

Make sure your compliments are grounded in reality.

organization. To come across as sincere, avoid exaggerating, and back up any compliments with specific points. In addition, readers often regard more restrained praise as being more sincere:

INSTEAD OF THIS	WRITE THIS
Words cannot express my appreciation for the great job you did. Thanks. No one could have done it better. You're terrific! You've made the whole firm sit up and take notice, and we are ecstatic to have you working here.	Thanks again for taking charge of the meeting in my absence. You did an excellent job. With just an hour's notice, you managed to pull the legal and public relations departments together so that we could present a united front in the negotiations. Your dedication and communication abilities have been noted and are truly appreciated.

Taking note of significant events in someone's personal life helps cement the business relationship.

Sending Congratulations One prime opportunity for sending goodwill messages is to congratulate someone for a significant business achievement—perhaps for being promoted or for attaining an important civic position. The congratulatory note in Figure 7.10 moves swiftly to the subject: the good news. It gives reasons for expecting success and avoids extravagances such as "Only you can do the job!"

Other reasons for sending congratulations include the highlights in people's personal lives—weddings, births, graduations, success in nonbusiness competitions. You may congratulate business acquaintances on their own achievements or on the accomplishments of a spouse or child. You may also take note of personal events, even if you don't know the reader well. If you're already friendly with the reader, a more personal tone is appropriate.

Some companies even develop a mailing list of potential customers by assigning an employee to clip newspaper announcements of births, engagements, weddings, and graduations or to obtain information on real estate transactions in the local community. Then they introduce themselves by sending out a form letter that might read like this:

> Congratulations on your new home! All of us at Klemper Security Solutions hope it brings you and your family many years of security and happiness.
>
> Please accept the enclosed *Homeowner's Guide to Home Security* with our compliments. It lists a number of simple steps you can take to keep your home, your family, and your possessions safe.

This simple message has a natural, friendly tone, even though the sender has never met the recipient.

An effective message of appreciation documents a person's contributions.

Sending Messages of Appreciation An important business quality is the ability to recognize the contributions of employees, colleagues, suppliers, and other associates. Your praise does more than just make the person feel good; it encourages further excellence. Moreover, a message of appreciation may become an important part of someone's personnel file. So when you write a message of appreciation, try to specifically mention the person or people you want to praise. The brief message that follows expresses gratitude and reveals the happy result:

> Thank you for sending the air-conditioning components by overnight delivery. You allowed us to satisfy the needs of two customers who were getting very impatient with the heat.
>
> Special thanks to Susan Brown, who answered our call for help and never said, "It can't be done." Her initiative on our behalf is greatly appreciated.

Plan

Analyze the Situation
Purpose is to foster goodwill with industry associates.

Gather Information
Gather information on specific accomplishments by the reader"s firm.

Select the Right Medium
The letter format gives this message an appropriate level of formality.

Organize the Information
The main idea is to offer congratulations; a direct approach is perfect for letters such as this.

1

Write

Adapt to Your Audience
Show sensitivity to audience needs with a "you" attitude, politeness, positive emphasis, and bias-free language.

Compose the Message
Style is positive but still respectful and businesslike.

2

Complete

Revise the Message
Evaluate content and review readability; avoid unnecessary details.

Produce the Message
Emphasize a clean, professional appearance appropriate for a letter on company stationery.

Proofread the Message
Review for errors in layout, spelling, and mechanics.

Distribute the Message
Deliver the message via postal mail.

3

FIGURE 7.10 Effective Letter Congratulating a Business Acquaintance

Office DEPOT, Inc.
2200 Old Germantown Road, Delray Beach, FL 33445 407/278-4800

March 3, 2005

Mr. Ralph Lambert, President
Lambert, Cutchen & Browt, Inc.
14355 Pasadena Parkway
Pasadena, TX 74229

Dear Mr. Lambert:

Congratulations on your firm's recent selection to design and print media advertisements for the National Association of Business Suppliers (ABS). Your appointment was announced at the national convention in Atlanta last month, and here at Office Depot, we can think of no better firm to help our industry achieve wide recognition.

Opens by immediately expressing the reason for congratulating the reader

Your success has been admirable in promoting associations of other industries, such as soft drinks, snack foods, and recycling. Your "Dream Vision 2004" ads for the bottling industry were both inspirational and effective in raising consumer awareness. The campaign you design for ABS is sure to yield similar positive responses.

Uses body to make compliment more effective by showing knowledge of the reader's work—without exaggeration

You can be sure we will follow your media campaign with great interest.

Closes by expressing interest in following the future success of the firm

Sincerely,

Janice McCarthy

Janice McCarthy
Director, Media Relations

tw

The primary purpose of condolence messages is to let the audience know that you and the organization you represent care about the person's loss.

Offering Condolences In times of serious trouble and deep sadness, well-written condolences and expressions of sympathy can mean a great deal to people who've experienced loss. Granted, this type of message is difficult to write, but don't let the difficulty of the task keep you from responding promptly. Those who have experienced a health problem, the death of a loved one, or a business misfortune appreciate knowing that others care.

Open condolences with a brief statement of sympathy, such as "I was deeply sorry to hear of your loss." In the body, mention the good qualities or the positive contributions made by the deceased. State what the person or business meant to you. In closing, you can offer your condolences and your best wishes. One considerate way to end this type of message is to say something that will give the reader a little lift, such as a reference to a brighter future. Here are a few general suggestions for writing condolence messages:

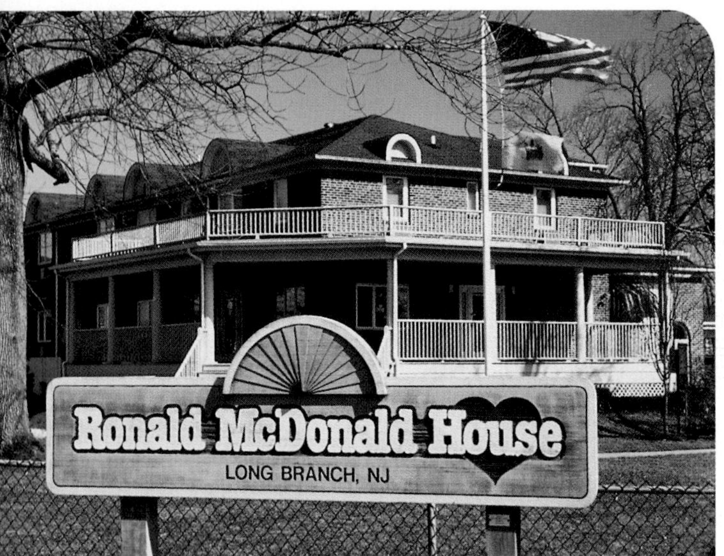

Ronald McDonald House has become known worldwide as a home away from home for the families of seriously ill children. But when employees of the global office send congratulations, thank-you notes, or condolences to associates inside or outside the organization, they don't boast about all the good their organization accomplishes; they focus on the situation of the person receiving the message.

- **Keep reminiscences brief.** Recount a memory or an anecdote (even a humorous one), but don't dwell on the details of the loss, lest you add to the reader's anguish.
- **Write in your own words.** Write as if you were speaking privately to the person. Don't quote "poetic" passages or use stilted or formal phrases. If the loss is a death, refer to it as such rather than as "passing away" or "departing."
- **Be tactful.** Mention your shock and dismay, but remember that bereaved and distressed loved ones take little comfort in lines such as "Richard was too young to die" or "Starting all over again will be so difficult." Try to strike a balance between superficial expressions of sympathy and painful references to a happier past or the likelihood of a bleak future.
- **Take special care.** Be sure to spell names correctly and to be accurate in your review of facts. Try to be prompt.
- **Write about special qualities of the deceased.** You may have to rely on reputation to do this, but let the grieving person know you valued his or her loved one.
- **Write about special qualities of the bereaved person.** A pat on the back helps a bereaved family member feel more confident about handling things during such a traumatic time.[5]

Supervisor George Bigalow sent the following condolence letter to his administrative assistant, Janice Case, after learning of the death of Janice's husband:

> My sympathy to you and your children. All your friends at Carter Electric were so very sorry to learn of John's death. Although I never had the opportunity to meet him, I do know how very special he was to you. Your tales of your family's camping trips and his rafting expeditions were always memorable.

To review the tasks involved in writing goodwill messages, see "Checklist: Sending Goodwill Messages."

CHECKLIST: Sending Goodwill Messages

- Be sincere and honest.
- Don't exaggerate or use vague, grandiose language; support positive statements with specific evidence.
- Use congratulatory messages to build goodwill with clients and colleagues.
- Send messages of appreciation to emphasize how much you value the work of others.
- When sending condolence messages, open with a brief statement of sympathy, followed by an expression of how much the deceased person meant to you or your firm (as appropriate), then close by offering your best wishes for the future.

COMMUNICATION CHALLENGES AT CONE, INC.

In addition to serving hot meals, the Kids Café program also provides a safe, nurturing environment that keeps kids out of trouble during the risky afternoon hours from 3:00 to 6:00. To make that time more valuable, many Kids Cafés have started offering sports, crafts, mentoring, and tutoring. These activities require qualified volunteers who are willing to spend a few hours each week working with the kids.

Individual Challenge: To staff the tutoring program, ConAgra has asked Cone to create a recruiting campaign that will attract volunteers qualified to help with math, English, and science homework. One of the most important recruiting tools will be a letter addressed to current monetary donors, asking them to give as little as three hours a month. Carol has asked you, her executive assistant, to draft the request letter. What key points should you include in the introduction, body, and close of the letter? Make a brief outline for your instructor.

Team Challenge: It's nine months later and the recruiting program has been a success: most Kids Cafés are now offering more tutoring sessions. Carol now asks you to draft a letter of appreciation, which is reviewed by executives at ConAgra. During this review process, ConAgra executives have suggested using the letter to ask volunteers to increase the amount of time they spend tutoring each month. With a small group, discuss the pros and cons of adding this request to your letter. In a brief paragraph, explain your team's conclusions.

SUMMARY OF LEARNING OBJECTIVES

1 **Apply the three-step writing process to routine and positive messages.** Even though routine messages are usually short and simple, they benefit from the three-step writing process. Planning routine messages may take only a few moments to (1) analyze your purpose and audience, (2) investigate your readers' needs and make sure that you have all the facts to satisfy them, and (3) adapt your message to your audience through your choice of medium and your use of the "you" attitude. When writing routine messages, use the direct approach, as long as your readers will be positive (or neutral) and have minimal cultural differences. Completing routine messages means making them as professional as possible by (1) revising for clarity and conciseness, (2) selecting appropriate design elements and delivery methods, and (3) careful proofreading.

2 **Illustrate an effective strategy for writing routine requests.** When writing a routine request, open by stating your specific request. At the same time, avoid being abrupt or tactless: pay attention to tone, assume your audience will comply, avoid personal introductions, end polite requests with a period, and be specific. Use the middle of a routine request to justify your request and explain its importance. Close routine requests by asking for specific action (including a deadline as often as possible), and expressing goodwill. Be sure to include all contact information so that your reader can respond easily.

3 **Explain how to ask for specific action in a courteous manner.** A courteous close contains three important elements: (1) a specific request, (2) information about

how you can be reached (if it isn't obvious), and (3) an expression of appreciation or goodwill.

4 **Illustrate a strategy for writing routine replies and positive messages.** First, open your message with a clear and concise statement of the main idea or your good news. Second, in the body of your message, provide the details and explanations necessary to meet the audience's information needs. If your message has a mix of positive and negative information, try to put the negative news in a positive context. If you are communicating with customers, you can also use the body of the message to share marketing and customer relationship information. Third, end your message with a courteous close that indicates to your audience that you have their best interests at heart.

5 **Discuss the importance of knowing who is responsible when granting claims and requests for adjustment.** Your response to a claim or a request for an adjustment can vary significantly depending on which party you determine to be at fault. If your company is at fault, your message should acknowledge receipt of the customer's claim or complaint, take responsibility, sympathize with the customer, explain how you will resolve the situation, take steps to repair the relationship, and keep the lines of communication open. If the customer is at fault, you have to decide whether to grant the claim in the interest of keeping the customer's business. If a third party is at fault, your response will be determined by whatever arrangements are in place between your company and the third party.

6 **Explain how creating informative messages differs from responding to information requests.** The key difference between creating informative messages and responding to information requests is a matter of who initiates the communication. When you create an informative message, your audience may or may not be expecting it and may or may not be motivated to read it, so you need to gauge their potential reaction and plan your message accordingly. In contrast, when someone else initiates the request, they will obviously be anticipating your response. The person may or may not like what you have to say, of course, but at least your message will not be unexpected.

7 **Describe the importance of goodwill messages, and explain how to make them effective.** Goodwill messages are important for building relationships with customers, colleagues, and other businesspeople. These friendly, unexpected notes have no direct business purpose, but they make people feel good about doing business with the sender. To make goodwill messages effective, make them honest and sincere. Avoid exaggerating, back up compliments with specific points, and give restrained praise.

Test Your Knowledge

1. When is a request routine?
2. What are some of the guidelines for asking a series of questions in a routine request?
3. What information should be included in an order request?
4. Should you use the direct or indirect approach for most routine messages? Why?
5. Where in a routine message should you state your actual request?
6. How does a claim differ from an adjustment?
7. How does the question of fault affect what you say in a message granting a claim?
8. What is the appropriate strategy for responding to a request for a recommendation about a job candidate whose performance was poor?
9. How can you avoid sounding insincere when writing a goodwill message?
10. What are some of the guidelines for writing condolence messages?

Apply Your Knowledge

1. When organizing request messages, why is it important to know whether any cultural differences exist between you and your audience? Explain.
2. Your company's error cost an important business customer a new client; you know it and your customer knows it. Do you apologize, or do you refer to the incident in a positive light without admitting any responsibility? Briefly explain.
3. You've been asked to write a letter of recommendation for an employee who is disabled and uses a wheelchair. The disability has no effect on the employee's ability to do the job, and you feel confident about writing the best recommendation possible. Nevertheless, you know the prospective company and its facilities aren't well suited to wheelchair access. Do you mention the employee's disability in your letter? Explain.
4. Every time you send a direct-request memo to Ted Jackson, who works in another department in your company, he delays or refuses to comply. You're beginning to get impatient. Should you send Jackson a memo to ask what's wrong? Complain to your supervisor about Jackson's uncooperative attitude? Arrange a face-to-face meeting with Jackson? Bring up the problem at the next staff meeting? Explain.
5. **Ethical Choices** You have a complaint against one of your suppliers, but you have no documentation to back it up. Should you request an adjustment anyway? Why or why not?

Practice Your Knowledge

Documents for Analysis

Read the following documents, then (1) analyze the strengths and weaknesses of each sentence, and (2) revise each document so that it follows this chapter's guidelines.

Document 7.A: Requesting Routine Information from a Business

Our college is closing its dining hall for financial reasons, so we want to do something to help the students prepare their own food in their dorm rooms if they so choose. Your colorful ad in *Collegiate Magazine* caught our eye. We need the following information before we make our decision.

- Would you be able to ship the microwaves by August 15th? I realize this is short notice, but our board of trustees just made the decision to close the dining hall last week and we're scrambling around trying to figure out what to do.
- Do they have any kind of a warranty? College students can be pretty hard on things, as you know, so we will need a good warranty.
- How much does it cost? Do you give a discount for a big order?
- Do we have to provide a special outlet?
- Will students know how to use them, or will we need to provide instructions?

As I said before, we're on a tight time frame and need good information from you as soon as possible to help us make our decision about ordering. You never know what the board might come up with next. I'm looking at several other companies, also, so please let us know ASAP.

Document 7.B: Making Claims and Requests for Adjustment

At a local business-supply store, I recently purchased your *Negotiator Pro* for my computer. I bought the CD because I saw your ad for it in *MacWorld* magazine, and it looked as if it might be an effective tool for use in my corporate seminar on negotiation.

Unfortunately, when I inserted it in my office computer, it wouldn't work. I returned it to the store, but since I had already opened it, they refused to exchange it for a CD that would work or give me a refund. They told me to contact you and that you might be able to send me a version that would work with my computer.

You can send the information to me at the letterhead address. If you cannot send me the correct disk, please refund my $79.95. Thanks in advance for any help you can give me in this matter.

Document 7.C: Responding to Claims and Adjustment Requests When the Customer Is at Fault

We read your letter requesting your deposit refund. We couldn't figure out why you hadn't received it, so we talked to our maintenance engineer as you suggested. He said you had left one of the doors off the hinges in your apartment in order to get a large sofa through the door. He also confirmed that you had paid him $5.00 to replace the door since you had to turn in the U-Haul trailer and were in a big hurry.

This entire situation really was caused by a lack of communication between our housekeeping inspector and the maintenance engineer. All we knew was that the door was off the hinges when it was inspected by Sally Tarnley. You know that our policy states that if anything is wrong with the apartment, we keep the deposit. We had no way of knowing that George just hadn't gotten around to replacing the door.

But we have good news. We approved the deposit refund, which will be mailed to you from our home office in Teaneck, New Jersey. I'm not sure how long that will take, however. If you don't receive the check by the end of next month, give me a call.

Next time, it's really a good idea to stay with your apartment until it's inspected as stipulated in your lease agreement. That way, you'll be sure to receive your refund when you expect it. Hope you have a good summer.

Document 7.D: Letter of Recommendation

Your letter to Kunitake Ando, President of Sony, was forwarded to me because I am the human resources director. In my job as head of HR, I have access to performance reviews for all of the Sony employees in the United States. This means, of course, that I would be the person best qualified to answer your request for information on Nick Oshinski.

In your letter of the 15th, you asked about Nick Oshinski's employment record with us because he has applied to work for your company. Mr. Oshinski was employed with us from January 5, 1995, until March 1, 2005. During that time, Mr. Oshinski received ratings ranging from 2.5 up to 9.6, with 10 being the top score. As you can see, he must have done better reporting to some managers than to others. In addition, he took all vacation days, which is a bit unusual. Although I did not know Mr. Oshinski personally, I know that our best workers seldom use all the vacation time they earn. I do not know if that applies in this case.

In summary, Nick Oshinski performed his tasks well depending on who managed him.

Exercises

For live links to all websites discussed in this chapter, visit this text's website at www.prenhall.com/bovee. Just log on, select Chapter 7, and click on "Featured Websites." Locate the page or the URL related to the material in the text.

7.1 Revising Messages: Directness and Conciseness Revise the following short e-mail messages so that they are more direct and concise; develop a subject line for each revised message.

a. I'm contacting you about your recent order for a High Country backpack. You didn't tell us which backpack you wanted, and you know we make a lot of different ones. We have the canvas models with the plastic frames and vinyl trim and we have the canvas models with leather trim, and we have the ones that have more pockets than the other ones. Plus they come in lots of different colors. Also they make the ones that are large for a big-boned person and the smaller versions for little women or kids.

b. Thank you for contacting us about the difficulty you had collecting your luggage at Denver International Airport. We are very sorry for the inconvenience this has caused you. As you know, traveling can create problems of this sort regardless of how careful the airline personnel might be. To receive compensation, please send us a detailed list of the items that you lost and complete the following questionnaire. You can e-mail it back to us.

c. Sorry it took us so long to get back to you. We were flooded with résumés. Anyway, your résumé made the final ten, and after meeting three hours yesterday, we've decided we'd like to meet with you. What is your schedule like for next week? Can you come in for an interview on June 15 at 3:00 P.M.? Please get back to us by the end of this work week and let us know if you will be able to attend. As you can imagine, this is our busy season.

d. We're letting you know that because we use over a ton of paper a year and because so much of that paper goes into the wastebasket to become so much more environmental waste, starting Monday, we're placing white plastic bins outside the elevators on every floor to recycle that paper and in the process, minimize pollution.

7.2 **Revising Messages: Directness and Conciseness** Rewrite the following sentences so that they are direct and concise.

a. We wanted to invite you to our special 40% off by-invitation-only sale. The sale is taking place on November 9.

b. We wanted to let you know that we are giving a tote bag and a free Phish CD with every $50 donation you make to our radio station.

c. The director planned to go to the meeting that will be held on Monday at a little before 11 A.M.

d. In today's meeting, we were happy to have the opportunity to welcome Paul Eccelson. He reviewed some of the newest types of order forms. If you have any questions about these new forms, feel free to call him at his office.

7.3 **Internet** Visit the Career eCards section of the Blue Mountain site at www.bluemountain.com and analyze one of the electronic greeting cards bearing a goodwill message of appreciation for good performance. Under what circumstances would you send this electronic message? How could you personalize it for the recipient and the occasion? What would be an appropriate close for this message?

7.4 **Teamwork** With another student, identify the purpose and select the most appropriate format for communicating these written messages. Next, consider how the audience is likely to respond to each message. Based on this audience analysis, determine whether the direct or indirect approach would be effective for each message, and explain your reasoning.

a. A notice to all employees about the placement of recycling bins by the elevator doors

b. The first late-payment notice to a good customer who usually pays his bills on time

7.5 **Revising Messages: Conciseness, Courteousness, and Specificity** Critique the following closing paragraphs. How would you rewrite each to be concise, courteous, and specific?

a. I need your response sometime soon so I can order the parts in time for your service appointment. Otherwise your air-conditioning system may not be in tip-top condition for the start of the summer season.

b. Thank you in advance for sending me as much information as you can about your products. I look forward to receiving your package in the very near future.

c. To schedule an appointment with one of our knowledgeable mortgage specialists in your area, you can always call our hotline at 1-800-555-8765. This is also the number to call if you have more questions about mortgage rates, closing procedures, or any other aspect of the mortgage process. Remember, we're here to make the home-buying experience as painless as possible.

7.6 **Ethical Choices** Your small supermarket chain has received dozens of complaints about the watery consistency of the ketchup sold under the chain's brand name. You don't want your customers to stop buying other store-brand foods, which are made and packaged for your chain by various suppliers, but you do want to address their concerns about the ketchup. In responding to these complaints, should you explain that the ketchup is actually manufactured by a local supplier and then name the supplier, who has already started bottling a thicker ketchup?

Expand Your Knowledge

For live links to the websites that follow, go to www.prenhall.com/bovee. When you log on, select Chapter 7, then select "Featured Websites," click on the URL of the website you wish to visit, and review the website to complete these exercises.

Exploring the Best of the Web

Recommended Advice for Recommendation Letters
www.about.com

Whether you're continuing on to graduate school or entering the workforce with your undergraduate degree, recommendation letters could play an important role in the next few steps of your career. From selecting the people to ask for recommendation letters to knowing what makes an effective letter, About.com extends the advice offered in this chapter with real-life examples and suggestions. Visit the site for "recommendation letters," read the advice you find, then answer the following questions:

1. What's a good process for identifying the best people to ask for recommendation letters?
2. What information should you provide to letter writers to help them produce a credible and compelling letter on your behalf?
3. What are the most common mistakes you need to avoid with recommendation letters?

Exploring the Web on Your Own

1. Learn how to write effective thank-you notes by reviewing the steps at www.globaltowne.com/aresume/thankyounotes.htm. (Looking for an easy way to stand out from other job candidates? Note the survey on this site that shows that only 12 percent of candidates bother to send a thank-you note after an interview.)
2. Need to write a press release but don't have time to become an expert? Learn from any expert at www.stetson.edu/~rhansen/prguide.html.
3. Get advice on writing sensitive condolence letters at www.ABusinessResource.com (search for "condolence letter").

Learn Interactively

Interactive Study Guide

Go to the Companion Website at www.prenhall.com/bovee. For Chapter 7, take advantage of the interactive "Study Guide" to test your knowledge of the chapter. Get instant feedback on whether you need additional studying.

Also, visit this site's "Study Hall," where you'll find an abundance of valuable resources that will help you succeed in this course.

Peak Performance Grammar and Mechanics

To improve your skill with sentences, visit www.prenhall.com/onekey, click "Peak Performance Grammar and Mechanics" then click "Sentences." Take the Pretest to determine whether you have any weak areas. Then review those areas in the Refresher Course. Take the Follow-Up Test to check your grasp of sentences. For an extra challenge or advanced practice, take the Advanced Test. Finally, for additional reinforcement in sentences, go to www.prenhall.com/bovee, where you will find "Improve Your Grammar, Mechanics, and Usage" exercises.

CASES

Applying the Three-Step Writing Process to Cases

Apply each step to the following cases, as assigned by your instructor

Plan

Analyze the Situation
Identify both your general purpose and your specific purpose. Clarify exactly what you want your audience to think, feel, or believe after receiving your message. Profile your primary audience, including their backgrounds, differences, similarities, and likely reactions to your message.

Gather Information
Identify the information your audience will need to receive, as well as other information you may need in order to craft an effective message.

Select the Right Medium
Make sure your medium is both acceptable to the audience and appropriate for the message.

Organize the Information
Choose a direct or indirect approach based on the audience and the message; most routine requests and routine and positive messages should use a direct approach. Identify your main idea, limit your scope, then outline necessary support points and other evidence.

1

Write

Adapt to Your Audience
Show sensitivity to audience needs with a "you" attitude, politeness, positive emphasis, and bias-free language. Understand how much credibility you already have—and how much you may need to establish. Project your company's image by maintaining an appropriate style and tone.

Compose the Message
Draft your message using powerful words, effective sentences, and coherent paragraphs.

2

Complete

Revise the Message
Evaluate content and review readability; then edit and rewrite for conciseness and clarity.

Produce the Message
Use effective design elements and suitable layout for a clean, professional appearance.

Proofread the Message
Review for errors in layout, spelling, and mechanics.

Distribute the Message
Deliver your message using the chosen medium; make sure all documents and all relevant files are distributed successfully.

3

ROUTINE REQUESTS

1. Step on it: Letter to Floorgraphics requesting information about underfoot advertising You work for Alberta Greenwood, owner of Better Bike and Ski Shop. Yesterday, Alberta met with the Schwinn sales representative, Tom Beeker, who urged her to sign a contract with Floorgraphics. That company leases floor space from retail stores, then creates and sells floor ads to manufacturers like Schwinn. Floorgraphics will pay Alberta a fee for leasing the floor space, as well as a percentage for every ad it sells. Alberta was definitely interested, and turned to you after Beeker left.

"Tom says that advertising decals on the floor in front of the product reach consumers right where they're standing when making a decision," explained Alberta. "He says the ads increase sales from 25 to 75 percent."

You both look down at the dusty floor, and Alberta laughs. "It seems funny that manufacturers will pay hard cash to put their names where customers are going to track dirt all over them! But if Tom's telling the truth, we could profit three ways: from the leasing fee, the increased sales, and the share in ad revenues. That's not so funny."

Your task: Alberta Greenwood asks you to write a letter for her signature to CEO Richard Rebh at Floorgraphics, Inc. (5 Vaughn Dr., Princeton, NJ 08540) asking for financial details and practical information about the ads. For example, how will you clean your floors? Who installs and removes the ads? Can you terminate the lease if you don't like them?[6]

2. Measuring suppliers: Memo requesting supplier reviews at Microsoft This meeting of the Employee Services Group was called by Roxanna Frost, group program manager from Microsoft's Executive Management and Development Group. "You already do reviews with employees to improve clarity in terms of goals and expectations." explained Frost. "These reviews give everyone the opportunity to talk about accomplishments and improvements—comparing results with goals and figuring out how better to achieve those goals." Frost paused a few moments before continuing. "Why can't the same be true for suppliers? There's a gap between what we want our suppliers to do and the feedback they're getting."

You think she's making perfect sense. Of the employee services that your group monitors—travel assistance, 401(k) programs, the library onsite at Microsoft's Redmond, Washington, campus—some 60 percent are outsourced to independent contractors. And many other departments at Microsoft outsource for services and products as well.

Frost asks you, as communications manager, to write a memo to all departments at Microsoft that use outside suppliers. You must ask them to evaluate each supplier for the same five qualities used to evaluate employees (financial value, delivery, quality, customer satisfaction, and innovation). Each quality should be rated on a scale of 1 (poor) to 5 (great). She wants the evaluations repeated every six months, and she wants them to be written up in a formal letter format for mailing to each supplier. The departments are to forward their supplier letters to Frost's office (for Microsoft record keeping), where her staff will handle all the mailing. She also suggests that your memo give managers some ideas for gently introducing this new policy to suppliers.

Your task: Write the memo to relevant departments. Think about reader benefits to suppress any concerns about the new procedure; for example, Microsoft's ratings may be more feedback than suppliers want, and the task will probably mean more work for department managers. As you begin planning your letter, your mind is already busy concocting a direct request memo that's friendly, helpful, and firm.[7]

3. Bolga boo-boo: E-mail to Getrade (Ghana) Ltd. from Pier 1 Imports The way you heard it, your employer, Pier 1 Imports, sent a buyer to Accra, Ghana, to find local handicrafts to slake your customers' insatiable thirst for African art. Free-market reforms in Ghana during the 1980s helped ease export procedures, but so far the local entrepreneurs who took advantage of the change are having trouble meeting demand from large-quantity buyers like Pier 1 (and rival, Cost Plus). The shipment that just arrived from Getrade (Ghana) Ltd., one of your best Ghanaian suppliers, is a good example of what's been going wrong.

Your customers love bowl-shaped Bolga baskets, traditionally woven by the Fra Fra people of northern Ghana. You can't keep the baskets in stock. So this was to be a huge shipment—3,000 Bolga baskets. You sympathize with Ladi Nylander, chairman and managing director of Getrade, who is trying hard to adapt to the specific tastes of his U.S. buyers. He's hiring local artisans to carve, shape, and weave all sorts of artifacts—often from designs provided by Pier 1. In this case, your order spelled out that Getrade was to ship 1,000 green, 1,000 yellow, and 1,000 magenta baskets in the traditional shape.

Your overseas buyer heard that the Body Shop ordered similar baskets but with mixed-color patterns and a flatter shape. Pier 1 may have received the Body Shop's order, because what you received was 3,000 mixed-color, flat Bolga baskets.

Your task: As assistant buyer, it's your job to compose the e-mail message alerting Getrade to the mix-up. You decide that if you want the mistake corrected, you'd better direct your message to Nylander at Nylander@Getrade.co.za. If you're lucky, it may be simply that the Body Shop got your order and you got theirs.[8]

4. Reverse migration: Letter requesting recommendation for "dot-com" dropout You were a part of the so-called "Great Migration" of executive talent to online companies. Like so many others, you left your job at a big company and plunged into the world of Internet commerce. Your position was creative services director at a well-funded dot-com company in your industry (travel services).

The first week wasn't so bad. You learned tons of new things and adapted readily to the seat-of-the-pants work style. You discovered with delight that at your new company, creativity and vision weren't considered terrifying traits of overachievers who had to be kept on a short leash; instead, your new company cultivated these traits. The more "out there" your ideas, the more attention they merited. That's because e-business moves fast and everybody needs to move fast with it.

You just didn't realize how long and how often you'd be expected to keep moving. That first week was only 50 hours. The second was 60. By the third week, 70 hours wasn't considered outlandish. Anyone who went home before 7 P.M. or who didn't show up on Saturday or Sunday was considered a loser and quickly disappeared from your workscape.

Your spouse was soon complaining about not recognizing you anymore. Your children told people at school functions that you were in the hospital, and you couldn't remember the last time you ate a meal without a computer screen, cell phone, or beeper a few inches from your plate. You love the fast decision making, and your CEO loves your exemplary work, but you are exhausted. Money is nice, you muse. But when will you enjoy the things it can buy? When will you live your life?

You read about others who had taken the Internet plunge only to quit after experiencing similar job stress. "Reverse migration" was the term the newspapers used to describe people who left dot-com jobs to return to the "normalcy" of the traditional workplace. One day you picked up your briefcase and left at 5 P.M. Horror registered on the few faces that lifted to see you go. Then their weary eyes shifted back to their computer screens.

Your task: You've already resigned. Now write a hard-copy letter to Glenna Evans, CEO of Yourtravel.com, asking for a letter of recommendation.[9]

5. Trans-global exchange: Instant message request for information from Chinese manufacturer Thank goodness your company, Diagonal Imports, chose the enterprise instant messaging software produced by IBM Lotus, called Sametime. Other products might allow you to carry on real-time exchanges with colleagues on the other side of the planet, but Sametime supports bidirectional machine translation, and you're going to need it.

The problem is that production on a popular line of decorative lighting appliances produced at your Chinese manufacturing plant inexplicably came to a halt last month. As the product manager in the United States, you have many resources you could call on to help, such as new sources for faulty parts. But you can't do anything if you don't know the details. You've tried telephoning top managers in China, but they're evasive, telling you only what they think you want to hear.

Finally, your friend Kuei-chen Tsao has returned from a business trip. You met her during your trip to China last year. She doesn't speak English, but she's the line engineer responsible for this particular product: a fiber-optic lighting display, featuring a plastic base with a rotating color-wheel. As the wheel turns, light emitted from the spray of fiber-optic threads changes color in soothing patterns. Product #3347XM is one of Diagonal's most popular items and you've got orders from novelty stores around the United States waiting to be filled. Kuei-chen should be able to explain the problem, determine whether you can help, and tell you how long before regular shipping resumes.

Your task: Write the first of what you hope will be a productive instant message exchange with Kuei-Chen. Remember your words will be machine-translated.[10]

ROUTINE ANNOUNCEMENTS

6. Temper, temper: E-mail to Metro Power employees about technology failures This is the third time in two months that your company, Metro Power, has had to escort an employee from the building after a violent episode. Frankly, everyone is a little frightened by this development, and as a human resources administrator, you have the unhappy task of trying to quell the storm.

Metro Power rarely fires employees, preferring to transfer them to new responsibilities, which may either draw out their finer points (and prove better for everyone in the long run) or help them decide to seek greener pastures. But in three cases, you had no choice. In one incident, a man punched out his computer screen after the system failed. In another, a man threw his keyboard across the room when he couldn't get access to the company's intranet. And in a third incident, a woman kicked a printer while screaming obscenities.

In all three cases, co-workers were terrified by these sudden outbursts. Too many disgruntled workers have committed too many violent acts against others in recent years, and whenever workers lose their temper on the job these days, it causes great fear—not to mention financial losses from the destruction of property and the disruption of work flow.

People are on edge at Metro Power right now. Rising energy costs, public and government scrutiny, and cries of price gouging are causing additional work and stress for all your employees. Plus, too much overtime, unrealistic expectations for overworked departments, and high demands on sensitive equipment are contributing to the problem. Tempers are frayed and nerves strained. You're concerned that these three incidents are just the tip of the iceberg.

Your department head suggests that you write a reminder to all employees about controlling tempers in the workplace. "Tell them that technology glitches are commonplace and not some unholy disaster. And remind them to report routine computer failures to Bart Stone. He'll get to them in due course."

You say nothing to contradict her idea, but you wonder how to do what she asks without sounding trite or condescending? You don't want to sound like some nagging parent—no one will pay attention to your message. You sigh deeply as your boss strolls calmly back to her office. You're fairly certain that every employee already knows about reporting computer failures to Bart Stone, assistant director of information services.

Even so, you can think of a few suggestions that might be helpful, such as taking a walk to cool down, or recognizing that machines, like humans, are not infallible. You want cooler heads to prevail, and that's just the sort of cliché you'd like to avoid in your message.

Your task: Write the e-mail message to all employees. Instead of uttering platitudes or wagging your finger, include preventive maintenance tips for office equipment, such as turning systems off at night, keeping food and liquids away from keyboards, making use of dusting sprays and special cloths, and so on. Your boss also asked you to make it clear that abusive behavior will be reprimanded, so include that point in a tactful way.[11]

7. Got it covered? Letter from American Express about SUV rentals You can always tell when fall arrives at American Express—you are deluged with complaints from customers who've just received their summer vacation bills. Often these angry calls are about a shock-inducing damage repair bill from a car rental agency. Vacation car rentals can be a lot more complicated than most people think. Here's what happens.

Your credit card customers are standing at the Hertz or Avis counter, ready to drive away, when the agent suggests an upgrade to, say, a Ford Expedition or another of those monstrous gas-eaters that families love to drive on city streets. Feeling happy-go-lucky on vacation, your customers say, "Why not?" and hand over their American Express card.

As they drive off in the lumbering, unfamiliar, supersize SUV, 9 out of 10 are unaware that the most common accidents among rental cars take place at low speeds in parking lots. Plus, the upgraded vehicle they're driving is no longer fully covered either by their regular auto insurance or by the secondary car rental insurance they expect from American Express. If they've agreed to pay the additional $10 to $25 a day for the car rental agency's "collision and liability damage wavier fee," they will be able to walk away from any accident with no liability. Otherwise, they're running a costly risk.

Soon they pull into a shopping mall with the kids to pick up the forgotten sunscreen and sodas, where they discover that this luxury van is not so easy to park in stalls designed when compact cars were all the rage. *Thwack*—there goes the door panel. *Crunch*—a rear bumper into a light post. *Wham!* There goes the family bank account, but they don't realize it yet—not until they receive the bill from the rental agency, the one that comes *after* their auto insurance and credit card companies have already paid as much as they're going to pay for damages.

Auto insurers typically provide the same coverage for rentals as you carry on your own car. When customers use their credit card to pay for car rentals, American Express offers secondary protection that generally covers any remaining, unpaid damages. But there are important exceptions.

Neither insurance nor credit card companies will pay the "loss of vehicle use fees" that car rental agencies always tack on. These fees can run into thousands of dollars, based on the agency's revenue losses while their car is in the repair shop. When your customers are billed for this fee, they invariably call you, angrily demanding to know why American Express won't pay it. And if they've rented an SUV, they're even angrier.

American Express Green and Gold cards provide secondary coverage up to $55,000, and the Platinum card extends that to $75,000. But large SUVs such as the Ford Expedition, GMC Yukon, and Chevrolet Suburban are not covered at all. Such exclusions are common. For instance, Diners Club specifically excludes "high-value, special interest or exotic cars"—such as the Ferraris, Maseratis, and even Rolls Royces that are urged on customers by rental agencies.

Your task: As assistant vice president of customer service, you'd like to keep the phone lines cooler this summer. It's April, so there's still time. Write a form letter to be sent to all American Express customers, urging them to check their rental car coverages, warning them to rent no vehicles larger than they require, and encouraging them to consider paying the rental agency's daily loss waiver fees.[12]

8. Time to grow: Memo at Wells Fargo about sabbatical selections San Francisco-based Wells Fargo Bank has actively implemented policies that help employees develop their full potential. Now the company has instituted a program that enables employees to take time off to pursue worthwhile personal objectives. The employees who qualify continue to receive salaries and benefits during the sabbaticals, and after their leave they can return to their old jobs or to positions at equivalent levels in the organization.

The program is designed to reward superior performers who have been with the bank for at least 10 years. The applicants must spend their leave time on projects that will enrich both themselves and their communities. Nancy Thompson, the program's director, says: "These are not larks. We eliminate people who want to take a cruise or go to Hawaii."

The bank has just approved sabbatical applications for the first two employees: Phyllis Jones, a bank operations officer who is studying Navajo rug weaving in New Mexico, and Patricia Lujan, a customer service representative who is preparing for a recital as a concert pianist.

Your task: Write a memo announcing the names of the first employees to participate in the program, and include details about the program so that other employees will want to apply.[13]

9. Stargazing: News release announcing new life for Mount Wilson Observatory Today, gazing at spectacular, four-color images of star clusters, nebulae, and galaxies requires only a click on the Internet, thanks to the Hubble Space Telescope and websites like the Hawaiian Astronomical Society's (www.hawastsoc.org/deepsky/index.html). But in 1929, Edwin P. Hubble searched the stars night after night, climbing up to a chilly wooden platform high in the dome that houses the 100-inch Hooker telescope at the Mount Wilson Observatory on the outskirts of Los Angeles. His computer-bereft studies of light from distant galaxies required endless analysis of crude photographic plates taken with the help of his assistant, a former mule skinner named Milton Humason. Their hard work paid off, however, and Hubble is credited with discovering the redshift that is the basis for the Big Bang theory of an expanding universe.

With the famous new space-based telescope named in his honor, we won't forget Hubble. But Mount Wilson and the Hooker telescope faded from importance as scientists rushed to larger scopes on bigger, darker mountains. In the 1980s, the Hooker was closed for eight years. Its 4.5-ton, green-glass mirror (built by a French wine-bottle manufacturer) became no more than a relic to curious visitors to the site in the San Gabriel Mountains, outside Pasadena.

Now the organization you work for, the Mount Wilson Institute in Pasadena, California, administers a reborn observatory, playing host to scientists from all over the map. And the Hooker telescope is once again making history.

For example, a team led by Dr. Laird Thompson of the University of Illinois is using the Hooker to test a computerized system of "laser adaptive optics." Adaptive optics have long been used to cancel the blur caused by atmospheric distortions, relying on natural guide stars to give computers a standard for making optical adjustments. But certain areas of space lack sufficient guide stars. Dr. Thompson's team is testing a 12-mile-high ultraviolet laser beam, sent into space at 333 pulses a second, as an artificial guide for adjustments. The resulting views are clearer than anything Hubble ever saw.

Mount Wilson also features an older, 60-inch telescope, a 60-foot solar tower operated by the University of Southern California for NASA, and a 150-foot solar tower run by the University of California at Los Angeles. A group headed by Dr. Harold A. McAlister (from Georgia State University) and another led by Nobel Prize–winning physicist Dr. Charles Townes (from the University of California at Berkeley) are both at the observatory conducting tests with "interferometry," using arrays of small telescopes to collect starlight simultaneously.

McAlister's team combines six small telescopes to mimic the effect of a single scope with an 1,100-foot mirror—impossible to build, but capable of detecting stellar details 200 times finer than the Hubble Space Telescope. Townes's group is using an array to make star surfaces visible beneath dust clouds.

Your task: Targeting science journalists, write a news release from the Mount Wilson Institute, a nonprofit, tax-exempt consortium of astronomers, educators, and private donors, which is directed by Dr. Robert Jastrow, former NASA scientist and author of astronomy books. You're hoping for news coverage of the observatory's new activities, which may attract donors. At the close of your release, invite journalists to sign up for a night tour with Dr. Jastrow and the scientists mentioned. Journalists can request a detailed science data sheet now or at the tour.[14]

ROUTINE REPLIES

10. Satellite farming: Letter granting credit from Deere & Company Arlen Ruestman in Toluca, Illinois, has asked for a line of credit to take advantage of new farming technology. Your company's new GreenStar system uses satellite technology originally developed by the defense department: the Global Positioning System (GPS). By using a series of satellites orbiting Earth, the system can pinpoint (to the meter) exactly where a farmer is positioned at any given moment as he drives his GreenStar-equipped combine over a field. For farmers like Reustman, that means a new ability to micromanage even 10,000 acres of corn or soybeans.

For instance, using the GreenStar system, farmers can map and analyze characteristics such as acidity, soil type, or crop yields from a given area. Using this information, they know exactly how much herbicide or fertilizer to spread over precisely which spot—eliminating waste and achieving better results. With cross-referencing and accumulated data, farmers can analyze why crops are performing well in some areas and not so well in others. Then they can program farm equipment to treat only the problem area—for example, spraying a new insect infestation two meters wide, 300 yards down the row.

Some farms have already saved as much as $10 an acre on fertilizers alone. For 10,000 acres, that's $100,000 a year. Once Ruestman retrofits your GreenStar precision package on his old combine and learns all its applications, he should have no problem saving enough to pay off the $7,350 credit account you're about to grant him.

Your task: Write a letter to Mr. Ruestman (P.O. Box 4067, Toluca, IL 61369), informing him of the good news.[15]

11. Auto-talk: E-mail messages for Highway Bytes computers to send automatically You are director of customer services at Highway Bytes, which markets a series of small, handlebar-mounted computers for bicyclists. These Cycle Computers do everything, from computing speed and distance traveled to displaying street maps. Serious cyclists love them, but your company is growing so fast that you can't keep up with all the customer service requests you receive every day. Your boss wants not only to speed up response time but also to reduce staffing costs and allow your technical experts the time they need to focus on the most difficult and important questions.

You've just been reading about automated response systems, and you quickly review a few articles before discussing the options with your boss. Artificial intelligence researchers have been working for decades to design systems that can actually converse with customers, ask questions, and respond to requests. Some of today's systems have vocabularies of thousands of words and the ability to understand simple sentences. For example, *chatterbots* are automated bots that can actually mimic human conversation. (You can see what it's like to carry on a conversation with some of these bots by visiting www.botspot.com, clicking on Artificial Life Bots, and then selecting Chatterbots.)

Unfortunately, even though chatterbots hold a lot of promise, human communication is so complex that a truly automated customer service agent could take years to perfect (and may even prove to be impossible). However, the simplest automated systems are called *autoresponders* or *e-mail–on-demand.* They are fast and extremely inexpensive. They have no built-in intelligence, so they do nothing more than send back the same reply to every message they receive.

You explain to your boss that although some of the messages you receive require the attention of your product specialists, many are simply requests for straightforward information. In fact, the customer service staff already answers some 70 percent of e-mail queries with three ready-made attachments:

- *Installing Your Cycle Computer.* Gives customers advice on installing the cycle computer the first time or reinstalling it on a new bike. In most cases, the computer and wheel sensor bolt directly to the bike without modification, but certain bikes do require extra work.
- *Troubleshooting Your Cycle Computer.* Provides a step-by-step guide to figuring out what might be wrong with a malfunctioning cycle computer. Most problems are simple, such as dead batteries or loose wires, but others are beyond the capabilities of your typical customer.
- *Upgrading the Software in Your Cycle Computer.* Tells customers how to attach the cycle computer to their home or office PC and download new software from Highway Bytes.

Your boss is enthusiastic when you explain that you can program your current e-mail system to look for specific words in incoming messages and then respond, based on what it finds. For example, if a customer message contains the word "installation," you can program the system to reply with the "Installing Your Cycle Computer" attachment. This reconfigured system should be able to handle a sizeable portion of the hundreds of e-mails your customer service group gets every week.

Your task: First, draft a list of keywords that you'll want your e-mail system to look for. You'll need to be creative and spend some time with a thesaurus. Identify all the words and word combinations that could identify a message as pertaining to one of the three subject areas. For instance, the word *attach* would probably indicate a need for the installation material, whereas *new software* would most likely suggest a need for the upgrade attachment.

Second, draft three short e-mail messages to accompany each ready-made attachment, explaining that the attached document answers the most common questions on a particular subject (installation, troubleshooting, or upgrading). Your messages should invite recipients to write back if the attached document doesn't solve the problem, and don't forget to provide the e-mail address: support2@highwaybytes.com.

Third, draft a fourth message to be sent out whenever your new system is unable to figure out what the customer is asking for. Simply thank the customer for writing and explain that the query will be passed on to a customer service specialist who will respond shortly.

12. The special courier: Letter of recommendation for an old friend In today's mail you get a letter from Non-Stop Messenger Service, 899 Sparks St., Ottawa, Ontario K1A 0G9, Canada. It concerns a friend of yours who has applied for a job. Here is the letter:

> Kathryn Norquist has applied for the position of special courier with our firm, and she has given us your name as a reference. Our special couriers convey materials of considerable value or confidentiality to their recipients. It is not an easy job. Special couriers must sometimes remain alert for periods of up to 20 hours, and they cannot expect to follow the usual "three square meals and eight hours' sleep" routine because they often travel long distances on short notice. On occasion, a special courier must react quickly and decisively to threatening situations.
>
> For this type of work, we hire only people of unquestioned integrity, as demonstrated both by their public records and by references from people, like you, who have known them personally or professionally.
>
> We would appreciate a letter from you, supplying detailed answers to the following questions: (1) How long and in what circumstances have you have known the applicant? (2) What qualities does she possess that would qualify her for the position of special courier? (3) What qualities might be improved before she is put on permanent assignment in this job?

As vice president of human resources at Airborne Express, you know how much weight a strong personal reference can carry, and you don't really mind that Kathryn never contacted you for permission to list your name—that's Kathryn. You met her during your sophomore year at San Diego State University—that would have been 1994—and you two were roommates for several years after. Her undergraduate degree was in journalism, and her investigative reporting was relentless. You have never known anyone who could match Kathryn's stamina when she was on a story. Of course, when she was between stories, she could sleep longer and do less than anyone else you have ever known.

After a few years reporting, Kathryn went back to school and earned her MBA from the University of San Diego, and after that you lost track of her for awhile. Somebody said that she had joined the FBI—or was it the CIA?—you never really knew. You received a couple of postcards from Paris and one from Madrid.

Two years ago, you met Kathryn for dinner. Only in town for the evening, she was on her way to Borneo to "do the text" for a photographer friend of hers who worked for National Geographic. You read the article last year on the shrinking habitat for orangutans. It was powerful.

Although you're in no position to say much about Kathryn's career accomplishments, you can certainly recommend her energy and enthusiasm, her ability to focus on a task or assignment, her devotion to ethics, and her style. She always seems unshakable—organized, thorough, and honorable, whether digging into political corruption or trudging the jungles of Borneo. You're not sure that her free spirit would flourish in a courier's position, and you wonder if she wouldn't be a bit overqualified for the job. But knowing Kathryn, you're confident she wouldn't apply for a position unless she truly wanted it.

Your task: Supplying any details you can think of, write as supportive a letter as possible about your friend Kathryn to Roscoe de la Penda, Human Resources Specialist, Non-Stop Messenger.

13. Shopping for talent: Memo at Clovine's recommending a promotion You enjoy your duties as manager of the women's sportswear at Clovine's—a growing chain of moderate to upscale department stores in South Florida. You especially enjoy being able to recommend someone for a promotion. Today, you received a memo from Rachel Cohen, head buyer for women's apparel. She is looking for a smart, aggressive employee to become assistant buyer for Clovine's women's sportswear division. Clovine's likes to promote from within, and Rachel is asking all managers and supervisors for likely candidates. You have just the person she's looking for.

Jennifer Ramirez, is a salesclerk in the designer sportswear boutique of your main store in Miami, and she has caught your attention. She's quick, friendly, and good at sizing up a customer's preferences. Moreover, at recent department meetings, she's made some intelligent remarks about new trends in South Florida.

Your task: Write a memo to Rachel Cohen, head buyer, women's sportswear, recommending Jennifer Ramirez, and evaluating her qualifications for the promotion. Rachel can check with the human resources department about Jennifer's educational and employment history; you're mainly interested in conveying your positive impression of Jennifer's potential for advancement.

14. Lighten up: E-mail reply to a website designer at Organizers Unlimited When Kendra Williams, owner of Organizers Unlimited, wanted to create a website to sell her Superclean Organizer, she asked you, her assistant, to find a designer. After some research, you found three promising individuals. Williams chose Pete Womack, whose résumé impressed both of you. Now he's e-mailed his first design proposal and Williams is not happy.

"I detest cluttered websites!" she explodes. "This homepage has too many graphics and animations, too much 'dancing baloney.' He must have included at least 500 kilobytes of bouncing cotton balls and jogging soap bars! Clever, maybe, but we don't want it! If the homepage takes too long to load, our customers won't wait for it and we'll lose sales."

Williams's dislike of clutter is what inspired her to invent the Superclean Organizer in the first place, a neat device for organizing bathroom items.

Your task: "You found him," says Williams, "now you can answer and tell him what's wrong with this design." Before you write the e-mail reply to Womack explaining the need for a simpler homepage, read some of the articles offering tips at www.sitepoint.com. On the homepage, under "Before You Code," select "Site Planning" and under "Design and Layout" select "Design Principles." Use these ideas to support your message.[16]

15. Yes, we do purple: Instant message from Lands' End When clothing retailer Lands' End offered its 2,500 telephone service representatives the chance to train on its new instant messaging system, "Lands' End Live," you jumped at the opportunity. As it turned out, so many volunteered for the new training that the company had to give preference to a few hundred who'd been on the job longest. You were one of the lucky ones.

Now you've had months of practice answering messages like the one you just received from a customer named Alicia. She wants to know if she can have a red Polartec Aircore-200 Scarf custom monogrammed—not in the standard, contrasting wheat-colored thread, but in radiant purple as a gift for her husband, whose favorite colors are red and purple. According to Alicia, her husband says, "Red & purple are feng shui symbols of wealth & prosperity."

On its website, Lands' End promises to fulfill nonstandard monogram requests "if technical limitations allow." You've done a quick check and yes, her husband can have his initials in bright purple on the red background.

Your task: Write the instant message reply to Alicia, telling her the good news.[17]

POSITIVE MESSAGES

16. Cold comfort: E-mail offering a regional sales position with Golight Winter in Nebraska ranch country is something to sneeze at—and to shiver over. That's why rancher Jerry Gohl invented the Golight, a portable spotlight that can be mounted on a car or truck roof and rotated 360 degrees horizontally and 70 degrees vertically *by remote control.* No more getting out of the truck in freezing, predawn temperatures to adjust a manual spotlight in order to check on his livestock in the dark. In fact, Gohl has hardly any time left to check the livestock these days: His invention has become so popular that Golight, Inc., expects to sell more than $2 million worth of the remote-controlled lights next year.

The company expanded fast, with Golights becoming popular not only with Nebraska ranchers but all over the world with hunters, boaters, commuters who fear dark-of-night roadside tire changes, and early-morning fishing enthusiasts who can scope out the best shoreline sites from inside their warm and cozy vehicles. Sales reps have been hired for every region except the Nebraska territory. Gohl has been holding out for just the right person to replace him—someone who knows what the local ranchers need and how they think.

Finally, last week he met Robert Victor, who grew up on a Nebraska ranch, helping his dad with those 4 A.M. chores. He's young, but he has felt the bite of Nebraska's cold, he knows the rancher mind, and best of all, he's been bringing in top dollar selling agricultural equipment in Montana for the past few years. Now he wants to return to his home state. Gohl liked him from the first moment they shook hands. "He's got the job if he wants it," the boss tells you. "Better send him some e-mail before someone else grabs him. He can start as soon as he's settled."

Your task: Compose the message communicating Gohl's offer to Robert Victor: salary plus commission as discussed, full benefits (paid vacation, health and dental insurance) if he's still around in six months. His e-mail address is rvictor@ism.net. Sign with your name, as Gohl's personnel manager.[18]

17. Our sympathy: Condolence letter to an Aetna underwriter As chief administrator for the underwriting department of Aetna Health Plans in Walnut Creek, California, you're facing a difficult task. One of your best underwriters, Hector Almeida, recently lost his wife in an automobile accident (he and his teenaged daughter weren't with her at the time). Since you're the boss, everyone in the close-knit department is looking to you to communicate the group's sympathy and concern.

Someone suggested a simple greeting card that everyone could sign, but that seems so impersonal for someone you've worked with every day for nearly five years. So you decided to write a personal note on behalf of the whole department. You met Hector's wife, Rosalia, at a few company functions although you knew her mostly through Hector's frequent references to her. Right now he's devastated by the loss. But if anyone can overcome this tragedy, Hector can. He's always determined to get a job done no matter what obstacles present themselves, and he does it with an upbeat attitude. That's why everyone in the office likes him so much.

You also plan to suggest that when he returns to work, he might like to move his schedule up an hour so that he'll have more time to spend with his daughter, Lisa, after school. It's your way of helping make things a little easier for them during this period of adjustment.

Your task: Write the letter to Hector Almeida, who lives at 47 West Ave., #10, Walnut Creek, CA 94596.[19]

18. Pizza promises: Memo from an unknown parent, VF Corporation Top VF Corporation executives have been moaning about a recent spot survey among 40,000 workers at your subsidiaries—the ones that produce Lee, Wrangler, Brittania, Jansport, and other brands. Apparently, few of these employees had heard of VF Corporation. According to the survey, these workers didn't even know they had a corporate parent.

"We'll fix 'em!" says your boss, the director of human relations at VF Corporation. He grins at you and continues. "If they think we're going to let them go on in ignorance, then they're wrong. And I know just what will get their attention."

As human relations assistant for the large Greensboro, North Carolina, apparel maker, you've learned that your boss likes to solve problems in a big, splashy way; that's one of the reasons that everyone likes him. He has a knack for turning corporate problems into opportunities for some new, wonderful development that no one else had thought of.

"You watch," your boss enthuses. "By tomorrow, they'll not only know who we are, they'll be singing our praises. And to think that you get to break the good news to them!" He gives you another winning smile. You love this job.

Your task: Write an e-mail message for companywide distribution explaining that tomorrow, 15,000 lunchtime pizzas (all shifts) will be delivered to the company's 40,000 employees, compliments of their no-longer-mysterious corporate parent. Try to reflect some of your boss's good nature when putting the point across, But remember: You're representing your company to every single employee.[20]

19. Boomerang back to us: E-mail from EDS to dot-com deserters "Now's our chance to get them back," announces director Tom Templeton at a human resources staff meeting. You're his assistant, and for a moment you're confused.

"Get who back?"

"Everyone who left to join dot-com start-ups. You know how many people we lost when the Internet's promise of overnight fortunes lured away some of our best employees. But now it's our turn."

"You mean invite back the 550 employees we lost to dot-coms in recent years?" you ask.

"Exactly. I read that 12,000 dot-com jobs were cut in a nine-month period last year. That number is probably higher now."

You see his point and smile. He'll save EDS considerable money and trouble if some of these individuals return. Finding and keeping good employees is one of the greatest costs of operating any business.

"As dot-coms fail, some of our best people may be out there looking for jobs," Templeton adds. "Are we going to let our competitors have them?"

Your task: After the meeting, Templeton asks you to create a form letter that he can send to ex-employees, telling them that EDS will welcome them back if their dot-com jobs haven't worked out as expected.[21]

20. Cooling it: Memo confirming details of a complex job As facilities manager, you're responsible for assigning and scheduling employees to various Public Works projects throughout the federal government installation at Pt. Mugu. Your department will be installing a central air-conditioning unit in one of Pt. Mugu's old office buildings.

The preliminary sheet-metal work has been done, and the main unit has arrived in your shop. You have scheduled a crew of three to install the unit and the vents, and you estimate the job will take about two weeks. The physicists working in the building have stated that it would be most convenient for them if you begin work on Saturday.

You want to tell everyone in the building that your crew will begin on Saturday, that the job will take at least two weeks, that the job will be a noisy one, and that you've made arrangements with security to give you access to the building through the front and side entrances from 8:15 A.M. until 4:15 P.M. Due to the age of the building, unforeseen delays may lengthen the project beyond the estimated two weeks.

Your task: Write a memo to the branch manager, Howard Steele. Confirm that Public Works employees will install the air-conditioning system beginning next Saturday and that they hope to have the job completed within two weeks.

chapter 8

Writing Negative Messages

LEARNING OBJECTIVES

After studying this chapter, you will be able to

1. Apply the three-step writing process to negative messages
2. Explain the differences between the direct and the indirect approaches to negative messages, including when it's appropriate to use each one
3. Identify the risks of using the indirect approach, and explain how to avoid such problems
4. Adapt your messages for internal and external audiences
5. Define defamation and explain how to avoid it in negative messages
6. Explain the role of communication in crisis management
7. List three guidelines for delivering negative news to job applicants and give a brief explanation of each one

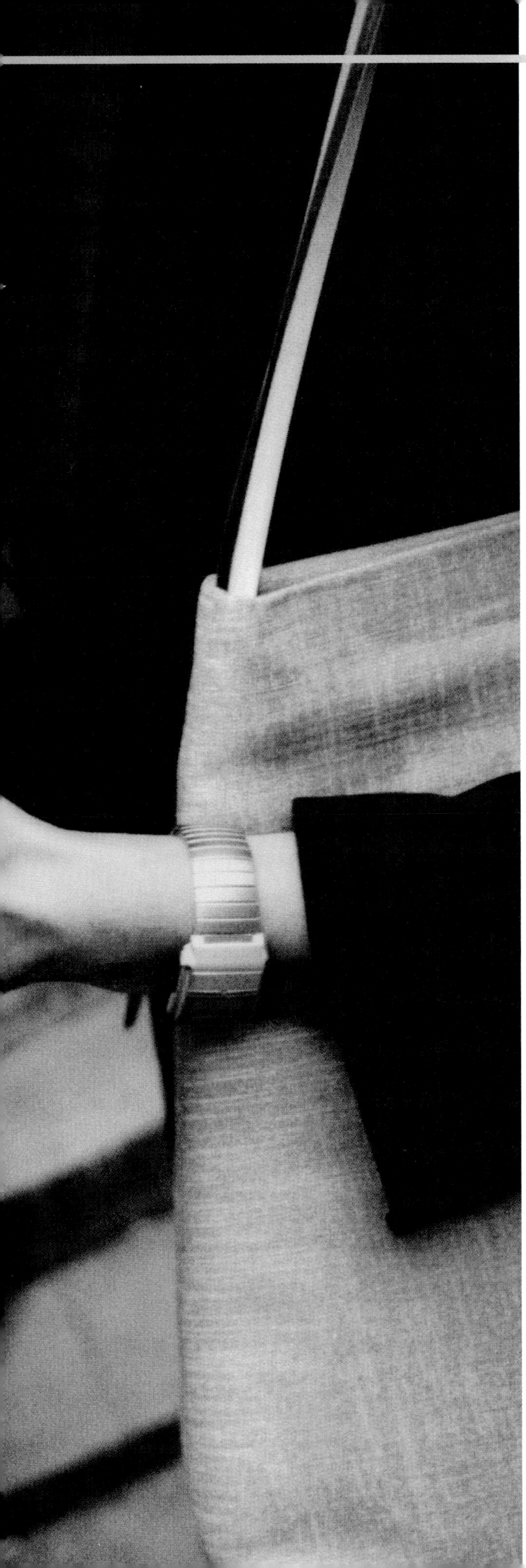

COMMUNICATION CLOSE-UP AT AGILENT TECHNOLOGIES

www.agilent.com

Nobody likes to deliver bad news, and telling people their jobs have disappeared is some of the worst news that managers ever have to share. Unfortunately, some managers handle these stressful situations by virtually disappearing from sight, delivering the bad news through faceless memos and e-mails—leaving shattered employees to wonder how much their bosses really cared in the first place.

Fortunately, there are exceptions, such as Edward "Ned" Barnholt, chairman, president, and CEO of Agilent Technologies, a company that develops advanced technology products used by scientists and engineers in a variety of industries. After it was spun off from computer giant Hewlett-Packard (HP) in 1999, Agilent enjoyed booming sales that led to rapid hiring. However, everything changed in 2001, when both the global economy and the telecommunications industry—a major Agilent customer—fell off rapidly.

The company took aggressive steps to cut its spending and avoid layoffs. Although laying off workers has always

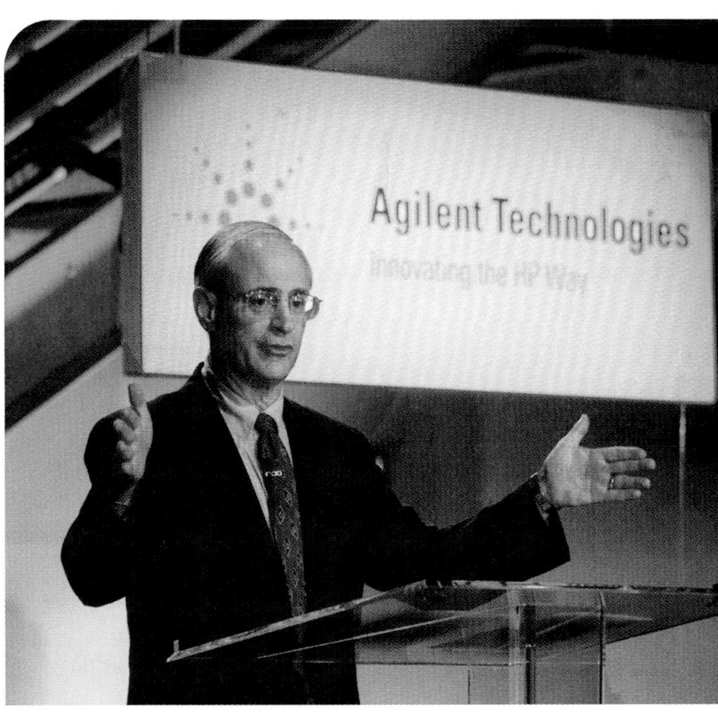

By focusing on honesty and compassion, Agilent CEO Ned Barnholt excelled in one of the toughest communication challenges that executives ever face—announcing the layoff of thousands of employees.

been a common cost-cutting solution in some industries, the practice had never been a part of Agilent's management approach. Nevertheless, the high-tech economy stayed in the doldrums for months on end, and Barnholt was eventually forced to order three rounds of layoffs that eliminated one-third of the company's employees.

Through it all, Barnholt was usually the first person to announce the bad news to both internal and external audiences, including employees, shareholders, and Wall Street analysts. He always told the employees first, traveling to tell them in person whenever possible and using the company's telephone and PA systems to reach Agilent facilities around the world. He knew employees would feel betrayed if they received this bad news first by the web, e-mail, or some external news source.

Even in the toughest times, Barnholt maintained a sense of empathy and a calm, candid style that earned him the 2003 Excellence in Communication Leadership award from the International Association of Business Communicators. In his acceptance speech, Ned offered some useful advice: "Good news travels fast. Bad news travels faster—so get out in front of it."[1]

---

1 LEARNING OBJECTIVE

Apply the three-step writing process to negative messages

USING THE THREE-STEP WRITING PROCESS FOR NEGATIVE MESSAGES

As Ned Barnholt can attest, nobody likes bad news. No one likes to get it, and no one likes to give it. Saying no to an idea from an employee, a proposal from a shareholder, a request from a customer, or even a well-meaning suggestion from a colleague can cause you and the other person considerable anxiety.

Five goals of negative messages:
- Give the bad news
- Ensure its acceptance
- Maintain reader's goodwill
- Maintain organization's good image
- Reduce future correspondence on the matter

Sending people negative messages from time to time will be a fact of life in your career. Just remember, whenever you deliver negative news, you have five main goals: (1) to convey the bad news, (2) to gain acceptance for it, (3) to maintain as much goodwill as possible with your audience, (4) to maintain a good image for your organization, and (5) to reduce or eliminate the need for future correspondence on the matter. That's a lot to accomplish in one message; however, by learning some simple techniques and following the three-step writing process, you'll develop negative messages that reduce the stress for everyone involved and improve the effectiveness of your communication efforts.

Step 1: Plan Your Message

Analysis, investigation, and adaptation help you avoid alienating your readers.

When planning negative messages, one stark but unavoidable fact influences your effort: Your audience does not want to hear what you have to say. To minimize the damage to business relationships and to encourage the acceptance of your message, start by analyzing the situation carefully. Only by understanding the context in which the recipient will process your message can you plan effectively.

Be sure to consider your purpose thoroughly—whether it's straightforward (such as rejecting a job application) or more complicated (such as drafting a negative performance review, in which you not only give the employee feedback on past performance but also help the person develop a plan to improve future performance).

Similarly, your audience profile can be simple and obvious in some situations (such as rejecting a credit request) and far more complex in others (such as turning down a non-profit organization's request to use your company offices for weekend meetings). Negative messages intended for large, diverse groups can trigger a wide range of possible reactions and complications.

In his role as director of Seattle's Pike Place Market, a vast farmer's market long considered the heart and soul of the city, Daniel Lieberman had to balance the competing interests of farmers, shop owners, real estate developers, city officials, historic preservationists, local residents, tourists, and others. During his four years in the position, Leiberman was credited with reducing the level of discord in this complex situation by doing a better job of listening to his diverse constituency and trying to consider every group's needs before communicating.[2]

With a clear purpose and your audience's needs in mind, identify and gather the information your audience will need to understand and accept your message. Negative messages can be intensely personal to the recipient, and in many cases recipients have a right to expect a thorough explanation of your answer (although this isn't always the case). For instance, if one of your hardest-working employees has asked for a raise and you don't think her performance warrants it, you can carefully explain the difference between hard work and productive results to help her accept your message.

Selecting the right medium is critical when delivering negative messages. For example, you might badly damage a working relationship if you use voice mail to reject a long-time employee's request for a promotion. Since the employee would surely have some important questions to ask, and you would certainly want to soothe hurt feelings, a face-to-face meeting would be the best choice for this situation. However, if your company receives ten thousand credit applications a month, you can't afford to engage every rejected applicant in a one-on-one conversation. A form letter that limits response options would be a better choice. Review the media selection guidelines in Chapter 4 if you're unsure of the best way to deliver your message.

As you'll see in this chapter, proper organization can mean the difference between an effective message and an unsuccessful one. Defining your main idea in a negative message is often more complicated than simply saying *no*. For instance, in the case of the hardworking employee who requested a raise, your message would go beyond saying no to explain how she can improve her performance by working smarter, not just harder. On the other hand, be sure to limit your scope and include only the information your audience needs. For example, a credit denial is not the place to lecture customers on better financial habits, nor should you divert attention to your own career struggles when denying someone a raise or a promotion. Before you outline your message, you need to select a direct or indirect approach—and because many negative messages result in emotionally charged situations, the right choice is vital. This chapter helps you explore both approaches in detail.

When Bausch & Lomb, maker of optics and healthcare products, was forced to reduce staff in recent years, President and CEO William Carpenter chose in-person communication to deliver the bad news because it gave employees the opportunity to ask questions and raise concerns.

Step 2: Write Your Message

When adapting a negative message to your audience, every aspect of effective, diplomatic writing is amplified; after all, your audience does not want to hear a negative message and might disagree strongly with you. Be sure to maintain a "you" attitude, strive for polite language that emphasizes the positive whenever appropriate, and make sure your word choice is without bias. For more advice, see "Adapting to Your Audience" later in this chapter on pages 231–232.

If your credibility hasn't already been established with an audience, lay out your qualifications for making the decision in question. Recipients of negative messages who don't think you are credible are more likely to challenge your decision. And as always, projecting and protecting your company's image is a prime concern; if you're not careful, a negative answer could spin out of control into negative feelings about your company.

When you use language that conveys respect and avoids an accusing tone, you protect your audience's pride. This kind of communication etiquette is always important, but it demands special care with negative messages. Moreover, you can ease the sense of disappointment by using positive words rather than negative, counterproductive ones (see Table 8.1). In fact, when refusing an adjustment or a claim, use third-person, impersonal, passive language to explain your audience's mistakes in an inoffensive way. This approach downplays the person, who is not specified, and emphasizes the action. Instead of saying, "The appliance won't work because you immersed it in water," say, "The appliance won't work after being immersed in water." When your audience is at fault, it's better to avoid the "you" attitude in a sentence that establishes blame.

Chances are you'll spend more time on word, sentence, and paragraph choices for negative messages than with any other type of business writing. People who receive negative messages often look for subtle shades of meaning, seeking flaws in your reasoning or other ways to challenge the decision. So if you use words that are open to multiple interpretations or construct illogical paragraphs, you are just asking for trouble. Fortunately, by writing clearly and sensitively, you can take some of the sting out of bad news and help your reader accept the decision and move on.

Communication Solution

With a workforce that numbers in the tens of thousands, Agilent's Ned Barnholt couldn't personally talk with every laid-off employee, but he announced layoffs either in-person or via telephone and public address systems at Agilent facilities, rather than hiding behind memos or assistants.

Choose the medium with care when preparing negative messages.

The appropriate organization helps readers accept your negative news.

Use positive rather than negative phrasing in negative messages.

Negative message can require more time to write than other messages.

TABLE 8.1 Choosing Positive Words

AVOID A NEGATIVE TONE	USE A POSITIVE TONE
I cannot understand what you mean.	Please clarify your request.
The *damage* won't be fixed for a week.	The item will be repaired next week.
There will be a *delay* in your order.	We will ship your order as soon as possible.
You are clearly *dissatisfied.*	We are doing what we can to make things right.
Your account is in *error.*	Corrections have been made to your account.
The breakage was not our *fault.*	The merchandise was broken during shipping.
Sorry for your inconvenience.	The enclosed coupon will save you $5 next time.
We *regret* the misunderstanding.	I'll try my best to be more clear from now on.
I was *shocked* to learn that you're unhappy.	Your letter reached me yesterday.
Unfortunately, we haven't received it.	It hasn't arrived yet.
The enclosed statement is *wrong.*	Please recheck the enclosed statement.

At Urban Terrain, a landscape design company, Hilberto Ortiz and his team try to play down negative messages. "When you have to say no, you want people to get the message," says Ortiz, "but you don't have to be harsh about it. Spend as little time as possible on the bad news and concentrate on the positive stuff."

Step 3: Complete Your Message

Your need for careful attention to detail continues as you complete your message. Revise your content to make sure everything is clear, complete, and concise—bearing in mind that even small flaws are magnified as readers react to your negative news. When you produce your message, stick with design and layout options that are clean and professional. People getting bad news will find flowery or playful designs a distraction at best and an insult at worst. Proofreading is important for every message, of course, but even more so for negative messages. Minor mistakes can be interpreted as carelessness—the last thing you need when readers might question your judgment. Finally, be especially sure that your negative messages are delivered promptly and successfully; waiting for bad news is hard enough without wondering whether a message was lost.

DEVELOPING NEGATIVE MESSAGES

As you apply the three-step writing process to develop negative messages, several key thoughts will help you craft effective messages quickly: First, before organizing the main points of a message, it is vital to choose a direct or an indirect approach. Second, before actually composing your message, be sensitive to variations across cultures or between internal and external audiences. And third, to fulfill the spirit of audience focus, be sure you maintain high ethical standards.

2 LEARNING OBJECTIVE

Explain the differences between the direct and the indirect approaches to negative messages, including when it's appropriate to use each one

Choosing the Best Approach

Without even thinking about it, you've probably been using both the direct and indirect approaches to deliver negative messages your entire life. When you come right out and tell somebody some bad news, you're using the direct approach. When you try to soften the impact by easing your way into the conversation before delivering the bad news, you're using the indirect approach. Chances are, you've already developed an instinctive feel for which approach to use in many situations. In your business writing, you'll need to make a similar choice whenever you deliver bad news; however, there are no clear guidelines to help you choose in every case. Some researchers even suggest that the way you organize the message is less important than achieving a personal tone.[3] Even so, you have to choose one approach or the other, so ask yourself the following questions:

You probably already have an instinctive feel for when to use direct or indirect approaches.

- **Will the bad news come as a shock?** The direct approach is fine for business situations in which people readily acknowledge the possibility of receiving bad news. You know you won't get every job you apply for or close every sales opportunity, and consumers realize that orders are sometimes delayed or mishandled. However, if the bad news might come as a shock to readers, use the indirect approach to help them prepare for it.
- **Does the reader prefer short messages that get right to the point?** If you know that your boss always wants brief messages that get right to the point, even when they deliver bad news, the direct approach is your best choice. If you don't know a reader's preferences, let the other questions in this list guide your choice.
- **How important is this news to the reader?** For minor or routine scenarios, the direct approach is nearly always best. When Amazon.com can't find an out-of-print book for a customer, the company sends a brief e-mail stating that fact directly. However, if the reader has an emotional investment in the situation or the consequences to the reader are considerable, the indirect approach is often best because it gives you a chance to prepare that reader to accept your news.
- **Do you need to maintain a close working relationship with the reader?** Pay attention to the relationship as you deliver your bad news. The indirect approach makes it easier to soften the blow of bad news and can therefore be the better choice when you need to preserve a good relationship.
- **Do you need to get the reader's attention?** If someone is ignoring repeated messages from you or is buried under hundreds of e-mails, instant messages, and memos, the direct approach can help you get his or her attention. In fact, a poorly written indirect message that obscures the bad news might be the reason the person has been ignoring you in the first place.
- **What is your organization's preferred style?** Some companies have a distinct communication style, often inherited from the founder or top manager. Blunt, direct messages could disturb or anger people in a company that's accustomed to a gentler, indirect style. Conversely, people accustomed to direct messages might grow impatient with, or even distrustful of, the indirect approach.
- **How much follow-up communication do you want?** If you want to discourage a response from your reader, the direct approach signals the finality of your message more effectively. However, if you use the indirect approach to list your reasons before announcing a decision, you leave the door open for a follow-up response from your reader—which might actually be the best strategy at times. For example, if you're rejecting a project team's request for funding, based on the information you currently have at hand, you might be wise to invite the team to provide any new information that could encourage you to reconsider your decision.

Use the direct approach when your negative answer or information will have minimal personal impact.

Using the Direct Approach Effectively

A negative message using the direct approach opens with the bad news, proceeds to the reasons for the situation or the decision, and ends with a positive statement aimed at maintaining a good relationship with the audience (see Figure 8.1). Depending on the circumstances, the message may also offer alternatives or a plan of action to fix the situation under discussion. Stating the bad news at the beginning can have two advantages: (1) It makes a shorter message possible, and (2) it requires less time for the audience to reach the main idea of the message.

Open with a Clear Statement of the Bad News Whether it's something relatively minor, such as telling a supplier that you're planning to reduce the size of your orders in the future, or something major, such as telling employees that revenues dropped the previous quarter, come right out and say it. Even if the news is devastating, maintain a calm,

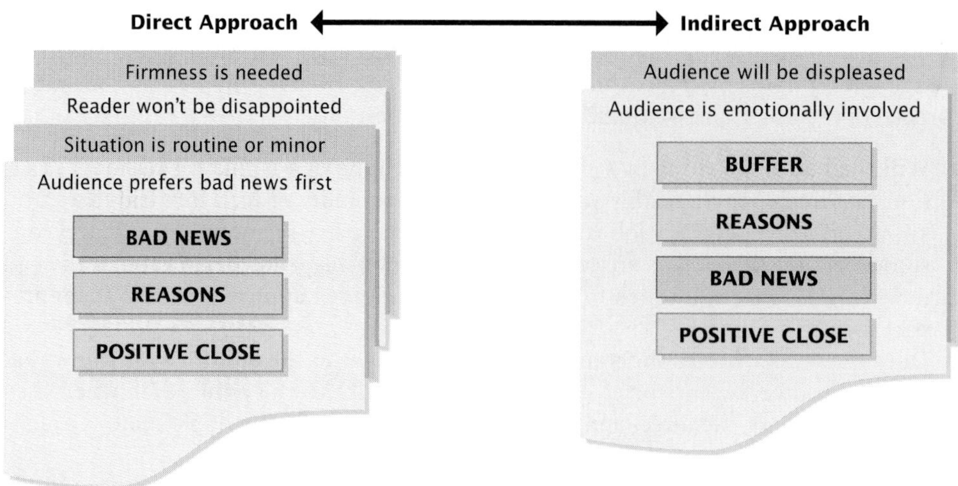

FIGURE 8.1
Choosing the Indirect or Direct Approach for Negative Messages

professional tone that keeps the focus on the news and not on individual failures. Also, if necessary, remind the reader why you're writing:

Reminds the reader that your company has a standing order, and announces the change immediately

> Please modify our standing order for the FL-205 shipping cases from 3,000 per month to 2,500 per month.

Reminds the reader that he or she applied for life insurance with your firm, and announces your decision

> Transnation Life is unable to grant your application for SafetyNet term life insurance.

Eases into the bad news with a personal acknowledgment to the staff, even though it delivers the news directly and immediately

> In spite of everyone's best efforts to close more sales this past quarter, revenue fell 14 percent compared to the third quarter last year.

Notice how the third example still manages to ease into the bad news, even though it delivers the bad new directly and quickly. In all three instances, the recipient gets the news immediately, without reading the reasons why the news is bad.

Provide Reasons and Additional Information In most cases, you'll follow the direct opening with an explanation of why the news is negative:

Reassures the reader that the product in question is still satisfactory but is no longer needed in the same quantity

> Please modify our standing order for the FL-205 shipping cases from 3,000 per month to 2,500 per month. The FL-205 continues to meet our needs for medical packaging, but our sales of that product line have leveled off.

Offers a general explanation as the reason the application was denied, and discourages further communication on the matter

> Transnation Life is unable to grant your application for SafetyNet term life insurance. The SafetyNet program has specific health history requirements that your application does not meet.

Lets readers know why the news is negative and reassures them that job performance is not the reason

> In spite of everyone's best efforts to close more sales this past quarter, revenue fell 14 percent compared to the third quarter last year. Reports from the field offices indicate that the economic downturn in Asia has reduced demand for our products.

The amount of detail you provide depends on your relationship with the audience.

The extent of your explanation depends on the nature of your news and your relationship with the reader. In the first example, a company wants to assure its long-time supplier that the product is still satisfactory. It's in the best interest of both parties to maintain a positive relationship even when circumstances between them are sometimes negative.

In the second example, the insurance company provides a general reason for the denial because listing a specific health issue (such as diabetes) might encourage additional communication from the reader to negotiate or to explain the situation ("My father had diabetes and lived to be 84"). The company's decision is final. Any further communication on the issue would be counterproductive for both parties.

In the third example, the explanation points out why the news is bad and also reassures employees that no one in the firm is personally responsible for the failure. Of course, if the bad news *were* a result of poor performance, this message would need to be revised appropriately.

In some situations, it's a good idea to follow the explanation with a statement of how you plan to correct or respond to the negative news. For instance, in the case of the sales decline, you might follow by telling the staff you plan to reduce prices or increase advertising to help stimulate sales. Alternatively, you might invite ideas from the staff. In any event, your readers will want to know how they should respond to the news, so additional information would be helpful.

Sometimes detailed reasons should not be provided.

You will encounter some situations in which explaining negative news is neither appropriate nor helpful, for example, when the reasons are confidential, excessively complicated, or irrelevant to the reader. To maintain a cordial working relationship with the reader, you might want to explain why you can't provide the information.

The decision whether to apologize depends on a number of factors.

Should you apologize when delivering bad news? The answer isn't quite as simple as one might think. The notion of *apology* is hard to pin down. To some people, it simply means an expression of sympathy that something negative has happened to another person. At the other extreme, it means a complete admission of fault and responsibility for specific compensations or corrections to atone for the mistake.

Some experts have advised that a company should never apologize, even when it knows it has made a mistake, as the apology might be taken as a confession of guilt. However, several states, including California, Georgia, Massachusetts, and Texas, recently passed laws that specifically prevent expressions of sympathy from being used as evidence of legal liability. In fact, judges, juries, and plaintiffs tend to be more forgiving of companies that express sympathy for wronged parties; moreover, the apology can help repair the company's reputation. The best general advice in the event of a serious mistake or accident is to immediately and sincerely express sympathy and even offer help, without admitting guilt; then seek the advice of your company's lawyers before elaborating. As one recent survey concluded, "The risks of making an apology are low, and the potential reward is high."[4]

Close your message in a positive but respectful tone.

Close on a Positive Note After you've explained the negative news, close the message in a positive, but still honest and respectful, manner:

> Please modify our standing order for the FL-205 shipping cases from 3,000 per month to 2,500 per month. The FL-205 continues to meet our needs for medical packaging, but our sales of that product line have leveled off. We appreciate the great service you continue to provide and look forward to doing business with you.

Reinforces the relationship you have with the reader and provides a positive view toward the future—without unduly promising a return to the old level of business

> Transnation Life is unable to grant your application for SafetyNet term life insurance. The SafetyNet program has specific health history requirements that your application does not meet. We wish you success in finding coverage through another provider.

Ends on a respectful note, knowing that life insurance is an important subject for the reader, but also makes it clear that the company's decision is final

> In spite of everyone's best efforts to close more sales this past quarter, revenue fell 14 percent compared to the third quarter last year. Reports from the field offices indicate that the economic downturn in Asia has reduced demand for our products. However, I continue to believe that we have the best product for these customers, and we'll continue to explore ways to boost sales in these key markets.

Helps readers respond to the news by letting them know that the company plans to fix the situation, even if the plan for doing so isn't clear yet

Notice how all three examples deliver bad news quickly and efficiently, without being unduly blunt or disrespectful, or overly apologetic. Consider offering your readers an alternative solution, if you can. For instance, if you know that another insurance company has a program for higher-risk policies, you can alert your reader to that opportunity.

3 LEARNING OBJECTIVE

Identify the risks of using the indirect approach, and explain how to avoid such problems

Using the Indirect Approach Effectively

The indirect approach helps readers prepare for the bad news by presenting the reasons for it first. However, don't assume that the indirect approach is meant to obscure bad news, delay it, or limit your responsibility. Rather, the purpose of this approach is to ease the blow and help readers accept the situation. When done poorly, the indirect approach can be disrespectful and even unethical. But when done well, it is a good example of "you" oriented communication crafted with attention to both ethics and etiquette.

Use the indirect approach when some preparation will help your audience accept your bad news.

A buffer establishes common ground with the reader.

Open with a Buffer The first step in using the indirect approach is to consider using a **buffer**, a neutral, noncontroversial statement that is closely related to the point of the message (look back at Figure 8.1 on page 226). A buffer establishes common ground with your reader; moreover, if you're responding to a request, a buffer validates that request. Some critics believe that using a buffer is manipulative and unethical, even dishonest. However, buffers are unethical only if they're insincere or deceptive. Showing consideration for the feelings of others is never dishonest.

Poorly written buffers mislead or insult the reader.

Good buffers can be difficult to write because you need to balance several important elements. A poorly written buffer might trivialize the reader's concerns, divert attention from the problem with insincere flattery or irrelevant material, or mislead the reader into thinking your message actually contains good news. A good buffer, on the other hand, can express your appreciation for being considered (if you're responding to a request), assure your reader of your attention to the request, or indicate your understanding of the reader's needs. A good buffer also needs to be relevant and sincere.

The following examples were all written in response to a manager of the order fulfillment department, who requested some temporary staffing help from your department (a request you won't be able to fulfill):

Establishes common ground with the reader and validates the concerns that prompted the original request—without promising a positive answer

Our department shares your goal of processing orders quickly and efficiently.

Establishes common ground, but in a negative way that downplays the recipient's concerns

Thanks to the last downsizing, every department in the company is running shorthanded.

Potentially misleads the reader into concluding that you will comply with the request

You folks are doing a great job over there, and I'd love to be able to help out.

Trivializes the readers concerns by opening with an irrelevant issue

Those new state labor regulations are driving me crazy over here; how about in your department?

Only the first of these buffers can be considered effective; the other three are likely to damage your relationship with the other manager—and to lower his or her opinion of you. Table 8.2 shows several types of effective buffers you could use to tactfully open a negative message.

Given the damage that a poorly composed buffer can do, consider each one carefully before you send it. Is it respectful? Is it relevant? Is it neutral, implying neither yes nor no? Does it provide a smooth transition to the reasons that follow? If you can answer yes to every question, you can proceed confidently to the next section of your message. However, if that little voice inside your head tells you that your buffer sounds insincere or misleading, it probably is, in which case you'll need to rewrite it.

Provide Reasons and Additional Information An effective buffer serves as a stepping stone to the next part of your message, in which you build up the explanations and information that will culminate in your negative news. The nature of the information you provide is similar to that of the direct approach—it depends on the audience and the situation—but the way you portray this information differs from any portrayal in a direct message because your reader doesn't know your conclusion yet.

Phrase your reasons to signal the negative news ahead.

An ideal explanation section leads readers to your conclusion before you come right out and say it. In other words, before you actually say no, the reader has followed your line

TABLE 8.2 Types of Buffers

BUFFER	STRATEGY	EXAMPLE
Agreement	Find a point on which you and the reader share similar views.	We both know how hard it is to make a profit in this industry.
Appreciation	Express sincere thanks for receiving something.	Your check for $127.17 arrived yesterday. Thank you.
Cooperation	Convey your willingness to help in any way you realistically can.	Employee Services is here to smooth the way for all of you who work to achieve company goals.
Fairness	Assure the reader that you've closely examined and carefully considered the problem, or mention an appropriate action that has already been taken.	For the past week, we have carefully monitored those using the photocopying machine to see whether we can detect any pattern of use that might explain its frequent breakdowns.
Good news	Start with the part of your message that is favorable.	A replacement knob for your range is on its way, shipped February 10 via UPS.
Praise	Find an attribute or an achievement to compliment.	Your résumé shows an admirable breadth of experience, which should serve you well as you progress in your career.
Resale	Favorably discuss the product or company related to the subject of the letter.	With their heavy-duty, full-suspension hardware and fine veneers, the desks and file cabinets in our Montclair line have become a hit with value-conscious professionals.
Understanding	Demonstrate that you understand the reader's goals and needs.	So that you can more easily find the printer with the features you need, we are enclosing a brochure that describes all the Panasonic printers currently available.

of reasoning and is ready for the answer. By giving your reasons effectively, you help maintain focus on the issues at hand and defuse the emotions that always accompany significantly bad news.

As you lay out your reasons, guide your readers' responses by starting with the most positive points first and moving forward to increasingly negative ones. Provide enough detail for the audience to understand your reasons, but be concise; a long, roundabout explanation will just make your audience impatient. Your reasons need to convince your audience that your decision is justified, fair, and logical.

If appropriate, you can use the explanation section to suggest how the negative news might in fact benefit your reader. Suppose you work for a multinational company that wants to hire an advertising agency to support your offices in a dozen different countries, and you receive a proposal from an agency that has offices in only one of those countries. In your list of reasons, you could indicate that you don't want to impose undue hardship on the agency by requiring significant amounts of international travel. However, use this technique with care; it's easy to insult readers by implying that they shouldn't be asking for the benefits or opportunities they were seeking in the first place.

Avoid hiding behind company policy to cushion your bad news. If you say, "Company policy forbids our hiring anyone who does not have two years' management experience," you imply that you won't consider anyone on his or her individual merits. Skilled and sympathetic communicators explain company policy (without referring to it as "policy") so that the audience can try to meet the requirements at a later time. Consider this response to an employee:

Don't hide behind "company policy" when you deliver bad news.

Because these management trainee positions are quite challenging, the human relations department has researched the qualifications needed to succeed in them. The findings show that the two most important qualifications are a bachelor's degree in business administration and two years' supervisory experience.

Shows the reader the decision is based on a methodical analysis of the company's needs and not on some arbitrary guideline

Establishes the criteria behind the decision and lets the reader know what to expect

Well-written reasons are
- Detailed
- Tactful
- Individualized
- Unapologetic
- Positive

The paragraph does a good job of stating reasons for the refusal:

- It provides enough detail to make the reason for the refusal logically acceptable.
- It implies that the applicant is better off avoiding a program in which he or she would probably fail, given the background of potential co-workers.
- It explains the company's policy as logical rather than arbitrary.
- It offers no apology for the decision because no one is at fault.
- It avoids negative personal expressions (such as "You do not meet our requirements").

Even valid, well-thought-out reasons won't convince every reader in every situation, but if you've done a good job of laying out your reasoning, then you've done everything you can to prepare the reader for the main idea, which is the negative news itself.

To handle bad news carefully
- De-emphasize the bad news visually and grammatically
- Use a conditional statement if appropriate
- Tell what you did do, not what you didn't do

Continue with a Clear Statement of the Bad News Now that you've laid out your reasons thoughtfully and logically, and now that readers are psychologically prepared to receive the bad news, your audience may still reject your message if the bad news is handled carelessly. Three techniques are especially useful for saying no as clearly and as kindly as possible. First, de-emphasize the bad news:

- Minimize the space or time devoted to the bad news—without trivializing it or withholding any important information.
- Subordinate bad news in a complex or compound sentence ("My department is already shorthanded, so I'll need all my staff for at least the next two months"). This construction pushes the bad news into the middle of the sentence, the point of least emphasis.
- Embed bad news in the middle of a paragraph or use parenthetical expressions ("Our profits, which are down, are only part of the picture").

However, keep in mind that it's possible to abuse de-emphasis. For instance, if the primary point of your message is that profits are down, it would be inappropriate to marginalize that news by burying it in the middle of a sentence. State the negative news clearly, then make a smooth transition to any positive news that might balance the story.

Second, use a conditional (*if* or *when*) statement to imply that the audience could have received, or might someday receive, a favorable answer ("When you have more managerial experience, you are welcome to reapply"). Such a statement could motivate applicants to improve their qualifications.

Third, emphasize what you can do or have done, rather than what you cannot do. Say, "We sell exclusively through retailers, and the one nearest you that carries our merchandise is . . ." rather than "We are unable to serve you, so please call your nearest dealer." By implying the bad news, you may not need to actually state it ("The five positions currently open have been filled with people whose qualifications match those uncovered in our research"). By focusing on the positive and implying the bad news, you make the impact less personal and soften the blow.

Don't disguise bad news when you emphasize the positive.

When implying bad news, be sure your audience understands the entire message—including the bad news. Withholding negative information or overemphasizing positive information is unethical and unfair to your reader. If an implied message might lead to uncertainty, state your decision in direct terms. Just be sure to avoid overly blunt statements that are likely to cause pain and anger:

INSTEAD OF THIS	USE THIS
I *must refuse* your request.	I will be out of town on the day you need me.
We *must deny* your application.	The position has been filled.
I *am unable* to grant your request.	Contact us again when you have established . . .
We *cannot afford to* continue the program.	The program will conclude on May 1.
Much as I would like to attend . . .	Our budget meeting ends too late for me to attend.

We *must reject* your proposal.	We've accepted the proposal from AAA Builders.
We *must turn down* your extension request.	Please send in your payment by June 14.

Close on a Positive Note As with the direct approach, the conclusion of the indirect approach is your opportunity to emphasize your respect for your audience, even though you've just delivered unpleasant news. Express best wishes without ending on a falsely upbeat note. If you can find a positive angle that's meaningful to your audience, by all means consider adding it to your conclusion. However, don't try to pretend that the negative news didn't happen or that it won't affect the reader. Suggest alternative solutions if such information is available. In a message to a customer or potential customer, an ending that includes resale information or sales promotion may also be appropriate. If you've asked readers to decide between alternatives or to take some action, make sure that they know what to do, when to do it, and how to do it with ease. Whatever type of conclusion you use, follow these guidelines:

A positive close
- Builds goodwill
- Offers a suggestion for action
- Provides a look toward the future

- **Keep it positive.** Don't refer to, repeat, or apologize for the bad news, and refrain from expressing any doubt that your reasons will be accepted (avoid statements such as "I trust our decision is satisfactory").
- **Limit future correspondence.** Encourage additional communication *only* if you're willing to discuss your decision further (if you're not, avoid wording such as "If you have further questions, please write").
- **Be optimistic about the future.** Don't anticipate problems (avoid statements such as "Should you have further problems, please let us know").
- **Be sincere.** Steer clear of clichés that are insincere in view of the bad news (avoid saying, "If we can be of any help, please contact us").
- **Be confident.** Don't show any doubt about keeping the person as a customer (avoid phrases such as "We hope you will continue to do business with us").

Finally, keep in mind that the closing is the last thing the audience has to remember you by. Try to make the memory a positive one.

Adapting to Your Audience

Even more than other business messages, negative messages require that you maintain your audience focus and be as sensitive as possible to audience needs. Therefore, you may need to adapt your message to cultural differences or to the differences between internal and external audiences.

Cultural Variations

Even though bad news is unwelcome in any language, the conventions for passing it on to business associates can vary considerably from country to country. For instance, French business letters are traditionally quite formal and writer-oriented, often without reference to audience needs or benefits. Moreover, when the news is bad, French writers take a direct approach. They open with a reference to the problem or previous correspondence and then state the bad news clearly. While they don't refer to the audience's needs, they often do apologize and express regret for the problem.[5]

Expectations for the handling of bad news vary from culture to culture.

In contrast, Japanese letters traditionally open with remarks about the season, business prosperity, or health. When the news is bad, these opening formalities serve as the buffer. Explanations and apologies follow, and then comes the bad news or refusal. Japanese writers protect their reader's feelings by wording the bad news ambiguously. Western readers may even misinterpret this vague language as a condition of acceptance rather than as the refusal it actually is.[6] In short, if you are communicating across cultures, you'll want to use the tone, organization, and other cultural conventions that your audience expects. Only then can you avoid the inappropriate or even offensive approaches that could jeopardize your business relationship.[7]

4 LEARNING OBJECTIVE

Adapt your messages for internal and external audiences

Communication Solution

As a sign of respect for his audience, Agilent's Ned Barnholt was always careful to share negative news with employees before it reached the public news media.

Internal Versus External Audiences

You'll want to adapt your negative messages according to whether your audience is inside or outside the organization. Recipients inside your company frequently have expectations for negative messages that differ from those of recipients outside the company. For example, an announcement of declining profits will spur decidedly different reactions between internal stakeholders such as employees and external stakeholders such as investors and suppliers.

Most employees will not only expect more detail, including how the decline might affect pay raises, promotions, and project funding, but will also expect to be informed before the general public is told. Plus, after several years of seemingly endless upheavals and bad news, from market collapses to financial scandals, many employees are less inclined to believe what they hear from management. Cynicism and distrust are rampant today, and employees are tired of discussing change.[8] They want to know more than how changes will help the company; they want to know how changes are going to affect them personally. Managers can rebuild trust only by communicating openly, honestly, and quickly in both good times and bad.

Sending bad news up the organizational chart is a difficult, but occasionally necessary, obligation for employees.

Of course, negative news must also flow upward in an organization, from lower-level employees up to higher-level managers. Even when employees are not at fault, the reluctance to give bad news to superiors can be strong. In corporate cultures that don't encourage open communication, employees who fear retribution may go to great lengths to avoid sending bad news messages. In such a dysfunctional environment, failure breeds still more failure because decision makers don't get the honest, objective information they need to make wise choices. In contrast, mangers in open cultures expect their employees to bring them bad news whenever it happens so that corrective action can be taken. Whatever the case, if you do need to transmit bad news up the organization chart, don't try to pin the blame on anyone in particular; emphasize the nature of the problem—and a solution, if possible. This tactic will help you earn a reputation as an alert problem solver, rather than as just a complainer.[9]

You may need to adjust the content of negative messages for different groups within an external audience.

Negative messages to outside audiences require attention to the diverse nature of your audience and the concern for confidentiality of internal information. As Daniel Lieberman of Seattle's Pike Place Market realized, a single message might have a half dozen or more separate audiences, all with differing opinions and agendas. You may not be able to explain things to the level of detail that some of these people want if doing so would release proprietary information such as future product plans.

Maintaining High Standards of Ethics and Etiquette

The difficulty we all face when sending and receiving negative messages leads to a natural human tendency to delay, downplay, or distort the bad news.[10] Unfortunately doing so may be unethical, if not illegal. In recent years, numerous companies have been sued by shareholders, consumers, employees, and government regulators for allegedly withholding negative information in such areas as company finances, environmental hazards, and product safety. When an organization has negative information that affects the well-being of others, it has an ethical obligation to communicate that information clearly and completely, even if doing so might harm careers or finances (see "Ethics Detective: Soft-Selling Bad News").

Delaying the delivery of negative news can be unethical in many situations.

This ethical obligation to communicate the facts also brings with it the responsibility to do so promptly. Bad news often means that people need to make other plans, whether it's an employee who needs to find a new job, consumers who need to stop using an unsafe product, or a community that needs to find safe drinking water when their supply has become polluted. The longer you wait to deliver bad news, the harder you make it for recipients to react and respond.

Negative news situations can put your sense of self-control and business etiquette to the test.

Some negative news scenarios will also test your self-control and sense of etiquette. An employee who lets you down, a supplier whose faulty parts damage your company's reputation, a business partner who violates the terms of your contract—such situations may tempt you to respond with a personal attack. However, whether maddening or completely warranted and necessary, negative messages can have a lasting impact on both the people

Ethics Detective

Soft-Selling Bad News

You and your colleagues are nervous. Sales have been on the decline for months, and you see evidence of budget tightening all over the place—the fruit and pastries have disappeared from the coffee stations, accountants are going over expense reports with magnifying glasses, and managers are slow to replace people who leave the company. Instant messages fly around the office; everyone wants to know if anyone has heard anything about layoffs.

The job market in your area is weak, and you know you might have to sell your house and move your family out of state to find another position in your field. If your job is eliminated, you're ready to cope with the loss, but you need as much time as possible. You breathe a sigh of relief when the following item from the CEO appears in the company's weekly e-mail newsletter:

> With news of workforce adjustments elsewhere in our industry, we realize many of you are concerned about the possibility here. I'd like to reassure all of you that we remain confident in the company's fundamental business strategy and the executive team is examining all facets of company operations to ensure our continued financial strength.

The message calms your fears. Should it?

ANALYSIS

A month later, the CEO announces a layoff of 20 percent of the company's workforce—nearly 700 people. You're shocked by the news because you felt reassured by the newsletter item from last month. In light of what happened, you retrieve a copy of the newsletter and re-read the CEO's message. Does it seem ethical now? Why or why not? If you were in charge of writing this newsletter item and your hands were tied because you couldn't come out and announce the layoffs yet, how would you have rewritten the message?

who receive them and the people who send them. As a communicator, it's your responsibility to minimize the negative impact of your negative messages through careful planning and sensitive, objective writing. As much as possible, focus on the actions or conditions that led to the negative news, not on personal shortcomings or character issues. Develop a reputation as a professional who can handle the toughest situations with dignity.

For a reminder of successful strategies for creating negative messages, see "Checklist: Creating Negative Messages."

DOCUMENT MAKEOVER

IMPROVE THIS MEMO

To practice correcting drafts of actual documents, visit www.prenhall.com/onekey on the web. Click "Document Makeovers" then click Chapter 8. You will find a memo that contains problems and errors relating to what you've learned in this chapter about handling bad-news messages. Use the Final Draft decision tool to create an improved version of this memo. Check the message for the use of buffers, apologies, explanations, subordination, embedding, positive action, conditional phrases, and upbeat perspectives.

EXPLORING COMMON EXAMPLES OF NEGATIVE MESSAGES

In the course of your business career, you might write a wide variety of negative messages, from announcing declines in revenue to giving negative performance reviews. The following sections offer examples of the most common negative messages, dealing with topics such as routine business matters, organizational news, and employment messages.

Sending Negative Messages on Routine Business Matters

Most companies receive numerous requests for information and donations or invitations to join community or industry organizations. As you progress in your career and become more visible in your industry and community, you will receive a wide variety of personal invitations to speak at private or public functions or to volunteer your time for a variety of organizations. In addition, routine business matters such as credit applications and requests for adjustment will often require negative responses. Neither you nor your company will be able to say yes to every request. So crafting negative responses quickly and graciously is an important skill for many professionals.

CHECKLIST: Creating Negative Messages

A. CHOOSE THE BEST APPROACH

- Use a direct approach when the audience is aware of the possibility of negative news, when the reader is not emotionally involved in the message, when you know that the reader would prefer the bad news first, when you know that firmness is necessary, and you want to discourage a response.
- Use an indirect approach when the news is likely to come as a shock or surprise and you want to maintain a good relationship with the audience.

B. FOR AN INDIRECT APPROACH, OPEN WITH AN EFFECTIVE BUFFER

- Establish common ground with the audience.
- Validate the request, if you are responding to a request.
- Don't trivialize the reader's concerns.
- Don't mislead the reader into thinking the coming news might be positive.

C. PROVIDE REASONS AND ADDITIONAL INFORMATION

- Explain why the news is negative.
- Adjust the amount of detail to fit the situation and the audience.
- Avoid explanations when the reasons are confidential, excessively complicated, or irrelevant to the reader.
- If appropriate, state how you plan to correct or respond to the negative news.
- Seek the advice of company lawyers if you're unsure what to say.

D. CLEARLY STATE THE BAD NEWS

- State the bad news as positively as possible, using tactful wording.
- De-emphasize bad news by minimizing the space devoted to it, subordinating it, or embedding it.
- If your response might change in the future if circumstances change, explain the conditions to the reader.
- Emphasize what you can or have done, rather than what you can't or won't do.

E. CLOSE ON A POSITIVE NOTE

- Express best wishes without being falsely positive.
- Suggest actions readers might take, if appropriate, and provide them with necessary information.
- Encourage further communication only if you're willing to discuss the situation further.
- Keep a positive outlook on the future.

Refusing Routine Requests

Routine requests may come both from groups and from individuals outside the company, as well as from colleagues inside the organization. When you aren't able to meet the request, your primary communication challenge is to give a clear negative response without generating negative feelings or damaging either your personal reputation or the company's. As simple as these messages may appear to be, they can test your skills as a communicator because you often need to deliver negative information while maintaining a positive relationship with the other party.

Saying no is a routine part of business and shouldn't reflect negatively on you. If you said yes to every request that crossed your desk, you'd never get any work done. The direct approach will work best for most routine negative responses. It not only helps your audience get your answer quickly and move on to other possibilities but also helps you save time, since the direct approach is often easier to write.

When turning down an invitation or a request for a favor, consider your relationship with the reader.

The indirect approach works best when the stakes are high for you or for the receiver, when you or your company has an established relationship with the person making the request, or when you're forced to decline a request that you might have said yes to in the past. May Yee Kwan used the indirect approach in her letter to Whittier Community College (see Figure 8.2). Her company has a long-standing relationship with the college and wants to maintain that positive relationship, but she can't meet this particular request. If Kwan and Wofford shared a closer relationship (if they worked together in a volunteer organization, for instance), the direct approach might have been more appropriate.

Consider the following points as you develop your routine negative messages:

- **Manage your time carefully.** Ironically, as you move upward in your career, you'll receive more and more requests—and have less and less time to answer them. Focus your limited time on the most-important relationships and requests, then get in the habit of crafting quick standard responses for less important situations.

Plan

Analyze the Situation
Purpose is to decline a request and offer alternatives; audience is likely to be surprised by the refusal.

Gather Information
Determine audience needs and obtain the information necessary to satisfy those needs.

Select the Right Medium
Choose the best medium for delivering your message; for formal messages, printed letters on company letterhead are best.

Organize the Information
Your main idea is to refuse the request so limit your scope to the problem at hand; select an indirect approach based on the audience and the situation.

1

Write

Adapt to Your Audience
Adjust the level of formality based on degree of familiarity with the audience; maintain a positive relationship by using the "you" attitude, politeness, positive emphasis, and bias-free language.

Compose the Message
Use a conversational but professional style and keep the message brief, clear, and as helpful as possible.

2

Complete

Revise the Message
Evaluate content and review readability to make sure the negative information won't be misinterpreted; make sure your tone stays positive without being artificial.

Produce the Message
Emphasize a clean, professional appearance on company letterhead.

Proofread the Message
Review for errors in layout, spelling, and mechanics.

Distribute the Message
Deliver your message using the chosen medium.

3

FIGURE 8.2 Effective Letter Declining a Favor

927 Dawson Valley Road, Tulsa, Oklahoma 74151
Voice: (918) 669-4428 Fax: (918) 669-4429
www.infotech.com

March 5, 2005

Dr. Sandra Wofford, President
Whittier Community College
333 Whittier Avenue
Tulsa, OK 74150

Dear Dr. Wofford:

Infotech has been happy to support Whittier Community College in many ways over the years, and we appreciate the opportunities you and your organization provide to so many deserving students. Thank you for considering our grounds for your graduation ceremony.

Buffers bad news by demonstrating respect and recapping request

Our company-wide sales meetings will be held during the weeks of May 31 and June 7. We will host over 200 sales representatives and their families, and activities will take place at both our corporate campus and the Ramada Renaissance. As a result, our support staff will be devoting all of their time and effort to these events.

States reason for the bad news explicitly and in detail

My assistant, Roberta Seagers, suggests you contact the Municipal Botanical Gardens as a possible graduation site. She recommends calling Jerry Kane, director of public relations. If we can help in any other way with graduation, please let us know.

Suggests an alternative—showing that Kwan cares about the college and has given the matter some thought

We remain firm in our commitment to you, President Wofford, and to the fine students you represent. We will continue to be a corporate partner to Whittier College and will support your efforts as you move forward.

Closes by renewing the corporation's future support

Sincerely,

May Yee Kwan

May Yee Kwan
Public Relations Director

lc

- **If the matter is closed, don't imply that it's still open.** If your answer is truly no, don't use phrases such as "Let me think about it and get back to you" as a way to delay saying no. Such delays waste time for you and the other party.
- **Offer alternative ideas if you can.** In her letter to Sandra Wofford, May Yee Kwan includes the name of someone to contact. However, remember to use your time wisely in such matters. Unless the relationship is vital to your company, you probably shouldn't spend time researching alternatives for the other person.

If you aren't in a position to offer additional information or assistance, don't imply that you are.

- **Don't imply that other assistance or information might be available if it isn't.** Don't close your negative message with a cheery but insincere "Please contact us if we can offer any additional assistance." An empty attempt to mollify hostile feelings could simply lead to another request you'll have to refuse. In Figure 8.2, Kwan makes such an offer in her letter because her company may indeed have other resources that could help the college with its graduation activities.

Handling Bad News About Transactions

For any number of reasons, businesses must sometimes convey bad news concerning the sale and delivery of products and services. Bad news about transactions is always unwelcome and usually unexpected. These messages have three goals: to modify the customer's expectations regarding the transaction, to explain how you plan to resolve the situation, and to repair whatever damage might've been done to the business relationship.

Some negative messages regarding transactions carry significant business ramifications.

The specific content and tone of each message can vary widely, depending on the nature of the transaction and your relationship with the customer. Telling an individual consumer that his new sweater will be arriving a week later than you promised is a much simpler task than telling General Motors that 30,000 transmission parts will be a week late,

FIGURE 8.3
Effective IM Chat Regarding Order Delays

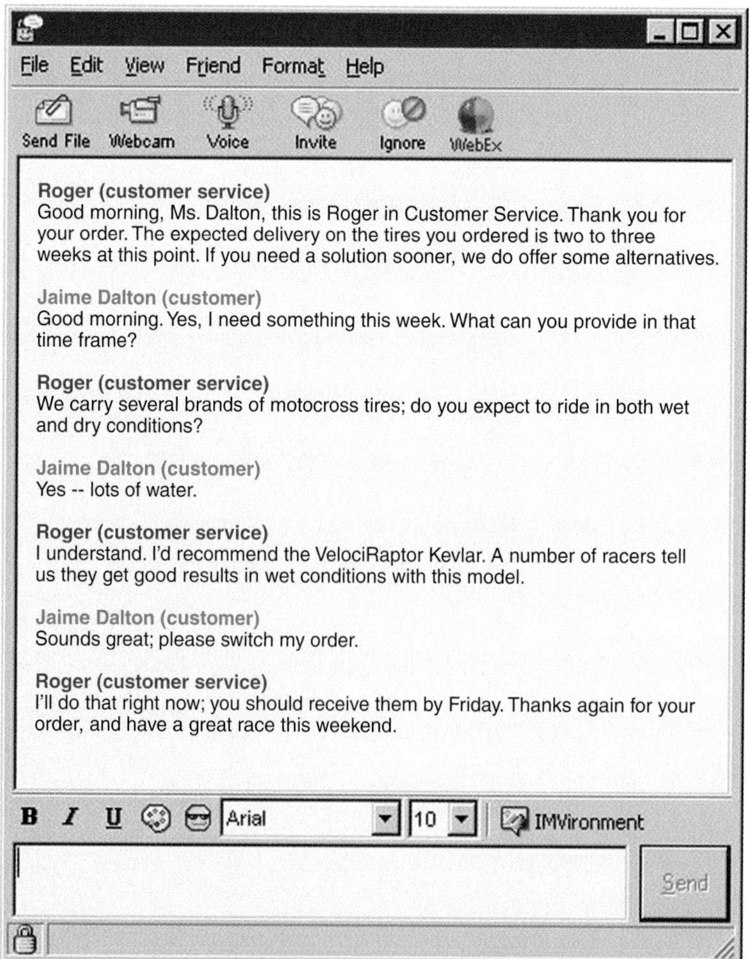

especially since you know the company will be forced to idle a multimillion-dollar production facility as a result. Negative messages concerning professional services can be particularly tricky since the person writing such a message is often the same person who performs the service; as a result, these messages can have an uncomfortably personal aspect to them.

Negative messages about transactions come in two basic flavors. If you haven't done anything specific to set the customer's expectations—such as promising delivery within 24 hours—the message simply needs to inform the customer, with little or no emphasis on apologies (see Figure 8.3). (Bear in mind, though, in this age of online ordering and overnight delivery, customers have been conditioned to expect instantaneous fulfillment of nearly every transaction, even if you haven't promised anything.) Notice how the e-mail message in Figure 8.4, which is combination of good and bad news, uses the indirect approach turning the good news into a buffer for the bad news. Because the customer wasn't promised delivery by a certain date, the writer simply informs the customer when to expect the rest of the order. The writer also took steps to repair the relationship and encourage future business with her firm.

Your approach to bad news about business transactions depends on the customer's expectations.

If you did set the customer's expectations and now find you can't meet them, your task is more complicated. In addition to resetting the customer's expectations and explaining how you'll resolve the problem, you may need to include an element of apology. The scope of the apology depends on the magnitude of the mistake. For the customer who ordered the sweater, a simple apology, followed by a clear statement of when the sweater will arrive, would probably be sufficient. An explanation is usually not required, although if a meaningful reason exists, and if stating it will help smooth over the situation without sounding like a feeble excuse, by all means include it. For example, if a snowstorm closed the highways and prevented your receiving necessary materials, say so; however, if you simply received more orders than you expected and promised more than you could deliver, the customer will be less sympathetic. For larger business-to-business transactions, the customer may want an explanation of what went wrong in order to determine whether you'll be able to perform as you promise in the future.

If you've fail to meet expectations that you set for the customer, an element of apology should be considered.

To help repair the damage to the relationship and encourage repeat business, many companies offer discounts on future purchases, free merchandise, or other considerations. Even modest efforts can go a long way to rebuilding the customer's confidence in your

FIGURE 8.4 Effective E-Mail Advising of a Back Order

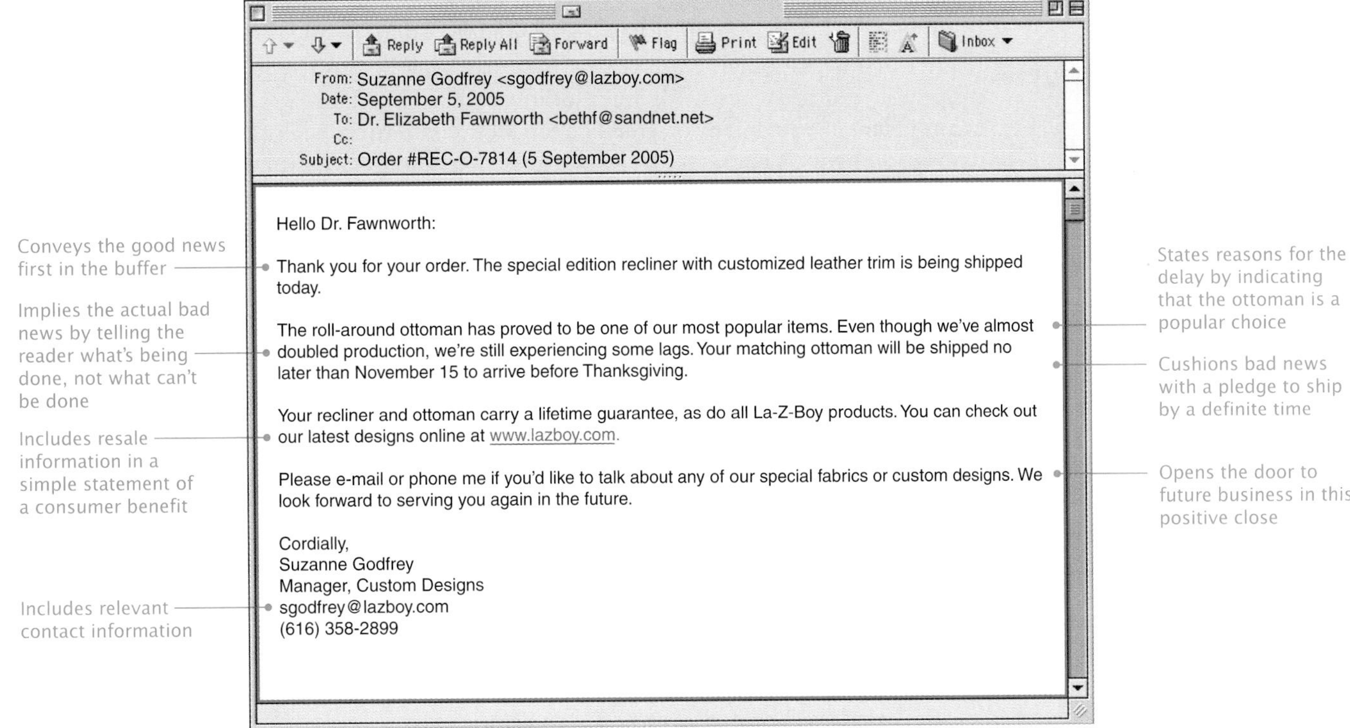

Reply
Reply All
Forward
Flag
Print
Edit
Inbox
From: Suzanne Godfrey <sgodfrey@lazboy.com>
Date: September 5, 2005
To: Dr. Elizabeth Fawnworth <bethf@sandnet.net>
Cc:
Subject: Order #REC-O-7814 (5 September 2005)
Hello Dr. Fawnworth:
Thank you for your order. The special edition recliner with customized leather trim is being shipped today.
The roll-around ottoman has proved to be one of our most popular items. Even though we've almost doubled production, we're still experiencing some lags. Your matching ottoman will be shipped no later than November 15 to arrive before Thanksgiving.
Your recliner and ottoman carry a lifetime guarantee, as do all La-Z-Boy products. You can check out our latest designs online at www.lazboy.com.
Please e-mail or phone me if you'd like to talk about any of our special fabrics or custom designs. We look forward to serving you again in the future.
Cordially,
Suzanne Godfrey
Manager, Custom Designs
sgodfrey@lazboy.com
(616) 358-2899
Conveys the good news first in the buffer
Implies the actual bad news by telling the reader what's being done, not what can't be done
Includes resale information in a simple statement of a consumer benefit
Includes relevant contact information
States reasons for the delay by indicating that the ottoman is a popular choice
Cushions bad news with a pledge to ship by a definite time
Opens the door to future business in this positive close

CHECKLIST: Handling Bad News About Transactions

- Reset the customer's expectations regarding the transaction.
- Explain what happened and why, if appropriate.
- Explain how you'll resolve the situation.
- Repair any damage done to the business relationship, perhaps offering future discounts, free merchandise, or other considerations.
- Offer a professional, businesslike expression of apology if your organization made a mistake.

company. However, you don't always have a choice. Business-to-business purchasing contracts often include performance clauses that legally entitle the customer to discounts or other restitution in the event of late delivery. Construction contracts sometimes specify penalties for every day the project extends past the original completion date. In such cases, a simple apology is clearly inadequate. To review the concepts covered in this section, see "Checklist: Handling Bad News About Transactions."

Refusing Claims and Requests for Adjustment

Use the indirect approach in most cases of refusing a claim.

Almost every customer who makes a claim or requests an adjustment is emotionally involved; therefore, the indirect method is usually the best approach for a refusal. Your job as a writer is to avoid accepting responsibility for the unfortunate situation and yet avoid blaming or accusing the customer. To steer clear of these pitfalls, pay special attention to the tone of your letter.

A tactful and courteous letter can build goodwill even while denying the claim. For example, Village Electronics recently received a letter from Daniel Lindmeier, who purchased a digital video camera a year ago. He wrote to say that the unit doesn't work correctly and to inquire about the warranty. Lindmeier believes that the warranty covers one year, when it actually covers only three months (see Figure 8.5).

When refusing a claim
- Demonstrate your understanding of the complaint
- Explain your refusal
- Suggest alternative action

When refusing a claim, avoid language that might have a negative impact on the reader. Instead, demonstrate that you understand and have considered the complaint carefully. Then, even if the claim is unreasonable, rationally explain why you are refusing the request. Remember, don't apologize and don't hide behind "company policy." End the letter on a respectful and action-oriented note.

5 LEARNING OBJECTIVE

Define defamation and explain how to avoid it in negative messages

If you deal with enough customers over a long enough period, chances are you'll get a request that is particularly outrageous. You may even be positive that the person is being dishonest. You must resist the temptation to call the person a crook, a swindler, or an incompetent. If you don't, you could be sued for **defamation**, a false statement that tends to damage someone's character or reputation. (Written defamation is called *libel;* spoken defamation is called *slander.*) Someone suing for defamation must prove (1) that the statement is false, (2) that the language is injurious to the person's reputation, and (3) that the statement has been published.

If you can prove that your accusations are true, you haven't defamed the person. The courts are likely to give you the benefit of the doubt because our society believes that ordinary business communication should not be hampered by fear of lawsuits. However, beware of the irate letter intended to let off steam: If the message has no necessary business purpose and is expressed in abusive language that hints of malice, you'll lose the case. To avoid being accused of defamation, follow these guidelines:

You can help avoid defamation by not responding emotionally.

- Avoid using any kind of abusive language or terms that could be considered defamatory.
- If you wish to express your own personal opinions about a sensitive matter, use your own stationery (not company letterhead), and don't include your job title or position. Just be aware that by doing so, you take responsibility for your own opinions, you are no longer acting within the scope of your duties with the company, and you are personally liable for any resulting legal action.
- Provide accurate information and stick to the facts.
- Never let anger or malice motivate your messages.

Plan

Analyze the Situation
Purpose is to refuse a warranty claim and offer repairs; audience's likely reaction will be disappointment and surprise.

Gather Information
Gather information on warranty policies and procedures, repair services, and resale information.

Select the Right Medium
Choose the best medium for delivering your message; for formal messages, printed letters on company letterhead are best.

Organize the Information
Your main idea is to refuse the claim and promote an alternative solution; select an indirect approach based on the audience and the situation.

1

Write

Adapt to Your Audience
Adjust the level of formality based on degree of familiarity with the audience; maintain a positive relationship by using the "you" attitude, politeness, positive emphasis, and bias-free language.

Compose the Message
Use a conversational but professional style and keep the message brief, clear, and as helpful as possible.

2

Complete

Revise the Message
Evaluate content and review readability to make sure the negative information won't be misinterpreted; make sure your tone stays positive without being artificial.

Produce the Message
Emphasize a clean, professional appearance appropriate for a letter on company stationery.

Proofread the Message
Review for errors in layout, spelling, nd mechanics.

Distribute the Message
Deliver your message using the chosen medium; make sure the reader receives any necessary support documents as well.

3

FIGURE 8.5 Effective Letter Refusing a Claim

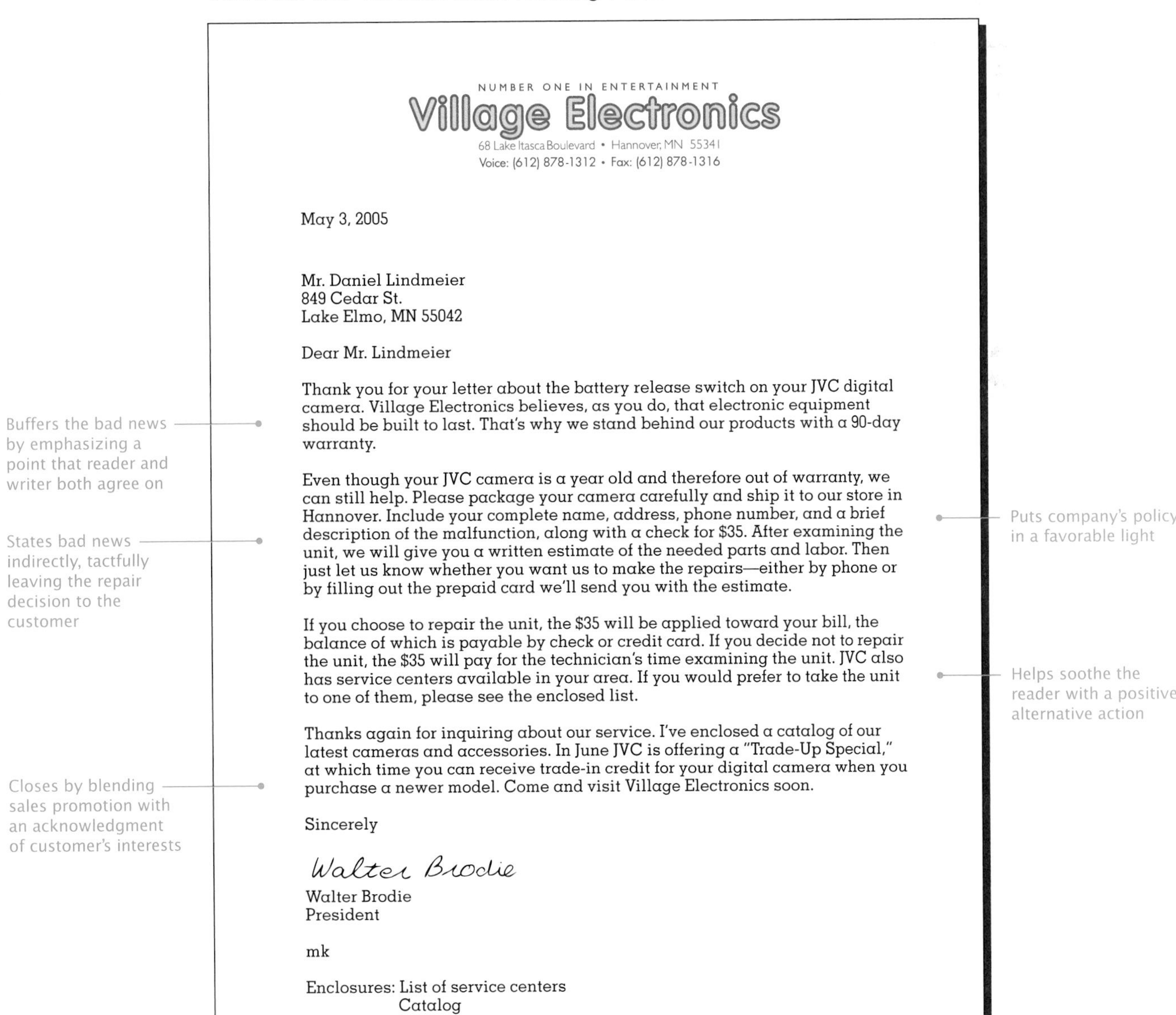

NUMBER ONE IN ENTERTAINMENT
Village Electronics
68 Lake Itasca Boulevard • Hannover, MN 55341
Voice: (612) 878-1312 • Fax: (612) 878-1316

May 3, 2005

Mr. Daniel Lindmeier
849 Cedar St.
Lake Elmo, MN 55042

Dear Mr. Lindmeier

Thank you for your letter about the battery release switch on your JVC digital camera. Village Electronics believes, as you do, that electronic equipment should be built to last. That's why we stand behind our products with a 90-day warranty.

Even though your JVC camera is a year old and therefore out of warranty, we can still help. Please package your camera carefully and ship it to our store in Hannover. Include your complete name, address, phone number, and a brief description of the malfunction, along with a check for $35. After examining the unit, we will give you a written estimate of the needed parts and labor. Then just let us know whether you want us to make the repairs—either by phone or by filling out the prepaid card we'll send you with the estimate.

If you choose to repair the unit, the $35 will be applied toward your bill, the balance of which is payable by check or credit card. If you decide not to repair the unit, the $35 will pay for the technician's time examining the unit. JVC also has service centers available in your area. If you would prefer to take the unit to one of them, please see the enclosed list.

Thanks again for inquiring about our service. I've enclosed a catalog of our latest cameras and accessories. In June JVC is offering a "Trade-Up Special," at which time you can receive trade-in credit for your digital camera when you purchase a newer model. Come and visit Village Electronics soon.

Sincerely

Walter Brodie

Walter Brodie
President

mk

Enclosures: List of service centers
Catalog

Buffers the bad news by emphasizing a point that reader and writer both agree on
States bad news indirectly, tactfully leaving the repair decision to the customer
Closes by blending sales promotion with an acknowledgment of customer's interests
Puts company's policy in a favorable light
Helps soothe the reader with a positive alternative action

CHECKLIST: Refusing Claims

- Use an indirect approach since the reader is expecting or hoping for a positive response.
- Indicate your full understanding of the nature of the complaint.
- Explain why you are refusing the request, without hiding behind company policy.
- Provide an accurate, factual account of the transaction.
- Emphasize ways things should have been handled, rather than dwelling on a reader's negligence.
- Avoid any appearance of defamation.
- Avoid expressing personal opinions.
- End with a positive, friendly, helpful close.
- Make any suggested action easy for readers to comply with.

- Consult your company's legal department or an attorney whenever you think a message might have legal consequences.
- Communicate honestly, and make sure that what you're saying is what you believe to be true.
- Emphasize a desire for a good relationship in the future.

Most important, remember that nothing positive can come out of antagonizing a customer, even a customer who has verbally abused you or your colleagues. Reject the claim or request for adjustment and move on to the next challenge. For a brief review of the tasks involved when refusing claims, see this chapter's "Checklist: Refusing Claims."

Sending Negative Organizational News

In addition to routine matters involving individual customers and other parties, you may encounter special cases that require you to issue negative announcements regarding some aspect of your products, services, or operations. Most of these scenarios have unique challenges that must be addressed on a case-by-case basis, but the general advice offered here applies to all of them. One key difference among all these messages is whether you have time to plan the announcement. The following section addresses those negative messages that you do have time to plan for, then "Communicating in a Crisis" offers advice on communication during emergencies.

Communicating Under Normal Circumstances

Even the best-run companies stumble on occasion, sometimes through their own actions and sometimes through the actions of someone else. At other times, the company needs to make decisions that are unpopular with customers (price increases, product cancellations, product recalls), with employees (layoffs, benefit reductions, plant closings), or with other groups (relocating to a new community, replacing a board member, canceling a contract with a supplier). The common characteristic of all these messages is the need to send negative announcements to one or more groups of people, rather than to a specific individual. Because you're using a single announcement to reach a variety of people, each of whom may react differently, these messages need to be planned with great care. A relatively simple announcement, such as a price increase, needs to be communicated to both customers on the outside and your sales force on the inside, neither of whom is likely to welcome the news.

Negative organizational messages to external audiences often require extensive planning.

A more significant event, such as a plant closing, can affect thousands of people in dozens of organizations. Employees need to find new jobs or get training in new skills. School districts may have to adjust budgets and staffing levels if many of your employees plan to move in search of new jobs. Your customers need to find new suppliers. Your suppliers may need to find other customers of their own. Government agencies may need to react to everything from a decrease in tax revenues to an influx of people seeking unemployment benefits.

When making negative announcements, follow these guidelines:

- **Match your approach to the situation.** A modest price increase won't shock most customers, so the direct approach is fine. However, canceling a product that people count on is another matter, so building up to the news via the indirect approach might be better.

- **Consider the unique needs of each group.** As the plant closing example illustrates, various people have different information needs.
- **Give each audience enough time to react as needed.** Most organizations operate on quarterly or annual budgeting cycles and need time to react to news. Employees, particularly higher-level executives, may need as much as six months or more to find new jobs.

Give people as much time as possible to react to negative news.

- **Plan the sequence of multiple announcements.** In addition to giving each group enough time, some groups will expect to be informed before others. For instance, if employees hear about a plant closing on the evening news or from a real estate agent, their trust in management will likely be destroyed. Tell insiders and the most-affected groups first.
- **Give yourself enough time to plan and manage a response.** Chances are you're going to be hit with complaints, questions, or product returns after you make your announcement, so make sure you're ready with answers and additional follow-up information.
- **Look for positive angles but don't exude false optimism.** Laying off 10,000 people does not give them "an opportunity to explore new horizons." It's a traumatic event that can affect employees, their families, and their communities for years. Phony optimism would only make a bad situation worse. The best you may be able to do is to thank people for their past support and to wish them well in the future. On the other hand, if eliminating a seldom-used employee benefit means the company doesn't have to deduct additional money from paychecks every month, by all means promote that positive angle.
- **Minimize the element of surprise whenever possible.** This step can require considerable judgment on your part, but if you recognize that current trends are pointing toward negative results sometime in the near future, it's often better to let your audience know ahead of time. For instance, a common complaint in many shareholder lawsuits is a claim that the company didn't let investors know business was deteriorating until it was too late.
- **Seek expert advice if you're not sure.** Many significant negative announcements have important technical, financial, or legal elements that require the expertise of lawyers, accountants, or other specialists. If you're not sure how to handle every aspect of the announcement, ask.

Ask for legal help and other assistance if you're not sure how to handle a significant negative announcement.

Negative scenarios such as these will test your skills both as a communicator and as a leader. People may turn to you and ask, "OK, so things are bad; now what do we do?" Inspirational leaders try to seize such opportunities as a chance to reshape or reinvigorate the organization, and they offer encouragement to those around them. Frank Leslie did just that in his e-mail message to Sybervantage employees (see Figure 8.6). Sybervantage had pursued licensing agreements with Warner and expected to enter into a mutually profitable arrangement. But when Warner rejected the deal, Leslie had to notify Sybervantage's sales force. Rather then dwell on the bad news, he focused on possible options for the future. The upbeat close diminishes the effect of the bad news without hiding or downplaying the news itself.

Communicating in a Crisis

6 LEARNING OBJECTIVE

Explain the role of communication in crisis management

The most extreme forms of business communication occur during a crisis, which can include a wide range of internal and external events, including an incident of product tampering, an industrial accident, a crime or scandal involving company employees, an on-site hostage situation, or a terrorist attack. During a crisis, employees, their families, the surrounding community, and others will demand information; plus, rumors can spread unpredictably and uncontrollably (see "Connecting with Technology: Controlling Rumors Online"). You can expect the news media to descend quickly as well, asking questions of anyone they can find.

Crisis communication is one of the most challenging jobs a business professional can ever face.

Although you can't predict these events, you can prepare for them. Companies that respond quickly with the information people need tend to fare much better in these

FIGURE 8.6 Effective E-Mail Providing Bad News About Company Operations

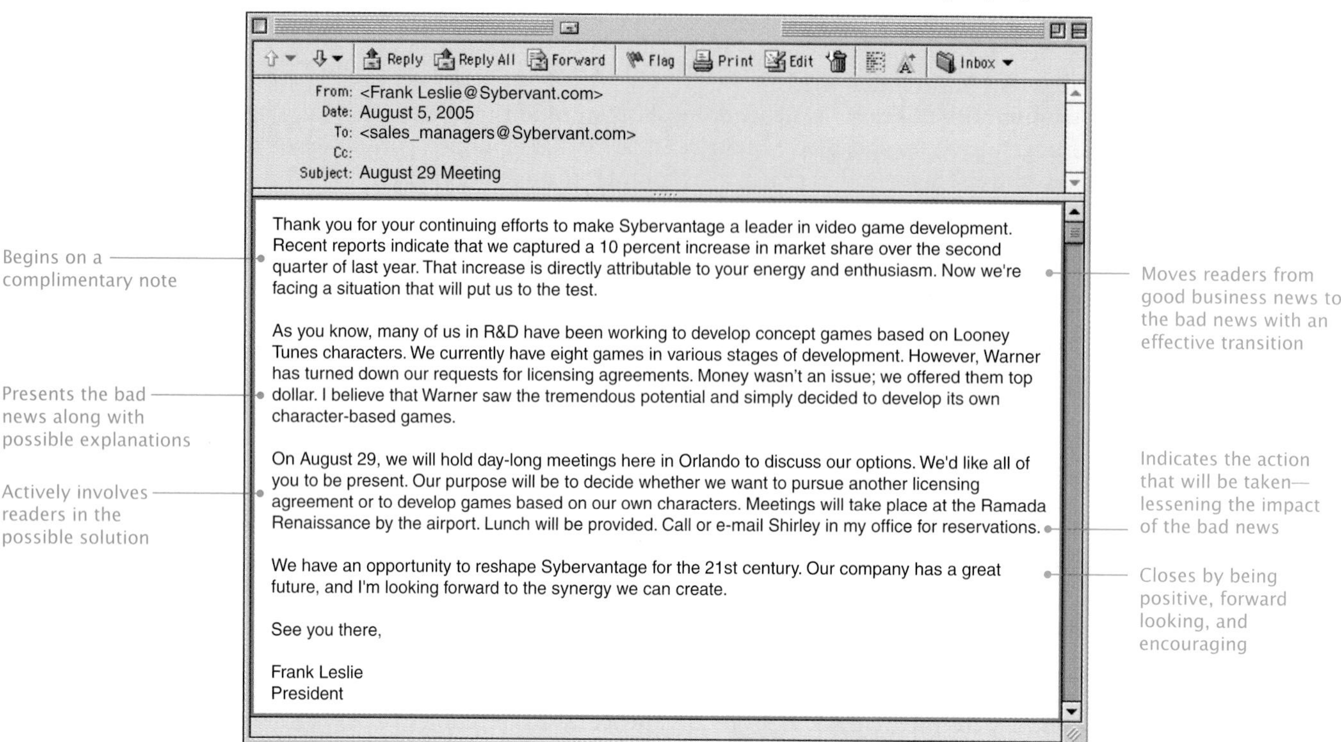
Reply
Reply All
Forward
Flag
Print
Edit
Inbox
Begins on a complimentary note
Presents the bad news along with possible explanations
Actively involves readers in the possible solution
Moves readers from good business news to the bad news with an effective transition
Indicates the action that will be taken—lessening the impact of the bad news
Closes by being positive, forward looking, and encouraging

From: <Frank Leslie@Sybervant.com>
Date: August 5, 2005
To: <sales_managers@Sybervant.com>
Cc:
Subject: August 29 Meeting

Thank you for your continuing efforts to make Sybervantage a leader in video game development. Recent reports indicate that we captured a 10 percent increase in market share over the second quarter of last year. That increase is directly attributable to your energy and enthusiasm. Now we're facing a situation that will put us to the test.

As you know, many of us in R&D have been working to develop concept games based on Looney Tunes characters. We currently have eight games in various stages of development. However, Warner has turned down our requests for licensing agreements. Money wasn't an issue; we offered them top dollar. I believe that Warner saw the tremendous potential and simply decided to develop its own character-based games.

On August 29, we will hold day-long meetings here in Orlando to discuss our options. We'd like all of you to be present. Our purpose will be to decide whether we want to pursue another licensing agreement or to develop games based on our own characters. Meetings will take place at the Ramada Renaissance by the airport. Lunch will be provided. Call or e-mail Shirley in my office for reservations.

We have an opportunity to reshape Sybervantage for the 21st century. Our company has a great future, and I'm looking forward to the synergy we can create.

See you there,

Frank Leslie
President

Connecting with Technology

Controlling Rumors Online

Ah, the miracles of the Internet: spam, viruses, spyware, stolen bandwidth, hacked databases full of confidential information—ruin and nuisance at the speed of light. If you work in corporate communications, you can add rapid-fire rumor mongering to that list.

Consumers can now share rumors and complaints through e-mail, instant messaging, blogs, chat rooms, newsgroups, and a variety of complaint websites such as Planet Feedback.com. On the positive side, consumers who feel they have been treated unfairly can use the public exposure as leverage. Many companies appreciate the feedback from these sites, too, and even buy complaint summaries so they can improve products and services.

On the negative side, many of these venues don't verify rumors or complaints. E-mail is probably the worst offender in this respect because messages are so easy to forward en masse. Among recent rumors spread via e-mail: products from Coca-Cola and PepsiCo are tainted, perfume samples arriving in the mail are poisonous, bananas from Costa Rica carry a flesh-eating bacteria, the small letter "k" on Snapple labels means the company supports the Ku Klux Klan, Carmex lip balm has (take your pick) addictive ingredients or either an acid or ground glass fibers that damage your lips so you have to use more. Every one of these rumors is false.

Controlling false rumors is difficult, but you help contain them by (1) responding quickly with clear information distributed in any way you can, (2) tracking down and responding to rumors wherever they appear, (3) enlisting the help of government agencies such as the Centers for Disease Control and Prevention and debunking sites such as www.urbanlegends.com, and (4) even digging back through e-mail threads and responding personally to everyone who passed the message along. Moreover, don't wait for bad news to find you; monitor complaint sites and newsgroups so that you can jump on false information faster.

CAREER APPLICATIONS

1. A legitimate complaint about one of your products on PlanetFeedback.com also contains a statement that your company "doesn't care about its customers." How should you respond?
2. A few e-mails are circulating with false information about your company, but it's not widespread. Should you jump on the problem now and tell the world the rumor is false—even though most people haven't heard it yet? Explain your answer.

TABLE 8.3 What to Do in a Crisis

WHEN A CRISIS HITS:	
DO	**DON'T**
Do prepare for trouble ahead of time by identifying potential problems, appointing and training a response team; and preparing and testing a crisis management plan. Do get top management involved as soon as the crisis hits. Do set up a news center for company representatives and the media, equipped with phones, computers, and other electronic tools for preparing news releases. • Issue at least two news updates a day, and have trained personnel to respond to questions around the clock. • Provide complete information packets to the media as soon as possible. • Prevent conflicting statements and provide continuity, appointing a single person, trained in advance; to speak for the company. • Tell receptionists to direct all calls to the news center. Do tell the whole story—openly, completely, and honestly. If you are at fault, apologize. Do demonstrate the company's concern by your statements and your actions.	Don't blame anyone for anything. Don't speculate in public. Don't refuse to answer questions. Don't release information that will violate anyone's right to privacy. Don't use the crisis to pitch products or services. Don't play favorites with media representatives.

circumstances than those who go into hiding or release bits and pieces of uncoordinated or inconsistent information. Companies such as Johnson & Johnson (in a Tylenol-tampering incident) emerged from crisis with renewed respect for their decisive action and responsive communication. In contrast, Exxon continues to be cited as a classic example of how not to communicate in a crisis—more than a quarter century after one of its tankers spilled 250,000 barrels of oil into Alaska's Prince William Sound. The company frustrated the media and the public with sketchy, inconsistent information and an adamant refusal to accept responsibility for the full extent of the environmental disaster. The company's CEO didn't talk to the media for nearly a week; other executives made contradictory statements, which further undermined public trust. The mistakes had a lasting impact on the company's reputation and consumers' willingness to buy its products.[11]

The key to successful communication efforts during a crisis is having a **crisis management plan**. In addition to defining operational procedures to deal with the crisis itself, the plan also outlines communication tasks and responsibilities, which can include everything from media contacts to news release templates (see Table 8.3). The plan should clearly specify which people are authorized to speak for the company, contact information for all key executives, and a list of the media outlets and technologies that will be used to disseminate information. Many companies now go one step further by regularly testing crisis communications in realistic practice drills lasting a full day or more.[12]

Anticipation and planning are key to successful communication in a crisis.

Sending Negative Employment Messages

Most managers must convey bad news about individual employees from time to time. You can use the direct approach when writing to job applicants or when communicating with other companies to send a negative reference to a prospective employer. But it's best to use the indirect approach when giving negative performance reviews to employees; they will most certainly be emotionally involved. In addition, choose the media you use for these messages with care. E-mail and other written forms let you control the message and avoid personal confrontation, but one-on-one conversations are more sensitive and facilitate questions and answers.

Refusing Requests for Recommendation Letters

Even though many states have passed laws to protect employers who provide open and honest job references for former employees, legal hazards persist.[13] That's why many former employers still refuse to write recommendation letters—especially for people whose job performance has been unsatisfactory. When sending refusals to prospective employers, your message may be brief and direct:

Implies that company policy prohibits the release of any more information but does provide what information is available

Ends on a positive note

> Our human resources department has authorized me to confirm that Yolanda Johnson worked for Tandy, Inc., for three years, from June 1999 to July 2001. Best of luck as you interview administrative applicants.

In letters informing prospective employers that you will not provide a recommendation, be direct, brief, and factual (to avoid legal pitfalls).

This message doesn't need to say, "We cannot comply with your request." It simply gets down to the business of giving readers the information that is allowable.

Refusing an applicant's direct request for a recommendation letter is another matter. Any refusal to cooperate may seem a personal slight and a threat to the applicant's future. Diplomacy and preparation help readers accept your refusal:

Uses the indirect approach since the other party is probably expecting a positive response

Announces that the writer cannot comply with the request, without explicitly blaming it on "policy"

Offers to fulfill as much of the request as possible, then offers an alternative suggestion that might address the requestor's needs

Ends on a positive note

> Thank you for letting me know about your job opportunity with Coca-Cola. Your internship there and the MBA you've worked so hard to earn should place you in an excellent position to land the marketing job.
>
> I can certainly send Coca-Cola a confirmation of your employment dates, although we do not send out formal recommendations here at PepsiCo. And if you haven't considered this already, be sure to ask several of your professors to write evaluations of your marketing skills. Best of luck to you in your career.

In letters telling job applicants that you will not write a recommendation, use the utmost tact.

This letter deftly and tactfully avoids hurting the reader's feelings, because it makes positive comments about the reader's recent activities, implies the refusal, suggests an alternative, and uses a polite close.

Rejecting Job Applications

Always respond to job applications.

Tactfully telling job applicants that you won't be offering them employment is another frequent communication challenge. But don't let the difficulty stop you from communicating the bad news. Failing to respond to applications is a shoddy business practice that will harm your company's reputation. At the same time, poorly written rejection letters have negative consequences, ranging from the loss of qualified candidates for future openings to the loss of potential customers (not only the rejected applicants but also their friends and family).[14] Poorly phrased rejection letters can even invite legal troubles. When delivering bad news to job applicants, follow three guidelines:[15]

7 LEARNING OBJECTIVE

List three guidelines for delivering negative news to job applicants, and give a brief explanation of each one

- **Open with the direct approach.** Job applicants know they won't get many of the positions they apply for, so negative news is not a shock. By trying to buffer the bad news that your reader is expecting, you will seem manipulative and insincere.[16]
- **Clearly state why the applicant was not selected.** Make your rejection less personal by stating that you hired someone with more experience or whose qualifications match the position requirements more closely.
- **Close by suggesting alternatives.** If you believe the applicant is qualified, mention other openings within your company. You might suggest professional organizations that could help the applicant find employment. Or you might simply mention that the applicant's résumé will be considered for future openings. Any of these positive

suggestions may help the applicant be less disappointed and view your company more positively.

A rejection letter need not be long. Remember, sending a well-written form letter that follows these three guidelines is better than not sending one at all. After all, the applicant wants to know only one thing: Did I land the job? Your brief message conveys the information clearly and with tactful consideration for the applicant's feelings. After Carol DeCicco interviewed with Bradley & Jackson, she was hopeful about receiving a job offer. Everything went well, and her résumé was in good shape. The e-mail in Figure 8.7 was drafted by Marvin Fichter to communicate the bad news to DeCicco. After reviewing the first draft, Ficher made several changes to improve the communication (see Figure 8.8). The revised e-mail helps DeCicco understand that (1) she would have been hired if she'd had more tax experience and (2) she shouldn't be discouraged.

Giving Negative Performance Reviews

A performance review is a manager's evaluation of an employee and may be formal or informal. Few other communication tasks require such a broad range of skills and strategy as those needed for performance reviews. The main purpose of these reviews is to improve employee performance by (1) emphasizing and clarifying job requirements, (2) giving employees feedback on their efforts toward fulfilling those requirements, and (3) guiding continued efforts by developing a plan of action, which includes rewards and opportunities. In addition to improving employee performance, performance reviews help companies set organizational standards and communicate organizational values.[17]

An important goal of any performance evaluation is giving the employee a plan of action for improving his or her performance.

Positive and negative performance reviews share several characteristics: The tone is objective and unbiased, the language is nonjudgmental, and the focus is problem resolution.[18] Also, to increase objectivity, more organizations are giving their employees feedback from multiple sources. In these "360-degree reviews," employees get feedback from all directions in the organization: above, below, and horizontally.[19]

It's difficult to criticize employees face to face, and it's just as hard to include criticism in written performance evaluations. Nevertheless, if you fire an employee for incompetence and the performance evaluations are all positive, the employee can sue your company, maintaining you had no cause to terminate employment.[20] Also, your company could be sued for negligence if an injury is caused by an employee who received a negative evaluation but received no corrective action (such as retraining).[21] So as difficult as it may be, make sure your performance evaluations are well balanced and honest.

When you need to give a negative performance review, follow these guidelines:[22]

- **Confront the problem right away.** Avoiding performance problems only makes them worse. Moreover, if you don't document problems when they occur, you may make it more difficult to terminate employment later on, if the situation comes to that.[23]
- **Plan your message.** Be clear about your concerns, and include examples of the employee's specific actions. Think about any possible biases you may have, and get feedback from others. Collect and verify all relevant facts (both strengths and weaknesses).
- **Deliver the message in private.** Whether in writing or in person, be sure to address the performance problem privately. Don't send performance reviews by e-mail or fax. If you're reviewing an employee's performance face to face, conduct that review in a meeting arranged expressly for that purpose, and consider holding that meeting in a conference room, the employee's office, or some other neutral area.

Address performance problems in private.

- **Focus on the problem.** Discuss the problems caused by the employee's behavior (without attacking the employee). Compare the employee's performance with what's expected, with company goals, or with job requirements (not with the performance of other employees). Identify the consequences of continuing poor performance, and show that you're committed to helping solve the problem.
- **Ask for a commitment from the employee.** Help the employee understand that planning for and making improvements are the employee's responsibility. However, finalize decisions jointly so that you can be sure any action to be taken is achievable. Set a schedule for improvement and for following up with evaluations of that improvement.

FIGURE 8.7 Ineffective E-Mail Rejecting a Job Application

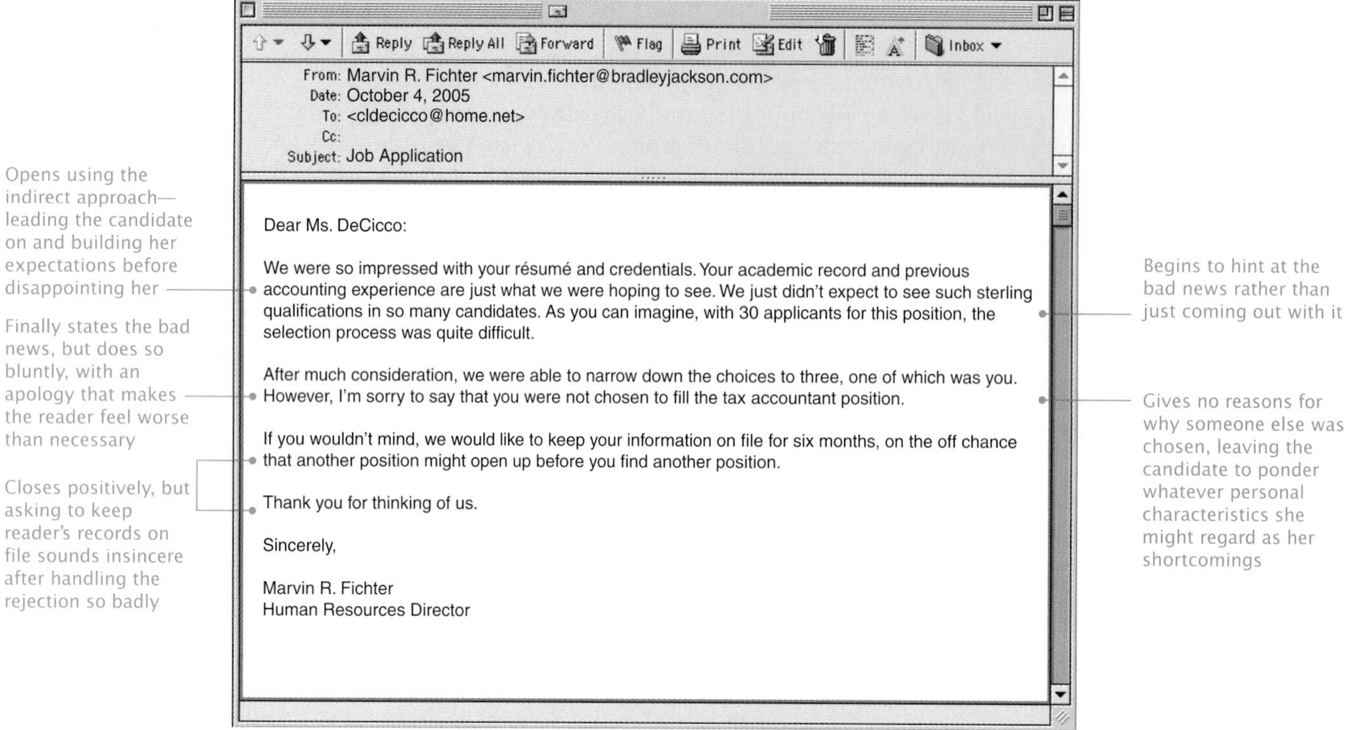

From: Marvin R. Fichter <marvin.fichter@bradleyjackson.com>
Date: October 4, 2005
To: <cldecicco@home.net>
Cc:
Subject: Job Application

Dear Ms. DeCicco:

We were so impressed with your résumé and credentials. Your academic record and previous accounting experience are just what we were hoping to see. We just didn't expect to see such sterling qualifications in so many candidates. As you can imagine, with 30 applicants for this position, the selection process was quite difficult.

After much consideration, we were able to narrow down the choices to three, one of which was you. However, I'm sorry to say that you were not chosen to fill the tax accountant position.

If you wouldn't mind, we would like to keep your information on file for six months, on the off chance that another position might open up before you find another position.

Thank you for thinking of us.

Sincerely,

Marvin R. Fichter
Human Resources Director

Opens using the indirect approach—leading the candidate on and building her expectations before disappointing her
Finally states the bad news, but does so bluntly, with an apology that makes the reader feel worse than necessary
Closes positively, but asking to keep reader's records on file sounds insincere after handling the rejection so badly
Begins to hint at the bad news rather than just coming out with it
Gives no reasons for why someone else was chosen, leaving the candidate to ponder whatever personal characteristics she might regard as her shortcomings

FIGURE 8.8 Effective E-Mail Rejecting a Job Application

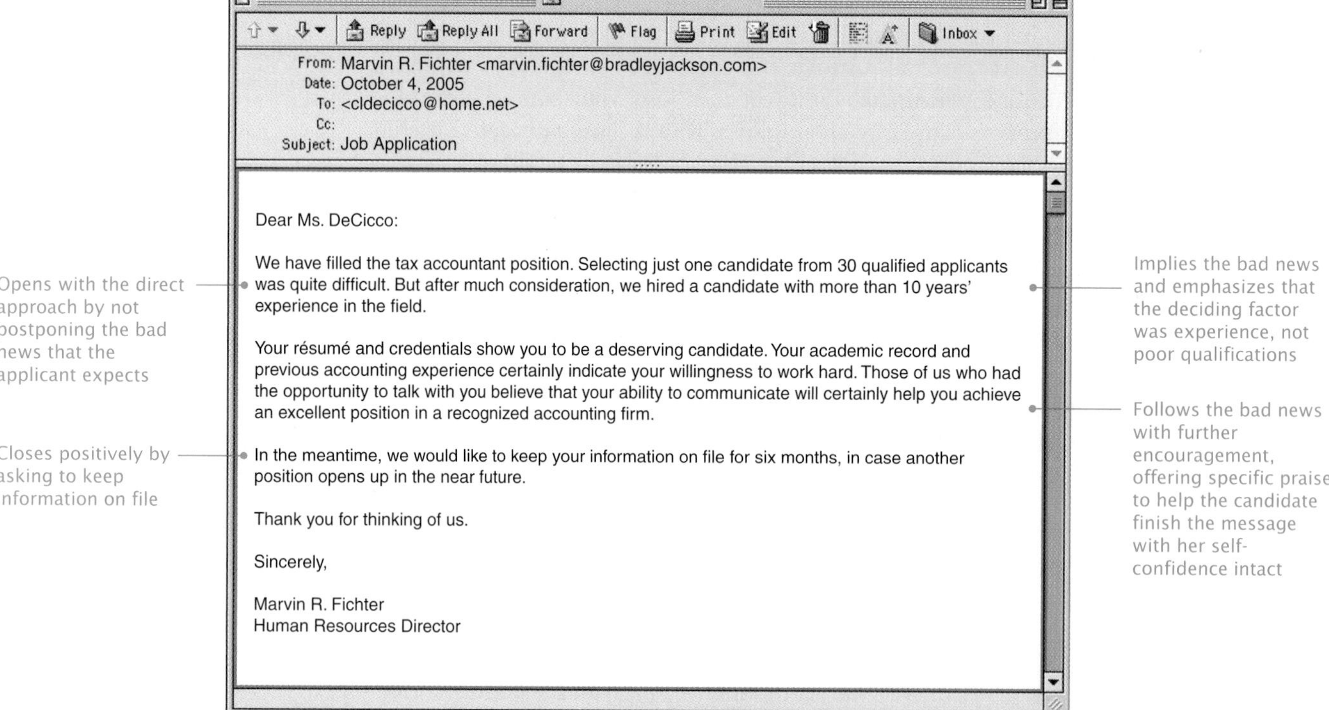

From: Marvin R. Fichter <marvin.fichter@bradleyjackson.com>
Date: October 4, 2005
To: <cldecicco@home.net>
Cc:
Subject: Job Application

Dear Ms. DeCicco:

We have filled the tax accountant position. Selecting just one candidate from 30 qualified applicants was quite difficult. But after much consideration, we hired a candidate with more than 10 years' experience in the field.

Your résumé and credentials show you to be a deserving candidate. Your academic record and previous accounting experience certainly indicate your willingness to work hard. Those of us who had the opportunity to talk with you believe that your ability to communicate will certainly help you achieve an excellent position in a recognized accounting firm.

In the meantime, we would like to keep your information on file for six months, in case another position opens up in the near future.

Thank you for thinking of us.

Sincerely,

Marvin R. Fichter
Human Resources Director

Opens with the direct approach by not postponing the bad news that the applicant expects
Closes positively by asking to keep information on file
Implies the bad news and emphasizes that the deciding factor was experience, not poor qualifications
Follows the bad news with further encouragement, offering specific praise to help the candidate finish the message with her self-confidence intact

Even if your employee's performance has been disappointing, you would do well to begin by mentioning some good points in your performance review. Then clearly and tactfully state how the employee can better meet the responsibilities of the job. If the performance review is to be effective, be sure to suggest ways that the employee can improve.[24] For example, instead of only telling an employee that he damaged some expensive machinery,

CHECKLIST: Negative Employment Messages

A. REFUSING REQUESTS FOR RECOMMENDATION LETTERS

- Don't feel obligated to write a recommendation letter if you don't feel comfortable doing so.
- Take a diplomatic approach to minimize hurt feelings.
- Compliment the reader's accomplishments.
- Suggest alternatives if available.

B. REJECTING JOB APPLICATIONS

- Always respond to applications.
- Use the direct approach.
- Clearly state why the applicant was rejected.
- Suggest alternatives if possible.

C. GIVING NEGATIVE PERFORMANCE REVIEWS

- Maintain an objective and unbiased tone.
- Use nonjudgmental language.
- Focus on problem resolution.
- Make sure negative feedback is documented and shared with the employee.
- Don't avoid confrontations by withholding negative feedback.
- Ask the employee for a commitment to improve.

D. TERMINATING EMPLOYMENT

- State your reasons accurately and make sure they are objectively verifiable.
- Avoid statements that might expose your company to a wrongful termination lawsuit.
- Consult company lawyers to clarify all terms of the separation.
- End the relationship on terms as positive as possible.

suggest that he take a refresher course in the correct operation of that machinery. The goal is to help the employee succeed.

Terminating Employment

Carefully word a termination letter to avoid creating undue ill will and grounds for legal action.

When writing a termination letter, you have three goals: (1) present the reasons for this difficult action, (2) avoid statements that might expose the company to a wrongful termination lawsuit, and (3) leave the relationship between the terminated employee and the firm as favorable as possible. For both legal and personal reasons, present specific justification for asking the employee to leave.[25] If the employee is working under contract, your company's lawyers will be able to tell you whether the employee's performance is legal grounds for termination.

Make sure that all your reasons are accurate and verifiable. Avoid words that are open to interpretation, such as *untidy* and *difficult.* Make sure the employee leaves with feelings that are as positive as the circumstances allow. You can do so by telling the truth about the termination and by helping as much as you can to make the employee's transition as smooth as possible.[26] To review the tasks involved in this type of message, see "Checklist: Negative Employment Messages."

COMMUNICATION CHALLENGES AT AGILENT TECHNOLOGIES

Agilent returned to profitability in late 2003 and eventually resumed hiring. You landed a job in the company's Corporate Communications group in Palo Alto, California, and are now responsible for handling Ned Barnholt's routine correspondence with people outside the company.

Individual Challenge: Today, Agilent is thriving and its growth has been covered widely in the business press. As a result, several universities are now asking Barnholt to speak at their graduation ceremonies. One invitation is from the president of your alma mater but, unfortunately, Barnholt will be in Japan that week. You've been asked to write a letter that declines the invitation but suggests another Agilent executive as speaker. You also learn that Barnholt and the school president attended Stanford University together. Should you use a direct or an indirect approach for your reply? Choose an approach and draft the refusal letter.

Team Challenge: Agilent has decided to sell its medical products group to Philips Electronics. One part of this group, the Heartstream division, was originally an independent company, then was acquired by HP, then spun off with Agilent, and now sold to Philips—its third owner in just a few years. With a small group, discuss the best way for Barnholt to tell Heartstream about the sale. Develop a list of the pros and cons of Barnholt's visiting the Heartstream offices in Seattle to deliver the message in person.

SUMMARY OF LEARNING OBJECTIVES

1 **Apply the three-step writing process to negative messages.** Because the way you say no can be far more damaging than the fact that you're saying it, planning your negative messages is crucial. Make sure your purpose is specific, necessary, and appropriate for written media. Find out how your audience prefers to receive bad news. Collect all the facts necessary to support your negative decision, and adapt your tone to the situation as well as to your audience. Negative messages may be organized according to the direct or the indirect approach, and your choice depends on audience preference as well as on the situation. In addition, carefully choose positive words to construct diplomatic sentences. Finally, revision, design, and proofreading are necessary to ensure that you are saying exactly what you want to say in the best possible way.

2 **Explain the differences between the direct and the indirect approaches to negative messages, including when it's appropriate to use each one.** The direct approach to negative messages puts the bad news up front, follows with the reasons (and perhaps offers an alternative), and closes with a positive statement. On the other hand, the indirect approach begins with a buffer (a neutral or positive statement), explains the reasons, clearly states the negative news (de-emphasizing it as much as possible), and closes with a positive statement. It's best to use the direct approach when you know your audience prefers receiving bad news up front or if the bad news will cause readers little pain or disappointment. Otherwise, the indirect approach is best.

3 **Identify the risks of using the indirect approach, and explain how to avoid such problems.** The indirect approach needs careful attention to avoid obscuring the bad news or misleading your audience into thinking you're actually delivering good news. The key to avoiding both problems is remembering that the purpose of the indirect approach is to cushion the blow, not to avoid delivering it. If you choose to start with a buffer, you must be sure it is neither deceptive nor insincere. If there's a risk it might be easier, skip the buffer entirely. To write an effective buffer, look for opportunities to express your appreciation for being considered, to assure your reader of your attention to the request, or to indicate your understanding of the reader's needs.

4 **Adapt your messages for internal and external audiences.** The key point to remember when considering internal versus external audiences is the issue of expectations. Internal audiences expect to get more detail in most cases, including information on how negative news affects their jobs. When messages will be sent to both internal and external audiences, internal audiences also expect to receive the message before it is sent to external audiences so they have time to prepare if necessary. Conversely, messages to external audiences may need a wider range of adaptation, given the diverse nature of many external audiences.

5 **Define *defamation* and explain how to avoid it in negative messages.** Defamation is a false statement that is damaging to a person's character or reputation. When written, defamation is called libel. When spoken, it's called slander. To avoid being accused of defamation, (1) never use abusive language, (2) express personal opinions without involving your company (using your own personal letterhead and excluding your title or position), (3) stick to the facts, (4) never write a message in anger, (5) seek legal advice about questionable messages, and (6) communicate honestly.

6 **Explain the role of communication in crisis management.** Preparation is key for successful crisis management. Although you can't anticipate the nature and circumstance of every possible crisis, you can prepare by deciding such issues as who is charge of communications, where the press and the public can get information, and what will be said in likely emergency scenarios. Rumor control is another important aspect; with the advent of instant messaging, text messaging on mobile phones, television, and other rapid communication vehicles, incorrect information can spread worldwide in seconds. A good crisis communication plan will also include such items as e-mail and phone lists for important media contacts, website templates for various emergency scenarios, and after-hours contact information for key personnel in the company.

7 List three guidelines for delivering bad news to job applicants, and give a brief explanation of each one. When rejecting job applicants, follow three guidelines: (1) Use the direct approach. Your readers probably assume that a letter from you is bad news, so don't build their suspense. (2) State clearly why your reader was not selected. This explanation can be specific without being personal if you explain that you hired someone with more experience or with qualifications that more closely match position requirements. (3) Suggest alternatives. Perhaps your company has other openings or you would be willing to consider the applicant for future openings.

Test Your Knowledge

1. What are the five main goals in delivering bad news?
2. Why is it particularly important to adapt your medium and tone to your audience's needs and preferences when writing a negative message?
3. What are the advantages of using the direct approach to deliver the negative news at the beginning of a message?
4. What is the sequence of elements in a negative message organized using the indirect approach?
5. What is a buffer, and why do some critics consider it unethical?
6. When using an indirect approach to announce a negative decision, what is the purpose of presenting your reasons before explaining the decision itself?
7. What are three techniques for de-emphasizing negative news?
8. What is defamation, and how does libel differ from slander?
9. What are three guidelines for writing rejection letters to job applicants?
10. When giving a negative review to an employee, what five steps should you follow?

Apply Your Knowledge

1. Why is it important to end your negative message on a positive note? Explain.
2. If company policy changes, should you explain those changes to employees and customers at about the same time, or should you explain them to employees first? Why?
3. If the purpose of your letter is to convey bad news, should you take the time to suggest alternatives to your reader? Why or why not?
4. When a company suffers a setback, should you soften the impact by letting out the bad news a little at a time? Why or why not?
5. **Ethical Choices** Is intentionally de-emphasizing bad news the same as distorting graphs and charts to de-emphasize unfavorable data? Why or why not?

Practice Your Knowledge

Documents for Analysis

Read the following documents, then (1) analyze the strengths and weaknesses of each sentence, and (2) revise each document so that it follows this chapter's guidelines.

Document 8.A: Providing Bad News About Products

Your spring fraternity party sounds like fun. We're glad you've again chosen us as your caterer. Unfortunately, we have changed a few of our policies, and I wanted you to know about these changes in advance so that we won't have any misunderstandings on the day of the party.

We will arrange the delivery of tables and chairs as usual the evening before the party. However, if you want us to set up, there is now a $100 charge for that service. Of course, you might want to get some of the brothers and pledges to do it, which would save you money. We've also added a small charge for cleanup. This is only $3 per person (you can estimate because I know a lot of people come and go later in the evening).

Other than that, all the arrangements will be the same. We'll provide the skirting for the band stage, tablecloths, bar setup, and, of course, the barbecue. Will you have the tubs of ice with soft drinks again? We can do that for you as well, but there will be a fee.

Please let me know if you have any problems with these changes and we'll try to work them out. I know it's going to be a great party.

Document 8.B: Refusing Requests for Claims and Adjustments

I am responding to your letter of about six weeks ago asking for an adjustment on your wireless hub, model WM39Z. We test all our products before they leave the factory; therefore, it could not have been our fault that your hub didn't work.

If you or someone in your office dropped the unit, it might have caused the damage. Or the damage could have been caused by the shipper if he dropped it. If so, you should file a claim with the shipper. At any rate, it wasn't our fault. The parts are already covered by warranty. However, we will provide labor for the repairs for $50, which is less than our cost, since you are a valued customer.

We will have a booth at the upcoming trade show there and hope to see you or someone from your office. We have many new models of office machines that we're sure you'll want to see. I've enclosed our latest catalog. Hope to see you there.

Document 8.C: Rejecting Job Applications

I regret to inform you that you were not selected for our summer intern program at Equifax. We had over a thousand résumés and cover letters to go through and simply could not get to them all. We have been asked to notify everyone that we have already selected students for the 25 positions based on those who applied early and were qualified.

We're sure you will be able to find a suitable position for summer work in your field and wish you the best of luck. We deeply regret any inconvenience associated with our reply.

Exercises

For live links to all websites discussed in this chapter, visit this text's website at www.prenhall.com/bovee. Just log on, select Chapter 8, and click on "Featured Websites." Locate the page or the URL related to the material in the text.

8.1 Selecting the Approach Select which approach you would use (direct or indirect) for the following negative messages:

a. A memo to your boss informing her that one of your key clients is taking its business to a different accounting firm

b. An e-mail message to a customer informing her that one of the books she ordered over the Internet is temporarily out of stock

c. A letter to a customer explaining that the DVD recorder he ordered for his new computer is on back order and that, as a consequence, the shipping of the entire order will be delayed

d. A memo to all employees notifying them that the company parking lot will be repaved during the first week of June and that the company will provide a shuttle service from a remote parking lot during that period

e. A letter from a travel agent to a customer stating that the airline will not refund her money for the flight she missed but that her tickets are valid for one year

f. A form letter from a U.S. airline to a customer explaining that they cannot extend the expiration date of the customer's frequent flyer miles even though the customer was living overseas for the past three years

g. A letter from an insurance company to a policyholder denying a claim for reimbursement for a special medical procedure that is not covered under the terms of the customer's policy

h. A letter from an electronics store stating that the customer will not be reimbursed for a malfunctioning cell phone still under warranty (the terms of the warranty do not cover damages to phones that were accidentally placed in the freezer overnight)

i. An announcement to the repairs department listing parts that are on back order and will be three weeks late

8.2 **Teamwork** Working alone, revise the following statements to de-emphasize the bad news. (*Hint:* Minimize the space devoted to the bad news, subordinate it, embed it, or use the passive voice.) Then team up with a classmate and read each other's revisions. Did you both use the same approach in every case? Which approach seems to be most effective for each of the revised statements?

a. The airline can't refund your money. The "Conditions" segment on the back of your ticket states that there are no refunds for missed flights. Sometimes the airline makes exceptions, but only when life and death are involved. Of course, your ticket is still valid and can be used on a flight to the same destination.

b. I'm sorry to tell you, we can't supply the custom decorations you requested. We called every supplier and none of them can do what you want on such short notice. You can, however, get a standard decorative package on the same theme in time. I found a supplier that stocks these. Of course, it won't have quite the flair you originally requested.

c. We can't refund your money for the malfunctioning lamp. You shouldn't have placed a 250-watt bulb in the fixture socket; it's guaranteed for a maximum of 75 watts.

8.3 **Using Buffers** As a customer service supervisor for a telephone company, you're in charge of responding to customers' requests for refunds. You've just received an e-mail from a customer who unwittingly ran up a $500 bill for long-distance calls after mistakenly configuring his laptop computer to dial an Internet access number that wasn't a local call. The customer says it wasn't his fault because he didn't realize he was dialing a long-distance number. However, you've dealt with this situation before; you know that the customer's Internet service provider warns its customers to choose a local access number, since customers are responsible for all long-distance charges. Draft a short buffer (1 to 2 sentences) for your e-mail reply, sympathizing with the customer's plight but preparing him for the bad news (company policy specifically prohibits refunds in such cases).

8.4 **Internet** Public companies occasionally need to issue news releases announcing or explaining downturns in sales, profits, demand, or other business factors. Search the Web to locate a company that has issued a press release that recently reported lower earnings or other bad news, and access the news release on that firm's website. Alternatively, find the type of press release you're seeking by reviewing press releases at www.prnewswire.com or www.businesswire.com. How does the headline relate to the main message of the release? Is the release organized according to the direct or the indirect approach? What does the company do to present the bad news in a favorable light—and does this effort seem sincere and ethical to you?

8.5 **Ethical Choices** The insurance company where you work is planning to raise all premiums for health-care coverage. Your boss has asked you to read a draft of her letter to customers announcing the new, higher rates. The first two paragraphs discuss some exciting medical advances and the expanded coverage offered by your company. Only in the final paragraph do customers learn that they will have to pay more for coverage starting next year. What are the ethical implications of this draft? What changes would you suggest?

Expand Your Knowledge

For live links to the websites that follow, go to www.prenhall.com/bovee. When you log on, select Chapter 8, then select "Featured Websites," click on the URL of the website you wish to visit, and review the website to complete these exercises.

Exploring the Best of the Web

Protect Yourself When Sending Negative Employment Messages
www.toolkit.cch.com

A visit to CCH's Business Owner's Toolkit can help you reduce your legal liability, whether you are laying off an employee, firing an employee, or contemplating a company-wide reduction in your workforce. Find out the safest way to fire someone from a legal standpoint before it's too late. Learn why it's important to document disciplinary actions. Discover why some bad news should be given face to face and never by a letter or over the phone. Read CCH's advice, and then answer these questions.

1. What should a manager communicate to an employee during a termination meeting?
2. Why is it important to document employee disciplinary actions?
3. What steps should you take before firing an employee for misconduct or poor work?

Exploring the Web on Your Own

Review these chapter-related websites on your own to learn more about the negative issues human resources departments are facing today.

1. Workforce magazine online, www.workforce.com, has the basics and the latest on human resource issues such as recruiting, laws, managing the workforce, incentives, strategies, and more. Read the current edition online.
2. HR.com, www4.hr.com, is the place to go to read about workplace trends, legislation affecting employers, recruiting, compensation, benefits, staffing, and more. Log on and learn.
3. BusinessTown.com, www.businesstown.com, offers information on a wide range of business topics, including advice on conducting successful employee performance reviews.

Learn Interactively

Interactive Study Guide

Go to the Companion Website at www.prenhall.com/bovee. For Chapter 8, take advantage of the interactive "Study Guide" to test your knowledge of the chapter. Get instant feedback on whether you need additional studying.

Also, visit this site's "Study Hall," where you'll find an abundance of valuable resources that will help you succeed in this course.

Peak Performance Grammar and Mechanics

To improve your skill with commas, semicolons, and colons, visit www.prenhall.com/onekey, click "Peak Performance Grammar and Mechanics," click "Punctuation," then click "Punctuation I." Take the Pretest to determine whether you have any weak areas. Then review those areas in the Refresher Course. Take the Follow-Up Test to check your grasp of commas, semicolons, and colons. For an extra challenge or advanced practice, take the Advanced Test. Finally, for additional reinforcement in commas, go to www.prenhall.com/bovee, where you will find "Improve Your Grammar, Mechanics, and Usage" exercises.

CASES

Applying the Three-Step Writing Process to Cases

Apply each step to the following cases, as assigned by your instructor.

Plan

Analyze the Situation
Identify both your general purpose and your specific purpose. Clarify exactly what you want your audience to think, feel, or believe after receiving your message. Profile your primary audience, including their backgrounds, differences, similarities, and likely reactions to your message.

Gather Information
Identify the information your audience will need to receive, as well as other information you may need in order to craft an effective message.

Select the Right Medium
Make sure your medium is both acceptable to the audience and appropriate for the message. Realize that written media are inappropriate for some negative messages.

Organize the Information
Choose a direct or indirect approach based on the audience and the message; many negative messages are best delivered with an indirect approach. If you use the indirect approach, carefully consider which type of buffer is best for the situation. Identify your main idea, limit your scope, and then outline necessary support points and other evidence.

1

Write

Adapt to Your Audience
Show sensitivity to audience needs with a "you" attitude, politeness, positive emphasis, and bias-free language. Understand how much credibility you already have—and how much you may need to establish. Project your company's image by maintaining an appropriate style and tone. Consider cultural variations and the differing needs of internal and external audiences.

Compose the Message
Draft your message using clear but sensitive words, effective sentences, and coherent paragraphs.

2

Complete

Revise the Message
Evaluate content and review readability; then edit and rewrite for conciseness and clarity.

Produce the Message
Use effective design elements and suitable layout for a clean, professional appearance.

Proofread the Message
Review for errors in layout, spelling, and mechanics.

Distribute the Message
Deliver your message using the chosen medium; make sure all documents and all relevant files are distributed successfully.

3

NEGATIVE REPLIES TO ROUTINE REQUESTS

1. No deal: Letter from Home Depot to faucet manufacturer As assistant to the vice president of sales for Atlanta-based Home Depot, you attended Home Depot's biannual product-line review, held at Tropicana Field in St. Petersburg, Florida. Also attending were hundreds of vendor hopefuls, eager to become one of the huge retail chain's 25,303 North American suppliers. During individual meetings with a panel of regional and national Home Depot merchandisers, these vendors did their best to win, keep, or expand their spot in the company's product lineup.

Vendors know that Home Depot holds all the cards, so if they want to play, they have to follow Home Depot rules, offering low wholesale prices and swift delivery. Once chosen, they're constantly re-evaluated—and quickly dropped for infractions such as requesting a price increase or planning to sell directly to consumers via the Internet. They also receive sharp critiques of past performance, which are not to be taken lightly.

A decade ago, General Electric failed to keep Home Depot stores supplied with light bulbs, causing shortages. Co-founder Bernard Marcus immediately stripped GE of its exclusive, 80-foot shelf-space and flew off to negotiate with its Netherlands competitor, Phillips. Two years later, after high-level negotiations, GE bulbs were back on Home Depot shelves—but in a position inferior to Phillips's.

Such cautionary tales aren't lost on vendors. But they know that despite tough negotiating, Home Depot is always looking for variety to please its customers' changing tastes and demands. The sales potential is so enormous that the compromises and concessions are worthwhile. If selected, vendors get immediate distribution in more than 1,700 stores (Home Depot, EXPO, and other subsidiary companies) across the United States, Canada, Mexico, and Puerto Rico.

Still, you've seen the stress on vendor reps' faces as they explain product enhancements and on-time delivery ideas in the review sessions. Their only consolation for this grueling process is that, although merchandisers won't say yes or no on the spot, they do let manufacturers know where they stand within a day or two. And the company is always willing to reconsider at the next product-line review—wherever it's held.

Your task: You're drafting some of the rejection letters, and the next one on your stack is to a faucet manufacturer, Roseway Manufacturing, 133 Industrial Ave., Gary, IN 46406. "Too expensive," "substandard plastic handles," and "a design not likely to appeal to Home Depot customers," say the panel's notes. (And knowing what its customers want has put Home Depot in the top 10 of the Fortune 500 list, with $40 billion in annual sales.) Find a way to soften the blow in your rejection letter to Roseway. After all, consumer tastes do change. Direct your letter to Pamela Wilson, operations manager.[27]

2. Suffering artists: Memo declining high-tech shoes at American Ballet Theatre Here at the American Ballet Theatre (ABT), where you're serving as assistant to Artistic Director Kevin McKenzie, the notion of suffering for the art form has been ingrained since the early 1800s, when the first ballerina rose up *en pointe.* Many entrepreneurs are viewing this painful situation with hopeful enthusiasm, especially when they discover that dancers worldwide spend about $150 million annually on their shoes—those "tiny torture chambers" of cardboard and satin (with glued linen or burlap to stiffen the toes). The pink monstrosities (about $50 a pair) rarely last beyond a single hard performance.

A company the size of ABT spends about $500,000 a year on point shoes—plus the cost of their staff physical therapist and all those trips to chiropractors, podiatrists, and surgeons to relieve bad necks, backs, knees, and feet. Entrepreneurs believe there must be room for improvement, given the current advantages of orthopedics, space-age materials, and high-tech solutions for contemporary athletes. There's no denying that ballerinas are among the hardest-working athletes in the world.

The latest entrepreneur to approach ABT is Eliza Minden of Gaynor Minden, Inc. She wants to provide a solution to the shoe problem. She approached Michael Kaiser, executive director and a member of ABT's Board of Governing Trustees, with a proposal for providing new, high-performance pointe shoes in exchange for an endorsement.

Minden's alternative pointe shoes offer high-impact support and toe cushions. They're only $90 a pair, and supposedly they can be blow dried (like Birkenstocks) back into shape after a performance. When the cost-conscious board member urged the company to give them a try, you were assigned to collect feedback from dancers.

So far, not so good. For example, after a brief trial one principal ballerina said she'd rather numb her feet in icy water, dance through "zingers" of toe pain, and make frequent visits to the physical therapist than wear Minden's shoes. The majority of others agree. Apparently, they *like* breaking in the traditional satin models with hammers and door slams and throwing them away after a single *Coppelia.* Too stiff, they say of the new shoes, and besides, they're simply not the shoes they grew up with and trained in. Only a few of the company's newest members, such as Gillian Murphy, liked Minden's high-tech shoes. That's not enough for a company endorsement.

You've seen those sinewy, wedge-shaped feet bleeding backstage. You feel sorry for Minden; it *was* a good idea—just a hard sell among the tradition-oriented dancers.

Your task: McKenzie has asked you to write an internal memo in his name to Michael Kaiser, executive director of the American Ballet Theatre, explaining the dancers' refusal to use the new high-tech Gaynor Minden pointe shoes. In your memo be sure to include the dancers' reasons as well as your own opinion regarding the matter. You'll need to decide whether to use the direct or the indirect approach; include a separate short note to your instructor justifying your selection of approach.[28]

3. Cyber-surveillance: Memo refusing claim from Silent Watch victim Your business is called Advertising Inflatables, and your specialty is designing and building the huge balloon replicas used for advertising atop retail stores, tire outlets, used car lots, fast-food outlets, fitness clubs, etc. You've built balloon re-creations of everything from a 50-foot King Kong to a "small" 10-foot pizza.

Not long ago, you installed the "cyber-surveillance" software, Silent Watch, to track and record employees' computer usage. At the time, you sent out a memo informing all employees that they should limit their computer use and e-mail to work projects only. You also informed them that their work would be monitored. You did not mention that Silent Watch would record every keystroke

of their work or that they could be monitored from a screen in your office.

As expected, Silent Watch caught two of the sales staff spending between 50 and 70 percent of their time surfing Internet sites unrelated to their jobs. You withheld their pay accordingly, without warning. You sent them a memo notifying them that they were not fired but were on probation. You considered this wise, because when they work, both employees are very good at what they do, and talent is hard to find.

But now salesman Jarod Harkington has sent you a letter demanding reinstatement of his pay and claiming he was "spied on illegally." On the contrary, company attorneys have assured you that the courts almost always side with employers on this issue, particularly after employees receive a warning such as the one you wrote. The computer equipment belongs to Advertising Inflatables, and employees are paid a fair price for their time.

Your task: Write a letter refusing Mr. Harkington's claim.[29]

4. Please try again: Letter from Ultra-Light Touring Shop about an incomplete order Manufacturer Chuck Harris didn't just talk about the need to recycle, to save the environment, and to use energy-saving transportation methods. He invested his creativity in a unique business—one you joined six months ago.

Harris owns the Ultra-Light Touring Shop in Gambier, Ohio, where he manufactures the kind of bicycle mirror that clips to a bike helmet or to a pair of eyeglasses so that riders can see what's coming up behind or beside them. But he makes his octagonal, 1-inch mirrors entirely from recycled materials, such as old bicycle spokes, plastic tubing from coat hangers, and aluminum and plastic litter culled from Ohio roadsides. He also shapes and polishes them on a pedal-powered grinder to save fuel, and ships them out in used, custom-shrunk plastic soda bottles.

After a glowing feature in *Garbage* magazine, orders for Harris's hand-made mirrors started pouring in from around the world, so he hired you to handle the customer communications. Trouble is, many of the orders don't include everything you need to know. For instance, you're looking at a message from Harold Lightwater in Reading, England. He got the prices right, and despite security risks, included his credit card number. He gave you his shipping address, but he didn't specify whether he wants his two mirrors to clip onto eyeglasses or helmets. He also failed to mention whether he prefers the standard embossed bicycle design on the mirror back, or whether he wants to take advantage of Harris's offer to emboss any design a customer requests.

Your task: Since Harris prefers snail mail and telephones, draft a bad-news letter informing Harold Lightwater (11 Moor Copse Close, Reading RG6 2NA, United Kingdom) that you can't ship his order until he clarifies his preferences.[30]

5. Navajo Joe's: Letter rejecting interior design proposal Atmosphere is everything at Navajo Joe's coffeehouse in Window Rock, Arizona, in the middle of a Navajo reservation the size of West Virginia. "We've got Starbucks and Hank Williams," brags owner Manny Wheeler, a 26-year-old art history graduate of Arizona State University who grew up on the "big rez." While a student, Wheeler used to hang out in coffeehouses all over Phoenix. When he came home, he took odd jobs but kept fine-tuning his business plan all the while. He knew Navajos loved their coffee as much as their fry bread, but as far as he was aware, nothing resembling an urban-style coffeehouse existed on any reservation. Finally, with a loan from his aunt, furniture from second-hand stores, and decor consisting of Wheeler's original art and cast-offs (an old saddle, rotting wagon harness, and so on) from his grandmother's yard, Navajo Joe's was born.

Wheeler has just hired you for your summer break from business school, and he's showing you around the place.

"I like the colors," says the 29-year-old musician whose band, Burn in Effigy, plays here on weekends. You look up at the black ceiling and yellow walls, then at the arrow holes in the back wall (no, not a sign of Navajo history, but left over from the archery store that once filled the space). One of Wheeler's paintings catches your eye: a black and gray abstract of a bronc rider painted on a slab of cardboard. "That's my Cubist phase," Wheeler explains. Another wall features Johnny Cash album covers and weird tabloid headlines: "Nude Sunbathers Attacked by Crazed Sea Gulls!" You can't help noticing the music; sometimes it's country and western, sometimes surf music, sometimes Native American music.

"I look at this coffeehouse as an art piece," Wheeler explains proudly. "You keep adding to it until you have a sense of what works."

Somehow Wheeler is appealing to Navajos of all generations. For the younger crowd, it's double lattes with a splash of hazelnut and late-night chess games. For the old timers, Wheeler keeps a warm pot of Farmer Bros. on hand. It works like a charm.

At the end of your first week, a pair of business partners from Albuquerque had heard of Wheeler's success and dropped by. Luther and Marilyn Busby own Native Design, a big-city interior-decorating firm that specializes in Southwestern decor for businesses. They loved Wheeler's operation and insisted on presenting him with a "cost-effective" proposal for sprucing up Navajo Joe's decor. "You'll triple your business," they assured him enthusiastically. You held your breath, but Wheeler was polite. He drawled, "Sure . . . send me a proposal."

Your task: The written proposal finally arrived and Wheeler's reaction was exactly as you expected. But what you didn't plan for was his insistence that you write the rejection letter. "You're a business student, aren't you?" he winks. "Tell 'em they don't know a thing about business on the rez . . . or whatever you think is an appropriate way to say, 'Not in my lifetime!'"[31]

6. Too anomalous: E-mail declining an invitation from the Disclosure Project As president of the Mid-State Flying Club, your job is to entice pilots to join your organization, which offers discounted flying lessons and plane rentals. Like most pilots, you're interested in anomalous aerial phenomena, but two club members have been pressuring you to sponsor an event you're just not comfortable with.

Both members are retired military pilots, and they volunteer for the Disclosure Project, a nonprofit research organization founded by Dr. Steven Greer. Once an emergency room physician, Greer gave up his doctor's salary to help document more than 400 "top-secret military, government, and other witnesses of UFO and extraterrestrial events." You watched the Project's videotape, and you were intrigued to see witnesses with impressive titles and affiliations discussing UFOs, secret government "black projects," and amazing technologies. One Disclosure Project goal is to convince Congress to hold open hearings and another is to release all information on "extraterrestrial technologies."

Apparently, your club members sent your club's contact information to Greer's Virginia headquarters, because now you've received an e-mail from him, inviting Mid-State to sponsor next week's free public "Campaign for Disclosure" event in Phoenix.

Your task: You're impressed by this businesslike effort to treat anomalous aerial phenomena seriously, but you're worried about the club's reputation. The last thing you want to hear is airport scuttlebutt about "those kooks over in Hangar 5." Keeping your personal views private, refuse the sponsorship invitation in a courteous e-mail to Dr. Steven Greer, inquiries@disclosureproject.org.[32]

7. Not this time: Letter denying debit adjustments to Union Bank of California customer You are an operations officer in the ATM Error Resolution Department at Union Bank of California. Your department often adjusts customer accounts for ATM debit errors. Mistakes are usually honest ones—such as a merchant swiping a customer's check debit card two or three times, thinking the first few swipes didn't "take," when they actually did.

Customers having problems on their statements are instructed to write a claim letter to your department that describes the situation and includes copies of receipts. Customers are notified of the outcome within 10 to 20 business days. Usually, you credit their account.

However, you've received a letter from Margaret Caldwell, who maintains several hefty joint accounts with her husband at your bank. Three debits to her checking account were processed on the same day and credited to the same market, Wilson's Gourmet. The debits carry the same transaction reference number, 1440022-22839837109, which is what caught Mrs. Caldwell's attention. But you know that number changes daily, not hourly, so multiple purchases made on the same day often carry the same number. Also, the debits are for different amounts ($23.02, $110.95, and $47.50), so these transactions were not a result of repeated card swipes. No receipts were enclosed.

Mrs. Caldwell writes that the store was trying to steal from her, but you doubt that and decide to contact Wilson's Gourmet. Manager Ronson Tibbits tells you that he's had no problems with his equipment, He also mentions that food shoppers commonly return at different times during the day to make additional purchases, particularly for beverages or merchandise they forgot the first time.

You decide that these charges did not the result from a bank or merchant error. It doesn't matter whether Mrs. Caldwell is merely confused or trying to commit an intentional fraud. Bank rules are clear for this situation: You must politely deny her request.

Your task: Write a letter to Margaret Caldwell, 2789 Aviara Pky., Carlsbad, CA 92008, explaining your refusal of her claim #7899. Keep in mind that you don't want to lose this wealthy customer's business.[33]

NEGATIVE ORGANIZATIONAL NEWS

8. More layoffs: Memo to Motorola employees "Success is a journey, not a destination," Motorola chairman and chief executive Christopher B. Galvin said a few years ago. That was when the battered company his grandfather started in 1928 first began its yo-yo pattern of rises and falls in profitability, reflecting big upsets in the markets it serves as manufacturer of semiconductors, cellular telephones, and other communications equipment.

Galvin turned the company upside down to keep it alive. You weren't a vice president at the Schaumburg, Illinois, headquarters at that time, but you are now—the result of much restructuring, plant closings, layoffs, and determined analysis of the world markets for high-tech communications. You were one of the lucky ones. Instead of being laid off, you rose to become director of technology and manufacturing. Others weren't so lucky. In one year alone, Galvin's company cut more than 30,000 jobs in its quest to modernize, streamline, and bring inventories down to realistic levels.

To keep up with competitors and respond quickly to changing consumer demand, Galvin's has already taken steps to reinvent Motorola's corporate culture. He's been transforming the company's cutthroat rivalry among executives into a new culture that rewards what might be called "cooperation for survival." But sales of cell phones and semiconductors have been sharply down for the past few years, and Motorola has been feeling the crunch—along with competitors and business partners such as Nokia, Cisco Systems, 3Com, and others. Galvin must do more to cut production, operating budgets, and inventory. Motorola must close and consolidate plant operations, make fewer but better products, and ultimately, eliminate jobs.

The good news is that Galvin's strategies are apparently working. Even more promising, the cell phone business has begun to rebound, a sign that Motorola may return to profitability soon. Financial analysts are hopeful. It may still be a roller-coaster ride for a while, but bets are on that Motorola will rise again.

You must announce another round of closings: two wafer fabrication lines at the Mesa, Arizona, plant. The phase-out will take place over the next two years, shutting down the MOS-6 line and Bipolar Manufacturing Center and affecting 1,200 employees.

Many of them will be offered positions at other Motorola plants in the Phoenix area—but not all. This consolidation is part of the continuing "manufacturing renewal process to improve asset management by investing in advanced technologies and consolidating older production facilities." That's what you're planning to tell the financial media.

Your task: Write the memo to employees in the Mesa, Arizona, plant. Use all the good communication techniques you can muster to make this difficult reality more palatable. Unfortunately, decisions about who will lose their jobs and who won't are currently unavailable. Such details will be released slowly over the next few months, on a case-by-case basis.[34]

9. Low-carb impact: E-mail announcing losses and new products at Monterey Pasta As marketing planning manager for Monterey Pasta Company, you're responsible for spotting social trends that could affect your company. Months ago, you suggested that your employer seriously consider the new low-carb diet craze, but your colleagues thought you were exaggerating the impact this trend would have on pasta sales. Now the figures bear you out: nationwide pasta sales have fallen dramatically as dieters in record numbers are avoiding high-carbohydrate and especially flour-based foods.

At Wal-Mart and Costco, the warehouse-style retail stores that make up Monterey Pasta's largest buyers, sales plummeted nearly 30 percent in the last few months. Your company is not alone; other traditional pasta makers are also showing losses because of the new diet preferences. In contrast, your major competitor, American Italian Pasta, introduced a line of low-carb pastas months ago. Their sales are still climbing.

Now management has asked you to issue a revised forecast for fourth-quarter earnings. Previous predictions were for fourth-quarter sales to increase over last year's figures by 7 to 10 percent. Today's forecast from chief financial officer Scott S. Wheeler is for a 3 to 5 percent *decrease* in revenue from last year's fourth-quarter earnings.

However, in the same message, management wants you to announce the release of Monterey Pasta's new "CARB-SMART line of fresh pastas, sauces, and prepared entrees. In a company meeting, Monterey Pasta president and CEO Jim Williams announced, "Americans love fresh pasta, but the current wave of low-carb diets has many consumers watching the amount of carbohydrates they consume. CARB-SMART responds to that trend by delivering the flavor and convenience of traditional fresh pasta, but with half the carbs. So carb-counting pasta lovers can now have their ravioli ... and eat it, too."

The new products include three prepared ravioli varieties, plus tortellini, linguine, fettucine, and a new low-carb, four-cheese sauce. Complete CARB-SMART product information will be posted on the Monterey Pasta website, www.montereypasta.com.

Your task: Write an e-mail to announce both the good news and the bad news. Your message will go to shareholders, retail customers, distributors, and other interested parties.[35]

10. Watch for symptoms: Memo at GTE announcing hepatitis outbreak Dr. Frank Provato, GTE's medical director, looks grim as he addresses the group of executives assembled for the Monday morning staff meeting. "We have another confirmed case of hepatitis," he says. "That brings the total to four. The city health department has traced the problem to a cafeteria worker who's employed by ARA Services, the food-vending contractor that supplies our cafeteria. We have to assume that anyone who has eaten in the cafeteria in the last month has been exposed to the virus. That means just about all 700 employees here at corporate headquarters could come down with the disease."

"Just how serious is this?" the human resources director wants to know.

"Pretty serious. The city health department thinks the virus is hepatitis A. That's good news and bad news. People don't usually die from hepatitis A, but it's the most contagious of the strains."

"So what should we do?" someone asks.

"First," Dr. Provato says, "we have to close the cafeteria until we're sure we can operate without posing any additional health threat. Second, we need to inform the employees of the problem and tell them what symptoms to watch out for. Finally, we need to offer gamma globulin shots, which will reduce the symptoms in anyone who has contracted the disease."

"What are the symptoms?" you ask, wondering whether the scratchy feeling in your throat is the beginning of something serious.

"Basically, you feel like you've got a bad, lingering case of the flu—fever, aches and pains, loss of appetite, loss of energy. After about a week or 10 days, you may notice a yellowing of the skin or the whites of the eyes. Some people are sick for a month or more; some recover more quickly. If you get a gamma globulin shot, you're usually back on your feet in a week or two."

"When and where can the employees get these gamma globulin shots?" asks someone else.

"I'll have the serum in my office starting at noon today," says Dr. Provato. "I strongly recommend a shot for anyone who has eaten in the cafeteria in the last month."

Your task: Your boss asks you to draft a memo informing GTE's employees of the hepatitis threat.[36]

11. Refinancing rules: Letter explaining changes at PeopleFirst.com When you began as a customer service representative at PeopleFirst.com, you worked with only five employees, helping to pioneer a web-based auto loan brokerage. Customers loved it.

From your website, they filled out a single application and faxed in any necessary verification documents. Then PeopleFirst matched them with the best loan for which they qualified, chosen from a variety of lenders. You mailed them a no-obligation "Blank Check®" to spend at any auto dealership, up to the amount for which they qualified. The loan didn't begin until they spent the check. Later, if rates dropped, they could come back to PeopleFirst.com for refinancing.

All that changed when huge Capital One Financial Corporation bought out PeopleFirst.com. They changed your name to Capital One Auto Finance and converted all loans to Capital One loans. Under its new policies, Capital One will not refinance its own loans. However, your existing customers aren't charged a prepayment penalty if they want to pay off their loans early by finding (on their own) another lender for refinancing. You might lose some business this way, but Capital One would lose a lot more if it refinanced all its loans every time rates drop.

Your task: Explain the new policy in a letter to Faviola and Mary Franzone (7200 Poplar Ave., Memphis, TN 38197), who have inquired about refinancing their auto loan at today's lower rates.[37]

12. Product recall: Letter from Perrigo Company about children's painkiller Your company is Perrigo, the leading manufacturer of more than 900 store-brand, over-the-counter (OTC) pharmaceuticals and nutritional products. These items are found beside brand-name products such as Tylenol, Motrin, Benadryl, NyQuil, Centrum, or Ex-Lax, but they're packaged under the name of the store that customers are shopping in. They're priced a bit lower and offer "comparable quality and effectiveness," as your sales literature proclaims. For retailers, selling Perrigo products yields a higher profit margin than name brands. For consumers, buying the store brands can mean significant savings.

However, your company has discovered that a batch of its cherry-flavored children's painkiller contains up to 29 percent more acetaminophen than the label indicates—enough to cause an overdose in the young children the product is designed for. Such overdoses can cause liver failure. As of this morning, your marketing department calculates that 6,500 four-ounce bottles of the "children's nonaspirin elixir" (a Tylenol look-alike) are already in the hands of consumers. That leaves some 1,288 bottles still on store shelves.

No one is telling you how this error happened, and it's only been found in lot number 1AD0228, but frankly, finding a guilty party is not so important to your job. You're more concerned about getting the word out fast. Such errors do happen, and the best move is immediate and direct, being completely honest with retailers and the public—so say your superiors in the Customer Support and Service Department. Full and prompt disclosure is especially crucial when consumers' health is involved, as it always is in your line of business.

The painkiller has been sold under the Kroger label at stores in Alabama, Arkansas, Georgia, Illinois, Indiana, Kentucky, Louisiana, Michigan, Mississippi, Missouri, North Carolina, Ohio, South Carolina, Tennessee, Texas, Virginia, and West Virginia. It was sold under the Hy-Vee label in Illinois, Iowa, Kansas, Minnesota, Missouri, Nebraska, and South Dakota, and under the Good Sense label at independent retail chains throughout the United States. Perrigo must notify consumers throughout the United States that they should not give the product to children, but rather should check the lot number and, if it's from the affected batch, return the bottle to the store they bought it from for a refund.

Your task: As Perrigo's customer service supervisor, you must notify retailers by letter. They've already been told verbally, but legal requirements mandate a written notification. That's good, because a form letter to your retail customers can also include follow-up instructions. Explain the circumstances behind the recall, and instruct stores to pull bottles from the shelves immediately for return to your company. Perrigo will, of course, reimburse the refunds provided to consumers. Questions should be directed to Perrigo at 1-800-321-0105—and it's okay if retailers give that number to consumers. Be sure to mention all that your company is doing, and use resale information.[38]

13. Cell phone violations: E-mail message to associates at Wilkes Artis law firm "Company policy states that personnel are not to conduct business using cell phones while driving," David Finch reminds you. He's a partner at the law firm of Wilkes Artis in Washington, D.C., where you work as his administrative assistant.

You nod, waiting for him to explain. He already issued a memo about this rule last year, after that 15-year-old girl was hit and killed by an attorney from another firm. Driving back from a client meeting, the attorney was distracted while talking on her cell phone. The girl's family sued the firm and won $30 million, but that's not the point. The point is that cell phones can cause people to be hurt, even killed.

Finch explains, "Yesterday one of our associates called his secretary while driving his car. We can't allow this. According to the National Highway Transportation Safety Administration, 20 to 30 percent of all driving accidents are related to cell phone usage. From now on, any violation of our cell phone policy will result in suspension without pay, unless the call is a genuine health or traffic emergency."

Your task: Finch asks you to write an e-mail message to all employees, announcing the new penalty for violating company policy.[39]

14. Safe selling: Memo about dangerous scooters at The Sports Authority You're not surprised that the Consumer Product Safety Commission (CPSC) has issued a consumer advisory on the dangers of motorized scooters. Unlike a motorcycle or bicycle, a scooter can be mastered by first-timers almost immediately. So both children and adults are hopping on, riding off—without helmets or other safety gear—and turning up with broken arms and legs, scraped faces, and bumped heads.

The popular electric or gas-powered scooters feature two wheels similar to in-line skates and travel 9 to 14 miles per hour. Over a six-month period, says the CPSC, emergency rooms around the country reported 2,250 motorized scooter injuries and three deaths. The riders who were killed (ages 6, 11, and 46), might all have lived if they'd been wearing helmets. As a result, some states have already enacted laws restricting scooter operations.

You are a merchandising assistant at The Sports Authority, which sells a wide selection of both the foot-powered ($25 to $150) and motorized scooters ($350 to $1,000). Your company is as concerned about the rise in injuries as they are about the CPSC advisory's potential negative effect on sales and legality. Thus, you've been assigned to a team that will brainstorm ideas for improving the situation. For example, one team member has suggested developing a safety brochure to give to customers; another wants to train salespeople to discuss safety issues with customers before they buy.

"We'd like to see increased sales of reflective gear ($6 to$15), helmets ($24), and elbow and knee pads ($19)," a store executive tells your team, "not to improve on our $1.5 billion annual revenue, but to save lives."

Your task: Working with classmates, discuss how The Sports Authority can use positive actions (including those mentioned in the case) to soften the effect of the CPSC advisory. Choose the best ideas and decide how to use them in a bad-news memo notifying the chain's 198 store managers about the consumer advisory. Then write the memo your team has outlined.[40]

NEGATIVE EMPLOYMENT MESSAGES

15. Bad news for 80: Form letter to unsuccessful job candidates The Dean's Selection Committee screened 85 applications for the position of dean of arts and sciences at your campus. After two rounds of eliminations, the top five candidates were invited to "airport interviews," where the committee managed to meet with each candidate for an hour. Then the top three candidates were invited to the campus to meet with students, faculty, and administrators.

The committee recommended to the university president that the job be given to Constance Pappas, who has a doctorate in American studies and has been chairperson of the history department at Minneapolis Metropolitan College for the past three years. The president agreed, and Dr. Pappas accepted the offer.

One final task remains before the work of the Dean's Selection Committee is finished: Letters must be sent to the 84 unsuccessful candidates. The four who reached the "airport interview" stage will receive personal letters from the chairperson of the committee. Your job, as secretary of the committee, is to draft the form letter that will be sent to the other 80 applicants.

Your task: Draft a letter of 100 to 200 words. All copies will be individually addressed to the recipients but will carry identical messages.

16. Try lady bugs: Letter rejecting an application at Fluker Farms cricket ranch Back in 1953, when Richard Fluker bought into a cricket ranch in Port Allen, Louisiana, he thought crickets were good fishing bait. After all, fishing was a long-entrenched Louisiana pastime. He never imagined that the company he passed on to his son, David Fluker, would one day be earning upwards of $6 million in annual sales.

Fluker Farms has grown along with a general interest in pets (particularly reptiles). The company ships live crickets, mealworms, and iguanas to pet stores, zoos, and universities around the world. It also sells "dry goods" (as in freeze-dried crickets), as well as reptile leashes and other accessories. Fluker Farms even markets chocolate-covered crickets for brave humans—a big hit at trade shows.

As the business has grown so has the number of applicants who want to work for Fluker Farms. You are the company's human resources manager, so it's your job to screen all applicants. Last week you interviewed about a dozen candidates for a job in research and development. The company is looking for other bugs it can profit from, testing them as pet food and evaluating their "shelf-life" potential in both live and freeze-dried forms. With pet stores expanding into superstores, the demand for new food varieties is also growing. So the researcher you hire has to understand the feeding habits of reptiles and birds, must be acquainted with insect life cycles, and must possess the kind of imagination that can come up with a new idea and figure out how to make it profitable. That's not an easy spot to fill.

Your task: The candidates you saw all carried excellent credentials, every one of them with multiple degrees and a research background. But only Maria Richter had the combination of imagination, knowledge, and resourcefulness you're seeking. In addition, she has five years of reptile research, a doctorate in zoology, and a bachelor's degree in marketing. You are writing rejection letters to the other candidates, and you're starting with a letter to Werner Speker, whom you liked personally but whose postgraduate work has been mostly with felines, not reptiles. He's at 4265 Broadview Rd., Baton Rouge, LA 70815.[41]

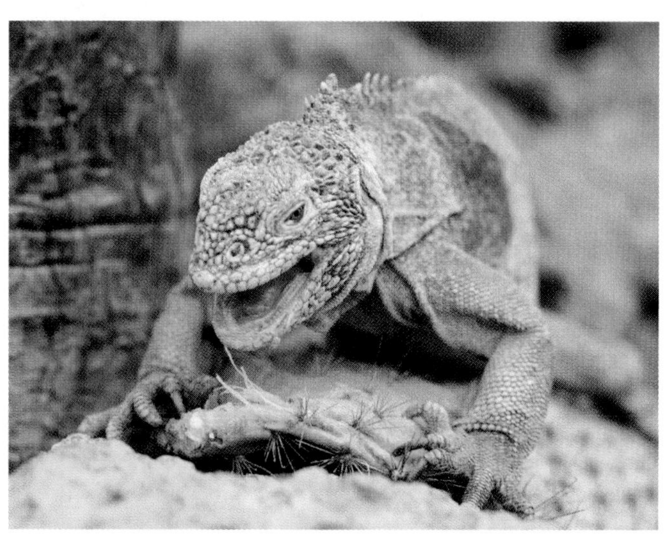

17. Too much *teléfono:* Memo giving a negative performance review at SBC Pacific Bell Because doing business in San Diego is a multicultural proposition, SBC Pacific Bell tries to be savvy about its diverse workforce, but it does not condone behaviors that interfere with the tasks at hand. In this case, the offender happens to be your 22-year-old nephew, and his offense is likely due to his Mexican American heritage—which won't get him off the hook, even though you may understand it better than anyone. You long ago joined your culture to his by marrying his mother's sibling.

You are supervisor of the billing adjustments department for SBC Pacific Bell. You and your staff ensure that every phone bill sent out by the company has been correctly calculated by your software and satisfies the ever-changing government tariffs. You didn't hire Jorge Gutierrez. That was done by a man one level below you, who found Gutierrez working as a temporary in another department and, with your approval, gave him a try.

Both of you have been pleased with his fast learning skills and innate understanding of the customer accounts associate job—a job that's been almost impossible to fill. Few employees could enter, verify price changes, and test computerized price-calculation formulas with the accuracy and speed that Gutierrez could. He's an extremely intelligent and skilled mathematician. With over 1 million customers, even tiny mistakes can be costly. Gutierrez was a real find—except for one problem he hasn't been able to surmount.

His supervisor, tells you that every morning your nephew receives a phone call from his Mexican American mother, who wants to be sure he's made it to work safely. Often his father also calls. Afternoon calls are from his baseball buddies—the ones he plays with in the Mexican league on weekends—and other family members. Then it's his girlfriend, also Mexican American. In one month's time, he asked permission to leave for "family emergencies" to (1) change his girlfriend's flat tire on the freeway, (2) deliver an extra car key because she locked herself out, and (3) defend her from an aggressive and unsavory boss at a job she quit that afternoon.

Gutierrez is fully aware of how these calls are interfering with his work, and he has asked friends and family not to call his office number—so they dial his cell phone instead. He still lives with his parents, which may be why they seem insensitive to his appeals.

Both you and his supervisor have given Gutierrez verbal warnings. You really can't afford to lose him, so you're hoping that a written, negative review will give him greater incentive to persuade friends and relatives. You'll deliver the letter in a meeting and help him find ways to resolve the issue within a mutually agreed-upon time frame.

As an "adopted" family member, you fully understand that Mexican American families tend to remain close-knit. Still, after six months on the job, Gutierrez should be better at balancing his family with his career.

Your task: Write the letter, using suggestions in this chapter and details in this case to help you put the bad news in a constructive light. Avoid culturally biased remarks or innuendo. Culture isn't really the issue; maturity is.

18. Career moves: E-mail refusing to write a recommendation Tom Weiss worked in the office at Opal Pools and Patios for four months, under your supervision (you're office manager). On the basis of what he told you he could do, you started him off as a word processor. However, his keyboard skills were inadequate for the job, so you transferred him to logging in accounts receivable, where he performed almost adequately. Because he assured you that his "real strength" was customer relations, you moved him to the complaint department. After he spent three weeks making angry customers even angrier, you were convinced that no place in your office was appropriate for the talents of Mr. Weiss. Five weeks ago, you encouraged him to resign before being formally fired.

Today's e-mail brings a request from Weiss asking you to write a letter recommending him for a sales position with a florist shop. You have no knowledge one way or the other of Weiss's sales abilities, but you do know him to be an incompetent word processor, a careless bookkeeper, and an insensitive customer service representative. Someone else is more likely to deserve the sales job, so you decide that you have done enough favors for Tom Weiss for one lifetime and plan to refuse his request.

Your task: Write an e-mail reply to Mr. Weiss (tomweiss@aol.com) indicating that you have chosen not to write a letter of recommendation for him.

19. Midair let-down: Instant message about flight cancellations at United Airlines It used to be that airline passengers didn't learn about cancelled connecting flights until after they'd landed. Sometimes a captain would announce cancellations just before touching down at a major hub, but how were passengers to notify waiting relatives or business associates on the ground?

As a customer service supervisor for United Airlines, you've just received information that all United flights from Chicago's O'Hare International Airport to Boston's Logan International have been cancelled until further notice. A late winter storm has already blanketed Boston with snow and freezing rain is expected overnight. The way the weather report looks, United will probably be lodging Boston-bound connecting passengers in Chicago-area hotels tonight. Meanwhile, you'll be using some of United's newest communication tools to notify travelers of the bad news.

United Airlines now partners with Verizon Airfone to provide JetConnect information services, giving travelers access to instant messaging and other resources while they're airborne. For a small fee, they can plug their laptop computers into the Airfone jack, activating their own instant messaging software to send and receive messages. If they've signed up for United's EasyUpdate flight status notification service, they'll also receive instant message alerts for flight cancellations, delays, seating upgrades, and so on.

Your task: Write the cancellation alert, staying within the 65-word limit of many instant-messaging programs. You might want to mention the airline's policy of providing overnight lodging for passengers who planned to use the Boston route as a connecting flight to complete journeys in progress.[42]

20. Quick answer: Instant message turning down employee request at Hewlett-Packard If she'd asked you a week ago, Lewinda Johnson might be granted her request to attend a conference on the use of "blogging" for business, which is being held in New York City next month. (Blogs are online documents written as a kind of journal posting; some businesses are testing them as a form of low-key promotion.) Instead, Johnson waited until you were stuck in this meeting, and she needs your response within the hour. She'll have to take no for an answer.

For one thing, you'd need budget approval from your group's vice president in order to green-light attendance at any conference longer than a day or farther than Denver, a short drive from your Colorado Springs office. The conference in question is not only being held in an expensive New York City hotel, it's going to last four days. Furthermore, Johnson hasn't given you sufficient justification for her attendance. You'd need a written document from her explaining how the use of business blogs relates to her job as marketing administrator.

Since she waited until precisely one hour before the application deadline, none of these issues can be addressed and you can't possibly say yes.

Your task: Write a 60 to 75 word instant message to Lewinda Johnson, declining her request. Decide whether the direct or indirect approach is appropriate.[43]

chapter 9

Writing Persuasive Messages

LEARNING OBJECTIVES

After studying this chapter, you will be able to

1. Apply the three-step writing process to persuasive messages
2. Identify seven ways to establish credibility in persuasive messages
3. Describe the AIDA model for persuasive messages
4. Distinguish between emotional and logical appeals and discuss how to balance them
5. Identify four common mistakes in writing persuasive messages
6. Discuss an effective approach to identifying selling points and audience benefits
7. Identify steps you can take to avoid ethical lapses in marketing and sales messages

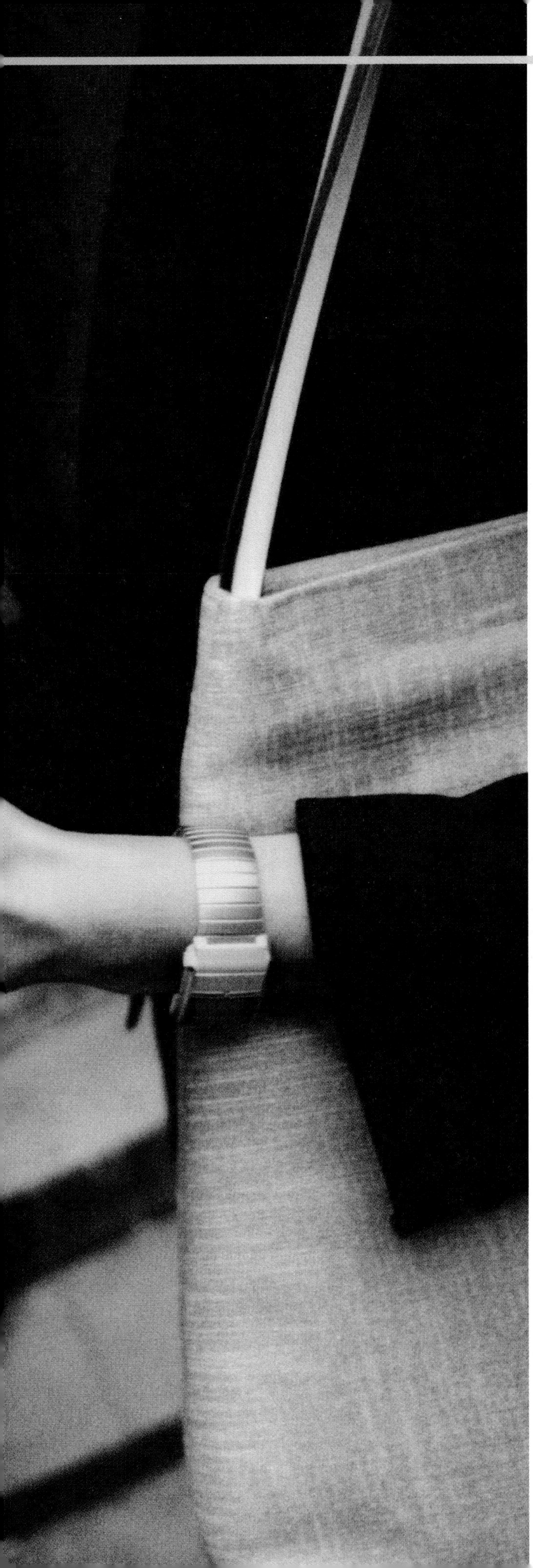

COMMUNICATION CLOSE-UP AT MARK BURNETT PRODUCTIONS

Think you can be as persuasive as Mark Burnett, a former member of Britain's elite Army Paratroop Regiment? His name may seem familiar: Burnett created the television series *Eco-Challenge—the Expedition Race* and was co-creator of the popular *Survivor* reality TV series. At 22, he left the military and moved to Los Angeles, where he needed just 24 hours to land a job as a Beverly Hills nanny-chauffeur. How? He appealed to the needs of his audience and convinced his employer that nobody could make neater beds or provide better security than a former British paratrooper.

Later on, driven by a fascination with adventure racing, Burnett used his persuasive powers to recruit team members, attract TV coverage, and launch *Eco-Challenge*. His powers of persuasion also helped him land TV contracts with MTV, ESPN, Discovery, and USA Network. In each case, he aligned his interests in television production with the business interests of each audience. Then came the idea for *Survivor*. The chairman of CBS said Burnett's *Survivor* pitch was the best he'd ever heard.

Burnett even persuaded renowned dealmaker Donald Trump, real estate mogul and author of a business bestseller, *The Art of the Deal,* to launch a television show. One night in

Once *Survivor* and *The Apprentice* had become hit TV shows, anyone could say that they seemed like great ideas. However, before these shows had any proof of success, Mark Burnett had to persuade television executives to give them a chance.

2002, Burnett was shooting a *Survivor* finale at an ice rink in Manhattan. Trump was there—he owns the rink—and Burnett walked up and introduced himself. He opened the discussion with some positive comments about Trump's book, then grabbed the opportunity to present his idea for a television show in which 16 ambitious young executives vie for a six-figure, one-year position in the Trump Organization. Ultimately, Burnett convinced Trump that he would enjoy starring in a new reality show of his own, and *The Apprentice* premiered on NBC in January 2004. The winner on that show?: Bill Rancic (www. billrancic.com), another persuasive businessperson.

Chances are your career won't involve hit television shows, but you can create some magic of your own by following Burnett's advice to understand your audiences and craft persuasive messages that meet their needs as well as your own.[1]

1 LEARNING OBJECTIVE

Apply the three-step writing process to persuasive messages

USING THE THREE-STEP WRITING PROCESS FOR PERSUASIVE MESSAGES

Persuasion is the attempt to change someone's attitudes, beliefs, or actions.

Professionals such as Mark Burnett realize that successful businesses rely on persuasive messages in both internal and external communication. Whether you're convincing your boss to open a new office in Europe or encouraging potential customers to try your products, you'll use many of the same techniques of **persuasion**—the attempt to change an audience's attitudes, beliefs, or actions.[2] Persuasive techniques are a cornerstone of marketing and selling, but even if you never write a single promotional message, you'll still need good persuasion skills to advance in your career. Successful professionals understand that persuasion is not about trickery or getting people to make choices that aren't in their best interest; rather, it lets your audience know they have a choice and helps them choose to agree with you.[3]

As with every type of business message, the three-step writing process improves persuasive messages. In addition, these messages require some specific techniques, which you have the opportunity to explore in this chapter.

Step 1: Plan Your Message

Unlike the routine positive messages discussed in Chapter 7, persuasive messages aim to influence audiences who may be inclined to resist at first. Even if they agree that your idea or product is attractive, they face so many options in today's crowded markets that you'll often need to use persuasive techniques to convince them that your choice is the best of all the attractive alternatives.

In today's message-saturated environment, it's not enough to have a great idea or a great product.

Having a great idea or a great product is no longer enough. Every day, untold numbers of good ideas go unnoticed and good products go unsold simply because of inept efforts to persuade people to accept them. If your company has a dozen or more possible retail sites for its next store, how do you convince management that the one you've selected is the best? How do you convince potential buyers that one out of the hundreds of personal computers or out of the thousands of vacation destinations is the best choice for them?

Creating successful persuasive messages in these challenging situations demands careful attention to all four tasks in the planning step, starting with an insightful analysis of your purpose and your audience.

Analyzing Your Situation

Failing to clarify your purpose is a common mistake with persuasive messages.

Your purpose might seem obvious—to persuade people to visit your website or buy your snowboards—but persuasive messages can suffer from three common mistakes related to purpose. The first mistake is failing to clarify your purpose before you continue with planning. Clarifying your purpose isn't as simple as you might think. Say that you want the city zoning commission to consider your request to build a new factory in an area zoned for retail. The best purpose to pursue might be to get the commission to change long-standing beliefs about the best uses of real estate in various parts of the city—rather than focusing the rezoning that will allow your single project to proceed. The second mistake is failing to clearly express your purpose to your audience. You may feel uncomfortable with the idea of asking others to give you time, money, or other considerations, but if you don't ask, you're not likely to get a positive response. The third mistake is failing to realize that the decision you want someone to make is too complicated or risky to make all in one leap.

You can't sell a $10 million office building by writing someone a letter and asking her to buy it. Your purpose in the first message might be to spark interest with a brief description of the facility or an analysis of lease income. If that message is successful, you might then offer a tour of the site, and so on until you finally ask for a decision. In complicated selling situations, you might need half a dozen or more carefully sequenced messages to accomplish your goal, and identifying the purpose of each message is crucial. If you try to accomplish too much with any single message, you risk confusing your audience or prompting them to say "no" before you've had a chance to build your case.

You can identify the number of messages and the nature of each one by analyzing your audience. Consider both the positives and the negatives—the wants, needs, and motivations of your audience (the reasons they might respond favorably to your message) as well as their concerns and objections (the reasons they might *not* respond favorably). With these two insights as guides, you can then work to find common ground with your audience, while emphasizing positive points and minimizing negative ones.

To persuade successfully, you need to consider both the positive and negative aspects of your proposed solution.

All of the aspects of creating an audience profile that you learned in Chapter 4 apply to persuasive messages. If your message is aimed at a single large organization, simply identifying all the people involved in the decision, and all their individual needs, can take days or weeks. In contrast, for a message aimed at a million consumers, you'll never know each one individually; the best you can do is sample a small number who represent the entire audience.

The best persuasive messages are closely connected to your audience's desires and interests.[4] Consider these important questions: Who is my audience? What are their needs? What do I want them to do? How might they resist? Are there alternative positions I need to examine? What does the decision maker consider the most important issue? How might the organization's culture influence my strategy?

Some theorists believe that certain needs have priority. Figure 9.1 represents psychologist Abraham Maslow's hierarchy of needs, with the most basic needs appearing at the bottom of the figure. Maslow suggests that only after lower-level needs have been met will a person seek to fulfill needs on higher levels.[5] Other theories exist as well, but the point here is that people have a variety of needs and that the most effective persuasive messages are aligned with the most important needs of every audience member.

Most persuasive communicators assume that their audiences have prioritized their own needs and desires.

For example, you want to pitch an idea for a high-risk, high-reward project to your boss. Even though this project could make you both look like heroes (an esteem and status need), your message won't be well received if your boss is currently fighting to keep his or her job (a survival or safety and security need that needs to be filled first).

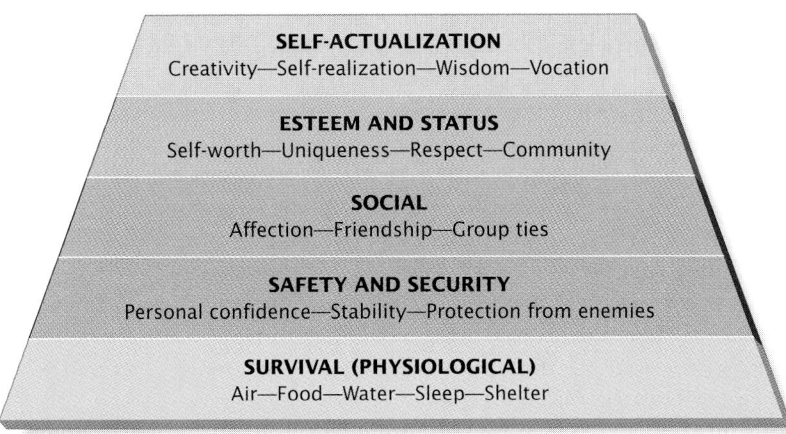

FIGURE 9.1
Maslow's Hierarchy of Needs

Demographics include characteristics such as age, gender, occupation, income, and education.

Psychographics include characteristics such as personality, attitudes, and lifestyle.

To understand and categorize audience needs, you can refer to specific information such as **demographics** (the age, gender, occupation, income, education, and other quantifiable characteristics of the people you're trying to persuade) and **psychographics** (personality, attitudes, lifestyle, and other psychological characteristics). Both types of information are strongly influenced by culture. When analyzing your audience, take into account their cultural expectations and practices so that you don't undermine your persuasive message by using an inappropriate appeal or by organizing your message in a way that seems unfamiliar or uncomfortable to your audience.

Gathering Information

Gather the information you need to close the gap between what your audience thinks or feels now and what you'd like them to think or feel in the future.

Once situation analysis is complete, gather the information necessary to close the gap between what your audience knows, believes, or feels right now and what you want them to know, believe, or feel as a result of receiving your message. Most persuasive messages are a combination of logical and emotional factors, but the ratio varies wildly from message to message. You can get a sense of this variation by comparing the websites of American Fastener Technology (industrial goods, www.americanfastener.com), Chrysler (automobiles, www.chrysler.com), and Lancôme (beauty products, www.lancome.com).

American Fasteners relies primarily on straightforward product information to convince buyers, whereas Lancôme tries to evoke a more emotional response through its visual and verbal imagery. Chrysler is somewhere in the middle, providing plenty of facts and figures about its cars but also including strong emotional messages about the joy of driving. By identifying the mix of factors that will most likely persuade your audience, you'll know what sort of information you need to gather. You'll learn more about the types of information to offer when you read "Developing Persuasive Messages" later in the chapter. Chapter 10 presents advice on how to find the information you need.

Selecting the Right Medium

Persuasive messages can be found in virtually every communication medium ever devised, from instant messages and computer animations to radio ads and skywriting. For persuasive business messages, your choice of medium will closely follow the guidelines presented in Chapter 4. However, for promotional messages, your options are far more numerous. In fact, advertising agencies employ media specialists whose only job is to analyze the media options available and select the most cost-effective combination for each client and each ad campaign.

You may need to employ multiple media to reach your entire audience.

To further complicate matters, various members of your audience might prefer different media for the same message. Some consumers like to do all their car shopping in person, whereas others do most of their research online. Some people don't mind promotional e-mails for products they're interested in; others resent every piece of commercial e-mail they receive. If you can't be sure you can reach most or all of your audience with a single medium, you'll need to use two or more, such as following up an e-mail campaign with printed letters.

Organizing Your Information

Be sure to give attention to all four aspects of organizing your information—defining your main idea, limiting your scope, choosing a direct or indirect approach, and grouping your points in a meaningful way. The most effective main ideas for persuasive messages have one thing in common: they are about the receiver, not the sender. Take a cue from a successful advertiser such as Nike. The company's ads are never about the company and often aren't even about the products; they're about the customer's experience when using Nike products. You can benefit from this same approach for all persuasive messages. If you're trying to convince another company to join yours in a business venture, explain how it will help them, not how it will help you.

Limit your scope to include only the information needed to help your audience take the next step toward making a favorable decision.

To limit the scope of each message effectively, include only the information needed to help your audience take the next step toward making the ultimate decision or taking the ultimate action you want. In simple scenarios such as persuading teammates to attend a special meeting, you might put everything you have to say into a single, short message. But if you want your company to invest several million dollars in your latest product idea, the scope of your first message might be limited to securing 10 minutes at the next executive committee meeting so that you can introduce your idea and get permission to explore it. You might not be in a position to actually ask for the money for weeks or months, after you've gathered support for the idea and collected enough information to make a compelling business case for it. Professional advertisers and sales experts spend days limiting the scope of their messages to make sure they can break through the clutter of competing messages and get the attention of their audiences.

As with routine and negative messages, the best organizational approach is based on your audience's likely reaction to your message. However, because the nature of persuasion is to convince your audience to change their attitudes, beliefs, or actions, most persuasive messages use an indirect approach. That means you'll want to explain your reasons and build interest before asking for a decision or for action—or perhaps even before revealing your purpose. You'll see several examples of the indirect approach in action later in this chapter, in the discussions of both persuasive business messages and promotional messages.

Use the direct approach if your audience is ready to hear your proposal.

Consider the direct approach whenever you know your audience is ready to hear your proposal. If your boss wants to change shipping companies and asks for your recommendation, you'll probably want to open with your choice, then provide your reasons as backup. Similarly, if there's a good chance your audience will agree with your message, don't force them to wade through pages of reasoning before seeing your main idea. If they happen not to agree with your pitch, they can move into your reasoning to see why you're promoting that particular idea. The direct approach is also called for if you've been building your case through several indirect messages and it's now time to make your request.

Bette McGiboney is administrative assistant to the athletic director of Auburn University. Each year, after season tickets have been mailed, the cost of the athletic department's toll-free phone number skyrockets as fans call with questions about their seats, complaints about receiving the wrong number of tickets, or orders for last-minute tickets. The August phone bill is usually over $3,000, in part because each customer is put on hold while operators serve others. McGiboney came up with an idea that could save the company money and save ticket holders time, so she composed an e-mail message that uses the direct approach (see Figure 9.2).

If you use the direct approach as McGiboney does in Figure 9.2, keep in mind that even though your audience may be easy to convince, you'll still want to include at least a brief justification or explanation. Don't expect your reader to accept your idea on blind faith. For example, consider the following two openers:

LESS EFFECTIVE	MORE EFFECTIVE
I recommend building our new retail outlet on the West Main Street site.	After comparing the four possible sites for our new retail outlet, I recommend West Main Street as the only site that fulfills our criteria for visibility, proximity to mass transportation, and square footage.

Choice of approach is also influenced by your position (or authority within the organization) relative to your audience's.

Your choice between the direct and indirect approaches is also influenced by the extent of your authority, expertise, or power in an organization. As a first-line manager writing a persuasive message to top management, you may try to be diplomatic and use an indirect approach. But your choice could backfire if some managers think your indirectness lacks confidence or even integrity. On the other hand, you may try to save your supervisors time by using a direct approach, which might be perceived as brash and presumptuous. Similarly, when writing a persuasive message to employees, you may use the indirect approach to ease into a major change, but your audience might see your message as weak, even wishy-washy. You need to think carefully about your corporate culture and what your audience expects before selecting your approach.

Step 2: Write Your Message

Persuasive messages are often unexpected or even unwelcome, so the "you" attitude is crucial.

The generally uninvited and occasionally even unwelcome nature of persuasive messages means the "you" attitude is more critical than ever. Most people won't even pay attention to

FIGURE 9.2 Effective E-Mail Message Presenting an Idea to a Boss

Reply
Reply All
Forward
Flag
Print
Edit
Inbox
From: "Bette McGiboney" mcgibon@ath.auburn.edu
Date: February 10, 2005
To: <housel@ath.auburn.edu>
Cc:
Subject: Savings on toll-free number
Attached: C:\Temp\NewPhoneMessage.doc
David:
We can save money, time, and frustration by modifying our toll-free message system. Currently, the bill for our toll-free number at the ticket office runs at least $3,000 for August (compared with $493 on average for the other 11 months). Plus, we're so busy fielding calls during August that our other work piles up. In addition, Tiger fans who call in August are frustrated by having to wait on hold at least five minutes and often longer.
By providing callers with an additional option, we can relieve a lot of the pressure. Under the new system, callers will hear all the same messages and have all the same options as before. But if no operator is available when a caller presses "0" for ticket information, a new message will request the caller's name and phone number so that we can return the call within the next two business days.
This new message system will help us
* Save money on our toll-free line
* Manage our time and stress levels
* Provide better customer service
Reducing the on-hold time should eliminate at least $2,000 from our August bill (according to a conversation with Tandy Robertson, our AT&T representative). Adding a new message option costs nothing, and we can implement the plan immediately. We will be able to manage our work more effectively by returning phone calls during quiet times of the day. And, not least important, Tiger fans can avoid the frustration of waiting on hold.
Our staff is enthusiastic about trying this new plan. If we implement it this August, then after football season, we could call a random selection of customers to see how they liked the new system.
Attached is a sheet with possible wording for the new message. Please let me know by the end of the month whether you'd like to give this a try.
Thanks,
Bette
Uses the subject line to announce that the proposal will save money
Grabs attention with the promise of saving money, time, and frustration
Creates more interest with an explanation of how the new plan will work
Creates desire by presenting supporting evidence
Shows audience focus by completing a chore that might have caused the reader to delay
Opens using the direct approach, but still introduces the idea briefly
Lists benefits to draw the reader into the meat of the message
Shows audience focus by including a method for measuring customer response
Makes a simple and direct request for action within a specific time frame

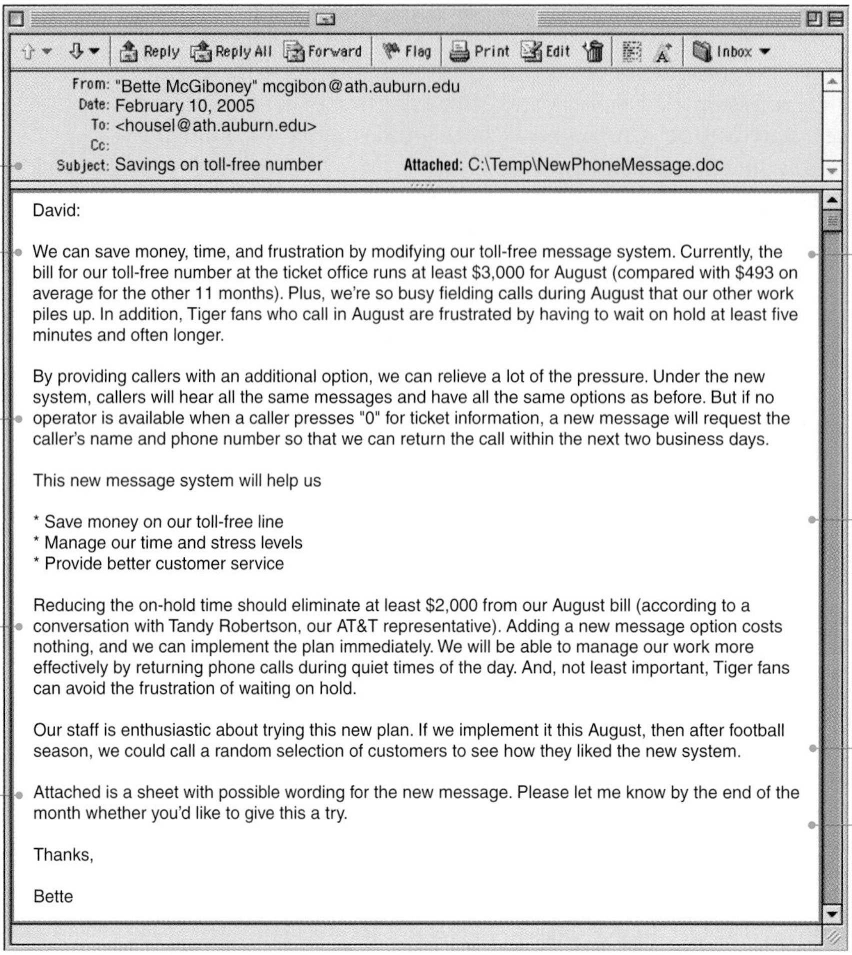

your message, much less respond to it, if it isn't about them. Positive language usually happens naturally with persuasive messages, since you're promoting an idea or product you believe in. However, polite language isn't as automatic, surprisingly enough. Some writers inadvertently insult their readers by implying that they've been making poor choices in the past or need the writer's keen insights to make a good choice in the current situation. Don't fall into the temptation of trying to make your readers' decisions for them; present your case and use your persuasive skills to let them see how making a particular choice is best for them.

Cultural differences influence your persuasion attempts.

Your understanding and respect for cultural differences will help you satisfy the needs of your audience and will help your audience respect you. That's because persuasion is different in different cultures. In France, using an aggressive, hard-sell technique is no way to win respect. Such an approach would probably antagonize your audience. In Germany, where people tend to focus on technical matters, plan on verifying any figures you use for support, and make sure they are exact. In Sweden, audiences tend to focus on theoretical questions and strategic implications, whereas U.S. audiences are usually concerned with more practical matters.[6]

As with individuals, an organization's culture or subculture heavily influences the effectiveness of messages. All the previous messages in an organization have established a tradition that defines persuasive writing within that culture. When you accept and implement these traditions, you establish one type of common ground with your audience. If you reject or never learn these traditions, you'll have difficulty achieving that common ground with your audience, which damages both your credibility and your persuasion attempts.

2 LEARNING OBJECTIVE

Identify seven ways to establish credibility in persuasive messages

When trying to persuade a skeptical or hostile audience, you must convince people that you know what you're talking about and that you're not trying to mislead them. Your credibility is even more important in persuasive messages than it is in other business messages (see Chapter 5). Without it, your efforts to persuade will seem ineffective at best and manipulative and worst. Research strongly suggests that most managers overestimate their own credibility—considerably.[7] Establishing your credibility in persuasive messages takes time. Chapter 5 lists characteristics essential to building and maintaining your credibility, including honesty, objectivity, awareness of audience needs, knowledge and expertise, endorsements, performance, and communication style. To establish credibility in persuasive messages, try to go beyond these characteristics by

- **Using simple language.** In most persuasive situations, your audience will be cautious, watching for fantastic claims, insupportable descriptions, and emotional manipulation. Speak plainly and simply.
- **Supporting your message with facts.** Documents, statistics, research results, and testimonials (from people who've made the choice you're advocating)—all provide objective evidence for what you have to say, which adds to your credibility. The more specific and relevant your proof, the better.
- **Naming your sources.** Telling your audience where your information comes from and who agrees with you always improves your credibility, especially if your sources are already respected by your audience.
- **Being an expert (or finding one to support your message).** Your knowledge of your message's subject area (or even of some other area) helps you give your audience the quality information necessary to make a decision. If you aren't an expert in the subject, try to get the support of someone who is.
- **Establishing common ground.** Those beliefs, attitudes, and background experiences that you have in common with members of your audience will help them identify with you.
- **Being objective.** Your ability to understand and acknowledge all sides of an issue helps you present fair and logical arguments in your persuasive message. Top executives often ask if their employees have considered all the possibilities before committing to a single choice.
- **Displaying your good intentions.** Show your audience your genuine concern, good faith, and truthfulness. Let them see how you are focusing on their needs. Your willingness to keep your audience's best interests at heart helps you create persuasive messages that are not only more effective but also more ethical (see "Ethics Detective: The Case of Incredible Credibility").

Audiences often respond unfavorably to over-the-top language, so keep your writing simple and straightforward.

Step 3: Complete Your Message

Professional advertisers may have a dozen or more people review a message before it's released to the public. Ads and commercial websites are often tested extensively with representative recipients to make sure the intended audience gets the information the sender intends. The pros know from experience that the details can make or break a persuasive message, so they're careful not to shortchange this part of the writing process.

When you evaluate your content, try to judge your argument objectively, and seriously appraise your credibility. When revising for clarity and conciseness, carefully match the purpose and organization to audience needs. If possible, ask an experienced colleague, preferably someone who knows your audience well, to review your draft. Your design elements must complement, not detract from, your argument. In addition, meticulous proofreading will identify any mechanical or spelling errors that would weaken your persuasive potential. Finally, make sure your distribution methods fit your audience's expectations as well as your purpose. Don't start your persuasive efforts on the wrong foot by annoying your audience with an unwelcome delivery method.

DEVELOPING PERSUASIVE MESSAGES

Your success as a businessperson is closely tied to your ability to convince others to accept new ideas, change old habits, or act on your recommendations. Even early in your career, you might have the opportunity to convince your manager to let you join an important

Your success in business will depend on writing persuasive messages effectively.

Ethics Detective

The Case of Incredible Credibility

As the director of human resources in your company, you're desperate for some help. You want to keep the costs of employee benefits under control while making sure you provide employees with a fair benefits package. However, you don't have time to research all the options for health insurance, wellness programs, retirement plans, family counseling, educational benefits, and everything else, so you decide to hire a consultant. You receive the following message from a consultant interested in working with you:

> I am considered the country's foremost authority on employee health insurance programs. My clients offer universally positive feedback on the programs I've designed for them. They also love how much time I save them—hundreds and hundreds of hours. I am absolutely confident that I can thoroughly analyze your needs and create a portfolio that realizes every degree of savings possible. I invite you to experience the same level of service that has generated such comments as "Best advice ever!" and "Saved us an unbelievable amount of money."

You'd love to get results like that, but the message almost sounds too good to be true. Is it?

ANALYSIS

The consultant's letter contains at least a dozen instances where this writer's credibility might be questioned. Identify as many as you can and explain how you would bolster reader confidence by providing additional or different information.

project team or to change a process that's wasting time and energy. As you progress into positions of greater responsibility, your persuasive messages could start to influence multimillion-dollar investments and the careers of hundreds of employees. Obviously, the increase in your persuasive skills needs to be matched by the care and thoroughness of your analysis and planning, so that the ideas you convince others to adopt are sound.

Persuasive messages constitute a broad and diverse category, from encouraging your fellow team members to adopt a different type of project management to encouraging customers to give your product or store a try. Your audiences for these messages can range from a single person in your own department to government agencies, investors, clients, community leaders, and other external groups. Most of your messages will consist of *persuasive business messages*, which are any persuasive messages designed to elicit a preferred response in a nonsales situation. You may also have the opportunity to write or at least help develop sales and marketing messages.

Persuasive Business Messages

The goal of your persuasive business message is to convince your reader that your request or idea is reasonable and that it will benefit your reader in some way. Within the context of the three-step process, effective persuasion involves four essential strategies: framing your arguments, balancing emotional and logical appeals, reinforcing your position, and anticipating objections.

Framing Your Arguments

3 LEARNING OBJECTIVE

Describe the AIDA model for persuasive messages

Organize persuasive messages using the AIDA model:
- Attention
- Interest
- Desire
- Action

Many persuasive messages follow some variation of the indirect approach. However, unlike the buffer in an indirect negative message, the opening in a persuasive message is designed to get your audience's attention. Similarly, the explanation section does more than present reasons, and it is expanded to two sections. The first raises your audience's interest, and the second attempts to change your audience's attitude. Finally, your close does more than end on a positive note; it emphasizes reader benefits and motivates readers to take specific action. This persuasive approach, called the **AIDA model**, organizes your presentation into those four phases: (1) **a**ttention, (2) **i**nterest, (3) **d**esire, and (4) **a**ction (see Table 9.1). Other models exist, but they all follow a similar pattern.

- **Attention.** Your first objective is to encourage your audience to want to hear about your problem, idea, new product—whatever your main idea is. Write a brief and

TABLE 9.1 The AIDA Model

PHASE	OBJECTIVE
Attention	Get the reader's attention with a benefit that is of real interest or value.
Interest	Build the reader's interest by further explaining benefits and appealing to his or her logic or emotions.
Desire	Build desire by showing how your offer can really help the reader.
Action	Give a strong and simple call to action and provide a convenient means for the reader to take the next step.

engaging opening sentence, with no extravagant claims or irrelevant points. And be sure to find some common ground on which to build your case. In the letter in Figure 9.3, Randy Thumwolt uses the AIDA model in a persuasive memo about his program that would try to reduce Host Marriott's annual plastics costs and try to curtail consumer complaints about the company's recycling record. Note also how Thumwolt "sells the problem" before attempting to sell the solution. Few people are interested in hearing about solutions to problems they don't know about or don't believe exist.

- **Interest.** Explain the relevance of your message to your audience. Continuing the theme you started with, paint a more detailed picture with words. Get your audience thinking. In Figure 9.3, Thumwolt's interest section introduces an additional, unforeseen problem with plastic product containers. Also, Thumwolt breaks out his suggestions into an easy-to-read list.
- **Desire.** Help audience members embrace your idea by explaining how the change will benefit them. Reduce resistance by identifying and answering in advance any questions the audience might have. If your idea is complex, you may need to explain how you would implement it. Back up your claims in order to increase audience willingness to take the action that you suggest in the next section. Just remember to make sure that all evidence is directly relevant to your point.
- **Action.** Suggest the action you want readers to take. Make it more than a statement such as "Please institute this program soon" or "Send me a refund." This is the opportunity to remind readers of the benefits of taking action. The secret of a successful action phase is making the action easy, so if possible, give your readers a couple of options for responding, such as a toll-free number to call and a website to visit. Include a deadline when applicable.

The AIDA plan is tailor-made for using the indirect approach, allowing you to save your main idea for the action phase. However, it can also be used for the direct approach, in which case you use your main idea as an attention-getter, build interest with your argument, create desire with your evidence, and emphasize your main idea in the action phase with the specific action you want your audience to take.

The AIDA model is ideal for the indirect approach.

When your AIDA message uses an indirect approach and is delivered by memo or e-mail, keep in mind that your subject line usually catches your readers' eye first. Your challenge is to make it interesting and relevant enough to capture reader attention without revealing your main idea. If you put your request in the subject line, you're likely to get a quick "no" before you've had a chance to present your arguments.

INSTEAD OF THIS	TRY THIS
Proposal to install new phone message system	Reducing the cost of our toll-free number

You can also see from the AIDA model why it's so important to have a concise, focused purpose for your persuasive messages. Otherwise, you'll find it nearly impossible to guide your reader through each phase from attention to action. Focus on your primary goal when presenting your case, and concentrate your efforts on accomplishing that one goal. For example, if your main idea is to convince your company to install a new phone-messaging system, leave discussions about switching long-distance carriers until another day—unless it's relevant to your argument.

Plan

Analyze the Situation
The purpose is to solve an ongoing problem, but the audience is uninterested.

Gather Information
Determine audience needs and obtain the necessary information on recycling problem areas.

Select the Right Medium
A printed letter is appropriate for this formal communication.

Organize the Information
Your main idea is to propose a recycling solution, so limit your scope to the problem at hand; use an indirect approach to lay out the extent of the problem.

1

Write

Adapt to Your Audience
Adjust the level of formality based on degree of familiarity with the audience; maintain a positive relationship by using the "you" attitude, politeness, positive emphasis, and bias-free language.

Compose the Message
Use a conversational but professional style and keep the message brief, clear, and as helpful as possible.

2

Complete

Revise the Message
Evaluate content and review readability to make sure the negative information won't be misinterpreted; make sure your tone stays positive without being artificial.

Produce the Message
Simple memo format is all the design this message needs.

Proofread the Message
Review for errors in layout, spelling, and mechanics.

Distribute the Message
Deliver your message using the chosen medium.

3

FIGURE 9.3 Persuasive Letter Using the AIDA Model Effectively

INTERNAL MEMORANDUM

TO: Eleanor Tran, Comptroller
FROM: Randy Thumwolt, Purchasing Director
DATE: May 10, 2005
SUBJECT: Cost Cutting in Plastics

In spite of our recent switch to purchasing plastic product containers in bulk, our costs for these containers are exorbitant. In my January 5 memo, I included all the figures showing that

- We purchase five tons of plastic product containers each year
- The price of the polyethylene terephthalate (PET) tends to rise and fall as petroleum costs fluctuate

In January I suggested that we purchase plastic containers in bulk during winter months, when petroleum prices tend to be lower. Because you approved that suggestion, we should realize a 10 percent saving this year. However, our costs are still out of line, around $2 million a year.

In addition to the cost in dollars of these plastic containers is the cost in image. We have recently been receiving an increasing number of consumer letters complaining about our lack of a recycling program for PET plastic containers, both on the airplanes and in the airport restaurants.

After conducting some preliminary research, I have come up with the following ideas:

- Provide recycling containers at all Host Marriott airport restaurants
- Offer financial incentives for the airlines to collect and separate PET containers
- Set up a specially designated dumpster at each airport for recycling plastics
- Contract with A-Batt Waste Management for collection

I've attached a detailed report of the costs involved. As you can see, our net savings the first year should run about $500,000. I've spoken to Ted Macy in marketing. If we adopt the recycling plan, he wants to build a PR campaign around it.

The PET recycling plan will help build our public image while improving our bottom line. If you agree, let's meet with Ted next week to get things started.

Grabs attention by clearly stating an ongoing problem and briefly providing background information that includes specific numbers

Reminds reader of important facts that have already been established by breaking them out into a list

Builds interest by introducing an additional problem with the plastic product containers

Makes suggestions in an easy-to-read list, providing detailed support in an attachment

Creates desire by providing another reader benefit

Urges action within a specific time frame

Balancing Emotional and Logical Appeals

Few persuasive appeals are purely logical or purely emotional. Even American Fasteners bolsters its fact-heavy website presentation with visual images of industrial-quality strength, such as massive bridges, military helicopters, and the Statue of Liberty. Without coming right out and saying so, the website shouts dependability, portraying employees as the people you can count on when you need to. Conversely, even though Lancôme's website is packed with emotional imagery, its product presentations are laced with facts and advice, from the vitamin content of moisturizing lipsticks to application techniques for various makeup products.

Imagine you're sitting at a control panel, with one knob labeled "logic" and another labeled "emotion." As you prepare your persuasive message, you carefully adjust each knob, tuning the message for maximum impact. Too little emotion, and your audience might not care enough to respond. Too much emotion, and your audience might think you haven't thought through the tough business questions. It's part art and part science, and the more messages you craft, the more confident you'll become in your adjustments.

To find the optimum balance, consider four factors: (1) the actions you hope to motivate, (2) your reader's expectations, (3) the degree of resistance you need to overcome, and (4) how far you feel empowered to go to sell your point of view.[8] When you're persuading someone to accept a complex idea, take a serious step, or make a large and important decision, lean toward logic and make your emotional appeal subtle. However, when you're persuading someone to purchase a product, join a cause, or change an attitude, you might rely a bit more heavily on emotion.

Emotional Appeals An **emotional appeal** calls on feelings, basing the argument on audience needs or sympathies; however, such an appeal must be subtle.[9] For instance, you can make use of the emotion surrounding certain words. The word *freedom* evokes strong feelings, as do words such as *success, prestige, compassion, free, value,* and *comfort.* Such words put your audience in a certain frame of mind and help them accept your message. However, emotional appeals aren't necessarily effective by themselves. For most business situations, the best use of emotion is working in tandem with logic. Even if your audience reaches a conclusion based on emotions, they'll look to you to provide logical support as well.

4 LEARNING OBJECTIVE

Distinguish between emotional and logical appeals, and discuss how to balance them

Communication Solution

Mark Burnett successfully blends emotional and logical appeals in his persuasive messages, adjusting the balance for each message and each audience. For example, when he promotes a reality show such as *Survivor* to contestants, the message emphasizes an emotional appeal (such as the thrill of competition and the opportunity for riches). However, when promoting that same show to television network executives, his message rests almost entirely on logical appeals (such as the attractive demographics of the show's target audience and the financial potential of selling advertising time during the show).

Emotional appeals attempt to connect with the reader's feelings or sympathies.

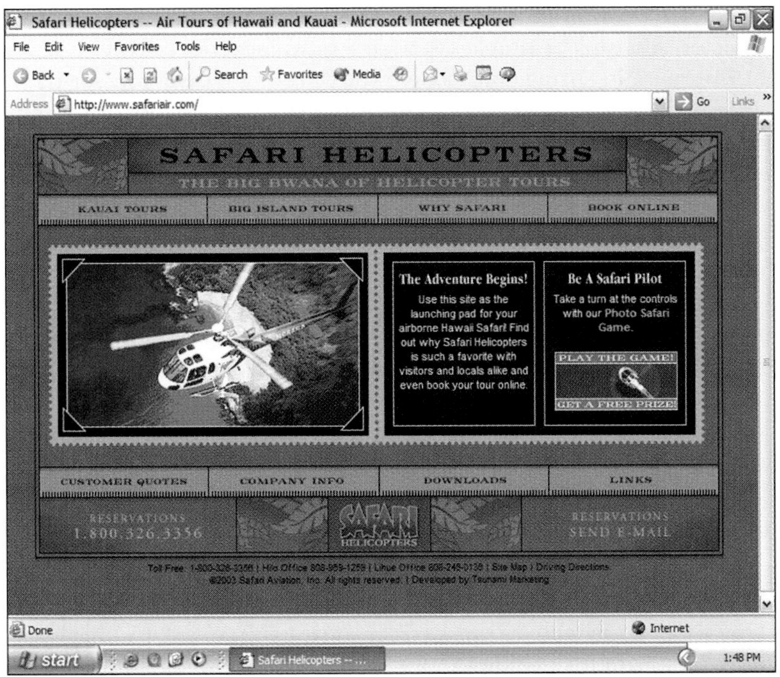

Starting its ads with the headline, "The Adventure Begins!" Safari Helicopters uses strong emotional appeals to interest visitors in helicopter tours of the Hawaiian Islands.

Logical appeals are based on the reader's notions of reason; these appeals can use analogy, induction, or deduction.

Logical Appeals A **logical appeal** calls on reason. In any argument you might use to persuade an audience, you make a claim and then support your claim with reasons or evidence. When appealing to your audience's logic, you might use three types of reasoning:

- **Analogy.** With analogy, you reason from specific evidence to specific evidence. For instance, to persuade reluctant employees to attend a planning session, you might use a town meeting analogy, comparing your company to a small community and your employees to valued members of that community.
- **Induction.** With inductive reasoning, you work from specific evidence to a general conclusion. To convince your team to change a certain production process, you could point out that every company who has adopted it has increased profits, so it must be a smart idea.
- **Deduction.** With deductive reasoning, you work from a generalization to a specific conclusion. To persuade your boss to hire additional customer support staff, you might point to industry surveys that show how crucial customer satisfaction is to corporate profits.

Every method of reasoning is vulnerable to misuse, both intentional and unintentional, so verify each of your rational arguments before you distribute your message. For example, in the case of the production process, are there any other factors that affect the integrity of your reasoning? What if that process works well only for small companies with few products, and your firm is a multinational behemoth with 10,000 products? To avoid faulty logic, practice the following guidelines:[10]

Logical flaws include hasty generalizations, circular reasoning, attacks on opponents, oversimplifications, assumptions of cause and effect, faulty analogies, and illogical support.

- **Avoid hasty generalizations.** Make sure you have plenty of evidence before drawing conclusions.
- **Avoid circular reasoning.** *Circular reasoning* is a logical fallacy in which you try to support your claim by restating it in different words. The statement "We know temporary workers cannot handle this task because temps are unqualified for it" doesn't prove anything because the claim and the supporting evidence are essentially identical. It doesn't prove *why* the temps are unqualified.
- **Avoid attacking an opponent.** Focus on the real question. Attack the argument your opponent is making, not your opponent's character.
- **Avoid oversimplifying a complex issue.** Make sure you present all the factors rather than relying on an "either/or" statement that makes it look as if only two choices are possible.
- **Avoid mistaken assumptions of cause and effect.** If you can't isolate the impact of a specific factor, you can't assume it's the cause of whatever effect you're discussing. The weather improves in spring, and people start playing baseball in spring. Does good weather cause baseball? No. There is a *correlation* between the two—meaning the data associated with them tend to rise and fall at the same time, but there is no *causation*—no proof that one causes the other. The complexity of many business situations makes cause and effect a particular challenge. You lowered prices and sales went up. Were lower prices the cause? Maybe, but it might've been caused by a competitor with delivery problems, a better advertising campaign, or any of a host of other factors.
- **Avoid faulty analogies.** Be sure that the two objects or situations being compared are similar enough for the analogy to hold. Even if A resembles B in one respect, it may not hold true in other important respects.
- **Avoid illogical support.** Make sure the connection between your claim and your support is truly logical and not based on a leap of faith, a missing premise, or irrelevant evidence.

Reinforcing Your Position

Choose your words carefully and use abstractions to enhance emotional content.

After you've worked out the basic elements of your argument, step back and look for ways to bolster the strength of your position. Can you find more powerful words to convey your message? For example, if your company is in serious financial trouble, talking about *survival* is more powerful than talking about *continued operations*. Using abstractions such as this along with basic facts and figures can bring your argument to life. You may have better luck collecting an overdue bill by mentioning honesty and fair play than by repeating the sum owed and the date it was due. As with any powerful tool, though, use vivid language and abstractions carefully and honestly.

In addition to individual word choices, consider using *metaphors* and other figures of speech. If you want to describe a quality-control system as being designed to catch every possible product flaw, you might call it a spider web to imply that it catches everything that comes its way. Similarly, anecdotes and stories can help your audience grasp the meaning and importance of your arguments. Instead of just listing the average failure rates of older model laptop computers, put a human face on the problem by describing what happened when your computer broke down during a critical presentation to your company's biggest customer.

Highlight the direct and indirect benefits of complying with your request.

Beyond the specific wording of your message, look for other forces and factors that can reinforce your position. When you're asking for something, your audience will find it easier to grant your request if they stand to benefit from it as well. For instance, if you're asking for more money to increase your staff, you might offer to lend those new employees to other managers during peak workloads in other departments. The timing of your message can also help. Virtually all organizations operate in cycles of some sort—incoming payments from major customers, outgoing tax payments, seasonal demand for products, and so on. Study these patterns to see whether they might work for or against you. For example, the best time to ask for additional staff might be right after a period of intense activity that prompted multiple customers to complain about poor service, when the experience is still fresh in everyone's mind. If you wait several months for the annual budgeting cycle, the emotional aspect of the experience will have faded, and your request will look like just another cost increase.

Anticipating Objections

Even powerful persuasive messages can encounter resistance from the audience.

Even the most powerful persuasive messages can expect to encounter some initial resistance. The best way to deal with audience resistance is to anticipate as many objections as you can and address them in your initial message before your audience can even bring them up. This anticipation is particularly important in written messages, when you don't have the opportunity to detect and respond to objections on the spot.

For instance, if you know that your proposal to switch to lower-cost materials will raise concerns about product quality and customer satisfaction, address these issues head-on in your message. If you wait until people raise the concern after reading your message, chances are they will already have gravitated toward a firm "no" before you have a chance to address their concerns. At the very least, waiting until people object will introduce additional rounds of communication that will delay the response you want to receive.

Present both sides to an issue when you expect to encounter strong resistance.

If you expect a hostile audience, one biased against your plan from the beginning, present all sides. As you cover each option, explain the pros and cons. You'll gain additional credibility if you present these options before presenting your recommendation or decision.[11]

To uncover audience objections, try some "What if?" scenarios. Poke holes in your own theories and ideas before your audience does. Then find solutions to the problems you've uncovered.

People are more likely to support what they help create, so ask your audience for their thoughts on the subject before you put your argument together. Let your audience recommend some solutions. With enough thought and effort, you may even be able to turn problems into opportunities; for example, you may show how your proposal will be more economical in the long run, even though it may cost more now. Just be sure to be thorough, open, and objective about all the facts and alternatives.

5 LEARNING OBJECTIVE

Identify four common mistakes in writing persuasive messages

When putting together persuasive arguments, avoid common mistakes such as these:[12]

- **Using an up-front hard sell.** Don't push. Setting out a strong position at the start of a persuasive message puts potential opponents on guard, giving them something to grab onto—and fight against.

CHECKLIST: Developing Persuasive Messages

A. GET YOUR READER'S ATTENTION

- Open with a reader benefit, a stimulating question, a problem, or an unexpected statement.
- Discuss something your audience can agree with (establishing common ground).
- Demonstrate that you understand the audience's concerns.

B. BUILD YOUR READER'S INTEREST

- Expand and support your opening claim or promise.
- Emphasize the relevance of your message to your audience.

C. INCREASE YOUR READER'S DESIRE

- Make audience members want to change by explaining how the change will benefit them.
- Back up your claims with relevant evidence.

D. MOTIVATE YOUR READER TO TAKE ACTION

- Suggest the action you want readers to take.
- Stress the positive results of the action.
- Make the desired action clear and easy.

E. BALANCE EMOTIONAL AND LOGICAL APPEALS

- Use emotional appeals to help the audience accept your message.
- Use logical appeals when presenting facts and evidence for complex ideas or recommendations.
- Avoid faulty logic.

F. REINFORCE YOUR POSITION

- Provide additional evidence of the benefits of your proposal and your own credibility in offering it.
- Use abstractions, metaphors, and other figures of speech to bring facts and figures to life.

G. ANTICIPATE OBJECTIONS

- Anticipate and answer potential objections.
- Present the pros and cons of all options if you anticipate a hostile reaction.

Avoid the common mistakes of using a hard sell, resisting compromise, relying solely on argumentation, and assuming persuasion is a one-time event.

- **Resisting compromise.** Don't dig your heels in. Persuasion is a process of give and take. As one expert points out, a persuader rarely changes another person's behavior or viewpoint without altering his or her own in the process.
- **Relying solely on great arguments.** Don't limit your tactics. In persuading people to change their minds, great arguments matter, but they are only one part of the equation. Your ability to create a mutually beneficial framework for your position, to connect with your audience on the right emotional level, and to communicate through vivid language are all just as important; they bring your argument to life.
- **Assuming persuasion is a one-shot effort.** Don't expect too much at once. Persuasion is a process, not a one-time event. More often than not, persuasion involves listening to people, testing a position, developing a new position that reflects new input, more testing, more compromise, and so on.

Your success with persuasive messages depends on your ability to frame your argument, balance emotional and logical appeals, reinforce your position, and overcome resistance. These strategies will help you craft strong persuasive messages, no matter what the situation. To review the steps involved in developing persuasive messages, refer to "Checklist: Developing Persuasive Messages."

DOCUMENT MAKEOVER

IMPROVE THIS E-MAIL MESSAGE

To practice correcting drafts of actual documents, visit www.prenhall.com/onekey on the web. Click "Document Makeovers" then click Chapter 9. You will find an e-mail message that contains problems and errors relating to what you've learned in this chapter about writing persuasive messages. Use the Final Draft decision tool to create an improved version of this e-mail. Check the message for its effectiveness at gaining attention, building interest, stimulating desire, motivating action, focusing on the primary goal, and dealing with resistance.

Common Examples of Persuasive Business Messages

Throughout your career, you'll have numerous opportunities to write persuasive messages within your organization: selling a supervisor on an idea for cutting costs, suggesting more efficient operating procedures, eliciting cooperation from competing departments, winning employee support for a new benefits package, requesting money for new equipment or funding for a special project. Similarly, you may send a variety of persuasive messages to people outside the organization: asking for information, soliciting funds and cooperation, collecting overdue debts, or requesting adjustments that go beyond a supplier's contractual obligations. In addition, many of the routine requests you studied in Chapter 7 can become persuasive messages if you want a nonroutine result or believe that you haven't received fair treatment. Most of these messages can be divided into persuasive requests for action, persuasive presentation of ideas, and persuasive claims and requests for adjustment.

Persuasive Requests for Action

When making a persuasive request for action, be sure to use the AIDA plan to frame your argument.

The bulk of your persuasive business messages will involve requests for action. In some cases, your request will be anticipated, so the direct approach is fine. In others, you'll need to introduce your intention indirectly, and the AIDA model is ideal for this purpose. Open with an attention-getting device and show readers that you know something about their concerns.

Use the interest and desire sections of your message to demonstrate that you have good reason for making such a request and to cover what you know about the situation: the facts and figures, the benefits of helping, and any history or experience that will enhance your appeal. Your goals are (1) to gain credibility (for yourself and your request) and (2) to make your readers believe that helping you will indeed help solve a significant problem.

Once you've demonstrated that your message is relevant to your reader, you can close with a request for some specific action, as Leslie Jorgensen did in the memo in Figure 9.4. She's excited about the new Airbus A380 and thinks that purchasing this plane for appropriate markets could help Qantas meet its growth needs while lowering its operating costs. She now needs her boss's approval for a study of the plane's market potential.

When requesting a favor that is routine (such as asking someone to attend a meeting in your absence), use the direct approach and the format for routine messages (see Chapter 7). However, when asking for a special favor (such as asking someone to chair an event or to serve as the team leader because you can no longer fill that role), use persuasive techniques to convince your reader of the value of the project. Include all necessary information about the project and any facts and figures that will convince your reader that his or her contribution will be enjoyable, easy, important, and of personal benefit.

Persuasive Presentation of Ideas

Most internal persuasive messages focus on getting the audience to make a specific decision or take some specific action. However, you will encounter situations in which you simply want to change attitudes or beliefs about a particular topic, without asking the audience to decide or do anything—at least not yet. In complicated, multistep persuasive efforts, the goal of your first message might be nothing more than convincing your audience to reexamine long-held opinions or admit the possibility of new ways of thinking.

For instance, you think your company is spending too much time processing payroll, and you've found an outside firm that can do it for less money than you now spend on internal staff and systems (a practice known an *outsourcing*). However, your company president is philosophically opposed to outsourcing any critical business function, saying that something as important as payroll should never be entrusted to outsiders. Until and unless you can bring about a change in the president's way of thinking, there is no point is pushing for a decision about outsourcing.

Another example is the effort to improve Internet access for people with visual disabilities and other conditions that hamper access. A campaign called the Web Accessibility Initiative has been launched by the Worldwide Web Consortium (a global association that defines many of the guidelines and technologies behind the World Wide Web). Although the Consortium's ultimate goal is making websites more accessible, a key interim goal is simply making website developers more aware of the need. Thus the Consortium developed a presentation that highlights issues such as the following:[13]

- The web's growing importance as a source of everything, including news and entertainment, workplace interaction, and government services
- The web's gradual displacement of traditional sources of these services

These marketing messages from Intel are not designed to evoke any immediate action from the target audience. Intel makes the processor chips used in most personal computers, which are made by other companies. So these posters simply remind buyers to look for the Intel name whenever they purchase new computers.

FIGURE 9.4 Effective Persuasive Memo Requesting Action

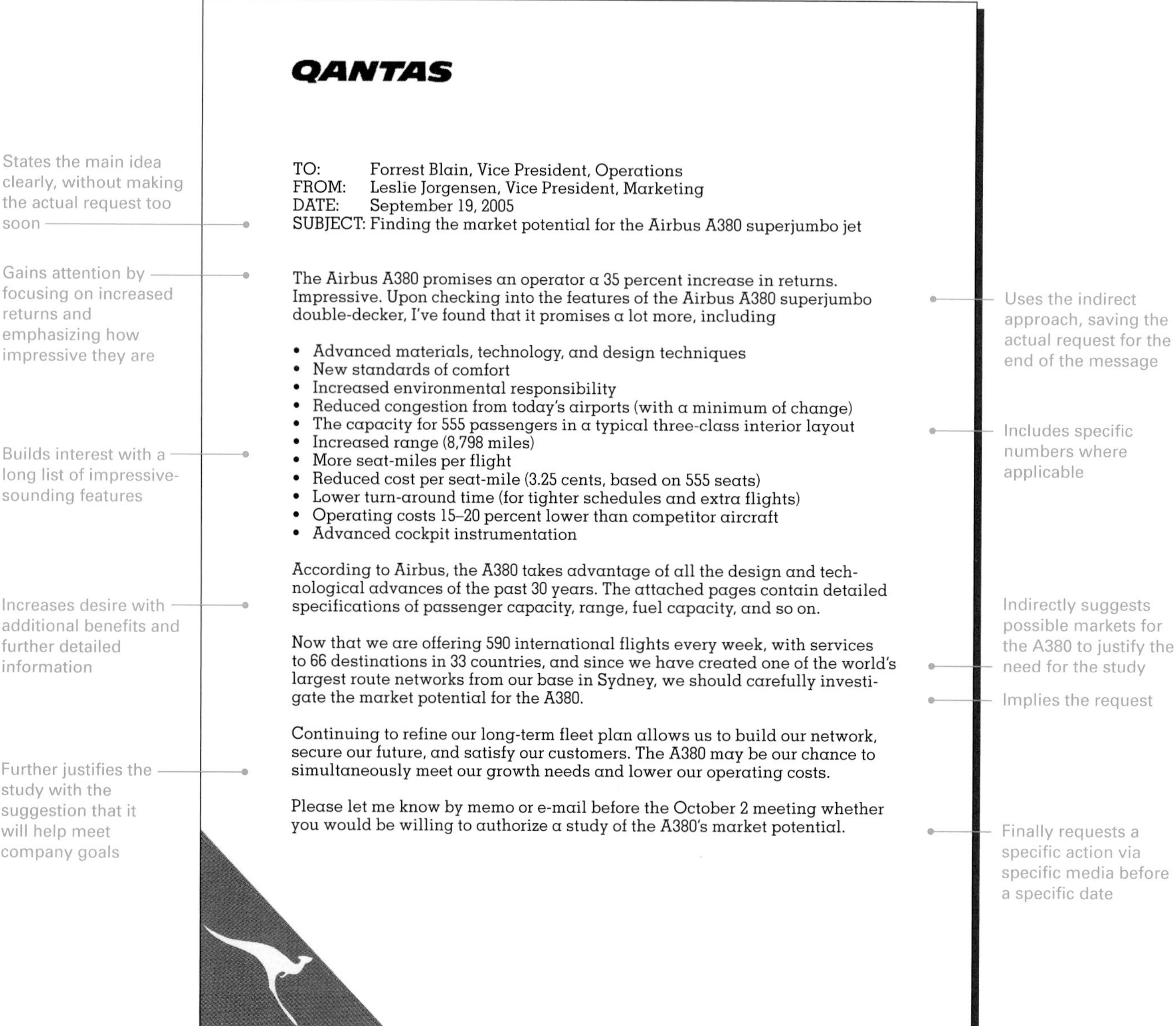

QANTAS

TO: Forrest Blain, Vice President, Operations
FROM: Leslie Jorgensen, Vice President, Marketing
DATE: September 19, 2005
SUBJECT: Finding the market potential for the Airbus A380 superjumbo jet

The Airbus A380 promises an operator a 35 percent increase in returns. Impressive. Upon checking into the features of the Airbus A380 superjumbo double-decker, I've found that it promises a lot more, including

- Advanced materials, technology, and design techniques
- New standards of comfort
- Increased environmental responsibility
- Reduced congestion from today's airports (with a minimum of change)
- The capacity for 555 passengers in a typical three-class interior layout
- Increased range (8,798 miles)
- More seat-miles per flight
- Reduced cost per seat-mile (3.25 cents, based on 555 seats)
- Lower turn-around time (for tighter schedules and extra flights)
- Operating costs 15–20 percent lower than competitor aircraft
- Advanced cockpit instrumentation

According to Airbus, the A380 takes advantage of all the design and technological advances of the past 30 years. The attached pages contain detailed specifications of passenger capacity, range, fuel capacity, and so on.

Now that we are offering 590 international flights every week, with services to 66 destinations in 33 countries, and since we have created one of the world's largest route networks from our base in Sydney, we should carefully investigate the market potential for the A380.

Continuing to refine our long-term fleet plan allows us to build our network, secure our future, and satisfy our customers. The A380 may be our chance to simultaneously meet our growth needs and lower our operating costs.

Please let me know by memo or e-mail before the October 2 meeting whether you would be willing to authorize a study of the A380's market potential.

States the main idea clearly, without making the actual request too soon
Gains attention by focusing on increased returns and emphasizing how impressive they are
Builds interest with a long list of impressive-sounding features
Increases desire with additional benefits and further detailed information
Further justifies the study with the suggestion that it will help meet company goals
Uses the indirect approach, saving the actual request for the end of the message
Includes specific numbers where applicable
Indirectly suggests possible markets for the A380 to justify the need for the study
Implies the request
Finally requests a specific action via specific media before a specific date

- The presence of barriers on the web for many types of disabilities
- The number of people whose disabilities affect their access to the web (the number is in the millions)
- The fact that accessible web designs can also help other users

Information on these specific issues can help open the eyes of website owners who may assume that standard web practices are sufficient for their audiences.

Persuasive Claims and Requests for Adjustments

Although persuasive claims and adjustment requests are sometimes referred to as complaint letters, you're not merely getting a complaint off your chest. Your goal is to persuade someone to make an adjustment in your favor. You work toward this goal by demonstrating the difference between what you expected and what you actually got.

Most claim letters are routine messages and use the direct approach discussed in Chapter 7. However, suppose you purchase something and, after the warranty expires, you discover that the item was defective. You write the company a routine request asking for a replacement, but your request is denied. You're not satisfied, and you still believe you have a strong case. Perhaps you just didn't communicate it well enough the first time. Persuasion is necessary in such cases.

You can't threaten to withhold payment, so try to convey the essentially negative information in a way that will get positive results. Fortunately, most people in business are open to settling your claim fairly. It's to their advantage to maintain your goodwill and to resolve your problem quickly.

The key ingredients of a good persuasive claim are a complete and specific review of the facts and a confident and positive tone. Assume that the other person is not trying to cheat you but that you also have the right to be satisfied with the transaction. Talk only about the complaint at hand, not about other issues involving similar products or other complaints about the company. Your goal is to solve a particular problem, and your audience is most likely to help if you focus on the audience benefits of doing so (rather than focusing on the disadvantages of neglecting your complaint).

Begin persuasive claims by stating the basic problem or reviewing what has been done about the problem so far. Include a statement that both you and your audience can agree with or that clarifies what you wish to convince your audience about. Be as specific as possible about what you want to happen. Next, give your reader a good reason for granting your claim. Show how your audience is responsible for the problem, and appeal to your reader's sense of fair play, goodwill, or moral responsibility. Explain how you feel about the problem, but don't get carried away, don't complain too much, and don't make threats. People generally respond more favorably to requests that are both calm and reasonable.

Marketing and Sales Messages

Marketing and sales messages use the same basic techniques as other persuasive messages, with the added emphasis of encouraging someone to participate in a commercial transaction. Although the terms *marketing message* and *sales message* are often used interchangeably, they do represent separate but related promotional efforts: Marketing messages usher potential buyers through the purchasing process without asking them to make an immediate decision; that's when sales messages take over. Marketing messages focus on such tasks as introducing new brands to the public, providing competitive comparison information, encouraging customers to visit websites for more information, and reminding buyers that a particular product or service is available. In contrast, a sales message makes a specific request for people to place an order for a particular product or service.

Marketing and sales messages use many of the same techniques as persuasive business messages.

Most promotional messages, particularly in larger companies, are created by professionals with specific training in marketing, advertising, and sales. However, you may be called on to review the work of these specialists or even to write promotional messages in smaller companies, so a good understanding of promotion fundamentals will help. The basic strategies to consider include assessing customer needs, analyzing your competition, determining key selling points and benefits, anticipating purchase objections, applying the AIDA model, and maintaining high standards of ethics, legal compliance, and etiquette. Also, keep in mind that marketing and sales campaigns often include the series of messages in a coordinated effort that can last for weeks or months. In these campaigns, your message planning might encompass a website, e-mails, letters, brochures, personal sales presentations, as well as a mix of print, online, and broadcast media.

Assessing Audience Needs

As with every other business message, successful marketing and sales messages start with an understanding of audience needs. For some products and services, this assessment is a simple matter. For instance, customers compare only a few basic attributes when purchasing copy or printer paper, including weight, brightness, color, and finish. In contrast, they might consider dozens of features when shopping for real estate, cars, professional services, and other complex purchases.

Purchasing decisions often involve more than just the basic product or service.

In addition, customer needs often extend beyond the basic product or service. Clothes do far more than simply keep you warm. What you wear makes a statement about who you are, which social groups you want to be associated with (or not), and how you view your relationship with the people around you. In fact, a simple pair of shoes can meet at least four levels in Maslow's hierarchy of needs.

For promotional messages, begin assessing audience needs, interests, and emotional concerns—just as you would for any business message. Try to form a mental image of the typical buyer for the product you wish to sell. Ask yourself what audience members might want to know about this product. How can your product help them? Are they driven by bottom-line pricing, or is quality more important to them?

Note the ads you're exposed to every day. They often focus on just one or two attributes or issues, even if the product or service has many different facets to consider. The purpose of these narrow marketing messages is to grab your attention and then raise your interest level enough to encourage you to conduct further research.

Analyzing Your Competition

Most marketing and sales messages have to compete for the audience's attention.

Marketing and sales messages nearly always compete with messages from other companies trying to reach the same audience. When Chrysler plans a sales letter to introduce a new model to current customers, the company knows that its audience has also been exposed to messages from Ford, Honda, Volkswagen, and numerous other car companies. In crowded markets, promotional writers sometimes have to search for words and phrases that other companies aren't already using. They might also want to avoid themes, writing styles, or creative approaches that are too similar to those of competitive messages.

6 LEARNING OBJECTIVE

Discuss an effective approach to identifying selling points and audience benefits

Determining Key Selling Points and Benefits

With some insight into audience needs and promotional messages from the competition, you're ready to decide which benefits and features of your product or service to highlight. For all but the simplest products, you'll want to prioritize the items you plan to discuss. You'll also want to distinguish between the features of the product and the benefits that those features offer the customers.

Selling points focus on the product; benefits focus on the user.

As Table 9.2 shows, **selling points** are the most attractive features of an idea or product, while **benefits** are the particular advantages that readers will realize from those features. Selling points focus on the product. Benefits focus on the user. For example, if you say that your snow shovel has "an ergonomically designed handle," you've described a good feature. But to persuade someone to buy that shovel, say "the ergonomically designed handle will reduce your risk of back injury." That's a benefit. For your message to be successful, your product's distinguishing benefit must correspond to your readers' primary needs or emotional concerns.

Consider how SecureAbel Alarms uses the AIDA model to persuade students to buy its dorm-room alarm system (see Figure 9.5). The features of the system are that it can be installed with a screwdriver, it has an activator that hooks to your key chain or belt loop,

TABLE 9.2 Features Versus Benefits

PRODUCT FEATURE (SELLING POINT)	CUSTOMER BENEFIT
No money down, no interest, payments for 24 months.	You can buy what you want right now at no additional costs.
This printer prints 17 pages a minute.	This printer can turn out one of your 100-page proposals in six minutes.
Our shelter provides 100 adult beds and 50 children's beds for the needy.	Your donation will provide temporary housing for 100 women who don't want to return to abusive husbands.
Your corporate sponsorship of the seminar will pay for the keynote speaker's travel and lodging.	Your corporate sponsorship of the seminar will allow your site manager a five-minute introduction at the beginning of the program to summarize your services.

Plan

1

Analyze the Situation
The purpose is to sell a product, therefore, the audience will be neutral, uninterested, or perhaps unwilling.

Gather Information
Determine audience needs and obtain the necessary information to present a persuasive message.

Select the Right Medium
A printed letter is appropriate for this formal communication.

Organize the Information
Your main idea is to offer a product for sale, so limit your scope to that issue; use the AIDA approach to propose the solution.

Write

2

Adapt to Your Audience
Adjust the level of formality based on degree of familiarity with the audience; maintain a positive relationship by using the "you" attitude, politeness, positive emphasis, and bias-free language.

Compose the Message
Use a conversational but professional style and keep the message brief, clear, and as helpful as possible.

Complete

3

Revise the Message
Evaluate content and review readability to make sure the negative information won't be misinterpreted; make sure your tone stays positive without being artificial.

Produce the Message
Emphasize a clean, professional appearance on company letterhead.

Proofread the Message
Review for errors in layout, spelling, and mechanics.

Distribute the Message
Deliver your message using the chosen medium.

FIGURE 9.5 **Effective Letter Selling a Product**

SecureAbel Alarms, Inc.

5654 Lakemont Drive • Altoona, PA 16602 • Voice: (814) 983-4424 • Fax: (814) 983-4422 • http://www.secure.com

October 11, 2005

Mr. Samuel Zolezzi
Penn State University, North Halls
104 Warnock Commons
State College, PA 16802

Dear Mr. Zolezzi:

Did you know that one out of four college students becomes a victim of theft? How would you feel if you returned to your dorm and discovered that your hard-earned stereo, computer, or microwave had been stolen? Remember, locked doors won't stop a determined thief.

> Draws the reader into the letter with a provocative question
>
> Raises reader's awareness of a need

My dorm room was burglarized when I was in college. That's why I've developed a portable security system for your dormitory room. This system works like an auto alarm and can be installed with an ordinary screwdriver. The small activator hooks to your key chain or belt loop. Just press the "lock" key. A "beep" tells you your room is secure, and a blinking red light warns intruders to stay away.

> Seeks to establish a common bond with the reader
>
> Explains how product works by comparing it to something familiar—a car alarm

If a thief tries to break in, a loud alarm sounds. Your possessions will be safe. And, even more important, you can activate the system from your bedside, so you're safe while you sleep.

> Mentions an additional threat (to personal safety), implying another benefit of the security system
>
> Uses both a logical appeal (protecting possessions) and an emotional appeal (personal safety)

You'd expect this peace of mind to cost a fortune—something most college students don't have. But we're offering the SecureAbel Dorm Alarm System for only $75. Here's what you'll receive by return mail:

- The patented alarm unit
- Two battery-operated programmable remote units
- A one-year warranty on all parts
- Complete and easy-to-follow installation instructions

Order additional alarm boxes to install on your window or bathroom door for only $50. Act now. Fill out the response card, and mail it along with your choice of payment method in the enclosed envelope. Don't give thieves and criminals a chance. Protect yourself and your belongings. Send in your card today.

> Creates the sense of added value
>
> Urges quick action

Sincerely,

Dan Abel

Dan Abel, President

Enclosures

and it has a blinking red light to warn intruders to stay away. The benefits are ease of installation, ease of activation, and a feeling of safety and security—all obtainable without investing in a permanently installed alarm system.

Anticipating Purchase Objections

Anticipating objections is crucial to effective marketing and sales messages.

As with persuasive business messages, marketing and sales messages often encounter objections, and once again, the best way to handle them is to identify them up front and try to address as many as you can in the original message (or messages, as the case may be). However, with promotional messages, you won't get a second chance to explain yourself or to present your case. Your boss might feel an obligation to let you explain what you meant in the third paragraph of your persuasive proposal, but potential customers feel no such responsibility. If your website for fashion jewelry aimed at college-age consumers strikes visitors as too juvenile, they'll click to another site within seconds and probably never come back to yours.

Objections can range from high price to low quality to a lack of compatibility with existing products. Perceived risk is another common objection. Consumers might worry that a car won't be safe enough for a family, that a jacket will make them look unattractive, or that a hair salon will botch a haircut. Business buyers might worry about disrupting operations or failing to realize the financial returns on a purchase.

Price can be a particularly tricky issue in any message, whether audience members are consumers or business customers. Whether you highlight or downplay the price of your product, prepare your readers for it. Words such as *luxurious* and *economical* provide unmistakable clues about how your price compares with that of competitors. Such words help your readers accept your price when you finally state it.

If the price is an attractive aspect of the proposed solution, emphasize it by featuring it prominently.

If price is a major selling point, give it a position of prominence, such as in the headline or as the last item in a paragraph. If price is not a major selling point, you can handle it in several ways. You could leave the price out altogether or deemphasize it by putting the figure in the middle of a paragraph that comes well after you've presented the benefits and selling points.

Emphasizes the rarity of the edition to signal value and thus prepare the reader for the big-ticket price that follows

Buries the actual price in the middle of a sentence and ties it in with another reminder of the exclusivity of the offer

Only 100 prints of this exclusive, limited-edition lithograph will be created. On June 15, they will be made available to the general public, but you can reserve one now for only $350, the special advance reservation price. Simply rush the enclosed reservation card back today so that your order is in before the June 15 publication date.

The pros also use two other techniques for minimizing price. One is to break a quantity price into units. Instead of saying that a case of motor oil costs $24, you might say that each bottle costs $2. The other technique is to compare your product's price with the cost of some other product or activity: "The cost of owning your own exercise equipment is less than you'd pay for a health-club membership." Your aim is to make the cost seem as small and affordable as possible, thereby minimizing price as a possible objection.

If you've done your homework up front and assessed your audience thoroughly, you should be aware of most of these concerns. You might not be able to address every one of them in your message—if the product or service isn't ideal for the customer, you're message can't fix that—but you will be prepared to do the best you can with the product or service you have to promote.

Applying the AIDA Model

Most marketing and sales messages are prepared according to the AIDA plan, or some variation of it. You begin with an attention-getting device, generate interest by describing some of the product or service's unique features, increase desire by highlighting the benefits that are most appealing to your audience, and close by suggesting the action you want the audience to take.

Getting Attention Not only do promotional messages open with an attention-getting device, but professionals use a wide range of techniques to attract their audience's attention:

You can employ a variety of attention-getting devices in promotional messages.

- **Your product's strongest benefit.** "iPod. 10,000 songs in your pocket."[14]
- **A point of common ground with the audience.** "An SUV adventurous enough to accommodate your spontaneity and the gear that comes with it."[15]
- **A piece of genuine news.** "In the past 60 days, mortgage rates have fallen to a 30-year low."
- **A personal appeal to the reader's emotions and values.** "The only thing worse than paying taxes is paying taxes when you don't have to."
- **The promise of insider information.** "You may be one of those people who dream of working and living in France and don't know how to go about simply doing it. This guide tells how—from the inside out—how others like yourself have managed to work within the French system."[16]
- **The promise of savings.** "Right now, you can get huge savings on a new camera phone."[17]
- **A sample or demonstration of the product.** "Here's your free sample of the new Romalite packing sheet."
- **A solution to a problem.** "This backpack's designed to endure all a kid's dropping and dragging."[18]

Of course, words aren't the only attention-getting device at your disposal. Strong, evocative images are a common attention getter. With online messages, you have even more options, including animation and music tracks.

Building Interest Use the interest section of your message to build on the interest you created with your opening. This section should also offer support for whatever claims or promises you might've made in the opening. For instance, after opening with the headline that claims "10,000 songs in your pocket," the Apple iPod webpage continues with[19]

To build interest, expand on and support the promises in your attention-getting opening.

> The new super-slim iPod once again redefines what a digital music player should be. It's lighter than 2 CDs, can hold up to 10,000 songs, thousands of digital photos, and works as a personal voice recorder. Now you can sync with iTunes for Mac and Windows at blazing speeds, and take your entire music collection with you wherever you go. Available for Mac and Windows starting at $299.

Using a powerful analogy to describe the product's weight, the webpage continues with additional features (all of which have obvious benefits)

Allays concerns of Windows users who may think an Apple product won't work with their computers

Emphasizes selling price by placing it prominently at the end of the paragraph

At this point in the message, Apple has offered enough information to help people understand how they might use the product, and it has answered a couple of potential objections as well (compatibility with Windows and the price). Anyone interested in a digital music player is probably intrigued enough to keep reading.

Increasing Desire To build desire for the product, continue to expand and explain what it offers, how it works, how customers can use it, and so on. In a printed letter, brochure, or other fixed piece, think carefully about the sequence of support points, and use plenty of subheadings and other devices to help people find the information they need quickly. For example, after reading this much about the iPod, some users might want to know more about the iTunes Music Store, whereas others will want technical specifications. You will want to make it easy to find the information each individual wants.

Add details and audience benefits to increase desire for the product or service.

Of course, with websites, e-mail, CD-ROMs, and other electronic formats, you can offer navigational links to let people access specific information almost instantly. The iPod product page continues with detailed discussions of various product features and benefits, but it also offers numerous links to pages with other kinds of support information. The ability to provide flexible access to information is just one of the reasons the

Connecting with Technology

The Power and Persuasion of Interactive Sales Tools

Have you ever booked a vacation hotel with great expectations, only to arrive and find the place nothing like what you thought it would be? Using words to describe the features and ambience of a physical space is a challenge for the best of writers. As a result, descriptions of hotels and conference centers tend to end up sounding an awful lot alike.

The possibility of making a poor choice can be a worry for vacationing consumers, but it's enough to keep corporate event planners awake at night. When you're responsible for planning and hosting events that could involve dozens, hundreds, even thousands of attendees, you need to know about everything from dining facilities to where people will register and pick up their name badges. Anything can cast a poor light on your planning efforts—from tacky interior decorating to overcrowded hallways that prevent people from moving comfortably between conference sessions. However, such factors are hard to judge from a printed brochure, and you won't always have the chance to visit every property ahead of time.

The South San Francisco Conference Center (www.ssfconf.com)is one of a growing number of facilities that offer virtual tours online. Potential visitors can experience what it's like to stand in the middle of various rooms and look around 360 degrees. By providing a virtual-reality experience that's the next best thing to being there, the center goes a long way toward removing an audience's perceived risks and accelerating a favorable purchase decision.

CAREER APPLICATIONS

1. What are the possible disadvantages of using these interactive tools?
2. How would you promote your college or university to prospective students using an interactive website?

web is such a powerful promotional medium (see "Connecting with Technology: The Power and Persuasion of Interactive Sales Tools").

Throughout the body of your message, remember to keep the focus on the audience, not on your company or your product. When you talk about product features, remember to stress the benefits and talk in terms that make sense to users. Listing the capacity of the iPod as 10,000 songs is a lot more meaningful for most readers than saying it has 40 gigabytes of memory. Action words give strength to any business message, but they are especially important in sales letters. Compare the following:

INSTEAD OF THIS	WRITE THIS
The NuForm desk chair is designed to support your lower back and relieve pressure on your legs.	The NuForm desk chair supports your lower back and relieves pressure on your legs.

The second version says the same thing in fewer words and emphasizes what the chair does for the user ("supports") rather than the intentions of the design team ("is designed to support").

To keep readers interested, use strong, colorful language without overdoing it.

To keep readers interested, use colorful verbs and adjectives that convey a dynamic image. Be careful, however, not to overdo it: If you say "Your factory floors will sparkle like diamonds," your audience will find it hard to believe, which may prevent them from believing the rest of your message.

To increase desire, as well as boost your credibility, provide support for your claims. You can't assume your audience will believe what you say just because you've said it in writing. You'll have to give them proof. Support is especially important if your product is complicated, costs a lot, or represents some unusual approach.

Creative marketers find many ways to provide support: testimonials from satisfied users, articles written by industry experts, competitive comparisons, product samples and free demonstrations, independent test results, even movies or computer animations that show a product in action. You can also highlight guarantees that demonstrate your faith in your product and your willingness to back it up ("Return it within 30 days if you're not satisfied"). Try to anticipate every question your audience may want to ask. Put yourself in your audience's place so that you can discover, and solve, all the "what if" scenarios.[20]

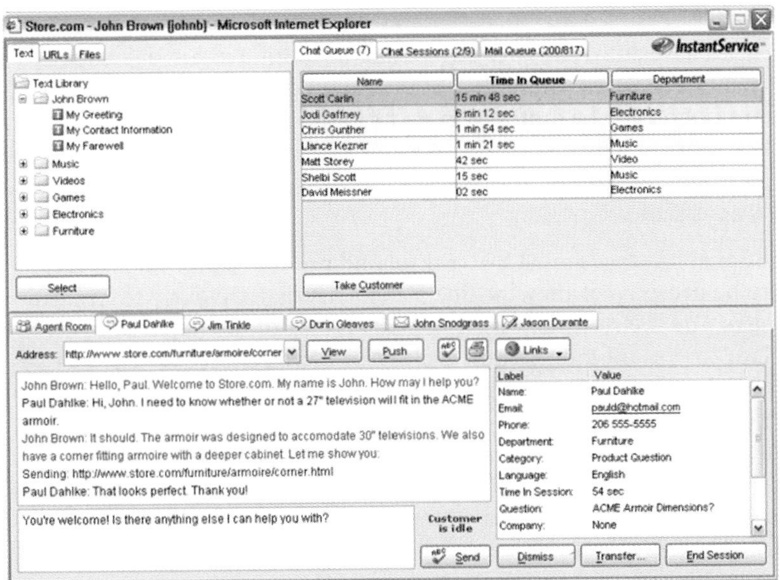

Chat software, such as this customer-service and sales solution from InstantService, gives websites an easy way to interact with their audiences. This screen shows what an online sales representative sees while communicating with customers: the current IM session (lower left corner), the queue of waiting customers (upper right corner), additional information about the current customer, and text files that the sales rep can access instantly to speed up the IM process.

Motivating Action After you have raised enough interest and built up the reader's desire for your offering, you're ready to ask your audience to take action. Whether you want people to pick up the phone to place an order or visit your website to download a free demo version of your software, try to persuade them to do it right away. You might offer a discount for the first 1,000 people to order, put a deadline on the offer, or simply remind them that the sooner they order, the sooner they'll be able to enjoy the product's benefits. Even potential buyers who want the product can get distracted or forget to respond, so the sooner you can encourage action, the better. Make the response action as simple and as risk-free as possible.

You can try to persuade readers to take the preferred action after you build up sufficient interest in and desire for the product or service.

Take care to maintain the respectful, professional tone you've been using up to this point. Don't resort to gimmicks and desperate-sounding pleas for the customer's business. Make sure your final impression is compelling and positive. For instance, in a sales letter, the postscript (P.S.) below your signature is often one of the first and last parts people read. Use this valuable space to emphasize the key benefit you have to offer and to emphasize the advantages of ordering soon.

Maintaining High Standards of Ethics, Legal Compliance, and Etiquette

7 LEARNING OBJECTIVE

Identify steps you can take to avoid ethical lapses in marketing and sales messages

The word *persuasion* has negative connotations for some people, especially in a marketing or sales context. They associate persuasion with dishonest and unethical practices that lead unsuspecting audiences into accepting unworthy ideas or buying unneeded products. However, effective businesspeople view persuasion as a positive force, aligning their own interests with what is best for their audiences. They influence audience members by providing information and aiding understanding, which allows audiences the freedom to choose.[21] Ethical businesspeople inform audiences of the benefits of an idea, an organization, a product, a donation, or an action so that these audiences can recognize just how well the idea, organization, product, donation, or action will satisfy a need they truly have. To maintain the highest standards of business ethics, make every attempt to persuade without manipulating. Choose words that won't be misinterpreted, and be sure you don't distort the truth. Adopt the "you" attitude by showing honest concern for your audience's needs and interests. Your consideration of audience needs is more than ethical; it's the proper use of persuasion. That consideration is likely to achieve the response you intend and to satisfy your audience's needs.

Persuasion has negative connotations for many people, a fact that you need to consider in your own persuasive writing.

As marketing and selling grow increasingly complex, so do the legal ramifications of promotional messages. In the United States, the Federal Trade Commission (FTC) has the authority to impose penalties (ranging from cease-and-desist orders to multimillion-dollar

Marketing and sales messages are covered by a wide range of laws and regulations.

fines) against advertisers who violate federal standards for truthful advertising.[22] Other federal agencies have authority over advertising in specific industries, such as transportation and financial services. Individual states have additional laws that apply. The legal aspects of promotion can be quite complex, from state to state and from country to country, and most companies require marketing and sales people to get clearance from company lawyers before sending promotional messages. In any event, pay close attention to the following legal aspects of promotion:

- **Promotional messages must be truthful and nondeceptive.** The FTC considers messages to be deceptive if they include statements that are likely to mislead reasonable customers, and the statement is an important part of the purchasing decision. Failing to include important information is also considered deceptive. The FTC also looks at *implied claims*, those you don't explicitly make but that can be inferred from what you do or don't say.
- **You must back up your claims with evidence.** According to the FTC, offering a money-back guarantee or providing letters from satisfied customers is not enough; you must still be able to support your claims with objective evidence such as a survey or scientific study. If you claim that your food product lowers cholesterol, you must have scientific evidence to support that claim.
- **Promotional messages are considered binding contracts in many states.** If you imply or make an offer and then can't fulfill your end of the bargain, you can be sued for breach of contract.
- **In most cases, you can't use a person's name, photograph, or other identity without permission.** Doing so is considered an invasion of privacy. You can use images of people considered to be public figures, as long as you don't unfairly imply that they endorse your message.

In both the United States and other countries, lawmakers are considering new legislation covering several other major aspects of promotion. Before you launch a promotional campaign, make sure you're up to date on the latest regulations affecting spam (or *unsolicited bulk e-mail,* as it's officially known), customer privacy, and data security. New laws are likely to appear in all three areas in the next few years.

Maintaining high ethical standards is a key aspect of good communication etiquette.

Meeting your ethical and legal obligations will go a long way toward maintaining good communication etiquette as well. However, you may still face etiquette decisions within ethical and legal boundaries. For instance, you can produce a marketing campaign that complies with all applicable laws and yet is still offensive or insulting to your audience. An audience-centered approach, involving respect for your readers and their values, should help you avoid any such etiquette missteps.

Common Examples of Marketing and Sales Messages

Even the most technologically advanced persuasive tools and media follow the basic guidelines of persuasive communication.

From simple letters to interactive kiosks, the variety of promotional messages in today's business environment is seemingly endless. However, no matter how advanced the technology becomes, successful promotion will always be built around the basics: understanding audience needs, out-communicating competitors, and providing clear, compelling information that encourages customers to make a decision in your favor. For instance, clothing retailer Lands' End (Figure 9.6) takes advantage of e-mail as a means to communicate with customers, but the company is careful to consider customers' wishes. To avoid the negative associations of spam, the newsletter is an *opt-in* mailing, meaning Lands' End sends it only to customers who request it. Recipients can also choose the categories of information they want to receive and how frequently they want to receive it. The newsletter itself combines friendly and informative text that addresses everyday customers' concerns, appealing photography of Lands' End products, and convenient links to the company's website for placing orders.

Saturn's website offers another example of the depth and breadth of information you can provide customers to help them make informed decisions. The product comparison

FIGURE 9.6 Opt-In E-Mail Newsletter

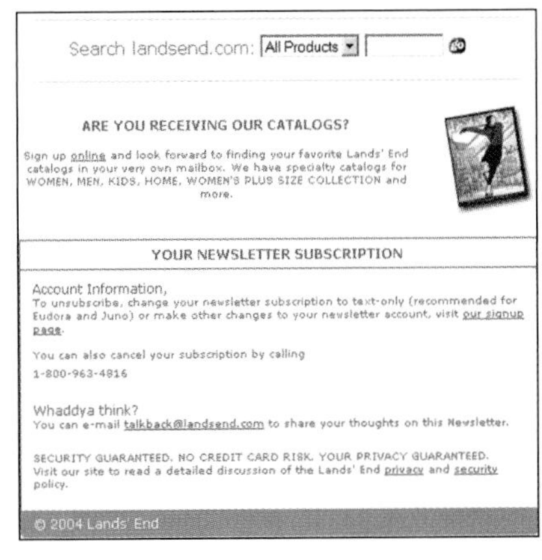

screen in Figure 9.7 lets car shoppers compare a Saturn model with competitive models—a task that is difficult and time-consuming with printed brochures. After selecting one or two competitors, the shopper is then presented with a comprehensive comparison of product features. Beyond the information itself, a presentation such as this sends two subtle messages to the reader. First, Saturn embraces the "you" attitude by giving consumers information that want, even if that means giving them information about Saturn's competitors. Second, by inviting comparisons with other cars, Saturn demonstrates confidence in its own products, which in turn helps it build credibility and inspire confidence among potential buyers.

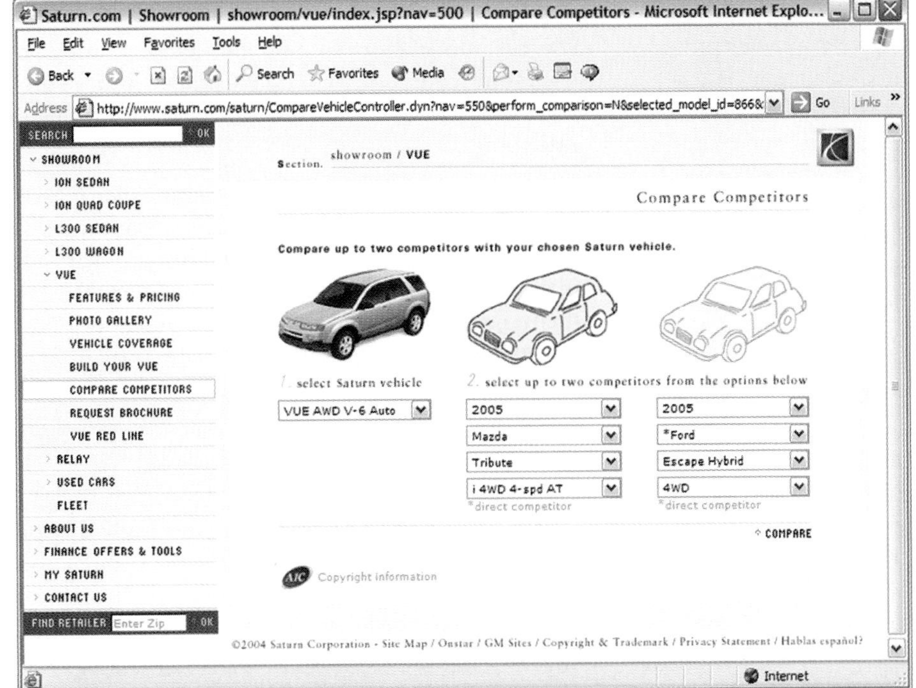

FIGURE 9.7
Saturn Website

COMMUNICATION CHALLENGES AT MARK BURNETT PRODUCTIONS

Mark Burnett is always looking for fresh new projects to develop, including more shows along the lines of *Survivor* and *The Apprentice*. Somehow, within your busy schedule as executive assistant, you've come up with an idea for a new reality show called *The Communicator*, to be set in a typical small business. Your idea for the prize is even more ambitious than that for *The Apprentice:* the winner will become the owner and manager of the business.

Individual Challenge: *The Communicator* should have the same high-stakes appeal of *The Apprentice*, but you recognize that the narrower focus on business communication (rather than the broader topic of business management) might be a challenge for the show's creators. Do people really care that much about communication in the workplace? Can you identify enough communication-related issues to sustain an entire season's worth of shows? Draft a one-page memo to Burnett persuading him that workplace communication is a universal issue that many television viewers will respond to.

Team Challenge: You know from previous summer jobs that small-business owners need solid persuasive skills. You've watched former bosses wrestle with persuasive writing projects that include sales letters, efforts to form a community business association, and presentations in front of the local zoning commission. You want the winner of *The Communicator* to be particularly good at persuasion. With a small team, brainstorm three persuasive skills challenges that the show could use to judge contestants in this important area. Describe the three challenges in an e-mail to your instructor.

SUMMARY OF LEARNING OBJECTIVES

1 **Apply the three-step writing process to persuasive messages.** The three-step process is easily adapted to promotional messages. These messages require careful planning since such messages are often unexpected and at times unwelcome. To plan successfully, truly clarify your purpose to make sure you focus on a single goal; clearly express your purpose to the audience so they are aware of what you would like them to feel, think, or do; and recognize that some audience decisions won't be made in a single step, and you'll need a series of persuasive messages to reach your ultimate objective. The information you need to gather involves a combination of emotional and logical elements, which you then blend together based on your knowledge of audience wants and needs. Most persuasive messages use an indirect approach to establish awareness and interest before asking the audience to take action, although the direct approach is often better for routine persuasive messages or when you're in a position of authority relative to the audience. The "you" attitude is critical in persuasive messages, and successful writers take care to adapt their appeals to the specific wants and needs of their audiences. They also work hard to establish credibility with their readers. The steps involved in completing persuasive messages are essentially the same as for other message types, although even small errors can damage credibility, so persuasive communicators need to be doubly careful with presentation and proofreading.

2 **Identify seven ways to establish credibility in persuasive messages.** The common ways to establish credibility include using simple language, supporting your message with factual evidence, naming your sources when you use information from others, demonstrating expertise (your own or others') establishing common ground with the audience, being objective, and displaying good intentions.

3 **Describe the AIDA model for persuasive messages.** When using the AIDA model, you open your message by getting *attention* with a reader benefit, a problem, a stimulating question, a piece of news, or an unexpected statement. You build *interest* with facts, details, and additional reader benefits. You increase *desire* by providing more evidence and reader benefits and by anticipating and answering possible objections. You conclude by motivating a specific *action*, emphasizing the positive results of that action, and making it easy for the reader to respond.

4 **Distinguish between emotional and logical appeals, and discuss how to balance them.** Emotional appeals call on human feelings, using arguments that are based on audience needs or sympathies. However, these appeals aren't effective by themselves. Logical appeals call on human reason (whether using analogy, induction, or deduction). If you're careful to avoid faulty logic, you can use logic together with emotion, thereby

supplying rational support for an idea that readers have already embraced emotionally. In general, logic will be your strongest appeal, with only subtle emotion. However, when persuading someone to purchase a product, join a cause, or make a donation, you can heighten emotional appeals a bit.

5 **Identify four common mistakes in writing persuasive messages.** Inexperienced writers often make one or more of these mistakes when writing persuasive messages: opening their messages with a hard sell, refusing to compromise, relying solely on great arguments while ignoring how to best present them, and assuming that persuasion is a one-time effort.

6 **Discuss an effective approach to identifying selling points and audience benefits.** Identifying selling points and audience benefits starts with deciding which *benefits* and *features* of your product or service to highlight, including prioritizing the items you want to discuss first. Also, be sure to distinguish between the features of the product, the *selling points*, and the benefits that those features offer the customers.

7 **Identify steps you can take to avoid ethical lapses in marketing and sales messages.** Effective and ethical persuasive communicators focus on aligning their interests with the interests of their audiences. They help audiences understand how their proposals will provide benefits to the audience, using language that is persuasive without being manipulative. They choose words that are less likely to be misinterpreted and take care not to distort the truth. Throughout, they maintain a "you" attitude with honest concern for the audience's needs and interests.

Test Your Knowledge

1. What are some questions to ask when gauging the audience's needs during the planning of a persuasive message?
2. What role do demographics and psychographics play in audience analysis during the planning of a persuasive message?
3. What are four of the ways you can build credibility with an audience when planning a persuasive message?
4. What is the AIDA plan, and how does it apply to persuasive messages?
5. How do emotional appeals differ from logical appeals?
6. What three types of reasoning can you use in logical appeals?
7. What are four common mistakes to avoid when developing a persuasive message to overcome resistance?
8. What are the similarities and differences between sales messages and fundraising messages?
9. How do benefits differ from features?
10. How does ethical behavior contribute to positive etiquette in persuasive messages?

Apply Your Knowledge

1. Why is it important to present both sides of an argument when writing a persuasive message to a potentially hostile audience?
2. How are persuasive messages different from routine messages?
3. When is it appropriate to use the direct organizational approach in persuasive messages?
4. As an employee, how many of your daily tasks require persuasion? List as many as you can think of. Who are your audiences, and how do their needs and characteristics affect the way you develop your persuasive messages at work?
5. **Ethical Choices** Are emotional appeals ethical? Why or why not?

Practice Your Knowledge

Documents for Analysis

Read the following documents, then (1) analyze the strengths and weaknesses of each sentence, and (2) revise each document so that it follows this chapter's guidelines.

Document 9.A: Writing Persuasive Requests for Action

At Tolson Auto Repair, we have been in business for over 25 years. We stay in business by always taking into account what the customer wants. That's why we are writing. We want to know your opinions to be able to better conduct our business.

Take a moment right now and fill out the enclosed questionnaire. We know everyone is busy, but this is just one way we have of making sure our people do their job correctly. Use the enclosed envelope to return the questionnaire.

And again, we're happy you chose Tolson Auto Repair. We want to take care of all your auto needs.

Document 9.B: Writing Persuasive Claims and Requests for Adjustment

Dear TechStar Computing:

I'm writing to you because of my disappointment with my new multimedia PC display. The display part works all right, but the audio volume is also set too high and the volume knob doesn't turn it down. It's driving us crazy. The volume knob doesn't seem to be connected to anything but simply spins around. I can't believe you would put out a product like this without testing it first.

I depend on my computer to run my small business and want to know what you are going to do about it. This reminds me of every time I buy electronic equipment from what seems like any company. Something is always wrong. I thought quality was supposed to be important, but I guess not.

Anyway, I need this fixed right away. Please tell me what you want me to do.

Document 9.C: Writing Sales Letters

We know how awful dining hall food can be, and that's why we've developed the "Mealaweek Club." Once a week, we'll deliver food to your dormitory or apartment. Our meals taste great. We have pizza, buffalo wings, hamburgers and curly fries, veggie roll-ups, and more!

When you sign up for just six months, we will ask what day you want your delivery. We'll ask you to fill out your selection of meals. And the rest is up to us. At "Mealaweek," we deliver! And payment is easy. We accept MasterCard and Visa or a personal check. It will save money especially when compared with eating out.

Just fill out the enclosed card and indicate your method of payment. As soon as we approve your credit or check, we'll begin delivery. Tell all your friends about Mealaweek. We're the best idea since sliced bread!

Exercises

For live links to all websites discussed in this chapter, visit this text's website at www.prenhall.com/bovee. Just log on, select Chapter 9, and click on "Featured Websites." Locate the page or the URL related to the material in the text.

9.1 **Teamwork** With another student, analyze the persuasive memo at Host Marriott (Figure 9.3 on page 272) by answering the following questions:
   a. What techniques are used to capture the reader's attention?
   b. Does the writer use the direct or the indirect organizational approach? Why?
   c. Is the subject line effective? Why or why not?
   d. Does the writer use an emotional or a logical appeal? Why?
   e. What reader benefits are included?
   f. How does the writer establish credibility?
   g. What tools does the writer use to reinforce his position?

9.2 **Composing Subject Lines** Compose effective subject lines for the following persuasive memos:
   a. A request to your supervisor to purchase a new high-speed laser printer for your office. You've been outsourcing quite a bit of your printing to AlphaGraphics, and you're certain this printer will pay for itself in six months.
   b. A direct mailing to area residents soliciting customers for your new business, "Meals à la Car," a carryout dining service that delivers from most of the local restaurants. All local restaurant menus are on the Internet. Mom and Dad can dine on egg rolls and chow mein while the kids munch on pepperoni pizza.
   c. A special request to the company president to allow managers to carry over their unused vacation days to the following year. Apparently, many managers canceled their fourth-quarter vacation plans to work on the installation of a new company computer system. Under their current contract, vacation days not used by December 31 aren't accruable.

9.3 **Ethical Choices** Your boss has asked you to draft a memo requesting that everyone in your department donate money to the company's favorite charity, an organization that operates a special summer camp for physically challenged children. You wind up writing a three-page memo packed with facts and heartwarming anecdotes about the camp and the children's experiences. When you must work that hard to persuade your audience to take an action such as donating money to a charity, aren't you being manipulative and unethical? Explain.

9.4 **Focusing on Benefits** Determine whether the following sentences focus on features or benefits; rewrite as necessary to focus all the sentences on benefits.
   a. All-Cook skillets are coated with a durable, patented nonstick surface.
   b. You can call anyone and talk as long as you like on Saturdays and Sundays with this new wireless telephone service.
   c. We need to raise $25 to provide each needy child with a backpack filled with school supplies.

9.5 **Internet** Visit the Federal Trade Commission website and read the "Catch the Bandit in Your Mailbox" consumer warning at www.ftc.gov/bcp/conline/pubs/tmarkg/bandit.htm. Select one or two sales or fundraising letters you've recently received and see whether they contain any of the suspicious content mentioned in the FTC warning. What does the FTC suggest you do with any materials that don't sound legitimate?

Expand Your Knowledge

For live links to the websites that follow, go to www.prenhall.com/bovee. When you log on, select Chapter 9, then select "Featured Websites," click on the URL of the website you wish to visit, and review the website to complete these exercises.

Exploring the Best of the Web

Influence an Official and Promote Your Cause
thomas.loc.gov

At the Thomas site compiled by the Library of Congress, you'll discover voluminous information about federal legislation, congressional members, and committee reports. You can also access committee homepages and numerous links to government agencies, current issues, and historical documents. You'll find all kinds of regulatory information, including laws and relevant issues that might affect you in the business world. Visit the site and stay informed. Maybe you'll want to convince a government official to support a business-related issue that affects you. Explore the data at the Thomas site, and find an issue you can use to practice your skills at writing a persuasive message.

1. What key ideas would you include in an e-mail message to persuade your congressional representative to support an issue important to you?
2. In a letter to a senator or member of Congress, what information would you include to convince the reader to vote for an issue supporting small business?
3. When sending a message to someone who daily receives hundreds of written appeals, what attention-getting techniques can you use? How can you get support for a cause that concerns you as a businessperson?

Exploring the Web on Your Own

Review these chapter-related websites on your own to learn more about writing persuasive messages.

1. Visit the Federal Trade Commission website, www.ftc.gov, to find out how consumers can cut down on the number of unsolicited mailings, calls, and e-mails they receive.
2. Explore some classic examples of persuasive messages at the National Archives' Powers of Persuasion online exhibit, www.archives.gov (enter the Exhibit Hall and find the Powers of Persuasion exhibit).
3. See how professional advertising copywriters use persuasive writing in their work; take the free tutorial at www.adcopywriting.com.

Learn Interactively

Interactive Study Guide

Go to the Companion Website at www.prenhall.com/bovee. For Chapter 9, take advantage of the interactive "Study Guide" to test your knowledge of the chapter. Get instant feedback on whether you need additional studying.

Also, visit this site's "Study Hall," where you'll find an abundance of valuable resources that will help you succeed in this course.

Peak Performance Grammar and Mechanics

In Chapter 8 you were referred to the Peak Performance Grammar and Mechanics activities on the web at www.prenhall.com/onekey to improve your skill with commas, semicolons, and colons. For additional reinforcement in semicolons and colons, go to www.prenhall.com/bovee, where you will find "Improve Your Grammar, Mechanics, and Usage" exercises.

CASES

Applying the Three-Step Writing Process to Cases

Apply each step to the following cases, as assigned by your instructor

Plan

Analyze the Situation
Identify both your general purpose and your specific purpose. Clarify exactly what you want your audience to think, feel, or believe after receiving your message. Profile your primary audience, including their backgrounds, differences, similarities, and likely reactions to your message.

Gather Information
Identify the information your audience will need to receive, as well as other information you may need in order to craft an effective message.

Select the Right Medium
Make sure your medium is both acceptable to the audience and appropriate for the message.

Organize the Information
Choose a direct or indirect approach based on the audience and the message; most persuasive messages employ an indirect approach (often following the AIDA model). Identify your main idea, limit your scope, then outline necessary support points and other evidence.

1

Write

Adapt to Your Audience
Show sensitivity to audience needs with a "you" attitude, politeness, positive emphasis, and bias-free language. Understand how much credibility you already have—and how much you may need to establish with any particular audience. Project your company's image by maintaining an appropriate style and tone.

Compose the Message
Draft your message using powerful words, effective sentences, and coherent paragraphs. Support your claims with objective evidence; balance emotional and logical arguments.

2

Complete

Revise the Message
Evaluate content and review readability; then edit and rewrite for conciseness and clarity.

Produce the Message
Use effective design elements and suitable layout for a clean, professional appearance.

Proofread the Message
Review for errors in layout, spelling, and mechanics.

Distribute the Message
Deliver your message using the chosen medium; make sure all documents and all relevant files are distributed successfully.

3

PERSUASIVE REQUESTS FOR ACTION

1. Travel turnaround: Memo convincing Travelfest boss to expand client services You are a successful agent with Travelfest, Inc., a full-service travel-management firm. Located in Austin, Texas, Travelfest has four offices and more than 50 employees. Headquarters are downtown, in the lobby of a 35-story office tower. The other three offices are located in major shopping centers in upscale suburbs. The company's business is made up of about 70 percent corporate and business travel and 30 percent leisure travel. However, much of the leisure business comes from corporate customers.

Your boss, Gary Hoover, has been working night and day to make up for declining revenues brought about by the loss of airline commissions. He has tried everything, from direct-mail campaigns to discount coupons to drawings for cruises and weekend getaways. Still, revenues remain flat.

You've been doing some research and analysis of your office's existing customer profiles. You find that many of your customers are middle- to high-income sophisticated travelers, that business travel is bouncing back (with an eye to cheaper fares and less costly accommodations), and that executives often make their own travel arrangements (now that many companies are cutting the cost of maintaining their own travel departments). Your research has triggered some ideas that you believe could substantially increase your revenue from existing customers.

You envision turning your headquarters office into a travel resource for corporate customers. First, you would like to provide as much information as you can on the most popular business destinations—both inside and outside the country. You could sell videos and audiotape courses in Spanish, French, German, Japanese, and other languages. And you'd like to introduce a line of travel products, including luggage, maps, travel guides, and electronics—all aimed at the business traveler. You might provide several computer terminals, where customers would have direct access to Internet sites providing on-the-spot weather reports, currency-exchange rates, and other important information about travel destinations. You're even thinking about a special area with videos and other educational materials on various cultures and business practices around the world.

You realize your ideas won't generate a lot of direct profit. However, you believe they will get business customers in the door, where you and other agents can sell them travel-management services. If Hoover is willing to try your idea and it works, he may want to do something similar in the suburb offices, perhaps with an emphasis on leisure travel.

Your task: Write a memo to Gary Hoover. Outline your ideas and suggest a meeting to discuss them further and determine what market research he'd like you to perform.[23]

2. Life's little hassles: E-mail requesting satisfaction It's hard to go through life without becoming annoyed at the way some things work. You have undoubtedly been dissatisfied with a product you've bought, a service you've received, or an action of some elected official or government agency.

Your task: Write a three- to five-paragraph persuasive e-mail request expressing your dissatisfaction in a particular case. Specify the action you want the reader to take.

3. Thanks-A-Bunch: Letter requesting continued funding At Thanks-A-Bunch flower shop in Chula Vista, California, former psychiatric patients can learn the skills—and regain the confidence—to reenter the workaday world. In a little over a dozen years, more than 400 people have successfully "graduated" from the innovative program. Once day-treatment patients suffering from hallucinations, these individuals are now functioning normally, thanks to the right psychotropic drugs rectifying certain chemical imbalances. However, functioning normally and rejoining society are sometimes two different matters. That's where Thanks-A-Bunch can help.

At the flower shop, the former patients become trainees, handling all the tasks necessary to operate the retail business. They assemble flowers, truck them to delivery sites, and handle cash sales. The trainees earn minimum wages—but the chance to work in a "safe environment" (where no one pushes too hard or demands too much) is priceless. "They won't get fired if they screw up," explains program director Nina Garcia.

Unfortunately, support from local businesses, who buy most of the shop's flower arrangements, isn't enough to pay for the costly program, so the shop depends on additional funding from San Diego County Mental Health Services (CMHS). Now, even though Thanks-A-Bunch has been used as a model for developing other rehabilitation centers throughout the county (breakfast cafés, furniture stores, ceramics shops, and bakeries), it's being threatened by county budget cuts. Garcia has received news that Thanks-A-Bunch may be targeted for elimination as the county board of supervisors weighs alternatives for stretching dwindling government funds.

Your task: Garcia spotted the business communication course you listed on your résumé and has asked you, her assistant, to write a strong letter to Morgan Cole, regional director for San Diego County Mental Health Services (1700 Pacific Highway, San Diego, CA 92186). You must convince him that Thanks-A-Bunch deserves to survive the impending budget cuts.[24]

4. Give me liberty: Letter persuading customers to remain loyal to Colbar Art For many people in the United States, the Statue of Liberty is a cliché, so much a part of New York City's tourist hype that it's taken for granted. But for most immigrants, the first sight of Liberty as they enter the city brings tears along with hopes for a new life. Ovidiu Colea knows the feeling. He immigrated to the United States in the early 1980s after a difficult past that included five long years in a Romanian hard-labor camp for trying to flee the communist regime.

Colea worked two years as a cab driver to save enough money to start Colbar Art, a company that produces up to 80,000 hand-crafted replicas of the Liberty statue each year. He now helps other immigrants get a start in their new country by hiring them to design and produce Liberty models. Colea pays a royalty to the Liberty–Ellis Island Foundation for using Liberty's image. In fact, during the first year of operation, that royalty amounted to $250,000.

Painstaking labor produces the acrylic and bonded marble statues with a hand-painted patina, and most of that work is done by the very immigrants lady Liberty welcomes to New York. Colea insists on keeping production in the United States. Although labor costs are cheaper outside the country, he refuses to produce the statues in countries "where there is no liberty or no Statue of Liberty." By keeping jobs in the United States, he's doing his share to keep the American Dream alive.

But the meticulous labor also costs precious production time. With recent high demand for the replicas, the company has fallen behind on orders. To increase production to 120,000 statues per year, the company is leasing more space and training new employees. Meanwhile, the production deficits may continue for several months.

Your task: You work for Colbar Art as assistant manager, and Colea has asked you to write a persuasive form letter to all your customers, explaining the current delays and requesting patience. Be sure to explain the steps the company is taking to solve these delays, and describe the quality and creativity that go into the replicas. You can quote Bradford Hill (owner of the Liberty Island gift shop), who says Colbar Art's models represent 65 percent of his sales. Make a convincing argument for your customers to remain loyal to Colbar Art.[25]

5. No more driving: Memo about telecommuting to Bachman, Trinity, and Smith Sitting in your Dallas office at the accounting firm of Bachman, Trinity, and Smith, clacking away on your calculator, it seems as though you could be doing this work from your home. You haven't spoken to any co-workers in more than two hours. As long as you complete your work on time, does your location matter?

As an entry-level accountant, you've participated in location audits at major companies for nearly a year now. If your bosses trust you to work while staying at a hotel, why not let you work from home, where you already have an office with computer, phone, and fax machine? You'd love to regain those two hours you lose commuting to and from work every day.

Your task: To support this idea, visit the website of the International Telework Association and Council website at www.telecommute.org. You'll find statistics and other support for a memo persuading your boss, senior partner Marjorie Bachman, to grant you a six-month trial as a telecommuter.[26]

6. Teachers' plea: Letter from TCTA urging reduced TV time Normally, the Texas Classroom Teachers Association (TCTA) is busy lobbying Texas legislators for better education laws or offering legal services to embattled teachers. When you got your hands on the results of a recent study conducted among children in Spain, you knew it called for a letter-writing campaign—but not one aimed at legislators. This time teachers would write to parents, begging them to treat their own children better.

The eight-month study involved parents of 221 children admitted to the pediatric ward of Santa Ana Hospital in Motril, Spain. The parents were asked to fill out a survey about family television viewing. By comparing injuries with hours of television watched, the researchers concluded that for every hour of television a child watched, the risk of injury rose by 34 percent. That seems a sizable increase to you, one that could easily be remedied.

Of course, scientific method demands further study before these results are fully accepted. On the other hand, every teacher you know would instantly chime in to say that television contributes to all sorts of social and behavioral problems and even impairs intellectual achievement by shortening attention spans, demeaning values, and presenting false images of life that children confuse with reality. Just opinions, mind you, but widely and firmly held—soon to be confirmed by science, you hope.

Meanwhile, the Spanish study is something the TCTA can sink its persuasive teeth into. If you can get parents to reduce their children's television viewing by only an hour or two a day, it could make a difference. Current estimates are that an average child today will have spent between 7 and 10 years watching television by the time he or she reaches the age of 70.

Jose Uberos Fernandez, author of the Spanish research program, stated in the *Archives of Pediatrics and Adolescent Medicine* professional journal, "Paradoxically, a child who spends more time watching television and devotes fewer hours to potentially more dangerous physical activities and games is at greater risk of experiencing events that cause physical injuries. . . . We believe that the depiction of a distorted reality on the television screen, which the child perceives as being real, may be of some help in explaining our findings." Later on in his paper, he adds, "Without any doubt, the effect of television on its viewers is directly related to the number of hours spent in watching per day and the content of the programs watched."

You had to convince the TCTA that parents should address this issue, not legislators. They finally agreed. Now, as director of communications, you've been assigned the task you'd hoped for.

Your task: Mold these study results into a persuasive letter to be sent on TCTA letterhead to all parents of school-age children in the state of Texas. Include TCTA's number (1-888-879-TCTA) for more information.[27]

7. Helping out: Memo to Whole Foods Market managers By swallowing up smaller health food stores, Whole Foods Market has grown into a 145-location chain of organic food stores spread across the United States. The stores are big and well lit, like their more traditional grocery store counterparts. They are also filled with a wide variety of attractively displayed foods and related products.

However, Whole Foods is different from the average supermarket. Its products include everything from granola sold in bulk to environmentally sensitive household products. The meats come from animals that were never fed antibiotics, and the cheese is from cows said to be raised on small farms and treated humanely.

Along with selling these products to upscale shoppers, the company makes a commitment "to the neighborhood and larger community that we serve and in which we live." Whole Foods not only donates 5 percent of after-tax profits to not-for-profit organizations but also financially supports employees who volunteer their time for community service projects. Many Whole Foods stores donate goods and supplies to soup kitchens in their local communities. Company executives want to encourage this type of activity, which reflects the "Whole Foods, Whole People, Whole Planet" corporate motto.

You are the manager of the Whole Foods Market on Ponce de Leon Avenue in Atlanta, Georgia. You've been very successful with a program you developed for donating surplus food to local food banks. You've been asked by higher-ups to help other Whole Foods stores coordinate this effort into a chain-wide food donation program, "Whole Foods for Life." Ideally, by streamlining the process chain-wide, the company would be able to increase the number of people it helps and to get more of its employees involved.

You don't have a great deal of extra money for the program, so the emphasis has to be on using resources already available to the stores. One idea is to use trucks from suburban branches to make the program "mobile." Another idea is to join forces with a retailing chain to give food and clothing to individuals. You've decided that the key will be to solicit input from the other stores so that they'll feel more involved in the final outcome as the larger food-donation program takes shape.

Your task: Send persuasive memos to all managers at Whole Foods Market, explaining the new program and requesting that they help by pooling ideas they've gleaned from their local experience. Even if they don't have food-donation programs currently in place, you want to hear ideas from them and their employees for this charitable project. With their help, you'll choose the best ideas to develop the new "Whole Foods For Life" program.[28]

8. Nap time: Memo requesting space for "day sleepers" at Phidias & Associates It's been one of those days . . . you were dragging by 10 A.M., ready to slump over onto your drafting table at Phidias & Associates architectural firm in San Francisco. Even that incredibly bright bay view outside the office windows hasn't helped perk you up, and the coffee is just giving you stomach pains. How are you supposed to be creatively inspired when you can barely get your eyes to focus and your head feels as if it's full of cotton? No, you weren't out partying last night; you've just been working long, late hours on a rush job for one of the firm's biggest clients. San Francisco is the Workaholic City, but this is too much. If only you could stretch out for a little catnap, you'd be good as new in 15 minutes.

Groggily, you recall an item you tore out of the *Wall Street Journal* a year ago. You saved it with the vague notion of presenting it during one of those officewide, corporate spirit "pep rallies" your employers are fond of. You rummage around in your desk drawer—ah, there it is. A paragraph or two in the "Work Week" column, all about a minitrend toward "nap rooms" in the workplace. At first, your work ethic was shocked at the concept, but then your creative self started to glow at the thought. After all, didn't they teach you in school that Thomas Edison kept a cot in his office and got his best ideas when he was napping? And the article quotes an expert, William A. Anthony, author of *The Art of Napping* and professor of rehabilitation counseling at Boston University. He says most people aren't sleep deprived, they're "nap ready."

There are plenty of other precedents and pioneers out there in the business world. At *Macworld Magazine,* the human resources director, Shelly Ginenthal, says their two-person nap room was installed in 1986 and usually has a waiting line. It must not be interfering with productivity if they're still using it 19 years later, you muse. And here's another firm, Yarde Metals in Bristol, Connecticut, whose president, Bruce Yarde, says, "A quick little nap can rejuvenate you." So he's fighting employee stress with a 25-person nap room. Wow. That's almost like your old kindergarten. And yet another—you like this one best—an architectural firm in Kansas City, Missouri, Gould Evans Goodman Associates, has plans on its drawing boards to add a nap space to its offices. If they can do it in Kansas City, why not here?

Your task: After you've had a good night's sleep, write a memo to Jonas T. Phidias, persuading the senior partner that the distinguished offices of Phidias & Associates could benefit from the addition of a corporate "nap room." Be sure you use your best persuasive skills, though, or you may send the wrong message to your employer. On a separate page, include a short note to your instructor justifying your organizational approach (direct or indirect) and your selection of delivery medium (e-mail or interoffice mail).[29]

PERSUASIVE CLAIMS AND REQUESTS FOR ADJUSTMENT

9. Too good to be true: E-mail to Page South requesting adjustment Page South offered its pager services for a mere $5 a month. You purchased an inexpensive pager and signed a contract for two years. After you thought your pager phone number was up and running for two weeks, you heard from co-workers and clients that they repeatedly get a busy signal when dialing your pager number. You call Page South, and they resolve the problem—but doing so takes an additional week. You don't want to be charged for the time the pager wasn't in service. After discussing the situation with the local manager, she asks you to contact Judy Hinkley at the company's regional business office.

Your task: Send an e-mail message to Hinkley at Judy@pgsouth.com and request an adjustment to your account. Request credit or partial credit for one month of service. Remember to write a summary of events in chronological order, supplying exact dates for maximum effectiveness.

10. Lock legends: Letter requesting refund and damages from Brookstone As a professional photographer, you travel the world for business, leaving from your home base in Williamstown, Massachusetts. Last month it was a trip to Australia, and you thought you'd finally found a way around the "no-locks-on-checked baggage" rules.

After the World Trade Center attacks of September 11, 2001, the United States' Travel Security Administration (TSA) forbid airline passengers to check locked luggage. TSA inspectors want easy access so that they can open and check bags for security purposes. But since you carry so much expensive equipment, including numerous camera bags, you've been nervous about the safety of your belongings—not to mention the loss of privacy.

So you were relieved when you read Joe Sharkey's "On the Road" column in the *New York Times* just before your trip. The columnist extolled a newly announced TSA program allowing airline travelers to lock their luggage *if they use special TSA-*

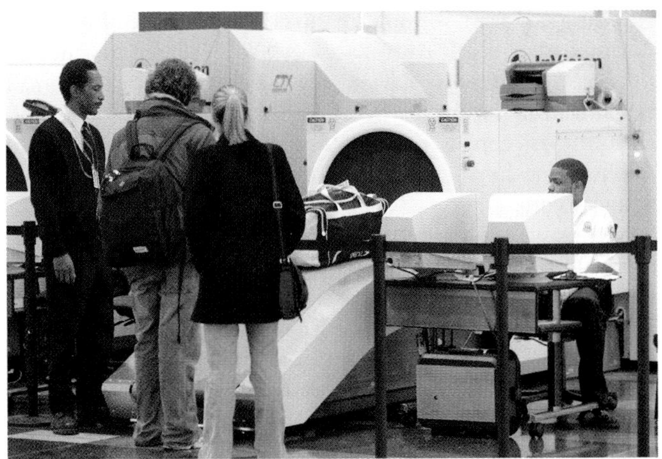

approved locks, certified by a company called Travel Sentry. You immediately went to the Brookstone store in Albany, after reading their web advertisement for "The luggage locks security won't cut off. Our Easycheck™ locks are certified by Travel Sentry™ and feature a secure system accepted and recognized by the Transportation Security Administration (TSA). Airport security personnel can now inspect and re-lock your bags quickly and easily." You bought eight locks, at $20 for each set of two.

When you left the Albany airport, TSA inspectors assured you that they had a master key for these locks, just as Mr. Sharkey's column had promised they would. But when you got to Melbourne after changing planes in Chicago and Los Angeles, you were stunned to discover the condition of your luggage. One bag was missing the new lock entirely; another was missing the lock and had a rip all along the seam—perhaps from an irritated inspector? Inside a third bag you found its broken Easycheck lock, with a terse TSA inspection notice reminding you that locked baggage is not allowed. On the return trip you tried again, using three of your remaining locks on camera bags. They arrived with no locks and no inspection notices.

You've now called the airports in Chicago and Cleveland, where TSA inspectors told you they'd "never heard of the program." Brookstone will replace the broken lock, but the woman on the phone wasn't sure about the ones that went missing entirely, since you have nothing left to bring into the store except your receipt.

Your task: After 10 minutes listening to bad music on hold for the TSA, you've abandoned the idea of a phone complaint to the government agency. You're going to write a letter to Brookstone (120 Washington Ave., Albany, NY 12203) requesting damages for the ripped luggage (a 24-inch Expandable Ballistic Suitor, $320) and a refund for all eight locks ($80). Six of them were ruined or missing and your last two are essentially useless![30]

11. Chintzy chairs: Letter requesting refunds from Office Depot Seven office assistants needed to be outfitted with decent desk chairs—that was your assignment last year. As office manager for Rinkert, Veldman, and D'Agostino, Attorneys at Law, you knew exactly what was required: seven Herman Miller Aeron chairs. They're top-of-the-line, ergonomically designed, and expensive ($1250 apiece)—but worth every penny for these hard-working individuals who spend most of their eight-hour days sitting down.

From their chairs they work on computers, answer phones, greet clients, make appointments, and flesh out letters their supervising attorneys have asked them to write. Although breaks are legally mandatory, you know these men and women rarely take them. The pressure's too high, and the workflow is too steady. They deserve the multi-adjustable, aerated, posture supporting, form-fitting chairs designed by Don Chadwick and Bill Stumpf. The fact that Herman Miller promotes the designers' names signifies the high status these chairs hold in the business world. In fact, that was part of your problem.

All the partners of Rinkert, Veldman, and D'Agostino sit in Aeron chairs. But you knew that buying the chairs for the other employees would more than pay for the out-of-pocket expense through their improved productivity, sustained and injury-free good health, and ultimate job satisfaction. Translation: The law firm would enjoy lower turnover among support staff, with fewer workmen's comp claims for back problems and carpal tunnel injuries.

Nevertheless the firm's partners immediately overruled your suggestion. The price tag horrified them. They insisted that you purchase seven Office Depot chairs, brand name unimportant as long as they cost $500 or less. Reluctantly you did as you were told, taking delivery on seven "OfficeBest 1600 High-Back Performance Task Chairs" with their "contoured cushions" and "one-touch seat-height adjustment." Negotiated price: $499.99 each, discounted from $570 because you ordered seven.

A year has passed, and if you didn't value your job so much, you could rightly say, "I told you so." Three of the chair seats have gone entirely flat, leaving your poor office assistants sitting on what amounts to fabric-covered steel, with all the stuffing pushed out to the sides (and none of these individuals are unusually overweight). In addition to the flattening seats, two others have broken arm rests, another has a broken seat-back adjustment knob, and the seventh chair just dumped your new hire unceremoniously on the floor when he tried the seat-tilt adjustment. The mechanism gave way and the seat tipped completely forward. Fortunately, he wasn't hurt other than bruised knees and a crushed ego.

Your bosses, mindful of potential lawsuits, have now granted you permission to order the Aeron chairs—as soon as you "take care of the Office Depot problem."

Your task: Your phone calls to Office Depot led nowhere; they seem reluctant to believe that all seven chairs are failing. You'll have to write a letter documenting the problem with each chair. You want the company to not only refund the full purchase price but bring their delivery truck and remove them from your sight the same way they delivered these low-budget chairs in the first place. Remind them of your frequent and abundant purchases from Office Depot, everything from legal pads and printer cartridges to reams of copy paper. You like their office supplies and the nearness of their store; it's the cheaply constructed furniture that you find troublesome.[31]

12. Broadband blues: Claim letter to ZippieNet about cable modem failures When your cable company offered ZippieNet—high-speed, cable modem Internet access—you signed up. You figured $49.95 a month was a bargain for Internet speed.

Your career as a freelance journalist requires you to compete with staff writers at the various publications that buy your work. So to meet short deadlines, you need to deliver stories fast. Plus, you were convinced that speedier access to Internet sources would make your work easier. You were ready to stop wasting all that time waiting for connections and downloads.

At first you were pleased. When the system worked, it worked beautifully. Then the problems began. Three days a week for four weeks, the system failed and you were stuck offline. When you called ZippieNet's support lines, you were put on hold for 30 minutes, and when someone finally answered, he seemed poorly trained and overworked. All you got were vague promises that the system was being repaired.

That was three months ago. Since then, you've experienced total shutdowns at least twice a month. During periods of high usage, the "zippy" speeds that ZippieNet promised slow down to a trickle—not much better than your old dial-up connection.

And now the unthinkable has happened. Last week you were working on an article that you had contracted to sell to *Arete* magazine for $1,000, and the system went down for more than 24 hours. You couldn't access critical information, your story was late, and you lost the sale. Moreover, the editor was so angry, he said he'll never work with you again.

Your task: Write a letter to ZippieNet (1203 West Barber Ave., Nashville, TN 37214), demanding a refund for your four months of service, plus $1,000 for lost income on the lost article sale (include a copy of your contract), and $3,000 toward the loss of future sales to the same publication. If ZippieNet pays the $1,000, you'll be satisfied, but don't tell them that. Instead, suggest that you will remain a customer if they can deliver improved service within three weeks. When it works, you love broadband.[32]

13. Double debit: Letter to Earthlink demanding an account adjustment In your part-time job for Maria's Pet-Sitting, you usually run errands or do the office work that Maria Pelaez doesn't have time for. She's too busy caring for people's pets or soliciting new business. This week Maria wants you to help her take on a giant: Earthlink Internet service provider.

As an automatic payment plan customer, Maria allows Earthlink to debit her bank account each month for their $21.95 fee. Earthlink then e-mails its invoice showing the debit and the transaction date. Since the amount and date are always the same, Maria debits the amount in her financial ledger on the first of every month. But this month, November, the invoice indicates a debit for $43.90. Maria called Earthlink in alarm.

The operator explained that back in March, Earthlink failed to debit accounts set up for automatic payment. They said she should have received a letter in August explaining the error, as well as Earthlink's plan to correct it in November by debiting her bank account twice. She hadn't received the letter and asked for a copy. She received a badly written, e-mailed version of what was purported to be the original letter.

Maria is angry about the cavalier way her bank account was accessed, and the sloppy handling of her subsequent inquiry. Her automatic payment plan is based on trust, she believes, and Earthlink has abused this access to her funds. She thinks they should refund the entire $43.90 as compensation for their mishandling and to restore her good faith.

Your task: Write the letter to Earthlink for Maria to sign.

14. Tangled web: E-mail to PurelySoftware regarding an online order duplication Last week you ordered new design software for your boss, Martin Soderburgh, at ArtAlive, the small art consulting business where you work. As he requested, you used his Visa card to order Adobe InDesign, Version 1.5, and Adobe Photoshop, Version 6.0, from an Internet vendor, Purely Software.com.

When you didn't receive the usual e-mail order confirmation, you called the company's toll-free number. The operator said the company's website was having problems, and he took a second order over the phone: $649.00 for Adobe InDesign, $564.00 for Adobe Photoshop, including tax and shipping. Four days later, ArtAlive received two shipments of the software, and your boss's credit card was debited twice for a total of $1,213.00.

Your task: Technically, you authorized both orders. But you understood during the phone call that the first order was cancelled, although you have no written proof. Send a persuasive e-mail to customerservice@purelysoftware.com, requesting (1) an immediate credit to your boss's Visa account and (2) a postage-paid return label for the duplicate order.[33]

15. Cow-spotty text: E-mail to Gateway requesting warranty extension Words Unlimited is a "microbusiness"—just two owners and you, the all-round office assistant. From a small office with two computers, you three provide editorial services to businesses.

When your employers, Tom and Miranda Goodman, decided to add a third computer, they ordered a Professional S1300 business system from Gateway, with a "flat screen" monitor that was supposed to offer superior visual display. They didn't realize that the monitor, recommended by salesman Chris Swanson, uses liquid crystal display (LCD) technology. That's great for graphics, but text is produced as disconnnected dots that are hard on the eyes. What they really need is an old-fashioned CRT monitor that displays text as a solid line.

They returned to the store and found one with a fast refresh rate, costing only $20 more, under Gateway's 30-day exchange

program. But when they got to the register, they discovered that their 30-day exchange period had run out five days before. Gateway wouldn't take back the LCD monitor, and the Goodmans would have to pay full price for the CRT.

"How did the time run out?" you ask when they return.

"Remember how Swanson forgot to include a modem in our original order and we had to wait for it to be delivered from the factory?" Tom says. "Then UPS delivered the package to the wrong address. When we finally retrieved it, the installation technician was out sick and we had to wait for his return."

Miranda adds, "And then it took Tom forever to set up the new system, between phone calls and other jobs. By the time we saw the flat screen in action, our 30 days had already elapsed."

"At least Swanson apologized," Tom adds. "He thinks his manager will extend our 30-day exchange period if we send her an e-mail."

Your task: Since your bosses are busy, they've asked you to draft the persuasive message to Ann Cameron, Manager, Gateway Country Store, Ann.Cameron@Gateway.com. So far Gateway employees have been courteous, quick, and eager to help, despite the mix-ups. You all have high hopes.[34]

SALES MESSAGES

16. Quotesmith.com: E-mail extolling a better way to buy insurance The great thing about Quotesmith.com is that no one is obligated to buy a thing. Consumers can log on to your website and ask for dozens of free insurance quotes, then go off and buy elsewhere. They can look at instant price-comparison quotes (from more than 300 insurers) for term life, dental, individual and family medical insurance, small group medical insurance, workers' compensation, short-term medical insurance, Medicare supplement insurance, "no-exam" whole life insurance, fixed annuity insurance, and (in a click-through arrangement with Progressive) private passenger automobile insurance. All rates are up-to-the-day accurate, and Quotesmith is the largest single source for comprehensive insurance price comparisons in the United States.

Once consumers see your price-comparison charts, many choose to fill out an easy insurance application request right on your site. Why deal with an insurance salesperson when you can see the price differences for yourself—especially over such a broad range of companies? Quotesmith backs up this application with toll-free customer-service lines operated by salaried representatives. They're not working on commission, but they know about insurance. And Quotesmith has based its new online service on a long history of serving the insurance industry.

The product pretty much sells itself, and that's what you love about your marketing job with Quotesmith. Consumers and computers do most of the work—and the results are at lightning speed, especially compared with what the insurance business was like just a few years ago. During peak periods, the site has been processing one quote request every four seconds, which leads, ultimately, to increased policy sales without an agent or intermediary.

Quotesmith advertises both in print and on TV, saying that it provides "the lowest term life rates in America or we'll overnight you $500." Your company also guarantees the accuracy of quotes against a $500 reward. Final rates depend on variables such as age, sex, state availability, hazardous activities, personal and family health history, driving records, and so on.

You're proud of the fact that Quotesmith has received positive press from *Nation's Business, Kiplinger's Personal Finance, Good Housekeeping, Los Angeles Times, Money, U.S. News & World Report,* and *Forbes* ("Quotesmith.com provides rock-bottom quotes")—your favorite. For every term-life quote, you even provide consumers with a look at how each insurer's ability to pay claims is rated by A.M. Best, Duff & Phelps, Moody's, Standard & Poor's, and Weiss Ratings, Inc.

And all of this is free. Too bad more people don't know about your services.

Your task: It's your job to lure more insurance customers to Quotesmith. You've decided to use direct e-mail marketing (using a list of consumers who have inquired about rates in the past but never committed to purchase anything). Write an e-mail sales message extolling the benefits of Quotesmith's services. Be sure your message is suited to an e-mail format, with an appropriate subject heading.[35]

17. Outsourcing: Letter from Kelly Services offering solutions In 1946, with his dynamic vision and pioneering spirit, William Russell Kelly started a new company to meet the office and clerical needs of Detroit-area businesses. Kelly temporary employees with skills in calculating, inventory, typing and copying were soon in great demand. During the 1960s, the Kelly Girl became a nationwide icon, synonymous with high-quality temporary employees. The company changed its name to Kelly Services, Inc. in 1966, reflecting the increasing diversity of its services, customers and employees.

Today, Kelly Services is a global Fortune 500 company that offers staffing solutions that include temporary services, staff leasing, outsourcing, vendor on-site and full-time placement. Kelly provides employees who have a wide range of skills across many disciplines including office services, accounting, engineering, information technology, law, science, marketing, light industrial, education, health care and home care.

Workforce needs, in terms of quantity and skills mix, fluctuate greatly. At the same time, employees have adaptable skills, and are far more mobile. The result is that more employers and employees alike want flexible staffing arrangements, and temporary staffing is often the best solution.

Companies use Kelly Services to strategically balance workload and workforce during peaks and valleys of demand, to handle special projects, and to evaluate employees prior to making a full-time hiring decision. This dramatic change in business has spurred the rapid growth of the contingent employment industry.

In turn, many individuals are choosing the flexibility of personal career management, increasing options of where, when, and how to work. It is now the desire of many employees to fit their work into their lifestyle, rather than fitting their lifestyle into their work. Therefore, more and more workers are becoming receptive to being a contract, temporary, or consulting employee.

There are advantages to both the company and the employee. Both have the opportunity to evaluate one another prior to making a long-term commitment. Kelly Services earns a fee when its employees are hired permanently, but employers find that it's a small price to pay for such valuable preview time, which saves everyone the cost and pain of a bad hiring decision.

Kelly has received many supplier awards for providing outstanding and cost-efficient staffing services, including DaimlerChrysler's Gold Award, Ford Motor Company's Q1 Preferred Quality Award, Intel Corporation's Supplier Continuous Quality Improvement (SCQI) Award and DuPont Legal's Challenge Award.

A job as a marketing manager with Kelly holds challenge and promise. With 2,500 offices in 26 countries, Kelly provides its customers with nearly 700,000 employees annually, with revenue of $4.3 billion in 2003. The company provides staffing solutions to more than 90 percent of the Fortune 500 companies.

As companies increasingly face new competitive pressures to provide better service and quality at lower prices, many are turning to outsourcing suppliers to deliver complete operational management of specific functions or support departments, allowing the company the necessary time to focus on its core competencies. One solution is to choose a single supplier such as the Kelly Management Services (KMS) division to deliver "full-service" outsourcing.

KMS combines management experience, people process improvements, technology enhancements, and industry expertise to optimize customer operations and reduce cost. KMS understands the unique challenges companies are facing in today's increasingly fast-paced business world and can provide customers with services across multiple functional offerings, including Call Center Operations, Warehousing, Distribution and Light Assembly, Back Office and Administrative functions, and Mail and Reprographic services. The result is a department staffed by employees that can fluctuate as a company's needs change.

KMS customers who have implemented one service often add others when they see KMS managed employees performing at high levels and producing substantial cost savings and operational efficiencies. By partnering with an outsourcing supplier such as KMS, companies will experience a greater value and cost savings than with in-house operations.

Your task: Write a sales letter to companies similar to DaimlerChrysler, Ford, Intel, and DuPont explaining what Kelly has to offer. For current information, visit the Kelly website at www.kellyservices.com.[36]

18. Greener Cleaners: Letter promoting "environmentally sound" Hangers franchise When you told everyone you aspired to work for an environmentally responsible business, you didn't imagine you'd end up in the dry-cleaning business. But now that you are Director of Franchise Development for Hangers Cleaners, you go home every night with a "clean conscience" (your favorite new pun).

Micell Technologies first invented the revolutionary "clean" technology used by Hanger's Cleaners, and then in 2001, sold all licensing, all intellectual property, and all interest in Hangers Cleaners to Cool Clean Technologies, which now manufactures the "CO2OL Clean" dry-cleaning machine that your franchise relies on. This breakthrough in dry-cleaning technology is the first in nearly 50 years—made by Micell co-founders Joseph DeSimone, James McClain, and Timothy Romack. Their new cleaning process uses liquid carbon dioxide (CO_2) and specially developed detergents to clean clothes. The process requires no heat and no further need for the toxic perchloroethylene (perc) or petroleum traditionally used in dry cleaning.

Hangers franchise owners don't have to deal with regulatory paperwork, zoning restrictions, or expensive insurance and taxes for hazardous waste disposal. And unlike petroleum-based solvents, the CO_2 used in the "CO2OL Clean" machine is noncombustible. It's the same substance that carbonates beverages, and it's captured from the waste stream of industries that produce it as a byproduct. Moreover, 98 percent of the CO_2 used in a Hangers outlet is recycled and used again, which helps keep prices competitive. The "CO2OL Clean" machine received accolades from the Environmental Protection Agency and was recently rated the best dry-cleaning alternative by a leading consumer products testing group.

You've already sold franchises in 60 locations, from Wilmington, North Carolina, to San Diego, California. Customers love the fact that their clothes don't carry toxic fumes after cleaning, and employees are happy to be working in a safe and cool environment. The process is actually gentler on clothes (no strong solvents or heat), reducing fading and shrinking and helping them last longer. You aren't dry cleaners; you are "garment care specialists."

And beyond the environmental boons, you simply love the design of Hangers stores. When Micell originally established the chain, it hired dry-cleaning experts and architects alike to come up with a sleek, modern, high-end retail "look" that features a cool, clean, light-filled interior and distinctive signage out front. It's more akin to a Starbucks than the overheated, toxic-smelling storefront most customers associate with dry cleaning. This high-end look is making it easier to establish Hangers as a national brand, attracting investors and franchisees rapidly as word spreads about the new "greener cleaner."

Your task: Develop a sales letter that can be mailed in response to preliminary inquiries from potential franchise owners. You'll include brochures covering franchise agreements and "CO2OL Clean" specifics, so focus on introducing and promoting the unique benefits of Hangers Cleaners. Your contact information is Hangers Cleaners, 3505 County Road 42 West, Burnsville, MN 55306-3803; phone 952-882-5000; toll-free 866-262-9274, or www.hangerscleaners.com.[37]

19. Always urgent: Memo pleading case for hosting a Red Cross blood drive Not many people realize that donated blood lasts for only 72 hours. So the mainstay of emergency blood supplies must be replenished in an ongoing effort. No one is more skilled, dedicated, or efficient in handling blood than the American Red Cross, which is responsible for half the nation's supply of blood and blood products.

This morning as you drove to work (as food services manager at the Pechanga Casino Entertainment Center in Temecula, California), you were concerned to hear on the radio that the local Red Cross chapter put out a call for blood because national supplies have fallen dangerously low. During a highly publicized disaster, people are emotional and eager to help out by donating blood. But in calm times, only 5 percent of eligible donors think of giving blood. You're one of those few.

Donated blood helps victims of accidents and disease, as well as surgery patients. Just yesterday you were reading about Melissa, who was diagnosed with multiple congenital heart defects and underwent her first open-heart surgery at one week old. Now five, she's used well over 50 units of donated blood, and she wouldn't be alive without them. In a thank-you letter, her

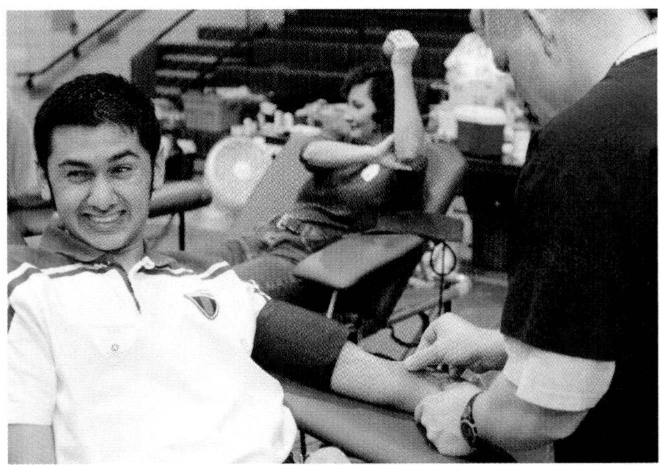

mother lauded the many strangers who had "given a piece of themselves" to save her precious daughter—and countless others. A donor's pint of blood benefits up to four people.

Today, you're going to do more than just roll up your own sleeve. You know the local Red Cross chapter takes its Blood Mobile to corporations, restaurants, even beauty salons—anyplace willing to host public blood drives. What if you could convince the board of directors to support a blood drive at the casino? The slot machines and gaming tables are usually full, hundreds of employees are on hand, and people who've never visited before might come down to donate blood. The positive publicity certainly couldn't hurt Pechanga's community image. With materials from the Red Cross, you're confident you can organize Pechanga's hosting effort and handle the promotion. (Last year you headed the casino's successful Toys for Tots drive.)

To give blood, one must be healthy, be at least 17 years old (with no upper age limit), and weigh at least 110 pounds. Donors can give every 56 days. You'll be urging Pechanga donors to eat well, drink water, and be rested before the Blood Mobile arrives.

The local chapter's mission statement says, in part, that the Red Cross is "a humanitarian organization led by volunteers and guided by the Fundamental Principles of the International Red Cross Movement" which will "prevent and alleviate human suffering wherever it may be found." All assistance is given free of charge, made possible by "contributions of people's time, money, and skills." And in the case of you and your co-workers, a piece of yourselves.

Your task: Write a memorandum persuading the Pechanga board of directors to host a public Red Cross blood drive. Ask the board to donate bottled water, orange juice, and snacks for donors. (You'll organize food service workers to handle the distribution.) To support your request, use a variety of appeals, mentioning both tangible and intangible benefits.[38]

20. Instant promotion: Text message from Hilton Hotels to frequent guests Hilton Hotels now uses an SMS (short messaging service) to send instant text promotions to customers who've signed up as "HHonors" members. But you work in marketing, and that means you're often struggling to condense elaborate travel packages into 65 enticing words (system maximum).

For example, today's promotion offers "A Golfer's Dream Come True: 'I just played a round of golf by the pyramids!'" For $575 (U.S.) per person per day (double room), valid through January 15, 2005, travelers can stay in the Hilton Pyramids Golf Resort in Cairo, Egypt, for 7 nights/8 days, including breakfast, service charge, and tax. They'll be met at the airport, given transportation to the resort, plus two rounds of golf per person at Dreamland Golf course and two rounds of golf per person at Soleimaneia Pyramids Golf & Country Club course. That's 88 words so far.

But you also need to convey that the Dreamland course wraps like a serpent around the Hilton resort. Its lush greens and lakes, designed by Karl Litten, contrast sharply with the golden desert, culminating in a stunning view of the great Pyramids of Giza, one of the seven wonders of the world. The Soleimaneia course features the "biggest floodlit driving course in Egypt." The travel package provides free transportation to this nearby course.

Rates, of course, are subject to availability and other restrictions may apply. But interested travelers should mention code G7 Pyramids Golf Special when they call Hilton Reservations Worldwide. They can also e-mail RM_PYRAMIDS_GOLF@hilton.com, or call the Cairo hotel directly at 20 2 8402402. That is, if you can entice them in 65 words.

Your task: Write the persuasive instant message.[39]

21. Helping children: Instant message holiday fund drive at IBM At IBM, you're one of the coordinators for the annual Employee Charitable Contributions Campaign. Since 1978, the company has helped employees contribute to more than 2,000 health and human service agencies. These groups may offer child care, treat substance abuse, provide health services, or fight illiteracy, homelessness, and hunger. Some offer disaster relief or care for the elderly. All deserve support. They're carefully screened by IBM, one of the largest corporate contributors of cash, equipment, and people to nonprofit organizations and educational institutions, both in the United States and around the world. As your literature states, the program "has engaged our employees more fully in the important mission of corporate citizenship."

During the winter holidays, you target agencies that cater to the needs of displaced families, women, and children. It's not difficult to raise enthusiasm. The prospect of helping children enjoy the holidays—children who otherwise might have nothing—usually awakens the spirit of your most distracted workers. But some of them wait until the last minute and then forget.

They have until Friday, December 16, to come forth with cash contributions. To make it in time for holiday deliveries, they can also bring in toys, food, and blankets through Tuesday, December 20. They shouldn't have any trouble finding the collection bins; they're everywhere, marked with bright red banners. But some will want to call you with questions or (hopefully) to make credit card contributions: 800-658-3899, ext. 3342.

Your task: It's December 14. Write a 75- to 100-word instant message encouraging last-minute gifts.[40]

PART 4

Finding and Communicating Information

CHAPTER 10

Finding, Evaluating, and Processing Information

CHAPTER 11

Communicating Information Through Visuals

chapter 10

Finding, Evaluating, and Processing Information

LEARNING OBJECTIVES

After studying this chapter, you will be able to

1. Describe an effective process for conducting business research
2. Define primary and secondary research and explain when you use each method
3. Name nine criteria for evaluating the credibility of an information source
4. Explain the complementary nature of search engines, web directories, and databases
5. Provide five guidelines for conducting an effective online search
6. Outline an effective process for planning and conducting information interviews
7. Explain the differences between drafting a summary, drawing a conclusion, and developing a recommendation

COMMUNICATION CLOSE-UP AT TOYOTA SCION

www.scion.com

If you're in your early twenties and in the market for your first new car, are you likely to rush out and buy the same car your parents drive? You know—that sensible, conventional car such as the Toyota they drive to the grocery store and to your little sister's soccer practice?

Toyota's Brian Bolain knows you probably won't, and he knows this because the company has already tried selling these conventional cars to your generation with conventional advertising messages. Over the past few decades, Toyota grew to a position of prominence in the United States by offering your parents refreshing alternatives to the cars that *their* parents drove; now Bolain and his colleagues want to continue that cycle of success with your generation.

But the problem is, what is the best way to craft unconventional products and messages that appeal to today's young adults? The solution was research, research, and more research. Even Toyota's approach to research was unconventional—for example, hiring 50 young Californians to record video diaries with their friends. The company even went so far as to learn how core groups of trendsetters discover new ideas and products before spreading them through the larger population. The research yielded a wide range of insights, including the emergence of Japan

With a shape that clearly says "this isn't your parents' car," the Toyota Scion was designed to attract younger buyers. Every aspect of Toyota's communication effort is researched carefully for maximum effectiveness.

as a new center of cool and the realization not only that young adults strongly resist being sold to but also that they put a high priority on individualism, self-expression, and authenticity.

The research results helped Toyota create a new line of cars called Scion, the most unconventional of which is the aggressively boxy xB model. Those research discoveries also shaped virtually every aspect of Toyota's communication efforts: The company downplays the "Toyota" name and shuns traditional mass-market advertising. Instead it favors small-scale, neighborhood-centered promotions that allow trendsetters to "discover" the Scion product line and share the word with other young adults (for example, putting posters near popular hangouts, bearing phrases such as "Ban Normality" and "No Clone Zone").

Toyota's extensive research offers a good lesson for all business communicators: Communication is successful only when it resonates with the priorities of your audience, and the only way to understand those priorities is through careful—and sometimes creative—research.[1]

SUPPORTING YOUR MESSAGES WITH SOLID RESEARCH

Many of your business reports will require some level of research.

Brian Bolain will be the first to tell you that audiences expect you to craft and support your business messages with solid research. Throughout your academic and business careers, you may be called upon to research everything from other companies and business trends to new technologies and tax laws. No matter what the task, successful research can be a rewarding activity if you follow productive research procedures:

1 LEARNING OBJECTIVE

Describe an effective process for conducting business research

1. **Plan your research.** Planning is the most important step of any research project; a solid plan yields better results in less time.
2. **Locate the data and information you need.** The research plan tells you *what* to look for, so your next step is to figure out *where* this data and information is and *how* to access it. Much of your business research will be done online, but other projects require personal interviews, surveys, and other techniques.
3. **Process the data and information you located.** The data and information you locate probably won't be in a form you can use immediately and will require some processing; this processing might involve anything from statistical analysis to resolving the differences between two or more expert opinions.
4. **Apply your findings.** You can apply your research findings in three ways: summarizing information for someone else's benefit, drawing conclusions based on what you've learned, or developing recommendations.
5. **Manage information efficiently.** Many companies today are trying to maximize the return on the time and money they invest in business research by collecting and sharing research results in a variety of computer-based systems.

Successful researchers follow a five-step process to acquire and use information.

Figure 10.1 lays out the steps and substeps in the research process; you'll learn about all of these tasks in the following sections. The amount of time you spend on each task will depend on your research objectives and the nature of the information you need.

FIGURE 10.1 The Research Process

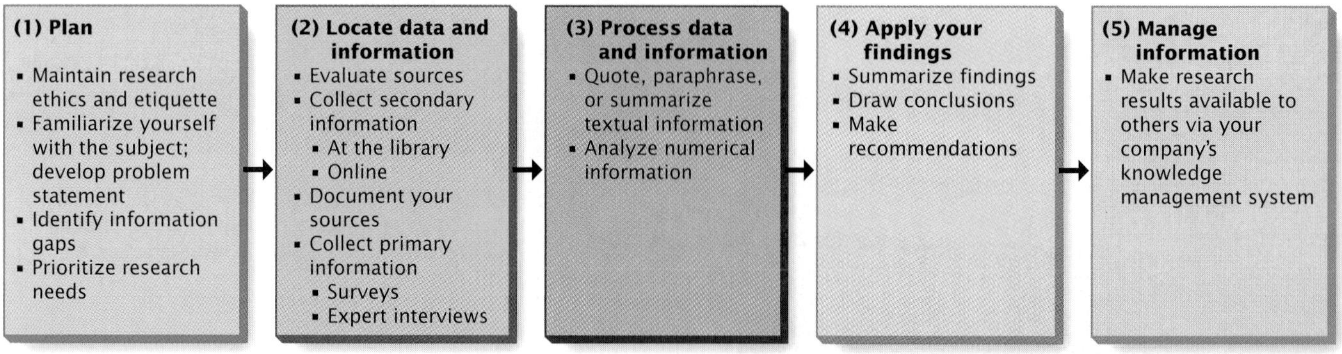

(1) Plan
- Maintain research ethics and etiquette
- Familiarize yourself with the subject; develop problem statement
- Identify information gaps
- Prioritize research needs

→

(2) Locate data and information
- Evaluate sources
- Collect secondary information
  - At the library
  - Online
- Document your sources
- Collect primary information
  - Surveys
  - Expert interviews

→

(3) Process data and information
- Quote, paraphrase, or summarize textual information
- Analyze numerical information

→

(4) Apply your findings
- Summarize findings
- Draw conclusions
- Make recommendations

→

(5) Manage information
- Make research results available to others via your company's knowledge management system

PLANNING YOUR RESEARCH

You've learned to resist the temptation to dive into a new writing project without thoughtful planning; now apply the same level of discipline to research. With so much information online these days, it's tempting just to punch some keywords into a search engine and then dig through the results looking for something, anything, that looks promising. However, such a lack of planning can limit both your effectiveness and your efficiency, and you can't afford either mistake in today's competitive business environment.

Researching without a plan can be ineffective for several reasons: Your favorite search engine might not index the websites that have the information you need, the engine might use different terms to identify the information you're looking for, the information might not be online, or the information might not even exist, in any form. Poor planning also limits your efficiency, and since you'll rarely have enough time to research as thoroughly as you'd like, you can't afford to waste any of it. If you don't frame the research challenge carefully before you start looking, chances are you'll discover something along the way that forces you to rethink the questions you're trying to answer or the approach you're taking. (Such discoveries often happen even when you are careful, but planning minimizes the chances.) Worse yet, you might move into the writing phase with inadequate information and waste additional time trying to construct a compelling message with insufficient support.

Researching without a plan wastes time and usually produces unsatisfactory results.

The goods news is you can minimize or avoid all these problems with a few well-considered planning steps: Familiarize yourself with the subject so that you can frame insightful questions, identify the most critical gaps in your information, and then prioritize your research needs. However, before launching any research project, take a moment or two to verify the ethics and etiquette of your approach.

Maintaining Ethics and Etiquette in Your Research

The number of potential ethical issues in business research might surprise you, but they all require attention to make sure that no ethical principles are violated in the pursuit of valuable information and insights. Your research tactics affect the people from whom you gather data and information, the people who read your results, and the people who are otherwise influenced by the way you present those results. To avoid ethical lapses, keep the following points in mind:

Business researchers can encounter a variety of ethical decisions.

- **Don't force a specific outcome by skewing your research.** If you set out to prove or disprove a particular point, you're more likely to find information that supports your position, but you may be overlooking contradictory points. If you go in with an open mind and are willing to accept whatever you find, your research will be more valuable.
- **Respect the privacy of your research participants.** Privacy is a contentious issue today. Businesses believe they have a right to protect confidential information from competitors, and consumers believe they have a right to protect personal information from businesses. While businesses are trying to design better products and market them more effectively by learning more about customers, those same customers are trying to protect their privacy. Notable ethical lapses to avoid include observing people without their consent or misleading them about the purposes of your research or about the ways you plan to use the information that people give you.[2]

Privacy is one the hottest issues in the research field today.

- **Document sources and give appropriate credit.** Whether you are using published documents, personal interviews, or company records, citing your sources is not only fair to the people who created and provided the information, but it also helps your audience confirm your information or explore it in more detail if they so chose.
- **Respect the intellectual property and digital rights of your sources.** *Intellectual property* refers to the ownership of unique ideas that have commercial value in the marketplace.[3] Your research might turn up a great new way to sell services online, but that doesn't mean you're free to implement that process. It might be protected by

one of the many patents that have been granted in recent years for business process models.

- **Don't extract more from your sources than they actually provide.** In other words, don't succumb to the temptation to put words in a source's mouth. For instance, if an industry expert says that a sales increase is a possibility, don't quote her as saying that a sales increase is likely.

In addition to ethics, research etiquette deserves careful attention, too. For example, respect the time of anyone who agrees to be interviewed or to be a research participant, and maintain courtesy throughout the interview or research process.

Familiarizing Yourself with the Subject

Sometimes you'll get a lucky break; you'll know exactly what kind of information to use in a report and where to find it. At other times, though, you won't be sure where to start. What if your California-based company wants to buy a firm in Colorado, and your boss asks you for a summary of the employment-related tax and regulatory issues the company will face when it takes over a business in that state? Would you know where to start? What if the request is even more challenging, such as "I need you to investigate ways we can grow this business"?

Familiarizing yourself with new subject areas before you start your research can save significant amounts of time.

Careful planning will help you avoid missteps caused by starting out too broadly or too narrowly or simply looking in the wrong direction. Give yourself some unstructured time at the beginning of the project to explore the general subject area, perhaps by reading industry publications, visiting competitors' websites, and interviewing experts within your organization. A quick online search can also be helpful at this point to identify the terminology people use, key organizations and experts, and other potential sources of information. Scan the contents and indexes of books on the subject. As you explore, keep a bibliographical list of the helpful resources you find, as well as a list of potentially significant phrases, terms, and key words that appear repeatedly.

Now use what you have learned so far to clarify your project. If you're conducting research at the request of someone else, make sure you both agree on the scope and purpose of the assignment. If you're conducting research for reasons of your own, use your preliminary information to make your purpose as clear and specific as possible. Develop a **problem statement** that defines the problem or purpose of your research—the decision you need to make or the conclusion you need to reach at the end of the process, even if it's a simple one. Phrase the statement as a question if that helps, such as "How can we improve customer satisfaction?" or "Does Nintendo's new system pose a competitive threat to us?" If someone assigned you the research project, you can take this question back and ask whether answering this specific question will meet his or her expectations.

The problem statement defines the purpose of your research and guides your investigation.

Identifying Information Gaps

Whether your research task is reasonably familiar or a complete mystery, the nature of the problem is the same: you don't have the information you need to make a decision or reach some important conclusion with confidence. **Information gap analysis** is an effective technique for identifying the specific pieces of information you need to acquire. Moreover, by focusing your effort, this type of analysis helps you make the best use of your limited research time (and money, if you're paying for research). The five columns in Table 10.1 represent the steps in gap analysis: (1) clarify the decision or conclusion to be reached, (2) identify any subquestions that would help you address that ultimate decision or conclusion, (3) identify the information you need in order answer those subquestions, (4) identify any existing information you and others in your organization already have that may provide at least a partial answer, and (5) "subtract" column 4 from column 3 to assess your *information gap*.

Information gap analysis helps focus your research on the most critical questions.

Assume you work for the owner of Antique & Collectible Autos in Buffalo, New York, a small company that sells replica parts for classic hot rods and sports cars (frames, electrical

TABLE 10.1 Information Gap Analysis

(1) TARGET CONCLUSION	(2) SUBQUESTIONS	(3) INFORMATION NEEDED	(4) INFORMATION AVAILABLE	(5) INFORMATION GAP
Would it be easier to sell more parts or more completed cars?	How easy would it be to sell more parts?	The number of existing customers who might want to buy more parts.	We know what each customer has purchased.	We don't know what other parts they might need.
		The total number of new customers who might want parts.	We know how many people attend the car builder shows every year. We've rented magazine mailing lists, so we know how many subscribe to enthusiast magazines.	We don't know how many people build cars but don't attend the shows or subscribe to magazines.
		The number of other companies trying to sell parts to this group.	We think we've identified all the major national suppliers.	What about local or regional companies?
	How easy would it be to sell more cars?	The number of existing customers who want to buy another car.	Doesn't seem likely that people will buy more than one.	We need to verify this assumption.
		(continued)	(continued)	(continued)

wiring, body parts, and so on) as well as complete cars, built to order. Your boss wants to know which would be the easier way to increase revenues: try to sell more parts to hobbyists who want to assemble their own cars, or try to sell more complete cars. Following the example in Table 10.1, the conclusion you want to reach is in column 1. This is a complicated question with no immediately obvious answer, so you simplify the task by breaking it down to two more-manageable subquestions (column 2): "How easy would it be to sell more parts?" and "How easy would it be to sell more cars?"

Next, identify the information that would help you answer each subquestion. For instance, you would need several pieces of information to know how easy it would be to sell more parts; these are listed in column 3. Column 4 then lists the information you already have that relates to those answers. For instance, regarding the total number of new customers who might want parts, you know how many people attend car shows and subscribe to related magazines, but this information doesn't give you a complete answer, so you list the information gap in column 5. This analysis takes some time, to be sure, but it saves time in the long run by making sure you focus on the most important research priorities.

By comparing what you need to know with what you (or others in your organization) already know, you can quickly identify research topics.

Prioritizing Research Needs

Research projects have a curious way of taking on lives of their own. As you analyze your questions, you'll probably think of other questions you'd like to ask. Colleagues might volunteer questions they'd like to have answered. You'll probably compile more questions than you have time or money to answer. Moreover, if you'll be interviewing or surveying people to gather information, you'll need to limit the number of questions you ask so that you don't consume more time than people are willing to give.

Professional researchers often divide questions into categories such as "need to know" and "nice to know," and then they toss out all the "nice to know" questions. If you started with a technique such as information gap analysis, you will have a clear idea of the information you truly need to collect.

You'll never have enough time or money to answer every question that comes to mind, so setting priorities is a must.

You may not have enough time even to answer all the "need to know" items. Scan your list of information gaps to decide which are (a) the most important to answer or (b) the least risky not to answer. In the example in Table 10.1, you might conclude that few people who have purchased a completed car would want another one. To save time, you remove this item from your list. You might also identify information gaps in which your partial answer, while incomplete, is safe enough to move ahead with. Naturally, experience and judgment are important when identifying these priorities, so call on experienced colleagues if necessary.

LOCATING DATA AND INFORMATION

2 LEARNING OBJECTIVE

Define primary and secondary research, and explain when you use each method

Primary research contains information that you gather specifically for a new research project; secondary research contains information that others have gathered (and published, in many cases).

A good plan and careful prioritization tells you *what* you need to know and *why* you need to know it; the next step is to identify *where* that information might exist and *how* to locate it. The range of sources available to business researchers today is remarkable, almost overwhelming at times. If you have a question about an industry, a company, a market, a new technology, or a financial topic, chances are somebody else has already researched the topic. Someone in your own company, in fact, might have already looked into the problem. Research materials previously created for another purpose are considered **secondary research**. Secondary sources include magazines, newspapers, public websites, books, and other reports. Don't let the name fool you, though; you want to start with secondary research because it can save considerable time and money for many projects. In contrast, **primary research** is new research done specifically for your current project. Primary sources include surveys, interviews, observations, and experiments. Before you use any sources, though, you need to know whether you can trust them.

Evaluating Sources

3 LEARNING OBJECTIVE

Name nine criteria for evaluating the credibility of an information source

Evaluate your sources carefully to avoid embarrassing and potentially damaging mistakes.

If you've ever searched for anything on the Internet, you already know that sources can range from documents published by reputable companies to highly suspect blogs and postings from anonymous sources and total strangers. No matter where you're searching, be sure to separate the quality from the rubbish so you don't taint your results or damage your reputation. Ask yourself the following questions about each piece of material:

- **Does the source have a reputation for honesty and reliability?** Naturally, you'll feel more comfortable using information from a publication that has a reputation for accuracy. Find out how the publication accepts articles and whether it has an editorial board. But don't let your guard down completely; even the finest reporters and editors make mistakes, reputation or not
- **Is the source potentially biased?** Depending on what an organization stands for, its messages may be written with a certain bias—which is neither bad nor unethical. In

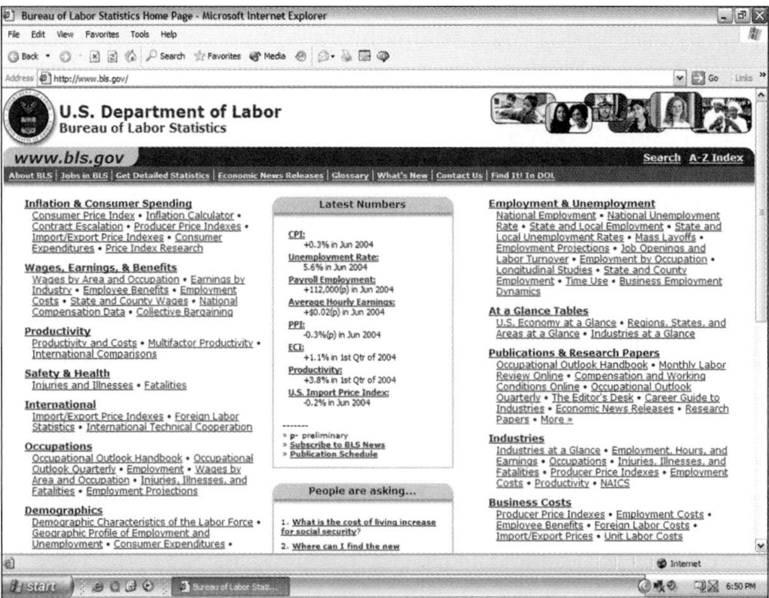

The U.S. Government's Bureau of Labor Statistics is a credible source of current economic and job-related data.

order to interpret an organization's information, you need to know its point of view. An organization's source of funding may also influence its information output.

- **What is the purpose of the material?** Was the material designed to inform others of new research, advance a position, or stimulate discussion? Was it designed to promote or sell a product? Be sure to distinguish between advertising and informing.
- **Is the author credible?** Find out whether the person or the publisher is well known in the field. Is the author an amateur? Merely someone with an opinion to air?
- **Where did the source get its information?** Many sources of secondary information get their material from other secondary sources, removing you even further from the original data. If a newspaper article says that pollutants in a local river dropped by 50 percent since last year, the reporter probably didn't measure those pollutants directly. If the accuracy of the measurement is critical for your purposes, find out who collected the data, the methods they used, their qualifications, and their professional reputation.
- **Can you verify the material independently?** Verification can uncover biases or mistakes—particularly important when the information goes beyond simple facts to include projections, interpretations, and estimates.
- **Is the material current?** Make sure you are using the most current information available by checking the publication date of a source. Many business-related fields change quickly, and published information can become obsolete in a matter of months or even weeks.
- **Is the material complete?** Have you accessed the entire document or only a selection from it? If it's a selection, which parts were excluded? Do you need more detail?
- **Do the source's claims stand up to scrutiny?** Step back and ask yourself whether the information makes sense. If a researcher claims that the market for a particular product will triple in the next five years, what would have to happen for that prediction to come true? Will three times as many customers buy the product? Will existing customers buy three times more than they currently buy?

You probably won't have time to conduct a thorough background check on all your sources, so focus your efforts on the most important or most suspicious pieces of information. If the material is from a website, take extra care to verify its accuracy and reliability; not all websites have the quality-control mechanisms common to traditional publishing.

Gathering Secondary Research

You'll want to start most projects by gathering secondary research first.

Even if you intend to eventually conduct primary research such as interviews or surveys, most projects start with a review of secondary research. Inside the company, you might be able to find a variety of reports, memos, and other documents that were prepared for other projects and that offer information relevant to your current project. Outside the company, business researchers can choose from a wide range of print and online resources, as you can see from the list in Table 10.2 (of course, this list represents a tiny fraction of the secondary resources available).[4] For instance, if you want to know more about a specific company, one of the first things you'll need to find out is whether the company is public (sells shares of stock to the general public) or private. Public companies, which are required to submit extensive financial reports to government agencies, generally have more information available than private companies. You can find a list of public companies in the *Directory of Companies Required to File Annual Reports with the Securities and Exchange Commission,* available in most public libraries. In fact, the best place to begin your search for secondary information is usually the nearest public or university library.

Finding Information at the Library

Even in the Internet age, libraries offer information and resources you can't find anywhere else—including specialized research librarians.

Libraries are where you'll find business books, electronic databases, newspapers, periodicals, directories, almanacs, and government publications. Many of these may be unavailable through a standard web search or may be available only with a subscription. Libraries are also where you'll find your most important resource: librarians. Reference librarians are trained in research techniques and spend their days managing information and helping people find materials. They can show you how to use the library's many databases, and they

TABLE 10.2 Major Business Resources

COMPANY, INDUSTRY, AND PRODUCT RESOURCES (PRINT)

- ***Brands and Their Companies/Companies and Their Brands.*** Data on over 281,000 consumer products and 51,000 manufacturers, importers, marketers, and distributors.
- ***Corporate and Industry Research Reports (CIRR).*** Collection of industry reports produced by industry analysts for investment purposes. Unique coverage includes industry profitability, comparative company sales, market share, profits, and forecasts.
- ***Directory of Companies Required to File Annual Reports with the Securities and Exchange Commission.*** Listing of U.S. publicly held firms.
- ***Dun's Directory of Service Companies.*** Information on 205,000 U.S. service companies.
- ***Forbes.*** Annual Report on American Industry published in first January issue of each year.
- ***Hoover's Handbook of American Business.*** Profiles of over 500 public and private corporations.
- ***Manufacturing USA.*** Data series listing nearly 25,000 companies, including detailed information on over 450 manufacturing industries.
- ***Market Share Report.*** Data covering products and service categories originating from trade journals, newsletters, and magazines.
- ***Moody's Industry Review.*** Data on 4,000 companies in about 150 industries. Ranks companies within industry by five financial statistics (revenue, net income, total assets, cash and marketable securities, and long-term debt) and includes key performance ratios.
- ***Moody's Manuals.*** Weekly manual of financial data in each of six business areas: industrials, transportation, public utilities, banks, finance, and over-the-counter (OTC) industrials.
- ***Service Industries USA.*** Comprehensive data on 2,100 services grouped into over 150 industries.
- ***Standard & Poor's Industry Surveys.*** Concise investment profiles for a broad range of industries. Coverage is extensive, with a focus on current situation and outlook. Includes some summary data on major companies in each industry.
- ***Standard & Poor's Register of Corporations, Directors and Executives.*** Index of major U.S. and international corporations. Lists officers, products, sales volume, and number of employees.
- ***Thomas's Register of American Manufacturers.*** Information on thousands of U.S. manufacturers indexed by company name and product.
- ***U.S. Industrial Outlook.*** Annual profiles of several hundred key U.S. industries. Each industry report covers several pages and includes tables, graphs, and charts that visually demonstrate how an industry compares with similar industries, including important component growth factors and other economic measures.

COMPANY, INDUSTRY, AND PRODUCT RESOURCES (ONLINE)

- ***CNN/Money*** http://money.cnn.com. News, analysis, and financial resources covering companies, industries, and world markets.
- ***Hoover's Online*** www.hoovers.com. Database of 12 million companies worldwide, including in-depth coverage of 35,000 leading companies around the world. Basic information available free; in-depth information requires subscription.
- ***NAICS Codes*** www.census.gov/naics. North American Industry Classification System.
- ***SEC filing*** www.sec.gov/edgar.shtml. SEC filings including 10Ks, 10Qs, annual reports, and prospectuses for 35,000 U.S. public firms.

DIRECTORIES AND INDEXES (PRINT)

- ***Books in Print.*** Index of 425,000 books in 62,000 subject categories currently available from U.S. publishers. Indexed by author and title.
- ***Directories in Print.*** Information on over 16,000 business and industrial directories.
- ***Encyclopedia of Associations.*** Index of thousands of associations listed by broad subject category, specific subject, association, and location.
- ***Reader's Guide to Periodical Literature.*** Periodical index categorized by subject and author.
- ***Ulrich's International Periodicals Directory.*** Listings by title, publisher, editor, phone, and address of over 140,000 publications such as popular magazines, trade journals, government documents, and newspapers. Great for locating hard-to-find trade publications.

PEOPLE (PRINT)

- ***Dun & Bradstreet's Reference Book of Corporate Management.*** Professional histories of people serving as the principal officers and directors of more than 12,000 U.S. companies.
- ***Who's Who in America.*** Biographies of living U.S. citizens who have gained prominence in their fields. Related book, *Who's Who in the World,* covers global achievers.

TRADEMARKS (PRINT/ONLINE)

- ***Official Gazette of the United Patent and Trademark Office.*** Weekly publication (one for trademarks and one for patents) providing official record of newly assigned trademarks and patents, product descriptions, and product names.
- ***United States Patent and Trademark Office*** www.uspto.gov. Trademark and patent information records.

TABLE 10.2 Continued

STATISTICS AND FACTS (PRINT)

- ***Industry Norms and Key Business Ratios*** **(Dun & Bradstreet).** Industry, financial, and performance ratios.
- ***Information Please Almanac.*** Compilation of broad-range statistical data with strong focus on labor force.
- ***Robert Morris Associates' Annual Statement Studies.*** Industry, financial, and performance ratios.
- ***Statistical Abstract of the United States.*** U.S. economic, social, political, and industrials statistics.
- ***The World Almanac and Book of Facts.*** Facts on economic, social, educational, and political events for major countries.

STATISTICS AND FACTS (ONLINE)

- **Bureau of Economic Analysis** www.bea.doc.gov. Large collection of economic and government data.
- **Europa—The European Union Online** www.europa.eu.int. A portal that provides up-to-date coverage of current affairs, legislation, policies and EU statistics.
- **FedStats** www.fedstats.gov. Access to full range of statistics and information from over 70 U.S. government agencies.
- **STAT-USA** www.census.gov. Large Collection of economic and government data.
- **U.S. Census Bureau** www.census.gov. Demographic data on both consumers and businesses based on 1990 census.
- **U.S. Bureau of Labor Statistics** www.bls.gov. Extensive national and regional information on labor and business, including employment, industry growth, productivity, Consumer Price Index (CPI), and overall U.S. economy.

COMMERCIAL DATABASES (REQUIRE SUBSCRIPTIONS)

- **Dialog.** Hundreds of databases that include areas such as business and finance, news and media, medicine, pharmaceuticals, reference, social sciences, government and regulation, science and technology, and more.
- **Ebsco Online Reference System.** Access to a variety of databases on a wide range of disciplines from leading information providers.
- **HighBeam.** Hundreds of full-text newspaper, magazine, newswire and articles, plus maps and photographs.
- **Gale Business & Company Resource Center.** A comprehensive research tool designed for undergraduate and graduate students, job searchers, and investors; offers a wide variety of information on companies and industries.
- **LexisNexis.** Several thousand databases covering legal, corporate, government, and academic subjects.
- **ProQuest.** Thousands of periodicals and newspapers; archives continue to expand with its program to digitize over five billion pages of microfilm.
- **SRDS Media Solutions** (Standard Rate and Data Service). A comprehensive database of magazine information and advertising rates, cataloging more than 100,000 U.S. and international media properties.

can help you find obscure information. Whether you're trying to locate information in printed materials or in databases, each type of resource serves a special function:

- **Newspapers and periodicals.** Libraries subscribe to only a select number of newspapers and store a limited number of back issues in print. However, they frequently subscribe to databases containing newspaper articles in full text (available online, on CD-ROM, or on microfilm). In addition, most newspapers today offer full-text or limited editions of their papers on the Internet, and archives are often searchable for subscribers. Most periodicals fall into one of four categories: (1) popular magazines (not intended for business, professional, or academic use), (2) trade journals (providing news and other facts about particular professions, industries, and occupations), (3) business magazines (covering all major industries and professions), and (4) academic journals (publishing data from professional researchers and educators). To locate a certain periodical, check your library's database.
- **Business books.** Although less timely than newspapers and periodicals, business books provide in-depth coverage of a variety of business topics. Because of budgetary constraints, public libraries must be selective about the books they put on their shelves, so you may have better luck finding specialized information at company libraries or at a college library (assuming the college offers courses in those subjects).
- **Directories.** Thousands of directories are published in print and electronic formats in the United States—covering everything from accountants to zoos. Many include membership information for all kinds of special-interest groups. For instance, business directories provide entries for companies, products, and individuals, and they include the name of key contact persons. Directories are considered invaluable for marketers, job seekers, and others who need to establish a prospect list.

- **Almanacs and statistical resources.** Almanacs are handy guides to factual and statistical information about countries, politics, the labor force, and so on. Also check out the *Statistical Abstract of the United States* (published annually by the U.S. Department of Commerce). This resource contains statistics about life, work, government, population patterns, health issues, business, crime, and the environment.

Local, state, and federal government agencies publish a huge array of information that is helpful to business researchers.

- **Government publications.** For information on a law, a court decision, or current population patterns and business trends, consult government documents. A librarian can direct you to the information you want. You'll need the name of the government agency you're interested in (U.S. Congress, Ninth Circuit Court of Appeals, or Department of Labor) and some identification for the specific information you need (Safe Drinking Water Act of 1974, *Price v. Shell Oil*, or the latest census). If you know the date and name of a publication, your search will be easier.
- **Electronic databases.** Databases offer computer-searchable collections of information, often categorized by subject area, such as business, law, science, technology, and education. Some libraries offer remote access to some or all databases; for others you'll need to visit in person. Databases offer quick access to billions of records of the world's published literature, but using one successfully requires knowledge of basic search techniques and a clear idea of what the database includes. For more information on databases, the following section covers "Understanding Search Engines, Web Directories, and Databases."

Finding Information Online

Conduct online research with extreme care; much of the information online has not be subjected to the same quality controls common in traditional offline publishing.

Experienced researchers know that the Internet can be a tremendous source of business information, much of it free and all of it available more or less instantly. They also know that the Internet can waste hours and hours of precious time and deliver inaccurate or biased information, exaggerated claims, and unsubstantiated rumors. You must remember that anyone (including you) can post virtually anything on a website, and much of that information will be unverified by the editorial boards and fact checkers commonly used in traditional publishing. If possible, try to learn something about an unfamiliar topic from a trusted source (such as an industry journal or an experienced colleague) before you start searching online. You'll be better able to detect skewed or erroneous information, and you can be more selective about which websites and documents to use.

One good place to start on the web is the Internet Public Library at www.ipl.org. Modeled after a real library, this site provides you with a carefully selected collection of links to high-quality business resources that offer such information as company profiles, trade data, business news, corporate tax and legal advice, small-business information, prepared forms and documents, biographies of executives, financial reports, job postings, online publications, and so on.

You can gather a lot of information on companies from their websites, but remember that such information is designed to present the company in a positive light.

If you're looking for specific company information, your best source may be the company's website (if it maintains one, which virtually all large and medium companies do, as well as many smaller companies). These websites generally include detailed information about a firm's products, services, history, mission, strategy, financial performance, and employment needs. Many sites provide links to related company information, such as SEC filings, news releases, and more. Reputable companies are careful about the information they put online, but beware of the possibility of biases and mistakes.

4 LEARNING OBJECTIVE

Explain the complementary nature of search engines, web directories, and databases

Understanding Search Engines, Web Directories, and Databases You've probably used one or more search engines, web directories, or databases for school and personal projects already. All three provide online access to secondary source material (and in some cases via CD-ROM), but each operates in a unique way and therefore offers distinct advantages and disadvantages for business researchers.

Search engines scan millions of webpages to find the terms you specify, but they can't access a lot of the information that is stored electronically.

Search engines identify individual webpages that contain a specific word or phrase you've asked for. Search engines have the advantage of scanning millions or billions of individual webpages, and the best engines use powerful ranking algorithms to present the pages that are probably the most relevant to your search request. Note that search engines don't actually search the web when you submit a query; doing so would be painfully slow.

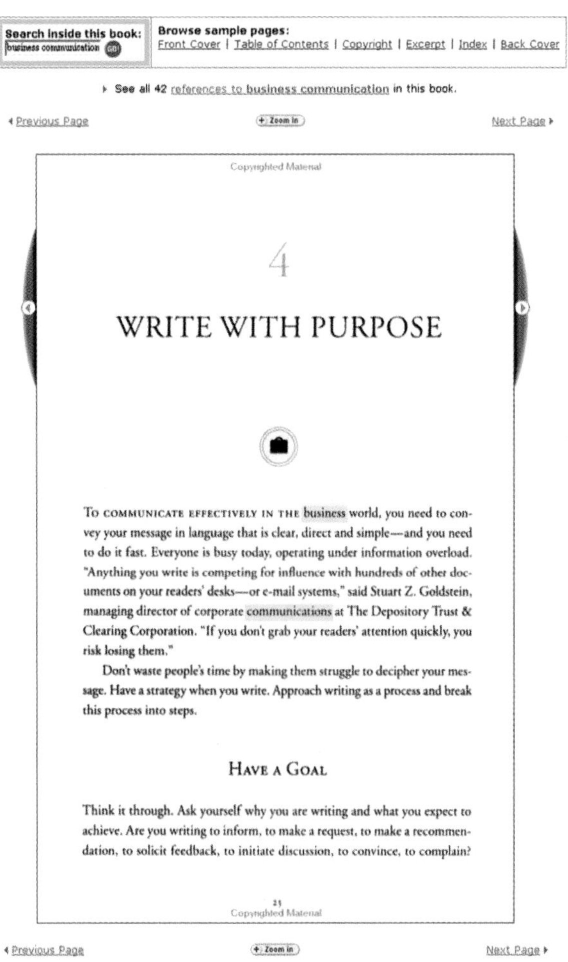

Search inside this book: business communication Go

Browse sample pages: Front Cover | Table of Contents | Copyright | Excerpt | Index | Back Cover

See all 42 references to business communication in this book.

Previous Page | Zoom in | Next Page

Copyrighted Material

4

WRITE WITH PURPOSE

TO COMMUNICATE EFFECTIVELY IN THE business world, you need to convey your message in language that is clear, direct and simple—and you need to do it fast. Everyone is busy today, operating under information overload. "Anything you write is competing for influence with hundreds of other documents on your readers' desks—or e-mail systems," said Stuart Z. Goldstein, managing director of corporate communications at The Depository Trust & Clearing Corporation. "If you don't grab your readers' attention quickly, you risk losing them."

Don't waste people's time by making them struggle to decipher your message. Have a strategy when you write. Approach writing as a process and break this process into steps.

HAVE A GOAL

Think it through. Ask yourself why you are writing and what you expect to achieve. Are you writing to inform, to make a request, to make a recommendation, to solicit feedback, to initiate discussion, to convince, to complain?

25

Copyrighted Material

Previous Page | Zoom in | Next Page

Amazon.com's "Search Inside" feature adds a powerful new dimension to online research by letting you look for specific words within the content of published books. The words highlighted in this example were the keywords in the search.

Instead, they search through an index of pages that the search engine updates periodically. This is why you occasionally see webpages listed in the search results that you can't access; they've been moved or deleted since the last index update.

For all the ease and power they offer, search engines have three disadvantages that could affect the quality of your research. First, the process that search engines use to find and present lists of webpages is computerized, with no human editors involved to evaluate the quality of the content you find on these pages. Second, search engines can't reach the content held in limited-access collections, such as the back issues of many newspapers, magazines, and professional journals. Third, various search engines use different techniques to find, classify, and present pages, so you might be able to find certain pages through one engine but not through another.

The good news is that you can get around all three shortcomings when conducting research—although doing so is sometimes expensive. **Web directories** address the first major shortcoming of search engines by using human editors to categorize and evaluate websites. Directories such as those offered by Yahoo!, About, and the Open Directory at dmoz.org present lists of websites chosen by a team of editors. For instance, the Open Directory lists more than 200,000 business-related websites by category, from individual companies to industry associations, all of which have been evaluated and selected by a team of volunteer editors.[5]

Web directories rely on human editors to evaluate and select websites.

Online databases address the second shortcoming of search engines by offering access to the newspapers, magazines, and journals that you're likely to need for many research projects. You can access such sources as *Business Week* and the *Wall Street Journal* either through the individual publisher's own sites or through a commercial database that offers access to multiple sources. Individual publisher sites usually require a subscription to that

Online databases give you access to the most important resource that searches engines usually can't reach: millions of newspaper, magazine, and journal articles.

The Internet Public Library is one of the most important web directories for business researchers.

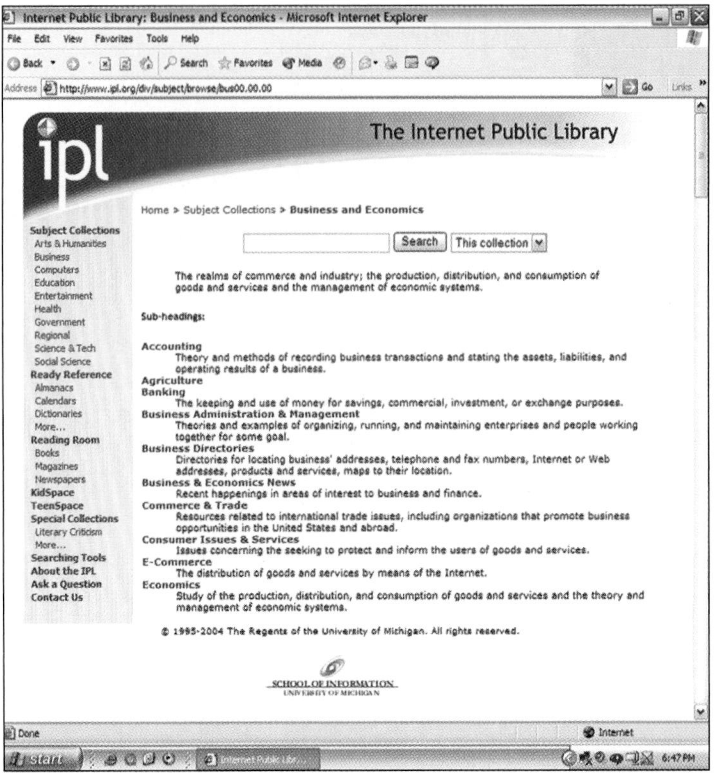

publication for anything beyond the current issue, and commercial databases require subscriptions to access all content. Some commercial databases, such as HighBeam (www.highbeam.com, formerly eLibrary), are priced to attract individual users, whereas others, such as LexisNexis and ProQuest, are intended for use by libraries and other institutions. In addition to databases that primarily feature content from newspapers and periodicals, specialized databases such as Hoover's (www.hoovers.com) and OneSource's CorpTech (www.corptech.com) offer detailed information on thousands of individual companies. You can obtain company news releases from the free databases maintained by PRNewswire (www.prnewswire.com) and Business Wire (www.businesswire.com). News releases are good places to look for announcements of new products, management changes, earnings, dividends, mergers, acquisitions, and other company information.

Metacrawlers can save you time by employing multiple search engines at once.

Metacrawlers or *metasearch engines* address the third shortcoming of search engines by formatting your search request for the specific requirements of multiple search engines and then telling you how many hits each engine was able to find for you. The more popular metacrawlers include DogPile.com and Mamma.com. Table 10.3 lists some of the most commonly used search engines, directories, and metacrawlers available today.

As often happens in technology and business, the lines between these three types of tools are beginning to blur. For instance, DogPile.com provides both metacrawler and directory functions, and LookSmart.com provides features of all three: a search engine, a directory, and a database of articles (although the database is limited to publications that provide free access to articles, which do not include major business publications such as *BusinessWeek* or *Fortune*).[6]

Make sure you know how each search engine, directory, database, or metacrawler works; they work in different ways and can produce unpredictable results if you don't know how each one operates.

Using Search Tools Effectively Search engines, metacrawlers, and databases offer a variety of ways to find information. That's the good news. The bad news is that no two of them work in exactly the same way, and many continue to refine and simplify their approaches, so you might have to modify your search techniques as you move from one tool to the next. The most basic form of searching is a *keyword search*, in which the engine or database attempts to find items that include all of the words you enter. A *Boolean search* expands on this capability by using search operators that let you define a query with greater precision. Common operators include AND (the search must include both words before and after the

TABLE 10.3 Best of Internet Searching

MAJOR SEARCH ENGINES			
A9 (Amazon)	www.a9.com	Google	www.google.com
AllTheWeb	www.alltheweb.com	Lycos	www.lycos.com
Alta Vista	www.altavista.com	MSN	http://search.msn.com
Ask Jeeves	www.askjeeves.com	Teoma	www.teoma.com
METACRAWLERS AND HYBRID SITES			
DogPile	www.dogpile.com	Query Server	www.queryserver.com
IXQuick	www.ixquick.com	Search.com	www.search.com
Kartoo	www.kartoo.com	Surfwax	www.surfwax.com
LookSmart	www.looksmart.com	Vivisimo	www.vivisimo.com
Mamma	www.mamma.com	Web Brain	www.webbrain.com
MetaCrawler	www.metacrawler.com	WebCrawler	www.webcrawler.com
Fazzle	www.fazzle.com	Yahoo!	www.yahoo.com
Infonetware RealTerm Search	www.infonetware.com	Zapmeta	www.zapmeta.com
ProFusion	www.profusion.com	Zworks	www.zworks.com
WEB DIRECTORIES			
About	www.about.com	Internet Public Library	www.ipl.org
Beaucoup	www.beaucoup.com	Open Directory	www.dmoz.com
NEWS SEARCH ENGINES			
AllTheWeb News	www.alltheweb.com/?cat=news	Newstrawler	www.newstrawler.com
AltaVista News	http://news.altavista.com	NewsTrove.com	www.newstrove.com
Daypop	www.daypop.com	World News Network	www.wn.com
Google News	http://news.google.com	Yahoo! News	http://news.yahoo.com
BLOG SEARCH ENGINES AND RSS NEWS FEEDS			
Bloglines	www.bloglines.com	Bloogz	www.bloogz.com
Blogsearchengine	www.blogsearchengine.com	Memigo	www.memigo.com
Boogleplay	www.boogleplay.com	Waypath	www.waypath.com
MAGAZINE AND PERIODICAL SEARCH ENGINES			
FindArticles.com	www.findarticles.com	MagPortal	www.magportal.com

AND), OR (it can include either or both words), or NOT (the search ignores items with whatever word comes after NOT). For example:

- *corporate AND profits* finds webpages or database entries that contain both *corporate* and *profits*
- *corporate OR profits* finds items that contain either *corporate* or *profit* but not necessarily both
- *corporate NOT profit* finds items that contain *corporate* but excludes all those that contain the word *profit*

Boolean searches can also include operators that let you find a particular word in close proximity to other words or that use *wildcards* to find similar spellings (such as *profit*, *profits*, and *profitability*).

To overcome the perceived complexity of Boolean searches, some search engines and databases offer *natural language searches*, which let you ask questions in normal, everyday English ("Which videogame companies are the most profitable?"). For instance, HighBeam lets you select either Boolean or natural language searches. However, if a site or database doesn't specifically say that it offers natural language searching, the results might be unpredictable.

Recently, search engines such as Google, Yahoo!, and AllTheWeb have implemented *forms-based searches* that help you create powerful queries without the need to learn any special techniques.[7] As the name implies, you simply fill out an online form that typically lets you specify such parameters as date ranges, words to include or exclude, language, Internet domain name, and even file and media types. To access these forms, look for "advanced search" or a similar option. (Note that these forms use Boolean and other techniques in the background, but you don't have to learn any special commands.)

5 LEARNING OBJECTIVE

Provide five guidelines for conducting an effective online search

To make the best use of any search engine or database, keep the following points in mind:

- **Read the instructions.** Unfortunately, there is no universal set of instructions that apply to every search tool. You can usually find a Help page that explains both basic and advanced functions, with advice on how to use a particular tool most effectively.
- **Pay attention to the details.** Details can make all the difference in a search. For instance, most search engines treat *AND* (upper case) as a Boolean search operator and look only for pages or entries that contain both words. In contrast, *and* (lower case) and similar basic words (called *stopwords*) are excluded from many searches because they are so common they'll show up in every webpage or database entry. Similarly, some engines and databases interpret the question mark as a wildcard to let you search for variations of a given word, but Google does not (Google searches for word variations automatically). Again, you need to know how to operate each search engine or database, and don't assume they all work in the same way.
- **Review the search and display options carefully.** Some sites and databases provide few options to control your queries, but others, such as AllTheWeb.com, let you make a variety of choices to include or exclude specific types of files and pages from specific sites. When the results are displayed, verify the presentation order. On Highbeam, for instance, you can choose to sort the results by either date or relevancy. If you're looking for an article that you know was recently published, it might not show up near the top of the list if the list is sorted by relevancy instead of date. Also, pay attention to whether you are searching in the title, subject, or document field of the database. Each will return different results.
- **Try variations of your terms.** If you can't find what you're looking for, try abbreviations (*CEO, CPA*), synonyms (*man, male*), related terms (*child, adolescent, youth*), different spellings (*dialog, dialogue*), singular and plural forms (*woman, women*), nouns and adjectives (*manager, management, managerial*), and open and compound forms (*online, on line, on-line*).
- **Adjust the scope of your search if needed.** If a search yields little or no information, broaden your search by specifying fewer terms. For example, "Sony" yields many more hits than "Sony PlayStation." Conversely, if you're inundated with too many hits, use more terms to narrow your search.

If you need to collect recurring information from online sources, consider using an RSS news aggregator.

Using Agents For years, Internet users have been dreaming of intelligent software agents that automatically prowl the online world and bring back high-quality information. Nothing like this is available quite yet, but the RSS (Rich Site Summary) technology mentioned as a delivery mechanism in Chapter 6 can also serve as a powerful research tool. RSS news aggregators such as NewsGator (www.newsgator.com) and NewzCrawler (www.newzcrawler.com) let you subscribe to channels at thousands of websites, blogs, and newsgroups. New information in the categories you specify is automatically delivered to your computer, saving you the trouble of searching multiple sites over and over again.[8]

Documenting Your Sources

Proper documentation of the sources you use is both ethical and an important resource for your readers.

Documenting the secondary sources you use in your writing serves three important functions: it properly and ethically credits the person who created the original material, it shows your audience that you have sufficient support for your message, and, as mentioned earlier, it helps your readers explore your topic in more detail if desired. Thorough documentation is particularly important if you're working in a large organization; your reports might be used by colleagues all around the world for years after you originally wrote them, and these people won't always have the opportunity to query you in person for more information. Be sure to take advantage of the source documentation tools in your word processor, rather than attempting to track source notes by hand. For instance, Microsoft Word automatically tracks and numbers endnotes for you, and you can use the "table of authorities" feature to create a bibliography of all the sources you've used. As computing technologies continue to advance, keep an eye out for other note-taking tools that can help you be a more efficient researcher. For example, software such as Microsoft's OneNote makes it easier to collect and organize notes wherever and however you find vital information, from meetings to websites to e-mail messages.[9]

You may document your sources through footnotes, endnotes, or some similar system (see Appendix B, "Documentation of Report Sources"). Whatever method you choose, documentation is necessary for books, articles, tables, charts, diagrams, song lyrics, scripted dialogue, letters, speeches—anything that you take from someone else, including ideas and information that you've re-expressed through paraphrasing or summarizing.

However, you do not have to cite a source for general knowledge or for specialized knowledge that's generally known among your readers. For example, most everyone knows that Microsoft is a large software company and that computers are pervasive in business today. You can say so on your own authority, even if you've read an article in which the author says the same thing.

Copyright law covers printed materials, audiovisual material, many forms of artistic expression, computer programs, maps, mailing lists, and even answering-machine messages. Copyright law does not protect

- titles, names, short phrases, and slogans
- familiar symbols or designs
- lists of ingredients or contents
- ideas, procedures, methods, systems, processes, concepts, principles, discoveries, or devices (although it does cover their description, explanation, or illustration)

A work is considered copyrighted as soon as it's put into fixed form, even if it hasn't been registered.[10]

Merely crediting the source is not always enough. According to the *fair use doctrine*, you can use other people's work only as long as you don't unfairly prevent them from benefiting as a result. For example, if you reproduce someone else's copyrighted questionnaire in a report you're writing, even if you identify the source thoroughly, you may be preventing the author from selling a copy of that questionnaire to your readers.

In general, avoid relying to such a great extent on someone else's work. However, when you can't avoid it, contact the copyright holder (usually the author or publisher) for permission to reprint. You'll usually be asked to pay a fee.

Gathering Primary Research

Surveys and interviews are the most common primary research techniques.

If secondary research can't provide the information and insights you need, your next choice is to gather the information yourself with primary research. The two most common primary research methods are surveys and interviews. (Other primary techniques

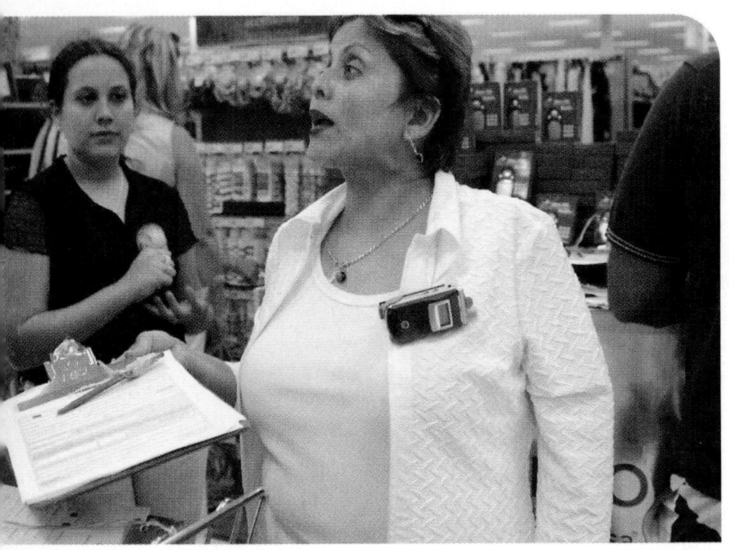

Marketing surveys are a common way of gathering data directly from customers.

are observations and experiments in special situations such as test marketing, but they're not commonly used for day-to-day business research.)

Conducting Surveys

A carefully prepared and conducted survey can provide invaluable insights on a wide variety of business topics. Of course, surveys are useful only when they're reliable and valid. A survey is *reliable* if it produces identical results when repeated. A survey is *valid* if it measures what it's intended to measure. To generate results that are both reliable and valid, you need to choose research participants carefully and develop an effective set of questions. (For surveys on high-risk or high-visibility topics, you're usually better off hiring a research specialist who knows how to avoid errors at each stage.)

For a survey to produce valid results, it must be based on a representative sample of respondents.

When selecting the people who'll participate in your survey, the most critical task is getting a representative sample of the entire population in question. For instance, if you want to know how U.S. consumers feel about a particular product or company, don't just randomly survey people in the local mall and assume their answers represent the opinions of everyone in the country. Different types of consumers shop at different times of the day and different days of the week, some consumers don't shop at malls regularly, and many who do won't stop to talk with researchers. The online surveys you see on many websites today potentially suffer from the same sampling bias; they capture only the opinions of people who visit the sites and want to participate, which might not represent the population that the site owner really needs to know about. A good handbook on survey research will help you select the right people for your survey, including selecting enough people to have a statistically valid survey.[11]

To develop an effective survey questionnaire, start with the prioritized information gaps you identified at the beginning of the research process. Then break these points into specific questions, choosing an appropriate type of question for each point (Figure 10.2 shows various types of survey questions). The following guidelines will help you produce results that are both valid and reliable:[12]

Provide clear instructions to prevent mistaken answers.

- **Provide clear instructions.** Respondents need to know exactly how to fill out your questionnaire.
- **Keep the questionnaire short and easy to answer.** Ask only questions that are relevant to your research. Remember that people are most likely to respond if they can complete your questionnaire within 10 to 15 minutes.
- **Whenever possible, formulate questions to provide answers that are easy to analyze.** Numbers and facts are easier to summarize than opinions, for instance. Professional researchers think through the entire process of post-survey analysis before they actually conduct the survey to make sure that none of the questions will create analysis problems.
- **Avoid leading questions.** Questions that lead to a particular answer will bias your survey. If you ask, "Do you prefer that we stay open in the evenings for customer convenience?" you'll no doubt get a "yes." Instead, ask, "What time of day do you normally do your shopping?"
- **Avoid ambiguous questions.** If you ask "Do you shop at the mall often?" some people might interpret *often* to mean "every day," whereas others might think it means "once a week" or "once a month."
- **Ask only one thing at a time.** A compound question such as "Do you read books and magazines?" doesn't allow for the respondent who reads one but not the other.

Be sure to test your survey before using it.

Before you conduct your survey, test it on a sample group to identify questions that might be confusing or that might generate answers you don't expect (see "Communication Miscues: The Art of the Question" on page 318).

FIGURE 10.2
Types of Survey Questions

QUESTION TYPE	EXAMPLE
Open-ended	How would you describe the flavor of this ice cream?
Either-or	Do you think this ice cream is too rich? _____ Yes _____ No
Multiple choice	Which description best fits the taste of this ice cream? (Choose only one.) a. Delicious b. Too fruity c. Too sweet d. Too intensely flavored e. Bland f. Stale
Scale	Please mark an X on the scale to indicate how you perceive the texture of this ice cream. ←——————————————→ Too light Light Creamy Too creamy
Checklist	Which flavors of ice cream have you had in the past 12 months? (Check all that apply.) _____ Vanilla _____ Chocolate _____ Strawberry _____ Chocolate chip _____ Coffee
Ranking	Rank these flavors in order of your preference, from 1 (most preferred) to 5 (least preferred): _____ Vanilla _____ Cherry _____ Maple nut _____ Chocolate ripple _____ Coconut
Short-answer	In the past month how many times did you buy ice cream in the supermarket? __________ In the past month how many times did you buy ice cream in ice cream shops? __________

The Internet is quickly becoming the preferred survey mechanism for many researchers, and dozens of companies now offer online survey services.[13] Compared to traditional mail and in-person techniques, online surveys are usually faster to create, easier to administer, faster to analyze, and less expensive overall. The interactive capabilities of the web can enhance all kinds of surveys, from simple opinion polls to complex purchase simulations. Many groupware systems now have polling features that make it easy to ask your fellow team members to vote on specific issues. However, don't let the speed and convenience of online surveys lower the requirements for careful planning; online surveys require the same care as any other type of survey, including being on guard against sampling bias.[14]

Conducting Interviews

Interviews are easy to conduct but require careful planning to produce useful results.

Getting information straight from an expert can be a great method for collecting primary information. Although interviews are relatively easy to conduct, they require careful

Communication Miscues

The Art of the Question

Poorly worded questions can render a survey useless. Even worse, they can produce subtle differences in answers from one respondent to the next that you didn't anticipate and don't take into account in your analysis. Assume you receive regular surveys from the human resources department in your company, dealing with such issues as productivity, employee satisfaction, and employee benefits. This month's survey contains the following questions:

1. How would you rate the food in the company cafeteria? (choose one)
 ____ Fantastic
 ____ Nutritious
 ____ Delicious
 ____ Filling
 ____ A good value for the money
2. What is your opinion of the improved insurance sign-up process we instituted last month?
3. If the dental benefits plan were modified relative to the current plan, wherein employees are expected to pay a $20 co-payment at the time of each visit, with benefits subject to the normal companywide 80% co-insurance standard, provided the co-insurance ratio did not drop, would you continue to participate in the plan if co-payment were increased to $50 but counterbalanced by a reduction in your monthly payroll deduction amount?
 ___ yes ___ no
4. Division supervisors continue to report problems with employees reporting for work late. Do the employees in your department tend to report for work
 ____ Always on time
 ____ Mostly on time
 ____ Usually on time
 ____ Occasionally late
 ____ Frequently late
5. How many times did you personally report for work late last year?
6. Do ever feel poorly trained or insufficiently motivated in your job?
 ___ yes ___ no

CAREER APPLICATIONS

1. Which of these questions might result in unusable information? Why?
2. How would you help the human resources manager rewrite them to improve the quality of information they generate?

planning to get the best results and make the best use of the other person's time. Planning an interview is similar to planning any other form of communication. You begin by analyzing your purpose, learning about the other person, and formulating your main idea. Then you decide on the length, style, and organization of the interview.

The answers you receive are influenced by the types of questions you ask, by the way you ask them, and by your subject's cultural and language background. Other influential factors include race, gender, age, educational level, and social status, so know your subject before you start writing questions.[15] In addition, be aware of ethical implications. For example, asking someone to divulge personal information about a co-worker may be asking that person to make an unethical choice. Always be careful about confidentiality, politics, and other sensitive issues.

Choose question types that will generate the specific information you need.

Ask **open-ended questions** to invite the expert to offer opinions, insights, and information, such as "Why do you believe that South America represents a better opportunity than Europe for this product line?" Bear in mind that although open-ended questions can extract significant amounts of information, they do give you less control over the interview. Someone might take 10 seconds or 10 minutes to answer a question, so plan to be flexible.

6 LEARNING OBJECTIVE

Outline an effective process for planning and conducting information interviews

Ask **closed questions** to elicit a specific answer, such as yes or no. However, including too many closed questions in an interview will make the experience feel more like a simple survey and won't take full advantage of the interview setting. When you do ask a question that implies a straightforward answer, such as "Do you think we should expand distribution in South America?" explore the reasoning behind the expert's answer.

The following guidelines will help you come up with a great set of interview questions:[16]

- **Think about sequence.** Arrange your questions in a way that helps uncover layers of information or that helps the subject tell you a complete story.
- **Rate your questions and highlight the ones you really need answers to.** If you start to run out of time during the interview, you may have to skip less important questions.
- **Ask smart questions.** If you ask a question that your subject perceives to be less than intelligent, the interview could go downhill in a hurry.
- **Limit the number of questions.** For a half-hour interview, plan on 15 to 20 questions, bearing in mind that open-ended questions can take far longer to answer than closed questions.
- **Edit your questions.** Try to make your questions as neutral and as easy to understand as possible. Then practice them several times to make sure you're ready for the interview.

A successful interview requires careful planning and organization to ensure you get the information you really need.

Consider providing the other person with a list of questions at least a day or two before the interview, especially if you'd like to quote your subject in writing or if your questions might require your subject to conduct research or think extensively about the answers. If you want to record the interview, ask the person ahead of time and respect his or her wishes.

As soon as possible after the interview, take a few moments to write down your thoughts, go over your notes, and organize your material. Look for important themes, helpful facts or statistics, and direct quotes. If you made a tape recording, *transcribe* it (take down word for word what the person said) or take notes from the tape just as you would while listening to someone in person.

Face-to-face interviews give you the opportunity to gauge nonverbal responses as well.

Face-to-face interviews give you the opportunity to gauge the reaction to your questions and observe the nonverbal signals that accompany the answers, but interviews don't necessarily have to take place in person. E-mail interviews are becoming more common, partly because they give subjects a chance to think through their responses thoroughly, rather than rushing to fit the time constraints of a face-to-face interview.[17] Also, e-mail interviews might be the only way you will be able to access some experts.

As a reminder of the tasks involved in interviews, see "Checklist: Conducting Effective Information Interviews."

DOCUMENT MAKEOVER

IMPROVE THIS LIST OF INTERVIEW QUESTIONS

To practice correcting drafts of actual documents, visit www.prenhall.com/onekey on the web. Click "Document Makeovers" then click Chapter 10. You will find a list of interview questions that contain problems and errors relating to what you've learned in this chapter about finding, evaluating, and processing information. Use the Final Draft decision tool to create an improved version of these questions. Check questions for sequencing, appropriateness, perceptiveness, and respect for ethical, confidential, political, or sensitive issues.

CHECKLIST: Conducting Effective Information Interviews

- Learn about the person you're interviewing.
- Formulate your main idea to ensure effective focus.
- Choose the length, style, and organization of the interview.
- Select question types to elicit the specific information you want.
- Design each question carefully to collect useful answers.
- Limit the number of questions you ask.
- Consider recording the interview if the subject permits.
- Review your notes as soon as the interview ends.

Communication Solution

Successfully processing research results was key to Toyota's efforts to craft effective messages for younger car buyers. For instance, the 50 individual video diaries produced a wide range of opinions, insights, and information. Brian Bolain and his team then needed to distill all that subjective input to find the most compelling recurring themes.

PROCESSING DATA AND INFORMATION

Once you've collected all the necessary secondary and primary information, the next step is transforming it into the specific content you need. For simpler projects, you may be able to drop your material directly into your report, presentation, or other application. However, when you have a significant amount of information or raw data from surveys, you'll need to process the material before you can use it. This step involves quoting, paraphrasing, and summarizing textual material or analyzing numerical data.

After you collect your research, the next step is converting it into usable information.

Quoting, Paraphrasing, and Summarizing

You can use information from secondary sources in three ways. *Quoting* a source means you reproduce it exactly as you found it, and you either set it off with quotation marks (for shorter passages) or extract it in an indented paragraph (for longer passages). Use direct quotations when the original language will enhance your argument or when rewording the passage would lessen its impact. However, try not to quote sources at great length. Too much quoting creates a choppy patchwork of varying styles and gives the impression that all you've done is piece together the work of other people. Moreover, remember that quotations are not meant to stand alone but to support your own ideas and arguments.

Quoting a source means reproducing the content exactly and indicating who created the information originally.

Paraphrasing is expressing someone else's ideas in your own words.

You can often maximize the impact of secondary material in your own writing by *paraphrasing* it, restating it in your own words and with your own sentence structures.[18] Paraphrasing helps you maintain consistent tone, present information using vocabulary more familiar to your audience, and avoid the choppy feel of too many quotations. Of course, you still need to credit the originator of the information, but not with quotation marks or indented paragraphs.

To paraphrase effectively, follow these tips:[19]

- Reread the original passage until you fully understand its meaning.
- Record your paraphrase on a note card or in an electronic format.
- Use business language and jargon that your audience is familiar with.
- Check your version with the original source to verify that you have not altered the meaning.
- Use quotation marks to identify any unique terms or phrases you have borrowed exactly from the source.
- Record the source (including the page number) so that you can give proper credit if you use this material in your report.

Summarizing is similar to paraphrasing but distills the content into fewer words.

Summarizing is similar to paraphrasing but presents the gist of the material in fewer words than the original. An effective summary identifies the main ideas and major support points from your source material, but leaves out most details, examples, and other information that is less critical to your audience. Like quotations and paraphrases, summaries also require complete documentation of your sources.

Plagiarism is the unethical presentation of someone else's words as your own.

Of course, all three approaches require careful attention to ethics. When quoting directly, take care not to distort the original intent of the material by quoting selectively or out of context. And never succumb to **plagiarism**, presenting someone else's words as your own, without proper credit. Movie advertisements are guilty of this from time to time, such as an ad reprinting the single word "Amazing" along with a critic's name, when the critic actually wrote something like "An amazing mess of a movie."

When paraphrasing and summarizing, take care not to distort the original intent as you express the ideas in your own words and sentences. Remember that the goal is to help your audience relate to material that supports your message. Double-check your writing to make sure you didn't subconsciously skew the other writer's message to fit your own needs (see "Ethics Detective: Finding What You're Looking For").

Analyzing Your Data

Business research, both secondary and primary, often produces numerical data—everything from sales figures to population statistics to survey answers. By themselves, these

Ethics Detective

Finding What You're Looking For

To deal with a growing problem of employee turnover, your company recently hired a research firm to survey employees to find out why more employees are leaving than in past years. You and a colleague were assigned to work with the consultants and present their findings to upper management. Neither one of you welcomed the assignment because you suspect you'll have to present information that is critical of the management team.

As you feared, the researchers deliver a mixture of news that is mostly negative:

- 78 percent of employees believe management cares more about profits than people
- 55 percent aren't sure what's expected of them anymore
- 40 percent believe wages at the company have not kept up with the industry average
- 38 percent think management has done a good job of responding to competitive advances
- 52 percent expect to finish their careers at the company
- 80 percent believe the economy is too slow to support a productive job search

While you're poring over the report, trying to figure out how you'll present the information tomorrow, an instant message from the CEO pops up on your partner's computer asking for a quick summary of the results. She types the following, then asks you to review it before she sends it:

> As you'd expect in a no-holds-barred investigation like this, the researchers did uncover some areas for improvements. The good news: only 20 percent of the workforce is even considering other options, and we could reasonably expect that only a fraction of that group will leave anytime soon.

ANALYSIS

You read your partner's summary twice, but something doesn't feel quite right. Does it present an accurate summary of the research? Why or why not? What's likely to happen when you present the complete research results to the CEO after first sending this IM?

numbers might not provide the insights you or your audience require. Are sales going up or going down? Are the age groups that represent our target markets growing or shrinking? What percentage of employees surveyed are so dissatisfied that they're ready to look for new jobs? These are the insights managers need in order to make good business decisions.

Gaining Insights

Even without advanced statistical techniques, you can use simple arithmetic to extract powerful insights from sets of research data. Table 10.4 shows some of the more common things you can learn about data you've collected. One useful way of looking at numerical data is to find measures that represent a group of numbers. Three useful measures are shown in Table 10.4. The **mean** (which is what most people refer to when they use the term "average") is the sum of all the items in the group divided by the number of items in that group. The **median** is the "middle of the road," or the midpoint of a series (with an equal number of items above and below). The **mode** is the number that occurs more often than any other in your sample. It's the best answer to a question such as "What is the usual amount?" Each of the three measures can tell you different things about a set of data.

Mean, median, and mode provide insight into sets of data.

It's also helpful to look for **trends**, any repeatable patterns taking place over time, including growth, decline, and cyclical trends that vary between growth and decline. Trend analysis is common in business. By looking at data over a period of time, you can detect patterns and relationships that will help you answer important questions.

Trends suggest patterns that repeat over time.

Summaries and trends identify *what* is happening. To help you understand *why* those things are happening, look at **causation** (the cause-and-effect linkage between two factors, where one of them causes the other to happen) and **correlation** (the simultaneous change in two variables that you're measuring, such as customer satisfaction dropping when product quality drops). As Chapter 9 points out, causation can be easy to assume but difficult to prove. The drop in customer satisfaction might have been caused by a new accounting system that fouled up customer invoices. In order to prove causation, you need to be able to isolate the suspected cause as the only potential source of the change in the measured effect. However, eliminating all but one possible cause isn't always feasible, so you often

Causation shows cause-and-effect relationships; *correlation* indicates simultaneous changes in two variables that may not necessarily be causally related.

TABLE 10.4 Three Types of Data Measures: Mean, Median, and Mode

SALESPERSON	SALES	
Wilson	$3,000	
Green	5,000	
Carrick	6,000	
Wimper	7,000	Mean
Keeble	7,500	Median
Kemble	8,500	Mode
O'Toole	8,500	Mode
Mannix	8,500	Mode
Caruso	9,000	
Total	$63,000	

have to apply careful judgment to correlations. Researchers frequently explore the relationships between subsets of data using a technique called **cross-tabulation**. For instance, if you're trying to figure out why total sales rose or fell, you might look separately at sales data by age, gender, location, and product type.

Guarding Against Mistakes and Misinterpretations

Numbers are easy to manipulate with spreadsheets and other computer tools—sometimes too easy—so be sure to guard against both computational errors and misinterpretation of results. Minor errors in spreadsheets can lead to major financial mistakes. Bowater, a pulp and paper company in South Carolina, discovered a $4.8 million error in its financial statements caused by one spreadsheet that computed interest monthly instead of quarterly.[20] Even though you might never be in a position to make mistakes of this magnitude, make sure to double-check all of your calculations and document the operation of any spreadsheets you plan to share with colleagues. Common spreadsheet mistakes to watch for include errors in math formulas, references to unintended cells in the spreadsheet (resulting in the inclusion of data you don't want or the exclusion of data you do want), failures to refresh calculations after data changes, and failures to verify the specific operation of the spreadsheet's built-in math functions.

Watch out for errors that might've crept in during collection and processing of data.

In addition to watching for computer errors, step back and look at your entire set of data before proceeding with any analysis. Do the numbers make sense based on what you know about the subject? Are there any individual data points that stand out as suspect? If the production numbers you've been measuring have never varied more than 10 percent month to month and then suddenly jumped 50 percent last month, is that number real or an erroneous measurement?

Even when your data points are accurate and your analysis is technically correct, it's still possible to misinterpret or misrepresent the results. Many analysis errors require statistical expertise to identify and fix, but even without advanced skills, you can always watch out for these common mistakes:

- **Avoid faulty comparisons.** Many of the reports and presentations you'll make in your career—and the data you collect through research—will involve comparisons of some sort. Are the employees in the consumer finance division as productive as those in commercial finance? Do we spend more for office space in Denver or in Kansas City? In order for such analyses to be meaningful, they have to be constructed to ensure fair comparisons; in other words, they must compare the same things. For instance, the office leasing costs in one city might be lower, but the parking may be so expensive that the company has to pay part of the employees' costs. Make sure you compare "apples to apples and not to oranges," whether you're comparing fruit or complex financial transactions.

- **Don't push research results beyond their limits.** The temptation to extract insights and assurances that aren't really there can be quite strong, particularly in situations of great uncertainty. For instance, if you're about to recommend that your company invest millions of dollars in developing a new product based on your consumer research, you're likely to find every possible justification in the data. A common mistake in these situations is assuming that people who like a product will actually buy it. Millions of people like Ferraris, but very few buy one. Another mistake of this sort is assuming that a trend in the past will continue in the future.
- **Steer clear of misleading presentations.** As you'll see in Chapter 11, there is a nearly endless variety of ways that valid data can be presented in invalid ways. Charts and graphs have a strange way of taking on lives of their own, and as the researcher behind the presentations, it's your responsibility to make sure the visual presentation is accurate.

APPLYING YOUR FINDINGS

7 LEARNING OBJECTIVE

Explain the differences between drafting a summary, drawing a conclusion, and developing a recommendation

After all your planning, researching, and processing, you're finally ready to apply your findings. Depending on the writing project, you may be summarizing your results, drawing conclusions based on your results, or making recommendations.

Summarizing Your Research

If your boss has asked you to summarize the competitive strengths and weaknesses of another company or the recent trends in a particular market, it's crucial that you provide an unbiased summary that is free of your own opinions, conclusions, or recommendations. If you do uncover something that sparks an idea or raises a concern, by all means communicate this but do so separately; don't include such information in your summary report.

Summarizing is not always a simple task, and your boss will be judging your ability to separate significant issues from less significant details. Identify the main idea and the key support points, and separate these from details, examples, and other supporting evidence (see Table 10.5). Focus your efforts on your audience, highlighting the information that is most important to the person who assigned the project or to those who will be reading the report.

However, don't interpret audience focus to mean that you're supposed to convey only information your audience wants to hear. A good summary might contain nothing but bad

TABLE 10.5 Summarizing Effectively

ORIGINAL MATERIAL (110 WORDS)	45-WORD SUMMARY	22-WORD SUMMARY
Our facilities costs spiraled out of control last year. The 23 percent jump was far ahead of every other cost category in the company and many times higher than the 4 percent average rise for commercial real estate in the Portland metropolitan area. The rise can be attributed to many factors, but the major factors include repairs (mostly electrical and structural problems at the downtown office), energy (most of our offices are heated by electricity, the price of which has been increasing much faster than for oil or gas), and last but not least, the loss of two sublease tenants whose rent payments made a substantial dent in our cost profile for the past five years.	Our facilities costs jumped 23 percent last year, far ahead of every other cost category in the company and many times higher than the 4 percent local average. The major factors contributing to the increase are repairs, energy, and the loss of two sublease tenants.	Our facilities costs jumped 23 percent last year, due mainly to rising repair and energy costs and the loss of sublease income.

Main idea
Major support points
Details

news or information that runs counter to majority assumptions in the organization. Even if the summary isn't pleasant, effective managers always appreciate and respect honest, complete, and perceptive information from their employees.

Drawing Conclusions

A conclusion is a logical interpretation of research results.

A **conclusion** is a logical interpretation of the facts and other information in your report. Reaching good conclusions based on the evidence at hand is one of the most important skills you can develop in your business career. A sound conclusion

- **is based strictly on the information included in your report.** Consider all the information in your report. Don't ignore anything—even if it doesn't support your conclusion. Moreover, don't introduce any new information in your conclusion. (After all, if something is that important, it should be in the body of your report.)
- **is logical.** A logical conclusion is one that follows accepted patterns of inductive or deductive reasoning. Avoid conclusions that are based on unproven premises, appeal to emotion, make hasty generalizations, or contain any other logical fallacies.

Even though conclusions need to be logical, they may not automatically or obviously flow from the evidence. Most business decisions require assumptions and judgment; relatively few are based strictly on the available evidence. In fact, the ability to see patterns and possibilities that others can't see is one of the hallmarks of innovative business leaders. Your personal values or the organization's values may also influence your conclusions (and differences between the two can create difficult ethical dilemmas). If your conclusion is potentially biased for any reason, you have an ethical responsibility to explain this to your audience. Also, don't expect all team members to examine the evidence and arrive at the same conclusion. One of the reasons for bringing additional people into a decision is to gain their unique perspective and experience.

Making Recommendations

A recommendation is a suggested course of action.

Whereas a conclusion interprets information, a **recommendation** suggests what to do about the information. The difference between a conclusion and a recommendation can be seen in the following example:

CONCLUSION	RECOMMENDATION
On the basis of its track record and current price, I conclude that this company is an attractive buy.	I recommend that we write a letter to the board of directors offering to buy the company at a 10 percent premium over the current market value of its stock.

If you've been asked to take the final step and translate your conclusions into recommendations, be sure to make the relationship between them clear. Remember, recommendations are inappropriate in a report when you're not expected to supply them. But when you do develop recommendations of your own, try not to let your assumptions and personal values influence them. To be credible, recommendations must be based on logical analysis and sound conclusions. They must also be practical and acceptable to your readers, the people who have to make your recommendations work. Finally, when making a recommendation, be certain that you have adequately described the steps that come next. Don't leave your readers wondering what they need to do in order to act on your recommendation.

MANAGING INFORMATION

Conducting your research well does more than provide strong support for your own writing projects; increasingly, your individual research is an important contribution to your organization's collective knowledge base. According to Meg Murphy, president of Inquisite,

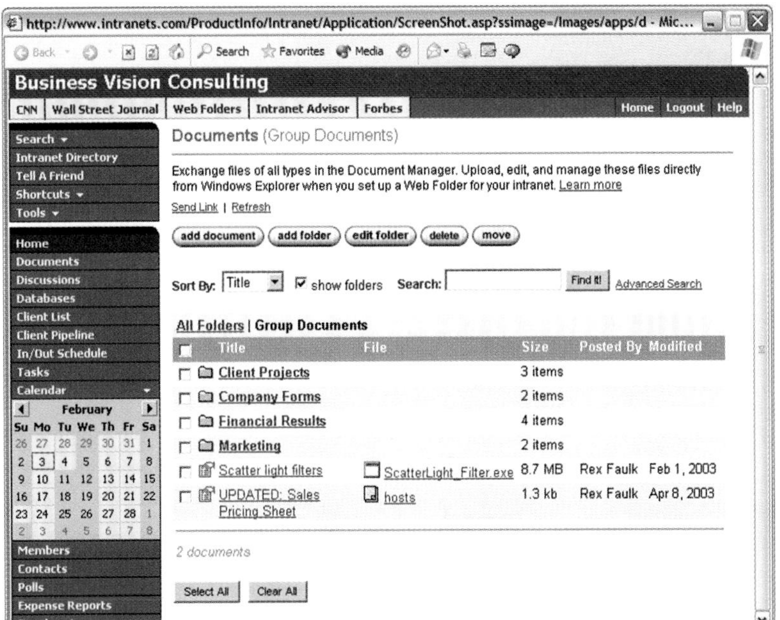

FIGURE 10.3
Knowledge Management Systems Software

an online survey company, "It's essential to take a big-picture approach to organizational knowledge and competencies."[21] That's why Inquisite is one of the many companies that have installed some form of **knowledge management system**, a means of capturing and sharing information throughout an organization (see Figure 10.3). Similar systems with a variety of names, including *enterprise content management systems, enterprise portals,* and *enterprise knowledge platforms,* all have the goal of getting maximum value from the information, insights, and experiences of their employees. Research results are one of the most important elements of value that these systems are designed to capture, so you can expect to see your work made available to colleagues all around the company. Even without a formal knowledge management system, teams can use such tools as shared workspaces to make sure people get access to important information.

Knowledge management systems help organizations share research results and other valuable information and insights.

COMMUNICATION CHALLENGES AT TOYOTA SCION

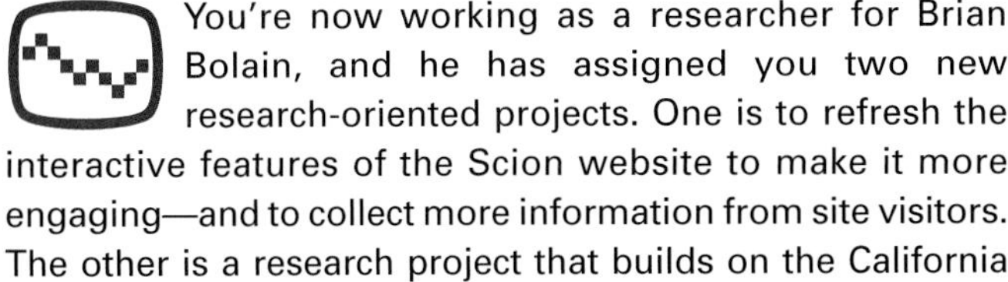

You're now working as a researcher for Brian Bolain, and he has assigned you two new research-oriented projects. One is to refresh the interactive features of the Scion website to make it more engaging—and to collect more information from site visitors. The other is a research project that builds on the California video diaries with consumer insights from other regions.

Individual Challenge: Visit www.scion.com or another website—marketing oriented, music related, shopping, whatever—that has interactive capabilities you can explore. What kinds of information did the site try to collect about you? If you had already registered with the site, what kinds of information did they ask for? How truthful were your responses? Compare the personal value of the data you provided to the value of the information or entertainment you get from the site. Who got the better value from the interaction, you or the website owner? Why?

Team Challenge: In a small group, discuss your experiences as a participant in marketing surveys or research projects. What were some of the most effective or creative methods the researchers used? What were some of the least effective methods? What advice would you give Bolain and Scion about conducting market research with the students on your campus? What are some of the local attitudes and biases they should be aware of?

SUMMARY OF LEARNING OBJECTIVES

1 **Describe an effective process for conducting business research.** Begin the research process with careful planning to make sure you focus on the most important questions and identify the best place to find answers. Then locate the data and information using primary and secondary research as needed. Process the results of your research, analyzing both textual and numerical information to extract averages, trends, and other insights. Apply your findings by summarizing information for someone else's benefit, drawing conclusions based on what you've learned, or developing recommendations. Lastly, manage information effectively so that you and others can retrieve it later and re-use it in other projects.

2 **Define primary and secondary research, and explain when you use each method.** Primary research is research that is being conducted for the first time, whereas secondary research involves information that was originally gathered for another research project or other effort. Secondary research is generally used first, both to save time in case someone else has already gathered the information needed and to offer additional insights into your research questions.

3 **Name nine criteria for evaluating the credibility of an information source.** Information should come from a credible source that has a reputation for being honest and reliable; the source should also be unbiased. The purpose of the material should be known, and the author should be credible. The information should include references to sources (if obtained elsewhere), and it should be independently verifiable. The material should be current, and it should be complete. Finally, the information should seem logical.

4 **Explain the complementary nature of search engines, web directories, and databases.** Search engines offer quick access to millions of web pages but don't offer (a) any filtering by human editors or (b) access to most private collections, such as newspaper and magazine archives. Web directories overcome the first limitation, and online databases overcome the second.

5 **Provide five guidelines for conducting an effective online search.** First and foremost, you need to read and understand the instructions for using each online research tool because they vary widely and may not search for or display results in the manner you expect. Second, pay attention to the details, since even minor aspects of searching can influence results dramatically. Third, review search and display options carefully to optimize results. Fourth, try variations on your search terms if you can't find what you're looking for. Fifth, try narrower or broader searches to adjust the scope of what you're looking for.

6 **Outline an effective process for planning and conducting information interviews.** Start by learning about the person(s) you plan to interview, then formulate your main idea to make sure your interview will stay focused. Choose the length, style, and organization of the interview, then select question types to elicit the sort of information you want, with each question designed to collect useful answers. Limit your questions to the most important queries. Record the interview if the person allows, and review your notes as soon as the interview ends.

7 **Explain the differences between drafting a summary, drawing a conclusion, and developing a recommendation.** A summary is a shortened version of one or more documents, research results, or other information; it filters out details and presents only the most important ideas. A conclusion is your analysis of what the findings mean (an interpretation of the facts). A recommendation is your opinion (based on reason and logic) about the course of action that should be taken.

Test Your Knowledge

1. When might a businessperson need to conduct research?
2. How does primary information differ from secondary information?
3. What are the main advantages of electronic databases?
4. How does a search engine differ from a directory?
5. What is the purpose of gap analysis?
6. How will you know when you are finished with the research process?
7. What is paraphrasing, and what is its purpose?
8. What is the difference between the mean, median, and mode?
9. What are the characteristics of a sound conclusion?
10. How does a conclusion differ from a recommendation?

Apply Your Knowledge

1. Why is browsing an important part of the research process?
2. Why must you be careful when citing information from a webpage?
3. Why do you need to evaluate your sources?
4. After an exhaustive study of an important problem, you have reached a conclusion that you believe your company's management will reject. What will you do? Explain your answer.
5. **Ethical Choices** Companies occasionally make mistakes that expose confidential information, such as when employees lose laptop computers containing sensitive data files or webmasters forget to protect confidential webpages from search engine indexes. If you conducted a Google search

that turned up competitive information on webpages that were clearly intended to be private, what would you do? Explain your answer.

Practice Your Knowledge

Document for Analysis

Writing Effective Interview Questions

The following set of interview questions were prepared for a manager of Whirlpool Corporation. The goal of the interview was to learn some basic information about Whirlpool's meeting practices. Read the questions, then (1) critique them, as a whole, indicating what you like or dislike about this series of questions; and (2) select five questions and revise them to make them more effective.

1. What is your position in the company?
2. To whom do you report?
3. Do you attend or run many meetings?
4. Do your meetings start on time? Run late?
5. Do you distribute or receive a meeting agenda several days in advance of the meeting?
6. Do you like your job?
7. Do you travel a lot for your job?
8. Has your company cut back on travel expenditures? If so, how and why?
9. Does your company use videoconferencing as an alternative to travel?
10. Does your company own its own videoconferencing equipment?
11. Are videoconferences more or less effective than face-to-face meetings?
12. How long have you worked for Whirlpool?
13. Is Sears your largest retail customer?
14. How often does your management team meet with the managers of Sears?
15. Does your company produce only household appliances?
16. How do you keep your meetings on track?
17. Does someone prepare written minutes of meetings? Are the minutes distributed to meeting members?

Exercises

For live links to all websites discussed in this chapter, visit this text's website at www.prenhall.com/bovee. Just log on, select Chapter 10, and click on "Featured Websites." Locate the page or the URL related to the material in the text.

10.1 Understanding Your Topic: Subquestions Your boss has asked you to do some research on franchising. Actually, he's thinking about purchasing a few Subway franchises, and he needs some information. Visit www.amazon.com and review the site. On the homepage, perform a keyword search on "franchises." Explore some of the books that you find by reading reviews and using the "search inside" feature.

a. Use the information to develop a list of subquestions to help you narrow your focus.
b. Write down the names of three books you might purchase for your boss.
c. How can this website assist you with your research efforts?

10.2 Finding Secondary Information Using online, database, or printed sources, find the following information. Be sure to properly cite your source using the formats discussed in Appendix B (*Hint:* Start with Table 10.2, Major Business Resources on pages 308–309.)

a. Contact information for the American Management Association
b. Median weekly earnings of men and women by occupation
c. Current market share for Perrier water
d. Performance ratios for office supply retailers
e. Annual stock performance for Hewlett-Packard
f. Number of franchise outlets in the United States
g. Composition of the U.S. workforce by profession

10.3 Finding Secondary Information Businesspeople have to know where to look for secondary information when they conduct research. Prepare a list of the most important magazines and professional journals in the following fields of study:

a. Marketing/advertising
b. Insurance
c. Telecommunications
d. Accounting

10.4 Finding Information: Industry Information Locate the NAICS codes for the following industries:

a. Hotels and motels
b. Breakfast cereals
c. Bottled water
d. Automatic vending machines

10.5 Finding Information: Company Information Select any public company and find the following information:

a. Names of the company's current officers
b. List of the company's products or services
c. Current issues in the company's industry
d. Outlook for the company's industry as a whole

10.6 Finding Information: Secondary Information You'd like to know if it's a good idea to buy banner ads on other websites to drive more traffic to your company's website. You're worried about the expense and difficulty of running an experiment to test banner effectiveness, so you decide to look for some secondary data. Using databases available through your library, identify three secondary sources that might offer helpful data on this question.

10.7 Finding Information: Search Techniques Analyze any recent school or work assignment that required you to conduct research. How did you approach your investigation? Did you rely mostly on sources of primary information or mostly on sources of secondary information? Now that you have studied this chapter, can you identify two ways to improve the research techniques you used during that assignment? Briefly explain.

10.8 Finding Information: Primary Information Deciding how to collect primary data is an important part of the research process. Which one or more of the five methods of data collection (examining documents, making observations, surveying people, conducting experiments, and performing interviews) would you use if you were researching these questions?

a. Has the litter problem on campus been reduced since the cafeteria began offering fewer take-out choices this year than in past years?

b. Has the school attracted more transfer students since it waived the formal application process and allowed students at other colleges simply to send their transcripts and a one-page letter of application?

c. Have the number of traffic accidents at the school's main entrance been reduced since a traffic light was installed?

d. Has student satisfaction with the campus bookstore improved now that students can order their books over the Internet and pick them up at several campus locations?

10.9 Finding Information: Surveys You work for a movie studio that is producing a young director's first motion picture, the story of a group of unknown musicians finding work and making a reputation in a competitive industry. Unfortunately, some of your friends leave the first complete screening, saying that the 132-minute movie is simply too long. Others said they couldn't imagine any sequences to cut out. Your boss wants to test the movie on a regular audience and ask viewers to complete a questionnaire that will help the director decide whether edits are needed and, if so, where. Design a questionnaire that you can use to solicit valid answers for a report to the director about how to handle the audience's reaction to the movie.

10.10 Finding Information: Interviews Plan an informational interview with a professional working in your chosen field of study. Plan the structure of the interview and create a set of interview questions. Conduct the interview. Using the information you gathered, write a memo to another student describing the tasks, advantages, and disadvantages of jobs in this field of study. (Your reader is a person who also plans to pursue a career in this field of study.)

10.11 Finding Information: Interviews You're conducting an information interview with a manager in another division of your company. Partway through the interview, the manager shows clear signs of impatience. How should you respond? What might you do differently to prevent this from happening in the future? Explain your answers.

10.12 Teamwork: Evaluating Sources Break into small groups and surf the Internet to find websites that provide business information such as company or industry news, trends, analysis, facts, or performance data. Using the criteria discussed under "Evaluating Your Sources," evaluate the credibility of the information presented at these websites.

10.13 Processing Information: Reading and Taking Notes Select an article from a business journal such as *Business Week*, *Fortune*, or *Forbes*. Read the article and highlight the article's key points. Summarize the article in less than 100 words, paraphrasing the key points.

10.14 Processing Information: Documenting Sources Select five business articles from sources such as journals, books, newspapers, or websites. Develop a resource list using Appendix B as a guideline.

10.15 Analyzing Data: Calculating the Mean Your boss has asked you to analyze and report on your division's sales for the first nine months of this year. Using the following data from company invoices, calculate the mean for each quarter and all averages for the year to date. Then identify and discuss the quarterly sales trends.

January	$ 24,600	June	$ 26,800
February	25,900	July	29,900
March	23,000	August	30,500
April	21,200	September	26,600
May	24,600		

Expand Your Knowledge

For live links to the websites that follow, go to www.prenhall.com/bovee. When you log on, select Chapter 10, then select "Featured Websites," click on the URL of the website you wish to visit, and review the website to complete these exercises.

Exploring the Best of the Web

Check Out This 24-Hour Library
www.ipl.org

Start your business research by visiting the Internet Public Library. Visit the reference center and explore the many online references available. These cover topics such as business, economics, law, government, science, technology, computers, education, and more. You can even submit questions for the IPL staff. Visit the reference center and explore the Business and Economics Reference section. Click on *Business Directories,* and then perform these tasks.

1. Select five companies and use the links provided to find contact information (address, phone, website, officers' names, and so on) for each company. What kinds of contact information did you find at the company websites?
2. Gather information about the U.S. budget by using one of the site's directories: A Business Researcher's Interests. Why is using a directory such as this one an efficient way to obtain information?
3. Go back to the library's main reference center and click on Reference. Follow some of the reference links. How might these links help you when performing business research?

Exploring the Web on Your Own

Review these chapter-related websites on your own to improve your research skills.

1. Visit Microsoft's Complete Internet Guide at www.microsoft.com/insider/internet/default.htm and take the web tutorial to improve your online researching skills.
2. Brush up on your business research by following the links at the Basic Business Research Methods webpage, www.mapnp.org/library/research/research.htm.
3. Find out what makes a website work and learn more about website design, speed, navigational structure, and standards at Usable Web, http://usableweb.com.

Learn Interactively

Interactive Study Guide

Go to the Companion Website at www.prenhall.com/bovee. For Chapter 10, take advantage of the interactive "Study Guide" to test your knowledge of the chapter. Get instant feedback on whether you need additional studying.

Also, visit this site's "Study Hall," where you'll find an abundance of valuable resources that will help you succeed in this course.

Peak Performance Grammar and Mechanics

To improve your skill with apostrophes, quotation marks, parentheses and brackets, question marks and exclamation points, dashes, hyphens, and ellipses, visit www.prenhall.com/onekey, click "Peak Performance Grammar and Mechanics," click "Punctuation," and then click "Punctuation II." Take the Pretest to determine whether you have any weak areas. Then review those areas in the Refresher Course. Take the Follow-Up Test to check your grasp of other types of punctuation. For an extra challenge or advanced practice, take the Advanced Test. Finally, for additional reinforcement in periods, question marks, and exclamation points, go to www.prenhall.com/bovee, where you will find "Improve Your Grammar, Mechanics, and Usage" exercises.

chapter 11

Communicating Information Through Visuals

LEARNING OBJECTIVES

After studying this chapter, you will be able to

1. Describe the communication power that visuals add to your writing
2. Explain how to choose which points in your message to illustrate
3. Describe the most common options for presenting data in a visual format
4. Identify the best applications for diagrams versus photographs
5. Discuss five principles of graphic design that can improve the quality of your visuals
6. Name three qualities to look for before including a visual in a report or presentation
7. Discuss the problem of deceptive visuals

COMMUNICATION CLOSE-UP AT STONE YAMASHITA PARTNERS

www.stoneyamashita.com

If you've ever wondered what a typical business consultant really does, Keith Yamashita isn't the best example—but he may be the most interesting. His biggest fans are executives at IBM, Nike, Gap, HP, and other firms who have worked with Keith and his company, Stone Yamashita Partners (SYP).

Yamashita and designer Robert Stone started SYP in 1994, after working together at Apple Computer. Gradually, they assembled a diverse team that includes designers, writers, technologists, a poet, a sociologist, and a former lawyer—and very few MBAs. This eclectic group specializes in helping companies examine, revamp, and sometimes reinvent their strategy, image, culture, and vision.

That kind of fundamental change affects everyone in a company, from the grayest senior executive to the greenest new hire. Of course, most people resist change, at least initially; however, communication that is effective and compelling can help turn such resistance into commitment.

Communication is SYP's specialty, but Yamashita's team never relies on words alone. Instead, they use strong visual elements to paint a picture—sometimes literally—of a company's new direction. Everything they produce is full of compelling visual cues, whether it's a short video, an interactive website, a pocket-sized book, a giant story scroll, or a

Compelling visual messages are critical to the success of consulting partners Keith Yamashita and Robert Stone.

full-sized store mockup. Highly visual content and off-beat presentation can make a message more tangible and thus more effective for employees, customers, and investors.

Why are visuals so important to the SYP team? "Strategy is not something that's done in a box with only a rational hat on," says Stone. "It needs to be visceral, human, and often emotional." Yamashita agrees, and adds, "We're trying to move people to a place where it makes sense to act." Both partners know that the right visuals can inspire people to move from resistance to commitment to action.[1]

1 LEARNING OBJECTIVE

Describe the communication power that visuals add to your writing

GAINING AN ADVANTAGE WITH VISUALS

Carefully crafted visuals enhance the power of your words.

Keith Yamashita knows that well-designed visuals can bring business messages to life and help communicators connect with their readers. Visuals enhance the communication power of textual messages. They can convey some message points (such as spatial relationships, correlations, and procedures) more effectively and more efficiently than words. Pictures are also an effective way to communicate with the diverse audiences that are common in today's business environment. In the numbers-oriented world of work, people rely heavily on trend lines, distribution curves, and percentages. An upward curve means good news in any language. Visuals attract and hold people's attention, helping your audience understand and remember your message. Busy readers often jump to visuals to try to get the gist of a message, and attractive visuals can draw readers deeper into your reports and presentations.

Communication Solution

Project teams from Stone Yamashita Partners look for new ways to connect and explore business ideas through creative visuals, often helping clients see important concepts and relationships that weren't obvious using textual communication alone.

However, for all their communication power, visuals need to be planned and designed carefully. Poorly chosen or badly designed visuals reduce the impact of your writing and delay the delivery of your message. As you identify which points in your document would benefit from a visual, make sure that each visual you decide on has a clear purpose (see Table 11.1). Moreover, unless language is an insurmountable barrier in a given situation, be sure to use visuals to supplement the written or spoken word, not to replace it.

Think about your visuals before you begin writing.

Consider creating your visuals first, before actually writing your document. Doing so has several advantages. First of all, chances are that much of your research and analytical work is already in tabular or graphic form, so sorting through and refining your visuals will help you decide exactly what you're going to say. Second, by starting with the visuals, you might be able to develop a graphic story line that supports your message

TABLE 11.1 When to Use Visuals

PURPOSE	APPLICATION
To clarify	Support text descriptions of "graphic" topics: quantitative or numerical information, explanations of trends, descriptions.
To simplify	Break complicated descriptions into components that can be depicted with conceptual models, flowcharts, organization charts, or diagrams.
To emphasize	Call attention to particularly important points by illustrating them with line, bar, and pie charts.
To summarize	Review major points in the narrative by providing a chart or table that sums up the data.
To reinforce	Present information in visual and written form to increase reader's retention.
To attract	Make material seem more interesting by decorating the cover or title page and by breaking up the text with visual aids.
To impress	Build credibility by putting ideas into visual form to convey the impression of authenticity and precision.
To unify	Depict the relationship among points—for example, with a flowchart.

from beginning to end. Third, because your text will explain and refer to any tables, charts, and diagrams you include, you save time by having those visuals ready when you begin composing your text, particularly if you plan to use quite a few visuals.

As you progress, be flexible in your approach. The process of writing is often a process of discovery, even after you've planned visuals and carefully outlined your text. You may find that a particular point you planned to present in writing isn't as easy to describe as you had hoped, or you might discover a new connection between two ideas that you hadn't recognized before. Leave enough time in your schedule and enough space in your presentation or report to allow for the possibility of introducing new visuals after you start writing.

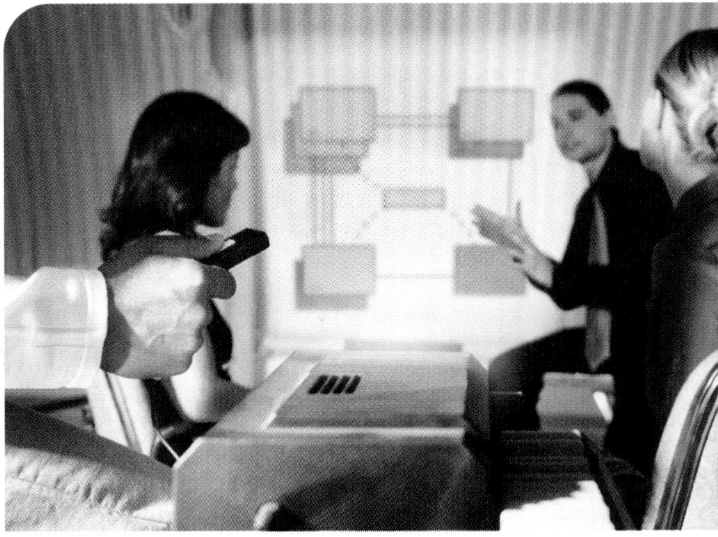

Our minds retain information shown as pictures better than information shown as words or numbers.

Identifying Points to Illustrate

2 LEARNING OBJECTIVE

Explain how to choose which points in your message to illustrate

To help identify which parts of your message can benefit from visual support, step back and consider the flow of your entire message from the audience's point of view. Which parts of the message are likely to seem complex, open to misinterpretation, or even just a little bit dull? Are there any connections between ideas or data sets that might not be obvious if they are addressed only in text? Is there a lot of numerical data or other discrete factual content that would be difficult to read if presented in paragraph form? Is there a chance that the main idea won't "jump off the page" if it's covered only in text? Will readers greet the message with skepticism and therefore look for plenty of supporting evidence?

Deciding which points to illustrate is one of the most important steps in planning your visuals.

If you answer yes to any of these questions, you probably need one or more visuals in your report or presentation. For instance, detailed facts and figures may be confusing and tedious in paragraph form, but tables and charts can conveniently organize and display such detail with clarity. Some points may require a detailed description of physical relationships or procedures, in which case you might want to use flowcharts, drawings, or photographs to clarify the discussion. Or you may simply want to draw attention to a particular fact or detail by reinforcing the message visually. When you're deciding which points to present visually, think of the five Cs:

Effective visuals are clear, complete, concise, connected, and compelling.

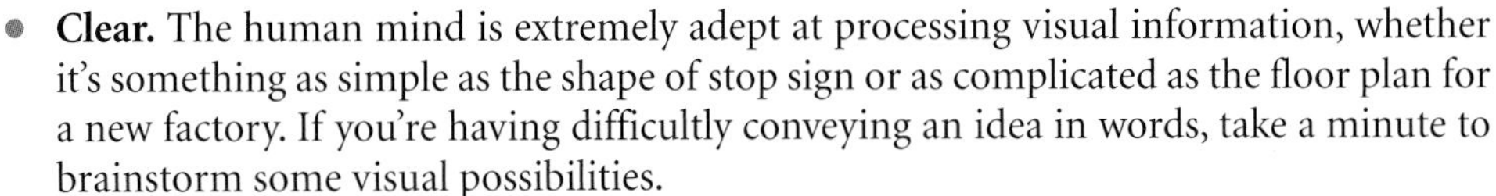

- **Clear.** The human mind is extremely adept at processing visual information, whether it's something as simple as the shape of stop sign or as complicated as the floor plan for a new factory. If you're having difficultly conveying an idea in words, take a minute to brainstorm some visual possibilities.
- **Complete.** Visuals, particularly tables, often serve to provide the supporting details for your main idea or recommendation. Moreover, the process of summarizing, concluding, or recommending often requires you to narrow down your material or exclude details; a table or other visual can provide these details without getting in the way of your main message.
- **Concise.** You've probably heard the phrase "A picture is worth a thousand words." If a particular section of your message seems to require extensive description or explanation, see whether there's a way to convey this information visually.
- **Connected.** A key purpose of many business messages is showing connections of some sort—similarities or differences, correlations, cause-and-effect relationships, and so on. Whenever you want readers to see such a connection, see whether a chart, diagram, or other illustration can help.
- **Compelling.** Your readers live in a highly visual world. Will one or more illustrations make your message more persuasive, more interesting, more likely to get read? You never want to insert visuals simply for decorative purposes, of course, but even if a particular point can be expressed equally well via text or visuals, consider adding the visual in order to make your report or presentation more compelling.

Maintaining a Balance Between Illustrations and Words

Maintain a balance between text and visuals, and pace your visuals in a way that emphasizes your key textual points.

Strong visuals enhance the descriptive and persuasive power of your writing, but it's important not to overdo them. Cramming too many visuals into a report can distract your readers in two ways. First, if you're constantly referring to tables, drawings, and other visual elements, the effort to switch back and forth from words to visuals can make it difficult for readers to maintain focus on the thread of your message. Second, the space occupied by visuals can disrupt the flow of text on the page or screen, which also creates additional work for the reader.

The pacing of visuals throughout the text is also important. For example, if you have a 50-page report with five illustrations in the first 10 pages, no illustrations for the next 30 pages, then five more in the final 10 pages, many readers will be tempted to focus on the 20 pages at the beginning and end of your report while skimming or even skipping the 30 pages in between. Granted, this might not be the best way for an audience to read important business documents, but with so much print and online material to read these days, businesspeople are always looking for ways to reduce their reading workload—and they might take shortcuts that reduce the impact of your message. In addition, the pacing of your visuals sends your readers a message (both intentional and unintentional) about the importance of various parts of the report or presentation.

Visuals need to be designed with your readers in mind.

As always, take your readers' specific needs into account. If you're addressing an audience with multiple language backgrounds or widely varying reading skills, you can shift the balance toward more visual elements to help get around any language barriers. The professional experience, education, and training of your audience should influence your approach as well. For instance, detailed statistical plots and math formulas are everyday reading material for quality control engineers but not for most salespeople or top executives.

SELECTING THE RIGHT VISUALS

You have many types of visuals to choose from, and each is best suited to particular communication tasks.

Once you've identified which points would benefit most from visual presentation, your next decision is choosing which type of visual to use for each message point. As you see in Figure 11.1, you have many choices for business graphics. For certain types of information, the decision is usually obvious. To present a large set of numerical values or detailed textual information, a table is the obvious choice in most cases. However, if you're presenting data broken down geographically, a color-coded map might be more effective to show overall patterns rather than individual data points. Also, certain visuals are used more commonly for certain applications, so you're audience is likely to expect line charts and bar charts to show trends. Line charts usually show data variations relative to a time axis (such as sales month by month), whereas bar charts more often compare discrete groups (such as sales by demographic segment). Although a bar chart can show the percentages that make up a whole, this job is usually reserved for pie charts.

The following sections explore the most common types of visuals in more detail, starting with visuals designed to present data.

3 LEARNING OBJECTIVE

Describe the most common options for presenting data in a visual format

Presenting Data

Business professionals have a tremendous number of choices for presenting data, from general purpose line, bar, and pie charts to specialized charts for product portfolios, financial analysis, and other professional functions. The visuals most commonly used to present data include tables, line and surface charts, bar charts, pictograms, Gantt charts, and pie charts.

Tables

Your options for presenting facts and figures include tables, line and surface charts, bar charts, pictograms, Gantt charts, and pie charts.

When you need to present detailed, specific information, choose a **table**, a systematic arrangement of data in columns and rows. Tables are ideal when your audience needs information that would be either difficult or tedious to handle in the main text.

Most tables contain the standard parts illustrated in Table 11.2 on page 336. Every table includes vertical columns and horizontal rows, with useful headings along the top and side.

FIGURE 11.1 Selecting the Best Visual

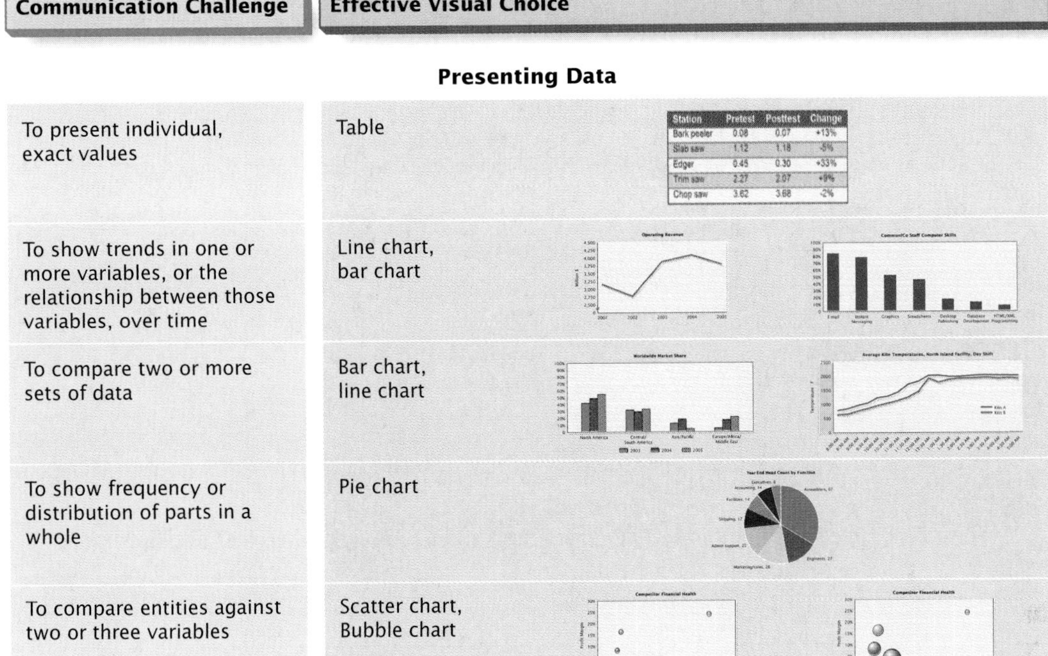

Communication Challenge
Effective Visual Choice
Presenting Data
To present individual, exact values
Table
To show trends in one or more variables, or the relationship between those variables, over time
Line chart, bar chart
To compare two or more sets of data
Bar chart, line chart
To show frequency or distribution of parts in a whole
Pie chart
To compare entities against two or three variables
Scatter chart, Bubble chart

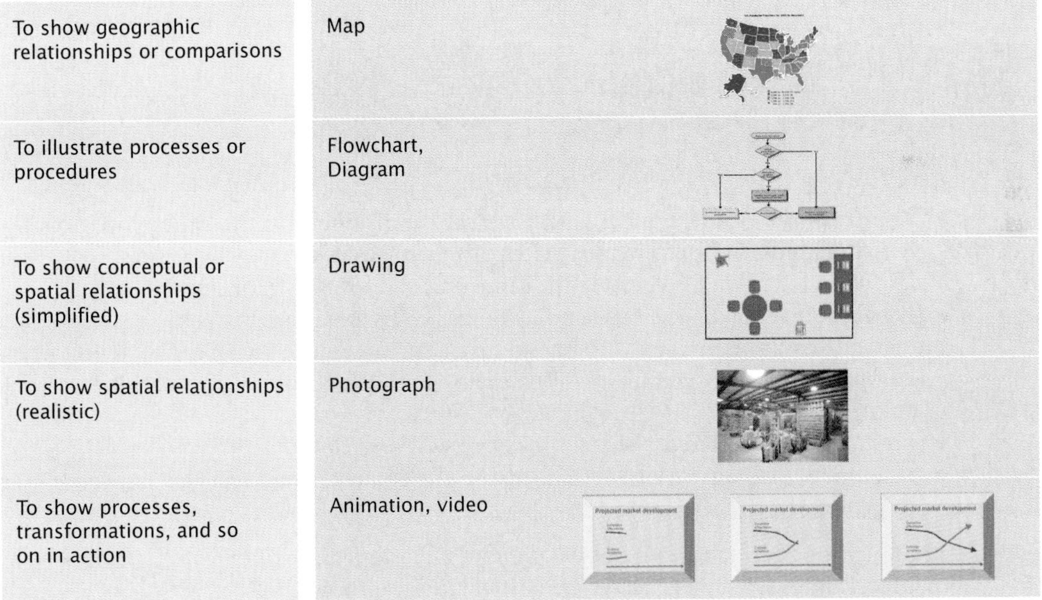

Presenting Information, Concepts, and Ideas
To show geographic relationships or comparisons
Map
To illustrate processes or procedures
Flowchart, Diagram
To show conceptual or spatial relationships (simplified)
Drawing
To show spatial relationships (realistic)
Photograph
To show processes, transformations, and so on in action
Animation, video

The number of columns and rows you can comfortably fit in a table depends on the medium. For printed documents, you can adjust font size and column/row spacing to fit a considerable amount of information on the page and still maintain readability. For online documents, you'll need to reduce the number of columns and rows to make sure your tables are easily readable online. Tables for oral presentations usually need to be the simplest of all, since you can't expect audiences to read detailed information from the screen.

Printed tables can display extensive amounts of data, but tables for online display and electronic presentations need to be simpler.

Although complex information may require formal tables that are set apart from the text, you can present some data more simply within the text. You make the table, in essence, a part of the paragraph, typed in tabular format. Such text tables are usually

TABLE 11.2 Parts of a Table

	MULTICOLUMN HEAD*			
STUB HEAD	SUBHEAD	SUBHEAD	SINGLE-COLUMN HEAD	SINGLE-COLUMN HEAD
Row head	XXX	XXX	XX	XX
Row head				
Subhead	XX	XXX	XX	X
Subhead	XX	XXX	XX	XX
Total	XXX	XXX	XX	XX

Source: (In the same format as a text footnote; see Appendix B.)

*Footnote (For an explanation of elements in the table, a superscript number or small letter may be used instead of an asterisk or other symbol.)

introduced with a sentence that leads directly into the tabulated information. Here's an example:[2]

This table compares the size of Outback Steakhouse and several of its leading competitors:

Feature	Outback Steakhouse	Applebee's	Carlson	Brinker	Darden
Chain name	Outback Steakhouse, Carrabba's	Applebee's	TGI Friday's	Chili's	Red Lobster, Olive Garden
Locations	950	1,500	700	920	1,270
Revenue (million $)	2,362	827	875	3,285	4,655

Source: Hoover's Online [accessed 30 December 2003] www.hoovers.com.

When you prepare tables, follow these guidelines to make your tables easy to read:

- Use common, understandable units, and clearly identify the units you're using, whether it's dollars, percentages, price per ton, or whatever.
- Express all items in a column in the same unit and round off for simplicity.
- Label column headings clearly and use a subhead if necessary.
- Separate columns or rows with lines or extra space to make the table easy to follow; in complex tables, consider highlighting every other row of column in a pale, contrasting color.
- Provide totals or averages of columns or rows when relevant.
- Document the source of the data using the same format as a text footnote (see Appendix B).

Although numerical tables are more common, tables can also contain words, symbols, or other facts and figures. Word tables are particularly appropriate for presenting survey findings or for comparing various items against a specific standard.

Line and Surface Charts

Line charts are commonly used to show trends over time or the relationship between two variables.

A **line chart** illustrates trends over time or plots the relationship of two variables. In line charts showing trends, the vertical, or *y*, axis shows the amount, and the horizontal, or *x*, axis shows the time or other quantity against which the amount is being measured (see Figure 11.2). Both axes often start at zero in the lower left hand corner, but you can exercise a fair amount of flexibility with both axes in order to present your data as clearly as possible. For instance, to show both positive and negative values (such as profit and loss), you can have the *y* axis span from a negative value up to a positive value, with zero somewhere in between. You want to avoid distorting the data, of course; see "Is the Visual Honest?" on page 352 for more information on this important topic.

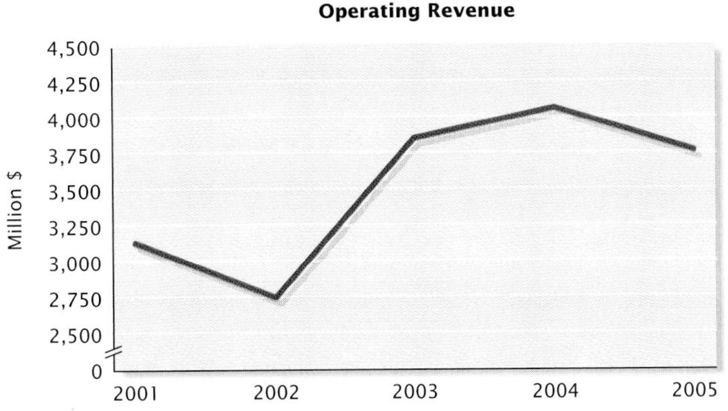

FIGURE 11.2
Line Chart

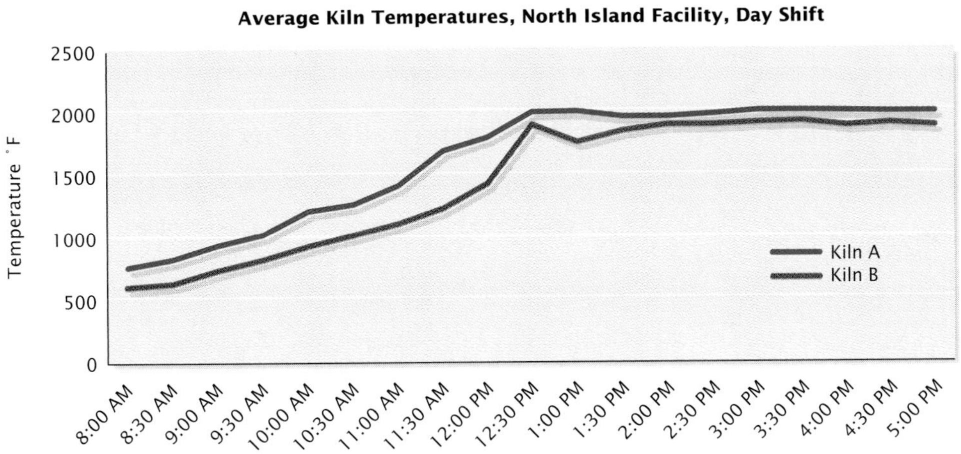

Average Kiln Temperatures, North Island Facility, Day Shift

FIGURE 11.3
Line Chart with Multiple Lines

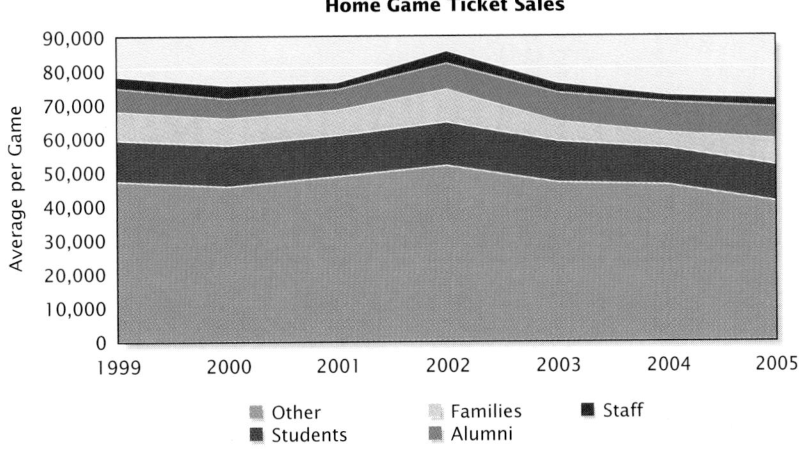

FIGURE 11.4
Surface Chart

If you need to compare two or more sets of data, you can plot them on the same chart for instant visual comparison (see Figure 11.3). Two or three lines on a single chart are usually easy to read, but beyond that, things can get confusing, particularly if the lines cross.

By their very nature, line charts often raise the question, "what happens next?" For instance, if you present sales data for the past 12 months, your audience may well ask what you think will happen in the next 12 months. Predicting the future is always a risky endeavor, but you can use your spreadsheet's forecasting tools to extend a line into the future (see "Connecting with Technology: Forecasting the Future").

A **surface chart**, also called an **area chart**, is a form of line chart with a cumulative effect; all the lines add up to the top line, which represents the total (see Figure 11.4). This form of chart helps you illustrate changes in the composition of something over time.

Connecting with Technology

Forecasting the Future

Because visuals such as line charts show what happened in the past, they almost automatically raise questions about the future. What will business look like tomorrow? Will that upward trend continue? Will we be able to reverse last year's decline?

Seeing into the future is one of the most vital skills in business. General Motors needs to know how many cars to build in order to keep a steady supply available for dealers. FootLocker needs to know how many pairs of each model of athletic shoe to order to satisfy customer demand. Microsoft needs to predict sales revenue to determine how many employees it can afford to hire.

The simple graphing functions in a spreadsheet don't take into account all the internal and external forces that might shape your company's future, but they can help you use your available data more effectively. Rather than simply "eyeballing" a line chart and guessing how it might continue in the future, you can use a technique called *regression analysis* to uncover patterns in your historical data and use those to make more informed guesses about future data.

Chart A shows a restaurant's weekly revenue for the last 12 weeks. The trend appears to be slightly upward, but the fluctuations make it difficult to predict what might happen in the future. If you try to draw a line to indicate the trend, would it look more like Line 1 or Line 2? Both seem like feasible guesses, but the difference could have considerable impact on the business's financial decisions.

Using the simplest form of regression analysis (*linear regression*), the spreadsheet suggests that the trend (the solid black line in Chart B) is closer to Line 2.

The software can also tell you how much confidence to put in the forecast week to week—not very much in this case, since the historical data fluctuate over such a wide range.

CAREER APPLICATIONS

1. In addition to historical sales data, what other variables would you take into account to forecast a restaurant's future sales revenues?
2. If you were to put a visual such as Chart B in a report to management, how should you document the chart?

Chart A

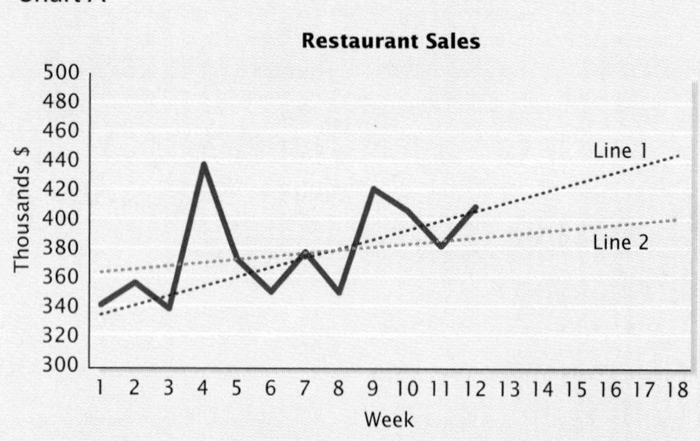

Chart B

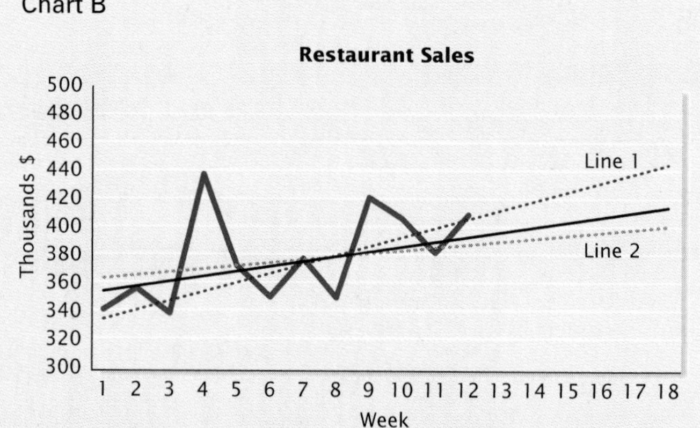

When preparing a surface chart, put the most important segment against the baseline, and restrict the number of strata to four or five.

Bar Charts, Pictograms, and Gantt Charts

A **bar chart** portrays numbers by the height or length of its rectangular bars, making a series of numbers easy to read or understand. Bar charts are particularly valuable when you want to

- compare the size of several items at one time
- show changes in one item over time
- indicate the composition of several items over time
- show the relative size of components of a whole

You can create bar charts in a wide variety of formats; choose the form that best illustrates the data and relationships in your message.

As the charts in Figure 11.5 show, bar charts can appear in various forms: *singular* (11.5a: "CommuniCo Staff Computer Skills"), *grouped* (11.5b: "Worldwide Market Share"), *deviation* (11.5c: "CommuniCo Stock Price"), *segmented* (11.5d: "CommuniCo

FIGURE 11.5
The Versatile Bar Chart

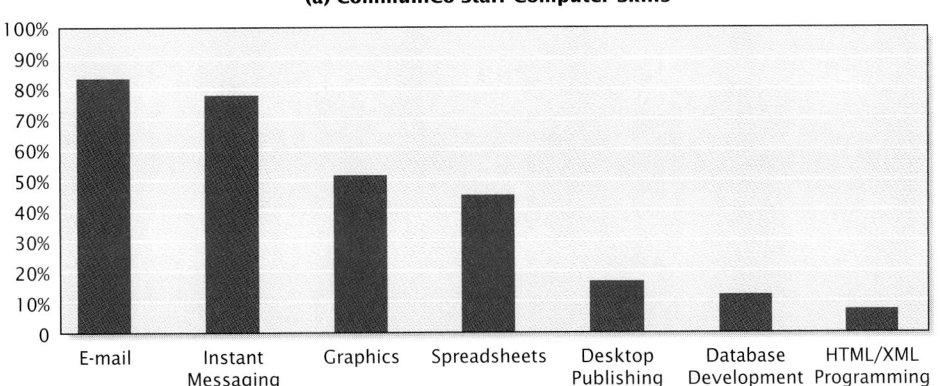

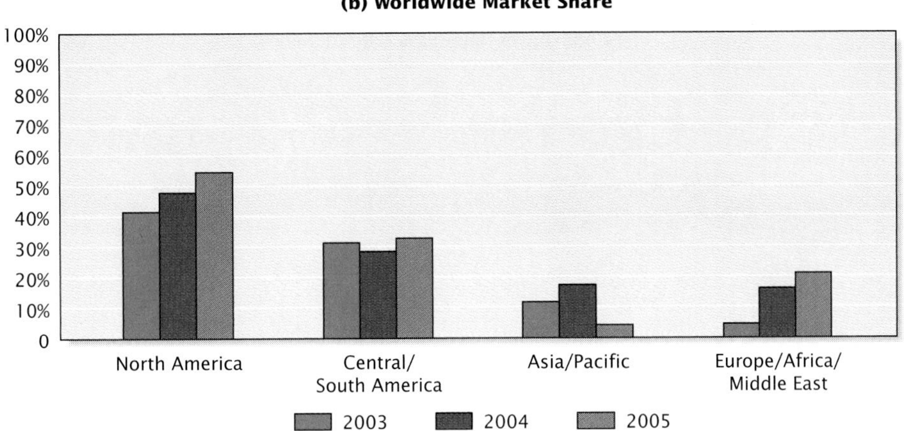

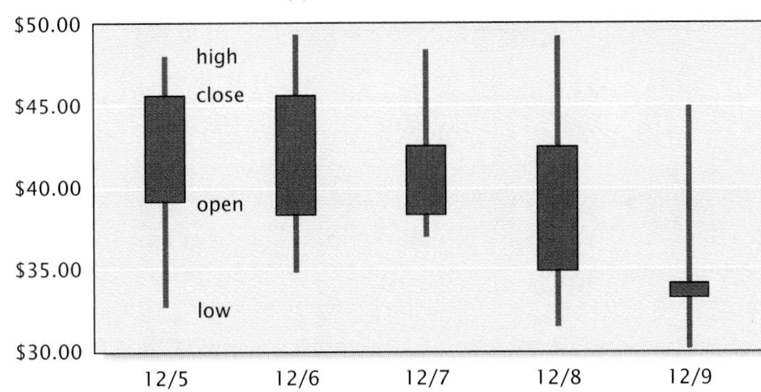

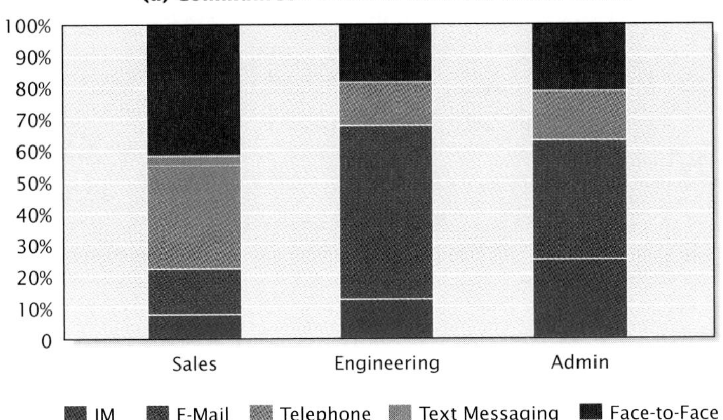

(continued)

FIGURE 11.5 (Continued)

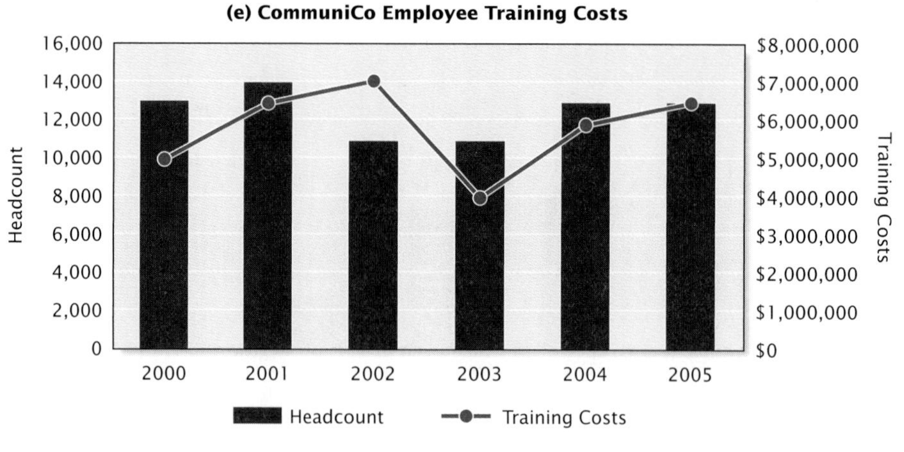

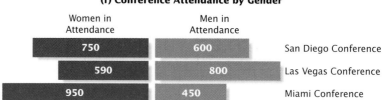

(f) Conference Attendance by Gender

Women in Attendance	Men in Attendance	
750	600	San Diego Conference
590	800	Las Vegas Conference
950	450	Miami Conference

Preferred Communication Media"), *combination* (11.5e: "CommuniCo Employee Training Costs"), and *paired* (11.5f: "Conference Attendance by Gender"). Grouped bar charts compare more than one set of data, using a different color or pattern for each set. Deviation bar charts identify positive and negative values, or winners and losers. Segmented bar charts, also known as stacked bar charts, show how individual components contribute to a total number, using a different color or pattern for each component. Combination bar and line charts compare quantities that require different intervals. Paired bar charts show the correlations between two items.

Figure 11.5 also shows how creative you can be with bar charts. You might align the bars either vertically or horizontally, or you might use bar charts to show both positive and negative quantities. Be careful, however, to keep all the bars in the chart the same width; different widths could suggest a relative importance to the viewer. In addition, space the bars evenly and place them in a logical order, such as chronological or alphabetical. Keep in mind that most computer software (such as Microsoft Excel) generates charts from data tables based on the order that is used in the table. So plan ahead, and if you don't like the way the computer displays your data, go back to the data table and adjust the order there.

You can also convert the bars into lines of symbols, so that the number or length of the symbols indicate the relative value of each item. A chart that portrays data as symbols instead of words or numbers is known as a **pictogram**. The chief value of pictograms is their novelty and ability to convey a more literal, visual message, but they tend to be more difficult to read and present a less professional tone than a straightforward bar chart.

Closely related to the bar chart is the **timeline chart**, which shows how much time is needed to complete each task in a given project. When you want to track progress toward completing a project, you can use a type of timeline chart known as a **Gantt chart** (named for management theorist Henry L. Gantt). The Gantt chart (see Figure 11.6) shows the activities involved in designing the prototype and conducting the marketing research for a new product. The maroon bars indicate completed tasks; the blue bars indicate activities not yet completed; the black diamond is a milestone—in this case the prototype's due date.

Scatter and Bubble Diagrams

If you need to compare several entities (companies, markets, employees, and so on) by two variables, such as revenue and profit margin, use a **scatter diagram**, also known as an **XY dia-**

FIGURE 11.6 Gantt Chart

ID	Project Timeline	Start Date	End Date	Duration	Percent Complete	2005: June	July	August	September
1	**Design Phase**	**6/20/05**	**8/31/05**	**73d**	**90.00%**				
2	Design Project	6/20/05	7/31/05	42d	100.00				
3	Prototype Design	8/3/05	8/21/05	19d	100.00				
4	Test Prototype	8/24/05	8/28/05	5d	0.00				
5	Prototype Complete	8/31/05	8/31/05	0d	0.00				
6	**Marketing Research Phase**	**8/3/05**	**9/25/05**	**54d**	**25.00**				
7	Preliminary Research	8/3/05	8/7/05	5d	100.00				
8	Conduct Focus Groups	8/10/05	8/11/05	2d	100.00				
9	Interviews	8/12/05	8/14/05	3d	100.00				
10	Secondary Research	8/17/05	8/28/05	12d	0.00				
11	Create Business Plan	8/31/05	9/25/05	26d	0.00				

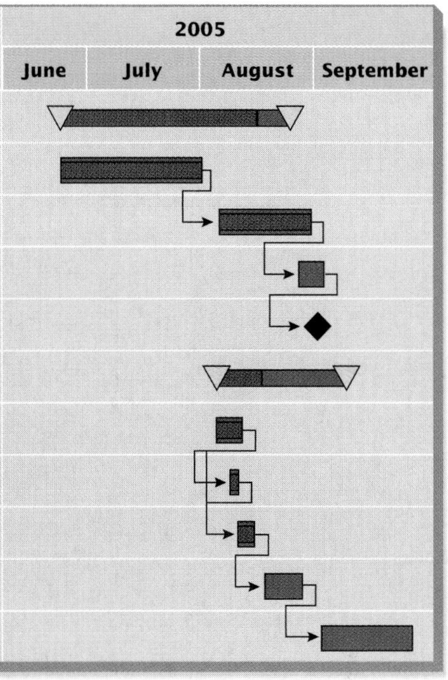

gram. This diagram is similar to a line chart in the sense that one variable is plotted along the *x* axis and another along the *y* axis. However, in a scatter diagram, individual points are plotted, not continuous lines. The **bubble diagram** expands to three variables, with the size of the bubble representing the third variable. In Figure 11.7, the rate of revenue growth is plotted on the *x* axis, profit margin is plotted on the *y* axis, and the size of the bubbles represents annual revenues. From this chart, you can see that MooreComp has the greatest revenues but the lowest profit margin, although it is growing faster than two of its three competitors.

Scatter diagrams compare entities against two variables; bubble diagrams compare them against three.

Pie Charts

Like segmented bar charts and area charts, a **pie chart** shows how the parts of a whole are distributed. However, pie charts have the advantage of familiarity; most people expect parts-of-a-whole to be displayed via a pie chart. Each segment represents a slice of a complete circle, or *pie*. As you can see in Figure 11.8, pie charts are an effective way to show percentages or to compare one segment with another. You can also combine pie charts with tables to expand the usefulness of such visuals.

Most readers expect pie charts to show the distribution of parts within a whole.

When composing pie charts, try to restrict the number of slices in the pie. Otherwise, the chart looks cluttered and is difficult to label. If necessary, lump the smallest pieces together in a "miscellaneous" category. Ideally, the largest or most important slice of the

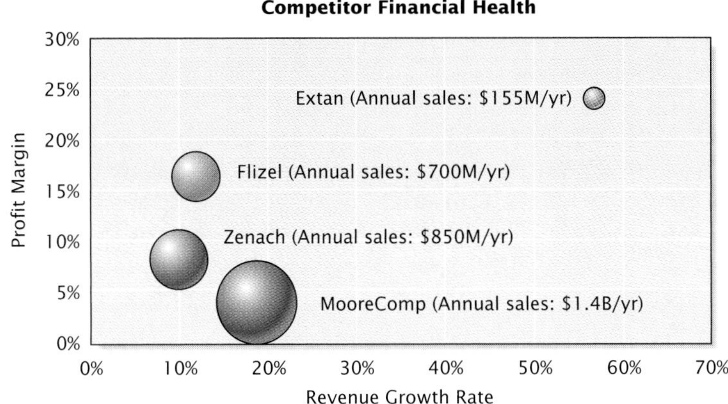

FIGURE 11.7 Bubble Diagram

FIGURE 11.8
Pie Chart Combined with Table

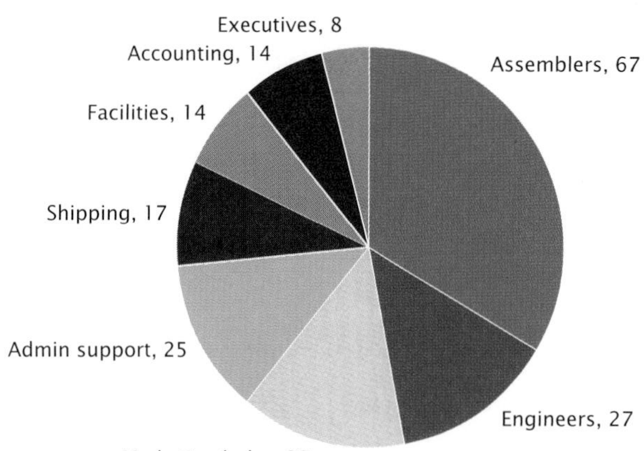

Function	Head Count
Assemblers	67
Engineers	27
Marketing/sales	28
Admin support	25
Shipping	17
Facilities	14
Accounting	14
Executives	8

pie, the segment you want to emphasize, is placed at the twelve o'clock position; the rest are arranged clockwise either in order of size or in some other logical progression.

Use different colors or patterns to distinguish the various pieces. If you want to draw attention to the segment that is of the greatest interest to your readers, use a brighter color for that segment, draw an arrow to the segment, or explode it; that is, pull the segment away from the rest of the pie. In any case, label all the segments and indicate their value in either percentages or units of measure so that your readers will be able to judge the value of the wedges. Remember, the segments must add up to 100 percent if percentages are used or to the total number if numbers are used.

Communication Solution

Keith Yamashita and his colleagues at SYP know that words aren't always the best way to communicate abstract or complex ideas, so they often look for visual solutions to complement or even replace textual information.

Presenting Information, Concepts, and Ideas

In addition to facts and figures, you'll need to present other types of information, from spatial relationships to abstract ideas. The most common types of visuals for these applications include flowcharts, organization charts, maps, drawings, diagrams, photographs, animation, and video.

Flowcharts and Organization Charts

Use flowcharts to show a series of steps or other sequential relationships.

If you need to show physical or conceptual relationships rather than numerical ones, you might want to use a flowchart or an organization chart. A **flowchart** (see Figure 11.9) illustrates a sequence of events from start to finish; it is indispensable when illustrating processes, procedures, and sequential relationships. For general business purposes, you don't need to be too concerned about the specific shapes, but keep them consistent. However, be aware that there is a formal flowchart "language" in which each shape has a specific meaning (diamonds are decision points, rectangles are process steps, and so on). If you're communicating with computer programmers and others who are accustomed to formal flowcharting, make sure you use the correct symbols in each case to avoid confusion. Graphics programs such as Microsoft Visio label the function of flowchart symbols for you, making it easy to use the right ones.

Use organization charts to depict the interrelationships among the parts of an organization or other whole.

As the name implies, an **organization chart** illustrates the positions, units, or functions of an organization and the way they interrelate. An organization's normal communication channels are almost impossible to describe without the benefit of a chart like the one in Figure 11.10 on page 344. These charts aren't limited to organizational structures, of course; as you saw Chapter 4, they can also be used to outline messages.

Maps

Use maps to represent statistics by geographic area and to show spatial relationships.

When your information has a geographic aspect, maps are often an ideal visual device. For example, Figure 11.11 on page 345 shows U.S. population projections state by state. This information could be presented in a table, of course, but a map makes the differences immediately obvious. In addition to presenting facts and figures, maps are useful for show-

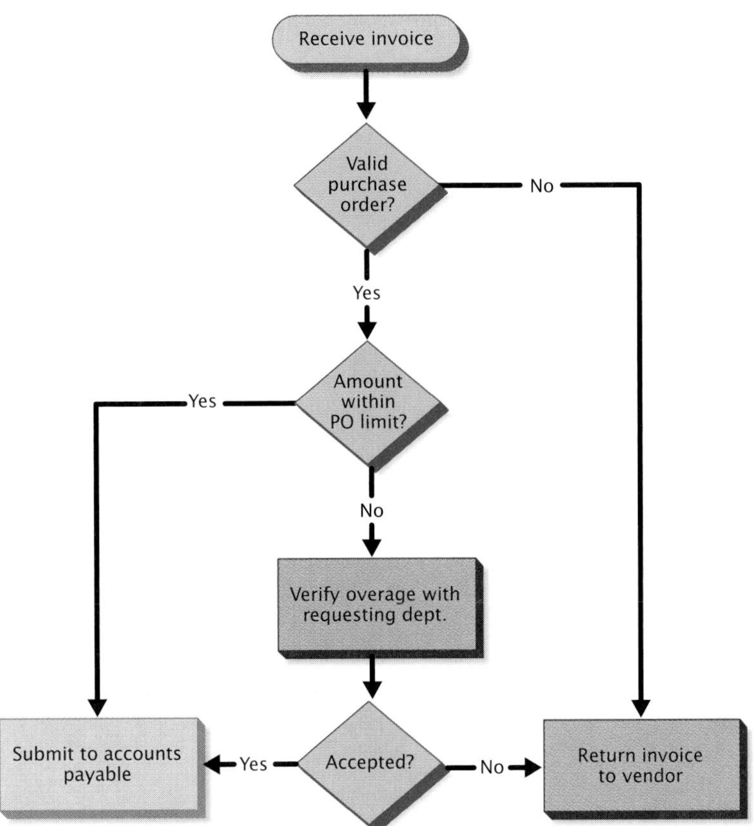

FIGURE 11.9
Flowchart

ing market territories, distribution routes, and facilities locations. Maps are sometimes used in conjunction with aerial photographs to illustrate such elements as land use.

Simple maps are available via clip art libraries for your word processor and presentation software, but more powerful uses (such as automatically generating color coded maps based on data inputs) usually require specialized software.

Drawings, Diagrams, and Photographs

4 LEARNING OBJECTIVE

Identify the best applications for diagrams versus photographs

Unless your career takes you into web design, advertising, technical writing, or another communication specialty, you probably won't need to create a large number of drawings, diagrams, or photographs to accompany your business messages. However, when you do have the opportunity, knowing some of the basics can help you make the most of these potentially compelling elements. Drawings and diagrams are most often used to show how something looks or operates. Figure 11.12 on page 345 was prepared using Microsoft Visio to compare the design of converged and traditional communication networks. Diagrams can be much clearer than words alone when it comes to giving your audience an idea of how an item looks or can be used.

Use drawings and diagrams to show how something works or how it is made or used; drawings are sometimes better than photographs because they let you focus on the most important details.

Word processors and presentation software provide basic drawing capabilities, but for more precise and professional illustrations you'll need a specialized package such as Visio or Adobe Illustrator. Moving a level beyond those programs, computer-aided design (CAD) systems such as Autodesk's Autocad can produce extremely detailed architectural and engineering drawings.

Use photographs for visual appeal and to show exact appearances.

Photographs offer both functional and decorative value. In the past their use was limited to specialized documents such as annual reports and product brochures; however, with low-cost digital photography now widely available, virtually all writers can have the ability to add photographs to print documents, presentations, and web pages. In addition, photo libraries such as Getty Images (www.gettyimages.com) and photo search engines such the one provided by AltaVista (www.altavista.com/image) make it easy to find digital photographs. Some of these photos are available for free, but the professional collections, such as Getty Images, require either a one-time payment for unlimited use (often called "royalty free") or an annual payment or other limited-use purchase (often called "rights managed").

FIGURE 11.10
Organization Chart

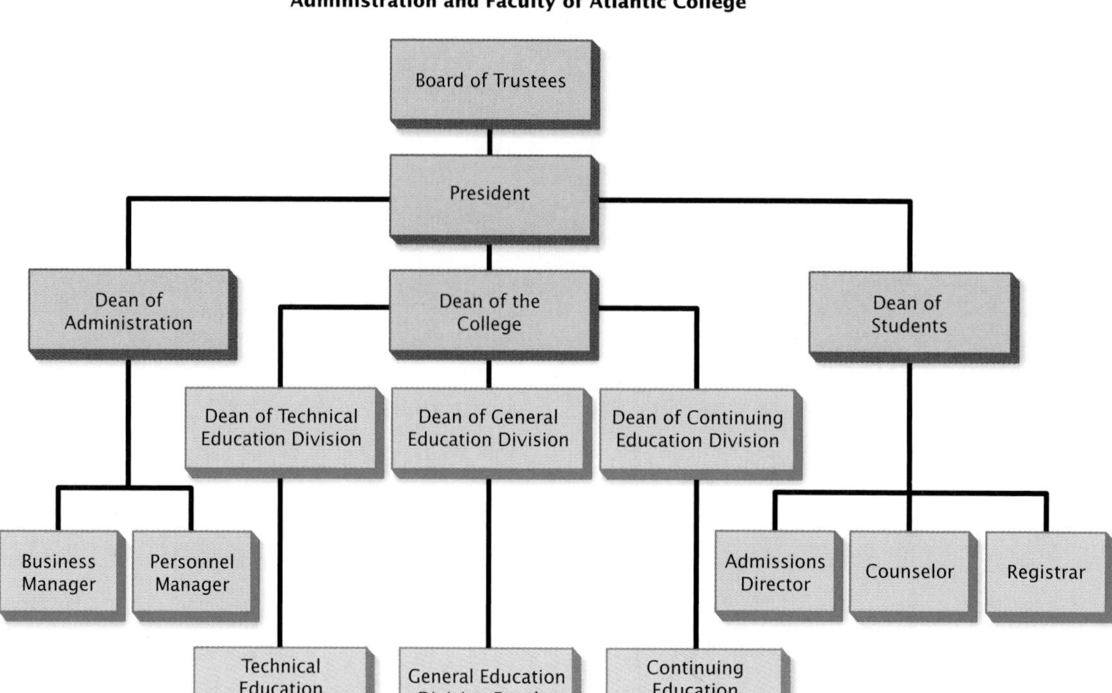

Learn how to use photographs and photo tools before trying to use them in your documents, presentations, or websites.

However, as with all computer advances, "easy" doesn't always mean "effective." To use photographs successfully, consider these guidelines:

- **Learn how to use basic image-processing tools.** For instance, you can drop photographs directly into your word processor or presentation files, then use that program to change the size of the file to fit the available space, but this isn't always the best approach. Rather than simply resizing, you might be better off *cropping*, or electronically cutting away part of the photo.
- **Match the file type to the application.** It's easy to capture a high-resolution image with a quality digital camera and transfer it directly to your website, but there's not much point in doing so. Even the best computer screens have limited resolution and can't display the details and nuances of high-resolution photos. This wouldn't be a problem except for file size, which increases geometrically as resolution increases; high-resolution photos create extremely large files, which of course take forever to download. If your software has a "save for web" function, use that to ensure appropriate resolution for online use. Conversely, low-resolution photographs can look awful in printed documents, since many printers have much higher resolution than computer screens.
- **Make sure the photographs have communication value.** Just because it's easy to drop photos into documents doesn't mean you should automatically do so, naturally. Judge photographs with the same discerning eye you use for every other element of your report or presentation.
- **Be aware of copyrights and model permissions.** Just as with the textual information that you find online, you can't simply insert online photographs into your documents. Unless they are specifically offered for free, you have to assume someone owns the photos and is entitled to payment or at least a photo credit. In addition, professional photographers are careful to have any person who poses in photos sign a model release form, which gives the photographer permission to use the person's image.

Nothing else can demonstrate the exact appearance of a new facility, a piece of property, a new product, or even a retiring co-worker the way a photograph can. However, in some situations a photograph may show too much detail, which is one reason that repair manuals frequently use drawings instead of photos, for instance. With a drawing, you can

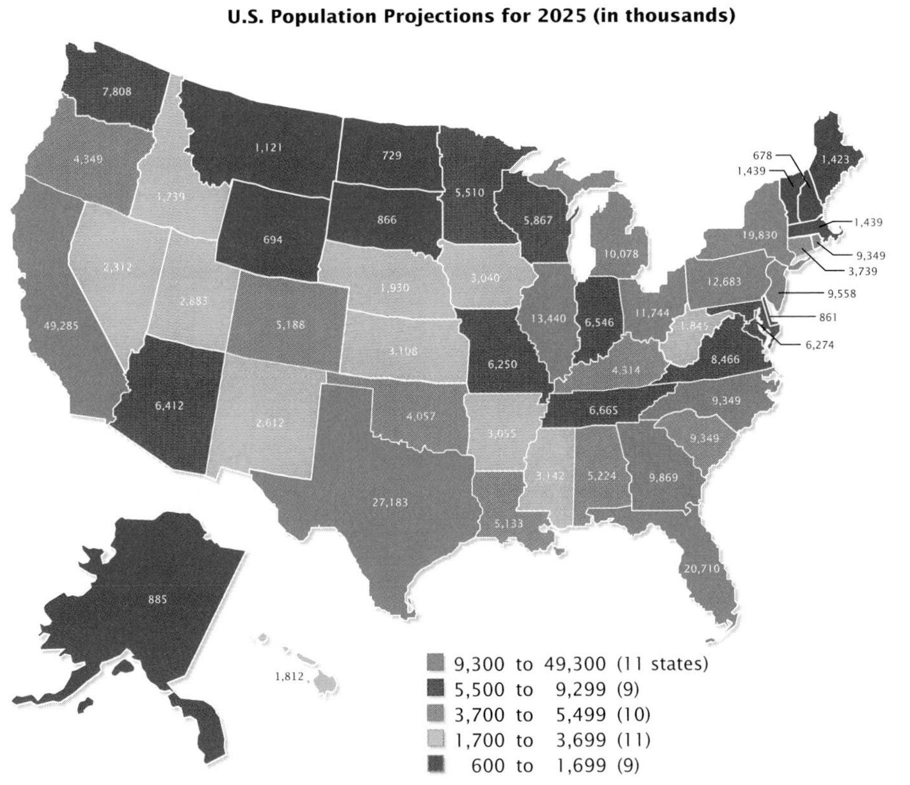

FIGURE 11.11
Map

select how much detail to show, and you can focus the reader's attention on particular parts or places. The disadvantage of such technical illustrations is the time, skill, and special tools often required to create them.

Technology makes it easier to use photographs in reports and presentations, but it also presents an important ethical concern. Software tools such as Photoshop and Paint Shop Pro allow you to easily make dramatic changes to photos—without leaving a clue that they've been altered. Altering photos in small ways has been possible for a long time (more than a few people have had blemishes airbrushed out of their yearbook photos), but computers make drastic changes easy and undetectable. You can remove people from photographs, put Person A's head on Person B's body, and make products look more attractive than they really are. Most people would agree that it's acceptable to make cosmetic improvements, such as brightening an underexposed photo to make it easier to view. But to

FIGURE 11.12 Diagram

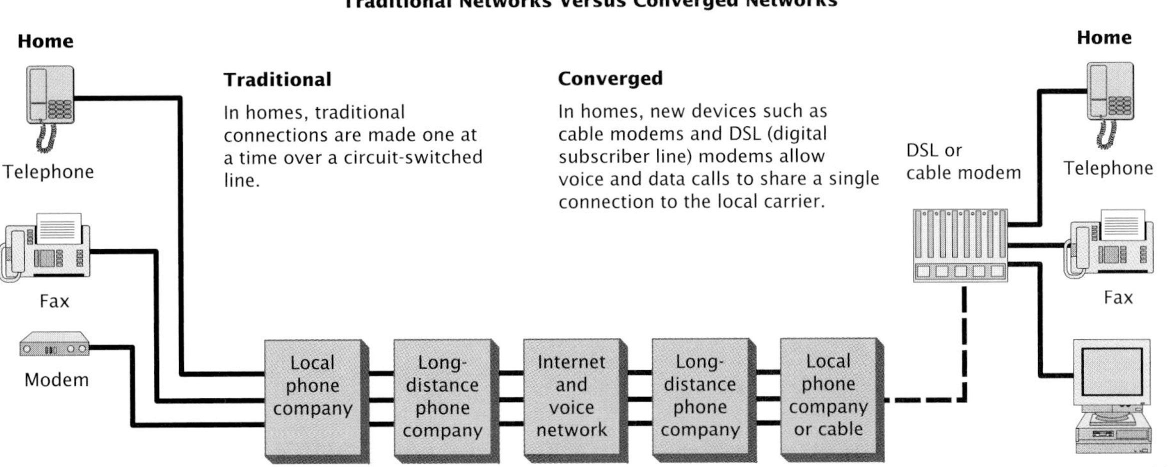

Today's software makes it easy to digitally alter photos. In the photo on the right, the bakery has been given a new name, the man's shirt has been changed to green, and a dog has been included. Is it ethical to change a photo without revealing the changes that were made to the original?

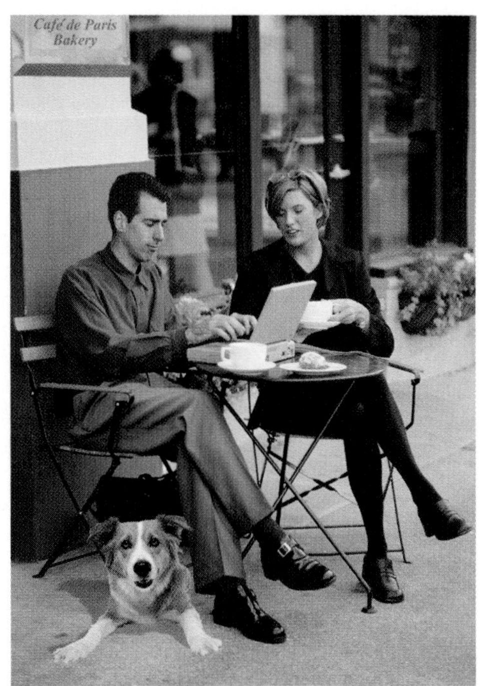

avoid ethical lapses, don't make any alterations that mislead the viewer or substantially change the message conveyed by the photo.[3]

Animation and Video

Computer animation and video are among the most specialized forms of business visuals. You won't encounter many situations that require them, but when they are appropriate and done well, they offer unparalleled visual impact. At a simple level, you can animate shapes and text within Microsoft PowerPoint, although the possibilities are somewhat limited—plus, it's easy to create animations that are more distracting than useful. At a more sophisticated level, software such as Macromedia Flash enables the creation of multimedia files that include computer animation, digital video, and other elements. A wide variety of tools are also available for digital video production. Chances are you won't have to use these tools yourself, but if you do employ a specialist to create animation or video for websites or presentations, make sure the results follow all the guidelines for effective business messages.

DESIGNING VISUALS FOR REPORTS AND PRESENTATIONS

Computer software offers a variety of tools but doesn't automatically give you the design sensibility that is needed for effective visuals.

Technology has put powerful graphics tools in the hands of virtually every business computer user, so you no longer have to rely on professional designers as much as businesspeople had to do only a few years ago. That's the good news. The bad news is that computers can't provide the specialized training and hands-on experience of a professional designer. Computers make it easy to create visuals, but they also make it easy to create ineffective, distracting, and even downright ugly visuals. However, by following some basic design principles, you can create all the basic visuals you need—visuals that are both attractive and effective.

Learning how to use your computer tools will help you save enormous amounts of time and produce better results.

Whether you're using the charting functions offered in a spreadsheet or the design features of a specialized graphics program, take a few minutes to familiarize yourself with the software's quirks and capabilities. For instance, popular spreadsheets can create charts with just a few clicks of the mouse, but the default colors, fonts, or other design elements might not be the best for your particular needs. If possible, have a professional designer set up a *template* for the various types of visuals you and your colleagues need to create. Not only does this help ensure an effective design, but it saves you the time of making numerous design decisions every time you create a chart or graphic.

However, be careful with templates, particularly with those that are included with some commercial software programs. Some are "overdesigned" and inappropriate for serious business uses, and some clutter the image with overly fancy borders and backgrounds that can distract an audience from your real message.

No matter which tools you're using, take care to match the style and quality of your visuals with the subject matter and the situation at hand. The style of your visuals communicates a subtle message about your relationship with the audience. A simple, hand-drawn diagram is fine for a working meeting but inappropriate for a formal presentation or report. On the other hand, elaborate, full-color visuals may be viewed as extravagant for an informal memo but may be entirely appropriate for a message to top management or influential outsiders.

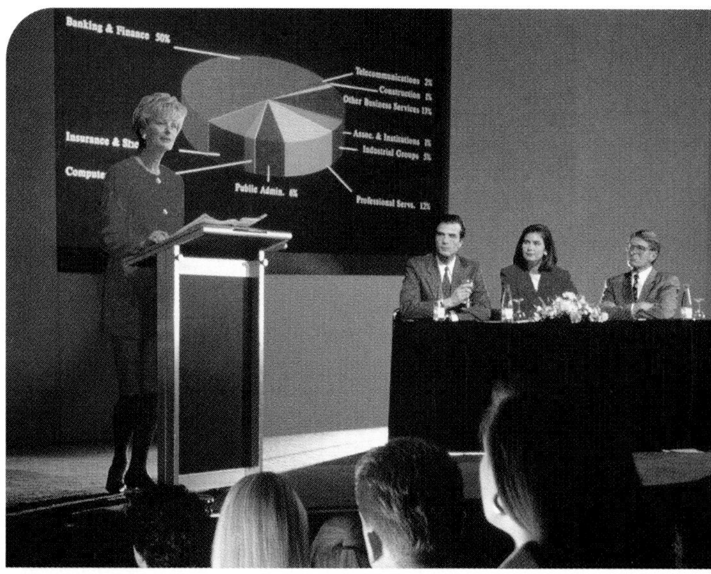

The use of color in visuals accelerates learning, retention, and recall between 55 and 78 percent; it increases motivation and audience participation up to 80 percent.

Understanding Graphic Design Principles

5 LEARNING OBJECTIVE

Discuss five principles of graphic design that can improve the quality of your visuals

Although you may not think of yourself as being the artistic type, chances are you have a better sense of design than you realize. Most people seem to subconsciously recognize good design when they see it, even if they don't know how to achieve the same effects on their own.[4]

However, few businesspeople have the opportunity to formally study the "language" of line, mass, space, size, color, pattern, and texture. When arranged in certain ways, these elements of visual design are pleasing to the eye. When you encounter visuals that you find appealing or unappealing, stop and ask yourself why, and see what you can learn from this to improve your own graphics. Bear in mind that design decisions can affect the meaning you convey with your visuals, too—sometimes in subtle ways. For instance, thick lines and square corners suggest power and strength, whereas thin lines and curves suggest lightness and grace. Colors have a language all their own as well.

The elements of design convey meaning in subtle ways.

To create effective visuals, learn both the aesthetic and the symbolic aspects of graphic art so that you won't send the wrong message or confuse your audience. Here are a few principles to be aware of:

When designing visuals, observe the principles of continuity; contrast; emphasis; simplicity; and, experience and expectations.

- **Continuity.** Readers view a series of visuals as a whole, assuming that design elements will be consistent from one page to the next. For instance, if your first chart shows results for Division A in blue, the audience will expect Division A to be shown in blue throughout the report or presentation. You'll confuse people if you make arbitrary changes in color, shape, size, texture, position, scale, or typeface.
- **Contrast.** Readers expect visual distinctions to match verbal ones. To emphasize differences, depict items in contrasting colors, such as red and blue, or black and white. But to emphasize similarities, make color difference more subtle. In a pie chart, you might show two similar items in two shades of blue and a dissimilar item in yellow. Keep in mind that accent colors draw attention to key elements, but they lose their effect if you overdo them.
- **Emphasis.** Readers assume that the most important point will receive the greatest visual emphasis. So present the key item on the chart in the most prominent way—through color, position, size, or whatever. Visually downplay less important items. Avoid using strong colors for unimportant data, and de-emphasize background features such as the grid lines on a chart.
- **Simplicity.** Limit the number of colors and design elements you use, and take care to avoid *chartjunk,* decorative elements that clutter documents (and confuse readers) without adding any relevant information.[5] Computers make it far too easy to add

FIGURE 11.13
The Power of Simplicity

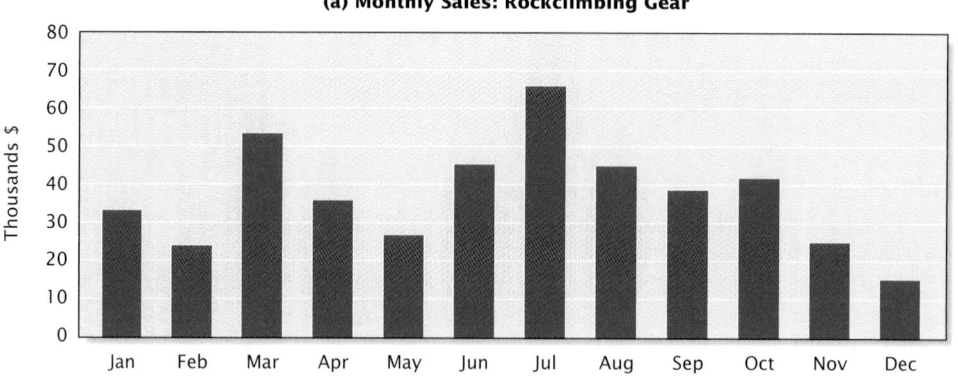

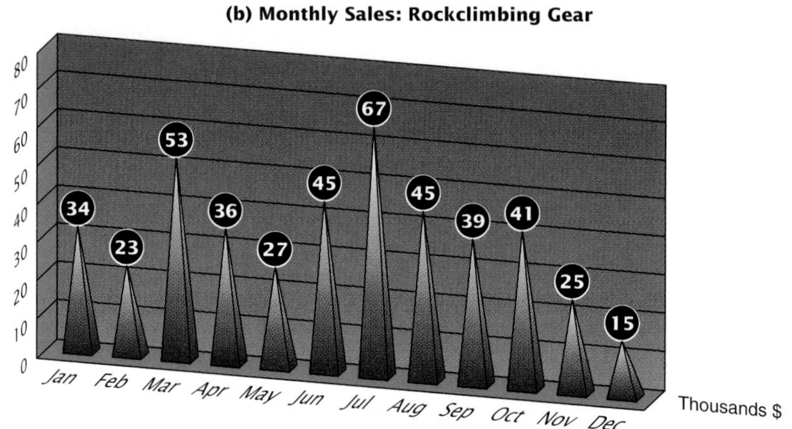

chartjunk, from clip art illustrations to three-dimensional bar charts that display only two dimensions of data. The two charts in Figure 11.13 show the same information, but the second one is cluttered with useless decoration and poor design choices. For example, the three-dimensional bars in Figure 11.13b don't show anything more than the simple two-dimensional bars in Figure 11.13a. As a result, the second chart is both much harder to read, and it conveys a sense of amateurism.

- **Experience and expectations.** Culture and education condition people to expect things to look a certain way, including visuals. For example, green may be associated with money in the United States, but not in countries whose currencies are different colors. Similarly, a red cross on a white background stands for emergency medical care in many countries. But the cross is also a Christian symbol, so the International Red Cross uses a red crescent in Islamic countries—even though the original Red Cross symbol is based on the flag of Switzerland and not on any religious icons.[6]

The best time to think about the principles of good design is before preparing your visuals; making changes after the fact increases the amount of time required to produce them.

Integrating Visuals into Your Text

Your approach to integrating text and visuals depends on the type of report you're preparing. If you're working on a glossy promotional document, handle the visuals as though they were illustrations in a magazine, positioning them to attract interest and tell a story of their own. However, in most business documents, the visuals clarify the text, so tie them closely to the discussion. Integrate your visuals into text in a manner that is convenient for your audience and practical from a production standpoint. Successful integration involves three decisions: the manner in which you refer to visuals in the text, the position you give visuals in the document, and the titles you write for the visuals.

To tie visuals to the text, introduce them in the text and place them near the points they illustrate.

Referencing Visuals

Unless a visual element clearly stands on its own, as in the *sidebars* you often see in magazines or the captioned photographs in this textbook, visuals should be clearly referred to by number in the text of your report. Some report writers refer to all visuals as "exhibits" and number them consecutively throughout the report; many others number tables and figures separately (everything that isn't a table is regarded as a figure). In a long report with numbered sections, illustrations may have a double number (separated by a period or a hyphen) representing the section number and the individual illustration number within that section. Whichever scheme you use, make sure it's clear and obvious to your readers.

Help your readers understand the significance of visuals by referring to them before readers encounter them in the document or on the screen. The following examples show how you can make this connection in the text:

Help your readers understand why each visual is important.

> Figure 1 summarizes the financial history of the motorcycle division over the past five years, with sales broken into four categories.
>
> Total sales were steady over this period, but the mix of sales by category changed dramatically (see Figure 2).
>
> The underlying reason for the remarkable growth in our sales of youth golf apparel is suggested by Table 4, which shows the growing interest in junior golf around the world.

When describing the data shown in your visuals, be sure to emphasize the main point you are trying to make. Don't make the mistake of simply repeating the data to be shown. Paragraphs that do are guaranteed to put the reader to sleep:

> Among women who replied to the survey, 17.4 percent earn less than $5 per hour; 26.4 percent earn $5 to $7; 25.7 percent, $8 to $12; 18.0 percent, $13 to $24; 9.6 percent, $25 to $49; and 2.9 percent, $50 and over.

The visual will (or at least should) provide all these details; there is no need to repeat them in the text. Instead, use round numbers that sum up the message:

> Over two-thirds of the women who replied earn less than $12 per hour.

Placing Visuals

Try to position your visuals so that your audience won't have to flip back and forth (in printed documents) or scroll (on screen) between the visuals and the text. Ideally, it's best to place each visual within, beside, or immediately after the paragraph it illustrates so that readers can consult the explanation and the visual at the same time. This scheme works well both in print and online. If at all possible, avoid bunching visuals at the end of a section or the end of a document; doing so asks a lot of the reader. (Bunching is unavoidable in some cases, such as when you have multiple visuals that accompany a single section of text.) Word processing and desktop publishing software let you place graphical elements virtually anywhere you wish, so take advantage of this flexibility (although you may have to learn the specific quirks of your software to achieve the best results).

Place each visual as close as possible to its in-text reference to help readers understand the illustration's relevance and to minimize the effort of reading.

Writing Titles, Captions, and Legends

Titles and legends provide two more opportunities to connect your visual messages with textual messages. A **title** is similar to a subheading, providing a short description that identifies the content and purpose of the visual, along with whatever label and number you're using to refer to the visual. A **caption** usually offers additional discussion of the visual's content and can be several sentences long if appropriate. Captions can also alert readers that additional discussion is available in the accompanying text. Titles usually appear above visuals and captions appear below, but effective designs can place these two elements in other positions. Sometimes titles and captions are combined in a single block of text as well. As with all design decisions, be consistent throughout your report or website. A **legend** helps readers "decode" the visual by explaining what various colors, symbols, or other design choices mean. Legends aren't necessary for simple graphs, such as a line chart or bar chart with only series of data, but they are invaluable with more complex graphics.

The title of a visual functions in the same way as a subheading, whereas the caption provides additional detail if needed.

DOCUMENT MAKEOVER

IMPROVE THIS REPORT SUMMARY AND VISUALS

To practice correcting drafts of actual documents, visit www.prenhall.com/onekey on the web. Click "Document Makeovers" then click Chapter 11. You will find a competitive analysis report summary that contains problems and errors relating to what you've learned in this chapter about communicating information through visuals. Use the Final Draft decision tool to create an improved version of this summary. Check the message for appropriate formatting of visuals and proper use of text with visuals.

CHECKLIST: Creating Effective Visuals

- Select the proper types of graphics for the information at hand and for the objective of the message.
- Be sure the visual contributes to overall understanding of the subject.
- Understand how to use your software tools to maximize effectiveness and efficiency.
- Emphasize visual continuity to connect parts of a whole.
- Avoid arbitrary changes of color, texture, typeface, position, or scale.
- Emphasize differences through design contrast.
- Strive for simplicity and clarity; don't clutter your visuals with meaningless decoration.
- Consider audience experience and cultural expectations.
- Integrate visuals to your text so that readers perceive a smoothly flowing unity throughout.
- Use titles, captions, and legends to help readers understand the meaning and importance of your visuals.

Descriptive titles simply identify the topic of an illustration; informative titles help the reader understand the conclusion to be drawn from the illustration.

By considering your word choices for all three of these textual elements, you can help readers link the visuals with the text and quickly grasp the most important points of each visual. Readers should be able to grasp the point of the visual without digging into the surrounding text. For instance, a title that says simply, "Refineries" doesn't say much at all. "Active Petroleum Refineries in the United States" provides a much better idea of what the chart is all about. You may also want to use informative titles, rather than basic descriptive titles. A **descriptive title** simply identifies the topic of the illustration, whereas an **informative title** calls attention to the conclusion that ought to be drawn from the data. Here's an example of the difference:

DESCRIPTIVE TITLE	INFORMATIVE TITLE
Relationship Between Petroleum Demand and Refinery Capacity in the United States	Shrinking Refinery Capacity Results from Stagnant Petroleum Demand

Regardless of whether your titles and legends are informative or descriptive, phrase them consistently throughout the report. For a review of the important points to remember when creating visuals, see "Checklist: Creating Effective Visuals."

6 LEARNING OBJECTIVE

Name three qualities to look for before including a visual in a report or presentation

Checking Over Visuals

Proof visuals as carefully as you proof text.

Even though visuals exist to support the message carried in your text, they have a particularly strong impact on your readers and on their perceptions of you and your work. Be sure to check visuals for mistakes such as typographical errors, inconsistent color treatment, confusing or undocumented symbols, and misaligned elements. Make sure that your computer hasn't done something unexpected, such as arranging pie chart slices in an order you don't want or plotting line charts in unusual colors. Also take a few extra minutes to make sure that your visuals are absolutely accurate, properly documented, and honest.

Is the Visual Accurate?

Errors are easy to make with computer generated visuals, so make sure that every piece of information is correct. Also verify that information in visuals and text matches. For data presentations, particularly if you're producing charts with a spreadsheet, verify any formulas used to generate the numbers, and make sure you've selected the right numbers for each chart. When you're in a hurry, it's easy to select the wrong column of numbers in a spreadsheet or the wrong set of numbers within a column. The software will happily create a chart for you, but it might be wildly inaccurate.

For flowcharts, organizational charts, diagrams, photos, and other visuals, compare the visuals you created with the visuals you had planned to create. Does each visual deliver your message accurately? Have you inserted the right photos, maps, or other files?

Is the Visual Properly Documented?

Cite the source of any data you use to create the visual.

As with the textual elements in your reports and presentations, visuals based on other people's research, information, and ideas require full citation. (Even if the graphical design is entirely yours, any underlying information taken from other sources needs to be documented.) Also, try to anticipate any questions or concerns your audience may have and address them with additional information as needed. For instance, if you're presenting the results of survey research, many readers will want to know who participated in the survey, how many people responded, and when the questions were asked. You could answer these questions with a note in the caption along the lines of "652 accountants, surveyed the week of January 17." Similarly, if you found a visual in a secondary source, list that source on or near the graphic to help readers assess the information. To avoid cluttering your graphic, you can use a shortened citation or note on the graphic itself and include a complete citation elsewhere in the report.

Is the Visual Honest?

Just as subtle word choices shade the meaning of your writing, so can seemingly minor design variations influence the message your readers take away from your business graphics. Visuals can suffer from distortions, both intentional and unintentional (see "Ethics Detective: Hiding Behind the Numbers"). Consider the line chart in Figure 11.14a, which shows impurities measured over the course of a 12-month period. The vertical scale is set from 0 to 120, sufficient to cover the range of variations in the data. However, what if you

To prevent your charts and visuals from creating a false impression, be sure to

- Include all key data points
- Mention any important outside influence on the data
- Maintain a consistent scale of measurement

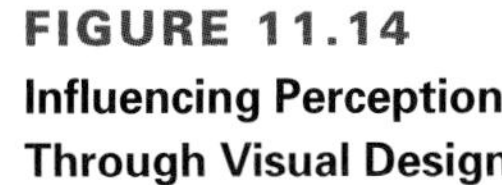

FIGURE 11.14
Influencing Perception Through Visual Design

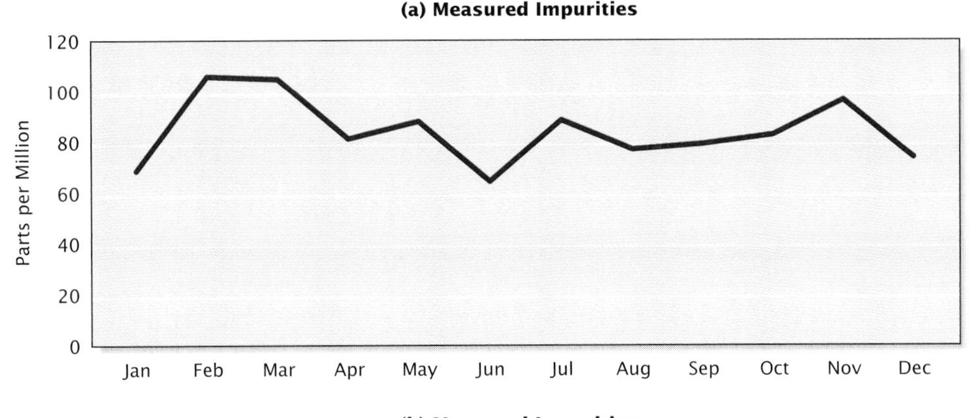

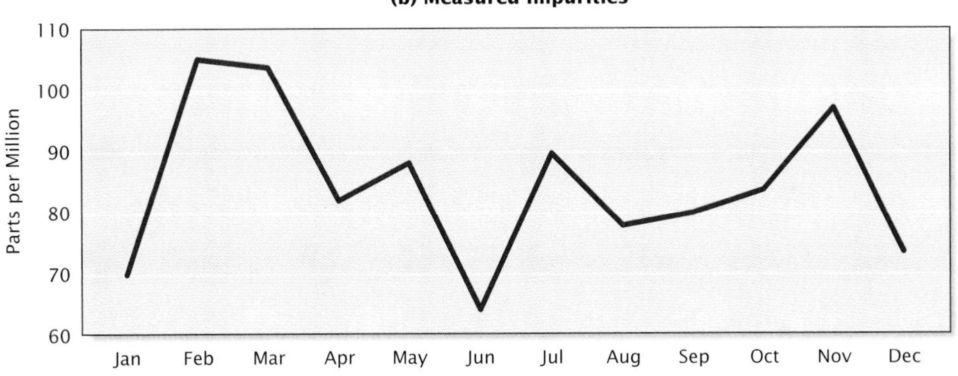

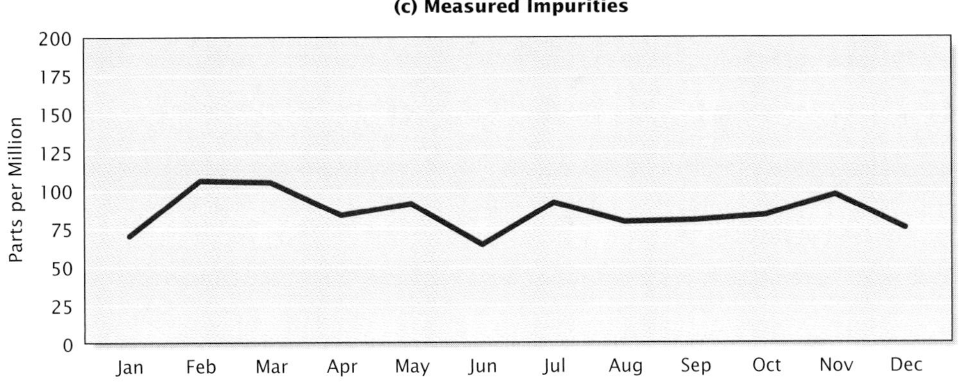

Ethics Detective

Hiding Behind the Numbers

You've been assigned to present the results of an industrywide study of the effects of insecticide. Your audience consists of the department heads in your company, whose experience and education backgrounds vary widely, from chemical engineers to insurance and legal experts. You're convinced you need to keep your report as simple and as jargon-free as possible. You'll then invite content-area specialists to contact you if they have technical questions.

You're not a scientific expert in insecticides, but your supervisor has introduced you to a scientist who works for a trade association that represents chemical producers, including your firm. The scientist is familiar with the study you'll be reporting on, and she has experience in communicating technical subjects to diverse audiences. You jumped at the chance to have such a knowledgeable person review your presentation for technical accuracy, but you're uncomfortable with some of her feedback. In particular, you question her advice to replace the following line chart, which shows the number of insecticide poisonings and deaths by age.

She suggests that this chart is too busy and too difficult for nonspecialists to read. As an alternative, she provides a bar chart that selects four specific ages from the entire range. She says this chart communicates the same basic idea the line chart but is much easier to read.

ANALYSIS

You agree with the scientist that the line chart is visually busy and takes more effort to process, but something bothers you about the bar chart. Does it present the insecticide situation accurately and honestly? Why or why not?

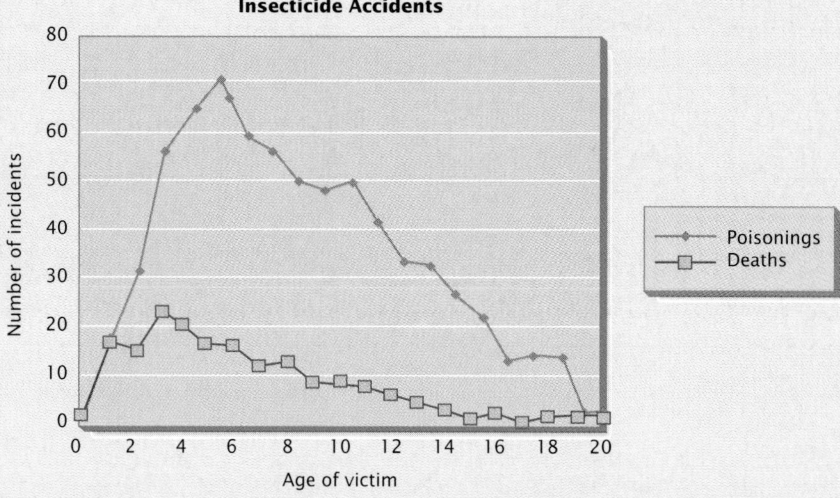

Chart B

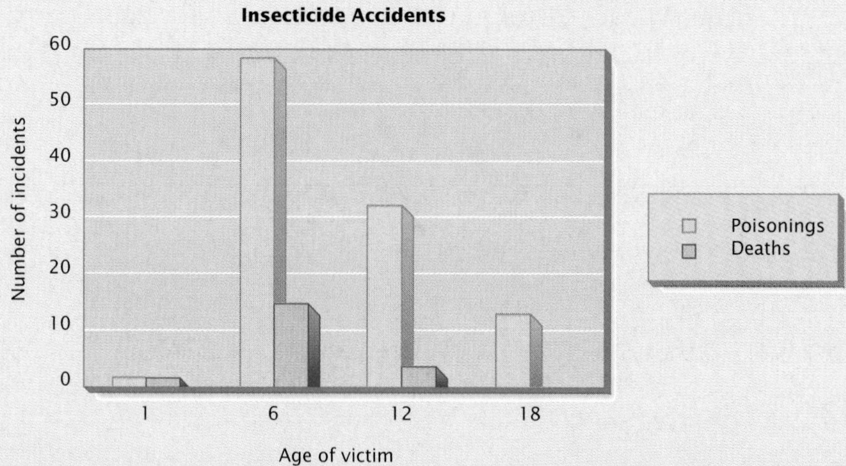

wanted to make the variations from month to month look more severe? Less severe? Figure 11.14b, with the scale "zoomed in" on 60 to 110, makes the variations look much more dramatic. The result could be a stronger emotional impact on the reader, creating the impression that these impurities are out of control. In contrast, Figure 11.14c expands the scale, from 0 to 200, which appears to minimize the variations in the data. This graph is visually "calmer," potentially creating the opposite impression—that there's really nothing to worry about. Of course, the data shown in all three graphs are identical, but they send three different messages to the reader.

7 LEARNING OBJECTIVE

Discuss the problem of deceptive visuals

If all three graphs in Figure 11.14 show the same data, which if any would be more honest than the others? The answer to this question depends on your intent and your audience's information needs. For instance, if dramatic swings in the measurement from month to month suggest a problem with the quality of your product or the safety of a process that affects the public, then visually minimizing the swings might well be considered dishonest.

Altering the scale of data charts is just one of many ways that visuals can be designed to emphasize or deemphasize certain aspects of information. For example, photographs can influence perceptions of physical size (and perhaps of quality, value, danger, or other associated variables), depending on the way the various elements are arranged in the picture. To increase the perceived size of a product, an advertiser might show a close-up of it being held by someone with smaller-than-average hands. Conversely, a large hand would make the product seem smaller. At the extreme, visuals can lie by hiding data or otherwise obscuring damaging information.

Review each visual to make sure it doesn't intentionally or unintentionally distort the meaning of the underlying information.

COMMUNICATION CHALLENGES AT STONE YAMASHITA PARTNERS

In Canada, the Tim Horton's chain is famous for its coffee and donuts. However, with over 2,200 shops, Tim's has saturated the Canadian market and is looking to grow in the United States, where it has just 160 shops. That growth won't be easy: Tim's will be facing Dunkin' Donuts, Krispy Kreme, and Starbucks in their home territory.

Individual Challenge: Tim's has hired SYP to help recruit franchise owners for its southward expansion, and Keith Yamashita is planning an event for the 100 most promising potential franchisees. To help illustrate the business opportunity, he has asked you, his newest employee, to create compelling visuals for the following items:

- The five-year trend in per capita donut consumption in the United States
- The five-year projected growth in the average price of coffee drinks in the United States
- Market share in coffee sales among Dunkin' Donuts, Peaberry's, Starbucks, and others
- The planned growth in the number of Tim's outlets in four U.S. regions (North, West, South, and East) over the next 10 years

Decide what kind of visual to use for each item. Create example visuals by making up any data you need.

Team Challenge: SYP often uses life-size mockups to help people visualize new possibilities, such as the interior layout of a Tim's franchise. In a small group, brainstorm the layout of a coffeehouse that you think would appeal to customers on or near your college campus. Write a brief e-mail explaining how you could "stage" a life-size mockup of your store layout to help potential franchisors see what a Tim's store is like inside.

SUMMARY OF LEARNING OBJECTIVES

1 **Describe the communication power that visuals add to your writing.** Visuals enhance the communication impact of your writing in three ways. First, visuals can convey some types of information better than text can. Second, visuals are an effective way to reach audiences of diverse professional and cultural backgrounds. Third, busy readers who may lack the time or inclination to

read your entire message often look to visuals to quickly grasp the essence of what you're trying to communicate.

2 **Explain how to choose which points in your message to illustrate.** To decide which points to illustrate, first step back and consider the overall flow of your message from the audience's point of view. Identify elements of the message that might be complex, vulnerable to misinterpretation, or even dull. Look for connections between ideas that should be highlighted or extensive collections of data and other discrete factual content that might be difficult to read in textual format.

3 **Describe the most common options for presenting data in a visual format.** The visuals most commonly used to present data include tables, line and surface charts, bar charts, pictograms, Gantt charts, and pie charts. You will probably use line, bar, and pie charts most often in your business communication efforts.

4 **Identify the best applications for diagrams versus photographs.** Diagrams and photographs are both useful for displaying spatial relations and other physical and conceptual concepts. Diagrams are often better when you want to highlight specific elements in a scene, such as a particular part in a complex machine. Photographs are better for realistic depictions, but can provide too much visual information in some cases.

5 **Discuss five principles of graphic design that can improve the quality of your visuals.** When preparing visuals, (1) use elements of design consistently so you don't confuse your audience; (2) use color and other elements to show contrast effectively; (3) use design elements to draw attention to key elements and to visually downplay less important items; (4) avoid clutter; and (5) try to match design selections with your audience's experience level and their professional and cultural expectations.

6 **Name three qualities to look for before including a visual in a report or presentation.** Before you include a visual, make sure it is accurate (there are no mistakes or missing information), properly documented (the creator of any underlying data used in the visual has been given complete credit), and honest (the visual honestly reveals the real meaning of the underlying data).

7 **Discuss the problem of deceptive visuals.** Visuals can be both intentionally and unintentionally deceptive, and the development of computerized image manipulation tools has raised the urgency of this problem even more. At a simple level, merely adjusting the vertical scaling of a line chart or bar chart can alter the meaning and emphasis of your message. At a more advanced level, image-processing software is so advanced now that both still and moving images can be altered in ways that are virtually undetectable. Moreover, audiences often lack the time, resources, or skill to recognize deceptive visual presentations. All of these factors increase the ethical burden on business communicators to ensure that all of their visuals are complete, honest, and truly representative of the underlying information.

Test Your Knowledge

1. What chart type would you use to compare one part with a whole?
2. What chart type would you use to present detailed, exact values?
3. What chart type would you use to compare one item with another?
4. What chart type would you use to illustrate trends over time?
5. When are combination bar and line charts used?
6. For what purposes are Gantt charts used?
7. How does a flowchart differ from an organization chart?
8. When would you use a bubble diagram instead of a scatter diagram?
9. What is the purpose of adding titles, captions, and legends to visuals in reports?
10. How do you check a visual for accuracy?

Apply Your Knowledge

1. What similarities do you see between visuals and nonverbal communication? Explain your answer.
2. You're writing a report to the director of human resources on implementing participative management throughout your company. You want to emphasize that since the new approaches were implemented six months ago, absenteeism and turnovers have been sharply reduced in all but two departments. How do you visually present your data in the most favorable light? Explain.
3. Besides telling readers why an illustration is important, why refer to it in the text of your document?
4. When you read a graph, how can you be sure that the visual impression you are receiving is an accurate reflection of reality? Please explain.
5. **Ethical Choices** What ethical issue is raised by the use of technology to alter photographs in reports?

Practice Your Knowledge

Documents for Analysis

Document 11.A

Examine the pie charts in Figure 11.15 and point out any problems or errors you notice.

Document 11.B

Examine the line chart in Figure 11.16 and point out any problems or errors you notice.

FIGURE 11.15 Pie Charts for Analysis

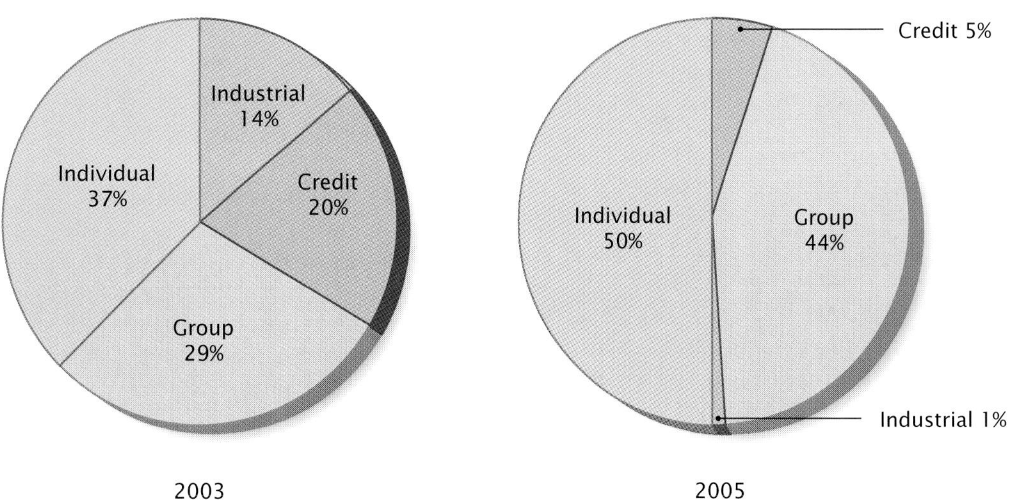

Exercises

For live links to all websites discussed in this chapter, visit this text's website at www.prenhall.com/bovee. Just log on, select Chapter 11, and click on "Featured Websites." Locate the page or the URL related to the material in the text.

11.1 Preparing Pie Charts As a market researcher for a statewide chain of car dealerships, you're examining car and truck ownership and lease patterns among single drivers in various age groups. By discovering which age groups have the highest percentages of owners, you will be better able to target advertising that promotes the leasing option. Using the table on page 356, prepare a bar chart comparing the number of owners with the number of leasers in each age category. Be sure to label your chart, and include combined totals for owners and leasers ("total drivers"). Then prepare a pie chart showing the proportion of owners and leasers in the one age group that you think holds the most promise for leasing a

FIGURE 11.16 Line Chart for Analysis

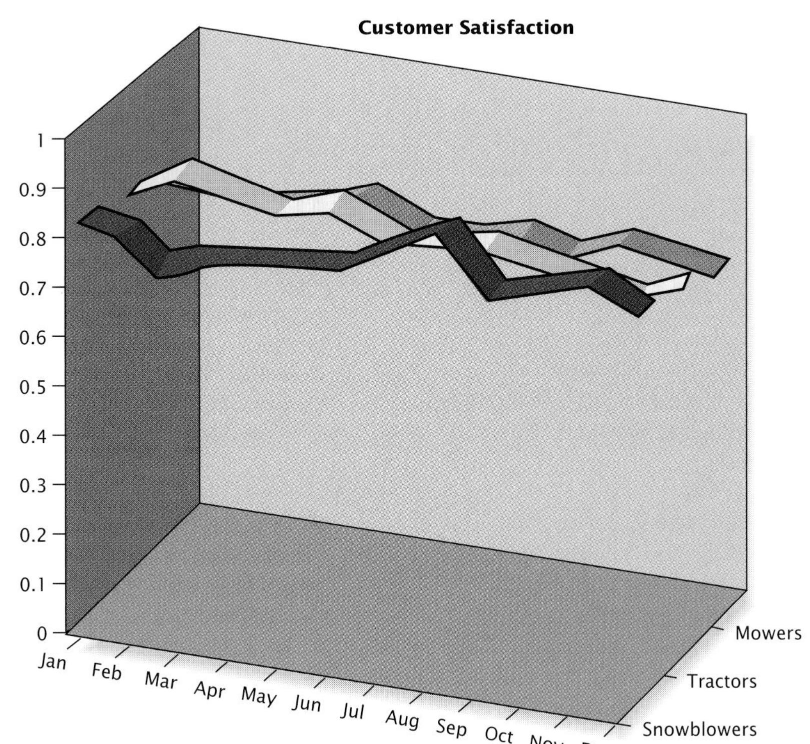

new vehicle. Write a sentence that prepares your company's management for the information shown in the pie chart.

Age group	Number of owners (in 000s)	Number of leasers (in 000s)
18–24	1,830	795
25–29	1,812	1,483
30–34	1,683	1,413
35–44	1,303	1,932
45–54	1,211	1,894
55–64	1,784	1,435
65–74	3,200	1,142
75+	3,431	854

11.2 **Preparing Pie Charts** As director of new business development for a growing advertising agency, you're interested in how companies spend their advertising dollars. Create a pie chart based on the following information, which shows U.S. national advertising spending by media category. Summarize these findings (in two or three sentences) for publication in a report to top management.

Media type	Expenditure (in $ billions)
Internet	1.9
Outdoor	2.0
Radio	2.9
Yellow Pages	12.7
Magazines	16.6
Newspapers	21.2
Television	45.1
Direct mail, promotions, special events	112.9
Total Advertising[7]	215.3

11.3 **Preparing Line Charts** The pet food manufacturer you work for is interested in the results of a recent poll of U.S. pet-owning households. Look at the statistics that follow and decide on the most appropriate scale for a chart; then create a line chart of the trends in cat ownership. What conclusions do you draw from the trend you've charted? Draft a paragraph or two discussing the results of this poll and the potential consequences for the pet food business. Support your conclusions by referring readers to your chart.

In 1990, 22 million U.S. households owned a cat. In 1995, 24 million households owned a cat. In 2000, 28 million households owned a cat. In 2005, 32 million households owned a cat.

11.4 **Selecting the Right Visual** You're preparing the annual report for FretCo Guitar Corporation. For each of the following types of information, select the right chart or visual to illustrate the text. Explain your choices.

a. Data on annual sales for the past 20 years
b. Comparison of FretCo sales, product by product (electric guitars, bass guitars, amplifiers, acoustic guitars), for this year and last year
c. Explanation of how a FretCo acoustic guitar is manufactured
d. Explanation of how the FretCo Guitar Corporation markets its guitars
e. Data on sales of FretCo products in each of 12 countries
f. Comparison of FretCo sales figures with sales figures for three competing guitar makers over the past 10 years

11.5 **Preparing Bar Charts** Team up with a classmate to design charts based on a comparison of the total tax burden of the U.S. taxpayer with that of people in other nations. One teammate should sketch a horizontal or vertical bar chart and the other should sketch a pictogram from the estimates that follow. Then exchange charts and analyze how well each conveys the situation of the U.S. taxpayer. Would the bar chart look best with vertical or horizontal bars? Why? What scale is best? How does the symbol used in the pictogram enhance or obscure the meaning or impact of the data? What suggestions can each student make for improving the other's visual aid?

Estimates show that Swedish taxpayers spend 51 percent of their incomes on taxes, British taxpayers spend 48 percent, French taxpayers spend 37 percent, Japanese taxpayers spend 28 percent, and U.S. taxpayers spend 27 percent.

11.6 **Selecting the Right Chart** Here are last year's sales figures for the appliance and electronics megastore where you work. Construct charts based on these figures that will help you explain to the store's general manager seasonal variations in each department.

Store Sales in 2004 (in $ thousands)

Month	Home Electronics	Computers	Appliances
January	$68	$39	$36
February	72	34	34
March	75	41	30
April	54	41	28
May	56	42	44
June	49	33	48
July	54	31	43
August	66	58	39
September	62	58	36
October	66	44	33
November	83	48	29
December	91	62	24

11.7 **Creating Maps** You work for C & S Holdings, a company that operates coin-activated, self-service car washes. Research shows that the farther customers live from a car wash, the less likely they are to visit. You know that 50 percent of customers at each of your car washes live within a 4-mile radius of the location, 65 percent live within 6 miles, 80 percent live within 8 miles, and 90 percent live within 10 miles. C & S's owner wants to open two new car washes in your city and has asked you to prepare a report recommending locations. Using a map of your city, choose two possible locations for car washes and create a visual depicting the customer base surrounding each location.

11.8 **Creating Organization Charts** Create an organization chart for your school. You will probably need to consult your school library or administration office for documents listing the various offices and departments. Figure 11.10 on page 344 can serve as a model for how to structure your chart.

11.9 **Creating Line Charts** Recreate the line chart in Figure 11.2 on page 337 as a bar chart and as a pie chart. Which of these three formats does the best job of conveying the information? Are any of the formats definitely inappropriate for this information? Explain your answers.

11.10 **Selecting the Right Chart** With a team of three or four other students, brainstorm and then sketch at least three types of charts you can use to compare the populations of all 50 states in the United States. You can use any of the graphic ideas presented in this chapter, as well as any ideas or examples you find from other sources.

11.11 **Internet** One of the best places to see how data can be presented visually is in government statistical publications, which are often available on the Internet. For example, the International Trade Administration (ITA), a branch of the U.S. Department of Commerce, publishes monthly reports about U.S. trade with other countries. Visit the report page of its website at www.ita.doc.gov and follow the link to the latest monthly trade update. Using what you learned in this chapter, evaluate the charts in the report. Do they present the data clearly? Are they missing any elements? What would you do to improve the charts? Print out a copy of the report to turn in with your answers, and indicate which charts you are evaluating.

11.12 **Ethical Choices** Create a bar or line chart using data you find online or in a business publication. Make of copy of your chart and alter the chart's scale. How does the altered chart distort the information? How might you detect whether a chart's scale has been altered?

Expand Your Knowledge

For live links to the websites that follow, go to www.prenhall.com/bovee. When you log on, select Chapter 11, then select "Featured Websites," click on the URL of the website you wish to visit, and review the website to complete these exercises.

Exploring the Best of the Web

Brush Up on Your Computer-Graphics Skills
graphicssoft.about.com
Need some help using graphics software? Get started at the About.com graphics software website. Take the tutorials and learn how to manage fonts, images, and a variety of graphics-related tasks. View the illustrated demonstrations. Read the instructional articles. Learn how to use the most common file formats for graphics. Expand your knowledge of the basic principles of graphic design. And master some advanced color tips and theory. Don't leave without following the links to recommended books and magazines. Before you leave, answer these questions:

1. What are the most common file formats for online visuals?
2. What does color depth mean in computer visuals?
3. What is dithering and how can it affect your visuals?

Exploring the Web on Your Own

Review these chapter-related websites on your own to learn more about creating charts, diagrams, and other visuals for written and oral reports.

1. Become an Excel pro by reading the Tips and Tricks and How-to Articles at the Microsoft Excel homepage, www.microsoft.com/excel. Click on Using Excel to get started.
2. Learn how to create effective diagrams at the Microsoft Visio website, www.microsoft.com/office/visio. Click on Using Visio to get started.
3. Check out the world's largest online encyclopedia of graphic symbols at Symbols.com, www.symbols.com.

Learn Interactively

Interactive Study Guide

Go to the Companion Website at www.prenhall.com/bovee. For Chapter 11, take advantage of the interactive "Study Guide" to test your knowledge of the chapter. Get instant feedback on whether you need additional studying.

Also, visit this site's "Study Hall," where you'll find an abundance of valuable resources that will help you succeed in this course.

Peak Performance Grammar and Mechanics

In Chapter 10 you were referred to the Peak Performance Grammar and Mechanics activities on the web at www.prenhall.com/onekey to improve your skill with apostrophes, quotation marks, parentheses and brackets, question marks and exclamation points, dashes, hyphens, and ellipses. For additional reinforcement in dashes and hyphens, go to www.prenhall.com/bovee, where you will find "Improve Your Grammar, Mechanics, and Usage" exercises.

PART 5

Planning, Writing, and Completing Reports and Proposals

chapter 12

Planning Reports and Proposals

LEARNING OBJECTIVES

After studying this chapter, you will be able to

1. Explain the differences between informational reports and analytical reports
2. Adapt the three-step writing process to reports and proposals
3. Explain the value of a work plan in the development of long reports
4. Describe the four major categories of informational reports and provide examples of each
5. Describe the three major categories of analytical reports and provide examples of each
6. Discuss three major ways to organize analytical reports
7. Explain how your approach to writing proposals should differ when you are responding to a formal request for proposals (RFP)

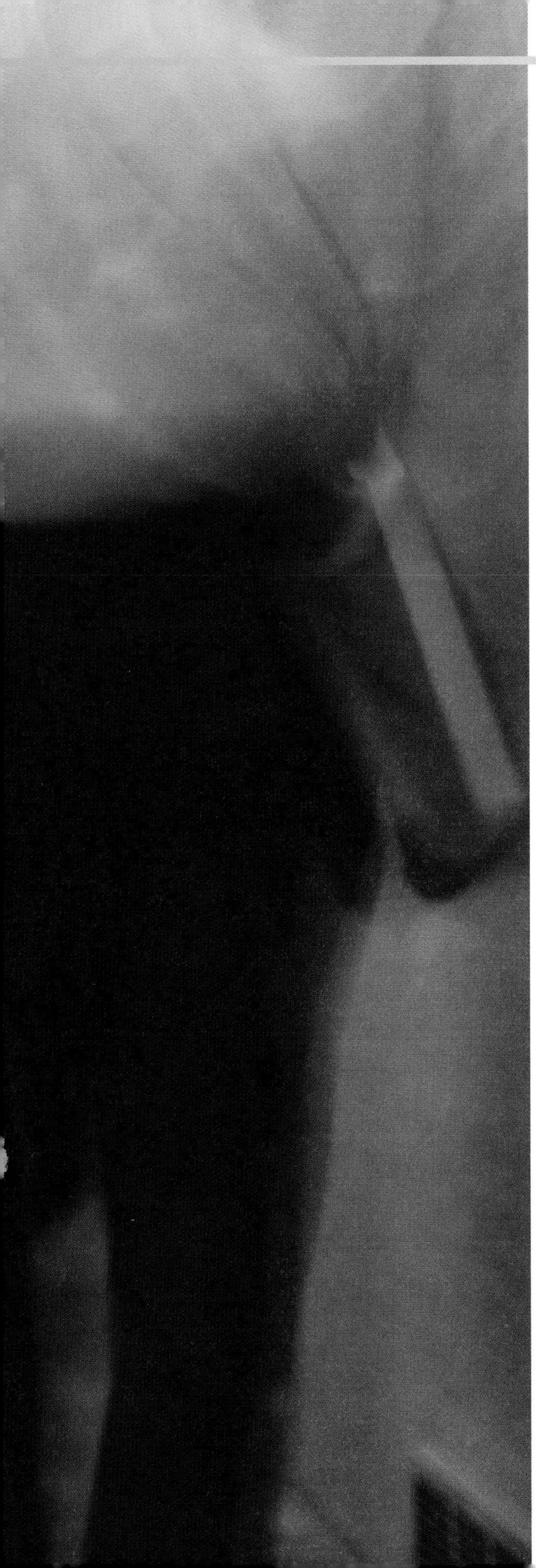

COMMUNICATION CLOSE-UP AT KENWOOD USA

www.kenwoodusa.com

When you try out the nonstop stream of new audio and video gadgets at your neighborhood electronics store, the last thing you're probably thinking about is business reports. However, if a particular set of features and functions catches your eye, chances are it owes its existence to a series of reports on marketing research.

For instance, Kenwood counts on reports from market specialist Dan Petersen, executive vice president, Consumer Electronics Sector at Kenwood USA, to help shape the features, functions, and appearance of next-wave products. Petersen and his team survey customers like you, monitor competitors, and track market trends—then they generate reports on all this information. These reports can contain anything from interviews with Kenwood dealers to hard numbers such as pricing statistics, all of which tell the designers what to include in upcoming products and how soon to jump on emerging trends.

Throughout 2002 and 2003, Petersen's team monitored the growth of new technologies in both terrestrial (ground-based transmission) and satellite radio in the U.S. market. Although fewer than 2 million drivers had satellite radio in

Kenwood's satellite car radio systems have been a hit with U.S. drivers, but the products would not have been successful without effective communication between the company's teams in the United States and Japan.

their cars at the time, Petersen knew from monitoring the consumer market that the technology was poised for growth and should be prominently featured in Kenwood's next generation of mobile audio products. However, adding the capability for improved terrestrial and satellite radio was not a simple matter: Kenwood had questions about competing satellite systems in the United States, acceptable pricing levels, auto dealer support, and other marketing issues. Petersen and his crew had to gather information on all these issues.

Thanks to frequent reports from market watchers like Petersen and regular communication with Japanese product designers, Kenwood managed to catch the terrrestrial radio trend and boost its sales. To make sure the information in the reports was interpreted correctly, Petersen and product developers made trans-Pacific trips and relied on teleconferences. "Communication is the key," says Petersen, "especially when you're dealing with somebody miles away who is from a different culture."[1]

CREATING EFFECTIVE REPORTS AND PROPOSALS

1 LEARNING OBJECTIVE

Explain the differences between informational reports and analytical reports

As with all business professionals, reports and proposals play a significant role in Dan Petersen's success. **Reports** are written factual accounts that objectively communicate information about some aspect of the business; **proposals** are a special category of reports that combine information delivery and persuasive communication. You'll encounter dozens of reports in all shapes and sizes throughout your career, but they all fall into three basic categories:

- **Informational reports** offer data, facts, feedback, and other types of information, without analysis or recommendations.
- **Analytical reports** offer both information and analysis, and they can also include recommendations.
- **Proposals** offer structured persuasion for internal or external audiences.

The purpose and content of business reports vary widely; in some cases you'll follow a strict guideline, but in others the organization and format will be up to you.

The nature of these reports will vary widely, depending on the circumstances surrounding them. Some of your reports will be voluntary, written at your own initiative and following the structure you find most effective. Other reports will be in response to a manager's or customer's request, and you may or may not receive guidance regarding the organization and content. You'll also write reports that follow strict, specific guidelines for content and layout, as with most reports that are required by government agencies. You may write some reports only once in your career; others you may write or update annually, monthly, weekly, or even daily.

Your audience will sometimes be internal, which gives you more freedom to discuss sensitive information with less regard for potential misinterpretation. At others times, your audience might include customers, investors, community members, or news media, any of which put additional demands on you as you present company information to these extrenal groups.

Finally, your reports will vary widely in length and complexity. You may write one-page reports that are simple, straightforward, and in memo format. Or you may write reports that cover complicated subjects, that run into hundreds or even thousands of pages, and that involve multiple writers and an array of technological tools.

No matter what the circumstances, these longer messages require all the skills and knowledge that you've gained throughout this course and will continue to gain on the job. Memos, e-mails, and other short messages will constitute most of your daily communication on the job, but writing reports and proposals is your chance to really shine.

Informational reports provide a solid foundation for many managerial discussions. The most effective reports present information in a logical, concise format and make it easy for management to locate needed facts without reading through the entire report.

Whatever your attitude has been toward school reports, try to view every business report as an opportunity to demonstrate your understanding of your audience's challenges and your ability to contribute to your organization's success.

APPLYING THE THREE-STEP WRITING PROCESS TO REPORTS AND PROPOSALS

2 LEARNING OBJECTIVE

Adapt the three-step writing process to reports and proposals

By carefully applying the three-step writing process (see Figure 12.1), you can reduce the time required to write effective reports and still produce documents that make a lasting and positive impression on your audience. The concepts are the same as those you explored in Chapters 4 to 6 and applied to shorter messages in Chapters 7 to 9; however, the emphasis on various substeps can vary considerably. For instance, the planning step alone can take days or weeks for a complex report or proposal.

Part 5 offers in-depth coverage of the three-step writing process for reports and proposals. This chapter discusses planning, Chapter 13 discusses writing, and Chapter 14 covers completing reports and proposals. Because much of the writing process is already covered in Chapters 4 to 6, Chapters 12 to 14 focus on those aspects that are unique to, or that require special attention for, longer messages.

Analyzing the Situation

The complexity of most reports and the magnitude of the work involved heighten the need to carefully analyze the situation. With an e-mail or other short message, you can change direction halfway through the first draft and perhaps lose only a few minutes of work. In contrast, if you change direction halfway through a major report, you could lose weeks or

FIGURE 12.1 Adapting the Three-Step Writing Process for Reports and Proposals

Plan

Analyze the Situation
Clarify the problem or opportunity at hand, define your purpose, develop an audience profile, and develop a work plan.

Gather Information
Determine audience needs and obtain the information necessary to satisfy those needs; conduct a research project if necessary.

Select the Right Medium
Choose the best medium for delivering your message; consider delivery through multiple media.

Organize the Information
Define your main idea, limit your scope, select a direct or an indirect approach, and outline your content using one of the models available for informational reports, analytical reports, or proposals.

1

Write

Adapt to Your Audience
Be sensitive to audience needs with a "you" attitude, politeness, positive emphasis, and bias-free language. Build a strong relationship with your audience by establishing your credibility and projecting your company's image. Control your style with a tone and voice appropriate to the situation.

Compose the Message
Choose strong words that will help you create effective sentences and coherent paragraphs throughout the introduction, body, and close of your report or proposal.

2

Complete

Revise the Message
Evaluate content and review readability; then edit and rewrite for conciseness and clarity.

Produce the Message
Use effective design elements and suitable layout for a clean, professional appearance; seamlessly combine textual and graphical elements.

Proofread the Message
Review for errors in layout, spelling, and mechanics.

Distribute the Message
Deliver your message using the chosen medium; make sure all documents and all relevant files are distributed successfully.

3

even months. To minimize the chances of wasting time, energy, and opportunities, pay special attention to your statement of purpose. In addition, for anything beyond the simplest reports, take the time to prepare a work plan before you start writing.

Defining Your Purpose

Informational reports often address a predetermined need and must meet specific audience expectations. For example, you may be asked to write reports that verify your company's compliance with government regulations (including dozens of different tax forms), that summarize sales, or that monitor a process—all of which have audiences who expect certain information in a certain format. You may also be asked to write other informational reports that require you to examine both audience needs and your own needs before defining the optimum purpose.

Analytical reports and proposals are almost always written in response to a perceived problem or a perceived opportunity. A clear statement of this problem or opportunity helps frame the communication challenge by identifying *what* you're going to write about, but it's insufficient to guide your writing efforts. To plan effectively, address the problem or opportunity with a clear **statement of purpose** that defines *why* you are preparing the report (see Table 12.1).

Given the length and complexity of many reports, it's crucial to define your purpose clearly so you don't waste time with unnecessary rework.

The most useful way to phrase your purpose statement is to begin with an infinitive phrase (*to* plus a verb). Using an infinitive phrase encourages you to take control and decide where you're going before you begin. When you choose an infinitive phrase (*to inform, to confirm, to analyze, to persuade, to recommend),* you pin down your general goal in preparing the report. For instance, in an informational report, your statement of purpose can be as simple as these:

To update clients on the progress of the research project (progress report)

To develop goals and objectives for the coming year (strategic plan)

To identify customers and explain how the company will service them (marketing plan)

To submit monthly sales statistics to management (operating report)

To summarize what occurred at the annual sales conference (personal activity report)

To explain building access procedures (policy implementation report)

To submit required information to the Securities and Exchange Commission (compliance report)

Longer reports may have several related purposes.

Your statement of purpose for an analytical report often needs to be more comprehensive than one for an informational report. Linda Moreno, the cost accounting manager for

TABLE 12.1 Problem Statements Versus Purpose Statements

PROBLEM STATEMENT	STATEMENT OF PURPOSE
Our company's market share is steadily declining.	To explore different ways of selling our products and to recommend the ones that will most likely increase our market share.
Our current computer network system is inefficient and cannot be upgraded to meet our future needs.	To analyze various computer network systems and to recommend the system that will best meet our company's current and future needs.
We need $2 million to launch our new product.	To convince investors that our new business would be a sound investment so that we can obtain desired financing.
Our current operations are too decentralized and expensive.	To justify the closing of the Newark plant and the transfer of East Coast operations to a single Midwest location in order to save the company money.

Electrovision, a high-tech company based in Los Gatos, California, was recently asked to find ways of reducing employee travel and entertainment costs (her complete report appears in Chapter 14). Because Moreno was supposed to suggest specific ways to solve a problem, she phrased her statement of purpose accordingly:

> . . . to analyze the T&E [travel and entertainment] budget, evaluate the impact of recent changes in airfares and hotel costs, and suggest ways to tighten management's control over T&E expenses.

If Moreno had been assigned an informational report instead, she might have stated her purpose differently:

> To summarize Electrovision's spending on travel and entertainment.

You can see from these two examples how much influence the purpose statement has on the scope of your report. If Moreno's manager had expected her to suggest ways to reduce costs but Moreno had collected only cost data, her report would have failed to meet expectations. Because she was assigned an analytical report rather than an informational report, Moreno had to go beyond merely collecting data; she had to draw conclusions and make recommendations.

Proposals must also be guided by a clear statement of purpose to help you focus on crafting a persuasive message. Here are several examples of internal and external proposals:

> To secure funding in next year's capital budget for a new conveyor system in the warehouse (funding proposal)
>
> To get management approval to reorganize the North American sales force (general project proposal)
>
> To secure $2 million in venture capital funding to complete design and production of the new titanium mountain bike (investment proposal)
>
> To convince CommuniCo to purchase a trial subscription to our latest database offering (sales proposal)

Remember, the more specific your purpose statement, the more useful it will be as a guide to planning your report. Furthermore, always double-check your statement of purpose with the person who authorized the report. Seeing the purpose written down in black and white, the authorizer may decide that the report needs to go in a different direction. Once your statement of purpose is confirmed, you're ready to prepare your work plan.

Preparing Your Work Plan

3 LEARNING OBJECTIVE

Explain the value of a work plan in the development of long reports

You're probably accustomed to some schedule pressure with school reports. This is good practice for your business career, when you'll be expected to produce quality reports quickly and efficiently. A carefully thought-out work plan is the best way to make sure you produce good work on schedule. By identifying all the tasks that must be performed, you ensure that nothing is overlooked.

If you are preparing the work plan for yourself, it can be relatively informal: a simple list of the steps you plan to take and an estimate of their sequence and timing. If you're conducting a lengthy, formal study, however, you'll want to develop a detailed work plan that can guide the performance of many tasks over a span of time. For consultants and others whose work output is a formal report, the work plan can become the basis for a contract if the proposal is accepted. A formal work plan might include the following elements (especially the first two):

A detailed work plan saves time and often produces more effective reports.

- **Statement of the problem or opportunity.** The problem statement clarifies the challenge you face, helps you (and anyone working with you) stay focused on the core issues, and helps everyone avoid the distractions that are likely to arise during report preparation.
- **Statement of the purpose and scope of your investigation.** The purpose statement describes what you plan to accomplish with this report and thus the boundaries of

your work. Stating which subjects you will cover and which you won't is especially important for complex, lengthy investigations.

- **Discussion of tasks to be accomplished.** Be sure to indicate your sources of information, the research necessary, and any constraints on time, money, personnel, or data. For simple reports, the list of tasks to be accomplished will be short and probably obvious. However, longer reports and complex investigations require an exhaustive list so that you can reserve time with customers, with executives, or for outside services such as pollsters or print shops.
- **Description of any products that will result from your investigation.** In many cases, the only product of your efforts will be the report itself. In other cases, you'll need to produce something beyond a report, perhaps a new marketing plan or even a tangible product. Make these expectations clear at the outset, and be sure to schedule enough time and resources to get the job done.
- **Review of project assignments, schedules, and resource requirements.** Indicate who will be responsible for what, when tasks will be completed, and how much the investigation will cost. If more than one person will be involved, you may also want to include a brief section on coordinating report writing and production. (Collaborative writing is discussed in detail in Chapter 2.)
- **Plans for following up after delivering the report.** Follow-up can be as simple as making sure people received the information they need or as complex as conducting additional research to evaluate the results of proposals included in your report. Even informal follow-up can help you improve your future reports and communicate that you care about your work's effectiveness and its impact on the organization.
- **Working outline.** Some work plans include a tentative outline of the report, as does the plan in Figure 12.2. This plan was developed for a report on whether to launch a company newsletter.

Communication Solution

Market researchers at Kenwood USA gather information from a wide variety of sources, including one-on-one interviews, surveys, anecdotal feedback from consumers and retailers, industry publications, and competitors' marketing materials.

Gathering Information

Some reports require formal research projects in order to gather all the necessary information.

The sheer volume of information in most reports and proposals requires careful planning—and may even require a separate research project just to acquire the data and information you need. To stay on schedule and on budget, be sure that you review both your statement of purpose and your audience's needs so that you collect all the information you need—and only the information you need. In some cases, you wont' be able to collect every piece of information you'd like, so prioritize your needs up front and focus on the most important questions. Experienced writers also try to avoid duplication of effort by using templates and boilerplate material whenever possible (not only for gathering information but also for writing).

Selecting the Right Medium

The best medium for a given report might be anything from a formal printed and bound document to an executive dashboard.

Expect to deliver many or most of your reports in electronic format.

Just as you would for other business messages, select the medium for your report based on the needs of your audience and the practical advantages and disadvantages of the choices available to you. In addition to the general media selection criteria discussed in Chapter 4, consider several points for reports and proposals. Start with what you know about audience expectations. For many reports and proposals, audiences have specific media requirements, and you might not have a choice. For instance, most government tax forms must be delivered on paper, although electronic filing (which delivers the same information as a paper form) is offered more and more often today. Conversely, executives in many corporations now expect to review reports via their in-house intranets, sometimes in conjunction with an *executive dashboard*, a customized online presentation of key operating variables such as revenue, profits, quality, customer satisfaction, and project progress.

Communication Solution

Dan Petersen knows that even the best-written reports can often benefit from in-person communication, so Kenwood employees in the United States and Japan discuss their reports frequently, via both teleconferences and meetings in both countries.

In other cases, your audience might be more flexible but still have preferences. If an audience of several managers is likely to make comments on your report, would they rather write on a paper copy or use the revision features in a word processor file? Will you or someone else be revising or updating the report? Given the multiple benefits of electronic reports (including low distribution costs, searchability, and easy archiving), expect to deliver many or even most of your reports in electronic format in the future.

FIGURE 12.2 Effective Work Plan for a Formal Study

STATEMENT OF THE PROBLEM
The rapid growth of our company over the past five years has reduced the sense of community among our staff. People no longer feel like part of an intimate organization where they matter as individuals.

States the problem clearly enough for anyone to understand without background research

PURPOSE AND SCOPE OF WORK
The purpose of this study is to determine whether a company newsletter would help rebuild employee identification with the organization. The study will evaluate the impact of newsletters in other companies and will attempt to identify features that might be desirable in our own newsletter. Such variables as length, frequency of distribution, types of articles, and graphic design will be considered. Costs will be estimated for several approaches. In addition, the study will analyze the personnel and the procedures required to produce a newsletter.

Lays out the tasks to be accomplished and does so in clear, simple terms

Delineates exactly what will be covered in the report

SOURCES AND METHODS OF DATA COLLECTION
Sample newsletters will be collected from 50 companies similar to ours in size, growth rate, and types of employees. The editors will be asked to comment on the impact of their publications on employee morale. Our own employees will be surveyed to determine their interest in a newsletter and their preferences for specific features. Production procedures and costs will be analyzed through conversations with newsletter editors and printers.

PRELIMINARY OUTLINE
The preliminary outline for this study is as follows:

I. Do newsletters affect morale?
   A. Do people read them?
   B. How do employees benefit?
   C. How does the company benefit?
II. What are the features of good newsletters?
   A. How long are they?
   B. What do they contain?
   C. How often are they published?
   D. How are they designed?
III. How should a newsletter be produced?
   A. Should it be written, edited, and printed internally?
   B. Should it be written internally and printed outside?
   C. Should it be totally produced outside?
IV. What would a newsletter cost?
   A. What would the personnel cost be?
   B. What would the materials costs be?
   C. What would outside services cost?
V. Should we publish a company newsletter?
VI. If so, what approach should we take?

Presents preliminary outline for guidance, even though no description of the end product is included

WORK PLAN
Each phase of this study will be completed by the following dates:

Collect/analyze newsletters	September 3 to September 14, 2005
Interview editors by phone	September 16 to September 20, 2005
Survey employees	September 23 to September 27, 2005
Develop sample	September 30 to October 7, 2005
Develop cost estimates	October 8 to October 11, 2005
Prepare report	October 14 to October 25, 2005
Submit final report	October 28, 2005

States the assignments and the schedules for completing them

Consider delivering your report via multiple media, too. You might provide a report both in hardcopy format for easy reading and in electronic format for logging into a knowledge management system. Similarly, you might be able to (or be asked to) deliver an oral presentation that covers the highlights of your written proposal. Again, the decision comes down to a balance of what's best for both you and your audience.

Whatever you decide, bear in mind that your choice of media also sends a message. A proposal that requests a venture capital investment of $5 million would look unimpressive as just a plain, coarsely formatted word processor document that could have been churned out on a manual typewriter. Conversely, a routine sales report dressed up in expensive multimedia will look like a waste of valuable company resources.

Organizing Your Information

The length and complexity of most reports and proposals require extra emphasis on clear, reader-oriented organization. Your readers might have the patience to struggle through a

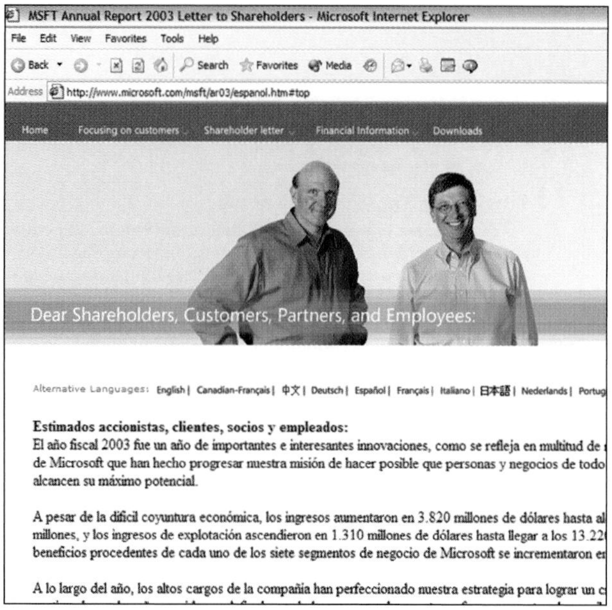

Global companies often post business reports on the web. Microsoft's annual report is prepared for investors and posted on the company's website in 11 languages (including French for Canadian readers and Portuguese for Brazilian readers). Readers simply click on the link for the language they want—and then read the report (see www.microsoft.com).

Most business reports use a direct approach.

disorganized e-mail message, but not through a poorly organized 200-page report. As discussed in Chapter 5, when an audience is considered either receptive or open-minded, use the direct approach: Lead off with a summary of your key findings, conclusions, recommendations, or proposal, as the case may be. This "up-front" arrangement is by far the most popular and convenient for business reports. It saves time and makes the rest of the report easier to follow. For those who have questions or want more information, later parts of the report provide complete findings and supporting details. The direct approach also produces a more forceful report. You sound sure of yourself when you state your conclusions confidently at the outset.

Use the indirect approach when you need to build support for your main idea or you want to avoid coming across as arrogant.

At times, however, confidence may be misconstrued as arrogance. If you're a junior member of a status-conscious organization or if your audience is skeptical or hostile, you may want to use the indirect approach: Introduce your complete findings and discuss all supporting details before presenting your conclusions and recommendations. The indirect approach gives you a chance to prove your points and gradually overcome your audience's reservations. By deferring the conclusions and recommendations to the end of your report, you imply that you've weighed the evidence objectively without prejudging the facts. You also imply that you're subordinating your judgment to that of the audience, whose members are capable of drawing their own conclusions when they have access to all the facts.

Although the indirect approach has its advantages, some readers will always be in a hurry to get to the answer and will immediately flip to the recommendations anyway, thus defeating your purpose. Therefore, consider length before choosing the direct or indirect approach. In general, the longer the message, the less effective an indirect approach is likely to be. Furthermore, an indirect argument is harder to follow than a direct one.

Long reports sometimes combine direct and indirect approaches, building support for interim conclusions or recommendations along the way.

Because both direct and indirect approaches have merit, businesspeople often combine them. They reveal their conclusions and recommendations as they go along, rather than putting them either first or last. Figure 12.3 presents the introductions from two reports with the same general outline. In the direct version, a series of statements summarizes the conclusion reached in relation to each main topic on the outline. In the indirect version, the same topics are introduced in the same order but without drawing any conclusions about them. Instead, the conclusions appear within the body of the report. Would you say that this second report is direct or indirect? Business reports are often difficult to classify.

Regardless of the format, length, or order of your report, you must still decide how your ideas will be subdivided and developed. Suppose you're writing a controversial report recommending that your company revise its policy on who reports to whom. You know that some of your readers will object to your ideas, so you decide to use indirect order, but how do you develop your argument? Your job is to choose the most logical

THE DIRECT APPROACH

Since the company's founding 25 years ago, we have provided regular repair service for all our electric appliances. This service has been an important selling point as well as a source of pride for our employees. However, we are paying a high price for our image. Last year, we lost $500,000 on our repair business.

Because of your concern over these losses, you have asked me to study the pros and cons of discontinuing our repair service. With the help of John Hudson and Susan Lefkowitz, I have studied the issue for the past two weeks and have come to the conclusion that we have been embracing an expensive, impractical tradition.

By withdrawing from the electric appliance repair business, we can substantially improve our financial performance without damaging our reputation with customers. This conclusion is based on three basic points that are covered in the following pages:

- It is highly unlikely that we will ever be able to make a profit in the repair business.
- Sevice is no longer an important selling point with customers.
- Closing down the service operation will create few internal problems.

THE INDIRECT APPROACH

Since the company's founding 25 years ago, we have provided repair service for all our electric appliances. This service has been an important selling point as well as a source of pride for our employees. However, the repair business itself has consistently lost money.

Because of your concern over these losses, you have asked me to study the pros and cons of discontinuing our repair service. With the help of John Hudson and Susan Lefkowitz, I have studied the issue for the past two weeks. The following pages present my findings for your review. Three basic questions are addressed:

- What is the extent of our losses, and what can we do to turn the business around?
- Would withdrawal hurt our sales of electrical appliances?
- What would be the internal repercussions of closing down the repair business?

FIGURE 12.3
Direct Approach Versus Indirect Approach in an Introduction

argument structure—the one that suits your topic and goals and that makes the most sense to your audience.

However you structure your argument, keep the following points in mind when organizing your report or proposal:

Audience expectations are one of the most important considerations when deciding on the organization of your report.

- **Understand and meet audience expectations.** Certain audiences expect (or even require) a specific organization, and your report might be rejected if it doesn't meet those requirements. Other audiences leave you room for some flexibility, as long as your report contains the right categories of information. Whenever possible, study an example of a successful report before writing a similar one. Such models will give you a feel not only for organization but also for content, emphasis, and tone.
- **Select a format that's appropriate to the task.** For reports of five pages or less, a memo (for internal audiences) or letter (for external audiences) is often sufficient. For longer reports, you'll want to include many of the elements of a formal report (see Chapter 14).
- **Keep it as short as possible.** Resist the temptation to load up your report with all the information you collect during the research phase. Reports place enough burden on busy readers already; don't make the task harder by including unnecessary information or inconsequential details. Your readers will appreciate your brevity, and you'll stand a better chance of getting your message across.
- **"Talk" your way through your outline.** When you outline your content, use informative ("talking") headings rather than simple descriptive ("topical") headings (see Table 12.2). When in question or summary form, informative headings force you to really think through the content, rather than simply identifying the general topic area. Using informative headings will not only help you plan more effectively but also will facilitate collaborative writing. A heading such as "Industry characteristics" could mean five different things to the five people on your writing team, so use a heading that conveys a single, unambiguous meaning, such as "Flour milling is a mature industry."

For a quick review of adapting the three-step process to long reports, refer to "Checklist: Adapting the Three-Step Writing Process to Informational and Analytical Reports." The following sections provide specific advice on how to plan informational reports, analytical reports, and proposals.

TABLE 12.2 Types of Outline Headings

DESCRIPTIVE (TOPICAL) OUTLINE	INFORMATIVE (TALKING) OUTLINE	
	QUESTION FORM	SUMMARY FORM
I. Industry Characteristics	I. What is the nature of the industry?	I. Flour milling is a mature industry.
A. Annual sales	A. What are the annual sales?	A. Market is large.
B. Profitability	B. Is the industry profitable?	B. Profit margins are narrow.
C. Growth rate	C. What is the pattern of growth?	C. Growth is modest.
1. Sales	1. Sales growth?	1. Sales growth averages less than 3 percent a year.
2. Profit	2. Profit growth?	2. Growth in profits is flat.

PLANNING INFORMATIONAL REPORTS

Informational reports provide the information that employees, managers, and others need in order to make decisions, take action, and respond to dynamic conditions both inside and outside the organization. Although there are dozens of particular formats for informational reports, they can be grouped into four general categories:

4 LEARNING OBJECTIVE

Describe the four major categories of informational reports and provide examples of each

- **Reports to monitor and control operations.** Just as doctors rely on medical reports to see how well the various systems in a patient's body are functioning, business managers rely on a wide range of reports to see how well the various systems inside their companies are functioning. *Plans* establish expectations and guidelines to direct future action. Plans can range from narrowly focused tactical plans covering short periods to high-level strategic plans that direct organizational activities over the course of several years. *Operating reports* provide feedback on a wide variety of an organization's functions, including sales, inventories, expenses, shipments, and so on. In many cases, operating reports are generated automatically by management information systems (MIS), which collect and disseminate operational data. *Personal activity reports* provide information regarding an individual's experiences during sales calls, industry conferences, market research trips, and so on. Managers frequently rely on individual employees to be the "eyes and ears" of the organization and to share what they've learned.

CHECKLIST: Adapting the Three-Step Writing Process to Informational and Analytical Reports

A. ANALYZE THE SITUATION
- Clearly define your purpose before you start writing.
- If you need to accomplish several goals in the report, identify all of them in advance.
- Prepare a work plan to guide your efforts.

B. GATHER INFORMATION
- Determine whether you need to launch a separate research project to collect the necessary information.
- Reuse or adapt existing material whenever possible.

C. SELECT THE RIGHT MEDIUM
- Base your decision on audience expectations (or requirements, as the case may be).
- Consider the need for commenting, revising, distributing, and storing.
- Remember that the medium you choose also sends a message.

D. ORGANIZE YOUR INFORMATION
- Use a direct approach if your audience is receptive.
- Use an indirect approach if your audience is skeptical.
- Use an indirect approach when you don't want to risk coming across as arrogant.
- Combine approaches if that will help build support for your primary message.

FIGURE 12.4 The Rich Variety of Reports and Proposals

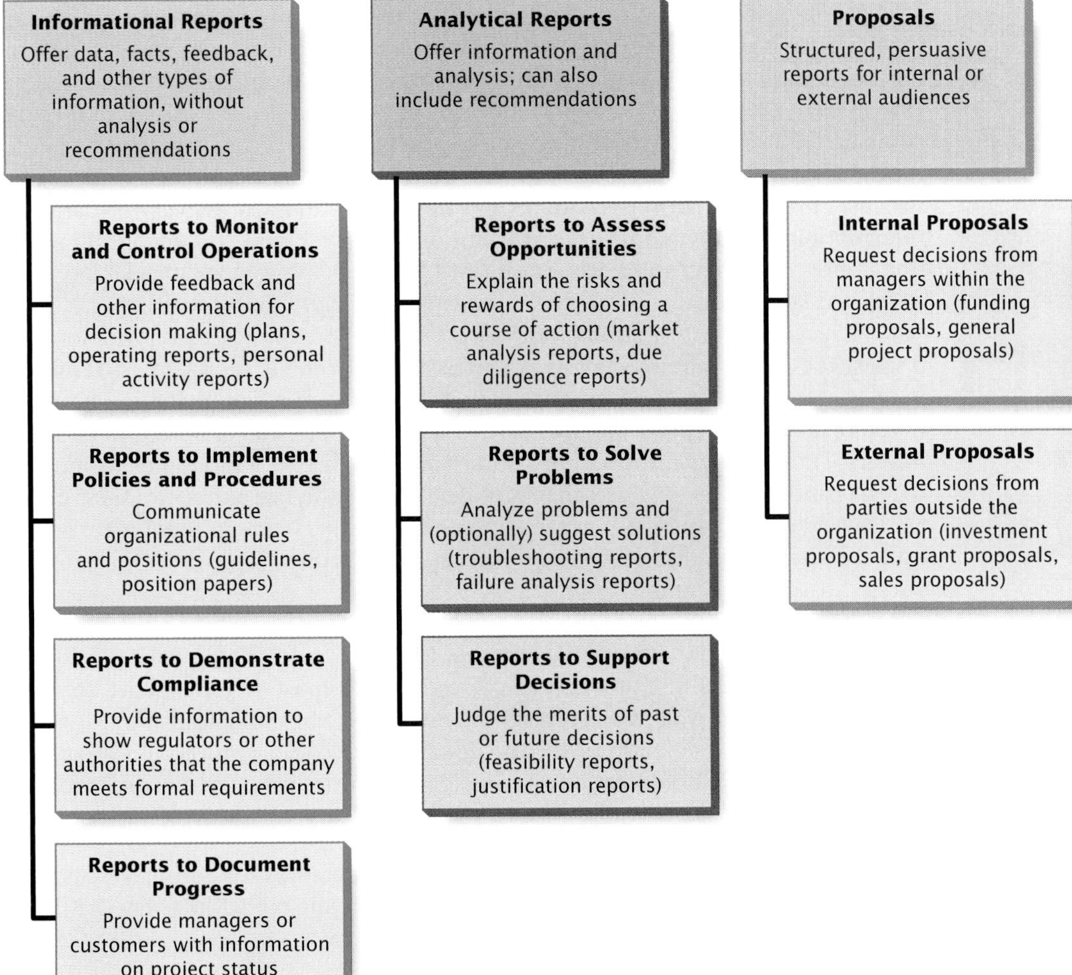

- **Reports to implement policies and procedures.** Reports are the most common vehicle for conveying guidelines, approved procedures, and other organizational decisions. In some cases, you may write *policy reports* that are as short as a page or two, such as to share a new procedure with your colleagues. In other cases, the report might be a handbook or policy manual that runs dozens or even hundreds of pages. *Position papers* are a special type of policy report that outlines an individual executive's (or the entire organization's) official position on issues that affect a company's success.
- **Reports to demonstrate compliance.** Even the smallest businesses are required to show that they are in compliance with government regulations of one sort or another. Some compliance reports, such as quarterly and annual tax reports, affect all businesses. Others concern particular industries, companies using hazardous materials, specific professional functions, or other special factors. Compliance reports are usually distributed in preprinted formats that must be followed precisely.
- **Reports to document progress.** Supervisors, investors, and customers frequently expect to be informed of the progress of projects and other activities. Progress reports range from simple updates in memo form to comprehensive reports that include such elements as measured progress toward goals, comparisons of budgeted versus actual expenses, and lists of ongoing concerns and risks.

Informational reports are used to monitor and control operations, to implement policies and procedures, to demonstrate compliance, and to document progress.

Figure 12.4 shows the major subcategories within each of the three major report categories, along with examples of the more common types. Specific titles may change depending on the company you're with, but chances are you'll be called upon to read nearly every one of these report types—and to write many of them, too.

At FedEx, reports of all kinds are used to track both system and employee performance, as well as to assemble information needed for making managerial decisions. Not only does CEO Frederick Smith read innumerable reports, he wrote a famous one in college, which detailed the idea of his air express delivery service and persuaded investors to fund him.

Organizational Strategies for Informational Reports

You can probably sense from the preceding list that informational reports can include extremely positive reports (such as a report on great sales results), neutral reports (a monitoring report that shows business as usual on the factory floor), and extremely negative reports (a report on customer satisfaction research that ranks the company quite poorly). Given the range of possibilities, the choice of direct or indirect approach warrants serious consideration before you start outlining in earnest. Because informational reports focus on the straightforward delivery of data and information, the direct approach is common. However, you will encounter situations when an indirect approach is more effective, such as when you need to build up a series of facts to help your readers understand the main idea of your report.

In one sense, informational reports are the least complicated reports to write because they don't require analysis or persuasion. Your job is simply to deliver information in an effective and efficient manner. However, that simplicity doesn't mean that informational reports are necessarily easy to prepare. You still need to evaluate, process, and organize information—sometimes hundreds or thousands of individual facts and figures—in a way that appeals to your audience and meets their needs. Moreover, because you're not expected to analyze or persuade in these reports, take care to remain objective throughout—a challenge if you're reporting on something you feel passionately about.

The messages conveyed by informational reports can range from extremely positive to extremely negative, so the approach you take warrants careful consideration.

When writing an informational report, you can let the nature of whatever you're describing dictate your structure. For example, if you're describing a manufacturing process, each stage in the process can correspond to a part of your report. If you're describing an event, you can approach the discussion chronologically. And if you're explaining how to do something, you can describe the steps in a process. Informational reports use a **topical organization**, arranging material according to one of the following topics:

A topical organization is built around the content itself, using such arrangements as comparison, importance, sequence, chronology, spatial orientation, geography, or category.

- **Comparison.** If you need to show similarities and differences (or advantages and disadvantages) between two or more entities, organize your report in a way that helps your readers see those similarities and differences clearly.
- **Importance.** If you're reviewing five product lines, you might organize your study according to the sales for each product line, beginning with the line that produces the most revenue and proceeding to the one that produces the least.
- **Sequence.** If you're studying a process, discuss it step by step—1, 2, 3, and so on.
- **Chronology.** When investigating a chain of events, organize the study according to what happened in January, what happened in February, and so on.
- **Spatial orientation.** If you're explaining how a physical object works or a physical space looks, describe it from left to right (or right to left in some cultures), top to bottom, or outside to inside—in whatever order makes the most sense; just be consistent.
- **Geography.** If location is important, organize your study according to geography, perhaps by region of the United States or by area of a city.
- **Category.** If you're asked to review several distinct aspects of a subject, look at one category at a time, such as sales, profit, cost, or investment.

Whichever pattern you choose, use it consistently so that readers can easily follow your discussion from start to finish. Of course, certain reports (such as compliance or monitor-and-control reports) must follow a prescribed flow. In such cases, you won't have the option of organizing information according to your own designs.

DOCUMENT MAKEOVER

IMPROVE THIS REPORT

To practice correcting drafts of actual documents, visit www.prenhall.com/onekey on the web. Click "Document Makeovers" then click Chapter 12. You will find an informational report that contains problems and errors relating to what you've learned in this chapter about planning business reports and proposals. Use the Final Draft decision tool to create an improved version of this report. Check the message for parallel construction, appropriate headings, suitable content, positive and bias-free language, and use of the "you" attitude.

Effective Informational Reports: An Example

Strong organization is only part of what makes informational reports effective. They must also be audience-

FIGURE 12.5 Ineffective Informational Report

MEMO

TO: Jeff Black and HR staff **DATE:** March 14, 2005
FROM: Carrie Andrews **SUBJECT:** Recruiting and hiring seminar

Last week I attended an American Management Association seminar on recruiting, screening, and hiring new employees. I got enough useful information to warrant updating our online personnel handbook and perhaps developing a quick training session for all interviewing teams to avoid some of the stupid mistakes we've made in the past. Here's a quick look at the things I learned.

We should avoid legal mistakes, screen and interview applicants more effectively, and measure applicants more accurately. We need to write recruiting ads that accurately portray job openings and that don't discriminate. We need to sort through résumés more efficiently, while still looking for telltale signs of false information. And we need more information on which types of preemployment tests are most effective.

I learned how best to comply with the Americans with Disabilities Act and how to use an employment agency effectively and safely (without risk of legal entanglements). The conference also covered how to screen and interview applicants more effectively, how to avoid interview questions that could get us into legal trouble, and when and how to check criminal records. In addition, I learned which drug-testing issues and recommendations affect us.

As you can see, the seminar addressed a lot of important information. I attended six sessions in all to gather exactly the information we needed. We covered the basic guidelines for much of this already, but a number of specific recommendations and legal concepts should be emphasized. Also, over the four-day conference, I attended three workshop lunches that addressed specific applications for much of what was presented during the regular sessions. I was amazed by the valuable information I received in addition to the cruise-ship-style buffet lunches. The food was fantastic.

It will take me a couple of weeks to get the personnel handbook updated, but we don't have any immediate hiring plans anyway. Contact me if you need any information before then. Everyone will have a lot to review to get up to speed. Also, we have a lot of new information that may well affect our need to train the interviewing team members.

Please don't hesitate to e-mail me or drop by for a chat.

Fails to state why Andrews attended the seminar

Does nothing to help readers focus on what is important

Fails to present pertinent material in a way that would be meaningful and useful to readers

Injects inappropriate personal opinion and criticism

Uses running text instead of bullets, making it difficult for readers to easily identify the new knowledge

Wastes time on some unimportant activities, such as how many sessions were offered during the seminar and what the lunches were like

centered, logical, focused, and easy to follow, with generous use of previews and summaries. They are complete, without being unnecessarily long or detailed. One of the tasks your audience expects you to do is to sort out the details and separate major points from minor points. In other words, readers expect you to put in all the thought and effort it takes to make the best use of their time. In addition, effective reports are honest and objective, but without being unduly harsh whenever negative information must be conveyed.

Compare the two versions of Carrie Andrews's personal activity report in Figures 12.5 and 12.6. At a quick glance, Figure 12.5 may seem to do a good job of meeting audience needs, but this report has a number of weaknesses that distract from the writer's intent and make readers work too hard to extract the main points.

PLANNING ANALYTICAL REPORTS

The purpose of analytical reports is to analyze, to understand, to explain—to think through a problem or an opportunity and figure out how it affects the company and how the company should respond. In many cases, you'll also be expected to make a recommendation

FIGURE 12.6 Effective Informational Report

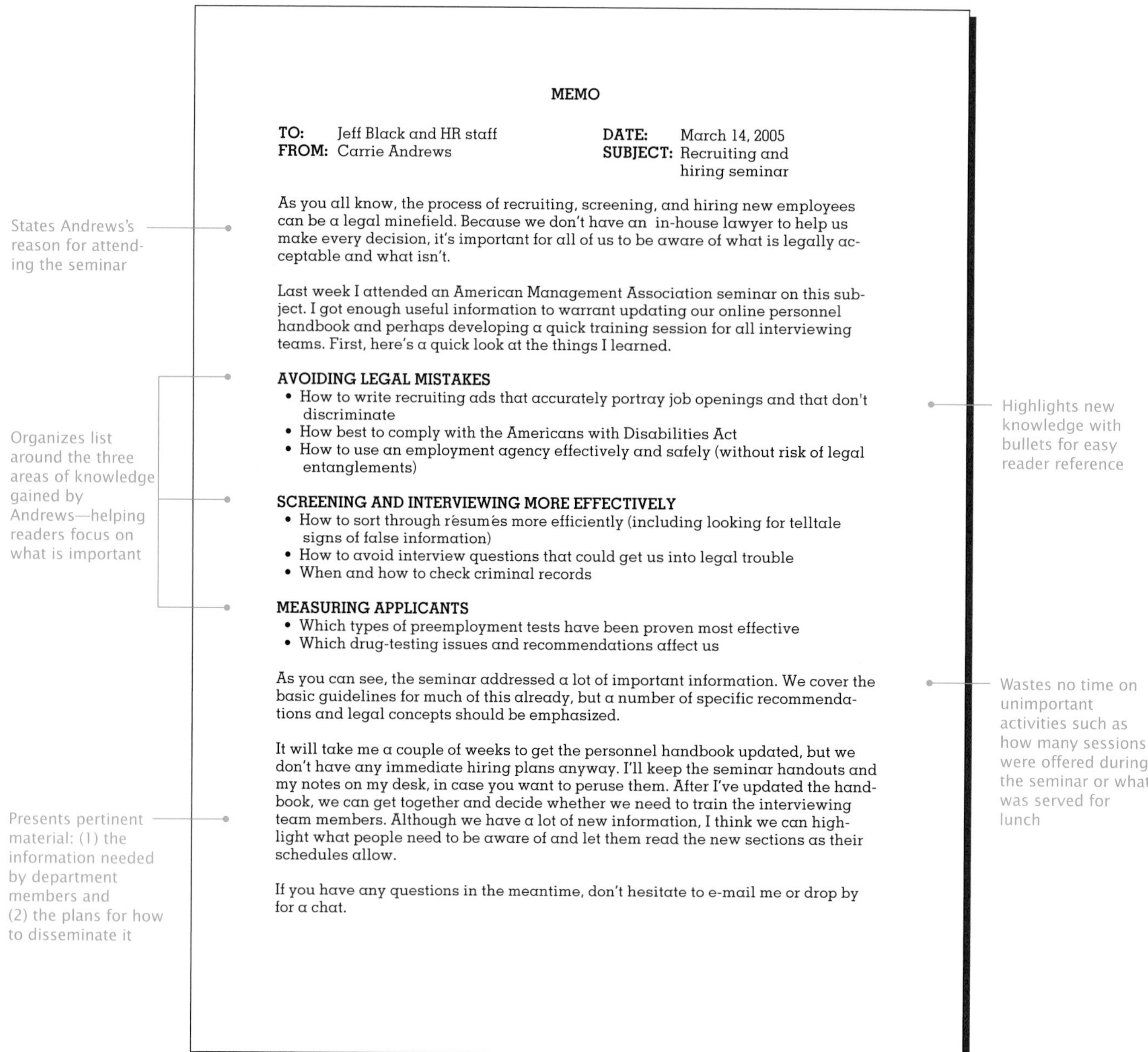

MEMO

TO: Jeff Black and HR staff
FROM: Carrie Andrews
DATE: March 14, 2005
SUBJECT: Recruiting and hiring seminar

As you all know, the process of recruiting, screening, and hiring new employees can be a legal minefield. Because we don't have an in-house lawyer to help us make every decision, it's important for all of us to be aware of what is legally acceptable and what isn't.

Last week I attended an American Management Association seminar on this subject. I got enough useful information to warrant updating our online personnel handbook and perhaps developing a quick training session for all interviewing teams. First, here's a quick look at the things I learned.

AVOIDING LEGAL MISTAKES
- How to write recruiting ads that accurately portray job openings and that don't discriminate
- How best to comply with the Americans with Disabilities Act
- How to use an employment agency effectively and safely (without risk of legal entanglements)

SCREENING AND INTERVIEWING MORE EFFECTIVELY
- How to sort through résumés more efficiently (including looking for telltale signs of false information)
- How to avoid interview questions that could get us into legal trouble
- When and how to check criminal records

MEASURING APPLICANTS
- Which types of preemployment tests have been proven most effective
- Which drug-testing issues and recommendations affect us

As you can see, the seminar addressed a lot of important information. We cover the basic guidelines for much of this already, but a number of specific recommendations and legal concepts should be emphasized.

It will take me a couple of weeks to get the personnel handbook updated, but we don't have any immediate hiring plans anyway. I'll keep the seminar handouts and my notes on my desk, in case you want to peruse them. After I've updated the handbook, we can get together and decide whether we need to train the interviewing team members. Although we have a lot of new information, I think we can highlight what people need to be aware of and let them read the new sections as their schedules allow.

If you have any questions in the meantime, don't hesitate to e-mail me or drop by for a chat.

States Andrews's reason for attending the seminar
Organizes list around the three areas of knowledge gained by Andrews—helping readers focus on what is important
Presents pertinent material: (1) the information needed by department members and (2) the plans for how to disseminate it
Highlights new knowledge with bullets for easy reader reference
Wastes no time on unimportant activities such as how many sessions were offered during the seminar or what was served for lunch

5 LEARNING OBJECTIVE

Describe the three major categories of analytical reports and provide examples of each

based on your analysis. As you saw in Figure 12.4 on page 369, analytical reports fall into three basic categories:

- **Reports to assess opportunities.** Every business opportunity carries some degree of risk and also requires a variety of decisions and actions in order to capitalize on the opportunity. You can use analytical reports to assess both risk and required decisions and actions. For instance, *market analysis reports* are used to judge the likelihood of success for new products or sales initiatives by suggesting potential opportunities in a given market and identifying competitive threats and other risks. *Due diligence reports* examine the financial aspects of a proposed decision, such as acquiring another company.
- **Reports to solve problems.** Managers often assign *troubleshooting reports* when they need to understand why something isn't working properly, from malfunctioning industrial processes to financial disappointments, and what needs to be done to fix it.

Communication Miscues

Suspect Reports Damage Wall Street Reputations

As the stock market soared in the late 1990s, wildly optimistic reports about new stock offerings provided a lot of fuel for the fire. However, when the market fell, the decline was led by many of the companies that had been touted in these enthusiastic reports—including some high-profile telecommunications and Internet companies. Some even went bankrupt. From pension funds to individual nest eggs, the financial devastation hit deep and hard.

Eliot Spitzer, the attorney general of New York State, was among those asking how this situation could possibly happen. Were those rosy reports misleading? And if so, was the deception intentional? His targets of investigation were some of the biggest names on Wall Street, including Goldman Sachs, Merrill Lynch, and Solomon Smith Barney.

Spitzer focused on possible conflicts of interest between the investment banking and research departments in each firm. Investment bankers represent companies that are making an initial public offering of stock. The bankers price the new stock, promote it to potential investors, and can earn huge fees for their efforts.

Research departments are supposed to operate independently. They evaluate a company's business outlook and issue reports that help investors make informed purchase decisions. If a banker were to pressure an analyst, it could reduce the analyst's objectivity.

Unfortunately, Spitzer did find evidence of bankers influencing analysts to write positive reports, even when the prevailing opinions in private meetings and internal e-mail messages were negative. Although no company admitted any wrongdoing, a dozen of them collectively agreed to pay $1.4 billion in fines and other costs. Most of these companies also agreed to add separate legal and compliance staff to their research departments.

A few individuals were also punished. Without admitting any wrongdoing, two of the best-known analysts agreed to pay multimillion dollar fines and accepted lifetime bans on working in the securities industry.

CAREER APPLICATIONS

1. An investment firm's reputation depends on its ability to earn and retain the trust of investors. In the aftermath of a scandal, how can companies, industry regulators, and the government restore that trust?
2. Every month, *Consumer Reports* publishes reviews of numerous products and services. The magazine prides itself on never accepting advertising from manufacturers or service providers. Is that policy a good idea? Why or why not?

A variation, the *failure analysis report,* studies events that happened in the past, with the hope of learning how to avoid similar failures in the future.

- **Reports to support decisions.** *Feasibility reports* are called for when managers need to explore the ramifications of a decision they're about to make (such as replacing an ad agency or switching materials used in a manufacturing process). *Justification reports* justify a decision that has already been made.

Analytical reports are used to assess opportunities, to solve problems, and to support decisions.

Writing analytical reports presents a greater challenge than writing informational reports, for three reasons: the quality of your reasoning, the quality of your writing, and the responsibility that comes with persuasion. First, you're doing more than simply delivering information—although that is of course critical—you're also thinking through a problem or opportunity and presenting your conclusions. The best writing in the world can't compensate for shaky analysis. Second, when your analysis is complete, you need to present your thinking in a compelling and persuasive manner. Third, by their very nature, analytical reports often convince other people to make significant financial and personnel decisions, so your reports carry the added responsibility of the consequences of these decisions (see "Communication Miscues: Suspect Reports Damage Wall Street Reputations").

In some cases, the problem or opportunity you address in an analytical report may be defined by the person who authorizes the report. In other cases, you will have to define it yourself. Be careful not to confuse a simple topic (campus parking) with a problem (the lack of enough campus parking). Moreover, if you're the only person who thinks a particular issue is a problem, your readers won't be very interested in your solution unless your report first convinces them that a problem does exists. Sometimes you need to "sell the problem" before you can sell the solution.

Clarify the problem in an analytical report by determining what you need to analyze, why the issue is important, who is involved, where the trouble is located, and how and when it started.

To help define the problem that your analytical report will address, answer these questions:

- What needs to be determined?
- Why is this issue important?
- Who is involved in the situation?
- Where is the trouble located?
- How did the situation originate?
- When did it start?

Not all these questions apply in every situation, but asking them helps you define the problem being addressed and limit the scope of your discussion.

Use problem factoring to divide a complex problem into more manageable pieces.

Also try breaking down the perceived problem into a series of logical, connected questions that try to identify cause and effect. This process is sometimes called **problem factoring**. You probably subconsciously approach most problems this way. When your car won't start, what do you do? You use the available evidence to organize your investigation, to start a search for cause-and-effect relationships. For example, if the engine doesn't turn over at all, you might suspect a dead battery. If the engine does turn over but won't fire, you can conclude that the battery is okay but perhaps you're out of gas. When you speculate on the cause of a problem, you're forming a **hypothesis**, a potential explanation that needs to be tested. By subdividing a problem and forming hypotheses based on available evidence, you can tackle even the most complex situations. With a clear picture of the problem or opportunity in mind, you're ready to consider the best structure for your report.

6 LEARNING OBJECTIVE

Discuss three major ways to organize analytical reports

Organizational Strategies for Analytical Reports

To create powerful analytical reports, consider your audience's likely reaction before choosing the most effective organizational strategy:

Before you choose an approach, determine whether your audience is receptive or skeptical.

- **Receptive audiences.** When you expect your audience to agree with you, use a structure that focuses attention on conclusions and recommendations (direct approach).
- **Skeptical audiences.** When you expect your audience to disagree with you or to be hostile, use a structure that focuses attention on the rationale behind your conclusions and recommendations (indirect approach).

The three most common structural approaches for analytical reports are (1) focusing on conclusions (direct), (2) focusing on recommendations (direct), and (3) focusing on logical argument (indirect). See Table 12.3.

TABLE 12.3 Common Ways to Structure Analytical Reports

		LOGICAL ARGUMENT		
ELEMENTS	CONCLUSIONS OR RECOMMENDATIONS	2 + 2 = 4	SCIENTIFIC	YARDSTICK
Readers	Are likely to accept	Are hostile or skeptical; need convincing	Need most convincing	Need most convincing
Order	Direct	Indirect	Indirect	Indirect
Writer credibility	High	Low	Low	Low
Advantages	Readers quickly grasp conclusions or recommendations	Readers follow writer's thinking process	Readers draw their own conclusions	Alternatives are all measured against same standards (criteria)
Drawbacks	Structure can make topic seem too simple	Structure can make report longer	Must discuss each alternative; very long	Must agree on criteria; can be boring; very long

Focusing on Conclusions

When writing an analytical report for people from your own organization who have asked you to study something, you're writing for your most receptive readers. They may know from experience that you'll do a thorough job, and they may trust your judgment. If they're likely to accept your conclusions—whatever they may be—you can structure your report around those conclusions, using a direct approach. Because your conclusions will often be the basis for management decisions, your audience counts on you to think carefully and write clearly.

Focusing on conclusions is often the best approach when you're addressing a receptive audience.

However, focusing directly on conclusions does have potential drawbacks. If your readers have reservations either about you or about your material, strong statements at the beginning may intensify reader resistance. Also, focusing on conclusions may make everything you say seem too simple. Your readers could criticize your report as being superficial: "Why didn't you consider this angle?" or "Where did you get this number?" You're generally better off taking the direct approach in a report only when your credibility is high—when your readers trust you and are willing to accept your conclusions.

Cynthia Zolonka works on the human resources staff of a bank in Houston, Texas. Her company decided to have an outside firm handle its employee training, and a year after the outsourcing arrangement was established, Zolonka was asked to evaluate the results. She explains: "Moving our training programs to an outside supplier was a tough—and controversial—decision for the entire company. Some people were convinced that outsourcing would never work; others thought it might save money but would hurt training quality. I took special care to do a thorough analysis of the data, and I supported my conclusion with objective answers, not personal opinions."

Figure 12.7 presents a preliminary outline of Zolonka's report. Her analysis shows that the outsourcing experiment was a success. She structured her report using a direct approach, as the outline illustrates.

You can use a similar structure, whether you're asked to analyze a problem or an opportunity. Readers who are interested mainly in your conclusions can grasp them

FIGURE 12.7 Preliminary Outline of a Research Report Focusing on Conclusions

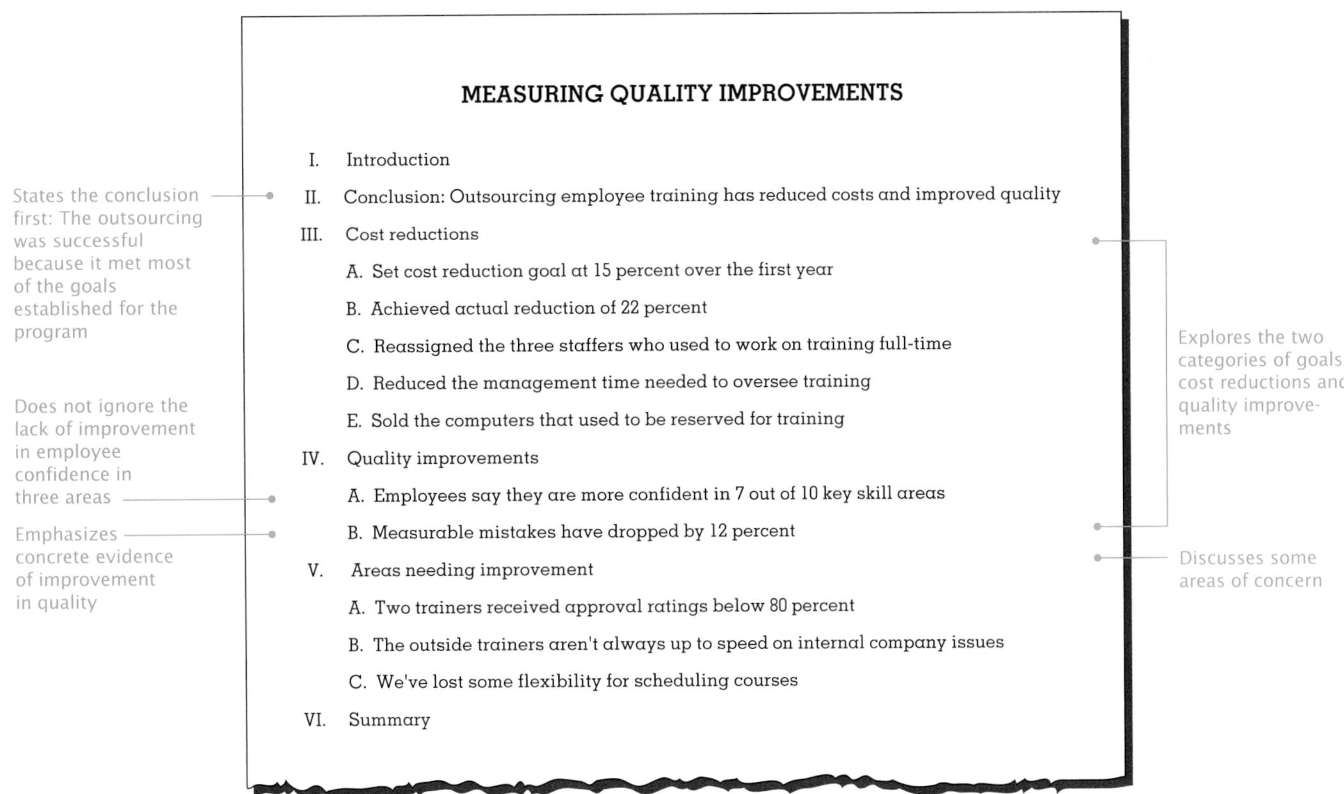

MEASURING QUALITY IMPROVEMENTS

I. Introduction

II. Conclusion: Outsourcing employee training has reduced costs and improved quality

III. Cost reductions

A. Set cost reduction goal at 15 percent over the first year

B. Achieved actual reduction of 22 percent

C. Reassigned the three staffers who used to work on training full-time

D. Reduced the management time needed to oversee training

E. Sold the computers that used to be reserved for training

IV. Quality improvements

A. Employees say they are more confident in 7 out of 10 key skill areas

B. Measurable mistakes have dropped by 12 percent

V. Areas needing improvement

A. Two trainers received approval ratings below 80 percent

B. The outside trainers aren't always up to speed on internal company issues

C. We've lost some flexibility for scheduling courses

VI. Summary

States the conclusion first: The outsourcing was successful because it met most of the goals established for the program
Does not ignore the lack of improvement in employee confidence in three areas
Emphasizes concrete evidence of improvement in quality
Explores the two categories of goals: cost reductions and quality improvements
Discusses some areas of concern

quickly, and readers who want to know more about your analysis can look at the data you provide.

Focusing on Recommendations

When readers want to know what you think they should do, organize your report to focus on recommendations.

A slightly different approach is useful when your readers want to know what they ought to do in a given situation (as opposed to what they ought to conclude). You'll often be asked to solve a problem or assess an opportunity, rather than just study it. The actions you want your readers to take become the main subdivisions of your report.

When structuring a report around recommendations, use the direct approach as you would for a report that focuses on conclusions. Then unfold your recommendations using a series of five steps:

1. Establish the need for action in the introduction, generally by briefly describing the problem or opportunity.
2. Introduce the benefit that can be achieved, without providing any details.
3. List the steps (recommendations) required to achieve the benefit, using action verbs for emphasis.
4. Explain each step more fully, giving details on procedures, costs, and benefits.
5. Summarize your recommendations.

Whenever a recommendation carries some element of risk, you owe it to your audience to make this clear.

If your recommendation carries any risks, be sure to clearly address those as well. Doing so not only makes your report more ethical but also offers you some protection in the event that your recommendation is implemented but doesn't work out as you had hoped. In short, make sure your readers know both the potential disadvantages as well as the potential benefits.

Focusing on Logical Arguments

Focusing on conclusions or recommendations is the most forceful and efficient way to structure an analytical report, but it isn't the best solution for every situation. You can sometimes achieve better results by encouraging readers to weigh all the facts before you present your conclusions or recommendations.

When your purpose is to collaborate with your audience and solve a problem or to persuade them to take a definite action, your structural approach must be indirect, highlighting logical arguments or focusing your audience's attention on what needs to be done. When you want your audience to concentrate on why your ideas make sense, use a logical organization: Arrange your ideas around the reasoning behind your report's conclusions and recommendations. Organize your material to reflect the thinking process that will lead readers to your conclusions.

Logical arguments can follow three basic approaches: 2 + 2 = 4 (adding everything up), the scientific method (proving or disproving one or more hypotheses), and the yardstick method (comparing ideas against a predetermined set of standards).

Three basic structural approaches may be used to argue your case: the *2 + 2 = 4 approach*, the *scientific method*, and the *yardstick approach*. These three approaches are not mutually exclusive. Essentially, you choose an approach that matches the reasoning process you used to arrive at your conclusions. That way you can lead readers along the same mental pathways you used, in hopes that they will follow you to the same conclusions.

In a long report, particularly, you may find it convenient to use differing organizational approaches for various sections. In general, however, simplicity of organization is a virtue. You need a clear, comprehensible argument in order to convince skeptical readers to accept your conclusions or recommendations.

The 2 + 2 = 4 Approach The **2 + 2 = 4 approach** is so named because it convinces readers of your point of view by demonstrating that everything adds up. The main points in your outline are the main reasons behind your conclusions and recommendations. You support each reason with the evidence you collected during your analysis.

Try using the 2 + 2 = 4 approach; it's familiar and easy to develop.

Because of its natural feel and versatility, the 2 + 2 = 4 approach is generally the most persuasive and efficient way to develop an analytical report for skeptical readers. When writing your own reports, try this structure first. You'll find that most of your arguments fall naturally into this pattern. However, not every problem or reporting situation can be handled with this organizational approach.

The Scientific Method When you're trying to discover whether an explanation is true, whether an option will solve your problem, or which one of several potential solutions or approaches will work best, you're likely to find the **scientific method** useful. You approach the problem by coming up with one or several possible solutions (hypotheses) and then conduct experiments or gather information to find the most effective one.

Use the scientific method when you need to prove, disprove, or select from alternatives.

Reports based on the scientific method begin with a statement of the problem and a brief description of the hypothetical solution or a list of possible solutions. The body of the report discusses each alternative in turn and offers evidence that will either confirm the alternative or rule it out. Because many problems have multiple causes and complex solutions, several alternatives may be relevant. The final section of the report summarizes the findings and indicates which solution or solutions are best. The report concludes with recommendations for solving the problem or eliminating the causes.

A troubleshooting report using a variation of the scientific method was prepared by Fredrik Swensen, an executive with a Miami restaurant management firm (see the outline in Figure 12.8). The purpose of Swensen's report is to help his company decide which of four franchise operations to invest in. "We wanted to buy 45 or 50 more franchise outlets across the country," says Swensen, "so this was a major investment decision. Our company already owns several hundred fast-food franchises, so we have a good idea of how to evaluate which ones are right for us."

By analyzing each alternative, Swensen hoped to unify a divided audience. Your chances of bringing about a consensus are much better when you show the strengths and weaknesses of all the ideas. However, the main drawback is that many of the alternatives may turn out to be irrelevant or unproductive, but you still have to discuss them all. The more ideas you discuss, the more confused your readers may become and the more trouble they may have comparing pros and cons.

The Yardstick Approach One way to reduce the confusion presented by having a lot of alternatives is to establish a yardstick for evaluating them. You begin by discussing the problem, as with the scientific method, but then you set up the conditions that must be met to solve the problem. These are the criteria against which you evaluate all possible solutions. The body of the report evaluates those alternatives in relation to the criteria. The main points of the outline are either the criteria themselves or the alternatives.

The yardstick approach compares alternatives to a set of predetermined standards, without conducting experiments or evaluating hypotheses.

Yardstick reports are similar in some respects to those based on the scientific method, but in criteria-based reports, all the alternatives are reviewed against the same standards. Another distinction is that criteria-based reports can be used to prove the need for action; that is, the current situation can be measured against the criteria and shown to be wanting.

The **yardstick approach** is useful for certain kinds of proposals because the client who requests the proposal often provides a list of criteria the solution must meet. Say that your company has been asked to bid on a contract to design and install a factory-floor distribution system for a large corporation. The client has listed the requirements (criteria) for the system, and you've developed a preliminary design to meet them. In the body of your proposal, you could use the client's list of requirements as the main headings and under each one explain how your preliminary design meets the requirement.

Figure 12.9 on page 379 is an outline of a feasibility report that uses the yardstick approach. The report was provided by J. C. Hartley, a market analyst for a large Sacramento company that makes irrigation equipment for farms and ranches. "We've been so successful in the agricultural market that we're starting to run out of customers to sell to," says Hartley. "To keep the company growing, we needed to find another market. Two obvious choices to consider were commercial buildings and residences." Hartley says that she was determined to make careful recommendations because, "even though I don't make the final decision, the information and the professional opinions that I provide in my report weigh heavily in the decision process."

The yardstick approach has two potential drawbacks. First, your audience needs to agree with the criteria you're using in your analysis. If they don't, they won't agree with the results of the evaluation. If you have any doubt about their agreement, build consensus before you start your report, if possible, or take extra care to explain why the criteria you're

FIGURE 12.8 Outline of a Troubleshooting Report Using the Scientific Method

Main Idea: We should purchase the 45 franchises currently for sale in the Burger World chain.

I. Statement of problem and purpose of this report
II. Scope of the investigation
III. Method used to compare the business opportunities
  A. Establish decision criteria
  B. Get input from consultants
  C. Gather secondary research
  D. Conduct market surveys for primary research
  E. Meet with franchisor management teams
  F. Analyze quantitative and qualitative data
  G. Prioritize and select the best opportunity
IV. Analysis of the four franchise operations
  A. Wacky Taco
    1. Description: Low-fat Mexican food; most locations in malls
    2. Pros: 58 units available within a year; consultants believe the concept has significant growth potential; operations easy to manage
    3. Cons: Company recently hit with employment discrimination lawsuit; franchise fees are 30 percent above average
    4. Conclusion: Priority = 3; lawsuit may be indicative of mismanagement; fees too high
  B. Thai in the Sky
    1. Description: Thai food served in New Age settings
    2. Pros: Healthy and interesting food; unusual theme concept; no franchised competition
    3. Cons: Complexity of food preparation; only 40 franchises available; franchisor's top management team replaced only six months ago
    4. Conclusion: Priority = 4; too risky and not enough units available
  C. Dog Tower
    1. Description: Gourmet hot dogs
    2. Pros: No nationwide competition; more than 60 franchises available within a year; easy to manage; fees lower than average
    3. Cons: Limited market appeal; many stores need updating
    4. Conclusion: Priority = 2; needs too much investment
  D. Burger World
    1. Description: Mainstream competitor to McDonald's and Burger King

Covers two major steps: (1) establishing the decision criteria and (2) testing each of four alternatives against those criteria

Assigns each of the four alternatives to an appropriate subdivision: description, pros, cons, and conclusion (priority)

    2. Pros: Aggressive franchisor willing to invest in national marketing; start-up costs are low; unique demographic target (teenagers and young adults; not a little kids' place)
    3. Cons: Fierce competition in burgers overall; some units in unproved locations
    4. Conclusion: Priority = 1; finances look good; research shows that teenagers will support a chain that doesn't cater to small children
V. Summary
VI. Appendixes
  A. Financial data
  B. Research results

Presents each of the four operations objectively by covering the same material for each one: a description, the pros, the cons, and Swensen's conclusion

FIGURE 12.9 Outline of an Analytical Report Using the Yardstick Approach

Main Idea: We should move into the commercial irrigation equipment market but not into the residential market.

I. Introduction
II. Criteria for entering new markets
  A. Size and growth
  B. Profit potential
  C. Ability to compete
  D. Distribution costs and opportunities
  E. Fit with current capabilities
III. Irrigation equipment trends
  A. Water shortages leading to demand for more efficient irrigation
  B. Labor costs encouraging automation
  C. More homeowners attempting do-it-yourself projects
IV. Comparison of new market opportunities
  A. Commercial landscapers and building owners
    1. Size and growth
    2. Profit potential
    3. Ability to compete
    4. Distribution costs and opportunities
    5. Fit with current capabilities
  B. Residential landscapers and homeowners
    1. Size and growth
    2. Profit potential
    3. Ability to compete
    4. Distribution costs and opportunities
    5. Fit with current capabilities
V. Recommendations
  A. Enter the commercial segment
    1. Select a test market
    2. Learn from the test and refine our approach
    3. Roll out product marketing nationwide
  B. Do not attempt to enter the residential market at this point

Introduces the report and explains the scope of the investigation

Defines the criteria for evaluating and choosing the market opportunities

Gives readers valuable background information for understanding this report and its recommendations

Recommendations clearly communicate the decision criteria—particularly important in yardstick evaluation reports so that readers will consciously evaluate the options using a consistent set of factors

using are the best ones in this particular case. Second, the yardstick approach can get a little boring when you have many options to consider or many criteria to compare them against. One way to minimize the repetition is to compare the options in tables and then highlight the more unusual or important aspects of each alternative in the text so that you get the best of both worlds. This approach allows you to compare all the alternatives against the same yardstick while calling attention to the most significant differences among them.

Effective Analytical Reports: An Example

As national sales manager of a New Hampshire sporting goods company, Binh Phan was concerned about his company's ability to sell to its largest customers. His boss, the vice president of marketing, shared these concerns and asked Phan to analyze the situation and recommend a solution. As Phan says, "We sell sporting goods to retail chains across the country. Large nationwide chains with superstores modeled after Toys "R" Us have been revolutionizing the industry, but we haven't had as much success with these big customers as we've had with smaller companies that operate strictly on a local or regional basis. With more and more of the industry in the hands of the large chains, we knew we had to fix the situation."

Phan's troubleshooting report appears in Figure 12.10. The main idea is that the company should establish separate sales teams for these major accounts, rather than continuing to service them through the company's four regional divisions. However, Phan knew his

FIGURE 12.10 Analytical Report Using the 2 + 2 = 4 Approach

MEMO

TO: Robert Mendoza, Vice President of Marketing
FROM: Binh Phan, National Sales Manager
DATE: September 12, 2005
SUBJECT: Major accounts sales problems

INTRODUCTION

As you requested on August 20, this report outlines the results of my investigation into the recent slowdown in sales to major accounts and the accompanying rise in sales- and service-related complaints from some of our largest customers.

Clarifies who requested the report, when it was requested, and who wrote it

Over the last four quarters, major account sales dropped 12 percent, whereas overall sales were up 7 percent. During the same time, we've all noticed an increase in both formal and informal complaints from larger customers, regarding how confusing and complicated it has become to do business with us.

States the reason the report was undertaken and supplies specific background figures

My investigation started with in-depth discussions with the four regional sales managers, first as a group and then individually. The tension I felt in the initial meeting eventually bubbled to the surface during my meetings with each manager. Staff members in each region are convinced that other regions are booking orders they don't deserve, with one region doing all the legwork only to see another region get the sale, the commission, and the quota credit.

Reviews how the information was gathered and under what conditions

I followed up these formal discussions by talking informally and exchanging e-mail with several sales reps from each region. Virtually everyone who is involved with our major national accounts has a story to share. No one is happy with the situation, and I sense that some reps are walking away from major customers because the process is so frustrating.

Describes follow-up efforts, emphasizing the deteriorating situation

The decline in sales to our major national customers and the increase in their complaints stem from two issues: (1) sales force organization and (2) commission policy.

Highlights two sets of issues that are discussed in the body

ORGANIZATIONAL ISSUES

When we divided the national sales force into four geographical regions last year, the idea was to focus our sales efforts and clarify responsibilities for each prospective and current customer. The regional managers have gotten to know their market territories very well, and sales have increased beyond even our most optimistic projections.

Keeps reader interest by showing success of current organization

However, while solving one problem, we have created another. In the past 12 to 18 months, several regional customers have grown to national status, and a few retailers have taken on (or expressed interest in) our products. As a result, a significant portion of both current sales and future opportunities lies with these large national accounts.

Points out how the market had changed in just over a year

(continued)

plan would be controversial because it required a big change in the company's organization and in the way sales reps are paid. His thinking had to be clear and easy to follow, so he used the 2 + 2 = 4 approach to focus on his reasons.

PLANNING PROPOSALS

Although the specific formats for proposals are innumerable, they can be grouped into two general categories:

- **Internal proposals.** Used to request decisions from managers within the organization, internal proposals may include *funding proposals,* which request funds and management support for new projects, and *general project proposals,* which request permission to take action on specific projects.
- **External proposals.** Used to request decisions from parties outside the organization, external proposals include *investment proposals,* which request funding from external investors such as venture capitalists; *grant proposals,* which request funds from government agencies and other sponsoring organizations; and *sales proposals,* which suggest individualized solutions for potential customers and request purchase decisions.

FIGURE 12.10 Continued

2

I uncovered more than a dozen cases in which sales reps from two or more regions found themselves competing with each other by pursuing the same customers from different locations. Moreover, the complaints from our major accounts about overlapping or nonexistent account coverage are a direct result of the regional organization. In some cases, customers aren't sure which of our reps they're supposed to call with problems and orders. In others, no one has been in contact with them for several months.

Explains organizational problems without going into unneeded detail

For example, having retail outlets across the lower tier of the country, AmeriSport received pitches from reps out of our West, South, and East regions. Because our regional offices have a lot of negotiating freedom, the three were offering different prices. But all AmeriSport buying decisions were made at the Tampa headquarters, so all we did was confuse the customer. The irony of the current organization is that we're often giving our weakest selling and support efforts to the largest customers in the country.

Supports the first main idea with evidence

COMMISSION ISSUES

The regional organization issues are compounded by the way we assign commissions and quota credit. Salespeople in one region can invest a lot of time in pursuing a sale, only to have the customer place the order in another region. So some sales rep in the second region ends up with the commission on a sale that was partly or even entirely earned by someone in the first region. Therefore, sales reps sometimes don't pursue leads in their regions, thinking that a rep in another region will get the commission.

Explains commission problems concisely

For example, Athletic Express, with outlets in 35 states spread across all four regions, finally got so frustrated with us that the company president called our headquarters. Athletic Express has been trying to place a large order for tennis and gold accessories, but none of our local reps seem interested in paying attention. I spoke with the rep responsible for Nashville, where the company is headquartered, and asked her why she wasn't working the account more actively. Her explanation was that last time she got involved with Athletic Express, the order was actually placed from their L.A. regional office, and she didn't get any commission after more than two weeks of selling time.

Supports the second main idea with evidence

RECOMMENDATIONS

Our sales organization should reflect the nature of our customer base. To accomplish that goal, we need a group of reps who are free to pursue accounts across regional borders—and who are compensated fairly for their work. The most sensible answer is to establish a national account group. Any customers whose operations place them in more than one region would automatically be assigned to the national group.

Further, we need to modify our commission policy to reward people for team selling. I'll talk with the sales managers to work out the details, but in general, we'll need to split

Presents advantages and recommended action

3

commissions whenever two or more reps help close a sale. This policy will also involve a "finder's fee" for a regional rep who pulls in national leads and passes them on to the national account team.

SUMMARY

The regional sales organization is effective at the regional and local levels but not at the national level. We should establish a national accounts group to handle sales that cross regional boundaries. Then we'll have one set of reps who are focused on the local and regional levels and another set who are pursuing national accounts.

To make sure that the sales reps (at both the regional and national levels) are adequately motivated and fairly compensated, we need to devise a system of commission splitting and finder's fees. Rather than working against each other, as they are now, the two groups will have incentive to work together.

Clearly and succinctly recaps recommendations and how the company will benefit from following them

Buyers solicit proposals by publishing a request for proposals (RFP).

The most significant factor in planning a proposal is whether the recipient has asked you to submit a proposal. *Solicited proposals* are generally prepared at the request of external parties that require a product or a service, but they may also be requested by such internal sources as management or the board of directors. Some external parties prepare a formal invitation to bid on their contract, called a **request for proposals (RFP)**, which includes instructions that specify the exact type of work to be performed or products to be delivered, along with budgets, deadlines, and other requirements. Say that the National Aeronautics and Space Administration (NASA) decides to develop a new satellite. The agency prepares an RFP that specifies exactly what the satellite should accomplish, and it sends the RFP to several aerospace companies, inviting them to bid on the job. You respond to RFPs by preparing a proposal that shows how you would meet the potential customer's needs. Responding to RFPs can be a significant task; fortunately, new software products are available to lighten the load considerably (see "Connecting with Technology: Proposals Get a Software Assist").

7 LEARNING OBJECTIVE

Explain how your approach to writing proposals should differ when you are responding to a formal request for proposals (RFP)

To attract a large pool of qualified bidders, organizations send RFPs to firms with good performance records in the field, print them in trade publications, and post them on the web. For example, FedBizOpps, www.fedbizopps.com, lists the federal government's requests for equipment, supplies, and services in amounts that exceed $25,000.[2] Regardless of how you obtain an RFP, you and your company must decide whether you're interested in the contract and whether you have a reasonable chance of winning it (since responding to each RFP can take weeks or months of work). When the proposal effort actually begins, you review the requirements, define the scope of the deliverables, determine the methods and procedures to be used, and estimate time requirements, personnel requirements, and costs.

Connecting with Technology

Proposals Get a Software Assist

Writing a new-business proposal should be an exciting time: a new opportunity is waiting for you, just out of reach. All you have to do is craft a document that explains how your company can meet customer needs better than anyone else, and the business is yours.

However, most businesspeople find proposal writing to be less than a wonderful opportunity and more of a chore. First of all, complicated proposals can involve dozens or even hundreds of detailed discussion points. In addition, the need to write a proposal is often unexpected, which means that you have to make room in your already-busy schedule. Also, deadlines are usually inflexible, which creates frequent last-minute rushes. To make matters worse, many proposals require similar information, so you end up writing the same thing, or nearly the same thing, over and over again.

Yet many companies live and die by proposals, so the chore of writing them is an ongoing part of doing business. Fortunately, a number of software companies have jumped in with promises to help beleaguered proposal writers. At the simplest level, you can use templates and cut-and-paste boilerplate text in your word processor. This method reduces the typing, but doing all these inserts manually is still tedious. Also, the possibility of errors is quite high (such as when you reuse a proposal and forget to change the name of the customer). Moreover, every time you need a new piece of information, you still need to track down the right expert in your company, draft the new material, then weave it into the proposal document.

Automated proposal solutions promise to solve all of these problems to one degree or another. Basic features include the ability to automatically personalize the proposal, ensure proper structure (making sure you don't forget any sections, for instance), and organize storage of all your boilerplate text. At a more advanced level, products such as Pragmatech's RFP Machine and Sant's RFPMaster can scan RFPs to identify questions and requirements, and then fill in potential answers from a centralized knowledge base that contains input from all the relevant experts in your company. Ideally, your job is then reduced to verifying the answers, modifying or replacing any that aren't quite right, and adding any personalized touches that are beyond the system's abilities. At last, you can spend a little more time profiting from that new business and less time struggling to get it.

CAREER APPLICATIONS

1. Research three commercially available software products that assist with proposal writing, then explain which one you think would be best for a small consulting firm.
2. Can you envision any disadvantages to using proposal writing software? If so, how might you overcome them?

Then you put it all on paper—exactly as specified in the RFP, following the exact format it requires and responding meticulously to every point it raises.[3] RFPs can seem surprisingly picky, even to the point of specifying the paper size to use and the number of copies to send, but you must follow every detail.

Unsolicited proposals are initiated by organizations attempting to obtain business or funding without a specific invitation from a potential client. Such proposals may also be initiated by employees or managers who wish to convince company insiders to adopt a program, policy, or idea. In other words, with an unsolicited proposal, the writer makes the first move. Even so, an unsolicited proposal should not come as a surprise to the recipient. According to management consultant Alan Weiss, the proposal should be the summation of a conversation that has been ongoing with the recipient.[4] Not only does this help ensure acceptance, but it gives you an opportunity to explore the recipient's needs and therefore craft your proposal around them.

Unsolicited proposals require additional persuasive elements because the audience isn't expecting the proposal and might not even be conscious of the problem the proposal is designed to solve.

Unsolicited proposals also differ from solicited proposals in another important respect: Your audience may not be aware of the problem you are addressing, so your proposal must first convince readers that a problem or opportunity exists before convincing them that you can address it. Thus, unsolicited proposals generally spend considerable time explaining why readers should take action and convincing them of the benefits of doing so.

Unsolicited proposals vary widely in form, length, and purpose. For example, a university seeking funding for a specific research project might submit an unsolicited proposal to a large local corporation. To be convincing, the university's proposal would show how the research could benefit the corporation and would demonstrate that the university has the resources and expertise to conduct the research.[5] Or an entrepreneur seeking funding for a new venture might modify a business plan to create a proposal that shows potential investors the return they should expect in exchange for the use of their funds. Such a proposal would try to convince investors of the viability of the new business.

With virtually any proposal, whether solicited or unsolicited, whether for internal audiences or external, keep in mind that you are competing for something—money, time, management attention, and so on. Even if yours is the only proposal on the table, you are still competing with all the other choices your audience could make.

Every proposal competes for something: money, time, attention, and so on.

Organizational Strategies for Proposals

As with informational and analytical reports, your choice of structure for proposals depends on whether your audience expects the proposal and, if they do, whether you expect them to be receptive. In general, your audience may be more receptive with solicited proposals, since the problem and the solution have already been identified. You submit a proposal for the solution specified in the RFP issued by the prospective client and structure the proposal using a direct approach, focusing on the recommendations.

Depending on the circumstances and your relationship with the recipient, the indirect approach may be a better choice for unsolicited proposals. When writing unsolicited proposals, you must first convince the audience that a problem exists and establish your credibility if you are unknown to the reader. To convince the reader that your recommendations are solid and logical, you unfold your solution to the problem using one of the logical arguments (2 + 2 = 4 approach, scientific method, or yardstick approach). As you unfold your solution, you have two goals: (1) to persuade readers to accept your idea and award you a contract, and (2) to spell out the terms of your proposal.

An indirect approach is a good way to build your case in an unsolicited proposal.

Effective Proposals: An Example

A good proposal explains why a project or course of action is needed, what it will involve, how much it will cost, and how the recipient will benefit. You can see all of these elements in Shandel Cohen's internal proposal for an automatic mail-response system (see Figure 12.11).

Cohen manages the customer-response section of the marketing department at a Midwest personal computer manufacturer. Her section sends out product information requested by customers and the field sales force. Cohen has observed that the demand for

FIGURE 12.11 Shandel Cohen's Internal Proposal

MEMO

TO: Jamie Engle
FROM: Shandel Cohen
DATE: July 8, 2005
SUBJECT: Proposed automatic mail-response system

THE PROBLEM:
SLOW RESPONSE TO CUSTOMER REQUESTS FOR INFORMATION

Describes the problem carefully in a positive light (in terms of the company's success) and shows why a new system is needed

Our new produce line has been very well received, and orders have surpassed our projections. This very success, however, has created a shortage of printed catalogs and data sheets, as well as considerable overtime for people in the customer response center. As we introduce upgrades and new options, our printed materials quickly become outdated. If we continue to rely on printed materials for customer information, we have two choices: Distribute existing materials (even though they are incomplete or inaccurate) or discard existing materials and print new ones.

THE SOLUTION:
AUTOMATED MAIL-RESPONSE SYSTEM

With minor modifications to our current computer system and very little additional software, we can set up an automated system to respond to customer requests for information. This system can save us time and money and can keep our distributed information current.

Automated mail-response systems have been tested and proven effective. Many companies already use this method to respond to customer information requests, so we won't have to worry about relying on untested technology. Both customer and company responses have been positive.

Hooks reader on solution by highlighting such economic and operational benefits as ease of implementation, affordability, cost and time savings, currency, and proven results

Uses headings to highlight the benefits of the solution

Ever-Current Information

Rather than discard and print new materials, we would need to update only the electronic files. We could be able to provide customers and our field sales organization with up-to-date, correct information as soon as the upgrades or options are available.

Instantaneous Delivery

Within a very short time of requesting information, customers would have that information in hand. Electronic delivery would be especially advantageous for our international customers. Regular mail to remote locations sometimes takes weeks to arrive, by which time the information may already be out of date. Both customers and field salespeople will appreciate the automatic mail-response system.

Minimized Waste

With our current method of sending printed information, we discard virtually tons of obsolete catalogs, data sheets, and other materials.

(continued)

information increases when a new product is released and that it diminishes as a product matures. This fluctuating demand causes drastic changes in her section's workload.

"Either we have more work than we can possibly handle," says Cohen, "or we don't have enough to keep us busy. But I don't want to get into a hiring-and-firing cycle." Cohen is also concerned about the amount of printed material that's discarded when products are upgraded or replaced.

Cohen's internal proposal seeks management's approval to install an automatic mail-response system. Because the company manufactures computers, she knows that her boss won't object to a computer solution. Also, since profits are always a concern, her report emphasizes the financial benefits of her proposal. Her report describes the problem, her proposed solutions, the benefits to the company, and the projected costs.

FIGURE 12.11 Continued

2

By maintaining and distributing the information electronically, we would eliminate this waste. We would also free up a considerable amount of floor space and shelving that is required for storing printed materials.

Of course, some of our customers may still prefer to receive printed materials, or they may not have access to electronic mail. For these customers, we could simply print copies of the files when we receive requests.

Lower Overtime Costs

Besides savings in paper and space, we would also realize considerable savings in wages. Because of the increased interest in our new products, we must continue to work overtime or hire new people to meet the demand. An automatic mail-response system would eliminate this need, allowing us to deal with fluctuating interest without a fluctuating workforce.

Setup and Operating Costs

Carefully explains the costs of the proposal

The necessary equipment and software costs approximately $15,000. System maintenance and upgrades are estimated at $5,000 per year.

We expect the following annual savings from eliminating printed information:

$100,000	Printing costs
25,000	Storage costs
5,000	Postage
20,000	Wages
$150,000	Total savings

Justifies the cost by detailing projected annual savings

CONCLUSION

Closes by offering to answer any questions management may have—rather than trying to anticipate management's questions and including unnecessary detail

I will be happy to answer any questions you have about this system. I believe that such an automated mail-response system would greatly benefit our company, in terms of both cost and customer satisfaction. If you approve, we can have it installed and running in six weeks.

COMMUNICATION CHALLENGES AT KENWOOD USA

Dan Petersen was so impressed by the opportunities in the emerging field of satellite radio that he left Kenwood USA for Sirius, one of the leading satellite radio services. Several key staff members followed him. Now Petersen's interim replacement, Mike Roberts, has to rebuild the sales and marketing staff, and he hired you as part of the market research team. Your group is currently discussing a proposal for a new mobile product: an in-dash video system that can play DVDs, receive and record high-definition television (HDTV) signals, and provide navigation information.

Individual Challenge: Recent research suggests that many consumers with children are interested in mobile DVD/HDTV systems. Kenwood dealers have reported rumors from Audiovox and Panasonic but neither has announced plans to introduce such a product. Roberts has asked you to write the product proposal, but he wants to review your working outline before you start writing.

Team Challenge: It will take about six weeks to complete the detailed proposal. In the interim, your department will continue to send its biweekly market intelligence reports to the developers in Japan. To lay the groundwork for the proposal, your group leader wants the next three reports to include market data that highlights the rising demand for mobile DVD/HDTV systems. In a small group, discuss the pros, cons, and ethics of dropping hints like this before sending your proposal.

SUMMARY OF LEARNING OBJECTIVES

1 **Explain the differences between informational reports and analytical reports.** Informational reports focus on the delivery of facts, figures, and other types of information, without making recommendations or proposing new ideas or solutions. In contrast, analytical reports assess a situation or problem and recommend a course of action in response.

2 **Adapt the three-step writing process to reports and proposals.** The comprehensive nature of the three-step process is ideal for the work involved in most reports and proposals. Use all of the advice you learned in Chapters 4 to 6, with added emphasis on a few specific points for longer documents: (1) identify your purpose clearly to avoid rework, (2) prepare a work plan to guide the research and writing tasks, (3) determine whether a separate research project might be needed to gather the necessary information, (4) choose the medium (or media, in some cases) that meets the needs of your audience, and (5) organize your information by selecting the best approach for an informational or analytical report.

3 **Explain the value of a work plan in the development of long reports.** A formal work plan makes the writing process more efficient and more effective by guiding you every step of the planning and writing process. Work plans usually include (1) a problem statement defining what you're going to investigate; (2) a statement of purpose defining *why* you are preparing the report; (3) the tasks to be accomplished and the sequence in which they should be performed; (4) a description of any product that will result from your study; (5) a review of responsibilities, assignments, schedules, and resource requirements; (6) plans for following up after delivering the report; and (7) a working outline.

4 **Describe the four major categories of informational reports and provide examples of each.** Informational reports include reports for monitoring and controlling operations, such as plans, operating reports, and personal activity reports; reports for implementing policies and procedures, such as policy reports and position papers; reports to demonstrate compliance, such as quarterly and annual income tax reports; and reports to document progress, such as status reports and lists of project risks and concerns.

5 **Describe the three major categories of analytical reports and provide examples of each.** The most common analytical reports are those written to assess opportunities, such as market analysis and due diligence reports; reports written to solve problems, including troubleshooting and failure analysis reports; and reports to support decisions, including feasibility and justification reports.

6 **Discuss three major ways to organize analytical reports.** The three most common ways to organize analytical reports are by focusing on conclusions, focusing on recommendations, and focusing on logical arguments.

7 **Explain how your approach to writing proposals should differ when you are responding to a formal request for proposals (RFP).** The most important point to consider when responding to an RFP is to follow the RFP's instructions down to the tiniest detail, since any deviation could be grounds for rejecting your proposal. With unsolicited proposals, you can have a considerable degree of freedom in deciding what information to include and how to organize it. However, when responding to an RFP, you must provide all the information requested and follow the organizational scheme dictated by the RFP.

Test Your Knowledge

1. How can your written reports influence your professional success?
2. What is the major difference between informational and analytical reports?
3. What does a statement of purpose convey?
4. What should you include in the work plan for a complex report or proposal?
5. How can you determine the best medium to use for a report?
6. How are reports for monitoring and controlling operations used?
7. What are the seven major ways to organize an informational report?
8. How does a feasibility report differ from a justification report?
9. What is problem factoring?
10. What is an RFP and how does it relate to proposal writing?

Apply Your Knowledge

1. Why are unsolicited proposals more challenging to write than solicited proposals?
2. What are the advantages and disadvantages of asking your employees to "fill in the blanks" on standardized reporting forms? Briefly explain.
3. If you want to make a specific recommendation in your report, should you include information that might support a different recommendation? Explain your answer.

4. If your report includes only factual information, is it objective? Please explain.
5. **Ethical Choices.** If you were writing a troubleshooting report to help management decide how to reduce quality problems at a manufacturing plant, what ethical issues might you face? How might these ethical issues conflict with your need to report all the relevant facts and to offer evidence for your conclusions? Explain briefly.

Practice Your Knowledge

Documents for Analysis

The Securities and Exchange Commission (SEC) requires all public companies to file a comprehensive annual report (form 10-K) electronically. Many companies post links to these reports on their websites along with links to other company reports. Visit the website of Dell at www.dell.com and find the company's most recent annual reports: 10-K and Year in Review. Compare the style and format of the two reports. For which audience(s) is the Year in Review targeted? Who besides the SEC might be interested in the Annual Report 10-K? Which report do you find easier to read? More interesting? More detailed?

Exercises

For live links to all websites discussed in this chapter, visit this text's website at www.prenhall.com/bovee. Just log on, select Chapter 12, and click on "Featured Websites." Locate the page or the URL related to the material in the text.

12.1 **Understanding Business Reports and Proposals: How Companies Use Reports** Interview several people working in a career you might like to enter, and ask them about the written reports they receive and prepare. How do these reports tie in to the decision-making process? Who reads the reports they prepare? Summarize your findings in writing, give them to your instructor, and be prepared to discuss them with the class.

12.2 **Understanding Business Reports and Proposals: Report Classification** Using the information presented in this chapter, identify the report type represented by each of the following examples. In addition, write a brief paragraph about each, explaining who the audience is likely to be, what type of data would be used, and whether conclusions and recommendations would be appropriate.

a. A statistical study of the pattern of violent crime in a large city during the last five years
b. A report prepared by a seed company demonstrating the benefits of its seed corn for farmers
c. A report prepared by an independent testing agency evaluating various types of nonprescription cold remedies
d. A trip report submitted at the end of a week by a traveling salesperson
e. A report indicating how 45 acres of undeveloped land could be converted into an industrial park
f. An annual report to be sent to the shareholders of a large corporation
g. A report from a U.S. National Park wildlife officer to Washington, D.C., headquarters showing the status of the California condor (an endangered species)
h. A written report by a police officer who has just completed an arrest

12.3 **Internet** Follow the step-by-step hints and examples for writing a funding proposal at www.learnerassociates.net/proposal. Review the writing hints and the entire sample proposal online. What details did the author decide to include in appendices? Why was this material placed in the appendices and not the main body of the report? According to the author's tips, when is the best time to prepare a Project Overview?

12.4 **Informational Reports: Personal Activity Report** Imagine you're the manager of campus recruiting for Nortel, a Canadian telecommunications firm. Each of your four recruiters interviews up to 11 college seniors every day. What kind of personal activity report can you design to track the results of these interviews? List the areas you would want each recruiter to report on, and explain how each would help you manage the recruiting process (and the recruiters) more effectively.

12.5 **Informational Reports: Policy Report** You're the vice president of operations for a Florida fast-food chain. In the aftermath of a major hurricane, you're drafting a report on the emergency procedures to be followed by personnel in each restaurant when storm warnings are in effect. Answer who, what, when, where, why, and how, and then prepare a one-page draft of your report.

12.6 **Unsolicited Proposal** You're getting ready to launch a new lawn-care business that offers mowing, fertilizing, weeding, and other services. The lawn surrounding a nearby shopping center looks as if it could use better care, so you target that business for your first unsolicited proposal. To help prepare this proposal, write your answers to these questions:

a. What questions will you need to answer before you can write a proposal to solve the reader's problem? Be as specific as possible.
b. What customer benefits will you include in your proposal?
c. Will you use a letter or memo format for your proposal? Explain your answer.

12.7 **Teamwork: Unsolicited Proposal** Break into small groups and identify an operational problem occurring at your campus involving either registration, university housing, food services, parking, or library services. Then develop a workable solution to that problem. Finally, develop a list of pertinent facts that your team will need to gather to convince the reader that the problem exists and that your solution will work.

12.8 **Analyzing the Situation: Statement of Purpose** Sales at The Style Shop, a clothing store for men, have declined for the third month in a row. Your boss is not sure if this decline is due to a weak economy or if it's due to another unknown reason. She has asked you to investigate the situation and to submit a report to her highlighting some possible reasons for the decline. Develop a statement of purpose for your report.

12.9 **Preparing the Work Plan** Using the situation described in Exercise 12.6, assume that you're the shopping center's facilities manager. You report to the general manager, who must approve any new contracts for lawn service. Before you contract for lawn care, you want to prepare a formal study of the current state of your lawn's health. The report will include conclusions and recommendations for your boss's consideration. Draft a work plan, including the problem statement, the statement of purpose and scope, a description of what will result from your investigation, the sources and methods of data collection, and a preliminary outline.

12.10 **Organizing Reports: Choosing the Direct or Indirect Approach** Of the organizational approaches introduced in the chapter, which is best suited for writing a report that answers the following questions? Briefly explain why. (Note, you will write one report for each question item.)

a. In which market segment—root beer, cola, or lemon-lime—should Fizz Drinks, Inc., introduce a new soft drink to take advantage of its enlarged research and development budget?

b. Should Major Manufacturing, Inc., close down operations of its antiquated Bellville, Arkansas, plant despite the adverse economic impact on the town that has grown up around the plant?

c. Should you and your partner adopt a new accounting method to make your financial statements look better to potential investors?

d. Should Grand Canyon Chemicals buy disposable test tubes to reduce labor costs associated with cleaning and sterilizing reusable test tubes?

e. What are some reasons for the recent data loss at the college computer center, and how can we avoid similar problems in the future?

12.11 **Choosing the Direct or Indirect Approach** Look through recent issues (print or online) of *Business Week, Fortune,* or other business publications for an article that describes how an executive's conclusions about his or her company's current situation or future opportunities led to changes in policy, plans, or products. Construct an outline of the material, using (a) direct order and (b) indirect order. Which approach do you think the executive would use when reporting these conclusions to stockholders? When reporting to other senior managers? Explain your answers.

12.12 **Organizing Reports: Deciding on Format** Go to the library or visit the Internet site www.annualreportservice.com and review the annual reports recently released by two corporations in the same industry. Analyze each report and be prepared to discuss the following questions in class:

a. What organizational differences, if any, do you see in the way each corporation discusses its annual performance? Are the data presented clearly so that shareholders can draw conclusions about how well the company performed?

b. What goals, challenges, and plans do top managers emphasize in their discussion of results?

c. How do the format and organization of each report enhance or detract from the information being presented?

12.13 **Organizing Reports: Structuring Informational Reports** Assume that your college president has received many student complaints about campus parking problems. You are appointed the chair of a student committee organized to investigate the problems and recommend solutions. The president gives you the file labeled "Parking: Complaints from Students," and you jot down the essence of the complaints as you inspect the contents. Your notes look like this:

- Inadequate student spaces at critical hours
- Poor night lighting near the computer center
- Inadequate attempts to keep resident neighbors from occupying spaces
- Dim marking lines
- Motorcycles taking up full spaces
- Discourteous security officers
- Spaces (usually empty) reserved for college officials
- Relatively high parking fees
- Full fees charged to night students even though they use the lots only during low-demand periods
- Vandalism to cars and a sense of personal danger
- Inadequate total space
- Resident harassment of students parking on the street in front of neighboring houses

Prepare an outline for an informational report to be submitted to committee members. Use a topical organization that categorizes this information.

12.14 **Organizing Reports: Structuring Analytical Reports** Three years ago, your company (a carpet manufacturer) modernized its Georgia plant in anticipation of increasing demand for carpets. Because of the depressed housing market, the increase in demand for new carpets has been slow to materialize. As a result, the company has excess capacity at both its Georgia and California plants. On the basis of your research, you have recommended that the company close the California plant. The company president, J. P. Lawrence, has asked you to prepare a justification report to support your recommendation. Here are the facts you gathered by interviewing the respective plant managers:

Operational Statistics

- Georgia plant: This plant has newer equipment, productivity is higher, employs 100 nonunion production workers, and ships $12 million in carpets a year. Hourly base wage is $16.
- California plant: California plant employs 80 union production workers and ships $8 million in carpets a year. Hourly base wage is $20.

Financial Implications

- Savings by closing California plant: (1) Increase productivity by 17%; (2) reduce labor costs by 20% (total labor savings would be $1 million per year; see assumptions); (3) annual local tax savings of $120,000 (Georgia has a more favorable tax climate).
- Sale of Pomona, California, land: Purchased in 1952 for $200,000. Current market value $2.5 million. Net profit (after capital gains tax) over $1 million.
- Sale of plant and equipment: Fully depreciated. Any proceeds a windfall.
- Costs of closing California plant: One-time deductible charge of $250,000 (relocation costs of $100,000 and severance payments totaling $150,000).

Assumptions

- Transfer 5 workers from California to Georgia.
- Hire 45 new workers in Georgia.
- Lay off 75 workers in California.
- Georgia plant would require a total of 150 workers to produce the combined volume of both plants.

a. Which approach (focus on conclusions, recommendations, or logical arguments) will you use to structure your report to the president? Why?

b. Suppose this report were to be circulated to plant managers and supervisors instead. What changes, if any, might you make in your approach?

c. List some conclusions that you might draw from the above information to use in your report.

d. Using the structure you selected for your report to the president, draft a final report outline with first- and second-level informative headings.

Expand Your Knowledge

For live links to the websites that follow, go to www.prenhall.com/bovee. When you log on, select Chapter 12, then select "Featured Websites," click on the URL of the website you wish to visit, and review the website to complete these exercises.

Exploring the Best of the Web

Better Ideas for Better Business Plans
www.bizplanit.com

What's involved in a business plan? BizPlanIt.Com offers tips and advice, consulting services, a free e-mail newsletter, and a sample virtual business plan. You'll find suggestions on what details and how much information to include in each section of a business plan. You can explore the site's numerous links to business plan books and software, online magazines, educational programs, government resources, women and minority resources, and even answers to your business plan questions. Review the articles on the site and answer the following questions:

1. Why is the executive summary such an important section of a business plan? What kind of information is contained in the executive summary?
2. What is the product/services section? What information should it contain? List some of the common errors to avoid when planning this part.
3. What type of business planning should you describe in the exit strategy section? Why?

Exploring the Web on Your Own

Review these chapter-related websites on your own to learn more about planning and using reports in the workplace.

1. If you need financial information on public companies, just ask Edgar, the Securities and Exchange Commission's online reporting warehouse at www.sec.gov/edgar.
2. Looking for a specific company, try SuperPages at www.bigbook.com where you'll find more than 16 million listings.
3. Compare annual report styles and formats from hundreds of publicly traded U.S. companies at the Report Gallery, www.reportgallery.com.

Learn Interactively

Interactive Study Guide

Go to the Companion Website at www.prenhall.com/bovee. For Chapter 12, take advantage of the interactive "Study Guide" to test your knowledge of the chapter. Get instant feedback on whether you need additional studying.

Also, visit this site's "Study Hall," where you'll find an abundance of valuable resources that will help you succeed in this course.

Peak Performance Grammar and Mechanics

In Chapter 10 you were referred to the Peak Performance Grammar and Mechanics activities on the web at www.prenhall.com/onekey to improve your skill with apostrophes, quotation marks, parentheses and brackets, question marks and exclamation points, dashes, hyphens, and ellipses. For additional reinforcement in quotation marks, parentheses, and ellipses, go to www.prenhall.com/bovee, where you will find "Improve Your Grammar, Mechanics, and Usage" exercises.

chapter 13

Writing Reports and Proposals

LEARNING OBJECTIVES

After studying this chapter, you will be able to

1. Explain how to adapt to your audiences when writing reports and proposals
2. List the topics commonly covered in introduction, body, and closing of informational or analytical reports
3. Name five characteristics of effective report content
4. Name six strategies to strengthen your proposal argument
5. List the topics commonly covered in a proposal's introduction, body, and closing
6. Briefly describe three report elements that can help readers find their way in long documents

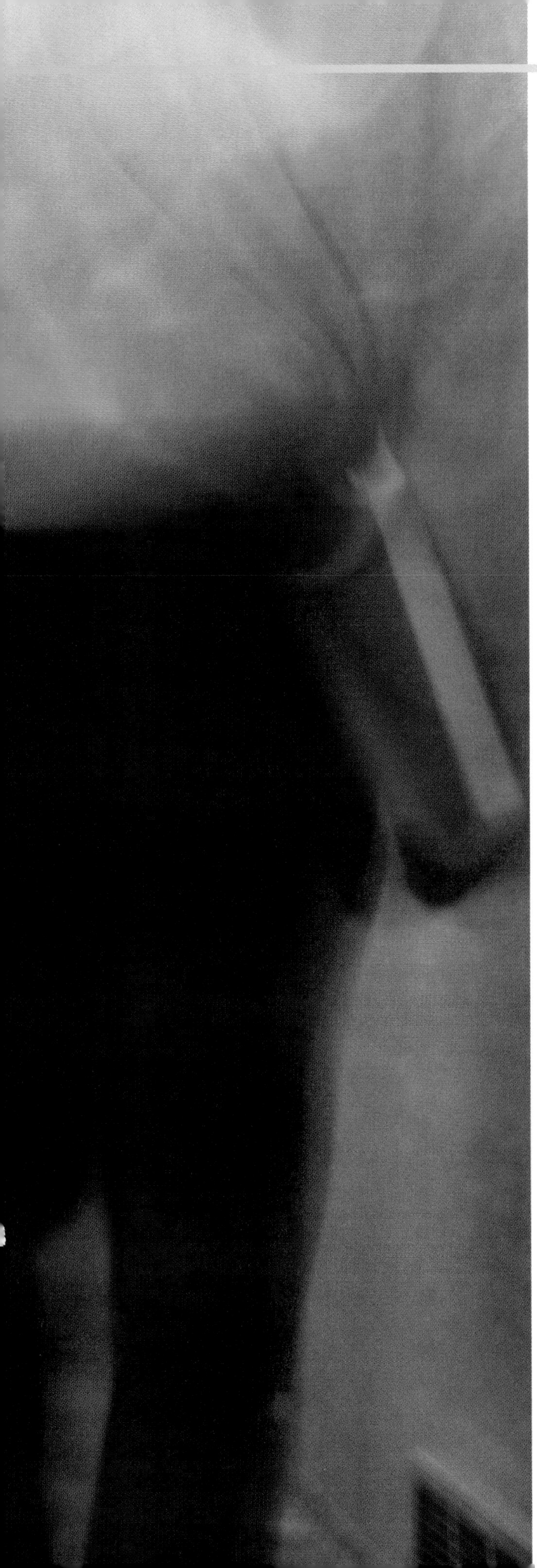

COMMUNICATION CLOSE-UP AT OMD WORLDWIDE

www.omdmedia.com

You've probably tried to talk with older family members or professors about some product that they've never even heard of. You're sure you've seen about a thousand ads for it, and you wonder, "How could they have missed it?" Pose this question to Beth Uyenco, and she could clear up the mystery with a two-part answer. First, media have become extremely fragmented in the United States, with an endless array of outlets spanning TV (broadcast, cable, and satellite), radio (AM, FM, and satellite), websites, magazines, newspapers, events, fashion, and more. So every year, the chances grow smaller that two people with different interests and habits will consume the same media. Second, new technologies let ad agencies develop unimaginably specific knowledge of audiences and their media preferences. Therefore these agencies can be more and more precise about placing the right ads in the right place at the right time.

The science behind all this insight is quite complicated. It relies on multiple databases, market segmentation (by age,

Beth Uyenco of OMD Worldwide relies on effective reports to help her clients understand complex issues involving the selection and purchase of advertising media.

gender, education, socioeconomic status, and so on), and detailed analyses of how and when various types of consumers interact with various media. Then once all this research has been completed and evaluated, it must be reported clearly and logically so that readers can act on the information. Uyenco is a superstar in this type of media research. She is the director of research at OMD Worldwide, an agency that provides media research, planning, and buying services for ad agencies and clients such as Dell Computer, FedEx, and PepsiCo.

Clients and colleagues praise Uyenco's rare ability to write reports and give presentations that explain the complexities of her work in plain, simple language, without confusing or frightening her audience. *Brandweek* magazine even named her its 2002 Media All-Star in Research. When asked about how she writes reports, Uyenco explained: "You can be the best researcher, but if you can't relate it to the business at hand, to the day-to-day demands that planners and media management face, or to the sales pressures that clients face, you'll be irrelevant."[1]

WRITING REPORTS AND PROPOSALS

Beth Uyenco will be the first to tell you how important the writing stage is in the development of successful reports and proposals. This chapter builds on the writing techniques and ideas you learned in Chapter 5 with issues that are particularly important when preparing longer message formats. As with shorter messages, take a few moments before you start writing to make sure you're ready to adapt your approach to your audience.

1 LEARNING OBJECTIVE

Explain how to adapt to your audiences when writing reports and proposals

ADAPTING TO YOUR AUDIENCE

Like all successful business messages, effective reports and proposals are adapted to the intended audience as much as possible. To ensure your own success with reports, be sensitive to audience needs, build strong relationships with your audience, and control your style and tone.

Communication Solution

One key to the success of Beth Uyenco's report writing is her emphasis on audience needs; she realizes her customers want practical, clearly understandable advice on creating effective advertising and choosing the best media to reach each audience—and they don't want to be bogged down with the technical intricacies of customer and media research.

Being Sensitive to Your Audience's Needs

Chapter 5 discusses four aspects of audience sensitivity, and all four apply to reports and proposals: adopting the "you" attitude, maintaining a strong sense of etiquette, emphasizing the positive, and using bias-free language. Reports and proposals that are highly technical, complex, or lengthy can put heavy demands on your readers, so the "you" attitude takes on even greater importance with these long messages. As you'll see later in this chapter, part of that attitude includes helping your readers find their way through your material so that they can understand critical information.

Long or complex reports demand a lot from readers, making the "you" attitude even more important.

In addition, various audience members can have widely different information needs. For instance, if you're reporting on the results of a customer satisfaction survey, the service manager might want every detail whereas the president may want only a top-level summary. With previews, summaries, appendixes, and other elements, you can meet the needs of a diverse audience—provided you plan for these elements in advance.

Building Strong Relationships with Your Audience

Your reports may continue to be read for months or years after you write them—and reach audiences you never envisioned.

Whether your report is intended for people inside or outside the company, be sure to plan how you will adapt your style and your language to reflect the image of your organization. Bear in mind that some reports can take on lives of their own, reaching a wider audience than you ever imagined and being read years after you wrote them, so choose your content and language with care. Since many companies have specific guidelines for communicating with public audiences, make sure you're aware of these preferences before you start writing.

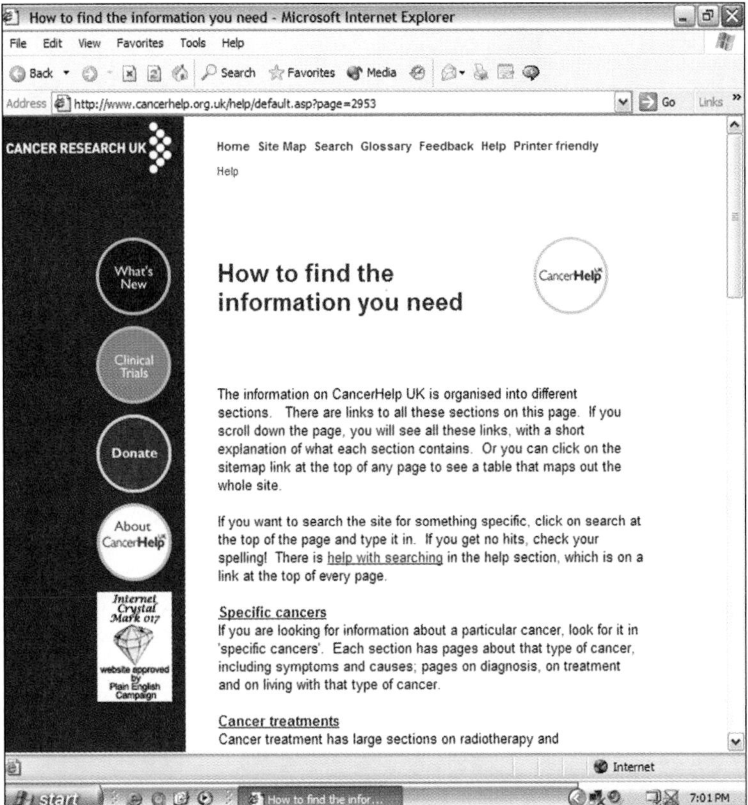

CancerHelp, a patient support organization in England, helps visitors to its website find needed information from a variety of online reports, even if they're new to the web.

As discussed in Chapter 5, establishing your credibility is vital to successful communication. To gain your audience's trust, research all sides of your topic, and document your findings with credible sources. Also, be aware that setting audience expectations too high can lead to problems with your credibility if you can't deliver everything people expect you to (see "Communication Miscues: Microsoft Slip Magnifies Criticism").

Controlling Your Style and Tone

Whether you're writing a report or a proposal, you'll need to decide on the appropriate style and tone. If you make your tone too informal, your audience might be put off by your casual approach. If you make it too formal, you could come across as impersonal and distant, perhaps too rigid to form a strong working relationship with others. Your level of formality is closely related to your document's format, length, and organization, as well as to your relationship with the audience.

If you know your readers reasonably well and your report is likely to meet with their approval, you can generally adopt a fairly informal tone. To make your tone less formal, speak to readers in the first person, refer to them as *you,* and refer to yourself as *I* (or *we* if there are multiple report authors). Such style choices create the more personal tone that is often (but not always) used in brief memo or letter reports.

To make your tone more formal, use the impersonal journalism style: Emphasize objectivity, ensure that content is free from personal opinion, and build your argument on provable facts. Naturally, an impersonal style does not automatically guarantee objective content. Your selection of facts is just as important as the way you phrase them, if not more so. If you omit crucial evidence, you're not being objective, even though your style is impersonal.

When creating a formal tone, you eliminate all references to *you* and *I* (including *we, us,* and *our*). However, be careful that avoiding personal pronouns doesn't lead to overusing phrases such as *there are* and *it is,* which sound dull and can lead to wordy sentence

Communication Miscues

Microsoft Slip Magnifies Criticism

Big companies are big targets, and software giant Microsoft has had to endure big headaches—customer tirades, competitor complaints, and government investigations. Worst of all, the company's widely used products are constantly being probed by hackers and virus writers looking for security flaws to exploit. In recent years, several widespread outbreaks of malicious software worms and viruses put Microsoft on the defensive. With every new software breach, critics accused Microsoft of rushing low-quality products to market and of taking too long to fix the problems.

The company responded with an internal initiative called Trustworthy Computing. Its main goal: improve software quality and make computing as dependable and secure as your electricity or telephone service. The word about Trustworthy Computing was spread throughout the company by Craig Mundie, chief technology officer, and the effort was supported by Chairman Bill Gates. But when Gates endorsed the idea in a position paper e-mailed to Microsoft's 50,000 full-time employees, someone leaked this internal document to the outside world, where it spread like a virus. Fortunately, the paper expressed noble goals—to create better software and to earn customer trust as it described the vision for Trustworthy Computing.

The leak seemed harmless enough . . . until the next major worm attack. Turns out that the very idea of Trustworthy Computing had raised customer expectations to a new high, and those expectations had only that much farther to fall after the latest attack. Critics hammered Microsoft even harder for unsatisfactory product quality and support practices. To counter these latest criticisms, Microsoft was forced to redouble quality efforts, even to the point of delaying the introduction of products that exhibit too many flaws during testing.

CAREER APPLICATIONS

1. This crisis came at a time when Microsoft was trying to sell more high-end software to businesses—which demand quality, reliability, and security. What else could Microsoft do to address the market's negative perceptions?
2. The leaked position paper created a lot of unplanned work for marketing and public relations personnel. Generalizing from this example, is any leak of an internal report truly harmless? Why or why not?

constructions. In addition, avoiding personal pronouns makes it easier to slip into the passive voice. Instead of saying "I think we should buy TramCo," you might end up saying "The financial analysis clearly shows that buying TramCo is the best alternative."

When you use an impersonal style, you impose a controlled distance between you and your readers. Your tone is not only objective but also businesslike and unemotional. Be careful to avoid jokes, similes, and metaphors, and try to minimize the use of colorful adjectives or adverbs.

A more formal tone is appropriate for longer reports, especially those dealing with controversial or complex information. You'll also use a more formal tone when your report will be sent to other parts of the organization or to outsiders, such as customers, suppliers, or members of the community. Yahoo! is known for using a playful, informal tone in its advertising, but the company's tone is more formal when communicating with the public on serious matters (see Figure 13.1).

Reports destined for audiences outside the United States often require a more formal tone to match the expectations of audiences in many other countries.

Communicating with people in other cultures often calls for more formality, for two reasons. First, the business environment outside the United States tends to be more formal in general, and that formality must be reflected in your communication. Second, the things you do to make a document informal (such as using humor and idiomatic language) tend to translate poorly or not at all from one culture to another. Using a less formal tone in cross-cultural reports and proposals increases the risk of offending people and the chance of miscommunicating information.

You can often tell what tone is appropriate for your readers by looking at other reports of a similar type in your company. If all the other reports on file are impersonal, you should probably adopt a formal tone yourself—unless you're confident that your readers prefer a document that is more personal and informal. However, most organizations expect business reports and proposals to be unobtrusive and impersonal, so your tone will often be formal.

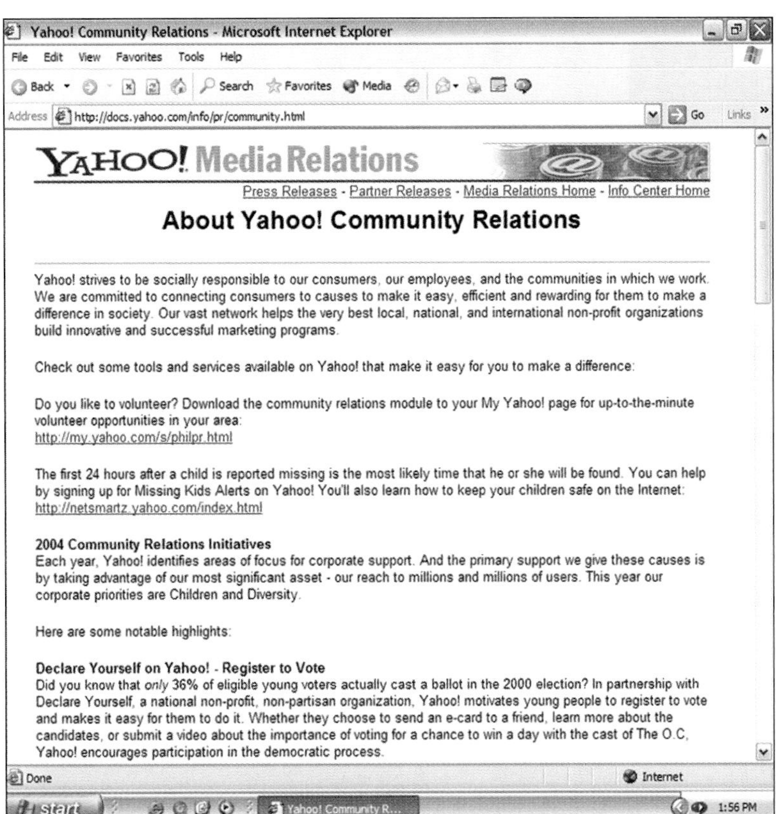

Yahoo! Community Relations - Microsoft Internet Explorer

File Edit View Favorites Tools Help

Address http://docs.yahoo.com/info/pr/community.html

YAHOO! Media Relations

Press Releases - Partner Releases - Media Relations Home - Info Center Home

About Yahoo! Community Relations

Yahoo! strives to be socially responsible to our consumers, our employees, and the communities in which we work. We are committed to connecting consumers to causes to make it easy, efficient and rewarding for them to make a difference in society. Our vast network helps the very best local, national, and international non-profit organizations build innovative and successful marketing programs.

Check out some tools and services available on Yahoo! that make it easy for you to make a difference:

Do you like to volunteer? Download the community relations module to your My Yahoo! page for up-to-the-minute volunteer opportunities in your area:
http://my.yahoo.com/s/philpr.html

The first 24 hours after a child is reported missing is the most likely time that he or she will be found. You can help by signing up for Missing Kids Alerts on Yahoo! You'll also learn how to keep your children safe on the Internet:
http://netsmartz.yahoo.com/index.html

2004 Community Relations Initiatives
Each year, Yahoo! identifies areas of focus for corporate support. And the primary support we give these causes is by taking advantage of our most significant asset - our reach to millions and millions of users. This year our corporate priorities are Children and Diversity.

Here are some notable highlights:

Declare Yourself on Yahoo! - Register to Vote
Did you know that *only* 36% of eligible young voters actually cast a ballot in the 2000 election? In partnership with Declare Yourself, a national non-profit, non-partisan organization, Yahoo! motivates young people to register to vote and makes it easy for them to do it. Whether they choose to send an e-card to a friend, learn more about the candidates, or submit a video about the importance of voting for a chance to win a day with the cast of The O.C, Yahoo! encourages participation in the democratic process.

Done Internet

start Yahoo! Community R... 1:56 PM

FIGURE 13.1
Choosing the Right Tone for Business Reports

COMPOSING REPORTS AND PROPOSALS

With a clear picture of how you need to adapt to your audience, you're ready to begin composing your first draft. Before you put those first words down on paper, though, review your outline one last time. Now that you've had a chance to think about your audience in detail, you might see some opportunities to improve the outline. For instance, you may decide to use an indirect approach instead of a direct one because now that you see your conclusions up front, you think that approach might be too forceful for your audience.

Fine-tuning your outline also gives you a chance to rephrase your headings to set the tone of your report. If you want a hard-hitting, direct tone, use informative phrasing. If you prefer an objective, indirect tone, use descriptive phrasing. You may even want to use your outline points as section headings for longer reports. Just be sure to use parallel construction when wording these points.

Give your outline another close look before you start writing; you can verify the organization of your information and start to craft final headings and subheadings.

This section not only discusses how to draft the content for your reports and proposals but also provides some examples of the types of content commonly included in each document. It also presents some strategies for making your content more readable, such as using a consistent time perspective and providing structural clues to help readers navigate your document. When you compose reports and proposals, follow the writing advice offered in Chapter 5: Select the best words, create the most effective sentences, and develop coherent paragraphs.

2 LEARNING OBJECTIVE

List the topics commonly covered in introduction, body, and closing of informational or analytical reports

As with other written business communications, the text of reports and proposals has three main sections: an introduction, a body, and a close. The content and length of each section varies with the type and purpose of the document, the document's organizational structure, the length and depth of the material, the document's degree of formality, and your relationship with your audience.

The *introduction* (or *opening*) is the first section in the text of any report or proposal. An effective introduction accomplishes at least four things:

Your introduction needs to put the report in context for the reader, introduce the subject, preview main ideas, and establish the tone of the document.

- Puts the report or proposal in a broader context by tying it to a problem or an assignment
- Introduces the subject or purpose of the report or proposal and indicates why the subject is important

FIGURE 13.2 Effective Problem-Solving Report Focusing on Recommendations

MEMO

TO: Board of Directors, Executive Committee members
FROM: Alycia Jenn, Business Development Manager
DATE: July 6, 2005
SUBJECT: World Wide Web retailing site

Clarifies the purpose and origin of the report in the introduction

In response to your request, my staff and I investigated the potential for establishing a retailing site on the World Wide Web. After analyzing the behavior of our customers and major competitors and studying the overall development of electronic retailing, we have three recommendations:

1. Yes, we should establish an online presence within the next six months.
2. We should engage a firm that specializes in online retailing to design and develop the website.
3. We must take care to integrate online retailing with our store-based and mail-order operations.

Clarifies what's needed by wording recommendations simply and to the point

WE SHOULD SET UP A WEBSITE

Presents logical and clear reasons for recommending that the firm establish a website

First, does a website make financial sense today? Studies suggest that our competitors are not currently generating significant revenue from their websites. Stallini's is the leader so far, but its sales haven't broken the $1 million mark. Moreover, at least half of our competitors' online sales are from current customers who would have purchased the same items in-store or by mail order. The cost of setting up a retailing site is around $120,000, so it isn't possible to justify a site solely on the basis of current financial return.

Second, do we need to establish a presence now in order to remain competitive in the future? The online situation is too fluid and unpredictable to answer this question in a quantitative profit-and-loss way, but a qualitative view of strategy indicates that we should set up a site:

- As younger consumers (more comfortable with online shopping) reach their peak earning years (ages 35–54), they'll be more likely to buy online than today's peak spenders.
- The web is erasing geographical shopping limits, presenting both a threat and an opportunity. Even though our customers can now shop websites anywhere in the world (so that we have thousands of competitors instead of a dozen), we can now target customers anywhere in the world.
- If the growth in online retailing continues, this will eventually be a viable market. Establishing a site now and working out any problems will prepare us for high-volume online business in the years ahead.

WE SHOULD ENGAGE A CONSULTANT TO IMPLEMENT THE SITE

Includes not only the recommendation to establish a website but also one to hire a consultant to implement the website and integrate it with existing systems

Implementing a competitive retailing site can take anywhere from 1,000 to 1,500 hours of design and programming time. We have some of the expertise needed in-house, but the marketing and information systems departments have only 300 person-hours in the next six months. I recommend that we engage a web design consultant to help us with the design and to do all the programming.

(continued)

- Previews the main ideas and the order in which they'll be covered
- Establishes the tone of the document and the writer's relationship with the audience

The body of your report presents, analyzes, and interprets the information you gathered during your investigation.

The *body* is the middle section in the text of your report or proposal. It consists of the major divisions or chapters (with various levels of headings for long documents). These divisions present, analyze, and interpret the information gathered during your investigation, and they support the recommendations or conclusions discussed in your document. The body contains the proof, the detailed information necessary to support your conclusions and recommendations. Notice how Alycia Jenn uses the body of her report to articulate her recommendation for establishing a retail website (see Figure 13.2). As Jenn puts it, "Retail websites might be common today, but setting up shop on the Internet is a big decision for our company. We don't have the big computer staffs that our larger competitors have, and our business development team is stretched rather thin already. On the other

FIGURE 13.2 Continued

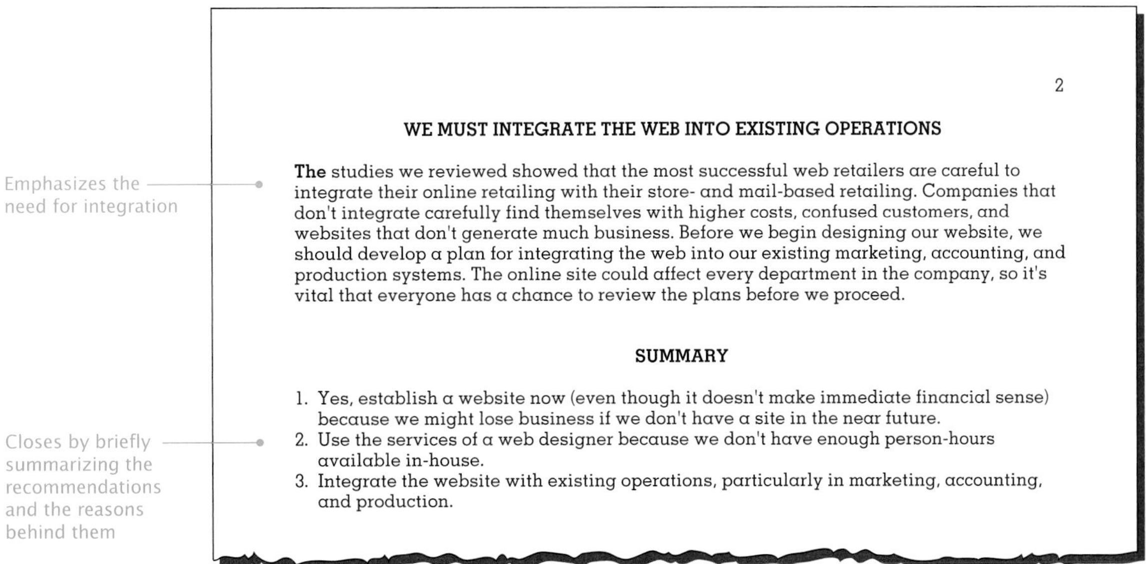

2

WE MUST INTEGRATE THE WEB INTO EXISTING OPERATIONS

The studies we reviewed showed that the most successful web retailers are careful to integrate their online retailing with their store- and mail-based retailing. Companies that don't integrate carefully find themselves with higher costs, confused customers, and websites that don't generate much business. Before we begin designing our website, we should develop a plan for integrating the web into our existing marketing, accounting, and production systems. The online site could affect every department in the company, so it's vital that everyone has a chance to review the plans before we proceed.

SUMMARY

1. Yes, establish a website now (even though it doesn't make immediate financial sense) because we might lose business if we don't have a site in the near future.
2. Use the services of a web designer because we don't have enough person-hours available in-house.
3. Integrate the website with existing operations, particularly in marketing, accounting, and production.

Emphasizes the need for integration
Closes by briefly summarizing the recommendations and the reasons behind them

hand, I know that more and more people are shopping online, and we don't want to be left out of this mode of retailing. After studying the issue for several weeks, I concluded that we should go ahead with a site, but we had to be careful about how we implement it." The body of her report provides enough information to support her argument, without burdening her high-level readership with a lot of tactical details.

The *close* is the final section in the text of your report or proposal. It has four important functions:

- Emphasizes the main points of the message
- Summarizes the benefits to the reader if the document suggests a change or some other course of action
- Refers back to all the pieces and reminds readers how those pieces fit together
- Brings all the action items together in one place and gives the details about who should do what, when, where, and how

Research shows that the final section of a report or proposal leaves a strong lasting impression. The close gives you one last chance to make sure that your report says what you intended.[2] In fact, readers who are in a hurry might skip the body of the report and read only the summary, so make sure it carries a strong, clear message.

The closing section of your report should emphasize the main message, summarize the benefits to the reader, remind the reader how the major pieces of information in the report relate to one another, and gather together all the action items (if any), and indicate responsibilities for each one.

The close might be the only part of your report some readers have time for, so make sure it conveys the full weight of your message.

Drafting Report Content

The content and quality of your reports can have a direct impact on your professional success because they show how well you think, gather and analyze data, draw conclusions, and develop and support your recommendations. In other words, your credibility and prospects for the future are at risk with every business report you write. You'll create more successful reports if your content is

3 LEARNING OBJECTIVE

Name five characteristics of effective report content

- **Accurate.** Information presented in a report must be factually correct and error-free. When writing reports, be sure to double-check your facts and references in addition to checking for typos. If an audience ever gets the inkling that your information is shaky, they'll start to view all your work with a skeptical eye.
- **Complete.** To help colleagues or supervisors make a decision, include all the information necessary for readers to understand the situation, problem, or proposal. Support all key assertions using an appropriate combination of illustrations, explanations, and facts.[3] But remember, time is precious, so tell your readers what they need to know—no more, no less—and present the information in a way that is geared to their needs.

- **Balanced.** Present all sides of the issue fairly and equitably, and include all the essential information, even if some of the information doesn't support your line of reasoning. Although you want to be as brief as possible, your readers need a minimum amount of information before they can grasp the issue being presented. Omitting relevant information or facts can bias your report.
- **Clear and logical.** Clear sentence structure and good transitions are essential.[4] Save your readers time by making sure your sentences are uncluttered, contain well-chosen words, and proceed logically. To help your readers move from one point to the next, make your transitions just as clear and logical. For a successful report, identify the ideas that belong together, and organize them in a way that's easy to understand.[5]
- **Documented properly.** If you use primary and secondary sources for your report or proposal, be sure to properly document and give credit to your sources, as Chapter 10 explains.

Keeping these points in mind will help you draft the most effective introduction, body, and close for your report. Note how Carlyce Johnson offers one client a complete, but efficient, update of her company's landscaping services (see an excerpt from her report in Figure 13.3). In addition to providing routine information, she also informs the client of progress on two

FIGURE 13.3 Effective Progress Report Offering Complete Content

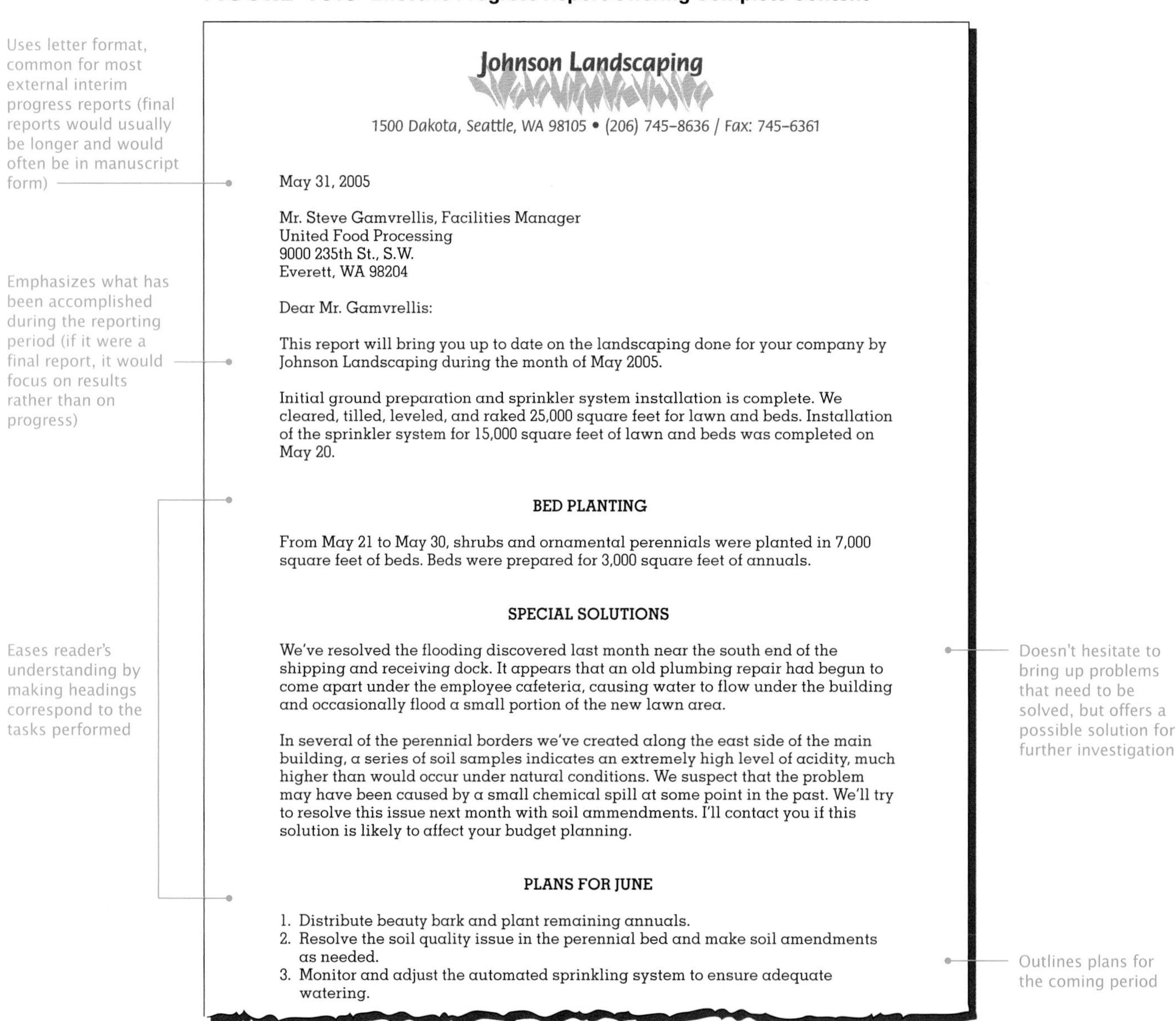

Johnson Landscaping

1500 Dakota, Seattle, WA 98105 • (206) 745-8636 / Fax: 745-6361

May 31, 2005

Mr. Steve Gamvrellis, Facilities Manager
United Food Processing
9000 235th St., S.W.
Everett, WA 98204

Dear Mr. Gamvrellis:

This report will bring you up to date on the landscaping done for your company by Johnson Landscaping during the month of May 2005.

Initial ground preparation and sprinkler system installation is complete. We cleared, tilled, leveled, and raked 25,000 square feet for lawn and beds. Installation of the sprinkler system for 15,000 square feet of lawn and beds was completed on May 20.

BED PLANTING

From May 21 to May 30, shrubs and ornamental perennials were planted in 7,000 square feet of beds. Beds were prepared for 3,000 square feet of annuals.

SPECIAL SOLUTIONS

We've resolved the flooding discovered last month near the south end of the shipping and receiving dock. It appears that an old plumbing repair had begun to come apart under the employee cafeteria, causing water to flow under the building and occasionally flood a small portion of the new lawn area.

In several of the perennial borders we've created along the east side of the main building, a series of soil samples indicates an extremely high level of acidity, much higher than would occur under natural conditions. We suspect that the problem may have been caused by a small chemical spill at some point in the past. We'll try to resolve this issue next month with soil ammendments. I'll contact you if this solution is likely to affect your budget planning.

PLANS FOR JUNE

1. Distribute beauty bark and plant remaining annuals.
2. Resolve the soil quality issue in the perennial bed and make soil amendments as needed.
3. Monitor and adjust the automated sprinkling system to ensure adequate watering.

Uses letter format, common for most external interim progress reports (final reports would usually be longer and would often be in manuscript form)
Emphasizes what has been accomplished during the reporting period (if it were a final report, it would focus on results rather than on progress)
Eases reader's understanding by making headings correspond to the tasks performed
Doesn't hesitate to bring up problems that need to be solved, but offers a possible solution for further investigation
Outlines plans for the coming period

problem areas, one that her firm has been able to resolve and one that they've just discovered. In the case of the problem with the soil, you might be tempted not to share any information with the client until you've resolved the problem, but doing so could affect the client's budgets and other plans. Johnson does the right thing by telling the client about the problem early.

Report Introduction

The specific elements you should include in an introduction depend on the nature and length of the report, the circumstances under which you're writing it, and your relationship with the audience. An introduction could contain all of the following topics, although you'll want to pick and choose the best ones to include with each report you write:

Carefully select the elements to include in your introduction; strive for a balance between necessary, expected information and brevity.

- **Authorization.** When, how, and by whom the report was authorized; who wrote it; and when it was submitted. This material is especially important when no letter of transmittal is included.
- **Problem/opportunity/purpose.** The reason for the report's existence and what is to be accomplished as a result of your having written the report.
- **Scope.** What is and what isn't going to be covered in the report. The scope indicates the report's size and complexity; it also helps with the critical job of setting the audience's expectations.
- **Background.** The historical conditions or factors that led up to the report. This section enables readers to understand how the problem, situation, or opportunity developed and what has been done about it so far.
- **Sources and methods.** The primary and secondary sources of information used. As appropriate, this section explains how samples were selected, how questionnaires were constructed (which should be included in an appendix with any cover letters), what follow-up was done, and so on. This section builds reader confidence in the work and in the sources and methods used.
- **Definitions.** A list of terms that might be unfamiliar to your audience, along with brief definitions. This section is unnecessary if readers are familiar with the terms you've used in your report—and they all agree on what the terms mean, which isn't always the case. If you have any question about reader knowledge, define any terms that might be misinterpreted. Terms may also be defined in the body, explanatory notes, or glossary.
- **Limitations.** Factors beyond your control that affect report quality, such as budget limitations, schedule constraints, or limited access to information or people. If appropriate, this section can also express any doubts you have about any aspect of your report. Such candor may be uncomfortable to you, but it helps your readers assess your information accurately, and it helps establish your report's integrity. However, always take care when expressing limitations. Don't apologize or try to explain away personal shortcomings (such as having put the report off until the last minute, so you weren't able to do a first-rate job on it).
- **Report organization.** The organization of the report (what topics are covered and in what order), along with a rationale for following this plan. This section is a road map that helps readers understand what's coming at each turn of the report and why.

In a relatively brief report, these topics may be discussed in only a paragraph or two. Here's an example of a brief indirect opening, taken from the introduction of a memo on why a new line of luggage has failed to sell well. The writer's ultimate goal is to recommend a shift in marketing strategy.

> The performance of the Venturer line can be improved. In the two years since its introduction, this product line has achieved a sales volume lower than we expected, resulting in a drain on the company's overall earnings. The purpose of this report is to review the luggage-buying habits of consumers in all markets where the Venturer line is sold, so that we can determine where to put our marketing emphasis.

This paragraph quickly introduces the subject (disappointing sales), tells why the problem is important (drain on earnings), and indicates the main points to be addressed in the body of the report (review of markets where the Venturer line is sold), without revealing what the conclusions and recommendations will be.

In a much longer formal report, the discussion of these topics may span several pages and constitute a significant section within the report.

Report Body

As with the introduction, the body of your report can require some tough decisions about which elements to include and how much detail to offer as supporting evidence. Here again, your decision depends on many variables, including the needs of your audience. Some audiences and situations require detailed coverage; others can be handled with more concise treatment. Provide only enough detail in the body to support your conclusions and recommendations; you can put additional detail in tables, charts, and appendixes.

As with the introduction, the report body should contain only enough information to convey your message in a convincing fashion; don't overload the body with interesting but unnecessary material.

The topics commonly covered in a report body include

- Explanations of a problem or opportunity
- Facts, statistical evidence, and trends
- Results of studies or investigations
- Discussion and analyses of potential courses of action
- Advantages, disadvantages, costs, and benefits of a particular course of action
- Procedures or steps in a process
- Methods and approaches
- Criteria for evaluating alternatives and options
- Conclusions and recommendations (in direct reports)
- Supporting reasons for conclusions or recommendations

For analytical reports using the direct organizational approach, you'll generally state your conclusions or recommendations in the introduction and use the body of your report to provide your evidence and support (as illustrated in Figures 13.2 on page 396 and 13.3 on page 398). If you're using the indirect organizational approach, you'll likely use the body to discuss your logic and reserve your conclusions or recommendations until the very end.

Report Close

The nature of your close depends on the type of report (informational, analytical, or proposal) and the approach (direct or indirect).

The content and length of your report close depend on your choice of direct or indirect order, among other variables. If your report is organized in the direct order, end with a summary of key points (usually not necessary in short memo-style reports), listed in the order they appear in the report body. If appropriate, briefly restate your conclusions or recommendations. If your report is organized in the indirect order, your conclusions or recommendations may be presented for the first time at the end. Just remember that a conclusion or recommendation isn't the place to introduce new facts; your audience should have all the information they need by the time they reach this point in your report.

If your report is intended to lead to action, use the ending to spell out exactly what should happen next. Readers may agree with everything you say in your report but still fail to take any action if you're vague about what should happen next. A key part of your job in the close is to make sure that your readers understand what's expected of them and that they have some appreciation of any difficulties that are likely to arise. Providing a schedule and specific task assignments is helpful because concrete plans have a way of commanding action. If you'll be taking all the actions yourself, make sure your readers understand this fact so that they'll know what to expect from you (see Figure 13.4).

For long reports, you may need to divide your close into separate sections for conclusions, recommendations, and actions.

In a short report, the close may be only a paragraph or two. However, the close of a long report may have separate sections for conclusions, recommendations, and actions. Using separate sections helps your reader locate this material and focus on each element. Such an arrangement also gives you a final opportunity to emphasize this important content. Combining conclusions and recommendations under one heading is perfectly fine; presenting a conclusion without implying a recommendation is often difficult.

If you have multiple conclusions, recommendations, or actions, you may want to number and list them. An appropriate lead-in to such a list might be, "The findings of this study lead to the following conclusions." A statement that could be used for a list of recommendations might be, "Based on the conclusions of this study, we make the following recommendations." A statement that could be used for actions might be, "In order to

FIGURE 13.4 Effective Report Expressing Action Plan in the Close

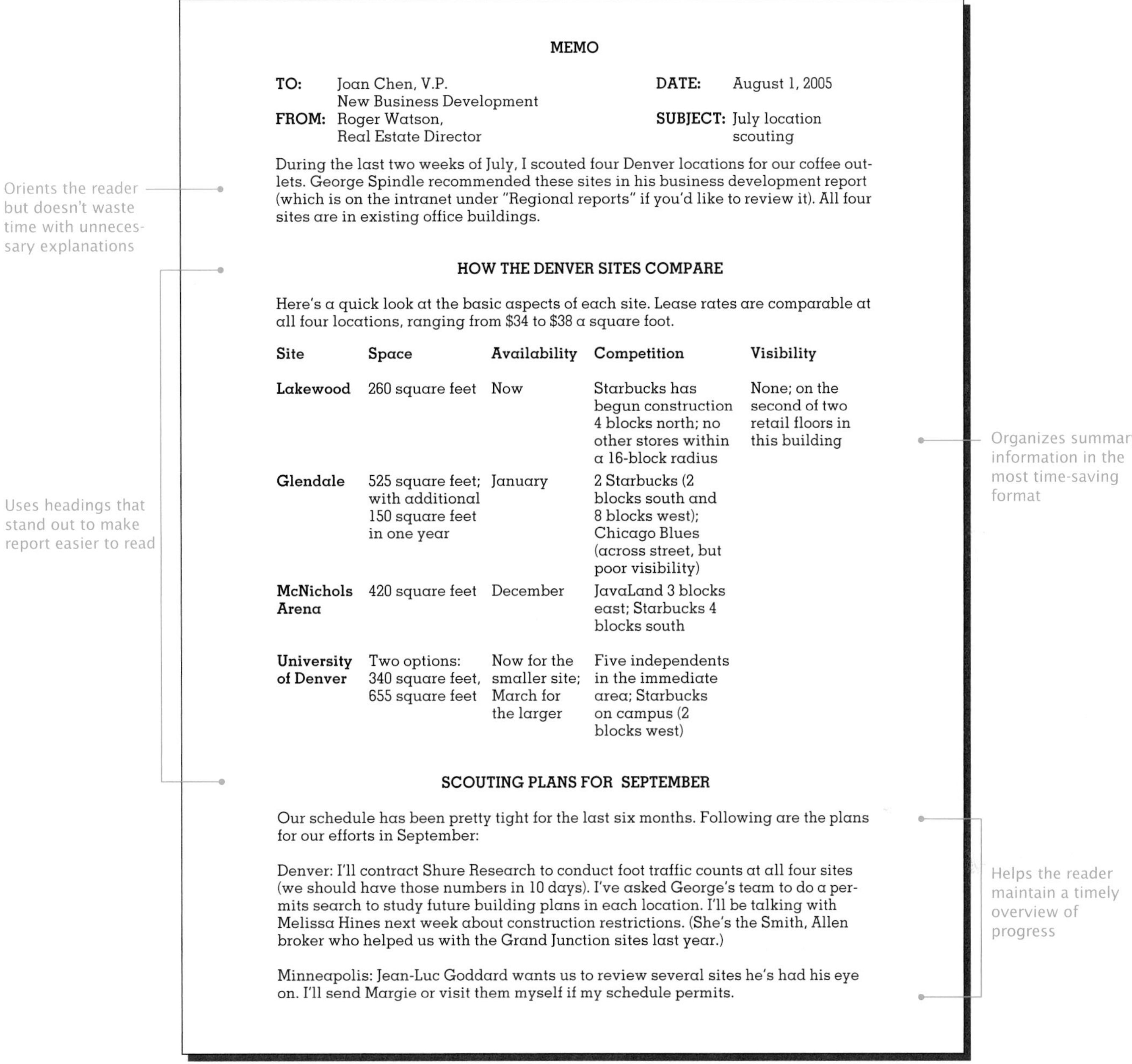

MEMO

TO: Joan Chen, V.P. New Business Development
FROM: Roger Watson, Real Estate Director
DATE: August 1, 2005
SUBJECT: July location scouting

During the last two weeks of July, I scouted four Denver locations for our coffee outlets. George Spindle recommended these sites in his business development report (which is on the intranet under "Regional reports" if you'd like to review it). All four sites are in existing office buildings.

HOW THE DENVER SITES COMPARE

Here's a quick look at the basic aspects of each site. Lease rates are comparable at all four locations, ranging from $34 to $38 a square foot.

Site	Space	Availability	Competition	Visibility
Lakewood	260 square feet	Now	Starbucks has begun construction 4 blocks north; no other stores within a 16-block radius	None; on the second of two retail floors in this building
Glendale	525 square feet; with additional 150 square feet in one year	January	2 Starbucks (2 blocks south and 8 blocks west); Chicago Blues (across street, but poor visibility)	
McNichols Arena	420 square feet	December	JavaLand 3 blocks east; Starbucks 4 blocks south	
University of Denver	Two options: 340 square feet, 655 square feet	Now for the smaller site; March for the larger	Five independents in the immediate area; Starbucks on campus (2 blocks west)	

SCOUTING PLANS FOR SEPTEMBER

Our schedule has been pretty tight for the last six months. Following are the plans for our efforts in September:

Denver: I'll contract Shure Research to conduct foot traffic counts at all four sites (we should have those numbers in 10 days). I've asked George's team to do a permits search to study future building plans in each location. I'll be talking with Melissa Hines next week about construction restrictions. (She's the Smith, Allen broker who helped us with the Grand Junction sites last year.)

Minneapolis: Jean-Luc Goddard wants us to review several sites he's had his eye on. I'll send Margie or visit them myself if my schedule permits.

Orients the reader but doesn't waste time with unnecessary explanations
Uses headings that stand out to make report easier to read
Organizes summary information in the most time-saving format
Helps the reader maintain a timely overview of progress

accomplish our goals on time, we must complete the following actions before the end of the year."

Drafting Proposal Content

Like reports, proposals have an introduction, a body, and a close. The content for each section is governed by many variables—the most important being the source of your proposal. If your proposal is unsolicited, you have some latitude in the scope and organization of content. However, the scope and organization of a solicited proposal are usually governed by the request for proposals. Most RFPs spell out precisely what you should cover and in what order so that all bids will be similar in form. This uniformity lets the recipient evaluate competing proposals in a systematic way. In many organizations a team of evaluators splits up the proposals and looks at various sections. An engineer might review the technical portions of all the proposals submitted, and an accountant might review the cost estimates.

Approach proposals the same way you approach persuasive messages.

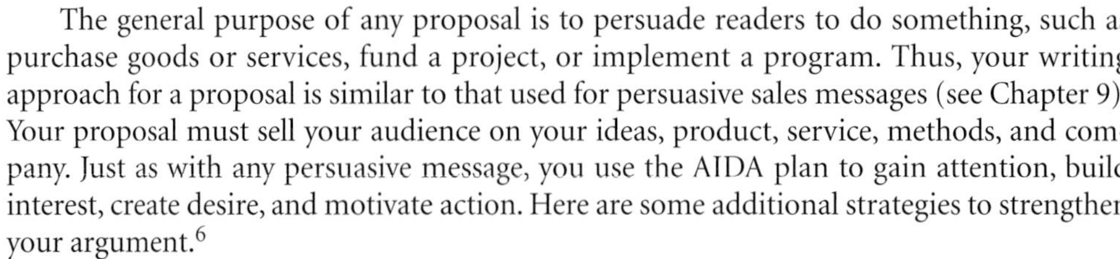

The general purpose of any proposal is to persuade readers to do something, such as purchase goods or services, fund a project, or implement a program. Thus, your writing approach for a proposal is similar to that used for persuasive sales messages (see Chapter 9). Your proposal must sell your audience on your ideas, product, service, methods, and company. Just as with any persuasive message, you use the AIDA plan to gain attention, build interest, create desire, and motivate action. Here are some additional strategies to strengthen your argument.[6]

4 LEARNING OBJECTIVE

Name six strategies to strengthen your proposal argument

Business proposals need to provide more than just attractive ideas—readers look for evidence of practical, achievable solutions.

- **Demonstrate your knowledge.** Everything you write should show your reader that you have the knowledge and experience to solve the problem or address the opportunity outlined in your proposal.
- **Provide concrete information and examples.** Enthusiasm and good intentions are no substitute for the hard facts readers will demand. Avoid vague, unsupported generalizations such as "We are losing money on this program." Instead, provide quantifiable details such as the amount of money being lost, how, why, and so on. Explain how much money your proposed solution will save. Spell out your plan and give details on how the job will be done. Such concrete information persuades readers; unsupported generalizations do not.
- **Research the competition.** If you're competing against other companies for a potential customer's business, use trade publications and the Internet to become familiar with the products, services, and prices of these other companies. Even if you're not competing against other companies, find out what alternatives your audience might choose over your proposal so that you can emphasize why your solution is the optimum choice.
- **Prove that your proposal is workable.** Your proposal must be appropriate and feasible for your audience. It should be consistent with your audience's capabilities. For instance, your proposal would be pointless if it recommended a plan of action that requires three times the number of employees or that doubles the budget.
- **Adopt a "you" attitude.** Relate your product, service, or personnel to the reader's exact needs, either as stated in the RFP for a solicited proposal or as discovered through your own investigation for an unsolicited proposal.
- **Package your proposal attractively.** Make sure your proposal is letter perfect, inviting, and readable. Readers will prejudge the quality of your products or services by the proposal you submit. Errors, omissions, or inconsistencies will work against you—and maybe even cost you important career and business opportunities.

When Karla Brown applied to the Small Business Association (SBA) for a microloan, she was facing stiff competition for the agency's limited resources. So Brown wrote a proposal using the AIDA plan and successfully persuaded the SBA to lend her $19,000 to start her business, Ashmont Flowers Plus.

Proposals in various industries often have their own special challenges as well. For instance, management consultants have to convince every potential client that they have the skills and knowledge to solve the client's problem—without giving the answer away for free in the proposal. In other industries, such as transportation services, bidders may be asked to compute hundreds or thousands of individual pricing scenarios. Hands-on experience goes a long way in deciding what to include and exclude in a report; whenever possible, get advice from a senior colleague who's been through it before.

5 LEARNING OBJECTIVE

List the topics commonly covered in a proposal's introduction, body, and closing

Proposal Introduction

The introduction presents and summarizes the problem you want to solve (or the opportunity you want to exploit), along with your proposed solution. It orients readers to the remainder of the text. If your proposal is solicited, its introduction should refer to the RFP so that readers know which RFP you're responding to. If your proposal is unsolicited, your introduction should mention any factors that led you to submit your proposal. You might mention mutual acquaintances, or you might refer to previous conversations you've had with readers. The following topics are commonly covered in a proposal introduction:

- **Background or statement of the problem.** Briefly reviews the reader's situation and establishes a need for action. Readers may not perceive a problem or opportunity the same way you do. In unsolicited proposals, you need to convince them that a problem or opportunity exists before you can convince them to accept your solution. In a way that is meaningful to your reader, discuss the current situation and explain how things could be better. Emphasize how your goals align with your audience's goals.
- **Solution.** Briefly describes the change you propose and highlights your key selling points and their benefits, showing how your proposal will help readers meet their business objectives. In long proposals, the heading for this section might also be "Preliminary Analysis," "Overview of Approach," or some other wording that will identify this section as a preview of your solution.
- **Scope.** States the boundaries of the proposal—what you will and will not do. Sometimes called "Delimitations."
- **Organization.** Orients the reader to the remainder of the proposal and calls attention to the major divisions of information.

In an unsolicited proposal, your introduction needs to convince readers that a problem or opportunity exists.

In short proposals, your discussion of these topics will be brief—perhaps only a sentence or two for each one. For long, formal proposals, each of these topics may warrant separate subheadings and several paragraphs of discussion.

Proposal Body

The proposal's body has the same purpose as the body of other reports: It gives complete details on the proposed solution and specifies what the anticipated results will be. Because a proposal is by definition a persuasive message, your audience expects you to promote your offering in a confident but professional manner. Even when you're expressing an idea that you believe in passionately, maintain an objective tone so that you don't risk overselling your message (see "Ethics Detective: Overselling the Solution").

Readers understand that a proposal is a persuasive message, so they're willing to accommodate a degree of promotional emphasis in your writing—as long as it is professional and focused on their needs.

Ethics Detective

Overselling the Solution

As the manager in charge of your company's New Ventures Group, you've read your share of proposals—hundreds, maybe thousands, of them. You've developed a sixth sense about these documents, an ability to separate cautious optimism from self-doubt and distinguish justified enthusiasm from insupportable hype.

Your company invests in promising smaller firms that could grow into beneficial business partners or even future acquisitions. In a typical scenario, a small company invents a new product but needs additional funding to manufacture and market it. You make the first major decision in this investment process, so your choices and recommendations to the board of directors are crucial.

Moreover, the risks are considerable. If one of your recommendations doesn't pan out, the company could lose all the money it invested (often millions), and that's only the start. Failures consume your team's precious time and energy and can even put the company at risk for shareholder lawsuits and other serious headaches. In other words, mistakes in your line of work are costly.

The proposal in front of you today is intriguing. A small company in Oklahoma has designed a product called the Wireless Shopping List, and you think the idea might appeal to upscale homeowners. Small touchscreens are placed around the house, wherever occupants are likely to think of things they need to buy on the next shopping trip: on the refrigerator door, in the media room (when somebody finishes off the popcorn), in the garage, in the gardening shed. The system collects all these inputs and prints out a handy shopping list on command. It's a clever idea, but one paragraph in the proposal bothers you:

> Everybody in our test market audience was absolutely stunned when we demonstrated the simulated system. They couldn't believe something like this was even possible. It was so handy and so convenient—everyone said it would change their lives forever. We haven't even settled on the price yet, but every single person in the room wanted to place an order, on the spot.

ANALYSIS

This proposal potentially oversells the idea in at least three different ways. Identify them and explain how they could lead you to decline the investment opportunity.

In addition to providing facts and evidence to support your conclusions, an effective body covers this information:

The work plan indicates exactly how you will accomplish the solution presented in the proposal.

- **Proposed approach.** Describes what you have to offer: your concept, product, or service. This section may also be titled "Technical Proposal," "Research Design," "Issues for Analysis," or "Work Statement." To convince readers that your proposal has merit, focus on the strengths of your offer in relation to reader needs. Stress the benefits of your product, service, or investment opportunity that are relevant to your readers' needs, and point out any advantages that you have over your competitors.
- **Work plan.** Describes how you'll accomplish what must be done (unless you'll provide a standard, off-the-shelf item). Explain the steps you'll take, their timing, the methods or resources you'll use, and the person(s) responsible. Specifically include when the work will begin, how it will be divided into stages, when you will finish, and whether any follow-up is involved. If appropriate, include a timeline or Gantt chart highlighting any critical dates. For solicited proposals, make sure your dates match those specified in the RFP. Keep in mind that if your proposal is accepted, the work plan is contractually binding, so don't promise to deliver more than you can realistically achieve within the stated time period.
- **Statement of qualifications.** Describes your organization's experience, personnel, and facilities—all in relation to reader needs. If you work for a large company that frequently submits proposals, you might borrow much of this section intact from previous proposals. However, be sure to tailor any boilerplate material to suit the situation. The qualifications section can be an important selling point, and it deserves to be handled carefully. You can supplement your qualifications by including a list of client references, but get permission ahead of time to use these references.
- **Costs.** Covers pricing, reimbursable expenses, discounts, and so on. Coverage can vary widely, from a single price amount to detailed breakdowns by part number, service category, and so on. If you're responding to an RFP, follow the instructions it contains. In other cases, your firm probably has a set policy for discussing costs. The amount of detail you provide depends on your relationship with your audience.

In an informal proposal, discussion of some or all of these elements may be grouped together and presented in a letter format, as the proposal in Figure 13.5 does. In a formal proposal, the discussion of these elements will be quite long and thorough. The format may resemble long reports with multiple parts, as Chapter 14 discusses.

Proposal Close

The close is your last chance to convince the reader of the merits of your proposal, so make doubly sure it's clear, compelling, and audience-oriented.

The final section of a proposal generally summarizes the key points, emphasizes the benefits that readers will realize from your solution, summarizes the merits of your approach, restates why you and your firm are the ones to perform the service or provide the products in question, and asks for a decision from the client. The close is your last opportunity to persuade readers to accept your proposal. In both formal and informal proposals, make this section relatively brief, assertive (but not brash or abrupt), and confident.

As you draft material for the introduction, body, and close of your reports and proposals, pay close attention to two issues that often cause problems for novice writers, especially in long documents: Be sure to maintain a consistent time perspective throughout your reports and help readers find their way through your material.

Establishing a Consistent Time Perspective

In what time frame will your report exist? Will you write in the past or present tense? The person who wrote this paragraph never decided:

> Of those interviewed, 25 percent <u>report</u> that they <u>are</u> dissatisfied with their present brand. The wealthiest participants <u>complained</u> most frequently, but all income categories <u>are</u> interested in trying a new brand. Only 5 percent of the interviewees <u>say</u> they <u>had</u> no interest in alternative products.

FIGURE 13.5 Effective Solicited Proposal in Letter Format

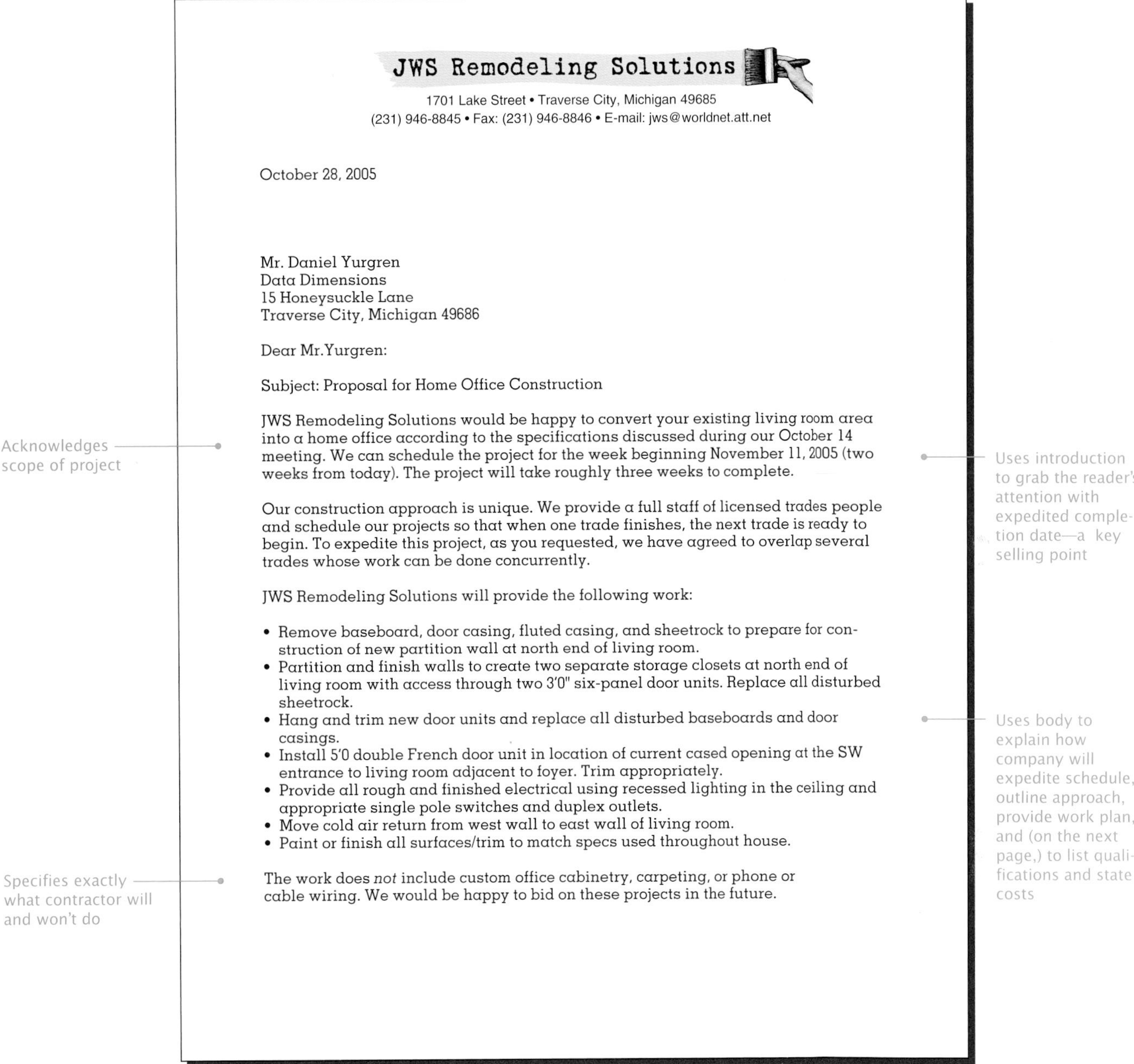

JWS Remodeling Solutions

1701 Lake Street • Traverse City, Michigan 49685
(231) 946-8845 • Fax: (231) 946-8846 • E-mail: jws@worldnet.att.net

October 28, 2005

Mr. Daniel Yurgren
Data Dimensions
15 Honeysuckle Lane
Traverse City, Michigan 49686

Dear Mr.Yurgren:

Subject: Proposal for Home Office Construction

JWS Remodeling Solutions would be happy to convert your existing living room area into a home office according to the specifications discussed during our October 14 meeting. We can schedule the project for the week beginning November 11, 2005 (two weeks from today). The project will take roughly three weeks to complete.

Our construction approach is unique. We provide a full staff of licensed trades people and schedule our projects so that when one trade finishes, the next trade is ready to begin. To expedite this project, as you requested, we have agreed to overlap several trades whose work can be done concurrently.

JWS Remodeling Solutions will provide the following work:

- Remove baseboard, door casing, fluted casing, and sheetrock to prepare for construction of new partition wall at north end of living room.
- Partition and finish walls to create two separate storage closets at north end of living room with access through two 3'0" six-panel door units. Replace all disturbed sheetrock.
- Hang and trim new door units and replace all disturbed baseboards and door casings.
- Install 5'0 double French door unit in location of current cased opening at the SW entrance to living room adjacent to foyer. Trim appropriately.
- Provide all rough and finished electrical using recessed lighting in the ceiling and appropriate single pole switches and duplex outlets.
- Move cold air return from west wall to east wall of living room.
- Paint or finish all surfaces/trim to match specs used throughout house.

The work does *not* include custom office cabinetry, carpeting, or phone or cable wiring. We would be happy to bid on these projects in the future.

Acknowledges scope of project
Uses introduction to grab the reader's attention with expedited completion date—a key selling point
Uses body to explain how company will expedite schedule, outline approach, provide work plan, and (on the next page,) to list qualifications and state costs
Specifies exactly what contractor will and won't do

(continued)

By flipping from tense to tense when describing the same research results, you can confuse your readers. Is the shift significant, they wonder, or are you just being careless? Eliminate the potential for such confusion by using tense consistently.

Also be careful to observe the chronological sequence of events in your report. If you're describing the history or development of something, start at the beginning and cover each event in the order of its occurrence. If you're explaining the steps in a process, take each step in proper sequence.

Unexplained shifts in time perspective can both confuse readers and lead them to question the thinking behind your proposal.

6 LEARNING OBJECTIVE

Briefly describe three report elements that can help readers find their way in long documents

Helping Readers Find Their Way

As you begin to compose the text for your report, remember that most readers have no idea how the various pieces of your report relate to one another (some readers will have an idea

FIGURE 13.5 Continued

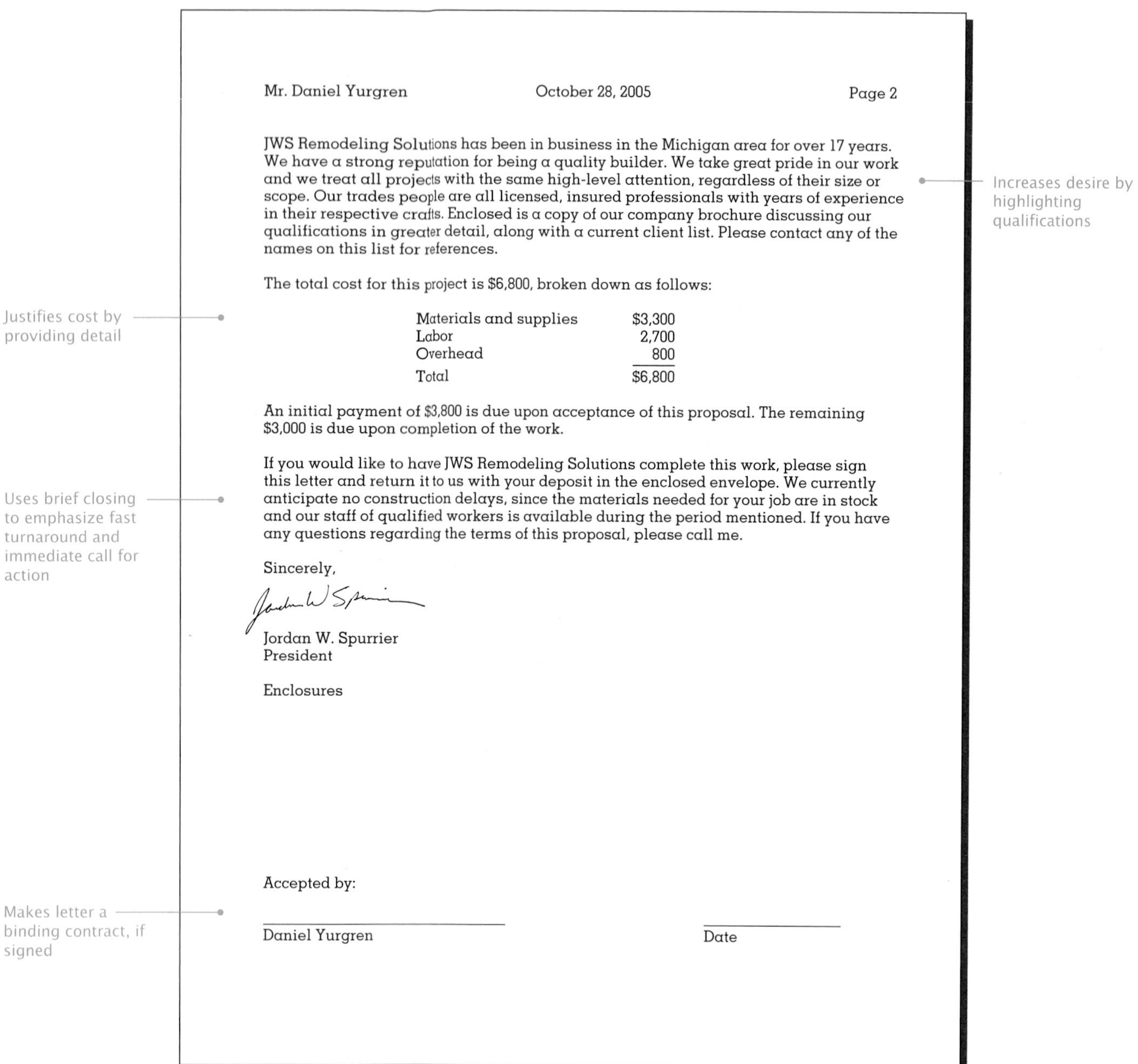

Mr. Daniel Yurgren October 28, 2005 Page 2

JWS Remodeling Solutions has been in business in the Michigan area for over 17 years. We have a strong reputation for being a quality builder. We take great pride in our work and we treat all projects with the same high-level attention, regardless of their size or scope. Our trades people are all licensed, insured professionals with years of experience in their respective crafts. Enclosed is a copy of our company brochure discussing our qualifications in greater detail, along with a current client list. Please contact any of the names on this list for references.

The total cost for this project is $6,800, broken down as follows:

Materials and supplies	$3,300
Labor	2,700
Overhead	800
Total	$6,800

An initial payment of $3,800 is due upon acceptance of this proposal. The remaining $3,000 is due upon completion of the work.

If you would like to have JWS Remodeling Solutions complete this work, please sign this letter and return it to us with your deposit in the enclosed envelope. We currently anticipate no construction delays, since the materials needed for your job are in stock and our staff of qualified workers is available during the period mentioned. If you have any questions regarding the terms of this proposal, please call me.

Sincerely,

Jordan W. Spurrier
President

Enclosures

Accepted by:

Daniel Yurgren Date

Increases desire by highlighting qualifications
Justifies cost by providing detail
Uses brief closing to emphasize fast turnaround and immediate call for action
Makes letter a binding contract, if signed

if they've specified the organization for you or if you're supposed to follow a predetermined organizational pattern). Because you have done the work, you have a sense of your document's wholeness and can see how each page fits into the overall structure. But readers see your report one page at a time. In a short report, readers are in little danger of getting lost; however, as the length of a report increases, so do the opportunities for readers to become confused and lose track of the relationships among ideas.

Report experts such as Beth Uyenco give their readers a preview or road map of a report's structure, clarifying how the various parts are related. If you fail to provide such clues to the structure of your report, readers might miss important points or give up before they reach critical destinations. Providing structural directions is especially important for people from other cultures and countries, whose language skills and business expectations may differ from yours.

Moreover, the accelerating pace of business and the increased familiarity with online information have raised reader expectations in another way. Readers today often lack the time or the inclination to plow through long reports page by page, word by word. They

want to browse quickly, find a section of interest, dive in for details, pull back out, browse for another section, and so on. In fact, it's often safer to assume that few if any audience members will read your entire report.

Navigational aids help your readers appreciate the organization of your thoughts—and can help you convey your message.

The best reports make the most important points easy to find so that everybody sees them. If you want readers to understand and accept your message, help them navigate your document. To give readers a sense of the overall structure of your document and to keep them on track as they read along, learn how to use three helpful tools: headings, smooth transitions, and previews and reviews.

Headings and Links

Headings are brief titles that cue readers about the content of the section that follows. They improve a document's readability and are especially useful markers for clarifying the framework of a report. Also, they visually indicate shifts from one idea to the next, and when you use a combination of headings and subheadings, you help readers see the relationship between subordinate and main ideas. In addition, busy readers can quickly understand the gist of a document simply by scanning the headings. (For a review of ways to write effective headings and subheadings, refer to Chapter 6.)

Many companies specify a format for headings, either through style guide handbooks or document templates; if yours does, use the recommended format. Otherwise, create a simple arrangement that clearly distinguishes levels and is applied consistently throughout your document. Figure 13.6 shows an example of a simple scheme that's easy for readers to follow. In any event, resist the temptation to dress up headings and subheadings with overly bright colors, odd font faces, or gigantic font sizes. They may well call attention to themselves, but they'll also make your report feel less professional.

Online reports can be more difficult to scan and browse through, so clear headings and subheadings are especially important.

For online reports, headings and subheads can be even more crucial, because it's difficult to scan long reports online in the same way readers can flip through printed materials. However, in online documents, any piece of text can be converted to a hyperlink, so you can further simplify reading by letting people jump from section to section, back and forth to the table of contents, and so on. As you probably know, hyperlinks are not limited to headings and subheadings. You can also link from within sections of text, perhaps to provide access to an appendix that provides supporting evidence for an argument you've made in the body of the report.

Transitions

Transitions connect ideas by helping readers move from one thought to the next.

Chapter 5 defines transitions as words or phrases that tie ideas together and show how one thought is related to another. Good report writers use transitions to help readers move from one section of a report to the next and from key point to key point within sections. Depending on the length of the report, such transitions can be words, sentences, or complete paragraphs. Here's an example:

> . . . As you can see, our profits have decreased by 12 percent over the past eight months.
>
> To counteract this decline in profits, we have three alternatives. First, we can raise our selling prices of existing products. Second, we can increase our offering by adding new products. Third, we can reduce our manufacturing costs. However, each of these alternatives has both advantages and disadvantages.

The phrase *As you can see* alerts readers to the fact that they are reading a summary of the information just presented. The phrase *this decline in profits* refers back to the previous paragraph to let readers know that the text will be saying something else about that topic. The words *first, second,* and *third* help readers stay on track as the three alternatives are introduced, and the word *however* alerts readers to the fact that evaluating the three alternatives requires some additional discussion. Effective transitions such as these can help readers summarize and remember what they've learned so far while giving them a mental framework to process new information.

Previews and Reviews

You may have heard the old saying, "Tell them what you're going to tell them, tell them, then tell them what you just told them." *Preview sections* introduce important topics by

FIGURE 13.6
Heading Format for Reports

TITLE

The title is centered at the top of the page in all capital letters, usually boldfaced (or underlined if typewritten), often in a large font (type size), and often using a sans serif typeface. When the title runs to more than one line, the lines are usually double-spaced and arranged as an inverted pyramid (longer line on the top).

FIRST-LEVEL HEADING

A first-level heading indicates what the following section is about, perhaps by describing the subdivisions. All first-level headings are grammatically parallel, with the possible exception of such headings as "Introduction," "Conclusions," and "Recommendations." Some text appears between every two headings, regardless of their levels. Still boldfaced and sans serif, the font may be smaller than that used in the title but still larger than the typeface used in the text and still in all capital letters.

Second-Level Heading

Like first-level headings, second-level headings indicate what the following material is about. All second-level headings within a section are grammatically parallel. Still boldfaced and sans serif, the font may either remain the same or shrink to the size used in the text, and the style is now initial capitals followed with lowercase. Never use only one second-level heading under a first-level heading. (The same is true for every other level of heading.)

Third-Level Heading

A third-level heading is worded to reflect the content of the material that follows. All third-level headings beneath a second-level heading should be grammatically parallel.

Fourth-Level Heading. Like all the other levels of heading, fourth-level headings reflect the subject that will be developed. All fourth-level headings within a subsection are parallel.

Fifth-level headings are generally the lowest level of heading used. However, you can indicate further breakdowns in your ideas by using a list:

1. *The first item in a list.* You may indent the entire item in block format to set it off visually. Numbers are optional.
2. *The second item in a list.* All lists have at least two items. An introductory phrase or sentence may be italicized for emphasis, as shown here.

DOCUMENT MAKEOVER

IMPROVE THIS POLICY REPORT

To practice correcting drafts of actual documents, visit www.prenhall.com/onekey on the web. Click "Document Makeovers" then click Chapter 13. You will find a policy eport that contains problems and errors relating to what u've learned in this chapter about writing business reports d proposals. Use the Final Draft decision tool to create an proved version of this report. Check the message for an ctive opening, consistent levels of formality or informalonsistent time perspective, and the use of headings, lists, sitions, and previews and reviews to help orient readers.

helping readers get ready for new information. Previews are particularly helpful when the information is complex, unexpected, or unfamiliar. You don't want readers to get halfway into a section before figuring out what it's all about. Think of a preview as an opportunity for readers to arrange their mental file folders before you start giving them information to put in those folders.

Review sections come after a body of material and summarize the information for your readers. Reviews help readers absorb details while keeping track of the big picture. Long reports and those dealing with complex subjects can often benefit from multiple review sections, one at the end of every major subject block, as well as a more comprehensive review at the very end of a document.

Swimming is a good analogy for using preview and review sections. Before you jump into the water, you look around, get your bearings, and get an idea of what you're about to dive into. A preview section serves the same purpose for your reader. After you dive in and

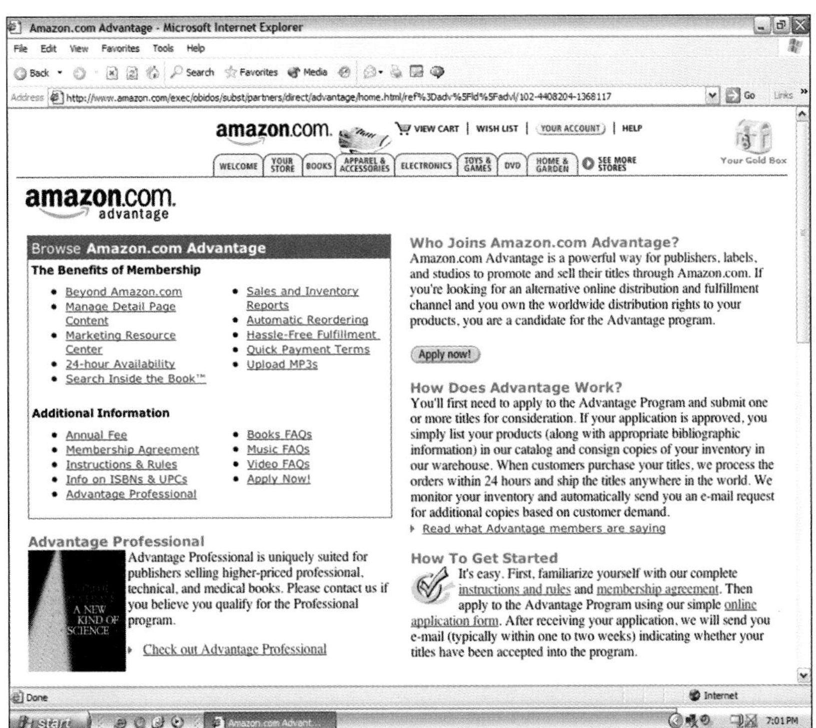

Amazon.com's Advantage program helps book publishers, music companies, and movie studios promote their products on Amazon.com. To help these audiences learn about the Advantage program quickly, an online informational report makes generous use of headings and links.

swim for a few moments, you come back up for air. You look around and get your bearings again. Whenever you've had your readers "swimming in details" for any length of time, bring them back to the surface with a review section so that they can get their bearings again. Keep in mind that your knowledge of the subject matter is probably more thorough and more current than your audience's knowledge of it. After you spend days or even weeks thinking about what you put in your report, the material may seem simple and obvious to you; however, it probably won't seem so easy to your readers.

Previews and reviews can be written in a sentence format, in bulleted lists, or a combination of the two. Both are effective, but bullets can increase your document's readability by adding white space to the document design. Consider the following preview, which is written using both formats:

SENTENCE FORMAT

The next section discusses the advantages of advertising on the Internet. Among them are currency, global reach, affordability, and interactivity.

BULLETED LIST

As the next section shows, advertising on the Internet has four advantages:

- Currency
- Global reach
- Affordability
- Interactivity

In long reports, bulleted lists may be worded to match actual paragraph headings. For a more in-depth discussion of how to write effective bullets and lists, see the section in Chapter 6 titled "Using Lists and Bullets for Clarifying and Emphasizing" on page 156. To review the tasks discussed in this section, see "Checklist: Composing Business Reports and Proposals."

USING TECHNOLOGY TO CRAFT REPORTS AND PROPOSALS

Look for ways to utilize technology to reduce the mechanical work involved in writing long reports.

Creating lengthy reports and proposals can be a huge task, so take advantage of technological tools to help throughout the process. You've read about some of these in earlier

CHECKLIST: Composing Business Reports and Proposals

A. REVIEW AND FINE-TUNE YOUR OUTLINE

- Match your parallel headings to the tone of your report.
- Understand how the introduction, body, and close work together to convey your message.

B. DRAFT REPORT CONTENT

- Use the introduction to establish the purpose, scope, and organization of your report.
- Use the body to present and interpret the information you gathered.
- Use the close to summarize major points, discuss conclusions, or make recommendations.

C. DRAFT PROPOSAL CONTENT

- Use the introduction to discuss the background or problem, your solution, the scope, and organization.
- Use the body to persuasively explain the benefits of your proposed approach.
- Use the close to emphasize reader benefits and summarize the merits of your approach.

D. ESTABLISH A CONSISTENT TIME FRAME

- Avoid flipping from tense to tense.
- Observe the chronological sequence of events.

E. HELP READERS FIND THEIR WAY

- Provide headings to improve readability and clarify the framework of your ideas.
- Use hyperlinks online to allow readers to jump from section to section.
- Create transitions that tie ideas together and show how one thought relates to another.
- Preview important topics to help readers get ready for new information.
- Review information to help readers absorb details and keep the big picture in mind.

chapters; here are some of the most important tools for developing reports and proposals:

- **Templates.** Beyond simply formatting documents, report templates can identify the specific sections required for each type of report. For instance, a marketing plan could include such sections as a competitive analysis, market analysis, launch plans, financial analysis, and promotional and customer support plans. The template would automatically insert headings for each section, with reminders of the content to include.
- **Linked and embedded documents.** Reports and proposals often include graphics, spreadsheets, databases, and other elements created in a variety of software packages. When you do combine files this way, make sure you know how the software handles the files or else you may receive some unpleasant surprises. For instance, in Microsoft Office, you can choose to either *link* or *embed* the incoming file, such as when you insert a spreadsheet table into a word processor document. If you link the table, it will get updated whenever you or someone else updates the spreadsheet. In contrast, if you embed it, the files are no longer connected; changes in the spreadsheet will not show up in the report document. Depending on what you expect to happen, this may or may not be good news. The choice you make when you combine files can have serious ramifications for file sharing or updating.
- **Electronic forms.** For recurring forms such as sales reports and compliance reports, consider creating a word processor file that combines boilerplate text for material that doesn't change from report to report. To accommodate information that does change (such as last week's sales results), use *form tools* such as text boxes (in which users can type new text) and check boxes (which can be used to select from a set of predetermined choices). The completed file can then be printed, e-mailed, or posted to an intranet, like any other document.
- **Electronic documents.** Portable Document Format (PDF) files have become a universal replacement for printed reports and proposals. With a copy of Adobe Acrobat (a separate product from the free Acrobat Reader), you can quickly convert reports and proposals to PDF files that are easy and safe to share electronically.
- **Multimedia documents.** When the written word isn't enough, combine your report with video clips, animation, presentation software slides, and other elements. As you'll see in Chapter 16, tools such as Microsoft Producer let you merge a variety of file types to create compelling multimedia presentations that supplement or replace traditional reports.

COMMUNICATION CHALLENGES AT OMD WORLDWIDE

Full-service advertising agencies once dominated the industry, and their creative departments called all the shots. However, the rise of specialist agencies such as OMD Worldwide has shifted the balance of power. With their detailed knowledge of consumer habits, some media research companies have been able to suggest ad concepts that would target specific consumers—suggestions that creative departments aren't always happy to get from outsiders.

Individual Challenge: You've spent the past year working for Beth Uyenco and have learned a lot about writing clear, effective reports. She recently assigned you to a project with PepsiCo, performing media research for a new campaign, which will be managed by an ad agency that is not affiliated with OMD. You've seen three initial ad concepts, and your research suggests that one concept will be more powerful than the others—and it can be made even more effective with one significant change. Beth has asked you to write a research report for PepsiCo that endorses the favored ad concept and suggests the enhancement. Briefly explain which type of logical argument you will use to structure your analytical report and why.

Team Challenge: In a small group, discuss which communication options (reports, proposals, presentations, or meetings) would be most effective for encouraging cooperation between the logic-based media researchers and the emotion-based advertising creative staff. Which options would be best for gaining approval from a client who might not want to hear the information you have to offer? Summarize your conclusions in a brief memo to your instructor.

SUMMARY OF LEARNING OBJECTIVES

1 **Explain how to adapt to your audiences when writing reports and proposals.** Adapt to your audience by demonstrating sensitivity to their needs (adopting the "you" attitude, maintaining a strong sense of etiquette, emphasizing the positive, and using bias-free language), building a strong relationship with your audience (make sure your writing reflects the desired image of your organization and build your credibility), and controlling your style and tone to achieve the appropriate degree of formality, given the nature of the material and your relationship with the audience.

2 **List the topics commonly covered in introduction, body, and closing of informational or analytical reports.** The introduction highlights who authorized the report, the purpose and scope of a report, necessary background material, the sources or methods used to gather information, important definitions, any limitations, and the order in which the various topics are covered. The body discusses such details as problems, opportunities, facts, evidence, trends, results of studies or investigations, analysis of potential courses of action, process procedures and steps, methods and approaches, evaluation criteria for options, conclusions, recommendations, and supporting reasons. The closing summarizes key points, restates conclusions and recommendations, and lists action items.

3 **Name five characteristics of effective report content.** Effective report content is accurate if it is factually correct and error-free. It is complete if it includes all necessary information and supports all key assertions. It is balanced if it presents all sides of an argument. It is clear and logical if it is well-written and organized logically. It is properly documented if credit is given to all primary and secondary sources of information used.

4 **Name six strategies to strengthen your proposal argument.** To strengthen your argument, you should demonstrate your knowledge, provide concrete examples, research the competition, prove that your proposal is workable, adopt a "you" attitude, and make your document attractive and error-free.

5 **List the topics commonly covered in a proposal's introduction, body, and closing.** The introduction discusses the background or existing problem, the solution to the problem, the scope of the proposal, and the order in which information is presented in the document. For solicited proposals, the introduction should also reference the RFP. The body discusses the proposed approach and benefits to the reader, the work plan, the organization's qualifications, and the costs of the proposal. The closing briefly summarizes the key points, the merits and benefits of the proposed approach, and the submitting firm's competencies.

6 Briefly describe three report elements that can help readers find their way in long documents. Effective reports help readers navigate the document by using these three elements: (1) Headings (and links for online reports) set off important ideas and provide the reader with clues as to the report's framework and shifts in discussion; (2) transitions tie ideas together and keep readers moving along; and (3) previews and reviews prepare readers for new information and summarize previously discussed information.

Test Your Knowledge

1. What writing choices can you make to adjust the formality of your reports?
2. What are your options for structuring an informational report?
3. What are your options for structuring an analytical report?
4. What steps should you follow when structuring a report around recommendations?
5. How does topical organization differ from logical organization?
6. What is the function of a report introduction?
7. What information might you include in the close of a report?
8. What information might you include in the introduction of a proposal?
9. Why is the work plan a key component of a proposal?
10. What tools can you use to help readers follow the structure and flow of information in a long report?

Apply Your Knowledge

1. Should a report always explain the writer's method of gathering evidence or solving a problem? Why or why not?
2. What are the risks of not explaining the purpose of a proposal within the introduction?
3. If you want readers to consider your reasoning in detail, should your close offer a concise summary of your recommendations in the close of your report?
4. If you want your audience to agree to a specific course of action, should you exclude any references to alternatives that you don't want the audience to consider? Why or why not?
5. **Ethical Choices** If a company receives a solicited formal proposal, is it ethical for the company to adopt the recommendations discussed in the proposal even though the company does not hire the submitting firm? Why or why not?

Practice Your Knowledge

Document for Analysis

Read Figure 13.7, a solicited memo proposal, then (1) analyze the strengths and weaknesses of this document, and (2) revise the document so that it follows this chapter's guidelines.

Exercises

For live links to all websites discussed in this chapter, visit this text's website at www.prenhall.com/bovee. Just log on, select Chapter 13, and click on "Featured Websites." Locate the page or the URL related to the material in the text.

13.1 **Adapting Reports to the Audience** Review the reports shown in Figures 13.1 to 13.3 on pages 395–398. Give specific examples of how each of these reports establishes a good relationship with the audience. Consider such things as using the "you" attitude, emphasizing the positive, establishing credibility, being polite, using bias-free language, and projecting a good company image.

13.2 **Composing Reports: Report Content** You are writing an analytical report on the U.S. sales of your newest product. Of the following topics, identify those that should be covered in the report's introduction, body, and close. Briefly explain your decisions:

a. Regional breakdowns of sales across the country
b. Date the product was released in the marketplace
c. Sales figures from competitors selling similar products worldwide
d. Predictions of how the struggling U.S. economy will affect sales over the next six months
e. Method used for obtaining the above predictions
f. The impact of similar products being sold in the United States by Japanese competitors
g. Your recommendation as to whether the company should sell this product internationally
h. Actions that must be completed by year end if the company decides to sell this product internationally

13.3 **Composing Reports** Find an article in a business newspaper or journal (in print or online) that recommends a solution to a problem. Identify the problem, the recommended solution(s), and the supporting evidence provided by the author to justify his or her recommendation(s). Did the author cite any formal or informal studies as evidence? What facts or statistics did the author include? Did the author cite any criteria for evaluating possible options? If so, what were they?

13.4 **Composing Reports: Time Perspective** Rewrite this section of text to give it a consistent time perspective:

Of those interviewed, 25 percent <u>report</u> that they <u>are</u> dissatisfied with their present brand. The wealthiest participants <u>complained</u> most frequently, but all income categories <u>are</u> interested in trying a new brand. Only 5 percent of the interviewees <u>say</u> they <u>had</u> no interest in alternative products.

13.5 **Composing Reports: Navigational Clues** Review a long business article in a journal or newspaper. Highlight examples of how the article uses headings, transitions, and previews and reviews to help the readers find their way.

FIGURE 13.7 Solicited Memo Proposal

MEMO

TO: Ken Estes, Northern Illinois Concrete
FROM: Kris Beiersdorf
DATE: April 19, 2005
PROJECT: IDOT Letting Item #83 Contract No. 79371 DuPage County

Memco Consruction proposes to furnish all labor, material, equipment, and supervision to provide Engineered Fill—Class II and IV for the following unit prices.

Engineered Fill – Class II and IV

Description	Unit	Quantity	Unit Price	Total
Mobilization*	Lump Sum	1	$4,500.00	$4,500.00
Engineered Fill Class II	Cubic Yards	1,267	$33.00	$41,811.00
Engineered Fill Class IV	Cubic Yards	1,394	$38.00	$52,972.00

* Mobilization includes one move-in. Additional move-ins to be billed at $1,100.00 each.

The following items clarify and qualify the scope of our subcontracting work:

1. All forms, earthwork, clearing, etc. to be provided and maintained by others at no cost to Memco Construction.
2. General Contractor shall provide location for staging, stockpiling material, equipment, and storage at the job site.
3. Memco Construction shall be paid strictly based upon the amount of material actually used on the job.
4. All prep work, including geotechnical fabrics, geomembrane liners, etc. to be done by others at no cost to Memco Construction.
5. Water is to be available at project site at no charge to Memco Construction.
6. Dewatering to be done by others at no cost to Memco Construction.
7. Traffic control setup, devices, maintenance, and flagmen are to be provided by others at no cost to Memco Construction.
8. Memco Construction LLC may withdraw this bid if we do not receive a written confirmation that we are the apparent low sub-bidder within 10 days of your receipt of this proposal.
9. Our F.E.I.N. is 36-4478095.
10. Bond is not included in above prices. Bond is available for an additional 1 percent.

If you have any questions, please contact me at the phone number listed below.

Kris Beiersdorf
Memco Construction
187 W. Euclid Avenue, Glenview, IL 60025
Office: (847) 352-9742, ext. 30
Fax: (847) 352-6595
E-mail: Kbeiersdorf@memco.com
www.memco.com

13.6 Ethical Choices Your boss has asked you to prepare a feasibility report to determine whether the company should advertise its custom-crafted cabinetry in the weekly neighborhood newspaper. Based on your primary research, you think they should. As you draft the introduction to your report, however, you discover that the survey administered to the neighborhood newspaper subscribers was flawed. Several of the questions were poorly written and misleading. You used the survey results, among other findings, to justify your recommendation. The report is due in three days. What actions might you want to take, if any, before you complete your report?

13.7 Composing Business Reports Your boss, Len Chow (vice president of corporate planning), has asked you to research opportunities in the cosmetics industry and to prepare a report that presents your findings and your recommendations for where you think the company should focus its marketing efforts. Here's a copy of your note cards (data were created for this exercise):

Sub: Demand ref:1.1
Industry grew through 1970s, 1980s, and early 1990s, fueled by per capita consumption
Sub: Competition ref:1.2
700 companies currently in cosmetics industry

Sub: Niches ref:1.3 Focusing on special niches avoids head-on competition with industry leaders
Sub: Competition ref: 1.4 Industry dominated by market leaders: Revlon, Procter & Gamble, Avon, Gillette
Sub: Demand ref: 1.5 Industry no longer recession-proof: Past year, sales sluggish; consumer spending is down; most affected were mid- to high-priced brands; consumers traded down to less expensive lines
Sub: Competition ref: 1.6 Smaller companies (Neutrogena, Mary Kay, Soft Soap, and Noxell) survive by specializing in niches, differentiating product line, focusing on market segment
Sub: Demand ref: 1.7 Consumption of cosmetics relatively flat for past five years
Sub: Competition ref: 1.8 Prices are constant while promotion budgets are increasing
Sub: Niches ref: 1.9 Men: 50% of adult population; account for one-fifth of cosmetic sales; market leaders have attempted this market but failed
Sub: Demand ref: 1.10 Cosmetic industry is near maturity but some segments may vary. Total market currently produces annual retail sales of $14.5 billion: Cosmetics/lotions/fragrances—$5.635 billion; Personal hygiene products—$4.375 billion; Hair-care products—$3.435 billion; shaving products—$1.055 billion
Sub: Niches ref: 1.11 Ethnic groups: Some firms specialize in products for African Americans; few firms oriented toward Hispanic, Asian, or Native Americans, which tend to be concentrated geographically
Sub: Demand ref: 1.12 Average annual expenditure per person for cosmetics is $58
Sub: Competition ref: 1.13 Competition is intensifying and dominant companies are putting pressure on smaller ones
Sub: Demand ref: 1.14 First quarter of current year, demand is beginning to revive; trend expected to continue well into next year
Sub: Niches ref: 1.15 Senior citizens: large growing segment of population; account for 6% of cosmetic sales; specialized needs for hair and skin not being met; interested in appearance
Sub: Demand ref: 1.16 Demographic trends: (1) Gradual maturing of baby-boomer generation will fuel growth by consuming greater quantities of shaving cream, hair-coloring agents, and skin creams; (2) population is increasing in the South and Southwest, where some brands have strong distribution

List the main idea of your message (your recommendation), the major points (your conclusions), and supporting evidence. Then construct a final report outline with first- and second-level informative headings focusing on your conclusions. Because Chow requested this report, you can feel free to use the direct approach. Finish by writing a draft of your memo report to Chow.

Expand Your Knowledge

For live links to the websites that follow, go to www.prenhall.com/bovee. When you log on, select Chapter 13, then select "Featured Websites," click on the URL of the website you wish to visit, and review the website to complete these exercises.

Exploring the Best of the Web

Research Before You Report

www.corporateinformation.com

Research your competition at Corporate Information, and find out what you need to know before you write your next report or proposal. This website has links to over 350,000 company profiles, data on 30 industries in 65 countries, and current economic information for over 100 countries. You'll also find research reports analyzing sales, dividends, earnings, and profit ratios on some 15,000 companies, current foreign exchange rates, and the definitions of commonly used global company extensions such as GmbH, SA, de CV, and more. Scan the site and answer these questions:

1. Select an industry of your choice from one of the listed countries and follow the links to reports, analyses, and data on that industry. What specific types of information did you find on the industry? How might you use this information when writing a report or proposal?
2. Read the online research reports for a company of your choice. What types of specific information are available in these reports? How might you use this information when writing a report or proposal?
3. What do the company extensions GmbH, KK, LLC, OHG, SA, and SNC mean?

Exploring the Web on Your Own

Review these chapter-related websites to learn more about writing reports and proposals.

1. Researching Companies Online, www.learnwebskills.com, has some good advice for finding company and industry information on the web. Take the tutorial.
2. Craft more-effective executive summaries by following the advice at the Harvard Business School's Working Knowledge website, http://hsbworkingknowledge.hsb.edu (look under Career Effectiveness).
3. The Spire Project, www.spireproject.com, claims to have a better way to find information on the web. Check it out.

Learn Interactively

Interactive Study Guide

Go to the Companion Website at www.prenhall.com/bovee. For Chapter 13, take advantage of the interactive "Study Guide" to test your knowledge of the chapter. Get instant feedback on whether you need additional studying.

Also, visit this site's "Study Hall," where you'll find an abundance of valuable resources that will help you succeed in this course.

Peak Performance Grammar and Mechanics

To improve your skill with mechanics, visit www.prenhall.com/onekey, click "Peak Performance Grammar and Mechanics" then click "Mechanics of Style." Take the Pretest to determine whether you have any weak areas. Then review those areas in the Refresher Course. Take the Follow-Up Test to check your grasp of mechanics. For an extra challenge or advanced practice, take the Advanced Test. Finally, for additional reinforcement in capitals, italics, and abbreviations, go to www.prenhall.com/bovee, where you will find "Improve Your Grammar, Mechanics, and Usage" exercises.

CASES

INFORMAL INFORMATIONAL REPORTS

1. My progress to date: Interim progress report on your academic career As you know, the bureaucratic process involved in getting a degree or certificate is nearly as challenging as any course you could take.

Your task: Prepare an interim progress report detailing the steps you've taken toward completing your graduation or certification requirements. After examining the requirements listed in your college catalog, indicate a realistic schedule for completing those that remain. In addition to course requirements, include steps such as completing the residency requirement, filing necessary papers, and paying necessary fees. Use memo format for your report, and address it to anyone who is helping or encouraging you through school.

2. Gavel to gavel: Personal activity report of a meeting Meetings, conferences, and conventions abound in the academic world, and you have probably attended your share.

Your task: Prepare a personal activity report on a meeting, convention, or conference that you recently attended. Use memo format, and direct the report to other students in your field who were not able to attend.

3. Check that price tag: Informational report on trends in college costs Are tuition costs going up, going down, or remaining the same? Your college's administration has asked you to compare your college's tuition costs with those of a nearby college and determine which has risen more quickly. Research the trend by checking your college's annual tuition costs for each of the most recent four years. Then research the four-year tuition trends for a neighboring college. For both colleges, calculate the percentage change in tuition costs from year to year and between the first and fourth year.

Your task: Prepare an informal report (using the letter format) presenting your findings and conclusions to the president of your college. Include graphics to explain and support your conclusions.

4. Get a move on it: Lasting guidelines for moving into college dormitories Moving into a college dormitory is one experience you weren't quite prepared for. In addition to lugging your earthly belongings up four flights of stairs in 90-degree heat, channeling electrical cords to the one room outlet tucked in the corner of the room, lofting your beds, and negotiating with your roommate over who gets the bigger closet, you had to hug your

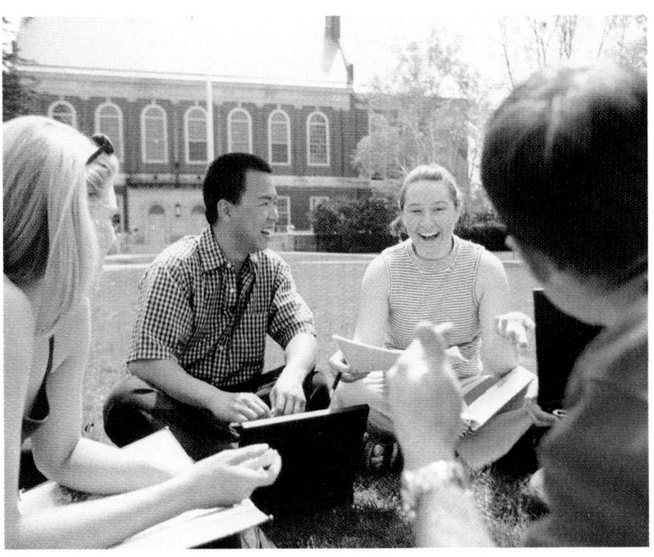

parents goodbye in the parking lot in front of the entire freshman class—or so it seemed. Now that you are a pro, you've offered to write some lasting guidelines for future freshmen so they know what is expected of them on moving day.

Your task: Prepare an informational report for future freshmen classes outlining the rules and procedures to follow when moving into a college dorm. Lay out the rules such as starting time, handling trash and empty boxes, items permitted and not permitted in dorm rooms, common courtesies, and so on. Be sure to mention what the policy is for removing furniture from the room, lofting beds, and overloading electrical circuits. Of course, any recommendations on how to handle disputes with roommates would be helpful. So would some brief advice on how to cope with anxious parents. Direct your memo report to the college dean.

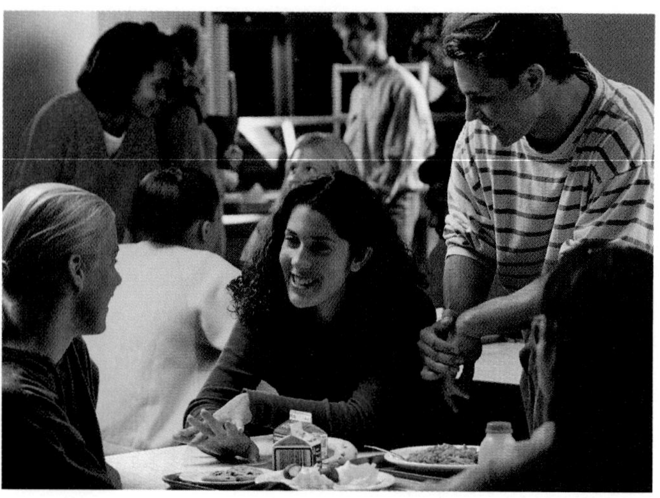

INFORMAL ANALYTICAL REPORTS

5. My next career move: Feasibility report organized around recommendations If you've ever given yourself a really good talking-to, you'll be quite comfortable with this project.

Your task: Write a memo report directed to yourself and signed with a fictitious name. Indicate a possible job that your college education will qualify you for, mention the advantages of the position in terms of your long-range goals, and then outline the actions you must take to get the job.

6. Staying the course: Unsolicited proposal using the 2 + 2 = 4 approach Think of a course you would love to see added to the core curriculum at your school. Conversely, if you would like to see a course offered as an elective rather than being required, write your e-mail report accordingly.

Your task: Write a short e-mail proposal using the 2 + 2 = 4 approach. Prepare your proposal to be submitted to the academic dean by e-mail. Be sure to include all the reasons supporting your idea.

7. Planning my program: Problem-solving report using the scientific method Assume that you will have time for only one course next term.

Your task: List the pros and cons of four or five courses that interest you, and use the scientific method to settle on the course that is best for you to take at this time. Write your report in memo format, addressing it to your academic adviser.

8. "Would you carry it?" Unsolicited sales proposal recommending a product to a retail outlet Select a product you are familiar with, and imagine that you are the manufacturer trying to get a local retail outlet to carry it. Use the Internet and other resources to gather information about the product.

Your task: Write an unsolicited sales proposal in letter format to the owner (or manager) of the store, proposing that the item be stocked. Use the information you gathered to describe some of the product's features and benefits to the store. Then make up some reasonable figures, highlighting what the item costs, what it can be sold for, and what services your company provides (return of unsold items, free replacement of unsatisfactory items, necessary repairs, and so on).

9. Restaurant review: Troubleshooting report on a restaurant's food and operations Visit any restaurant, possibly your school cafeteria. The workers and fellow customers will assume that you are an ordinary customer, but you are really a spy for the owner.

Your task: After your visit, write a short memo to the owner, explaining (a) what you did and what you observed, (b) any violations of policy that you observed, and (c) your recommendations for improvement. The first part of your report (what you did and what you observed) will be the longest. Include a description of the premises, inside and out. Tell how long it took for each step of ordering and receiving your meal. Describe the service and food thoroughly. You are interested in both the good and bad aspects of the establishment's décor, service, and food. For the second section (violations of policy), use some common sense. If all the servers but one have their hair covered, you may assume that policy requires hair to be covered; a dirty window or restroom obviously violates policy. The last section (recommendations for improvement) involves professional judgment. What management actions will improve the restaurant?

10. On the books: Troubleshooting report on improving the campus bookstore Imagine that you are a consultant hired to improve the profits of your campus bookstore.

Your task: Visit the bookstore and look critically at its operations. Then draft a memo to the bookstore manager, offering recommendations that would make the store more profitable, perhaps suggesting products it should carry, hours that it should remain open, or added services that it should make available to students. Be sure to support your recommendations.

11. Press 1 for efficiency: Unsolicited proposal on a telephone interviewing system How can a firm be thorough yet efficient when considering dozens of applicants for each position? One tool that just may help is IntelliView, a 10-minute question-and-answer session conducted by Touch-Tone telephone. The company recruiter dials up the IntelliView computer and then leaves the room. The candidate punches in answers to roughly 100 questions about work attitudes and other issues. In a few minutes, the recruiter can call Pinkerton, which offers the service, and find out the results. On the basis of what the IntelliView interview revealed, the recruiter can delve more deeply into certain areas and, ultimately, have more information on which to base the hiring decision.

Your task: As a recruiter for Curtis Box and Crate, you think that IntelliView might help your firm. Write a brief memo to Wallace Jefferson, the director of human resources, in which you suggest a test of the IntelliView system. Your memo should tell your boss why you believe your firm should test the system before making a long-term commitment.[7]

12. Day and night: Problem-solving report on stocking a 24-hour convenience store When a store is open all day, every day, when's the best time to restock the shelves? That's the challenge at Store 24, a retail chain that never closes. Imagine you're the assistant manager of a Store 24 branch that just opened near your campus. You want to set up a restocking schedule that won't conflict with prime shopping hours. Think about the number of customers you're likely to serve in the morning, afternoon, evening, and overnight hours. Consider, too, how many employees you might have during these four periods.

Your task: Using the scientific approach, write a problem-solving report in letter form to the store manager (Isabel Chu) and the regional manager (Eric Angstrom), who must agree on a solution to this problem. Discuss the pros and cons of each of the four periods, and include your recommendation for restocking the shelves.

chapter 14

Completing Reports and Proposals

LEARNING OBJECTIVES

After studying this chapter, you will be able to

1. Characterize the four tasks involved in completing business reports and proposals
2. Explain how computers have both simplified and complicated the report-production process
3. Identify the circumstances in which you should include letters of authorization and letters of acceptance in your reports
4. Explain the difference between a synopsis and an executive summary
5. Describe the three supplementary parts of a formal report
6. Identify the major components to include in a request for proposals (RFP)

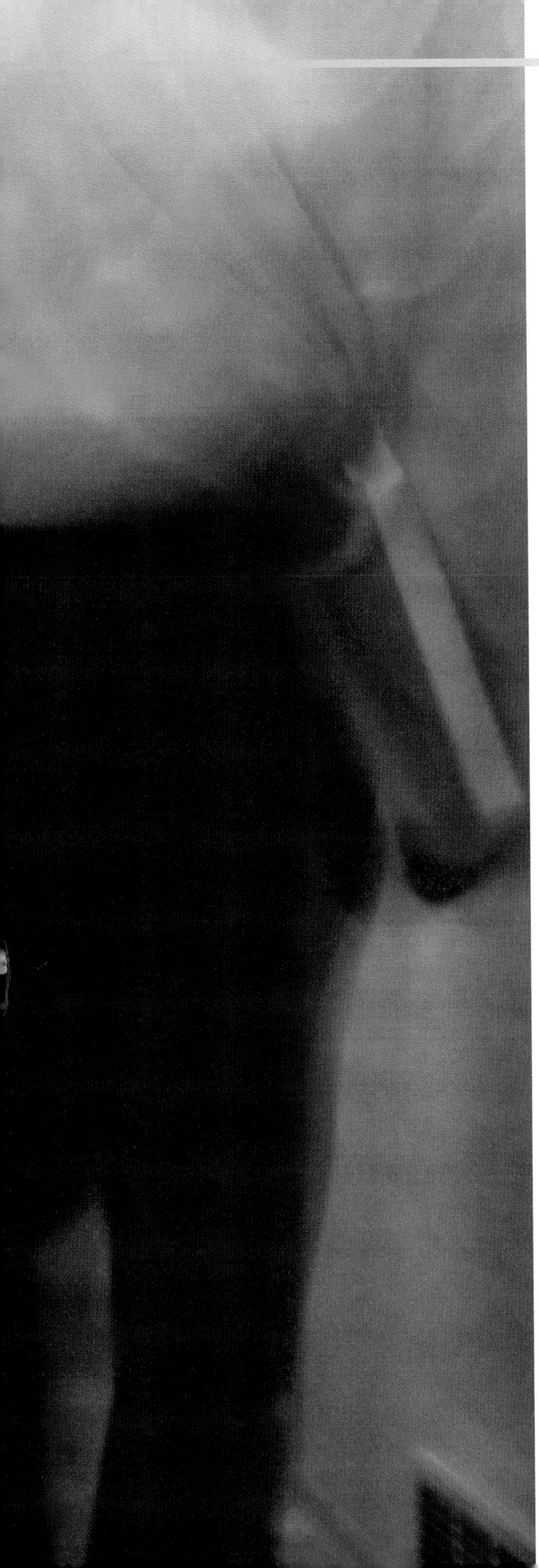

COMMUNICATION CLOSE-UP AT THE BILL AND MELINDA GATES FOUNDATION

www.gatesfoundation.org

If you were the richest person in the world, what would you do with all that money? Would you try to help less-fortunate people? Bill Gates, co-founder of software giant Microsoft, is using his wealth to do just that. With his wife, Melinda, he created the Bill and Melinda Gates Foundation, which aims to make lasting improvements in health and learning around the world. With billions of dollars in assets, it's the largest foundation in history.

In 2002 the foundation hired Dr. Richard Klausner, an award-winning scientist, to be its executive director of global health. His mission is to donate more than $500 million every year in pursuit of solutions to health problems such as HIV, AIDS, and malaria the world over. The foundation receives nearly 3,000 formal grant requests every month, and the review process is a thorough one. Klausner's staff scrutinizes the health-related proposals carefully. Successful proposals are free of mistakes not only in content but also in grammar and appearance. Staff members submit their top picks to Klausner and other foundation senior executives for consideration. (For major grant requests, Bill and Melinda also review the proposal.)

"A well-written grant [proposal] is a beautiful thing," says Klausner. "You have a really smart person saying,

Written reports play a key role in virtually every aspect of operations at the Bill and Melinda Gates Foundation, which has become one of the world's most significant charitable organizations.

'I have this idea.' It's a wonderful story." He examines proposals from various angles, listening to his colleagues' perspectives and asking all sorts of questions: Is this really the best approach? What's going to make the biggest difference? Could this proposal be a catalyst that attracts other organizations to participate?

A successful grant proposal is just the beginning of the communication process between the foundation and the grant recipient. Klausner's team treats each grant like an investment, staying involved, setting specific milestones, and expecting progress reports in return. If the recipients can't show tangible progress, they risk losing their funding. This ongoing accountability creates an impact that lasts long after a proposal's goals are achieved. And that's why each report must be as carefully prepared and completed as the initial proposal.[1]

1 LEARNING OBJECTIVE

Characterize the four tasks involved in completing business reports and proposals

COMPLETING REPORTS AND PROPOSALS

You're almost there. You've researched, planned, and written your report or proposal, and now it's time to finalize it, package it, and get it into the hands of your readers. As the last step in the three-step writing process, completing reports and proposals involves four tasks: revising, producing, proofreading, and distributing. With careful planning and a bit of luck, you still have enough time in your schedule to address each of these tasks thoroughly.

Don't rush through the completion stage and risk making mistakes that could undo your days or weeks of hard work.

Compared to your research and writing efforts, some of these final activities may seem minor, but they can make or break your success in report writing. Although the tasks covered in this chapter are similar in concept to those you studied in Chapter 6, the amount of work involved in completing reports and proposals can vary dramatically from the work described earlier for short message formats. Production alone can take several days for a complex report. And as you've probably experienced with school reports already, computers, copiers, and other resources have an uncanny knack for going haywire at the last minute, when you're frantic to finish and have no time to spare. If at all possible, leave yourself double or triple the amount of time you think you'll need to complete your project. With interruptions, system glitches, and last-minute corrections, you'll probably need all that time and then some.

As Airbus ramps up to produce the world's largest aircraft (holding nearly 600 passengers), CEO Noel Forgeard sets priorities and focus on his goals by reading a lot of reports. With each report, he expects the introduction to (1) give him perspective on where the report fits into the overall picture, (2) clearly state its purpose, (3) preview the contents, and (4) establish a tone that defines its relationship with its readers.

By the time you're ready to complete your report or proposal, the amount of work you have left to do depends on your project's formality, length, and complexity. Most of the discussion in this chapter applies to *formal* reports and proposals, those documents that require an extra measure of polish and professionalism—whether because of audience expectations, company tradition, or even marketing needs. Even so, few reports and proposals require every component described in this chapter; just be sure to carefully select the elements you want to include in each document.

Depending on your job and the industry you work in, you may prepare many formal reports and proposals over the course of your career. For instance, management consultants routinely prepare formal documents, both formal proposals to solicit new projects and formal reports to communicate the results of those projects to their clients. Although some reports and proposals don't require the grand treatment of formal documents, many others do, so it's good to know which pieces to include and how to prepare them. This chapter addresses all four completion tasks (revising, producing, proofreading, and distributing) and concludes with a brief look at writing requests for proposals.

REVISING YOUR REPORTS AND PROPOSALS

Experienced business communicators such Richard Klausner recognize that the process of writing a report or proposal doesn't end with a first draft. As Chapter 5 points out, when you compose a first draft, you simply try to get your ideas on paper with some semblance of organization, and you often save any strengthening, tightening, and polishing for second and final drafts.

The revision process is essentially the same for reports as for any business message, although it may take considerably longer, depending on the length of your document. Evaluate your organization, style, and tone, making sure that you've said what you want to say and that you've said it in the most logical order and in a way that responds to your audience's needs. Then work to improve the report's readability by varying sentence length, keeping paragraphs short, using lists and bullets, and adding headings and subheadings. Keep revising the content until it is clear, concise, and compelling.

The revision process for long reports is the same as for short messages, although it can take considerably longer.

PRODUCING YOUR REPORTS AND PROPOSALS

Once you are satisfied with your text, you're ready to produce your report by incorporating the design elements discussed in Chapter 6. Headings, captions, typographical devices (such as capital letters, italics, and boldface type), margins, line justifications, and white space are just some of the techniques and tools you can use to present your material effectively. At this point you also start to add in charts, graphs, and other visuals, as well as any missing textual elements such as previews and reviews. Many organizations have format guidelines that make your decisions easier, but the goal is always to focus readers' attention on major points and on the flow of ideas.

In some organizations, you'll be able to rely on the help of specialists in design and production, particularly for important, high-visibility reports or proposals. You may also have clerical help available to assist with the mechanical assembly and distribution. However, for most reports in many of today's lean-staffed companies, you should count on doing most or all of the production work yourself.

The good news is that computer tools are now generally easy enough for the average businessperson to use productively. A software suite such as Microsoft Office or Sun StarOffice lets you produce reports that incorporate graphics, tables, spreadsheet data, and database records. Even advanced report features such as photography are relatively simple these days, with the advent of low-cost digital cameras, color desktop scanners, and inexpensive color printers with near-photo-quality output.

2 LEARNING OBJECTIVE

Explain how computers have both simplified and complicated the report-production process

The bad news is that continually improving computer tools increases your audience's expectations. People are influenced by packaging, so a handsomely bound report with full-color graphics will impress your audience more than a plain, typewritten-style report, even though the two documents contain the same information. The competition is even tougher when your report must contend with electronic reports that are filled with multimedia effects and hypertext links. In some cases, sending a custom-made CD-ROM containing your new business proposal might be your best option.

Computer tools have made it easy for virtually anyone to create handsome reports, but they've also raised the expectations of business audiences.

Components of a Formal Report

The parts you include in a report depend on the type of report you are writing, how long it is, what your audience expects and requires, and what your organization dictates. At the Gates Foundation, Richard Klausner pays close attention to his readers' needs, whether those readers are employees, customers, or members of the community. From the style of the report to the language used, Klausner targets his readers' preferences and familiarity, including only the parts that are appropriate for each audience. The components listed in Figure 14.1 fall into three categories, depending on where they are found in a report: prefatory parts, text of the report, and supplementary parts. For an illustration of how the various parts fit together, see Linda Moreno's Electrovision report in the "Report Writer's Notebook: Analyzing a Formal Report."

Length, audience expectations, and organizational traditions all dictate what you should include in a formal report.

Many of the components in a formal report start on a new page, but not always. Inserting page breaks consumes more paper and adds to the bulk of your report. On the other hand, starting a section on a new page helps your readers navigate the report and recognize transitions between major sections or features.

FIGURE 14.1 Parts of a Formal Report

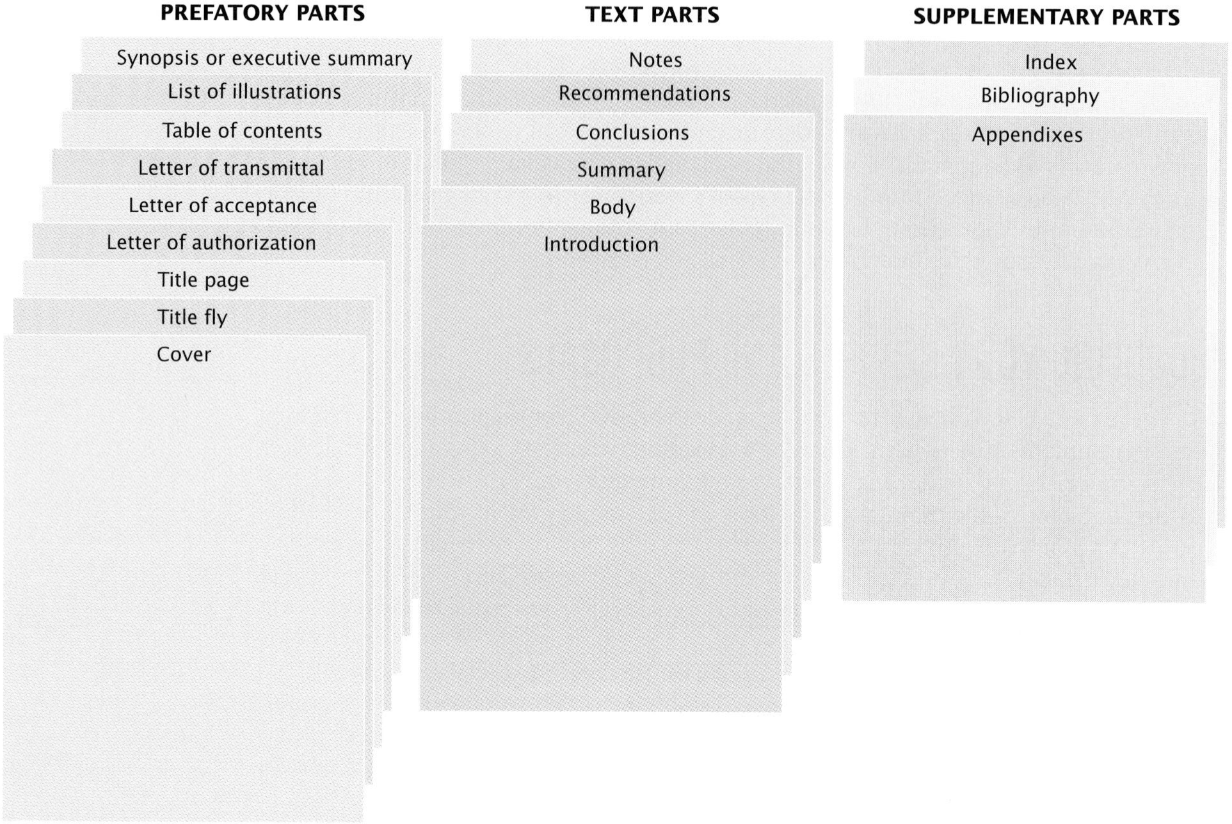

PREFATORY PARTS	TEXT PARTS	SUPPLEMENTARY PARTS
Synopsis or executive summary	Notes	Index
List of illustrations	Recommendations	Bibliography
Table of contents	Conclusions	Appendixes
Letter of transmittal	Summary	
Letter of acceptance	Body	
Letter of authorization	Introduction	
Title page		
Title fly		
Cover		

When you want a particular section to stand apart, you'll generally start it and the material after it on new pages. Most prefatory parts (such as the table of contents) should also be placed on their own pages. However, the various parts in the report text are often run together and seldom stand alone. If your introduction is only a paragraph long, don't bother with a page break before moving into the body of your report. If the introduction runs longer than a page, however, a page break can signal the reader that a major shift is about to occur in the flow of the report.

You can use this textbook as a model for deciding where to put page breaks. Each chapter starts on a new page, which provides a clear break between chapters. On the other hand, the vignette that opens each story flows right into the chapter content without a page break.

Prefatory Parts

Formal reports can contain a variety of prefatory parts, from a cover page to a synopsis or executive summary.

Prefatory parts are front-end materials that provide key preliminary information so that readers can decide whether and how to read the report.[2] Although these parts are placed before the text of the report, you may not want to write them until after you've written the text. Many of these parts—such as the table of contents, list of illustrations, and executive summary—are easier to prepare after the text has been completed, because they directly reflect the contents. When your text is complete, you can also use your word processor to automatically compile the table of contents and the list of illustrations. Other parts can be prepared at almost any time.

Cover Many companies have standard covers for reports, made of heavy paper and imprinted with the company's name and logo. Report titles are either printed on these covers or attached with gummed labels. If your company has no standard covers, you can usually find something suitable in a good stationery store. Look for a **cover** that is attractive, convenient, and appropriate to the subject matter. Also, make sure it can be labeled with the report title, the writer's name (optional), and the submission date (also optional).

(continued on page 442)

Report Writer's Notebook

Analyzing a Formal Report

The report presented in the following pages was prepared by Linda Moreno, manager of the cost accounting department at Electrovision, a high-tech company based in Los Gatos, California. Electrovision's main product is optical character recognition equipment, which is used by the U.S. Postal Service for sorting mail. Moreno's job is to help analyze the company's costs. She has this to say about the background of the report:

> For the past three or four years, Electrovision has been on a roll. Our A-12 optical character reader was a real breakthrough, and the post office grabbed up as many as we could make. Our sales and profits kept climbing, and morale was fantastic. Everybody seemed to think that the good times would last forever. Unfortunately, everybody was wrong. When the Postal Service announced that it was postponing all new equipment purchases because of cuts in its budget, we woke up to the fact that we are essentially a one-product company with one customer. At that point, management started scrambling around looking for ways to cut costs until we could diversify our business a bit.
>
> The vice president of operations, Dennis McWilliams, asked me to help identify cost-cutting opportunities in travel and entertainment. On the basis of his personal observations, he felt that Electrovision was overly generous in its travel policies and that we might be able to save a significant amount by controlling these costs more carefully. My investigation confirmed his suspicion.
>
> I was reasonably confident that my report would be well received. I've worked with Dennis for several years and know what he likes: plenty of facts, clearly stated conclusions, and specific recommendations for what should be done next. I also knew that my report would be passed on to other Electrovision executives, so I wanted to create a good impression. I wanted the report to be accurate and thorough, visually appealing, readable, and appropriate in tone.

When writing the analytical report that follows, Moreno based the organization on conclusions and recommendations presented in direct order. The first two sections of the report correspond to Moreno's two main conclusions: that Electrovision's travel and entertainment costs are too high and that cuts are essential. The third section presents recommendations for achieving better control over travel and entertainment expenses. As you review the report, analyze both the mechanical aspects and the way Moreno presents her ideas. Be prepared to discuss the way the various components convey and reinforce the main message.

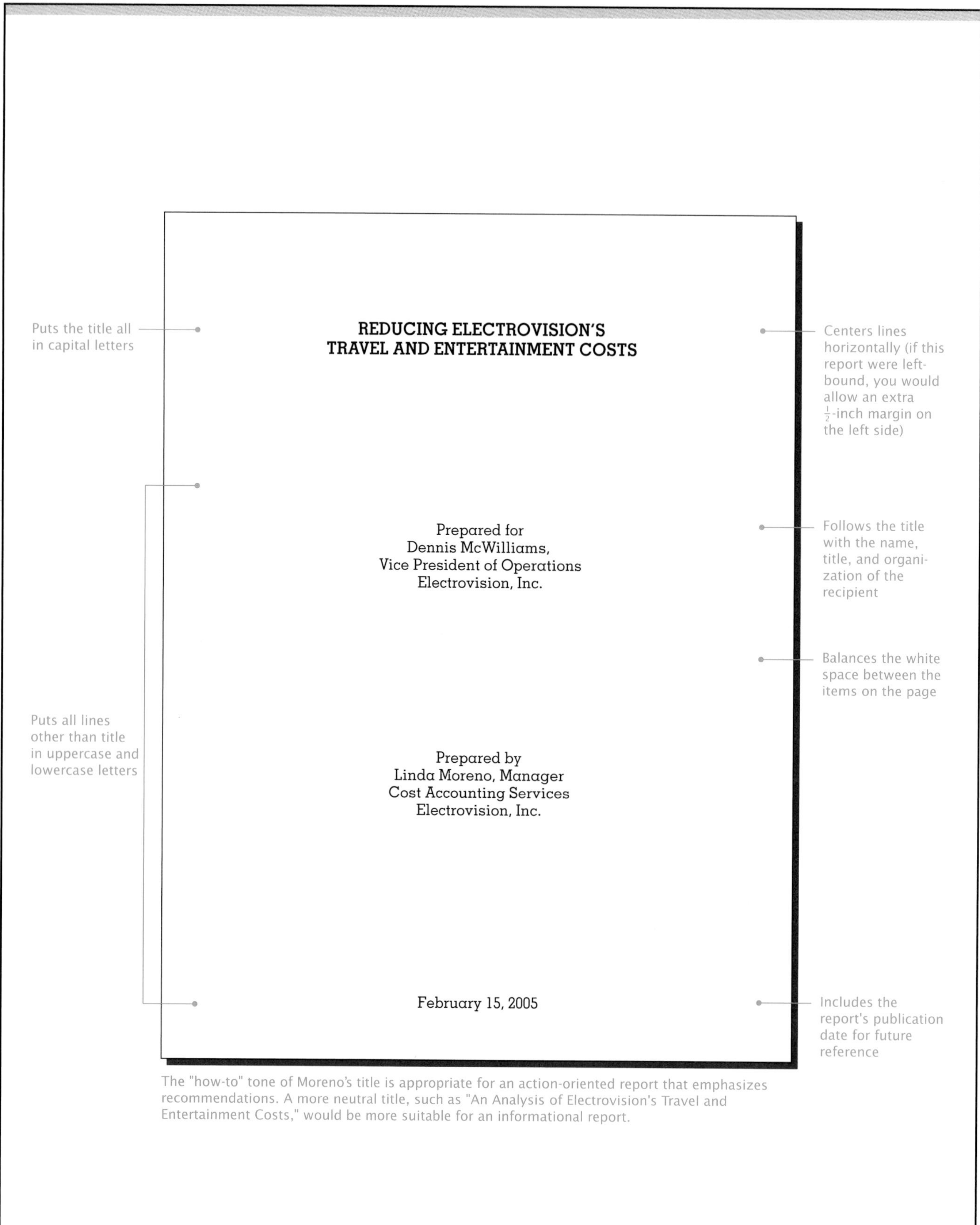
Puts the title all in capital letters
REDUCING ELECTROVISION'S
TRAVEL AND ENTERTAINMENT COSTS
Centers lines horizontally (if this report were left-bound, you would allow an extra ½-inch margin on the left side)
Prepared for
Dennis McWilliams,
Vice President of Operations
Electrovision, Inc.
Follows the title with the name, title, and organization of the recipient
Balances the white space between the items on the page
Puts all lines other than title in uppercase and lowercase letters
Prepared by
Linda Moreno, Manager
Cost Accounting Services
Electrovision, Inc.
February 15, 2005
Includes the report's publication date for future reference

The "how-to" tone of Moreno's title is appropriate for an action-oriented report that emphasizes recommendations. A more neutral title, such as "An Analysis of Electrovision's Travel and Entertainment Costs," would be more suitable for an informational report.

Uses memo format for transmitting this internal report; otherwise, letter format would be used for transmitting external reports

MEMORANDUM

TO: Dennis McWilliams, Vice President of Operations

FROM: Linda Moreno, Manager of Cost Accounting Services

DATE: February 15, 2005

SUBJECT: Reducing Electrovision's Travel and Entertainment Costs

Here is the report you requested January 30 on Electrovision's travel and entertainment costs.

Your suspicion was right. We are spending far too much on business travel. Our unwritten policy has been "anything goes," leaving us with no real control over T&E expenses. Although this hands-off approach may have been understandable when Electrovision's profits were high, we can no longer afford the luxury of going first class.

Presents the main conclusion right away (because Moreno expects a positive response)

The solutions to the problem seem rather clear. We need to have someone with centralized responsibility for travel and entertainment costs, a clear statement of policy, an effective control system, and a business-oriented travel service that can optimize our travel arrangements. We should also investigate alternatives to travel, such as videoconferencing. Perhaps more important, we need to change our attitude. Instead of viewing travel funds as a bottomless supply of money, all traveling employees need to act as though they were paying the bills themselves.

Uses an informal, conversational style

Getting people to economize is not going to be easy. In the course of researching this issue, I've found that our employees are exceedingly attached to their first-class travel privileges. I think they would almost prefer a cut in pay to a loss in travel status. We'll need a lot of top management involvement to sell people on the need for moderation. One thing is clear: People will be very bitter if we create a two-class system in which top executives get special privileges while the rest of the employees make the sacrifices.

I'm grateful to Mary Lehman and Connie McIlvain for their help in rounding up and sorting through five years' worth of expense reports. Their efforts were truly Herculean.

Acknowledges help that has been received

Thanks for giving me the opportunity to work on this assignment. It's been a real education. If you have any questions about the report, please give me a call.

Closes with thanks and an offer to discuss results (when appropriate, you could also include an offer to help with future projects)

In this report, Moreno decided to write a brief memo of transmittal and include a separate executive summary. Short reports (fewer than 10 pages) often combine the synopsis or executive summary with the memo or letter of transmittal.

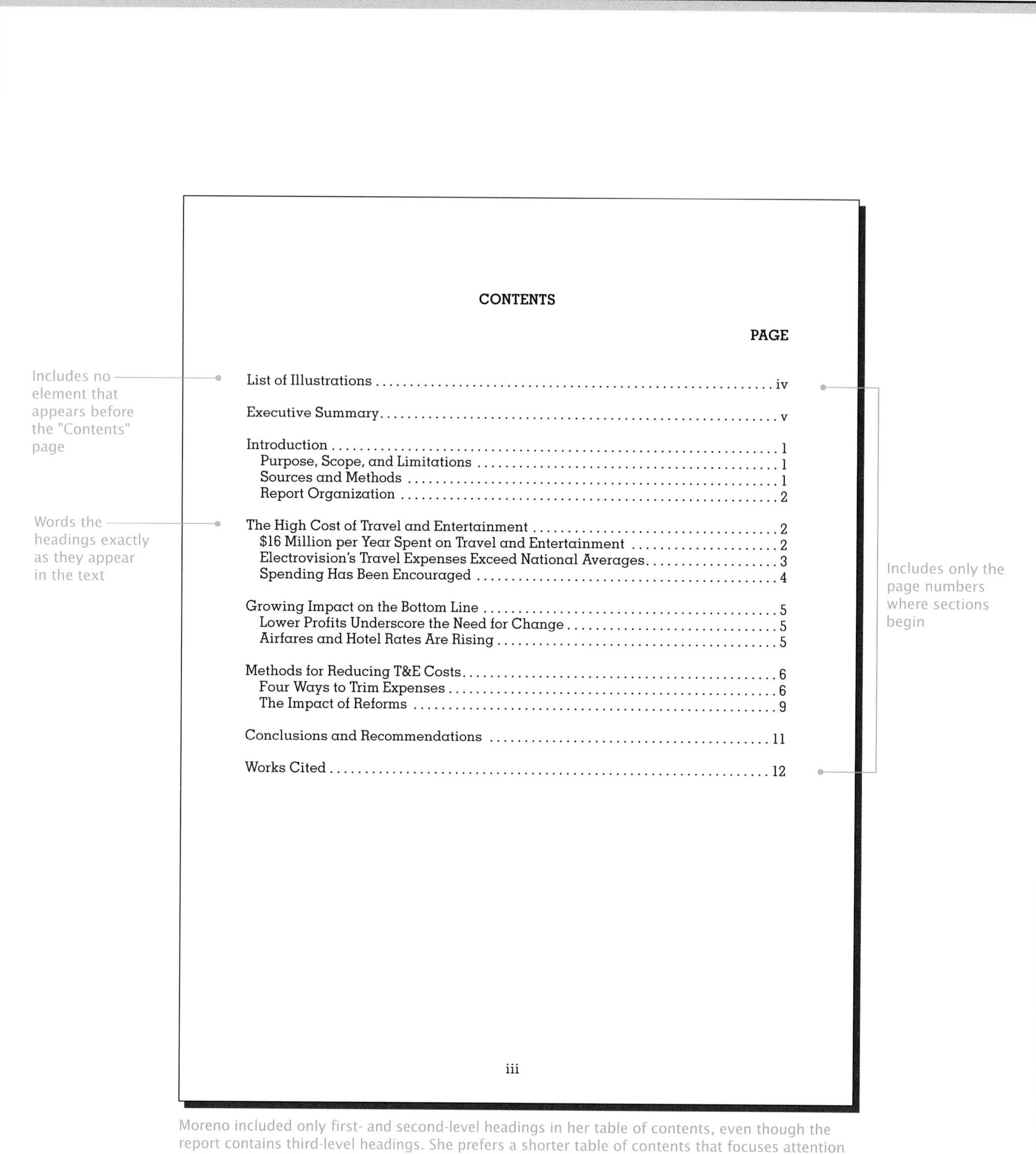

CONTENTS

iii

Includes no element that appears before the "Contents" page
Words the headings exactly as they appear in the text
Includes only the page numbers where sections begin

Moreno included only first- and second-level headings in her table of contents, even though the report contains third-level headings. She prefers a shorter table of contents that focuses attention on the main divisions of thought. She used informative titles, which are appropriate for a report to a receptive audience.

Numbers figures consecutively throughout the report

LIST OF ILLUSTRATIONS

FIGURE **PAGE**

TABLE

iv

Numbers the contents pages with lowercase roman numerals centered at the bottom margin

Because figures and tables were numbered separately in the text, Moreno listed them separately here. If all were labeled as exhibits, a single list of illustrations would have been appropriate.

Begins by stating the purpose of the report

Presents the points in the executive summary in the same order as they appear in the report

EXECUTIVE SUMMARY

This report analyzes Electrovision's travel and entertainment (T&E) costs and presents recommendations for reducing those costs.

Travel and Entertainment Costs Are Too High

Travel and entertainment is a large and growing expense category for Electrovision. The company spends over $16 million per year on business travel, and these costs have been increasing by 12 percent annually. Company employees make roughly 3,390 trips each year at an average cost per trip of $4,720. Airfares are the biggest expense, followed by hotels, meals, and rental cars.

The nature of Electrovision's business does require extensive travel, but the company's costs appear to be excessive. Every year Electrovision employees spend more than twice as much on T&E as the average business traveler. Although the location of the company's facilities may partly explain this discrepancy, the main reason for Electrovision's high costs is the firm's philosophy and managerial style. Electrovision's tradition and its hands-off style almost invite employees to go first class and pay relatively little attention to travel costs.

Cuts Are Essential

Uses subheadings that summarize the content of the main sections of the report without repeating what appears in the text

Although Electrovision has traditionally been casual about travel and entertainment expenses, management now recognizes the need to gain more control over this element of costs. The company is currently entering a period of declining profits, prompting management to look for every opportunity to reduce spending. At the same time, rising airfares and hotel rates are making travel and entertainment expenses more important to the bottom line.

Electrovision Can Save $6 Million per Year

Fortunately, Electrovision has a number of excellent opportunities for reducing its travel and entertainment costs. Savings of up to $6 million per year should be achievable, judging by the experience of other companies. American Express suggests that a sensible travel-management program can save companies as much as 35 percent a year (Gilligan 39–40). Given that we purchase many more first-class tickets than the average company, we should be able to achieve even greater savings. The first priority should be to hire a director of travel and entertainment to assume overall responsibility for T&E spending. This individual should establish a written travel and entertainment policy and a cost-control

v

Appears in the same typeface and type style as the text of the report. Uses single-spacing because the report is single-spaced, and follows the text's format for margins, paragraph indentions, and headings

Moreno decided to include an executive summary because her report was aimed at a mixed audience. She knew that some readers would be interested in the details of her report and some would prefer to focus on the big picture. The executive summary was aimed at the "big picture" group. Moreno wanted to give these readers enough information to make a decision without burdening them with the task of reading the entire report.

system. The director should also retain a nationwide travel agency to handle our reservations and should lead an investigation into electronic alternatives to travel.

Targets a receptive audience with a hard-hitting tone in the executive summary (a more neutral approach would be better for hostile or skeptical readers)

At the same time, Electrovision should make employees aware of the need for moderation in travel and entertainment spending. People should be encouraged to forgo any unnecessary travel and to economize on airline tickets, hotels, meals, rental cars, and other expenses.

In addition to economizing on an individual basis, Electrovision should look for ways to reduce costs by negotiating preferential rates with travel providers. Once retained, a travel agency should be able to accomplish this.

Finally, the company should look into alternatives to travel. Although we may have to invest money in videoconferencing systems or other equipment, we may be able to recover these costs through decreased travel expenses. I recommend that the new travel director undertake this investigation to make sure it is well integrated with the rest of the travel program.

As necessary as these changes are, they will likely hurt morale, at least in the short term. Management will need to make a determined effort to explain the rationale for reduced spending. By exercising moderation in their own travel arrangements, Electrovision executives can set a good example and help other employees accept the changes. On the plus side, cutting back on travel with videoconferencing or other alternatives will reduce the travel burden on many employees and help them balance their business and personal lives.

Continues numbering the executive summary pages with lowercase roman numerals centered about 1 inch from the bottom of the page

vi

This executive summary is written in an impersonal style, which adds to the formality of the report. Some writers prefer a more personal approach. Generally speaking, you should gear your choice of style to your relationship with the readers. Moreno chose the formal approach because several members of her audience were considerably higher up in the organization. She did not want to sound too familiar. In addition, she wanted the executive summary and the text to be compatible, and her company prefers the impersonal style for formal reports.

Centers the title of the report on the first page of the text, 2 inches from the top of the page ($2\frac{1}{2}$ inches if top-bound)

REDUCING ELECTROVISION'S TRAVEL AND ENTERTAINMENT COSTS

INTRODUCTION

Electrovision has always encouraged a significant amount of business travel, believing that it is an effective way of operating. To compensate employees for the inconvenience and stress of frequent trips, management has authorized generous travel and entertainment (T&E) allowances. This philosophy has been good for morale, but the company has paid a price. Last year Electrovision spent $16 million on T&E—$7 million more than it spent on research and development.

Begins the introduction by establishing the need for action

This year the cost of travel and entertainment will have a bigger impact on profits, owing to changes in airfares and hotel rates. The timing of these changes is unfortunate because the company anticipates that profits will be relatively weak for a variety of other reasons. In light of these profit pressures, Dennis McWilliams, Vice President of Operations, has asked the accounting department to take a closer look at the T&E budget.

Purpose, Scope, and Limitations

The purpose of this report is to analyze the T&E budget, evaluate the impact of recent changes in airfares and hotel costs, and suggest ways to tighten management's control over T&E expenses. Although the report outlines a number of steps that could reduce Electrovision's expenses, the precise financial impact of these measures is difficult to project. The estimates presented in the report provide a "best guess" view of what Electrovision can expect to save. Until the company actually implements these steps, however, we won't know exactly how much the travel and entertainment budget can be reduced.

Sources and Methods

In preparing this report, the accounting department analyzed internal expense reports for the past five years to determine how much Electrovision spends on travel and entertainment. These figures were then compared with average statistics compiled by Dow Jones (publisher of *The Wall Street Journal*) and presented as the Dow Jones Travel Index. We also analyzed trends and suggestions published in a variety of business journal articles to see how other companies are coping with the high cost of business travel.

Mentions sources and methods to increase credibility and to give readers a complete picture of the study's background

Uses the arabic numeral 1 for the first page, centering the number about 1 inch from the bottom of the page

1

In a brief introduction such as this one, some writers would omit the subheadings within the introduction and rely on topic sentences and on transitional words and phrases to indicate that they are discussing subjects such as the purpose, scope, and limitations of the study. Moreno decided to use headings because they help readers scan the document. Also, to conserve space, Moreno used single spacing and 1-inch side margins.

2

Uses arabic numerals to number the second and succeeding pages of the text in the upper right-hand corner where the top and right-hand margins meet

Report Organization

This report reviews the size and composition of Electrovision's travel and entertainment expenses, analyzes trends in travel costs, and recommends steps for reducing the T&E budget.

THE HIGH COST OF TRAVEL AND ENTERTAINMENT

Although many companies view travel and entertainment as an "incidental" cost of doing business, the dollars add up. At Electrovision the bill for airfares, hotels, rental cars, meals, and entertainment totaled $16 million last year. Our T&E budget has increased by 12 percent per year for the past five years. Compared with the average U.S. business's travel expenditures, Electrovision's expenditures are high, largely because of management's generous policy on travel benefits.

$16 Million per Year Spent on Travel and Entertainment

Electrovision's annual budget for travel and entertainment is only 8 percent of sales. Because this is a relatively small expense category compared with such things as salaries and commissions, it is tempting to dismiss T&E costs as insignificant. However, T&E is Electrovision's third-largest controllable expense, directly behind salaries and information systems.

Last year Electrovision personnel made about 3,390 trips at an average cost per trip of $4,720. The typical trip involved a round-trip flight of 3,000 miles, meals and hotel accommodations for two or three days, and a rental car. Roughly 80 percent of the trips were made by 20 percent of the staff—top management and sales personnel traveled most, averaging 18 trips per year.

Places the visual aid as close as possible to the point it illustrates

Figure 1 illustrates how the travel and entertainment budget is spent. The largest categories are airfares and lodging, which together account for $7 out of every

Gives each visual aid a title that clearly indicates what it's about

Figure 1
Airfares and Lodging Account for Over Two-Thirds of Electrovision's T&E Budget

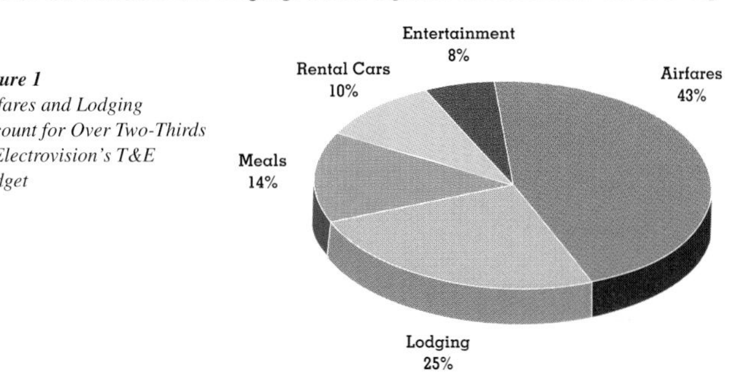

Makes placement of visual aid titles consistent throughout the report (options for placement include above, below, or beside the visual)

Moreno opened the first main section of the body with a topic sentence that introduces an important fact about the subject of the section. Then she oriented the reader to the three major points developed in the section.

$10 that employees spend on travel and entertainment. This spending breakdown has been relatively steady for the past five years and is consistent with the distribution of expenses experienced by other companies.

Although the composition of the T&E budget has been consistent, its size has not. As mentioned earlier, these expenditures have increased by about 12 percent per year for the past five years, roughly twice the rate of the company's growth in sales (see Figure 2). This rate of growth makes T&E Electrovision's fastest-growing expense item.

Introduces visual aids before they appear and indicates what readers should notice about the data

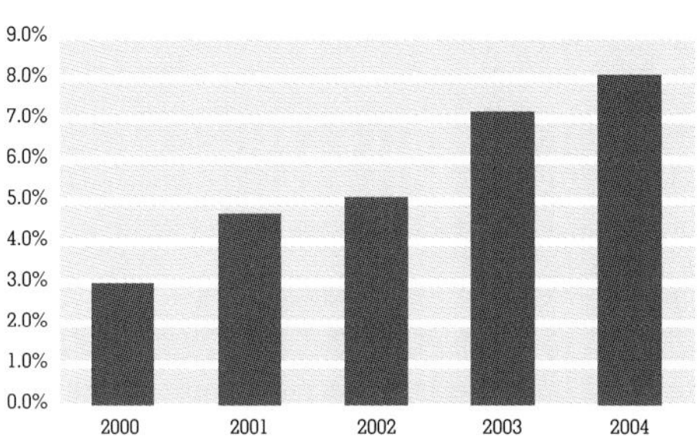

Figure 2
Travel and Entertainment Expenses Have Increased as a Percentage of Sales

Numbers the visual aids consecutively and refers to them in the text by their numbers (if your report is a book-length document, you may number the visual aids by chapter; for example, Figure 4-2 would be the second figure in the fourth chapter)

Electrovision's Travel Expenses Exceed National Averages

Much of our travel budget is justified. Two major factors contribute to Electrovision's high travel and entertainment budget:

- With our headquarters on the West Coast and our major customer on the East Coast, we naturally spend a lot on cross-country flights.
- A great deal of travel takes place between our headquarters here on the West Coast and the manufacturing operations in Detroit, Boston, and Dallas. Corporate managers and division personnel make frequent trips to coordinate these disparate operations.

However, even though a good portion of Electrovision's travel budget is justifiable, our travelers spend considerably more on T&E than the average business traveler (see Figure 3).

Moreno originally drew the bar chart in Figure 2 as a line chart, showing both sales and T&E expenses in absolute dollars. However, the comparison was difficult to interpret because sales were so much greater than T&E expenses. Switching to a bar chart expressed in percentage terms made the main idea much easier to grasp.

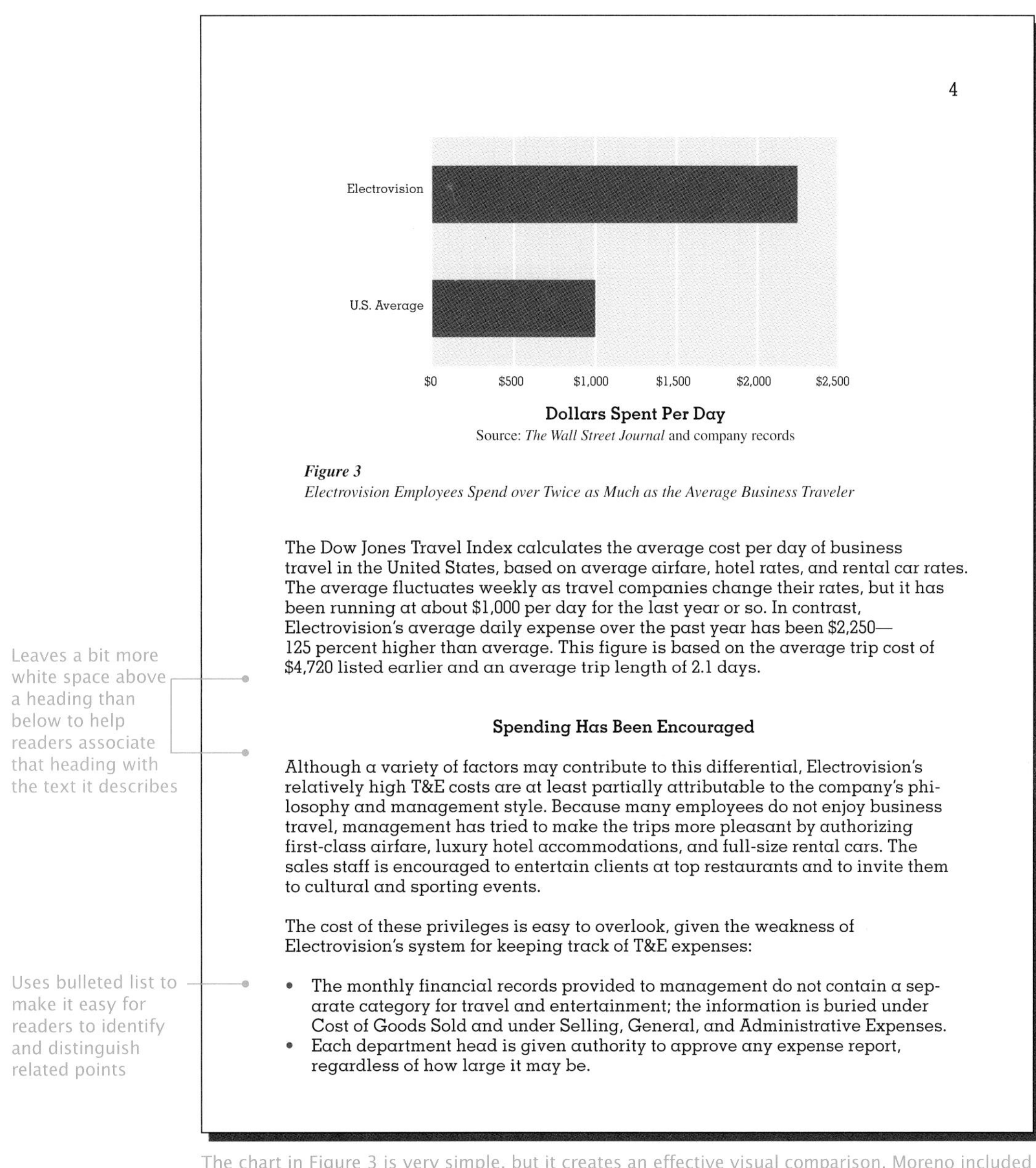

4

Figure 3
Electrovision Employees Spend over Twice as Much as the Average Business Traveler

The Dow Jones Travel Index calculates the average cost per day of business travel in the United States, based on average airfare, hotel rates, and rental car rates. The average fluctuates weekly as travel companies change their rates, but it has been running at about $1,000 per day for the last year or so. In contrast, Electrovision's average daily expense over the past year has been $2,250—125 percent higher than average. This figure is based on the average trip cost of $4,720 listed earlier and an average trip length of 2.1 days.

Spending Has Been Encouraged

Although a variety of factors may contribute to this differential, Electrovision's relatively high T&E costs are at least partially attributable to the company's philosophy and management style. Because many employees do not enjoy business travel, management has tried to make the trips more pleasant by authorizing first-class airfare, luxury hotel accommodations, and full-size rental cars. The sales staff is encouraged to entertain clients at top restaurants and to invite them to cultural and sporting events.

The cost of these privileges is easy to overlook, given the weakness of Electrovision's system for keeping track of T&E expenses:

- The monthly financial records provided to management do not contain a separate category for travel and entertainment; the information is buried under Cost of Goods Sold and under Selling, General, and Administrative Expenses.
- Each department head is given authority to approve any expense report, regardless of how large it may be.

Leaves a bit more white space above a heading than below to help readers associate that heading with the text it describes

Uses bulleted list to make it easy for readers to identify and distinguish related points

The chart in Figure 3 is very simple, but it creates an effective visual comparison. Moreno included just enough data to make her point. Moreno was as careful about the appearance of her report as she was about its content.

5

- Receipts are not required for expenditures of less than $100.
- Individuals are allowed to make their own travel arrangements.
- No one is charged with the responsibility for controlling the company's total spending on travel and entertainment.

Uses informative headings to focus reader attention on the main points (such headings are appropriate when a report is in direct order and intended for a receptive audience; however, descriptive headings are more effective when a report is in indirect order and readers are less receptive)

GROWING IMPACT ON THE BOTTOM LINE

During the past three years, the company's healthy profits have resulted in relatively little pressure to push for tighter controls over all aspects of the business. However, as we all know, the situation is changing. We're projecting flat to declining profits for the next two years, a situation that has prompted all of us to search for ways to cut costs. At the same time, rising airfares and hotel rates have increased the impact of T&E expenses on the company's financial results.

Lower Profits Underscore the Need for Change

The next two years promise to be difficult for Electrovision. After several years of steady increases in spending, the Postal Service is tightening procurement policies for automated mail-handling equipment. Funding for the A-12 optical character reader has been canceled. As a consequence, the marketing department expects sales to drop by 15 percent. Although Electrovision is negotiating several promising R&D contracts with nongovernment clients, the marketing department does not foresee any major procurements for the next two to three years.

At the same time, Electrovision is facing cost increases on several fronts. As we've known for several months, the new production facility now under construction in Salt Lake City is behind schedule and over budget. Labor contracts in Boston and Dallas expire within the next six months, and plant managers there anticipate that significant salary and benefits concessions may be necessary to avoid strikes.

Moreover, marketing and advertising costs are expected to increase as we attempt to strengthen these activities to better cope with competitive pressures. Given the expected decline in revenues and increase in costs, the Executive Committee's prediction that profits will fall by 12 percent in the coming fiscal year does not seem overly pessimistic.

Airfares and Hotel Rates Are Rising

Business travelers have grown accustomed to frequent fare wars and discounting in the travel industry in recent years. Excess capacity and aggressive price competition, particularly in the airline business, made travel a relative bargain.

Because airfares represent Electrovision's biggest T&E expense, Moreno included a subsection that deals with the possible impact of trends in the airline industry. Airfares are rising, so it is especially important to gain more control over employees' air travel arrangements.

6

However, that situation has changed, as weaker competitors have been forced out and the remaining players have grown stronger and smarter. Airlines and hotels are better at managing inventory and keeping occupancy rates high, and high occupancy translates into higher prices because suppliers have less reason to compete on price. Last year saw some of the steepest rate hikes in years. Business airfares (tickets most likely to be purchased by business travelers) jumped over 40 percent in many markets. The trend is expected to continue, with rates increasing another 5 to 10 percent overall (Phillips 331; "Travel Costs Under Pressure" 30; Dahl B6).

Documents the facts to add weight to Moreno's argument

Given the fact that airfare and hotel costs account for 70 percent of Electrovision's T&E budget, the trend toward higher prices in these two categories will have serious consequences on the company's expenses unless management takes action to control these costs.

METHODS FOR REDUCING T&E COSTS

By implementing a number of reforms, management can expect to reduce Electrovision's T&E budget by as much as 40 percent. This estimate is based on the general assessment made by American Express (Gilligan 39–40) and the fact that we have an opportunity to significantly reduce air travel costs by reducing or eliminating first-class travel. However, these measures are likely to be unpopular with employees. To gain acceptance for such changes, management will need to sell employees on the need for moderation in travel and entertainment allowances.

Gives recommendations an objective flavor by pointing out both the benefits and the risks of taking action

Four Ways to Trim Expenses

By researching what other companies are doing to curb travel and entertainment expenses, the accounting department has identified four prominent opportunities that should enable Electrovision to save about $6 million annually in travel-related costs.

Institute Tighter Spending Controls

A single individual should be appointed director of travel and entertainment to spearhead the effort to gain control of the T&E budget. More than a third of all U.S. companies now employ travel managers in an effort to keep costs in line ("Businesses Use Savvy Managers" 4). The director should be familiar with the travel industry and should be well versed in both accounting and information technology. The director should also report to the vice president of operations. The director's first priorities should be to establish a written travel and entertainment policy and to implement a system for controlling travel and entertainment costs.

Electrovision currently has no written policy on travel and entertainment, a step

Moreno created a forceful tone by using action verbs in the third-level subheadings of this section. This approach is appropriate to the nature of the study and the attitude of the audience. However, in a status-conscious organization, the imperative verbs might sound a bit too presumptuous coming from a junior member of the staff.

7

widely recommended by air travel experts (Smith D4). Creating a policy would clarify management's position and serve as a vehicle for communicating the need for moderation. At a minimum, the policy should include the following provisions:

- All travel and entertainment should be strictly related to business and should be approved in advance.
- Except under special circumstances to be approved on a case-by-case basis, employees should travel by coach and stay in mid-range business hotels.
- The travel and entertainment policy should apply equally to employees at all levels in the organization. No special benefits should be allowed for top executives.

Breaks up text with bulleted lists, which not only call attention to important points but also add visual interest (you can also use visual aids, headings, and direct quotations to break up large, solid blocks of print)

To implement the new policy, Electrovision will need to create a system for controlling travel and entertainment expenses. Each department should prepare an annual T&E budget as part of its operating plan. These budgets should be presented in detail so that management can evaluate how travel and entertainment dollars will be spent and recommend appropriate cuts.

To help management monitor performance relative to these budgets, the director of travel should prepare monthly financial statements showing actual travel and entertainment expenditures by department. The system for capturing this information should be computerized and should be capable of identifying individuals who consistently exceed approved spending levels. The recommended average should range between $2,000 and $2,500 per month for each professional employee, depending on the individual's role in the company. Because they make frequent trips, sales and top management personnel can be expected to have relatively high travel expenses.

Specifies the steps required to implement recommendations

The director of travel should also be responsible for retaining a business-oriented travel service that will schedule all employee business trips and look for the best travel deals, particularly in airfares. In addition to centralizing Electrovision's reservation and ticketing activities, the agency will negotiate reduced group rates with hotels and rental car agencies. The agency selected should have offices nationwide so that all Electrovision facilities can channel their reservations through the same company. By consolidating its travel planning in this way, Electrovision can increase its control over costs and achieve economies of scale. This is particularly important in light of the dizzying array of often wildly different airfares available between some cities. It's not uncommon to find dozens of fares along commonly traveled routes (Rowe 30).

The director should also work with the agency to explore low-cost alternatives, such as buying tickets from airfare consolidators (the air travel equivalent of factory outlet malls). In addition, the director can help coordinate travel across the company to secure group discounts whenever possible (Barker 31; Miller B6).

Moreno decided to single-space her report to create a formal, finished look; however, double-spacing can make the text of a long report somewhat easier to read and provide more space for readers to write comments.

8

Reduce Unnecessary Travel and Entertainment

One of the easiest ways to reduce expenses is to reduce the amount of traveling and entertaining that occurs. An analysis of last year's expenditures suggests that as much as 30 percent of Electrovision's travel and entertainment is discretionary. The professional staff spent $2.8 million attending seminars and conferences last year. Although some of these gatherings are undoubtedly beneficial, the company could save money by sending fewer representatives to each function and by eliminating some of the less valuable seminars.

Similarly, Electrovision could economize on trips between headquarters and divisions by reducing the frequency of such visits and by sending fewer people on each trip. Although there is often no substitute for face-to-face meetings, management could try to resolve more internal issues through telephone, electronic, and written communication.

Electrovision can also reduce spending by urging employees to economize. Instead of flying first class, employees can fly tourist class or take advantage of discount fares. Instead of taking clients to dinner, Electrovision personnel can hold breakfast meetings, which tend to be less costly. Rather than ordering a $50 bottle of wine, employees can select a less-expensive bottle or dispense with alcohol entirely. People can book rooms at moderately priced hotels and drive smaller rental cars. In general, employees should be urged to spend the company's money as though it were their own.

Obtain Lowest Rates from Travel Providers

Apart from urging individual employees to economize, Electrovision can also save money by searching for the lowest available airfares, hotel rates, and rental car fees. Currently, few Electrovision employees have the time or specialized knowledge to seek out travel bargains. When they need to travel, they make the most convenient and most comfortable arrangements. However, if Electrovision contracts with a professional travel service, the company will have access to professionals who can more efficiently obtain the lower rates from travel providers.

Judging by the experience of other companies, Electrovision may be able to trim as much as 30 to 40 percent from the travel budget by looking for bargains in airfares and negotiating group rates with hotels and rental car companies. Electrovision should be able to achieve these economies by analyzing its travel patterns, identifying frequently visited locations, and selecting a few hotels that are willing to reduce rates in exchange for guaranteed business. At the same time, the company should be able to save up to 40 percent on rental car charges by negotiating a corporate rate.

Note how Moreno made the transition from section to section. The first sentence under the second heading on this page refers to the subject of the previous paragraph and signals a shift in thought.

The possibilities for economizing are promising, but it's worth noting that making the best arrangements is a complicated undertaking, requiring many trade-offs such as the following:

- The best fares might not always be the lowest. Indirect flights are often less expensive than direct flights, but they take longer and may end up costing more in lost work time.
- The cheapest tickets may have to be booked 30 days in advance, often impossible for us.
- Discount tickets may be nonrefundable, which is a real drawback if the trip has to be canceled at the last minute.

Electrovision is currently ill-equipped to make these and other trade-offs. However, by employing a business-oriented travel service, the company will have access to computerized systems that can optimize its choices.

Replace Travel with Technological Alternatives

Points out possible difficulties to show that all angles have been considered and to build reader confidence in the writer's judgment

We might be able to replace a significant portion of our interdivisional travel with electronic meetings that utilize videoconferencing, real-time document sharing on PC screens, and other alternatives. Naturally, we don't want to reduce employee or team effectiveness, but many companies are using these new tools to cut costs and reduce wear and tear on employees.

Rather than make specific recommendations in this report, I suggest that the new travel director conduct an in-depth study of the company's travel patterns as part of an overall cost-containment effort. A thorough analysis of why employees travel and what they accomplish will highlight any opportunities for replacing face-to-face meetings. Part of this study should include limited-scope tests of various communication systems as a way of measuring their impact on both workplace effectiveness and overall costs.

The Impact of Reforms

By implementing tighter controls, reducing unnecessary expenses, negotiating more favorable rates, and exploring "electronic travel," Electrovision should be able to reduce its travel and entertainment budget significantly. As Table 1 illustrates, the combined savings should be in the neighborhood of $6 million, although the precise figures are somewhat difficult to project.

Note how Moreno calls attention in the last paragraph to items in the following table without repeating the information in the table.

Uses informative title in the table, which is consistent with the way headings are handled and is appropriate for a report to a receptive audience

Uses complete sentence to help readers focus immediately on the point of the illustrations

Includes dollar figures to help management envision the impact of the suggestions, even though estimated savings are difficult to project

10

Table 1
Electrovision Can Trim Travel and Entertainment Costs
by an Estimated $6 Million per Year

SOURCE OF SAVINGS	AMOUNT SAVED
Switching from first-class to coach airfare	$2,300,000
Negotiating preferred hotel rates	940,000
Negotiating preferred rental car rates	460,000
Systematically searching for lower airfares	375,000
Reducing interdivisional travel	675,000
Reducing seminar and conference attendance	1,250,000
TOTAL POTENTIAL SAVINGS	$6,000,000

To achieve the economies outlined in the table, Electrovision will incur expenses for hiring a director of travel and for implementing a T&E cost-control system. These costs are projected at $95,000: $85,000 per year in salary and benefits for the new employee and a one-time expense of $10,000 for the cost-control system. The cost of retaining a full-service travel agency is negligible because agencies normally receive a commission from travel providers rather than a fee from clients.

The measures required to achieve these savings are likely to be unpopular with employees. Electrovision personnel are accustomed to generous travel and entertainment allowances, and they are likely to resent having these privileges curtailed. To alleviate their disappointment

- Management should make a determined effort to explain why the changes are necessary.
- The director of corporate communication should be asked to develop a multifaceted campaign that will communicate the importance of curtailing travel and entertainment costs.
- Management should set a positive example by adhering strictly to the new policies.
- The limitations should apply equally to employees at all levels in the organization.

The table on this page puts Moreno's recommendations in perspective. Moreno called attention to the most important sources of savings and spells out the costs required to achieve those results.

11

Uses a descriptive heading for the last section of the text (in informational reports, this section is often called "Summary"; in analytical reports, it is called "Conclusions" or "Conclusions and Recommendations")

CONCLUSIONS AND RECOMMENDATIONS

Summarizes conclusions in the first two paragraphs—a good approach because Moreno organized her report around conclusions and recommendations, so readers have already been introduced to them

Electrovision is currently spending $16 million per year on travel and entertainment. Although much of this spending is justified, the company's costs appear to be high relative to competitors', mainly because Electrovision has been generous with its travel benefits.

Electrovision's liberal approach to travel and entertainment was understandable during years of high profitability; however, the company is facing the prospect of declining profits for the next several years. Management is therefore motivated to cut costs in all areas of the business. Reducing T&E spending is particularly important because the bottom-line impact of these costs will increase as airline fares increase.

Electrovision should be able to reduce travel and entertainment costs by as much as 40 percent by taking four important steps:

Emphasizes the recommendations by presenting them in list format

1. *Institute tighter spending controls.* Management should hire a director of travel and entertainment who will assume overall responsibility for T&E activities. Within the next six months, this director should develop a written travel policy, institute a T&E budget and a cost-control system, and retain a professional, business-oriented travel agency that will optimize arrangements with travel providers.

2. *Reduce unnecessary travel and entertainment.* Electrovision should encourage employees to economize on travel and entertainment spending. Management can accomplish this by authorizing fewer trips and by urging employees to be more conservative in their spending.

3. *Obtain lowest rates from travel providers.* Electrovision should also focus on obtaining the best rates on airline tickets, hotel rooms, and rental cars. By channeling all arrangements through a professional travel agency, the company can optimize its choices and gain clout in negotiating preferred rates.

4. *Replace travel with technological alternatives.* With the number of computers already installed in our facilities, it seems likely that we could take advantage of desktop videoconferencing and other distance-meeting tools. This won't be quite as feasible with customer sites, since these systems require compatible equipment at both ends of a connection, but it is certainly a possibility for communication with Electrovision's own sites.

Because these measures may be unpopular with employees, management should make a concerted effort to explain the importance of reducing travel costs. The director of corporate communication should be given responsibility for developing a plan to communicate the need for employee cooperation.

Morena introduced no new facts in this entire section. In a longer report she might have divided this section into subsections, labeled "Conclusions" and "Recommendations," to distinguish between the two. If the report had been organized around logical arguments, this section would have been the readers' first exposure to the conclusions and recommendations, and Moreno would have needed to develop them more fully.

12

WORKS CITED

Lists references alphabetically by the author's last name, and when the author is unknown, by the title of the reference (see Appendix II for additional details on preparing reference lists)

Barker, Julie. "How to Rein in Group Travel Costs." *Successful Meetings* Feb. 2004: 31.

"Businesses Use Savvy Managers to Keep Travel Costs Down." *Christian Science Monitor* 17 July 2004: 4.

Dahl, Jonathan. "2000: The Year Travel Costs Took Off." *Wall Street Journal* 29 Dec. 2004: B6.

Gilligan, Edward P. "Trimming Your T&E Is Easier Than You Think." *Managing Office Technology* Nov. 2004: 39–40.

Miller, Lisa. "Attention, Airline Ticket Shoppers." *Wall Street Journal* 7 July 2004: B6.

Phillips, Edward H. "Airlines Post Record Traffic." *Aviation Week & Space Technology* 8 Jan. 2005: 331.

Rowe, Irene Vlitos. "Global Solution for Cutting Travel Costs." *European* 12 Oct. 2004: 30.

Smith, Carol. "Rising, Erratic Air Fares Make Company Policy Vital." *Los Angeles Times* 2 Nov. 2004: D4.

"Travel Costs Under Pressure." *Purchasing* 15 Feb. 2004: 30.

Moreno's list of references follows the style recommended in *The MLA Style Manual.*

Think carefully about the title you put on the cover. A business report is not a mystery novel, so give your readers all the information they need: the who, what, when, where, why, and how of the subject. At the same time, try to be concise. You don't want to intimidate your audience with a title that's too long or awkward. You can reduce the length of your title by eliminating phrases such as *A Report of*, *A Study of*, or *A Survey of*.

Title Fly and Title Page The **title fly** is a plain sheet of paper with only the title of the report on it. You don't really need one, but it adds a touch of formality.

The **title page** includes four blocks of information, as shown in Moreno's Electrovision report: (1) the title of the report; (2) the name, title, and address of the person, group, or organization that authorized the report (if anyone); (3) the name, title, and address of the person, group, or organization that prepared the report; and (4) the date on which the report was submitted. On some title pages the second block of information is preceded by the words *Prepared for* or *Submitted to*, and the third block of information is preceded by *Prepared by* or *Submitted by*. In some cases the title page serves as the cover of the report, especially if the report is relatively short and is intended solely for internal use.

3 LEARNING OBJECTIVE

Identify the circumstances in which you should include letters of authorization and letters of acceptance in your reports

In the most formal report situations, you might have both a letter of authorization from the person who authorized the report and your response, which is called a letter of acceptance.

Letter of Authorization and Letter of Acceptance If you received written authorization to prepare the report, you may want to include that letter or memo in your report. This **letter of authorization** (or *memo of authorization*) is a document you received, asking or directing you to prepare the report. If you wrote a **letter of acceptance** (or *memo of acceptance*) in response to that communication, accepting the assignment and clarifying any conditions or limitations, you might also include that letter here in the report's prefatory parts. If there is any chance that your audience's expectations might not align with the actual work you did on the report, the letter of acceptance can show your readers what you agreed to do and why.

In general, the letters of authorization and acceptance are included in only the most formal reports. However, in any case in which a significant amount of time has passed since you received the letter of authorization, or you do not have a close working relationship with the audience, consider including both letters to make sure everyone is clear about the report's intent and the approach you took to create it. You don't want your weeks or months of work to be diminished by any such misunderstandings.

Letter of Transmittal The **letter of transmittal** (or *memo of transmittal*), a specialized form of a cover letter, introduces your report to your audience. (In a book, this section is called the preface.) The letter of transmittal says what you'd say if you were handing the report directly to the person who authorized it, so the style is less formal than the rest of the report. For example, the letter would use personal pronouns (*you, I, we*) and conversational language. Moreno's Electrovision report includes a one-page transmittal memo from Moreno to her boss (the person who requested the report).

The transmittal letter usually appears right before the table of contents. If your report will be widely distributed, however, you may decide to include the letter of transmittal only in selected copies so that you can make certain comments to a specific audience. If your report discusses layoffs or other issues that affect people in the organization, you might want to discuss your recommendations privately in a letter of transmittal to top management. If your audience is likely to be skeptical of or even hostile to something in your report, the transmittal letter is a good opportunity to acknowledge their concerns and explain how the report addresses the issues they care about.

Depending on the nature of your report, your letter of transmittal can follow either the direct approach for routine or positive messages described in Chapter 7 or the indirect approach for negative messages described in Chapter 8. Open by officially conveying the report to your readers and summarizing its purpose. Such a letter typically begins with a statement such as "Here is the report you asked me to prepare on . . ." The rest of the introduction includes information about the scope of the report, the methods used to complete the study, and the limitations that became apparent. In the body of the transmittal letter, you may also highlight important points or sections of the report, make comments on side issues, give suggestions for follow-up studies, and offer any details that will help readers understand and use the report. You may also wish to acknowledge help given by others—if your report is extensive, chances are you received assistance from many people, and this letter is a high-visibility way to thank them. The conclusion of the transmittal letter is a note of thanks for having been given the report assignment, an expression of willingness to discuss the report, and an offer to assist with future projects.

If the report does not have a synopsis, the letter of transmittal may summarize the major findings, conclusions, and recommendations. This material would be placed after the opening of the letter.

If you don't include a synopsis, you can summarize the report's content in your letter of transmittal.

Table of Contents The **table of contents** (titled simply "Contents") indicates in outline form the coverage, sequence, and relative importance of the information in the report. The headings used in the text of the report are the basis for the table of contents. Depending on the length and complexity of the report, you may need to decide how many levels of headings to show in the contents; it's a trade-off between simplicity and completeness. Contents that show only first-level heads are easy to scan but could frustrate people looking for specific subsections in the report. Conversely, contents that show every level of heading—down to fourth or fifth level in detailed reports—identify all the sections but can intimidate readers and blur the focus by detracting from your most important message points. In extreme cases, where the detailed table of contents could have dozens or even hundreds of entries, consider including two tables: a high-level table that shows only major headings, followed by a detailed table that includes everything (as this and many other textbooks do). No matter how many levels you include, make sure readers can easily distinguish between them (Look back at Figure 13.6 on page 408 for examples of various levels of headings).

Also, take extra care to ensure that your table of contents is accurate, consistent, and complete. Even minor errors could damage your credibility if readers turn to a given page expecting to find something that isn't there, of if they find headings that seem similar to the table of contents but aren't worded quite the same. To ensure accuracy, construct the table of contents after your report is complete, thoroughly edited, and proofed. This way, the headings and subheadings aren't likely to change or move from page to page.

If at all possible, use the automatic features in your word processor to generate the table of contents—not only does this help improve accuracy by eliminating typing mistakes, but it keeps your table current in the event you do have to repaginate or revise headings late in the process. In Microsoft Word, for instance, you can automatically create a table of contents based on the heading levels identified in your style sheet. As long as you use styles consistently throughout the report, the process is quick and painless. However, discipline is paramount. If you or any of your co-authors deviate from the style sheet (say, by manually formatting a line of regular text to look like a major heading, without using the heading style), those entries will be missing from your table of contents. Naturally, to make sure your contents are accurate and complete, be sure to proofread them even if they are automatically generated.

Use the table of contents generator in your word processor whenever possible; it will reduce the amount of work involved and reduce the chance of errors as well.

List of Illustrations If you have more than a handful of illustrations in your report, or you want to call attention to your illustrations, include a **list of illustrations** after the table of contents. For simplicity's sake, some reports refer to all visuals as *illustrations* or *exhibits*. In other reports, as in Moreno's Electrovision report, tables are labeled separately from other types of visuals, which are called *figures*. Regardless of the system you use, be sure to include titles and page numbers.

If you have enough space on a single page, include the list of illustrations directly beneath the table of contents. Otherwise, put the list on the page after the contents page. When tables and figures are numbered separately, they should also be listed separately. The two lists can appear on the same page if they fit; otherwise, start each list on a separate page.

Synopsis or Executive Summary A **synopsis** is a brief overview (one page or less) of a report's most important points, designed to give readers a quick preview of the contents. It's often included in long informational reports dealing with technical, professional, or

Take time writing your synopsis or executive summary; it's one of the most important parts of your report.

The introductory page of this AT&T online report serves as a synopsis, giving readers a brief overview of the main points covered.

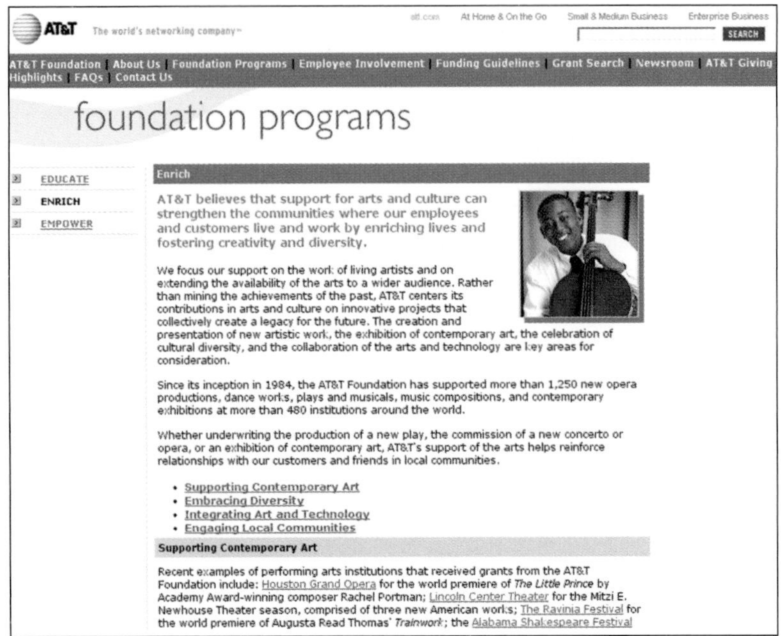

academic subjects and can also be called an **abstract**. Because it's a concise representation of the whole report, it may be distributed separately to a wide audience; then interested readers can request a copy of the entire report.

Think carefully about the wording of your synopsis or abstract. Not only does it establish readers' expectations for the entire report, but this piece of text might also be indexed as a separate entry in either internal or external databases. People researching the subject area may run across your abstract in a list of results and use it to decide whether or not to read your report.

The phrasing of a synopsis can be either informative or descriptive, depending on whether the report is in direct or indirect order. In an informative synopsis, you present the main points of the report in the order in which they appear in the text. A descriptive synopsis, on the other hand, simply tells what the report is about, using only moderately greater detail than the table of contents; the actual findings of the report are omitted. Here are examples of statements from each type:

INFORMATIVE SYNOPSIS	DESCRIPTIVE SYNOPSIS
Sales of super-premium ice cream make up 11 percent of the total ice cream market.	This report contains information about super-premium ice cream and its share of the market.

The way you handle a synopsis reflects the approach you use in the text. If you're using an indirect approach in your report, you're better off with a descriptive synopsis. An informative synopsis, with its focus on conclusions and key points, may be too confrontational if your audience is skeptical. You don't want to derail the communication process by providing a controversial beginning. No matter which type of synopsis you use, be sure to present an accurate picture of the report's contents.[3]

4 LEARNING OBJECTIVE

Explain the difference between a synopsis and an executive summary

A synopsis and an executive summary both summarize a report's content, but an executive summary is more comprehensive.

Many business report writers prefer to include an **executive summary** instead of a synopsis or an abstract. Whereas a synopsis is a prose table of contents that outlines the main points of the report, an executive summary is a fully developed "mini" version of the report itself. Executive summaries are more comprehensive than a synopsis; many contain headings, well-developed transitions, and even visual elements. A good executive summary opens a window into the body of the report and allows the reader to quickly see how well you have managed your message. It is often organized in the same way as the report, using a direct or an indirect approach, depending on the audience's receptivity. However, executive summaries can also deviate from the sequence of material in the remainder of the report.

Executive summaries are intended for readers who lack the time or motivation to study the complete text. As a general rule, keep the length of an executive summary proportionate to the length of the report. A brief business report may have only a one-page or shorter executive summary. Longer business reports may have a two- or three-page summary. Anything longer, however, might cease to be a summary.[4]

Linda Moreno's Electrovision report provides one example of an executive summary. After reading the summary, audience members know the essentials of the report and are in a position to make a decision. Later, when time permits, they may read certain parts of the report to obtain additional detail. However, from daily newspapers to websites, businesspeople are getting swamped with more and more data and information. They are looking for ways to cut through all the clutter, and reading executive summaries is a popular shortcut. Because you can usually assume that many of your readers will not read the main text of your report, make sure you cover all your important points (along with significant supporting information) in the executive summary.

Many reports require neither a synopsis nor an executive summary. Length is usually the determining factor. Most reports of fewer than 10 pages either omit such a preview or combine it with the letter of transmittal. However, if your report is over 20 or 30 pages long, you'll probably want to include either a synopsis or an executive summary as a convenience for readers. Which one you'll provide depends on the traditions of your organization.

Text of the Report

Although reports may contain a variety of components, the heart of a report is always composed of three main parts: an introduction, a body, and a close (which may consist of a summary, conclusions, or recommendations, or some combination of the three). As Chapter 13 points out, the length and content of each of these parts varies with the length and type of report, the organizational structure, and the reader's familiarity with the topic. Following is a brief review of the three major parts of the report text. See Chapter 13 for a more detailed discussion of composing these parts.

Introduction A good introduction prepares your readers to follow and comprehend the information that follows. It invites the audience to continue reading by telling them what the report is about, why they should be concerned, and how the report is organized. If your report has a synopsis or an executive summary, minimize redundancy by balancing the introduction with the material in your summary—as Linda Moreno does in her Electrovision report. For example, Moreno's executive summary is fairly detailed, so she keeps her introduction brief. If you believe that your introduction needs to repeat information that has already been covered in one of the prefatory parts, try to vary the wording to minimize the feeling of repetition.

Body This section contains the information that supports your conclusions and recommendations as well as your analysis, logic, and interpretation of the information. See the body of Linda Moreno's Electrovision report for an example of the types of supporting detail commonly included in this section. Pay close attention to her effective use of visuals. Most inexperienced writers have a tendency to include too much data in their reports or place too much data in paragraph format instead of using tables and charts. Such treatment increases the chance of boring or losing an audience. If you find yourself with too much information, include only the essential supporting data in the body, use visuals, and place any additional information in an appendix.

Close The close of your report should summarize your main ideas, highlight your conclusions or recommendations (if any), and list any courses of action that you expect readers to take or that you will be taking yourself. In a long report, this section may be labeled "Summary," or "Conclusions and Recommendations." If you have organized your report in a direct pattern, your close should be relatively brief, like Linda Moreno's. With an indirect organization, you may be using this section to present your conclusions and recommendations for the first time, in which case this section might be fairly extensive.

5 LEARNING OBJECTIVE

Describe the three supplementary parts of a formal report

Supplementary Parts

Supplementary parts follow the text of the report and provide information for readers who seek more detailed discussion. For online reports, you can put supplements on separate webpages and allow readers link to them from the main report pages. Supplements are more common in long reports than in short ones, and they typically include appendixes, a bibliography, and an index.

Put into an appendix materials that are
- Bulky or lengthy
- Not directly relevant to the text

Appendixes An **appendix** contains materials related to the report but not included in the text because they are too lengthy, are too bulky, or lack direct relevance. However, don't include too much ancillary material. Keep your reports straightforward and concise. Well-designed appendixes provide enough but not too much additional information for those readers who want it. If your company has an intranet or other means of storing and accessing information online, consider putting your detailed supporting evidence there and referring readers to those sources for more detail.

The content of report appendixes varies widely, including any sample questionnaires and cover letters, sample forms, computer printouts, statistical formulas, financial statements and spreadsheets, copies of important documents, and complex illustrations. You might also include a glossary as an appendix or as a separate supplementary part. Of course, the best place to include visual aids is in the text body nearest the point of discussion, but if any visuals are too large to fit on one page or are only indirectly relevant to your report, they too may be put in an appendix.

If you have multiple categories of supporting material, give each type a separate appendix. Appendixes are usually identified with a letter and a short, descriptive title—for example, "Appendix A: Questionnaire," "Appendix B: Computer Printout of Raw Data," and so on. All appendixes should be mentioned in the text and listed in the table of contents.

If possible, consult other reports like yours to see what method of source citations your audience expects.

Bibliography To fulfill your ethical and legal obligation to credit other people for their work, and to assist readers who may wish to research your topic further, include a **bibliography**, a list of the secondary sources you consulted when preparing your report. In her Electrovision report, Linda Moreno labeled her bibliography "Works Cited" because she listed only the works that were mentioned in the report. You might call this section "Sources" or "References" if it includes works consulted but not mentioned in your report. Linda Moreno's Electrovision report uses the author-date system. An alternative is to use numbered footnotes (bottom of the page) or endnotes (end of the report). For more information on citing sources, see Appendix B, "Documentation of Report Sources."

In addition to providing a bibliography, some authors prefer to cite references in the report text. Acknowledging your sources in the body of your report demonstrates that you have thoroughly researched your topic. Furthermore, mentioning the names of well-known or important authorities on the subject helps build credibility for your message. It's often a good idea to mention a credible source's name several times if you need to persuade your audience. On the other hand, you don't want to make your report read like an academic treatise, dragging along from citation to citation. The source references should be handled as conveniently and inconspicuously as possible. One approach, especially for internal reports, is simply to mention a source in the text:

> According to Dr. Lewis Morgan of Northwestern Hospital, hip replacement operations account for 7 percent of all surgery performed on women age 65 and over.

However, if your report will be distributed to outsiders, include additional information on where you obtained the data. Most college students are familiar with citation methods suggested by the Modern Language Association (MLA) or the American Psychological Association (APA). *The Chicago Manual of Style* is a reference often used by typesetters and publishers. All of these sources encourage the use of in-text citations (inserting the author's last name and a year of publication or a page number directly into the text).

Index An **index** is an alphabetical list of names, places, and subjects mentioned in your report, along with the pages on which they occur (see the indexes in this book for examples). If you think your readers will need to access specific points of information in a lengthy report, consider including an index that lists all key topics, product names, markets, important persons—whatever is relevant to your subject matter. As with your table of contents, accuracy is critical. The good news is that you can also use your word processor to compile the index. Just be sure to update the index (and any automatically generated elements, for that matter), right before you print the report or convert it to PDF or other electronic format. Have another person spot-check the index, too, to make sure your entries are correct and easy to follow.

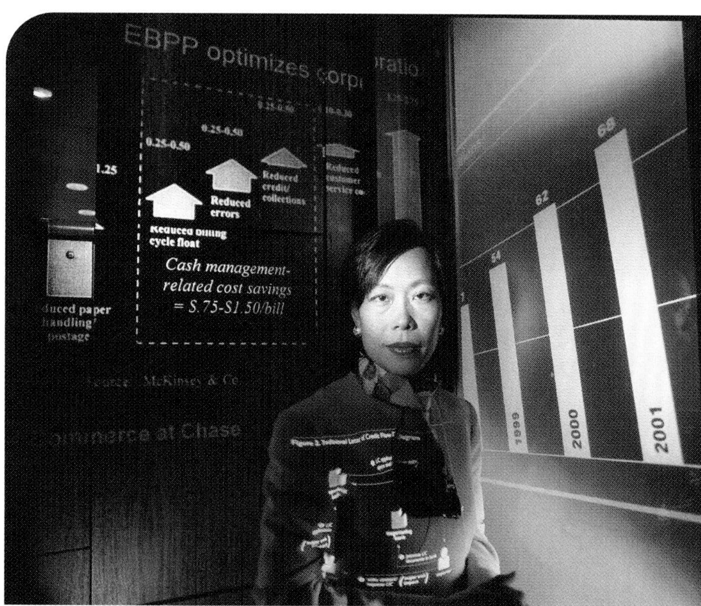

Senior Vice President June Yee Felix solicited proposals from consultants and research firms when she needed to start a service for online bill payment at Chase Manhattan Bank. The RFP stated her criteria and detailed requirements for selecting a service provider.

Components of a Formal Proposal

The goal of a proposal is to impress readers with your professionalism and to make your offering and your company stand out. Consequently, proposals addressed to external audiences, including potential customers and investors, are nearly always formal. For smaller projects and situations where you already have a working relationship with the audience, the proposal can be less formal and skip some of the components described in this section.

Formal proposals contain many of the same components as other formal reports (see Figure 14.2). The difference lies mostly in the text, although a few of the prefatory parts are also different. With the exception of an occasional appendix, most proposals have few supplementary parts. As always, if you're responding to an RFP, follow its specifications to the letter, being sure to include everything it asks for and nothing it doesn't ask for.

FIGURE 14.2 Parts of a Formal Proposal

PREFATORY PARTS	TEXT PARTS	SUPPLEMENTARY PARTS
Synopsis or executive summary	Summary	Appendixes
List of illustrations	Body	
Table of contents	Introduction	
Letter of transmittal		
Request for proposals		
Title page		
Title fly		
Cover		

Prefatory Parts

The cover, title fly, title page, table of contents, and list of illustrations are handled the same as in other formal reports. However, you'll want to handle other prefatory parts a bit differently, such as the copy of the RFP, the synopsis or executive summary, and the letter of transmittal.

DOCUMENT MAKEOVER

IMPROVE THIS EXECUTIVE SUMMARY

To practice correcting drafts of actual documents, visit www.prenhall.com/onekey on the web. Click "Document Makeovers" then click Chapter 14. You will find an excerpt from an executive summary that contains problems and errors relating to what you've learned in this chapter about completing formal reports and proposals. Use the Final Draft decision tool to create an improved version of this excerpt. Check the message for an appropriate degree of formality, parallel structures, the skillful inclusion or exclusion of detail, and a consistent time perspective.

Copy of the RFP Instead of having a letter of authorization, a formal proposal may have a copy of the request for proposals (RFP), which is a letter or memo soliciting a proposal or a bid for a particular project. If the RFP includes detailed specifications, it may be too long to bind into the proposal; in that case, you may want to include only the introductory portion of the RFP. Another option is to omit the RFP and simply refer to it in your letter of transmittal. However, as with the letter of authorization for a formal report, if there is likely to be any doubt or confusion over what exactly your proposal is responding to, make sure your readers have ready access to the specifications spelled out in the RFP.

If there's likely to be any confusion over which RFP you're responding to, include the RFP in your proposal. If the RFP is long, include just its introductory sections.

Synopsis or Executive Summary Although you may include a synopsis or an executive summary for your reader's convenience when your proposal is quite long, these components are often less useful in a formal proposal than they are in a formal report. If your proposal is unsolicited, your transmittal letter will already have caught the reader's interest, making a synopsis or an executive summary pointless. It may also be less important if your proposal is solicited, because the reader is already committed to studying your proposal to find out how you intend to satisfy the terms of a contract. The introduction of a solicited proposal would provide an adequate preview of the contents.

Letter of Transmittal The way you handle the letter of transmittal depends on whether the proposal is solicited or unsolicited. If the proposal is solicited, the transmittal letter follows the pattern for good-news messages, highlighting those aspects of your proposal that may give you a competitive advantage. If the proposal is unsolicited, the transmittal letter follows the pattern for persuasive messages (see Chapter 9). The letter must persuade the reader that you have something worthwhile to offer, something that justifies the time required to read the entire proposal. Because the transmittal letter may be all that the client reads, it must be especially convincing. However, bear in mind that even unsolicited proposals should not come as a surprise to the recipient; they should be the end result of an ongoing dialog about the other party's needs.

Text of the Proposal

Just as with reports, the text of a proposal is composed of three main parts: an introduction, body, and close. The content and depth of each part depend on whether the proposal is solicited or unsolicited, formal or informal. See Chapter 13 for a more detailed discussion of the topics covered in each part. Here's a brief review:[5]

- **Introduction.** This section presents and summarizes the problem you intend to solve and your solution to that problem, including any benefits the reader will receive from your solution.
- **Body.** This section explains the complete details of the solution: how the job will be done, how it will be broken into tasks, what method will be used to do it (including the required equipment, material, and personnel), when the work will begin and end, how much the entire job will cost (including a detailed breakdown, if required or requested), and why your company is qualified.
- **Close.** This section emphasizes the benefits that readers will realize from your solution, and it urges readers to act.

FIGURE 14.3 Dixon O'Donnell's Informal Solicited Proposal

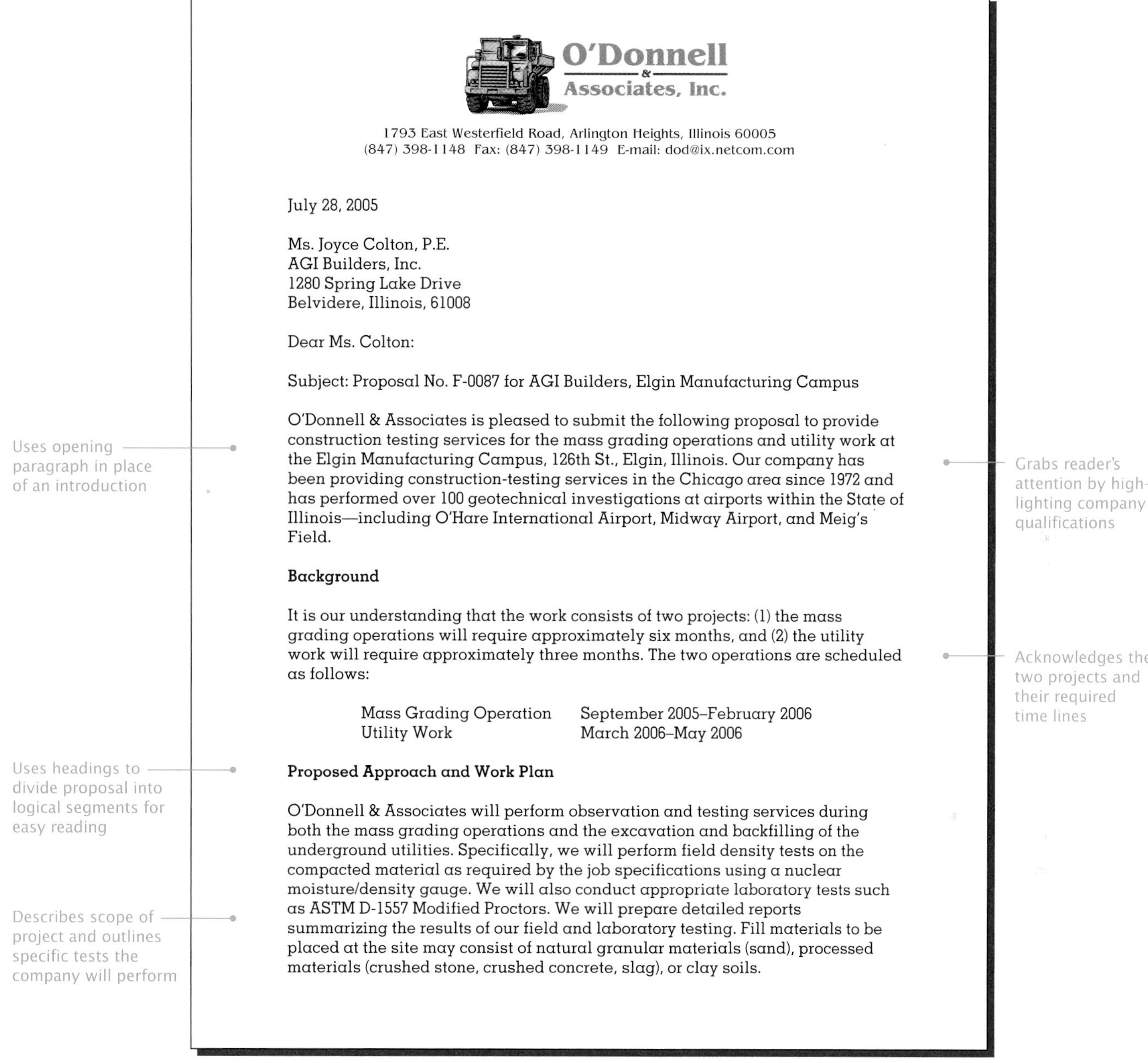

O'Donnell & Associates, Inc.

1793 East Westerfield Road, Arlington Heights, Illinois 60005
(847) 398-1148 Fax: (847) 398-1149 E-mail: dod@ix.netcom.com

July 28, 2005

Ms. Joyce Colton, P.E.
AGI Builders, Inc.
1280 Spring Lake Drive
Belvidere, Illinois, 61008

Dear Ms. Colton:

Subject: Proposal No. F-0087 for AGI Builders, Elgin Manufacturing Campus

O'Donnell & Associates is pleased to submit the following proposal to provide construction testing services for the mass grading operations and utility work at the Elgin Manufacturing Campus, 126th St., Elgin, Illinois. Our company has been providing construction-testing services in the Chicago area since 1972 and has performed over 100 geotechnical investigations at airports within the State of Illinois—including O'Hare International Airport, Midway Airport, and Meig's Field.

Background

It is our understanding that the work consists of two projects: (1) the mass grading operations will require approximately six months, and (2) the utility work will require approximately three months. The two operations are scheduled as follows:

Mass Grading Operation	September 2005–February 2006
Utility Work	March 2006–May 2006

Proposed Approach and Work Plan

O'Donnell & Associates will perform observation and testing services during both the mass grading operations and the excavation and backfilling of the underground utilities. Specifically, we will perform field density tests on the compacted material as required by the job specifications using a nuclear moisture/density gauge. We will also conduct appropriate laboratory tests such as ASTM D-1557 Modified Proctors. We will prepare detailed reports summarizing the results of our field and laboratory testing. Fill materials to be placed at the site may consist of natural granular materials (sand), processed materials (crushed stone, crushed concrete, slag), or clay soils.

Uses opening paragraph in place of an introduction
Grabs reader's attention by highlighting company qualifications
Acknowledges the two projects and their required time lines
Uses headings to divide proposal into logical segments for easy reading
Describes scope of project and outlines specific tests the company will perform

(continued)

Figure 14.3 is an informal proposal submitted by Dixon O'Donnell, vice president of O'Donnell & Associates, a geotechnical engineering firm that conducts a variety of environmental testing services. The company is bidding on the mass grading and utility work specified by AGI Builders. As you review this document, pay close attention to the specific items addressed in the proposal's introduction, body, and close.

PROOFREADING YOUR REPORTS AND PROPOSALS

Once you have assembled all the various components of your report or proposal, revised the entire document's content for clarity and conciseness, and designed the document to ensure readability and a positive impression on your readers, you have essentially

FIGURE 14.3 Continued

O'Donnell & Associates, Inc. July 28, 2005 Page 2

Explains who will be responsible for the various tasks

O'Donnell & Associates will provide qualified personnel to perform the necessary testing. Mr. Kevin Patel will be the lead field technician responsible for the project. A copy of Mr. Patel's résumé is included with this proposal for your review. Kevin will coordinate field activities with your job site superintendent and make sure that appropriate personnel are assigned to the job site. Overall project management will be the responsibility of Mr. Joseph Proesel. Project engineering services will be performed under the direction of Mr. Dixon O'Donnell, P.E. All field personnel assigned to the site will be familiar with and abide by the Project Site Health and Safety Plan prepared by Carlson Environmental, Inc., dated April 2005.

Encloses résumé rather than list qualifications in the document

Qualifications

O'Donnell & Associates has been providing quality professional services since 1972 in the areas of

- Geotechnical engineering
- Materials testing and inspection
- Pavement evaluation
- Environmental services
- Engineering and technical support (CADD) services

Grabs attention by mentioning distinguishing qualifications

The company provides Phase I and Phase II environmental site assessments, preparation of LUST site closure reports, installation of groundwater monitoring wells, and testing of soil/groundwater samples of environmental contaminants. Geotechnical services include all phases of soil mechanics and foundation engineering, including foundation and lateral load analysis, slope stability analysis, site preparation recommendations, seepage analysis, pavement design, and settlement analysis.

O'Donnell & Associates materials testing laboratory is certified by AASHTO Accreditation Program for the testing of Soils, Aggregate, Hot Mix Asphalt and Portland Cement Concrete. A copy of our laboratory certification is included with this proposal. In addition to in-house training, field and laboratory technicians participate in a variety of certification programs, including those sponsored by the American Concrete Institute (ACI) and the Illinois Department of Transportation (IDOT).

Gains credibility by describing certifications

Costs

On the basis of our understanding of the scope of the work, we estimate the total cost of the two projects to be $100,260.00, as follows:

(continued)

produced your document in its final form. Now you need to review it thoroughly one last time, looking for inconsistencies, errors, and missing components. For instance, if you changed a heading in the report's text part, make sure that you also changed the corresponding heading in the table of contents and in all references to that heading in your report. Proofing can catch minor flaws that might diminish your credibility—and major flaws that might damage your career (see "Communication Miscues: Error-Riddled Study Guides Embarrass School District" on page 453).

Proofreading the textual part of your report is essentially the same as proofreading any business message—you check for typos, spelling errors, and mistakes in punctuation. However, reports often have elements that may not be included in other messages, so don't forget to proof your visuals thoroughly, as Chapter 11 points out, and make sure they are

FIGURE 14.3 Continued

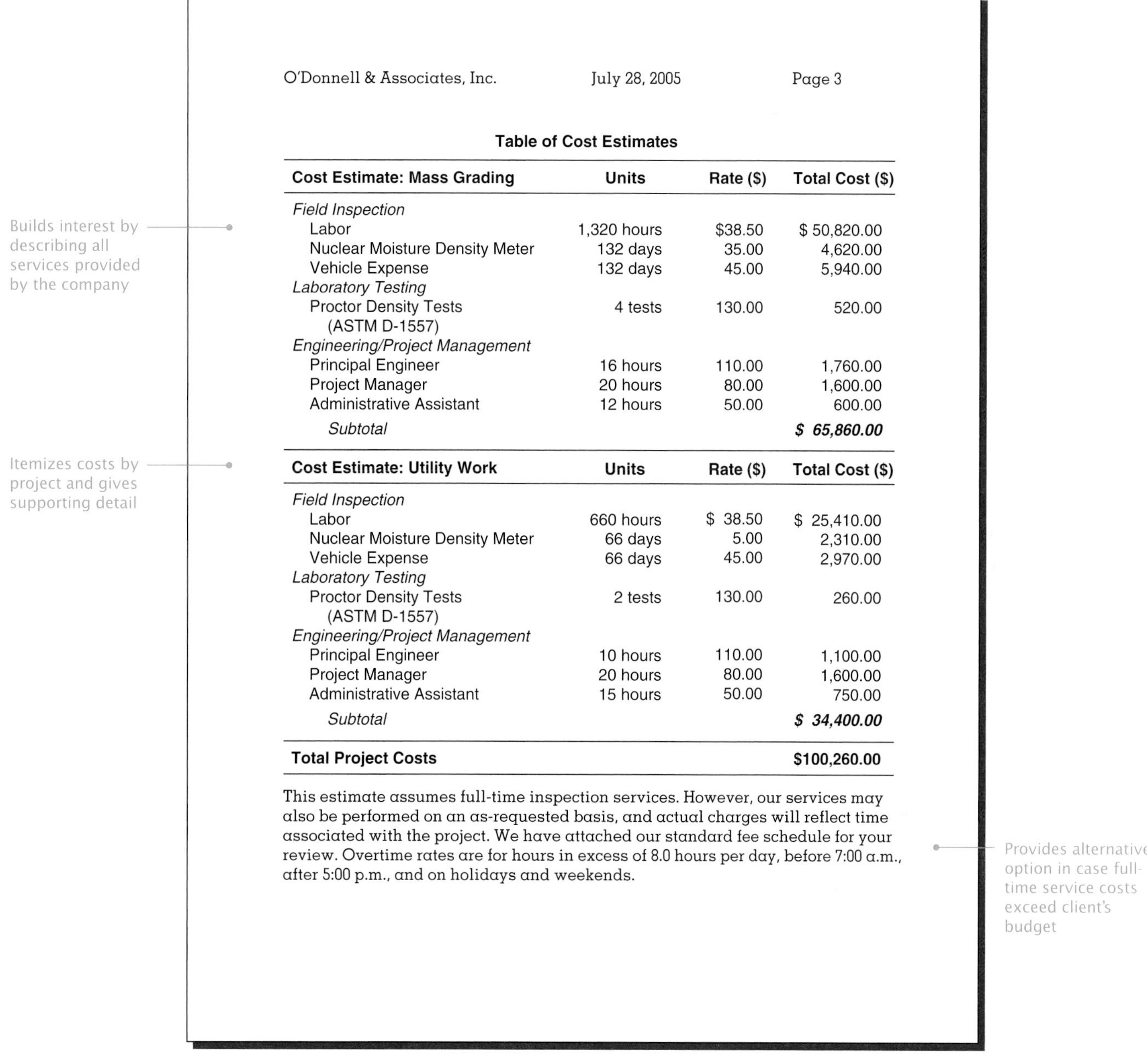

O'Donnell & Associates, Inc. July 28, 2005 Page 3

Table of Cost Estimates

Cost Estimate: Mass Grading	Units	Rate ($)	Total Cost ($)
Field Inspection			
Labor	1,320 hours	$38.50	$ 50,820.00
Nuclear Moisture Density Meter	132 days	35.00	4,620.00
Vehicle Expense	132 days	45.00	5,940.00
Laboratory Testing			
Proctor Density Tests (ASTM D-1557)	4 tests	130.00	520.00
Engineering/Project Management			
Principal Engineer	16 hours	110.00	1,760.00
Project Manager	20 hours	80.00	1,600.00
Administrative Assistant	12 hours	50.00	600.00
Subtotal			***$ 65,860.00***
Cost Estimate: Utility Work	**Units**	**Rate ($)**	**Total Cost ($)**
Field Inspection			
Labor	660 hours	$ 38.50	$ 25,410.00
Nuclear Moisture Density Meter	66 days	5.00	2,310.00
Vehicle Expense	66 days	45.00	2,970.00
Laboratory Testing			
Proctor Density Tests (ASTM D-1557)	2 tests	130.00	260.00
Engineering/Project Management			
Principal Engineer	10 hours	110.00	1,100.00
Project Manager	20 hours	80.00	1,600.00
Administrative Assistant	15 hours	50.00	750.00
Subtotal			***$ 34,400.00***
Total Project Costs			**$100,260.00**

This estimate assumes full-time inspection services. However, our services may also be performed on an as-requested basis, and actual charges will reflect time associated with the project. We have attached our standard fee schedule for your review. Overtime rates are for hours in excess of 8.0 hours per day, before 7:00 a.m., after 5:00 p.m., and on holidays and weekends.

Builds interest by describing all services provided by the company
Itemizes costs by project and gives supporting detail
Provides alternative option in case full-time service costs exceed client's budget

(continued)

positioned correctly. If you need specific tips on proofreading documents, look back at Chapter 6 for some reminders on what to look for when proofreading text and how to proofread like a pro.

Ask for proofreading assistance from someone who hasn't been involved in the development of your proposal; he or she might see errors that you've been overlooking.

Whenever possible, arrange for someone with "fresh eyes" to proofread the report, somebody who hasn't been involved with the text so far. At this point in the process, you are so familiar with the content that your mind will fill in missing words, fix misspelled words, and subconsciously compensate for other flaws without you even being aware of it. Someone with fresh eyes might see mistakes that you've passed over a dozen times without noticing. An ideal approach is to have two people review it, one who is an expert in the subject matter and one who isn't. The first person can ensure its technical accuracy, and the second can ensure that a wide range of readers will understand it.[6]

FIGURE 14.3 Continued

O'Donnell & Associates, Inc. July 28, 2005 Page 4

Authorization

Uses brief closing to emphasize qualifications and ask for client decision

With a staff of over 30 personnel, including registered professional engineers, resident engineers, geologists, construction inspectors, laboratory technicians, and drillers, we are convinced that O'Donnell & Associates is capable of providing the services required for a project of this magnitude.

If you would like our firm to provide the services as outlined in this proposal, please sign this letter and return it to us along with a certified check in the amount of $10,000 (our retainer) by August 15, 2005. Please call me if you have any questions regarding the terms of this proposal or our approach.

Provides deadline and makes response easy

Sincerely,

Dixon O'Donnell

Dixon O'Donnell
Vice President

Enclosures

Accepted for AGI BUILDERS, INC.

By______________________ Date ______________________

Makes letter a binding contract, if signed

DISTRIBUTING YOUR REPORTS AND PROPOSALS

All of the distribution issues you explored in Chapter 6 apply to reports and proposals, as long as you pay particular attention to the length and complexity of your documents. For physical distribution, consider spending the few extra dollars for a professional courier or package delivery service, if that will help your document stand apart from the crowd. The online tracking offered by FedEx, UPS, and other services can verify that your document arrived safely. On the other hand, if you've prepared the document for a single person or small group, delivering it in person can be a nice touch. Not only can you answer any immediate questions about it, but you can also promote the results in person—reminding the recipient of the benefits contained in your report or proposal.

For electronic distribution, unless your audience specifically requests a word processor file, provide documents in PDF format. Most people are reluctant to open word processor files these days, particularly from outsiders, given their vulnerability to macro viruses and other contaminations. Moreover, PDF format lets you control how your doc-

Communication Miscues

Error-Riddled Study Guides Embarrass School District

Governments and parents often rely on standardized tests to gauge the performance of students and schools. It's no wonder, then, that many school districts make an effort to help students prepare for such tests. But what if they provide study materials that are riddled with errors?

The Washington, D.C., public school district recently created a 20-page study guide to help its elementary school students prepare for the Stanford 9 test. When Chief Academic Officer Mary H. Gill reviewed the booklet, she found incorrect illustrations, inaccurate information, and numerous spelling and grammatical errors.

Gill ordered a recall, but more than 100 schools had already received the booklets—and some had distributed them to students. News of the botched booklet soon appeared in the local media, leaving administrators red-faced and school board members outraged.

Duvon Winborne, executive director of educational accountability, headed the department that produced the booklet. When quizzed by a reporter, Winborne said his group was responsible for the typos but blamed another department for the factual errors. He also suggested that the booklet would not adversely affect test scores: "Most of the children throw these things away, so it's not really a major problem in terms of outcomes."

Gill initially placed Winborne on administrative leave with pay and launched an investigation. A few days later she fired him, citing not only his department's failure to follow proper review procedures but also his indifferent and evasive attitude, as well as his comment that the booklet is "not really a major problem."

The district soon hired new editors for its communications department and required them to review all materials sent to students' homes. Even so, the embarrassment was repeated in 2003 when new study guides were issued with fresh errors. The cause? In their rush to complete the guides before spring break—so that students could study during the holiday—study guide creators never sent their material to the editors.

CAREER APPLICATIONS

1. Winborne was also quoted as saying, "We missed a few things. It's a mistake, human error." Would you ever adopt this attitude in your business communications? Explain your answer.
2. You face a dilemma: (a) to deliver an error-riddled report right before a long holiday or (b) to provide error-free materials shortly after the break. When would each answer be the better solution? Why?

ument is displayed on your audience's computer, ensuring that your readers see your document as you intended. It would be a shame to build your entire report around a particular chart or table, only to learn that it didn't display properly on your readers' computer screens. PDFs display your document exactly as you formatted it on your computer. In addition, making documents available as downloadable PDF files is almost universally expected these days, if only for the sake of convenience.

Many businesses use the Adobe Portable Document Format (PDF) to distribute reports electronically.

If your company or client expects you to distribute your reports via a web-based content management system, intranet, or extranet, be sure to upload the correct file(s) to the correct online location. Verify the on-screen display of your report after you've posted it, too; make sure graphics, charts, links, and other elements are in place and operational.

Once you've completed your formal report and sent it off to your audience, you'll naturally expect a positive response, and quite often you'll get one—but not always. You may get halfhearted praise or no action on your conclusions and recommendations. Even worse, you may get some serious criticism. Try to learn from these experiences. Sometimes you won't get any response at all. If you don't hear from your readers within a week or two, you might want to ask politely whether the report arrived. (Some RFPs specify a response timeframe. If so, *don't* pester the recipient ahead of schedule; you'll hurt your chances.) In hope of stimulating a response, you might ask a question about the report, such as "How do you think accounting will react to the proposed budget increase?" You might also offer to answer any questions or provide additional information. To review the ideas presented in this chapter, see "Checklist: Completing Formal Reports and Proposals."

Communication Solution

In order to manage the high volume of requests for funding, the Gates Foundation makes extensive use of RFPs. The foundation's education program does not accept unsolicited proposals, so grant proposals must be written in response to a published RFP. The health program also emphasizes RFPs but does invite inquiries regarding other projects that align with its funding priorities. In these cases, organizations are asked to submit a letter of inquiry (LOI) via an online form. If an LOI is accepted, the organization is then invited to submit a grant proposal.

WRITING REQUESTS FOR PROPOSALS

At some point in your career, you might be the one receiving proposals. The skills you've developed as a writer of reports and proposals will help you understand how to request a

CHECKLIST: Completing Formal Reports and Proposals

A. PREFATORY PARTS

- Use your company's standard report covers, if available.
- Include a concise, descriptive title on the cover.
- Include a title fly only if you want an extra-formal touch.
- On the title page, list (1) report title; (2) name, title, and address of the group or person who authorized the report; (3) name, title, and address of the group or person who prepared the report; and (4) date of submission.
- Include a copy of letter of authorization or request for proposals, if appropriate.
- Include a copy of the RFP (or its introduction only if the document is long), if appropriate.
- Include a letter of transmittal that introduces the report.
- Provide a table of contents in outline form, with headings worded exactly as they appear in the body of the report.
- Include a list of illustrations if the report contains a large number of them.
- Include a synopsis (brief summary of the report) or executive summary (a condensed, "mini" version of the report) for longer reports.

B. TEXT OF THE REPORT

- Draft an introduction that prepares the reader for the content that follows.
- Provide the information that supports your conclusions, recommendations, or proposals in the body of the report.
- Don't overload the body with unnecessary detail.
- Close with a summary of your main idea.

C. SUPPLEMENTARY PARTS

- Use appendixes to provide supplementary information or supporting evidence.
- List any secondary sources you used in a bibliography.
- Provide an index if your report contains a large number of terms or ideas and is likely to be consulted over time.

proposal. An RFP is more than just a request, it's an informational report that provides potential bidders with the information they need to craft effective proposals.

Drafting an RFP is more than just a writing process; it must also include a thorough analysis of your company's needs.

Writing an RFP demands careful consideration because it starts a process that leads to a proposal, a contract, and eventually the delivery of a product or the performance of a service. In other words, any mistakes at the RFP stage can ripple throughout the process and cause huge headaches for everyone involved.

An RFP's specific content will vary widely from industry to industry, but all RFPs should include some combination of the following elements:[7]

6 LEARNING OBJECTIVE

Identify the major components to include in a request for proposals (RFP)

Give potential bidders everything they need to know to propose meaningful solutions to your business problems.

- **Company background.** Give potential bidders some background information on your organization, your business priorities, and other information they might need in order to respond in an informed manner.
- **Project description.** Put your requirements in context; are you seeking bids for routine supplies or services, or do you need a major computer system?
- **Project requirements.** The requirements section should spell out everything you expect from potential vendors; don't leave anything to unstated assumptions. Will potential vendors provide key equipment, or will you? Will you expect vendors to work under confidentiality restrictions, such as a nondisclosure agreement? Who will pay if costs run higher than expected? Will you require ongoing service or support? For instance, if you are requesting proposals for a corporate website project, you would specify everything, including how much experience your company has with websites, what type of design and technical requirements you have, who will develop the website content, and what type of service and maintenance will be provided after the site is set up.[8] As you can imagine, the details of your requirements can run to many pages and necessitate the input of numerous subject-area experts throughout your company. Providing this information can be a lot of work, but again, overlooking anything at this point is likely to create considerable problems once the project gets rolling.
- **Decision criteria.** Let bidders know how you'll be making the decision. Is quality more important than cost? Will you consider only certain types of vendors or only those that use certain processes or technologies? Will you entertain bids from companies that have never worked in your particular industry? The answers to such questions not only help bidders determine whether they're right for your project but also help them craft proposals that meet your needs.

- **Proposal requirements.** Explain exactly what you expect to see in the proposal itself—which sections, what media, how many copies, and so on.
- **Submission and contact information.** A well-written RFP answers most potential questions, and it also tells people when, where, and how to respond. In addition, effective RFPs always give bidders a contact name within the organization who can answer detailed questions.

A smart approach to managing RFPs can minimize the work involved for everyone and maximize the effectiveness of the RFP. First identify your decision criteria, then brainstorm the information you need to measure against those criteria. Don't ask bidders to submit information about every aspect of their operations if such details aren't relevant to your decision. Making such unreasonable demands is unfair to bidders, will unnecessarily complicate your review process, and will discourage some potentially attractive bidders from responding.

Second, to get quality responses that match your unique business needs, give bidders plenty of time to respond. Good companies are usually busy responding to other RFPs and working on other projects. Therefore, you can't expect them to drop everything to focus solely on your RFP.

Third, if your company generates numerous RFPs, tracking proposals can become a full-time job. Consider establishing an online system for tracking responses automatically.[9]

COMMUNICATION CHALLENGES AT THE BILL AND MELINDA GATES FOUNDATION

Dr. Richard Klausner and his colleagues at the Bill and Melinda Gates Foundation not only read numerous reports and proposals every year, they also write and produce many reports, for both internal and external audiences. In fact, communication is one of the foundation's most important functions as it seeks to improve the health and education of children worldwide. In addition, the foundation is known as one of the most efficiently managed charities in the world, so cost-effectiveness is a vital concern in every phase of the communication process. Dr. Klausner recently hired you as an assistant director of communication, and your responsibilities include developing new ways for the foundation to produce effective reports as efficiently as possible.

Individual Challenge: Review several of the reports and other publications posted online (as PDF files) at www.gatesfoundation.org. Compare the design and layout of these documents. Do you see evidence of standardized design across documents? Write a brief e-mail to Dr. Klausner explaining the financial advantages of using a single design scheme for all external foundation documents.

Team Challenge: As a champion of new technologies, Bill Gates has a strong interest in applying information technology to the challenge of global communication. In a small team, research the opportunities for electronic delivery of health information to remote villages in India. Prepare a one-page report summarizing your findings.

SUMMARY OF LEARNING OBJECTIVES

1 **Characterize the four tasks involved in completing business reports and proposals.** To complete business reports and proposals, you first need to revise, produce, and proofread the document just as you would with any other business message. Revising reports and proposals involves evaluating content, style, organization, and tone; reviewing for readability; and editing for clarity and conciseness. After you've verified the reports quality, the fourth step is distributing the report and all supporting materials to the intended audience.

2 **Explain how computers have both simplified and complicated the report-production process.** Computers have simplified report preparation by giving all businesspeople production and distribution capabilities that only a few years ago either required specialized skills and expensive equipment or weren't possible at all. The downside is

that so many audiences have seen these highly polished reports that they have come to expect a high level of production quality in nearly all business reports.

3 **Identify the circumstances in which you should include letters of authorization and letters of acceptance in your reports.** If you received a letter of authorization to begin work on a report and you wrote a letter of acceptance when you took on the assignment, it's a good idea to include both items in your report whenever there's a chance that your audience might not expect the material you're about to deliver. Either or both of these documents can help clarify what you did and why you did it.

4 **Explain the difference between a synopsis and an executive summary.** A synopsis is a brief overview of the entire report and may either highlight the main points as they appear in the text or simply tell the reader what the report is about. It is designed to entice the audience to read the report, but is not intended to replace the report. By contrast, an executive summary is more comprehensive than a synopsis. It may contain headings, visual aids, and enough information to help busy executives make quick decisions. Although executive summaries are not designed to replace the report, in some cases it may be the only thing that a busy executive reads carefully.

5 **Describe the three supplementary parts of a formal report.** Formal reports may include an appendix, a bibliography, and an index. The appendix contains a variety of additional information that is useful but not critical to the report. Some of this material may be too detailed or bulky to be included in the report body. A bibliography is a list of secondary sources consulted when preparing the report; these sources may or may not be mentioned in the report body. An index is an alphabetical list of names, places, and subjects mentioned in the report along with their corresponding pages.

6 **Identify the major components to include in a request for proposals (RFP).** The content of RFPs varies widely from industry to industry and project to project, but most will include background on your company, a description of the project, your solution requirements, the criteria you'll use to make your selection decisions, your expectations for submitted proposals, and any relevant submission and contact information.

Test Your Knowledge

1. What are the tasks involved in revising a report or proposal?
2. When should you start a report section on a new page?
3. What information is included on the title page of a report?
4. What is the difference between a letter of authorization and a letter of acceptance?
5. What is a letter of transmittal, and where is it positioned within a report?
6. When are executive summaries useful?
7. What are three supplementary parts often included in formal reports?
8. What types of material does an appendix contain?
9. Why do some writers cite references in the report text?
10. What is the equivalent of a letter of authorization for a proposal?

Apply Your Knowledge

1. Is an executive summary a persuasive message? Explain your answer.
2. Under what circumstances would you include more than one index in a lengthy report?
3. If you were submitting a solicited proposal to build an indoor pool, would you include as references the names and addresses of other clients for whom you recently built similar pools? Would you include these references in an unsolicited proposal? Where in either proposal would you include these references? Why?
4. If you included a bibliography in your report, would you also need to include in-text citations? Please explain.
5. **Ethical Choices** How would you report on a confidential survey in which employees rated their managers' capabilities? Both employees and managers expect to see the results. Would you give the same report to employees and managers? What components would you include or exclude for each audience? Explain your choices.

Practice Your Knowledge

Document for Analysis

Visit the website of the U.S. Citizenship and Immigration Services (a division of the U.S. Department of Homeland Security) at http://uscis.gov. Find a report entitled "Triennial Comprehensive Report on Immigration" and follow the link to the executive summary. Using the information in this chapter, analyze the executive summary and offer specific suggestions for revising it.

Exercises

For live links to all websites discussed in this chapter, visit this text's website at www.prenhall.com/bovee. Just log on, select Chapter 14, and click on "Featured Websites." Locate the page or the URL related to the material in the text.

14.1 Teamwork You and a classmate are helping Linda Moreno prepare her report on Electrovision's travel and entertainment costs (see "Report Writer's Notebook"). This time, however, the report is to be informational rather than analytical, so it will not include recommendations. Review the existing report and determine what changes would be needed to make it an informational report. Be as specific as possible. For example, if your team decides the report needs a new title, what title would you use? Now draft a transmittal memo for Moreno to use in conveying this informational report to Dennis McWilliams, Electrovision's vice president of operations.

14.2 Producing Reports: Letter of Transmittal You are president of the Friends of the Library, a nonprofit group that raises funds and provides volunteers to support your local library. Every February, you send a report of the previous year's activities and accomplishments to the County Arts Council, which provides an annual grant of $1,000 toward your group's summer reading festival. Now it's February 6, and you've completed your formal report. Here are the highlights:

- Back-to-school book sale raised $2,000.
- Holiday craft fair raised $1,100.
- Promotion and prizes for summer reading festival cost $1,450.
- Materials for children's program featuring local author cost $125.
- New reference databases for library's career center cost $850.
- Bookmarks promoting library's website cost $200.

Write a letter of transmittal to Erica Maki, the council's director. Because she is expecting this report, you can use the direct approach. Be sure to express gratitude for the council's ongoing financial support.

14.3 Internet Government reports vary in purpose and structure. Read through the Department of Education's report, "Helping Your Child Become a Reader," available online at www.ed.gov. What is the purpose of this document? Does the title communicate this purpose? What type of report is this, and what is the report's structure? Which prefatory and supplementary parts are included? Now analyze the visuals. What types are included in this report? Are they all necessary? Are the titles and legends sufficiently informative? How does this report take advantage of the online medium to enhance readability?

14.4 Ethical Choices: Team Challenge You submitted what you thought was a masterful report to your boss over three weeks ago. The report analyzes current department productivity and recommends several steps that you think will improve employee output without increasing individual workloads. Brilliant, you thought. But you haven't heard a word from your boss. Did you overstep your boundaries by making recommendations that might imply that she has not been doing a good job? Did you overwhelm her with your ideas? You'd like some feedback. In your last e-mail to her, you asked if she had read your report. So far you've received no reply. Then yesterday, you overheard the company vice president talk about some productivity changes in your department. The changes were ones that you had recommended in your report. Now you're worried that your boss submitted your report to senior management and will take full credit for your terrific ideas. What, if anything, should you do? Should you confront your boss about this? Should you ask to meet with the company vice president? Discuss this situation among your teammates and develop a solution to this sticky situation. Present your solution to the class, explaining the rationale behind your decision.

Expand Your Knowledge

For live links to the websites that follow, go to www.prenhall.com/bovee. When you log on, select Chapter 14, then select "Featured Websites," click on the URL of the website you wish to visit, and review the website to complete these exercises.

Exploring the Best of the Web

Preview Before You Produce
www.ixquick.com
A good way to get ideas for the best style, organization, and format of a report is by looking at copies of professional business reports. To find samples of various types of reports, you can use a metasearch engine such as Ixquick Metasearch. Enter the phrase *business reports*, then choose a report and review it. Answer the following questions:

1. What is the purpose of the report you read? Who is its target audience? Explain why the structure and style of the report make it easy or difficult to follow the main idea.
2. What type of report did you read? Briefly describe the main message. Is the information well organized? If you answer yes, explain how you can use the report as a guide for a report you might write. If you answer no, explain why the report is not helpful.
3. Drawing on what you know about the qualities of a good business report, review a report and describe what features contribute to its readability.

Exploring the Web on Your Own

Review these chapter-related websites to learn more about writing reports and proposals.

1. Plan your way to profit by learning how to write effective business plans. Refer to the Business Planning section on the Small Business Administration website, www.sba.gov (look under "Starting Your Business").
2. Improve the quality of your reports by following an effective proofreading strategy. Visit Purdue University's Online Writing Lab, http://owl.english.purdue.edu, and search for "Editing and Proofreading Strategies."
3. Resolve any grammar question you come across in your proofreading by consulting the online grammar directory at www.clearenglish.net.

Learn Interactively

Interactive Study Guide

Go to the Companion Website at www.prenhall.com/bovee. For Chapter 14, take advantage of the interactive "Study Guide" to test your knowledge of the chapter. Get instant feedback on whether you need additional studying.

Also, visit this site's "Study Hall," where you'll find an abundance of valuable resources that will help you succeed in this course.

Peak Performance Grammar and Mechanics

In Chapter 13 you were referred to the Peak Performance Grammar and Mechanics activities on the web at www.prenhall.com/onekey to improve your skill with mechanics. For additional reinforcement in numbers, go to www. prenhall.com/bovee, where you will find "Improve Your Grammar, Mechanics, and Usage" exercises.

CASES

SHORT FORMAL REPORTS REQUIRING NO ADDITIONAL RESEARCH

1. Giving it the online try: Report analyzing the advantages and disadvantages of corporate online learning As the newest member of the corporate training division of Paper Products, Inc., you have been asked to investigate and analyze the merits of establishing Internet courses (e-learning) for the company's employees. The president of your company thinks e-learning might be a good employee benefit as well as a terrific way for employees to learn new skills that they can use on the job. You've already done your research and here's a copy of your notes:

Online courses open up new horizons for working adults, who often find it difficult to juggle conventional classes with jobs and families.
Adults over 25 now represent nearly half of higher-ed students; most are employed and want more education to advance their careers.
Some experts believe that online learning will never be as good as face-to-face instruction.
Online learning requires no commute and is appealing for employees who travel regularly.
Enrollment in courses offered online by postsecondary institutions is expected to increase from 2 million students in 2001 to 5 million students in 2006.
E-learning is a cost-effective way to get better-educated employees.
Corporate spending on e-learning is expected to more than quadruple by 2005, to $18 billion.
At IBM, some 200,000 employees received education or training online last year, and 75 percent of the company's Basic Blue course for new managers is online. E-learning cut IBM's training bill by $350 million last year—mostly because online courses don't require travel.
There are no national statistics, but a recent report from the *Chronicle of Higher Education* found that institutions are seeing dropout rates that range from 20 to 50 percent for online learners. The research does not adequately explain why the dropout rates for e-learners are higher.
A recent study of corporate online learners reported that employees want the following things from their online courses: college credit or a certificate; active correspondence with an online facilitator who has frequent virtual office hours; access to 24-hour, seven-day-a-week technical support; and the ability to start a course anytime.
Corporate e-learners said that their top reason for dropping a course was lack of time. Many had trouble completing courses from their desktops because of frequent distractions caused by co-workers. Some said they could only access courses through the company's intranet, so they couldn't finish their assignments from home.
Besides lack of time, corporate e-learners cited the following as e-learning disadvantages: lack of management oversight; lack of motivation; problems with technology; lack of student support; individual learning preferences; poorly designed courses; substandard/inexperienced instructors.
A recent study by GE Capital found that finishing a corporate online course was dependent on whether managers gave reinforcement on attendance, how important employees were made to feel, and whether employee progress in the course was tracked.
Sun Microsystems found that interactivity can be a critical success factor for online courses. Company studies showed that only 25 percent of employees finish classes that are strictly self-paced. But 75 percent finish when given similar assignments and access to tutors through e-mail, phone, or threaded discussion.
Too often companies dump courses on their employees and wonder why they don't finish them.
Company managers must supervise e-learning just as they would any other important initiative.
For online learning to work, companies must develop a culture that takes online learning just as seriously as classroom training.
For many e-learners, studying at home is optimal. Whenever possible, companies should offer courses through the Internet or provide intranet access at home. Having employees studying on their own time will more than cover any added costs.
Corporate e-learning has flared into a $2.3 billion market, making it one of the fastest-growing segments of the education industry.
Rather than fly trainers to 7,000 dealerships, General Motors University now uses interactive satellite broadcasts to teach salespeople the best way to highlight features on the new Buick.
Fast and cheap, e-training can shave companies' training costs while it saves employees travel time.
Pharmaceutical companies such as Merck are conducting live, interactive classes over the web, allowing sales reps to learn about the latest product information at home rather than fly them to a conference center.
McDonald's trainers can log into Hamburger University to learn such skills as how to assemble a made-to-order burger or properly place the drink on a tray.
One obstacle to the spread of online corporate training is the mismatch between what employees really need—customized courses that are tailored to a firm's products and its unique corporate culture—and what employers can afford.
80 percent of companies prefer developing their own online training courses in-house. But creating even one customized e-course can take months, involve armies of experts, and cost anywhere from $25,000 to $50,000. Thus, most companies either stick with classroom training or buy generic courses on such topics as how to give performance appraisals, understanding basic business ethics, and so on. Employers can choose from a wide selection of noncustomized electronic courses.
For online learning to be effective, content must be broken into short "chunks" with lots of pop quizzes, online discussion groups, and other interactive features that let students demonstrate what they've learned. For instance, Circuit City's tutorial on digital camcorders consists of three 20-minute segments. Each contains audio demonstrations of how to handle customer product queries, tests on terminology, and "try-its" that propel trainees back onto the floor to practice what they've learned.

Your task: Write a short (3 to 5 pages) memo report to the director of human resources, Kerry Simmons, presenting the advantages and disadvantages of e-learning and making a recommendation as to whether Paper Products, Inc., should invest time and money in training its employees this way. Be sure to organize your information so that it is clear, concise, and logically presented. Simmons likes to read the "bottom line" first, so be direct: Present your recommendation up front and support your recommendation with your findings.[10]

2. Grumbling in the ranks: When departments can't agree on the value of work You've been in your new job as human resources director for only a week, and already you have a major personnel crisis on your hands. Some employees in the marketing department got their hands on a confidential salary report, only to learn that, on average, marketing employees earn less than engineering employees. In addition, several top performers in the engineering group make significantly more than anybody in marketing. The report was passed around the company instantly by e-mail, and now everyone is discussing the situation. You'll deal with the data security issue later; for now, you need to address the dissatisfaction in the marketing group.

Table 14.1 lists the salary and employment data you were able to pull from the employee database. You also had the opportunity to interview the engineering and marketing directors to get their opinions on the pay situation; their answers are listed in Table 14.2.

Your task: The CEO has asked for a short report summarizing whatever data and information you have on engineering and marketing salaries. Feel free to offer your own interpretation of the situation as well (make up any information you need), but keep in mind that as a new manager with almost no experience in the company, your opinion might not have a lot of influence.

TABLE 14.1 Selected Employment Data for Engineers and Marketing Staff

EMPLOYMENT STATISTIC	ENGINEERING DEPARTMENT	MARKETING DEPARTMENT
Average number of years of work experience	18.2	16.3
Average number of years of experience in current profession	17.8	8.6
Average number of years with company	12.4	7.9
Average number of years of college education	6.9	4.8
Average number of years between promotions	6.7	4.3
Salary range	$58–165k	$45–85k
Median salary	$77k	$62k

3. Building a new magazine: Finding opportunity in the remodeling craze Spurred on in part by the success of such hit shows as *Changing Rooms*, *Trading Spaces*, and *Designers' Challenge*, homeowners across the country are redecorating, remodeling, and rebuilding. Many people are content with superficial changes, such as new paint or new accessories, but some are more ambitious. These homeowners want to move walls, add rooms, redesign kitchens, convert garages to home theaters—the big stuff.

TABLE 14.2 Summary Statements from Department Director Interviews

QUESTION	ENGINEERING DIRECTOR	MARKETING DIRECTOR
1. Should engineering and marketing professionals receive roughly similar pay?	In general, yes, but we need to make allowances for the special nature of the engineering profession. In some cases, it's entirely appropriate for an engineer to earn more than a marketing person.	Yes.
2. Why or why not?	Several reasons: (1) top engineers are extremely hard to find and we need to offer competitive salaries; (2) the structure of the engineering department doesn't provide as many promotional opportunities, so we can't use promotions as a motivator the way marketing can; (3) many of our engineers have advanced degrees and nearly all pursue continuous education to stay on top of the technology.	Without marketing, the products the engineers create wouldn't reach customers and the company wouldn't have any revenue. The two teams make equal contributions to the company's success.
3. If we decide to balance pay between the two departments, how should we do it?	If we do anything to cap or reduce engineering salaries, we'll lose key people to the competition.	If we can't increase payroll immediately to raise marketing salaries, the only fair thing to do is freeze raises in engineering and gradually raise marketing salaries over the next few years.

TABLE 14.3 Rooms Most Frequently Remodeled by DIYers

ROOM	PERCENT OF SURVEYED HOMEOWNERS WHO HAVE TACKLED OR PLAN TO TACKLE AT LEAST A PARTIAL REMODEL
Kitchen	60
Bathroom	48
Home office/study	44
Bedroom	38
Media room/home theater	31
Den/recreation room	28
Living room	27
Dining room	12
Sun room/solarium	8

TABLE 14.4 Average Amount Spent on Remodeling Projects

ESTIMATED AMOUNT	PERCENT OF SURVEYED HOMEOWNERS
Under $5k	5
$5–10k	21
$10–20k	39
$20–50k	22
More than $50k	13

TABLE 14.5 Tasks Performed by Homeowner on a Typical Remodeling Project

TASK	PERCENT OF SURVEYED HOMEOWNERS WHO PERFORM OR PLAN TO PERFORM MOST OR ALL OF THIS TASK THEMSELVES
Conceptual design	90
Technical design/ architecture	34
Demolition	98
Foundation work	62
Framing	88
Plumbing	91
Electrical	55
Heating/cooling	22
Finish carpentry	85
Tile work	90
Painting	100
Interior design	52

As with many consumer trends, publishers try to create magazines that appeal to carefully identified groups of potential readers and the advertisers who'd like to reach them. The do-it-yourself (DIY) market is already served by numerous magazines, but you see an opportunity in those homeowners who tackle the heavy-duty projects. Tables 14.3 through 14.5 summarize the results of some preliminary research you asked your company's research staff to conduct.

Your task: You think the data show a real opportunity for a "big projects" DIY magazine, although you'll need more extensive research to confirm the size of the market and refine the editorial direction of the magazine. Prepare a brief analytical report that presents the data you have, identifies the opportunity or opportunities you've found (suggest your own ideas based on the Tables 14.3 through 14.5), and requests funding from the editorial board to pursue further research.

SHORT FORMAL REPORTS REQUIRING ADDITIONAL RESEARCH

4. Picking the better path: Research report assisting a client in a career choice You are employed by Open Options, a career-counseling firm, where your main function is to help clients make career choices. Today a client with the same name as yours (a truly curious coincidence!) came to your office and asked for help deciding between two careers—careers that you yourself had been interested in (an even greater coincidence!).

Your task: Do some research on the two careers and then prepare a short report that your client can study. Your report should compare at least five major areas, such as salary, working conditions, and education required. Interview the client to understand her or his personal preferences regarding each of the five areas. For example, what is the minimum salary the client will accept? By comparing the client's preferences with the research material you collect, such as salary data, you will have a basis for concluding which of the two careers is best. The report should end with a career recommendation. (Note: One good place for career-related information is the Occupational Outlook Handbook, published by the U.S. Bureau of Labor Statistics, available in print and online at http://stats.bls.gov/oco/ocoiab.htm.)

5. Selling overseas: Research report on the prospects for marketing a product in another country Select (a) a product and (b) a country. The product might be a novelty item that you own (an inexpensive but accurate watch or clock, a desk organizer, or a coin bank). The country should be one that you are not currently familiar with. Imagine that you are with the international sales department of the company that manufactures and sells the novelty item and that you are proposing to make it available in the country you have selected.

The first step is to learn as much as possible about the country where you plan to market the product. Check almanacs, encyclopedias, the Internet, and library databases for the most recent information, paying particular attention to descriptions of the social life of the inhabitants, their economic conditions, and cultural traditions that would encourage or discourage use of the product.

Your task: Write a short report that describes the product you plan to market abroad, briefly describes the country you have selected, indicates the types of people in this country who would find the product attractive, explains how the product would be transported into the country (or possibly manufactured there if materials and labor are available), recommends a location for a regional sales center, and suggests how the product should be sold. Your report is to be submitted to the chief operating officer of the company, whose name you can either make up or find in a corporate directory. The report should include your conclusions (how the product will do in this new environment) and your recommendations for marketing (steps the company should take immediately and those it should develop later).

6. A ready-made business: Finding the right franchise opportunity After 15 years in the corporate world, you're ready to strike out on your own. Rather than building a business from the ground up, however, you think that buying a franchise is a better idea. Unfortunately, some of the most lucrative franchise opportunities, such as the major fast food chains, require significant start-up costs—some more than a half million dollars. Fortunately, you've met several potential investors who seem willing to help you get started in exchange for a share of ownership. Between your own savings and these investors, you estimate that you can raise from $350,000 to $600,000, depending on how much of an ownership you want to concede to the investors.

You've worked in several functional areas already, including sales and manufacturing, so you have a fairly well-rounded business résumé. You're open to just about any type of business, too, as long as it provides the opportunity to grow; you don't want to be so tied down to the first operation that you can't turn it over to a hired manager and expand into another market.

Your task: In order to convene a formal meeting with the investor group, you need to first draft a report outlining the types of franchise opportunities you'd like to pursue. Write a brief report identifying five franchises that you would like to explore further (choose five based on your own personal interests and the criteria identified above). For each possibility, identify the nature of the business, the financial requirements, the level of support the company provides, and a brief statement of why you could run such a business successfully (make up any details you need). Be sure to carefully review the information you find about each franchise company to make sure you can quality for it. For instance, McDonald's doesn't allow investment partnerships to buy franchises, so you won't be able to start up a McDonald's outlet until you have enough money to do it on your own.

For a quick introduction to franchising, see How Stuff Works (www.howstuffworks.com/franchising). You can learn more about the business of franchising at Franchising.com (www.franchising. com) and search for specific franchise opportunities at FranCorp Connect (www.francorpconnect.com). In addition, many companies that sell franchises, such as Subway, offer additional information on their websites.

LONG FORMAL REPORTS REQUIRING NO ADDITIONAL RESEARCH

7. You can get anything online these days: Shopping for automobiles on the Internet As a researcher in your state's consumer protection agency, you're frequently called on to investigate consumer topics and write reports for the agency's website. Thousands of consumers have arranged the purchase of cars online, and millions more do at least some of their research online before heading to the dealership. Some want to save time and money, some want to be armed with as much information as possible before talking to a dealer, while others want to completely avoid the often-uncomfortable experience of negotiating prices with car salespeople. In response, a variety of online services have emerged to meet these consumer needs. Some let you compare information on various car models, some connect you to local dealers to complete the transaction, and some complete nearly all of the transaction details for you, including negotiating the price. Some search the inventory of thousands of dealers, whereas other search only a single dealership or a network of affiliated dealers. In other words, a slew of new tools are available for car buyers, but it's not always easy to figure out where to go and what to expect. That's where your report will help.

By visiting a variety of car-related websites and reading magazine and newspaper articles on the car-buying process, you've compiled a variety of notes related to the subject:

- **Process overview:** The process is relatively straightforward and fairly similar to other online shopping experiences, with two key differences. In general, a consumer identifies the make and model of car he or she wants, then the online car buying service searches the inventories of car dealers nationwide and presents the available choices. The consumer chooses a particular car from that list, then the service handles the communication and purchase details with the dealer. When the paperwork is finished, the consumer then visits the dealership and picks up the car. The two biggest differences with online auto buying are that (1) you can't actually complete the purchase over the Internet (in most cases, you must visit a local dealer to pick up the car and sign the papers, although in some cities, a dealer or a local car buying service will deliver it to your home) and (2) in most states, it's illegal to purchase a new car from anyone other than a franchise dealer (i.e., you can't buy directly from the manufacturer, the way you can buy a Dell computer directly from Dell).
- **Information you can find online (not all information is available at all sites):** makes, models, colors, options, option packages (often, specific options are available only as part of a package; you need to know these constraints before you select your options), photos, specifications (everything from engine size to interior space), mileage estimates, performance data, safety information, predicted resale value, reviews, comparable models, insurance costs, consumer ratings, repair and reliability histories, available buyer incentives and rebates, true ownership costs (which include fuel, maintenance, repair, etc.), warranty, loan and lease payments, and maintenance requirements.
- **Advantages of shopping online:** Shopping from the comfort and convenience of home, none of the dreaded negotiating at the dealership (in many cases), the ability to search

far and wide for a specific car (even nationwide on many sites), the rapid access to considerable amounts of data and information, reviews from both professional automotive journalists and other consumers. In general, online auto shopping reduces a key advantage that auto dealers used to have, which was control of most of the information in the purchase transaction. Now consumers can find out how reliable each model is, how quickly it will depreciate, how often it is likely to need repairs, what other drivers think of it, how much the dealer paid the manufacturer for it, and so on.

- **Changing nature of the business.** The relationship between "third-party" websites (such as CarsDirect.com and Vehix.com) continues to evolve. At first, the relationship was more antagonistic, as some third-party sites and dealers frequently competed for the same customers, and both sides made bold proclamations about driving the other out of business. However, the relationship is more collaborative in many cases now, with dealers realizing that some third-party sites already have wide brand awareness and nationwide audiences. As the percentage of new car sales that originate via the Internet continue to increase, dealers are more receptive to working with third-party sites.
- **Compare information from multiple sources.** Consumers shouldn't rely solely on the information from a single website. Each site has its own way of organizing information and many have their own ways of evaluating car models and connecting buyers with sellers.
- **Understand what each site is doing.** For instance, some search thousands of dealers, regardless of ownership connections. Others, such as AutoNation, search only affiliated dealers. A search for a specific model might yield only a half dozen cars on one site but dozens of cars on another site. Find out who owns the site and what their business objectives are, if you can; this will help you assess the information you receive.
- **Leading websites.** Consumers can check out a wide variety of websites, some of which are full-service operations, offering everything from research to negotiation; others provide more specific and limited services. For instance, CarsDirect (www.carsdirect.com) provides a full range of services, whereas Carfax (www.carfax.com) specializes in uncovering the repair histories of individual used cars. Table 14.6 lists some of the leading car-related websites.

Your task: Write an informational report based on your research notes. The purpose of the report is to introduce consumers to the basic concepts of integrating the Internet into their car-buying activities and to educate them about important issues.[11]

TABLE 14.6 Leading Automotive Websites

SITE	URL
AutoAdvice	www.autoadvice.com
Autobytel	www.autobytel.com
AutoDirectory.com	www.autodirectory.com
Autos.com	www.autos.com
AutoVantage	www.autovantage.com
Autoweb	www.autoweb.com
CarBargains	www.carbargains.com
Carfax	www.carfax.com
CarPrices.com	www.carprices.com
Cars.com	www.cars.com
CarsDirect	www.carsdirect.com
CarSmart	www.carsmart.com
Consumer Reports	www.consumerreports.com
eBay Motors	www.ebaymotors.com
Edmunds	www.edmunds.com
iMotors	www.imotors.com
IntelliChoice	www.intellichoice.com
InvoiceDealers	www.invoicedealers.com
J.D. Power	www.jdpower.com
Kelly Blue Book	www.kbb.com
MSN Autos	www.autos.msn.com
PickupTruck.com	www.pickuptruck.com
The Car Connection	www.thecarconnection.com
Vehix.com	www.vehix.com
Yahoo! Autos	www.autos.yahoo.com

8. Moving the Workforce: Understanding commute patterns Your company is the largest private employer in your metropolitan area, and the 43,500 employees in your workforce have a tremendous impact on local traffic. A group of city and county transportation officials recently approached your CEO with a request to explore ways to reduce this impact. The CEO has assigned you the task of analyzing the workforce's transportation habits and attitudes as a first step toward identifying potential solutions. He's willing to consider anything from subsidized bus passes to company-owned shuttle buses to telecommuting, but the decision requires a thorough understanding of employee transportation needs. Tables 14.7 through 14.11 summarize data you collected in an employee survey.

Your task: Present the results of your survey in an informational report using the data provided in Tables 14.7 through 14.11.

TABLE 14.7 Employee Carpool Habits

FREQUENCY OF USE: CARPOOLING	PORTION OF WORKFORCE
Every day, every week	10,138 (23%)
Certain days, every week	4,361 (10%)
Randomly	983 (2%)
Never	28,018 (64%)

TABLE 14.8 Use of Public Transportation

FREQUENCY OF USE: PUBLIC TRANSPORTATION	PORTION OF WORKFORCE
Every day, every week	23,556 (54%)
Certain days, every week	2,029 (5%)
Randomly	5,862 (13%)
Never	12,053 (28%)

TABLE 14.9 Effect of Potential Improvements to Public Transportation

WHICH OF THE FOLLOWING WOULD ENCOURAGE YOU TO USE PUBLIC TRANSPORTATION MORE FREQUENTLY (CHECK ALL THAT APPLY)	PORTION OF RESPONDENTS
Increased perceptions of safety	4,932 (28%)
Improved cleanliness	852 (5%)
Reduced commute times	7,285 (41%)
Greater convenience: fewer transfers	3,278 (18%)
Greater convenience: more stops	1,155 (6%)
Lower (or subsidized) fares	5,634 (31%)
Nothing could encourage me to take public transportation	8,294 (46%)

Note: This question was asked of those respondents who use public transportation randomly or never, a subgroup that represents 17,915 employees or 41 percent of the workforce

TABLE 14.10 Distance Traveled to/from Work

DISTANCE YOU TRAVEL TO WORK (ONE WAY)	PORTION OF WORKFORCE
Less than 1 mile	531 (1%)
1–3 miles	6,874 (16%)
4–10 miles	22,951 (53%)
11–20 miles	10,605 (24%)
More than 20 miles	2,539 (6%)

TABLE 14.11 Is Telecommuting an Option?

DOES THE NATURE OF YOUR WORK MAKE TELECOMMUTING A REALISTIC OPTION?	PORTION OF WORKFORCE
Yes, every day	3,460 (8%)
Yes, several days a week	8,521 (20%)
Yes, random days	12,918 (30%)
No	18,601 (43%)

LONG FORMAL REPORTS REQUIRING ADDITIONAL RESEARCH

9. Face-off: Informational report comparing and contrasting two companies in the same industry Your boss, Dana Hansell, has been searching for some solid companies to personally invest in for the long term. After reviewing security analysts' reports and financial statements for several candidates, Hansell has narrowed the list to these leading industry competitors:

- Boeing; Airbus (aerospace and airline industry)
- Gateway; Dell (computers and software industry)
- Merrill Lynch; Schwab (finance, banking, and insurance industry)
- Barnes & Noble; Amazon.com (book industry—retail and wholesale)
- UPS; FedEx (trucking and freight industry)

According to Hansell, all of these candidates have about the same financial outlook for the future, so she is not interested in obtaining more financial performance detail. Instead, your boss is looking for more substantive information, such as

- Fundamental philosophical differences in management styles, launching and handling products and services, marketing products and services, and approach to e-commerce that sets one rival company apart from the other
- Future challenges that each competitor faces
- Important decisions made by the two competitors and how those decisions affected their company
- Fundamental differences in each company's vision of their industry's future (for instance, do they both agree on what consumers want, what products to deliver, and so on?)
- Specific competitive advantages held by each rival
- Past challenges each competitor has faced and how each met those challenges
- Strategic moves made by one rival that might affect the other
- Company success stories
- Brief company background information (Hansell already has some from the brokers' reports)

- Brief comparative statistics such as annual sales, market share, number of employees, number of stores, types of equipment, number of customers, sources of revenue, and so on

Hansell has heard that you are the department's most proficient researcher and an effective writer. You have been assigned the task of preparing a formal, long informational report for her. You need not make a recommendation or come to any conclusions; Hansell will do that based on the informational content of your report.

Your task: Select two industry competitors from the above list (or another list provided by your instructor) and write a long formal informational report comparing and contrasting how the two companies are addressing the topics outlined by Hansell. Of course, not every topic will apply to each company, and some will be more important than others—depending on the companies you select. Hansell will invest in only one of the two companies in your report. (Note: Because these topics require considerable research, your instructor may choose to make this a team project.)

10. Is there any justice? Report critiquing legislation Plenty of people complain about their state legislators, but few are specific about their complaints. Here's your chance.

Your task: Write a long formal report about a law that you believe should not have been enacted or should be enacted. Be objective. Write the report using specific facts to support your beliefs. Reach conclusions and offer your recommendation at the end of the report. As a final step, send a copy of the report to an appropriate state official or legislator.

11. Travel opportunities: Report comparing two destinations You are planning to take a two-week trip abroad sometime within the next year. Because there are a couple of destinations that appeal to you, you are going to have to do some research before you can make a decision.

Your task: Prepare a lengthy comparative study of two countries that you would like to visit. Begin by making a list of important questions you will need to answer. Do you want a relaxing vacation or an educational experience? What types of services will you require? What will your transportation needs be? Where will you have the least difficulty with the language? Using resources in your library, the Internet, and perhaps travel agencies, analyze the suitability of these two destinations with respect to your own travel criteria. At the end of the report, recommend the better country to visit this year.

12. Secondary sources: Report based on library and online research As a college student and active consumer, you may have considered one or more of the following questions at some point in the past few years:

a. What criteria distinguish the top-rated MBA programs in the country? How well do these criteria correspond to the needs and expectations of business? Are the criteria fair for students, employers, business schools?
b. Which of three companies you might like to work for has the strongest corporate ethics policies?
c. What will the music industry look like in the future? What's next after online stores such as Apple iTunes and digital players such as the iPod?
d. Which industries and job categories are forecast to experience the greatest growth—and therefore the greatest demands for workers—in the next 10 years?
e. What has been the impact of Starbucks' aggressive growth on small, independent coffee shops? On midsized chains or franchises? In the United States or in another country?
f. How large is the "industry" of major college sports? How much do the major football or basketball programs contribute—directly or indirectly—to other parts of a typical university?
g. How much have minor league sports—baseball, hockey, arena football—grown in small- and medium-market cities? What is the local economic impact when these municipalities build stadiums and arenas?

Your task: Answer one of those questions using secondary research sources for information. Be sure to document your sources in the correct form. Give conclusions and offer recommendations where appropriate.

13. Doing business abroad: Report summarizing the social and business customs of a foreign country Your company would like to sell its products overseas. Before they begin negotiating on the international horizon, however, management must have a clear understanding of the social and business customs of the countries where they intend to do business.

Your task: Choose a non-English-speaking country and write a long formal report summarizing the country's social and business customs. Review Chapter 3 and use Table 3.1 on page 75 as a guide to the types of information you should include in your report.

FORMAL PROPOSALS

14. Polishing the presenters: Offering your services as presentation trainer Presentations can make—or break—both careers and businesses. A good presentation can bring in millions of dollars in new sales or fresh investment capital. A bad presentation might cause any number of troubles, from turning away potential customers to upsetting fellow employees to derailing key projects. To help business professionals plan, create, and deliver more effective presentations, you offer a three-day workshop that covers the essentials of good presentations:

- Understanding your audience's needs and expectations
- Formulating your presentation objectives
- Choosing an organizational approach
- Writing openings that catch your audience's attention
- Creating effective graphics and slides
- Practicing and delivering your presentation
- Leaving a positive impression on your audience
- Avoiding common mistakes with Microsoft PowerPoint
- Handling questions and arguments from the audience
- Overcoming the top 10 worries of public speaking (including *How can I overcome stage fright?* and *I'm not the performing type; can I still give an effective presentation?*)

Workshop benefits: Students will learn how to prepare better presentations in less time and deliver them more effectively.

Who should attend: Top executives, project managers, employment recruiters, sales professionals, and anyone else who gives important presentations to internal or external audiences.

Your qualifications: 18 years of business experience, including 14 years in sales and 12 years in public speaking. Experience speaking to audiences as large as 5,000 people. More than a dozen speech-related articles published in professional journals. Have conducted successful workshops for nearly 100 companies.

Workshop details: Three-day workshop (9 A.M. to 3:30 P.M.) that combines lectures, practice presentations, and both individual and group feedback. Minimum number of students: 6. Maximum number of students per workshop: 12

Pricing: The cost is $3,500, plus $100 per student. 10 percent discount for additional workshops.

Other information: Each attendee will have the opportunity to give three practice presentations that will last from three to five minutes. Everyone is encouraged to bring PowerPoint files containing slides from actual business presentations. Each attendee will also receive a workbook and a digital video recording of his or her final class presentation on DVD. You'll also be available for phone or e-mail coaching for six months after the workshop.

Your task: Identify a company in your local area that might be a good candidate for your services. Learn more about them by visiting their website so you can personalize your proposal. Using the information listed above, prepare a sales proposal that explains the benefits of your training and what students can expect during the workshop.

15. Healthy alternatives: Proposal to sell snacks and beverages at local high schools For years, a controversy has been brewing over the amount of junk food and soft drinks being sold through vending machines in local schools. Schools benefit from revenue-sharing arrangements, but many parents and health experts are concerned about the negative effects of these snacks and beverages. You and your brother have almost a decade of experience running espresso and juice stands in malls and on street corners, and you'd love to find some way to expand your business into schools. After a quick brainstorming session, the two of you craft a plan that makes good business sense while meeting the financial concerns of school administrators and the nutritional concerns of parents and dieticians. Here are the notes from your brainstorming session:

- Set up portable juice bars on school campuses, offering healthy fruit and vegetable drinks along with simple, healthy snacks
- Offers schools 30 percent of profits in exchange for free space and long-term contracts
- Provide job training opportunities for students (during athletic events, etc.)
- Provide detailed dietary analysis of all products sold
- Establish a nutritional advisory board composed of parents, students, and at least one certified health professional
- Assure schools and parents that all products are safe (e.g., no stimulant drinks, no dietary supplements, and so on)
- Support local farmers and specialty food preparers by buying locally and giving these vendors the opportunity to test market new products at your stands

Your task: Based on the ideas listed, draft a formal proposal to the local school board, outlining your plan to offer healthier alternatives to soft drinks and prepackaged snack foods. Invent any details you need to complete your proposal.

16. Career connections: Helping employees get the advice they need to move ahead Seems like everybody in the firm is frustrated. On the one hand, top executives complain about the number of lower-level employees who want promotions but just don't seem to "get it" when it comes to dealing with customers and the public, recognizing when to speak out and when to be quiet, knowing how to push new ideas through the appropriate channels, and performing other essential but difficult-to-teach tasks. On the other hand, ambitious employees who'd like to learn more feel that they have nowhere to turn for career advice from people who've been there. In between, a variety of managers and mid-level executives are overwhelmed by the growing number of mentoring requests they're getting, sometimes from employees they don't even know.

You've been assigned the challenge of proposing a formal mentoring program—and a considerable challenge it is:

- The number of employees who want mentoring relationships far exceeds the number of managers and executives willing and able to be mentoring; how will you select people for the program?
- The people most in demand for mentoring also tend to be some of the busiest people in the organization.
- After several years of belt tightening and staff reductions, the entire company feels overworked; few people can imagine adding another recurring task to their seemingly endless to-do lists.
- What's in it for the mentors? Why would they be motivated to help lower-level employees?
- How will you measure success or failure of the mentoring effort?

Your task: Identify potential solutions to the issues (make up any information you need), then draft a proposal to the executive committee for a formal, company-wide mentoring program that would match selected employees with successful managers and executives.

PART 6

Designing and Delivering Oral Presentations

CHAPTER 15
Planning, Writing, and Completing Oral Presentations

CHAPTER 16
Enhancing Presentations with Slides and Transparencies

chapter 15

Planning, Writing, and Completing Oral Presentations

LEARNING OBJECTIVES

After studying this chapter, you will be able to

1. Explain the importance of oral presentations in your career success
2. Explain how to adapt the three-step writing process to oral presentations
3. Identify the two primary reasons why limiting your scope is especially important for oral presentations
4. Distinguish a planning outline from a speaking outline and explain the purpose of each
5. Discuss the three functions of an effective introduction
6. Identify four ways to keep your audience's attention during your presentation
7. Describe the techniques you can use to appear more confident in front of an audience

COMMUNICATION CLOSE-UP AT FITCH

www.fitch.com

Figure out what your audience expects to get from your presentation—and then don't give it to them? A risky strategy, indeed, but it's working for Fitch, a global, diversified design consultancy with offices in North America, Europe, and Asia. Fitch designs everything from restaurant layouts and consumer products to corporate events and marketing campaigns.

For most professional services firms, a sales presentation follows a predictable pattern: speak about your capabilities, introduce a small army of talented people to impress the client, present examples of work you've done for other clients, then ask the client to hire you. Most presenters prefer this approach because they get to speak from a position of confidence (based on all the great work they've done for other clients) and their level of risk is low (they don't have to present any new ideas until they get a contract).

Even though potential clients expect a traditional "pitch" with all this information, Fitch doesn't offer it. Instead, the company's designers study the client's business, develop a strong point of view regarding the challenge at hand, then work on a design concept—all before making a presentation. When it comes time for a presentation, Fitch essentially says, "Here's the design we think is right for you. Love it or leave it." According to Eric Ashworth, a Fitch marketing executive, the goal is to inspire an "A-ha!" moment

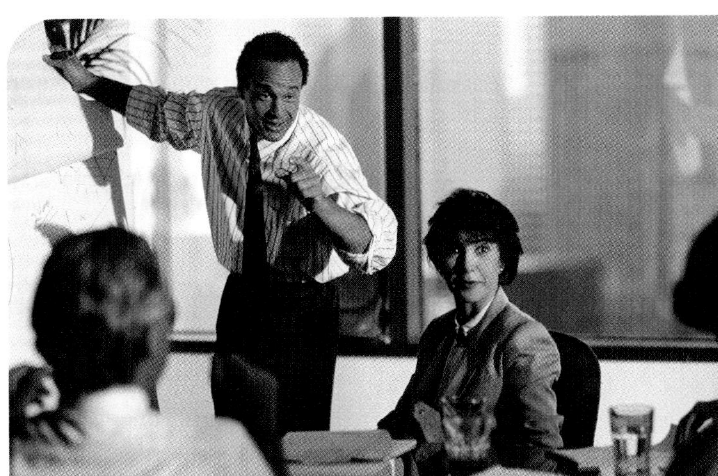

Presenters at Fitch often take chances in their presentations by going against audience expectations. The strategy works if it stimulates new thinking and ultimately meets audience needs.

that makes the audience excited—and maybe just a little nervous.

Does this brash approach work? Ashworth says this style of presentation is 30 percent more effective in generating sales and has led to contracts with such clients as 3M, LEGO, Nissan, and Nokia. However, he does offer a caution: the approach can work wonders—or "get you pushed out of the room."[1]

1 LEARNING OBJECTIVE

Explain the importance of oral presentations in your career success

BUILDING YOUR CAREER WITH ORAL PRESENTATIONS

Oral presentations involve all of your communication skills, from research through nonverbal communication.

No matter how expected or unexpected your next presentation might be, Eric Ashworth can verify that oral presentations offer you important opportunities to put all your communication skills on display—not only in research, planning, writing, and visual design, but also in interpersonal and nonverbal communication. Oral presentations can also give you a chance to demonstrate your ability to think on your feet, grasp complex issues, and handle challenging situations—all attributes that executives look for when searching for talented employees to promote within the organization. Perhaps best of all, oral presentations let your personality shine through in ways that even the best-written reports can't provide.

The nature and frequency of the presentations you make will vary widely, depending on your career path. For instance, if you move into sales or professional services, you might give several presentations a week or even several a day. In other situations, you might give weekly or monthly status updates to your colleagues or quarterly and annual financial updates to investors and stock market analysts. If you work in the human resources department, you may give orientation briefings to new employees or explain company policies, procedures, and benefits at companywide meetings. If you're a technical expert, you may conduct training programs. If you give regular, recurring presentations, you will usually follow the same format, and your biggest challenge will be simply to update the necessary information. In contrast, if you are called on to give a one-of-a-kind presentation, all your creative instincts will be put to the test, from audience analysis through visual design.

Feeling nervous is perfectly normal when you're faced with an oral presentation; the good news is there are positive steps you can take to reduce your anxiety.

If the thought of giving a speech or presentation makes you nervous, try to keep three points in mind. First, everybody gets nervous when speaking in front of a group. Even professional speakers and entertainers get nervous after years of experience. Second, being nervous is actually a good thing; it means you care about the topic, your audience, and your career success. With practice, you can convert those nervous feelings into positive energy. Third, you don't have to be a victim of your own emotions when it comes to oral presentations. You can take control of the situation by using the planning and development techniques that you'll learn in this chapter—starting with how to adapt the three-step writing process to the unique challenges of oral presentations.

2 LEARNING OBJECTIVE

Explain how to adapt the three-step writing process to oral presentations

ADAPTING THE THREE-STEP PROCESS FOR ORAL PRESENTATIONS

While you don't usually write your oral presentations word for word, the three-step writing process is easily adaptable to oral presentations.

You don't often write out a presentation word for word; nevertheless, nearly every task in the three-step writing process applies to oral presentations, with some modifications (see Figure 15.1). In addition, a few extra steps will help you prepare both your material and yourself for the actual presentation. As with written reports, people often judge the quality of the content by the quality of the presentation, so your delivery style and the packaging of any visual support materials can be as important as your message. This chapter walks you through the three-step development process, then Chapter 16 offers advice on creating visual materials to enhance your presentation.

FIGURE 15.1 The Three-Step Process for Developing Oral Presentations

Plan	Write	Complete
Analyze the Situation Define your purpose and develop a profile of your audience, including their emotional states and language preferences. **Gather Information** Determine audience needs and obtain the information necessary to satisfy those needs. **Select the Right Medium** Choose the best medium or combination of media for delivering your presentation. **Organize the Information** Define your main idea, limit your scope and verify timing, select a direct or an indirect approach, and outline your content.	**Adapt to Your Audience** Be sensitive to audience needs and expectations with a "you" attitude, politeness, positive emphasis, and bias-free language. Build a strong relationship with your audience by establishing your credibility and projecting your company's image. Adjust your delivery style to fit the situation, from casual to formal. **Compose the Message** Outline an effective introduction, body, and close. Prepare any visual aids necessary to support your argument or clarify concepts.	**Revise the Message** Evaluate your content and speaking notes. **Produce the Message** Choose your delivery mode and practice your presentation. **Proofread the Message** Verify facilities and equipment; hire an interpreter if necessary. **Distribute the Message** Take steps to feel more confident and appear more confident on stage.
1	2	3

STEP 1: PLANNING YOUR PRESENTATION

Planning oral presentations is much like planning any other business message: You (1) analyze the situation, (2) gather information, (3) select the right medium, and (4) organize the information. Gathering information for oral presentations is essentially the same as it is for written communication projects (see Chapter 10). The other three planning tasks have some special applications when it comes to oral presentations; they are covered in the following sections.

The purpose of most business presentations is to inform or persuade; you may also give presentations designed primarily to collaborate with others.

Analyzing the Situation

As with written communications, analyzing the situation involves defining your purpose and developing an audience profile. The purpose of most of your presentations will be to inform or to persuade, although you may occasionally need to make a collaborative presentation, such as when you're leading a problem-solving or brainstorming session. The guidelines in Chapter 4 will help you identify and refine your purpose. In rare circumstances, the purpose of a business presentation will be to entertain the audience, but most companies hire professional speakers for that sort of presentation.

When you develop your audience profile, start with the advice in Chapter 4 and then consider two other issues that are particularly important for oral presentations. First, try to anticipate what sort of emotional state your audience members are likely to be in. Will they accept your message automatically, or will they fight you every step of the way? Even though such concerns apply to written messages as well, they become even more important in live-audience situations, because individual emotions can play off one another. In a worst-case scenario, a herd mentality can take over, and people who might accept your message in a calm, one-on-one setting wind up rejecting it under the influence of the crowd's emotions.

Second, when developing your audience profile, determine whether your audience is comfortable listening to the language you speak. Listening to an unfamiliar language is

Communication Solution

With Fitch's unusual presentation strategy, the company skips something the audience expects to hear (descriptions of work done in the past) in order to focus on something the audience really wants to hear (how Fitch can help them in the future).

Knowing your audience's state of mind will help you adjust both your message and your delivery.

Communicating Across Cultures

Five Tips for Making Presentations Around the World

When making presentations to international audiences, language fluency might vary widely. So take special care to ensure clear communication:

1. **Speak slowly and distinctly.** The most common complaint of international audiences is that English speakers talk too fast. Articulate every word carefully, emphasize consonants for clarity, and pause frequently.
2. **Repeat key words and phrases.** When audiences are less familiar with your language, they need to hear important information more than once. Also, they may not be familiar with synonyms, so word key points in the same way throughout your presentation.
3. **Aim for clarity.** Keep your message simple. Eliminate complex sentence structure, abbreviations, and acronyms. Replace two-word verbs with one-word alternatives (such as *review* instead of *look over*). Such verbs are confusing because the definition of each separate word differs from the meaning of the two words combined. Avoid cultural idioms, such as *once in a blue moon,* which may be unfamiliar to an international audience.
4. **Communicate with body language.** Emphasize and clarify verbal information with gestures and facial expressions. For instance, smile to emphasize positive points and use gestures to illustrate the meaning of words such as *up, down,* or *under.*
5. **Support your oral message with visual aids.** For most audiences, visual messages support and clarify spoken words. As Chapter 16 discusses in detail, handouts, flip charts, overheads, and electronic slides can help you describe your key points. To eliminate problems with rapid speech, unclear pronunciations, or strange accents, prepare captions both in English and in your audience's native language.

CAREER APPLICATIONS

1. One of the most important changes speakers need to make when addressing audiences in other cultures is to avoid colloquial figures of speech. Replace each of these phrases with wording that is more likely to be understood by non-native English speakers or audiences in other countries: "hit one out of the park," "go for broke," and "get your ducks lined up."
2. Make a list of 10 two-word verbs. How does the meaning of each separate word differ from the definition of the combined words? Replace each two-word verb with a single, specific word that will be clearer to an international audience.

much harder than reading that language, so an audience that might be able to read a written report might not be able to understand an oral presentation covering the same material (see "Communicating Across Cultures: Five Tips for Making Presentations Around the World").

Try to learn as much as you can about the setting and circumstances of your presentation, from the size of the audience to potential interruptions.

As you analyze the situation, also consider the specific circumstances in which you'll be making your presentation. Will you speak to five people in a conference room, where you can control everything from light to sound to temperature? Or will you be demonstrating a product on the floor of a trade show, where you might have anywhere from five people to five hundred and little control over the environment? Will everyone be in the same room, or will some or all of your audience participate from remote locations via the Internet? What equipment will you have at your disposal—a complete multimedia presentation system or a humble overhead projector (or perhaps no equipment at all)? All these variables can influence not only the style of your presentation but even the content itself. For instance, in a public environment full of distractions and uncertainties, you're probably better off keeping your content simple and short because chances are you won't be able to keep everyone's attention for the duration of your presentation.

Table 15.1 offers a summary of the key steps in analyzing an audience for oral presentations. For even more insight into audience evaluation (including emotional and cultural issues), consult a good public-speaking textbook.

Selecting the Right Medium

The task of selecting the right medium might seem obvious—after all, you are speaking, so it's an oral medium. However, technology offers an array of choices these days, ranging

TABLE 15.1 Analyzing an Audience for Oral Presentations

TASK	ACTIONS
To determine audience size and composition	1. Estimate how many people will attend. 2. Consider whether they have some political, religious, professional, or other affiliation in common. 3. Analyze the mix of men and women, age ranges, socioeconomic and ethnic groups, occupations, and geographic regions represented.
To predict the audience's probable reaction	1. Analyze why audience members are attending the presentation. 2. Determine the audience's general attitude toward the topic: interested, moderately interested, unconcerned, open-minded, or hostile. 3. Analyze the mood that people will be in when you speak to them. 4. Find out what kind of backup information will most impress the audience: technical data, historical information, financial data, demonstrations, samples, and so on. 5. Consider whether the audience has any biases that might work against you. 6. Anticipate possible objections or questions.
To gauge the audience's experience.	1. Analyze whether everybody has the same background and level of understanding. 2. Determine what the audience already knows about the subject. 3. Decide what background information the audience will need to better understand the subject. 4. Consider whether the audience is familiar with your vocabulary. 5. Analyze what the audience expects from you. 6. Think about the mix of general concepts and specific details you will need to present.

from live, in-person presentations to webcasts that people view on your website whenever it fits their individual schedules. Explore these options early on so that you can take full advantage of the ones at your disposal. For example, to reach an international audience, you might want to conduct a live presentation with a question-and-answer session for the

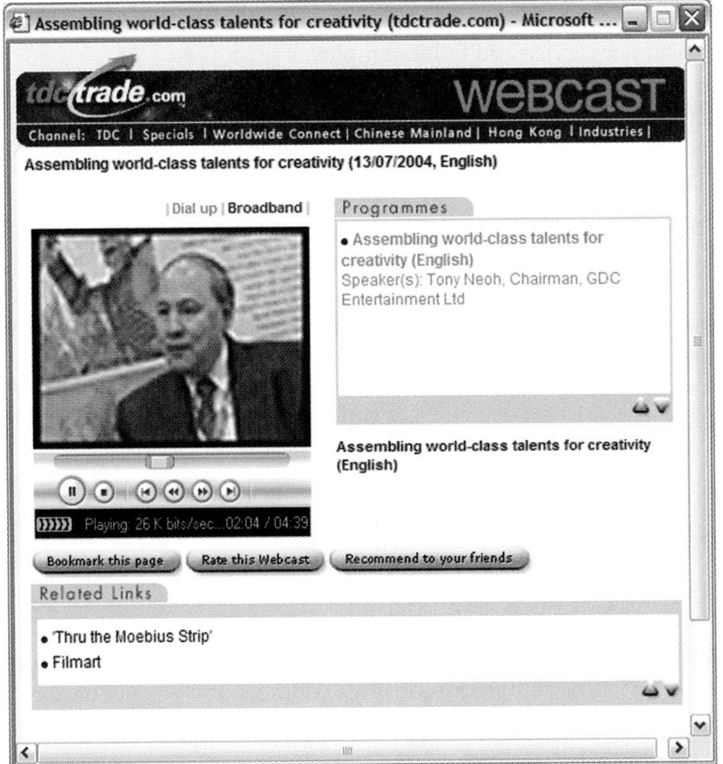

Organizations such as the Hong Kong Trade Development Council, Nike, Sears, and Avon use webcast speeches to make live announcements of financial news, new products, and management changes, as shown on the Yahoo! Broadcast site. Unlike ordinary speeches that address a particular audience at a particular time and place, webcast speeches can be viewed and listened to long after the speaker has left the podium.

audience members in your home office, and then you may want to post a video archive of this meeting on your website for audience members in other time zones. Again, planning ahead is the key to media selection.

Organizing Your Presentation

Organizing a presentation involves the same tasks as organizing a written message: Define your main idea, limit your scope, select a direct or an indirect approach, and outline your content. As you work through these tasks, keep in mind that oral media have certain restraints. When reading written reports, audiences can skip back and forth, backing up if they miss a point or become confused and jumping ahead if they aren't interested in a particular part or are already familiar with the content. However, audiences for oral presentations are more or less trapped in your timeframe and sequence. Other than interrupting you, they have no choice but to listen to your content in the exact order in which you present it.

For instance, say that your presentation is a proposal and that you believe your audience will be hostile to both your proposal and to you. So you plan to structure your proposal using an indirect approach. Simple enough, until . . . surprise—the members of your audience have already heard of your idea through other channels, and they like it. Now they have to sit through an extended presentation of your reasons so that you can convince them to accept an idea they already accept. With a printed report, your audience would simply skip ahead, but they can't do that with an oral presentation. Consequently, organizing your presentation becomes even more important.

Define Your Main Idea

If you've ever heard a speaker struggle to get his or her main point across ("What I really mean to say is . . ."), you know how frustrating such an experience can be for an audience. To avoid that struggle, figure out the one message you want audience members to walk away with. Know what you want them to do after listening to you. Then compose a one-sentence summary that links your subject and purpose to your audience's frame of reference, much as an advertising slogan points out how a product can benefit consumers. Here are some examples of how to word your main idea:

If you can't express your main idea in a single sentence, you probably haven't defined it clearly enough.

- Convince management that reorganizing the technical support department will improve customer service and reduce employee turnover
- Convince the board of directors that we should build a new plant in Texas to eliminate manufacturing bottlenecks and improve production quality
- Address employee concerns regarding a new health-care plan by showing how the plan will reduce costs and improve the quality of their care

Each of these statements puts a particular slant on the subject, one that directly relates to the audience's interests. By focusing on your audience's needs and using the "you" attitude, you help keep their attention and convince them that your points are relevant. For example, a group of new employees will be much more responsive to your discussion of plant safety procedures if you focus on how the procedures can save lives and prevent injuries, rather than focusing on company rules, saving the company money, or conforming to Occupational Safety and Health Administration (OSHA) guidelines.

3 LEARNING OBJECTIVE

Identify the two primary reasons why limiting your scope is especially important for oral presentations

Limit Your Scope

Limiting you scope is important for two reasons: to ensure that your presentation fits the allotted time and to make sure your content meets audience needs and expectations.

Effective presentations not only focus on the audience's needs but also tailor the material to the time allowed, which is often strictly regulated. Moreover, in many situations, multiple presenters are scheduled to speak one right after the other, so time allotments are rigid, permitting little or no flexibility. If you overestimate the amount of material you can cover within your allotted time, you're left with only unpleasant alternatives, such as rushing through your presentation, skipping some of the information you've so carefully prepared, or trying to steal a few minutes from the next presenter. Or if don't have enough material prepared to fill your time slot (generally, a much rarer problem), you might be left standing in front of the audience trying to ad lib information you haven't prepared.

Limiting your scope also involves matching your message with your audience's needs and expectations. For instance, if you're training your teammates on a new web publishing system, you'll need to cover both basic and advanced techniques. Many of your colleagues may need to spend some time practicing the basics in order to fully internalize them and use them as a foundation for the advanced techniques. So if you try to cover both basic and advanced material in a single session, the training may be less effective than it could've been. Trying to cover too many details in a presentation can produce similar results. Often the best approach is to explain important concepts in your oral presentation and refer your audience to a printed document for supporting details.

Once you've decided on the right amount of information to cover, do your best to estimate the time required to present that material or to estimate the amount of material you can cover within a fixed amount of time The only sure way to do this is to practice—always a great idea anyway. By running through your presentation (preferably with a test audience), you'll not only get a fairly accurate idea of how long it will take, but you might also get feedback that could help you improve your content and delivery.

The only sure way to measure the length of your presentation is to complete a practice run.

As an alternative to a complete practice run, you can try several alternatives for estimating time requirements. First, if you're in one of those rare situations in which you're reciting your material verbatim or reading from a prepared script (more on this later in the chapter), you can divide your word count by 125 (if you speak slower than average) or 150 (if you're faster than average) to get a rough idea of how many minutes you'll need. Most speakers can comfortably deliver between 125 and 150 words per minute. Second, you can measure how long it takes to talk through a small portion of your presentation, then extrapolate how long the entire presentation will take. This method isn't terribly accurate, but it can help identify major timing problems. Third, after you get some experience giving presentations with either overhead transparencies or electronic slides, you'll get a feel for the time you typically need to cover a single slide. As a general guideline, figure on three or even four minutes per slide.[2] For instance, if you have 20 minutes, plan on roughly six or seven slides. If you're whipping through slides faster than that, chances are your slides are too simple or you're not engaging the audience with enough discussion about each one.

Of course, be sure to factor in time for introductions, coffee breaks, demonstrations, question-and-answer sessions, and anything else that takes away from your speaking time.

Choose Your Approach

With a well-defined main idea to guide you and a clear idea about the scope of your presentation, you can begin to arrange your message. If you have 10 minutes or less to deliver your message, organize your presentation much as you would a letter or a brief memo: Use the direct approach if the subject involves routine information or good news, and use the indirect approach if the subject involves bad news or persuasion. Plan your introduction to arouse interest and to give a preview of what's to come. For the body of the presentation, be prepared to explain the who, what, when, where, why, and how of your subject. In the final paragraph or two, review the points you've made, and close with a statement that will help your audience remember the subject of your speech. Figure 15.2 presents an outline of a short presentation that updates management on the status of a key project; the presenter has some bad news to deliver, so she opted for an indirect approach to lay out the reasons for the delay before sharing the news of the schedule slip.

Organize short presentations the same way you would a letter or brief memo.

Longer presentations are organized like reports. If the purpose is to entertain, motivate, or inform, use direct order and a structure imposed naturally by the subject: importance, sequence, chronology, spatial orientation, geography, or category (as discussed in Chapter 13). If your purpose is to analyze, persuade, or collaborate, organize your material around conclusions and recommendations or around a logical argument. Use direct order if the audience is receptive and indirect if you expect resistance.

As you develop your approach, keep in mind that oral reports have one important advantage over written reports: you can adjust your outline on the fly if you need to. Identify the critical points in your presentation and ask yourself some "what if" questions

FIGURE 15.2
Effective Outline for a 10-Minute Progress Report

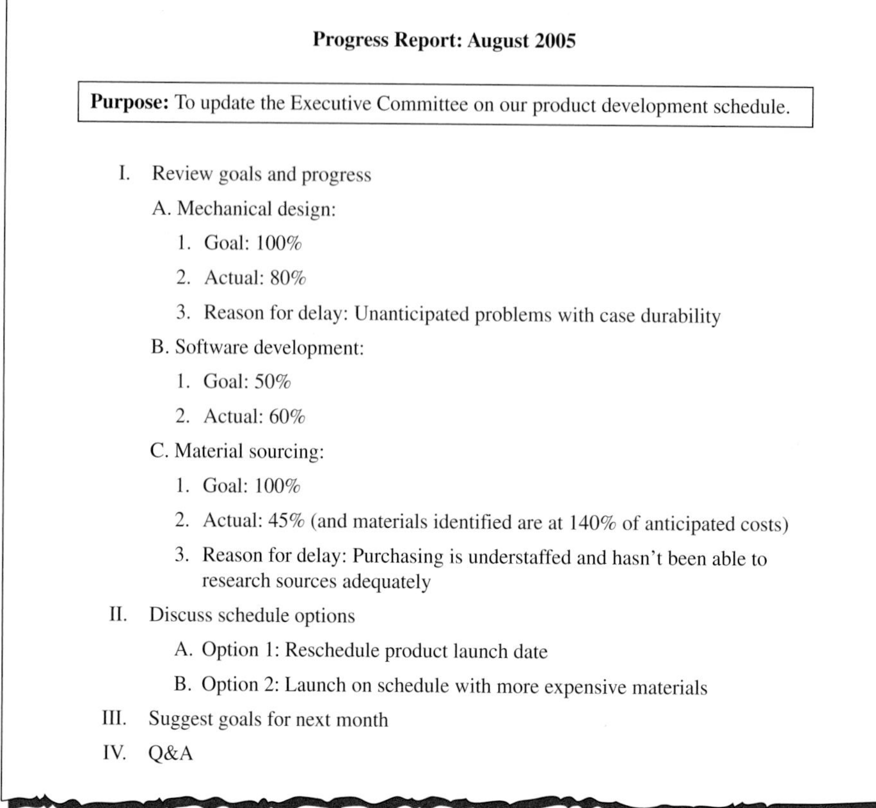
Progress Report: August 2005

Purpose: To update the Executive Committee on our product development schedule.

I. Review goals and progress
   A. Mechanical design:
      1. Goal: 100%
      2. Actual: 80%
      3. Reason for delay: Unanticipated problems with case durability
   B. Software development:
      1. Goal: 50%
      2. Actual: 60%
   C. Material sourcing:
      1. Goal: 100%
      2. Actual: 45% (and materials identified are at 140% of anticipated costs)
      3. Reason for delay: Purchasing is understaffed and hasn't been able to research sources adequately
II. Discuss schedule options
   A. Option 1: Reschedule product launch date
   B. Option 2: Launch on schedule with more expensive materials
III. Suggest goals for next month
IV. Q&A

to consider possible audience reactions. For instance, if you're worried that the audience might not agree with the financial assumptions you've made, you might prepare a detailed analysis that you can include in your presentation if you sense that a negative reaction is building in the audience or if someone openly questions you about it. As you'll see in Chapter 16, presentation software such as Microsoft PowerPoint makes it easy to adjust your presentation as you move along, allowing you the chance to skip over any parts you decide not to use or to insert backup material at the last minute.

Simplicity is critical in the organization of oral presentations.

Regardless of the length of your presentation, remember that simplicity of organization is especially valuable in oral communication. If listeners lose the thread of your presentation, they'll have a hard time catching up and following your message in the remainder of your speech. Look for the most obvious and natural way to organize your ideas, using a direct approach whenever possible. Explain at the beginning how you've organized your material, and try to limit the number of main points to three or four—even when the speech or presentation is lengthy.

Prepare Your Outline

In addition to planning your speech, a presentation outline helps you plan your speaking notes as well.

A presentation outline performs the same all-important function as an outline for a written report: helping you organize the message in way that maximizes its impact on your audience. However, a presentation outline can also serve as the foundation of your speaking notes, so as you write your outline, start thinking about the words you'll want to use when you deliver your speech. To ensure effective organization, prepare your outline in several stages:[3]

- **State your purpose and main idea.** As you develop your outline, check frequently to be sure that the points, organization, connections, and title relate to your purpose and main idea.
- **Organize your major points and subpoints.** Express each major point as a single, complete sentence to help you keep track of the one specific idea you want to convey in that point. Then look at the order of points to make sure their arrangement is logical and effective.

- **Identify your introduction, body, and close.** Start with the body, numbering each major point and subpoint according to its level in your outline. Then lay out the points for your introduction and close.
- **Show your connections.** Write out in sentence form the transitions you plan to use to move from one part to the next. Remember to include additional transitions between major points in the body of your speech.
- **Show your sources.** Prepare your bibliography, making sure that it reads easily, follows a consistent format, and includes all the details needed to identify your various sources.
- **Choose a title.** Not all speeches have a title. However, a title can be useful if your speech will be publicized ahead of time or introduced by someone else. The title sets everyone's expectations, so make it compelling and audience-centered.

Figure 15.3 is an outline for a 30-minute analytical presentation. It is organized around conclusions and presented in direct order. This outline is based on Chapter 14's Electrovision report, written by Linda Moreno.

Many speakers like to prepare both a detailed *planning outline* and a simpler *speaking outline* that provides all the cues and reminders they need to present their material.[4] To prepare an effective speaking outline, follow these steps:[5]

4 **LEARNING OBJECTIVE**

Distinguish a planning outline from a speaking outline, and explain the purpose of each

You may find it helpful to create a simpler speaking outline from your planning outline.

- **Follow the planning outline.** Follow the same format as you used for your planning outline (so that you can see at a glance where you are in your speech and how each part and point relates to the one before and after). However, strip away anything you don't plan to say to your audience (statements of general purpose, specific purpose, main idea, bibliography, etc.)
- **Condense points and transitions to keywords.** Choose words that will prompt you to remember what each point is about so that you can speak fluently. Be sure to write out statistics, quotations, and other specifics so that you don't stumble over them. You may also want to write complete sentences for transitions that connect main points or for critical points in your introduction or your close. Aim for the shortest outline you can comfortably use.
- **Add delivery cues.** During rehearsals, note the places in your outline where you plan to pause for emphasis, speak more slowly, use a visual aid, and so on. You might use colored ink to highlight your delivery cues. However, avoid cluttering your outline; include only the most important cues.
- **Arrange your notes.** Whether you hand-print or type your speaking outline on paper or note cards, make sure your final version is legible and accessible so that you can refer to it as you speak. Number your cards (or sheets of paper) so that you can keep them in order.

If you plan to use PowerPoint or other presentation software, you can also use the "notes" field on each slide for speaking notes.

STEP 2: WRITING YOUR PRESENTATION

Although you may never actually write out a presentation word for word, you still engage in the writing process—developing your ideas, structuring support points, phrasing your transitions, and so on. Depending on the situation and your personal style, your actual presentation might follow these initial words closely or might express your thoughts in fresh, spontaneous language. Because you get to the actual writing phase, consider how you should adapt your style to your audience.

Adapting to Your Audience

What does your audience expect from your presentation? Will you stage a formal presentation in an impressive setting with professionally produced visual aids? Or will you lead a casual, roll-up-your-sleeves working session? Adapt your approach to fit the occasion. Your audience's size, your subject, your purpose, your budget, and the time available for prepa-

Adapting to your audience addresses a number of issues, from speaking style to technology choices.

FIGURE 15.3 Effective Outline for a 30-Minute Presentation

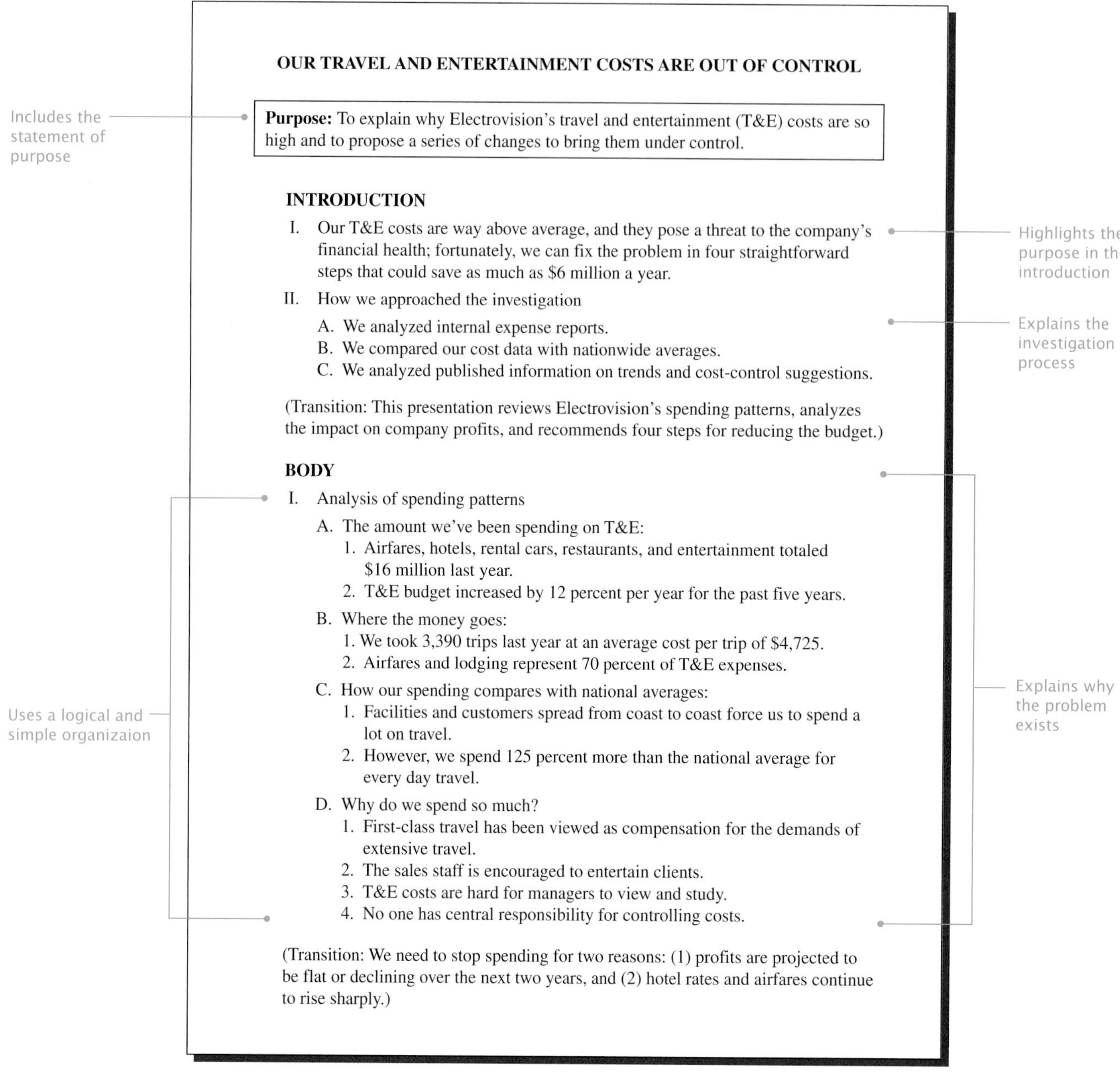
OUR TRAVEL AND ENTERTAINMENT COSTS ARE OUT OF CONTROL

Purpose: To explain why Electrovision's travel and entertainment (T&E) costs are so high and to propose a series of changes to bring them under control.

INTRODUCTION

I. Our T&E costs are way above average, and they pose a threat to the company's financial health; fortunately, we can fix the problem in four straightforward steps that could save as much as $6 million a year.

II. How we approached the investigation
   A. We analyzed internal expense reports.
   B. We compared our cost data with nationwide averages.
   C. We analyzed published information on trends and cost-control suggestions.

(Transition: This presentation reviews Electrovision's spending patterns, analyzes the impact on company profits, and recommends four steps for reducing the budget.)

BODY

I. Analysis of spending patterns
   A. The amount we've been spending on T&E:
      1. Airfares, hotels, rental cars, restaurants, and entertainment totaled $16 million last year.
      2. T&E budget increased by 12 percent per year for the past five years.
   B. Where the money goes:
      1. We took 3,390 trips last year at an average cost per trip of $4,725.
      2. Airfares and lodging represent 70 percent of T&E expenses.
   C. How our spending compares with national averages:
      1. Facilities and customers spread from coast to coast force us to spend a lot on travel.
      2. However, we spend 125 percent more than the national average for every day travel.
   D. Why do we spend so much?
      1. First-class travel has been viewed as compensation for the demands of extensive travel.
      2. The sales staff is encouraged to entertain clients.
      3. T&E costs are hard for managers to view and study.
      4. No one has central responsibility for controlling costs.

(Transition: We need to stop spending for two reasons: (1) profits are projected to be flat or declining over the next two years, and (2) hotel rates and airfares continue to rise sharply.)

Includes the statement of purpose
Highlights the purpose in the introduction
Explains the investigation process
Uses a logical and simple organizaion
Explains why the problem exists

(continued)

ration all influence the style of your presentation. Your style sends a message, and that message is open to interpretation. For example, a glitzy, multimedia presentation might attract trendy new clients, but it might cause potential investors to question your fiscal prudence.

If you're speaking to a small group, particularly people you already know, you can use a casual style that encourages audience participation. A small conference room, with your audience seated around a table, may be appropriate. Use simple visual aids, and invite your audience to interject comments. Deliver your remarks in a conversational tone, using notes to jog your memory if necessary.

If you're addressing a large audience and the event is an important one, you'll want to establish a more formal atmosphere. A formal style is well suited to announcements about mergers or acquisitions, new products, financial results, and other business milestones. During formal presentations, speakers are often located on a stage or platform, standing behind a lectern and using a microphone so that their remarks can be heard throughout

FIGURE 15.3 Continued

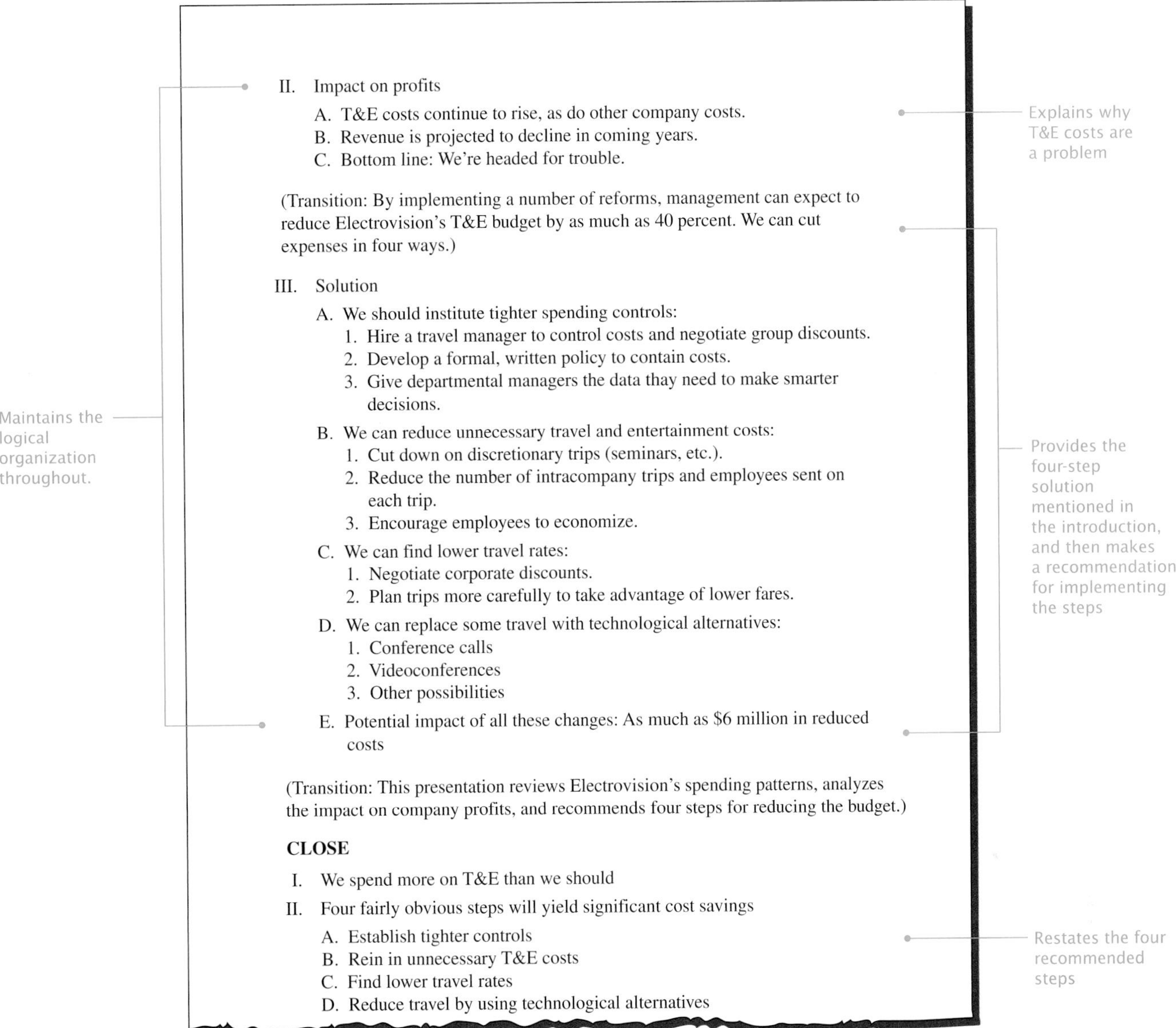
II. Impact on profits

A. T&E costs continue to rise, as do other company costs.
B. Revenue is projected to decline in coming years.
C. Bottom line: We're headed for trouble.

(Transition: By implementing a number of reforms, management can expect to reduce Electrovision's T&E budget by as much as 40 percent. We can cut expenses in four ways.)

III. Solution

A. We should institute tighter spending controls:
1. Hire a travel manager to control costs and negotiate group discounts.
2. Develop a formal, written policy to contain costs.
3. Give departmental managers the data thay need to make smarter decisions.

B. We can reduce unnecessary travel and entertainment costs:
1. Cut down on discretionary trips (seminars, etc.).
2. Reduce the number of intracompany trips and employees sent on each trip.
3. Encourage employees to economize.

C. We can find lower travel rates:
1. Negotiate corporate discounts.
2. Plan trips more carefully to take advantage of lower fares.

D. We can replace some travel with technological alternatives:
1. Conference calls
2. Videoconferences
3. Other possibilities

E. Potential impact of all these changes: As much as $6 million in reduced costs

(Transition: This presentation reviews Electrovision's spending patterns, analyzes the impact on company profits, and recommends four steps for reducing the budget.)

CLOSE

I. We spend more on T&E than we should

II. Four fairly obvious steps will yield significant cost savings

A. Establish tighter controls
B. Rein in unnecessary T&E costs
C. Find lower travel rates
D. Reduce travel by using technological alternatives

Explains why T&E costs are a problem
Maintains the logical organization throughout.
Provides the four-step solution mentioned in the introduction, and then makes a recommendation for implementing the steps
Restates the four recommended steps

the room. These presentations are often accompanied by slides and other visual aids showcasing major products, technological breakthroughs, and other information that the speakers want audience members to remember.

Whether your presentation is formal or informal, always choose your words carefully. If you try to impress your audience with obscure or unfamiliar vocabulary, your message will be lost. Make sure you can define all the words you use. And keep things simple. If you repeatedly stumble over a word as you rehearse, use a different one.[6]

Finally, when you're pondering how you'll adapt to your audience, take public speaking etiquette into account. Show consideration for your audience by making good use of their time, addressing them respectfully, and maintaining a professional presence during your speech.

Composing Your Presentation

Just like written documents, oral presentations are composed of distinct elements: the introduction, the body, and the close.

5 LEARNING OBJECTIVE

Discuss the three functions of an effective introduction

Introduction

A good introduction arouses the audience's interest in your topic, establishes your credibility, and prepares the audience for what will follow. That's a lot to pack into the first few minutes of your presentation, so give yourself plenty of time to develop the words and visuals you'll use to get your presentation off to a great start.

An effective introduction arouses interest in your topic, establishes your credibility, and prepares the audience for the body of your presentation.

Arousing Audience Interest Some subjects are naturally more interesting than others. If you will be discussing a matter of profound significance that will personally affect the members of your audience, chances are they'll listen regardless of how you begin. All you really have to do is announce your topic, and you'll have their attention.

If your audience isn't likely to be naturally interested in your topic, your introduction will need to build interest by relating the subject to their personal concerns.

Other subjects call for more imagination. How do you get people to listen if you're explaining your pension program to a group of new clerical employees, none of whom will be fully eligible for the program for another five years and many of whom might leave the company within two? The best approach to dealing with an uninterested audience is to appeal to human nature and encourage people to take the subject personally. Show them how they'll be affected as individuals. For example, you might begin by addressing the new clerical employees like this:

> If somebody offered to give you $200,000 in exchange for $5 per week, would you be interested? That's the amount you can expect to collect during your retirement years if you choose to contribute to the voluntary pension plan. During the next two weeks, you will have to decide whether you want to participate. Although retirement is many years away for most of you, it is an important financial decision. During the next 20 minutes, I hope to give you the information you need to make a decision that's best for you and your families.

Another way to arouse the audience's interest is to draw out ideas and encourage comments from the audience throughout your presentation. Of course, this technique works better with a small group of co-workers than it does when you're addressing a large audience—particularly if the members of that large audience are hostile or unknown to you. When addressing large audiences, responding to questions and comments can interrupt the flow of information, weaken your argument, and reduce your control of the situation. In such situations, it's best to ask people to hold their questions until after you have concluded your remarks. Just be sure to allow ample time for audience questions at the end of your presentation, as this chapter discusses later.

Table 15.2 suggests several techniques you can use to arouse audience interest and keep listeners involved. Regardless of which technique you choose, always make sure that the introduction matches the tone of your presentation. If the occasion is supposed to be fun, you might begin with something light, but if you're talking business to a group of executives, don't waste their time with cute openings. Avoid jokes and personal anecdotes when you're discussing a serious problem. If you're giving a routine oral report, don't be overly dramatic. Most of all, be natural. Nothing turns off the average audience faster than a trite, staged beginning.

Building Your Credibility In addition to grabbing the audience's attention, your introduction also has to establish your credibility. If you're a well-known expert in the subject matter or have earned your audience's trust in other situations, you're already ahead of the game. However, if you have no working relationship with your audience or if you're speaking in an area outside your presumed expertise, you need to establish your credibility and do so quickly; people tend to decide within a few minutes whether you're worth listening to.[7]

Movie stars and world champion athletes such as Oscar de la Hoya may have instant credibility, but if you're like most public speakers, you will have to establish your credibility in a short period of time. Use your introduction to highlight a few personal accomplishments that your audience will value and respect.

Techniques for building credibility vary depending on whether you will be introducing yourself or having someone else introduce you. If a master of ceremonies, conference chair, or other person will introduce you, he or she can present your credentials so that you won't appear boastful. However, make sure that the person introducing you doesn't exaggerate your qualifications—some members of the audience are likely to bristle if you're billed as being the world's greatest authority on your subject.

If you will be introducing yourself, keep your comments simple. At the same time, don't be afraid to mention your accomplishments. Your listeners will be curious about

TABLE 15.2 Five Ways to Get Attention and Keep It

Use humor	Even though the subject of most business presentations is serious, including a light comment now and then can perk up the audience. Just be sure the humor is relevant to the presentation and not offensive to the audience.
Tell a story	Slice-of-life stories are naturally interesting and can be compelling. Be sure your story illustrates an important point.
Pass around a sample	Psychologists say that you can get people to remember your points by appealing to their senses. The best way to do so is to pass around a sample. If your company is in the textile business, let the audience handle some of your fabrics. If you sell chocolates, give everybody a taste.
Ask a question	Asking questions will get the audience actively involved in your presentation and, at the same time, will give you information about them and their needs.
State a startling statistic	People love details. If you can interject an interesting statistic, you can often wake up your audience.

your qualifications, so tell them briefly who you are and why you're there. Generally, you need to mention only a few aspects of your background: your position in an organization, your profession, the name of your company. You might say something like this:

> I'm Karen Whitney, a market research analyst with Information Resources Corporation. For the past five years, I've specialized in studying high-technology markets. Your director of engineering, John LaBarre, has asked me to talk to you about recent trends in computer-aided design so that you'll have a better idea of how to direct your research efforts.

This speaker establishes credibility by tying her credentials to the purpose of her presentation. By mentioning her company's name, her specialization and position, and the name of the audience's boss, she lets her listeners know immediately that she is qualified to tell them something they need to know. She connects her background to their concerns.

Communication Solution

Most professional services firms try to build credibility with a new audience by focusing on their own credentials (primarily through work they've done for other clients). In contrast, Fitch seeks to build credibility by showing how well its designers understand the audience's business needs.

Previewing Your Message In addition to arousing audience interest and building your credibility, a good introduction gives your audience a preview of what's ahead, helping them understand the structure and content of your message. A reader can get an idea of the structure and content of a report by looking at the table of contents and scanning the headings. However, in an oral presentation, you provide that framework with a preview. Without cues from the speaker, the audience may be unable to figure out how the main points of the message fit together.

Your preview should summarize the main idea of your presentation, identify major supporting points, and indicate the order in which you'll develop those points. Tell your listeners in so many words, "This is the subject, and these are the points I will cover." Once you've established the framework, you can be confident that the audience will understand how the individual facts and figures are related to your main idea as you move into the body of your presentation.

Use the preview to help your audience understand the importance, the structure, and the content of your message.

Body

The bulk of your speech or presentation is devoted to a discussion of the three or four main points in your outline. Use the same organizational patterns you'd use in a letter, memo, or report, but keep things simple. As Eric Ashworth of Fitch can tell you, your goals are to make sure that (1) the organization of your presentation is clear and (2) your presentation holds the audience's attention.

Connecting Your Ideas Making sure your audience doesn't get lost is always important, but clarity is doubly critical with spoken communication for the simple reason that your

When attempting to hold an audience's attention, public speakers sometimes face distractions in the background. It takes a focused speaker to overcome such physical interruptions and get his or her message across.

audience can't back up and reread if they get confused. In written documents, you can show how ideas are related on the page or screen by employing a variety of design clues: headings, paragraph indentions, white space, and lists. However, with oral communication—particularly when you aren't using visual aids for support—you have to rely primarily on words to link various parts and ideas.

For the small links between sentences and paragraphs, use one or two transitional words: *therefore, because, in addition, in contrast, moreover, for example, consequently, nevertheless,* or *finally.* To link major sections of a presentation, use complete sentences or paragraphs, such as "Now that we've reviewed the problem, let's take a look at some solutions." Every time you shift topics, be sure to stress the connection between ideas. Summarize what's been said, then preview what's to come.

The longer your presentation, the more important your transitions become. If you will be presenting many ideas, audience members may have trouble absorbing them and seeing the relationships among them. Your listeners need clear transitions to guide them to the most important points. Furthermore, they'll appreciate brief, interim summaries to pick up any ideas they may have missed. So by repeating key ideas in your transitions, you can compensate for lapses in your audience's attention. When you actually give your presentation, you might also want to call attention to the transitions by using gestures, changing your tone of voice, or introducing a visual aid, as Chapter 16 points out.

Use transitions to repeat key ideas, particularly in longer presentations.

6 LEARNING OBJECTIVE

Identify four ways to keep your audience's attention during your presentation

Holding Your Audience's Attention An important part of helping your audience connect your ideas is to hold their attention from start to finish. In addition to the general challenge of keeping readers interested, you have to compensate for another inescapable fact of oral presentations: your audience can think and read faster than you can speak. If you don't keep their minds engaged, they'll start thinking of other pressing subjects, reading ahead through your handouts, checking e-mail on wireless handhelds, or doing a thousand other things besides paying attention to you. Here are a few helpful tips for keeping the audience tuned into your message:

The most important way to hold an audience's attention is to show how your message relates to their individual needs and concerns.

- **Relate your subject to your audience's needs.** People are interested in things that affect them personally. As much as possible, present every point in light of your audience's needs and values.
- **Anticipate your audience's questions.** Try to anticipate as many questions as you can, and address these questions in the body of your presentation. You'll also want to prepare and reserve additional material to use during the question-and-answer period should the audience ask for greater detail.
- **Use clear, vivid language.** People become bored quickly when they don't understand the speaker. If your presentation will involve abstract ideas, show how those abstractions connect with everyday life. Use familiar words, short sentences, and concrete examples. Be sure to throw in some variety as well; repeating the same words and phrases over and over puts people to sleep.
- **Explain the relationship between your subject and familiar ideas.** Show how your subject is related to ideas that audience members already understand, and give people a way to categorize and remember your points.[8]
- **Ask for opinions or pause occasionally for questions or comments.** Audience feedback helps you determine whether your listeners understand a key point before you launch into another section. Feedback also gives your audience a chance to switch for a time from listening to participating, which helps them engage with your message and develop a sense of shared ownership.

- **Illustrate your ideas with visual aids.** As Chapter 16 discusses, you may wish to develop visual aids for your presentation and coordinate them with your delivery. Visuals enliven your message, help you connect with audience members, and help them remember your message more effectively.

Close

The close of a speech or presentation is critical for two reasons: First, audience attention tends to peak at this point because they anticipate moving on to the next activity in their busy day, and second, audience members will leave with your final words ringing in their ears. Before closing your presentation, tell listeners that you're about to finish so that they'll make one final effort to listen intently. Don't be afraid to sound obvious. Consider saying something such as "In conclusion" or "To sum it all up." You want people to know that this is the final segment of your presentation.

Restating Your Main Points Once you've decided how to announce your close, repeat your main idea. Emphasize what you want your audience to do or to think, and stress the key motivating factor that will encourage them to respond that way. Finally, reinforce your theme by restating your main supporting points. A few sentences are generally enough to refresh people's memories. One speaker ended a presentation on the company's executive compensation program by repeating his four specific recommendations and then concluding with a memorable statement that would motivate his audience to take action:

Plan your close carefully so that your audience leaves with your main idea fresh in their minds.

> We can all be proud of the way our company has grown. However, if we want to continue that growth, we need to adjust our executive compensation program to reflect competitive practices. If we don't, our best people will look for opportunities elsewhere.
>
> In summary, our survey has shown that we need to do four things to improve executive compensation:
>
> - Increase the overall level of compensation
> - Install a cash bonus program
> - Offer a variety of stock-based incentives
> - Improve our health insurance and pension benefits
>
> By making these improvements, we can help our company cross the threshold of growth to face our industry's largest competitors.

Such repetition of key ideas greatly improves the chance that your audience will hear your message in the way you intended.

Describing Next Steps Some presentations require the audience to reach a decision or agree to take specific action, in which case the close provides a clear wrap-up. If the audience agrees on an issue covered in the presentation, you'll want to review the consensus in a sentence or two. If they don't agree, you'll want to make the lack of consensus clear by saying something like "We seem to have some fundamental disagreement on this question." Then be ready to suggest a method of resolving the differences. If you're not sure in advance how your audience will respond, prepare alternative closes. Few things in public speaking are more embarrassing than trying to launch into a rousing, positive finish when you know you've lost your audience somewhere along the way.

If you need to have the audience make a decision or agree to take action, make sure the responsibilities for doing so are clear.

If you expect any action to occur as a result of your speech, be sure to explain who is responsible for doing what. One effective technique is to list the action items, with an estimated completion date and the name of the person or team responsible. You can present this list in a visual aid and ask each person on the list to agree to accomplish his or her assigned task by the target date. This public commitment to action is good insurance that something will happen.

If the required action is likely to be difficult, make sure that everyone understands the problems involved. You don't want people to leave the presentation thinking their tasks will be easy, only to discover later that the jobs are quite demanding. You'll want everyone to have a realistic attitude and to be prepared to handle whatever arises. So when composing

DOCUMENT MAKEOVER

IMPROVE THIS SPEECH

To practice correcting drafts of actual documents, visit www.prenhall.com/onekey on the web. Click "Document Makeovers" then click Chapter 15. You will find a speech that contains problems and errors relating to what you've learned in this chapter about preparing effective speeches and oral presentations. Use the Final Draft decision tool to create an improved version of this speech. Check the message for effective choices in scope, style, opening, use of transitions, and closing.

your presentation, use the close to alert people to potential difficulties or pitfalls.

Ending on a Strong Note Make sure that your final remarks are encouraging and memorable. After summarizing the key points of your presentation, conclude with a quote, a call to action, or some encouraging words. For instance, you might stress the benefits of action or express confidence in the listeners' ability to accomplish the work ahead. An alternative is to end with a question or a statement that will leave your audience thinking.

At the completion of your presentation, your audience should feel satisfied. The close is not the place to introduce new ideas or to alter the mood of the presentation. Even if parts of your presentation are downbeat, you will want to close on a positive note. Also, avoid using a staged finale—keep it natural. As with everything else in your oral presentation, compose your closing remarks carefully. You don't want to wind up on stage with nothing to say but "Well, I guess that's it."

Plan your final statement carefully so you can end on a strong, positive note.

STEP 3: COMPLETING YOUR PRESENTATION

With a draft of your presentation in hand, you're ready to complete the development of your presentation. As with written communication, this third step starts with the all-important task of revising your message to ensure appropriate content. Edit your presentation for clarity and conciseness as you would any business message. For presentations, you'll go beyond these now familiar tasks and pay special attention to four special tasks: mastering the art of delivery, preparing to speak, overcoming anxiety, and handling questions responsively.

Mastering the Art of Delivery

Once you've written your presentation and created the visuals you will use, you're ready to begin practicing your delivery. You have a variety of delivery methods to choose from, some of which are easier to handle than others:

- **Memorizing.** Unless you're a trained actor, avoid memorizing your speech, especially a long one. In the best of circumstances you'll probably sound stilted; in the worst, you might forget your lines. Besides, you'll often need to address audience questions during your speech, so you must be flexible enough to adjust your speech as you go. However, memorizing a quotation, an opening paragraph, or a few concluding remarks can bolster your confidence and strengthen your delivery.
- **Reading.** If you're delivering a technical or complex presentation, you may want to read it. Policy statements by government officials are sometimes read because the wording may be critical. But unless you're required or expected to read your presentation verbatim, think twice about doing so. After all, if all you're doing is reading, why not just write a report and let your audience read it themselves? If you do plan to read your speech, practice enough so that you can still maintain eye contact with your audience. Triple-spaced copy, wide margins, and large type will help. You might even want to include stage cues, such as *pause, raise hands, lower voice.*
- **Speaking from notes.** Making a presentation with the help of an outline, note cards, or visual aids is usually the most effective and easiest delivery mode. This approach gives you something to refer to and still allows for plenty of eye contact, interaction with the audience, and improvisation in response to audience feedback. (When speaking from notes, be sure to use stiff note cards; nervousness is more easily exposed by shaking sheets of paper.)

Speaking from carefully prepared notes is the easiest and most effective delivery mode for most speakers.

- **Impromptu speaking.** From time to time, you may have to give an impromptu, or unrehearsed, speech: you may be called on to speak unexpectedly or circumstances may prevent you from preparing a planned speech. If you have the option, avoid speaking unprepared unless you're well versed in the topic or have lots of experience at improvising in front of a live audience. When you're asked to speak "off the cuff," take a moment to think through what you'll say and then focus on your key points. If you absolutely cannot say something intelligent and effective on the subject at hand, it's usually better to explain that you can't and ask for an opportunity to prepare some remarks for a later time or date.

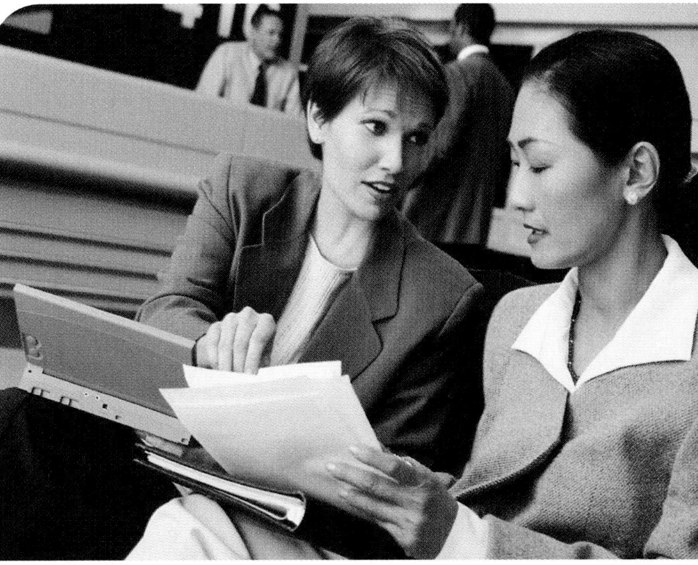

Practicing your oral presentation with a co-worker or a friend is a terrific way to polish your public-speaking skills in a relaxed setting.

Regardless of which delivery mode you use, be sure that you're thoroughly familiar with your subject. Knowing what you're speaking about is the best way to build your self-confidence. If you stumble, get interrupted, or suffer equipment failures, your expertise will help you restart and get back on track.

Practice is key to success as a presenter, especially if you haven't had much experience with public speaking. If you rehearse in front of a mirror, try to visualize the room filled with listeners. Try to record your speech to check the sound of your voice, as well as your timing, phrasing, and emphasis. And if possible, rehearse on video to see yourself as your audience will.

Schedule plenty of practice time whenever you're developing a high-profile presentation.

Preparing to Speak

In addition to knowing your material and practicing your delivery, you can build confidence in other ways. First, know that your location is ready and that you will have everything you'll need. Second, make sure you're prepared to address audiences from other cultures.

Whenever you can, check the location for your presentation in advance. Check the seating arrangements to make sure they're appropriate for both your needs and the audience's. Verify the availability and operation of all the equipment and supplies you're counting, from a laptop and LCD projector to simple but vital necessities such as flipcharts and marking pens. Many corporate conference rooms now have permanent projection systems that require you to e-mail your presentation file or bring it on disk. Just make sure that you know what to expect in advance.

If possible, visit the speaking venue ahead of time to familiarize yourself with the facilities and the equipment.

If you're addressing an audience that doesn't speak your language, consider using an interpreter. Working with an interpreter does constrain your presentation somewhat. For one thing, you must speak slowly enough for the interpreter to keep up with you; however, don't speak so slowly that the rest of your audience loses interest. Send your interpreter a copy of your speech and visual aids as far in advance of your presentation as possible. If your audience is likely to include persons with hearing impairments, be sure to team up with a sign-language translator as well.

Any time you deliver an oral presentation to people from other cultures, you may need to adapt the content of your presentation. It is also important to take into account any cultural differences in appearance, mannerisms, and other customs. Your interpreter or host will be able to suggest appropriate changes for a specific audience or particular occasion.

Overcoming Anxiety

If you're nervous about facing an audience and you experience stage fright, you're not alone. Even speakers with years of experience feel some anxiety about getting up in front of an audience. Although you might not be able to make your nervous feelings disappear, you can learn to cope with your anxiety and even to use that nervous energy to your advantage.

Feeling More Confident

Preparation is the best antidote for anxiety.

For starters, think of nervousness as an indication that you care about your audience, your topic, and the occasion. If your palms get wet or your mouth goes dry, don't think of nerves, think of excitement. Such stimulation can give you the extra energy you need to make your presentation sparkle. Here are some ways to harness your nervous energy to become a more confident speaker.[9]

- **Prepare more material than necessary.** Combined with a genuine interest in your topic, extra knowledge will reduce your anxiety.
- **Rehearse.** The more familiar you are with your material, the less panic you'll feel.
- **Think positively.** See yourself as polished and professional, and your audience will too.
- **Visualize your success.** Use the few minutes before you actually begin speaking to tell yourself you're on and you're ready. Visualize mental images of yourself in front of the audience, feeling confident, prepared, and able to handle any situation that might arise.[10]
- **Take a few deep breaths.** Before you begin to speak, remember that your audience is silently wishing you success.
- **Be ready.** Have your first sentence memorized and on the tip of your tongue.
- **Be comfortable.** Dress appropriately for the situation but as comfortably as possible. Drink plenty of water before your scheduled presentation time to ensure that your voice is well hydrated (bring a bottle of water with you, too). If possible, adjust the temperature in the room to your personal preference. The fewer physical distractions you have, the better you'll perform.
- **Don't panic.** If you feel that you're losing your audience during your speech, try to pull them back by involving them in the action; ask for their opinions or pause for questions. Realize that most audiences want you to succeed.
- **Concentrate on your message and your audience, not on yourself.** When you're busy thinking about your subject and observing your audience's response, you tend to forget your fears.
- **Keep going.** Things usually get better as you move along, with each successful minute giving you more and more confidence.

No one welcomes mistakes, equipment failures, and other troubles, but they are survivable. To learn how several experienced presenters have overcome some serious glitches, see "Communication Miscues: Recovering from Disasters."

7 LEARNING OBJECTIVE

Describe the techniques you can use to appear more confident in front of an audience

Appearing More Confident

Most of the steps you take to feel more confident will also make you appear more confident to your audience. In addition to that advice, try to be aware of the nonverbal signals you're transmitting throughout your presentation. Regardless of how you feel inside, your effectiveness depends to a large degree on how you look and sound.

Nonverbal signals tell the audience how you're feeling, so pay attention to the signals you send.

Well-delivered presentations start with your first minute at the podium, so don't rush. As you approach the speaker's lectern, walk with confidence, breathe deeply, and stand up straight. Face your audience, adjust the microphone and other equipment as needed, count to three slowly, and then survey the room. When you find a friendly face, make eye contact and smile. Count to three again and then begin your presentation.[11] If you are nervous, this slow, controlled beginning will help you establish rapport and appear more confident.

Once your presentation is under way, be particularly careful to maintain eye contact with your audience. Pick out several people positioned around the room, and shift your gaze from one to another. Looking directly at your listeners will make you appear sincere, confident, and trustworthy. It also helps you get an idea of the impression you're creating. If you sense that you're starting to race—a natural response when you're nervous—stop for a second and arrange your notes or perform some other small task while taking several deep breaths. Then start again at your normal pace.

Communication Miscues

Recovering from Disasters

You've researched your topic, analyzed your audience, prepared a compelling message, crafted eye-catching visuals, and practiced until you're running like a smooth machine. You're ready to go.

Then you wake up with a sore throat and half a voice. You grab a few lozenges, hope for the best, and drive to the conference facility in plenty of time to set up your equipment. Oops, somebody forgot to tell you that your presentation has been moved up by an hour, and your audience is already in the room waiting for you. You scramble to turn on your laptop and get it connected to the projector, only to discover that you forgot to pack the power cord for you laptop and your battery is low on juice. But that won't be a problem: your laptop is dead anyway. Feeling smart, you pull out a floppy disk with a backup copy of your PowerPoint slides and ask to use one of the half dozen laptops you see scattered around the room. Nice idea, but they're equipped only with CD-ROM drives. The audience is getting restless; a few people get up to leave. You keep hoping you'll wake up from this bad dream so that your great day can really start. Sorry; this is your day.

Ask any business speaker with a few years of experience, and you'll hear all these horror stories and no doubt a few more. People who've driven to the wrong conference center, hit themselves in the head with a microphone, tripped over wires, started with a sure-fire joke that generated nothing but cold stares, or been rendered speechless by tough questions. Hoping you'll be spared isn't an effective response. You must be prepared when—not if—something goes wrong.

If you assume something will go wrong at some point, you can make peace with the possibility and focus on backup planning. Experts suggest you make a list of every major problem you might encounter and imagine how you'll respond when these calamities strike you on the day of a big presentation. As much as possible, create a backup plan, such as calling ahead to reserve a second projector in the event yours gets lost in transit. You won't be able to put backup resources in place for every possible glitch, but by at least thinking through the possibilities, you can decide how you'll respond. When disaster does strike, you'll look like a polished pro instead of a befuddled novice.

CAREER APPLICATIONS

1. If you spy trouble ahead in your presentation, such as noticing that your laptop battery is about to go dead or that you somehow have an old copy of the presentation file, should you tell your audience what's wrong? Or should you try to "wing it"? Explain your answer.
2. What steps can you take to make absolutely sure that you have a usable backup copy of your electronic presentation slides outside your office? Why is this important?

Your posture is also important in projecting more confidence. Stand tall, with your weight on both feet and your shoulders back. Avoid gripping the lectern or other physical structure. In fact, you might step out from behind the lectern to help your audience feel more comfortable with you and to express your own comfort and confidence in what you're saying. Use your hands to emphasize your remarks with appropriate gestures. Meanwhile, vary your facial expressions to make the message more dynamic.

Finally, think about the sound of your voice. Studies indicate that people who speak with lower vocal tones at a slightly faster than average rate are perceived as being more credible.[12] Speak in a normal, conversational tone but with enough volume for everyone to hear you. Try to sound poised and confident, varying your pitch and speaking rate to add emphasis. Don't ramble. Speak clearly and crisply, articulating all the syllables, and sound enthusiastic about what you're saying. Use silence instead of meaningless filler words such as *um, you know, okay,* and *like.* Silence adds dramatic punch and gives the audience time to think about your message. That slight pause might feel like it lasts an hour when you're in the spotlight, but it'll seem natural to your audience.

Handling Questions Responsively

The question-and-answer period is one of the most important parts of an oral presentation. Questions give you a chance to obtain important information, to emphasize your main idea and supporting points, and to build enthusiasm for your point of view. Without questions, you might just as well write a report. If you don't expect to interact with the audience, you're wasting the chief advantage of an oral format. In addition to giving you

Don't leave the question-and-answer period to chance: anticipate likely questions and think through your answers.

During meetings at Tellme.com, polished speakers use question-and-answer sessions to reinforce their ideas and credibility.

valuable feedback, this period gives you a chance to emphasize the points you made earlier, work in any material that didn't fit into the formal presentation, and try to identify and overcome audience resistance.

Many speakers do well delivering their oral presentation only to falter during the question-and-answer period. But since you've already spent time anticipating the questions that audience members might ask, you are ready with answers. Some experts recommend that you hold back some dramatic statistics as ammunition for the question-and-answer session.[13] If your message is unpopular, you should also be prepared for hostile questions. Treat them as legitimate requests for information. Maintaining your professionalism will improve your credibility.

Focus on the Questioner

When someone poses a question, focus your attention on that individual. Pay attention to the questioner's body language and facial expression to help determine what the person really means. Nod your head to acknowledge the question; then repeat it aloud to confirm your understanding and to ensure that the entire audience has heard it. If the question is vague or confusing, ask for clarification; then give a simple, direct answer. If you're asked to choose between two alternatives, don't feel you must do so. Offer your own choice instead, if it makes more sense.[14]

Respond Appropriately

This might sound like obvious advice, but be sure to answer the question you're asked. Don't sidestep it, ignore it, laugh it off, or get so caught up in the situation that you forget to respond. Gauge the length of your response to the importance of the question, the status of the questioner, and the time you have left. If giving an adequate answer would take too long, simply say, "I'm sorry, we don't have time to get into that issue right now, but if you'll see me after the presentation, I'll be happy to discuss it with you." If you don't know the answer, don't pretend that you do. Instead, say something like "I don't have those figures. I'll get them for you as quickly as possible." In some cases, you won't have time to answer every question that is asked; if possible, arrange another means to give people the information they need.

Maintain Control

Maintaining control during the question-and-answer session can be a challenge, particularly if any audience members outrank you in the corporate hierarchy.

Unlike the delivery phase of your presentation, you have less control over the proceedings during the question and answer session. However, you can help maintain control during this period by establishing some ground rules up front. Before you begin, announce a time limit or a question limit per person. Establishing limits will protect you from getting into a heated exchange with one member of the audience and from allowing one or two people to monopolize the question period. Give as many audience members as possible a chance to participate by calling on people from different parts of the room. If the same person keeps angling for attention, restate the question limit or say something like "Several other people have questions; I'll get back to you if time permits."

If audience members try to turn a question into an opportunity to make their own mini-presentations, remember that's it's up to you to stay in control. You might ask people to identify themselves before they ask questions. People are more likely to behave themselves when everyone present knows their name.[15] You might admit that you and the questioner have differing opinions and, before calling on someone else, offer to get back to the questioner once you've done more research. Or you might simply respond with a brief answer, avoiding a lengthy debate or additional questions.[16] Finally, you might thank the person for the comments and then remind everyone that you were looking for specific questions.

Survive the Hot Seat

If a question ever puts you on the hot seat, respond honestly, but remember to keep your cool. Look the person in the eye, answer the question as well as you can, and try not to show your feelings. Whatever the situation, avoid getting into a heated argument. Even if you win, you'll leave the audience feeling both uncomfortable about the situation and your ability to handle conflict. Recognize that questioners who challenge your ideas, logic, or facts may just be trying to push you into overreacting. Defuse hostility by paraphrasing the question and asking the questioner to confirm that you've understood it correctly. Break long, complicated questions into parts that you can answer simply. State your response accurately and factually; then move on to the next question. Avoid postures or gestures that might seem antagonistic. Maintain a businesslike tone of voice and a pleasant expression.[17] Don't indulge in put-downs—they may backfire and make the audience more sympathetic to the questioner.

If you ever face hostile questions, don't duck; respond honestly and directly while keeping your cool.

Encourage Questions

Although exactly the opposite of a noisy, confrontational audience, listeners who are deadly quiet can be just as uncomfortable. If there's a chance your audience will be too timid or too hostile to ask questions, consider arranging a few questions ahead of time with a cooperative member of the audience. If a friend or the meeting organizer gets the ball rolling, other people in the audience will probably join in. You might ask a question yourself: "Would you like to know more about . . ." If someone in the audience answers, act as if the question came from that person in the first place. When all else fails, say something like "I know from experience that most questions are asked after the question period. So I'll be around afterward to talk."[18]

Conclude Your Presentation

When the time allotted for your presentation is up, call a halt to the question-and-answer session, even if more people want to talk. Prepare the audience for the end by saying, "Our time is almost up. Let's have one more question." After you've made your reply, summarize the main idea of the presentation and thank people for their attention. Conclude the way you opened: by looking around the room and making eye contact. Then gather your notes and leave the podium, maintaining the same confident demeanor you've had from the beginning.

No matter how the presentation has gone, conclude in a strong, confident manner.

For a reminder of the steps to take in developing an oral presentation, refer to "Checklist: Developing Oral Presentations."

CHECKLIST: Developing Oral Presentations

A. PLAN YOUR ORAL PRESENTATION

- Analyze the situation by defining your purpose and developing an audience profile.
- Select the right medium.
- Organize your presentation by defining the main idea, limiting the scope, choosing your approach, and preparing your outline.

B. WRITE YOUR ORAL PRESENTATION

- Adapt to your audience by tailoring your style and language.
- Compose your presentation by preparing an introduction, body, and close.
- Use your introduction to arouse audience interest, build your credibility, and preview your message.
- Use the body to connect your ideas and hold your audience's attention.
- Use the close to restate your main points and describe the next steps.

C. COMPLETE YOUR ORAL PRESENTATION

- Master the art of delivery by choosing a delivery method, knowing your material, and practicing your delivery.
- Check the location and equipment in advance.
- Determine whether you should use an interpreter.
- Overcome anxiety by preparing thoroughly.
- Handle questions responsively.

COMMUNICATION CHALLENGES AT FITCH

Pacific Theaters, a Southern California movie-theater operator, is preparing to launch a new chain called ArcLight Cinemas (www.arclight.com). The company wants to present ArcLight as a more enjoyable, upscale move-going experience, something clearly differentiated from the run-of-the mill theaters across the country. Yesterday, Fitch's Eric Ashworth met with Pacific Theaters' management to discuss the possibility of creating a compelling image for ArcLight. Today, he selected you and three others to form the account team and asked that the group start developing ideas. From his meeting notes, it's clear the client envisions a typical presentation about logos, marketing slogans, and color schemes—the usual stuff in a traditional agency pitch. Not the Fitch way, for sure.

Individual Challenge: Two weeks have passed and, true to the Fitch mentality, you and your teammates have developed a strong vision for ArcLight. Your concept centers on the notion of recapturing the old-time glamour and excitement of going to the movies—back when going to the movies was a special event. Now it's time to outline your sales presentation, from introduction to body to close. How will you grab and hold the audience's attention? How can you make them excited and inspire the big "A-ha!" that Fitch aims for? Prepare a one-page outline.

Team Challenge: In a small group, brainstorm ways to describe the glamour of old-time Hollywood to younger audiences who may have grown up on teen comedies and horror movies. Assume you're going to speak to a group of young managers at Pacific Theaters and outline a short presentation that would help them get a sense of what Hollywood was like in the days of Clark Gable, Vivien Leigh, Rita Hayworth, and Cary Grant. Provide your instructor with an outline and a brief description of the visuals aids you might use.

SUMMARY OF LEARNING OBJECTIVES

1 **Explain the importance of oral presentations in your career success.** Oral presentations give the opportunity to use all of your communication skills, from research to writing to speaking. Presentations also demonstrate your ability to think quickly, to adapt to challenging situations, and to handle touchy questions and complex issues. They also let your personality shine through in ways that aren't always possible in written media.

2 **Explain how to adapt the three-step writing process to oral presentations.** Although you rarely want to write out your presentation word for the word, the three-step writing process is easy to adapt to oral presentations. The steps you take in planning oral presentations are generally the same as with any other business message: (1) analyzing the situation (be sure to gauge the audience's likely emotional state and their comfort level with your language), (2) gathering information, (3) selecting the right medium (electronic media play an increasing role in business presentations today), and (4) organizing the information (you may want to create a speaking outline in addition to your planning outline). To write your presentation, you don't actually "write" your presentation in most cases, but rather plan your word and phrase choices so you can speak in a way that delivers planned messages in a spontaneous way. This step also includes creating whatever visual support materials you plan to use. And, of course, adapting to your audience is every bit as important with oral messages as with written messages. Completing the third step in the three-step process is where oral presentations differ the most from written messages. You still want to revise carefully and proofread all handouts and visual materials to ensure clarity and accuracy. You also need to practice and perfect your delivery, prepare to speak by verifying facilities and equipment (and working with an interpreter if needed), take steps to manage anxiety, and plan your approach to handling questions.

3 **Identify the two primary reasons why limiting your scope is especially important for oral presentations.** Limiting the scope of presentations is crucial because (1) you generally have a fixed amount of time in which to speak, so you need to fit your material to the time allotted, and (2) if you don't align your content with your audience's needs and expectations, they may not understand it or bother to listen to it.

4 **Distinguish a planning outline from a speaking outline and explain the purpose of each.** A planning outline identifies and organizes the content of your presentation, whereas a speaking outline emphasizes the cues and reminders you'll use to present your material.

5 **Discuss the three functions of an effective introduction.** An effective introduction arouses audience interest in your topic, builds your credibility, and offers your audience a preview of your message. If your topic doesn't naturally interest the audience, you need to work extra hard in your introduction (and throughout the presentation) to relate the material to the audience in as personal a manner as possible. Speaker credibility is a crucial aspect of any presentation because audiences are more likely to pay attention to messages coming from someone they perceive to be an expert in the subject area. If you can't demonstrate credibility in your subject area, you "borrow" credibility from recognized experts by incorporating their insights and opinions into your presentation (giving proper credit, of course). Previewing your message in the introduction helps the audience recognize the importance of your material and gives them a chance to prepare for it by understanding how you plan to present it.

6 **Identify four ways to keep your audience's attention during your presentation.** To hold your audience's attention after you've captured it with a compelling introduction, continue to relate your subject to your audience's needs, anticipate audience questions and prepare effective responses, use clear and vivid language, and relate your subject to ideas the audience is already familiar and comfortable with.

7 **Describe the techniques you can use to appear more confident in front of an audience.** To overcome anxiety and feel more confident as a speaker, prepare more material than necessary so that the extra knowledge will reduce your nervousness. Rehearse your oral presentation to become as familiar as possible with your topic. Think positively and see yourself as a polished professional. Right before speaking, visualize your success and tell yourself you're ready. Take a few deep breaths and remember that your audience actually wants you to succeed. Be ready by memorizing your first sentence. Be comfortable by sipping some water. If you feel you're losing your audience, don't panic; instead, pull them back by asking for their opinions or questions and involving them in the action. Keep going no matter what, because you'll get better as you go.

Test Your Knowledge

1. What issues do you need to consider when planning an oral presentation?
2. What are the two most common purposes for giving oral presentations?
3. Why do you have to limit your scope when planning a presentation?
4. Why is simplicity of organization important in oral communication?
5. How can outlines help you with the writing and delivery of an oral presentation?
6. What three goals should you accomplish during the introduction of an oral presentation?
7. How can you get and keep the audience's attention?
8. How does the delivery method of impromptu speaking differ from the delivery method of speaking from notes?
9. As a speaker, what nonverbal signals can you send to appear more confident?
10. What can speakers do to maintain control during the question-and-answer period of a presentation?

Apply Your Knowledge

1. Would you rather (a) deliver an oral presentation to an outside audience, (b) be interviewed for a news story, or (c) make a presentation to a departmental meeting? Why? How do the communication skills differ among those situations? Explain.
2. How might the audience's attitude affect the amount of audience interaction during or after a presentation? Explain your answer.
3. If you were giving an oral presentation on the performance of a company product, what three attention-getters might you use to enliven your speech?
4. From the speaker's perspective, what are the advantages and disadvantages of responding to questions from the audience throughout an oral presentation, rather than just afterward? From the listener's perspective, which approach would you prefer? Why?
5. **Ethical Choices** Business speakers don't always have the luxury of complete confidence in the material they have to present. For instance, sales forecasts for new products are notoriously difficult to make because they depend on so many factors in the marketplace. If you were presenting a forecast that was the best available answer but not one that you had much confidence in, should you still follow this chapter's guidelines for appearing confident in front of your audience? Explain your answer.

Practice Your Knowledge

Document for Analysis

Pick a speech from *Vital Speeches of the Day*, a publication containing recent speeches on timely and topical subjects. As an alternative, select a speech from an online source such as the speech archives of NASA, www.nasa.gov, or AT&T, www.att.com (look under Investor Relations). Examine both the introduction and the close; then analyze how these two sections work together to emphasize the main idea. Does the speaker want the audience to take any specific actions? To change any particular beliefs or feelings?

Next, identify the transitional sentences or phrases that clarify the speech's structure for the listener, especially those that help the speaker shift between supporting points. Using these transitions as clues, list the main message and supporting points; then indicate how each transitional phrase links the current supporting point to the succeeding one. Finally, prepare a brief (two- to three-minute) oral presentation summarizing your analysis for your class.

Exercises

For live links to all websites discussed in this chapter, visit this text's website at www.prenhall.com/bovee. Just log on, select Chapter 15, and click on "Featured Websites." Locate the page or the URL related to the material in the text.

15.1 Internet For many years, Toastmasters has been dedicated to helping its members give speeches. Instruction, good speakers as models, and practice sessions aim to teach members to convey information in lively and informative ways. Visit the Toastmasters website at www.toastmasters.org, and review the organization's vision and mission statements. Evaluate the information and outline a three-minute presentation to your class, telling why Toastmasters would or would not help you and your classmates write and deliver an effective speech.

15.2 Mastering Delivery: Analysis Attend a presentation at your school or in your town, or watch a speech on television. Categorize the speech as one that motivates or entertains, one that informs or analyzes, or one that persuades or urges collaboration. Then compare the speaker's delivery with this chapter's "Checklist: Developing Oral Presentations" on page 487. Write a two-page report analyzing the speaker's performance and suggesting improvements.

15.3 Mastering Delivery: Nonverbal Signals Observe and analyze the delivery of a speaker in a school, work, or other setting. What type of delivery did the speaker use? Was this delivery appropriate for the occasion? What nonverbal signals did the speaker use to emphasize key points? Were these signals effective? Which nonverbal signals would you suggest to further enhance the delivery of this oral presentation—and why?

15.4 Ethical Choices Think again about the oral presentation you observed and analyzed in 15.3. How could the speaker have used nonverbal signals to unethically manipulate the audience's attitudes or actions?

15.5 Teamwork You've been asked to give an informative 10-minute presentation on vacation opportunities in your home state. Draft your introduction, which should last no more than 2 minutes. Then pair off with a classmate and analyze each other's introductions. How well do these two introductions arouse the audience's interest, build credibility, and preview the presentation? Suggest how these introductions might be improved.

15.6 Completing Oral Presentations: Self-Assessment How good are you at planning, writing, and delivering oral presentations? Rate yourself on each of the following elements of the oral presentation process. Then examine your ratings to identify where you are strongest and where you can improve, using the tips in this chapter.

Element of Presentation Process	Always	Frequently	Occasionally	Never
1. I start by defining my purpose.	_____	_____	_____	_____
2. I analyze my audience before writing an oral presentation.	_____	_____	_____	_____
3. I match my presentation length to the allotted time.	_____	_____	_____	_____
4. I begin my oral presentations with an attention-getting introduction.	_____	_____	_____	_____
5. I look for ways to build credibility as a speaker.	_____	_____	_____	_____
6. I cover only a few main points in the body of my presentation.	_____	_____	_____	_____
7. I use transitions to help listeners follow my ideas.	_____	_____	_____	_____
8. I review main points and describe next steps in the close.	_____	_____	_____	_____
9. I practice my presentation beforehand.	_____	_____	_____	_____
10. I prepare in advance for questions and objections.	_____	_____	_____	_____
11. I conclude oral presentations by summarizing my main idea.	_____	_____	_____	_____

Expand Your Knowledge

For live links to the websites that follow, go to www.prenhall.com/bovee. When you log on, select Chapter 15, then select "Featured Websites," click on the URL of the website you wish to visit, and review the website to complete these exercises.

Exploring the Best of the Web

Speak with Flair

www.ukans.edu/cwis/units/coms2/vpa/vpa.htm

The Virtual Presentation Assistant offers abundant resources with related links to other websites that contain useful articles, reviews, or supplemental materials for planning presentations. You can also connect to popular media and library pages with worldwide research information. You'll find examples of presentation types, suggestions for selecting and focusing your topic, tips on audience analysis, delivery, use of visual aids, and various other guidelines to help you prepare and deliver an effective oral presentation. Check out this site, then answer the following questions:

1. Suppose you have been asked to prepare an oral presentation on a business issue currently in the news. How could you use what you've discovered at the VPA site to help you select a topic? How could you use this site to find additional information or supplementary materials related to your topic?
2. According to this website, what factors should you consider when analyzing your audience?
3. What topics or information will entice you to return to this site or its links? (If you don't find the Virtual Presentation Assistant useful, explain why.)

Exploring the Web on Your Own

Review these chapter-related websites on your own to enhance your oral presentation skills and knowledge.

1. Visit Abraham Lincoln Online, http://showcase.netins.net/web/creative/Lincoln, to retrieve some of President Lincoln's classic speeches. Not only can you see examples of great writing, but you can also see how speechwriting has changed in the past century and a half.
2. Visit the Advanced Public Speaking Institute, at www.public-speaking.org, and learn how to be the best public speaker you can be.
3. Learn to prepare, write, and polish your oral presentations at SpeechTips.com, www.speechtips.com.

Learn Interactively

Interactive Study Guide

Go to the Companion Website at www.prenhall.com/bovee. For Chapter 15, take advantage of the interactive "Study Guide" to test your knowledge of the chapter. Get instant feedback on whether you need additional studying.

Also, visit this site's "Study Hall," where you'll find an abundance of valuable resources that will help you succeed in this course.

Peak Performance Grammar and Mechanics

To improve your skill with vocabulary, visit www.prenhall.com/onekey, click "Peak Performance Grammar and Mechanics," click "Vocabulary," then click "Vocabulary I." Take the Pretest to determine whether you have any weak areas. Then review those areas in the Refresher Course. Take the Follow-Up Test to check your grasp of frequently confused words.

chapter 16

Enhancing Presentations with Slides and Transparencies

LEARNING OBJECTIVES

After studying this chapter, you will be able to

1. Explain how visuals enhance oral presentations, and list several popular types of visuals
2. Describe the steps needed to write readable content for slides
3. Explain the importance of design consistency in electronic slides and other visuals
4. Explain the use of hyperlinks in electronic presentations
5. Discuss the steps you can take to develop a clear structure for your presentation to make sure your audience never gets lost or confused
6. List the six questions you should ask yourself to determine whether or not you're ready to give your presentation
7. Highlight seven major issues to consider when you're preparing to give a presentation online

COMMUNICATION CLOSE-UP AT HEWLETT-PACKARD

www.hp.com

Presentations make everyone nervous, but imagine how nervous you might be if you were making a presentation with millions, even billions, of dollars on the line. That situation is business as usual for Dan Talbott, a senior leader in Hewlett-Packard's (HP's) computer services organization, a unit that manages computer operations for other companies. After HP's controversial acquisition of Compaq, it was desperate for a major contract that would highlight the capabilities of both firms.

Against that backdrop, Talbott was asked to pursue a huge deal with Procter & Gamble (P&G), the consumer-products giant that markets over 300 brands, including Charmin, Crest, and Tide. P&G was looking to lower its costs by hiring someone outside its organization to take over the operation of its global computer systems. HP was facing two tough competitors for the contract, Electronic Data Systems and IBM. Conditions got even tougher when P&G published a 10,000-page request for proposals (RFP) and limited the response time to just 56 days (nine months is typical on projects of this magnitude).

Talbott's team moved into an HP office near P&G's Cincinnati headquarters, tapped the brainpower of 80 colleagues from around the world, and began developing the series of presentations that were specified in the RFP. Knowing that every interaction with P&G could nudge HP

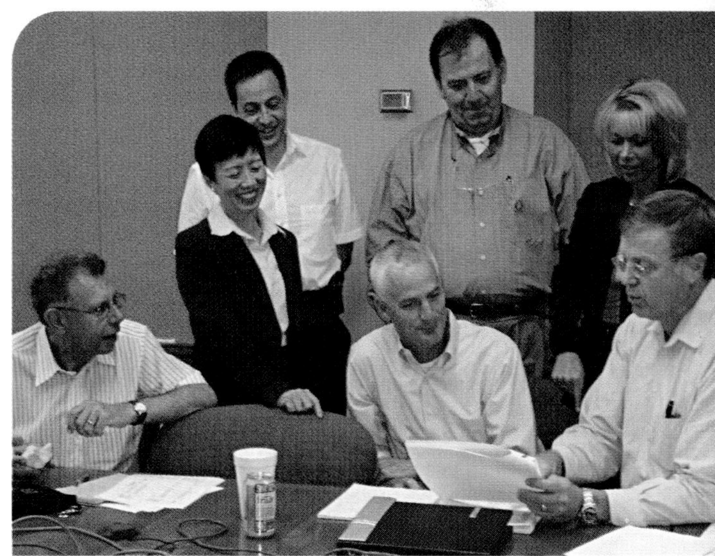

Dan Talbott (far right) led a team whose presentation skills helped land a multimillion-dollar contract for Hewlett-Packard.

closer to its goal, Talbott told the group, "Our job is to ensure that every conversation is a win." However, HP's initial presentation was shaky, so Talbott asked the presenters to print their PowerPoint slides—over 200 in all—and post them on the walls of a conference room. He conducted a slide-by-slide critique, questioning every slide that lacked a clear message. The team revised and kept revising until the presentation was audience centered and crystal clear from beginning to end.

That rigorous review produced a string of successful presentations that ultimately helped HP win a 10-year contract worth $3 billion. You may never be on stage with $3 billion at stake, but your own presentation visuals will surely benefit from the same degree of care.[1]

1 LEARNING OBJECTIVE

Explain how visuals enhance oral presentations, and list several popular types of visuals

PLANNING YOUR PRESENTATION VISUALS

Your presentations may never be as grand and complex as Dan Talbott's, but chances are that yours will often involve some degree of visual support. By following the three-step development process in Chapter 15, you'll have a well-designed, audience-focused message. The techniques in this chapter will help you enhance the delivery of that message with creative and effective visuals.

Thoughtfully designed visuals create interest, illustrate complex points in your message, add variety, and help the audience absorb and remember information.

Visual aids can improve the quality and impact of your oral presentation by creating interest, illustrating points that are difficult to explain in words alone, adding variety, and increasing the audience's ability to absorb and remember information. Behavioral research has shown that visual aids can improve learning by up to 400 percent because humans can process visuals 60,000 times faster than text.[2]

As a speaker, you'll find that visual aids can help you remember the details of the message (no small feat in a lengthy presentation) and improve your professional image: Speakers who use presentation visuals generally appear better prepared and more knowledgeable than speakers who do not.

An effective electronic presentation can significantly boost the retention level of audience members.

Selecting the Type of Visuals to Use

You can select from a variety of visual aids to enhance oral presentations, each with unique advantages and disadvantages:

- **Overhead transparencies.** Overhead transparencies have been the workhorses of business presentations for decades (you've no doubt seen a few thousand during your school years as well). Some business professionals still prefer them to electronic presentations. You can create overheads using software such as Microsoft PowerPoint, other graphics programs, your word processor, a typewriter, or even a pen. Moreover, simple transparencies don't require the latest computer or projection equipment. You can write on them during a presentation, and they never crash on you—as computers have been known to do. On the downside, they're limited to static displays, they're impossible to edit once you've printed them, and you or a partner are forced to stand next to the projector throughout your entire presentation.
- **Electronic presentations.** Easy-to-use software and affordable hardware have made electronic presentations the visual aid of choice in most business situations today. An **electronic presentation** or *slide show* consists of a series of **electronic slides** composed using popular computer software such as Microsoft PowerPoint or Sun StarOffice. To display an electronic presentation, you simply connect your computer to a portable projector (some are now small enough to carry around in a briefcase) or a built-in unit that's part of a multimedia system in a conference room. Electronic presentations have numerous advantages: They are easy to edit and update (right up to the last second before your presentation starts); you can add sound, photos, video, and animation; they can be incorporated into online meetings, webcasts, and *webinars* (a common term for web-based seminars); and you can record self-running presentations for trade shows, websites, and other uses. The primary disadvantages are the cost of equipment, the potential complexity involved in creating multimedia presentations, and the risk, however slight these days, that your hardware or software won't cooperate when it's show time.

In most businesses, electronic presentations are now the presentation technology of choice, although they're certainly not the only option.

Plus, the extreme flexibility of electronic presentations makes it that much easier for inexperienced users to create poorly designed slides full of distracting special effects.

- **Chalkboards and whiteboards.** Chalkboards and whiteboards are effective tools for recording points made during small-group sessions. Because these visual aids are produced on the spot, they are great for the flexible, spontaneous nature of workshops and brainstorming sessions. New electronic whiteboards can overcome the biggest drawback of their mechanical counterparts: capturing the information written on them. After you and your team brainstorm a complex product design or a long list of marketing ideas, you simply hit a button to print a hardcopy or distribute an electronic version via e-mail.
- **Flip charts.** Large sheets of paper attached at the top like a tablet can be propped on an easel so that you can flip the pages as you speak, with each chart illustrating or clarifying a point. You might have a few lines from your outline on one, a graph or diagram on another, and so on. By using felt-tip markers of various colors, you can also record ideas generated during a discussion. Flip charts are also great for recording comments and questions during your presentation or for creating a "group memory" during brainstorming sessions, keeping track of all the ideas the team generates. Flip charts are about as low tech as you can get, but they're inexpensive and 100 percent dependable.
- **Other visual aids.** Be creative when choosing visuals to support your presentation. A videotape of a focus group talking about your company can have a lot more impact than a series of slides that summarize what they said. In technical or scientific presentations, a sample of a product or type of material lets your audience experience your subject directly. Designers and architects use mockups and models to help people envision what a final creation will look like.

Sometimes the best strategy is to use a combination of visuals, such as electronic slides to present your ideas to the audience and a flip chart to record their feedback. This chapter focuses on electronic presentations, the mainstay of business presentations today, although most of these design tips apply to overhead transparencies as well.

Team members generally plan, write, and edit group oral presentations together.

Enhancing Your Presentations with Effective Visuals

Think through your presentation outline carefully before designing your visuals.

Once you've decided on the form your visuals will take, think through your presentation plan carefully before you start creating anything. Visuals are powerful devices, and that power can just as easily harm your efforts as help. Above all, remember that visuals support your spoken message; they should never replace it or overshadow it. Don't have your audience leaving the room impressed with your multimedia show but confused about what you said. In addition, don't expect your visuals to rescue a weak message. A discerning audience—the sort of people who can influence the direction of your career—are not easily fooled by visual razzle-dazzle. If your analysis is shaky or your conclusions suspect, an over-the-top visual production won't help your presentation succeed.

As you approach each visual, whether it's a PowerPoint slide, a physical model, or something else, ask yourself how it will help your audience understand and appreciate your message. This simple test alone can eliminate that scourge of the modern conference room—PowerPoint presentations festooned with flying objects, dancing text, swirling transitions, meaningless sound effects, and other electronic distractions. Think through the words you'll use while displaying each visual and make sure your words and visuals will work in harmony. Also take the time to double-check any cultural assumptions that might be inappropriate. Are you highlighting with a color that has negative emotional connotations in your audience's culture? Are you too playful for a serious audience? Too serious for an audience that values creativity?

Accuracy and simplicity are keys to effective visuals.

When it comes time to make design choices, from selecting fonts to deciding whether or not to include a photo, let accuracy and simplicity guide you. Doing so has several advantages. First, it takes less time to create simple materials, and time is the most precious commodity in today's business environment. Second, simple visuals reduce the chances of distraction and misinterpretation. Third, the more "bells and whistles" you have in your presentation, the more likely it is that something will go wrong. That funny video clip you found on the Internet might not load when you click on it, or in the heat of the moment, you might forget how to talk the audience through the impressively complicated animation sequence around which you built your entire presentation.

Finally, use your time wisely. Presentation software in particular has an uncanny knack for eating up hours and hours of time you probably don't have. You can spend days trying to fine-tune and adjust a single presentation, whether you're trying to change a simple color block to a multicolor blend, add drop shadows behind all your photographs, or incorporate one of the other endless possibilities from today's software. Based on your audience and situation, decide up front how much sophistication is good enough, then stop when you get there. Use the time you'll save to rehearse your presentation and get a good night's sleep before the big day.

CREATING EFFECTIVE SLIDES

Creating effective slides can be a challenge because you need both your rational and creative instincts. You want to create presentations that are visually attractive but without compromising your message. To maintain audience focus, get into the habit of starting with the text and making sure that your content is easy to read and easy to understand before you move on to graphic elements, animation, or special effects.

Develop the textual part of your message first, so that special effects and other visuals don't become the focus of your presentation.

If you start with special effects or eye-catching multimedia, these aspects are likely to become the focus of your slides, rather than the message. So get your text in place first, then think about graphics. This approach can rescue you from schedule nightmares, too; if you run out of time, at least you'll have the message in place, even if you didn't have time to dress it up with as many graphic elements as you had planned.

2 LEARNING OBJECTIVE

Describe the steps needed to write readable content for slides

Writing Readable Content

One of the biggest mistakes you can make when writing text visuals is to overload them with too much information. People do so for two reasons: (1) They believe that every word or concept they wish to convey should be illustrated by a slide, and (2) they use their slides as speaker's notes—focusing on their own needs instead of the needs of their audience. Text slides are not intended to display your entire script or highlight each point you make.[3]

Communication Solution

When HP's first presentation to Procter & Gamble was not as successful as he had hoped, Dan Talbott reviewed and edited every single one of more than 200 slides to make sure each one carried a clear, audience-focused message.

Effective text slides supplement your words. They help your audience follow the flow of ideas. They are simplified outlines of your presentation and are used to highlight key points, summarize and preview your message, signal major shifts in thought, illustrate concepts, or help create interest in your oral message. They are not the presentation itself.

Packing slides with too much information is a common beginner's mistake; use slide text to emphasize key points, not to convey your entire message.

Slides with too much text, long sentences, or wordy bullets are difficult to read from a distance and difficult to understand. They confuse and distract the audience, and they diminish your credibility as a speaker.[4] If you overload your slides with content, members of the audience will assume that you are afraid to look at them and interact with them.

When writing content for text slides, keep your message short and simple:

- Limit each slide to one thought, concept, or idea.
- Limit the content to about 40 words—with no more than six lines of text containing about six or seven words per line.
- Write short bulleted phrases rather than long sentences or paragraph-length blocks of text.
- Phrase list items in parallel grammatical form to facilitate quick reading.

FIGURE 16.1 Writing Readable Content

What Is Supply-Chain Management?

Developing long-term partnerships among channel members working together to create a distribution system that reduces inefficiencies, costs, and redundancies while creating a competitive advantage and satisfying customers

Figure 16.1a—Inappropriate paragraph style

What Is Supply-Chain Management?

- Partnering with channel members
- Reducing channel inefficiencies
- Creating a competitive advantage
- Satisfying customers

Figure 16.1b—Appropriate bulleted phrases

The definition provided in Figure 16.1a was taken from a persuasive report written by the speaker. The paragraph style is inappropriate for slides and difficult to read. Figure 16.1b restates the definition in short phrases that highlight the key point of the definition. The speaker will explain these points while showing the slide.

Figure 16.1c—Inappropriate wordy bullets

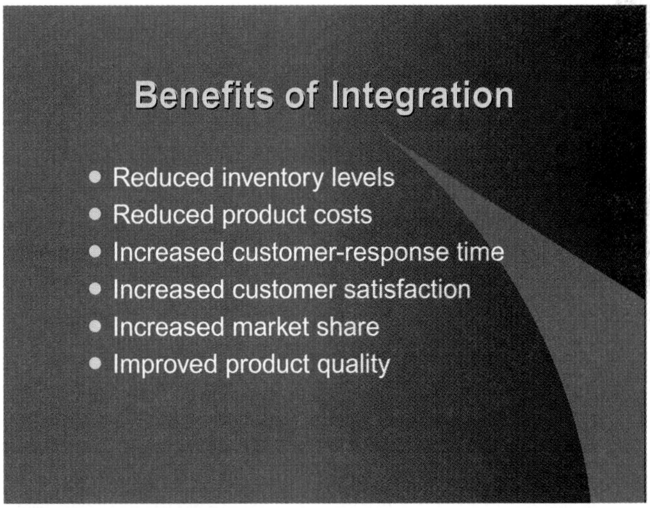

Benefits of Integration

- Reduced inventory levels
- Reduced product costs
- Increased customer-response time
- Increased customer satisfaction
- Increased market share
- Improved product quality

Figure 16.1d—Appropriate concise bullets

Although Figure 16.1c falls within acceptable word-count guidelines, unnecessary words still make the slide difficult to read. Figure 16.1d is an improved version of Figure 16.1c: The sentences are converted to short, parallel phrases and the slide's title is condensed.

- Make your slides easy to read by using the active voice.
- Include short informative titles.

Figure 16.1 is a good example of text slides that have been revised according to these principles to make their content more readable.

Modifying Graphics for Slides

The old saying "A picture is worth a thousand words" is especially true when it comes to creating effective slides. Graphic visuals can be an effective way to clarify a concept, show a process, or highlight important information. They can help your audience absorb information in a short time, and they can increase their interest and retention.

FIGURE 16.2 Modifying Graphs for Slides

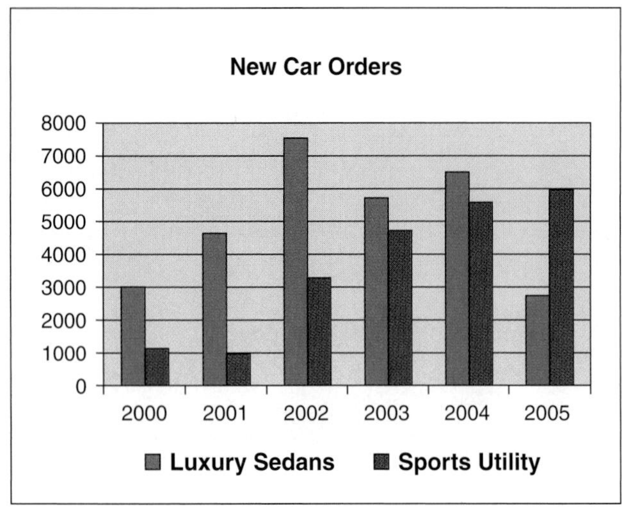

Figure 16.2a—Graph included in printed report

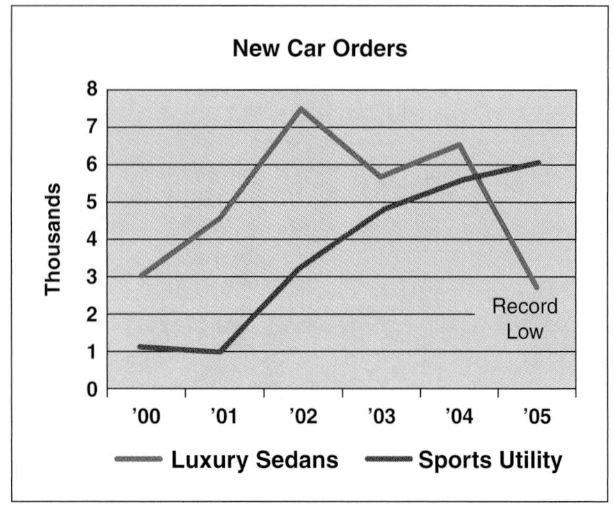

Figure 16.2b—Graph simplified for overhead

The graph shown in Figure 16.2a has too much detail for a presentation visual aid. It was copied from the 2005 annual sales report for Bressler Toyota car dealership, where it filled an entire page. Scaled down to fit a slide format, Figure 16.2a crams too much data into too little space. Figure 16.2b simplifies the graph for an electronic slide by shortening the numbers, adding a title to the Y axis, changing the format from bars to trend lines, and highlighting a key segment of the graph with the words "record low."

Many graphics that work quite well in printed form need to be simplified for use in presentations because they are too dense and too complicated to be easily viewed on screen.

The techniques you learned in Chapter 11 for creating effective charts, diagrams, maps, drawings, and tables for written documents still apply, but with an important caution: visuals for oral presentations need to be much simpler. If you're adapting visuals originally created for a written report, you will probably need to simplify them. Detailed visuals that might look fine on the printed page can be too dense and complicated for presentations. You can create effective presentation visuals by following these guidelines:

- **Reduce the detail.** Eliminate anything that is not absolutely essential to the message. Show only key numbers on a chart. If people need to see only trends, then show only the trend line and not the numbers. If necessary, break information into more than one graphic illustration.
- **Avoid repeating text.** Don't repeat the same word five times. Minimize repetition by including the word in a title, subtitle, label, or legend.
- **Shorten numbers.** On graphs, use 05 for the year 2005; round off numbers such as $12,500.72 to $12 or $12.5, and then label the axis to indicate thousands.
- **Limit data.** Try not to use more than five lines or five sets of bars on one chart.
- **Highlight key points.** Use arrows, boldface type, and color to direct your audience's eyes to the main point of a visual. Summarize the intent of the graphic in one clear phrase or sentence, such as "Earnings have increased by 15 percent."
- **Adjust the size and design.** Modify the size of the graphic to accommodate the size of a slide. Leave plenty of white space (area with no text or graphics) so that audience members can view and interpret content from a distance. Use colors that stand out from the slide's background, and choose a font that's clear and easy to read.

Note how the sales chart in Figure 16.2 was modified for use in a presentation. Not only were the numbers simplified, but the switch from a bar chart to a line chart makes trends easier to spot.

Simplicity is critical, but don't oversimplify to the extent that the audience doesn't get the important nuances or connections in your message.

However, you must guard against simplifying text or graphic information so much that your audience can't grasp the entire message. In recent years, a number of critics have begun to blame PowerPoint for encouraging the fracturing of, and the oversimplification of, complex ideas (see "Communication Miscues: Is PowerPoint Destroying Communication?"). If you have text or graphic information that is too complex to display on a slide, be sure to supplement your presentation with printed handouts that offer complete information—and connect your presentation to the information in the handouts.

Communication Miscues

Is PowerPoint Destroying Communication?

For a software program that started out as a way to help businesspeople create presentations more efficiently, Microsoft PowerPoint is taking a lot of criticism these days, for problems ranging from dull business meetings to even contributing to the tragic loss of the Space Shuttle *Columbia* and her crew. A closer look at the criticism might help you design more effective slides.

The criticism of PowerPoint focuses on the abbreviated text used in bulleted lists and on simplified charts. In February 2003, *Columbia* was destroyed while re-entering Earth's atmosphere; experts suspect the primary cause was a large piece of foam insulation that broke free and damaged a wing. A crucial piece of test information should have warned shuttle managers about the potential danger from large pieces of loose foam, but that information was buried in a bullet point at the bottom of a slide that was packed with technical details. Moreover, the bullet item was worded in such a way that the full impact of its warning might not have been immediately obvious.

Critics use this case as an example of how bulleted PowerPoint slides fracture complex ideas and allow speakers to dodge the responsibility of crafting complete, cohesive narratives—the kind of text that public speakers had to craft before they had the luxury of relying on PowerPoint slides. Well-known information theorist Edward Tufte is particularly critical of templates with multilevel bullet lists, which he says "usually weaken verbal and spatial reasoning, and almost always corrupt statistical analysis."

On the other side of the argument, Microsoft and its supporters contend that PowerPoint is simply a tool and that it's up to users to employ the tool appropriately and intelligently. The controversy continues, but one thing is clear: Using the wrong communication tool or using the right tool poorly can have tragic consequences.

CAREER APPLICATIONS

1. You've probably picked up on an important dilemma here: You've been told not to put full paragraphs on your slides because they're hard to read, but now you're being told not to break those paragraphs into bullets because doing so destroys the narrative cohesiveness of your message. Explain how to get around this dilemma.
2. Search online for the PowerPoint slide discussed in the *Columbia* case. Do you think the fault lies with PowerPoint? The people who created the slide? The people who viewed the slide? Explain your answer.

Selecting Design Elements

Once you've composed the text and graphic elements of your slides, you're ready to focus on their design. Nothing detracts from good content as much as poorly designed slides. However, by paying attention to a few design basics, you can transform a dull presentation into one that is not only dynamic but also readable.

Chapter 11 highlights five principles of effective design: continuity, contrast, emphasis, simplicity, and experience. Pay close attention to these principles as you select the color, background design, artwork, fonts, and typestyles for your slides. Then once you have selected the best design elements for your slides, stick with them throughout your presentation.

To design effective slides, you need to consider five principles of effective design: continuity, contrast, emphasis, simplicity, and audience experience.

Color

Color is a critical design element. It grabs the viewer's attention, emphasizes important ideas, creates contrast, and isolates slide elements. Color can make your slides more attractive, lively, and professional. It can also play a key role in the overall acceptance of your message. Research shows that color visuals can account for 60 percent of an audience's acceptance or rejection of an idea. Color can increase willingness to read by up to 80 percent, and it can enhance learning and improve retention by more than 75 percent.[5]

Your color choices can also stimulate various emotions, as Table 16.1 suggests. For instance, if you wish to excite your audience, add some warm colors such as red and orange to your slides. If you wish to achieve a more relaxed and receptive environment, blue would be a better choice.[6] Remember, color may have a different meaning in certain cultures (see Chapter 3). So if you are creating slides for international audiences, be sensitive to cultural differences.

Color is more than just decoration; colors have meanings themselves, based on both cultural experience and the relationships that you establish between the colors in your designs.

TABLE 16.1 Color and Emotion

COLOR	EMOTIONAL ASSOCIATIONS	BEST USE
	Peaceful, soothing, tranquil, cool, trusting	Background for electronic business presentations (usually dark blue); safe and conservative
	Neutral, innocent, pure, intelligent	Font color of choice for most electronic business presentations with a dark background
	Warm, bright, cheerful, enthusiastic	Text bullets and subheadings with a dark background
	Losses in business; passion, danger, action, pain	Promote action or stimulate audience; seldom used as a background
	Money, growth, assertiveness, prosperity, envy, relaxation	Highlight and accent color

When selecting color, limit your choices to a few complementary ones, and keep in mind that some colors work better together than others. Contrasting colors, for example, increase readability. So when selecting color for backgrounds, titles, and text, avoid choosing colors that are close in hue: yellow text on a white background, brown on green, blue on black, blue on purple, and so on.[7] Because most electronic presentations are shown in a dark room, use dark colors such as blue for the background, a midrange of brightness for illustrations, and light colors for text. If you are showing overhead transparencies in well-lit rooms, reverse the colors: Use light colors for the background and dark colors for text (see Figure 16.3). When changing colors from slide to slide, don't switch back and forth from very dark to very bright; the effect is jarring to the audience's eyes.[8]

Background Designs and Artwork

Electronic slides have two layers or levels of graphic design: the background and foreground. The background is the equivalent of paper in a printed report and normally stays the same from slide to slide. The foreground contains the unique text and graphic elements that make up each individual slide.

FIGURE 16.3 Adjusting Color for Lighting Differences

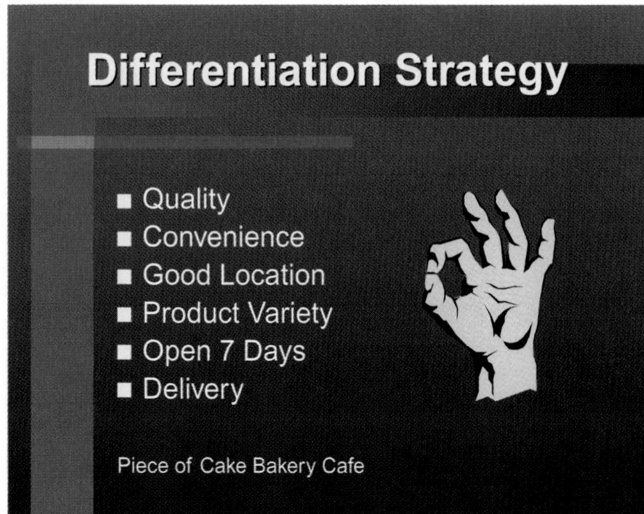

Figure 16.3a—Electronic slide for darkened rooms

Differentiation Strategy

▶ **Quality**
▶ **Convenience**
▶ **Good Location**
▶ **Product Variety**
▶ **Open 7 Days**
▶ **Delivery**

Piece of Cake Bakery Cafe

Figure 16.3b—Overhead transparency or electronic slide for well-lit rooms

Figure 16.3a uses a dark background with light text suitable for projecting in a dark room. Figure 16.3b reverses the colors, using a light background with dark text suitable for projecting in a well-lit room or for use as an overhead transparency.

Generally speaking, the less your background does, the better. Cluttered or flashy backgrounds tend to distract from your message. Look through the design templates next time you use PowerPoint; you'll find a selection of designs with backgrounds that range from subtle and visually "quiet" to extremely colorful, flashy, and too playful for business use. When in doubt, go for subtle and simple; no one will fault you for using a background that's "boring." (A boring foreground is another matter; more on that in a minute.) In fact, for many presentations, a single color in the background might be all you really need in terms of design.

Some of the predesigned backgrounds available in PowerPoint are cluttered with distracting imagery and multiple colors; a good background should stay in the background.

You may also want to add a company logo, the date, the presentation title, and a running slide number to help both you and the audience follow along. Just be sure to keep all these elements small and unobtrusive. Also, be sure to check whether your company has a standard design; many companies now have custom-designed PowerPoint templates that ensure consistency for all their presentations.

In the foreground, artwork can be either functional or decorative. Functional artwork includes photos, technical drawings, charts, and other visual elements containing information that's part of your message. In contrast, decorative artwork is there simply to enhance the look of your slides. Decorative artwork is the least important element of any slide, but it tends to cause the most trouble for anyone inexperienced in designing slides.

Artwork in the foreground of your slides can be either decorative or functional; use decorative artwork sparingly.

Clip art is probably the biggest troublemaker in decorative art because it is so easy to use and therefore so easy to misuse. You can find thousands and thousands of pieces of clip art, but few of them add any information value. Use them judiciously, or they'll add a cartoony feel to your slides. In general, keep clip art small—treat it like jewelry, not clothing. For title slides and other instances where you don't have a lot of information on a slide, you can sometimes get away with larger clip art (see Figure 16.4). In any event, don't use clip art just because you see it in a lot of other presentations; use it only if it helps make your presentation more appealing to your audience.

You don't need to use clip art on every one of your slides—or on any of your slides—if it doesn't make your presentation more effective and compelling.

Avoid the temptation to find a piece of clip art for every slide in your presentation. Unless you have access to a comprehensive, high-quality collection of artwork, chances are you won't find a good image for every single slide. At the very least, you'll spend a lot of time trying to fit images to slide content, and that time is probably better spent on other tasks.

Fonts and Type Styles

The selection of fonts available on computer today is immense. However, even though decorative fonts appear attractive, few of them project well on screen. That's because print on

Many of the fonts available on your computer are difficult to read on screen, so they aren't good choices for presentation slides.

FIGURE 16.4 Using Clip Art Effectively

Figure 16.4a

Figure 16.4b

Both of these slides use clip art effectively. In Figure 16.4a, placing the small target in the title adds visual interest without distracting from the busy text area of the slide. Figure 16.4b is a title slide, so using a similar piece of clip art emphasizes the theme of the presentation. The clip art can be larger in this case because there is no competing text.

FIGURE 16.5 Selecting Readable Fonts and Type Styles

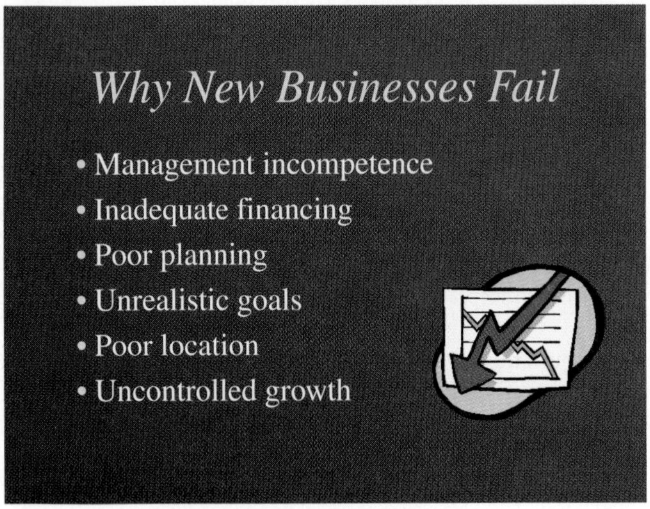

Why New Businesses Fail

- Management incompetence
- Inadequate financing
- Poor planning
- Unrealistic goals
- Poor location
- Uncontrolled growth

Figure 16.5a Times New Roman font

Why New Businesses Fail

- Management incompetence
- Inadequate financing
- Poor planning
- Unrealistic goals
- Poor location
- Uncontrolled growth

Figure 16.5b Arial font

Times New Roman is a standard font for many print documents; however, as Figure 16.5a demonstrates, the serifs at the end of each letter make is difficult to read on screen, and so does the italicized type. As Figure 16.5b shows, san serif fonts such as Arial are a better choice for slides; they are clearer and easier to read from a distance.

screen has a much lower resolution than print on a page. When selecting fonts and type styles for slides, follow these guidelines:

- Avoid script or decorative fonts.
- Limit your fonts to one or two per slide (if two fonts are used, reserve one for headings and the other for slide text).
- For thinner fonts, use boldface type so that letters won't look washed out.
- Avoid italicized type because it is difficult to read when projected.
- Use both uppercase and lowercase letters, with extra white space between lines of text.
- Be consistent in your use of fonts.

Keep in mind that bigger is not always better when it comes to type size. Large type can force text from one line to two and diminish the slide's white space. A good rule of thumb is to use between 24- and 36-point type for electronic presentations, reserving the larger size for titles and the smaller size for text items. Headings of the same level of importance should use the same font, type size, and color. Once you have selected your fonts and type styles, test them for readability by viewing sample slides from a distance (see Figure 16.5).

3 LEARNING OBJECTIVE

Explain the importance of design consistency in electronic slides and other visuals

Achieving Design Consistency

Audiences start to assign meaning to visual elements beginning with the first slide. For instance, if the first slide presents the most important information in bright yellow, 36-point Arial, your audience will expect the same font treatment for the most important information on the second and third slides as well, so when choosing fonts and point size, be consistent. Also be consistent in your layout. Make sure items that repeat on every slide, such as the date and the company logo, are in the same location on every slide. Otherwise, you'll distract your readers as they try to figure out the arrangement of each new slide.

Design inconsistencies confuse and annoy audiences; don't change colors and other design elements randomly throughout your presentation.

Fortunately, software designed specifically for presentations (as opposed to general graphics software) makes consistency easy to achieve. You simply create the slide master using the colors, fonts, and other design elements you've chosen, then these choices automatically show up on every slide in the presentation (see Figure 16.6). In addition, you can maintain consistency by choosing a predefined layout from those available in your software—which helps ensure that bulleted lists, charts, graphics, and other elements show up in predictable places on each slide. Something as simple as switching from a single column of bullet points to two columns can throw readers off as they try to figure out the meaning

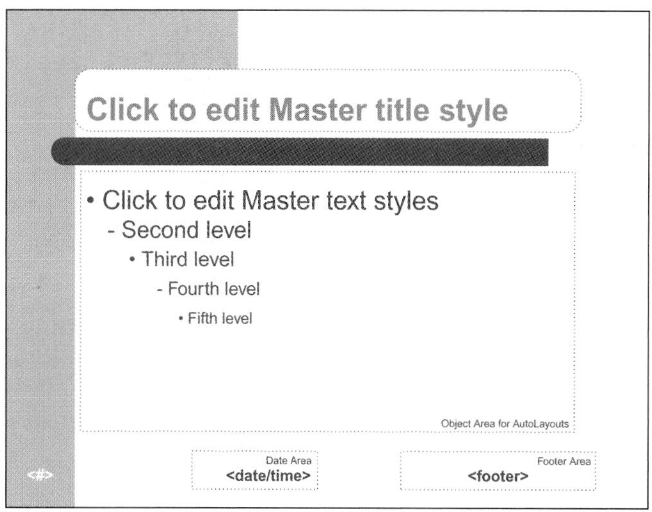

FIGURE 16.6
PowerPoint Slide Master

Whenever you want to change all the slides in a presentation in exactly the same way, use the slide master. Be sure to apply a design template before viewing the slide master so that you can see the fonts and color choices that will be applied to every slide (you can always override these selections on individual slides).

of the new arrangement. The less that readers have to work to interpret your slide designs, the more attention they can pay to your message.

Now, after all this advice about simplicity and consistency, a word of caution: Too much of a good thing can make your slides dull and lifeless. Particularly in a long presentation, one identical-looking slide after another can lull your audience to sleep. By adding some carefully planned animation and other special effects to your slides, you can keep your audience involved without distracting them from your message.

With some practice (as both a presenter and an audience member), you'll get a feel for how much consistency is too much—when a design goes from being cohesive to being bland and uninteresting.

Adding Animation and Special Effects

Today's presentation software offers a wide array of options for livening up your slides, including sound, animation, video clips, transition effects from one slide to the next, and hyperlinks to websites and other resources. The trick is to make sure that any effects you use support your message. You wouldn't slap a photo of a volcano into the middle of a text slide just because it looks exciting, and neither would you launch words across the screen or add amusing sound effects just because you find them entertaining. As always, think about the impact that all these effects will have on your audience and use only those special effects that support your message.[9]

You can group animation and special effects into four categories: functional animation, transitions and builds, hyperlinks, and multimedia. These capabilities are briefly discussed in the following sections, but to learn more about them, consult the Help menu in your software or some of the many online resources that offer advice on using PowerPoint. For a look at some of the amazing ways technology is extending the reach and capability of PowerPoint see "Connecting with Technology: Creating High-Octane Presentations."

Functional Animation

PowerPoint and other presentation packages now offer a mind-boggling set of tools for moving and changing things on the screen. You can have a block of text cartwheel in from outer space, change colors, change font and font size, spin around in circles, blink on and off, wave back and forth, crawl around the screen following an intricate, predefined path, then disappear one letter at a time like some sort of erasing typewriter. You *can* do all this, but *should* you?

You can animate just about everything in a PowerPoint presentation; resist the temptation to do so—make sure the animation has a purpose.

Just as static graphic elements can be either functional or decorative, so too can animated elements. For instance, having each bullet point fly in from the left side of the screen doesn't add any functional value to your communication effort. In contrast, a highlight arrow or color bar that moves around the screen to emphasize specific points in a technical diagram can be an effective use of animation and a welcome alternative to a laser pointer. You can control every aspect of the animation, so it's easy to coordinate the movement with the points you're making in your presentation. Controlled animation is also a great way to demonstrate sequences and procedures. For a training session on machinery repair, for example, you can show a schematic diagram of the machinery and walk your audience through each step of the

Connecting with Technology

Creating High-Octane Presentations

The board of directors wants to know how your division is doing: revenues, profits, employee satisfaction, customer satisfaction, and some half a dozen other metrics. You have all the data—for all 10,000 of your customers in 38 countries, which are supported by 58 offices staffed by nearly 2,000 employees. Data isn't the problem. The problem is time: the board has given you 10 minutes on this month's agenda. How can you possibly summarize so many important issues in so little time? And what if the directors ask questions about any one of the thousands of pieces of underlying data; how can you access all your supporting information quickly?

Despair not, brave presenter: a new generation of software tools can help. As one of the many examples now available, Xcelsius from Infommersion lets you create eye-catching, interactive visuals based on data contained in Excel spreadsheets. For instance, you can use it to create the "gas gauge" style graphs that are popular in executive dashboard displays or the interactive bar and pie charts that let you click through reams of data in seconds. And because the charts and graphs are "live" (always connected to updated data in your spreadsheet), you can continue to update the data over time without having to recreate your presentation visuals.

What about those globe-trotting executives who want to hear your presentation but can't attend the meeting or log in remotely? With a solution such as Anystream's Apreso, you can capture your entire presentation—audio, video, and presentation slides—and put it on a website for remote viewing at any time. Moreover, you and your team can build keyword-searchable archives of your brainstorming sessions and other meetings so that you can go back and find the great idea that somebody had that one time, which nobody can quite remember.

Xcelsius and Apreso are just two of the many tools that can amplify the impact of your presentations and make sure your message gets through. For the latest tools available, visit Microsoft's PowerPoint information online or search the web for "PowerPoint add-ins."

CAREER APPLICATIONS

1. Research one of the executive dashboard tools available for Excel or PowerPoint and explain how your college's placement office could use it to display information on the job market facing this year's graduates.
2. Discuss the potential risks of presenting complex data as simple graphic elements.

troubleshooting process, highlighting each step on screen as you address it verbally. Similarly, when addressing a group of data input clerks, you can not only show them where to type specific pieces of information in an online form but also liven up the presentation and emphasize your message by having each piece of data slide into the correct location on the form. Again, use animation in support of your message, not simply for animation's sake.

Transitions and Builds

Many of the slide transitions available in PowerPoint are distracting and can quickly begin to annoy audiences.

In addition to animating specific elements on your slides, PowerPoint also provides options for adding motion between slides. These **transitions** control how one slide replaces another on screen. Subtle transitions can ease your viewers' gaze from one slide to the next—such as having the current slide gently fade out before the next slide fades in. However, most of the transitions currently available (such as checkerboards, pinwheels, and spinning "newsflashes") are like miniature animated shows themselves and therefore too distracting. You can even add sound effects, from drumrolls to explosions. These exaggerated transition effects not only disrupt the flow of your presentation, but they can give your entire presentation an air of amateurism.

Carefully designed builds can be a great way to present information in easy-to-process pieces.

Similar to transitions, **builds** control the release of text, graphics, and other elements on individual slides. With builds you can make your bullet points appear one at a time rather than having all of them appear on a slide at once, which makes it difficult to focus on a single point. This controlled release of information helps draw the audience's attention to the point being discussed and prevents the audience from reading ahead.

As with transitions, stick with the subtle, basic options for builds. The point of a build, after all, is to release information in a controlled fashion, not to make the text dance around the screen. Another useful option is to change the color of bullet points as you discuss each one. For instance, if your primary text color is a strong blue, you might have the text in each bullet change to a light gray after you've finished talking about it. This adds some subtle activity to the screen and keeps the audience's attention focused on the current bullet point.

Once you've assigned builds to your slides, control the motion with a mouse or a remote control device, if you have one. For instance, click the mouse and the slide's title appears. Click again, and the first bullet point appears. Keep clicking to display each programmed element of your slide. You can even build graphs section by section. Say that you have a graph that illustrates how sales have taken off in the past year. You could show the whole graph all at one time and verbally emphasize the spike in the final quarter. Or you could add the bars to the graph one at a time, building up to the spike in the final quarter.

As with all design elements, you'll generally want to use the same transitions and builds throughout your presentation. Don't introduce text that builds left to right on one slide and from top to bottom on the next.

Hyperlinks and Action Buttons

4 LEARNING OBJECTIVE

Explain the use of hyperlinks in electronic presentations

Hyperlinks and action buttons can be real lifesavers when you need flexibility in your presentations or want to share different kinds of files with the audience. A **hyperlink** instructs your computer to jump to another slide in your presentation, to a website, or to another program entirely. Hyperlinks can be either simple underlined text (like most of the links you see on a website) or they can be assigned to **action buttons**, which are a variety of preprogrammed hyperlink icons available in PowerPoint. Action buttons let you perform such common tasks as jumping forward or backward to a specific slide or opening a Word document or an Excel spreadsheet.

You can increase the flexibility of your presentation slides with hyperlinks that let you jump to different slides, websites, or other displays at will.

In addition to navigating through your presentation, showing other files, and visiting websites, hyperlinks are a great way to customize your presentations in advance. For instance, if you work in sales and call on a variety of customers, you can never be sure what sort of situation you'll encounter at each customer's site. You might be prepared to give an in-depth technical presentation to a group of engineers, only to have the company president walk in and request a five-minute overview. Or you might prepare a set of detailed technical slides but not show them unless the audience asks detailed questions. Another common situation is finding out at the last minute that you have only a fraction of the time you thought you had to make your presentation. With some foresight and planning, you won't need to rush through your entire presentation or scramble on the spot to find the most important slides. Instead, you can simply click an action button labeled "Five-minute overview" and jump right to the two or three most important slides in your presentation. With hyperlinks, you can even switch from an indirect approach to a direct approach or vice versa, based on the response you're getting from your audience. By building in links that accommodate these various scenarios, you can adjust your presentation at a moment's notice—and look polished and professional while you do it (see Figure 16.7).

Multimedia Elements

For the ultimate in active presentations, consider adding video clips. Say that a few words from your company president would help bolster your argument but she's not available to speak at your presentation. Don't worry, you can capture her on video beforehand, include the video clip in your PowerPoint file, and insert the video clip file as an object on your slide. Then all you need to decide is whether you want to activate the clip manually or have it play automatically whenever you show that slide. As you'll see on page 511 (under "Giving Presentations Online"), the combination of video and electronic slides offers a great way to give presentations over the Internet. For more advanced digital video, you can turn to such specialized products as Adobe Premiere Pro or Macromedia Director (samples of which can be viewed at the respective companies' website).

If you have access to video clips, they can add memorable, engaging content to your presentations, as long as they are relevant, interesting, and brief.

COMPLETING SLIDES AND SUPPORT MATERIALS

Just as you would review any written message for content, style, tone, readability, clarity, and conciseness, apply the same quality control to your slides and other visuals. As you look over your presentation for the final time, make sure that all visuals are

Review each slide carefully to make sure it is clear and readable.

- **Readable.** Are the font sizes large enough? Too large? Can they be seen from the back of the room? Does the font color stand out from the background?

FIGURE 16.7 Building Slides with Hyperlinks

Figure 16.7a

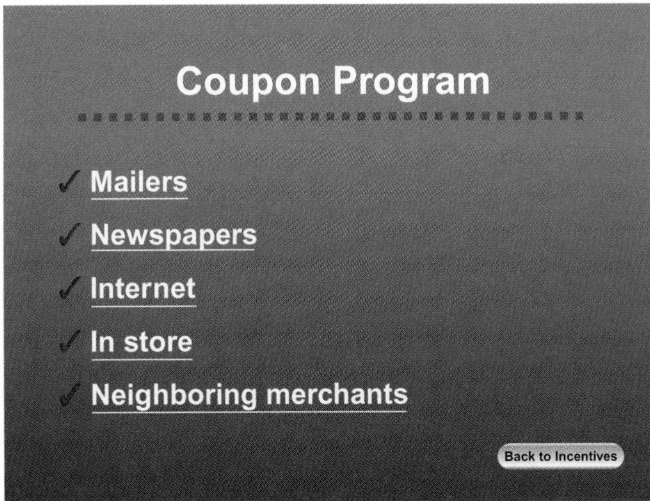

Figure 16.7b

Both of these slides contain multiple hyperlinks embedded in the text of bullet points, making it easy for the speaker to navigate in and out of detail slides based on questions from the audience. By clicking on any of the bullets in Figure 16.7a, the speaker advances to a new slide explaining the details of that particular program. For instance, if the speaker clicks on *Coupons*, the slide show will advance to Figure 16.7b, that outlines the coupon program. Each of the bullets in Figure 16.7b is also formatted as a hyperlink, so the speaker can advance further into the details of each type of coupon. The *Internet* bullet links to a live website that shows the audience how the online coupon program works. To return to Figure 16.7a, the speaker clicks *Back to Incentives* in the lower right corner.

- **Consistent.** Are colors and design elements used consistently?
- **Simple.** Should some information be illustrated by a chart, diagram, or picture? Should some information be eliminated or moved to handouts or backup slides? Should some slides be eliminated altogether?
- **Audience centered.** Are design elements such as clip art and color appropriate for your audience?
- **Clear.** Is the main point of a slide obvious? Easy to understand? Can the audience grasp the main point in five to eight seconds?
- **Concise and grammatical.** Is text written in concise phrases? Are the phrases parallel?
- **Focused.** Does each slide cover only one thought, concept, or idea? Does the slide grab the viewer's attention in the right place and support the key points of the message? Are arrows, symbols, or other techniques used to draw the audience's attention to the key sections of a chart or diagram?
- **Fully operational.** Have you verified every slide in your presentation? Do all the animations and other special effects work as you intended?

Remember, you want the audience to listen to you, not study the slides. So unless you keep things simple, your slides will be distracting.

Use the slide sorter view to verify and modify the organization of your slides.

Electronic presentation software can help you during the editing and revision process. As Figure 16.8 shows, the *slide sorter view* lets you see a file's batch of slides, either all at once or in significant portions (for lengthy presentations). Thus using slide sorter makes it easy to add and delete slides, reposition slides, and check slides for design consistency. You can also use this view to preview animation and transition effects and experiment with design elements. For instance, if you wish to experiment with a different background design or different font, select a new design element and preview it in your slides. If you choose to keep the new design, execute the "apply all" command to update all existing slides and to change the slide master, which applies the design changes to any new slides you create. Of course, it's always a good idea to rename and save a copy of your file before making such irreversible changes.

With your slides working properly and in clear, logical order, you're just a few steps away from being ready. Now is a good time to think about a backup plan. What will you do if your laptop won't boot up or the projector dies? Can you get by without your slides? For important

FIGURE 16.8 Slide Sorter View

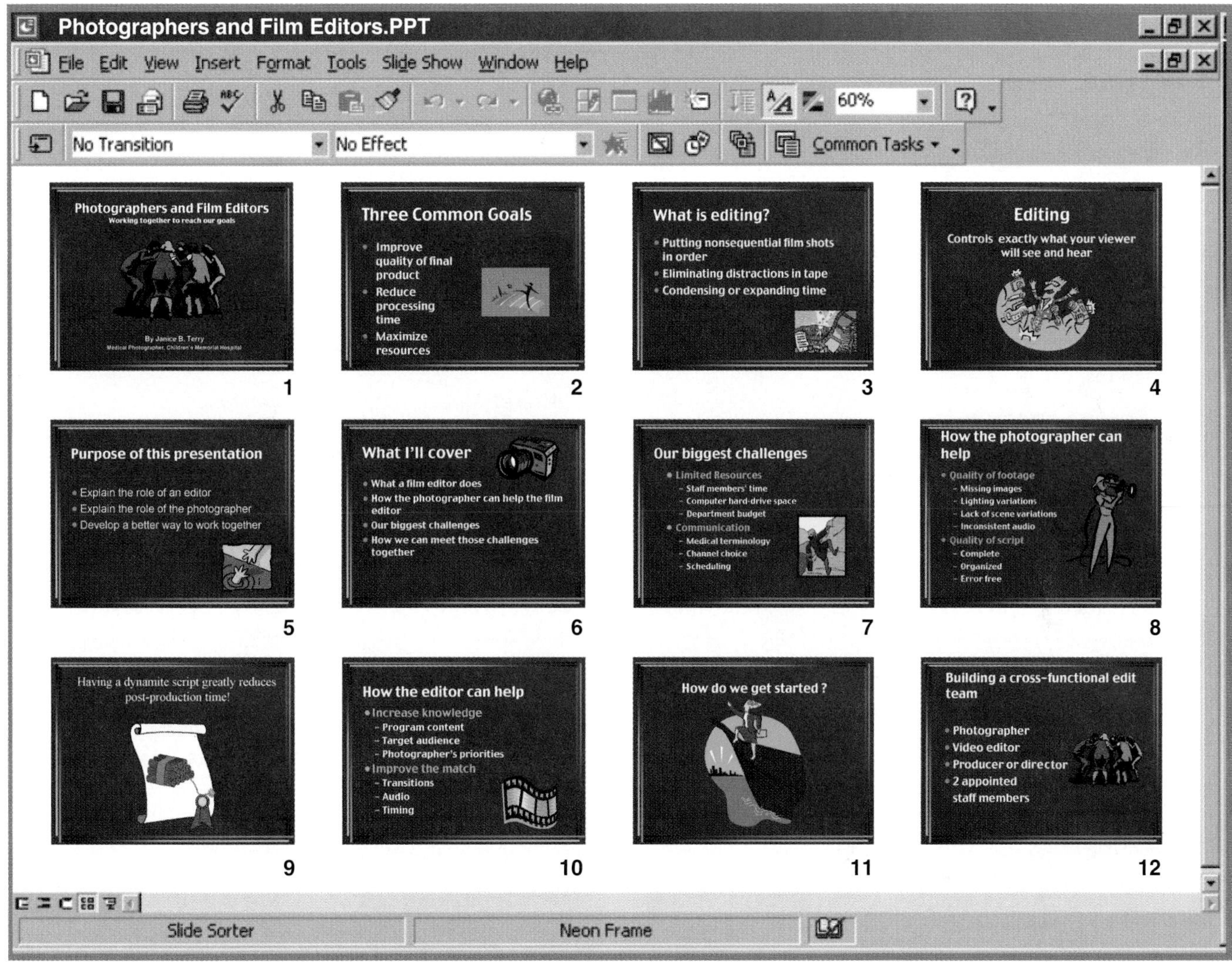

Examining thumbnails of slides on one screen is the best way to check the overall design of your final product. The slide sorter also makes it easy to ponder the order and organization of your presentation; you can change the position of any slide simply by clicking and dragging it to a new position.

presentations, consider having backup equipment on standby, loaded with your presentation, and ready to go. At the very least, have enough printed handouts ready to give the audience so that, as a last resort, you can give your presentation "on paper." Then once your backup plans are in place, you can complete your slides and support materials by performing tasks such as developing a clear structure, creating handouts, and practicing your delivery.

Developing a Clear Structure for Slide Presentations

In addition to delivering content, your slides can help both you and your audience follow the flow of your presentation. To help your audience stay on track, you'll want to identify what you're talking about, why, and in what order. You can clarify this structure throughout your presentation by using three types of *navigational slides:*

- **Cover slides.** Make a good first impression on your audience with a cover slide, the equivalent of a report's title page (see Figure 16.9a). Cover slides should contain the title of your presentation, a subtitle if appropriate, your name (as presenter), and your company affiliation (if you're addressing an audience outside your firm). You may also include the presentation date and an appropriate graphic element.

5 LEARNING OBJECTIVE

Discuss the steps you can take to develop a clear structure for your presentation to make sure your audience never gets lost or confused

Navigational slides help your audience keep track of what you've covered already and what you plan to cover next.

FIGURE 16.9 Cover and Introduction Slides

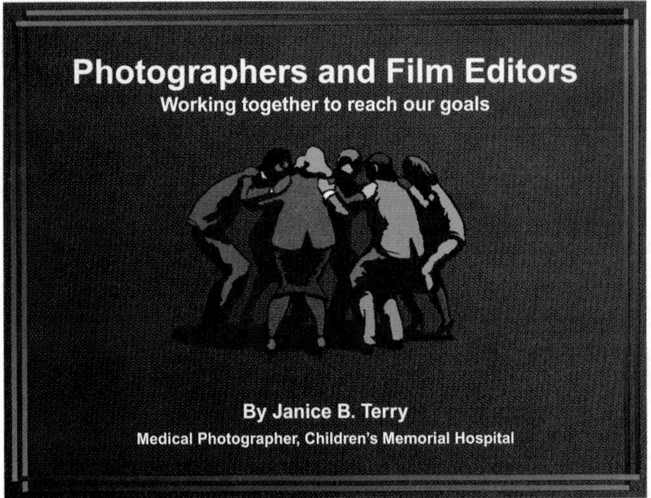

Figure 16.9a Cover slide

Figure 16.9b Introduction slide—clarify topic

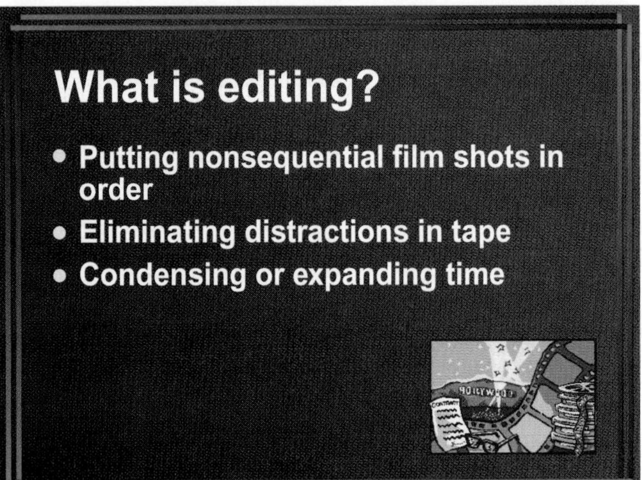

Figure 16.9c Introduction slide—clarify topic

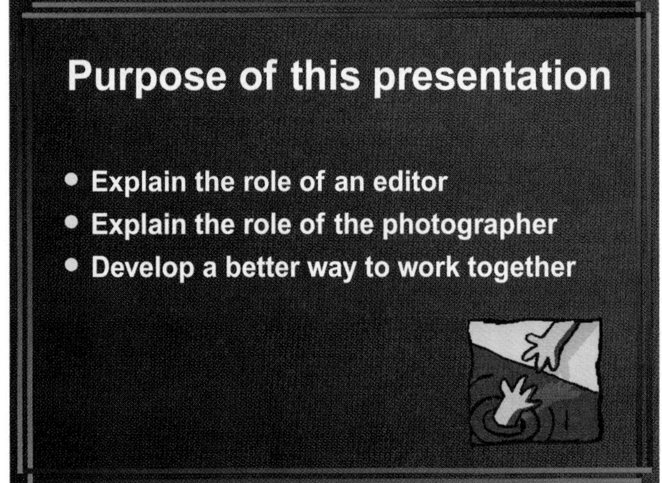

Figure 16.9b Introduction slide—explain purpose

Effective presentations begin with an inviting cover slide, followed by several introduction slides that define key terms, clarify the topic, and explain the purpose of the presentation.

- **Introduction slides.** As Figure 16.9 shows, introduction slides define the topic of your presentation, clarify the topic, emphasize why you are speaking on this topic, and establish any expectations you may have of the audience. Are you going to ask them to make a decision or take some action? Or are you simply explaining a new company policy?[10]
- **Blueprint slides.** To tell your audience where you're going and where you've been, use a blueprint slide, which serves as your agenda and provides a road map of your presentation. Use it at the beginning of your presentation to identify the major points you will cover. Then as you progress through your presentation, insert copies of it, known as **moving blueprint slides**, to indicate where you are (see Figure 16.10). Generally speaking, use one moving blueprint slide at the beginning of each major section to indicate what you've covered so far and what you'll cover next. You can also use moving blueprint slides at the end of the presentation to summarize and review the presentation's key points.

In addition to blueprint slides, you can use a special type of heading called an *eyebrow* along the top of every slide to remind your audience where you are in your presentation. Eyebrows serve the same function as the chapter number and name you see listed in run-

FIGURE 16.10 Blueprint Slides

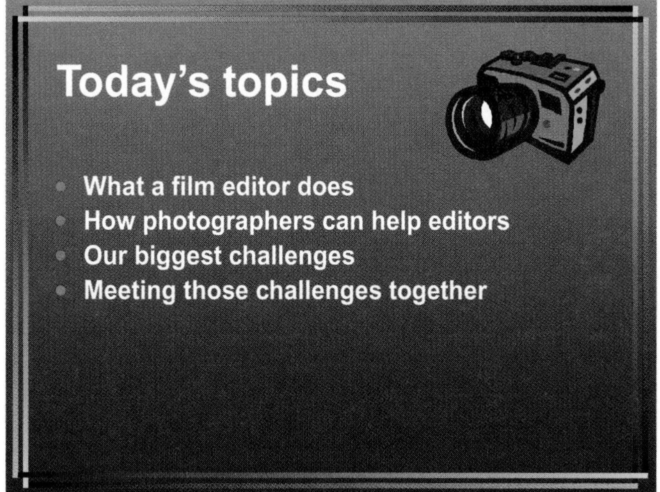

Figure 16.10a Blueprint slide

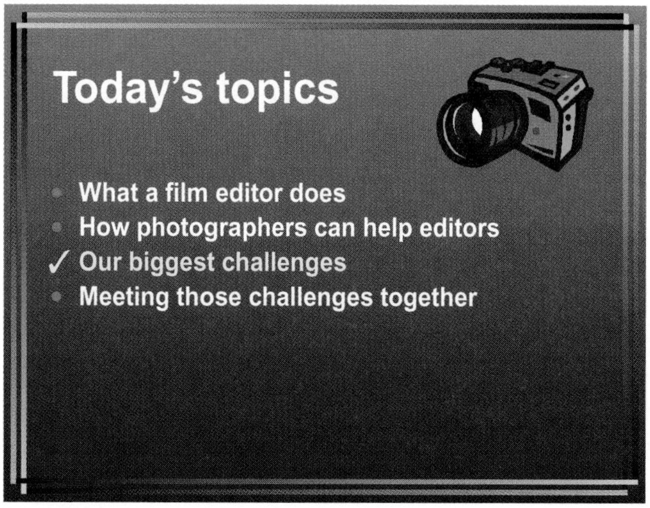

Figure 16.10b Moving blueprint slide

A blueprint slide near the beginning of a presentation, such as Figure 16.10a, defines the structure of the presentation so that the audience knows where the speaker is going. As the speaker finishes each subsection, the blueprint is then shown again and updated to indicate progress. For instance, the yellow checkmark and text in Figure 16.10b highlights the speaker's next topic. Blueprint slides share the same design elements as other slides in the presentation, but they can have a slightly different background design or use of different colors to distinguish them from other slides in the presentation.

ning heads at the top of textbook pages. Although eyebrows aren't necessary in short presentations, they can be quite useful in long ones. Finally, if your presentation will include product demonstrations or other activities in addition to your slides, include a simple slide that indicates the nature of the activity (such as "Software Demonstration" or "Group Discussion"). You can use this slide to introduce the activity to the audience, and the slide can remind you to stop at the right point in the presentation to initiate it.

Creating Effective Handouts

Use handout materials to support the points made in your presentation and to offer the audience additional information on your topic.

Handouts are a terrific way to offer your audience additional material without overloading your slides with information. Possibilities for good handout materials include the following:[11]

- **Complex charts and diagrams.** Charts and tables that are too unwieldy for the screen or that demand thorough analysis make good handouts. A common approach is to create a stripped-down version of a chart or graphic for the presentation slide and include a more detailed version in your handouts.
- **Articles and technical papers.** Magazine articles that supplement the information in your presentation make good handout materials, as do technical papers that provide in-depth coverage of the material you've highlighted in your presentation.
- **Case studies.** Summaries of case studies along with references and contact information make good supplemental reading material.
- **Websites.** Lists of websites related to your topic are useful. In addition to the URL address, annotate each item with a one- or two-sentence summary of each site's content.
- **Copies of presentation slides.** In many cases, audiences like to have small print versions of the slides used by a speaker, containing the speaker's comments about each slide and blank lines for note taking. PowerPoint gives you several options for printing handouts, from a single slide per page to as many as nine per page.

Other good handout materials include brochures, pictures, outlines, and a copy of the presentation agenda. Make sure the information is all useful and relevant.

Timing the distribution of handouts is a difficult decision that depends on the content of your handouts, the nature of your presentation, and your personal preference. Some

Learning to focus on the audience and interact with them while using electronic slides or other visual aids takes practice.

speakers prefer to distribute handout copies of their slides before the presentation begins so that the audience can take notes. The downside of doing so is that it allows your audience to read ahead instead of listening to you, which could backfire if your subject is a touchy one and you've chosen an indirect approach. Other speakers simply advise the audience of the types of information they are including in handouts but delay distributing anything until they have finished speaking.

Practicing Your Delivery

You're now just one step away from giving your presentation, and it's a step that too many novice presenters overlook: practicing the delivery of your presentation. So many things can go wrong in a major presentation, including equipment glitches, confusing slides, and the unpleasant discovery that you're out of time but only halfway through your material. That's why experienced speakers always practice important presentations. If you can arrange an audience of several helpful colleagues, by all means do so. They can tell you if your slides are understandable and whether your delivery is effective. A day or two before you're ready to step on stage for an important talk, make sure you can give a positive response to the following questions:

The more you practice, the more confidence you'll have in yourself and your material.

6 LEARNING OBJECTIVE

List the six questions you should ask yourself to determine whether or not you're ready to give your presentation

- **Can you present your material naturally, without reading your slides word-for-word?** Your audience wants you to talk to them, not read to them. In fact, reading your slides is generally considered one of the worst mistakes a presenter can make. If you need to refer to your speaking notes, either print a copy or take advantage of the "Presenter View" feature in Microsoft PowerPoint. With Presenter View (which requires a PC capable of displaying on two monitors at once), you can see your notes privately on your own PC screen while your audience sees your regular slides on the presentation screen. (Presenter View is found in the "Set Up Show" dialog box in the Slide Show menu.)

Make sure you're comfortable with the equipment you'll be expected to use; you don't want to be fumbling with controls while the audience is watching and waiting.

- **Is the equipment working—and do you know how to work it?** Verify that your computer will work with the projector; sometimes you need to adjust the resolution of your computer screen to make it compatible with a particular projector. Also, some conference rooms are now equipped with sophisticated wireless remote controls and other high-tech devices. You don't want to find yourself struggling to turn on the projector in front of a restless audience. Some presentation tools, such as wireless remote controls for your laptop computer, need to have software installed on your computer before they'll operate, so don't bring some fancy new gadget to the conference room without trying it out first.
- **Is your timing on track?** Your practice runs, particularly if you can arrange to speak in front of a test audience, will give you a good idea of how much time you'll need. Now is the time to trim, not when you're live on stage.
- **Can you easily pronounce all the words you plan to use?** Everyone stumbles over certain words, and your tongue is more likely to get tied up when you're under pressure and your mouth is dry.
- **Have you decided how you're going to introduce your slides?** Effective speakers usually introduce the slide before they show it. Doing so allows you to set the stage before your audience starts reading the slide and jumping to their own conclusions.
- **Have you anticipated likely questions and objections?** Put yourself in the audience's shoes and try to imagine what issues they might have about your content, then think through your answers ahead of time. Don't assume you can handle whatever comes up.[12]

You'll know you've practiced enough when you can present the material at a comfortable pace and in a conversational tone, without the need to read your slides or constantly refer to your notes.

With experience, you'll get a feel for how much practice is enough in any given situation. If you find yourself constantly stumbling with the software and hardware or referring to your slides to remind yourself of key points, you need more practice. For an important presentation, four or five practice runs is not excessive. Your credibility is dramatically enhanced when you move seamlessly through your presentation, matching effective words with each slide. Practicing helps keep you on track, helps you maintain a conversational tone with your audience, and boosts your confidence and composure.

DOCUMENT MAKEOVER

IMPROVE THESE SLIDES

To practice correcting drafts of actual documents, visit www.prenhall.com/onekey on the web. Click "Document Makeovers" then click Chapter 16. You will find a series of slides containing problems and errors relating to what you've learned in this chapter about enhancing oral presentations with electronic slide shows and overhead transparencies. Use the Final Draft decision tool to create an improved version of these slides. Check the slides for wordiness, clarity, consistency, complexity, necessity, readability, active versus passive voice, appropriateness of ideas, spelling, and grammar.

GIVING PRESENTATIONS ONLINE

With the global reach of today's business organizations, you can expect that at some point in your career, you'll be asked to deliver a presentation online. In some companies, online presentations have already become a routine matter, conducted via internal groupware, virtual meeting systems (see Chapter 2), or webcast systems designed specifically for online presentations. Capabilities vary from one system to another, so it's a good idea, well in advance of your presentation, to make sure you're familiar with the system you'll be using. In most cases, you'll communicate through some combination of audio, video, and data presentations (for instance, your PowerPoint slides). Your audience will view your presentation either on their individual computer screens or via a projector in a conference room.

The benefits of online presentations are considerable, including the opportunity to communicate with a geographically dispersed audience at a fraction of the cost of travel and the ability for a project team or an entire organization to meet at a moment's notice. Online presentations can also be less disruptive for the members of your audience, giving them the options of viewing your presentation from their desk and listening to only those parts that apply to them. However, the challenges for a presenter can be considerable, thanks to that layer of technology between you and your audience. Many of those "human moments" that guide and encourage you through an in-person presentation won't travel across the digital divide. Moreover, the technology itself can be a source of trouble from time to time, with dropped Internet connections, untrained users, and other problems. However, online systems continue to improve, and presenters who master this new mode of communication will definitely have an advantage in tomorrow's business environment.

Online presentations give you a way to reach more people in less time, but they require special preparation and skills.

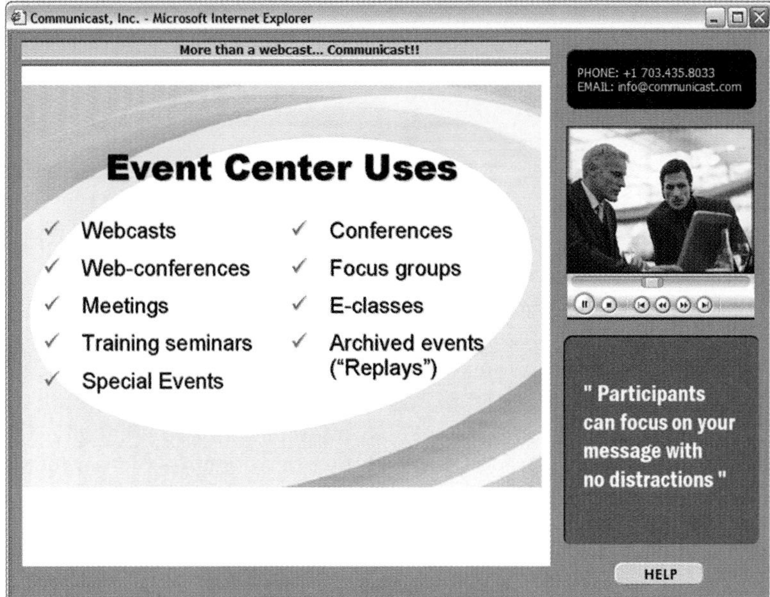

Online meetings can dramatically reduce travel costs and personnel disruptions. Webcasting services such as Communicast help businesses host live meetings over the Internet. The meetings can also be archived and replayed at a later date.

7 LEARNING OBJECTIVE

Highlight seven major issues to consider when you're preparing to give a presentation online

To ensure successful online presentations, regardless of the system you're using, keep the following advice in mind:

- **Consider sending preview study materials ahead of time.** If your presentation covers complicated or unfamiliar material, consider sending a brief message ahead of time so that your audience can familiarize themselves with any important background information.
- **Keep your content—and your presentation of it—as simple as possible.** Break complicated slides down into multiple slides if necessary and keep the direction of your discussion clear so that no one gets lost. Moreover, make sure any streaming video presentations are short; viewers have expressed strong opinions about sitting through long speeches online.[13]
- **Ask for feedback frequently.** You won't have as much of the visual feedback that alerts you when audience members are confused (such as perplexed looks or blank stares), and many online viewers will be reluctant to call attention to themselves by interrupting you to ask for clarification. So you'll have to draw out feedback as you go.
- **Consider the viewing experience from the audience's side.** Will they be able to see what you think they can see? For instance, webcast video is typically displayed in a comparatively tiny window on screen. (Viewers can expand the size of the window, but then they lose visual resolution.) Consequently, if you try to use video to demonstrate the detailed operation of a piece of equipment, your audience might not even be able to see those details.
- **Improve any sections of your presentation that might be slow or difficult.** When people are viewing you from their desks, potential distractions abound: e-mail, instant messaging, stacks of paperwork, and so on. Moreover, they might be more inclined to succumb to those temptations if they know you can't watch them. You need to work even harder than usual to make sure you keep everyone interested and involved in what you're saying.
- **Make sure your audience can receive the sort of content you intend to use.** For instance, some corporate firewalls (electronic "safety gates" on corporate networks) don't allow streaming media, so your webcast video might not survive the trip.[14]
- **Allow plenty of time for everyone to get connected and familiar with the screen they're viewing.** Build extra time into your schedule to ensure that everyone is connected, particularly if some are connecting from dial-up lines in hotel rooms, wireless hot spots, and other remote locations.

Once you master the technology, you can spend less time thinking about it and more time thinking about the most important elements of the presentation: your message and your audience.

Last but not least, don't get lost in the technology. With virtual white boards, real-time polling, collaborative editing, and other powerful features, electronic communication systems have lots of gadgets that can distract both you and your audience. Use these tools whenever they'll help, but remember that the most important aspect of any presentation is getting the audience to receive, understand, and embrace your message.

COMMUNICATION CHALLENGES AT HEWLETT-PACKARD

HP continues to pursue major contracts with other global companies. This time, Dan Talbott is pursuing a big project with Walt Disney Imagineering, the organization that unites the artistic, engineering, production, and installation teams responsible for creating Disney theme parks. As with the Procter & Gamble deal, Talbott has assembled a team—including you—in an HP sales office near Disney's headquarters in Burbank, California.

Individual Challenge: In his first meeting with the team, Tablott mentioned two significant links between the companies. First, in 1939 when HP was just starting out (as a maker of electronic instrumentation), Disney was one of its first customers, buying equipment that was used in the production of the movie *Fantasia*. Second, both companies value innovation, imagination, and creativity. To help prepare your part of the presentation—and get ready for Dan's rigorous review—create a list of the images and electronic presentation capabilities that can help convey HP's passion for innovation.

Team Challenge: In a small group, discuss the risks and rewards of using visual effects, sound effects, and animation in an electronic presentation when you'll be facing a visually sophisticated audience such as Walt Disney Imagineering. List the major pros and cons in a brief memo to your instructor.

SUMMARY OF LEARNING OBJECTIVES

1 **Explain how visuals enhance oral presentations, and list several popular types of visuals.** Visual aids create interest, illustrate and clarify important points, add variety, and help the listener absorb the information you're presenting. In most businesses today, electronic presentations are the most common tool, but you might also use overhead transparencies, chalkboards and whiteboards (including electronic whiteboards), flipcharts, product samples, models, and videotapes.

2 **Describe the steps needed to write readable content for slides.** The key point to keep in mind when drafting textual content slides is that you can't use as many words as you would in a printed message covering the same material. Follow these steps to make sure your text slides are easy for the audience: limit each slide to one thought or message point, limit content to 40 words or so (six lines of six words each is a good baseline), use short bulleted phrases rather than sentences or paragraphs, phrase list items in parallel grammatical form, use the active voice, and include short informative titles.

3 **Explain the importance of design consistency in electronic slides and other visuals.** Consistency is important because your audience looks for patterns in the way you use color, font size, and other design elements. If the first slide shows major points in blue text and minor points in green text, your audience will expect that pattern to continue throughout the presentation. If you change color assignments from slide to slide, you'll lose their attention as they try to figure out what's important on each slide. Anything that distracts the audience diminishes the concentration they can direct toward your presentation.

4 **Explain the use of hyperlinks in electronic presentations.** Hyperlinks can give you instant access to other slides within the current presentation, other presentation files, websites, word processor documents, word processor or spreadsheet files, or other software applications. You can use these links to quickly show your audience other information or to customize your slide presentation for each audience.

5 **Discuss the steps you can take to develop a clear structure for your presentation to make sure your audience never gets lost or confused.** First, you can use three types of navigational slides to help your audience keep track of where you've been and where you're going: (1) a cover slide, which provides basic information about the presentation and is the equivalent of a report's title page; (2) introductory slides, which define and clarify the presentation topic and explain the purpose of the presentation; and (3) blueprint slides, which list the main segments to be addressed during the presentation and guide the audience from one segment to the next. Second, you can use an eyebrow heading on each slide, much like the chapter name and number that appear at the top or bottom of the page in many books, to remind the audience which section you're currently covering.

6 **List the six questions you should ask yourself to determine whether or not you're ready to give your presentation.** A day or two before every major presentation, ask yourself these questions: (1) Can you present your material naturally, without reading your slides word-for-word? (2) Is the equipment working—and do you know how to work it? (3) Does the timing of your presentation match the time allotted to you? (4) Can you easily pronounce all the words you plan to use? (5) Have you decided how you're going to introduce your slides (whether you discuss the slide before you show it or show the slide first)? (6) Have you anticipated likely questions and objections, and have you prepared responses to these issues?

7 **Highlight seven major issues to consider when you're preparing to give a presentation online.** Review these points to help plan a successful online presentation: (1) Consider sending preview materials ahead of time so your audience can familiarize themselves with the issues you plan to discuss. (2) Keep your content and presentation as simple as possible. (3) Plan to ask for feedback frequently since you might not get all the nonverbal signals that normally alert you to confusion or disagreement. (4) Consider the viewing experience from the audience's side to make sure your displayed content is easy to view. (5) Improve any sections of your presentation that might be slow or difficult because they'll be even harder to mange long-distance. (6) Make sure your audience can receive the sort of content you intend to use. (7) Allow plenty of time for everyone to get connected and familiar with the screen they're viewing.

Test Your Knowledge

1. When creating slides for oral presentations, which should you do first: select the background design for your slides or write your bulleted phrases? Explain your answer.
2. What is the recommended number of fonts you should use per slide?
3. How can hyperlinks be used in electronic slides?
4. How does *slide sorter view* facilitate the editing process for an electronic presentation?
5. How is a blueprint slide used in an oral presentation?
6. When should you distribute handouts? Why?
7. What is the difference between decorative and functional artwork and animation?
8. What is the advantage of practicing an oral presentation with visual aids before a live audience?
9. When should you introduce slides?
10. On average, how many slides should you create for a 30-minute presentation?

Apply Your Knowledge

1. Why do presenters sometimes include too much information on their slides?
2. How might you modify a graph appearing in a printed document to make it appropriate for a slide?
3. What should you strive for when selecting background designs, fonts, and type styles for your slides?
4. How can you use slide master to enhance the effectiveness of your slides?
5. **Ethical Choices** Is it ethical to use design elements and special effects to persuade an audience? Why or why not?

Practice Your Knowledge

Documents for Analysis

Document 16.A

Examine the slide in Figure 16.11 and point out any problems you notice. How would you correct these problems?

Document 16.B

Examine the graph in Figure 16.12 and explain how to modify it for an electronic presentation using the guidelines discussed in this chapter.

Exercises

For live links to all websites discussed in this chapter, visit this text's website at www.prenhall.com/bovee. Just log on, select Chapter 16, and click on "Featured Websites." Locate the page or the URL related to the material in the text.

16.1 **Creating Effective Slides: Content** Look through recent issues (print or online) of *Business Week, Fortune,* or other business publications for articles discussing issues a specific company or industry is facing. Using the articles and the guidelines discussed in this chapter, create three to five text or graphic slides summarizing these issues. If you don't have access to computer presentation software or a word processor, you can draw the slides on plain paper.

16.2 **Creating Effective Slides: Content and Design** You've been asked to give an informative 10-minute talk to a group of conventioneers on great things to see and do while visiting your hometown. Write the content for

FIGURE 16.11 Piece of Cake Bakery Electronic Slide #8

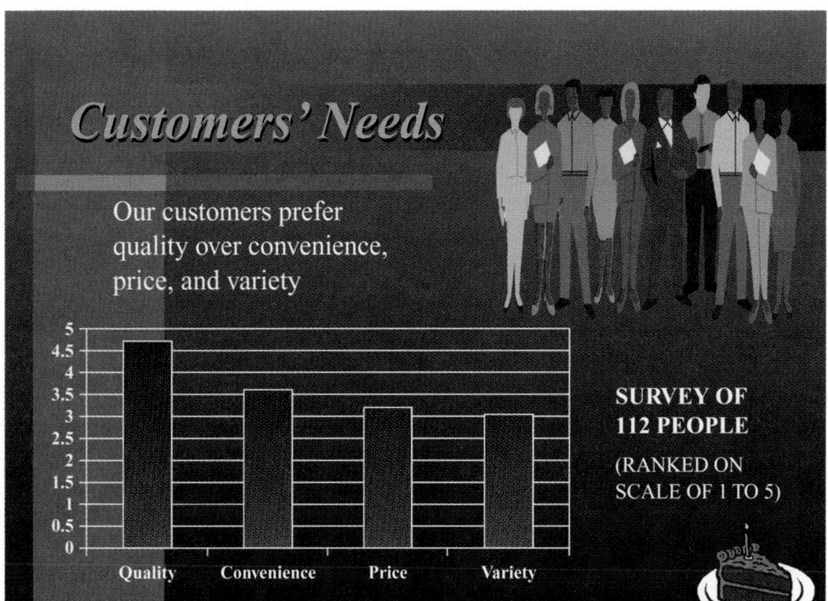

FIGURE 16.12 CommuniCo Employee Training Costs

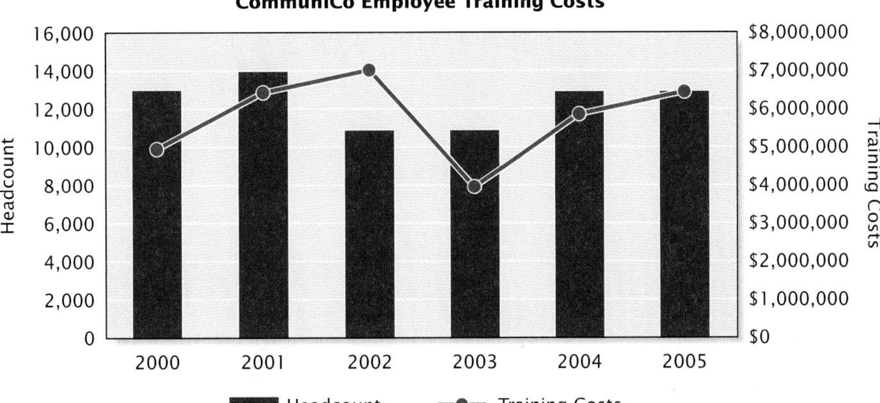

three or four slides (including a cover slide). Then think about the design elements for your slides. Describe design choices you would make, particularly in terms of colors, fonts, drawings, and photography.

16.3 **Completing Electronic Presentations: Slide Sorter View** PowerPoint comes with a number of content templates for presentations. Use the software's AutoContent Wizard to create a short presentation by selecting a presentation type and supplying information for the slide templates (feel free to make up material). Then use the *slide sorter view* to critique the content, layout, and design elements of your presentation. Edit and revise the slides to improve their overall effectiveness.

16.4 **Creating Effective Slides: Design Elements** Most personal computers offer a large selection of fonts. Review the fonts available to you and select three to five fonts suitable for electronic slides or overhead transparencies. Explain the criteria you use for your selections.

16.5 **Internet** Creating hyperlinks to live websites can perk up an electronic presentation, but it also means being prepared for the unexpected. What are some of the obstacles you might encounter when creating live Internet links? How can you prepare in advance to overcome such obstacles?

Expand Your Knowledge

For live links to the websites that follow, go to www.prenhall.com/bovee. When you log on, select Chapter 16, then select "Featured Websites," click on the URL of the website you wish to visit, and review the website to complete these exercises.

Exploring the Best of the Web

Look Smart in Your Electronic Presentations
www.3m.com/meetingnetwork/presentations
Visit the presentation center at 3M, and follow the expert advice on creating and delivering effective oral presentations. Find out why a bad presentation can kill even the best idea. Did you pick the right colors? Is your presentation too long? Too wordy? Find out why a strong template is the key to positive first impressions. Review the five tips for better presentations. Download some templates and look smart. Log on and learn the secrets from the pros, then address these questions:

1. What three questions should you answer for a successful presentation?
2. What common PowerPoint pitfalls should you avoid?
3. What are the two common causes of presentation paralysis?

Exploring the Web on Your Own

Review these chapter-related websites on your own to learn more about creating effective slides for oral presentations.

1. Save time with PowerPoint tips and tricks at the Microsoft PowerPoint homepage, www.microsoft.com/powerpoint.
2. Take the online tutorial at the KU Medical Center, www.kumc.edu/SAH/OTEd/jradel/effective.html, and learn how to design effective visual aids.
3. Develop better presentations with the helpful advice at Presenters Online, www.presentersonline.com.

Learn Interactively

Interactive Study Guide

Go to the Companion Website at www.prenhall.com/bovee. For Chapter 16, take advantage of the interactive "Study Guide" to test your knowledge of the chapter. Get instant feedback on whether you need additional studying.

Also, visit this site's "Study Hall," where you'll find an abundance of valuable resources that will help you succeed in this course.

Peak Performance Grammar and Mechanics

To continue improving your skill with vocabulary, visit www.prenhall.com/onekey, click "Peak Performance Grammar and Mechanics," click "Vocabulary," then click "Vocabulary II." Take the Pretest to determine whether you have any weak areas. Then review those areas in the Refresher Course. Take the Follow-Up Test to check your grasp of frequently misused words.

PART 7

Writing Employment Messages and Interviewing for Jobs

chapter 17

Building Careers and Writing Résumés

LEARNING OBJECTIVES

After studying this chapter, you will be able to

1. Discuss how employers view today's job market
2. List three things you can do before you graduate and while you're job hunting that will make you more valuable to employers
3. Describe the approach most employers take to finding potential new employees
4. Discuss how to choose the appropriate résumé organization, and list the advantages or disadvantages of the three common options
5. List the major sections of a traditional résumé
6. Describe what you should do to adapt your résumé to a scannable format

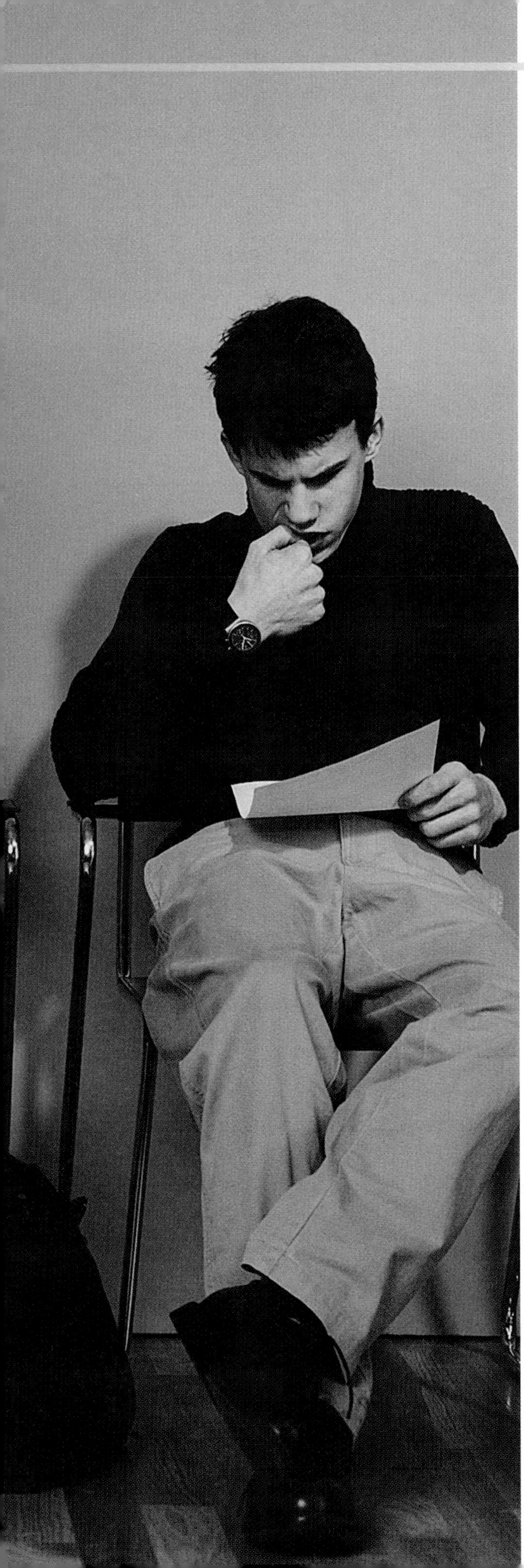

COMMUNICATION CLOSE-UP AT E*TRADE FINANCIAL

www.etrade.com

To get a job interview, your résumé has to catch the eye of someone like Armnon Geshuri, director of global staffing at E*Trade Financial. If Geshuri and his staff don't see your résumé, you won't see the inside of E*Trade. Geshuri wants to see the résumé of every qualified candidate, and he devotes considerable time, money, and creative energy to making sure that E*Trade gets to see the best candidates as quickly as possible.

Like many companies these days, E*Trade uses advanced technology to filter résumés, spot qualified candidates, conduct personality and skill tests, and even handle background checks. The company uses these solutions in good times and bad, whether the talent pool is empty or overflowing. "In any market, finding the right talent is key," says Geshuri. "Effective applicant tracking and screening is what differentiates companies and creates a competitive advantage."

Using technology creatively is another key to success. Early computer-based systems emphasized the fairly simple ability to search on keywords in résumés and applications. However, organizations that relied too heavily on keywords discovered they were often overlooking highly qualified candidates. The latest applicant-tracking programs do much

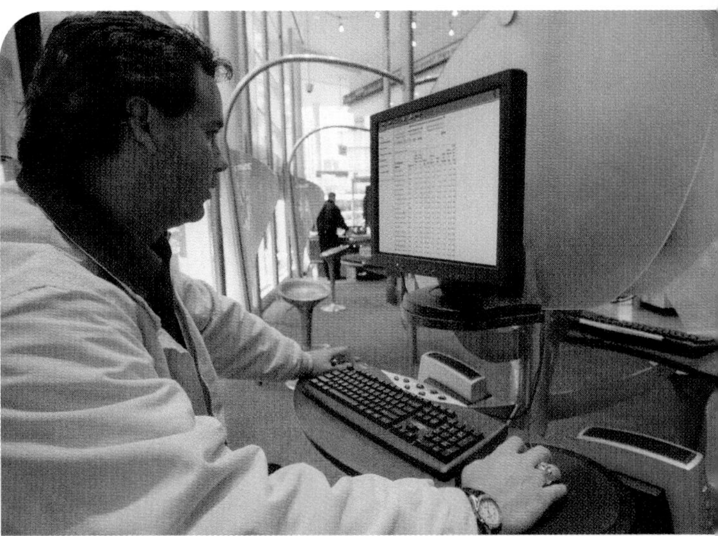

E*Trade achieved a strong position in the online trading market through a combination of innovative technology and effective workforce recruiting.

more, letting recruiters analyze various words and rank them according to how (and how often) they're used.

In the end, though, people like Geshuri still have the final say. They read the résumés the programs select, choose who gets a phone call, perform the interviews, and decide who to hire. So no matter how advanced the technology gets, getting in the door still depends on a well-written résumé.[1]

BUILDING A CAREER WITH YOUR COMMUNICATION SKILLS

Successful job hunters view the search as a comprehensive process—and put all of their communication skills to work.

As Armnon Geshuri will tell you, getting the job that's right for you takes more than sending out a few résumés and application letters. As you get ready to enter (or reenter) the workplace, explore the wide range of actions you can take to maximize your perceived value and find the ideal career opportunities. The skills you've learned in research, planning, and writing will help you every step of the way.

Understanding Today's Dynamic Workplace

If you've spent any time in the workplace recently, you know it's a tumultuous place these days. Moreover, social, political, and financial events change workplace conditions from year to year, so the job market you read about this year might not be the same market you try to enter a year from now. However, you can count on a few forces that are likely to affect your entry into the job market and your career success in years to come:[2]

For many workers, the employment picture is less stable than it was just a few years ago.

- **Stability.** Your career probably won't be as stable as careers were in your parents' generation. In today's business world, your career will be affected by globalization, mergers and acquisitions, short-term mentality driven by the demands of stockholders, ethical upheavals, and the relentless quest for lower costs.
- **Single firm employment.** The idea of lifetime employment with a single firm is all but gone in many industries. Even stalwarts such as Hewlett-Packard (which prided itself for decades on never laying off a single employee) have been forced to join the layoff parade in recent years as business faltered. In addition, employees seem less willing to stay in one career track forever, even when they have the opportunity to do so. In fact, most U.S. employees will not only change employers multiple times but will even change careers anywhere from three to five times over their working lives.
- **Growth of small business.** Small business continues to be the primary engine of job creation in the United States, so chances are good that you'll work for a small firm at some point. One expert predicts that before long, 80 percent of the U.S. labor force will be working for firms employing fewer than 200 people.
- **Increase in independent contractors.** The nature of employment itself is changing for many people. As companies try to become more flexible, more employees are going solo and setting up shop as independent contractors, sometimes selling their services back to the very companies they just left.
- **Changing view of job-hopping.** Given all these changes, job-hopping doesn't have quite the negative connotation it once had. Even so, you still need to be careful about jumping at every new opportunity that promises more money or prestige. Recruiting and integrating new employees takes time and costs money, and most employers are reluctant to invest in someone who has a history of switching jobs numerous times.

Changes in the job market mean you need to take charge of your career, rather than counting on a single employer to look out for you.

What do all these forces mean to you? First, take charge of your career—and stay in charge of it. Understand your options and don't count on others to watch out for your future. Second, as you've learned throughout this course, understanding your audience is key to successful communication. As you pursue your career, you'll be communicating with potential employers. You'll need to understand how they view the dynamic job market and how they're handling it so that you can adjust your communication efforts appropriately.

How Employers View Today's Job Market

1 LEARNING OBJECTIVE

Discuss how employers view today's job market

From the employer's perspective, the employment process is always a question of balance. Maintaining a stable workforce can improve practically every aspect of business performance, and yet many employers feel they need the flexibility to shrink and expand payrolls as business conditions change. Employers obviously want to attract the best talent, but the best talent is more expensive and more vulnerable to offers from competitors, so there are always financial trade-offs to consider.

The nature of the job market fluctuates with the ups and downs of the economy.

Employers also struggle with the ups and downs of the economy, just as employees do. When unemployment is low, the balance of power shifts to employees, and employers have to compete to attract and keep top talent. In the Internet boom of the late 1990s, companies were practically throwing money at hot, young talent, sometimes even paying new hires more than seasoned professionals. Unfortunately, many of those high-flying jobs evaporated almost overnight, so the party didn't last long.[3] When unemployment is high, the power shifts back to employers, who can afford to be more selective and less accommodating. In other words, pay attention to the economy whenever you're job hunting; there are times when you can be more aggressive and times when you should be more accommodating.

As discussed in the previous section, employment today is generally more flexible than in the past. Rather than looking for lifelong employees for every position, many employers now fill some needs by hiring temporary workers or engaging contractors on a project-by-project basis. Many U.S. employers are now also more willing to move jobs to cheaper labor markets outside the country and to recruit globally to fill positions in the United States. Both trends have stirred controversy, especially in the technology sector, as U.S. firms recruited top engineers and scientists from other countries while shifting mid- and low-range jobs to India, China, Russia, and other countries with lower wage structures.[4]

What Employers Look for in Job Applicants

Given the forces in the contemporary workplace, employers such as E*Trade are looking for people who are able and willing to adapt to the new dynamics of the business world, can survive and thrive in fluid and uncertain situations, and continue to learn throughout their careers. Companies want team players with strong work records, leaders who are versatile, and employees with diversified skills and varied job experience.[5] In addition, most employers expect college graduates to be sensitive to intercultural differences and to have a sound understanding of international affairs.[6] In fact, in some cases, your chances of being hired are better if you've studied abroad, learned another language, or can otherwise demonstrate an appreciation of other cultures.

Communication Solution

E*Trade's résumé-tracking and candidate-evaluation system works in large part because the company has clear and consistent criteria for new employees. As a result, the system is able to identify those applicants most likely to fit the company's needs, making the process far more efficient than it would be otherwise.

Adapting to Today's Job Market

Adapting to the workplace is a lifelong process of seeking the best fit between what you want to do and what employers are willing to pay you to do. For instance, if money is more important to you than anything else, you can certainly pursue jobs that promise high pay; just be aware that most of these jobs require years of experience and many produce a lot of stress, require frequent travel, or have other drawbacks you'll want to consider. In contrast, if location, life-style, intriguing work, or other factors are more important to you, you may well have to sacrifice some level of pay to achieve them. The important thing is to know what you want to do, what you have to offer, and how to make yourself more attractive to employers.

Most employers value employees who are flexible, adaptable, and sensitive to the complex dynamics of today's business world.

What Do You Want to Do?

Economic necessities and the vagaries of the marketplace will influence much of what happens in your career, of course; nevertheless, it's wise to start your employment search by examining your own values and interests. Identify what you want to do first, then see whether you can find a position that satisfies you at a personal level while also meeting your financial needs.

Have you thought long and hard about what you really want to do in your career? The choices you make now could influence your life for years to come.

- **What would you like to do every day?** Conduct research into occupations that interest you. Find out what people really do every day. Ask friends, relatives, or alumni from your school. On the web, visit Career One Stop, www.careeronestop.com, which offers a vast array of career resources, including short online videos of real people doing real work in hundreds of different professions.

- **How would you like to work?** Consider how much independence you want on the job, how much variety you like, and whether you prefer to work with products, machines, people, ideas, figures, or some combination thereof. Do you like physical work, mental work, or a mix? Constant change or a predictable role?
- **What specific compensation do you expect?** What do you hope to earn in your first year? What kind of pay increase do you expect each year? What's your ultimate earnings goal? Would you be comfortable getting paid on commission, or do you prefer a steady paycheck? Are you willing to settle for less money in order to do something you really love?
- **Can you establish some general career goals?** Consider where you'd like to start, where you'd like to go from there, and the ultimate position you'd like to attain. Do you want to be a corporate executive or a technical specialist? How important are power and influence to you?
- **What size company would you prefer?** Do you like the idea of working for a small, entrepreneurial operation? Would you prefer a large corporation? Do you want to work on your own?
- **What type of operation is appealing to you?** Would you prefer to work for a profit-making company or a nonprofit organization? Are you interested in service or manufacturing? Do you require regular, predictable hours or can you handle a flexible or unpredictable schedule? Do you prefer consistent work throughout the year or seasonal cycles (as in education, accounting, or retailing)?
- **What facilities do you envision?** Would you prefer a downtown high-rise building, an office park in the suburbs, a shop on Main Street in a small town—or perhaps no office at all?
- **What sort of corporate culture are you most comfortable with?** Would you be happy in a formal hierarchy with clear reporting relationships? Or do you prefer less structure? Teamwork or individualism? Do you like a competitive environment? What qualities do you want in a boss?
- **What location would you like?** Would you like to work in a city, a suburb, a small town, an industrial area, or an uptown setting? Do you favor a particular part of the country? Do you like working indoors or outdoors? In other country? (See "Communicating Across Cultures: Looking for Work Around the World.")

What Do You Have to Offer?

No matter what profession you're in, you are a valuable package of skills and capabilities; make sure you have a clear picture of your own strengths.

Knowing what you *want* to do is one thing. Knowing what you *can* do is another. You may already have a good idea of what you can offer employers. If not, some brainstorming can help you identify your skills, interests, and characteristics. Start by jotting down 10 achievements you're proud of, such as learning to ski, taking a prize-winning photo, tutoring a child, or editing your school paper. Think carefully about what specific skills these achievements demanded of you. For example, leadership skills, speaking ability, and artistic talent may have helped you coordinate a winning presentation to your school's administration. As you analyze your achievements, you'll begin to recognize a pattern of skills. Which of them might be valuable to potential employers?

Next, look at your educational preparation, work experience, and extracurricular activities. What do your knowledge and experience qualify you to do? What have you learned from volunteer work or class projects that could benefit you on the job? Have you held any offices, won any awards or scholarships, mastered a second language?

Take stock of your personal characteristics. Are you aggressive, a born leader? Or would you rather follow? Are you outgoing, articulate, great with people? Or do you prefer working alone? Make a list of what you believe are your four or five most important qualities. Ask a relative or friend to rate your traits as well.

Your college placement office can point you to a variety of tests to gauge your interest and suitability for a variety of career possibilities.

If you're having difficulty figuring out your interests, characteristics, or capabilities, consult your college placement office. Many campuses administer a variety of tests to help you identify interests, aptitudes, and personality traits. These tests won't reveal

Communication Across Cultures

Looking for Work Around the World

With his eyes fixed on a career in international law, University of Michigan graduate Andrew Jaynes knew that overseas work experience would help his law school admission chances and expand his intercultural background.

Jaynes started with the Overseas Opportunities Office at UM's International Center, which offers UM students extensive information on its website and access to advisors and students who have international work experience. With that information as a starting point, he signed on with one of several companies that offer students assistance with foreign work permits and provide housing and job leads. He eventually found a job on his own, working at the American Library in Paris. "It took longer than I expected, but every day I learned more about the real lives of working Parisians—an awareness you can't get as a tourist."

To help ensure success in your own search for employment abroad, keep these points in mind:

- **Give yourself plenty of time.** Finding a job in another country is a complicated process that requires extensive and time-consuming research.
- **Research thoroughly, both online and off.** In addition to your school's resources, you can find numerous websites that offer advice, job listings, and other information. For a good look at the range of international opportunities, visit www.InternAbroad.com, www.VolunteerAbroad.com, www.TeachAbroad.com, and www.JobsAbroad.com. However, Jaynes and others with international experience will tell you that you can't limit your research to the web. Like any job search, networking is crucial, so join cultural societies with international interests, volunteer with exchange student programs, or find other ways to connect with people who have international experience.
- **Consider all the possibilities.** Keep an open mind when you're exploring your options; you'll probably run across situations you hadn't considered at the beginning of your search. For instance, you might find that an unpaid internship in your future profession would help your career prospects more than a paying position in some other industry.
- **Be flexible.** If you have to settle for something less than that dream job, focus on the big picture, which for most students is the cultural opportunity.

Finding a job in another country can be a lot of work, but the rewards can be considerable. "I had studied abroad for a year and traveled through many countries around the world," Jaynes says, "but nothing gives you the same feel for a culture as working in it."

CAREER APPLICATIONS

1. How might international work experience help you in a career in the United States, even if you never work abroad again?
2. If your work history involves religious or political activities, either paid or volunteer, explain how you might present this information on a curriculum vitae intended for international readers?

your "perfect" job, but they'll help you focus on the types of work best suited to your personality.

How Can You Make Yourself More Valuable?

2 LEARNING OBJECTIVE

List three things you can do before you graduate and while you're job hunting that will make you more valuable to employers

While you're figuring out what you want from a job and what you can offer an employer, you can take positive steps toward actually building your career. You can do a lot before you graduate from college and even while you are seeking employment:

Take an active approach to making yourself a more attractive job candidate—and it's never too early to start.

- **Keep an employment portfolio.** Collect anything that shows your ability to perform, whether it's in school, on the job, or in other venues. Your portfolio is a great resource for writing your résumé, and it gives employers tangible evidence of your professionalism. Many colleges now offer students the chance to create an *e-portfolio*, a multimedia presentation of your skills and experiences. It's an extensive résumé that links to an electronic collection of your student papers, solutions to tough problems, internship and work projects, and anything else that demonstrates your accomplishments and activities.[7] To distribute the portfolio to potential employers, you can burn a CD-ROM or store your portfolio on a website—whether it's a personal site, your college's site (if student pages are available), or a site such as www.collegegrad.com. (However, you *must* check with an employer before including any items that belong to the company or contain sensitive information.)

- **Take interim assignments.** As you search for a permanent job, consider temporary jobs, freelance work, or internships. These temporary assignments not only help you gain valuable experience and relevant contacts but also provide you with important references and with items for your portfolio.[8]
- **Continue to polish and update your skills.** Join networks of professional colleagues and friends who can help you keep up with your occupation and industry. Many professional societies have student chapters or offer students discounted memberships. Take courses and pursue other educational or life experiences that would be hard to get while working full-time.

Keep your eyes and your mind open as you approach every experience in school, part-time jobs, and social engagements; you can learn a remarkable number of things that will help you in your career.

Even after an employer hires you, continue improving your skills to distinguish yourself from your peers and to make yourself more valuable to current and potential employers:[9]

- Acquire as much technical knowledge as you can, build broad-based life experience, and develop your social skills.
- Learn to respond to change in positive, constructive ways; this will help you adapt if your "perfect" career path eludes your grasp.
- Keep up with developments in your industry and the economy at large; read widely and subscribe to free e-mail newsletters.
- Learn to see each job, even so-called entry-level jobs, as an opportunity to learn more and to expand your knowledge, experience, and social skills.
- Take on as much responsibility as you can outside your job description.
- Share what you know with others instead of hoarding knowledge in the hope of becoming indispensable; helping others excel is a skill, too.
- Understand the big picture; knowing your own job inside and out isn't enough any more.
- Understand that what counts isn't only who you know but also what you know and who knows you.

Securing Employment in Today's Job Market

After you've armed yourself with knowledge of today's workplace and your potential role in it, it's time to launch an efficient, productive process to find that ideal position. Figure 17.1 shows the six most important tasks in the job search process. This chapter discusses the first two, and Chapter 18 explores the final four. The more you know about this process, the more successful you'll be in your job search. Plus, it's important to keep in mind that employers and job candidates approach the process differently.

FIGURE 17.1
The Employment Search

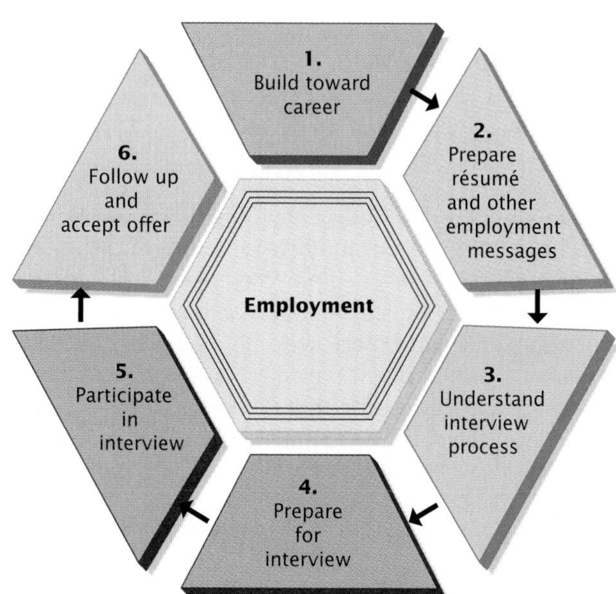

FIGURE 17.2 How Organizations Prefer to Find New Employees

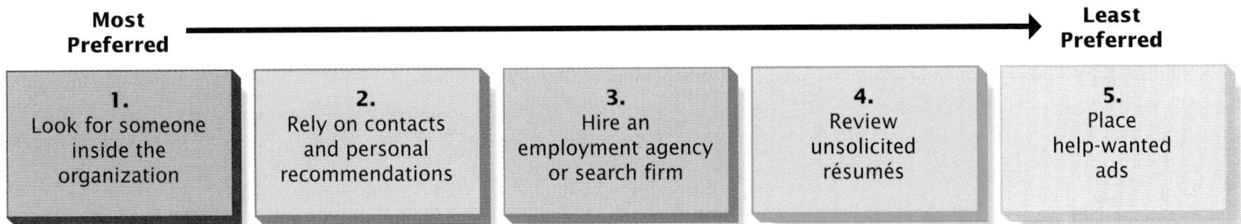
Most Preferred
Least Preferred
1. Look for someone inside the organization
2. Rely on contacts and personal recommendations
3. Hire an employment agency or search firm
4. Review unsolicited résumés
5. Place help-wanted ads

Understanding Employers' Approach to the Employment Process

3 LEARNING OBJECTIVE

Describe the approach most employers take to finding potential new employees

You can save considerable time and effort by understanding how employers approach the recruiting process (see Figure 17.2). Generally, employers prefer to look for candidates within their own organization or through referrals from people they know and trust. In fact, personal contacts appear to be the prime source of jobs, regardless of whether a candidate has just graduated from college or has been out of school for several years.[10]

Many employers send representatives to college campuses to conduct student interviews, which are usually coordinated by the campus placement office. In addition, many employers accept unsolicited résumés, and most keep unsolicited résumés on file or in a database. Employers recruit candidates through employment agencies, state employment services, temporary staffing services, and the employment bureaus operated by some trade associations. They also post jobs through ads in newspapers, trade magazines, campus publications, their own websites, and job sites such as Monster.com. Some companies even use nontraditional recruiting media, such as radio and television.[11]

Look again at Figure 17.2, and you'll notice that the easiest way for you to find out about new opportunities—through the employer's outside advertising—is the employer's least-preferred way of finding new employees. As many as 80 percent of all job openings are never advertised, a phenomenon known as the hidden job market.[12] In other words, employers have looked in quite a few other places before they come looking for you. To find the best opportunities, it's up to you to take action to get yourself noticed.

It's important to understand that the easiest way for you to find jobs (through companies' help-wanted advertising) is the least-preferred channel for many companies to find new employees.

Organizing Your Approach to the Employment Process

The employment process can consume many hours of your time over weeks or months, so organize your efforts in a logical, careful manner to save time. Begin by finding out where the job opportunities are, which industries are strong, which parts of the country are booming, and which specific job categories offer the best prospects for the future. From there you can investigate individual organizations, doing your best to learn as much about them as possible.

Staying Abreast of Business and Financial News If you don't already do so, subscribe to a major newspaper (print or online editions) and scan the business pages every day. Watch some of the television programs that focus on business, such as *Wall Street Week*, and use a news aggregator (see Chapter 10) to automatically receive updates on interesting professions and companies. You can find information about the future of specific jobs in the *Dictionary of Occupational Titles* (U.S. Employment Service), the employment publications of Science Research Associates, and the *Occupational Outlook Handbook* (U.S. Bureau of Labor Statistics). This last reference is available both in print and online at www.bls.gov. Of course, with all the business information available today, it's easy to get lost in the details. Try not to get too caught up in the daily particulars of business. Start by examining "big picture" topics—trends, issues, industrywide challenges, and careers—before delving into specific companies that look attractive.

With so many print and electronic resources available today, it's easy to stay in touch with what's happening in the business world; however, don't get too caught up in the details too early in your search.

Researching Specific Companies Chapter 10 discusses how to find information on individual industries and companies, and it provides a list of popular business resources.

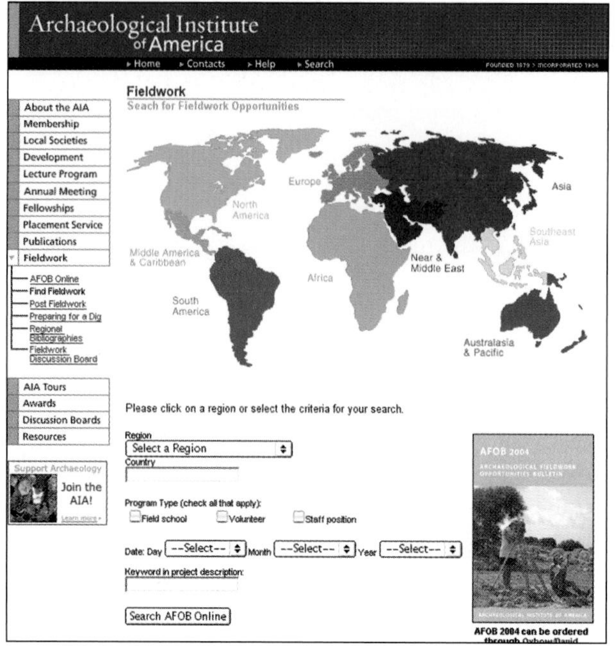

Looking for a career off the beaten path? The Archaeological Institute of America's website is one of the hundreds of specialized job board sites that help people in specific fields find employment opportunities.

Review those sources, as well as professional and trade journals in the fields that interest you. Once you've identified a promising industry and career field, consult directories of employers at your college library, at your career center, or on the Internet and compile a list of specific organizations that appeal to you.

As you probably already know, a staggering amount of company and employment information is available online. In addition to gaining detailed information about your prospective employers, you can use the web to look for and respond to job openings:

Go beyond every company's own communication materials; find out what others in their industries and communities think about them.

- **Learn about the organization.** Most companies, even small firms, offer at least basic information about themselves on their websites. Look for the "About Us" or "Company" part of the site to find a company profile, executive biographies, press releases, financial information, and information on employment opportunities. You'll often find information about an organization's mission, products, annual reports, and employee benefits. You can also e-mail organizations and ask for annual reports, descriptive brochures, or newsletters. Look for outside sources as well, including the business sections of local newspapers and trade publications that cover the company's industries and markets.
- **Look for job openings.** Newspapers remain a popular source of information about job openings, but an increasing number of employers and employees connect online via job boards such as Monster.com, CareerBuilder.com, and Yahoo Hotjobs (http://hotjobs.yahoo.com). Refer to Table 17.1 for more sites. Your college placement office probably maintains an up-to-date list as well.
- **Respond to job openings.** You can respond directly to job postings without going through recruiters, post tailor-made résumés (that match the qualifications required by a particular position), send résumés quickly and cheaply through e-mail, and send focused cover letters directly to the executives doing the hiring. Be ready to respond quickly when you see job postings online; some new openings get flooded with hundreds of résumés within hours.[13]

Keep in mind that because e-mailing résumés is so easy, companies are getting thousands of electronic résumés a day—and not all employers appreciate the flood. Thus, in some cases you may want to try a more personal touch such as a printed letter or phone call. In addition to using the web to look for job openings, you'll still want to use other techniques for finding employment, such as looking in local and major newspapers and signing up for campus interviews. Two effective techniques are networking and finding career counseling.

TABLE 17.1 Netting a Job on the Web

WEBSITE*	URL	HIGHLIGHTS
Riley Guide	www.rileyguide.com	Vast collection of links to both general and specialized job sites for every career imaginable; don't miss this one—it'll save you hours or days of searching
America's CareerOneStop	www.careeronestop.org	Comprehensive, government-funded site that includes America's Career InfoNet and America's Job Bank; learn more about the workplace in general as well as specific careers; offers information on typical wages and employment trends and identifies education, knowledge, and skills requirements for most occupations
Monster	www.monster.com	World's largest job site with hundreds of thousands of openings, many from hard-to-find smaller companies; extensive collection of advice on the job search process
MonsterTrak	www.monstertrak.com	Focused on job searches for new college grads; your school's career center site probably links here
Yahoo! Hotjobs	http://hotjobs.yahoo.com	Another leading job board, formed by recent merger of Hotjobs and Yahoo! Careers
CareerBuilder	www.careerbuilder.com	Fast-growing site affiliated with more than 100 local newspapers around the country
USA Jobs	www.usajobs.opm.gov	The official job search site for the U.S. government, featuring everything from economists to astronauts to Border patrol agents
IMDiversity	www.imdiversity.com	Good resource on diversity in the workplace, with job postings from companies that have made a special commitment to promoting diversity in their workforces
Dice.com	www.dice.com	One of the best sites for high-technology jobs
Net-Temps	www.nettemps.com	Popular site for contractor and freelancers looking for short-term assignments
InternshipPrograms.com	www.internships.wetfeet.com	Posts listings from companies looking for interns in a wide variety of professions

* Note: This list represents only a small fraction of the job-posting sites and other resources available online; be sure to check with your college's career center for the latest information.

Networking **Networking** is the process of making informal connections with a broad sphere of mutually beneficial business contacts. According to one recent survey, networking is the most common way that employees find jobs.[14] Networking takes place wherever and whenever people talk: at industry functions, social gatherings, sports events and recreational activities, online chat rooms, alumni reunions, and so on.

Novice job seekers sometimes misunderstand networking and unknowingly commit breaches of etiquette. Networking isn't a matter of walking up to strangers at social events, handing over your résumé, and asking them to find you a job. Rather, it involves the sharing of information between people who might be able to offer mutual help at some point in the future. Think of it as an organic process, in which you cultivate the possibility of finding that perfect opportunity. Networking can take time, and it can operate in unpredictable ways. You may not get results for months, so it's important to start early and make it part of your lifelong program of career management.

Networking can be a time-consuming process, but it can also uncover some of the best job opportunities.

To become a valued network member, you need to be able to help others in some way. You may not have any influential contacts yet, but because you're actively researching a number of industries and trends in your own job search, you probably have valuable information you can share. Or you might simply be able to connect one person with another person who can help. The more you network, the more valuable you become in your network—and the more valuable your network becomes to you.

Start thinking like a networker now; your classmates could turn out to be some of your most important business contacts.

Look for networking opportunities wherever people with similar interests gather, both online and in person. Read news sites, blogs, and other online sources. Plus, you may be able to network with executives in your field by joining or participating in student business organizations, especially those with ties to professional organizations such as the American Marketing Association or the American Management Association.

Recruiters at this job fair in Austin, Texas, explain the benefits of working at their respective companies.

You might try visiting some organizations, contacting their personnel departments, and talking with key employees. Also, visit trade shows that cater to an industry you're interested in. Not only will you learn plenty about that sector of the workplace, but you'll rub shoulders with people who actually work in the industry.[15] Hundreds of trade shows are held every year around the country, and many are open to the public for free or for a nominal fee.

Moreover, don't overlook volunteering, an important source of networking contacts. Millions of businesspeople volunteer in social, civic, and religious organizations. As a volunteer, you not only meet people but also demonstrate your ability to solve problems, plan projects, and so on. You can do some good while creating a network for yourself.

Be sure to keep records of all your contacts and their interests. You can do this with anything from a simple address book to a spreadsheet or one of the several contact management programs now available.

Don't overlook the many resources available through your college's placement office.

Seeking Career Counseling College placement offices offer individual counseling, credential services, job fairs, on-campus interviews, and job listings. They can give you advice on résumé-writing software and provide workshops in job-search techniques, résumé preparation, interview techniques, and more.[16] You can also find job counseling online. You might begin your self-assessment, for example, with the Keirsey Temperament Sorter, an online personality test at www.advisorteam.com. For excellent job-seeking pointers and counseling, visit college- and university-run online career centers. Major online job boards such as Monster.com also offer a variety of career planning resources.

PREPARING RÉSUMÉS

To distinguish yourself from all the other people looking for work, you need to start with a well-written résumé. In fact, your success in finding a job will depend on how carefully you plan, write, and complete your résumé. Some job searchers are intimidated by the prospect of writing a résumé, but your résumé is really just another specialized business message. Follow the three-step writing process, and it'll be easier than you thought (see Figure 17.3).

Planning Your Résumé

Your résumé must be more than a simple list of the jobs you've held. As with other business messages, planning a résumé means analyzing your purpose and your audience, gathering information, choosing the best medium, and organizing your content. Although this chapter refers to your résumé in the singular, be prepared to craft several or perhaps many versions of your résumé. By making some simple changes in wording or organization, you'll probably be able to match your value more closely to the specific opportunities offered by particular employers.

FIGURE 17.3 Three-Step Writing Process for Résumés

Plan

Analyze the Situation
Recognize that the purpose of your résumé is to get an interview, not to get a job.

Gather Information
Research target industries and companies so that you know what they're looking for in new hires; learn about various jobs and what to expect.

Select the Right Medium
Start with a traditional paper résumé and develop scannable or plain text versions as needed.

Organize the Information
Choose an organizational model that highlights your strengths and downplays your shortcomings.

1

Write

Adapt to Your Audience
Plan your wording carefully so that you can catch a recruiter's eye within seconds; translate your history into attributes that mean something to an employer.

Compose the Message
Write clearly and succinctly, using active, powerful language that is appropriate to the industries and companies you're targeting; use a professional tone in all communications, even via e-mail.

2

Complete

Revise the Message
Evaluate your content and review readability, clarity, and accuracy.

Produce the Message
Use effective design elements and suitable layout for a clean, professional appearance.

Proofread the Message
Review for errors in layout, spelling, and mechanics; mistakes can cost you interview opportunities.

Distribute the Message
Deliver your résumé following the instructions of each specific employer or job board site.

3

Analyzing Your Purpose and Audience

A **résumé** is a structured, written summary of a person's education, employment background, and job qualifications. Although many people have misconceptions about résumés (see Table 17.2), the fact is that a résumé is a form of persuasive communication—an advertisement intended to stimulate an employer's interest in meeting you and learning more about you. A successful résumé inspires a prospective employer to invite you to interview with the company. Thus, your purpose in writing your résumé is to create interest—*not* to tell readers everything about you. In fact, it may be best to only hint at some things and leave the reader wanting more. The potential employer will then have even more reason to contact you.[17]

Once you view your résumé as a persuasive business message, it's easier to decide what should and shouldn't be in it.

By the way, if employers ask to see your "CV," they're referring to your *curriculum vitae*, the term used instead of *résumé* in some professions and in many countries outside the United States. Résumés and CVs are essentially the same, although CVs can be more detailed. If you need to adapt a U.S.-style résumé to CV format, or vice versa, Monster.com has helpful guidelines on the subject.

TABLE 17.2 Fallacies and Facts About Résumés

FALLACY	FACT
⊗ The purpose of a résumé is to list all your skills and abilities.	☑ The purpose of a résumé is to kindle employer interest and generate an interview.
⊗ A good résumé will get you the job you want.	☑ All a résumé can do is get you in the door.
⊗ Your résumé will be read carefully and thoroughly by an interested employer.	☑ Your résumé probably has less than 45 seconds to make an impression.
⊗ The more good information you present about yourself in your résumé, the better.	☑ Too much information on a résumé may actually kill the reader's appetite to know more.
⊗ If you want a really good résumé, have it prepared by a résumé service.	☑ Prepare your own résumé—unless the position is especially high-level or specialized. Even then, you should check carefully before using a service.

Gathering Pertinent Information

Since you've already completed a good deal of research on specific companies, you should know quite a bit about the organizations you'll be applying to. But take some time now to learn what you can about the individuals who may be reading your résumé. If you're applying to a *Fortune* 500 company, you may have to make some educated guesses about the people in the human resources department and what their needs might be. But in smaller companies, you may be able to learn the name of the recruiter or manager you'll be addressing. If you learned of an opportunity through your networking efforts, chances are you'll have both a name and some personalized advice to help tune your writing. Either way, try to put yourself in your audience's position so that you'll be able to tailor your résumé to satisfy your audience's needs. Why would they be interested in learning more about you?

If you haven't been keeping a log or journal of your accomplishments in your academic career and in any jobs you've held so far, you may need to do some research on yourself. Gather all the pertinent personal history you can think of, including all the specific dates, duties, and accomplishments of any previous jobs you've held. Collect every piece of relevant educational experience that adds to your qualifications—formal degrees, skills certificates, academic awards, or scholarships. Also, gather any relevant information about personal endeavors: dates of your membership in an association, offices you may have held in a club or professional organization, any presentations you might have given to a community group. You probably won't use every piece of information you come up with, but you'll want to have it at your fingertips before you begin composing your résumé.

Selecting the Best Medium

Selecting the medium for your résumé used to be a simple matter: it was typed on paper. These days, though, your job search might involve various forms, including an uploaded Word document, a plain text document that you paste into an online form, or a multimedia résumé available online or on CD-ROM. Your choice of medium involves whatever is available to you, the requirements of your target employers (many have specific instructions on their websites, which you must follow to the letter), and the skills and attributes that you're trying to promote. For instance, if you're applying for a sales position, a video clip of yourself on CD-ROM can be a strong persuader.

However, as impressive as personal websites and CD-ROM e-portfolios are, it's always a good idea to prepare a basic paper résumé and keep copies on hand. You'll never know when someone might ask for it, and not every employer wants to bother with electronic media when all they want to know is your basic profile. In addition, starting with a traditional paper résumé is a great way to organize your background information and identify your unique strengths.

4 LEARNING OBJECTIVE

Discuss how to choose the appropriate résumé organization, and list the advantages or disadvantages of the three common options

Organizing Your Résumé Around Your Strengths

The key to organizing a résumé is aligning your personal strengths with both the general and specific qualities that your target employers are looking for.

The most successful résumés convey seven qualities that employers seek: they demonstrate that you (1) think in terms of results, (2) know how to get things done, (3) are well rounded, (4) show signs of career progress and professional development, (5) have personal standards of excellence, (6) are flexible and willing to try new things, and (7) communicate effectively. Organizing your résumé is a question of portraying these seven attributes in the strongest possible light.

Although you may want to include a little information in all categories, you'll naturally want to emphasize the information that does the best job of aligning your career objectives with the needs of your target employers—and that does so without distorting or misrepresenting the facts.[18] Do you have something in your history that might trigger an employer's red flag? Here are some common problems and some quick suggestions for overcoming them:[19]

- **Frequent job changes.** If you've had a number of short-term jobs of a similar nature, such as independent contracting and temporary assignments, see if you can group them under a single heading. Also, if you were a victim of circumstances in positions that were eliminated as a result of mergers or other factors beyond your control, find a subtle way to convey that information (if not in your résumé, then in your cover letter). Given the number of business upheavals in recent years, reasonable employers understand that many otherwise stable employees have been forced to job hop.

- **Gaps in work history.** Mention relevant experience and education you gained during employment gaps, such as volunteer or community work. If gaps are due to personal problems such as drug or alcohol abuse or mental illness, offer honest but general explanations about your absences ("I had serious health concerns and had to take time off to fully recover").
- **Inexperience.** Mention related volunteer work. List relevant course work and internships. Also, offer hiring incentives such as "willing to work nights and weekends."
- **Overqualification.** Tone down your résumé, focusing exclusively on the experience and skills that relate to the position.
- **Long-term employment with one company.** Itemize each position held at the firm to show "interior mobility" and increased responsibilities.
- **Job termination for cause.** Be honest with interviewers. Show that you're a hard-working employee and counter their concerns with proof, such as recommendations and examples of completed projects.
- **Criminal record.** Consider sending out a "broadcast letter" about your skills and experience, rather than a résumé and cover letter. Prepare answers to questions that interviewers will probably pose ("You may wonder whether I will be a trustworthy employee. I'd like to offer you a list of references from previous bosses and co-workers who will attest to my integrity. I learned some hard lessons during that difficult time in my life, and now I'm fully rehabilitated").

Frequent job changes and gaps in your work history are two of the more common issues that employers may perceive as weaknesses, so plan to address these if they pertain to you.

To focus attention on your strongest points, adopt the appropriate organizational approach—make your résumé chronological, functional, or a combination of the two. The "right" choice depends on your background and your goals.

The Chronological Résumé In a **chronological résumé,** the work-experience section dominates and is placed in the most prominent slot, immediately after the name and address and optional objective. You develop this section by listing your jobs sequentially in reverse order, beginning with the most recent position and working backward toward earlier jobs. Under each listing, describe your responsibilities and accomplishments, giving the most space to the most recent positions. If you're just graduating from college with limited professional experience, you can vary this chronological approach by putting your educational qualifications before your experience, thereby focusing attention on your academic credentials.

The chronological approach is the most common way to organize a résumé, and many employers prefer it. This approach has three key advantages: (1) Employers are familiar with it and can easily find information, (2) it highlights growth and career progression, and (3) it highlights employment continuity and stability.[20] As vice president with Korn/Ferry International, Robert Nesbit speaks for many recruiters: "Unless you have a really compelling reason, don't use any but the standard chronological format. Your résumé should not read like a treasure map, full of minute clues to the whereabouts of your jobs and experience. I want to be able to grasp quickly where a candidate has worked, how long, and in what capacities."[21]

The chronological résumé is the most common approach, but it might not be right for you at a particular stage in your career.

The chronological approach is especially appropriate if you have a strong employment history and are aiming for a job that builds on your current career path. This is the case for Roberto Cortez. Compare the ineffective and effective versions of Cortez's résumé in Figures 17.4 and 17.5.

The Functional Résumé A **functional résumé,** sometimes called a *skills résumé*, emphasizes your skills and capabilities, identifying employers and academic experience in subordinate sections. This pattern stresses individual areas of competence, so it's useful for people who are just entering the job market, want to redirect their careers, or have little continuous career-related experience. The functional approach also has three advantages:

FIGURE 17.4 Ineffective Chronological Résumé

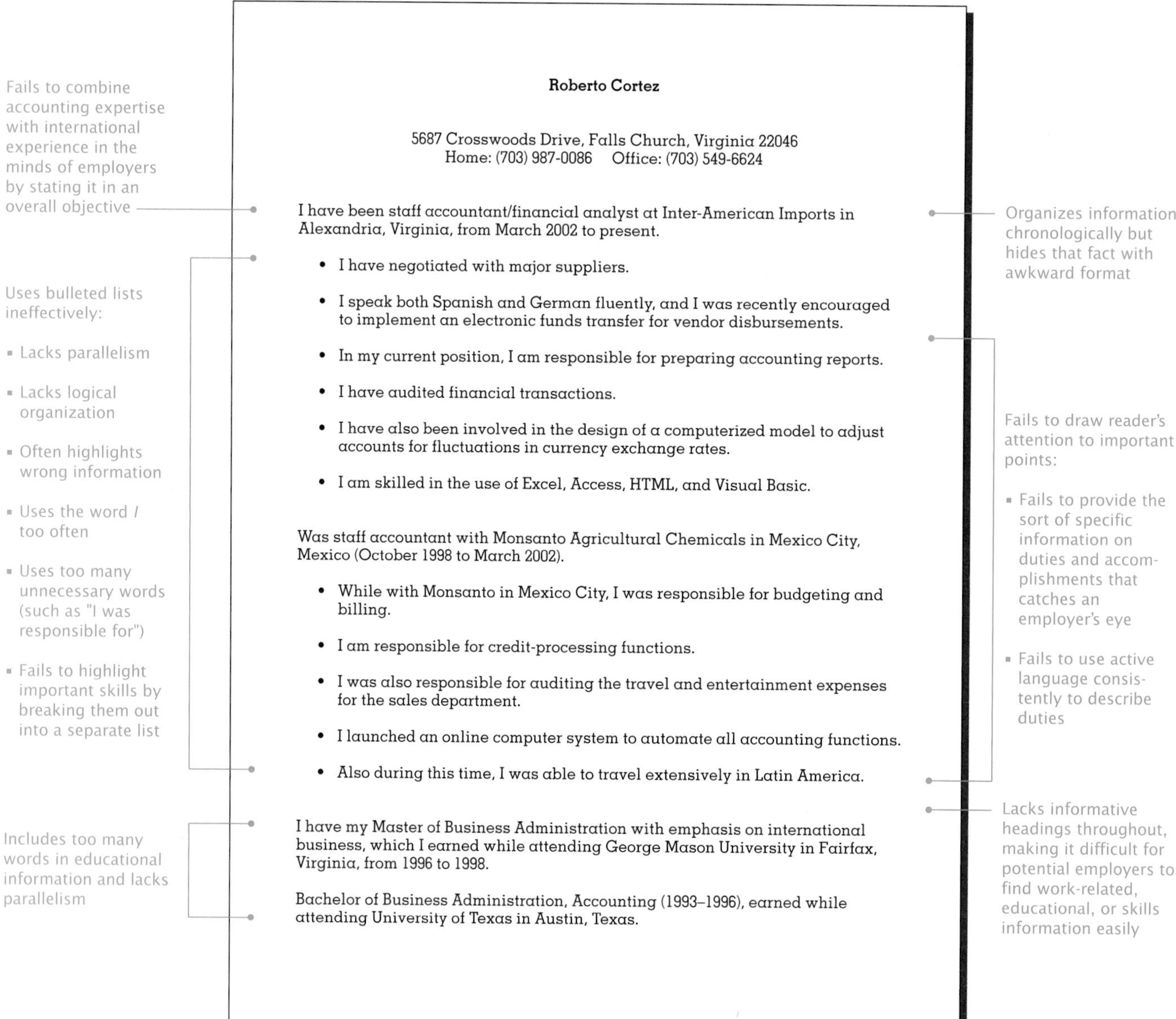
Fails to combine accounting expertise with international experience in the minds of employers by stating it in an overall objective
Uses bulleted lists ineffectively:
▪ Lacks parallelism
▪ Lacks logical organization
▪ Often highlights wrong information
▪ Uses the word I too often
▪ Uses too many unnecessary words (such as "I was responsible for")
▪ Fails to highlight important skills by breaking them out into a separate list
Includes too many words in educational information and lacks parallelism
Organizes information chronologically but hides that fact with awkward format
Fails to draw reader's attention to important points:
▪ Fails to provide the sort of specific information on duties and accomplishments that catches an employer's eye
▪ Fails to use active language consistently to describe duties
Lacks informative headings throughout, making it difficult for potential employers to find work-related, educational, or skills information easily

Roberto Cortez

5687 Crosswoods Drive, Falls Church, Virginia 22046
Home: (703) 987-0086 Office: (703) 549-6624

I have been staff accountant/financial analyst at Inter-American Imports in Alexandria, Virginia, from March 2002 to present.

- I have negotiated with major suppliers.
- I speak both Spanish and German fluently, and I was recently encouraged to implement an electronic funds transfer for vendor disbursements.
- In my current position, I am responsible for preparing accounting reports.
- I have audited financial transactions.
- I have also been involved in the design of a computerized model to adjust accounts for fluctuations in currency exchange rates.
- I am skilled in the use of Excel, Access, HTML, and Visual Basic.

Was staff accountant with Monsanto Agricultural Chemicals in Mexico City, Mexico (October 1998 to March 2002).

- While with Monsanto in Mexico City, I was responsible for budgeting and billing.
- I am responsible for credit-processing functions.
- I was also responsible for auditing the travel and entertainment expenses for the sales department.
- I launched an online computer system to automate all accounting functions.
- Also during this time, I was able to travel extensively in Latin America.

I have my Master of Business Administration with emphasis on international business, which I earned while attending George Mason University in Fairfax, Virginia, from 1996 to 1998.

Bachelor of Business Administration, Accounting (1993–1996), earned while attending University of Texas in Austin, Texas.

The functional résumé is often considered by people with little employment history to show or gaps in their work history, but some employers suspect that people who use this approach are trying to hide weaknesses in their backgrounds.

(1) Without having to read through job descriptions, employers can see what you can do for them, (2) you can emphasize earlier job experience, and (3) you can de-emphasize any lack of career progress or lengthy unemployment. However, you should be aware that not all employers like the functional résumé, perhaps partly because it can obscure your work history and partly because it's less common. In any event, many seasoned employment professionals are suspicious of this résumé style, and some assume that candidates who use it are trying to hide something. In fact, Monster.com lists the functional résumé as one of employers' "Top 10 Pet Peeves."[22] If you don't have a strong, uninterrupted history of relevant work, the combination résumé might be a better choice.

If you don't have a lot of work history to show, consider a combination résumé to highlight your skills while still providing a chronological history of your employment.

The Combination Résumé A **combination résumé** includes the best features of the chronological and functional approaches. Nevertheless, it is not commonly used, and it has two major disadvantages: (1) It tends to be longer, and (2) it can be repetitious if you have to list your accomplishments and skills in both the functional section and the chronological job descriptions.[23] When Erica Vorkamp developed her résumé, she chose not to use a chronological pattern, which would focus attention on her lack of recent work experience.

Plan

1

Analyze the Situation
Decide on the best way to combine finance and international experience.

Gather Information
Research target positions to identify key employer needs.

Select the Right Medium
Start with a traditional paper résumé and develop scannable or plain text versions as needed.

Organize the Information
A chronological format fits this strong employment history perfectly.

Write

2

Adapt to Your Audience
Include points of experience that translate into general qualifications that any international company can relate to.

Compose the Message
Write clearly and succinctly, using active, powerful language that is appropriate to financial management profession.

Complete

3

Revise the Message
Evaluate your content and review readability, clarity, and accuracy.

Produce the Message
Use effective design elements and suitable layout for a clean, professional appearance.

Proofread the Message
Review for errors in layout, spelling, and mechanics.

Distribute the Message
Deliver your résumé and other employment messages following the instructions of each specific employer or job board site.

FIGURE 17.5 Effective Chronological Résumé

ROBERTO CORTEZ
5687 Crosswoods Drive
Falls Church, Virginia 22046
Home: (703) 987-0086 Office: (703) 549-6624 RCortez@silvernet.com

OBJECTIVE

Accounting management position requiring a knowledge of international finance

EXPERIENCE

March 2002 to present — **Staff Accountant/Financial Analyst,** Inter-American Imports (Alexandria, Virginia)
- Prepare accounting reports for wholesale giftware importer ($15 million annual sales)
- Audit financial transactions with suppliers in 12 Latin American countries
- Created a computerized model to adjust accounts for fluctuations in currency exchange rates
- Negotiated joint-venture agreements with major suppliers in Mexico and Colombia
- Implemented electronic funds transfer for vendor disbursements, improving cash flow and eliminating payables clerk position

October 1998 to March 2002 — **Staff Accountant,** Monsanto Agricultural Chemicals (Mexico City, Mexico)
- Handled budgeting, billing, and credit-processing functions for the Mexico City branch
- Audited travel/entertainment expenses for Monsanto's 30-member Latin American sales force
- Assisted in launching an online computer system to automate all accounting functions

EDUCATION

1996 to 1998 — Master of Business Administration with emphasis in international business
George Mason University (Fairfax, Virginia)

1993 to 1996 — Bachelor of Business Administration, Accounting, University of Texas, Austin

INTERCULTURAL AND TECHNICAL SKILLS

- Fluent in Spanish and German
- Traveled extensively in Latin America
- Excel • Access • HTML • Visual Basic

Combines accounting expertise with international experience in the minds of employers by stating it in an overall objective

Organizes information chronologically and emphasizes that organization with format

Makes each description concise, easy to read, and informative:
- Avoids the word "I" throughout
- Uses no unnecessary words

Highlights important skills by breaking them out into a list in a separate section

Includes e-mail address

Draws reader's attention to important points:
- Provides the sort of specific information on duties and accomplishments that catches an employer's eye
- Highlights duties and work achievements in bulleted lists
- Uses active language to describe duties

Includes informative headings throughout, making it easy for potential employers to find work-related, educational, or skills information

FIGURE 17.6 Combination Résumé

Erica Vorkamp

993 Church Street, Barrington, Illinois 60010
(847) 884-2153

OBJECTIVE

To obtain a position as a special event coordinator that will utilize my skills and experience

SKILLS AND CAPABILITIES

- Plan and coordinate large-scale public events
- Develop community support for concerts, festivals, and the arts
- Manage publicity for major events
- Coordinate activities of diverse community groups
- Establish and maintain financial controls for public events
- Negotiate contracts with performers, carpenters, electricians, and suppliers

SPECIAL EVENT EXPERIENCE

- Arranged 2003's week-long Arts and Entertainment Festival for the Barrington Public Library, involving performances by 25 musicians, dancers, actors, magicians, and artists
- Supervised the 2002 PTA Halloween Carnival, an all-day festival with game booths, live bands, contests, and food service that raised $7,600 for the PTA
- Organized the 2001 Midwestern convention for 800 members of the League of Women Voters, which extended over a three-day period and required arrangements for hotels, meals, speakers, and special tours
- Served as chairperson for the 2000 to 2002 Children's Home Society Fashion Show, a luncheon for 400–500 that raised $5,000–$6,700 for orphans and abused children

EDUCATION

- Associate of Applied Science, Administrative Assistant program with specialization in General Business, Lincoln School of Commerce (Lincoln, Nebraska), 1998

EMPLOYMENT HISTORY

- First National Bank of Chicago, 1998 to 2000, operations processor; processed checks with a lost/stolen status, contacted customers by phone, inspected checks to determine risk characteristics, processed payment amounts, verified receipt reports, researched check authenticity, managed orientation program for entry-level trainees
- Lincoln School of Commerce, 1996 to 1998, part-time administrative assistant for admissions (Business Department)

Relates all capabilities and experience to the specific job objective, giving a selective picture of the candidate's abilities

Includes event attendance statistics and fundraising results to quantify accomplishments

Includes work history (even though it has little bearing on job target) because Vorkamp believes recruiters want to see evidence that she's held a paying position

As Figure 17.6 shows, she used a combination approach to emphasize her abilities, skills, and accomplishments while also including a complete job history.

As you look at a number of sample résumés, you'll probably notice variations on the three basic formats presented here. Study these other options in light of effective communication principles; if you find one that seems like the best fit for your unique situation, by all means use it.

Writing Your Résumé

Until employers meet you in person, your résumé (and perhaps your cover letter) is usually the only information they have about you, so make sure that information is clear and compelling.

Your résumé is one of the most important documents you'll ever write. Even so, you needn't work yourself into a panic—all the advice you'll need to write effective résumés is presented in this chapter. Follow the three-step process and help ensure success by remembering four things: First, treat your résumé with the respect it deserves. Until you're able to meet with employers in person, your résumé is all they have of you. Until that first personal contact occurs, you *are* your résumé, and a single mistake or oversight can cost you interview opportunities. Second, give yourself plenty of time. Don't put off preparing your résumé until the last second and then try to write it in one sitting. Let this special document stew and try out different ideas and phrases until you hit on the right combination. Third, learn from good models. You can find thousands of sample résumés online at college websites and job sites such as Monster.com. Fourth, don't get frustrated by the conflicting advice you'll read about résumés; they are more art than science. Consider the alternatives and choose the approach that makes the most sense to you, given everything you know about successful business communication.

If you feel uncomfortable writing about yourself, you're not alone. Many people, even accomplished writers, find it difficult to write their own résumés. So if you're stuck, find a classmate or friend who's also writing a résumé and swap projects for a while. By working on each other's résumés, you might be able to speed up the process for both of you.

Keeping Your Résumé Honest

At some point in the writing process, you're sure to run into the question of honesty. A claim may be clearly wrong ("So what if I didn't get those last two credits—I got the same education as people who did graduate, so it's OK to say that I graduated too"). Or a rationalization may be more subtle ("Even though the task was to organize the company picnic, I did a good job, so it should qualify as 'project management' "). Either way, the information is dishonest.

Résumé fraud has reached epidemic proportions, but employers are fighting back with more rigorous screening techniques.

Somehow, the idea that "everybody lies on their résumés" has crept into popular consciousness, and dishonesty in the job search process has reached epidemic proportions. As many as half of the résumés now sent to employers contain false information. And it's not just the simple fudging of a fact here and there. Dishonest applicants are getting creative—and bold. Don't have the college degree you want? You can buy a degree from one of the websites that now offer fake diplomas. Better yet, pay a computer hacker to insert your name into a prestigious university's graduation records, in case somebody checks. Aren't really working in that impressive job at a well-known company? You can always list it on your résumé and sign up for a service that provides phony employment verification.[24]

Applicants with integrity know they don't need to stoop to lying to compete in the job market. If you are tempted to stretch the truth, bear in mind that professional recruiters have seen every trick in the book, and employers who are fed up with the dishonesty are getting more aggressive at uncovering the truth. Roughly 80 percent now contact references and conduct criminal background checks, and many do credit checks when the job involves financial responsibility.[25] And even if you get past these filters with fraudulent information, you'll probably be exposed on the job when you can't live up to your own résumé. Such fabrications have been known to catch up to people many years into their careers, with embarrassing consequences. See "Ethics Detective: The Dream Employee?"

To maintain a high standard of honesty in your résumé, subject any questionable entries to two simple tests: First, if something is not true, don't include it—don't try to rationalize it, excuse it, or make it sound better than it is; simply leave it out. A second and more subtle test, helpful for those borderline issues, is asking whether you'd be comfortable sharing a particular piece of information face to face. If you wouldn't be comfortable saying in it person, don't say it in your résumé. These tests will help ensure a factual résumé that represents who you are and leads you toward jobs that are truly right for you.

Adapting Your Résumé to Your Audience

One of the biggest challenges in writing a résumé is to make your unique qualities apparent to a reader quickly; they won't search through details if you don't look like an appealing candidate.

Your résumé needs to make a positive impression in a matter of seconds, so be sure to adopt a "you" attitude and think about your résumé from the employer's perspective. Ask yourself: What key qualifications will this employer be looking for? Which of these qualifications are your greatest strengths? What quality would set you apart from other candidates in the eyes of a potential employer? What are three or four of your greatest accomplishments, and what resulted from these accomplishments? No matter which format you use or what information you include, the single most important concept to keep in mind as you write is to translate your past accomplishments into perceived future potential. In other

Ethics Detective

The Dream Employee?

You've been poring over résumés for hours, searching for the ideal candidate to fill an opening on your sales staff. Your company sells golf simulators to retail stores, fitness clubs, driving ranges, and other facilities where golfers congregate. These machines use the latest in laser sensors and artificial reality software to let customers "play" some of the world's most famous courses—from inside a 10' x 20' booth.

The job requires a host of skills, from knowledge of golf's storied past to personal selling to technical competence. You're about to give up when you spy a résumé that lists everything you want and then some:

- B.A. in Physical Education, UCLA, 1983
- Electrical engineer, Unisys Corporation, 1984–1991
- Golf club designer, Reebok Sports, 1991–1994
- Graduated with honors from the University of Seattle's acclaimed master's program in sports management, 1993
- Top sales rep for Nike golf clubs in Western U.S. Sales Region; 1994, 1995, and 1997
- Have maintained an official golf handicap index between 10.0 and 12.0 ever since high school
- Winner, 1994 U.S. Amateur Golf Championship
- Co-authored the Scotland chapter in Arnold Palmer's best-selling world golf guide, *Global Golf.*

You're so excited by this candidate that you walk the résumé across the hall to your boss, the company president. She quickly scans the items you highlighted, then looks back at you like you've lost your mind. What did she see that you didn't?

ANALYSIS

Take another look the items that caught your eye in this candidate's résumé, then log onto the Internet and do some research. Can you find any inaccuracies?

words, employers are certainly interested in what you've done in the past, but they're more interested in what you can do for them in the future.

A good résumé is flexible and can be customized for various situations and employers. If you're applying for a marketing job at an international company such as Hewlett-Packard, the first skill on your list might be your ability to speak French. However, if you're applying for a sales position at Frito-Lay, the first skill on your list might be your summer job building product displays at a local grocery store. It's perfectly fine to have several résumés, each tailored for a different type of position or company.

Keep in mind that you may need to "translate" your skills and experiences into the terminology of the hiring organization. For instance, military experience can develop a number of skills that are valuable in business, but military terminology can sound like a foreign language to people who aren't familiar with it. Isolate the important general concepts and present them in common business language. Similarly, educational achievements in other countries might not align with the standard U.S. definitions of high schools, community colleges, technical and trade schools, and universities. If necessary, include a brief statement explaining how your degree or certificate relates to U.S. expectations—or how your U.S. degree relates to expectations in other countries, if you're applying for work abroad.

Although your résumé is a highly factual document, it should still tell the "story of you," giving readers a clear picture of the sort of employee you are.

Regardless of your background, it's up to you to combine your experiences into a straightforward message that communicates what you can do for your potential employer.[26] Think in terms of an image or a theme you'd like to project. Are you academically gifted? A campus leader? A well-rounded person? A creative genius? A technical wizard? Don't exaggerate, and don't alter the past or claim skills you don't have. However, don't dwell on negatives, either. By knowing yourself and your audience, you'll focus successfully on the strengths needed by potential employers.

Composing Your Résumé

Use short, crisp phrases built around strong verbs and nouns.

To save readers time and to state your information as forcefully as possible, write your résumé using a simple and direct style (you may need to modify your approach for other countries). Use short, crisp phrases instead of whole sentences, and focus on what your reader needs to know. Avoid using the word *I*, which can sound both self-involved and repetitious by the time you outline all your skills and accomplishments. Instead, start your phrases with strong action verbs such as these:[27]

accomplished	coordinated	initiated	participated	set up
achieved	created	installed	performed	simplified
administered	demonstrated	introduced	planned	sparked
approved	developed	investigated	presented	streamlined
arranged	directed	joined	proposed	strengthened
assisted	established	launched	raised	succeeded
assumed	explored	maintained	recommended	supervised
budgeted	forecasted	managed	reduced	systematized
chaired	generated	motivated	reorganized	targeted
changed	identified	operated	resolved	trained
compiled	implemented	organized	saved	transformed
completed	improved	oversaw	served	upgraded

For instance, you might say, "Coached a Little League team to the regional playoffs" or "Managed a fast-food restaurant and four employees." Here are some additional examples of how to phrase your accomplishments using active statements that show results:

AVOID WEAK STATEMENTS	USE ACTIVE STATEMENTS THAT SHOW RESULTS
Responsible for developing a new filing system	Developed a new filing system that reduced paperwork by 50 percent
I was in charge of customer complaints and all ordering problems	Handled all customer complaints and resolved all product order discrepancies
I won a trip to Europe for opening the most new customer accounts in my department	Generated the highest number of new customer accounts in my department
Member of special campus task force to resolve student problems with existing cafeteria assignments	Assisted in implementing new campus dining program that balances student wishes with cafeteria capacity

In addition to presenting your accomplishments effectively, think carefully about the way you provide your name and contact information, educational credentials, employment history, activities and achievements, and relevant personal data.

5 LEARNING OBJECTIVE

List the major sections of a traditional résumé

Name and Contact Information The first thing an employer needs to know is who you are and where you can be reached. Your name and contact information constitute the heading of your résumé, so include the following:

Be sure to provide complete and accurate contact information; mistakes in this section of the résumé are surprisingly common.

- Your name
- Physical address (both permanent and temporary if you're likely to move during the job search process)
- E-mail address
- Phone number(s)
- The URL of your personal webpage if you have one

Be sure that everything in your résumé heading is well-organized and clearly laid out on the page.

If the only e-mail address you have is through your current employer, get a free personal e-mail address from one of the many services that offer them, such a Hotmail or Yahoo!. It's not fair to your current employer to use company resources for a job search; moreover, it sends a bad signal to potential employers. Also, if your personal e-mail address

Get a professional-sounding e-mail address for business correspondence (such as *firstname.lastname@something.com*), if you don't already have one.

is anything like *precious.princess@something.com* or *PsychoDawg@something.com*, get a new e-mail address for your business correspondence.

Career Objective or Summary of Qualifications Experts disagree about the need to state a career objective on your résumé. Some argue that your objective is obvious from your qualifications, so stating your objective seems redundant. Some also maintain that such a statement labels you as being interested in only one thing and thus limits your possibilities as a candidate (especially if you want to be considered for a variety of openings). Other experts argue that employers will try to categorize you anyway, so you might as well make sure they attach the right label. They maintain that stating your objective up front gives employers an immediate idea of what you're all about.

Whether you choose to open with a career objective or a summary of qualifications, remember that the important point is to generate interest immediately.

Remember, your goal is to generate interest immediately. Consider the situation and the qualities the employer is looking for. If a stated objective will help you look like the perfect fit, then you should definitely consider adding it. Consider the following objectives:

> A software sales position in a growing company requiring international experience
>
> Advertising assistant with print media emphasis requiring strong customer-contact skills

With some careful writing, you can phrase your career objective in terms that highlight the reader's needs.

Both these objectives have an important aspect: even though they are stating "your" objective, they are really about the employer's needs. Avoid such self-absorbed (but all too common) statements such as "A fulfilling position that provides ample opportunity for career growth and personal satisfaction." Writers who include such statements have completely forgotten about audience focus and the "you" attitude.

Instead of stating your objective, you might summarize your qualifications in a brief statement that highlights your strongest points, particularly if you have had a good deal of varied experience. Use a short, simple phrase:

> Summary of qualifications: Ten years of experience in commission selling with track record of generating new customer leads through creative advertising and community leadership positions

If you have different types of qualifications (such as a certificate in a specific professional specialty but two years' experience in a different profession), prepare separate résumés, each with a different objective. The career objective or summary of qualifications may be the only section that employers read fully, so if you include either one, make it strong, concise, and convincing.

Your education might be one of your strongest selling points, so think carefully about how you will present it.

Education If you're still in school, education is probably your strongest selling point. Present your educational background in depth, choosing facts that support your "theme." Give this section a heading such as "Education," "Technical Training," or "Academic Preparation," as appropriate. Then, starting with the most recent, list the name and location of each school you attended, along with the term of your enrollment (in months and years), your major and minor fields of study, significant skills and abilities you've developed in your course work, and the degrees or certificates you've earned. If you're working on an uncompleted degree, include in parentheses the expected date of completion. Showcase your qualifications by listing courses that have directly equipped you for the job you are seeking, and indicate any scholarships, awards, or academic honors you've received.

The education section also includes off-campus training sponsored by business or government. Include any relevant seminars or workshops you've attended, as well as the certificates or other documents you've received. Mention high school or military training only if the associated achievements are pertinent to your career goals.

Whether you list your grade point average depends on the job you want and the quality of your grades. If you choose to show a grade-point average, be sure to mention the scale, especially if a five-point scale is used instead of a four-point scale. If you don't show your GPA on your résumé—and there's no rule saying you have to—be prepared to answer questions about it during the interview process, because many employers will assume that your GPA is not spectacular if you didn't show it on your résumé. If your grades are better within your major than in other courses, you can also list your GPA as "Major GPA" and include only those courses within your major (that D you received in scuba diving or Sanskrit doesn't need to hurt your accounting career).

Education is usually given less emphasis in a résumé after you've worked in your chosen field for a year or more. If work experience is your strongest qualification, save the section on education for later in the résumé and provide less detail.

Work Experience, Skills, and Accomplishments Like the education section, the work-experience section should focus on your overall theme. Align your past experience with your target employer's future. Call attention to the skills you've developed on the job and to your ability to handle increasing responsibility.

When you describe past job responsibilities, be sure to relate them to the needs of potential employers—identify the skills and knowledge from these previous jobs that you can apply to a future job.

List your jobs in reverse chronological order and include any part-time, summer, or intern positions, even if unrelated to your current career objective. Employers will see that you have the ability to get and hold a job—an important qualification in itself. If you have worked your way through school and contributed significantly to your education expenses, say so. Many employers interpret this accomplishment as a sign of both character and the ability to manage your time.

In each listing include the name and location of the employer. If readers are unlikely to recognize the organization, briefly describe what it does. When you want to keep the name of your current employer confidential, you can identify the firm by industry only ("a large film-processing laboratory"). Alternatively, you might use the firm's name and request confidentiality in your application letter or include an underlined note at the top or bottom of your résumé: "Résumé submitted in confidence." If an organization's name or location has changed since your worked there, state the current name and location, and then include the old information as "formerly . . . "

Before or after each job listing, state your functional title, such as "records clerk" or "salesperson." If you were a dishwasher, say so. Don't try to make your role seem more important by glamorizing your job title, functions, or achievements. Employers know better. Indicate how long you worked on each job, from month/year to month/year. Use the phrase "to present" to denote current employment. If a job was part-time, say so.

Devote the most space to the jobs that are related to your target position. If you were personally responsible for something significant, be sure to mention it ("Devised a new collection system that accelerated payment of overdue receivables"). Facts about your skills and accomplishments are the most important information you can give a prospective employer, so quantify them whenever possible:

Whenever you can, quantify your accomplishments in numerical terms: sales increases, customer satisfaction scores, measured productivity, and so on.

Designed a new ad that increased sales by 9 percent

Raised $2,500 in 15 days for cancer research

You may also include information describing other aspects of your background that pertain to your career objective. If you were applying for a position with a multinational organization, you could mention your command of another language or your travel experience. If you have an array of special skills, group them together and include them near your education or work-experience section. You might categorize such additional information as "Special Skills," "Work-Related Skills," "Other Experience," "Language Skills," or "Computer Skills."

If samples of your work might increase your chances of getting the job, insert a line at the end of your résumé offering to supply them on request, or indicate they're available in your e-portfolio. You may put "References available upon request" at the end of your résumé, but doing so is not necessary; the availability of references is usually assumed. Don't include actual names of references, but have them available.

Activities and Achievements Your résumé should describe any volunteer activities that demonstrate your abilities. List projects that require leadership, organization, teamwork, and cooperation. Emphasize career-related activities such as "member of the Student Marketing Association." List skills you learned in these activities, and explain how these skills are related to the job you're applying for. Include speaking, writing, or tutoring experience; participation in athletics or creative projects; fundraising or community-service activities; and offices held in academic or professional organizations. (However, mention of political or religious organizations may be a red flag to someone with differing views, so use your judgment.)

Don't overlook any personal accomplishments that indicate special skills or qualities, but make sure they are relevant to the jobs you're seeking.

Note any awards you've received. Again, quantify your achievements whenever possible. Instead of saying that you addressed various student groups, state how many and the approximate audience sizes. If your activities have been extensive, you may want to group them into divisions such as "College Activities," "Community Service," "Professional Associations," "Seminars and Workshops," and "Speaking Activities." An alternative is to divide them into two categories: "Service Activities" and "Achievements, Awards, and Honors."

Personal Data Personal data is another common source of confusion with résumés. Most experts advise you to skip personal interests unless including them enhances the employer's understanding of why you would be the best candidate for the job.[28] Do personal interests and accomplishments relate to the employer's business, culture, or customers? For instance, your achievements as an amateur artist could appeal to an advertising agency, even if you're applying for a technical or business position, because its shows an appreciation for the creative process. Similarly, an interest in sports and outdoor activities could show that you'll fit in nicely at a company such as REI, Nike, or Patagonia.

Some information is best excluded from your résumé. Civil rights laws prohibit employers from discriminating on the basis of gender, marital or family status, age (although only persons aged 40 to 70 are protected), race, religion, national origin, and physical or mental disability. So be sure to exclude any items that could encourage discrimination, even subconsciously. Experts also recommend excluding salary information, reasons for leaving jobs, names of previous supervisors, your Social Security number, and other identification codes. Save these items for the interview, and then offer them only if the employer specifically requests them.

If military service is relevant to the position, you may list it in this section (or under "Education" or "Work Experience"). List the date of induction, the branch of service, where you served, the highest rank you achieved, any accomplishments related to your career goals, and the date you were discharged.

Completing Your Résumé

The last step in the three-step writing process is no less important than the other two. As with any other business message, you need to revise your résumé, produce it in an appropriate form, and proofread it for any errors before distributing it to your target employers.

Try to keep your résumé to one page. If you have a great deal of experience and are applying for a higher-level position, you may need to prepare a somewhat longer résumé. The important thing is to have enough space to present a persuasive, accurate, and concise portrait of your skills and accomplishments.

Revising Your Résumé

Avoid the common errors that will get your résumé excluded from consideration.

Ask professional recruiters to list the most common mistakes they see on résumés, and you'll hear the same things over and over again. Keep your résumé out of the recycling bin by avoiding these flaws:

- **Too long.** The résumé is not concise, relevant, and to the point.
- **Too short or sketchy.** The résumé does not give enough information for a proper evaluation of the applicant.
- **Hard to read.** The résumé lacks enough white space and devices such as indentions and boldfacing to make the reader's job easier.
- **Wordy.** Descriptions are verbose, using numerous words describing simple concepts.
- **Too slick.** The résumé appears to have been written by someone other than the applicant, which raises the question of whether the qualifications have been exaggerated.
- **Amateurish.** The résumé includes the wrong information or presents it awkwardly, which indicates that the applicant has little understanding of the business world or of a particular industry.
- **Poorly produced.** The print is faint and difficult to read or the paper is cheap and inappropriate.

- **Misspelled and ungrammatical throughout.** The document contains spelling and grammar mistakes that indicate the candidate lacks the verbal skills that are so important on the job.
- **Boastful.** The overconfident tone makes the reader wonder whether the applicant's self-evaluation is realistic.
- **Gimmicky.** The words, structure, decoration, or material used in the résumé depart so far from the usual as to make the résumé ineffective.

Producing Your Résumé

With less than a minute to make a good impression, your résumé needs to look sharp and grab a recruiter's interest in the first few lines. A typical recruiter devotes 45 seconds to each résumé before tossing it into either the "maybe" or the "reject" pile. Most recruiters scan a résumé rather than read it from top to bottom. If yours doesn't stand out—or stands out in a negative way—chances are a recruiter won't look at it long enough to judge your qualifications.[29]

Effective résumé designs are simple, clean, and professional—not gaudy, clever, or cute.

Good design is a must, and it's not hard to achieve. As you can see in Figures 17.4, 17.5, and 17.6, good designs feature simplicity, order, plenty of white space, and straightforward typefaces such as Times Roman or Arial (most of the fonts on your computer are not appropriate for a résumé). Make your subheadings easy to find and easy to read, placing them either above each section or in the left margin. Use lists to itemize your most important qualifications, and leave plenty of white space, even if doing so forces you to use two pages rather than one. Color is not necessary by any means, but if you add color, make it subtle and sophisticated, such as in a thin horizontal line under your name and address. The most common way to get into trouble with résumé design is going overboard. If any part of the design "jumps out at you," get rid of it. You want people to be impressed with the information on your résumé, not the number of colors in your printer. To see how jarring and unprofessional a poor design looks to an employer, compare Figures 17.4, 17.5, and 17.6 with the "creative" design in Figure 17.7.

Start with a traditional printed résumé, but realize that you may need to create several other versions during your job search.

Until just a few years ago, producing résumés was a simple matter: you printed or photocopied as many as you needed and mailed them out. Not any more. Depending on the companies you apply to, you might want to produce your résumé in as many as six forms:

- **Printed traditional résumé.** Format your traditional résumé simply but elegantly to make the best impression on your employer. Naturally, printed versions must be delivered by hand or through the post.
- **Printed scannable résumé.** Prepare a printed version of your résumé that is unformatted and thus electronically scannable so that employers can store your information in their database.
- **Electronic plain-text file.** Create an electronic plain-text file to use when uploading your résumé information into web forms or inserting it into e-mail messages.
- **Microsoft Word file.** Keep a Microsoft Word file of your traditional résumé so that you can upload it on certain websites.
- **HTML format.** By creating an HTML version, you can post your résumé on your own website, on a page provided by your college, or some of the many job board sites now available.
- **PDF file.** This is an optional step, but a PDF file of your traditional résumé provides a simple, safe format to attach to e-mail messages. Creating PDFs requires Adobe Acrobat software, but a PDF can be a helpful item to have on hand in case an employer asks you to e-mail your résumé.

Don't panic; most of these versions are easy to do, as you'll see in the following sections.

Strive for a clean, classy look in your printed résumé, using professional-grade paper and a clean, high-quality printer.

Printing a Traditional Résumé The traditional paper résumé still has a place in this world of electronic job searches, if only to have a few ready whenever one of your networking contacts asks for a copy. Spend a few minutes in the paper aisle at an office supply store, and you'll notice that paper falls into three general categories: basic white bond paper used for photocopying and printing (avoid these; they make your résumé look cheap), predesigned papers with borders and backgrounds (avoid these; they make your résumé look gimmicky), and heavier, higher-quality papers designed specifically for résumés and other important documents. Choose a white or off-white paper from this third category; these papers are more expensive, but you don't need much, and it's a worthwhile investment.

FIGURE 17.7 Ineffective Résumé Design

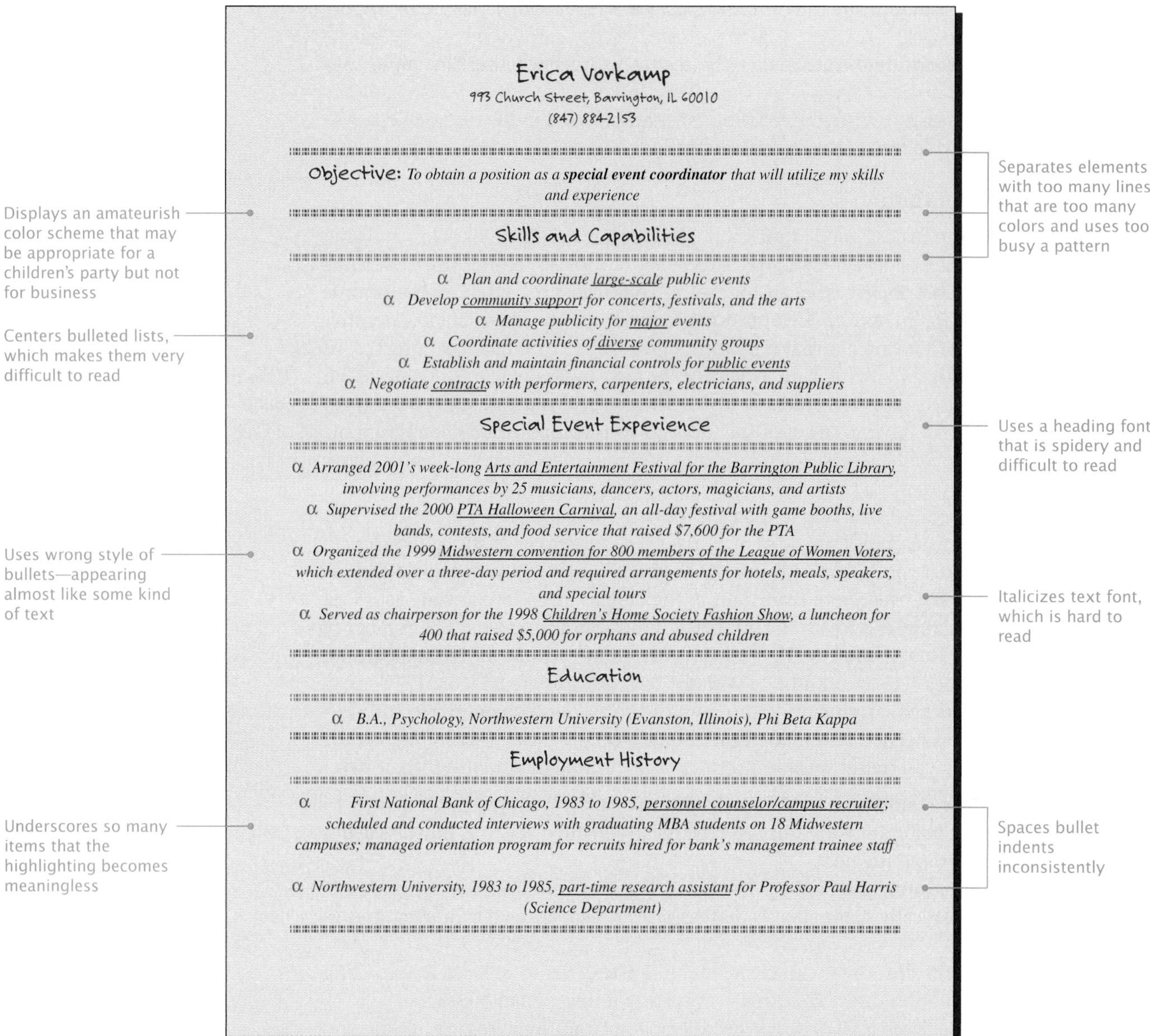
Erica Vorkamp
993 Church Street, Barrington, IL 60010
(847) 884-2153

Objective: *To obtain a position as a* ***special event coordinator*** *that will utilize my skills and experience*

Skills and Capabilities

α *Plan and coordinate large-scale public events*
α *Develop community support for concerts, festivals, and the arts*
α *Manage publicity for major events*
α *Coordinate activities of diverse community groups*
α *Establish and maintain financial controls for public events*
α *Negotiate contracts with performers, carpenters, electricians, and suppliers*

Special Event Experience

α *Arranged 2001's week-long Arts and Entertainment Festival for the Barrington Public Library, involving performances by 25 musicians, dancers, actors, magicians, and artists*
α *Supervised the 2000 PTA Halloween Carnival, an all-day festival with game booths, live bands, contests, and food service that raised $7,600 for the PTA*
α *Organized the 1999 Midwestern convention for 800 members of the League of Women Voters, which extended over a three-day period and required arrangements for hotels, meals, speakers, and special tours*
α *Served as chairperson for the 1998 Children's Home Society Fashion Show, a luncheon for 400 that raised $5,000 for orphans and abused children*

Education

α *B.A., Psychology, Northwestern University (Evanston, Illinois), Phi Beta Kappa*

Employment History

α *First National Bank of Chicago, 1983 to 1985, personnel counselor/campus recruiter; scheduled and conducted interviews with graduating MBA students on 18 Midwestern campuses; managed orientation program for recruits hired for bank's management trainee staff*

α *Northwestern University, 1983 to 1985, part-time research assistant for Professor Paul Harris (Science Department)*

Communication Solution

E*Trade's résumé analysis software goes beyond simple keyword analysis to study how important words are used in each résumé; Armnon Geshuri's recruiting team uses these results to make sure they find the best candidates for each position.

6 LEARNING OBJECTIVE

Describe what you should do to adapt your résumé to a scannable format

When you're ready to print your résumé, find a well-maintained, quality printer. Don't tolerate any streaks, stray lines, or poor print quality. You wouldn't walk into an interview looking messy, so make sure your résumé doesn't look that way, either.

Printing a Scannable Résumé To cope with the flood of unsolicited paper résumés in recent years, many companies now optically scan incoming résumés into a database. When hiring managers want to interview candidates for job openings, they search the database for the most attractive candidates, using keywords appropriate to a specific position. The system then displays a list of possible candidates, each with a percentage score indicating how closely the résumé reflects the employer's requirements.[30] Nearly all large companies now use these systems, as do many mid-sized companies and even some smaller firms.[31]

The emergence of such scanning systems has important implications for your résumé. First, computers are interested only in matching information to search parameters, not in artistic attempts at résumé design. A human being may never actually see the résumé as you submitted it, so don't worry about it looking depressingly dull; computers prefer it that way. Second, *optical character recognition (OCR) software* doesn't technically "read" anything; it merely looks for shapes that match stored profiles of characters. Although printing your name in some gothic font might look grand to you, it will look like nonsense to the OCR software. If the OCR software can't make sense of your fancy fonts or creative page layout, it will enter gibberish into the database (for instance, your name might go in as "W{$..3r ?00!#" instead of "Walter Jones"). Third, even the most sophisticated databases cannot conduct a search with the nuance and intuition of an experienced human recruiter. Therefore, choosing the keywords for your résumé is a critical step. A human might know that "data-driven webpage design" means that you know XML, but the database probably won't make that connection.

Converting your résumé to scannable format is easy to do—and extremely important.

The solution to these issues is twofold: (1) use a plain font and simplified design, and (2) compile your list of keywords carefully.

A scannable résumé contains the same information as your traditional résumé but is formatted to be OCR-friendly (see Figure 17.8):[32]

- Use a clean, common sans serif font such as Optima or Arial, and size it between 10 and 14 points.
- Make sure that characters do not touch one another (whether numbers, letters, or symbols—including the slash [/]).
- Don't use side-by-side columns (the OCR software reads one line all the way across the page).
- Don't use ampersands (&), percent signs (%), foreign-language characters (such as é and ö), or bullet symbols (use a dash—not a lower-case 'o'—in place of a bullet symbol).
- Put each phone number and e-mail address on its own line.
- Print on white, plain paper (speckles and other background coloration can confuse the OCR software).

Your scannable résumé will probably be longer than your traditional résumé because you can't compress text into columns and because you need plenty of white space between headings and sections. If your scannable résumé runs more than one page, make sure your name appears on every subsequent page (in case the pages become separated). Before sending a scannable résumé, check the company's website or call the human resources department to see whether it has any specific requirements other than those discussed here.

When adding a keyword summary to your résumé, keep your audience in mind. Employers generally search for nouns (since verbs tend to be generic rather than specific to a particular position or skill), so make your keywords nouns as well. Use abbreviations sparingly and only when they are well-known and unambiguous, such as *MBA*. List 20 to 30 words and phrases that define your skills, experience, education, professional affiliations, and so on. Place this list right after your name and address. Figure 17.8 offers an example of a keyword summary for an accountant.

One good way to identify which keywords to include in your summary is to underline all the skills listed in ads for the types of jobs you're interested in. (Another advantage of staying current by reading periodicals, networking, and so on is that you'll develop a good ear for current terminology.) Be sure to include only those keywords that correspond with your skills and experience. Trying to get ahead of the competition by listing skills you don't have is unethical; moreover, your efforts will be quickly exposed when your keywords don't match your job experience or educational background.

Think carefully about the keywords you include in your scannable résumé; they need to appeal to recruiters and reflect your qualities accurately.

Creating a Plain-Text File of Your Résumé An increasingly common way to get your information into an employer's database is by entering a *plain-text* version (sometimes referred to as an *ASCII text version*) of your résumé into an online form. This approach has the same goal as a scannable résumé, but it's faster, easier, and less prone to errors than the scanning process. If you have the option of mailing a scannable résumé or submitting plain text online, go with plain text.

A plain-text version of your résumé is simply a computer file without any of the formatting that you typically apply using a word processor.

In addition, when employers or networking contacts ask you to e-mail your résumé, they'll often want to receive it in plain text format in the body of your e-mail message. Thanks to the prevalence of computer viruses these days, many employers will refuse to open an e-mail attachment.

Plain text is just what it sounds like: no font selections, no bullet symbols, no colors, no lines or boxes, and so on. A plain-text version is easy to create with your word processor. Start

FIGURE 17.8 Scannable Résumé

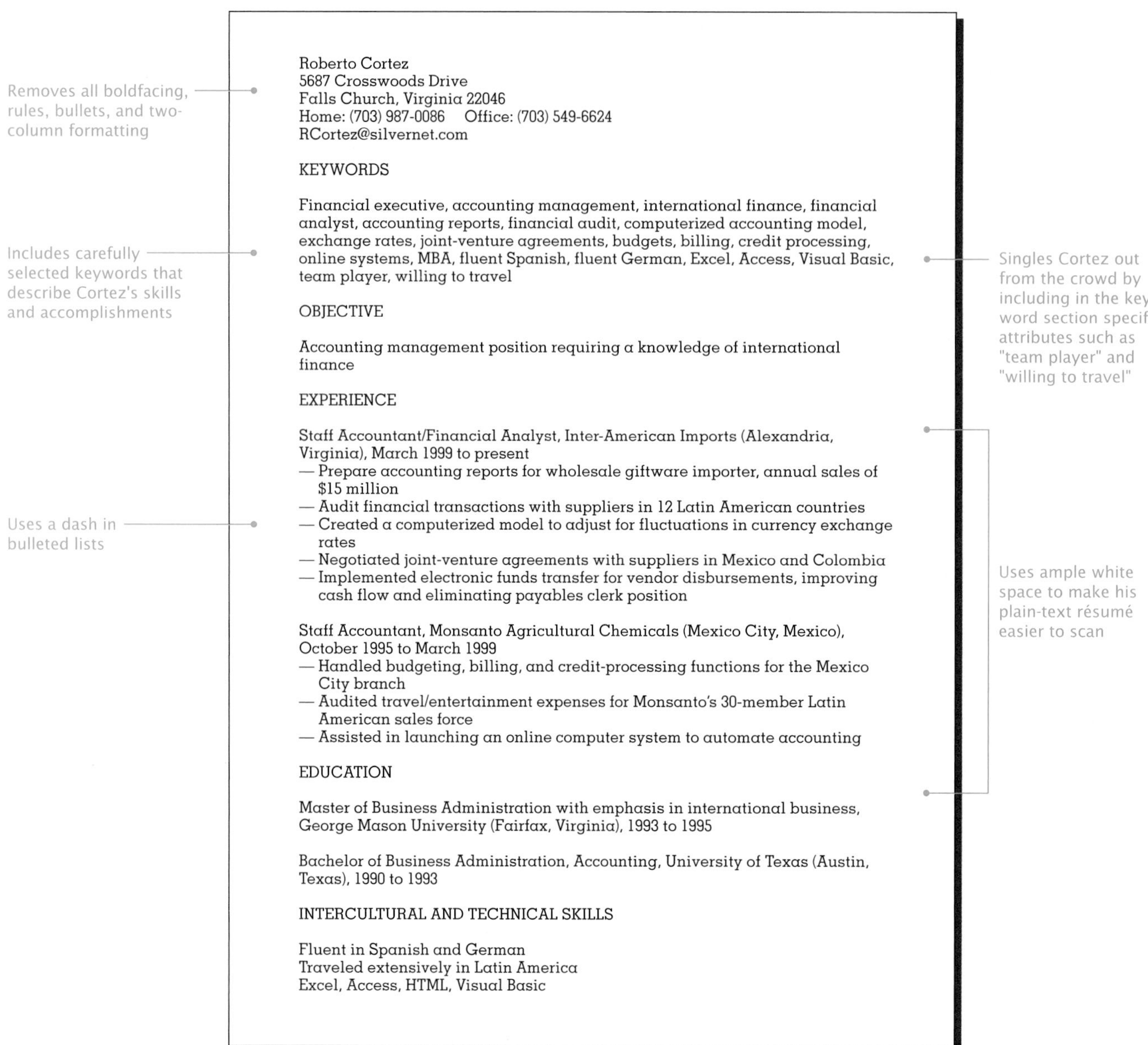
Roberto Cortez
5687 Crosswoods Drive
Falls Church, Virginia 22046
Home: (703) 987-0086 Office: (703) 549-6624
RCortez@silvernet.com

KEYWORDS

Financial executive, accounting management, international finance, financial analyst, accounting reports, financial audit, computerized accounting model, exchange rates, joint-venture agreements, budgets, billing, credit processing, online systems, MBA, fluent Spanish, fluent German, Excel, Access, Visual Basic, team player, willing to travel

OBJECTIVE

Accounting management position requiring a knowledge of international finance

EXPERIENCE

Staff Accountant/Financial Analyst, Inter-American Imports (Alexandria, Virginia), March 1999 to present
— Prepare accounting reports for wholesale giftware importer, annual sales of $15 million
— Audit financial transactions with suppliers in 12 Latin American countries
— Created a computerized model to adjust for fluctuations in currency exchange rates
— Negotiated joint-venture agreements with suppliers in Mexico and Colombia
— Implemented electronic funds transfer for vendor disbursements, improving cash flow and eliminating payables clerk position

Staff Accountant, Monsanto Agricultural Chemicals (Mexico City, Mexico), October 1995 to March 1999
— Handled budgeting, billing, and credit-processing functions for the Mexico City branch
— Audited travel/entertainment expenses for Monsanto's 30-member Latin American sales force
— Assisted in launching an online computer system to automate accounting

EDUCATION

Master of Business Administration with emphasis in international business, George Mason University (Fairfax, Virginia), 1993 to 1995

Bachelor of Business Administration, Accounting, University of Texas (Austin, Texas), 1990 to 1993

INTERCULTURAL AND TECHNICAL SKILLS

Fluent in Spanish and German
Traveled extensively in Latin America
Excel, Access, HTML, Visual Basic

Removes all boldfacing, rules, bullets, and two-column formatting
Includes carefully selected keywords that describe Cortez's skills and accomplishments
Uses a dash in bulleted lists
Singles Cortez out from the crowd by including in the keyword section specific attributes such as "team player" and "willing to travel"
Uses ample white space to make his plain-text résumé easier to scan

Make sure you verify the plain-text file that you output from your word processor; it might need a few manual adjustments (make these using a text editor such as Notepad, not your word processor).

with the file you used to create your traditional printed résumé, use the *save as* choice to save it as "plain text" or whichever similarly labeled option your software has, then verify the result.

The verification step is crucial because you can never be quite sure what happens to your layout. Open the text file to view the layout, but don't use your word processor; instead, open the file with a basic text editor (such as Microsoft's Notepad). If necessary, reformat the page manually, moving text and inserting spaces as needed. For simplicity's sake, left justify all your headings, rather than trying to center them manually. You can put headings in all caps or underline them with a row of dashes to separate them from blocks of text.

Creating a Word File of Your Traditional Résumé In some cases, an employer or job-posting website will let you upload a Microsoft Word file directly. (Although there are certainly other word processors on the market, particularly on Apple and Linux systems, Microsoft Word is the de facto standard in business these days.) This method of transferring information preserves the design and layout of your traditional printed résumé and saves you the trouble of creating a plain text version. However, read the instructions carefully. For instance, you can upload a Word résumé to Monster.com, but the site asks you to follow some specific formatting instructions to make sure your file isn't garbled.[33]

Before you submit a Word file to anyone, make sure your system is free from viruses. Infecting a potential employer's PC is probably not the way to make a good first impression.

Creating an HTML Version of Your Résumé You can probably find several uses for an HTML version of your résumé, including sending it as a fully formatted e-mail message (which is less risky than sending a Word file) and posting it on your personal webpage. Employers probably won't try to find you via a search engine, but if you send an e-mail to a potential employer, you can include the URL that links back to your site. Plus, you can provide links to supporting details and other materials from within your résumé. You can also use the HTML file in your e-portfolio, if you choose to create one. Even if you don't have HTML experience, you can save your résumé as a webpage from within Word.

You have several options for posting your résumé online, but remember that you could be displaying your personal information for all the world to see, so think carefully about privacy and security.

As you design your website résumé, think of important keywords to use as hyperlinks—words that will grab an employer's attention and make the recruiter want to click on that hyperlink to learn more about you. You can link to papers you've written, recommendations you've received, and sound or video clips that directly support your résumé. However, don't distract potential employers from your credentials by providing hyperlinks to other organizations or other websites (unless you designed a website and want to show it to recruiters). Also, in addition to the HTML version of your résumé, include a plain-text version on your webpage so that prospective employers can download it into their company's database.

Proofreading Your Résumé

Employers view your résumé as a concrete example of how you will prepare material on the job. It doesn't need to be good or pretty good; it needs to be perfect. Job seekers have committed every error from forgetting to put their own names on their résumés to misspelling "Education."[34] Not only is your résumé one of the most important documents you'll ever write, it's also one of the shortest, so there's every reason to make it perfect. Check all headings and lists for clarity and parallelism, and be sure that your grammar, spelling, and punctuation are correct. Ask at least three or four other people to read it, too. As the creator of the material, you could stare at a mistake for weeks and not see it.

Your résumé can't be "pretty good" or "almost perfect"—it needs to be perfect, so proofread it thoroughly and ask several other people to verify it, too.

You also need to make sure your résumé works in every format you create, so double- and triple-check your scannable and plain-text résumés closely. Many personal computer users now have low-cost scanners with OCR software, so you can even test the scannability of your résumé. These OCR tools aren't as accurate as commercial systems, but you'll get a rough idea of what your résumé will look like on the other end of the scanning process. And always test your plain-text version. Simply copy it into an e-mail message and send it to yourself and several friends on different e-mail systems. Doing so will tell you if previously hidden characters are suddenly showing up or if your formatting fell apart.

Once your résumé is complete, update it continuously. As flexible as employment has become these days, you'll probably want or need to change employers several times in your career. You'll also need a current résumé to apply for membership to professional organizations and to apply for a promotion. Moreover, updating your résumé frequently helps you see how your career is progressing. Some people even create "future résumés" that list skills and experience they'd like to have. By pursuing those attributes, they can become the person they want to be, the one in that résumé.

DOCUMENT MAKEOVER

IMPROVE THIS RÉSUMÉ

To practice correcting drafts of actual documents, visit www.prenhall.com/onekey on the web. Click "Document Makeovers" then click Chapter 17. You will find a résumé that contains problems and errors relating to what you've learned in this chapter about writing effective résumés. Use the Final Draft decision tool to create an improved version of this résumé. Check the document for spelling and grammatical errors, effective use of verbs and pronouns, inclusion of unnecessary information, and omission of important facts.

Distributing Your Résumé

What you do to distribute your résumé depends on the number of employers you target and their preferences for receiving résumés. Employers usually list their preferences on their websites, so verify this information to make sure that your résumé ends up in the right format and in the right channel. Beyond that, here are some general delivery tips:

- **Mailing your traditional and scannable résumés.** Take some care with the packaging. Spend a few extra cents to mail these documents in a flat 9 × 12 envelope, or better yet,

The most important advice you can get about distributing your résumé is to pay close attention to the specific wishes of each organization, whether it's an individual company or a job site online; some want printed résumés, some want Microsoft Word files, some want plain text in an online form, and so on.

use Priority Mail, which gives you a sturdy cardboard mailer and faster delivery for just a few more dollars. Consider sending both formats to each employer. In your cover letter, explain that for the employer's convenience, you're sending both standard and scannable versions.

- **Faxing your traditional and scannable résumés.** If you know that an employer prefers résumés via fax, be sure to include a standard fax cover sheet, along with your cover letter, followed by your résumé(s). Set the fax machine to "fine" mode to help ensure a high-quality printout on the receiving end.
- **E-mailing your résumé.** Unless someone specifically asks for a Word document as an attachment, don't send it—it probably won't be opened. Instead, insert plain text into the body of the e-mail message or simply include a hyperlink in the e-mail that links back to your webpage résumé (or do both). If you know a reference number or a job ad number, include it in your e-mail subject line.
- **Submitting your résumé online.** The details of submitting résumés online vary from site to site, so be sure to read the instructions thoroughly. Some sites let you grab a file from your hard disk and upload it as is; others instruct you to cut and paste blocks of plain text into specific fields in an online form. Whenever you do this, be sure to cut and paste, rather than re-typing information; you've already proofed this material, and you don't want to create any new mistakes while re-keying it.
- **Posting a résumé on your website.** If you wish to post your résumé on your website, you'll need to find some way of providing potential employers with your URL; most recruiters won't take the time to use search engines to find your site.[35]
- **Posting your résumé with an index service or job site.** Make sure you explore all your online options. Websites such as Monster.com, CareerBuilder.com, and Yahoo Hotjobs have rapidly become a major force in recruiting. Don't forget to check specialty sites as well, such as those maintained by professional societies in your fields of interest. However, before you upload your résumé to any site, learn about its confidentiality protection. Some sites allow you to specify levels of confidentiality, such as letting employers search your qualifications without seeing your personal contact information or preventing your current employer from seeing your résumé. In any case, carefully limit the amount of personal information you provide online. Never put your Social Security number, student ID number, or driver's license number online.

For a quick summary of the steps to take when planning, writing, and completing your résumé, refer to "Checklist: Writing an Effective Résumé."

CHECKLIST: Writing an Effective Résumé

A. PLAN YOUR RÉSUMÉ

- Analyze your purpose and audience carefully to make sure your message meets employers' needs.
- Gather pertinent information about your target companies.
- Select the best medium by researching the website and preferences of each employer.
- Organize your résumé around your strengths, choosing the chronological, functional, or combination structure (be careful about using the functional structure).

B. WRITE YOUR RÉSUMÉ

- Keep your résumé honest.
- Adapt your résumé to your audience to highlight the qualifications employers are looking for.
- Use powerful language to convey your name and contact information, career objective or summary of qualifications, education, work experience, skills, work or school accomplishments, and personal activities and achievements.

C. COMPLETE YOUR RÉSUMÉ

- Revise your résumé until it is clear, concise, and compelling.
- Produce your résumé in all the formats you might need: traditional printed résumé, scannable plain text file, Microsoft Word file, or HTML format.
- Proofread your résumé to make sure it is letter perfect.
- Distribute your résumé using the means that each employer prefers.

COMMUNICATION CHALLENGES AT E*TRADE FINANCIAL

E*Trade Financial is creating a division that will offer home mortgages and auto loans. To staff this effort, Armnon Geshuri has been asked to launch a hiring program that will attract recent college graduates. E*Trade knows that its most successful employees fit a consistent profile: They are highly energetic risk takers who thrive on chaos, act quickly, and adjust their work methods as often as needed.

Individual Challenge: To evaluate how candidates approach problems, Armnon wants to give interviewees a homework assignment to complete before their face-to-face interview. He asked you to develop the assignment, and you've decided to ask candidates to visit the E*Trade website and prepare a brief report that summarizes their observations, comments, and suggestions. (As background, visit www.etrade.com and explore the "products" and "about us" sections.) Decide how to evaluate their reports so that E*Trade can get a sense of how well interviewees fit the desired profile.

Team Challenge: Some hiring experts suggest reviewing résumés in teams. In a group of four to five, have each person give a copy of his or her résumé to everyone else. After reading all of the résumés, go around the group, reviewing the résumés one at a time and discussing your comments, observations, and suggestions. Look carefully for any of the "red flag" problems described in this chapter.

SUMMARY OF LEARNING OBJECTIVES

1 **Discuss how employers view today's job market.** The question of balance is vital to most employers today, as they try to balance the quality and cost of talent, as well as the size of their workforces in the face of fluctuating business requirements. Most employers view employment as being more flexible than in the past; many hire temporary workers and consultants on a project-by-project basis or try to shift jobs into cheaper labor markets in other countries. At the same time, many employers are now more understanding of applicants who've had nontraditional career paths, extensive self-employment, or multiple short-duration jobs.

2 **List three things you can do before you graduate and while you're jobhunting that will make you more valuable to employers.** To build toward a successful career, take the following actions: (1) Keep an employment portfolio of anything that shows your ability to perform, so that you can use it when writing your résumé and show it to employers as tangible evidence of your professionalism. (2) Take interim assignments (such as freelance work or internships) to gain valuable experience, relevant contacts, and important references. (3) Work on polishing and updating your skills by joining professional networks, taking a computer course, or seeking out other educational or life experiences.

3 **Describe the approach most employers take to finding potential new employees.** Employers look for new employees in as many as five different sources, and most have definite preferences from among these five. The preferred source is the employer's current workforce (most employers try to promote and hire from within before looking anywhere else), followed by the hiring manager's own personal contacts and personal recommendations from other trusted professionals. If these sources don't yield the right candidates or enough of them, employers will consider hiring an employment agency or search firm (sometimes called a "headhunter") and begin to review unsolicited résumés (often with the computerized assistance of a résumé database). Finally, employers will solicit applications from the general public, through their own websites, job boards such as Monster.com, and a variety of advertising efforts.

4 **Discuss how to choose the appropriate résumé organization, and list the advantages or disadvantages of the three common options.** Each organizational approach emphasizes different strengths. If you have a lot of employment experience, you would choose the chronological approach because it focuses on your work history. The advantages of the chronological résumé are (1) it helps employers easily locate necessary information, (2) it highlights your professional growth and career progress, and (3) it emphasizes continuity and stability in your employment background. The functional approach focuses on particular skills and competencies you've developed. The advantages of the functional résumé are (1) it helps employers easily see what you can do for them, (2) it allows you to emphasize earlier job experience, and (3) it lets you downplay any lengthy periods of unemployment or a lack of career progress. However,

many employers are suspicious of the functional résumé for this very reason. The combination approach uses the best features of the other two, but it has two disadvantages: (1) It tends to be longer, and (2) it can be repetitious if you must list accomplishments and skills in the functional section as well as in the individual job descriptions.

5 **List the major sections of a traditional résumé.** Your résumé must include three sections: (1) your contact information (including name, address, telephone, and e-mail), (2) your education background (with related skills and accomplishments), and (3) your work experience (with related skills and accomplishments). Options include listing your career objective or a summary of qualifications, describing related activities and achievements, and perhaps (although not necessarily recommended) providing relevant personal data.

6 **Describe what you should do to adapt your résumé to a scannable format.** A scannable résumé requires two significant changes to the traditional printed format: removing all formatting (including multiple columns of bullet points) and adding a list of keywords. You can remove all the formatting manually, but it's easier to just save a plain text version of your traditional résumé file, then verify its appearance using a simple text editor such as NotePad. You may need to move a few items around and insert or remove blank lines and spaces to make sure all the items line up appropriately. Then add a list of keywords (nouns) that define your skills, experience, and education. Make sure it also includes important jargon that is characteristic of the language in your field.

Test Your Knowledge

1. What are some of the most important qualities that employers look for in job applicants?
2. What is the purpose of maintaining an employment portfolio?
3. In what ways can job seekers use the Internet during their career and employment search?
4. What is a résumé, and why is it important to adopt a "you" attitude when preparing one?
5. How does a chronological résumé differ from a functional résumé, and when is each appropriate?
6. Why are some employers suspicious of the functional résumé?
7. What elements are commonly included in a résumé?
8. What are some of the most common problems with résumés?
9. Why is it important to provide a keyword summary in a scannable or electronic résumé?
10. Should you include personal data on a résumé? Explain your answer.

Apply Your Knowledge

1. If you're still a year or two away from graduation, should you worry about your job search? Explain your answer.
2. One of the disadvantages of résumé scanning is that some qualified applicants will be missed because the technology isn't perfect. However, more companies are using this approach. Do you think that résumé scanning is a good idea? Please explain.
3. Stating your career objective on a résumé or application might limit your opportunities by labeling you too narrowly. Not stating your objective, however, might lead an employer to categorize you incorrectly. Which outcome is riskier? Do summaries of qualifications overcome such drawbacks? If so, how? Explain briefly.
4. Some people don't have a clear career path when they enter the job market. If you're in the situation, how would your uncertainty affect the way your write your résumé?
5. **Ethical Choices** Between your sophomore and junior year, you quit school for a year to earn the money to finish college. You worked as a clerk in a finance company, checking references on loan applications, typing, and filing. Your manager made a lot of the fact that he had never attended college. He seemed to resent you for pursuing your education, but he never criticized your work, so you thought you were doing okay. After you'd been working there for six months, he fired you, saying that you failed to be thorough enough in your credit checks. You were actually glad to leave, and you found another job right away at a bank doing similar duties. Now that you've graduated from college, you're writing your résumé. Will you include the finance company job in your work history? Please explain.

Practice Your Knowledge

Document for Analysis

Read the following résumé information, then (1) analyze the strengths or weaknesses of the information, and (2) create a résumé that follows the guidelines presented in this chapter.

Document 17.A: Writing a Résumé

Sylvia Manchester
765 Belle Fleur Blvd.
New Orleans, LA 70113
(504) 312-9504
smanchester@rcnmail.com

PERSONAL: Single, excellent health, 5'8", 116 lbs.; hobbies include cooking, dancing, and reading.

JOB OBJECTIVE: To obtain a responsible position in marketing or sales with a good company.

Education: BA degree in biology, University of Louisiana. Graduated with a 3.0 average. Member of the varsity cheerleading squad. President of Panhellenic League. Homecoming queen.

WORK EXPERIENCE

<u>Fisher Scientific Instruments, 2000 to present, field sales representative.</u> Responsible for calling on customers and explaining the

features of Fisher's line of laboratory instruments. Also responsible for writing sales letters, attending trade shows, and preparing weekly sales reports.

Fisher Scientific Instruments, 1997–99, customer service representative. Was responsible for handling incoming phone calls from customers who had questions about delivery, quality, or operation of Fisher's line of laboratory instruments. Also handled miscellaneous correspondence with customers.

Medical Electronics, Inc., 1994–97, administrative assistant to the vice president of marketing. In addition to handling typical secretarial chores for the vice president of marketing, I was in charge of compiling the monthly sales reports, using figures provided by members of the field sales force. I also was given responsibility for doing various market research activities.

New Orleans Convention and Visitors Bureau, 1991–94, summers, tour guide. During the summers of my college years, I led tours of New Orleans for tourists visiting the city. My duties included greeting conventioneers and their spouses at hotels, explaining the history and features of the city during an all-day sight-seeing tour, and answering questions about New Orleans and its attractions. During my fourth summer with the bureau, I was asked to help train the new tour guides. I prepared a handbook that provided interesting facts about the various tourist attractions, as well as answers to the most commonly asked tourist questions. The Bureau was so impressed with the handbook they had it printed up so that it could be given as a gift to visitors.

University of Louisiana, 1991–94, part-time clerk in admissions office. While I was a student in college, I worked 15 hours a week in the admissions office. My duties included filing, processing applications, and handling correspondence with high school students and administrators.

Exercises

For live links to all websites discussed in this chapter, visit this text's website at www.prenhall.com/bovee. Just log on, select Chapter 17, and click on "Featured Websites." Locate the name of the page or the URL related to the material in the text.

17.1 Work-Related Preferences: Self-Assessment What work-related activities and situations do you prefer? Evaluate your preferences in each of the following areas. Use the results as a good start for guiding your job search.

Activity or Situation	Strongly Agree	Agree	Disagree	No Preference
1. I want to work independently.	_____	_____	_____	_____
2. I want variety in my work.	_____	_____	_____	_____
3. I want to work with people.	_____	_____	_____	_____
4. I want to work with products or machines.	_____	_____	_____	_____
5. I want physical work.	_____	_____	_____	_____
6. I want mental work.	_____	_____	_____	_____
7. I want to work for a large organization.	_____	_____	_____	_____
8. I want to work for a nonprofit organization.	_____	_____	_____	_____
9. I want to work for a small family business.	_____	_____	_____	_____
10. I want to work for a service business.	_____	_____	_____	_____
11. I want regular, predictable work hours.	_____	_____	_____	_____
12. I want to work in a city location.	_____	_____	_____	_____
13. I want to work in a small town or suburb.	_____	_____	_____	_____
14. I want to work in another country.	_____	_____	_____	_____
15. I want to work outdoors.	_____	_____	_____	_____
16. I want to work in a structured environment.	_____	_____	_____	_____

17.2 Internet Based on the preferences you identified in the self-assessment (Exercise 17.1) and the academic, professional, and personal qualities you have to offer, perform an Internet search for an appropriate career, using any of the websites listed in Table 17.1 on page 525. Draft a brief report indicating how the careers you select and job openings you find match your strengths and preferences.

17.3 Teamwork Working with another student, change the following statements to make them more effective for a traditional résumé by using action verbs.

a. Have some experience with database design.
b. Assigned to a project to analyze the cost accounting methods for a large manufacturer.
c. I was part of a team that developed a new inventory control system.

d. Am responsible for preparing the quarterly department budget.
e. Was a manager of a department with seven employees working for me.
f. Was responsible for developing a spreadsheet to analyze monthly sales by department.
g. Put in place a new program for ordering supplies.

17.4 **Résumé Preparation: Work Accomplishments** Using your team's answers to Exercise 17.3, make the statements stronger by quantifying them (make up any numbers you need).

17.5 **Ethical Choices** Assume that you achieved all the tasks shown in Exercise 17.3 not as an individual employee, but as part of a work team. In your résumé, must you mention other team members? Explain your answer.

17.6 **Résumé Preparation: Electronic Version** Using your revised version of Document for Analysis 17.A, prepare a fully formatted print résumé. What formatting changes would Sylvia Manchester need to make if she were sending her résumé electronically? Develop a keyword summary and make all the changes needed to complete this electronic résumé.

Expand Your Knowledge

For live links to the websites that follow, go to www.prenhall.com/bovee. When you log on, select Chapter 17, then select "Featured Websites," click on the URL of the website you wish to visit, and review the website to complete these exercises.

Exploring the Best of the Web

Post an Online Résumé
www.careerbuilder.com
At CareerBuilder, you'll find sample résumés, tips on preparing different types of résumés (including scannable ones), links to additional articles, and expert advice on creating résumés that bring positive results. After you've polished your résumé-writing skills, you can search for jobs online using the site's numerous links to national and international industry-specific websites. You can access the information at CareerBuilder to develop your résumé and then post it with prospective employers—all free of charge. Take advantage of what this site offers, and get ideas for writing or improving a new résumé.

1. Before writing a new résumé, make a list of action verbs that describe your skills and experience.
2. Describe the advantages and disadvantages of chronological and functional résumé formats. Do you think a combination résumé would be an appropriate format for your new résumé? Explain why or why not.
3. List some of the tips you learned for preparing an electronic résumé.

Exploring the Web on Your Own

Review these chapter-related websites on your own to learn more about writing résumés and cover letters.

1. To find out what happens when résumés are scanned, log on to Proven Résumés, www.provenresumes.com/reswkshps/electronic/scnres.html.
2. Take measures to ensure that your e-mail résumé arrives intact by following the helpful advice at www.businessweek.com/careers/content/nov2001/ca20011113_7790.html.
3. Accepted.com, www.accepted.com, can give you advice on getting into graduate school or on writing the perfect résumé.

Learn Interactively

Interactive Study Guide

Go to the Companion Website at www.prenhall.com/bovee. For Chapter 17, take advantage of the interactive "Study Guide" to test your knowledge of the chapter. Get instant feedback on whether you need additional studying.

Also, visit this site's "Study Hall," where you'll find an abundance of valuable resources that will help you succeed in this course.

Peak Performance Grammar and Mechanics

To improve your skill with spelling, visit www.prenhall.com/onekey, click "Peak Performance Grammar and Mechanics," then click "Spelling." Take the Pretest to determine whether you have any weak areas. Then review those areas in the Refresher Course. Take the Follow-Up Test to check your grasp of spelling. Finally, for additional reinforcement in frequently confused, misused, and misspelled words, go to www.prenhall.com/bovee, where you will find "Improve Your Grammar, Mechanics, and Usage" exercises.

CASES

BUILDING TOWARD A BETTER CAREER

1. Taking stock and taking aim: Résumé tailored for the right job Think about yourself. What are some things that come easily to you? What do you enjoy doing? In what part of the country would you like to live? Do you like to work indoors? Outdoors? A combination of the two? How much do you like to travel? Would you like to spend considerable time on the road? Do you like to work closely with others or more independently? What conditions make a job unpleasant? Do you delegate responsibility easily, or do you like to do things yourself? Are you better with words or numbers? Better at speaking or writing? Do you like to work under fixed deadlines? How important is job security to you? Do you want your supervisor to state clearly what is expected of you, or do you like the freedom to make many of your own decisions?

Your task: After answering these questions, gather information about possible jobs that suit your profile by consulting reference materials (from your college library or placement center) and by searching the Internet (using some of the search strategies discussed in Chapter 10). Next, choose a location, a company, and a job that interests you. With guidance from your instructor, decide whether to apply for a job you're qualified for now or one you'll be qualified for with additional education. Then, as directed by your instructor, write a résumé.

2. Scanning the possibilities: Résumé for the Internet In your search for a position, you discover Career Magazine, a website that lists hundreds of companies advertising on the Internet. Your chances of getting an interview with a leading company will be enhanced if you submit your résumé and cover letter electronically. On the web, explore www. careermag.com.

Your task: Prepare a scannable résumé that could be submitted to one of the companies advertising at the Career Magazine website. Print out the résumé for your instructor.

WRITING A RÉSUMÉ AND AN APPLICATION LETTER

3. "Help wanted": Application for a job listed in the classified section Among the jobs listed in today's *Chicago Tribune* (435 N. Michigan Avenue, Chicago, IL 60641) are the following:

Accounting Assistant

Established leader in the vacation ownership industry has immediate opening in its Northbrook corp. accounting dept. for an Accounting Assistant. Responsibilities include: bank reconciliation, preparation of deposits, AP, and cash receipt posting. Join our fast-growing company and enjoy our great benefits package. Flex work hours, medical, dental insurance. Fax résumé to Lisa: 847-564-3876.

Administrative Assistant

Fast-paced Wood Dale office seeks professional with strong computer skills. Proficient in MS Word & Excel, PowerPoint a plus. Must be detail oriented, able to handle multiple tasks, and possess strong communication skills. Excellent benefits, salary, and work environment. Fax résumé to 630-350-8649.

Customer Service

A nationally known computer software developer has an exciting opportunity in customer service and inside sales support in its fast-paced downtown Chicago office. You'll help resolve customer problems over the phone, provide information, assist in account management, and administer orders. If you're friendly, self-motivated, energetic, and have 2 years of experience, excellent problem-solving skills, organizational, communication, and PC skills, and communicate well over the phone, send résumé to J. Haber, 233 North Lake Shore Drive, Chicago, IL 60641.

Sales-Account Manager

MidCity Baking Company is seeking an Account Manager to sell and coordinate our programs to major accounts in the Chicago market. The candidate should possess strong analytical and selling skills and demonstrate computer proficiency. Previous sales experience with major account level assignment desired. A degree in business or equivalent experience preferred. For confidential consideration please mail résumé to Steven Crane, Director of Sales, MidCity Baking Company, 133 N. Railroad Avenue, Northlake IL 60614.

Your task: Write a résumé for one of these potential employers.

chapter 18

Applying and Interviewing for Employment

LEARNING OBJECTIVES

After studying this chapter, you will be able to

1. Define the purpose of application letters, and explain how to apply the AIDA organizational approach to them
2. Describe the typical sequence of job interviews
3. Describe briefly what employers look for during an employment interview
4. List six tasks you need to complete to prepare for a successful job interview
5. Explain the three stages of a successful employment interview
6. Identify the most common employment messages that follow an interview, and explain when you would use each one

COMMUNICATION CLOSE-UP AT GOOGLE

www.google.com

When you prepare for an interview, your research often yields useful clues about the hiring company and the types of people it wants. Those clues can also help you decide which skills, traits, and successes to highlight during the interview. You'll find them especially helpful when interviewing with companies that have strong corporate personalities and specific ideas about hiring and management—companies such as Google.

For example, to maintain its lead in search-engine technology, Google pursues exceptionally talented software engineers. Most are either young risk takers with adventurous outside interests or experienced superstars from top research labs. Hiring such divergent personalities creates a tension between risk and caution that helps Google quickly try, kill, or improve new ideas—and the company believes that even the best technology can always be improved.

Google also believes that talented people can manage themselves. "There's faith here in the ability of smart, well-motivated people to do the right thing," says Wayne Rosing, head of Google's engineers. "Anything that gets in the way of that is evil," including middle managers. They're no longer part of Google's engineering hierarchy because they tended to stifle innovation and creativity. Instead,

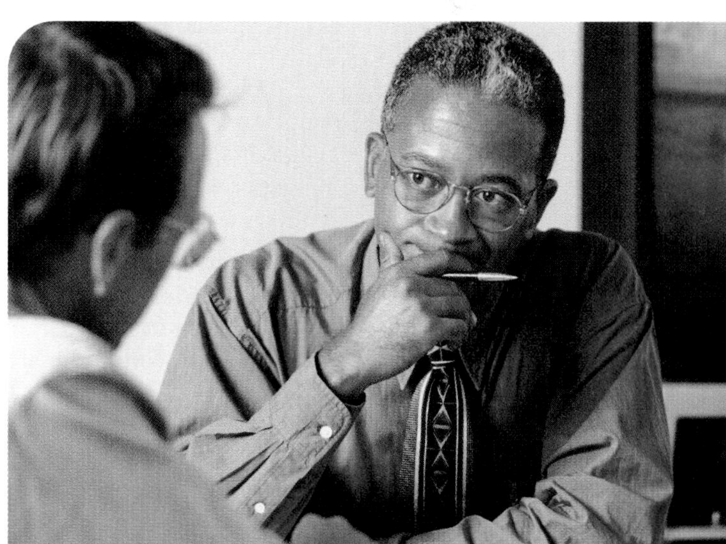

Technical talent is so crucial to Google's success that the company expects its engineers to spend as much as 20 percent of their time interviewing job candidates.

Rosing now assigns engineers to small teams and rotates project leadership within the group.

In addition to working on their projects, engineers are expected to spend 20 percent of their time interviewing outside job candidates. These interviews help them stay abreast of new thinking, and it helps the company cope with the deluge of over 1,000 résumés per day.

You may never apply to Google, but similar insights about the companies you are interested in will give you a competitive edge. And here's a hint: information like this isn't usually posted on a company's website. However, some extra digging in magazines, newsgroups, and other sources can unearth insights that will help you prepare for every stage of the employment search process.[1]

PREPARING OTHER TYPES OF EMPLOYMENT MESSAGES

Your résumé (see Chapter 17) is the centerpiece of your job search package, but it needs support from several other employment messages, including application letters, job-inquiry letters, application forms, and follow-up notes.

Application Letters

1 LEARNING OBJECTIVE

Define the purpose of application letters, and explain how to apply the AIDA organizational approach to them

Always accompany your résumé with an application letter that explains what you're sending, why you're sending it, and how the reader can benefit from reading your material.

Resist the temptation to stand out with gimmicky letters; they almost never work. Impress with knowledge and professionalism instead.

The casual e-mail communication style you may be accustomed to with your friends is considered unacceptable by most business professionals, particularly when you're making your initial contacts.

Whenever you submit your résumé, accompany it with a cover, or application, letter to let readers know what you're sending, why you're sending it, and how they can benefit from reading it. Always send your résumé and application letter together because each has a unique job to perform. The purpose of your résumé is to get employers interested enough to contact you for an interview. The purpose of your application letter is to get employers interested enough to read your résumé.

Before drafting a letter, learn something about the organization you're applying to, then focus on your audience so that you can show you've done your homework. Imagine yourself in the recruiter's situation, and show how your background and talents will solve a particular problem or fill a specific need the company has. The more you can learn about the organization, the better you'll be able to capture the reader's attention and convey your interest in the company.[2] During your research, find out the name, title, and department of the person you're writing to. Reaching and addressing the right person is the most effective way to gain attention. Avoid canned phrases such as "To Whom It May Concern" or gender-limited phrases such as "Dear Sir." If you can't find a specific name, use something like "Dear Hiring Manager."[3]

When putting yourself in your reader's shoes, remember that this person's in-box is probably overflowing with résumés and cover letters. So respect your reader's time. Steer clear of gimmicks, which almost never work, and don't waste time covering information that already appears in your résumé. Keep your letter straightforward, fact-based, short, upbeat, and professional. Some quick tips for cover letters include the following:[4]

- **Be specific.** Avoid general objectives. Be as clear as possible about the kind of opportunity and industry you're looking for. Show that you understand the company and the position by echoing the key messages you picked up from the job ad, company brochure, or other information source.
- **Never volunteer salary information unless an employer asks for it.** And even if you are asked, you probably don't want to pin down a specific number at this point in the process. See "Discussing Salary" on page 574 for more information.
- **Keep it short—and keep e-mail cover letters even shorter.** In just two or three paragraphs, convey how your strengths and character would fit the position. If you find you need more space, you probably haven't thought through the opportunity sufficiently. When sending a cover letter by e-mail, make it even shorter than traditional application letters. Remember, e-mail readers want the gist as quickly as possible.
- **Show some personality.** Because your application letter is in your own style (rather than the choppy, shorthand style of your résumé), make the most of your chance to reveal not only your excellent communication skills but also some of your personality.
- **Aim for high quality.** Meticulously check your spelling, mechanics, and grammar. Recruiters are complaining about the declining quality of written communication,

FIGURE 18.1 Effective Solicited Application Letter

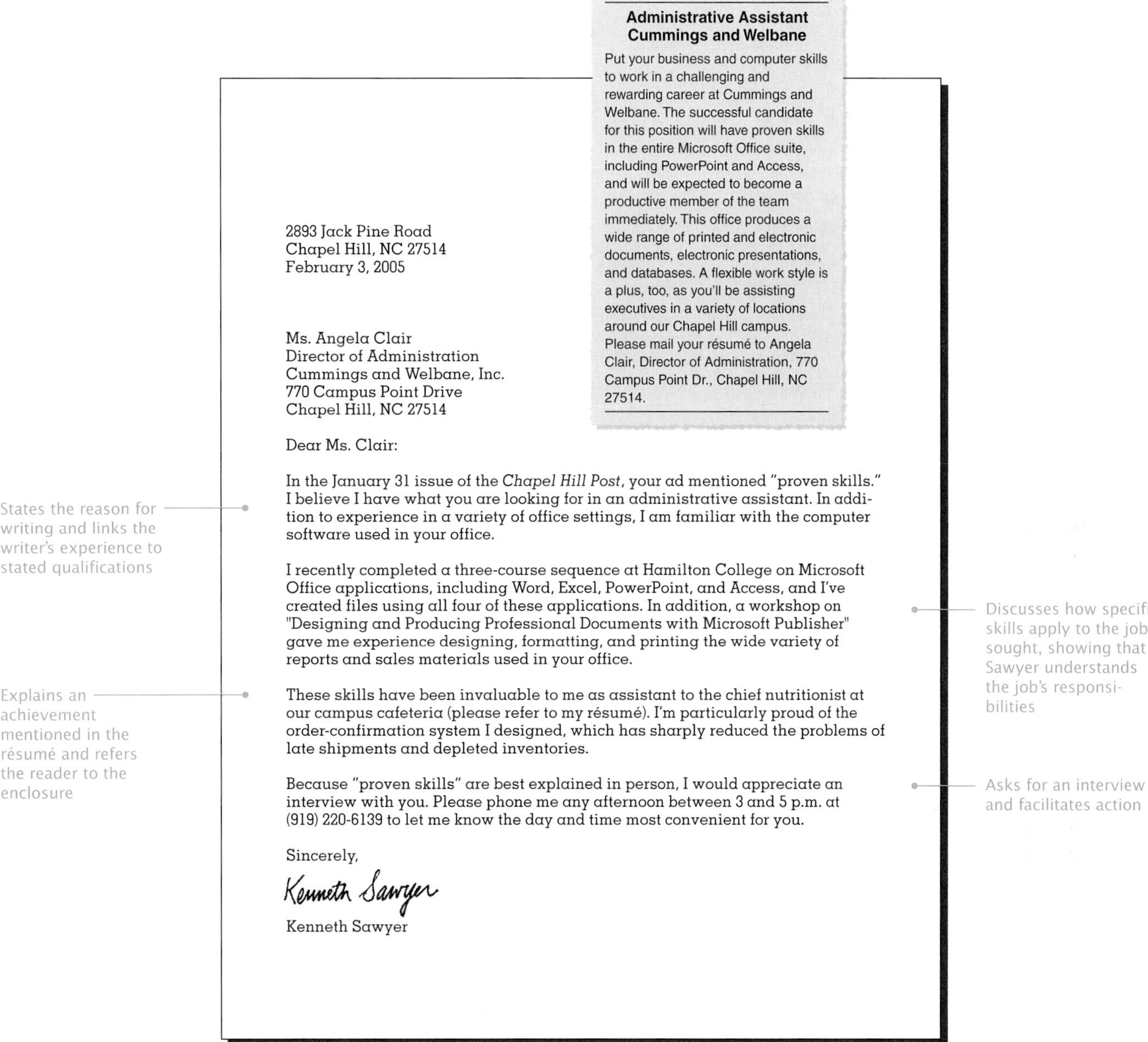

Administrative Assistant
Cummings and Welbane

Put your business and computer skills to work in a challenging and rewarding career at Cummings and Welbane. The successful candidate for this position will have proven skills in the entire Microsoft Office suite, including PowerPoint and Access, and will be expected to become a productive member of the team immediately. This office produces a wide range of printed and electronic documents, electronic presentations, and databases. A flexible work style is a plus, too, as you'll be assisting executives in a variety of locations around our Chapel Hill campus. Please mail your résumé to Angela Clair, Director of Administration, 770 Campus Point Dr., Chapel Hill, NC 27514.

2893 Jack Pine Road
Chapel Hill, NC 27514
February 3, 2005

Ms. Angela Clair
Director of Administration
Cummings and Welbane, Inc.
770 Campus Point Drive
Chapel Hill, NC 27514

Dear Ms. Clair:

In the January 31 issue of the *Chapel Hill Post*, your ad mentioned "proven skills." I believe I have what you are looking for in an administrative assistant. In addition to experience in a variety of office settings, I am familiar with the computer software used in your office.

I recently completed a three-course sequence at Hamilton College on Microsoft Office applications, including Word, Excel, PowerPoint, and Access, and I've created files using all four of these applications. In addition, a workshop on "Designing and Producing Professional Documents with Microsoft Publisher" gave me experience designing, formatting, and printing the wide variety of reports and sales materials used in your office.

These skills have been invaluable to me as assistant to the chief nutritionist at our campus cafeteria (please refer to my résumé). I'm particularly proud of the order-confirmation system I designed, which has sharply reduced the problems of late shipments and depleted inventories.

Because "proven skills" are best explained in person, I would appreciate an interview with you. Please phone me any afternoon between 3 and 5 p.m. at (919) 220-6139 to let me know the day and time most convenient for you.

Sincerely,

Kenneth Sawyer

Kenneth Sawyer

States the reason for writing and links the writer's experience to stated qualifications
Discusses how specific skills apply to the job sought, showing that Sawyer understands the job's responsibilities
Explains an achievement mentioned in the résumé and refers the reader to the enclosure
Asks for an interview and facilitates action

including cover letters. Since spellcheckers are only a mouse click away, there's really no excuse for misspelled words. Don't think that typos don't matter, either; readers equate typos with writing ability. Second, don't let the ease and speed of e-mail lull you into thinking it's a casual medium. Recruiters who complain about writing quality specifically mention sloppy e-mail cover letters from younger applicants who are accustomed to casual online communication with their friends but who don't seem to recognize that expectations in the business world are much different. At least until potential employers get to know you, they treat your e-mail messages every bit as seriously as formal, printed letters.[5]

If you're sending a **solicited application letter** in response to an announced job opening, you'll usually know what qualifications the organization is seeking. You'll also face more competition for the position because hundreds of other job seekers will have seen the listing and may be sending applications too. The letter in Figure 18.1 was written in response to a help-wanted ad. Sawyer highlights his chief qualifications and mirrors the requirements specified in the ad. He actually grabs attention by focusing on the phrase

FIGURE 18.2 Effective Unsolicited Application Letter

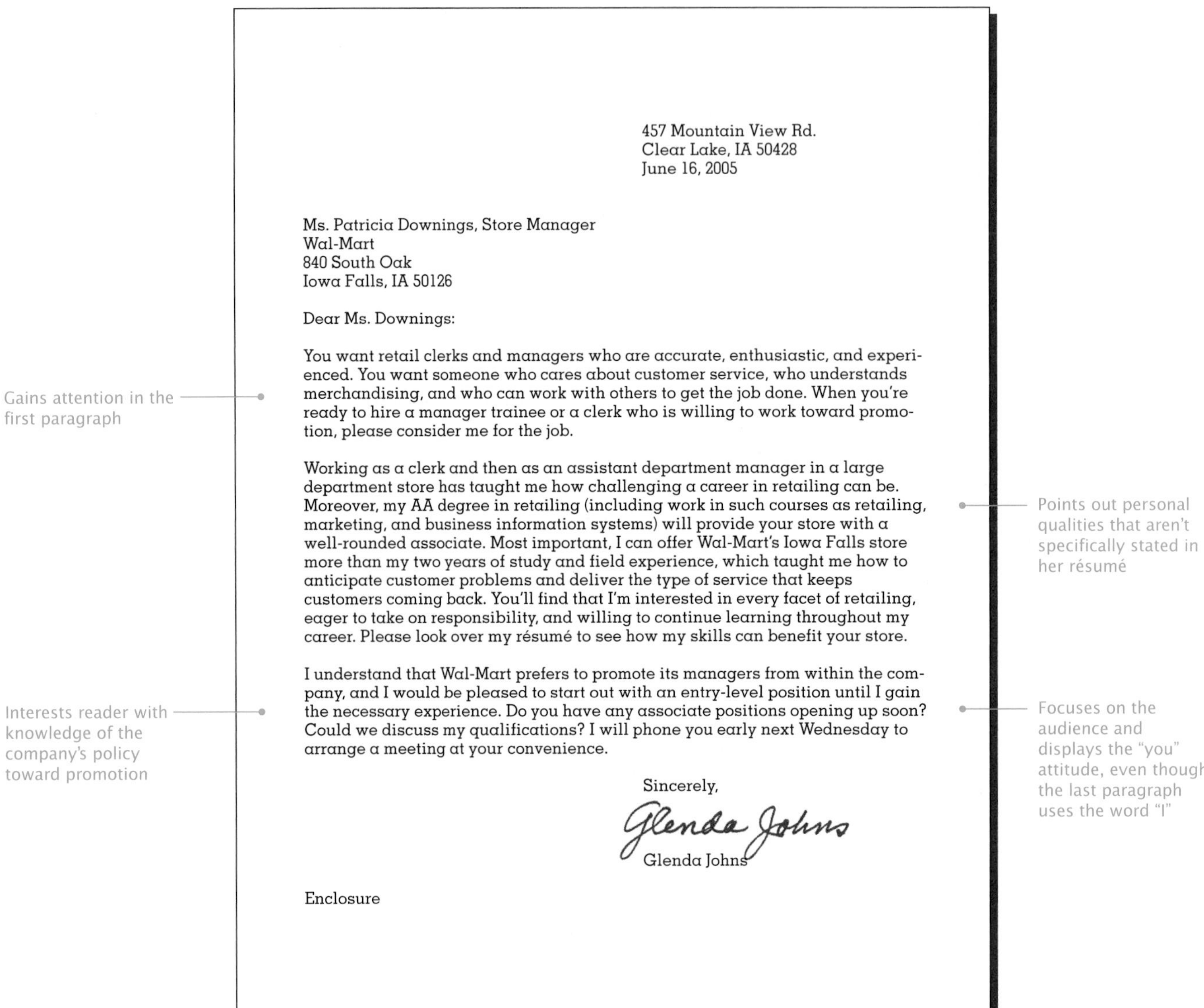

457 Mountain View Rd.
Clear Lake, IA 50428
June 16, 2005

Ms. Patricia Downings, Store Manager
Wal-Mart
840 South Oak
Iowa Falls, IA 50126

Dear Ms. Downings:

You want retail clerks and managers who are accurate, enthusiastic, and experienced. You want someone who cares about customer service, who understands merchandising, and who can work with others to get the job done. When you're ready to hire a manager trainee or a clerk who is willing to work toward promotion, please consider me for the job.

Working as a clerk and then as an assistant department manager in a large department store has taught me how challenging a career in retailing can be. Moreover, my AA degree in retailing (including work in such courses as retailing, marketing, and business information systems) will provide your store with a well-rounded associate. Most important, I can offer Wal-Mart's Iowa Falls store more than my two years of study and field experience, which taught me how to anticipate customer problems and deliver the type of service that keeps customers coming back. You'll find that I'm interested in every facet of retailing, eager to take on responsibility, and willing to continue learning throughout my career. Please look over my résumé to see how my skills can benefit your store.

I understand that Wal-Mart prefers to promote its managers from within the company, and I would be pleased to start out with an entry-level position until I gain the necessary experience. Do you have any associate positions opening up soon? Could we discuss my qualifications? I will phone you early next Wednesday to arrange a meeting at your convenience.

Sincerely,

Glenda Johns

Glenda Johns

Enclosure

Gains attention in the first paragraph
Points out personal qualities that aren't specifically stated in her résumé
Interests reader with knowledge of the company's policy toward promotion
Focuses on the audience and displays the "you" attitude, even though the last paragraph uses the word "I"

"proven skills," which was used in the ad: He not only elaborates on his own proven skills throughout the letter but even mentions the term in his closing paragraph.

If you're sending an **unsolicited letter** to an organization that has not announced an opening, it may actually have a better chance of being read and receiving individualized attention. In her unsolicited application letter in Figure 18.2, Glenda Johns manages to give a snapshot of her qualifications and skills without repeating what is said in her résumé. She gains attention by focusing on the needs of the employer.

Both solicited and unsolicited application letters present your qualifications similarly. The main difference is in the opening paragraph. In a solicited letter, you need no special attention-getter because you have been invited to apply. In an unsolicited letter, you need to start by capturing the reader's attention and interest.

Getting Attention

Like your résumé, your application letter is a form of advertising, so organize it as you would a sales letter: Use the AIDA approach, focus on your audience, and emphasize reader benefits (as discussed in Chapter 9). Make sure your style projects confidence, without being arrogant. To sell a potential employer on your merits, you must believe in yourself and sound as though you do.

TABLE 18.1 Tips for Getting Attention in Application Letters

TIP	EXAMPLE
UNSOLICITED APPLICATION LETTERS	
• Show how your strongest skills will benefit the organization. A 20-year-old in her third year of college might begin like this:	When you need a secretary in your export division who can take shorthand at 125 words a minute and transcribe notes at 70—in English, Spanish, or Portuguese—call me.
• Describe your understanding of the job's requirements and then show how well your qualifications fit-them	Your annual report states that Mobil Corporation runs employee-training programs about workforce diversity. The difficulties involved in running such programs can be significant, as I learned while tutoring inner-city high school students last summer. My 12 pupils were enrolled in vocational training programs and came from diverse ethnic and racial backgrounds. The one thing they had in common was a lack of familiarity with the typical employer's expectations. To help them learn the "rules of the game," I developed exercises that cast them in various roles: boss, customer, new recruit, and coworker. Of the 12 students, 10 subsequently found full-time jobs and have called or written to tell me how much they gained from the workshop.
• Mention the name of a person known to and highly regarded by the reader	When Janice McHugh of your franchise sales division spoke to our business communication class last week, she said you often need promising new marketing graduates at this time of year.
• Refer to publicized company activities, achievements, changes, or new procedures	Today's issue of the *Detroit News* reports that you may need the expertise of computer programmers versed in robotics when your Lansing tire plant automates this spring.
• Use a question to demonstrate your understanding of the organization's needs	Can your fast-growing market research division use an interviewer with 1½ years of field survey experience, a B.A. in public relations, and a real desire to succeed? If so, please consider me for the position.
• Use a catchphrase opening if the job requires ingenuity and imagination	*Haut monde*—whether said in French, Italian, or Arabic, it still means "high society." As an interior designer for your Beverly Hills showroom, not only could I serve and sell to your distinguished clientele, but I could do it in all these languages. I speak, read, and write them fluently.
SOLICITED APPLICATION LETTERS	
• Identify the publication in which the ad ran; describe what you have to offer	Your ad in the April issue of *Travel & Leisure* for a cruise-line social director caught my eye. My eight years of experience as a social director in the travel industry would allow me to serve your new Caribbean cruise division well.

The opening paragraph of your application letter has two important jobs to do: (1) clearly stating your reason for writing and (2) giving the recipient a reason to keep reading. Why would a recruiter want to keep reading your letter instead of the hundred others piling up on his or her desk? Because you show some immediate potential for meeting the company's needs. You've researched the company and the position, and you know something about the industry and its current challenges. Consider this opening:

The opening paragraph of your application letter needs to clearly convey the reason you're writing and give the recipient a compelling reason to keep reading.

> With the recent slowdown in corporate purchasing, I can certainly appreciate the challenge of new fleet sales in this business environment. With my high energy level and 16 months of new-car sales experience, I believe I can produce the results you listed as vital in your September 23 ad in the *Baltimore Sun.*

This applicant does a smooth job of mirroring the company's stated needs while highlighting his personal qualifications along with evidence that he understands the broader market. Although 16 months may not be considered a lot of experience, the letter balances that shortfall with enthusiasm and genuine interest in the position.

Use the subject line in your e-mail message or cover letter to get the employer's attention: simply identify the job you are applying for. Table 18.1 highlights some other ways that you can spark interest and grab attention in your opening paragraph. All these openings demonstrate the "you" attitude, and many indicate how the applicant can serve the employer.

Building Interest and Increasing Desire

Use the middle section of your letter to expand on your opening, presenting a more complete picture of your strengths.

The middle section of your application letter presents your strongest selling points in terms of their potential benefit to the organization, thereby building interest in you and creating a desire to interview you. Don't repeat whatever selling points you may have used in your opening, but rather use this section to create a more rounded picture of your potential to contribute to the organization. As with the opening, the more specific you can be, the better. And back up your assertions with some convincing evidence of your ability to perform:

> **Poor:** I completed three college courses in business communication, earning an A in each course, and have worked for the past year at Imperial Construction.
>
> **Improved:** Using the skills gained from three semesters of college training in business communication, I developed a collection system for Imperial Construction that reduced annual bad-debt losses by 25 percent. By emphasizing a win-win scenario for the company and its clients with incentives for on-time payment, the system was also credited with improving customer satisfaction.

When writing a solicited letter in response to an advertisement, be sure to discuss each requirement specified in the ad. If you are deficient in any of these requirements, stress other solid selling points to help strengthen your overall presentation.

Don't restrict your message to just core job duties, either. Also highlight personal characteristics, as long as they apply to the targeted position, such as your diligence or your ability to work hard, learn quickly, handle responsibility, or get along with people:

> While attending college full-time, I trained 3 hours a day with the varsity track team. In addition, I worked part-time during the school year and up to 60 hours a week each summer in order to be totally self-supporting while in college. I can offer your organization the same level of effort and perseverance.

Don't bring up salary in your application letter unless the recipient has previously asked you to include your requirements.

Another matter you might bring up in this section is your salary requirements—but *only* if the organization has asked you to state them. If you don't know the salary that's appropriate for the position and someone with your qualifications, you can find salary ranges for hundreds of jobs at the Bureau of Labor Statistics website, www.bls.gov or a number of commercial sites, including Monster.com. If you do state a target salary, tie it to the benefits you would bring to the organization (much as you would handle price in a sales letter):

> For the past two years, I have been helping a company similar to yours organize its database marketing efforts. I would therefore like to receive a salary in the same range (the mid-40s) for helping your company set up a more efficient customer database.

Toward the end of this section, refer the reader to your résumé by citing a specific fact or general point covered there:

> As you can see in the attached résumé, I've been working part-time with a local publisher since my sophomore year. During that time, I've used client interactions as an opportunity to build strong customer service skills.

Motivating Action

The final paragraph of your application letter has two important functions: to ask the reader for a specific action and to facilitate a reply. In almost all cases, the action you request is an interview. Don't demand it, however; try to sound natural and appreciative. Offer to come to the employer's office at a convenient time or, if the firm is some distance away, to meet with its nearest representative or arrange a telephone interview. Make the request easy to fulfill by stating your phone number and the best time to reach you—or, if you wish to be in control, by mentioning that you will follow up with a phone call in a few days. Refer again to your strongest selling point and, if desired, your date of availability:

In the final paragraph of your application letter, respectfully ask for specific action and make it easy for the reader to respond.

> After you have reviewed my qualifications, could we discuss the possibility of putting my marketing skills to work for your company? Because I will be on spring break the week of

CHECKLIST: Writing Application Letters

- Open the letter by capturing the reader's attention in a businesslike way.
- Use specific language to clearly state your interests and objectives.
- Build interest and desire in your potential contribution by presenting your key qualifications for the job.
- Link your education, experience, and personal qualities to the job requirements.
- Outline salary requirements only if the organization has requested that you provide them.
- Request an interview at a time and place that is convenient for the reader.
- Make it easy to comply with your request by providing your complete contact information and good times to reach you.
- Adapt your style for cultural variations if required.

> March 8, I would like to arrange a time to talk then. I will call in late February to schedule a convenient time when we could discuss employment opportunities at your company.

Once you have edited and proofread your application letter, mail it and your résumé promptly, especially if they have been solicited.

Adapting Your Style and Approach to Cultural Variations

The AIDA approach isn't appropriate for job seekers in every culture. If you're applying for a job abroad or want to work with a U.S. subsidiary of an organization based in another country, you may need to adjust your tone. Blatant self-promotion is considered bad form in some cultures. Other cultures stress group performance over individual contributions. As for format, recruiters in some countries prefer handwritten letters to printed or typed ones—another good reason to research a company carefully before drafting your application letter.

For U.S. and Canadian companies, let your letter reflect your personal style. Be yourself, but be businesslike too; avoid sounding cute. Don't use slang or a gimmicky layout. The only time to be unusually creative in content or format is when the job you're seeking requires imagination, such as a position in advertising. Compare your own letters with the tasks in "Checklist: Writing Application Letters."

Job-Inquiry Letters

Before considering you for a position, some organizations require you to fill out and submit an **application form,** a standardized data sheet that simplifies the comparison of applicants' qualifications. To request such a form, send a job-inquiry letter and include enough information about yourself in the letter to show that you have at least some of the requirements for the position you are seeking:

A letter requesting an application form can also convey some of your key strengths.

> Please send me an application form for work as an interior designer in your home furnishings department. For my certificate in design, I took courses in retail merchandising and customer relations. I have also had part-time sales experience at Capwell's department store.

Instead of writing a letter of this kind, you may want to drop in at the office you're applying to. You probably won't be able to talk to anyone other than the receptionist or a human resources assistant, but you can pick up the form, get an impression of the organization, and demonstrate your initiative and energy.

Organizations will use your application form as a convenient one-page source for information about your qualifications. So try to be thorough and accurate when filling it out. Have your résumé with you to remind you of important information, and if you can't remember something and have no record of it, provide the closest estimate possible. If you cannot provide some of the information because you have no such background (military experience, for example), write "Not applicable." When filling out applications, use a pen (unless specifically requested to use a pencil) and print legibly.

Use the application form to communicate as many of your strengths as you can, but ask if you can submit a résumé and application letter as well.

Application forms rarely give you enough space or ask you the right questions to reflect your unique skills and abilities accurately. Nevertheless, show your cooperation by doing your best to fill out the form completely. If you get an interview, you'll have an opportunity to fill in the gaps. Ask whether you might submit a résumé and an application letter along with the application. At the very least, take your résumé with you if you are asked back for an interview.

Application Follow-Ups

If your application letter and résumé fail to bring a response within a month or so, follow up with a second letter to keep your file active. This follow-up letter also gives you a chance to update your original application with any recent job-related information:

> Since applying to you on May 3 for an executive assistant position, I have completed a course in office management at South River Community College and received straight A's. I am now a proficient user of MS Word, including macros and other complex functions.
>
> Please keep my application in your active file, and let me know when you need a skilled executive assistant.

Even if you've received a letter acknowledging your application and saying that it will be kept on file, don't hesitate to send a follow-up letter three months later to show that you are still interested:

> Three months have elapsed since I applied to you for an underwriting position, but I want to let you know that I am still very interested in joining your company.
>
> I recently completed a four-week temporary work assignment at a large local insurance agency. I learned several new verification techniques and gained experience in using the online computer system. This experience could increase my value to your underwriting department.
>
> Please keep my application in your active file, and let me know when a position opens for a capable underwriter.

Think creatively about a follow-up letter; show that you've continued to add to your skills or that you've learned more about the company or the industry.

Even if you have no new accomplishments to share, such as the fact that you've taken a relevant course or gotten more experience in the field, you can still write this sort of follow-up message. Do some quick research on the company and its industry to find something that you can feature in your message ("I've been reading about the new technical challenges facing your industry . . ."). Your initiative and knowledge will impress recruiters. Without a follow-up communication from you, the human resources office is likely to assume that you've already found a job and are no longer interested in the organization. Moreover, a company's requirements change. A follow-up letter can demonstrate that you're sincerely interested in working for the organization, persistent in pursuing your goals, and committed to upgrading your skills. And it might just get you an interview.

Finding a compatible company culture is an important aspect of your job search. Paul Eichen and his team at Rokenbok Toys rely on a casual atmosphere in which a creative gang of workers come and go, focusing hard on work and life (rather than on politics and protocol).

UNDERSTANDING THE INTERVIEWING PROCESS

Like Google's Wayne Rosing, all recruiters have a list of qualities and accomplishments they are looking for in job candidates. An **employment interview** is a formal meeting during which both you and the prospective employer ask questions and exchange information. These meetings have a dual purpose: (1) The organization's main objective is to find the best person available for the job by determining whether you and the organization are a good match, and (2) your main objective is to find the job best suited to your goals and capabilities. While recruiters such as those at Google are trying to decide whether you are right for them, you must decide whether Google or any other company is right for you.

An employment interview is a formal meeting in which both employer and applicant ask questions and exchange information to learn more about each other.

Large organizations that hire hundreds of new employees every year typically take a more systematic approach to the recruiting and interviewing process than small local businesses that hire only a few new people each year. You'll need to adjust your job search according to the company's size and hiring practices. Table 18.2 contrasts the recruiting procedures of large companies with those of smaller companies and provides tips for increasing your chances of getting an interview with either type of employer. In general, the easiest way to connect with a big company is through your campus placement office; the most efficient way to approach a smaller business is by contacting the company directly.

Regardless of which path you choose, interviewing takes time, so start seeking jobs well in advance of the date you want to start work. Some students begin their job search as much as nine months before graduation. During downturns in the economy, early planning is even more crucial. Many employers become more selective and many corporations reduce their campus visits and campus hiring programs, so more of the job-search burden falls on you. As you plan your job-search strategy, keep in mind that it can take an average of 10 interviews to get one job offer. Thus, if you hope to have several offers to choose from, expect to go through 20 or 30 interviews.[6]

In a typical job search, you can expect to have many interviews before you accept a job offer.

The Typical Sequence of Interviews

2 LEARNING OBJECTIVE

Describe the typical sequence of job interviews

Not all organizations interview potential candidates the same way. At Southwest Airlines, for example, a candidate undergoes a rigorous interview process that can take as long as six weeks.[7] However, most employers interview an applicant two or three times before deciding to make a job offer. Applicants often face a sequence of interviews, each with a different purpose.

First is the preliminary *screening stage,* which is generally held on campus for new college hires and which helps employers screen out unqualified applicants. Those candidates who best meet the organization's requirements are invited to visit company offices for further evaluation. Interviews at the screening stage are fairly structured, so applicants are often asked roughly the same questions. Many companies use standardized evaluation sheets to "grade" the applicants so that all the candidates will be measured against the same criteria. In some cases, technology has transformed the initial, get-to-know-you interview, allowing employers to screen candidates by phone, video interview, or computer.[8]

Most organizations interview an applicant several times before extending a job offer:

- Screening stage
- Selection stage
- Final stage

Your best approach to an interview at the screening stage is to follow the interviewer's lead. Keep your responses short and to the point. Time is limited, so talking too much can be a big mistake. However, to give the interviewer a way to differentiate you from other candidates and to demonstrate your strengths and qualifications, try to emphasize the "theme" you used in developing your résumé.

During the selection stage of interviews, you may interview with several people, perhaps even all at once.

The next stage of interviews helps the organization narrow the field a little further. Typically, if you're invited to visit a company, you will talk with several people: a member of the human resources department, one or two potential colleagues, and your potential supervisor. You might face a panel of several interviewers who ask you questions during a single session. By noting how you listen, think, and express yourself, they can decide how likely you are to get along with colleagues. Your best approach during this *selection stage* of interviews is to show interest in the job, relate your skills and experience to the organization's needs, listen attentively, ask insightful questions, and display enthusiasm.

During the screening stage of interviews, try to differentiate yourself from other candidates.

If the interviewers agree that you're a good candidate, you may receive a job offer, either on the spot or a few days later by phone or mail. In other cases, you may be invited back for a final evaluation by a higher-ranking executive who has the authority to make the hiring decision and to decide on your compensation. An underlying objective of the *final stage* is often to sell you on the advantages of joining the organization.

During the final stage, the interviewer may try to sell you on working for the firm.

Common Types of Interviews

Organizations use various types of interviews to discover as much as possible about you and other applicants. A **structured interview** is generally used in the screening stage. The

A structured interview is controlled by the interviewer to gather facts.

TABLE 18.2 Recruiting Procedures of Big Versus Small Companies: The Best Way to Get Your Foot in the Door

	BIG COMPANIES	SMALL COMPANIES
Number and type of applicants sought	Consistently hire thousands of new employees each year; have relatively specific hiring criteria depending on the position; tend to be highly selective	Hire a handful of new people each year, but requirements fluctuate widely depending on ups and downs in the business; may have specific requirements but are often looking for flexibility, versatility; are often somewhat more open-minded than big corporations about candidate's background
Person or department in charge of recruiting	Handled by human resources or personnel department	Companies at large end of the small-company scale (500 employees) may have a specialized human resources department, but many depend on line managers to staff their own functions; in really small companies, the founder/top manager makes all hiring decisions
General recruiting and interviewing style	Governed by formal policies and procedures; typically, involves series of several interviews on campus and at company facility; approach is generally systematic, well planned, and well financed	Conducted informally on an as-needed basis without a standard procedure; hiring decision may be made after first interview or may drag on for several months; company generally lacks budget/motive for conducting elaborate recruiting programs
Where/how they advertise	Use national and local newspapers, trade, journals, campus placement offices, word of mouth, company websites	Rely heavily on word of mouth and local newspapers; may post openings at local colleges or at a few colleges whose graduates have specific qualifications; online job banks
Use of employment agencies, search firms	Roughly 60 percent use employment agencies, whereas 40 percent use executive search firms; however, new college graduates are generally recruited directly without help of intermediaries	Agency use varies widely among small companies; cost may be a factor
Responsiveness to unsolicited resumes	Receive hundreds of unsolicited résumés, which typically get less attention than résumés obtained through department's own planned recruiting program; most companies will scan unsolicited résumés into a database if they maintain one; best to send résumé directly to line manager or potential co-worker in department where you want to work	Receive relatively few unsolicited résumés, so they pay close attention to them; however, given limited hiring needs, chances are slim that your résumé will arrive when company has a corresponding opening
Reliance on campus recruiting	Roughly 80 percent rely heavily on campus recruiting programs to fill entry-level professional, technical, and managerial positions; however, most limit their recruiting to a relatively small number of campuses	Companies at large end of small company scale (500 employees) may have limited campus recruiting programs; the smaller the company, the less likely it is to recruit in this manner, and the fewer schools it is likely to visit
Best way for candidate to approach company	Use campus placement office to schedule interviews with companies that recruit on your campus; if these interviews are by invitation only, send a letter and resume to company asking to be included on its schedule; if company does not recruit on your campus, call the person in charge of college recruiting; explain your situation, and ask for advice on best way to get an interview	Check with campus placement office; try to make direct personal contact with owner/manager or department head; get names and addresses from chamber of commerce, business directories, or local economic development agency; send résumé and application letter; follow up with phone call

employer controls the interview by asking a series of prepared questions in a set order. Working from a checklist, the interviewer asks you each question, staying within an allotted time period. All answers are noted. Although useful for gathering facts, the structured interview is generally regarded as a poor measure of an applicant's personal qualities. Nevertheless, some companies use structured interviews to create uniformity in their hiring process.[9]

By contrast, the **open-ended interview** is less formal and unstructured, with a relaxed format. The interviewer poses broad, open-ended questions and encourages you to talk freely. This type of interview is good for bringing out your personality and for testing professional judgment. However, some candidates reveal too much, rambling on about personal or family problems that have nothing to do with their qualifications for employment, their ability to get along with co-workers, or any personal interests that could benefit their performance on the job. So be careful. You need to strike a balance between being friendly and remembering that you're in a business situation.

In an open-ended interview, the recruiter encourages you to speak freely.

Some organizations perform **group interviews**, meeting with several candidates simultaneously to see how they interact. This type of interview is useful for judging interpersonal skills. For example, The Walt Disney Company uses group interviews when hiring people for its theme parks. During a 45-minute session, the Disney recruiter watches how three candidates relate to one another. Do they smile? Are they supportive of one another's comments? Do they try to score points at each other's expense?[10]

Group interviews help recruiters see how candidates interact with one another.

The most unnerving type of interview is the **stress interview**, during which you might be asked pointed questions designed to irk or unsettle you, or you might be subjected to long periods of silence, criticisms of your appearance, deliberate interruptions, and abrupt or even hostile reactions by the interviewer. The theory behind this approach is that you'll reveal how well you handle stressful situations, although some experts find the technique of dubious value—particularly if the stress induced during the interview has no relationship to the job in question.[11] If you find yourself in a stress interview, pause for a few seconds to collect your thoughts, then continue knowing what the interviewer is up to.

Stress interviews help recruiters see how you handle yourself under pressure.

As employers try to cut travel costs, the **video interview** is becoming more popular. Many large companies use videoconferencing systems to screen middle-management candidates or to interview new recruits at universities. Experts recommend that candidates prepare a bit differently for a video interview than for an in-person meeting:[12]

Video interviews require some special preparation.

- Ask for a preliminary phone conversation to establish rapport with the interviewer.
- Arrive early enough to get used to the equipment and setting.
- During the interview, speak clearly but not more slowly than normal.
- Sit straight.
- Look up but not down.
- Keep your mannerisms lively without looking forced or fake.

Another modern twist is the **situational interview** or *behavioral interview*, in which an interviewer may describe a situation and ask, "How would you handle this?" or may ask you to describe how you handled some situation in your past. Many companies have learned that no correlation exists between how well people answer interview questions in a traditional interview and how well they perform on the job. In response, firms such as Kraft Foods, Delta Air Lines, AT&T, and Procter & Gamble rely on situational interviews. Proponents of this approach claim that interviewing is about the job, not about a candidate's five-year goals, weaknesses or strengths, challenging experiences, or greatest accomplishment. The situational interview is a hands-on, at-work meeting between an employer who needs a job done and a worker who must be fully prepared to do the work.[13]

In situational interviews, you're asked to explain how you would handle a specific set of circumstances.

Regardless of the type of interview you may face, a personal interview is vital because your résumé can't show whether you're lively and outgoing or subdued and low key, able to take direction or able to take charge. Each job requires a different mix of personality traits. The interviewer's task is to find out whether you will be effective on the job.

3 LEARNING OBJECTIVE

Describe briefly what employers look for during an employment interview

What Employers Look For in an Interview

Chapter 17 pointed out the attributes employers look for when reviewing résumés. The interview gives them a chance to go beyond this basic data to see what sort of person you

TABLE 18.3 What's Your EQ?

☑ Think clearly and stay focused on the task at hand while under pressure.
☑ Admit to your own mistakes.
☑ Meet commitments and keep promises.
☑ Hold yourself accountable for meeting your goals.
☑ Seek new ideas from a variety of sources.
☑ Handle multiple demands and changing priorities.
☑ Make sacrifices to meet an important organizational goal.
☑ Cut through red tape and bend outdated rules when necessary.
☑ Seek fresh perspectives, even if that means trying something totally new.
☑ Operate from an expectation of success rather than a fear of failure.
☑ Try to learn how to improve your performance.
☑ Set challenging goals and take calculated risks to reach them.

Communication Solution

Google looks for a specific type of employee—highly talented, creative, and independent-thinking—so its interview process is geared toward exposing those qualities. The company views interviewing with such importance that all software engineers are expected to devote a significant portion of their time to interviewing Google candidates.

Compatibility with the organization is judged on the basis of personal background, attitudes, and style.

are and whether you are a fit for the organization. For instance, Southwest Airlines recruiters put a high priority on a sense of humor because they believe that people who don't take themselves too seriously are better able to cope with the stress of airline work. Southwest also wants employees who are self-motivated, enthusiastic, not afraid to make decisions, willing to take risks, intelligent, good communicators, and considerate of others.[14]

Current research shows that employees with certain personality traits tend to be more successful at their job. As a result, many employers today seek candidates with high "emotional intelligence" or EQ (emotional quotient), defined as the ability to recognize one's own emotions and those of others. People with a high EQ generally possess self-awareness, good impulse control, persistence, confidence, self-motivation, and empathy, as well as the abilities to persuade, articulate a mission, interpret the mood of a group, and communicate with people in terms they understand (see Table 18.3). The theory behind the emphasis on EQ is that success in teamwork, customer support, and other vital business endeavors requires a broader range of capabilities than the traditional, narrow definitions of academic intelligence.

When it comes down to it, every job has basic qualifications. Employers first look for two things: evidence that a candidate will fit in with the organization and proof that the person can handle a specific job. In addition, many employers conduct preemployment testing.

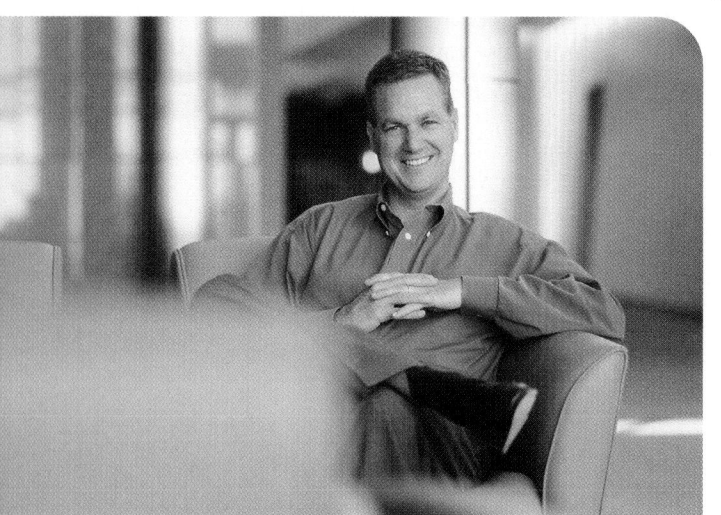

TechTarget CEO Greg Strakosch offers his employees extraordinary amounts of freedom, so he works hard to find employees who can handle the responsibility of setting their own schedules.

A Good Fit with the Organization

Most interviewers put a high priority on discovering the basic dimensions of your personality so that they can judge whether you will be compatible with other people in the organization and with the corporate culture in general. For instance, TechTarget, an interactive media company, gives employees an unusual amount of freedom, including the freedom to set their own hours and take as many days off for illness, personal matters, and vacation as they want or need—provided they meet their work objectives. It may sound like a wonderful arrangement, but CEO Greg Strakosch recognizes some people can't handle the responsibility that comes with such independence. As a result, TechTarget's hiring process is focused on filtering out candidates who need a more structured environment.[15]

Some interviewers believe that personal background indicates how well the candidate will fit in, so they might ask

TABLE 18.4 Checking Out New Hires

PERCENTAGE OF EMPLOYERS THAT CONDUCT BACKGROUND CHECKS	
Employment verification	86%
Criminal records check	81%
Drug screen	78%
Reference checks	70%
Education verification	70%
Motor vehicle records	56%

about your interests, hobbies, awareness of world events, and so forth. You can expand your potential along these lines by reading widely, making an effort to meet new people, and participating in discussion groups, seminars, and workshops.

Beyond your organizational fit, interviewers are likely to consider your personal style as well. You're likely to impress an employer by being open, enthusiastic, and interested. Some interviewers also look for courtesy, sincerity, willingness to learn, and a style that is positive and self-confident. All of these qualities help a new employee adapt to a new workplace and new responsibilities.

Impress employers by being open, enthusiastic, and interested.

Qualifications for the Job

When you're invited to interview for a position, the interviewer may already have some idea of whether you have the right qualifications based on a review of your résumé. But during the interview, you'll be asked to describe your education and previous jobs in more depth so that the interviewer can determine how well your skills match the requirements. In many cases, the interviewer will be seeking someone with the flexibility to apply diverse skills in several areas.[16]

When describing your skills, be honest. If you don't know how to do something, say so. Given the high cost of hiring unsuitable employees, more and more companies are performing background checks (see Table 18.4). In addition, many employers administer preemployment tests.[17] Such tests verify candidates' job skills and determine whether applicants are suited to the job and whether they'll be worth the expense of hiring and training.

Suitability for the specific job is judged on the basis of
- Academic preparation
- Work experience
- Job-related personality traits

Preemployment Testing

In an effort to improve the predictability of the selection process, many employers now conduct a variety of preemployment tests to assess such factors as integrity, personality, job skills, and substance use. Testing is a complex topic that varies widely by industry and position, and it also involves a wide range of legal and ethical issues, including discrimination and privacy. For instance, any testing that can be construed as a preemployment medical examination is prohibited by the Americans with Disabilities Act. One national retailer was successfully sued by applicants for a preemployment test that included questions designed to uncover applicants' sexual orientation.[18] Although a simple summary is unrealistic, here is an overview of the most common types of tests:

Preemployment tests attempt to provide objective, quantitative information about a candidate's skills, attitudes, and habits.

- **Integrity tests.** You might not think that a test could identify job candidates who are more likely to steal from their employers or commit other ethical or legal infractions, but employers have had some success in using integrity tests. For example, one nationwide retailer found that preemployment integrity screening reduced its inventory shrinkage by 35 percent (*shrinkage* is an umbrella term for all inventory items that disappear before they can be sold).[19]
- **Personality tests.** Personality tests are used to assess either general character or suitability for the demands of a specific profession. General tests attempt to profile overall

intellectual ability, attitudes toward work, interests, and managerial potential as well as such characteristics as dependability, commitment, honesty, and motivation. The specific tests evaluate whether a candidate is suited to the emotional rigors of demanding positions, such as flight crews, air marshalls, police and fire services, and nuclear power plant operators (in fact, federal law requires such tests for nuclear plant candidates).[20]

- **Job skills tests.** The most common type of preemployment tests are those designed to assess the competency or specific abilities needed to perform a job. The skills you might be tested on vary according to the position, naturally, but the most frequently tested include basic computer skills, clerical tasks, basic business financial tasks, and legal and medical terminology.[21]
- **Substance tests.** Drug and alcohol testing is one of the most controversial issues in business today. Some employers believe such testing is absolutely necessary to maintain workplace safety, whereas others view it as an invasion of employee privacy and a sign of disrespect. Even within a single industry, you can find widely divergent opinions on the subject. Computer maker Dell tests every employee, whereas rival HP doesn't test anyone. Some companies test only applicants, but not employees.[22] Nationwide, nearly half of all companies now require applicants to undergo drug and alcohol testing, and this percentage is expected to rise for two reasons: (1) to cut the costs (approximately $100 billion a year) and the reduced productivity associated with drug abuse, and (2) to reduce the number of accidents (substance abusers have two to four times as many accidents as other employees, and drug use is linked to 40 percent of industrial fatalities).[23] Moreover, companies are liable for negligent hiring practices if an employee harms an innocent party on the job. Thus drug testing will probably increase, even though the direct financial payback of these programs is unclear.[24]
- **Background checks.** Although not a test in the usual sense, a background check also helps employers learn more about you. A background check might be used to verify the credentials on your résumé, to see how well you manage credit, or even to learn if you have a criminal history. These investigations can generate considerable controversy, since some people consider them an invasion of privacy. However, many employers believe they have no choice, given the magnitude of the risks they now face. Employers can be held liable for the actions of employees who obtained jobs under false pretenses—and lying on résumés and in interviews has reached epidemic proportions. In one recent survey of more than 2 million job applicants, 44 percent lied about their employment history, 41 percent lied about their education, and 23 percent claimed to have professional credentials or licenses they didn't have.[25]

If you're concerned about any preemployment test, ask the employer for more information or ask your college placement office for advice. You can also get more information from the Equal Employment Opportunity Commission at www.eeoc.gov.

4 LEARNING OBJECTIVE

List six tasks you need to complete to prepare for a successful job interview

PREPARING FOR A JOB INTERVIEW

Just as written messages need planning, employment interviews need preparation.

Preparation will help you perform better under pressure; moreover, the more prepared you are, the less nervous you'll be about the interviewing process. Be sure to consider any cultural differences when preparing for interviews, and base your approach on what your audience expects (see "Communicating Across Cultures: Successfully Interviewing Across Borders"). To prepare for a successful interview, learn about the organization, think ahead about questions, bolster your confidence, polish your interview style, plan to look good, and be ready when you arrive.

Learn About the Organization

Today's companies expect serious candidates to demonstrate an understanding of the company's operations, its markets, and its strategic and tactical challenges.[26] When you were planning your employment search, you probably already researched the companies you

Communicating Across Cultures

Successfully Interviewing Across Borders

Interviewing for a job in another country can be one of the most exciting steps in your career. To succeed, you need to pay even closer attention to the important elements of the interviewing process, including personal appearance, an awareness of what interviewers are really trying to learn about you, and what you should learn about the organization you're hoping to join.

Some countries and cultures place a much higher importance on dress and personal grooming than many employees in the United States are accustomed to; moreover, expectations of personal appearance can vary dramatically from country to country. Ask people who've been to the country before and observe local businesspeople when you arrive. Many people interpret inappropriate dress as more than a simple fashion mistake; they view it as an inability or unwillingness to understand another culture.

Whether or not these things should matter isn't the question; they do matter, and successful job candidates learn how to respond to differing expectations. For instance, business image consultant Ashley Rothschild points out that you could get away with wearing a boldly colored suit in Italy but probably not in Japan; Business professionals do tend to dress formally in Italy, but as a worldwide fashion leader, the country has a broad definition of what is appropriate businesswear.

Smart U.S. recruiters always analyze both nonverbal signals and verbal messages to judge whether an applicant truly has the qualities necessary for a job. In international employment situations, you'll probably be under even closer scrutiny. Recruiters abroad will want to know if you really have what it takes to succeed in unfamiliar social settings, how your family will handle the transition, and whether you can adapt your personal work style and habits enough to blend in with the hiring organization.

Remember to ask plenty of questions and do your research, both before and after the interview. Some employees view overseas postings as grand adventures, only to collide headfirst with the reality of what it's like to live and work in a completely different culture. For instance, if you've grown accustomed to the independent work style you enjoy in your current job or in school, could you handle a more structured work environment with a hierarchical chain of command? Make sure to get a sense of the culture both within the company and within its social community before you commit to a job in another country.

CAREER APPLICATIONS

1. Explain how you could find out what is appropriate dress for a job interview in South Africa.
2. Would it be appropriate to ask an interviewer to describe the culture in his or her country? Explain your answer.

sent your résumé to. But now that you've been invited for an interview, you'll want to fine-tune your research and brush up on the facts you've collected. You can review Chapters 10 and 17 for ideas on where to look for information.

Think Ahead About Questions

Planning ahead for the interviewer's questions will help you handle them more confidently and intelligently. Moreover, you will want to prepare insightful questions of your own.

Planning for the Employer's Questions

Employers usually gear their interview questions to specific organizational needs. You can expect to be asked about your skills, achievements, and goals, as well as about your attitude toward work and school, your relationships with others (work supervisors, colleagues, and fellow students), and occasionally your hobbies and interests. You'll also need to anticipate and give a little extra thought to a few particularly tough questions, such as these:

Be prepared to relate your qualifications to the organization's needs.

- **What was the toughest decision you ever had to make?** Be prepared with a good example, explaining why the decision was difficult and how you finally made it.
- **What are your greatest weaknesses?** Describe a weakness so that it sounds like a virtue—honestly revealing something about yourself while showing how it works to an

employer's advantage. If you sometimes drive yourself too hard, explain that it has helped when you've had to meet deadlines.

- **What didn't you like about previous jobs you've held?** State what you didn't like and discuss what the experience taught you. Avoid making slighting references to former employers or colleagues.
- **Where do you want to be five years from now?** This question tests (1) whether you're merely using this job as a stopover until something better comes along and (2) whether you've given thought to your long-term goals. Saying that you'd like to be company president is unrealistic, and yet few employers want people who are content to sit still. Your answer should reflect your long-term goals and the organization's advancement opportunities.
- **Tell me something about yourself.** Answer that you'll be happy to talk about yourself, and ask what the interviewer wants to know. If this point is clarified, respond. If it isn't, explain how your skills can contribute to the job and the organization. This is a great chance to sell yourself.

You might be asked to collaborate on a decision or to develop a group presentation. Trained observers evaluate the candidates' performance using predetermined criteria and then advise management on how well each person is likely to handle the challenges normally faced on the job.[27]

Practice answering interview questions.

For a look at the types of questions often asked, see Table 18.5. Jot down a brief answer to each one. Then read over the answers until you feel comfortable with each of them. Although practicing your answers will help you feel prepared and confident, you don't want to memorize responses or sound overrehearsed. You might also give a list of interview questions to a friend or relative and have that person ask you various questions at random. This method helps you learn to articulate answers and to look at the person as you answer.

Planning Questions of Your Own

Remember that the interview is a two-way street: the questions you ask are just as important as the answers you provide. By asking insightful questions, you can demonstrate your understanding of the organization, you can steer the discussion into those areas that allow you to present your qualifications to best advantage, and you can verify for yourself whether this is the right opportunity for you. Before the interview, prepare a list of about a dozen questions you need answered in order to evaluate the organization and the job.

You are responsible for deciding whether the work and the organization are compatible with your goals and values.

Don't limit your questions to those you think will impress the interviewer, or you won't get the information you'll need to make a wise decision if and when you're offered the job. Here's a list of some things you might want to find out:

- **Are these my kind of people?** Observe the interviewer, and if you can, arrange to talk with other employees.
- **Can I do this work?** Compare your qualifications with the requirements described by the interviewer.
- **Will I enjoy the work?** Know yourself and what's important to you. Will you find the work challenging? Will it give you feelings of accomplishment, of satisfaction, and of making a real contribution?
- **Is the job what I want?** You may never find a job that fulfills all your wants, but the position you accept should satisfy at least your primary ones. Will it make use of your best capabilities? Does it offer a career path to the long-term goals you've set?
- **Does the job pay what I'm worth?** By comparing jobs and salaries before you're interviewed, you'll know what's reasonable for someone with your skills in your industry.
- **What kind of person would I be working for?** If the interviewer is your prospective boss, watch how others interact with that person, tactfully query other employees, or pose a careful question or two during the interview. If your prospective boss is someone else, ask for that person's name, job title, and responsibilities. Try to learn all you can.

TABLE 18.5 Twenty-Five Common Interview Questions

QUESTIONS ABOUT COLLEGE
1. What courses in college did you like most? Least? Why?
2. Do you think your extracurricular activities in college were worth the time you spent on them? Why or why not?
3. When did you choose your college major? Did you ever change your major? If so, why?
4. Do you feel you did the best scholastic work you are capable of?
5. Which of your college years was the toughest? Why?
QUESTIONS ABOUT EMPLOYERS AND JOBS
6. What jobs have you held? Why did you leave?
7. What percentage of your college expenses did you earn? How?
8. Why did you choose your particular field of work?
9. What are the disadvantages of your chosen field?
10. Have you served in the military? What rank did you achieve? What jobs did you perform?
11. What do you think about how this industry operates today?
12. Why do you think you would like this particular type of job?
QUESTIONS ABOUT PERSONAL ATTITUDES AND PREFERENCES
13. Do you prefer to work in any specific geographic location? If so, why?
14. How much money do you hope to be earning in 5 years? In 10 years?
15. What do you think determines a person's progress in a good organization?
16. What personal characteristics do you feel are necessary for success in your chosen field?
17. Tell me a story.
18. Do you like to travel?
19. Do you think grades should be considered by employers? Why or why not?
QUESTIONS ABOUT WORK HABITS
20. Do you prefer working with others or by yourself?
21. What type of boss do you prefer?
22. Have you ever had any difficulty getting along with colleagues or supervisors? With instructors? With other students?
23. Would you prefer to work in a large or a small organization? Why?
24. How do you feel about overtime work?
25. What have you done that shows initiative and willingness to work?

- **What sort of future can I expect with this organization?** How healthy is the organization? Can you look forward to advancement? Does the organization offer insurance, pension, vacation, or other benefits?

Rather than bombarding the interviewer with these questions the minute you walk in the room, work them into the conversation naturally, without trying to take control of the interview. For a list of good questions you might use as a starting point, see Table 18.6.

You don't necessarily have to wait until the interviewer asks if you have any questions of your own; look for smooth ways to work prepared questions into the conversation.

TABLE 18.6 Fifteen Questions to Ask the Interviewer

QUESTIONS ABOUT THE JOB	QUESTIONS ABOUT THE ORGANIZATION
What are the job's major responsibilities?	Who are your organization's major competitors, and what are their strengths and weaknesses?
What qualities do you want in the person who fills this position?	What makes your organization different from others in the industry?
Do you want to know more about my related training?	What are your organization's major markets?
What is the first problem that needs the attention of the person you hire?	Does the organization have any plans for new products? Acquisitions?
Would relocation be required now or in the future?	How would you define your organization's managerial philosophy?
Why is this job now vacant?	What additional training does your organization provide?
What can you tell me about the person I would report to?	Do employees have an opportunity to continue their education with help from the organization?
How do you measure success for someone in this position?	

Impress the interviewer with your ability to organize and be thorough by bringing a list of questions to the job interview.

Write your list of questions on a notepad and take it to the interview. If you need to, jot down brief notes during the meeting, and be sure to record answers in more detail afterward. Having a list of questions should impress the interviewer with your organization and thoroughness. It will also show that you're there to evaluate the organization and the job as well as to promote yourself.

Bolster Your Confidence

By building your confidence, you'll make a better impression and make the whole process less stressful. The best way to counteract any apprehension is to remove its source. You may feel shy or self-conscious because you think you have some flaw that will prompt others to reject you. Bear in mind, however, that you're often much more conscious of your limitations than other people are.

If you feel shy or self-conscious, remember that recruiters are human too.

If some aspect of your appearance or background makes you uneasy, correct it or offset it by emphasizing positive traits such as warmth, wit, intelligence, or charm. Instead of dwelling on your weaknesses, focus on your strengths. Instead of worrying about how you will perform in the interview, focus on how you can help the organization succeed. Remember that all the other candidates for the job are just as nervous as you are. The interviewers may be nervous, too; after all, they're judged on how well they assess candidates, so help them see your positive qualities clearly.

Polish Your Interview Style

Competence and confidence are the foundation of your interviewing style, and you can enhance those by giving the interviewer an impression of poise, good manners, and good judgment. Some job seekers hire professional coaches and image consultants to create just the right impression. Charging anywhere from $125 to $500 an hour, these professionals spend a majority of their time teaching clients how to adopt appropriate communication styles, and to do so they use role-playing, videotaping, and audio taping.[28] You can use these techniques too.

Staging mock interviews with a friend is a good way to hone your style.

You can develop an adept style by staging mock interviews with a friend. After each practice session, try to identify opportunities for improvement. Have your friend critique your performance, using the list of interview faults shown in Table 18.7. You can tape-

TABLE 18.7 What Employers Don't Like to See in Candidates

WHAT EMPLOYERS DON'T LIKE TO SEE IN CANDIDATES
☑ Poor personal appearance
☑ Overbearing, overaggressive, conceited demeanor; a "superiority complex"; "know it all" attitude
☑ Inability to express ideas clearly; poor voice, diction, grammar
☑ Lack of knowledge or experience
☑ Poor preparation for the interview
☑ Lack of interest in the job
☑ Lack of planning for career; lack of purpose, goals
☑ Lack of enthusiasm; passive and indifferent demeanor
☑ Lack of confidence and poise; appearance of being nervous and ill at ease
☑ Insufficient evidence of achievement
☑ Failure to participate in extracurricular activities
☑ Overemphasis on money; interest only in the best dollar offer
☑ Poor scholastic record; just got by
☑ Unwillingness to start at the bottom; expecting too much too soon
☑ Tendency to make excuses
☑ Evasive answers; hedges on unfavorable factors in record
☑ Lack of tact
☑ Lack of maturity
☑ Lack of courtesy; ill-mannered
☑ Condemnation of past employers
☑ Lack of social skills
☑ Marked dislike for schoolwork
☑ Lack of vitality
☑ Failure to look interviewer in the eye
☑ Limp, weak handshake

record or videotape these mock interviews and then evaluate them yourself. The taping process can be intimidating, but it helps you work out any problems before you begin actual job interviews. Your career center may have computer-based systems for practicing interviews as well, or you might consider one of the commercially available systems such as that offered by Perfect Interview, www.perfectinterview.com. To find others, search online for "practice interviews" or "interview simulators."

As you stage your mock interviews, pay particular attention to your nonverbal behavior. In the United States, you are more likely to have a successful interview if you maintain eye contact, smile frequently, sit in an attentive position, and use frequent hand gestures. These nonverbal signals convince the interviewer that you're alert, assertive, dependable, confident, responsible, and energetic.[29] Some companies based in the United States are owned and managed by people from other cultures, so during your research, find out about the company's cultural background and preferences regarding nonverbal behavior.

Nonverbal behavior has a significant effect on the interviewer's opinion of you.

The sound of your voice can also have a major impact on your success in a job interview.[30] You can work with a tape recorder to overcome voice problems. If you tend to speak

The way you speak is almost as important as what you say.

too rapidly, practice speaking more slowly. If your voice sounds too loud or too soft, practice adjusting it. Work on eliminating speech mannerisms such as *you know, like,* and *um,* which might make you sound inarticulate.

When Patricia Washington interviews potential employees, she looks for people who communicate well. Part of good communication is being prepared with résumés and work samples; another part is knowing how to look. Applicants show more than their job skills—they also demonstrate their ability to communicate and their concern for a professional appearance.

Plan to Look Good

Physical appearance is important because clothing and grooming reveal something about a candidate's personality, professionalism, and ability to sense the unspoken "rules" of a situation. When it comes to clothing, the best policy is to dress conservatively. Wear the best-quality businesslike clothing you can, preferably in a dark, solid color. However, wearing clothes that are appropriate and clean is far more important than wearing clothes that are expensive. Avoid flamboyant styles, colors, and prints. Even in companies where interviewers may dress casually, it's important to show good judgment by dressing—and acting—in a professional manner. Even minor points of etiquette can make a lasting impression on recruiters.

Some candidates ask interviewers ahead of time what they should wear. One human resources executive tells job seekers to dress business casual because dressing in a suit, for example, looks awkward at his company.[31] However, in other companies, business casual would be completely out of place in a job interview. Your research into various industries and professions should give you insight into expectations for business attire, too. If you're not sure, being a little too formal is a better guess than being too casual.

Good grooming makes any style of clothing look better. Make sure your clothes are clean and unwrinkled, your shoes unscuffed and well shined, your hair neatly styled and combed, your fingernails clean, and your breath fresh. If possible, check your appearance in a mirror before entering the room for the interview. Finally, remember that one of the best ways to look good is to smile at appropriate moments.

Dress conservatively and be well groomed for every interview; there's plenty of time to be casual after you get the job.

Make professional appearance and habits a routine part of your day after you land that first job, too. Some students fail to recognize the need to adjust their dress and personal habits when they make the transition to professional life. Behaviors you may not think about, such as showing up five minutes late to every meeting or wearing a T-shirt to a client's office, could limit your career potential. Again, these may seem like minor issues, but many people are sensitive to these points of business etiquette and consider them a sign of mutual respect.

Be Ready When You Arrive

Be ready to go the minute you arrive at the interviewing site; don't fumble around for your résumé or your list of questions.

When you go to your interview, take a small notebook, a pen, a list of the questions you want to ask, two copies of your résumé (protected in a folder), an outline of what you have learned about the organization, and any past correspondence about the position. You may also want to take a small calendar, a transcript of your college grades, a list of references, and a portfolio containing samples of your work, performance reviews, and certificates of achievement. In an era when many people exaggerate their qualifications, visible proof of your abilities carries a lot of weight.[32]

Be sure you know when and where the interview will be held. The worst way to start any interview is to be late. Check the route you will take, even if it means phoning ahead to ask. Find out how much time it takes to get there; then plan to arrive early. Allow a little extra time in case you run into a problem on the way.

Once you arrive, relax. You may have to wait a little while, so bring along something business-oriented to read. If company literature is available in the lobby, read it while you wait. In every case, show respect for everyone you encounter. If the opportunity presents itself, ask a few questions about the organization or express enthusiasm for the job. Refrain from smoking before the interview (nonsmokers can smell smoke on the clothing of interviewees), and avoid chewing gum or otherwise eating in the waiting room. Anything you do or say while you wait may well get back to the interviewer, so make sure your best qualities show from the moment you enter the premises. That way you'll be ready for the inter-

CHECKLIST: Planning for a Successful Job Interview

- Learn about the organization, including its operations, markets, and challenges.
- Plan for the employer's questions, including questions about tough decisions you've made, your weaknesses, what you didn't like about previous jobs, and your career plans.
- Plan questions of your own to find out whether this is really the job and the organization for you, and to show that you've done your research.
- Bolster your confidence by removing as many sources of apprehension as you can.
- Polish your interview style by staging mock interviews.
- Plan to look good with appropriate dress and grooming.
- Be ready when you arrive, and bring along a pen, paper, list of questions, two résumés, an outline of your research on the company, and any correspondence you've had regarding the position.
- Double-check the location and time of the interview and map out the route beforehand.
- Relax and be flexible; the schedule and interview arrangements may change when you arrive.

view itself once it actually begins. To review the steps for planning a successful interview, see "Checklist: Planning for a Successful Job Interview."

INTERVIEWING FOR SUCCESS

Your approach to interviews evolves as you move through each stage of the process. The techniques for success are similar throughout, even though the focus and purpose of the interviews do change—both for you and for the employer. To increase your chances of success, follow the tips from successful interviewers about how to make a positive impression by avoiding mistakes (see "Communication Miscues: Talking Yourself out of a Job").

Present a memorable "headline" during an interview at the screening stage.

If you're being interviewed for the first time, your main objective is to differentiate yourself from the many other candidates who are also being screened. Without resorting to gimmicks, call attention to one key aspect of your personal or professional background so that the recruiter can say, "Oh yes, I remember Brenda Jones—the one who built a computerized home weather station to wake her up a few minutes early whenever it snowed overnight." Just be sure the trait you accentuate is relevant to the job in question. In addition, you'll want to be prepared in case an employer expects you to demonstrate a particular skill (perhaps problem solving) during the screening interview.

Cover all your strengths during an interview at the selection stage.

If you progress to the initial selection interview, broaden your promotional message. Instead of telegraphing the "headline," give the interviewer the whole story. Touch briefly on all your strengths, but explain three or four of your best qualifications in depth. At the same time, probe for information that will help you evaluate the position objectively.

Emphasize your personality during a final interview.

If you're asked back for a final visit, your chances of being offered a position have improved considerably. At this point, you'll probably talk to a person who has the authority to make an offer and negotiate terms. This individual may have already concluded that your background is right for the job and may be more concerned with sizing up your personality. Both you and the employer need to find out whether there is a good psychological fit. Be honest about your motivations and values. If the interview goes well, your objective should be to clinch the deal on the best possible terms.

Regardless of where you are in the interview process, every interview will proceed through three stages: the warm-up, the question-and-answer session, and the close.

5 LEARNING OBJECTIVE

Explain the three stages of a successful employment interview

The Warm-Up

The first minute of the interview is crucial.

Of the three stages, the warm-up is the most important, even though it may account for only a small fraction of the time you spend in the interview. Psychologists say that 50 percent of an interviewer's decision is made within the first 30 to 60 seconds, and another 25 percent is made within 15 minutes. If you get off to a bad start, it's extremely difficult to turn the interview around.[33] Don't let your guard down if it appears the interviewer wants

Communication Miscues

Talking Yourself out of a Job

Even well-qualified applicants sometimes talk themselves right out of an opportunity by making avoidable blunders during the job interview. As you develop your interviewing style, take care to avoid these all-too-common mistakes:

- **Being defensive.** An interview isn't an interrogation, and the interviewer isn't out to get you. Treat interviews as business conversations, an exchange of information in which both sides have something of value to share. You'll give (and get) better information that way.
- **Failing to ask questions.** Interviewers expect you to ask questions, both during the interview and at its conclusion when they ask if you have any questions. If you have nothing to ask, you come across as someone who isn't really interested in the job or the company. Prepare a list of questions before every interview.
- **Failing to answer questions—or trying to bluff your way through difficult questions.** If you simply can't answer a question, don't try to talk your way around it or fake your way through it. Remember that sometimes interviewers ask strange questions just to see how you'll respond. What kind of fish would you like to be? How would you go about nailing jelly to the ceiling? Why are manhole covers round? Some of these questions are designed to test your grace under pressure, whereas others actually expect you to think through a logical answer (manhole covers are round because that's the only shape that can't fall through an open hole, by the way). Don't act like the question is stupid or refuse to answer it. Sit quietly for a few seconds, try to imagine why the interviewer has asked the question, then frame an answer that links your strengths to the company's needs.
- **Freezing up.** The human brain seems to have the capacity to just freeze up under stressful situations. An interviewer might've asked you a simple question, or perhaps you were halfway through an intelligent answer, and poof—all your thoughts disappear and you can't organize words in any logical order. Try to quickly replay the last few seconds of the conversation in your mind to see if you can recapture the conversational thread. If that fails, you're probably better off explaining to the interviewer that your mind has gone blank and asking him or her to repeat the question. Doing so is embarrassing, but not as embarrassing as chattering on and on with no idea of what you're saying, hoping you'll stumble back onto the topic.
- **Failing to understand your potential to contribute to the organization.** Interviewers care less about your history than about how you can help their organization in the future. Unless you've inventoried your own skills, researched their needs, and found a match between the two, you won't be able to answer these questions quickly and intelligently.

CAREER APPLICATIONS

1. What should you do if you if you suddenly realize that something you said earlier in the interview is incorrect or incomplete? Explain your answer.
2. How would you answer the following question: "How do you respond to colleagues who make you angry?" Explain your answer.

to engage in what feels like small talk; these exchanges are every bit as important as structured questions.

Body language is important at this point. Because you won't have time to say much in the first minute or two, you must sell yourself nonverbally. Begin by using the interviewer's name if you're sure you can pronounce it correctly. If the interviewer extends a hand, respond with a firm but not overpowering handshake, and wait until you're asked to be seated. Let the interviewer start the discussion, and listen for cues that tell you what he or she is interested in knowing about you as a potential employee.

The Question-and-Answer Stage

Questions and answers will consume the greatest part of the interview. The interviewer will ask you about your qualifications and discuss many of the points mentioned in your résumé. You'll also be asking questions of your own.

Dealing with Questions

Tailor your answers to emphasize your strengths.

Let the interviewer lead the conversation, and never answer a question before he or she has finished asking it—the last few words of the question might alter how you respond. As questions are asked, tailor your answers to make a favorable impression. Don't limit yourself to yes-or-no answers. If you're asked a difficult question, be sure you pause to think before responding. The recruiter may know that you can't answer a question and only wants to know how you'll respond.

If you periodically ask a question or two from the list you've prepared, you'll not only learn something but also demonstrate your interest. Probe for what the company is looking for in its new employees so that you can show how you meet the firm's needs. Also try to zero in on any reservations the interviewer might have about you so that you can dispel them.

Listening to the Interviewer

Paying attention when the interviewer speaks can be as important as giving good answers or asking good questions. Review the tips on listening offered in Chapter 2.

The interviewer's facial expressions, eye movements, gestures, and posture may tell you the real meaning of what is being said. Be especially aware of how your comments are received. Does the interviewer nod in agreement or smile to show approval? If so, you're making progress. If not, you might want to introduce another topic or modify your approach.

Paying attention to both interviewer's verbal and nonverbal messages can help you turn the question-and-answer stage to your advantage.

Fielding Discriminatory Questions

Employers cannot legally discriminate against a job candidate on the basis of race, color, gender, age (at least if you're between 40 and 70), marital status, religion, national origin, or disability. In general, the following topics should not be directly or indirectly introduced by an interviewer:[34]

Well-trained interviewers are aware of questions they shouldn't ask.

- Your religious affiliation or organizations and lodges you belong to
- Your national origin, age, marital status, or former name
- Your spouse, spouse's employment or salary, dependents, children, or child-care arrangements
- Your height, weight, gender, pregnancy, or any health conditions or disabilities that are not reasonably related to job performance
- Arrests or criminal convictions that are not related to job performance

Although federal law does not specifically prohibit questions that touch on these areas, the Equal Employment Opportunity Commission considers such questions with "extreme disfavor." Individual states and cities have also enacted laws concerning interview questions, so you may have additional protections beyond the federal standards.[35] Table 18.8 compares specific questions that may and may not be asked during an employment interview.

TABLE 18.8 Interview Questions That May and May Not Be Asked

INTERVIEWER MAY ASK THIS . . .	BUT NOT THIS
What is your name?	What was your maiden name?
Are you over 18?	When were you born?
Did you graduate from high school?	When did you graduate from high school?
[No questions about race are allowed.]	What is your race?
Can you perform [specific tasks]?	Do you have physical or mental disabilities?
	Do you have a drug or alcohol problem?
	Are you taking any prescription drugs?
Would you be able to meet the job's requirement to frequently work weekends?	Would working on weekends conflict with your religion?
Do you have the legal right to work in the United States?	What country are you a citizen of?
Have you ever been convicted of a felony?	Have you ever been arrested?
This job requires that you speak Spanish. Do you?	What language did you speak in your home when you were growing up?

Think about how you might respond if you are asked to a potentially unlawful question.

How to Respond If your interviewer asks these personal questions, how you respond depends on how badly you want the job, how you feel about revealing the information asked for, what you think the interviewer will do with the information, and whether you want to work for a company that asks such questions. Remember that you always have the option of simply refusing to answer or of telling the interviewer that you think a particular question is unethical—although either of these responses is likely to leave an unfavorable impression.[36] If you do want the job, you might (1) ask how the question is related to your qualifications, (2) explain that the information is personal, (3) respond to what you think is the interviewer's real concern, or (4) answer both the question and the concern.

If you do answer an unethical or unlawful question, you run the risk that your answer may hurt your chances, so think carefully before answering.[37] In any event, don't forget the two-way nature of the interview process: the organization is learning about you and you're learning about the organization. Would you want to work for an organization that condones illegal or discriminatory questions or that doesn't train its employees enough to avoid them?

Where to File a Complaint When a business can show that the safety of its employees or customers is at stake, it may be allowed to ask questions that would seem discriminatory in another context. Despite this exception, if you believe an interviewer's questions are unreasonable, unrelated to the job, or an attempt to discriminate, you may complain to the nearest field office of the EEOC (find offices online at www.eeoc.gov) or to the state agency that regulates fair employment practices. To report discrimination on the basis of age or physical disability, contact the employer's equal opportunity officer or the U.S. Department of Labor. If you file a complaint, be prepared to spend a lot of time and effort on it—and keep in mind that you may not win.[38]

The Close

Like the warm up, the end of the interview is more important than its brief duration would indicate. In the last few minutes, you need to evaluate how well you've done. You also need to correct any misconceptions the interviewer might have.

Concluding Gracefully

Conclude the interview with courtesy and enthusiasm.

You can generally tell when the interviewer is trying to conclude the session. He or she may ask whether you have any more questions, sum up the discussion, change position, or indicate with a gesture that the interview is over. When you get the signal, respond promptly, but don't rush. Be sure to thank the interviewer for the opportunity and express an interest in the organization. If you can do so comfortably, try to pin down what will happen next, but don't press for an immediate decision.

If this is your second or third visit to the organization, the interview may culminate with an offer of employment. You have two options: Accept it or request time to think it over. The best course is usually to wait. If no job offer is made, the interviewer may not have reached a decision yet, but you may tactfully ask when you can expect to know the decision.

Discussing Salary

Be realistic in your salary expectations and diplomatic in your negotiations.

Research salary ranges in your job, industry, and geographic region before you try to negotiate salary.

If you do receive an offer during the interview, you'll naturally want to discuss salary. However, let the interviewer raise the subject. If asked your salary requirements during the interview or on a job application, you can say that your salary requirements are open or negotiable or that you would expect a competitive compensation package.[39] If you have added qualifications, point them out: "With my 18 months of experience in the field, I would expect to start in the middle of the normal salary range." As Chapter 17 pointed out, you can find industry salary ranges at the Bureau of Labor Statistics website, www.bls.gov, or at several of the popular job websites.

When to Negotiate If you don't like the offer, you might try to negotiate, provided you're in a good bargaining position and the organization has the flexibility to accommodate you. You'll be in a fairly strong position if your skills are in short supply and you have several other offers. It also helps if you're the favorite candidate and the organization is booming. However, many organizations are relatively rigid in their salary practices, particularly at the entry level. In the United States and some European countries, it is perfectly acceptable to ask, "Is there any room for negotiation?"

Negotiating benefits may be one way to get more value from an employment package.

What to Negotiate Salary will probably be the most important component of your compensation and benefits package, but it's not the only factor by any means. And even if salary isn't negotiable, you may find flexibility in a signing bonus, profit sharing, pension and other retirement benefits, health coverage, vacation time, stock options, and other factors.[40] The value of negotiating can be significant because benefits often cost the employer 25 to 45 percent of your salary.

In other words, if you're offered an annual salary of $40,000, you'll ordinarily get an additional $10,000 to $18,000 in benefits: life, health, and disability insurance; pension and savings plans; vacation time; or even tuition reimbursement.[41] If you can trade one benefit for another, you may be able to enhance the value of the total package. For example, life insurance may be relatively unimportant to you if you're single, whereas extra vacation time might be very valuable indeed. Review the important tips for successful interviews in "Checklist: Making a Positive Impression in Job Interviews."

Interview Notes

Keep a written record of your job interviews.

If yours is a typical job search, you'll have many interviews before you accept an offer. For that reason, keeping a notebook or binder of interview notes can help you refresh your memory of each conversation. As soon as you leave the interview facility, jot down the names and titles of the people you met. Briefly summarize the interviewer's answers to your questions. Then quickly evaluate your performance during the interview, listing what you handled well and what you didn't. Going over these notes can help you improve your performance in the future.[42] In addition to improving your performance during

CHECKLIST: Making a Positive Impression in Job Interviews

A. THE WARM-UP

- Stay on your toes; even initial small talk is part of the interviewing process.
- Greet the interviewer by name, with a smile and direct eye contact.
- Offer a firm (not crushing) handshake if the interviewer extends a hand.
- Take a seat only after the interviewer invites you to sit or has taken his or her own seat.
- Listen for cues about what the questions are trying to reveal about you and your qualifications.

B. THE QUESTION-AND-ANSWER STAGE

- Let the interviewer lead the conversation.
- Never answer a question before the interviewer finishes asking it.
- Listen carefully to the interviewer and watch for nonverbal signals.
- Don't limit yourself to simple yes or no answers; expand on the answer to show your knowledge of the company (but don't ramble on).
- If you encounter a potentially discriminatory question, decide how you want to respond before you say anything.
- When you have the opportunity, ask questions from the list you've prepared; remember that interviewers expect you to ask questions.

C. THE CLOSE

- Watch and listen for signs that the interview is about to end.
- Quickly evaluate how well you've done and correct any misperceptions the interviewer might have.
- If you receive an offer and aren't ready to decide, it's entirely appropriate to ask for time to think about it.
- Don't bring up salary, but be prepared to discuss it if the interviewer raises the subject.
- End with a warm smile and a handshake, and thank the interviewer for meeting with you.

interviews, interview notes will help you keep track of any follow-up messages you'll need to send.

6 LEARNING OBJECTIVE

Identify the most common employment messages that follow an interview, and explain when you would use each one

FOLLOWING UP AFTER THE INTERVIEW

Touching base with the prospective employer after the interview, either by phone or in writing, shows that you really want the job and are determined to get it. This also gives you another chance to demonstrate your communication skills and sense of business etiquette. Following up brings your name to the interviewer's attention once again and reminds him or her that you're actively looking and waiting for the decision.

The two most common forms of follow-up are the thank-you message and the inquiry. These messages are often handled by letter, but an e-mail or a phone call can be just as effective, particularly if the employer seems to favor a casual, personal style. Other types of follow-up messages are sent only in certain cases—letters requesting a time extension, letters of acceptance, letters declining a job offer, and letters of resignation. These four types of employment messages are best handled in writing to document any official actions relating to your employment.

Six types of follow-up messages:
- Thank-you message
- Message of inquiry
- Request for a time extension
- Letter of acceptance
- Letter declining a job offer
- Letter of resignation

Thank-You Message

A note or phone call thanking the interviewer should be organized like a routine message and close with a request for a decision or future consideration.

Express your thanks within two days after the interview, even if you feel you have little chance for the job; not only is this good etiquette, but it leaves a positive impression. Acknowledge the interviewer's time and courtesy, and be sure to restate the specific job you're applying for. Convey your continued interest, then ask politely for a decision.

Keep your thank-you message brief (less than five minutes for a phone call or only one page for a letter), and organize it like a routine message. Demonstrate the "you" attitude, and sound positive without sounding overconfident. The following sample thank-you letter shows how to achieve all this in three brief paragraphs:

When Michael Espinosa followed up after a recent job interview, he sent his thank-you message by e-mail the same day.

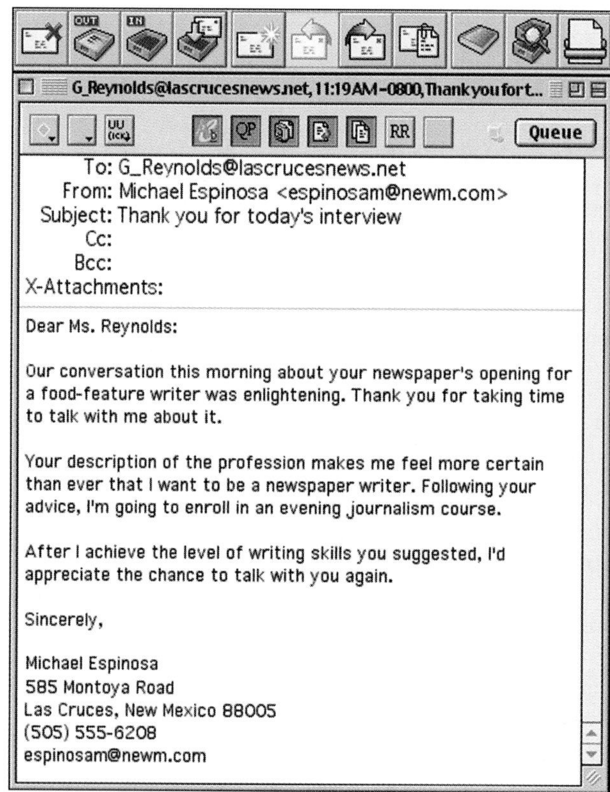
G_Reynolds@lascrucesnews.net, 11:19AM-0800, Thankyou fort...

To: G_Reynolds@lascrucesnews.net
From: Michael Espinosa <espinosam@newm.com>
Subject: Thank you for today's interview
Cc:
Bcc:
X-Attachments:

Dear Ms. Reynolds:

Our conversation this morning about your newspaper's opening for a food-feature writer was enlightening. Thank you for taking time to talk with me about it.

Your description of the profession makes me feel more certain than ever that I want to be a newspaper writer. Following your advice, I'm going to enroll in an evening journalism course.

After I achieve the level of writing skills you suggested, I'd appreciate the chance to talk with you again.

Sincerely,

Michael Espinosa
585 Montoya Road
Las Cruces, New Mexico 88005
(505) 555-6208
espinosam@newm.com

After talking with you yesterday, touring your sets, and watching the television commercials being filmed, I remain enthusiastic about the possibility of joining your staff as a television/film production assistant. Thanks for taking so much time to show me around.

During our meeting, I said that I would prefer not to relocate, but I've reconsidered the matter. I would be pleased to relocate wherever you need my skills in set decoration and prop design.

Now that you've explained the details of your operation, I feel quite strongly that I can make a contribution to the sorts of productions you're lining up. You can also count on me to be an energetic employee and a positive addition to your crew. Please let me know your decision as soon as possible.

Reminds the interviewer of the reasons for meeting and graciously acknowledges the consideration shown to the applicant

Indicates the writer's flexibility and commitment to the job if hired

Reminds the recruiter of special qualifications

Closes on a confident, you-oriented note

Ends with a request for decision

Even if the interviewer has said that you are unqualified for the job, a thank-you message may keep the door open.

Message of Inquiry

If you're not advised of the interviewer's decision by the promised date or within two weeks, you might make an inquiry. A letter of inquiry is particularly appropriate if you've received a job offer from a second firm and don't want to accept it before you have an answer from the first. The following letter illustrates the general plan for a direct request; the writer assumes that a simple oversight, and not outright rejection, is the reason for the delay:

An inquiry about a hiring decision follows the model for a direct request.

When we talked on April 7 about the fashion coordinator position in your Park Avenue showroom, you indicated that a decision would be made by May 1. I am still enthusiastic about the position and eager to know what conclusion you've reached.

To complicate matters, another firm has now offered me a position and has asked that I reply within the next two weeks.

Because your company seems to offer a greater challenge, I would appreciate knowing about your decision by Thursday, May 12. If you need more information before then, please let me know.

Identifies the position and introduces the main idea

Places the reason for the request second

Makes a courteous request for specific action last, while clearly stating a preference for this organization

Request for a Time Extension

If you receive a job offer while other interviews are still pending, you'll probably want more time to decide, so write to the offering organization and ask for a time extension. Employers understand that candidates often interview with several companies. They want you to be sure you're making the right decision, so most are happy to accommodate you with a reasonable extension.

Preface your request with a friendly opening. Ask for more time, stressing your enthusiasm for the organization. Conclude by allowing for a quick decision if your request for additional time is denied. Ask for a prompt reply confirming the time extension if the organization grants it. This type of letter is, in essence, a direct request. However, because the recipient may be disappointed, be sure to temper your request for an extension with statements indicating your continued interest. The letter in Figure 18.3 is a good example of an effective request for a time extension.

DOCUMENT MAKEOVER

IMPROVE THIS LETTER

To practice correcting drafts of actual documents, visit www.prenhall.com/onekey on the web. Click "Document Makeovers" and then click Chapter 18. You will find a letter that contains problems and errors relating to what you've learned in this chapter about interviewing for employment and following up. Use the "Final Draft" decision tool to create an improved version of this letter. Check the message to make sure it reassures the potential employer, asks for the extension, explains the reasons for the request, offers to compromise, and facilitates a quick reply.

FIGURE 18.3 Effective Request for a Time Extension

1448 Solsbury Avenue
Thunderhawk, SD 57655
January 6, 2005

Mr. Frank Lapuzo, Vice President
Customer Relations
Lone Star Foods
7499 Hackberry Parkway
San Antonio, TX 78210

Dear Mr. Lapuzo:

Begins with a strong statement of interest in the job

The customer relations position in your snack foods division seems like an exciting challenge and a great opportunity. I'm very pleased that you offered it to me.

Emphasizes specific reasons for preferring the first job offer to help reassure the reader of sincerity

Stresses professional obligations, not the desire to learn what the other company may offer

Because of another commitment, I would appreciate your giving me until February 15 to make a decision. Before our interview, I scheduled a follow-up interview with another company. I'm interested in your organization because of its impressive quality-control procedures and friendly, attractive work environment. But I do feel obligated to keep my appointment.

Closes with expression of willingness to yield or compromise, conveying continued interest in the position

If you need my decision immediately, I'll gladly let you know. However, If you can allow me the added time to fulfill the earlier commitment, I'd be grateful. Please let me know right away by telephoning me at (605) 234-6897.

Sincerely,

Chang Li

Chang Li

Letter of Acceptance

Use the model for positive messages when you write a letter of acceptance.

When you receive a job offer that you want to accept, reply within five days. Begin by accepting the position and expressing thanks. Identify the job that you're accepting. In the next paragraph, cover any necessary details. Conclude by saying that you look forward to reporting for work. As always, a positive letter should convey your enthusiasm and eagerness to cooperate:

Confirms the specific terms of the offer with a good-news statement at the beginning

I'm delighted to accept the graphic design position in your advertising department at the salary of $2,175 a month.

Covers miscellaneous details in the middle

Enclosed are the health insurance forms you asked me to complete and sign. I've already given notice to my current employer and will be able to start work on Monday, January 18.

Closes with another reference to the good news and a look toward the future

The prospect of joining your firm is exciting. Thank you for giving me this opportunity for what I'm sure will be a challenging future.

Be aware that a job offer and a written acceptance of that offer can constitute a legally binding contract, for both you and the employer. Before you write an acceptance letter, be sure you want the job.

Written acceptance of a job offer can be considered a legally binding contract, so make sure this is really the job you want.

Letter Declining a Job Offer

After all your interviews, you may find that you need to write a letter declining a job offer. The bad-news plan is ideally suited to this type of letter. Open warmly, state the reasons for refusing the offer, decline the offer explicitly, and close on a pleasant note, expressing gratitude. By taking the time to write a sincere, tactful letter, you leave the door open for future contact:

A letter declining a job offer follows the model for negative messages.

> One of the most interesting interviews I have ever had was the one last month at your Durham textile plant. I'm flattered that you would offer me the computer analyst position that we talked about.
>
> During my job search, I applied to five highly rated firms like your own, each one a leader in its field. Both your company and another offered me a position. Because my desire to work abroad can more readily be satisfied by the other company, I have accepted that job offer.
>
> I deeply appreciate the time you spent talking with me. Thank you again for your consideration and kindness.

Makes the opening paragraph a buffer

Precedes the bad news with tactfully phrased reasons for the applicant's unfavorable decision, and leaves the door open

Lets the reader down gently with a sincere and cordial ending

Letter of Resignation

If you get a job offer and are currently employed, you can maintain good relations with your current employer by writing a letter of resignation to your immediate supervisor. Follow the bad-news plan, and make the letter sound positive, regardless of how you feel. Say something favorable about the organization, the people you work with, or what you've learned on the job. Then state your intention to leave and give the date of your last day on the job. Be sure you give your current employer at least two weeks' notice:

Letters of resignation should always be written in a gracious and professional style; criticizing your employer or your colleagues serves no legitimate purpose, and it can come back to haunt you later in your career.

> My sincere thanks to you and to all the other Emblem Corporation employees for helping me learn so much about serving the public these past 11 months. You have given me untold help and encouragement.
>
> You may recall that when you first interviewed me, my goal was to become a customer relations supervisor. Because that opportunity has been offered to me by another organization, I am submitting my resignation. I will miss all of you, but I want to take advantage of this opportunity.
>
> I would like to terminate my work here two weeks from today but can arrange to work an additional week if you want me to train a replacement.
>
> My sincere thanks and best wishes to all of you.

Uses on appreciative opening to serve as a buffer

States reasons before the bad news itself, using tactful phrasing to help keep the relationship friendly, should the writer later want letters of recommendation

Discusses necessary details in an extra paragraph

Tempers any disappointment with a cordial close

To verify the content and style of your follow-up messages, consult the tips in "Checklist: Writing Follow-up Messages."

CHECKLIST: Writing Follow-Up Messages

A. THANK-YOU MESSAGES

- Write a brief thank-you letter within two days of the interview.
- Acknowledge the interviewer's time and courtesy.
- Restate the specific job you're applying for.
- Express your enthusiasm about the organization and the job.
- Add any new facts that may help your chances.
- Politely ask for a decision.

B. MESSAGES OF INQUIRY

- If you haven't heard from the interviewer by the promised date, write a brief message of inquiry.
- Use a direct approach: main idea, necessary details, specific request.

C. REQUESTS FOR A TIME EXTENSION

- Request an extension if you have pending interviews and need time to decide about an offer.
- Open on a friendly note.
- Explain why you need more time and express continued interest in the company.
- In the close, promise a quick decision if your request is denied, and ask for a confirmation if your request is granted.

D. LETTERS OF ACCEPTANCE

- Send this message within five days of receiving the offer.
- State clearly that you accept the offer, identify the job you're accepting, and confirm vital details such as salary and the start date.
- Make sure you want the job; an acceptance letter can be treated as a legally binding contract.

E. LETTERS DECLINING A JOB OFFER

- Use the model for negative messages.
- Open on a warm and appreciative note, then explain why you are refusing the offer.
- End on a sincere, positive note.

F. LETTERS OF RESIGNATION

- Send a letter of resignation to your current employer as soon as possible.
- Begin with an appreciative buffer.
- In the middle section, state your reasons for leaving, and actually state that you are resigning.
- Close cordially.

COMMUNICATION CHALLENGES AT GOOGLE

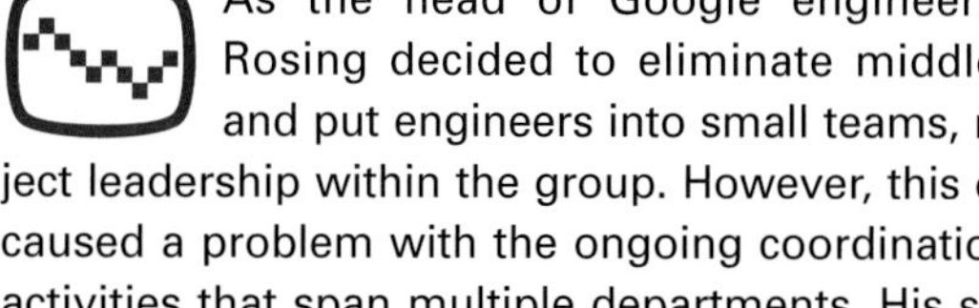

As the head of Google engineering, Wayne Rosing decided to eliminate middle managers and put engineers into small teams, rotating project leadership within the group. However, this decision has caused a problem with the ongoing coordination of project activities that span multiple departments. His solution is to hire five "project coordinators" who will provide administrative help to the engineering teams and also serve as liaisons to other departments.

Individual Challenge: After a few years of experience in the human resources department of a publishing company, you recently joined Google's HR team. Today, Rosing asked you to help with the recruiting and hiring of the project coordinators. He is looking for experienced administrative support people who remain calm when things get chaotic and are flexible enough to interact successfully not only with engineers but also with accountants, marketing managers, sales people, facilities staff, and others. With those requirements in mind, create a list of three or four questions to use during the screening interviews for project coordinators.

Team Challenge: Seven candidates survived the screening process and now you're planning the onsite interviews. In a small group, discuss the types of people to include on the interview team (consult a management textbook if you're unfamiliar with positions in a typical corporation): Who should serve as host and handle the warm-up stage? Who should be involved in the question-and-answer stage? Who should handle the close? In all cases, explain why.

SUMMARY OF LEARNING OBJECTIVES

1 **Define the purpose of application letters, and explain how to apply the AIDA organizational approach to them.** In addition to explaining why you're sending a résumé, the purpose of an application letter is to convince readers to look at your résumé. This makes application letters a type of sales letter, so you'll want to use the AIDA organizational approach. Get attention in the opening paragraph by showing how your work skills could benefit the organization, by explaining how your qualifications fit the job, or by demonstrating an understanding of the organization's needs. Build interest and desire by showing how you can meet the job requirements, and be sure to refer your reader to your résumé near the end of this section. Finally, motivate action by making your request easy to fulfill and by including all necessary contact information.

2 **Describe the typical sequence of job interviews.** The typical sequence of interviews involves three stages. During the first or *screening stage,* employers administer fairly structured interviews to eliminate unqualified applicants. During the second or *selection stage,* the pool of applicants is narrowed considerably. The employer administers a series of structured and unstructured interviews to find the best candidates for the job. Those candidates who advance to the third or *final stage* of the sequence have a good chance of receiving a job offer. During this stage, candidates meet with executives who have the authority to offer the job and set compensation. The underlying objective of this final stage is to select the final candidate(s) and convince the candidate(s) to accept a job offer.

3 **Describe briefly what employers look for during an employment interview.** Employers look for two things during an employment interview. First, they seek evidence that an applicant will be compatible with the other people in the organization. Whether interviewers focus on personal background or personal style, they are interested in finding someone who will easily adapt to a new workplace and new responsibilities. Second, employers seek evidence that an applicant is qualified for the position. Even though interviewers have already reviewed your résumé, they want to see how well your skills match their requirements and perhaps even get a sense of your ability to be flexible and apply diverse skills in more than one area. Sometimes, interviewers will use preemployment tests to help them gather the evidence they need to make a decision.

4 **List six tasks you need to complete to prepare for a successful job interview.** To prepare for a successful job interview, begin by (1) refining the research you did when planning your résumé. Knowing as much as you can about the company and its needs helps you highlight the aspects of your background and qualifications that will appeal to the organization. (2) Next, think ahead about questions—both those you'll need to answer and those you'll want to ask. (3) Bolster your confidence by focusing on your strengths to overcome any apprehension. (4) Polish your style by staging mock interviews and paying close attention to nonverbal behaviors, including voice problems. (5) Plan to look your best with businesslike clothing and good grooming. And (6) arrive on time and ready to begin.

5 **Explain the three stages of a successful employment interview.** All employment interviews have three stages. The warm-up stage is the most important, because first impressions greatly influence an interviewer's decision. The question-and-answer stage is the longest, during which you will answer and ask questions. Listening carefully and watching the interviewer's nonverbal cues help you determine how the interview is going. The close is also important because you need to evaluate your performance to see whether the interviewer has any misconceptions that you must correct.

6 **Identify the most common employment messages that follow an interview, and explain when you would use each one.** The two most common types of follow-up messages are usually in letter form but can also be effective by phone or e-mail. You send the *thank-you* message within two days after your interview to show appreciation, express your continued interest in the job, and politely ask for a decision. You send an *inquiry* if you haven't received the interviewer's decision by the date promised or within two weeks of the interview—especially if you've received a job offer from another firm. The remaining four employment messages are best sent in letter form, to document any official action. You request a *time extension* if you receive a job offer while other interviews are pending and you want more time to complete those interviews before making a decision. You send a *letter of acceptance* within five days of receiving a job offer that you want to take. You send a *letter declining a job offer* when you want to refuse an offer tactfully and leave the door open for future contact. You send a *letter of resignation* when you receive a job offer that you want to accept while you are currently employed.

Test Your Knowledge

1. How does the AIDA model apply to an application letter?
2. How does a structured interview differ from an open-ended interview and a situational interview?
3. What typically occurs during a stress interview?
4. Why do employers conduct preemployment testing?
5. Why are the questions you ask during an interview as important as the answers you give to the interviewer's questions?
6. What are the three stages of every interview, and which is the most important?
7. How should you respond if an interviewer at a company where you want to work asks you a question that seems too personal or unethical?
8. What should you say in a thank-you message after an interview?
9. What is the purpose of sending a letter of inquiry after an interview?
10. What is the legal significance of a letter of acceptance?

Apply Your Knowledge

1. How can you distinguish yourself from other candidates in a screening interview and still keep your responses short and to the point? Explain.
2. What can you do to make a favorable impression when you discover that an open-ended interview has turned into a stress interview? Briefly explain your answer.
3. If you want to switch jobs because you can't work with your supervisor, how can you explain this situation to a prospective employer? Give an example.
4. During a group interview you notice that one of the other candidates is trying to monopolize the conversation. He's always the first to answer, his answer is the longest, and he even interrupts the other candidates while they are talking. The interviewer doesn't seem to be concerned about his behavior, but you are. You would like to have more time to speak so that the interviewer could get to know you better. What should you do?
5. **Ethical Choices** Why is it important to distinguish unethical or illegal interview questions from acceptable questions? Explain.

Practice Your Knowledge

Documents for Analysis

Read the following documents, then (1) analyze the strengths or weaknesses of each document, and (2) revise each document so that it follows this chapter's guidelines.

Document 18.A: Writing an Application Letter

I'm writing to let you know about my availability for the brand manager job you advertised. As you can see from my enclosed résumé, my background is perfect for the position. Even though I don't have any real job experience, my grades have been outstanding considering that I went to a top-ranked business school.

I did many things during my undergraduate years to prepare me for this job:

- Earned a 3.4 out of a 4.0 with a 3.8 in my business courses
- Elected representative to the student governing association
- Selected to receive the Lamar Franklin Award
- Worked to earn a portion of my tuition

I am sending my résumé to all the top firms, but I like yours better than any of the rest. Your reputation is tops in the industry, and I want to be associated with a business that can pridefully say it's the best.

If you wish for me to come in for an interview, I can come on a Friday afternoon or anytime on weekends when I don't have classes. Again, thanks for considering me for your brand manager position.

Document 18.B: Writing Application Follow-Up Messages

Did you receive my résumé? I sent it to you at least two months ago and haven't heard anything. I know you keep résumés on file, but I just want to be sure that you keep me in mind. I heard you are hiring health-care managers and certainly would like to be considered for one of those positions.

Since I last wrote you, I've worked in a variety of positions that have helped prepare me for management. To wit I've become lunch manager at the restaurant where I work, which involved a raise in pay. I now manage a waitstaff of 12 girls and take the lunch receipts to the bank every day.

Of course, I'd much rather be working at a real job, and that's why I'm writing again. Is there anything else you would like to know about me or my background? I would really like to know more about your company. Is there any literature you could send me? If so, I would really appreciate it.

I think one reason I haven't been hired yet is that I don't want to leave Atlanta. So I hope when you think of me, it's for a position that wouldn't require moving. Thanks again for considering my application.

Document 18.C: Thank-You Message

Thank you for the really marvelous opportunity to meet you and your colleagues at Starret Engine Company. I really enjoyed touring your facilities and talking with all the people there. You have quite a crew! Some of the other companies I have visited have been so rigid and uptight that I can't imagine how I would fit in. It's a relief to run into a group of people who seem to enjoy their work as much as all of you do.

I know that you must be looking at many other candidates for this job, and I know that some of them will probably be more experienced than I am. But I do want to emphasize that my two-year hitch in the Navy involved a good deal of engineering work. I don't think I mentioned all my shipboard responsibilities during the interview. Please give me a call within the next week to let me know your decision. You can usually find me at my dormitory in the evening after dinner (phone: 877-9080).

Document 18.D: Letter of Inquiry

I have recently received a very attractive job offer from the Warrington Company. But before I let them know one way or another, I would like to consider any offer that your firm may extend. I was quite impressed with your company during my recent interview, and I am still very interested in a career there.

I don't mean to pressure you, but Warrington has asked for my decision within 10 days. Could you let me know by Tuesday whether you plan to offer me a position? That would give me enough time to compare the two offers.

Document 18.E: Letter Declining a Job Offer

I'm writing to say that I must decline your job offer. Another company has made me a more generous offer, and I have decided to accept. However, if things don't work out for me there, I will let you know. I sincerely appreciate your interest in me.

Exercises

For live links to all websites discussed in this chapter, visit this text's website at www.prenhall.com/bovee. Just log on, select Chapter 18, and click on "Student Resources." Locate the name of the page or the URL related to the material in the text.

18.1 Internet Select a large company (one that you can easily find information on) where you might like to work. Use Internet sources to gather some preliminary research on the company; don't limit your search to the company's own website.

1. What did you learn about this organization that would help you during an interview there?
2. What Internet sources did you use to obtain this information?
3. Armed with this information, what aspects of your background do you think might appeal to this company's recruiters?
4. If you choose to apply for a job with this company, what keywords would you include on your résumé, and why?

18.2 Teamwork Divide the class into two groups. Half the class will be recruiters for a large chain of national department stores looking to fill manager trainee positions (there are 15 openings). The other half of the class will be candidates for the job. The company is specifically looking for candidates who demonstrate these three qualities: initiative, dependability, and willingness to assume responsibility.

1. Have each recruiter select and interview an applicant for 10 minutes.
2. Have all the recruiters discuss how they assessed the applicant in each of the three desired qualities. What questions did they ask or what did they use as an indicator to determine whether the candidate possessed the quality?
3. Have all the applicants discuss what they said to convince the recruiters that they possessed each of these qualities.

18.3 Interviews: Understanding Qualifications Write a short memo to your instructor, discussing what you believe are your greatest strengths and weaknesses from an employment perspective. Next, explain how these strengths and weaknesses would be viewed by interviewers evaluating your qualifications.

18.4 Interviews: Being Prepared Prepare written answers to 10 of the questions listed in Table 18.5 on page 567, "Twenty-Five Common Interview Questions."

18.5 Ethical Choices You have decided to accept a new position with a competitor of your company. Write a letter of resignation to your supervisor, announcing your decision.

1. Will you notify your employer that you are joining a competing firm? Please explain.
2. Will you use the direct or the indirect approach? Please explain.
3. Will you send your letter by e-mail, send it by regular mail, or place it on your supervisor's desk?

Expand Your Knowledge

URLs for all Internet exercises are provided at the website for this book, www.prenhall.com/bovee. When you log on to the text website, select Chapter 18, then select "Student Resources," click on the name of the featured website, and review the website to complete these exercises.

Exploring the Best of the Web

Planning for a Successful Interview
www.job-interview.net

How can you practice for a job interview? What are some questions that you might be asked, and how should you respond? What questions are you not obligated to answer? Job-interview.net, www.job-interview.net, provides mock interviews based on actual job openings. It provides job descriptions, questions and answers for specific careers and jobs, and links to company guides and annual reports. You'll find a step-by-step plan that outlines key job requirements, lists practice interview questions, and helps you put together practice interviews. The site offers tips on the keywords to look for in a job description, which will help you narrow your search and anticipate the questions you might be asked on your first or next job interview. Have a look around, then answer these questions:

1. What are some problem questions you might be asked during a job interview? How would you handle these questions?
2. Choose a job title from the list, and read more about it. What did you learn that could help during an actual interview for the job you selected?
3. Developing an "interview game plan" ahead of time helps you make a strong, positive impression during an interview. What are some of the things you can practice to help make everything you do during an interview seem to come naturally?

Exploring the Web on Your Own

Review these chapter-related websites on your own to learn more about interviewing for jobs.

1. Get over 2,000 pages of career advice at Monster.com, www.monster.com, and talk to career experts in your choice of industry or profession.
2. For a humorous—but effective take on cover letters, visit www.soyouwanna.com, click on Work, then find the article about cover letters.
3. Among the many helpful pages of advice you'll find at the Online Writing Lab is a section on writing cover letters; check it out at http://owl.english.purdue.edu/handouts/pw/p_applettr.html.

Learn Interactively

Interactive Study Guide

Go to the Companion Website at www.prenhall.com/bovee. For Chapter 18, take advantage of the interactive "Study Guide" to test your knowledge of the chapter. Get instant feedback on whether you need additional studying.

Also, visit this site's "Study Hall," where you'll find an abundance of valuable resources that will help you succeed in this course.

Peak Performance Grammar and Mechanics

To review the grammar and mechanics skills that you've learned throughout this course, visit www.prenhall.com/onekey, and click "Peak Performance Grammar and Mechanics." Re-take the Pretests, Follow-Up Tests, and even the Advanced Tests to measure your progress, and review weak areas in the Refresher Courses.

CASES

PREPARING OTHER TYPES OF EMPLOYMENT MESSAGES

1. Online application: Electronic cover letter introducing a résumé While researching a digital camera purchase, you stumble on the webzine *Megapixel* (www.megapixel.com), which offers product reviews on a wide array of camera models. The quality of the reviews and the stunning examples of photography on the site inspire you to a new part-time business idea—you'd like to write a regular column for *Megapixel.* The webzine does a great job addressing the information needs of experienced camera users, but you see an opportunity to write for "newbies," people who are new to digital photography and need a more basic level of information.

Your task: Write an e-mail message that will serve as your cover letter and address your message to Denys Bouton, who edits the English edition of *Megapixel* (it is also published in French). Try to limit your message to one screen (generally 20–25 lines). You'll need a creative "hook" and a reassuring approach that identifies you as the right person to launch this new feature in the webzine (make up any details about your background that you may need to complete the letter).

2. Crashing the last frontier: Letter of inquiry about jobs in Alaska Your friend can't understand why you would want to move to Alaska. So you explain: "What really decided it for me was that I'd never seen the northern lights."

"But what about the bears? The 60-degree-below winters? The permafrost?" asks your friend.

"No problem. Anchorage doesn't get much colder than Buffalo does. It is just windier and wetter. Anyhow, I want to live near Fairbanks, which is near the gold-mining area—and the university is there. Fairbanks has lots of small businesses, like a frontier town in the West about 150 years ago. I think it still has homesteading tracts for people who want to do their own building and are willing to stay for a certain number of years."

"Your plans seem a little hasty," your friend warns. "Maybe you should write for information before you just take off. How do you know you could get a job?"

Your task: Take your friend's advice and write to the Chamber of Commerce, Fairbanks, AK 99701. Ask what types of employment are available to someone with your education and experience, and ask who specifically is hiring year-round employees.

INTERVIEWING WITH POTENTIAL EMPLOYERS

3. Interviewers and interviewees: Classroom exercise in interviewing Interviewing is clearly an interactive process involving at least two people. The best way to practice for interviews is to work with others.

Your task: You and all other members of your class are to write letters of application for an entry-level or management-trainee position requiring a pleasant personality and intelligence but a minimum of specialized education or experience. Sign your letter with a fictitious name that conceals your identity. Next, polish (or prepare) a résumé that accurately identifies you and your educational and professional accomplishments.

Now, three members of the class who volunteer as interviewers divide up all the anonymously written application letters. Then each interviewer selects a candidate who seems the most pleasant and convincing in his or her letter. At this time the selected candidates identify themselves and give the interviewers their résumés.

Each interviewer then interviews his or her chosen candidate in front of the class, seeking to understand how the items on the résumé qualify the candidate for the job. At the end of the interviews, the class may decide who gets the job and discuss why this candidate was successful. Afterward, retrieve your letter, sign it with the right name, and submit it to the instructor for credit.

4. Internet interview: Exercise in interviewing Using the Web 100 site at www.web100.com, locate the homepage of a company you would like to work for. Then identify a position within the company for which you would like to apply. Study the company, using any of the online business resources discussed in Chapter 10, and prepare for an interview with that company.

Your task: Working with a classmate, take turns interviewing each other for your chosen positions. Interviewers should take notes during the interview. Once the interview is complete, critique each other's performance (interviewers should critique how well candidates prepared for the interview and answered the questions; interviewees should critique the quality of the questions asked). Write a follow-up letter thanking your interviewer and submit the letter to your instructor.

FOLLOWING UP AFTER THE INTERVIEW

5. A slight error in timing: Letter asking for delay of an employment decision You botched your timing and applied for your third-choice job before going after what you really wanted. What you want to do is work in retail marketing with Neiman Marcus in Dallas; what you have been offered is a similar job with Longhorn Leather and Lumber, 55 dry and dusty miles away in Commerce, just south of the Oklahoma panhandle.

You review your notes. Your Longhorn interview was three weeks ago with the human resources manager, R. P. Bronson, a congenial person who has just written to offer you the position. The store's address is 27 Sam Rayburn Drive, Commerce, TX 75428. Mr. Bronson notes that he can hold the position open for 10 days. You have an interview scheduled with Neiman Marcus next week, but it is unlikely that you will know the store's decision within this 10-day period.

Your task: Write to R. P. Bronson, requesting a reasonable delay in your consideration of his job offer.

6. Job hunt: Set of employment-related letters to a single company Where would you like to work? Pick a real or an imagined company, and assume that a month ago you sent your résumé and application letter. Not long afterward, you were invited to come for an interview, which seemed to go very well.

Your task: Use your imagination to write the following: (a) a thank-you letter for the interview, (b) a note of inquiry, (c) a request for more time to decide, (d) a letter of acceptance, and (e) a letter declining the job offer.

Appendix A
Format and Layout of Business Documents

The format and layout of business documents vary from country to country; they even vary within regions of the United States. In addition, many organizations develop their own variations of standard styles, adapting documents to the types of messages they send and the kinds of audiences they communicate with. The formats described here are more common than others.

First Impressions

Your documents tell readers a lot about you and about your company's professionalism. So all your documents must look neat, present a professional image, and be easy to read. Your audience's first impression of a document comes from the quality of its paper, the way it is customized, and its general appearance.

Paper

To give a quality impression, businesspeople consider carefully the paper they use. Several aspects of paper contribute to the overall impression:

- **Weight.** Paper quality is judged by the weight of four reams (each a 500-sheet package) of letter-size paper. The weight most commonly used by U.S. business organizations is 20-pound paper, but 16- and 24-pound versions are also used.
- **Cotton content.** Paper quality is also judged by the percentage of cotton in the paper. Cotton doesn't yellow over time the way wood pulp does, plus it's both strong and soft. For letters and outside reports, use paper with a 25 percent cotton content. For memos and other internal documents, you can use a lighter-weight paper with lower cotton content. Airmail-weight paper may save money for international correspondence, but make sure it isn't too flimsy.[1]
- **Size.** In the United States, the standard paper size for business documents is $8^1/_2$ by 11 inches. Standard legal documents are $8^1/_2$ by 14 inches. Executives sometimes have heavier 7-by-10-inch paper on hand (with matching envelopes) for personal messages such as congratulations and recommendations.[2] They may also have a box of note cards imprinted with their initials and a box of plain folded notes for condolences or for acknowledging formal invitations.
- **Color.** White is the standard color for business purposes, although neutral colors such as gray and ivory are sometimes used. Memos can be produced on pastel-colored paper to distinguish them from external correspondence. In addition, memos are sometimes produced on various colors of paper for routing to separate departments. Light-colored papers are appropriate, but bright or dark colors make reading difficult and may appear too frivolous.

Customization

For letters to outsiders, U.S. businesses commonly use letterhead stationery, which may be either professionally printed or designed in-house using word-processing templates and graphics. The letterhead includes the company's name and address, usually at the top of the page but sometimes along the left side or even at the bottom. Other information may be included in the letterhead as well: the company's telephone number, fax number, cable address, website address, product lines, date of establishment, officers and directors, slogan, and symbol (logo). Well-designed letterhead gives readers[3]

- Pertinent reference data
- A favorable image of the company
- A good idea of what the company does

For as much as it's meant to accomplish, the letterhead should be as simple as possible. Too much information makes the page look cluttered, occupies space needed for the message, and might become outdated before all the stationery can be used. If you correspond frequently with people abroad, your letterhead must be intelligible to foreigners. It must include the name of your country in addition to your cable, telex, e-mail, or fax information.

In the United States, businesses always use letterhead for the first page of a letter. Successive pages are usually plain sheets of paper that match the letterhead in color and quality. Some companies use a specially printed second-page letterhead that bears only the company's name. Other countries have other conventions.

Many companies also design and print standardized forms for memos and frequently written reports that always require the same sort of information (such as sales reports and expense reports). These forms may be printed in sets for use with carbon paper or in carbonless-copy sets that produce multiple copies automatically. More and more organizations use computers to generate their standardized forms, which can save them both money and time.[4]

Appearance

Produce almost all of your business documents using either a printer (letter-quality, not a dot matrix) or a typewriter. Certain documents, however, should be handwritten (such as a short informal memo or a note of condolence). Be sure to handwrite, print, or type the envelope to match the document. However, even a letter on the best-quality paper with the best-designed letterhead may look unprofessional if it's poorly produced. So pay close attention to all the factors affecting appearance, including the following:

- **Margins.** Companies in the United States make sure that documents (especially external ones) are centered on the page, with margins of at least an inch all around. Using word-processing software, you can achieve this balance simply by defining the format parameters. When using a typewriter, either establish a standard line length (usually about 6 inches) or establish a "picture frame."
- **Line length.** Lines are rarely justified, because the resulting text looks too much like a form letter and can be hard to read (even with proportional spacing). Varying line length makes the document look more personal and interesting. Pica type (12 points) gives you 60 characters in a line; elite type (10 points) gives you 72 characters in a line.
- **Line spacing.** You can adjust the number of blank lines between elements (such as between the date and the inside address) to ensure that a short document fills the page vertically or that a longer document extends at least two lines of the body onto the last page.
- **Character spacing.** Use proper spacing between characters and after punctuation. For example, U.S. conventions include leaving one space after commas, semicolons, colons, and sentence-ending periods. Each letter in a person's initials is followed by a period and a single space. However, abbreviations such as U.S.A. or MBA may or may not have periods, but they never have internal spaces.
- **Special symbols.** When using a computer, use appropriate symbols to give your document a professional look (see Table A.1 for examples). When using a typewriter, use a hyphen for the en dash, and use two hyphens (with no space before, between, or after) for the em dash. Find other details of this sort in your company's style book or in most secretarial handbooks.
- **Corrections.** Messy corrections are obvious and unacceptable in business documents. Reprint or retype any letter, report, or memo requiring a lot of corrections. Word-processing software and self-correcting typewriters can produce correction-free documents at the push of a button.

Letters

All business letters have certain elements in common. Several of these elements appear in every letter; others appear only when desirable or appropriate. In addition, these letter parts are usually arranged in one of three basic formats.

TABLE A.1 Special Symbols on Computer

	COMPUTER SYMBOL	TYPED SYMBOL
Case fractions	½	1/2
Copyright	©	(c)
Registered trademark	®	(R)
Cents	¢	None
British pound	£	None
Paragraph	¶	None
Bullets	●,◆,■,□, ✓,☑,⊗	*, #, 0
Em dash	—	-- (two hyphens)
En dash	—	- (one hyphen)

Standard Letter Parts

The letter in Figure A.1 shows the placement of standard letter parts. The writer of this business letter had no letterhead available but correctly included a heading. All business letters typically include these seven elements.

Heading

Letterhead (the usual heading) shows the organization's name, full address, telephone number (almost always), and e-mail address (often). Executive letterhead also bears the name of an individual within the organization. Computers allow you to design your own letterhead (either one to use for all correspondence or a new one for each piece of correspondence). If letterhead stationery is not available, the heading includes a return address (but no name) and starts 13 lines from the top of the page, which leaves a two-inch top margin.

Date

If you're using letterhead, place the date at least one blank line beneath the lowest part of the letterhead. Without letterhead, place the date immediately below the return address. The standard method of writing the date in the United States uses the full name of the month (no abbreviations), followed by the day (in numerals, without *st, nd, rd,* or *th*), a comma, and then the year: July 14, 2003 (7/14/03). Some organizations follow other conventions (see Table A.2). To maintain the utmost clarity in international correspondence, always spell out the name of the month in dates.[5]

When communicating internationally, you may also experience some confusion over time. Some companies in the United States refer to morning (A.M.) and afternoon (P.M.), dividing a 24-hour day into 12-hour blocks so that they refer to four o'clock in the morning (4:00 A.M.) or four o'clock in the afternoon (4:00 P.M.). The U.S. military and European companies refer to one 24-hour period so that 0400 hours (4:00 A.M.) is always in the morning and 1600 hours (4:00 P.M.) is always in the afternoon.[6] Make sure your references to time are as clear as possible, and be sure you clearly understand your audience's time references.

FIGURE A.1 Standard Letter Parts

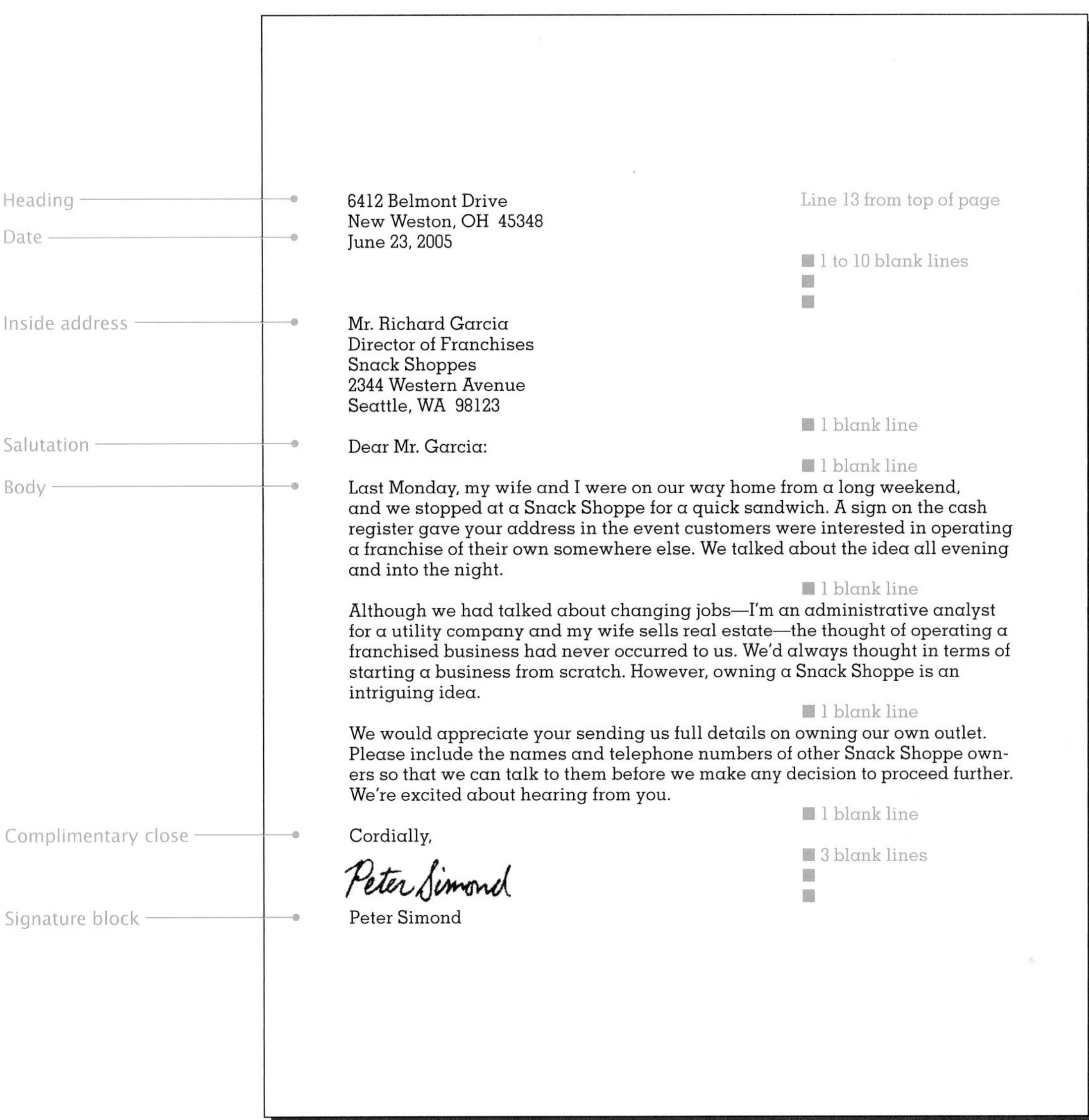

Inside Address

The inside address identifies the recipient of the letter. For U.S. correspondence, begin the inside address at least one line below the date. Precede the addressee's name with a courtesy title, such as *Dr., Mr.,* or *Ms.* The accepted courtesy title for women in business is *Ms.*, although a woman known to prefer the title *Miss* or *Mrs.* is always accommodated. If you don't know whether a person is a man or a woman (and you have no way of finding out), omit the courtesy title. For example, *Terry Smith* could be either a man or a woman. The first line of the inside address would be just *Terry Smith*, and the salutation would be *Dear Terry*

TABLE A.2 Common Date Forms

CONVENTION	DESCRIPTION	DATE—MIXED	DATE—ALL NUMERALS
U.S. standard	Month (spelled out) day, year	July 14, 2003	7/14/03
U.S. government and some U.S. industries	Day (in numerals) month (spelled out) year	14 July 2003	14/7/03
European	Replace U.S. solidus (diagonal line) with periods	14 July 2003	14.7.2003
International standard	Year month day	2003 July 14	2003,7,14

TABLE A.3 Forms of Address

PERSON	IN ADDRESS	IN SALUTATION
PERSONAL TITLES		
Man	Mr. [first & last name]	Dear Mr. [last name]:
Woman (marital status unknown)	Ms. [first & last name]	Dear Ms. [last name]:
Woman (single)	Ms. *or* Miss [first & last name]	Dear Ms. *or* Miss [last name]:
Woman (married)	Ms. *or* Mrs. [wife's first & last name] *or*	Dear Ms. *or* Mrs. [last name]: Mrs. [husband's first & last name]
Woman (widowed)	Ms. *or* Mrs. [wife's first name & last name]	Dear Ms. *or* Mrs. [last name]:
Woman (separated or divorced)	Ms. *or* Mrs. [first & last name]	Dear Ms. *or* Mrs. [last name]:
Two men (or more)	Mr. [first & last name] and Mr. [first & last name]	Dear Mr. [last name] and Mr. [last name] *or* Messrs. [last name] and [last name]:
Two women (or more)	Ms. [first & last name] and Ms. [first & last name] *or*	Dear Ms. [last name] and Ms. [last name] *or* Mses. [last name] and [last name]:
	Mrs. [first & last name] and Mrs. [first & last name]	Dear Mrs. [last name] and Mrs. [last name]: *or* Dear Mesdames [last name] and [last name] *or* Mesdames:
	Miss [first & last name] Mrs. [first & last name]	Dear Miss [last name] and Mrs. [last name]:
One woman and one man	Ms. [first & last name] and Mr. [first & last name]	Dear Ms. [last name] and Mr. [last name]:
Couple (married)	Mr. and Mrs. [husband's first & last name]	Dear Mr. and Mrs. [last name]:
Couple (married with different last names)	[title] [first & last name of husband] [title] [first & last name of wife]	Dear [title] [husband's last name] and [title] [wife's first & last name]:
Couple (married professionals with same title and same last name)	[title in plural form] [husband's first name] and [wife's first & last name]	Dear [title in plural form] [last name]:
Couple (married professionals with different titles and same last name)	[title] [first & last name of husband] and [title] [first & last name of wife]	Dear [title] and [title] [last name]:

(continued)

Smith. The same is true if you know only a person's initials, as in *S. J. Adams.*

Spell out and capitalize titles that precede a person's name, such as *Professor* or *General* (see Table A.3 for the proper forms of address). The person's organizational title, such as *Director,* may be included on this first line (if it is short) or on the line below; the name of a department may follow. In addresses and signature lines, don't forget to capitalize any professional title that follows a person's name:

> Mr. Ray Johnson, Dean
>
> Ms. Patricia T. Higgins
>
> Assistant Vice President

However, professional titles not appearing in an address or signature line are capitalized only when they directly precede the name.

> President Kenneth Johanson will deliver the speech.
>
> Maria Morales, president of ABC Enterprises, will deliver the speech.
>
> The Honorable Helen Masters, senator from Arizona, will deliver the speech.

If the name of a specific person is unavailable, you may address the letter to the department or to a specific position within the department. Also, be sure to spell out company

TABLE A.3 Continued

PERSON	IN ADDRESS	IN SALUTATION
PROFESSIONAL TITLES		
President of a college or university (doctor)	Dr. [first & last name], President	Dear Dr. [last name]:
Dean of a school of college	Dean [first & last name] *or* Dr., Mr., Mrs., *or* Miss [first & last name] Dean of (title)	Dear Dean [last name]: Dear Dr., Mr., Ms., Mrs., *or* Miss [last name]:
Professor	Professor [first & last name]	Dear Professor [last name]:
Physician	[first & last name], M.D.	Dear Dr. [last name]:
Lawyer	Mr., Ms., Mrs., *or* Miss [first & last name]	Dear Mr., Ms., Mrs., *or* Miss [last name]:
Service personnel	[full rank, first & last name, abbreviation of service designation] (add *Retired* if applicable)	Dear [rank] [last name]:
Company or corporation	[name of organization]	Ladies and Gentlemen *or* Gentlemen and Ladies
GOVERNMENTAL TITLES		
President of the United States	The President	Dear Mr. *or* Madam President:
Senator of the United States	Honorable [first & last name]	Dear Senator [last name]:
Cabinet member Postmaster General Attorney General	Honorable [first & last name]	Dear Mr. *or* Madam Secretary: Dear Mr. *or* Madam Postmaster General: Dear Mr. *or* Madam Attorney General:
Mayor	Honorable [first & last name] Mayor of [name of city]	Dear Mayor [last name]:
Judge	The Honorable	Dear Judge [last name]:
RELIGIOUS TITLES		
Priest	The Reverend [first & last name], [initials of order, if any]	Reverend Sir: (formal) *or* Dear Father [last name]: (informal)
Rabbi	Rabbi & [first & last name]	Dear Rabbi [last name]:
Minister	The Reverend [first & last name] [title, if any]	Dear Reverend [last name]:

names in full, unless the company itself uses abbreviations in its official name.

Other address information includes the treatment of buildings, house numbers, and compass directions (see Table A.4 on page A-6). The following example shows all the information that may be included in the inside address and its proper order for U.S. correspondence:

Ms. Linda Coolidge, Vice President
Corporate Planning Department
Midwest Airlines
Kowalski Building, Suite 21-A
7279 Bristol Ave.
Toledo, OH 43617

Canadian addresses are similar, except that the name of the province is usually spelled out:

Dr. H. C. Armstrong
Research and Development
Commonwealth Mining Consortium
The Chelton Building, Suite 301
585 Second St. SW
Calgary, Alberta T2P 2P5

The order and layout of address information vary from country to country. So when addressing correspondence for other countries, carefully follow the format and information that appear in the company's letterhead.

TABLE A.4 Inside Address Information

DESCRIPTION	EXAMPLE
Capitalize building names.	Empire State Building
Capitalize locations within buildings (apartments, suites, rooms).	Suite 1073
Use numerals for all house or building numbers, except the number one.	One Trinity Lane 637 Adams Ave., Apt. 7
Spell out compass directions that fall within a street address.	1074 West Connover St.
Abbreviate compass directions that follow the street address.	783 Main St. N.E., Apt. 27

However, when you're sending mail from the United States, be sure that the name of the destination country appears on the last line of the address in capital letters. Use the English version of the country name so that your mail is routed from the United States to the right country. Then, to be sure your mail is routed correctly within the destination country, use the foreign spelling of the city name (using the characters and diacritical marks that would be commonly used in the region). For example, the following address uses *Köln* instead of *Cologne*:

H. R. Veith, Director	Addressee
Eisfieren Glaswerk	Company Name
Blaubachstrasse 13	Street address
Postfach 10 80 07	Post office box
D-5000 Köln I	District, city
GERMANY	Country

For additional examples of international addresses, see Table A.5.

Be sure to use organizational titles correctly when addressing international correspondence. Job designations vary around the world. In England, for example, a managing director is often what a U.S. company would call its chief executive officer or president, and a British deputy is the equivalent of a vice president. In France, responsibilities are assigned to individuals without regard to title or organizational structure, and in China the title *project manager* has meaning, but the title *sales manager* may not.

To make matters worse, businesspeople in some countries sign correspondence without their names typed below. In Germany, for example, the belief is that employees represent the company, so it's inappropriate to emphasize personal names.[7] Use the examples in Table A.5 as guidelines when addressing correspondence to countries outside the United States.

Salutation

In the salutation of your letter, follow the style of the first line of the inside address. If the first line is a person's name, the salutation is *Dear Mr.* or *Ms. Name.* The formality of the salutation depends on your relationship with the addressee. If in conversation you would say "Mary," your letter's salutation should be *Dear Mary,* followed by a colon. Otherwise, include the courtesy title and last name, followed by a colon. Presuming to write *Dear Lewis* instead of *Dear Professor Chang* demonstrates a disrespectful familiarity that the recipient will probably resent.

If the first line of the inside address is a position title such as *Director of Personnel,* then use *Dear Director.* If the addressee is unknown, use a polite description, such as *Dear Alumnus, Dear SPCA Supporter,* or *Dear Voter.* If the first line is plural (a department or company), then use *Ladies and Gentlemen* (look again at Table A.3). When you do not know whether you're writing to an individual or a group (for example, when writing a reference or a letter of recommendation), use *To whom it may concern.*

In the United States some letter writers use a "salutopening" on the salutation line. A salutopening omits *Dear* but includes the first few words of the opening paragraph along with the recipient's name. After this line, the sentence continues a double space below as part of the body of the letter, as in these examples:

Thank you, Mr. Brown,	Salutopening
for your prompt payment of your bill.	Body
Congratulations, Ms. Lake!	Salutopening
Your promotion is well deserved.	Body

Whether your salutation is informal or formal, be especially careful that names are spelled right. A misspelled name is glaring evidence of carelessness, and it belies the personal interest you're trying to express.

Body

The body of the letter is your message. Almost all letters are single-spaced, with one blank line before and after the salutation or salutopening, between paragraphs, and before the complimentary close. The body may include indented lists, entire paragraphs indented for emphasis, and even subheadings. If it does, all similar elements should be treated in the same way. Your department or company may select a format to use for all letters.

Complimentary Close

The complimentary close begins on the second line below the body of the letter. Alternatives for wording are available, but currently the trend seems to be toward using one-word closes, such as *Sincerely* and *Cordially.* In any case, the complimentary close reflects the relationship between you and the person you're writing to. Avoid cute closes, such as *Yours*

TABLE A.5 International Addresses and Salutations

COUNTRY	POSTAL ADDRESS	ADDRESS ELEMENTS	SALUTATIONS
Argentina	Sr. Juan Pérez Editorial Internacional S.A. Av. Sarmiento 1337, 8° P. C. C1035AAB BUENOS AIRES – CF ARGENTINA	S.A. = Sociedad Anónima (corporation) Av. Sarmiento (name of street) 1337 (building number) 8°= 8th. P = Piso (floor) C (room or suite) C1035AAB (postcode + city) CF = Capital Federal (federal capital)	Sr. = Señor (Mr.) Sra. = Señora (Mrs.) Srta. = Señorita (Miss) Don't use given names except with people you know well.
Australia	Mr. Roger Lewis International Publishing Pty. Ltd. 166 Kent Street, Level 9 GPO Box 3542 SYDNEY NSW 2001 AUSTRALIA	Pty. Ltd. = Proprietory Limited (corp.) 166 (building number) Kent Street (name of street) Level (floor) GPO Box (post office box) city + state (abbrev.) + postcode	Mr. and Mrs. used on first contact. Ms. not common (avoid use). Business is informal—use given name freely.
Austria	Herrn Dipl.-Ing. J. Gerdenitsch International Verlag Ges.m.b.H. Glockengasse 159 1010 WIEN AUSTRIA	Herrn = To Mr. (separate line) Dipl.-Ing. (engineering degree) Ges.m.b.H. (a corporation) Glockengasse (street name) 159 (building number) 1010 (postcode + city) WIEN (Vienna)	Herr (Mr.) Frau (Mrs.) Fräulein (Miss) obsolete in business, so do not use. Given names are almost never used in business.
Brazil	Ilmo. Sr. Gilberto Rabello Ribeiro Editores Internacionais S.A. Rua da Ajuda, 228–6° Andar Caixa Postal 2574 20040–000 RIO DE JANEIRO – RJ BRAZIL	Ilmo. = Ilustrissimo (honorific) Ilma. = Ilustrissima (hon. female) S.A. = Sociedade Anônima (corporation) Rua = street, da Ajuda (street name) 228 (building number) 6° = 6th. Andar (floor) Caixa Postal (P.O. box) 20040–000 (postcode + city) - RJ (state abbrev.)	Sr. = Senhor (Mr.) Sra. = Senhora (Mrs.) Srta. = Senhorita (Miss) Family name at end, e.g., Senhor Ribeiro (Rabello is mother's family—as in Portugal) Given names readily used in business.
China	Xia Zhiyi International Publishing Ltd. 14 Jianguolu Chaoyangqu BEIJING 100025 CHINA	Ltd. (limited liability corporation) 14 (building number) Jianguolu (street name), lu (street) Chaoyangqu (district name) (city + postcode)	Family name (single syllable) first. Given name (2 syllables) second, sometimes reversed. Use Mr. or Ms. at all times (Mr. Xia).
France	Monsieur LEFÈVRE Alain Éditions Internationales S.A. Siège Social Immeuble Le Bonaparte 64–68, av. Galliéni B.P. 154 75942 PARIS CEDEX 19 FRANCE	S.A. = Société Anonyme Siège Social (head office) Immeuble (building + name) 64–68 (building occupies 64, 66, 68) av. = avenue (no initial capital) B.P. = Boîte Postale (P.O. box) 75942 (postcode) CEDEX (postcode for P.O. box)	Monsieur (Mr.) Madame (Mrs.) Mademoiselle (Miss) Best not to abbreviate. Family name is sometimes in all caps with given name following.
Germany	Herrn Gerhardt Schneider International Verlag GmbH Schillerstraβe 159 44147 DORTMUND GERMANY	Herrn = To Herr (on a separate line) GmbH (inc.—incorporated) -straβe (street—'β' often written 'ss') 159 (building number) 44147 (postcode + city)	Herr (Mr.) Frau (Mrs.) Fräulein (Miss) obsolete in business. Business is formal: (1) do not use given names unless invited, and (2) use academic titles precisely.
India	Sr. Shyam Lal Gupta International Publishing (Pvt.) Ltd. 1820 Rehaja Centre 214, Darussalam Road Andheri East BOMBAY – 400049 INDIA	(Pvt.) (privately owned) Ltd. (limited liability corporation) 1820 (possibly office #20 on 18th floor) Rehaja Centre (building name) 214 (building number) Andheri East (suburb name) (city + hyphen + postcode)	Shri (Mr.), Shrimati (Mrs.) but English is common business language, so use Mr., Mrs., Miss. Given names are used only by family and close friends.

(continued)

TABLE A.5 Continued

COUNTRY	POSTAL ADDRESS	ADDRESS ELEMENTS	SALUTATIONS
Italy	Egr. Sig. Giacomo Mariotti Edizioni Internazionali S.p.A. Via Terenzio, 21 20138 MILANO ITALY	Egr. = Egregio (honorific) Sig. = Signor (not nec. a separate line) S.p.A. = Società per Azioni (corp.) Via (street) 21 (building number) 20138 (postcode + city)	Sig. = Signore (Mr.) Sig.ra = Signora (Mrs.) Sig.a (Ms.) Women in business are addressed as Signora. Use given name only when invited.
Japan	Mr. Taro Tanaka Kokusai Shuppan K.K. 10–23, 5-chome, Minamiazabu Minato-ku TOKYO 106 JAPAN	K.K. = Kabushiki Kaisha (corporation) 10 (lot number) 23 (building number) 5-chome (area #5) Minamiazabu (neighborhood name) Minato-ku (city district) (city + postcode)	Given names not used in business. Use family name + job title. Or use family name + "-san" (Tanaka-san) or more respectfully, add "-sama" or "-dono."
Korea	Mr. Kim Chang-ik International Publishers Ltd. Room 206, Korea Building 33–4 Nonhyon-dong Kangnam-ku SEOUL 135–010 KOREA	English company names common Ltd. (a corporation) 206 (office number inside the building) 33–4 (area 4 of subdivision 33) -dong (city neighborhood name) -ku (subdivision of city) (city + postcode)	Family name is normally first but sometimes placed after given name. A two-part name is the given name. Use Mr. or Mrs. in letters, but use job title in speech.
Mexico	Sr. Francisco Pérez Martínez Editores Internacionales S.A. Independencia No.322 Col. Juárez 06050 MEXICO D.F.	S.A. = Sociedad Anónima (corporation) Independencia (street name) No. = Número (number) 322 (building number) Col. = Colonia (city district) Juárez (locality name) 06050 (postcode + city) D.F. = Distrito Federal (federal capital)	Sr. = Señor (Mr.) Sra. = Señora (Mrs.) Srta. = Señorita (Miss) Family name in middle: e.g., Sr. Pérez (Martínez is mother's family). Given names are used in business.
South Africa	Mr. Mandla Ntuli International Publishing (Pty.) Ltd. Private Bag X2581 JOHANNESBURG 2000 SOUTH AFRICA	Pty. = Proprietory (privately owned) Ltd. (a corporation) Private Bag (P.O. Box) (city + postcode) or (postcode + city)	Mnr. = Meneer (Mr.) Mev. = Mevrou (Mrs.) Mejuffrou (Miss) is not used in business. Business is becoming less formal, so the use of given names is possible.
United Kingdom	Mr. N. J. Lancaster International Publishing Ltd. Kingsbury House 12 Kingsbury Road EDGEWARE Middlesex HA8 9XG ENGLAND	N. J. (initials of given names) Ltd. (limited liability corporation) Kingsbury House (building name) 12 (building number) Kingsbury Road (name of street/road) EDGEWARE (city—all caps) Middlesex (county—not all caps) HA8 9XG (postcode)	Mr. and Ms. used mostly. Mrs. and Miss sometimes used in North and by older women. Given names—called Christian names—are used in business after some time. Wait to be invited.

for bigger profits. If your audience doesn't know you well, your sense of humor may be misunderstood.

Signature Block

Leave three blank lines for a written signature below the complimentary close, and then include the sender's name (unless it appears in the letterhead). The person's title may appear on the same line as the name or on the line below:

Cordially,

Raymond Dunnigan
Director of Personnel

Your letterhead indicates that you're representing your company. However, if your letter is on plain paper or runs to a second page, you may want to emphasize that you're speaking legally for the company. The accepted way of doing that is to place the company's name in capital letters a double space below the complimentary close and then include the sender's name and title four lines below that:

Sincerely,

WENTWORTH INDUSTRIES

(Mrs.) Helen B. Taylor
President

FIGURE A.2 Additional Letter Parts

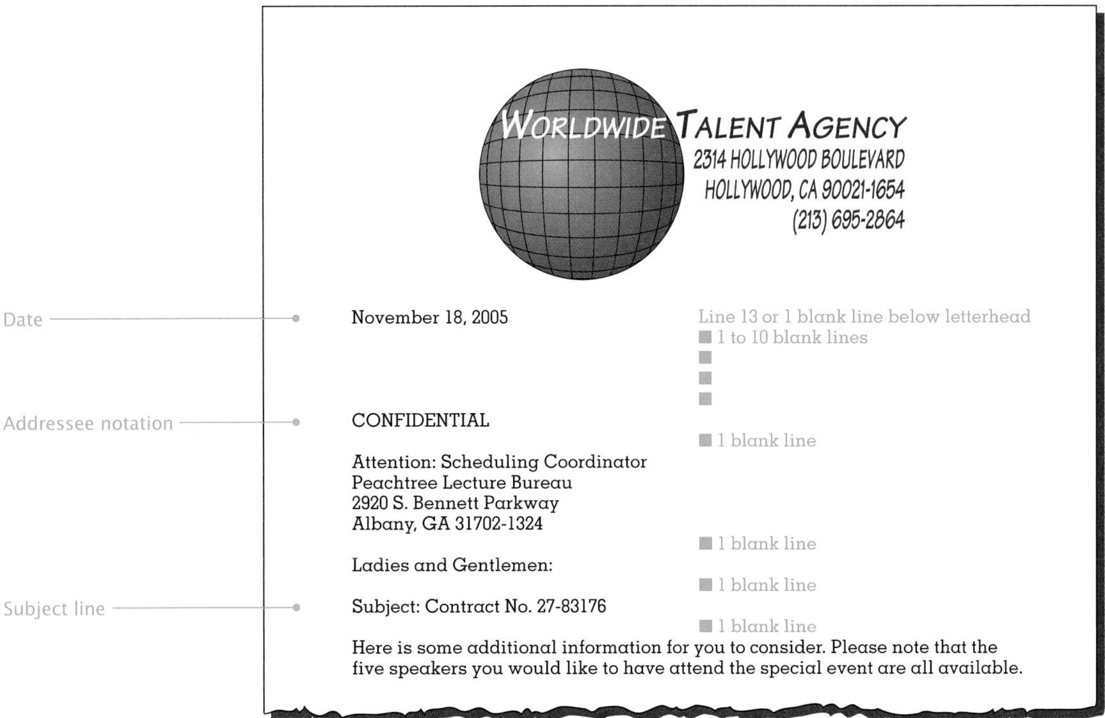
WORLDWIDE TALENT AGENCY
2314 HOLLYWOOD BOULEVARD
HOLLYWOOD, CA 90021-1654
(213) 695-2864

November 18, 2005

CONFIDENTIAL

Attention: Scheduling Coordinator
Peachtree Lecture Bureau
2920 S. Bennett Parkway
Albany, GA 31702-1324

Ladies and Gentlemen:

Subject: Contract No. 27-83176

Here is some additional information for you to consider. Please note that the five speakers you would like to have attend the special event are all available.

If your name could be taken for either a man's or a woman's, a courtesy title indicating gender should be included, with or without parentheses. Also, women who prefer a particular courtesy title should include it:

Mrs. Nancy Winters

(Miss) Juana Flores

Ms. Pat Li

(Mr.) Jamie Saunders

Additional Letter Parts

Letters vary greatly in subject matter and thus in the identifying information they need and the format they adopt. The letter in Figure A.2 shows how these additional parts should be arranged. The following elements may be used in any combination, depending on the requirements of the particular letter:

- **Addressee notation.** Letters that have a restricted readership or that must be handled in a special way should include such addressee notations as *Personal, Confidential,* or *Please Forward.* This sort of notation appears a double space above the inside address, in all-capital letters.
- **Attention line.** Although not commonly used today, an attention line can be used if you know only the last name of the person you're writing to. It can also direct a letter to a position title or department. Place the attention line on the first line of the inside address and put the company name on the second.[8] Match the address on the envelope with the style of the inside address. An attention line may take any of the following forms or variants of them:

  Attention: Dr. McHenry

  Attention Director of Marketing

  Attention Marketing Department
- **Subject line.** The subject line tells recipients at a glance what the letter is about (and indicates where to file the letter for future reference). It usually appears below the salutation, either against the left margin, indented (as a paragraph in the body), or centered. It can be placed above the salutation or at the very top of the page, and it can be underscored. Some businesses omit the word *Subject,* and some organizations replace it with *Re:* or *In re:* (meaning "concerning" or "in the matter of"). The subject line may take a variety of forms, including the following:

  Subject: RainMaster Sprinklers

  About your February 2, 2003, order

  FALL 1998 SALES MEETING

  Reference Order No. 27920
- **Second-page heading.** Use a second-page heading whenever an additional page is required. Some companies have second-page letterhead (with the company name and address on one line and in a smaller typeface). The heading bears the name (person or organization) from the first line of the inside address, the page number, the date, and perhaps a reference number. Leave two blank lines before the body. Make sure that at least two lines of a continued paragraph appear on the first and

FIGURE A.2 (Continued)

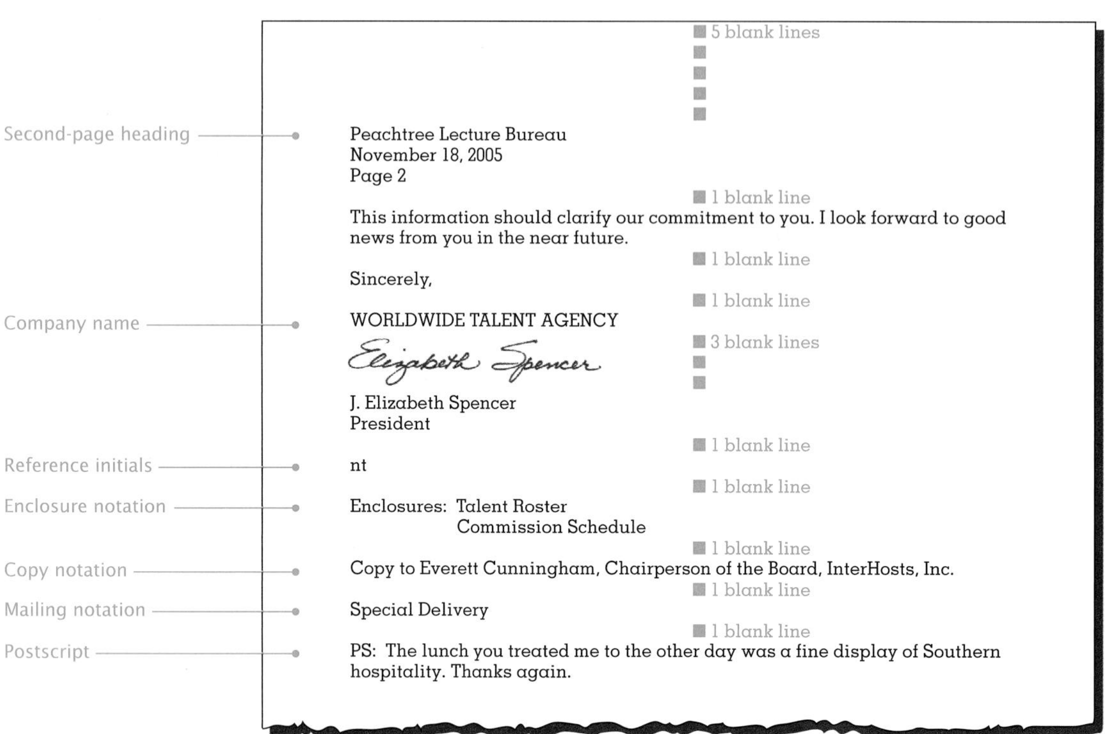

Peachtree Lecture Bureau
November 18, 2005
Page 2

This information should clarify our commitment to you. I look forward to good news from you in the near future.

Sincerely,

WORLDWIDE TALENT AGENCY

J. Elizabeth Spencer
President

nt

Enclosures: Talent Roster
Commission Schedule

Copy to Everett Cunningham, Chairperson of the Board, InterHosts, Inc.

Special Delivery

PS: The lunch you treated me to the other day was a fine display of Southern hospitality. Thanks again.

second pages. Never allow the closing lines to appear alone on a continued page. Precede the complimentary close or signature lines with at least two lines of the body. Also, don't hyphenate the last word on a page. All the following are acceptable forms for second-page headings:

Ms. Melissa Baker

May 10, 2003

Page 2

Ms. Melissa Baker, May 10, 2003, Page 2

Ms. Melissa Baker -2- May 10, 2003

- **Company name.** If you include the company's name in the signature block, put it all in capital letters a double space below the complimentary close. You usually include the company's name in the signature block only when the writer is serving as the company's official spokesperson or when letterhead has not been used.
- **Reference initials.** When businesspeople keyboard their own letters, reference initials are unnecessary, so they are becoming rare. When one person dictates a letter and another person produces it, reference initials show who helped prepare it. Place initials at the left margin, a double space below the signature block. When the signature block includes the writer's name, use only the preparer's initials. If the signature block includes only the department, use both sets of initials, usually in one of the following forms: *RSR/sm*, *RSR:sm*, or *RSR:SM* (writer/preparer). When the writer and the signer are different people, at least the file copy should bear both their initials as well as the typist's: *JFS/RSR/sm* (signer/writer/preparer).
- **Enclosure notation.** Enclosure notations appear at the bottom of a letter, one or two lines below the reference initials. Some common forms include the following:

Enclosure

Enclosures (2)

Enclosures: Résumé

Photograph

Attachment

- **Copy notation.** Copy notations may follow reference initials or enclosure notations. They indicate who's receiving a *courtesy copy* (*cc*). Some companies indicate copies made on a photocopier (*pc*), or they simply use *copy* (*c*). Recipients are listed in order of rank or (rank being equal) in alphabetical order. Among the forms used are the following:

cc: David Wentworth, Vice President

pc: Dr. Martha Littlefield

Copy to Hans Vogel

748 Chesterton Rd.

Snowhomish, WA 98290

c: Joseph Martinez with brochure and technical sheet

When sending copies to readers without other recipients knowing about it, put *bc*, *bcc*, or *bpc* ("blind copy,"

FIGURE A.3 Block Letter Format

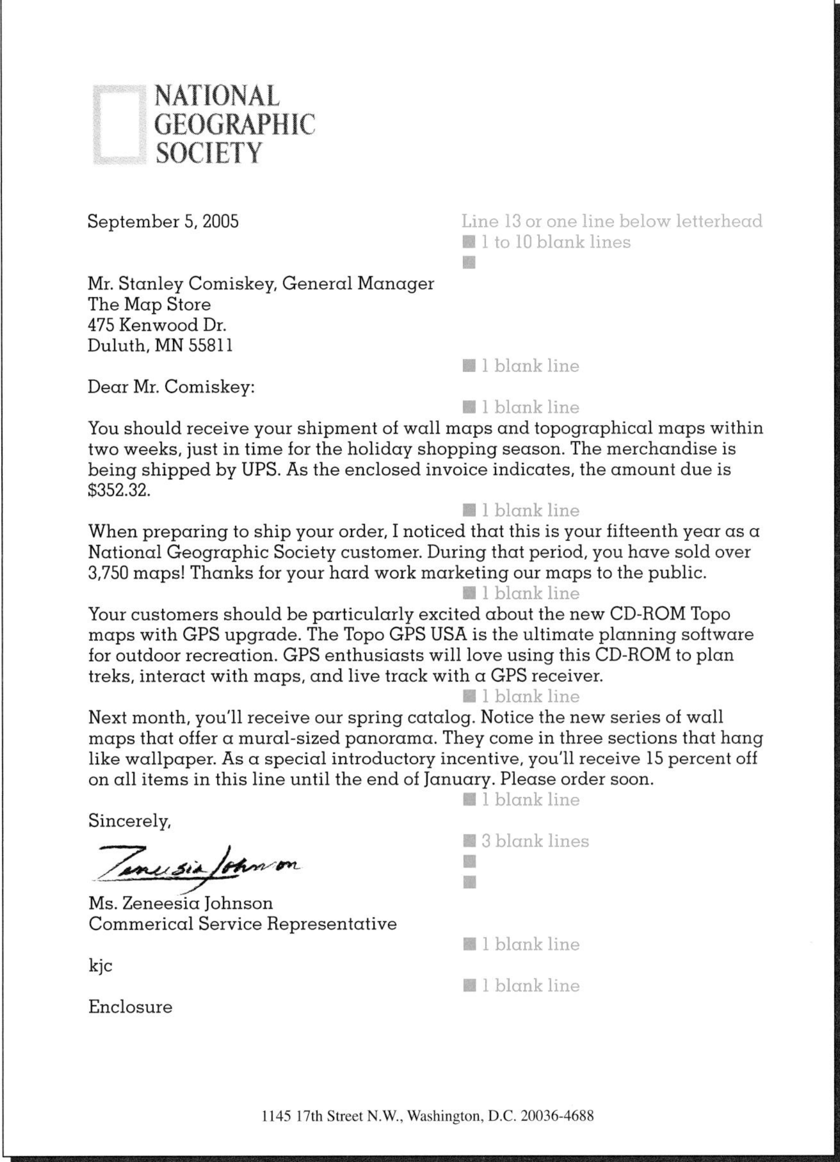

NATIONAL
GEOGRAPHIC
SOCIETY

September 5, 2005 — Line 13 or one line below letterhead

■ 1 to 10 blank lines
■

Mr. Stanley Comiskey, General Manager
The Map Store
475 Kenwood Dr.
Duluth, MN 55811

■ 1 blank line

Dear Mr. Comiskey:

■ 1 blank line

You should receive your shipment of wall maps and topographical maps within two weeks, just in time for the holiday shopping season. The merchandise is being shipped by UPS. As the enclosed invoice indicates, the amount due is $352.32.

■ 1 blank line

When preparing to ship your order, I noticed that this is your fifteenth year as a National Geographic Society customer. During that period, you have sold over 3,750 maps! Thanks for your hard work marketing our maps to the public.

■ 1 blank line

Your customers should be particularly excited about the new CD-ROM Topo maps with GPS upgrade. The Topo GPS USA is the ultimate planning software for outdoor recreation. GPS enthusiasts will love using this CD-ROM to plan treks, interact with maps, and live track with a GPS receiver.

■ 1 blank line

Next month, you'll receive our spring catalog. Notice the new series of wall maps that offer a mural-sized panorama. They come in three sections that hang like wallpaper. As a special introductory incentive, you'll receive 15 percent off on all items in this line until the end of January. Please order soon.

■ 1 blank line

Sincerely,

■ 3 blank lines
■
■

Ms. Zeneesia Johnson
Commerical Service Representative

■ 1 blank line

kjc

■ 1 blank line

Enclosure

1145 17th Street N.W., Washington, D.C. 20036-4688

"blind courtesy copy," or "blind photocopy") along with the name and any other information only on the copy, not on the original.

- **Mailing notation.** You may place a mailing notation (such as *Special Delivery* or *Registered Mail*) at the bottom of the letter, after reference initials or enclosure notations (whichever is last) and before copy notations. Or you may place it at the top of the letter, either above the inside address on the left side or just below the date on the right side. For greater visibility, mailing notations may appear in capital letters.
- **Postscript.** A postscript is an afterthought to the letter, a message that requires emphasis, or a personal note. It is usually the last thing on any letter and may be preceded by *P.S.*, *PS.*, *PS:*, or nothing at all. A second afterthought would be designated *P.P.S.* (post postscript). Since postscripts usually indicate poor planning, generally avoid them. However, they're common in sales letters as a punch line to remind readers of a benefit for taking advantage of the offer.

Letter Formats

A letter format is the way of arranging all the basic letter parts. Sometimes a company adopts a certain format as its policy; sometimes the individual letter writer or preparer is allowed to choose the most appropriate format. In the United States, three major letter formats are commonly used:

- **Block format.** Each letter part begins at the left margin. The main advantage is quick and efficient preparation (see Figure A.3).
- **Modified block format.** Same as block format, except that the date, complimentary close, and signature block

FIGURE A.4 Modified Block Letter Format

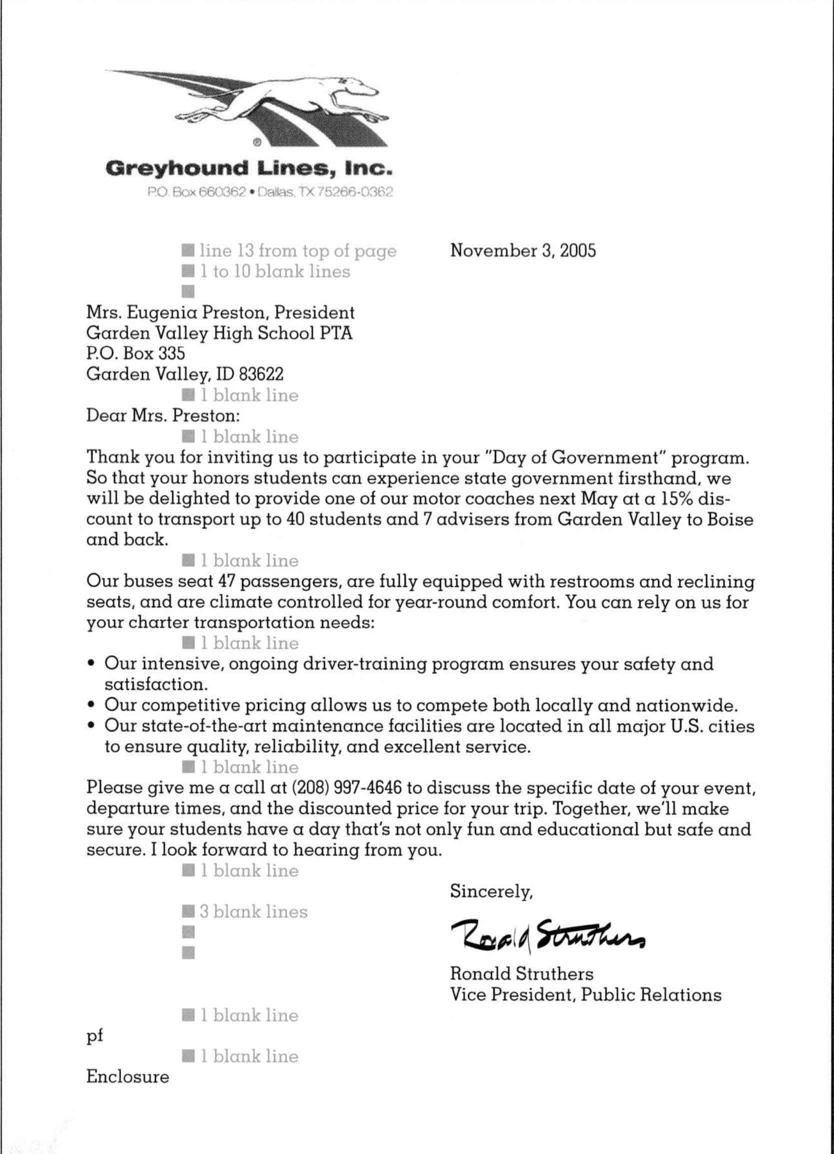
Greyhound Lines, Inc.
P.O. Box 660362 • Dallas, TX 75266-0362

■ line 13 from top of page November 3, 2005
■ 1 to 10 blank lines
■

Mrs. Eugenia Preston, President
Garden Valley High School PTA
P.O. Box 335
Garden Valley, ID 83622
■ 1 blank line
Dear Mrs. Preston:
■ 1 blank line
Thank you for inviting us to participate in your "Day of Government" program. So that your honors students can experience state government firsthand, we will be delighted to provide one of our motor coaches next May at a 15% discount to transport up to 40 students and 7 advisers from Garden Valley to Boise and back.
■ 1 blank line
Our buses seat 47 passengers, are fully equipped with restrooms and reclining seats, and are climate controlled for year-round comfort. You can rely on us for your charter transportation needs:
■ 1 blank line
- Our intensive, ongoing driver-training program ensures your safety and satisfaction.
- Our competitive pricing allows us to compete both locally and nationwide.
- Our state-of-the-art maintenance facilities are located in all major U.S. cities to ensure quality, reliability, and excellent service.

■ 1 blank line
Please give me a call at (208) 997-4646 to discuss the specific date of your event, departure times, and the discounted price for your trip. Together, we'll make sure your students have a day that's not only fun and educational but safe and secure. I look forward to hearing from you.
■ 1 blank line
Sincerely,
■ 3 blank lines
■
■
Ronald Struthers
Vice President, Public Relations
■ 1 blank line
pf
■ 1 blank line
Enclosure

start near the center of the page (see Figure A.4). The modified block format does permit indentions as an option. This format mixes preparation speed with traditional placement of some letter parts. It also looks more balanced on the page than the block format does.

- **Simplified format.** Instead of using a salutation, this format often weaves the reader's name into the first line or two of the body and often includes a subject line in capital letters (see Figure A.5). With no complimentary close, your signature appears after the body, followed by your printed (or typewritten) name (usually in all capital letters). This format is convenient when you don't know the reader's name; however, some people object to it as mechanical and impersonal (a drawback you can overcome with a warm writing style). Because certain letter parts are eliminated, some line spacing is changed.

These three formats differ in the way paragraphs are indented, in the way letter parts are placed, and in some punctuation. However, the elements are always separated by at least one blank line, and the printed (or typewritten) name is always separated from the line above by at least three blank lines to allow space for a signature. If paragraphs are indented, the indention is normally five spaces. The most common formats for intercultural business letters are the block style and the modified block style.

In addition to these three letter formats, letters may also be classified according to their style of punctuation. *Standard,* or *mixed, punctuation* uses a colon after the salutation (a comma if the letter is social or personal) and a comma after the complimentary close. *Open punctuation* uses no colon or comma after the salutation or the complimentary close. Although the most popular style in business communi-

FIGURE A.5 Simplified Letter Format

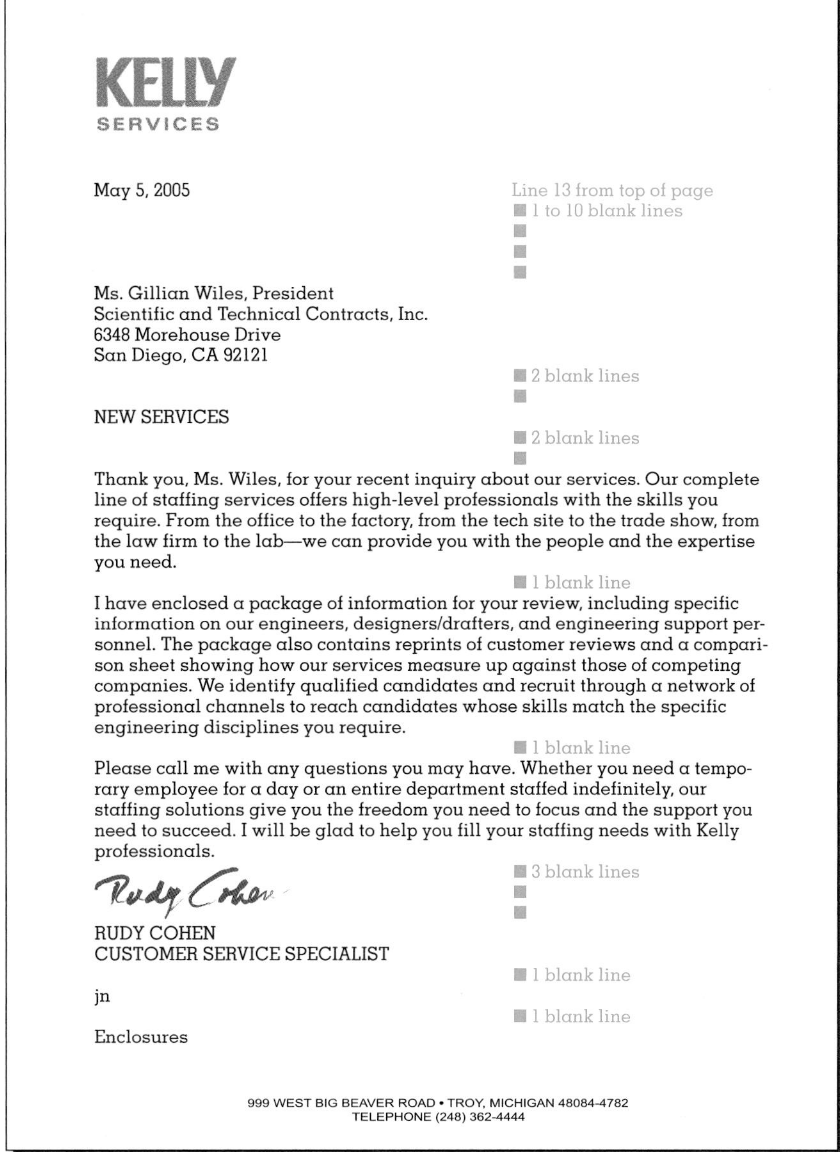
KELLY
SERVICES

May 5, 2005

Ms. Gillian Wiles, President
Scientific and Technical Contracts, Inc.
6348 Morehouse Drive
San Diego, CA 92121

NEW SERVICES

Thank you, Ms. Wiles, for your recent inquiry about our services. Our complete line of staffing services offers high-level professionals with the skills you require. From the office to the factory, from the tech site to the trade show, from the law firm to the lab—we can provide you with the people and the expertise you need.

I have enclosed a package of information for your review, including specific information on our engineers, designers/drafters, and engineering support personnel. The package also contains reprints of customer reviews and a comparison sheet showing how our services measure up against those of competing companies. We identify qualified candidates and recruit through a network of professional channels to reach candidates whose skills match the specific engineering disciplines you require.

Please call me with any questions you may have. Whether you need a temporary employee for a day or an entire department staffed indefinitely, our staffing solutions give you the freedom you need to focus and the support you need to succeed. I will be glad to help you fill your staffing needs with Kelly professionals.

Rudy Cohen

RUDY COHEN
CUSTOMER SERVICE SPECIALIST

jn

Enclosures

999 WEST BIG BEAVER ROAD • TROY, MICHIGAN 48084-4782
TELEPHONE (248) 362-4444

cation is mixed punctuation, either style of punctuation may be used with block or modified block letter formats. Because the simplified letter format has no salutation or complimentary close, the style of punctuation is irrelevant.

Envelopes

For a first impression, the quality of the envelope is just as important as the quality of the stationery. Letterhead and envelopes should be of the same paper stock, have the same color ink, and be imprinted with the same address and logo. Most envelopes used by U.S. businesses are No. 10 envelopes ($9^1/_2$ inches long), which are sized for an $8^1/_2$-by-11-inch piece of paper folded in thirds. Some occasions call for a smaller, No. $6^3/_4$, envelope or for envelopes proportioned to fit special stationery. Figure A.6 shows the two most common sizes.

Addressing the Envelope

No matter what size the envelope, the address is always single-spaced with all lines aligned on the left. The address on the envelope is in the same style as the inside address and presents the same information. The order to follow is from the smallest division to the largest:

1. Name and title of recipient
2. Name of department or subgroup
3. Name of organization
4. Name of building
5. Street address and suite number, or post office box number
6. City, state or province, and ZIP code or postal code
7. Name of country (if the letter is being sent abroad)

Because the U.S. Postal Service uses optical scanners to sort mail, envelopes for quantity mailings, in particular,

FIGURE A.6 Prescribed Envelope Format

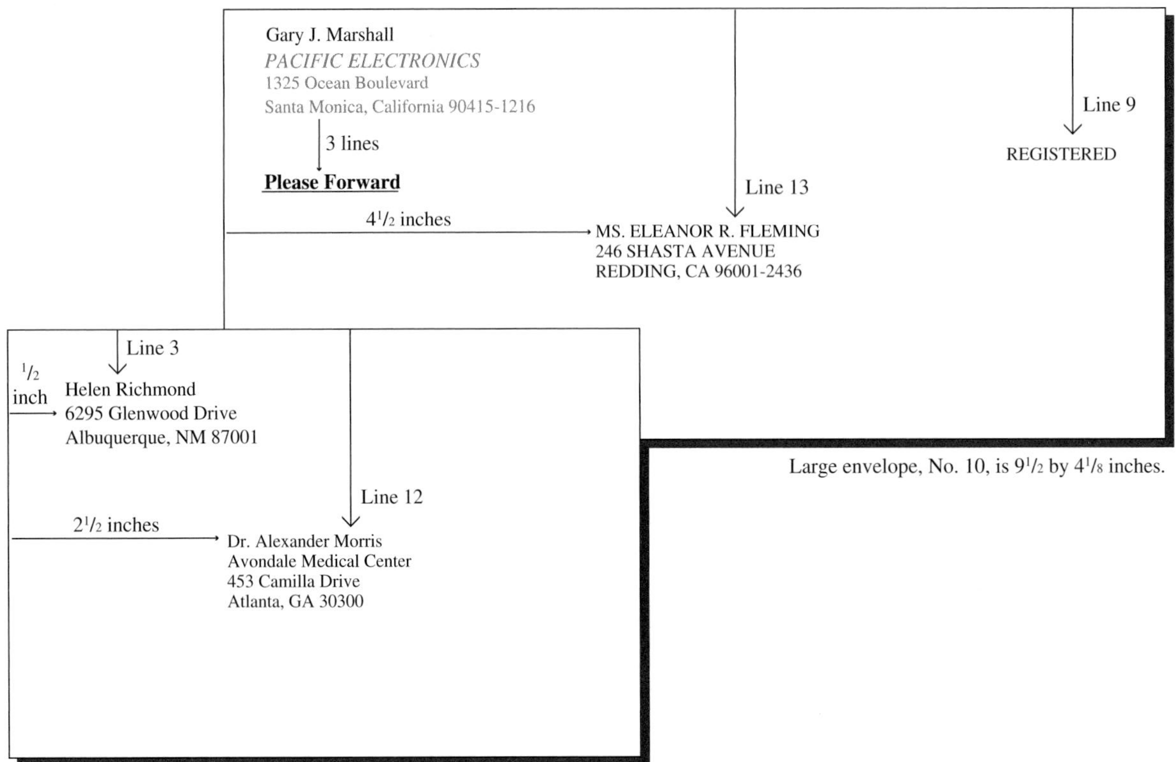

Gary J. Marshall
PACIFIC ELECTRONICS
1325 Ocean Boulevard
Santa Monica, California 90415-1216
3 lines
Please Forward
Line 13
Line 9
REGISTERED
4 1/2 inches
MS. ELEANOR R. FLEMING
246 SHASTA AVENUE
REDDING, CA 96001-2436
Line 3
1/2 inch
Helen Richmond
6295 Glenwood Drive
Albuquerque, NM 87001
Line 12
2 1/2 inches
Dr. Alexander Morris
Avondale Medical Center
453 Camilla Drive
Atlanta, GA 30300

Large envelope, No. 10, is 9 1/2 by 4 1/8 inches.

Small envelope, No. 6 3/4, is 6 1/2 by 3 5/8 inches.

should be addressed in the prescribed format. Everything is in capital letters, no punctuation is included, and all mailing instructions of interest to the post office are placed above the address area (see Figure A.6). Canada Post requires a similar format, except that only the city is all in capitals, and the postal code is placed on the line below the name of the city. The post office scanners read addresses from the bottom up, so if a letter is to be sent to a post office box rather than to a street address, the street address should appear on the line above the box number. Figure A.6 also shows the proper spacing for addresses and return addresses.

The U.S. Postal Service and the Canada Post Corporation have published lists of two-letter mailing abbreviations for states, provinces, and territories (see Table A.6). Postal authorities prefer no punctuation with these abbreviations, but some executives prefer to have state and province names spelled out in full and set off from city names by a comma. The issue is unresolved, although the comma is most often included. Quantity mailings follow post office requirements. For other letters, a reasonable compromise is to use traditional punctuation, uppercase and lowercase letters for names and street addresses, but two-letter state or province abbreviations, as shown here:

Mr. Kevin Kennedy

2107 E. Packer Dr.

Amarillo, TX 79108

For all out-of-office correspondence, use ZIP and postal codes that have been assigned to speed mail delivery. The U.S. Postal Service has divided the United States and its territories into 10 zones (0 to 9); this digit comes first in the ZIP code. The second and third digits represent smaller geographical areas within a state, and the last two digits identify a "local delivery area." Canadian postal codes are alphanumeric, with a three-character "area code" and a three-character "local code" separated by a single space (K2P 5A5). ZIP codes should be separated from state and province names by one space. Canadian postal codes may be treated the same or may be put in the bottom line of the address all by itself.

The U.S. Postal Service has added ZIP + 4 codes, which add a hyphen and four more numbers to the standard ZIP codes. The first two of the new numbers may identify an area as small as a single large building, and the last two digits may identify one floor in a large building or even a specific department of an organization. The ZIP + 4 codes are especially useful for business correspondence. The Canada Post Corporation achieves the same result with special postal codes assigned to buildings and organizations that receive a large volume of mail.

Folding to Fit

The way a letter is folded also contributes to the recipient's overall impression of your organization's professionalism. When sending a standard-size piece of paper in a No. 10

TABLE A.6 Two-Letter Mailing Abbreviations for the United States and Canada

STATE/ TERRITORY/ PROVINCE	ABBREVIATION	STATE/ TERRITORY/ PROVINCE	ABBREVIATION	STATE/ TERRITORY/ PROVINCE	ABBREVIATION
United States		Massachusetts	MA	Texas	TX
Alabama	AL	Michigan	MI	Utah	UT
Alaska	AK	Minnesota	MN	Vermont	VT
American Samoa	AS	Mississippi	MS	Virginia	VA
Arizona	AZ	Missouri	MO	Virgin Islands	VI
Arkansas	AR	Montana	MT	Washington	WA
California	CA	Nebraska	NE	West Virginia	WV
Canal Zone	CZ	Nevada	NV	Wisconsin	WI
Colorado	CO	New Hampshire	NH	Wyoming	WY
Connecticut	CT	New Jersey	NJ	**Canada**	
Delaware	DE	New Mexico	NM	Alberta	AB
District of Columbia	DC	New York	NY	British Columbia	BC
Florida	FL	North Carolina	NC	Labrador	NL
Georgia	GA	North Dakota	ND	Manitoba	MB
Guam	GU	Northern Mariana	MP	New Brunswick	NB
Hawaii	HI	Ohio	OH	Newfoundland	NL
Idaho	ID	Oklahoma	OK	Northwest Territories	NT
Illinois	IL	Oregon	OR	Nova Scotia	NS
Indiana	IN	Pennsylvania	PA	Nunavut	NU
Iowa	IA	Puerto Rico	PR	Ontario	ON
Kansas	KS	Rhode Island	RI	Prince Edward Island	PE
Kentucky	KY	South Carolina	SC	Quebec	QC
Louisiana	LA	South Dakota	SD	Saskatchewan	SK
Maine	ME	Tennessee	TN	Yukon Territory	YT
Maryland	MD	Trust Territories	TT		

envelope, fold it in thirds, with the bottom folded up first and the top folded down over it (see Figure A.7 on page A-16); the open end should be at the top of the envelope and facing out. Fit smaller stationery neatly into the appropriate envelope simply by folding it in half or in thirds. When sending a standard-size letterhead in a No. 6$^{3}/_{4}$ envelope, fold it in half from top to bottom and then in thirds from side to side.

International Mail

Postal service differs from country to country. For example, street addresses are uncommon in India, and the mail there is unreliable.[9] It's usually a good idea to send international correspondence by airmail and to ask that responses be sent that way as well. Also, remember to check the postage; rates for sending mail to most other countries differ from the rates for sending mail within your own country.

International mail falls into three main categories:

- **LC mail.** An abbreviation of the French *Lettres et Cartes* ("letters and cards"), this category consists of letters, letter packages, aerograms, and postcards.
- **AO mail.** An abbreviation of the French *Autres Objets* ("other articles"), this category includes regular printed matter, books and sheet music, matter for the blind, small packets, and publishers' periodicals (second class).
- **CP mail.** An abbreviation of the French *Colis Postaux* ("parcel post"), this category resembles fourth-class mail, including packages of merchandise or any other articles not required to be mailed at letter rates.

FIGURE A.7 Folding Standard-Size Letterhead

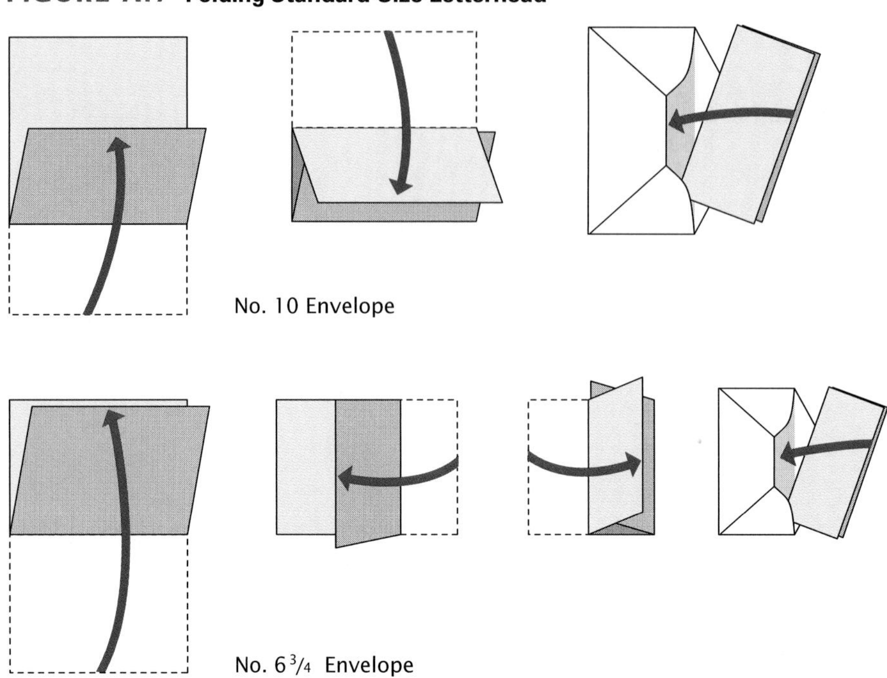

Along with several optional special services, the U.S. Postal Service also offers the following:

- **Express Mail International Service (EMS).** A high-speed mail service to many countries
- **International Priority Airmail (IPA).** An international service that's as fast as or faster than regular airmail service
- **International Surface Air Lift (ISAL).** A service providing quicker delivery and lower cost for all kinds of printed matter
- **Bulk Letter Service to Canada.** An economical airmail service for letters weighing 1 ounce or less
- **VALUEPOST/CANADA.** A reduced postage rate for bulk mailings
- **International Electronic Post (INTELPOST).** A service offering same- or next-day delivery of fax documents
- **International Postal Money Orders.** A service for transferring funds to other countries

To prepare your mail for international delivery, follow the instructions in the U.S. Postal Service Publication 51, *International Postal Rates and Fees.* Be sure to note instructions for the address, return address, and size limits. Envelopes and wrappers must be clearly marked to show their classification (letter, small packet, printed matter, airmail). All registered letters, letter packages, and parcel post packages must be securely sealed. Printed matter may be sealed only if postage is paid by permit imprint, postage meter, precanceled stamps, or second-class imprint. Otherwise, prepare contents so that they're protected without hindering inspection. Finally, because international mail is subject to customs examination in the country of destination, the contents and value must be declared on special forms.

Memos

Many organizations have memo forms preprinted, with labeled spaces for the recipient's name (or sometimes a checklist of all departments in an organization or all persons in a department), the sender's name, the date, and the subject (see Figure A.8). If such forms don't exist, you can use a memo template (which comes with word-processing software and provides margin settings, headings, and special formats), or you can use plain paper.

On your document, include a title such as *MEMO* or *INTEROFFICE CORRESPONDENCE* (all in capitals) centered at the top of the page or aligned with the left margin. Also at the top, include the words *To, From, Date,* and *Subject*—followed by the appropriate information—with a blank line between, as shown here:

MEMO

TO:

FROM:

DATE:

SUBJECT:

Sometimes the heading is organized like this:

MEMO

TO: DATE:

FROM: SUBJECT:

You can arrange these four pieces of information in almost any order. The date sometimes appears without the heading *Date.* The subject may be presented with the letters *Re:* (in place of *SUBJECT:*) or may even be presented without any

FIGURE A.8 Preprinted Memo Form

MEMO

TO: ______________

DEPT: ______________ FROM: ______________

DATE: ______________ TELEPHONE: ______________

SUBJECT: ______________ For your ☐ APPROVAL ☐ INFORMATION ☐ COMMENT

heading (but in capital letters so that it stands out clearly). You may want to include a file or reference number, introduced by the word *File.*

The following guidelines will help you effectively format specific memo elements:

- **Addressees.** When sending a memo to a long list of people, include the notation *See distribution list* or *See below* in the *To* position at the top; then list the names at the end of the memo. Arrange this list alphabetically, except when high-ranking officials deserve more prominent placement. You can also address memos to groups of people—*All Sales Representatives, Production Group, New Product Team.*
- **Courtesy titles.** You need not use courtesy titles anywhere in a memo; first initials and last names, first names, or even initials alone are often sufficient. However, use a courtesy title if you would use one in a face-to-face encounter with the person.
- **Subject line.** The subject line of a memo helps busy colleagues quickly find out what your memo is about. Although the subject "line" may overflow onto a second line, it's most helpful when it's short (but still informative).
- **Body.** Start the body of the memo on the second or third line below the heading. Like the body of a letter, it's usually single-spaced with blank lines between paragraphs. Indenting paragraphs is optional. Handle lists, important passages, and subheadings as you do in letters. If the memo is very short, you may double-space it.
- **Second page.** If the memo carries over to a second page, head the second page just as you head the second page of a letter.
- **Writer's initials.** Unlike a letter, a memo doesn't require a complimentary close or a signature, because your name is already prominent at the top. However, you may initial the memo—either beside the name appearing at the top of the memo or at the bottom of the memo—or you may even sign your name at the bottom, particularly if the memo deals with money or confidential matters.
- **Other elements.** Treat elements such as reference initials, enclosure notations, and copy notations just as you would in a letter.

Memos may be delivered by hand, by the post office (when the recipient works at a different location), or through interoffice mail. Interoffice mail may require the use of special reusable envelopes that have spaces for the recipient's name and department or room number; the name of the previous recipient is simply crossed out. If a regular envelope is used, the words *Interoffice Mail* appear where the stamp normally goes, so that it won't accidentally be stamped and mailed with the rest of the office correspondence.

Informal, routine, or brief reports for distribution within a company are often presented in memo form (see Chapter 10). Don't include report parts such as a table of contents and appendixes, but write the body of the memo report just as carefully as you'd write a formal report.

E-Mail

Because e-mail messages can act both as memos (carrying information within your company) and as letters (carrying information outside your company and around the world), their format depends on your audience and purpose. You may choose to have your e-mail resemble a formal letter or a detailed report, or you may decide to keep things as simple as an interoffice memo. A modified memo format is appropriate for most e-mail messages.[10] All e-mail programs include two major elements: the header and the body (see Figure A.9 on the following page).

Header

The e-mail header depends on the particular program you use. Some programs even allow you to choose between a shorter and a longer version. However, most headers contain similar information.

- **To:** Contains the audience's e-mail address (see Figure A.10 on page A-19). Most e-mail programs also allow you to send mail to an entire group of people all at once. First, you create a distribution list. Then you type the name of the list in the *To:* line instead of typing the addresses of every person in the group.[11] The most common e-mail addresses are addresses such as

  nmaa.betsy@c.si.edu (Smithsonian Institute's National Museum of American Art)

  webwsj@dowjones.com (*Wall Street Journal*'s home page)

  relpubli@mairie-toulouse.mipnet.fr (Municipal Services, Toulouse, France)

FIGURE A.9 A Typical E-Mail Message

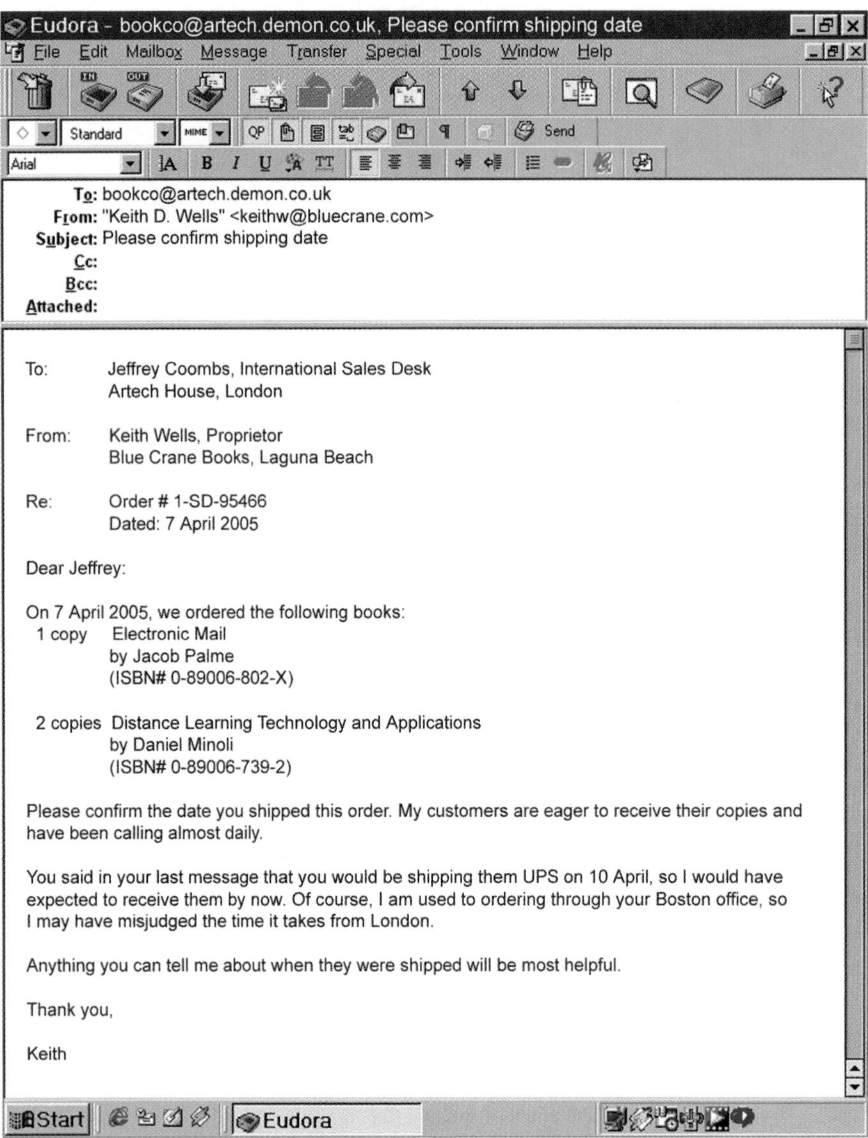
Eudora - bookco@artech.demon.co.uk, Please confirm shipping date

To: bookco@artech.demon.co.uk
From: "Keith D. Wells" <keithw@bluecrane.com>
Subject: Please confirm shipping date
Cc:
Bcc:
Attached:

To: Jeffrey Coombs, International Sales Desk
Artech House, London

From: Keith Wells, Proprietor
Blue Crane Books, Laguna Beach

Re: Order # 1-SD-95466
Dated: 7 April 2005

Dear Jeffrey:

On 7 April 2005, we ordered the following books:
1 copy Electronic Mail
by Jacob Palme
(ISBN# 0-89006-802-X)

2 copies Distance Learning Technology and Applications
by Daniel Minoli
(ISBN# 0-89006-739-2)

Please confirm the date you shipped this order. My customers are eager to receive their copies and have been calling almost daily.

You said in your last message that you would be shipping them UPS on 10 April, so I would have expected to receive them by now. Of course, I am used to ordering through your Boston office, so I may have misjudged the time it takes from London.

Anything you can tell me about when they were shipped will be most helpful.

Thank you,

Keith

- **From:** Contains your e-mail address.
- **Date:** Contains the day of the week, date (day, month, year), time, and time zone.
- **Subject:** Describes the content of the message and presents an opportunity for you to build interest in your message.
- **Cc:** Allows you to send copies of a message to more than one person at a time. It also allows everyone on the list to see who else received the same message.
- **Bcc:** Lets you send copies to people without the other recipients knowing—a practice considered unethical by some.[12]
- **Attachments:** Contains the name(s) of the file(s) you attach to your e-mail message. The file can be a word-processing document, a digital image, an audio or video message, a spreadsheet, or a software program.[13]

Most e-mail programs now allow you the choice of hiding or revealing other lines that contain more detailed information, including

- **Message-Id:** The exact location of this e-mail message on the sender's system
- **X-mailer:** The version of the e-mail program being used
- **Content type:** A description of the text and character set that is contained in the message
- **Received:** Information about each of the systems your e-mail passed through en route to your mailbox.[14]

Body

The rest of the space below the header is for the body of your message. In the *To:* and *From:* lines, some headers actually print out the names of the sender and receiver (in addition to their e-mail addresses). Other headers do not. If your mail program includes only the e-mail addresses, you might consider including your own memo-type header in the body of your message, as in Figure A.9. The writer even included a second, more specific subject line in his

FIGURE A.10 Anatomy of an E-Mail Address

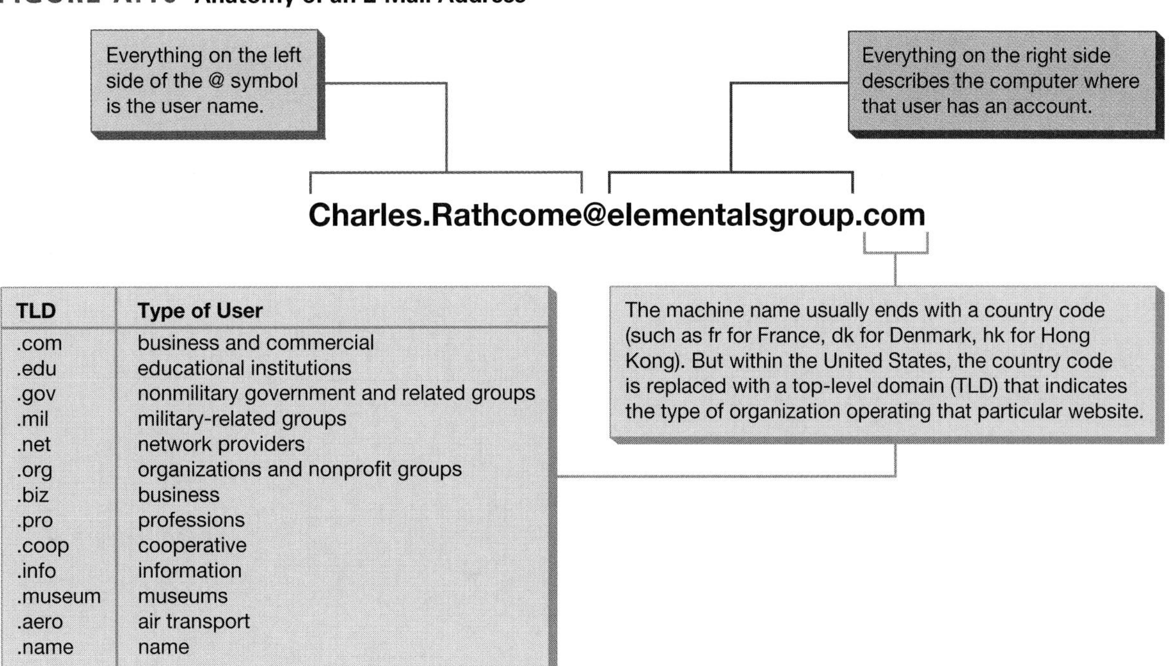

memo-type header. Some recipients may applaud the clarity of such second headers; however, others will criticize the space it takes. Your decision depends on how formal you want to be.

Everything on the left side of the @ symbol is the user name.
Everything on the right side describes the computer where that user has an account.
Charles.Rathcome@elementalsgroup.com
TLD
Type of User
.com business and commercial
.edu educational institutions
.gov nonmilitary government and related groups
.mil military-related groups
.net network providers
.org organizations and nonprofit groups
.biz business
.pro professions
.coop cooperative
.info information
.museum museums
.aero air transport
.name name
The machine name usually ends with a country code (such as fr for France, dk for Denmark, hk for Hong Kong). But within the United States, the country code is replaced with a top-level domain (TLD) that indicates the type of organization operating that particular website.

Do include a greeting in your e-mail. As pointed out in Chapter 6, greetings personalize your message. Leave one line space above and below your greeting to set it off from the rest of your message. You may end your greeting with a colon (formal), a comma (conversational), or even two hyphens (informal)—depending on the level of formality you want.

Your message begins one blank line space below your greeting. Just as in memos and letters, skip one line space between paragraphs and include headings, numbered lists, bulleted lists, and embedded lists when appropriate. Limit your line lengths to a maximum of 80 characters by inserting a hard return at the end of each line.

One blank line space below your message, include a simple closing, often just one word. A blank line space below that, include your signature. Whether you type your name or use a signature file, including your signature personalizes your message.

Reports

Enhance your report's effectiveness by paying careful attention to its appearance and layout. Follow whatever guidelines your organization prefers, always being neat and consistent throughout. If it's up to you to decide formatting questions, the following conventions may help you decide how to handle margins, headings, spacing and indention, and page numbers.

Margins

All margins on a report page are at least 1 inch wide. For double-spaced pages, use 1-inch margins; for single-spaced pages, set margins between $1^1/_4$ and $1^1/_2$ inches. The top, left, and right margins are usually the same, but the bottom margins can be $1^1/_2$ times deeper. Some special pages also have deeper top margins. Set top margins as deep as 2 inches for pages that contain major titles: prefatory parts (such as the table of contents or the executive summary), supplementary parts (such as the reference notes or bibliography), and textual parts (such as the first page of the text or the first page of each chapter).

If you're going to bind your report at the left or at the top, add half an inch to the margin on the bound edge (see Figure A.11). The space taken by the binding on left-bound reports makes the center point of the text a quarter inch to the right of the center of the paper. Be sure to center headings between the margins, not between the edges of the paper. Computers can do this for you automatically. Other guidelines for report formats are in the Chapter 12 samples.

Headings

Headings of various levels provide visual clues to a report's organization. Figure 11–16, on page 378, illustrates one good system for showing these levels, but many variations exist. No matter which system you use, be sure to be consistent.

Spacing and Indentions

If your report is double-spaced (perhaps to ease comprehension of technical material), indent all paragraphs five character spaces (or about $^1/_2$ inch). In single-spaced reports, block

FIGURE A.11 Margins for Formal Reports

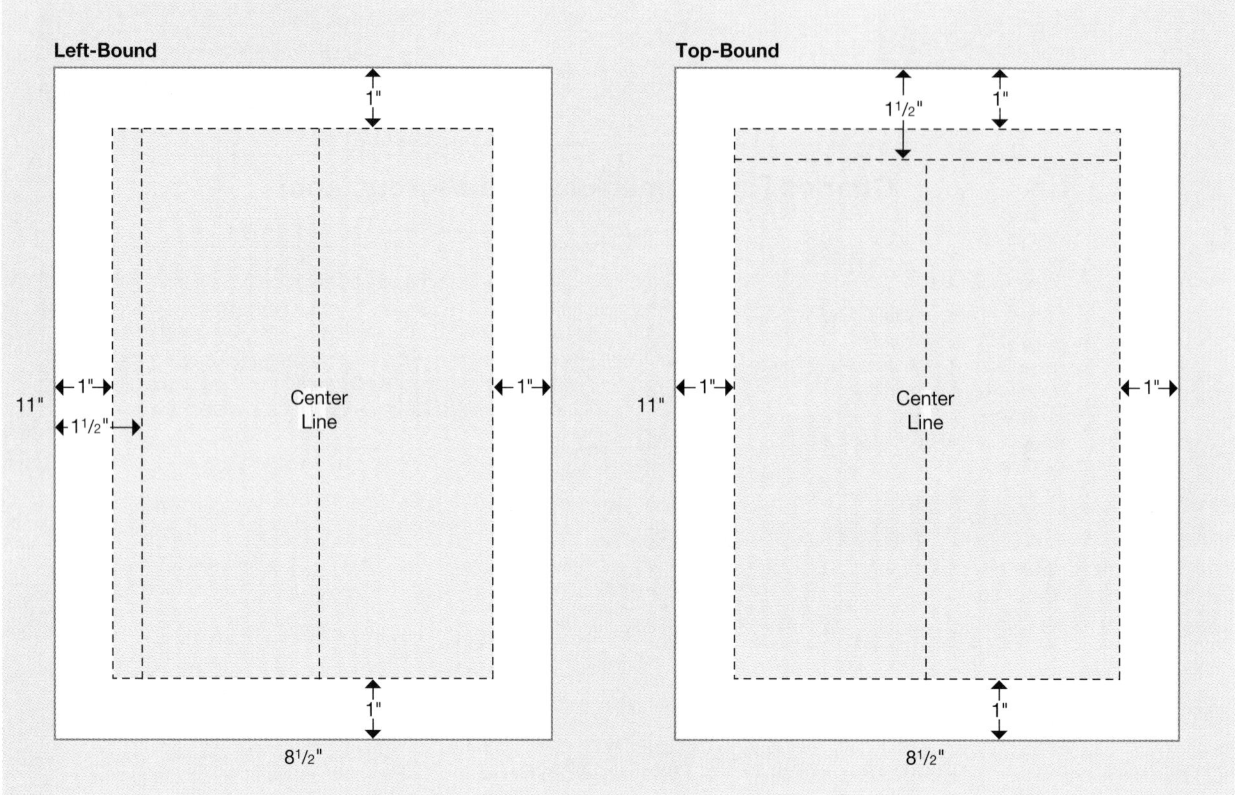

the paragraphs (no indentions) and leave one blank line between them.

Make sure the material on the title page is centered and well balanced, as on the title page of the sample report in Chapter 14. When using a typewriter, proper spacing takes some calculation. To center text in left-bound reports, start a quarter inch to the right of the paper's center. From that point, backspace once for each two letters in the line. The line will appear centered once the report is bound.

To place lines of type vertically on the title page, follow these steps:

1. Count the number of lines in each block of copy, including blank lines.
2. Subtract that total from 66 (the number of lines on an 11-inch page); the result is the number of unused lines.
3. Divide the number of unused lines by the number of blank areas (always one more than the number of blocks of copy). The result is the number of blank lines to allocate above, between, and below the blocks of copy.

A computer with a good word-processing program will do these calculations for you at the click of a mouse.

Page Numbers

Remember that every page in the report is counted; however, not all pages show numbers. The first page of the report, normally the title page, is unnumbered. All other pages in the prefatory section are numbered with a lowercase roman numeral, beginning with *ii* and continuing with *iii, iv, v,* and so on. The unadorned (no dashes, no period) page number is centered at the bottom margin.

Number the first page of the text of the report with the unadorned arabic numeral 1, centered at the bottom margin (double- or triple-spaced below the text). In left-bound reports, number the following pages (including the supplementary parts) consecutively with unadorned arabic numerals (2, 3, and so on), placed at the top right-hand margin (double- or triple-spaced above the text). For top-bound reports and for special pages having 2-inch top margins, center the page numbers at the bottom margin.

Appendix B
Documentation of Report Sources

Documenting a report is too important a task to undertake haphazardly. By providing information about your sources, you improve your own credibility as well as the credibility of the facts and opinions you present. Documentation gives readers the means for checking your findings and pursuing the subject further. Also, documenting your report is the accepted way to give credit to the people whose work you have drawn from.

What style should you use to document your report? Experts recommend various forms, depending on your field or discipline. Moreover, your employer or client may use a form different from those the experts suggest. Don't let this discrepancy confuse you. If your employer specifies a form, use it; the standardized form is easier for colleagues to understand. However, if the choice of form is left to you, adopt one of the styles described here. Whatever style you choose, be consistent within any given report, using the same order, punctuation, and format from one reference citation or bibliography entry to the next.

A wide variety of style manuals provide detailed information on documentation. Here is a brief annotated list:

- American Psychological Association, *Publication Manual of the American Psychological Association,* 5th ed. (Washington, DC: American Psychological Association, 2001). Details the author-date system, which is preferred in the social sciences and often in the natural sciences as well.
- *The Chicago Manual of Style,* 15th ed. (Chicago: University of Chicago Press, 1993). Often referred to only as *Chicago* and widely used in the publishing industry; provides detailed treatment of documentation in Chapters 15 and 16.
- Joseph Gibaldi, *MLA Style Manual and Guide to Scholarly Publishing,* 2d ed. (New York: Modern Language Association, 1998). Serves as the basis for the note and bibliography style used in much academic writing and is recommended in many college textbooks on writing term papers; provides a lot of examples in the humanities.
- Andrew Harnack and Eugene Kleppinger, *Online! A Reference Guide to Using Internet Sources—2000* (New York: St. Martin's Press, 2000). Offers an approach to style for citing online references.

Although many schemes have been proposed for organizing the information in source notes, all of them break the information into parts: (1) information about the author (name), (2) information about the work (title, edition, volume number), (3) information about the publication (place, publisher), (4) information about the date, and (5) information on relevant page ranges.

In the following sections, we summarize the major conventions for documenting sources in three styles: *The Chicago Manual of Style* (Chicago), the *Publication Manual of the American Psychological Association* (APA), and the *MLA Style Manual* (MLA).

Chicago Humanities Style

The Chicago Manual of Style recommends two types of documentation systems. The *documentary-note,* or *humanities,* style gives bibliographic citations in notes—either footnotes (when printed at the bottom of a page) or endnotes (when printed at the end of the report). The humanities system is often used in literature, history, and the arts. The other system strongly recommended by Chicago is the *author-date* system, which cites the author's last name and the date of publication in the text, usually in parentheses, reserving full documentation for the reference list (or bibliography). For the purpose of comparing styles, we will concentrate on the humanities system, which is described in detail in Chicago.

In-Text Citation—Chicago Humanities Style

To document report sources in text, the humanities system relies on superscripts—arabic numerals placed just above the line of type at the end of the reference:

> Toward the end of his speech, Myers sounded a note of caution, saying that even though the economy is expected to grow, it could easily slow a bit.[10]

The superscript lets the reader know how to look for source information in either a footnote or an endnote (see Figure B.1 on the following page). Some readers prefer footnotes so that they can simply glance at the bottom of the page for information. Others prefer endnotes so that they can read the text without a clutter of notes on the page. Also, endnotes relieve the writer from worrying about how long each note will be and how much space it will take away from the page. Both footnotes and endnotes are handled automatically by today's word-processing software.

For the reader's convenience, you can use footnotes for **content notes** (which may supplement your main text with asides about a particular issue or event, provide a cross-reference to another section of your report, or direct

FIGURE B.1 Sample Endnotes—Chicago Humanities Style

NOTES

Journal article with volume and issue numbers	1. James Assira, "Are They Speaking English in Japan?" *Journal of Business Communication* 36, no. 4 (Fall 2002): 72.
Brochure	2. BestTemp Staffing Services, *An Employer's Guide to Staffing Services,* 2d ed. (Denver: BestTemp Information Center, 2000), 31.
Newspaper article, no author	3. "Buying Asian Supplies on the Net," *Los Angeles Times,* 12 February 2000, sec. D, p. 3.
Annual report	4. Eurotec, *2001 Annual Report* (New York: Eurotec, Inc., 2001), 48.
Magazine article	5. Holly Graves, "Prospecting Online," *Business Week,* 17 November 2002, 43–5.
Television broadcast	6. Daniel Han, "Trade Wars Heating Up Around the Globe," *CNN Headline News* (Atlanta: CNN, 5 March 2002).
Internet, World Wide Web	7. "Intel—Company Capsule," Hoover's Online [cited 8 March 2003], 3 screens; available from www.hoovers.com/capsules/13787.html.
Book, component parts	8. Sonja Kuntz, "Moving Beyond Benefits," in *Our Changing Workforce,* ed. Randolf Jacobson (New York: Citadel Press, 2001), 213–27.
Unpublished dissertation or thesis	9. George H. Morales, "The Economic Pressures on Industrialized Nations in a Global Economy" (Ph.D. diss., University of San Diego, 2001), 32–47.
Paper presented at a meeting	10. Charles Myers, "HMOs in Today's Environment" (paper presented at the Conference on Medical Insurance Solution, Chicago, Ill., August 2001), 16–17.
Online magazine article	11. Preston Norwalk, "Training Managers to Help Employees Accept Change," in *Business Line* [online] (San Francisco, 2002 [updated 17 September 2002; cited 3 October 2001]); available from www.busline.com/news.
CD-ROM encyclopedia article,one author	12. Robert Parkings, "George Eastman," *The Concise Columbia Encyclopedia* (New York: Columbia University Press, 1998) [CD-ROM].
Interview	13. Georgia Stainer, general manager, Day Cable and Communications, interview by author, Topeka, Kan., 2 March 2000.
Newspaper article, one author	14. Evelyn Standish, "Global Market Crushes OPEC's Delicate Balance of Interests," *Wall Street Journal,* 19 January 2002, sec. A, p. 1.
Book, two authors	15. Miriam Toller and Jay Fielding, *Global Business for Smaller Companies* (Rocklin, Calif.: Prima Publishing, 2001), 102–3.
Government publication	16. U.S. Department of Defense, *Stretching Research Dollars: Survival Advice for Universities and Government Labs* (Washington, D.C.: GPO, 2002), 126.

the reader to a related source). Then you can use endnotes for **source notes** (which document direct quotations, paraphrased passages, and visual aids). Consider which type of note is most common in your report, and then choose whether to present these notes all as endnotes or all as footnotes. Regardless of the method you choose for referencing textual information in your report, notes for visual aids (both content notes and source notes) are placed on the same page as the visual.

Bibliography—Chicago Humanities Style

The humanities system may or may not be accompanied by a bibliography (because the notes give all the necessary bibliographic information). However, endnotes are arranged in order of appearance in the text, so an alphabetical bibliography can be valuable to your readers. The bibliography may be titled *Bibliography, Reference List, Sources, Works Cited* (if you include only those sources you actually cited in your report), or *Works Consulted* (if you include uncited sources as well). This list of sources may also serve as a reading list for those who want to pursue the subject of your report further, so you may want to annotate each entry—that is, comment on the subject matter and viewpoint of the source, as well as on its usefulness to readers. Annotations may be written in either complete or incomplete sentences. (See the annotated list of style manuals early in this appendix.) A bibliography may also be more manageable if you subdivide it into categories (a classified bibliography), either by type of reference (such as

FIGURE B.2 Sample Bibliography—Chicago Humanities Style

BIBLIOGRAPHY

Journal article with volume and issue numbers	Assira, James. "Are They Speaking English in Japan?" *Journal of Business Communication* 36, no. 4 (Fall 2002): 72.
Brochure	BestTemp Staffing Services. *An Employer's Guide to Staffing Services.* 2d ed. Denver: BestTemp Information Center, 2000.
Newspaper article, no author	"Buying Asian Supplies on the Net." *Los Angeles Times,* 12 February 2000, sec. D, p. 3.
Annual report	Eurotec. *2000 Annual Report.* New York: Eurotec, Inc., 2001.
Magazine article	Graves, Holly. "Prospecting Online." *Business Week,* 17 November 2002, 43–5.
Television broadcast	Han, Daniel. "Trade Wars Heating Up Around the Globe." *CNN Headline News.* Atlanta: CNN, 5 March 2002.
Internet, World Wide Web	"Intel—Company Capsule." *Hoover's Online* [cited 8 March 2003]. 3 screens; Available from www.hoovers.com/capsules/13787.html.
Book, component parts	Kuntz, Sonja. "Moving Beyond Benefits." In *Our Changing Workforce*, edited by Randolf Jacobson. New York: Citadel Press, 2001.
Unpublished dissertation or thesis	Morales, George H. "The Economic Pressures on Industrialized Nations in a Global Economy." Ph.D. diss., University of San Diego, 2001.
Paper presented at a meeting	Myers, Charles. "HMOs in Today's Environment." Paper presented at the Conference on Medical Insurance Solutions, Chicago, Ill., August 2001.
Online magazine article	Norwalk, Preston. "Training Managers to Help Employees Accept Change." In *Business Line* [online]. San Francisco, 2002 [updated 17 September 2002; cited 3 October 2002]. Available from www.busline.com/news.
CD-ROM encyclopedia article, one author	Parkings, Robert. "George Eastman." *The Concise Columbia Encyclopedia.* New York: Columbia University Press, 1998. [CD-ROM].
Interview	Stainer, Georgia, general manager, Day Cable and Communications. Interview by author. Topeka, Kan., 2 March 2000.
Newspaper article, one author	Standish, Evelyn. "Global Market Crushes OPEC's Delicate Balance of Interests." *Wall Street Journal,* 19 January 2002, sec. A, p. 1.
Book, two authors	Toller, Miriam, and Jay Fielding. *Global Business for Smaller Companies.* Rocklin, Calif.: Prima Publishing, 2001.
Government publication	U.S. Department of Defense. *Stretching Research Dollars: Survival Advice for Universities and Government Labs.* Washington, D.C.: GPO, 2002.

books, articles, and unpublished material) or by subject matter (such as government regulation, market forces, and so on). Following are the major conventions for developing a bibliography according to Chicago style (see Figure B.2):

- Exclude any page numbers that may be cited in source notes, except for journals, periodicals, and newspapers.
- Alphabetize entries by the last name of the lead author (listing last name first). The names of second and succeeding authors are listed in normal order. Entries without an author name are alphabetized by the first important word in the title.
- Format entries as hanging indents (indent second and succeeding lines three to five spaces).
- Arrange entries in the following general order: (1) author name, (2) title information, (3) publication information, (4) date, (5) periodical page range.
- Use quotation marks around the titles of articles from magazines, newspapers, and journals—capitalizing the first and last words, as well as all other important words (except prepositions, articles, and coordinating conjunctions).
- Use italics to set off the names of books, newspapers, journals, and other complete publications—capitalizing the first and last words, as well as all other important words.
- For journal articles, include the volume number and the issue number (if necessary). Include the year of publication inside parentheses and follow with a colon

and the page range of the article: *Journal of Business Communication* 36, no. 4 (2001): 72. (In this source, the volume is 36, the number is 4, and the page is 72.)
- Use brackets to identify all electronic references: [Online database] or [CD-ROM].
- Explain how electronic references can be reached: Available from www.spaceless.com/WWWVL.
- Give the citation date for online references: Cited 23 August 2002.
- For additional information about documenting online sources, go to www.lib.ohio-state.edu/guides/chicagogd.html.

APA Style

The American Psychological Association (APA) recommends the author-date system of documentation, which is popular in the physical, natural, and social sciences. When using this system, you simply insert the author's last name and the year of publication within parentheses following the text discussion of the material cited. Include a page number if you use a direct quote. This approach briefly identifies the source so that readers can locate complete information in the alphabetical reference list at the end of the report. The author-date system is both brief and clear, saving readers time and effort.

In-Text Citation—APA Style

To document report sources in text using APA style, insert the author's surname and the date of publication at the end of a statement. Enclose this information in parentheses. If the author's name is referred to in the text itself, then the number can be omitted from parenthetical material.

> Some experts recommend both translation and back-translation when dealing with any non-English-speaking culture (Assira, 2001).
>
> Toller and Fielding (2000) make a strong case for small companies succeeding in global business.

Personal communications and interviews conducted by the author would not be listed in the reference list at all. Such citations would appear in the text only.

> Increasing the role of cable companies is high on the list of Georgia Stainer, general manager at Day Cable and Communications (personal communication, March 2, 2001).

List of References—APA Style

For APA style, list only those works actually cited in the text (so you would not include works for background or for further reading). Report writers must choose their references judiciously. Following are the major conventions for developing a reference list according to APA style (see Figure B.3):

- Format entries as hanging indents.
- List all author names in reversed order (last name first), and use only initials for the first and middle names.
- Arrange entries in the following general order: (1) author name, (2) date, (3) title information, (4) publication information, (5) periodical page range.
- Follow the author name with the date of publication in parentheses.
- List titles of articles from magazines, newspapers, and journals without underlines or quotation marks. Capitalize only the first word of the title, any proper nouns, and the first word to follow an internal colon.
- Italicize titles of books, capitalizing only the first word, any proper nouns, and the first word to follow a colon.
- Italicize names of magazines, newspapers, journals, and other complete publications—capitalizing all the important words.
- For journal articles, include the volume number (in italics) and, if necessary, the issue number (in parentheses). Finally, include the page range of the article: *Journal of Business Communication, 36*(4), 72. (In this example, the volume is 36, the number is 4, and the page number is 72.)
- Include personal communications (such as letters, memos, e-mail, and conversations) only in text, not in reference lists.
- Electronic references include author, date of publication, title of article, name of publication (if one), volume, date of retrieval (month, day, year), and the source.
- For electronic references, indicate the actual year of publication, and the exact date of retrieval.
- For electronic references, specify the URL, leave periods off the ends of URLs.
- For additional information about documenting online sources, go to www.apastyle.org/elecref.html.

MLA Style

The style recommended by the Modern Language Association of America is used widely in the humanities, especially in the study of language and literature. Like APA style, MLA style uses brief parenthetical citations in the text. However, instead of including author name and year, MLA citations include author name and page reference.

In-Text Citation—MLA Style

To document report sources in text using MLA style, insert the author's last name and a page reference inside parentheses following the cited material: (Matthews 63). If the author's name is mentioned in the text reference, the name can be omitted from the parenthetical citation: (63). The citation indicates that the reference came from page 63 of a work by Matthews. With the author's name, readers can find complete publication information in the alphabetically arranged list of works cited that comes at the end of the report.

> Some experts recommend both translation and back-translation when dealing with any non-English-speaking culture (Assira 72).
>
> Toller and Fielding make a strong case for small companies succeeding in global business (102–03).

List of Works Cited—MLA Style

The *MLA Style Manual* recommends preparing the list of works cited first so that you will know what information to

FIGURE B.3 Sample References—APA Style

REFERENCES

Journal article with volume and issue numbers	Assira, J. (2002). Are they speaking English in Japan? *Journal of Business Communication, 36*(4), 72.
Brochure	BestTemp Staffing Services. (2000). *An employer's guide to staffing services* (2d ed.) [Brochure]. Denver: BestTemp Information Center.
Newspaper article, no author	Buying Asian supplies on the net. (2000, February 12). *Los Angeles Times*, p. D3.
Annual report	Eurotec. (2001). *2001 annual report*. New York: Eurotec.
Magazine article	Graves, H. (2002, November 17). Prospecting online. *Business Week*, 43–45.
Television broadcast	Han, D. (2002, March 5). Trade wars heating up around the globe. *CNN Headline News*. [Television broadcast]. Atlanta, GA: CNN.
Internet, World Wide Web	Hoover's Online. (2003). *Intel—Company Capsule*. Retrieved March 8, 2003, from http://www.hoovers.com/capsules/13787.html
Book, component parts	Kuntz, S. (2001). Moving beyond benefits. In Randolph Jacobson (Ed.), *Our changing workforce* (pp. 213–227). New York: Citadel Press.
Unpublished dissertation or thesis	Morales, G. H. (2001). *The economic pressures on industrialized nations in a global economy*. Unpublished doctoral dissertation, University of San Diego.
Paper presented at a meeting	Myers, C. (2001, August). *HMOs in today's environment*. Paper presented at the Conference on Medical Insurance Solutions, Chicago, IL.
Online magazine article	Norwalk, P. (2002, July 17). Training managers to help employees accept change. *Business Line*. Retrieved March 8, 2003, from http://www.busline.com/news
CD-ROM encyclopedia article, one author	Parkings, R. (1998). George Eastman. On *The concise Columbia encyclopedia*. [CD-ROM]. New York: Columbia University Press.
Interview	*Cited in text only, not in the list of references.*
Newspaper article, one author	Standish, E. (2002, January 19). Global market crushes OPEC's delicate balance of interests. *Wall Street Journal*, p. A1.
Book, two authors	Toller, M., & Fielding, J. (2001). *Global business for smaller companies*. Rocklin, CA: Prima Publishing.
Government publication	U.S. Department of Defense. (2002). *Stretching research dollars: Survival advice for universities and government labs*. Washington, DC: U.S. Government Printing Office.

give in the parenthetical citation (for example, whether to add a short title if you're citing more than one work by the same author, or whether to give an initial or first name if you're citing two authors who have the same last name). The list of works cited appears at the end of your report, contains all the works that you cite in your text, and lists them in alphabetical order. Following are the major conventions for developing a reference list according to MLA style (see Figure B.4):

- Format entries as hanging indents.
- Arrange entries in the following general order: (1) author name, (2) title information, (3) publication information, (4) date, (5) periodical page range.
- List the lead author's name in reverse order (last name first), using either full first names or initials. List second and succeeding author names in normal order.
- Use quotation marks around the titles of articles from magazines, newspapers, and journals—capitalize all important words.
- Italicize the names of books, newspapers, journals and other complete publications, capitalizing all main words in the title.
- For journal articles, include the volume number and the issue number (if necessary). Include the year of publication inside parentheses and follow with a colon and the page range of the article: *Journal of Business Communication* 36.4 (2001): 72. (In this source, the volume is 36, the number is 4, and the page is 72.)
- Electronic sources are less fixed than print sources, and they may not be readily accessible to readers. So citations for electronic sources must provide more information. Always try to be as comprehensive as possible, citing whatever information is available.

FIGURE B.4 Sample Works Cited—MLA Style

WORKS CITED

Journal article with volume and issue numbers	Assira, James. "Are They Speaking English in Japan?" *Journal of Business Communication* 36.4 (2002): 72.
Brochure	BestTemp Staffing Services. *An Employer's Guide to Staffing Services*. 2d ed. Denver: BestTemp Information Center, 2000.
Newspaper article, no author	"Buying Asian Supplies on the Net." *Los Angeles Times* 12 Feb. 2000: D3.
Annual report	Eurotec. *2001 Annual Report*. New York: Eurotec, Inc., 2001.
Magazine article	Graves, Holly. "Prospecting Online." *Business Week* 17 Nov. 2002: 43–45.
Television broadcast	Han, Daniel. "Trade Wars Heating Up Around the Globe." *CNN Headline News*. CNN, Atlanta. 5 Mar. 2002.
Internet, World Wide Web	"Intel—Company Capsule." *Hoover's Online*. 2003. Hoover's Company Information. 8 Mar. 2003 <http://www.hoovers.com/capsules/13787.html>.
Book, component parts	Kuntz, Sonja. "Moving Beyond Benefits." *Our Changing Workforce*. Ed. Randolf Jacobson. New York: Citadel Press, 2001. 213–27.
Unpublished dissertation or thesis	Morales, George H. "The Economic Pressures on Industrialized Nations in a Global Economy." Diss. U of San Diego, 2001.
Paper presented at a meeting	Myers, Charles. "HMOs in Today's Environment." Conference on Medical Insurance Solutions. Chicago. 13 Aug. 2001.
Online magazine article	Norwalk, Preston. "Training Managers to Help Employees Accept Change." *Business Line* 17 July 2002. 8 Mar. 2003 <http://www.busline.com/news>.
CD-ROM encyclopedia article, one author	Parkings, Robert. "George Eastman." *The Concise Columbia Encyclopedia*. CD-ROM. New York: Columbia UP, 1998.
Interview	Stainer, Georgia, general manager, Day Cable and Communications. Telephone interview. 2 Mar. 2000.
Newspaper article, one author	Standish, Evelyn. "Global Market Crushes OPEC's Delicate Balance of Interests." *Wall Street Journal* 19 Jan. 2002: A1.
Book, two authors	Toller, Miriam, and Jay Fielding. *Global Business for Smaller Companies*. Rocklin, CA: Prima Publishing, 2001.
Government publication	United States. Department of Defense. *Stretching Research Dollars: Survival Advice for Universities and Government Labs*. Washington: GPO, 2002.

- The date for electronic sources should contain both the date assigned in the source and the date accessed by the researcher.
- The URL for electronic sources must be as accurate and complete as possible, from access-mode indentifier (http, ftp, gopher, telnet) to all relevant directory and file names. Be sure to enclose this path inside angle brackets: <http://www.hoovers.com/capsules/13787.html>.
- For additional information about documenting online sources, go to http://owl.english.purdue.edu/handouts/research/r_mla.html#Electronic

A number of websites contain useful information about the most common styles for documenting online sources. Here is a brief list:

Columbia Guide to Online Style (CGOS)
www.columbia.edu/cu/cup/cgos/idx_basic.html

Long Island University, C.W. Post Campus, B. Davis Schwartz Memorial Library
www.liu.edu/cwis/cwp/library/workshop/citation.htm

Ithaca College Library Reference Guide
www.ithaca.edu/library/htmls/citing.html

Citation Styles Online
www.bedfordstmartins.com/online/citex.html

Duke Libraries—Guide to Library Research
www.lib.duke.edu/libguide/works_cited.htm

Appendix C
Correction Symbols

Instructors often use these short, easy-to-remember correction symbols and abbreviations when evaluating students' writing. You can use them too, to understand your instructor's suggestions and to revise and proofread your own letters, memos, and reports. Refer to the Handbook of Grammar, Mechanics, and Usage (pp. H-1–H-23) for further information.

Content and Style

Acc	Accuracy. Check to be sure information is correct.
ACE	Avoid copying examples.
ACP	Avoid copying problems.
Adp	Adapt. Tailor message to reader.
App	Follow proper organization approach. (Refer to Chapter 4.)
Assign	Assignment. Review instructions for assignment.
AV	Active verb. Substitute active for passive.
Awk	Awkward phrasing. Rewrite.
BC	Be consistent.
BMS	Be more sincere.
Chop	Choppy sentences. Use longer sentences and more transitional phrases.
Con	Condense. Use fewer words.
CT	Conversational tone. Avoid using overly formal language.
Depers	Depersonalize. Avoid attributing credit or blame to any individual or group.
Dev	Develop. Provide greater detail.
Dir	Direct. Use direct approach; get to the point.
Emph	Emphasize. Develop this point more fully.
EW	Explanation weak. Check logic; provide more proof.
Fl	Flattery. Avoid compliments that are insincere.
FS	Figure of speech. Find a more accurate expression.
GNF	Good news first. Use direct order.
GRF	Give reasons first. Use indirect order.
GW	Goodwill. Put more emphasis on expressions of goodwill.
H/E	Honesty/ethics. Revise statement to reflect good business practices.
Imp	Imply. Avoid being direct.
Inc	Incomplete. Develop further.
Jar	Jargon. Use less specialized language.
Log	Logic. Check development of argument.
Neg	Negative. Use more positive approach or expression.
Obv	Obvious. Do not state point in such detail.
OC	Overconfident. Adopt humbler language.
OM	Omission.
Org	Organization. Strengthen outline.
OS	Off the subject. Close with point on main subject.
Par	Parallel. Use same structure.
Pom	Pompous. Rephrase in down-to-earth terms.
PV	Point of view. Make statement from reader's perspective rather than your own.
RB	Reader benefit. Explain what reader stands to gain.
Red	Redundant. Reduce number of times this point is made.
Ref	Reference. Cite source of information.
Rep	Repetitive. Provide different expression.
RS	Resale. Reassure reader that he or she has made a good choice.
SA	Service attitude. Put more emphasis on helping reader.
Sin	Sincerity. Avoid sounding glib or uncaring.
SL	Stereotyped language. Focus on individual's characteristics instead of on false generalizations.
Spec	Specific. Provide more specific statement.
SPM	Sales promotion material. Tell reader about related goods or services.
Stet	Let stand in original form.
Sub	Subordinate. Make this point less important.
SX	Sexist. Avoid language that contributes to gender stereotypes.
Tone	Tone needs improvement.
Trans	Transition. Show connection between points.
UAE	Use action ending. Close by stating what reader should do next.
UAS	Use appropriate salutation.
UAV	Use active voice.
Unc	Unclear. Rewrite to clarify meaning.
UPV	Use passive voice.

USS	Use shorter sentences.
V	Variety. Use different expression or sentence pattern.
W	Wordy. Eliminate unnecessary words.
WC	Word choice. Find a more appropriate word.
YA	"You" attitude. Rewrite to emphasize reader's needs.

Grammar, Mechanics, and Usage

Ab	Abbreviation. Avoid abbreviations in most cases; use correct abbreviation.
Adj	Adjective. Use adjective instead.
Adv	Adverb. Use adverb instead.
Agr	Agreement. Make subject and verb or noun and pronoun agree.
Ap	Appearance. Improve appearance.
Apos	Apostrophe. Check use of apostrophe.
Art	Article. Use correct article.
BC	Be consistent.
Cap	Capitalize.
Case	Use cases correctly.
CoAdj	Coordinate adjective. Insert comma between coordinate adjectives; delete comma between adjective and compound noun.
CS	Comma splice. Use period or semicolon to separate clauses.
DM	Dangling modifier. Rewrite so that modifier clearly relates to subject of sentence.
Exp	Expletive. Avoid expletive beginnings, such as it is, there are, there is, this is, and these are.
F	Format. Improve layout of document.
Frag	Fragment. Rewrite as complete sentence.
Gram	Grammar. Correct grammatical error.
HCA	Hyphenate compound adjective.
lc	Lowercase. Do not use capital letter.
M	Margins. Improve frame around document.
MM	Misplaced modifier. Place modifier close to word it modifies.
NRC	Nonrestrictive clause (or phrase). Separate from rest of sentence with commas.
P	Punctuation. Use correct punctuation.
Par	Parallel. Use same structure.
PH	Place higher. Move document up on page.
PL	Place lower. Move document down on page.
Prep	Preposition. Use correct preposition.
RC	Restrictive clause (or phrase). Remove commas that separate clause from rest of sentence.
RO	Run-on sentence. Separate two sentences with comma and coordinating conjunction or with semicolon.
SC	Series comma. Add comma before *and.*
SI	Split infinitive. Do not separate *to* from rest of verb.
Sp	Spelling error. Consult dictionary.
S-V	Subject-verb pair. Do not separate with comma.
Syl	Syllabification. Divide word between syllables.
WD	Word division. Check dictionary for proper end-of-line hyphenation.
WW	Wrong word. Replace with another word.

Proofreading Marks

Symbol	Meaning	Symbol Used in Context	Corrected Copy
	Align horizontally	meaningful result	meaningful result
	Align vertically	1. Power cable 2. Keyboard	1. Power cable 2. Keyboard
(bf)	Boldface	Recommendations (bf)	**Recommendations**
	Capitalize	Pepsico, Inc.	PepsiCo, Inc.
	Center	Awards Banquet	Awards Banquet
	Close up space	self- confidence	self-confidence
	Delete	harrassment and abuse	harassment
(ds)	Double-space	text in first line text in second line (ds)	text in first line text in second line
	Insert	trquoise shirts (u, and white)	turquoise and white shirts
	Insert apostrophe	our teams goals	our team's goals
	Insert comma	a, b and c	a, b, and c
	Insert hyphen	third quarter sales	third-quarter sales
	Insert period	Harrigan et al	Harrigan et al.
	Insert quotation marks	This team isn't cooperating.	This "team" isn't cooperating.
#	Insert space	realestate testcase	real estate test case
(ital)	Italics	Quarterly Report (ital)	*Quarterly Report*
/	Lowercase	TULSA, South of here	Tulsa, south of here
	Move down	Sincerely,	Sincerely,
	Move left	Attention: Security	Attention: Security
	Move right	February 2, 2003	February 2, 2003
	Move up	THIRD-QUARTER SALES	THIRD-QUARTER SALES
(STET)	Restore	staff talked openly and frankly (STET)	staff talked openly
	Run lines together	Manager, Distribution	Manager, Distribution
(ss)	Single space	(ss) text in first line text in second line	text in first line text in second line
	Spell out	COD	cash on delivery
(sp)	Spell out	(sp) Assn. of Biochem. Engrs.	Association of Biochemical Engineers
	Start new line	Marla Fenton, Manager, Distri- bution	Marla Fenton, Manager, Distribution
¶	Start new paragraph	¶ The solution is easy to determine but difficult to implement in a competitive environment like the one we now face.	The solution is easy to determine but difficult to implement in a competitive environment like the one we now face.
	Transpose	airy, light, casaul tone	light, airy, casual tone

Video Guide: Applications and Exercises

Your instructor may elect to show you one or more of the videos described on the following pages. These programs supplement course concepts with real-life examples of businesspeople meeting important communication challenges. This video guide includes several review and analysis questions as well as exercises for each video. Be sure to review the appropriate page ahead of time so that you'll know what to look for when you watch the video.

Ethical Communication

Learning Objectives

After viewing this video, you will be able to

1. Describe a process for deciding what is ethical or unethical
2. Explain the importance of meeting your personal and professional responsibilities in an ethical manner
3. Discuss the possible consequences of ethical and unethical choices and talk about the impact of these choices on direct and related audiences

Background Information

Communication is ethical when it includes all relevant information, when it's true in every sense, and when it isn't deceptive in any way. In contrast, communication is unethical when it includes false information, fails to include important information, or otherwise misleads an audience. To avoid unethical choices in your communication efforts, you must consider not only legal issues but also the needs of your audience and the expectations of society and your employer. In turn, companies that demonstrate high standards of ethics maintain credibility with employees, customers, and other stakeholders.

The Video

This video identifies two important tools in a communicator's toolbox: honesty and objectivity. These tools help businesspeople resolve ethical dilemmas and avoid ethical lapses, both within the company and during interactions with outside audiences. Poor ethical choices can damage a company's credibility and put employees, customers, and the surrounding community at risk. Unfortunately, some ethical choices are neither clear nor simple, and you may face situations in which the needs of one group or individual must be weighed against the needs of another.

Discussion Questions

1. Would you ever consider compromising your ethics for self-gain? If so, under what circumstances? If not, why?
2. The video mentions the role of misrepresentations in the collapse of Enron. If you were the head of communications at Enron and had some knowledge of the true nature of the company's financial condition, what would you have done?
3. Identify risks involved when you choose to act in an unethical manner.
4. How can you be an effective business communicator without credibility?
5. Is it ethical to call in sick to work, even though you are not ill? What happens to your credibility if someone finds out you were not sick?

Follow-Up Assignment

Many businesses, from small companies to large corporations, formulate codes of ethics that outline ethical standards for employees. Review IBM's guidelines, which are posted on its website at www.ibm.com/investor/corpgovernance/cgbcg.phtml. Now answer the following questions:

1. What does IBM want employees to do if they are aware of unethical situations within the organization?
2. How does IBM view misleading statements or innuendos about competitors?
3. What advice does IBM give employees on the subject of receiving gifts from people outside the company?

For Further Research

Advertising communications, particularly advertising aimed at children, can present a variety of ethical concerns. The article provided at www.mediascope.org/pubs/ibriefs/cha.htm reports statistics on the advertising of alcohol and tobacco products and discusses the negative effect these advertisements can have on children. To what extent was it ethical for Anheuser Busch to use the Budweiser frog or for Philip Morris to use Joe Camel in its advertisements, given that many children were able to identify with both characters?

Learning to Listen: Second City Communications

Learning Objectives

After viewing this video, you will be able to

1. Understand the functions of interpersonal communication in the workplace
2. Identify the ways to overcome barriers to effective communication
3. Discuss the importance of active listening both socially and professionally

Background Information

Chicago's Second City Improv is more than the world's best-known comedy theater. Second City now brings its famous brand of humor to corporate giants such as Coca-Cola, Motorola, and Microsoft. With over 40 years of experience in corporate services, Second City's teachers help business professionals develop communication skills through lessons in improvisational theater. Business Communications Training is Second City's fastest growing practice, fueled by the demands of more than two hundred Fortune 500 companies. Workshops are tailored to client's needs in such areas as listening and giving presentations, collaborative leadership and team skills, interviewing, breaking down barriers to successful communication, and using humor to convey important messages. The next time you watch improvisational sketch comedy, ask yourself how a lesson in the art of "improv" might give your career a boost.

The Video

In these two video segments, you'll see Second City's training techniques in action. The first segment addresses the need to listen actively, and the second explores techniques for encouraging innovation. The second clip is less focused on communication, but you can see how the techniques for stimulating innovation work equally well for fostering meaningful, two-way conversation that encourages people to open up rather than shut down.

Discussion Questions

1. How do the exercises featured in this video address the contrasting needs of the trial lawyer, the divorce lawyer, and the media buyer?
2. Would ABC's talkative guest Kay Jarman, the 47-year-old award winning salesperson, be a good candidate for Second City's training workshop?
3. What other workshops might Tom Yorton want to offer companies in response to the current economic and political climate?
4. How might the "yes and" rule of improvisation be used to train customer service representatives at an L.L. Bean or a Dell computer call center? Without physical cues, such as facial expression and body language, is the "yes and" rule still effective?
5. As President and Managing Director of Second City Communications, Tom Yorton says the following: "You have to be willing to fail to be able to get the results you want...to connect with an audience." Do you agree that this statement is as true in business as it is in comedy? Support your chosen position.

Follow-Up Assignment

Enjoy Second City Communication's website at www.secondcity.com. If you are a loyal fan, you might want to check out the book titles offered and read more about the group's history. Now explore Second City's Corporate Services: Scan the client roster, read the testimonials, and then select a case study that you find compelling. If you are currently employed, which workshop would be most beneficial to you and to your work team? Explain your choice. If you are not currently employed, how might you and your fellow business students benefit from a Second City workshop? Which workshop would you most like to participate in? Explain how you think it might help you in terms of your social life, your career planning, and your interviewing skills.

For Further Research

The importance of active listening is at the core of *consultative selling*, an approach that emphasizes posing questions to the potential buyer in order to identify needs and expectations—rather than rattling off a prepared sales speech. PublicSpeakingSkills.com (www.publicspeakingskills.com) is one of many companies that offer training in consultative selling. Review the description of the company's Consultative Selling and Negotiating Skills course. Do the principles espoused match the concept of the "you" attitude and the elements of ethical communication that you've learned so far?

Communicating in the Global Workplace

Learning Objectives

After viewing this video, you will be able to

1. Discuss the challenges of communicating in the global workplace
2. Identify barriers to effective communication across borders
3. Explain the critical role of time in global communication efforts

Background Information

Many businesses are crossing national boundaries to engage in international business. However, operating in a global environment presents a variety of challenges related to culture and communication. Understanding and respecting these challenges can mean the difference between success and failure, so executives must make sure that employees are educated on cultural issues before attempting to do business in other countries.

The Video

This video identifies the challenges to effective communication in the global marketplace, including the barriers posed by language, culture, time, and technology. You will see that a significant amount of research needs to be conducted before a company can engage in successful global business ventures. For instance, if communicators are unaware of differences in gestures, expressions, and dialect, they can inadvertently offend or confuse their audiences. In addition, time zone differences require organizations to plan carefully in advance so that they can develop, translate, and deliver information in a timely manner.

Discussion Questions

1. Language can be a barrier to effective communication. What steps can a company take to minimize language barriers across borders?
2. What characteristics of a country's culture need to be researched to ensure business success across borders?
3. How does a company ensure that a message is properly translated into the local language and dialect of the people it conducts business with?
4. What challenges does a company face when trying to hold a conference call or video meeting with affiliates and employees around the world?
5. The video mentions that some companies have trusted contacts in a country they wish to do business with, while other companies rely on a significant amount of research to learn more about culture and other local characteristics. What method do you feel is most effective for gathering useful, accurate, and up-to-date information regarding cultural issues?

Follow-Up Assignment

The Coca-Cola Company has local operations in more than 200 countries throughout the world. Visit www.coca-cola.com to learn more about the company's business activities in a variety of countries. What steps does Coke take to communicate through its website with customers around the world? Does the company strive to develop products that meet local tastes and needs? If so, how and why?

For Further Research

Choose a country other than the United States, and research your selection using both online and library resources to identify important cultural characteristics specific to that country. For example, you may want to gather information about gestures and other nonverbal communication that would be considered offensive, about work habits, or about laws related to conducting business in that country. The characteristics you identify should be useful and accurate.

Based on what you've learned about this country and your personal beliefs, values, and life experiences, is there any risk that you might have a prejudiced or ethnocentric viewpoint regarding people from this country? Why or why not?

Impact of Culture on Business: Spotlight on Latin America

Learning Objectives

After viewing this video, you will be able to

1. List key aspects of Latin American culture and indicate the influences on their development
2. Identify factors that might lead to cultural change in Latin America
3. Explain some of the major cultural contrasts within Latin America and their impact on international business operations

Background Information

To a large degree, culture defines the way all human beings interpret and respond to life's changing circumstances. When you interact with people from your own culture, your shared experiences and expectations usually enhance the communication process by providing a common language and frame of reference. However, when you communicate across cultural boundaries, a lack of awareness of your audience's culture—and the subconscious ways that your own culture shapes your perceptions—can result in partial or even total failure of the communication process. Moreover, culture is rarely static, so impressions you may have gathered at one point in your life may need to be revisited and revised over time.

The Video

This video takes a broad look at Latin America's various countries and cultures and explores the business implications of cultural similarities and differences. You'll learn how cultural groups that may appear identical on the surface can in fact have subtle but profound differences. Although communication is just one of many topics discussed in the video, you will get a sense of just how important—and challenging—communication can be when conducting business across cultural boundaries.

Discussion Questions

1. Explain what the video means when it says that your own culture can "sneak up on you."
2. How is business influencing the economic gulf between urban and rural populations in Latin America?
3. How have imperial conquests and slavery affected the populations and cultures of Latin America?
4. How do many outsiders view the issue of business and government corruption in Latin America?
5. Is business etiquette in most of Latin America considered relatively formal or relatively informal?

Follow-Up Assignment

The World Bank plays an important role in today's fast-changing, closely meshed global economy. Visit the bank's website at www.worldbank.org and explore the initiatives programs underway in the Latin American region. How is the bank using this website to foster better communication between Latin America and the rest of the world?

For Further Research

In today's global marketplace, knowing as much as possible about your international customers' business practices and customs could give you a strategic advantage. To help you successfully conduct business around the globe, navigate the resources at the U.S. Government Export Portal. Start at www.export.gov, then click on "Market Research" and then on "Country Information—Quick Reference (TIC)." Click anywhere on the world map to learn more about each country.

How can resources such as this website help U.S. businesses communicate more successfully with customers, employees, and other groups in Latin America?

Technology and the Tools of Communication

Learning Objectives

After viewing this video, you will be able to

1. Identify technology-related issues to consider when developing communication strategies
2. Identify advantages of using technology as a tool for effective communication
3. Differentiate between "push" and "pull" communication

Background Information

From instant messaging to online meetings, technology has become an integral element of business communication. When used with care, technological tools can help you reach more people in less time with more effective messages. However, when technology is misused or misunderstood, it can cause more problems than it solves. Knowing which technologies to use in every situation—and knowing how to use each one—are vital to your success.

The Video

This video discusses how the Internet, e-mail, voicemail, and other devices have revolutionized the way people communicate. These technological tools increase the speed, frequency, and range of business communication. The video also discusses factors to consider when choosing the most appropriate vehicle for your communication, including the all-important challenge of getting and keeping your audience's attention. The advantages of using technological communication tools are presented throughout the video.

Discussion Questions

1. Identify six questions you need to consider when choosing a technology vehicle for your messages.
2. List the advantages of communicating via e-mail within an organization.
3. What role does technology play in ensuring effective communication within an organization?
4. What are some of the more common challenges that business communicators can encounter when they use technology for communication purposes?
5. Identify the difference between "push" and "pull" communications, and provide an example of each method.

Follow-Up Assignment

VolResource (at www.volresource.org.uk/samples/olcomms.htm) provides practical and informative resources for volunteer organizations that are trying to develop online communication strategies. The VolResource website further details questions that need to be addressed in the process of developing an effective communication strategy for any organization. What issues do you think are the most important to consider? Why?

For Further Exploration

Visit the Yellow Freight website at www.yellowfreight.com and explore the various e-commerce tools this company utilizes to communicate effectively with its customers. Examine these tools and consider their effectiveness. What are some of the advantages of these online communication tools? How do they benefit the client? How do they benefit Yellow Freight?

Handbook of Grammar, Mechanics, and Usage

Grammar and mechanics are nothing more than the way words are combined into sentences. Usage is the way words are used by a network of people—in this case, the community of businesspeople who use English. You'll find it easier to get along in this community if you know the accepted standards of grammar, mechanics, and usage. This handbook offers you valuable opportunities in two sections:

- **Diagnostic Test of English Skills.** Testing your current knowledge of grammar, mechanics, and usage helps you find out where your strengths and weaknesses lie. This test offers 60 items taken from the topics included in this Handbook.
- **Assessment of English Skills.** After completing the diagnostic test, use the assessment form to highlight those areas you most need to review.

To quickly review the basics, you can visit www.prenhall.com/bovee and select "Handbook of Grammar, Mechanics, and Usage Practice Sessions." Test yourself and reinforce what you learn. Use this essential review not only to study and improve your English skills but also as a reference for any questions you may have during this course.

Without a firm grasp of the basics of grammar, punctuation, mechanics, and vocabulary, you risk being misunderstood, damaging your company's image, losing money for your company, and possibly even losing your job. However, once you develop strong English skills, you will create clear and concise messages, you will enhance your company's image as well as your own, and you will not only increase your company's profits but expand your own chances of success.

Diagnostic Test of English Skills

Use this test to help you determine whether you need more practice with grammar, punctuation, mechanics, or vocabulary. When you've answered all the questions, ask your instructor for an answer sheet so that you can score the test. On the Assessment of English Skills form (page H-3), record the number of questions you answered correctly in each section.

The following choices apply to items 1–10. In each blank, write the letter of the choice that best describes the problem with each sentence.

A. sentence incomplete
B. too many phrases/clauses strung together
C. modifying elements misplaced (dangling)
D. structure not parallel
E. nothing wrong

____ **1.** Stop here.

____ **2.** Your duties are interviewing, hiring, and also to fire employees.

____ **3.** After their presentation, I was still undecided.

____ **4.** Speaking freely, the stock was considered a bargain.

____ **5.** Margaret, pressed for time, turned in unusually sloppy work.

____ **6.** Typing and filing, routine office chores.

____ **7.** With care, edit the report.

____ **8.** When Paul came to work here, he brought some outmoded ideas, now he has accepted our modern methods.

____ **9.** To plan is better than improvising.

____ **10.** Hoping to improve performance, practice is advisable.

The following choices apply to items 11–20. In each blank, write the letter of the choice that identifies the underlined word(s) in each sentence.

A. subject
B. predicate (verb)
C. object
D. modifier
E. conjunction/preposition

____ **11.** Take his memo upstairs.

____ **12.** Before leaving, he repaired the photocopier.

____ **13.** Velnor, Inc., will soon introduce a new product line.

____ **14.** We must hire only qualified, ambitious graduates.

____ **15.** They are having trouble with their quality control systems.

____ **16.** After she wrote the report, Jill waited eagerly for a response.

____ **17.** The route to the plant isn't paved yet.

____ **18.** See me after the meeting.

____ **19.** Your new home is ready and waiting.

____ **20.** BFL is large but caring.

In the blanks for items 21–30, write the letter of the word that best completes each sentence.

_____ **21.** Starbucks (A. is, B. are) opening five new stores in San Diego in the next year.

_____ **22.** There (A. is, B. are) 50 applicants for the job opening.

_____ **23.** Anyone who wants to be (A. their, B. his or her) own boss should think about owning a franchise.

_____ **24.** Neither of us (A. was, B. were) prepared for the meeting.

_____ **25.** Another characteristic of a small business is that (A. they tend, B. it tends) to be more innovative than larger firms.

_____ **26.** After he had (A. saw, B. seen) the revised budget, Raymond knew he wouldn't be getting a new desk.

_____ **27.** The number of women-owned small businesses (A. has, B. have) increased sharply in the past two decades.

_____ **28.** If I (A. was, B. were) you, I'd stop sending personal e-mails at work.

_____ **29.** Eugene (A. lay, B. laid) the files on the desk.

_____ **30.** Either FedEx or UPS (A. has, B. have) been chosen as our preferred shipping service.

The following choices apply to items 31–40. In each blank, write the letter of the choice that best describes each sentence.

A. all punctuation used correctly
B. some punctuation used incorrectly or incorrectly omitted

_____ **31.** The president who rarely gave interviews, agreed to write an article for the company newsletter.

_____ **32.** Give the assignment to Karen Schiff, the new technical writer.

_____ **33.** Could you please send a replacement for Item No. 3–303.

_____ **34.** Debbie said that, "technicians must have technical degrees."

_____ **35.** We'll have branches in Bakersfield, California, Reno, Nevada, and Medford, Oregon.

_____ **36.** Before leaving her secretary finished typing the memo.

_____ **37.** How many of you consider yourselves "computer literate?"

_____ **38.** This, then, is our goal: to increase market share by 50 percent.

_____ **39.** They plan to move soon, however, they still should be invited.

_____ **40.** Health, wealth, and happiness—those are my personal goals.

The following choices apply to items 41–50. In each blank, write the letter of the choice that best describes the problem with each sentence.

A. error in punctuation
B. error in use of abbreviations or symbols
C. error in use of numbers
D. error in capitalization
E. no errors

_____ **41.** Most of last year's sales came from the midwest.

_____ **42.** We can provide the items you are looking for @ $2 each.

_____ **43.** Alex noted: "few of our competitors have tried this approach."

_____ **44.** Address the letter to professor Elliott Barker, Psychology Department, North Dakota State University.

_____ **45.** They've recorded 22 complaints since yesterday, all of them from long-time employees.

_____ **46.** Leslie's presentation—"New Markets for the Nineties"—was well organized.

_____ **47.** We're having a sale in the childrens' department, beginning Wednesday, August 15.

_____ **48.** About 50 of the newly inducted members will be present.

_____ **49.** Mister Spencer has asked me to find ten volunteers.

_____ **50.** Let's meet in Beth and Larry's office at one o'clock.

In the blanks for items 51–60, write the letter of the word that best completes each sentence.

_____ **51.** Will having a degree (A. affect, B. effect) my chances for promotion?

_____ **52.** Place the latest drawings (A. beside, B. besides) the others.

_____ **53.** Try not to (A. loose, B. lose) this key; we will charge you a fee to replace it.

_____ **54.** Let us help you choose the right tie to (A. complement, B. compliment) your look.

_____ **55.** The five interviewers should discuss the candidates' qualifications (A. among, B. between) themselves.

_____ **56.** New employees spend their time looking for (A. perspective, B. prospective) clients.

_____ **57.** Are the goods you received different (A. from, B. than) the goods you ordered?

_____ **58.** He took those courses to (A. farther, B. further) his career.

_____ **59.** We are (A. anxious, B. eager) to see you next Thursday.

_____ **60.** All commissions will be (A. disbursed, B. dispensed, C. dispersed) on the second Friday of every month.

Assessment of English Skills

In the space provided below, record the number of questions you answered correctly.

QUESTION	NUMBER YOU GOT CORRECT	SKILL AREA
1–10	_______	Sentence structure
11–20	_______	Grammar: Parts of speech
21–30	_______	Grammar: Verbs and agreement
31–40	_______	Punctuation
41–50	_______	Punctuation and mechanics
51–60	_______	Vocabulary

If you scored 8 or lower in any of the skills areas, focus on those areas in the appropriate sections of this Handbook.

Essentials of Grammar, Mechanics, and Usage

The sentence below looks innocent, but is it really?

> We sell tuxedos as well as rent.

You might sell rent, but it's highly unlikely. Whatever you're selling, some people will ignore your message because of a blunder like this. The following sentence has a similar problem:

> Vice President Eldon Neale told his chief engineer that he would no longer be with Avix, Inc., as of June 30.

Is Eldon or the engineer leaving? No matter which side the facts are on, the sentence can be read the other way. Now look at this sentence:

> The year before we budgeted more for advertising sales were up.

Confused? Perhaps this is what you meant:

> The year before, we budgeted more for advertising. Sales were up.

Maybe you meant this:

> The year before we budgeted more for advertising, sales were up.

The meaning of language falls into bundles called sentences. A listener or reader can take only so much meaning before filing a sentence away and getting ready for the next one. So, as a business writer, you have to know what a sentence is. You need to know where one ends and the next one begins.

If you want to know what a sentence is, you have to find out what goes into it, what its ingredients are. Luckily, the basic ingredients of an English sentence are simple: The parts of speech combine with punctuation, mechanics, and vocabulary to convey meaning.

1.0 Grammar

Grammar is the study of how words come together to form sentences. Categorized by meaning, form, and function, English words fall into various parts of speech: nouns, pronouns, verbs, adjectives, adverbs, prepositions, conjunctions, articles, and interjections. You will communicate more clearly if you understand how each of these parts of speech operates in a sentence.

1.1 Nouns

A noun names a person, place, or thing. Anything you can see or detect with one of your other senses has a noun to name it. Some things you can't see or sense are also nouns—ions, for example, or space. So are things that exist as ideas, such as accuracy and height. (You can see that something is accurate or that a building is tall, but you can't see the idea of accuracy or the idea of height.) These names for ideas are known as abstract nouns. The simplest nouns are the names of things you can see or touch: car, building, cloud, brick.

1.1.1 Proper Nouns and Common Nouns

So far, all the examples of nouns have been common nouns, referring to general classes of things. The word *building* refers to a whole class of structures. Common nouns such as *building* are not capitalized.

If you want to talk about one particular building, however, you might refer to the Glazier Building. The name is capitalized, indicating that *Glazier Building* is a proper noun.

Here are three sets of common and proper nouns for comparison:

Common	Proper
city	Kansas City
company	Blaisden Company
store	Books Galore

1.1.2 Nouns as Subject and Object

Nouns may be used in sentences as subjects or objects. That is, the person, place, idea, or thing that is being or doing (subject) is represented by a noun. So is the person, place, idea, or thing that is being acted on (object). In the following sentence, the nouns are underlined.

> The <u>secretary</u> keyboarded the <u>report</u>.

The secretary (subject) is acting in a way that affects the report (object). The following sentence is more complicated:

> The <u>installer</u> delivered the <u>carpeting</u> to the <u>customer</u>.

Installer is the subject. *Carpeting* is the object of the main part of the sentence (acted on by the installer), whereas *customer* is the object of the phrase *to the customer.* Nevertheless, both *carpeting* and *customer* are objects.

1.1.3 Plural Nouns

Nouns can be either singular or plural. The usual way to make a plural noun is to add *s* to the singular form of the word:

Singular	**Plural**
rock	rocks
picture	pictures
song	songs

Many nouns have other ways of forming the plural. Letters, numbers, and words used as words are sometimes made plural by adding an apostrophe and an *s*. Very often, *'s* is used with abbreviations that have periods, lowercase letters that stand alone, and capital letters that might be confused with words when made into plurals:

Spell out all *St.*'s and *Ave.*'s.

He divided the page with a row of *x*'s.

Sarah will register the *A*'s through the *G*'s at the convention.

In other cases, however, the apostrophe may be left out:

They'll review their ABCs.

The stock market climbed through most of the 1980s.

Circle all *thes* in the paragraph.

In some of these examples, the letters used as letters and words used as words are *italicized* (a mechanics issue that is discussed later).

Other nouns, such as those below, are so-called irregular nouns; they form the plural in some way other than by simply adding *s:*

Singular	**Plural**
tax	taxes
specialty	specialties
cargo	cargoes
shelf	shelves
child	children
woman	women
tooth	teeth
mouse	mice
parenthesis	parentheses
son-in-law	sons-in-law
editor-in-chief	editors-in-chief

Rather than memorize a lot of rules about forming plurals, use a dictionary. If the dictionary says nothing about the plural of a word, it's formed the usual way: by adding *s*. If the plural is formed in some irregular way, the dictionary often shows the plural spelling.

1.1.4 Possessive Nouns

A noun becomes possessive when it's used to show the ownership of something. Then you add *'s* to the word:

the man's car   the woman's apartment

However, ownership does not need to be legal:

the secretary's desk   the company's assets

Also, ownership may be nothing more than an automatic association:

a day's work   the job's prestige

An exception to the rule about adding *'s* to make a noun possessive occurs when the word is singular and already has two "s" sounds at the end. In cases like the following, an apostrophe is all that's needed:

crisis' dimensions   Mr. Moses' application

When the noun has only one "s" sound at the end, however, retain the *'s:*

Chris's book   Carolyn Nuss's office

With hyphenated nouns (compound nouns), add *'s* to the last word:

Hyphenated Noun	**Possessive Noun**
mother-in-law	mother-in-law's
mayor-elect	mayor-elect's

To form the possessive of plural nouns, just begin by following the same rule as with singular nouns: add *'s*. However, if the plural noun already ends in an *s* (as most do), drop the one you've added, leaving only the apostrophe:

the clients' complaints   employees' benefits

1.2 Pronouns

A pronoun is a word that stands for a noun; it saves repeating the noun:

Drivers have some choice of weeks for vacation, but *they* must notify this office of *their* preference by March 1.

The pronouns *they* and *their* stand in for the noun *drivers*. The noun that a pronoun stands for is called the antecedent of the pronoun; *drivers* is the antecedent of *they* and *their.*

When the antecedent is plural, the pronoun that stands in for it has to be plural; *they* and *their* are plural pronouns because *drivers* is plural. Likewise, when the antecedent is singular, the pronoun has to be singular:

We thought the *contract* had expired, but we soon learned that *it* had not.

1.2.1 Multiple Antecedents

Sometimes a pronoun has a double (or even a triple) antecedent:

Kathryn Boettcher and *Luis Gutierrez* went beyond *their* sales quotas for January.

If taken alone, *Kathryn Boettcher* is a singular antecedent. So is *Luis Gutierrez.* However, when together they are the plural antecedent of a pronoun, so the pronoun has to be plural. Thus the pronoun is *their* instead of *her* or *his.*

1.2.2 Unclear Antecedents

In some sentences the pronoun's antecedent is unclear:

Sandy Wright sent Jane Brougham *her* production figures for the previous year. *She* thought they were too low.

To which person does the pronoun *her* refer? Someone who knew Sandy and Jane and knew their business relationship might be able to figure out the antecedent for *her.* Even with such an advantage, however, a reader might receive the wrong meaning. Also, it would be nearly impossible for any reader to know which name is the antecedent of *she.*

The best way to clarify an ambiguous pronoun is usually to rewrite the sentence, repeating nouns when needed for clarity:

> Sandy Wright sent her production figures for the previous year to Jane Brougham. *Jane* thought they were too low.

The noun needs to be repeated only when the antecedent is unclear.

1.2.3 Gender-Neutral Pronouns

The pronouns that stand for males are *he, his,* and *him.* The pronouns that stand for females are *she, hers,* and *her.* However, you'll often be faced with the problem of choosing a pronoun for a noun that refers to both females and males:

> Each manager must make up (his, her, his or her, its, their) own mind about stocking this item and about the quantity that (he, she, he or she, it, they) can sell.

This sentence calls for a pronoun that's neither masculine nor feminine. The issue of gender-neutral pronouns responds to efforts to treat females and males evenhandedly. Here are some possible ways to deal with this issue:

> Each manager must make up *his* . . .
>
> (Not all managers are men.)

> Each manager must make up *her* . . .
>
> (Not all managers are women.)

> Each manager must make up *his* or *her* . . .
>
> (This solution is acceptable but becomes awkward when repeated more than once or twice in a document.)

> Each manager must make up *her* . . . Every manager will receive *his* . . . A manager may send *her* . . .
>
> (A manager's gender does not alternate like a windshield wiper!)

> Each manager must make up *their* . . .
>
> (The pronoun can't be plural when the antecedent is singular.)

> Each manager must make up *its* . . .
>
> (*It* never refers to people.)

The best solution is to make the noun plural or to revise the passage altogether:

> Managers must make up *their* minds . . .
>
> Each manager must decide whether . . .

Be careful not to change the original meaning.

1.2.4 Case of Pronouns

The case of a pronoun tells whether it's acting or acted upon:

> *She sells* an average of five packages each week.

In this sentence, *she* is doing the selling. Because *she* is acting, *she* is said to be in the nominative case. Now consider what happens when the pronoun is acted upon:

> After six months, Ms. Browning promoted *her.*

In this sentence, the pronoun *her* is acted upon. The pronoun *her* is thus said to be in the objective case.

Contrast the nominative and objective pronouns in this list:

Nominative	**Objective**
I	me
we	us
he	him
she	her
they	them
who	whom
whoever	whomever

Objective pronouns may be used as either the object of a verb (such as *promoted*) or the object of a preposition (such as *with*):

> Rob worked with *them* until the order was filled.

In this example, *them* is the object of the preposition *with* because Rob acted upon—worked with—them. Here's a sentence with three pronouns, the first one nominative, the second the object of a verb, and the third the object of a preposition:

> *He* paid *us* as soon as the check came from *them.*

He is nominative; *us* is objective because it's the object of the verb *paid; them* is objective because it's the object of the preposition *from.*

Every writer sometimes wonders whether to use *who* or *whom:*

> (Who, Whom) will you hire?

Because this sentence is a question, it's difficult to see that *whom* is the object of the verb *hire.* You can figure out which pronoun to use if you rearrange the question and temporarily try *she* and *her* in place of *who* and *whom:* "Will you hire *she?*" or "Will you hire *her?*" *Her* and *whom* are both objective, so the correct choice is "*Whom* will you hire?" Here's a different example:

> (Who, Whom) logged so much travel time?

Turning the question into a statement, you get:

> *He* logged so much travel time.

Therefore, the correct statement is:

> *Who* logged so much travel time?

1.2.5 Possessive Pronouns

Possessive pronouns work like possessive nouns: They show ownership or automatic association.

her job	their preferences
his account	its equipment

However, possessive pronouns are different from possessive nouns in the way they are written. That is, possessive pronouns never have an apostrophe.

Possessive Noun	Possessive Pronoun
the woman's estate	her estate
Roger Franklin's plans	his plans
the shareholders' feelings	their feelings
the vacuum cleaner's attachments	its attachments

The word *its* is the possessive of *it.* Like all other possessive pronouns, its has no apostrophe. Some people confuse *its* with *it's,* the contraction of *it is.* Contractions are discussed later.

1.3 Verbs

A verb describes an action:

They all *quit* in disgust.

It may also describe a state of being:

Working conditions *were* substandard.

The English language is full of action verbs. Here are a few you'll often run across in the business world:

verify	perform	fulfill
hire	succeed	send
leave	improve	receive
accept	develop	pay

You could undoubtedly list many more.

The most common verb describing a state of being instead of an action is *to be* and all its forms:

I *am, was,* or *will be;* you *are, were,* or *will be*

Other verbs also describe a state of being:

It *seemed* a good plan at the time.

She *sounds* impressive at a meeting.

These verbs link what comes before them in the sentence with what comes after; no action is involved. (See Section 1.7.5 for a fuller discussion of linking verbs.)

1.3.1 Verb Tenses

English has three simple verb tenses: present, past, and future.

Present: Our branches in Hawaii *stock* other items.

Past: We *stocked* Purquil pens for a short time.

Future: Rotex Tire Stores *will stock* your line of tires when you begin a program of effective national advertising.

With most verbs (the regular ones), the past tense ends in *ed,* and the future tense always has *will* or *shall* in front of it. But the present tense is more complex, depending on the subject:

	First Person	Second Person	Third Person
Singular	I stock	you stock	he/she/it stocks
Plural	we stock	you stock	they stock

The basic form, *stock,* takes an additional *s* when *he, she,* or *it* precedes it. (See section 1.3.4 for more on subject-verb agreement.)

In addition to the three simple tenses, there are three perfect tenses using forms of the helping verb *have.* The present perfect tense uses the past participle (regularly the past tense) of the main verb, *stocked,* and adds the present-tense *have* or *has* to the front of it:

(I, we, you, they) *have stocked.*

(He, she, it) *has stocked.*

The past perfect tense uses the past participle of the main verb, *stocked,* and adds the past-tense *had* to the front of it:

(I, you, he, she, it, we, they) *had stocked.*

The future perfect tense also uses the past participle of the main verb, *stocked,* but adds the future-tense *will have:*

(I, you, he, she, it, we, they) *will have stocked.*

Keep verbs in the same tense when the actions occur at the same time:

When the payroll checks *came* in, everyone *showed* up for work.

We *have found* that everyone *has pitched* in to help.

When the actions occur at different times, you may change tense accordingly:

The shipment *came* last Wednesday, so if another one *comes* in today, please *return* it.

The new employee *had been* ill at ease, but now she *has become* a full-fledged member of the team.

1.3.2 Irregular Verbs

Many verbs don't follow in every detail the patterns already described. The most irregular of these verbs is *to be:*

Tense	Singular	Plural
Present:	I *am*	we *are*
	you *are*	you *are*
	he, she, it *is*	they *are*
Past:	I *was*	we *were*
	you *were*	you *were*
	he, she, it *was*	they *were*

The future tense of *to be* is formed in the same way that the future tense of a regular verb is formed.

The perfect tenses of *to be* are also formed as they would be for a regular verb, except that the past participle is a special form, *been,* instead of just the past tense:

Present perfect: you have been

Past perfect: you had been

Future perfect: you will have been

Here's a sampling of other irregular verbs:

Present	Past	Past Participle
begin	began	begun
shrink	shrank	shrunk
know	knew	known
rise	rose	risen
become	became	become
go	went	gone
do	did	done

Dictionaries list the various forms of other irregular verbs.

1.3.3 Transitive and Intransitive Verbs

Many people are confused by three particular sets of verbs:

lie/lay sit/set rise/raise

Using these verbs correctly is much easier when you learn the difference between transitive and intransitive verbs.

Transitive verbs convey their action to an object; they "transfer" their action to an object. Intransitive verbs do not. Here are some sample uses of transitive and intransitive verbs:

Intransitive	Transitive
We should include in our new offices a place to *lie* down for a nap.	The workers will be here on Monday to *lay* new carpeting.
Even the way an interviewee *sits* is important.	That crate is full of stemware, so *set* it down carefully.
Salaries at Compu-Link, Inc., *rise* swiftly.	They *raise* their level of production every year.

The workers *lay* carpeting, you *set* down the crate, they *raise* production; each action is transferred to something. In the intransitive sentences, one *lies* down, an interviewee *sits,* and salaries *rise* without (at least grammatically) affecting anything else. Intransitive sentences are complete with only a subject and a verb; transitive sentences are not complete unless they also include an object, or something to transfer the action to.

Tenses are a confusing element of the *lie/lay* problem:

Present	Past	Past Participle
I lie	I lay	I have lain
I lay (something down)	I laid (something down)	I have laid (somthing down)

The past tense of *lie* and the present tense of *lay* look and sound alike, even though they're different verbs.

1.3.4 Subject-Verb Agreement

Whether regular or irregular, every verb must agree with its subject, both in person (first, second, or third) and in number (singular or plural).

	First Person	Second Person	Third Person
Singular	I *am;* I *write*	you *are;* you *write*	he/she/it *is;* he/she/it *writes*
Plural	we *are;* we *write*	you *are;* you *write*	they *are;* they *write*

In a simple sentence, making a verb agree with its subject is a straightforward task:

Hector Ruiz *is* a strong competitor. (third-person singular)

We *write* to you every month. (first-person plural)

Confusion sometimes arises when sentences are a bit more complicated. For example, be sure to avoid agreement problems when words come between the subject and verb. In the following examples, the verb appears in italics, and its subject is underlined:

The <u>analysis</u> of existing documents *takes* a full week.

Even though *documents* is a plural, the verb is in the singular form. That's because the subject of the sentence is *analysis,* a singular noun. The phrase *of existing documents* can be disregarded. Here is another example:

The <u>answers</u> for this exercise *are* in the study guide.

Take away the phrase *for this exercise* and you are left with the plural subject *answers.* Therefore, the verb takes the plural form.

Verb agreement is also complicated when the subject is not a specific noun or pronoun and when the subject may be considered either singular or plural. In such cases, you have to analyze the surrounding sentence to determine which verb form to use.

The <u>staff</u> *is* quartered in the warehouse.

The <u>staff</u> *are* at their desks in the warehouse.

The <u>computers</u> and the <u>staff</u> *are* in the warehouse.

Neither the staff nor the <u>computers</u> *are* in the warehouse.

<u>Every</u> computer *is* in the warehouse.

Many a <u>computer</u> *is* in the warehouse.

Did you notice that words such as *every* use the singular verb form? In addition, when an *either/or* or a *neither/nor* phrase combines singular and plural nouns, the verb takes the form that matches the noun closest to it.

In the business world, some subjects require extra attention. Company names, for example, are considered singular and therefore take a singular verb in most cases—even if they contain plural words:

<u>Stater Brothers</u> *offers* convenient grocery shopping.

In addition, quantities are sometimes considered singular and sometimes plural. If a quantity refers to a total amount, it takes a singular verb; if a quantity refers to individual, countable units, it takes a plural verb:

Three <u>hours</u> *is* a long time.

The eight <u>dollars</u> we collected for the fund *are* tacked on the bulletin board.

Fractions may also be singular or plural, depending on the noun that accompanies them:

One-third of the <u>warehouse</u> *is* devoted to this product line.

One-third of the <u>products</u> *are* defective.

For a related discussion, see Section 1.7.2, "Longer Sentences," later in this Handbook.

1.3.5 Voice of Verbs

Verbs have two voices, active and passive. When the subject comes first, the voice is active. When the object comes first, the voice is passive:

Active: The buyer paid a large amount.

Passive: A large amount was paid by the buyer.

The passive voice uses a form of the verb *to be,* which adds words to a sentence. In the example, the passive-voice sentence uses eight words, whereas the active-voice sentence uses only six to say the same thing. The words *was* and *by* are unnecessary to convey the meaning of the sentence. In fact, extra words usually clog meaning. So be sure to opt for the active voice when you have a choice.

At times, however, you have no choice:

Several items *have been taken,* but so far we don't know who took them.

The passive voice becomes necessary when you don't know (or don't want to say) who performed the action; the active voice is bolder and more direct.

1.3.6 Mood of Verbs

You have three moods to choose from, depending on your intentions. Most of the time you use the indicative mood to make a statement or to ask a question:

The secretary *mailed* a letter to each supplier.

Did the secretary *mail* a letter to each supplier?

When you wish to command or request, use the imperative mood:

Please *mail* a letter to each supplier.

Sometimes, especially in business, a courteous request is stated like a question; in that case, however, no question mark is required:

Would you *mail* a letter to each supplier.

The subjunctive mood, most often used in formal writing or in presenting bad news, expresses a possibility or a recommendation. The subjunctive is usually signaled by a word such as *if* or *that.* In these examples, the subjunctive mood uses special verb forms:

If the secretary *were to mail* a letter to each supplier, we might save some money.

I suggested that the secretary *mail* a letter to each supplier.

Although the subjunctive mood is not used as often as it once was, it's still found in such expressions as *Come what may* and *If I were you.* In general, it is used to convey an idea that is contrary to fact: If iron *were* lighter than air.

1.4 Adjectives

An adjective modifies (tells something about) a noun or pronoun. Each of the following phrases says more about the noun or pronoun than the noun or pronoun would say alone.

an *efficient* staff | a *heavy* price

brisk trade | *poor* you

Adjectives always tell us something that we wouldn't know without them. So you don't need to use adjectives when the noun alone, or a different noun, will give the meaning:

a *company* employee
(An employee ordinarily works for a company.)

a *crate-type* container
(*Crate* gives the entire meaning.)

Verbs in the *ing* (present participle) form can be used as adjectives:

A *boring* job can sometimes turn into a *fascinating* career.

So can the past participle of verbs:

A freshly *painted* house is a *sold* house.

Adjectives modify nouns more often than they modify pronouns. When adjectives do modify pronouns, however, the sentence usually has a linking verb:

They were *attentive.* | It looked *appropriate.*

He seems *interested.* | You are *skillful.*

At times, a series of adjectives precedes a noun:

It was a *long* and *active* workday.

Such strings of adjectives are acceptable as long as they all convey a different part of the phrase's meaning. However, adjectives often pile up in front of a noun, like this:

The *superficial, obvious* answer was the one she gave.

The most valuable animal on the ranch is a *small black* horse.

The question is whether a comma should be used to separate the adjectives. The answer is to use a comma when the two adjectives independently modify the noun; do not use a comma when one of the adjectives is closely identified with the noun. In the first example above, the answer was both superficial and obvious. But in the second example, the black horse is small.

Another way to think about this is to use the word *and* as a replacement for the comma. Study the following example:

We recommend a diet of leafy green vegetables.

We recommend a diet of green, leafy vegetables.

Because some green vegetables are not leafy (cucumbers and zucchini, for example), it is correct to leave out the comma in the first example so that you know which kind of green vegetables are being discussed. But because all leafy vegetables are also green (green and leafy), the comma must be included in the second example.

You might also try switching the adjectives. If the order of the adjectives can be reversed without changing the meaning of the phrase, you should use a comma. If the order cannot be reversed, you should not use a comma. Consider these examples:

Here's our *simplified credit* application.

Here's our *simplified, easy-to-complete* application.

Here's our *easy-to-complete, simplified* application.

A credit application may be simple or complex; however, you cannot talk about a credit, simplified application; therefore, leave the comma out of the first example. The application in the second and third examples is both simplified and easy to complete, no matter how you arrange the words, so include the comma in these examples.

1.4.1 Comparative Degree

Most adjectives can take three forms: simple, comparative, and superlative. The simple form modifies a single noun or pronoun. Use the comparative form when comparing two items. When comparing three or more items, use the superlative form.

Simple	Comparative	Superlative
hard	harder	hardest
safe	safer	safest
dry	drier	driest

The comparative form adds *er* to the simple form, and the superlative form adds *est.* (The *y* at the end of a word changes to *i* before the *er* or *est* is added.)

A small number of adjectives are irregular, including these:

Simple	Comparative	Superlative
good	better	best
bad	worse	worst
little	less	least

When the simple form of an adjective is two or more syllables, you usually add *more* to form the comparative and *most* to form the superlative:

Simple	Comparative	Superlative
useful	more useful	most useful
exhausting	more exhausting	most exhausting
expensive	more expensive	most expensive

The most common exceptions are two-syllable adjectives that end in *y:*

Simple	Comparative	Superlative
happy	happier	happiest
costly	costlier	costliest

If you choose this option, change the *y* to *i,* and tack *er* or *est* onto the end.

Some adjectives cannot be used to make comparisons because they themselves indicate the extreme. For example, if something is perfect, nothing can be more perfect. If something is unique or ultimate, nothing can be more unique or more ultimate.

1.4.2 Hyphenated Adjectives

Many adjectives used in the business world are actually combinations of words: *up-to-date* report, *last-minute* effort, *fifth-floor* suite, *well-built* engine. As you can see, they are hyphenated when they come before the noun they modify. However, when they come after the noun they modify, they are not hyphenated. In the following example, the adjectives appear in italics, and the nouns they modify are underlined:

> The <u>report</u> is *up to date* because of our team's *last-minute* <u>efforts</u>.

Hyphens are not used when part of the combination is a word ending in *ly* (because that word is usually not an adjective). Hyphens are also omitted from word combinations that are used frequently.

> We live in a *rapidly shrinking* world.
>
> Our *highly motivated* employees will be well paid.
>
> Please consider renewing your *credit card* account.
>
> Send those figures to our *data processing* department.
>
> Our new intern is a *high school* student.

1.5 Adverbs

An adverb modifies a verb, an adjective, or another adverb:

Modifying a verb:	Our marketing department works *efficiently.*
Modifying an adjective:	She was not dependable, although she was *highly* intelligent.
Modifying another adverb:	His territory was *too* broadly diversified, so he moved *extremely* cautiously.

Most of the adverbs mentioned are adjectives turned into adverbs by adding *ly,* which is how many adverbs are formed:

Adjective	Adverb
efficient	efficiently
extreme	extremely
high	highly
official	officially
separate	separately
special	specially

Some adverbs are made by dropping or changing the final letter of the adjective and then adding *ly:*

Adjective	Adverb
due	duly
busy	busily

Other adverbs don't end in *ly* at all. Here are a few examples of this type:

often	fast	too
soon	very	so

Some adverbs are difficult to distinguish from adjectives. For example, in the following sentences, is the underlined word an adverb or an adjective?

> They worked <u>well</u>.
>
> The baby is <u>well</u>.

In the first sentence, *well* is an adverb modifying the verb worked. In the second sentence, *well* is an adjective modifying the noun *baby.* To choose correctly between adverbs and adjectives, remember that verbs of being link a noun to an adjective describing the noun. In contrast, you would use an adverb to describe an action verb.

Adjective	Adverb
He is a *good* worker. (What kind of worker is he?)	He works *well.* (How does he work?)
It is a *real* computer. (What kind of computer is it?)	It *really* is a computer. (To what extent is it a computer?)
The traffic is *slow.* (What quality does the traffic have?)	The traffic moves *slowly.* (How does the traffic move?)

1.5.1 Negative Adverbs

Negative adverbs (such as *neither, no, not, scarcely,* and *seldom*) are powerful words and therefore do not need any help in conveying a negative thought. In fact, using double negatives gives a strong impression of illiteracy, so avoid sentences like these:

I don't want no mistakes.
(Correct: "I don't want any mistakes," or "I want no mistakes.")

They couldn't hardly read the report.
(Correct: "They could hardly read the report," or "They couldn't read the report.")

They scarcely noticed neither one.
(Correct: "They scarcely noticed either one," or "They noticed neither one.")

1.5.2 Comparative Degree

Like adjectives, adverbs can be used to compare items. Generally, the basic adverb is combined with *more* or *most,* just as long adjectives are. However, some adverbs have one-word comparative forms:

One Item	Two Items	Three Items
quickly	more quickly	most quickly
sincerely	less sincerely	least sincerely
fast	faster	fastest
well	better	best

1.6 Other Parts of Speech

Nouns, pronouns, verbs, adjectives, and adverbs carry most of the meaning in a sentence. Four other parts of speech link them together in sentences: prepositions, conjunctions, articles, and interjections.

1.6.1 Prepositions

Prepositions are words like these:

of	to	for	with
at	by	from	about

Some prepositions consist of more than one word—like these:

because of   in addition to   out of   except for

And some prepositions are closely linked with a verb. When using phrases such as *look up* and *wipe out,* keep the phrase intact and do not insert anything between the verb and the preposition.

Prepositions most often begin prepositional phrases, which function like adjectives and adverbs by telling more about a pronoun, noun, or verb:

of a type	*by* Friday
to the point	*with* characteristic flair

To prevent misreading, prepositional phrases should be placed near the element they modify:

Of all our technicians, she is the best trained.

They couldn't see the merit *in my proposal.*

Someone left a folder *on my desk.*

It was once considered totally unacceptable to put a preposition at the end of a sentence. Now you may:

I couldn't tell what they were interested in.

What did she attribute it to?

However, be careful not to place prepositions at the end of sentences when doing so is unnecessary. In fact, avoid using any unnecessary preposition. In the following examples, the prepositions in parentheses should be omitted:

All (of) the staff members were present.

I almost fell off (of) my chair with surprise.

Where was Mr. Steuben going (to)?

They couldn't help (from) wondering.

The opposite problem is failing to include a preposition when you should. Consider the two sentences that follow:

Sales were over $100,000 for Linda and Bill.

Sales were over $100,000 for Linda and for Bill.

The first sentence indicates that Linda and Bill had combined sales over $100,000; the second, that Linda and Bill each had sales over $100,000, for a combined total in excess of $200,000. The preposition *for* is critical here.

Prepositions are also required in sentences like this one:

Which type of personal computer do you prefer?

Certain prepositions are used with certain words. When the same preposition can be used for two or more words in a sentence without affecting the meaning, only the last preposition is required:

We are familiar (*with*) and satisfied *with* your company's products.

But when different prepositions are normally used with the words, all the prepositions must be included:

We are familiar *with* and interested *in* your company's products.

Here is a partial list of prepositions that are used in a particular way with particular words:

among/between: *Among* is used to refer to three or more (*Circulate the memo among the staff*); *between* is used to refer to two (*Put the copy machine between Judy and Dan*).

as if/like: *As if* is used before a clause (*It seems as if we should be doing something*); *like* is used before a noun or pronoun (*He seems like a nice guy*).

have/of: *Have* is a verb used in verb phrases (*They should have checked first*); *of* is a preposition and is never used in such cases.

in/into: *In* is used to refer to a static position (*The file is in the cabinet*); *into* is used to refer to movement toward a position (*Put the file into the cabinet*).

And here is a partial list of some prepositions that have come to be used with certain words:

according to
agree to (a proposal)
agree with (a person)
buy from
capable of
comply with
conform to
differ from (things)
differ with (person)
different from
get from (receive)
get off (dismount)
in accordance with
in search of
independent of
inferior to
plan to
prefer to
prior to
reason with
responsible for
similar to
talk to (without interaction)
talk with (with interaction)
wait for (person or thing)
wait on (like a waiter)

1.6.2 Conjunctions

Conjunctions connect the parts of a sentence: words, phrases, and clauses. You are probably most familiar with coordinating conjunctions such as the following:

and	for	or	yet
but	nor	so	

Conjunctions may be used to connect clauses (which have both a subject and a predicate) with other clauses, to connect clauses with phrases (which do not have both a subject and a predicate), and to connect words with words:

We sell designer clothing *and* linens.
(Words with words)

Their products are expensive *but* still appeal to value-conscious consumers.
(Clauses with phrases)

I will call her on the phone today, *or* I will visit her office tomorrow.
(Clauses with clauses)

Some conjunctions are used in pairs:

both . . . and	neither . . . nor	whether . . . or
either . . . or	not only . . . but also	

With paired conjunctions, you must be careful to construct each phrase in the same way.

They *not only* are out of racquets *but also* are out of balls.

They are *not only* out of racquets *but also* out of balls.

They are out of *not only* racquets *but also* balls.

In other words, the construction that follows each part of the pair must be parallel, containing the same verbs, prepositions, and so on. The same need for parallelism exists when using conjunctions to join the other parts of speech:

He is listed in *either* your roster *or* my roster.

He is listed *neither* in your roster nor *on* the master list.

They *both* gave *and* received notice.

A certain type of conjunction is used to join clauses that are unequal—that is, to join a main clause to one that is subordinate or dependent. Here is a partial list of conjunctions used to introduce dependent clauses:

although	before	once	unless
as soon as	even though	so that	until
because	if	that	when

Using conjunctions is also discussed in sections 1.7.3 and 1.7.4.

1.6.3 Articles and Interjections

Only three articles exist in English: *the, a,* and *an.* These words are used, like adjectives, to specify which item you are talking about.

Interjections are words that express no solid information, only emotion:

Wow!	Well, well!
Oh, no!	Good!

Such purely emotional language has its place in private life and advertising copy, but it only weakens the effect of most business writing.

1.7 Sentences

Sentences are constructed with the major building blocks, the parts of speech.

Money talks.

This two-word sentence consists of a noun (*money*) and a verb (*talks*). When used in this way, the noun works as the first requirement for a sentence, the subject, and the verb works as the second requirement, the predicate. Now look at this sentence:

They merged.

The subject in this case is a pronoun (*they*), and the predicate is a verb (*merged*). This is a sentence because it has a subject and a predicate. Here is yet another kind of sentence:

The plans are ready.

This sentence has a more complicated subject, the noun *plans* and the article *the;* the complete predicate is a state-of-being verb (*are*) and an adjective (*ready*).

Without a subject (who or what does something) and a predicate (the doing of it), you have merely a collection of words, not a sentence.

1.7.1 Commands

In commands, the subject (always *you*) is only understood, not stated:

(You) Move your desk to the better office.

(You) Please try to finish by six o'clock.

1.7.2 Longer Sentences

More complicated sentences have more complicated subjects and predicates, but they still have a simple subject and a predicate verb. In the following examples, the subject is underlined once, the predicate verb twice:

Marex and Contron enjoy higher earnings each quarter.

(*Marex* [and] *Contron* do something; *enjoy* is what they do.)

My interview, coming minutes after my freeway accident, did not impress or move anyone.

(*Interview* is what did something. What did it do? It *did* [not] *impress* [or] *move.*)

In terms of usable space, a steel warehouse, with its extremely long span of roof unsupported by pillars, makes more sense.

(*Warehouse* is what *makes.*)

These three sentences demonstrate several things. First, in all three sentences, the simple subject and predicate verb are the "bare bones" of the sentence, the parts that carry the core idea of the sentence. When trying to find the subject and predicate verb, disregard all prepositional phrases, modifiers, conjunctions, and articles.

Second, in the third sentence the verb is singular (*makes*) because the subject is singular (*warehouse*). Even though the plural noun *pillars* is closer to the verb, *warehouse* is the subject. So *warehouse* determines whether the verb is singular or plural. Subject and predicate must agree.

Third, the subject in the first sentence is compound (*Marex* [and] *Contron*). A compound subject, when connected by *and,* requires a plural verb (*enjoy*). Also in the second sentence, compound predicates are possible (*did* [not] *impress* [or] *move*).

Fourth, the second sentence incorporates a group of words—*coming minutes after my freeway accident*—containing a form of a verb (*coming*) and a noun (*accident*). Yet this group of words is not a complete sentence for two reasons:

- Not all nouns are subjects: *Accident* is not the subject of *coming.*
- Not all verbs are predicates: A verb that ends in *ing* can never be the predicate of a sentence (unless preceded by a form of *to be,* as in *was coming*).

Because they don't contain a subject and a predicate, the words *coming minutes after my freeway accident* (called a phrase) can't be written as a sentence. That is, the phrase cannot stand alone; it cannot begin with a capital letter and end with a period. So a phrase must always be just one part of a sentence.

Sometimes a sentence incorporates two or more groups of words that do contain a subject and a predicate; these word groups are called clauses:

My *interview,* because it came minutes after my freeway accident, did not impress or move anyone.

The independent clause is the portion of the sentence that could stand alone without revision:

My interview did not impress or move anyone.

The other part of the sentence could stand alone only by removing *because:*

(because) It came minutes after my freeway accident.

This part of the sentence is known as a dependent clause; although it has a subject and a predicate (just as an independent clause does), it's linked to the main part of the sentence by a word (*because*) showing its dependence.

In summary, the two types of clauses—dependent and independent—both have a subject and a predicate. Dependent clauses, however, do not bear the main meaning of the sentence and are therefore linked to an independent clause. Nor can phrases stand alone, because they lack both a subject and a predicate. Only independent clauses can be written as sentences without revision.

1.7.3 Sentence Fragments

An incomplete sentence (a phrase or a dependent clause) that is written as though it were a complete sentence is called a fragment. Consider the following sentence fragments:

Marilyn Sanders, having had pilferage problems in her store for the past year. Refuses to accept the results of our investigation.

This serious error can easily be corrected by putting the two fragments together:

Marilyn Sanders, having had pilferage problems in her store for the past year, refuses to accept the results of our investigation.

Not all fragments can be corrected so easily. Here's more information on Sanders's pilferage problem.

Employees a part of it. No authority or discipline.

Only the writer knows the intended meaning of those two phrases. Perhaps the employees are taking part in the pilferage. If so, the sentence should read:

Some employees are part of the pilferage problem.

On the other hand, it's possible that some employees are helping with the investigation. Then the sentence would read:

> Some employees are taking part in our investigation.

It's just as likely, however, that the employees are not only taking part in the pilferage but are also being analyzed:

> Those employees who are part of the pilferage problem will accept no authority or discipline.

Even more meanings could be read into these fragments. Because fragments can mean so many things, they mean nothing. No well-written memo, letter, or report ever demands the reader to be an imaginative genius.

One more type of fragment exists, the kind represented by a dependent clause. Note what *because* does to change what was once a unified sentence:

> Our stock of sprinklers is depleted.
>
> Because our stock of sprinklers is depleted.

Although the second version contains a subject and a predicate, adding *because* makes it a fragment. Words such as *because* form a special group of words called subordinating conjunctions. Here's a partial list:

after	if	unless
although	since	whenever
even if	though	while

When a word of this type begins a clause, the clause is dependent and cannot stand alone as a sentence. However, if a dependent clause is combined with an independent clause, it can convey a complete meaning. The independent clause may come before or after the dependent clause:

> We are unable to fill your order because our stock of sprinklers is depleted.
>
> Because our stock of sprinklers is depleted, we are unable to fill your order.

Also, to fix a fragment that is a dependent clause, remove the subordinating conjunction. Doing so leaves a simple but complete sentence:

> Our stock of sprinklers is depleted.

The actual details of a situation will determine the best way for you to remedy a fragment problem.

The ban on fragments has one exception. Some advertising copy contains sentence fragments, written knowingly to convey a certain rhythm. However, advertising is the only area of business in which fragments are acceptable.

1.7.4 Fused Sentences and Comma Splices

Just as there can be too little in a group of words to make it a sentence, there can also be too much:

> All our mail is run through a postage meter every afternoon someone picks it up.

This example contains two sentences, not one, but the two have been blended so that it's hard to tell where one ends and the next begins. Is the mail run through a meter every afternoon? If so, the sentences should read:

> All our mail is run through a postage meter every afternoon. Someone picks it up.

Perhaps the mail is run through a meter at some other time (morning, for example) and is picked up every afternoon:

> All our mail is run through a postage meter. Every afternoon someone picks it up.

The order of words is the same in all three cases; sentence division makes all the difference. Either of the last two cases is grammatically correct. The choice depends on the facts of the situation.

Sometimes these so-called fused sentences have a more obvious point of separation:

> Several large orders arrived within a few days of one another, too many came in for us to process by the end of the month.

Here the comma has been put between two independent clauses in an attempt to link them. When a lowly comma separates two complete sentences, the result is called a comma splice. A comma splice can be remedied in one of three ways:

- Replace the comma with a period and capitalize the next word: ". . . one another. Too many . . . "
- Replace the comma with a semicolon and do not capitalize the next word: ". . . one another; too many . . . " This remedy works only when the two sentences have closely related meanings.
- Change one of the sentences so that it becomes a phrase or a dependent clause. This remedy often produces the best writing, but it takes more work.

The third alternative can be carried out in several ways. One is to begin the blended sentence with a subordinating conjunction:

> Whenever several large orders arrived within a few days of one another, too many came in for us to process by the end of the month.

Another way is to remove part of the subject or the predicate verb from one of the independent clauses, thereby creating a phrase:

> Several large orders arrived within a few days of one another, too many for us to process by the end of the month.

Finally, you can change one of the predicate verbs to its *ing* form:

> Several large orders arrived within a few days of one another, too many coming in for us to process by the end of the month.

At other times a simple coordinating conjunction (such as *or, and,* or *but*) can separate fused sentences:

> You can fire them, or you can make better use of their abilities.

Margaret drew up the designs, and Matt carried them out.

We will have three strong months, but after that sales will taper off.

Be careful using coordinating conjunctions: Use them only to join simple sentences that express similar ideas.

Also, because they say relatively little about the relationship between the two clauses they join, avoid using coordinating conjunctions too often: *and* is merely an addition sign; *but* is just a turn signal; *or* only points to an alternative. Subordinating conjunctions such as *because* and *whenever* tell the reader a lot more.

1.7.5 Sentences with Linking Verbs

Linking verbs were discussed briefly in the section on verbs (Section 1.3). Here you can see more fully the way they function in a sentence. The following is a model of any sentence with a linking verb:

A (*verb*) B.

Although words such as *seems* and *feels* can also be linking verbs, let's assume that the verb is a form of *to be:*

A *is* B.

In such a sentence, A and B are always nouns, pronouns, or adjectives. When one is a noun and the other is a pronoun, or when both are nouns, the sentence says that one is the same as the other:

She is president.

Rachel is president.

When one is an adjective, it modifies or describes the other:

She is forceful.

Remember that when one is an adjective, it modifies the other as any adjective modifies a noun or pronoun, except that a linking verb stands between the adjective and the word it modifies.

1.7.6 Misplaced Modifiers

The position of a modifier in a sentence is important. The movement of *only* changes the meaning in the following sentences:

Only we are obliged to supply those items specified in your contract.

We are obliged only to supply those items specified in your contract.

We are obliged to supply only those items specified in your contract.

We are obliged to supply those items specified only in your contract.

In any particular set of circumstances, only one of those sentences would be accurate. The others would very likely cause problems. To prevent misunderstanding, place such modifiers as close as possible to the noun or verb they modify.

For similar reasons, whole phrases that are modifiers must be placed near the right noun or verb. Mistakes in placement create ludicrous meanings.

Antia Information Systems has bought new computer chairs for the programmers *with more comfortable seats.*

The anatomy of programmers is not normally a concern of business writers. Obviously, the comfort of the chairs was the issue:

Antia Information Systems has bought new computer chairs *with more comfortable seats* for the programmers.

Here is another example:

I asked him to file all the letters in the cabinet that had been answered.

In this ridiculous sentence the cabinet has been answered, even though no cabinet in history is known to have asked a question.

That had been answered is too far from *letters* and too close to *cabinet.* Here's an improvement:

I asked him to file in the cabinet all the letters that had been answered.

In some cases, instead of moving the modifying phrase closer to the word it modifies, the best solution is to move the word closer to the modifying phrase.

2.0 Punctuation

On the highway, signs tell you when to slow down or stop, where to turn, when to merge. In similar fashion, punctuation helps readers negotiate your prose. The proper use of punctuation keeps readers from losing track of your meaning.

2.1 Periods

Use a period (1) to end any sentence that is not a question, (2) with certain abbreviations, and (3) between dollars and cents in an amount of money.

2.2 Question Marks

Use a question mark after any direct question that requests an answer:

Are you planning to enclose a check, or shall we bill you?

Don't use a question mark with commands phrased as questions for the sake of politeness:

Will you send us a check today.

2.3 Exclamation Points

Use exclamation points after highly emotional language. Because business writing almost never calls for emotional language, you will seldom use exclamation points.

2.4 Semicolons

Semicolons have three main uses. One is to separate two closely related independent clauses:

> The outline for the report is due within a week; the report itself is due at the end of the month.

A semicolon should also be used instead of a comma when the items in a series have commas within them:

> Our previous meetings were on November 11, 1998; February 20, 1999; and April 28, 2000.

Finally, a semicolon should be used to separate independent clauses when the second one begins with a word such as *however, therefore,* or *nevertheless* or a phrase such as *for example* or *in that case:*

> Our supplier has been out of part D712 for 10 weeks; however, we have found another source that can ship the part right away.

> His test scores were quite low; on the other hand, he has a lot of relevant experience.

Section 4.4 has more information on using transitional words and phrases.

2.5 Colons

Use a colon after the salutation in a business letter. You also use a colon at the end of a sentence or phrase introducing a list or (sometimes) a quotation:

> Our study included the three most critical problems: insufficient capital, incompetent management, and inappropriate location.

In some introductory sentences, phrases such as *the following* or *that is* are implied by using a colon.

A colon should not be used when the list, quotation, or idea is a direct object or part of the introductory sentence:

> We are able to supply
> staples
> wood screws
> nails
> toggle bolts

> This shipment includes 9 videotapes, 12 CDs, and 14 cassette tapes.

Another way you can use a colon is to separate the main clause and another sentence element when the second explains, illustrates, or amplifies the first:

> Management was unprepared for the union representatives' demands: this fact alone accounts for their arguing well into the night.

However, in contemporary usage, such clauses are frequently separated by a semicolon.

2.6 Commas

Commas have many uses; the most common is to separate items in a series:

> He took the job, learned it well, worked hard, and succeeded.

> Put paper, pencils, and paper clips on the requisition list.

Company style often dictates omitting the final comma in a series. However, if you have a choice, use the final comma; it's often necessary to prevent misunderstanding.

A second place to use a comma is between independent clauses that are joined by a coordinating conjunction (*and, but,* or *or*) unless one or both are very short:

> She spoke to the sales staff, and he spoke to the production staff.

> I was advised to proceed and I did.

A third use for the comma is to separate a dependent clause at the beginning of a sentence from an independent clause:

> Because of our lead in the market, we may be able to risk introducing a new product.

However, a dependent clause at the end of a sentence is separated from the independent clause by a comma only when the dependent clause is unnecessary to the main meaning of the sentence:

> We may be able to introduce a new product, although it may involve some risk.

A fourth use for the comma is after an introductory phrase or word:

> Starting with this amount of capital, we can survive in the red for one year.

> Through more careful planning, we may be able to serve more people.

> Yes, you may proceed as originally planned.

However, with short introductory prepositional phrases and some one-syllable words (such as *hence* and *thus*), the comma is often omitted:

> Before January 1 we must complete the inventory.

> Thus we may not need to hire anyone.

> In short the move to Tulsa was a good idea.

Fifth, commas are used to surround nonrestrictive phrases or words (expressions that can be removed from the sentence without changing the meaning):

> The new owners, the Kowacks, are pleased with their purchase.

Sixth, commas are used between adjectives modifying the same noun (coordinate adjectives):

> She left Monday for a long, difficult recruiting trip.

To test the appropriateness of such a comma, try reversing the order of the adjectives: *a difficult, long recruiting trip.* If the order cannot be reversed, leave out the comma (*a good old friend* isn't the same as *an old good friend*). A comma is also not used when one of the adjectives is part of the noun. Compare these two phrases:

> a distinguished, well-known figure

> a distinguished public figure

The adjective-noun combination of *public* and *figure* has been used together so often that it has come to be considered a single thing: *public figure*. So no comma is required.

Seventh, commas are used both before and after the year in sentences that include month, day, and year:

> It will be sent by December 15, 1999, from our Cincinnati plant.

Some companies write dates in another form: 15 December 2000. No commas should be used in that case. Nor is a comma needed when only the month and year are present (December 2000).

Eighth, commas are used to set off a variety of parenthetical words and phrases within sentences, including state names, dates, abbreviations, transitional expressions, and contrasted elements:

> They were, in fact, prepared to submit a bid.
>
> Our best programmer is Ken, who joined the company just a month ago.
>
> Habermacher, Inc., went public in 1999.
>
> Our goal was increased profits, not increased market share.
>
> Service, then, is our main concern.
>
> The factory was completed in Chattanooga, Tennessee, just three weeks ago.
>
> Joanne Dubiik, M.D., has applied for a loan from First Savings.
>
> I started work here on March 1, 2001, and soon received my first promotion.

Ninth, a comma is used to separate a quotation from the rest of the sentence:

> Your warranty reads, "These conditions remain in effect for one year from date of purchase."

However, the comma is left out when the quotation as a whole is built into the structure of the sentence:

> He hurried off with an angry "Look where you're going."

Finally, a comma should be used whenever it's needed to avoid confusion or an unintended meaning. Compare the following:

> Ever since they have planned new ventures more carefully.
>
> Ever since, they have planned new ventures more carefully.

2.7 Dashes

Use a dash to surround a comment that is a sudden turn in thought:

> Membership in the IBSA—it's expensive but worth it—may be obtained by applying to our New York office.

A dash can also be used to emphasize a parenthetical word or phrase:

> Third-quarter profits—in excess of $2 million—are up sharply.

Finally, use dashes to set off a phrase that contains commas:

> All our offices—Milwaukee, New Orleans, and Phoenix—have sent representatives.

Don't confuse a dash with a hyphen. A dash separates and emphasizes words, phrases, and clauses more strongly than a comma or parentheses can; a hyphen ties two words so tightly that they almost become one word.

On computer, use the em dash symbol. When typing a dash in e-mail or on a typewriter, type two hyphens with no space before, between, or after.

2.8 Hyphens

Hyphens are mainly used in three ways. The first is to separate the parts of compound words beginning with such prefixes as *self-*, *ex-*, *quasi-*, and *all-*:

self-assured	quasi-official
ex-wife	all-important

However, omit hyphens from and close up those words that have prefixes such as *pro, anti, non, re, pre, un, inter,* and *extra:*

prolabor	nonunion
antifascist	interdepartmental

Exceptions occur when (1) the prefix occurs before a proper noun, or (2) the vowel at the end of the prefix is the same as the first letter of the root word:

pro-Republican	anti-American
anti-inflammatory	extra-atmospheric

When in doubt, consult your dictionary.

Hyphens are also used in some compound adjectives, which are adjectives made up of two or more words. Specifically, you should use hyphens in compound adjectives that come before the noun:

> an interest-bearing account   well-informed executives

However, you need not hyphenate when the adjective follows a linking verb:

> This account is interest bearing.
>
> Their executives are well informed.

You can shorten sentences that list similar hyphenated words by dropping the common part from all but the last word:

> Check the costs of first-, second-, and third-class postage.

Finally, hyphens may be used to divide words at the end of a typed line. Such hyphenation is best avoided, but when you have to divide words at the end of a line, do so correctly (see Section 3.5). A dictionary will show how words are divided into syllables.

2.9 Apostrophes

Use an apostrophe in the possessive form of a noun (but not in a pronoun):

> On *his* desk was a reply to Bette *Ainsley's* application for the *manager's* position.

Apostrophes are also used in place of the missing letter(s) of a contraction:

Whole Words	**Contraction**
we will	we'll
do not	don't
they are	they're

2.10 Quotation Marks

Use quotation marks to surround words that are repeated exactly as they were said or written:

> The collection letter ended by saying, "This is your third and final notice."

Remember: (1) When the quoted material is a complete sentence, the first word is capitalized. (2) The final comma or period goes inside the closing quotation marks.

Quotation marks are also used to set off the title of a newspaper story, magazine article, or book chapter:

> You should read "Legal Aspects of the Collection Letter" in *Today's Credit.*

The book title is shown here in italics. When typewritten, the title is underlined. The same treatment is proper for newspaper and magazine titles. (Appendix B explains documentation style in more detail.)

Quotation marks may also be used to indicate special treatment for words or phrases, such as terms that you're using in an unusual or ironic way:

> Our management "team" spends more time squabbling than working to solve company problems.

When you are defining a word, put the definition in quotation marks:

> The abbreviation *etc.* means "and so forth."

When using quotation marks, take care to insert the closing marks as well as the opening ones.

Although periods and commas go inside any quotation marks, colons and semicolons go outside them. A question mark goes inside the quotation marks only if the quotation is a question:

> All that day we wondered, "Is he with us?"

If the quotation is not a question but the entire sentence is, the question mark goes outside:

> What did she mean by "You will hear from me"?

2.11 Parentheses

Use parentheses to surround comments that are entirely incidental:

> Our figures do not match yours, although (if my calculations are correct) they are closer than we thought.

Parentheses are also used in legal documents to surround figures in arabic numerals that follow the same amount in words:

> Remittance will be One Thousand Two Hundred Dollars ($1,200).

Be careful to put punctuation (period, comma, and so on) outside the parentheses unless it is part of the statement in parentheses.

2.12 Ellipses

Use ellipsis points, or dots, to indicate that material has been left out of a direct quotation. Use them only in direct quotations and only at the point where material was left out. In the following example, the first sentence is quoted in the second:

> The Dow Jones Industrial Average, which skidded 38.17 points in the previous five sessions, gained 4.61 to end at 2213.84.

> According to the Honolulu *Star Bulletin*, "The Dow Jones Industrial Average . . . gained 4.61" on June 10.

The number of dots in ellipses is not optional; always use three. Occasionally, the points of ellipsis come at the end of a sentence, where they seem to grow a fourth dot. Don't be fooled: One of the dots is a period.

3.0 Mechanics

The most obvious and least tolerable mistakes that a business writer makes are probably those related to grammar and punctuation. However, a number of small details, known as writing mechanics, demonstrate the writer's polish and reflect on the company's professionalism.

3.1 Capitals

Capitals are used at the beginning of certain word groups:

- **Complete sentence:** *Before* hanging up, he said, "*We'll* meet here on Wednesday at noon."
- **Formal statement following a colon:** She has a favorite motto: Where there's a will, there's a way. (Otherwise, the first word after a colon should not be capitalized—see Section 2.5.)
- **Phrase used as sentence:** Absolutely not!
- **Quoted sentence embedded in another sentence:** Scot said, "Nobody was here during lunch hour except me."
- **List of items set off from text:** Three preliminary steps are involved:
  Design review
  Budgeting
  Scheduling

Capitalize proper adjectives and proper nouns (the names of particular persons, places, and things):

> Darrell Greene lived in a Victorian mansion.

> We sent Ms. Larson an application form, informing her that not all applicants are interviewed.

> Let's consider opening a branch in the West, perhaps at the west end of Tucson, Arizona.

> As office buildings go, the Kinney Building is a pleasant setting for TDG Office Equipment.

Ms. Larson's name is capitalized because she is a particular applicant, whereas the general term *applicant* is left uncapitalized.

Likewise, *West* is capitalized when it refers to a particular place but not when it means a direction. In the same way, *office* and *building* are not capitalized when they are general terms (common nouns), but they are capitalized when they are part of the title of a particular office or building (proper nouns).

Titles within families, governments, or companies may also be capitalized:

> I turned down Uncle David when he offered me a job, since I wouldn't be comfortable working for one of my relatives.
>
> We've never had a president quite like President Sweeney.

People's titles are capitalized when they are used in addressing a person, especially in a formal context. They are not usually capitalized, however, when they are used merely to identify the person:

> Address the letter to Chairperson Anna Palmer.
>
> I wish to thank Chairperson Anna Palmer for her assistance.
>
> Please deliver these documents to board chairperson Anna Palmer.
>
> Anna Palmer, chairperson of the board, took the podium.

Also capitalize titles if they are used by themselves in addressing a person:

> Thank you, Doctor, for your donation.

Always capitalize the first word of the salutation and complimentary close of a letter:

> *Dear* Mr. Andrews: *Yours* very truly,

The names of organizations are capitalized, of course; so are the official names of their departments and divisions. However, do not use capitals when referring in general terms to a department or division, especially one in another organization:

> Route this memo to Personnel.
>
> Larry Tien was transferred to the Microchip Division,
>
> Will you be enrolled in the Psychology Department?
>
> Someone from the engineering department at EnerTech stopped by the booth.
>
> Our production department has reorganized for efficiency.
>
> Send a copy to their school of business administration.

Capitalization is unnecessary when using a word like *company, corporation,* or *university* alone:

> The corporation plans to issue 50,000 shares of common stock.

Likewise, the names of specific products are capitalized, although the names of general product types are not:

> Compaq computer   Tide laundry detergent

One problem that often arises in writing about places is the treatment of two or more proper nouns of the same type. When the common word comes before the specific names, it is capitalized; when it comes after the specific names, it is not:

> Lakes Ontario and Huron
>
> Allegheny and Monongahela rivers

The names of languages, races, and ethnic groups are capitalized: *Japanese, Caucasian, Hispanic.* But racial terms that denote only skin color are not capitalized: *black, white.*

When referring to the titles of books, articles, magazines, newspapers, reports, movies, and so on, you should capitalize the first and last words and all nouns, pronouns, adjectives, verbs, adverbs, and prepositions and conjunctions with five letters or more. Except for the first and last words, do not capitalize articles:

> *Economics During the Great War*
>
> "An Investigation into the Market for Long-Distance Services"
>
> "What Successes Are Made Of"

When *the* is part of the official name of a newspaper or magazine, it should be treated this way too: *The Wall Street Journal.*

References to specific pages, paragraphs, lines, and the like are not capitalized: *page 73, line 3.* However, in most other numbered or lettered references, the identifying term is capitalized: *Chapter 4, Serial No. 382–2203, Item B-11.*

Finally, the names of academic degrees are capitalized when they follow a person's name but are not capitalized when used in a general sense:

> I received a bachelor of science degree.
>
> Thomas Whitelaw, Doctor of Philosophy, will attend.

Similarly, general courses of study are not capitalized, but the names of specific classes are:

> She studied accounting as an undergraduate.
>
> She is enrolled in Accounting 201.

3.2 Underscores and Italics

Usually a line typed underneath a word or phrase either provides emphasis or indicates the title of a book, magazine, or newspaper. If possible, use italics instead of an underscore. Italics (or underlining) should also be used for defining terms and for discussing words as words:

> In this report *net sales* refers to after-tax sales dollars.
>
> The word *building* is a common noun and should not be capitalized.

3.3 Abbreviations

Abbreviations are used heavily in tables, charts, lists, and forms. They're used sparingly in prose paragraphs, however. Here are some abbreviations often used in business writing:

Abbreviation	Full Term
b/l	bill of lading
ca.	circa (about)
dol., dols.	dollar, dollars
etc.	et cetera (and so on)
FDIC	Federal Deposit Insurance Corporation
Inc.	Incorporated
L.f.	Ledger folio
Ltd.	Limited
mgr.	manager
NSF or N/S	not sufficient funds
P&L or P/L	profit and loss
reg.	regular
whsle.	wholesale

One way to handle an abbreviation that you want to use throughout a document is to spell it out the first time you use it, follow it with the abbreviation in parentheses, and then use the abbreviation in the remainder of the document.

Because *etc.* contains a word meaning "and," never write *and etc.* In fact, try to limit your use of such abbreviations to tables and parenthetical material.

3.4 Numbers

Numbers may be correctly handled many ways in business writing, so follow company style. In the absence of a set style, however, generally spell out all numbers from one to nine and use arabic numerals for the rest.

There are some exceptions to this general rule. For example, never begin a sentence with a numeral:

> *Twenty* of us produced *641* units per week in the first *12* weeks of the year.

Use numerals for the numbers one through ten if they're in the same list as larger numbers:

> Our weekly quota rose from *9* to *15* to *27*.

Use numerals for percentages, time of day (except with *o'clock*), dates, and (in general) dollar amounts.

> Our division is responsible for *7* percent of total sales.
>
> The meeting is scheduled for *8:30* A.M. on August *2*.
>
> Add *$3* for postage and handling.

Use a comma in numbers expressing thousands (*1,257*), unless your company specifies another style. When dealing with numbers in the millions and billions, combine words and figures: *7.3 million, 2 billion.*

When writing dollar amounts, use a decimal point only if cents are included. In lists of two or more dollar amounts, use the decimal point either for all or for none:

> He sent two checks, one for *$67.92* and one for *$90.00.*

When two numbers fall next to each other in a sentence, use figures for the number that is largest, most difficult to spell, or part of a physical measurement; use words for the other:

> I have learned to manage a classroom of 30 twelve-year-olds.
>
> She's won a bonus for selling 24 thirty-volume sets.
>
> You'll need twenty 3-inch bolts.

In addresses, all street numbers except *One* are in figures. So are suite and room numbers and ZIP codes. For street names that are numbered, practice varies so widely that you should use the form specified on an organization's letterhead or in a reliable directory. All of the following examples are correct:

> One Fifth Avenue   297 Ninth Street
>
> 1839 44th Street   11026 West 78 Place

Telephone numbers are always expressed in figures. Parentheses may separate the area code from the rest of the number, but a slash or a dash may be used instead, especially if the entire phone number is enclosed in parentheses:

> 382–8329   (602/382–8329)   602–382–8329

Percentages are always expressed in figures. The word *percent* is used in most cases, but % may be used in tables, forms, and statistical writing.

Physical measurements such as distance, weight, and volume are also often expressed in figures: *9 kilometers, 5 feet 3 inches, 7 pounds 10 ounces.*

Ages are usually expressed in words—except when a parenthetical reference to age follows someone's name:

> Mrs. Margaret Sanderson is seventy-two.
>
> Mrs. Margaret Sanderson, 72, swims daily.

Also, ages expressed in years and months are treated like physical measurements that combine two units of measure: *5 years 6 months.*

Decimal numbers are always written in figures. In most cases, add a zero to the left of the decimal point if the number is less than one and does not already start with a zero:

> 1.38   .07   0.2

In a series of related decimal numbers with at least one number greater than one, make sure that all numbers smaller than one have a zero to the left of the decimal point: *1.20, 0.21, 0.09.* Also, express all decimal numbers in a series to the same number of places by adding zeroes at the end:

> The responses were Yes, 37.2 percent; No, 51.0; Not Sure, 11.8.

Simple fractions are written in words, but more complicated fractions are expressed in figures or, if easier to read, in figures and words:

two-thirds   9/32   2 hundredths

A combination of whole numbers and a fraction should always be written in figures. Note that a hyphen is used to separate the fraction from the whole number when a slash is used for the fraction: *2–11/16.*

3.5 Word Division

In general, avoid dividing words at the ends of lines. When you must do so, follow these rules:

- Don't divide one-syllable words (such as *since, walked,* and *thought*); abbreviations (*mgr.*); contractions (*isn't*); or numbers expressed in numerals (*117,500*).
- Divide words between syllables, as specified in a dictionary or word-division manual.
- Make sure that at least three letters of the divided word are moved to the second line: *sin-cerely* instead of *sincere-ly.*
- Do not end a page or more than three consecutive lines with hyphens.
- Leave syllables consisting of a single vowel at the end of the first line (*impedi-ment* instead of *imped-iment*), except when the single vowel is part of a suffix such as *-able, -ible, -ical,* or *-ity* (*re-spons-ible* instead of *re-sponsi-ble*).
- Divide between double letters (*tomor-row*), except when the root word ends in double letters (*call-ing* instead of *cal-ling*).
- Wherever possible, divide hyphenated words at the hyphen only: instead of *anti-inde-pendence,* use *anti-independence.*

4.0 Vocabulary

Using the right word in the right place is a crucial skill in business communication. However, many pitfalls await the unwary.

4.1 Frequently Confused Words

Because the following sets of words sound similar, be careful not to use one when you mean to use the other:

Word	Meaning
accede exceed	to comply with to go beyond
accept except	to take to exclude
access excess	admittance too much
advice advise	suggestion to suggest
affect effect	to influence the result
allot a lot	to distribute much or many
all ready already	completely prepared completed earlier
born borne	given birth to carried
capital capitol	money; chief city a government building
cite sight site	to quote a view a location
complement compliment	complete amount; to go well with expression of esteem; to flatter
corespondent correspondent	party in a divorce suit letter writer
council counsel	a panel of people advice; a lawyer
defer differ	to put off until later to be different
device devise	a mechanism to plan
die dye	to stop living; a tool to color
discreet discrete	careful separate
envelop envelope	to surround a covering for a letter
forth fourth	forward number four
holey holy wholly	full of holes sacred completely
human humane	of people kindly
incidence incidents	frequency events
instance instants	example moments
interstate intrastate	between states within a state
later latter	afterward the second of two
lead led	a metal; to guide guided

lean	to rest at an angle
lien	a claim
levee	embankment
levy	tax
loath	reluctant
loathe	to hate
loose	free; not tight
lose	to mislay
material	substance
materiel	equipment
miner	mineworker
minor	underage person
moral	virtuous; a lesson
morale	sense of well-being
ordinance	law
ordnance	weapons
overdo	to do in excess
overdue	past due
peace	lack of conflict
piece	a fragment
pedal	a foot lever
peddle	to sell
persecute	to torment
prosecute	to sue
personal	private
personnel	employees
precedence	priority
precedents	previous events
principal	sum of money; chief; main
principle	general rule
rap	to knock
wrap	to cover
residence	home
residents	inhabitants
right	correct
rite	ceremony
write	to form words on a surface
role	a part to play
roll	to tumble; a list
root	part of a plant
rout	to defeat
route	a traveler's way
shear	to cut
sheer	thin, steep
stationary	immovable
stationery	paper
than	as compared with
then	at that time
their	belonging to them
there	in that place
they're	they are
to	a preposition
too	excessively; also
two	the number
waive	to set aside
wave	a swell of water; a gesture
weather	atmospheric conditions
whether	if
who's	contraction of "who is" or "who has"
whose	possessive form of who

In the preceding list, only enough of each word's meaning is given to help you distinguish between the words in each group. Several meanings are left out entirely. For more complete definitions, consult a dictionary.

4.2 Frequently Misused Words

The following words tend to be misused for reasons other than their sound. Reference books (including the *Random House College Dictionary*, revised edition; Follett's *Modern American Usage;* and Fowler's *Modern English Usage*) can help you with similar questions of usage.

a lot: When the writer means "many," *a lot* is always two separate words, never one.

correspond with: Use this phrase when you are talking about exchanging letters. Use *correspond to* when you mean "similar to." Use either *correspond with* or *correspond to* when you mean "relate to."

disinterested: This word means "fair, unbiased, having no favorites, impartial." If you mean "bored" or "not interested," use *uninterested.*

etc.: This abbreviated form of the Latin phrase *et cetera* means "and so on" or "and so forth." The current tendency among business writers is to use English rather than Latin.

imply/infer: Both refer to hints. Their great difference lies in who is acting. The writer implies; the reader infers, sees between the lines.

lay: This word is a transitive verb. Never use it for the intransitive *lie.* (See Section 1.3.3.)

less: Use *less* for uncountable quantities (such as amounts of water, air, sugar, and oil). Use *fewer* for countable quantities (such as numbers of jars, saws, words, pages, and humans). The same distinction applies to *much* and *little* (uncountable) versus *many* and *few* (countable).

like: Use *like* only when the word that follows is just a noun or a pronoun. Use *as* or *as if* when a phrase or clause follows:

She looks like him.

She did just as he had expected.

It seems as if she had plenty of time.

many/much: See *less.*

regardless: The *less* ending is the negative part. No word needs two negative parts, so don't add *ir* (a negative prefix) to the beginning. There is no such word as *irregardless.*

to me/personally: Use these phrases only when personal reactions, apart from company policy, are being stated (not often the case in business writing).

try: Always follow with *to,* never *and.*

verbal: People in the business community who are careful with language frown on those who use *verbal* to mean "spoken" or "oral." Many others do say "verbal agreement." Strictly speaking, *verbal* means "of words" and therefore includes both spoken and written words. Follow company usage in this matter.

4.3 Frequently Misspelled Words

All of us, even the world's best spellers, sometimes have to check a dictionary for the spelling of some words. People who have never memorized the spelling of commonly used words must look up so many that they grow exasperated and give up on spelling words correctly.

Don't expect perfection, and don't surrender. If you can memorize the spelling of just the words listed here, you'll need the dictionary far less often, and you'll write with more confidence.

absence
absorption
accessible
accommodate
accumulate
achieve
advantageous
affiliated
aggressive
alignment
aluminum
ambience
analyze
apparent
appropriate
argument
asphalt
assistant
asterisk
auditor

bankruptcy
believable
brilliant
bulletin

calendar
campaign
category
ceiling
changeable
clientele
collateral
committee
comparative
competitor
concede
congratulations
connoisseur
consensus
convenient
convertible
corroborate
criticism

definitely
description
desirable
dilemma
disappear
disappoint
disbursement
discrepancy
dissatisfied
dissipate

eligible
embarrassing
endorsement
exaggerate
exceed
exhaust
existence
extraordinary

fallacy
familiar
flexible
fluctuation
forty

gesture
grievous

haphazard
harassment
holiday

illegible
immigrant
incidentally
indelible
independent
indispensable
insistent
intermediary
irresistible

jewelry
judgment
judicial

labeling
legitimate
leisure
license
litigation

maintenance
mathematics
mediocre
minimum
necessary
negligence
negotiable
newsstand
noticeable

occurrence
omission

parallel
pastime
peaceable
permanent
perseverance
persistent
personnel
persuade
possesses
precede
predictable
preferred
privilege
procedure
proceed
pronunciation
psychology
pursue

questionnaire

receive
recommend
repetition
rescind
rhythmical
ridiculous

salable
secretary
seize
separate
sincerely
succeed
suddenness
superintendent
supersede
surprise

tangible
tariff
technique
tenant
truly

unanimous
until

vacillate
vacuum
vicious

4.4 Transitional Words and Phrases

The following sentences don't communicate as well as they might because they lack a transitional word or phrase:

> Production delays are inevitable. Our current lag time in filling orders is one month.

A semicolon between the two sentences would signal a close relationship between their meanings, but it wouldn't even hint at what that relationship is. Here are the sentences again, now linked by means of a semicolon, with a space for a transitional word or phrase:

> Production delays are inevitable; ______________ , our current lag time in filling orders is one month.

Now read the sentence with *nevertheless* in the blank space. Now try *therefore, incidentally, in fact,* and *at any rate* in the blank. Each substitution changes the meaning of the sentence.

Here are some transitional words (called conjunctive adverbs) that will help you write more clearly:

accordingly	furthermore	moreover
anyway	however	otherwise
besides	incidentally	still
consequently	likewise	therefore
finally	meanwhile	

The following transitional phrases are used in the same way:

as a result	in other words
at any rate	in the second place
for example	on the other hand
in fact	to the contrary

When one of these words or phrases joins two independent clauses, it should be preceded by a semicolon and followed by a comma, as shown here:

> The consultant recommended a complete reorganization; moreover, she suggested that we drop several products.

CHAPTER 1

1. Kara Parlin, "Reaching Out to Customers," *Internet World*, February 2003, 26; "American Airlines Federal Credit Union Deploys LivePerson MultiCARE Solution," 11 June 2002 [accessed 15 October 2003] www.liveperson.com; "American Airlines Federal Credit Union and LivePerson Make Customer Service a Profitable Investment," 4 September 2002 [accessed 15 October 2003] www.liveperson.com; "Banking Companies Realize Customers Want One-on-One Attention," *Dallas Morning News*, February 2003 [accessed 15 October 2003] www.elibrary.com.
2. Richard L. Daft, *Management*, 6th ed. (Cincinnati: Thomson South-Western, 2003), 580.
3. Daft, *Management*, 147.
4. Gareth R. Jones and Jennifer M. George, *Contemporary Management*, 3rd ed. (New York: McGraw-Hill Irwin, 2003), 512, 517.
5. Paula Jacobs, "Strong Writing Skills Essential for Success, Even in IT," *InfoWorld*, 6 July 1998, 86.
6. Philip C. Kolin, *Successful Writing at Work*, 6th ed. (Boston: Houghton Mifflin, 2001), 17–23.
7. Donald O. Wilson, "Diagonal Communication Links with Organizations," *Journal of Business Communication* 29, no. 2 (Spring 1992): 129–143.
8. J. David Johnson, William A. Donohoe, Charles K. Atkin, and Sally Johnson, "Differences Between Formal and Informal Communication Channels," *Journal of Business Communication* 31, no. 2 (1994): 111–122.
9. David Pescovitz, "Technology of the Year: Social Network Applications," *Business 2.0*, November 2003, 113–114.
10. Daft, *Management*, 107.
11. J. Michael Sproule, *Communication Today* (Glenview, Ill.: Scott Foresman, 1981), 329.
12. Carol Hymowitz, "If the Walls Had Ears You Wouldn't Have Any Less Privacy," *Wall Street Journal*, 19 May 1998, B1.
13. Kenneth Hein, "Hungry for Feedback," *Incentive*, September 1997, 9+.
14. Daft, *Management*, 614; James M. Citrin and Thomas J. Neff, "Digital Leadership," *Strategy and Business*, First Quarter 2000, 42–50; Gary L. Neilson, Bruce A. Pasternack, and Albert J. Viscio, "Up the E-Organization," *Strategy and Business*, First Quarter 2000, 52–61.
15. Thomas S. Bateman and Scott A. Snell, *Management: Competing in the New Era* (New York: McGraw-Hill Irwin, 2002), 472, 474; Gretel Johnston, "We've Got Mail: 60 Billion Daily," PC World.com [accessed 2 October 2002] www.pcworld.com/news/article/0%2Caid%2C105525%2C00.asp.
16. Chuck Williams, *Management*, 2nd ed. (Cincinnati: Thomson/South-Western, 2002), 690.
17. Don Hellriegel, Susan E. Jackson, and John W. Slocum, Jr., *Management: A Competency-Based Approach*, (Cincinnati: Thomson/South-Western, 2002), 447.
18. Shirley Duglin Kennedy, "Finding a Cure for Information Anxiety," *Information Today*, May 2001, 40+.
19. Hellriegel et al., *Management: A Competency-Based Approach*, 451.
20. John Owens, "Good Communication in Workplace Is Basic to Getting Any Job Done," *Knight Ridder Tribune Business News*, 9 July 2003, 1.
21. Tamar Lewin, "Study Finds Widespread Neglect of Writing Skills," *Desert Sun*, 26 April 2003, A12.
22. Williams, *Management*, 706–707.
23. Jane Spencer, "The Annoying New Face of Customer Service—Virtual Phone Reps Replace the Old Touch-Tone Menus; Making Claire Less Irritating," *Wall Street Journal*, 21 January 2003, D1; Allison Fass, "Speak Easy," *Forbes*, 6 January 2003, 135.
24. "FNB Moves to Quell Fears (uses SMS)," News24.com, 24 July 2003 [accessed 12 August 2003] www.news24.com/News24/Finance/Companies/0,,2-8-24_1392154,00.html; Daft, *Management*, 701–702.
25. Gregory A Maciag, "Finding the Right Medium for the Message," *National Underwriter*, 20 October 1997, 19–21.
26. Weld Royal, "Is Your CEO a Computer Geek?" *Industry Week*, 5 March 2001, 26+.
27. A. Thomas Young, "Ethics in Business: Business of Ethics," *Vital Speeches*, 15 September 1992, 725–730.
28. Kolin, *Successful Writing at Work*, 24–30.
29. David Grier, "Confronting Ethical Dilemmas: The View from Inside—A Practitioner's Perspective," *Vital Speeches*, 1 December 1989, 100–104.
30. Anthony Breznican, "Fake Movie Reviews Prompt Investigation," *Washington Times*, 7 June 2001, C6.
31. Daft, *Management*, 155.
32. Daft, *Management*, 157.
33. Maryann Napoli, "Rx News: Dietary Supplement Labels Are Found Wanting," *HealthFacts*, 1 June 2003, 5.
34. Based in part on Robert Kreitner, *Management*, 9th ed. (Boston: Houghton Mifflin), 163.

CHAPTER 2

1. Mike Duff, "Top-Shelf Employees Keep Container Store on Track," *DSN Retailing Today*, 8 March 2004, 49; Holly Hayes, "Container Store Brings Clutter Control to San Jose, Calif.," *San Jose Mercury News*, 17 October 2003, 1F; "Performance Through People Award" press release, 10 September 2003; David Lipke, "Container Store's CEO: People Are Most Valued Asset," *HFN*, 13 January 2003 [accessed 9 March 2004] www.highbeam.com; Lorrie Grant, "Container Store's Workers Huddle Up To Help You Out," *USA Today*, 30 April 2002, B.1; "Learn About Us," The Container Store Website, [accessed 23 October 2003], www.containerstore.com.
2. Michael H. Mescon, Courtland L. Bovée, and John V. Thill, *Business Today* (Upper Saddle River, N.J.: Prentice Hall, 1999), 203.
3. Ellen Neuborne, "Companies Save, But Workers Pay," *USA Today*, 25 February 1997, B1; Richard L. Daft, *Management*, 6th ed. (Cincinnati: Thomson South-Western, 2003), 594–595; Stephen P. Robbins and David A. DeCenzo, *Fundamentals of Management*, 2d ed. (Upper Saddle River, N.J.: Prentice Hall, 1998), 336–338.
4. Daft, *Management*, 614.
5. "Five Case Studies on Successful Teams," *HR Focus*, April 2002, 18+.
6. Lynda McDermott, Bill Waite, and Nolan Brawley, "Executive Teamwork," *Executive Excellence*, May 1999, 15.
7. Larry Cole and Michael Cole, "Why Is the Teamwork Buzz Word Not Working?" *Communication World*, February–March 1999, 29; Patricia Buhler, "Managing in the 90s: Creating Flexibility in Today's Workplace," *Supervision*, January 1997, 24+; Allison

W. Amason, Allen C. Hochwarter, Wayne A. Thompson, and Kenneth R. Harrison, "Conflict: An Important Dimension in Successful Management Teams," *Organizational Dynamics*, Autumn 1995, 20+.

8. Daft, *Management*, 614.
9. Vijay Govindarajan and Anil K. Gupta, "Building an Effective Global Business Team," *MIT Sloan Management Review*, Summer 2001, 63+.
10. Stephen R. Robbins, *Essentials of Organizational Behavior*, 6th ed. (Upper Saddle River, N.J.: Prentice Hall, 2000), 98.
11. Jon Hanke, "Presenting as a Team," *Presentations*, January 1998, 74–82.
12. William P. Galle, Jr., Beverly H. Nelson, Donna W. Luse, and Maurice F. Villere, *Business Communication: A Technology-Based Approach* (Chicago: Irwin, 1996), 260.
13. Mary Beth Debs, "Recent Research on Collaborative Writing in Industry," *Technical Communication* November 1991, 476–484.
14. B. Aubrey Fisher, *Small Group Decision Making: Communication and the Group Process*, 2d ed. (New York: McGraw-Hill, 1980), 145–149; Robbins and DeCenzo, *Fundamentals of Management*, 334–335; Daft, *Management*, 602–603.
15. Daft, *Management*, 609–612.
16. Thomas K. Capozzoli, "Conflict Resolution—A Key Ingredient in Successful Teams," *Supervision*, November 1999, 14–16.
17. Janis Graham, "Sharpen Your Negotiating Skills," *Sylvia Porter's Personal Finance*, December 1985, 54–58.
18. Amason, Hochwarter, Thompson, and Harrison, "Conflict."
19. Jesse S. Nirenberg, *Getting Through to People* (Paramus, N.J.: Prentice Hall, 1973), 134–142.
20. Nirenberg, *Getting Through to People.*
21. Nirenberg, *Getting Through to People.*
22. Dana May Casperson, *Power Etiquette: What You Don't Know Can Kill Your Career* (New York: AMACOM, 1999), 9.
23. Marilyn Pincus, *Everyday Business Etiquette* (Hauppauge, N.Y.: Barron's Educational Series, 1996), 7, 133.
24. Pincus, *Everyday Business Etiquette*, 136.
25. Casperson, *Power Etiquette: What You Don't Know Can Kill Your Career*, 23.
26. Gerald H. Graham, Jeanne Unrue, and Paul Jennings, "The Impact of Nonverbal Communication in Organizations: A Survey of Perceptions," *Journal of Business Communication* 28, no. 1 (Winter 1991): 45–62.
27. Pincus, *Everyday Business Etiquette*, 100–101.
28. Alf Nucifora, "Voice Mail Demands Good Etiquette from Both Sides," *Puget Sound Business Journal*, 5–11 September 2003, 24; Ruth Davidhizar and Ruth Shearer, "The Effective Voice Mail Message," *Hospital Material Management Quarterly*, 45–49; "How to Get the Most Out of Voice Mail," *The CPA Journal*, February 2000, 11.
29. Maggie Jackson, "Turn Off That Cellphone. It's Meeting Time," *New York Times*, 2 March 2003, 3.12.
30. Casperson, *Power Etiquette: What You Don't Know Can Kill Your Career*, 10–14; Ellyn Spragins, "Introducing Politeness," *Fortune Small Business*, November 2001, 30.
31. Tanya Mohn, "The Social Graces As a Business Tool," *New York Times*, 10 November 2002, 3.12.
32. Casperson, *Power Etiquette: What You Don't Know Can Kill Your Career*, 19; Pincus, *Everyday Business Etiquette*, 7–8.
33. Casperson, *Power Etiquette: What You Don't Know Can Kill Your Career*, 44–46.
34. Casperson, *Power Etiquette: What You Don't Know Can Kill Your Career*, 109–110.
35. "Better Meetings Benefit Everyone: How to Make Yours More Productive," *Working Communicator Bonus Report*, July 1998, 1.
36. Ken Blanchard, "Meetings Can Be Effective," *Supervisory Management*, October 1992, 5.
37. "Better Meetings Benefit Everyone."
38. Kathleen Melymuka, "Far from the Mothership," *Computerworld*, 9 December 2002, 47.
39. Jefferson Graham, "Instant Messaging Programs Are No Longer Just for Messages," *USA Today*, 20 October 2003, 5D; Todd R. Weiss, "Microsoft Targets Corporate Instant Messaging Customers," *Computerworld*, 18 November 2002, 12; "Banks Adopt Instant Messaging to Create a Global Business Network," *Computer Weekly*, 25 April 2002, 40; Michael D. Osterman, "Instant Messaging in the Enterprise," *Business Communications Review*, January 2003, 59–62; John Pallato, "Instant Messaging Unites Work Groups and Inspires Collaboration," *Internet World*, December 2002, 14+.
40. Mark Gibbs, "Racing to Instant Messaging," *NetworkWorld*, 17 February 2003, 74.
41. Christine Y. Chen, "The IM Invasion," *Fortune*, 26 May 2003, 135–138; Yudhijit Bhattacharjee, "A Swarm of Little Notes," *Time*, September 2002, A3–A8; Mark Bruno, "Taming the Wild Frontiers of Instant Messaging," *Bank Technology News*, December 2002, 30–31; Richard Grigonis, "Enterprise-Strength Instant Messaging," *Convergence.com*, 10–15 [accessed March 2003] www.convergence.com.
42. Pallato, "Instant Messaging Unites Work Groups and Inspires Collaboration," 14+.
43. Anita Hamilton, "You've Got Spim!" *Time*, 2 February 2004, [accessed 1 March 2004] www.time.com.
44. Tony Kontzer, "Learning to Share," *InformationWeek*, 5 May 2003, 28; Jon Udell, "Uniting Under Groove," *InfoWorld*, 17 February 2003 [accessed 9 September 2003] www.elibrary.com; Alison Overholt, "Virtually There?" *Fast Company*, 14 February 2002, 108.
45. Nicole Ridgway, "A Safer Place to Meet," *Forbes*, 28 April 2003, 97.
46. Judi Brownell, *Listening*, 2d edition (Boston: Allyn and Bacon, 2002), 9, 10.
47. Augusta M. Simon, "Effective Listening: Barriers to Listening in a Diverse Business Environment," *Bulletin of the Association for Business Communication* 54, no. 3 (September 1991): 73–74.
48. Robyn D. Clarke, "Do You Hear What I Hear?" *Black Enterprise*, May 1998, 129.
49. Larry Barker and Kittie Watson, *Listen Up*, (New York: St. Martin's, 2000), 24–27.
50. Dennis M. Kratz and Abby Robinson Kratz, *Effective Listening Skills* (New York: McGraw-Hill, 1995), 45–53; J. Michael Sproule, *Communication Today* (Glenview, Ill.: Scott, Foresman, 1981), 69.
51. Brownell, *Listening*, 230–231.
52. Kratz and Kratz, *Effective Listening Skills*, 78–79; Sproule, *Communication Today.*
53. Bob Lamons, "Good Listeners Are Better Communicators," *Marketing News*, 11 September 1995, 13+; Phillip Morgan and H. Kent Baker, "Building a Professional Image: Improving Listening Behavior," *Supervisory Management*, November 1985, 35–36.
54. Clarke, "Do You Hear What I Hear?"; Dot Yandle, "Listening to Understand," *Pryor Report Management Newsletter Supplement* 15, no. 8 (August 1998): 13.
55. Brownell, *Listening*, 14; Kratz and Kratz, *Effective Listening Skills*, 8–9; Sherwyn P. Morreale and Courtland L. Bovée, *Excellence in Public Speaking* (Orlando, Fla.: Harcourt Brace, 1998), 72–76; Lyman K. Steil, Larry L. Barker, and Kittie W. Watson, *Effective Listening: Key to Your Success* (Reading, Mass.: Addison-Wesley, 1983), 21–22.
56. Patrick J. Collins, *Say It with Power and Confidence* (Upper Saddle River, N.J.: Prentice Hall, 1997), 40–45.
57. Morreale and Bovée, *Excellence in Public Speaking*, 296.
58. Judee K. Burgoon, David B. Butler, and W. Gill Woodall, *Nonverbal Communication: The Unspoken Dialog*, (New York: McGraw-Hill, 1996), 137.
59. Dale G. Leathers, *Successful Nonverbal Communication: Principles and Applications* (New York: Macmillan, 1986), 19.

60. Gerald H. Graham, Jeanne Unrue, and Paul Jennings, "The Impact of Nonverbal Communication in Organizations: A Survey of Perceptions," *Journal of Business Communication* 28, no. 1 (Winter 1991): 45–62.
61. Virginia P. Richmond and James C. McCroskey, *Nonverbal Behavior in Interpersonal Relations,* (Boston: Allyn and Bacon, 2000), 153–157.
62. Richmond and McCroskey, *Nonverbal Behavior in Interpersonal Relations,* 2–3.

CHAPTER 3

1. Software Development, E-SoftSys website [accessed 30 May 2004] www.e-softsys.com/swdevelopment.htm; Bob Davis, With Software Jobs Migrating to India, Think Long Term, 6 October 2003, *The Wall Street Journal Online* [accessed 6 October 2003] http://online.wsj.com; Carolyn A. April, App-Dev Megatrends: New Tools And Techniques Take The Drudgery out of Development Work, 15 September 2003, *VAR Business,* 28; Larry Dignan, How to Manage A Globally Staffed Project, 1 September 2003, *Baseline,* 17.
2. Ford Motor Co. website [accessed 16 September 2003] www.ford.com.
3. Pgymy Boats website [accessed 16 September 2003] www.pygmyboats.com.
4. Pens.it website [accessed 22 October 2003] www.pens.it.
5. Anne Papmehl, "Diversity in Workforce Paying Off, IBM Finds," *Toronto Star,* 7 October 2002 [accessed 4 November 2003] www.elibrary.com.
6. Rona Gindin, "Dealing with a Multicultural Workforce," *Nation's Restaurant News,* September–October 1998, 31, 83; Howard Gleckman, "A Rich Stew in the Melting Pot," *Business Week,* 31 August 1998, 76+; Toby B. Gooley, "A World of Difference," *Logistics Management and Distribution Report,* June 2000, 51–55; William H. Miller, "Beneath the Surface," *Industry Week,* 20 September 1999, 13–16.
7. Linda Beamer and Iris Varner, *Intercultural Communication in the Workplace,* 2d ed. (New York: McGraw-Hill Irwin, 2001), xiii.
8. Tracy Novinger, *Intercultural Communication, A Practical Guide* (Austin, TX: University of Texas Press, 2001), 15.
9. Beamer and Varner, *Intercultural Communication in the Workplace,* 3.
10. Philip R. Harris and Robert T. Moran, *Managing Cultural Differences,* 3rd ed. (Houston: Gulf, 1991), 394–397, 429–430.
11. Lillian H. Chaney and Jeanette S. Martin, *Intercultural Business Communication* (Upper Saddle River, N.J.: Prentice Hall, 2000), 6.
12. Beamer and Varner, *Intercultural Communication in the Workplace,* 4.
13. Chaney and Martin, *Intercultural Business Communication,* 9.
14. Richard L. Daft, *Management,* 6th ed. (Cincinnati: Thomson South-Western, 2003), 455.
15. Larry A. Samovar and Richard E. Porter, "Basic Principles of Intercultural Communication," in *Intercultural Communication: A Reader,* 6th ed., edited by Larry A. Samovar and Richard E. Porter (Belmont, Calif.: Wadsworth, 1991), 12.
16. Lalita Khosla, "You Say Tomato," *Forbes Best of the Web,* 21 May 2001, 36.
17. Lionel Laroche, "Cultural Miscues Lose Top Staff," *Canadian HR Reporter,* 21 April 2003, 4.
18. Chaney and Martin, *Intercultural Business Communication,* 159.
19. Linda Beamer, "Teaching English Business Writing to Chinese-Speaking Business Students," *Bulletin of the Association for Business Communication* 57, no. 1 (1994): 12–18.
20. Edward T. Hall, "Context and Meaning," in *Intercultural Communication,* edited by Samovar and Porter, 46–55.
21. Daft, *Management,* 459.
22. Beamer, "Teaching English Business Writing to Chinese-Speaking Business Students."
23. Charley H. Dodd, *Dynamics of Intercultural Communication,* 3rd ed. (Dubuque, Iowa: Brown, 1991), 69–70.
24. Daft, *Management,* 459.
25. Beamer and Varner, *Intercultural Communication in the Workplace,* 230–233.
26. Beamer and Varner, *Intercultural Communication in the Workplace,* 236.
27. Beamer and Varner, *Intercultural Communication in the Workplace,* 252–261.
28. James Wilfong and Toni Seger, *Taking Your Business Global* (Franklin Lakes, N.J.: Career Press, 1997), 277–278.
29. Harris and Moran, *Managing Cultural Differences,* 260.
30. Skip Kaltenheuser, "Bribery Is Being Outlawed Virtually Worldwide," *Business Ethics,* May–June 1998, 11; Thomas Omestad, "Bye-Bye to Bribes," *U.S. News & World Report,* 22 December 1997, 39, 42–44.
31. "Big Oil's Dirty Secrets," *The Economist,* 10 May 2003, 62; Skip Kaltenheuser, "A Little Dab Will Do You?" *World Trade,* January 1999, 58-63; James Walsh, "A World War on Bribery," *Time,* 22 June 1998, 16.
32. Guo-Ming Chen and William J. Starosta, *Foundations of Intercultural Communication* (Boston: Allyn & Bacon, 1998), 288–289.
33. Mary A. DeVries, *Internationally Yours* (New York: Houghton Mifflin, 1994), 194.
34. Robert O. Joy, "Cultural and Procedural Differences That Influence Business Strategies and Operations in the People's Republic of China," *SAM Advanced Management Journal* (Summer 1989): 29–33.
35. Chaney and Martin, *Intercultural Business Communication,* 122–123.
36. Novinger, *Intercultural Communicatio: A Practical Guide,* 54.
37. Beamer and Varner, *Intercultural Communication in the Workplace,* 107–108.
38. Beamer and Varner, *Intercultural Communication in the Workplace,* 107–108.
39. Daft, *Management,* 448.
40. Tonya Vinas, "A Place At the Table," *Industry Week,* 1 July 2003, 22.
41. Daft, *Management,* 445.
42. John Gray, *Mars and Venus in the Workplace* (New York: Harper Collins, 2002), 10, 25–27, 61–63.
43. Craig S. Smith, "Beware of Green Hats in China and Other Cross-Cultural Faux Pas," *New York Times,* 30 April 2002, C11.
44. Francesca Bargiela-Chiappini, Anne Marie Bülow-Møller, Catherine Nickerson, Gina Poncini, and Yunxia Zhu, "Five Perspectives on Intercultural Business Communication," *Business Communication Quarterly* (September 2003): 73-96.
45. Justin Fox, "The Triumph of English," *Fortune,* 18 September 2000, 209–212.
46. Miki Fujii, "English: Bane or Blessing? English Transforms Nissan, Mazda Culture," *Yomiuri Shimbun,* 1 April 2000, 1.
47. "Less Yiddish, More Tagalog," *U.S. News & World Report,* 10 May 1993, 16; Gary Levin, "Marketers Learning New Languages for Ads," *Advertising Age,* 10 May 1993, 33.
48. Mary Beth Sheridan, "Learning the New Language of Labor," *Washington Post,* 20 August 2002, A1.
49. Bob Nelson, "Motivating Workers Worldwide," *Global Workforce,* November 1998, 25–27.
50. Mona Casady and Lynn Wasson, "Written Communication Skills of International Business Persons," *Bulletin of the Association for Business Communication* 57, no. 4 (1994): 36–40.
51. Myron W. Lustig and Jolene Koester, *Intercultural Competence,* 4th ed. (Boston: Allyn and Bacon, 2003), 196.
52. Daren Fonda, "Selling in Tongues," *Time,* 26 November 2001, B12+.
53. Wilfong and Seger, *Taking Your Business Global,* 232.
54. Sheridan Prasso (ed.), "It's All Greek to These Sites," *Business Week,* 22 July 2002, 18.

55. Jennifer Vogelson, "Online Translation Services Deliver Uneven Performance," *Knight Ridder Tribune Business News*, 15 August 2003, 1.

CHAPTER 4

1. Chris Taylor, "One-Minute Photo Smile!," *Time*, 23 December 2002, 80; "Writers Seek Simple Ways To Describe New Products," *Washington Times*, 7 November 2002 [accessed 28 October 2003] www.elibrary.com; Caroline E. Mayer, "Why Won't We Read the Manual?" *Washington Post*, 26 May 2002, H01.
2. Sanford Kaye, "Writing Under Pressure," *Soundview Executive Book Summaries* 10, no. 12, part 2 (December 1988): 1–8.
3. Peter Bracher, "Process, Pedagogy, and Business Writing," *Journal of Business Communication* 24, no. 1 (Winter 1987): 43–50.
4. Iris I. Varner, "Internationalizing Business Communication Courses," *Bulletin of the Association for Business Communication* 50, no. 4 (December 1987): 7–11.
5. Laurey Berk and Phillip G. Clampitt, "Finding the Right Path in the Communication Maze," *IABC Communication World*, October 1991, 28–32.
6. Berk and Clampitt, "Finding the Right Path in the Communication Maze."
7. Jon Van, "Technology Notebook Column," *Chicago Tribune*, 13 March 2004 [accessed 19 March 2004] www.ebsco.com.
8. Mike Bransby, "Voice Mail Makes a Difference," *Journal of Business Strategy* (January–February 1990): 7–10.
9. Mary Munter, Priscilla S. Rogers, Jone Rymer, "Business E-Mail: Guidelines for Users," *Business Communication Quarterly* (March 2003): 26-40.
10. Tim McCollum, "The Net Result of Computer Links," *Nation's Business*, March 1998, 55–58.
11. Berk and Clampitt, "Finding the Right Path in the Communication Maze."
12. Berk and Clampitt, "Finding the Right Path in the Communication Maze."
13. Berk and Clampitt, "Finding the Right Path in the Communication Maze."
14. Raymond M. Olderman, *10 Minute Guide to Business Communication* (New York: Alpha Books, 1997), 19–20.
15. Mohan R. Limaye and David A. Victor, "Cross-Cultural Business Communication Research: State of the Art and Hypotheses for the 1990s," *Journal of Business Communication* 28, no. 3 (Summer 1991): 277–299.
16. Based on the Pyramid Model developed by Barbara Minto of McKinsey & Company, management consultants.

CHAPTER 5

1. "Frequently Asked Questions," Algenix website [accessed 4 November 2003] www.algenix.com; "Who We Are," Algenix website [accessed 4 November 2003] www.algenix.com; Jenni Swenson, Helen Constantinides, and Laura Gurak, "Audience-Driven Web Site Design: An Application to Medical Web Sites," *Technical Communication*, August 2002, 340; Josephine Marcotty, "The Genesis of an Artificial Liver," *Star Tribune*, 15 March 2000 [accessed 4 November 2003] www.elibrary.com.
2. Elizabeth Blackburn and Kelly Belanger, "You-Attitude and Positive Emphasis: Testing Received Wisdom in Business Communication," *Bulletin of the Association for Business Communication* 56, no. 2 (June 1993): 1–9.
3. Placard at Alaska Airlines ticket counters, Seattle-Tacoma International Airport, 3 October 2003.
4. Annette N. Shelby and N. Lamar Reinsch, Jr., "Positive Emphasis and You Attitude: An Empirical Study," *Journal of Business Communication* 32, no. 4 (1995): 303–322.
5. Judy E. Pickens, "Terms of Equality: A Guide to Bias-Free Language," *Personnel Journal*, August 1985, 24.
6. Lisa Taylor, "Communicating About People with Disabilities: Does the Language We Use Make a Difference?" *Bulletin of the Association for Business Communication* 53, no. 3 (September 1990): 65–67.
7. Susan Benjamin, *Words at Work* (Reading, Mass.: Addison-Wesley, 1997), 136–137.
8. Plain English Campaign website [accessed 3 October 2003] www.plainenglish.co.uk.
9. Plain English Campaign website [accessed 3 October 2003].
10. Securities and Exchange Commission website [accessed 3 October 2003] www.sec.gov/news/extra/handbook.htm; Deloitte Consulting website [accessed 3 October 2003] www.dc.com/insights/bullfighter/index.asp.
11. Peter Crow, "Plain English: What Counts Besides Readability?" *Journal of Business Communication* 25, no. 1 (Winter 1988): 87–95.
12. Alinda Drury, "Evaluating Readability," *IEEE Transactions on Professional Communication* PC-28 (December 1985): 12.
13. Portions of this section are adapted from Courtland L. Bovée, *Techniques of Writing Business Letters, Memos, and Reports* (Sherman Oaks, Calif.: Banner Books International, 1978), 13–90.
14. Robert Hartwell Fiske, *Thesaurus of Alternatives to Worn-Out Words and Phrases* (Cincinnati: Writer's Digest Books, 1994), 171.
15. Iris I. Varner, "Internationalizing Business Communication Courses," *Bulletin of the Association for Business Communication* 50, no. 4 (December 1987): 7–11.
16. Matt Cain, "Managing E-Mail Hygiene," ZD Net Tech Update, 5 February 2004 [accessed 19 March 2004] www.techupdate.zdnet.com.
17. Renee B. Horowitz and Marian G. Barchilon, "Stylistic Guidelines for E-Mail," *IEEE Transactions on Professional Communication* 37, no. 4 (December 1994): 207–212; Angell and Heslop, *The Elements of E-Mail Style*, 22.
18. Jill H. Ellsworth and Matthew V. Ellsworth, *The Internet Business Book* (New York: Wiley, 1994), 91.
19. Angell and Heslop, *The Elements of E-Mail Style*, 18–19.
20. Horowitz and Barchilon, "Stylistic Guidelines for E-Mail"; Lance Cohen, "How to Improve Your E-Mail Messages," [accessed April 14, 2004] galazy.einet/galaxy/Business-and-Commerce/Management/Communications/How_to_Improve_YourEmail.html.
21. Lance Cohen, "How to Improve Your E-Mail Messages."
22. Milton Moskowitz, Michael Katz, and Robert Levering, eds., *Everybody's Business: An Almanac* (San Francisco: Harper & Row, 1980), 131.

CHAPTER 6

1. Allison Fass, "Reality Bites," *Forbes*, 25 November 2002, 242; Lisa Granatstein, "Not Fade Away," *Brandweek*, 21 October 2002, SR6; Jenna Schnuer, "Launch of the Year," *Advertising Age*, October 21, 2002, S8; Michael Grossman, "Rolling Revisions," *Folio*, October 2002, 66; Anthony Violanti, "Rolling Stone Losing the Youth Battle," *Buffalo News*, 21 June 2002, C.1.
2. Susan Benjamin, *Words at Work* (Reading, Mass.: Addison-Wesley, 1997), 71.
3. William Zinsser, *On Writing Well*, 5th ed. (New York: HarperCollins, 1994), 9.
4. "Message Lost in Some Memos," *USA Today*, 25 March 1987, 1A.
5. Zinsser, *On Writing Well*, 7, 17.
6. Mary A. DeVries, *Internationally Yours* (Boston: Houghton Mifflin, 1994), 160.
7. Zinsser, *On Writing Well*, 126.
8. William Wresch, Donald Pattow, and James Gifford, *Writing for the Twenty-First Century: Computers and Research Writing* (New York: McGraw-Hill, 1988), 192–211; Melissa E. Barth, *Strategies for Writing with the Computer* (New York: McGraw-Hill, 1988), 108–109, 140, 172–177.

9. Patsy Nichols, "Desktop Packaging," *Bulletin of the Association for Business Communication* 54, no. 1 (March 1991): 43–45; Raymond W. Beswick, "Designing Documents for Legibility," *Bulletin of the Association for Business Communication* 50, no. 4 (December 1987): 34–35.
10. Debbie Weil, "5 Key Questions (You've Been Dying) to Ask About Business Blogs," *Wordbiz Report*, 25 June 2003 [accessed 27 October 2003] www.wordbiz.com; Jonathan Eisenzopf, "Making Headlines with RSS: Using Rich Site Summaries to Draw New Visitors," *New Architect* website [accessed 28 October 2003] www.webtechniques.com.
11. Benjamin, *Words at Work*, 121.

CHAPTER 7

1. Feeding Children Better website, [accessed 25 November 2003] www.feedingchildrenbetter.org; "Awards & Accolades," Cone Inc. website, [accessed 25 November 2003], www.coneinc.com; "Platinum PR Award Winner: Cause-Related Marketing; ConAgra Program Combats Child Hunger," 13 October 2003, *PR News*, 1; Jennifer Comiteau, "Do Do-Gooders Do Better?" 29 September 2003, *AdWeek*, 24; "ConAgra Foods Donates Refrigerated Trucks from Former Dot-com Webvan to Help Feed Hungry Americans," 2 May 2002, *PR Newswire*, 1.
2. Susan Stobaugh, "Watch Your Language," *Inc.*, May 1985, 156.
3. *Techniques for Communicators* (Chicago: Lawrence Ragan Communication, 1995), 34, 36.
4. John A. Byrne, "Jack," *Business Week*, 8 June 1998, 91–112.
5. Donna Larcen, "Authors Share the Words of Condolence," *Los Angeles Times*, 20 December 1991, E11.
6. Adapted from Floorgraphics website [accessed 18 June 2001] www.floorgraphics.com; John Grossman, "It's an Ad, Ad, Ad, Ad World," *Inc.*, March 2000, 23–26; David Wellman, "Floor 'Toons," *Supermarket Business*, 15 November 1999, 47; "Floorshow," *Dallas Morning News*, 4 September 1998, 11D.
7. "How Microsoft Reviews Suppliers," *Fast Company*, no. 17 [accessed 3 September 1998] http://fastcompany. com/online/17/msoftreviews.html.
8. Michael M. Phillips, "Carving Out an Export Industry, and Hope, in Africa," *Wall Street Journal*, 18 July 1996, A8.
9. Adapted from George Anders, "Voyage to the New Economy," *Fast Company* 36:142 [accessed 11 July 2000], http://fastcompany.com/online/36/migration2. html; Pamela Kruger, "Stop the Insanity!" *Fast Company* 36: 240 [accessed 11 July 2000], www. fastcompany.com/online/36/stopinsanity.html; Anna Muoio, "Should I Go.Com?" *Fast Company* 36:164 [accessed 11 July 2000], www.fastcompany.com/online/36/stein.html.
10. Adapted from Lisa DiCarlo, "IBM Gets the Message—Instantly," Forbes.com, 7 July 2002 [accessed 22 July 2003], www.forbes. com/home/2002/07/0723ibm. html; "IBM Introduces Breakthrough Messaging Technology for Customers and Business Partners," *M2 Presswire*, 19 February 2003 [accessed 24 July 2003] www.proquest. com; "IBM and America Online Team for Instant Messaging Pilot," *M2Presswire*, 4 February 2003 [accessed 24 July 2003] www. proquest.com.
11. Adapted from Michael Mescon, Courtland Bovée, and John Thill, *Business Today*, 10th ed. (Upper Saddle River, NJ: Prentice Hall, 2002), 220.
12. Adapted from Jane Costello, "Check Your Insurance Before Renting an SUV," *Wall Street Journal*, 13 June 2001 [accessed 14 June 2001], http://interactive.wsj. com/articles/SB991402678854239871.htm.
13. Adapted from William Dunn, "Sabbaticals Aim to Cool Job Burnout," *USA Today*, 25 July 1986, 1B, 2B.
14. Adapted from John Noble Wilford, "An Old Observatory Finds a New Life," *New York Times*, 3 July 2001 [accessed on 3 July 2001], www.nytimes.com/2001/07/03/science/03WILS.html.
15. Adapted from Barbara Carton, "Farmers Begin Harvesting Satellite Data to Boost Yields," *Wall Street Journal*, 11 July 1996, B4.
16. Adapted from Dylan Tweney, "The Defogger: Slim Down That Homepage," *Business 2.0*, 13 July 2001 [accessed 1 August 2001] www.business2.com/ articles/web/0,1653,16483,FF.html
17. Adapted from Davide Dukcevich, "Instant Business: Retailer Lands' End Profits from Online Chat," Forbes.com, Special to ABCNEWS.com, 29 July 2002 [accessed 21 July 2003], http://abcnews.go.com/ sections/business/DailyNews/forbes_landsend.com; Lands' End website [accessed 5 December 2003], www.landsend.com; Forbes.com staff, "Instant Messaging at Work," Forbes.com, 26 July 2002 [accessed 21 July 2003] www.forbes.com/2002/07/ 23/0723im/html; Tischelle George and Sandra Swanson with Christopher T. Heun, "Not Just Kid Stuff," *InformationWeek*, 3 September 2001 [accessed 21 July 2003], www.informationweek.com/story/ IWK20010830S0030.
18. "Entrepreneurs Across America," *Entrepreneur Magazine Online* [accessed 12 June 1997] www. entrepreneurmag.com/entmag/50states5.hts#top.
19. Adapted from Donna Larcen, "Authors Share the Words of Condolence," *Los Angeles Times*, 20 December 1991, E11.
20. Carl Quintanilla, "Work Week: Pizza, Pizza," *Wall Street Journal*, 18 August 1998, A1.
21. Adapted from Carol Vinzant, "They Want You Back," *Fortune*, 2 October 2000, 271–2; Stephanie Armour, "Companies Recruiting Former Employees," *USA Today*, 2 February 2000, B1.

CHAPTER 8

1. Jane Naczynski and Shel Holtz, "Toronto 2003: The Inside Scoop On IABC's Biggest Annual Event," Communication World, 1 August 2003, 20; Natasha Spring, "Communicating Under Pressure," *Communication World*, 1 August 2003, 36; "IABC Recognizes Agilent Technologies' CEO with Excellence in Communication Leadership Award," press release, IABC website [accessed 9 October 2003] www.iabc.com; Daniel Roth, "How To Cut Pay, Lay Off 8,000 People and Still Have Workers Who Love You," Fortune, 4 February 2002, 62.
2. Greg Lamm, "Pike Place Market Head Leaving After 4 Years in 'Very Contentious Job,'" *Seattle Times*, 29 November 2003 [accessed 29 November 2003] www.seattletimes.com.
3. Carol David and Margaret Ann Baker, "Rereading Bad News: Compliance-Gaining Features in Management Memos," *Journal of Business Communication*, October 1994 [accessed 1 December 2003] www.elibrary.com.
4. Ameeta Patel and Lamar Reinsch, "Companies Can Apologize: Corporate Apologies and Legal Liability," *Business Communication Quarterly*, March 2003 [accessed 1 December 2003] www.elibrary.com.
5. Iris I. Varner, "A Comparison of American and French Business Correspondence," *Journal of Business Communication* 24, no. 4 (Fall 1988): 55–65.
6. Susan Jenkins and John Hinds, "Business Letter Writing: English, French, and Japanese," *TESOL Quarterly* 21, no. 2 (June 1987): 327–349; Saburo Haneda and Hiosuke Shima, "Japanese Communication Behavior As Reflected in Letter Writing," *Journal of Business Communication* 19, no. 1 (1982): 19–32.
7. James Calvert Scott and Diana J. Green, "British Perspectives on Organizing Bad-News Letters: Organizational Patterns Used by Major U.K. Companies," *Bulletin of the Association for Business Communication* 55, no. 1 (March 1992): 17–19.
8. "Need To Deliver Bad News? How and Why to Tell It Like It Is," *HR Focus*, November 2003 [accessed 1 December 2003] www.elibrary.com.
9. Walter Kiechel III, "Breaking Bad News to the Boss," *Fortune*, 9 April 1990 [accessed 2 December 2003] www.elibrary.com.

10. "Advice From the Pros On the Best Way To Deliver Bad News," *Report on Customer Relationship Management*, 1 February 2003 [accessed 1 December 2003] www.elibrary.com.
11. Courtand L. Bovée, John V. Thill, George P. Dovel, and Marian Burk Wood, *Advertising Excellence* (New York: McGraw-Hill, 1995) 508–509; John Holusha, "Exxon's Public-Relations Problem," *New York Times*, 12 April 1989, D1.
12. "Throw Out the Old Handbook in Favor of Today's Crisis Drills," *PR News*, 27 January 2003, 1.
13. Maura Dolan and Stuart Silverstein, "Court Broadens Liability for Job References," *Los Angeles Times*, 28 January 1997, A1, A11; Frances A. McMorris, "Ex-Bosses Face Less Peril Giving Honest Job References," *Wall Street Journal*, 8 July 1996, B1, B8.
14. Thomas S. Brice and Marie Waung, "Applicant Rejection Letters: Are Businesses Sending the Wrong Message?" *Business Horizons*, March–April 1995, 59–62.
15. Gwendolyn N. Smith, Rebecca F. Nolan, and Yong Dai, "Job-Refusal Letters: Readers' Affective Responses to Direct and Indirect Organizational Plans," *Business Communication Quarterly* 59, no. 1 (1996): 67–73; Brice and Waung, "Applicant Rejection Letters."
16. Korey A. Wilson, "Put Rejection Up-Front," *Black Enterprise*, November 1999, 69.
17. Judi Brownell, "The Performance Appraisal Interviews: A Multipurpose Communication Assignment," *Bulletin of the Association for Business Communication* 57, no. 2 (1994): 11–21.
18. Brownell, "The Performance Appraisal Interviews."
19. Stephanie Gruner, "Feedback from Everyone," *Inc.*, February 1997, 102–103.
20. Howard M. Bloom, "Performance Evaluations," *New England Business*, December 1991, 14.
21. David I. Rosen, "Appraisals Can Make—or Break—Your Court Case," *Personnel Journal*, November 1992, 113.
22. Patricia A. McLagan, "Advice for Bad-News Bearers: How to Tell Employees They're Not Hacking It and Get Results," *Industry Week*, 15 February 1993, 42; Michael Lee Smith, "Give Feedback, Not Criticism," *Supervisory Management*, 1993, 4; "A Checklist for Conducting Problem Performer Appraisals," *Supervisory Management*, December 1993, 7–9.
23. Carrie Brodzinski, "Avoiding Wrongful Termination Suits," *National Underwriter Property & Casualty-Risk & Benefits Management*, 13 October 2003 [accessed 2 December 2003] www.elibrary.com.
24. Jane R. Goodson, Gail W. McGee, and Anson Seers, "Giving Appropriate Performance Feedback to Managers: An Empirical Test of Content and Outcomes," *Journal of Business Communication* 29, no. 4 (1992): 329–342.
25. Craig Cox, "On the Firing Line," *Business Ethics*, May–June 1992, 33–34.
26. Cox, "On the Firing Line."
27. Adapted from Michael H. Mescon, Courtland L. Bovée, and John V. Thill, *Business Today*, 10th ed. (Upper Saddle River, N.J.: Prentice Hall, 2002), 369; Bruce Upbin, "Profit in a Big Orange Box," *Forbes*, 165, no. 2, 24 January 2000 [accessed 2 August 2001] www.forbes.com/forbes/2000/0124/6502122a.html.
28. Michelle Higgins, "The Ballet Shoe Gets a Makeover, But Few Yet See the Pointe," *Wall Street Journal*, 8 August 1998, A1, A6; Gaynor Minden website [accessed 17 December 2003] www.dancer.com; American Ballet Theatre website [accessed 17 December 2003] www.abt.org.
29. Adapted from Wolf Blitzer, "More Employers Taking Advantages of New Cyber-Surveillance Software," *CNN.com*, 10 July 2000 [accessed 11 July 2000] www. cnn.com/2000/US/07/10/workplace.eprivacy/index.html.
30. Adapted from Hannah Holmes, "Keepers: Better Bike Mirror," *Garbage*, June–July 1993, 53.
31. Leo W. Banks, "Not Your Average Joe," *Los Angeles Times*, 7 January 1997, E1, E6.
32. Adapted from the Disclosure Project website [accessed 20 August 2001] www.disclosureproject.org; Katelynn Raymer and David Ruppe, "UFOs, Aliens and Secrets," ABCNews.com, 10 May 2001 [accessed 20 August 2001] http://more.abcnews.go.com/sections/scitech/DailyNews/ufo010509.html; Rachael Myer, "UFO Probe Sought," *Las Vegas Review-Journal*, 11 May 2001 [accessed 20 August 2001] www.lvrj.com/cgi-bin/printable.cgi?/lvrj_home/2001/May-11-Fri-2001/ news/16064080.html.
33. Adapted from Union Bank of California teleservices, personal communication, 16 August 2001.
34. Adapted from "Motorola to Cut Arizona Jobs," CNNfn website, 15 August 2001 [accessed 15 August 2001] http://cnnfn.cnn.com/2001/18/15/companies/motorola; Barnaby J. Feder, "Motorola Says It Expects Loss in Third Quarter," *New York Times*, 13 July 2001, C4; David Barboza, "Motorola Cuts 3% of Its Jobs as Chip Demand Cools Off," *New York Times*, 10 February 2001, C2; Dave Carpenter, "Motorola to Lop Another 4,000," *Chicago Sun-Times*, 13 July 2001, 49; Roger O. Crockett, "Motorola Can't Seem to Get Out of Its Own Way," *Business Week*, 22 January 2001, 72; Roger O. Crockett, "A New Company Called Motorola," *Business Week*, 17 April 2000, 86–92.
35. Adapted from Alyce Lomax, "Monterey's High-Carb Woes," The Motley Fool, 23 December 2003 [accessed 23 December 2003] www.fool.com/News/mft/ 2003/mft03122312.htm; "Monterey Pasta Announces Quarterly Sales Decline of 3%–5% Expected When Compared to Fourth Quarter, 2002" Monterey Pasta corporate press release, 23 December 2003 [accessed 23 December 2003] www.montereypasta.com/Company/PressReleases/index.cfm?ID=84; "Monterey Pasta Company Introduces Reduced Carbohydrate Product Line," Monterey Pasta corporate press release, 23 December 2003 [accessed 23 December 2003] www.montereypasta.com/Company/PressReleases.
36. Adapted from "GTE Headquarters in Connecticut Hit by Hepatitis," *Wall Street Journal*, 20 October 1989, A9.
37. Adapted from Capital One Auto Finance (formerly PeopleFirst.com) website [accessed 23 December 2003] www.capitaloneautofinance.com
38. Adapted from Associated Press, "Children's Painkiller Recalled," CNN.com/Health website, 16 August 2001 [accessed 22 August 2001] www.cnn.com/2001/HEALTH/parenting/08/16/kids.drug.recalled.ap/index.html; Perrigo Company website [accessed 29 August 2001] www.perrigo.com.
39. Adapted from Associated Press, "Employers Restricting Use of Cell Phones in Cars," CNN.com/Sci-Tech, 27 August 2001 [accessed 27 August 2001]www.cnn. com/2001/TECH/08/27/cell-phones.cars.ap/index.html; Julie Vallese, "Study: All Cell Phones Distract Drivers," CNN.com/U.S., 16 August 2001 [accessed 7 September 2001] www.cnn.com/2001/ US/08/16/cell.phone. driving/index.html.
40. Adapted from Julie Vallese, "Motorized Scooter Injuries on the Rise," CNN.com/U.S., 22 August 2001 [accessed 22 August 2001] www.cnn.com/2001/US/08/22/scooter. advisory/index.html; The Sports Authority website [accessed 28 August 2001] www. thesportauthority.com.
41. "Entrepreneurs Across America," [accessed 25 June 1997] *Entrepreneur Magazine Online*, www.enterpreneurmag.com/entmag/50states2.hts.
42. Adapted from United Airlines website [accessed 31 December 2003] www.united.com; "United Airlines First To Offer Inflight Email on Domestic Flights: Verizon Airfone Outfits UAL's Fleet with JetConnect," United Airlines press release [accessed 21 July 2003] www.ual.com/press/detail/o,1442,51106,00.html; "Laptops Sprout Wings with Verizon Airfone JetConnect Service," *PR Newswire*, 24 September 2002 [accessed 21 July 2003] www.proquest.com; "Verizon Hopes Data Flies with Airfone JetConnect," *Wireless Data News*, 7 May 2003 [accessed 24 July 2003] www.proquest.com.

43. Adapted from Sean Doherty, "Dynamic Communications," *Network Computing*, 3 April 2003, 26 [accessed 24 July 2003] search.epnet.com/direct.asp?an-9463336&db=bsh&tg=AN; Todd Wasserman, "Post-Merger HP Invents New Image to Challenge Tech Foes IBM and Dell," *Brandweek*, 18 November 2002, [accessed 24 July 2003] search.epnet.com/direct.asp?an=8887152&db=bsh&tg=AN; R. P. Srikanth, "IM Tools Are Latest Tech Toys for Corporate Users," *Express Computer*, 1 July 2002 [accessed 21 July 2003] www.expresscomputeronline.com/20020701/ indtrend1.shtml.

CHAPTER 9

1. Nellie Andreeva, "Commando Nanny Gets a Sitcom on WB," *Hollywood Reporter*, October 2003, 21–27, 4; Abby Ellin, "'Survivor' Meets Millionaire, and a Show Is Born," *New York Times*, 19 October 2003, sec. 3, 4; Kelli Anderson, "Out of the Wild," *Sports Illustrated*, 12 May 2003, A6; Maggie Sieger, "Paddle Faster, Mom," *Time*, 5 May 2003, 85; Bill Carter, "Survival of the Pushiest," *New York Times Magazine*, 28 January 2001, 22.
2. Jay A. Conger, "The Necessary Art of Persuasion," *Harvard Business Review*, May–June 1998, 84–95; Jeanette W. Gilsdorf, "Write Me Your Best Case for . . ." *Bulletin of the Association for Business Communication* 54, no. 1 (March 1991): 7–12.
3. "Vital Skill for Today's Managers: Persuading, Not Ordering Others," *Soundview Executive Book Summaries*, September 1998, 1.
4. Mary Cross, "Aristotle and Business Writing: Why We Need to Teach Persuasion," *Bulletin of the Association for Business Communication* 54, no. 1 (March 1991): 3–6.
5. Abraham H. Maslow, *Motivation and Personality* (New York: Harper & Row, 1954), 12, 19.
6. Robert T. Moran, "Tips on Making Speeches to International Audiences," *International Management*, April 1980, 58–59.
7. Conger, "The Necessary Art of Persuasion."
8. Raymond M. Olderman, *10-Minute Guide to Business Communication* (New York: Macmillan Spectrum/Alpha Books, 1997), 57–61.
9. Gilsdorf, "Write Me Your Best Case for . . ."
10. John D. Ramage and John C. Bean, *Writing Arguments: A Rhetoric with Readings*, 3d ed. (Boston: Allyn & Bacon, 1995), 430–442.
11. Dianna Booher, *Communicate with Confidence* (New York: McGraw-Hill, 1994), 102.
12. Conger, "The Necessary Art of Persuasion."
13. Overview of the Web Accessibility Initiative, W3C website [accessed 8 December 2003] www.w3.org.
14. iPod product page, Apple Computer website [accessed 8 December 2003] www.apple.com/ipod.
15. Saturn VUE product page, Saturn website [accessed 8 December 2003] www.saturn.com.
16. Working and Living in France: The Ins and Outs product page, Insider Paris Guides webpage [accessed 8 December 2003] www.insiderparisguides.com.
17. Verizon Wireless sales letter, received 1 December 2003.
18. Fast Break Backpack product page, Lands End website [accessed 8 December 2003] www.landsend.com.
19. iPod product page.
20. William North Jayme, quoted in Albert Haas, Jr., "How to Sell Almost Anything by Direct Mail," *Across the Board*, November 1986, 50.
21. Gilsdorf, "Write Me Your Best Case for . . ."
22. *Frequently Asked Advertising Questions: A Guide for Small Business*, U.S. Federal Trade Commission website [accessed 9 December 2003] www.ftc.gov.
23. John Case and Jerry Useem, "Six Characters in Search of a Strategy," *Inc.*, March 1996, 46–49.
24. Adapted from David A. Avila, "Mentally Ill Find Health in Flowers," *Los Angeles Times*, 15 January 1992, B2.
25. Adapted from Norimitsu Onishi, "Making Liberty His Business: Ex-Political Prisoner Turns Freedom's Icon into a Career," *New York Times*, 18 April 1996, B1; Colbar Art website [accessed 9 January 2004] www.colbarart.com.
26. Adapted from Michael H. Mescon, Courtland L. Bovée, and John V. Thill, *Business Today*, 10th ed. (Upper Saddle River, N.J.: Prentice Hall, 2002), 272–274; Jason Roberson, "Rush-hour Rebellion," *Dallas Business Journal*, 22 June 2001, 31; Carole Hawkins, "Ready, Set, Go Home," *Black Enterprise*, August 2001, 118–124; Wayne Tompkins, "Telecommuting in Transition," *Courier-Journal*, 9 July 2001, 01C.
27. Reuters Limited, "Kids Who Watch More TV Get Hurt More, Study Says," CNN Custom News, CNN Interactive, 14 July 1998; customnews.com/cnews/ pna.show_s..t_type=190294&p_sub-cat=Authors&p_ category, accessed 16 July 1998; Texas Classroom Teachers Association website [accessed 30 September 1998] www.tcta.org/geninfo.htm.
28. Adapted from Andrew Ferguson, "Supermarket of the Vanities," *Fortune*, 10 June 1996, 30, 32; Whole Foods Market website [accessed 9 January 2004] www.wholefoodsmarket.com.
29. Albert R. Karr, "Work Week: Wake Up and Read This," *Wall Street Journal*, 6 May 1997, A1.
30. Adapted from Joe Sharkey, "Luggage Lock Plan Revisited, Again," *New York Times*, 6 January 2004 [accessed 6 January 2004] www.nytimes.com; Brookstone website [accessed 13 January 2004] www.brookstone.com.
31. Adapted from Herman Miller website [accessed 13 January 2004] www.hermanmiller.com; Office Depot website [accessed 13 January 2004] www.officedepot.com.
32. Adapted from Bruce Haring, "Trouble Getting up to Speed," *USA Today*, 27 December 1999, D3, D2; Mike Rogoway, "AT&T Seeks to Improve Internet Connections," *Columbian*, 9 March 2001, E1.
33. Adapted from CNET Shopper.com [accessed 1 October 2001] http://shopper.cnet.com/shopping/0-1257. html?tag=sh.
34. Adapted from Gateway website [accessed 2 October 2001] www.gateway.com; Gateway customer service sales representative, 1-800-GATEWAY, personal interview, 10 October 2001.
35. Adapted from Quotesmith.com website, Investor Overview and FAQ [accessed 31 August 2000] http://investor.quotesmith.com/ireye/ir_site.zhtml?ticker=QUOT&script=2100.
36. Provided by Kelly Services, Inc. June 2004
37. Adapted from Charles Fishman, "The Greener Cleaners," *Fast Company*, 36, 54 [accessed 11 July 2000] fastcompany.com/online/36/greenclean.html; Micell Technologies website [accessed 1 September 2000] www.micell.com/08142000.htm; Hangers Cleaners website [accessed 1 September 2000] www.hangersdrycleaners.com/about/corp/triplebottomline.htm; Hangers Cleaners website [accessed 9 January 2004] www.hangerscleaners. com; Cool Clean Technologies, Inc., website [accessed 9 January 2004] www.co2olclean.com.
38. Adapted from the American Red Cross website [accessed 3 October 2001] www.redcross.org; American Red Cross San Diego Chapter website [accessed 3 October 2001] www.sdarc.org/blood.htm.
39. Adapted from Sarah Plaskitt, "Case Study: Hilton Uses SMS with Success," *B&T Marketing & Media*, 27 June 2002 [accessed 22 July 2003] www.bandt.com.au/articles/ce/0c00eace.asp; "Wireless Messaging Briefs," *Instant Messaging Planet*, 4 October 2002 [accessed 22 July 2003] www.instantmessagingplanet.com/wireless/print.php/10766_1476111; Hilton Hotels Corporation, *Hoover's Company Capsules*, 1 July 2003 [accessed 24 July 2003] www.proquest.com; Matthew G. Nelson, "Hilton Takes Reservations Wireless," *InformationWeek*, 25 June 2001, 99 [accessed 24 July 2003] www.web22.epnet.com; Hilton Hotels website [accessed 15 January 2004] www.hilton.com.
40. Adapted from IBM website [accessed 15 January 2004] www.ibm.com/ibm/ibmgives; IBM website, "DAS Faces an Assured Future with IBM" [accessed 16 January 2004] www-306.ibm.com/software/success/ cssdb.nsf/CS/DNSD-5S6KTF; IBM website, "Sametime" [accessed 16 January 2004] www.lotus.com/products/lotussametime.nsf/wdocs/homepage.

CHAPTER 10

1. Dan Lienert, "What's New? With Toyota's Scion, Youth Must Be Served," *New York Times*, 19 October 2003 [accessed 12 November 2003] www.nytimes.com; Fara Warner, "Learning How to Speak to Gen Y," *Fast Company*, July 2003, 36; Darren Fonda, "Baby, You Can Drive My Car," *Time*, 30 June 2003, 46; Christopher Palmeri, Ben Elgin, Kathleen Kerwin, "Toyota's Scion: Dude, Here's Your Car," *Business Week*, 9 June 2003, 44; Jonathan Fahey, "For the Discriminating Body Piercer," *Forbes*, 12 May 2003, 136; George Raine, "Courting Generation Y," *San Francisco Chronicle*, 11 May 2003, 13.
2. Courtland L. Bovée, Michael J. Houston, and John V. Thill, *Marketing*, 2d ed., (New York: McGraw-Hill, 1995), 194–196.
3. Legal-Definitions.com [accessed 17 December 2003] www.legal-definitions.com.
4. Information for this section was obtained from "Finding Industry Information" [accessed 3 November 1998] www.pitt.edu/~buslibry/industries.htm; Thomas P. Bergman, Stephen M. Garrison, and Gregory M. Scott, *The Business Student Writer's Manual and Guide to the Internet* (Upper Saddle River, N.J.: Prentice Hall, 1998), 67–80; Ernest L. Maier, Anthony J. Faria, Peter Kaatrude, and Elizabeth Wood, *The Business Library and How to Use It* (Detroit: Omnigraphics, 1996), 53–76; Sherwyn P. Morreale and Courtland L. Bovée, *Excellence in Public Speaking* (Fort Worth: Harcourt Brace College Publishers, 1998), 166–171.
5. Open Directory [accessed 13 December 2003] www.dmoz.com.
6. LookSmart.com [accessed 13 December 2003] www.looksmart.com.
7. AllTheWeb.com advanced search page [accessed 13 December 2003] www.alltheweb.com; Google advanced search page [accessed 13 December 2003] www.google.com; Yahoo! advanced search page [accessed 13 December 2003] www.yahoo.com.
8. NewsGator website [accessed 13 December 2003] www.newsgator.com, NewzCrawler website [accessed 13 December 2003] www.newzcrawler.com.
9. "Top 10 Benefits of OneNote 2003," Microsoft website [accessed 21 June 2004], www.microsoft.com.
10. Dorothy Geisler, "How to Avoid Copyright Lawsuits," *IABC Communication World*, June 1984, 34–37.
11. A. B. Blankenship and George Edward Breen, *State of the Art Marketing Research*, (Chicago: NTC Business Books, 1993), 136.
12. "How to Design and Conduct a Study," *Credit Union Magazine*, October 1983, 36–46.
13. American Marketing Association [accessed 14 December 2003] www.marketingpower.com.
14. Karen J. Bannan, "Companies Save Time, Money with Online Surveys," *B to B*, 9 June 2003, 1+; Allen Hogg, "Online Research Overview," on American Marketing Association website [accessed 15 December 2003] www.marketingpower.com.
15. Morreale and Bovée, *Excellence in Public Speaking*, 177.
16. Morreale and Bovée, *Excellence in Public Speaking*, 178–180.
17. Morreale and Bovée, *Excellence in Public Speaking*, 182.
18. Lynn Quitman Troyka, *Simon & Schuster Handbook for Writers*, 6th ed. (Upper Saddle River, NJ: Simon & Schuster, 2002), 481.
19. "How to Paraphrase Effectively: 6 Steps to Follow," Researchpaper.com [accessed 26 October 1998] www.researchpaper.com/writing_center/30.html.
20. Tony Mecia, "Greenville, S.C.-Based Bowater to Restate Earnings," *Charlotte Observer*, 12 July 2002 [accessed online 16 December 2003] www.ebsco.com.
21. Samuel Greengard, "What's in Store for 2004," *Workforce Management*, December 2003, 34+.

CHAPTER 11

1. "Overview," SYP website [accessed 8 October 2003] www.stoneyamashita.com; "Approach," SYP website [accessed 8 October 2003] www.stoneyamashita.com; Christine Dyrness, "Expert Talks to Raleigh, N.C., Businesses About Fusion of Work, Creativity," *News & Observer*, 20 March 2003 [accessed 3 December 2003] www.elibrary.com; Polly LaBere, "Keith Yamashita Wants to Reinvent Your Company," *Fast Company*, November 2002, 88; James Aley, "Big Ideas For Hire," *Fortune*, 28 October 2002, 178; Pui-Wing Tam, "The Corporate Strategist," *Wall Street Journal*, 13 May 2002, R8.
2. Hoover's Online [accessed 30 December 2003] www.hoovers.com.
3. Sheri Rosen, "What Is Truth?" *IABC Communication World*, March 1995, 40.
4. Maureen Jones, "Getting Good Graphs," *PC Magazine*, 23 July 1985, 217.
5. Edward R. Tufte, *The Visual Display of Quantitative Information* (Cheshire, Conn.: Graphic Press, 1983), 113.
6. Courtland L. Bovée, Michael J. Houston, and John V. Thill, *Marketing*, 2d ed. (New York: McGraw-Hill, 1995), 250.
7. "Leading National Advertisers," *Advertising Age*, 25 September 2000, S4.

CHAPTER 12

1. Amy Gilroy, "Vendors Retool Lines to Combat Sales Slump," *TWICE*, 13 October 2003, 28; Amy Gilroy, "Car Audio In Double-Digit Slump," *TWICE*, 7 July 2003, 8; Martin Fackler, "Japan Profiles: Haruo Kawahara, Kenwood Chief," Dow Jones Newswires; *Far Eastern Economic Review*, 24 September 2003 [accessed 9 December 2003] http://online.wsj.com; Corey Goldman, "Satellite Radio's Future Still Up in the Air," *Toronto Star*, 11 August 2003 [accessed 9 December 2003] www.elibrary.com; Denis Storey, "Kenwood Chief Touts Turnaround," *Mobile Radio Technology* website 1 February 2003, [accessed 9 December 2003] www.iwce-mrt.com; Erin Strout, "Ask SMM," *Sales and Marketing Management*, October 2002, 59.
2. FedBizOpps.com [accessed 12 January 2003] www.fedbizopps.com.
3. Iris Varner, *Contemporary Business Report Writing*, 2nd ed. (Chicago: Dryden Press, 1991), 170.
4. Curt Kampmeier, "How To Write a Proposal That's Accepted Every Time," *Consulting to Management*, September 2000, 62.
5. Varner, *Contemporary Business Report Writing*, 178.

CHAPTER 13

1. Richard Linnett and Wayne Friedman, "OMD Plans Strategy to Challenge Upfront," *Advertising Age*, 23 June 2003, 1; Katy Bachman, "Research: Beth Uyenco," *Brandweek*, 9 December 2003, SR24; Kate Fitzgerald, "Communication Architects," *Advertising Age*, 5 August 2002, S6; Katy Bachman, "Research: Tony Jarvis," *Mediaweek*, 3 December 2001, SR20.
2. A. S. C. Ehrenberg, "Report Writing—Six Simple Rules for Better Business Documents," *Admap*, June 1992, 39–42.
3. Michael Netzley and Craig Snow, *Guide to Report Writing* (Upper Saddle River, N.J.: Prentice Hall, 2001), 15.
4. Claudia Mon Pere McIsaac, "Improving Student Summaries Through Sequencing," *Bulletin of the Association for Business Communication* (September 1987): 17–20.
5. David A. Hayes, "Helping Students GRASP the Knack of Writing Summaries," *Journal of Reading* (November 1989): 96–101.
6. Philip C. Kolin, *Successful Writing at Work*, 6th ed. (Boston: Houghton Mifflin, 2001), 552–555.
7. Adapted from Bob Smith, "The Evolution of Pinkerton," *Management Review*, September 1993, 54–58.

CHAPTER 14

1. "Richard Klausner Spends to Save Lives," *Fast Company*, November 2002, 128; "Letter from Bill and Melinda Gates," Gates Foundation website [accessed 6 October 2003] www.gatesfoundation.org; "Foundation Leadership," Gates Foundation Web site [accessed 6 October 2003] www.gatesfoundation.org.

2. Michael Netzley and Craig Snow, *Guide to Report Writing* (Upper Saddle River, N.J.: Prentice Hall, 2001), 57.
3. Oswald M. T. Ratteray, "Hit the Mark with Better Summaries," *Supervisory Management,* September 1989, 43–45.
4. Netzley and Snow, *Guide to Report Writing,* 43.
5. Alice Reid, "A Practical Guide For Writing Proposals" [accessed 31 May 2001] http://members.dca.net/ areid/proposal.htm.
6. Toby B. Gooley, "Ocean Shipping: RFPs That Get Results," *Logistics Management,* July 2003, 47–52.
7. Andrea Obana, "How to Write a Request for Proposal (RFP)," Fine Brand Media website [accessed 22 January 2004] www.finebrand.com; Gooley, "Ocean Shipping: RFPs that Get Results," 47–52.
8. Obana, "How to Write a Request for Proposal (RFP)."
9. Obana, "How to Write a Request for Proposal (RFP)"; Gooley, "Ocean Shipping: RFPs that Get Results," 47–52; "Writing a Good RFP," *Infrastructure Issues,* September 1998, Mead & Hunt website [accessed 23 January 2004] www.meadhunt.com.
10. Adapted from William C. Symonds, "Giving It the Old Online Try," *Business Week,* 3 December 2001, 76–80; Karen Frankola, "Why Online Learners Drop Out," *Workforce,* October 2001, 52–60; Mary Lord, "They're Online and on the Job; Managers and Hamburger Flippers Are Being E-Trained at Work," *U.S. News & World Report,* 15 October 2001, 72–77.
11. Ieva M. Augstumes, "Buyers Take the Driver's Seat," *Dallas Morning News,* 20 February 2004 [accessed 30 June 2004] www.highbeam.com; Jill Amadio, "A Click Away: Automotive Webs Are Revved Up and Ready to Help You Buy," *Entrepreneur,* 1 August 2003 [accessed 30 June 2004] www.highbeam.com; Dawn C. Chmielewski, "Car Sites Lend Feel-Good Info for Haggling," *San Jose Mercury News,* 1 August 2003 [accessed 30 June 2004] www.highbeam.com; Cromwell Schubarth, "Autoheroes Handle Hassle of Haggling," *Boston Herald,* 24 July 2003 [accessed 30 June 2004] www.highbeam.com; Rick Popely, "Internet Doesn't Change Basic Shopping Rules," *Chicago Tribune,* 28 February 2004 [accessed 30 June 2004] www.highbeam.com; Matt Nauman, "Walnut Creek, Calif., Firm Prospers as Online Car Buying Becomes More Popular," *San Jose Mercury News,* 21 June 2004 [accessed 30 June 2004] www.highbeam.com; Cliff Banks, "e-Dealer 100," *Ward's Dealer Business,* 1 April 2004 [accessed 30 June 2004] www.highbeam.com; Cars.com website [accessed 30 June 2004] www.cars.com; CarsDirect.com website [accessed 30 June 2004] www.carsdirect.com.

CHAPTER 15

1. "Fitch: Worldwide—A Different View," company brochure, Fitch website [accessed 15 December 2003] www.fitchworldwide.com; "About Fitch: Worldwide," Fitch website [accessed 10 October 2003] www.fitchworldwide.com; Fara Warner, "How Fitch Makes Its (Fast) Pitch," *Fast Company,* March 2002, 126.
2. Sarah Lary and Karen Pruente, "Powerless Point: Common PowerPoint Mistakes to Avoid," *Public Relations Tactics,* February 2004, 28.
3. Sherwyn P. Morreale and Courtland L. Bovée, *Excellence in Public Speaking* (Fort Worth: Harcourt Brace, 1998), 234–7.
4. Morreale and Bovée, *Excellence in Public Speaking,* 230.
5. Morreale and Bovée, *Excellence in Public Speaking,* 241–3.
6. "Choose and Use Your Words Deliberately," *Soundview Executive Book Summaries,* 20, no. 6, pt. 2 (June 1998): 3.
7. Walter Kiechel III, "How to Give a Speech," *Fortune,* 8 June 1987, 180.
8. *Communication and Leadership Program* (Santa Ana, Calif.: Toastmasters International, 1980), 44, 45.
9. Morreale and Bovée, *Excellence in Public Speaking,* 24–25.
10. Jennifer Rotondo and Mike Rotondo, Jr., *Presentation Skills for Managers,* (New York: McGraw-Hill, 2002), 9.
11. Judy Linscott, "Getting On and Off the Podium," *Savvy,* October 1985, 44.
12. Iris R. Johnson, "Before You Approach the Podium," *MW,* January–February 1989, 7.
13. Sandra Moyer, "Braving No Woman's Land," *The Toastmaster,* August 1986, 13.
14. "Control the Question-and-Answer Session," *Soundview Executive Book Summaries* 20, no. 6, pt. 2 (June 1998): 4.
15. "Control the Question-and-Answer Session."
16. Teresa Brady, "Fielding Abrasive Questions During Presentations," *Supervisory Management,* February 1993, 6.
17. Robert L. Montgomery, "Listening on Your Feet," *The Toastmaster,* July 1987, 14–15.
18. Adapted from Ronald L. Applebaum and Karl W. E. Anatol, *Effective Oral Communication: For Business and the Professions* (Chicago: Science Research Associates, 1982), 240–244.

CHAPTER 16

1. Bill Breen, "The Big Score," September 2003, *Fast Company,* 64; "HP Finalizes $3 Billion Outsourcing Agreement to Manage Procter & Gamble's IT Infrastructure," press release, HP website, 6 May 2003 [accessed 10 October 2003] www.hp.com; "HP Selected by P&G for $3 Billion, 10-Year Services Contract," press release, HP website, 11 April 2003 [accessed 10 October 2003] www.hp.com.
2. "Polishing Your Presentation," 3M Meeting Network [accessed 8 June 2001] www.mmm.com/meetingnetwork/readingroom/meetingguide_pres.html.
3. Claudyne Wilder and David Fine, *Point, Click & Wow* (San Francisco: Jossey-Bass Pfeiffer, 1996), 50.
4. Allbee, personal communication.
5. Margo Halverson, "Choosing the Right Colors for Your Next Presentation," 3M Meeting Network [accessed 8 June 2001] www.mmm.com/meetingnetwork/ readingroom/meetingguide_right_color.html.
6. Carol Klinger and Joel G. Siegel, "Computer Multimedia Presentations," *CPA Journal,* June 1996, 46.
7. Jon Hanke, "Five Tips for Better Visuals," 3M Meeting Network [accessed 8 June 2001] www.mmm.com/meetingnetwork/presentations/pmag_better_visuals.html.
8. Hanke, "Five Tips for Better Visuals."
9. Sarah Lary and Karen Pruente, "Powerless Point: Common PowerPoint Mistakes to Avoid," *Public Relations Tactics,* February 2004, 28.
10. Edward P. Bailey, *Writing and Speaking at Work* (Upper Saddle River, N.J.: Prentice Hall, 1999), 138–145.
11. Ted Simons, "Handouts That Won't Get Trashed," *Presentations,* February 1999, 47–50.
12. Jennifer Rotondo and Mike Rotondo, Jr., *Presentation Skills for Managers,* (New York: McGraw-Hill, 2002), 151.
13. Jeff Yocom, " TechRepublic Survey Yields Advice on Streaming Video," TechRepublic website [accessed 16 February 2004] www.techrepublic.com.
14. "Webcasting Tips & Advice," Spider Eye Solutions [accessed 13 February 2004] www.spidereye.com.

CHAPTER 17

1. "Who We Are," E*Trade website [accessed 24 December 2003] www.etrade.com; Samuel Greengard, "Smarter Screening Takes Technology and HR Savvy," *Fast Company,* June 2002, 56; Alison Overholt, "Job Search 101," *Fast Company,* April 2002, 122–125; Pierre Mornell, "Zero Defect Hiring," *Inc.,* March 1998, 74.
2. "Firm Predicts Top 10 Workforce/Workplace Trends for 2004," *Enterprise,* 8–14 December 2003, 1–2; Scott Hudson, "Keeping Employees Happy," *Community Banker,* September 2003, 34+; Marvin J. Cetron and Owen Davies, "Trends Now Changing the World: Technology, the Workplace, Management, and Institutions," *Futurist* 35, no. 2 (March/ April 2001): 27–42.
3. Steve Crabtree, "Beyond the Dot-Com Bust; How Managers Can Help Younger Workers Regain Their Lost Momentum," *Gallup Management Journal,* 11 December 2003, 11.

4. Jim Puzzanghera, "Coalition of High-Tech Firms to Urge Officials to Help Keep U.S. Competitive," *San Jose Mercury News*, 8 January 2004 [accessed online 17 February 2004] www.ebscohost.com.
5. Amanda Bennett, "GE Redesigns Rungs of Career Ladder," *Wall Street Journal*, 15 March 1993, B1, B3.
6. Robin White Goode, "International and Foreign Language Skills Have an Edge," *Black Enterprise*, May 1995, 53.
7. Jeffrey R. Young, "'E-Portfolios' Could Give Students a New Sense of Their Accomplishments," *The Chronicle of Higher Education*, 8 March 2002, A31.
8. Nancy M. Somerick, "Managing a Communication Internship Program," *Bulletin of the Association for Business Communication* 56, no. 3 (1993): 10–20.
9. Joan Lloyd, "Changing Workplace Requires You to Alter Your Career Outlook," *Milwaukee Journal Sentinel*, 4 July 1999, 1; DeBell, "Ninety Years in the World of Work in America."
10. Robert J. Gerberg, *Robert Gerberg's Job Changing System*, summarized by Macmillan Book Clubs, Inc., in the "Macmillan Executive Summary Program," April 1987, 4.
11. Christopher Caggiano, "Recruiting Secrets," *Inc.*, October 1998, 29–42.
12. Caroline A. Drakeley, "Viral Networking: Tactics in Today's Job Market," *Intercom*, September–October 2003, 4–7.
13. Ted Mitchner," Job Search (column), *Oregonian*, 8 February 2004 [accessed 16 February 2004] www.ebscohost.com.
14. Drakeley, "Viral Networking: Tactics in Today's Job Market," 5.
15. Anne Fisher, "Greener Pastures in a New Field," *Fortune*, 26 January 2004, 48.
16. Cheryl L. Noll, "Collaborating with the Career Planning and Placement Center in the Job-Search Project," *Business Communication Quarterly* 58, no. 3 (1995): 53–55.
17. Rockport Institute, "How to Write a Masterpiece of a Résumé" [accessed 16 October 1998] www.rockportinstitute.com/résumés.html.
18. Pam Stanley-Weigand, "Organizing the Writing of Your Resume," *Bulletin of the Association for Business Communication* 54, no. 3 (September 1991): 11–12.
19. Susan Vaughn, "Answer the Hard Questions Before Asked," *Los Angeles Times*, 29 July 2001, W1–W2.
20. Richard H. Beatty and Nicholas C. Burkholder, *The Executive Career Guide for MBAs* (New York: Wiley, 1996), 133.
21. Adapted from Burdette E. Bostwick, *How to Find the Job You've Always Wanted* (New York: Wiley, 1982), 69–70.
22. Norma Mushkat Gaffin, "Recruiters' Top 10 Resume Pet Peeves," Monster.com [accessed 19 February 2004] www.monster.com; Beatty and Burkholder, *The Executive Career Guide for MBAs*, 151.
23. Rockport Institute, "How to Write a Masterpiece of a Résumé."
24. "Resume Fraud Gets Slicker and Easier," CNN.com [accessed 11 March 2004] www.cnn.com.
25. "Resume Fraud Gets Slicker and Easier"; Employment Screening Resources website [accessed 18 March 2004] www.erscheck.com.
26. Sal Divita, "If You're Thinking Résumé, Think Creatively," *Marketing News*, 14 September 1992, 29.
27. Rockport Institute, "How to Write a Masterpiece of a Résumé."
28. Rockport Institute, "How to Write a Masterpiece of a Résumé."
29. Beverly Culwell-Block and Jean Anna Sellers, "Résumé Content and Format—Do the Authorities Agree?" *Bulletin of the Association for Business Communication* 57, no. 4 (1994): 27–30.
30. Ellen Joe Pollock, "Sir: Your Application for a Job Is Rejected; Sincerely, Hal 9000," *Wall Street Journal*, 30 July 1998, A1, A12.
31. "Scannable Resume Design," ResumeEdge.com [accessed 19 February 2004] www.resumeedge.com.
32. Kim Isaacs, "Tips for Creating a Scannable Resume," Monster.com [accessed 19 February 2004] www.monster.com.
33. Kim Isaacs, "Enhance Your Resume for Monster Upload," Monster.com [accessed 19 February 2004] www.monster.com.
34. "The Rogue's Gallery of 25 Awful Résumé Mistakes," CareerExplorer.net [accessed 19 February 2004] www.careerexplorer.net.
35. Regina Pontow, "Electronic Résumé Writing Tips," Proven Résumés.com [accessed 18 October 1998] www.provenresumes.com/reswkshps/electronic/scnres.html.

CHAPTER 18

1. "Top 10 Reasons To Work at Google," Google website [accessed 24 December 2003] www.google.com; Fred Vogelstein, "Can Google Grow Up?" *Fortune*, 8 December 2003, 102; Quentin Hardy, "All Eyes on Google," *Forbes*, 26 May 2003, 100; Keith H. Hammonds, "Growth Search," *Fast Company*, April 2003, 74–81; Stanley Bing, "How Not to Success *(sic)* in Business," *Fortune*, 30 December 2002, 210; Pierre Mornell, "Zero Defect Hiring," *Inc.*, March 1998, 74.
2. William J. Banis, "The Art of Writing Job-Search Letters," *CPC Annual*, 36th ed., no. 2 (1992): 42–50.
3. "The Writer Approach," *Los Angeles Times*, 17 November 2002, W1.
4. Toni Logan, "The Perfect Cover Story," *Kinko's Impress* 2 (2000): 32, 34; James Gonyea, "Money Talks: Salary History Versus Salary Requirements," Monster.com [accessed 19 October 2004] www.monster.com.
5. Marguerite Higgins, "Tech-Savvy Job Hunters Not So Suave in Writing; E-Mail Résumés Appall Employers," *Washington Times*, 17 December 2002 [accessed 22 February 2004] www.highbeam.com; "Keep Goal in Mind When Crafting a Résumé," *Register-Guard* (Eugene, Ore.), 3 August 2003 [accessed 22 February 2004] www.highbeam.com; Anis F. McClin, "Effects of Spelling Errors on the Perception of Writers," *Journal of General Psychology*, January 2002 [accessed 22 February 2004] www.highbeam.com.
6. Sylvia Porter, "Your Money: How to Prepare for Job Interviews," *San Francisco Chronicle*, 3 November 1981, 54.
7. George Donnelly, "Recruiting, Retention & Returns," *cfonet*, March 2000 [accessed 10 April 2000] www.cfonet. com/html/Articles/CFO/2000/00Marecr.html.
8. Stephanie Armour, "The New Interview Etiquette," *USA Today*, 23 November 1999, B1, B2.
9. Samuel Greengard, "Are You Well Armed to Screen Applicants?" *Personnel Journal*, December 1995, 84–95.
10. Charlene Marmer Solomon, "How Does Disney Do It?" *Personnel Journal*, December 1989, 53.
11. William Poundstone, "Beware the Interview Inquisition," *Harvard Business Review*, May 2003, 18+.
12. Marcia Vickers, "Don't Touch That Dial: Why Should I Hire You?" *New York Times*, 13 April 1997, F11.
13. Terry McKenna, "Behavior-Based Interviewing," *National Petroleum News*, January 2004, 16; Nancy K. Austin, "Goodbye Gimmicks," *Incentive*, May 1996, 241.
14. "Southwest Is Picky," *Soundview Executive Book Summaries*, September 1998, 5.
15. Patrick J. Sauer, "Open-Door Management," *Inc.*, June 2003, 44.
16. Joel Russell, "Finding Solid Ground," *Hispanic Business*, February 1992, 42–44, 46.
17. Michael P. Cronin, "This Is a Test," *Inc.*, August 1993, 64–68.
18. Steven Mitchell Sack, "The Working Woman's Legal Survival Guide: Testing," FindLaw.com [accessed 22 February 2004] www.findlaw.com; David W. Arnold and John W. Jones, "Who the Devil's Applying Now?" *Security Management*, March 2002, 85–88.
19. Arnold and Jones, "Who the Devil's Applying Now?" 86.
20. Arnold and Jones, "Who the Devil's Applying Now?" 86.
21. Adam Agard, "Preemployment Skills Testing: An Important Step in the Hiring Process," *Supervision*, June 2003, 7+.
22. Andy Meisler, "Negative Results," *Workforce Management*, October 2003, 35+.
23. Tyler D. Hartwell, Paul D. Steele, and Nathaniel F. Rodman, "Workplace Alcohol-Testing Programs: Prevalence and Trends,"

Monthly Labor Review, June 1998, 27–34; "Substance Abuse in the Workplace," *HR Focus,* February 1997, 1, 4+.

24. Meisler, "Negative Results," 35+.
25. Thomas A. Buckhoff, "Preventing Fraud by Conducting Background Checks," *CPA Journal,* November 2003, 52.
26. Austin, "Goodbye Gimmicks."
27. Peter Rea, Julie Rea, and Charles Moonmaw, "Training: Use Assessment Centers in Skill Development," *Personnel Journal,* April 1990, 126–131; Greengard, "Are You Well Armed to Screen Applicants?"
28. Anne Field, "Coach, Help Me Out with This Interview," *Business Week,* 22 October 2001, 134E2, 134E4.
29. Robert Gifford, Cheuk Fan Ng, and Margaret Wilkinson, "Nonverbal Cues in the Employment Interview: Links Between Applicant Qualities and Interviewer Judgments," *Journal of Applied Psychology* 70, no. 4 (1985): 729.
30. Dale G. Leathers, *Successful Nonverbal Communication* (New York: Macmillan, 1986), 225.
31. Armour, "The New Interview Etiquette."
32. Shirley J. Shepherd, "How to Get That Job in 60 Minutes or Less," *Working Woman,* March 1986, 119.
33. Shepherd, "How to Get That Job in 60 Minutes or Less," 118.
34. H. Anthony Medley, *Sweaty Palms: The Neglected Art of Being Interviewed* (Berkeley, Calif.: Ten Speed Press, 1993), 179.
35. Steven Mitchell Sack, "The Working Woman's Legal Survival Guide: Illegal Job Interview Questions," FindLaw.com [accessed 22 February 2004] www.findlaw.com.
36. Gerald L. Wilson, "Preparing Students for Responding to Illegal Selection Interview Questions," *Bulletin of the Association for Business Communication* 54, no. 2 (1991): 44–49.
37. Jeff Springston and Joann Keyton, "Interview Response Training," *Bulletin of the Association for Business Communication* 54, no. 3 (1991): 28–30; Gerald L. Wilson, "An Analysis of Instructional Strategies for Responding to Illegal Selection Interview Questions," *Bulletin of the Association for Business Communication* 54, no. 3 (1991): 31–35.
38. Stephen J. Pullum, "Illegal Questions in the Selection Process: Going Beyond Contemporary Business and Professional Communication Textbooks," *Bulletin of the Association for Business Communication* 54, no. 3 (1991): 36–43; Alicia Kitsuse, "Have You Ever Been Arrested?" *Across the Board,* November 1992, 46–49; Christina L. Greathouse, "Ten Common Hiring Mistakes," *Industry Week,* 20 January 1992, 22–23, 26.
39. "Negotiating Salary: An Introduction," *InformationWeek* online [accessed 22 February 2004] www.infoweek.com.
40. "Negotiating Salary: An Introduction."
41. Marilyn Moats Kennedy, "Are You Getting Paid What You're Worth?" *New Woman,* November 1984, 110.
42. Harold H. Hellwig, "Job Interviewing: Process and Practice," *Bulletin of the Association for Business Communication* 55, no. 2 (1992): 8–14.

TEXT

5 (Communication Miscues: The High Cost of Failure) Adapted from Allison Hoffman and Olga R. Rodriguez, "Railroad Vows to Aid Recovery: Union Pacific Says It Will Directly Handle Claims from Derailment," *Los Angeles Times,* 27 June 2003, B1; "City Officials Condemn Lack Of Warning Of Derailment," *Augusta Chronicle,* 22 June 2003, A8. **17 (Connecting with Technology: Extreme Telecommuting)** Adapted from Rick Whiting, "Innovation: Videoconferencing's Virtual Room," *InformationWeek,* 1 April 2002, 14; Mark Alpert, "Long-Distance Robots," *Scientific American,* December 2001, 94; Teliris website, [accessed 8 August 2003] www.teliris.com. **53 (Communicating Across Cultures: Actions Speak Louder Than Words All Around the World)** Adapted from David A. Victor, *International Business Communication* (New York: HarperCollins, 1992); David Wallace, "Mind Your Manners," *World Trade,* October 1992, 52, 54–55; Hannele Duvfa, "Innocents Abroad: The Politics of Cross-Cultural Communication," *Communication and Discourse Across Cultures and Languages,* 1991, 73–89; M. Katherine Glover, "Do's and Taboos: Cultural Aspects of International Business," *Business America,* 13 August 1990, 2–6; C. Barnum and N. Woniansky, "Taking Cues from Body Language," *Management Review,* June 1989, 59–60. **55 (Checklist: Improving Nonverbal Communication Skills)** Source: Gerald H. Graham, Jeanne Unrue, and Paul Jennings, "The Impact of Nonverbal Communication in Organizations: A Survey of Perceptions," *Journal of Business Communication* 28, no. 1 (Winter 1991): 45–62; Dianna Booher, *Communicate with Confidence* (New York: McGraw-Hill, 1994), 363–370. **67 (Communicating Across Cultures: Test Your Intercultural Knowledge)** Adapted from David A. Ricks, "International Business Blunders: An Update," *Business & Economic Review,* January–March 1988, 25; Valerie Frazee, "Keeping Up on Chinese Culture," *Global Workforce,* October 1996, 16–17; Valerie Frazee, "Establishing Relations in Germany," *Global Workforce,* April 1997, 16–17; James Wilfong and Toni Seger, *Taking Your Business Global* (Franklin Lakes, N.J.: Career Press, 1997), 282. **81 (Connecting with Technology: The Gist of Machine Translation)** Adapted from Sheridan Prasso, ed., "It's All Greek to These Sites," *Business Week,* 22 July 2002, 18; Alis Technologies website [accessed 4 November 2003] www.alis.com; WorldLingo website [accessed 4 November 2003] www.worldlingo.com. **95 (Ethics Detective: Telling Only Half the Story)** Adapted in part from product warning message at the Minwax website [accessed 1 November 2003] www.minwax.com. **108 (Connecting with Technology: Create and Collaborate with Powerful Outlining Tools)** Adapted from Microsoft Word Help text; Microsoft website [accessed 2 December 2003] www.microsoft.com/office; "What Electronic Outlining Tools Can Do for You," Web Writing That Works website [accessed 7 March 2004] www.webwritingthatworks.com. **129 (Communicating Across Cultures: Communicating with a Global Audience on the Web)** Adapted from Laura Morelli, "Writing for a Global Audience on the Web," *Marketing News,* 17 August 1998, 16; Yuri and Anna Radzievsky, "Successful Global Web Sites Look Through Eyes of the Audience," *Advertising Age's Business Marketing,* January 1998, 17; Sari Kalin, "The Importance of Being Multiculturally Correct," *Computerworld,* 6 October 1997, G16–G17; B. G. Yovovich, "Making Sense of All the Web's Numbers," *Editor & Publisher,* November 1998, 30–31; David Wilford, "Are We All Speaking the Same Language?" *The Times,* (London), 20 April 2000, 4. **131 (Communication Miscues: When Words Kill: Hidden Dangers in Food Labels)** Food Allergy Initiative website [accessed 4 October 2003] www.foodallergyinitiative.org; Diana Keough, "Snacks That Can Kill; Schools Take Steps to Protect Kids Who Have Severe Allergies to Nuts," *Plain Dealer,* 15 July 2003, E1; "Dawdling Over Food Labels," *New York Times,* 2 June 2003, A16; Sheila McNulty, "A Matter of Life and Death, *Financial Times,* 10 September 2003, 14. **174 (Communication Miscues: Sending Messages Where They Don't Belong)** Sharon Salyer, "State Group Urges Hospital Policy Checks," 22 June 2003, *Everett Herald* [accessed 20 October 2003] www.heraldnet.com; Sharon Salyer, "Providence Tightens Up Its Fax Policy," *Everett Herald,* 13 June 2003 [accessed 20 October 2003] www.heraldnet.com; Sharon Salyer, "Faxed Medical Records Go Astray," *Everett Herald,* 10 June 2003 [accessed 20 October 2003] www.heraldnet.com; "Kaiser Misdirected Patient Medical Info," *Employee Benefit News,* 15 September 2000, 93. **183 (Communicating Across Cultures: How Direct Is Too Direct?)** Adapted from Mary A. DeVries, *Internationally Yours* (Boston: Houghton Mifflin, 1994), 195; Myron W. Lustig and Jolene Koester, *Intercultural Competence* (New York: HarperCollins, 1993), 66–72; Mary Munter, "Cross-Cultural Communication for Managers," *Business Horizons,* May–June 1993, 69–78; David A. Victor, *International Business Communication* (New York: HarperCollins, 1992), 137–168; Larry A. Samovar and Richard E. Porter, *Intercultural Communication: A Reader,* 6th ed. (Belmont, Calif.: Wadsworth, 1991), 109–110; Larry A. Samovar and Richard E. Porter, *Communication Between Cultures* (Belmont, Calif.: Wadsworth, 1991), 235–244; Carley H. Dodd, *Dynamics of Intercultural Communication,* 3d ed. (Dubuque, Iowa: Wm. C. Brown, 1989), 69–73. **242 (Connecting with Technology: Controlling Rumors Online)** Adapted from PlanetFeedback.com [accessed 3 December 2003] www.planetfeedback.com/consumer; "Health Related Hoaxes and Rumors," Centers for Disease Control [accessed 3 December 2003] www.cdc.gov; UrbanLegends.com [accessed 3 December 2003] www.urbanlegends.com; "Pranksters, Activists and Rogues: Know Your Adversaries and Where They Surf," *PR News,* 26 June 2000 [accessed 3 December 2003] www.elibrary.com. **284 (Connecting with Technology: The Power and Persuasion of Interactive Sales Tools)** South San Francisco Conference Center [accessed 24 June 2004] www.ssfconf.com. **352 (Ethics Detective: Hiding Behind the Numbers)** Adapted from A. S. C. Ehrenberg, "The Problem of Numeracy," *Admap,* February 1992, 37–40; Mary S. Auvil and Kenneth W. Auvil, *Introduction to Business Graphics: Concepts and Applications* (Cincinnati: South-Western, 1992), 40, 192–193; Peter H. Selby, *Using Graphs and Tables: A Self-Teaching Guide* (New York: Wiley, 1979), 8–9. **373 (Communication Miscues: Suspect Reports Damage Wall Street Reputations)** Adapted from Greg Farrell, "Merrill Lynch: Regulators Cite 'Misleading' Reports," *USA Today,* 29 April 2003, 3B; Emily Thornton, Heather Timmons, Mike McNamee, "Dirty Research: Not Only Analysts Are To Blame," *Business Week,* 20 January 2003, 59; "It Just Gets Worse," *Economist.com* [accessed 14 January 2003] www.proquest.com; Emily Thornton, Peter Elstrom, and Mike McNamee, "Trying to Build a Wall on Wall Street," *BusinessWeek,* 29 April 2002, 40. **382 (Connecting with Technology: Proposals Get a Software Assist)** Adapted from Dan MacDougall, "Orchestrating Your Proposal," *Canadian Consulting Engineer,* March–April 2003, 51–56; Sant Corporation website [accessed 23 January 2004] www.santcorp.com; Pragmatech Software website [accessed 23 January 2004] www.pragmattech.com. **394 (Communication Miscues: Microsoft Slip Magnifies Criticism)** Adapted from Bill Breen, "Can Microsoft Finally Kill All the Bugs?" October 2003, *Fast Company,* 82;

Craig Mundie, "Q&A: Inside Trustworthy Computing," 3 February 2003, *Computerworld*, 28; Dennis Fisher, "A Super Response?" 30 September 2002, *eWeek*, 25; John Foley, "Different Views Of Microsoft," 20 May 2002, *InformationWeek*, 104; Bob Evans, "Bashing The Bill Bashers," 28 January 2002, *InformationWeek*, 106; Bill Gates, "Memo from Bill Gates," *InformationWeek* website, 21 January 2002 [accessed 21 January 2004] www.informationweek.com. **453 (Communication Miscues: Error-Riddled Study Guides Embarrass School District)** Adapted from David H. Price, "Outcome-Based Tyranny: Teaching Compliance While Testing Like A State," *Anthropological Quarterly*, Fall 2003, 715; Justin Bloom, "D.C. Study Guides Problematic," *Washington Post*, 15 April 2003, B01; Metro In Brief, "Homework Errors Lead To Official's Firing," *The Washington Post*, 25 April 2002, B03; Justin Bloom, "D.C. Schools Still Need Help With Homework," *The Washington Post*, 13 April 2002, B01. **470 (Communicating Across Cultures: Five Tips for Making Presentations Around the World)** Adapted from Patricia L. Kurtz, *The Global Speaker* (New York: AMACOM, 1995), 35–47, 56–68, 75–82, 87–100; David A. Victor, *International Business Communication* (New York: HarperCollins Publishers, 1992), 39–45; Lalita Khosla, "You Say Tomato," *Forbes*, 21 May 2001, 36; Stephen Dolainski, "Are Expats Getting Lost in the Translation?" *Workforce*, February 1997, 32–39. **485 (Communication Miscues: Recovering from Disasters)** Adapted from C. Peter Guiliano and Frank J. Currilo, "Going Blank in the Boardroom," *Public Relations Quarterly*, Winter 2003, 35+; Jennifer Rotondo and Mike Rotondo, Jr., *Presentation Skills for Managers*, (New York: McGraw-Hill, 2002), 160–162; Mark Merritt, "No More Nightmares," *Presentations*, April 2001, 44+. **499 (Communication Miscues: Is PowerPoint Destroying Communication?)** Adapted from Edward Tufte, "*ET on Columbia Evidence—Analysis of Key Slide*" [accessed 15 February 2004] www.edwardtufte.com; Edward Tufte, [introduction to] "Essay: The Cognitive Style of PowerPoint" [accessed 15 February 2004] www.edwardtufte.com; Clive Thompson, "PowerPoint Makes You Dumb," *New York Times Magazine*, 14 December 2003, 88; Mark Gibbs, "Blame the Workman," *Network World*, 2 February 2004, 50. **504 (Connecting with Technology: Creating High-Octane Presentations)** Adapted from Connecting with Technology: Infommersion website [accessed 15 February 2004] www.informmersion.com; Anystream website [accessed 15 February 2004] www.anystream.com; Serious Magic website [accessed 15 February 2004] www.seriousmagic.com. **521 (Communication Across Cultures: Looking for Work Around the World)** Adapted from University of Michigan International Center Website [accessed 18 February 2004] www.umich.edu; Allan Hoffman, "Five Strategies for Finding Work Abroad," Monster.com [accessed 18 February 2004] www.monster.com; Personal communication, Andrew Jaynes, 18 February 2004. **565 (Communication Across Cultures: Successfully Interviewing Across Borders)** Adapted from Jean-Marc Hachey, "Interviewing for an International Job," excerpt from *The Canadian Guide to Working and Living Overseas*, 3rd edition [accessed 23 February 2004] www.workingoverseas.com; Rebecca Falkoff, "Dress to Impress the World: International Business Fashion," Monster.com [accessed 23 February 2004] www.monster.com; Mary Ellen Slater, "Navigating the Details of Landing an Overseas Job," *Washington Post*, 11 November 2002, E4. **572 (Communication Miscues: Talking Yourself out of a Job)** Adapted from Thomas Pack, "Good Answers to Job Interview Questions," *Information Today*, January 2004, 35+; John Lees, "Make Them Believe You Are the Best," *The Times* (United Kingdom), 21 January 2004, 3; "Six Interview Mistakes," Monster.com [accessed 23 February 2004] www.monster.com.

FIGURES AND TABLES

46 (Figure 2.4) From http://messenger.yahoo.com/messenger/ business/products/msg/sshot.php. Copyright © 2003 Yahoo! Inc. All rights reserved. **47 (Figure 2.5)** From www.microsoft.com/office/editions/ prodinfo/technologies/sharepoint.mspx. © 2004 Microsoft Corporation. All rights reserved. **48 (Figure 2.6)** From www.webex.com/press_kit. html. **51 (Table 2.2)** Madelyn Burley-Allen, *Listening: The Forgotten Skill*, (New York: Wiley, 1995), 70–71, 119–120; Judi Brownell, *Listening: Attitudes, Principles, and Skills*, (Boston: Allyn and Bacon, 2002); 3, 9, 83, 89, 125; Larry Barker and Kittie Watson, *Listen Up*, (New York: St. Martin's, 2000), 8, 9, 64. **63 (Figure 3.1)** Source: Going Global Has Its Barriers, *USA Today*, 3 May 2000, B1. **68 (Figure 3.2)** Source: Mary O'Hara-Devereaux and Robert Johansen, *Global Work: Bridging Distance, Culture, and Time* (San Francisco: Jossey-Bass, 1994), 55, 59. **70 (Figure 3.3)** Source: "New ILO Study Highlights Labour Trends Worldwide," International Labour Organization [accessed 15 September 2003] www.ilo.org/public/ english/bureau/inf/ pr/2003/40.htm. **71 (Figure 3.4)** Source: Roger Axtell, *Gestures: The Do's and Taboos of Body Language Around the World* (New York: Wiley, 1991), 117–119. **76 (Table 3.2)** Source: Guo-Ming Chen and William J. Starosta, *Foundations of Intercultural Communication* (Boston: Allyn and Bacon, 1998), 66. **187 (Figure 7.2)** Courtesy Ace Hardware. **195 (Figure 7.6)** Courtesy Herman Miller. **200 (Figure 7.8)** Courtesy Discovery Communications. **265 (Figure 9.1)** Adapted from Abraham H. Maslow, *Motivation and Personality* (New York: Harper & Row, 1954), 12, 19. Copyright © 1970 by Abraham H. Maslow. Reprinted by permission of HarperCollins Publishers. **325 (Figure 10.3)** Source: From www.thebrain.com/BrainEKPtour/ ekptour.htm. Copyright 2004, The Brain Technologies Corporation. All rights reserved. **308–309 (Table 10.2)** Source: Adapted from Subscribed Sites page, Sno-Isle Regional Library System [accessed 18 December 2003] www.-sno-isle.org; "Finding Industry Information" [accessed 3 November 1998] www.pitt.edu/~buslibry/industries.htm; Thomas P. Bergman, Stephen M. Garrison, and Gregory M. Scott, *The Business Student Writer's Manual and Guide to the Internet* (Paramus, N.J.: Prentice Hall, 1998), 67–80; Ernest L. Maier, Anthony J. Faria, Peter Kaatrude, and Elizabeth Wood, *The Business Library and How to Use It* (Detroit: Omnigraphics, 1996), 53–76. **335 (Figure 11.1)** Source: From www.census.gov/statab/ranks/pg05.txt. **337 (Figure 11.2)** Source: "How the Networks Deliver the Goods," *BusinessWeek*, 6 April 1998, 91–92. **479 (Table 15.2)** Source: Adapted from Eric J. Adams, "Management Focus: User-Friendly Presentation Software," *World Trade*, March 1995, 92. **500 (Table 16.1)** Source: Adapted from Claudyne Wilder and David Fine, *Point, Click & Wow* (San Francisco: Jossey-Bass Pfeiffer, 1996), 63, 527. **503 (Figure 16.6)** Source: Microsoft PowerPoint2002 software. **525 (Table 17.1)** Sources: Bethany McLean, "A Scary Monster," *Fortune*, 22 December 2003, 19+; Alan Cohen, "Best Job Hunting Sites," *Yahoo! Internet Life*, May 2002, 90–92; Richard N. Bolles, "Career Strategizing or, What Color Is Your Web Parachute?" *Yahoo! Internet Life*, May 1998, 116, 121; Tara Weingarten, "The All-Day, All-Night, Global, No-Trouble Job Search," *Newsweek*, 6 April 1998, 17; Michele Himmelberg, "Internet an Important Tool in Employment Search," *San Diego Union-Tribune*, 7 September 1998, D2; Gina Imperato, "35 Ways to Land a Job Online," *Fast Company*, August 1998, 192–197; Roberta Maynard, "Casting the Net for Job Seekers," *Nation's Business*, March 1997, 28–29. **523 (Figure 17.2)** Source: Adapted from Richard Nelson Bolles, *What Color Is Your Parachute?* (Berkeley, Calif.: Ten Speed Press, 1997), 67. **562 (Table 18.3)** Sources: Adapted from Anne Fisher, "Success Secret: A High Emotional IQ," *Fortune*, 26 October 1998, 293–298; Laura Lyne McMurchie, "Careers Can Rise and Fall with an EQ," *Computing Canada*, September 1998, 18, 21. **563 (Table 18.4)** Source: USA Today Snapshot "Checking Out New Hires," *USA Today*, 18 May 2000, B1. **567 (Table 18.5)** Source: Adapted from *The Northwestern Endicott Report* (Evanston, Ill.: Northwestern University Placement Center). **568 (Table 18.6)** Sources: Adapted from Marilyn Sherman, "Questions R Us: What to Ask at a Job Interview," *Career World*, January 2004, 20; H. Lee Rust, *Job Search: The Completion Manual for Jobseekers* (New York: American Management Association, 1979), 56. **569 (Table 18.7)** Source: Adapted from *The Northwestern Endicott Report* (Evanston: Ill.: Northwestern University Placement Center). **573 (Table 18.8)** Source: "Dangerous Questions," *Nation's Business*, May 1999, 22.

PHOTO CREDITS

3 PictureQuest 11 PhotoEdit 12 Danny Turner Photography 18 Ethan Hill 18 Dell, Inc. 18 Belkin Corporation 18 Digital Vision Ltd. 18 PhotoEdit 18 Ezonics Corporation 19 3M 19 Ethan Hill 19 AGE Fotostock America, Inc. 20 Masterfile Corporation 20 United Parcel Service 20 AGE Fotostock America, Inc. 20 FEDEX Corporation 20 Corbis/SABA Press Photos, Inc. 21 Photolibrary.Com 21 Masterfile Corporation 21 Staples, Inc. 21 Getty Images, Inc. – Taxi 22 The Image Works 33 AP Wide World Photos 35 Andy Freeberg Photography 40 Michael L. Abramson Photography 50 Masterfile Corporation 54 Photolibrary.Com 61 E-SoftSys 63 Brian Coats Photography 71 PhotoEdit 72 AGE Fotostock America, Inc. 80 Kyodo News International, Inc. 87 Alpha Books/Penguin Group, USA 91 Jamaican Hut Foods, Inc. 93 Mark Richards 97 PhotoEdit 117 Corbis/Bettmann 118 Evan Kafka 126 Ward-Williams Inc. 136 Corbis/Bettmann 151 Corbis/Bettmann 157 Alamy Images 181 Cone, Inc. 184 Philip Saltonstall 186 Jyoti Cuisine India 202 B. Smith Enterprises 206 The Image Works 212 Rowhouse Pictures, Inc. 214 Ford Motor Company 217 AP Wide World Photos 218 Alamy Images 221 AP Wide World Photos 223 AP Wide World Photos 224 Corbis/Bettmann 254 Corbis/Bettmann 256 Masterfile Corporation 258 AP Wide World Photos 258 Corbis/Bettmann 263 Corbis/SABA Press Photos, Inc. 277 Corbis/Bettmann 292 Corbis/Bettmann 294 Getty Images, Inc.—Liaison 296 PhotoEdit 298 AP Wide World Photos 301 Toyota Motor Sales, USA, Inc. 319 Corbis/Bettmann 331 Stone Yamashita Partners 333 Inmagine Corporation LLC 346 Getty Images, Inc.—Photodisc 347 Getty Images 359 AP Wide World Photos 360 Corbis/Bettmann 370 Corbis/Sygma 391 OMD Worldwide 415 Corbis/Bettmann 416 Alamy Images Royalty Free 419 NewsCom 420 AP Wide World Photos 447 Peter Gregoire 463 Landov LLC 464 Getty Images Inc.—Image Bank 467 Getty Images 478 Bozell Worldwide, Inc. 480 PhotoEdit 483 Getty Images, Inc.—Liaison 486 Mark Richards 493 Hewlett Packard 494 Getty Images 495 Corbis/Stock Market 510 Index Stock Imagery, Inc. 517 Richard B. Levine/Frances M. Roberts 526 The Image Works 551 Corbis/Bettmann 558 Michael Grecco Photography, Inc. 562 David Carmack Photography 570 The Image Works

Organization/ Brand/Company Index

Subject Index

XYZ